PRAISE FOR THE ULTIMATE SCHOLARSHIP BOOK
BY GEN AND KELLY TANABE

"Upbeat, well-organized and engaging, this comprehensive tool is an exceptional investment for the college-bound."

—*PUBLISHERS WEEKLY*

"Gen and Kelly Tanabe are by far the best experts on winning scholarships. Not only will their books help you find scholarships that you qualify for, they will show you how to win them. Soon after applying the strategies in their book, I won a $1,000 scholarship. I couldn't have done it without them. The Tanabes can help you win scholarships too!"

—*DOUG WONG, UNIVERSITY OF CALIFORNIA, SAN DIEGO*

"A present for anxious parents."

—*THE HONOLULU ADVERTISER*

"Upbeat tone and clear, practical advice."

—*BOOK NEWS*

"Unlike other authors, the Tanabes use their experiences and those of other students to guide high school and college students and their parents through the scholarship and financial aid process."

—*PALO ALTO DAILY NEWS*

"If the Tanabes could earn over $100,000 in scholarships and graduate from an Ivy League institution owing nothing, others can, too."

—*STAR-BULLETIN*

"This is a helpful, well-organized guide. A good resource for all students."

—*KLIATT*

"A common sense approach to scholarship searches. *The Ultimate Scholarship Book* gives a down to earth step by step method of finding, applying for and winning scholarships. The scholarship list has many opportunities for students to showcase their talents for financial reward."

—*LYNDA McGEE, COLLEGE COUNSELOR, DOWNTOWN MAGNETS HIGH SCHOOL, LOS ANGELES*

"This guide (has) ... practical tips on where to find scholarships; how to write effective applications, resumes and winning essays; and how to get glowing recommendations and ace scholarship interviews."

—*C.E. KING, IOWA STATE UNIVERSITY, CHOICE MAGAZINE*

"Getting into college is only half of the game. How to pay for it offers the second big challenge. Whether they qualify for financial need or are just looking for ways to help their parents with this heavy burden, all students will profit from *The Ultimate Scholarship Book* which both outlines the process of finding financial help for college as well as it provides an extensive and up to date list of current scholarship sources.

"Take these important tips from two experienced writers who are nationally recognized for their expertise on all facets of the college application process. Both members of this impressive husband and wife team paid for their Harvard educations by following the precepts which they share with you now in this easy to read guidebook."

—*DAVID MILLER, DIRECTOR OF COLLEGE COUNSELING, STEVENSON SCHOOL, PEBBLE BEACH, CALIFORNIA*

Dedication

To our families for shaping who we are.

To Harvard for four of the best years of our lives.

To the many students and friends who made this book possible by sharing their scholarship experiences, secrets, successes and failures.

To all the students and parents who understand that paying for college is a challenging but worthwhile endeavor.

The Ultimate Scholarship Book 2023

Billions of Dollars in Scholarships, Grants and Prizes

Gen and Kelly Tanabe

Winners of over $100,000 in college scholarships and award-winning authors of
Get Free Cash for College and *How to Write a Winning Scholarship Essay*

- Comprehensive scholarship directory to over 1.5 million awards worth more than $2 billion
- Scholarships for high school and college students of every background, talent and achievement level
- Easy to use indexes to quickly find the best matching scholarships

The Ultimate Scholarship Book 2023: Billions of Dollars in Scholarships, Grants and Prizes

By Gen and Kelly Tanabe

Published by SuperCollege
2713 Newlands Avenue
Belmont, CA 94002
650-395-9655
editor@supercollege.com
www.supercollege.com

The Ultimate Scholarship Book is the #1 bestselling scholarship guide based on Nielsen/BookScan sales data of the 2022 editions of comparable titles.

Special Sales: For information on using SuperCollege books in the classroom or special prices for bulk quantities, please contact our Special Sales Department at sales@supercollege.com.

ISBN-13: 978-1-61760-172-9
ISBN-10: 1-61760-172-1

Manufactured in the United States of America
10 9 8 7 6 5 4 3 2 1

Library of Congress ISSN (International Standard Serial Number)
The ultimate scholarship book
ISSN 2644-0555

CONTENTS

How to Use the Ultimate Scholarship Book

chapter 1

A Scholarship Book That's Better Than a Website

Is it crazy to say that a bound stack of paper and glue is superior to the high speed bits and bytes of a scholarship website? Absolutely not! Because it is true.

Let us explain.

Unless you're starting out, you've probably used a scholarship website. Typically you fill out a profile questionnaire to provide information about yourself before hitting the "search" button. So far, this seems much easier than using a book.

Until you get your results.

No matter what website you use, there will be an unusually large number of scholarships that aren't good matches. After reading the eligibility requirements, you will discover that only a small handful are worth your time to apply.

You've just discovered the first major weakness of every scholarship website: your life (background, experiences, goals, talents, awards, interests and accomplishments) cannot be defined or summarized by a computer-generated questionnaire.

Your Life is MORE Than a 30-Question Profile

The simple truth is that no computer can match you to scholarships as well as you can. You are a complex individual with a variety of passions, interests and goals. Nothing—person or machine—knows you better than you know yourself.

And think about that profile form. That's the only information the computer has about you. But what if you don't know all the answers? Are you really set on becoming an orthopedic surgeon, or did that just sound cool? Even worse, you are limited by the choices provided on that profile questionnaire. Imagine that you wrote a poem that was published in your town's community newspaper. Should you select "poet" as a future career? Will that trigger a great poetry scholarship? Or maybe under hobbies, you should select "writing and journalism"? Of course, that might trigger a flood of journalism scholarships that wouldn't apply to you. Or maybe, even though your school doesn't have a poetry club, you should still tell the computer that you are a member of one in order to trick it into showing you a sweet poetry award?

Do you see where we're going?

The very fact that you need to give the computer information about yourself while only using the choices the computer provides, without any clue about how those answers will affect your results, almost guarantees that you are going to miss out on some good scholarships. How do you know that because you answered a single question in the way that you did, that you are not missing out on some fantastic scholarship opportunities?

The answer is, you don't.

About Your Authors

What makes us qualified to write *The Ultimate Scholarship Book*? Primarily it's because at one time we were exactly where you are now. We needed money to pay for college, and scholarships turned out to be our only answer. Not only did we do pretty well (winning more than $100,000 in free cash for college) but since then, we've continued to help thousands of students do the same.

Here's our story:

Kelly grew up in Los Angeles and when she got accepted to Harvard (which costs about $80,000 per year!), her family just didn't have the money to pay for it. Gen grew up in Hawaii and faced a similar financial crunch when he got into Harvard. In fact, his father even tried to bribe him to attend his state university by offering him a new car if he would give up his idea of attending the ivy-league college. Even considering the cost of a brand new car, it would have been cheaper for Gen's family to make car payments than pay Harvard tuition!

Since we both had our hearts set on attending a very expensive college that our families could not afford, we had little choice but to become fanatics about applying for scholarships. While we made a lot of beginner mistakes and it was by no means a quick or easy process, we were ultimately successful in winning more than $100,000 in scholarships. It was only because of this money that we were able to attend Harvard and were both able to graduate from college debt free.

As you may have guessed by now, we met while at college. We were actually next door neighbors in the dorm, and we were married a few years after we graduated from Harvard. Knowing first-hand how hard it can be for families to pay for college, we decided to share what we had learned as a result of our own pursuits to find funds for tuition. Our first books were about how to win scholarships and get financial aid. In fact, you can find *1001 Ways to Pay for College* and *How to Write a Winning Scholarship Essay* in bookstores. But despite the success of these books, we found that whenever we spoke to groups of students or parents, the number one question they asked was, "Do you know of scholarships for such-and-such a student?"

At the same time, we were also noticing a growing dissatisfaction from students who only relied on websites for scholarship information. This was somewhat of a mystery to us since we knew of thousands of great scholarships that were available. Why weren't these awards being found? Why wasn't every student applying for these scholarships?

All of this led to our decision to build our own database of scholarships and publish the results in *The Ultimate Scholarship Book*. We have a team of researchers who help us investigate scholarships, verify awards and ensure that the scholarships that make it into the book are the best and most up-to-date possible.

So that's our story and why we feel so passionate about what we write in this book. It's not just a collection of words on paper; it's really the collective experience and intelligence of our own quest for scholarships along with thousands of hours of research by our scholarship staff.

How This Book Overcomes the Disadvantages of Websites

A book has certain advantages over websites; for example, a book can work for you without the necessity of input. In many ways, a book is more flexible than a computer site because you are not penalized for not having an answer to a specific question that is worded in a narrow and inflexible way. Likewise, you are not forced to fit yourself into a predetermined, inflexible category. A book also lets you do the matching, a tool which we have found to be far better than outsourcing that work to some machine.

The Ultimate Scholarship Book is designed to be browsed. Spend an hour with this book and you will be able to evaluate hundreds of scholarships quickly and efficiently. By scanning the descriptions, you (not some computer) can decide if you have the right combination of background, interests or skills to qualify. By seeing all of the possibilities, you remain in control of how you prioritize which awards are right for you.

Now it is true that this is a slower process than using a website. But the trade-off is that it is far more accurate, and accuracy is what it's all about. You're not trying to find hundreds of awards that you may or may not win. Who has time to apply for that many scholarships anyway?! Your goal is to find the best awards that you have highest chances of winning. So while you'll invest more time in the finding of scholarships by using a book, we guarantee that the payoff (which in this case is literally thousands of extra dollars in scholarships) will be worth it.

If the time aspect of using a book versus a website still bothers you, here's one more thought. You can use books practically anywhere—especially when you have downtime. In other words, you can transform the natural wasted time during your day into highly productive scholarship time.

A Dirty Secret of Websites: They're Out-of-Date

It's natural to assume that anything online is more current than something printed on paper. But is this really true? Use a few scholarship websites and you'll soon realize that many are horribly out of date. Does it make you angry? Do you want to demand a refund? Of course not! Most scholarship websites are free services! Now it is true that many so-called "free" websites do actually make money by reselling your information; and once they get this from your profile form, you are of little value to the site. This is very annoying. However, we digress. Our point is that as a free service, there is really very little incentive for the website to maintain a high level of accuracy in their data. You really do get what you pay for with most scholarship websites!

It's a lot different with a book. There are two strong incentives that ensure the data in this book is up-to-date and accurate. The first is that we know once we commit something to paper, it's permanent. That creates a very strong desire to get it right the first time. This degree of permanence—the finality of words on paper—is a huge responsibility for us. Once the book goes to press, it is very difficult and expensive to update a mistake. The second powerful incentive is that you're paying hard earned money for this book! It's not free. Because of this, you expect to receive only the best product. If we don't deliver, we'll hear from you!

Together, these two incentives guarantee that each award in this book has been checked and re-checked. We have a small army of researchers whose only job is to verify each award in the book before it goes to press. We also send out communication twice a year to every scholarship listed to ask the providers themselves to verify and update their information. The end result is that this book is extremely accurate and up-to-date.

We also never keep this book in print for longer than a year—which is what we have found to be the typical time in which scholarships change. So as long as you are buying this book new, you are guaranteed to have the latest information possible.

Given how diligent and thorough our researchers are and the rigorous process we apply to every award we publish, we would happily pit this book against any website!

Another Dirty Secret of Websites: They Don't Actually List Millions of Awards

Here's a controversial statement: Websites often claim to list millions of awards worth billions of dollars, but the truth is that these numbers are just marketing hype. To arrive at these numbers, the websites use the most liberal definitions possible. For example, the Coca-Cola Foundation awards $3.55 million per year to 1,400 students. So the website counts their single listing of the Coca-Cola Foundation Scholarship as being 1,400 awards valued at $3.55 million. Or consider that the Jack Kent Cooke Foundation awards about 100 scholarships for $40,000 each. The total value of $4 million is added to the website's sum even though you can only win up to $40,000 of this amount. The results are highly inflated numbers.

Now before we claim the high road in this debate, we have to admit that we do the exact same thing! Take a look at the front cover of this book. Our numbers are just as impressive as many scholarship websites. But unlike the websites, we don't hide reality. All you need to do is pick up our book and see how thick it is to know how many awards we have inside. But you can't do this with a website. There is no way to know (and the website will never tell you) how many actual awards they have. They want you to think that they have millions when in reality they often contain no more—and often much less—than what you'll find in this book!

The Bottom Line: Books Can Beat Websites

It should be obvious by now that we are just a little bothered when we hear that websites—just because they are online—are superior to books.

It's just not true.

This is not to say that websites don't have any value. They absolutely do and inside this book, we list a number of websites that we think are worth your time. However, you need to understand that you must go beyond websites if you hope to find the best scholarships. In fact, you need to go beyond books too! The entire next chapter is dedicated to places in which to find scholarships other than books and websites. We highly recommend that you explore all these sources in order to find the best scholarships for you.

Why Choose *This* Book?

We know that there are other books that provide directories of scholarships, so why choose this one?

- Discover the best scholarships for you with awards in the humanities, academics, public service, extracurricular activities, talents, athletics, religion, ethnicity, social science and science based on career goals and more.

- Find scholarships that are not based on grades.

- Get all the information you need in one place with the application details, eligibility requirements, deadlines, contact information and website addresses.

- Find scholarships you can use at any college.

- Avoid wasting money on scholarship competitions that require a fee to enter.

- Save time and find the best scholarships that fit you with the easy-to-use indexes.

- Access the most up-to-date information that has been checked and double-checked.

- Learn not only how to find scholarships but how to win them! Get insider advice from judges and scholarship winners.

Common Scholarship Myths Busted

Now that we've cleared up some of the misconceptions about books and websites, let's debunk some of the common scholarship myths. We hate these myths because not only are they untrue, but they often prevent students from applying for scholarships.

Myth: You need to be financially destitute to be eligible to apply for scholarships.

Busted: While it is true that financial need is a consideration for some scholarships, the definition of "need" varies considerably. Given the cost of a college education, many families who consider themselves to be "middle class" actually qualify for some need-based scholarships. In addition, there are many scholarships where financial need is not even a factor. These "merit-based" scholarships are based on achievements, skills, career goals, family background and a host of other considerations that have nothing to do with a family's financial situation. You could actually be the son or daughter of Bill Gates and still win a "merit-based" scholarship.

Myth: You can only win scholarships as a high school senior.

Busted: It is never too early or too late to apply for scholarships. There are awards for students as young as seventh grade. If you win, the money is usually held in an account until it is time for you to actually go to college. But even if there are not as many awards for younger students as there are for seniors, it doesn't mean it's not important to look. Finding awards that you can apply for next year or even two years from now is a huge advantage. Keep a list of these awards since you are going to be super busy as a senior (think college apps and AP classes!) and you are going to be so thankful when you can just refer to your file of previously found awards and don't have to spend time searching. At the same time, you also don't want to stop applying for scholarships after you graduate from high school. There are many awards for college students. Once you are in college, you should continue to apply for scholarships, especially those geared toward specific majors and careers.

Myth: Only star athletes get college scholarships.

Busted: While star running backs receiving full-tuition scholarships are often what make the news, the majority of scholarships awarded by colleges are not for athletics. As you will see in this book, there are literally thousands of scholarships for those of us who don't know the difference between a touchdown and a touchback. Even if you are an athlete, you might also be surprised to know that many colleges give scholarships to student athletes who may not be destined to become the next Steph Curry. The needs of a college's athletic program depend on the level of their competition. You may find that at one college your soccer skill wouldn't earn you a place on the team as a bench warmer; but at another school, you might not only be a starter but also earn a half-tuition scholarship.

Myth: You need straight A's to win money for college.

Busted: While straight A's certainly don't hurt, most students mistakenly assume that grades are the primary determinate for selecting scholarship winners. This is just not true. Most scholarships are based on criteria other than grades and reward specific skills or talents such as linguistic, athletic or artistic ability. Even for scholarships in which grades are considered, GPAs are often not the most important factor. What's more relevant is that you best match the qualities the scholarship committee seeks. Don't let the lack of a perfect transcript prevent you from applying for scholarships.

Myth: You should get involved in as many extracurricular activities as possible to win a scholarship.

Busted: Scholarship competitions are not pie eating contests where you win through volume. They are more like baking contests in which you create an exquisite dessert with an appearance and flavor that matches the tastes of the judges. Scholarships are won by quality, not quantity. Scholarship judges are looking for students who have made quality contributions. For example, for a public service scholarship, the judges would be more impressed if you organized a school-wide volunteer day than if you were a member of 20 volunteer organizations but did little to distinguish yourself in any one of them.

Myth: If you qualify for financial aid, you don't need to apply for scholarships.

Busted: Financial aid and scholarships are not mutually exclusive but complimentary. You need to do both—apply for financial aid and scholarships—at the same time! Relying only on financial aid is dangerous. First, financial aid is "need based" which means if you're a middle or upper middle class family, you may not receive any free money (i.e. grants) but only student loans which you need to pay back. Even if you do qualify for grants, it may not be enough. The maximum Pell Grant, for example, is $6,495 per year, which is still far short of what tuition plus room and board costs at most schools. While financial aid is important, we consider scholarships to be far superior. With few, if any, strings attached, scholarships represent free cash that does not have to be paid back and which you can use at almost any school. Best of all, you can win scholarships regardless of your family's income!

Myth: You should apply to every scholarship that you find.

Busted: When you turn 35, you technically are eligible to run for President of the United States. This hardly means you should start packing your bags for the White House. Let's apply that same logic to scholarships. Just because you are technically eligible for a scholarship does not mean you should start filling out the paperwork for it. Why? You have a limited amount of time to spend on scholarship applications. It is necessary to allocate your time to those that you have the best chance of winning. You may find that you are eligible for 500 scholarships. Unless you're willing to make applying to scholarships your full-time avocation, it's unlikely that you can apply for more than several dozen awards. Thus, you need to be selective about which scholarships fit you the best. One caveat: This does not mean that you should only apply to two or three scholarships. You should still apply to as many scholarships as you can—just make sure you have them prioritized.

How a Solid Scholarship Strategy Helps Win You Money

Back in high school, Kelly applied for a scholarship from her father's employer. She was confident she would win since academically she had both high grades and test scores—which she diligently listed on the application. After turning in her application, she eagerly waited for the check to arrive. But the check never came. In fact, when Kelly found out who did win, she was surprised to learn that he had lower grades and lower test scores. What happened? How did this guy win instead of Kelly?

The answer was that Kelly relied solely on grades and test scores to win while the other applicant clearly used the entire application to stand out. That was when Kelly learned the importance of having a strategy.

So what does it take to win a scholarship?

The answer is that scholarship winners are not superstars. Rather, they are the students who have prepared—those young men and women that have invested the time to create applications that highlight their strengths. It's really sad to see students who don't apply for scholarships because they mistakenly assume that they don't have a chance to win.

Unlike a lottery, scholarships are not based on luck. To win scholarships, you need to show the scholarship judges how you fit the award. Often this is through the scholarship application, essay and interview. In fact, almost all scholarship competitions come down to one key factor—how well you can show that you fit the purpose of the scholarship. In this respect, you have power over the outcome. Through what you choose to highlight (and ignore) in the scholarship application, you are able to construct a case for why you deserve to win.

In the following chapters we will lay out what we found to be the keys to a winning strategy. Now turn the page and let's get started!

Where to Find the Best Scholarships

chapter 2

Scholarships Beyond this Book

We know you bought this book because it's the largest and most up-to-date directory of scholarships available. However, we do want to show you how to find even more scholarships above and beyond the ones listed in this book.

We learned how to find scholarships through trial and often painful error. For example, when we first started to search for scholarships, we spent a lot of time tracking down scholarships that we later discovered were listed in our high school counseling office. But we did learn from each mistake and slowly developed an efficient strategy for finding scholarships.

Our approach to finding scholarships consists of two important steps. First, you must create a list of as many scholarships as possible that fit you. Second, once you have a big list of scholarships, prioritize the awards. Here is where you will do some detective work that will show you which scholarships are worth your time to fill out.

By following this two-step approach, you will end up with a prioritized list of scholarships that are closely matched to your background and achievements. So, even before you fill out a single scholarship application form, you will have greatly improved your chances of winning. Plus, you saved time by not wasting energy on awards that you won't win.

Start Your Scholarship Search in Your Own Backyard

When we began looking for scholarships, we made what is perhaps the biggest mistake of the novice scholarship hunter—we started by looking as far away as possible. We were mesmerized by the big prizes of the large (and often well-publicized) national awards. We thought, "If I won just one of these national scholarship competitions, I'd be set and could end my search." This turned out to be a big mistake and an even bigger time-waster. It seemed that everyone and his brother, sister and cousin were also applying to these competitions. The Coca-Cola scholarship competition, for example, receives more than 100,000 applications each year.

It turned out that the last place we looked for scholarships was our most lucrative source. Best of all, this place turned out to be in our own backyard!

What are backyard scholarships and where do you find them? Think about all the civic groups, clubs, businesses, churches and organizations in your community. Each of these is a potential source for scholarships. (If you are already in college, you have two communities: your hometown and the city in which you go to school.) Since these awards are usually only available to students in your community, the competition is a lot less fierce.

You may be thinking, "What good is a $500 Lions Club scholarship when my college costs 20 grand a year?" It's true that local scholarships don't award the huge prizes that some of the national competitions do. You already know that we won over $100,000 in scholarships. What we haven't told you is that the majority of this money came from local scholarships! We literally won $500 here and $1,500 there. By the time we graduated from Harvard and added up all the awards, it turned out to be a huge amount. Plus, some of the local scholarships that we won were "renewable," which meant that we received that money each year we were in college. So a $500 renewable scholarship was really worth $2,000 over four years.

If you still can't get excited because these local awards seem small compared to the cost of tuition, try this exercise: Take the amount of the award and divide it by the time you invested in the application. For the $500 Lions Club award, let's say that you spent one hour each night for three days to complete the application and write the essay. Take $500 and divide it by three hours. That works out to a little over $166 per hour. (Now imagine that the award was for $1,000 instead. That would make it $333 per hour!) Not bad by any measure. If you can find a job that pays you more than $166 an hour, then take it and forget applying to scholarships. If not, get back to applying for scholarships–even the little ones!

Let's get specific and look at all of the places in your backyard to find scholarships.

✔ High school counselor or college financial aid officer

If you are a high school student, start with your counselor. Ask if he or she has a list of scholarship opportunities. Most counselors have a binder filled with local scholarships. It's helpful if before your meeting, you prepare information about your family's financial background as well as special interests or talents you have that would make you eligible for scholarships. Don't forget that your own high school will have a variety of scholarships from such places as the parent-teacher organization, alumni group and athletic booster clubs.

If you are a college student, make an appointment with your school's financial aid office. Before the appointment, think about what interests and talents you have and what field you may want to enter after graduation. Take a copy of your Free Application for Federal Student Aid (FAFSA) as background (https://studentaid.ed.gov). Mention any special circumstances about your family's financial situation. Ask the financial aid officer for recommendations of scholarships offered by the college or by community organizations.

Also, if you have already declared a major, check with the department's administrative assistant or chair for any awards that you might be eligible to win.

It's important whenever you speak to a counselor (either in high school or college) that you inquire about any scholarships that require nomination. Often these scholarships are easier to win since the applicant pool is smaller. You have nothing to lose by asking, and if anything, it shows how serious you are about financing your education.

✓ High school websites

You may not visit your school's website daily, but when you are looking for scholarships, it pays to search the site for lists of scholarships. Most high schools post scholarship opportunities for students on their websites. (You may have to dig down a few levels to find this list.)

✓ Other high school websites

If your school does not post scholarship opportunities, surf over to the websites of other high schools in the area. You'll find that many offer a wealth of scholarship resources.

✓ Nearby colleges

While your college has great scholarship resources, wouldn't it be great if you had double or triple these resources? You can. Simply seek the resources of other local colleges. Ask permission first, but you'll find that most neighboring schools are more than willing to help you. If you are in high school, nothing prevents you from visiting a local college and asking for scholarship information. Because you are a prospective student, the college will often be happy to provide whatever assistance it can.

✓ Student clubs and organizations

Here's a reason to enjoy your extracurricular activities even more. One benefit of participating may be a scholarship sponsored by the organization. Inquire with the officers or advisors of the organization about scholarship funds. Bands, newspapers, academic clubs, athletic organizations and service organizations often have scholarships that are awarded to outstanding members. If the organization has a national parent organization (e.g. National Honor Society) visit the national organization website. There are often awards that are given by the parent organization for members of local chapters.

✓ Community organizations

Maybe you've wondered why community organizations have so many breakfast fundraisers—one reason is that some provide money for scholarships.

You usually don't have to be a member of these organizations to apply. In fact, many community groups sponsor scholarships that are open to all students who live in the area. As we have mentioned, college students really have two communities: their hometown and where they go to college. Don't neglect either of these places.

How do you find these organizations? Many local government websites list them. Visit the websites for your town, city and state. Also visit or call your community association or center. You can search online to look up organizations and a calendar of annual events that are sponsored by various civic groups. Finally, don't forget to pay a visit to the public library and ask the reference librarian for help. Here is a brief list of some of the more common civic groups to track down:

- Altrusa
- American Legion and American Legion Auxiliary
- American Red Cross
- Association of Junior Leagues International
- Boys and Girls Clubs
- Boy Scouts and Girl Scouts
- Circle K
- Civitan
- Elks Club
- Lions Club
- 4-H Clubs
- Fraternal Order of Eagles
- Friends of the Library
- Kiwanis International
- Knights of Columbus
- National Exchange Club
- National Grange
- Optimist International
- Performing Arts Center
- Rotary Club
- Rotaract and Interact
- Ruritan
- Sertoma International

- Soroptimist International of the Americas
- U.S. Jaycees
- USA Freedom Corps
- Veterans of Foreign Wars
- YMCA and YWCA
- Zonta International

✔ Local businesses

Businesses like to return some of their profits to employees and students in the community. Many offer scholarships as a way to reward students who both study and work. Ask your manager if your employer has a scholarship fund and how you can apply. Some companies—particularly large conglomerates that have offices, distributorships or factories in your community—offer scholarships that all students in the community are eligible to win. Check with the chamber of commerce for a list of the largest companies in the area. You can call the public relations or community outreach department in these companies to inquire about any scholarship opportunities. Visit the large department and chain stores in the area and ask the store manager or customer service manager about scholarships.

✔ Parents' employer

Your parents may hate their jobs, but they'll love the fact that many companies award scholarships to the children of employees as a benefit. They should speak with someone in the human resources department or with their direct managers about scholarships and other educational programs offered by their company.

✔ Parents' or grandparents' military service

If your parents or grandparents served in the U.S. Armed Forces, you may qualify for a scholarship from a military association. Each branch of the service and even specific divisions within each branch have associations. Speak with your parents and grandparents about their military service and see if they belong to or know of these military associations.

✔ Your employer

Flipping burgers may have an up side. Even if you work only part-time, you may qualify for an educational scholarship given by your employer. For example, McDonald's offers the Archways to Opportunity tuition assistance to reward the accomplishments of its student-employees. If you have a full- or part-time job, ask your employer about scholarships.

✔ Parents' union

Don't know if your parents are in a union? Ask and find out. Some unions sponsor scholarships for the children of their members. Ask your parents to speak with the union officers about scholarships and other educational programs sponsored by their union.

✔ Interest clubs

Performing arts centers, city orchestras, equestrian associations and amateur sports leagues are just a few of the many special interest clubs that may offer scholarships. While some limit their awards to members, many simply look for students who are interested in what they support. A city performing arts center, for example, may offer an award for a talented performing artist in the community.

✔ Professional sports teams

They may not have won a World Series since the 1950s, but don't discount them as a viable scholarship source. Many local professional athletic teams offer community awards (and not necessarily for athletes) as a way to contribute to the cities in which they are based.

✔ Church or religious organizations

Religious organizations may provide scholarships for members. If you or your parents are members of a religious organization, check with the leaders to see if a scholarship is offered.

✔ Local government

Some cities and counties provide scholarships specifically designated for local students. Often, local city council members and state representatives sponsor a scholarship fund. Even if you didn't vote for them, call their offices and ask if they offer a scholarship.

✔ Local newspaper

Local newspapers often print announcements about students who win scholarships. Keep a record of the scholarships featured or go to the library or look online at back issues of the newspaper. Check last year's spring issues (between March and June) for announcements of scholarship recipients. Contact the sponsoring organizations to see if you're eligible to enter the next competition.

Is There a Magic Number of Scholarships?

We often are asked, "How many scholarships should I apply to?" The truth is that there is no magic number of scholarships for which you should apply. But you should avoid the extremes. Don't select only a couple of scholarships with the intention of spending countless hours crafting the perfect application. While it is true that to win you need to turn in quality applications, there is also a certain amount of subjective decision making. So even with the perfect application, you may not win. This means that you need to apply to more than a few scholarships. On the other hand, don't apply for 75 awards, sending in the same application to each. You'll just waste your time. You need to strike a balance between quantity and quality.

Searching Beyond Your Backyard

Once you have exhausted the opportunities in the community, it is time to broaden your search. Although the applicant pool is often larger with national awards, you shouldn't rule them out. Because many national award programs have marketing budgets, finding these awards may actually be easier than local awards. Most national awards will be advertised and the following places will help you track them down:

✔ Internet

Forget the time-wasting social networks, and let's use the Internet for something productive. We recommend that you use as many online scholarship databases as possible as long as they are free. There are enough quality free databases that you should not have to pay for any online search. Here are a few we recommend:

- SuperCollege (www.supercollege.com)

- Verified Scholarships (www.verifiedscholarships.com)

- moolahSPOT (www.moolahspot.com)

- Sallie Mae (www.salliemae.com/scholarships)

- FastWeb (www.fastweb.com)

- CollegeXpress (www.collegexpress.com)

- The College Board (www.collegeboard.org)

- Scholarships.com (www.scholarships.com)

- Chegg (https://www.chegg.com/scholarships)

Just remember that while many online databases claim to have billions of dollars in scholarships listed, they represent only a tiny fraction of what is available. We have personally used nearly every free scholarship database on the Internet and know from experience that none of them (including our own at www.supercollege.com) lists every scholarship that you might win. Think of these databases as starting points, and remember that they are not the only places to find awards.

✔ Professional associations

There is an association for every profession you can imagine. Whether you want to be a doctor, teacher or helicopter pilot, there are professional organizations that exist not only to advance the profession, but also to encourage students to enter that field by awarding grants and scholarships.

To find these associations, contact people who are already in the profession. If you think you want to become a computer programmer, ask computer programmers about the associations to which they belong. Also look at the trade magazines that exist for the profession since they have advertisements for various professional organizations.

Another way to find associations is through books like *The Encyclopedia of Associations*. This multi-volume set found at most college libraries lists nearly every professional association in the United States. Once you find these associations, contact them or visit their websites to see if they offer scholarships.

Professional associations often provide scholarships for upper-level college students, graduate school or advanced training. But even high school students who know what they want to do after college can find money from associations.

✔ Big business

If you've never received a personal "thank you" from large companies like Coca-Cola, Tylenol or Microsoft, here it is. A lot of these have charitable foundations that award scholarships. Companies give these awards to give something back to the community (and the positive PR sure doesn't hurt either). When you visit company websites, look for links to their foundations, which often manage the scholarship programs.

Many companies offer similar types of scholarships. What if you're a student film maker? Think about all the companies that make money or sell products to you from cameras to editing software to tripods. Are you into industrial music? What special equipment or instruments do you use? Consider the companies that will benefit from more people using their products and services. Some companies also offer awards to attract future employees. For example, Microsoft, the software company, sponsors a scholarship program for student programmers. Be sure to investigate companies that employ people in your field of study—especially if it is highly competitive—to see if they offer scholarships.

✓ Colleges

You may think that checks only travel from your pocket to your college to pay for tuition. But colleges actually give a lot of money to students. Some of this money comes from the college itself while other money is from generous donations of alumni. Every college administers a number of scholarships, some based on financial need and some based on merit. What many students don't know is that often a student's application for admission is also used by the college to determine if he or she may win a scholarship. This is one reason it is worth the submission of any optional essay suggested on a college application. Even if the essay does not impact your admission, it could be used to award you some scholarship dollars.

Don't Look for Scholarships Alone

One of the biggest mistakes we made when looking for scholarships was that we did so alone. Maybe we didn't want to share what we found with our friends and thereby increase competition, or perhaps we just didn't see the benefits of working In groups. Whatever the reason, it probably cost us a ton of money.

Since then we've met thousands of students who have won scholarships. Of these the most successful are those who did not look for scholarships alone. In fact, they made it the biggest group project imaginable.

Take for example the three guys we met in Los Angeles. Essentially, all three young men are going to college for free because they were able to win way more money than they could ever use! How did they do it? They formed a "scholarship group". Every Saturday morning they met at Starbucks and one of their parents agreed to pick up the tab for Frappuccinos. The only rule was that each had to bring at least two new scholarships. What happened was that one guy might find an award that was not right for him but was perfect for someone else in the group. This sharing of information was a tremendous advantage over laboring individually and literally tripled their chances of finding scholarships.

Another benefit was that working in a group kept these guys motivated. There certainly must have been weeks when searches were fruitless and the scholarship pickings were slim. The guys might have been tempted to give up, but being in a group brings with it a sense of responsibility not to disappoint the other members of the unit. Searching for scholarships alone is very difficult and it's so easy to just quit. But when you work in a group, you keep one another motivated and you have a natural support base that keeps you going when you feel like quitting.

So did these guys increase the competition by sharing scholarships? In some cases they did. But this was far outweighed by the sheer number of scholarships that they found collectively that they never would have found working alone.

As a general rule, students who worked with others discovered that by sharing the awards they found and pooling their resources, they were able to find more scholarships in less time than they would have found individually. The end result was that these students had more scholarships to apply to and more time to focus on their applications. Hence, they won more money.

Let this be a lesson to all of us. Look around you and find others who are also hunting for scholarships. Convince them that the way to really win lots of free money for college is to work in groups.

Prioritize the Scholarships You Find

Until now, we have focused on where to find scholarships. If you invest time exploring these areas, you should have a fairly long list of potential scholarships. It may be tempting to start cranking out applications. We actually have a name for the methodology used by students that apply to anything and everything they find—it's called the "shotgun" approach and it never works. Just because you find an award for which you qualify does not mean that you should immediately apply. You want to focus your energies (and limited time) only on those awards that you have the best chance of winning.

It would save a lot of time if you knew beforehand which scholarships you'd win and which you wouldn't. With this information, you'd only spend time applying for the scholarships that you knew would result in cash in your pocket. While there is no way to be 100 percent certain that you'll win any scholarship, you can do some research and make an educated guess.

Here are the steps you should take with each scholarship to determine if you have a reasonable chance of winning it. By prioritizing your list based on these criteria, you'll be able to focus time on awards that you have the best odds of winning while not wasting time on the ones where being a match is a long shot.

Step 1   Learn the Purpose

Nobody, and we mean nobody, gives away money without a reason. Every sponsor of a scholarship has a concrete reason for giving away their hard-earned cash to students like you. For example, a teachers' organization might award a scholarship to encourage students to enter the teaching profession. An environmental group might sponsor a scholarship with the purpose of promoting environmental awareness, or it might reward students who have done environmental work in school. A local bank might give money to a student who has done a great deal of public service as a way to give back to the community in which it does business.

Your job is to uncover the purpose of every scholarship on your list. If you're lucky, it will be stated in the description of the award. Look at the eligibility requirements to see what kind of questions the scholarship sponsors are asking. Is there a GPA requirement? If there is and it's relatively high, academic achievement is probably important. If the GPA requirement is low, then grades are probably not important. Does the application ask for a list of extracurricular activities? If so, they are probably a significant part of the selection criteria. Do you need to submit an essay on a specific topic or a project to demonstrate proficiency in a field of study? All these requirements are clues about what the scholarship judges think will (and won't) be important.

For example, the sole purpose of a public service scholarship may be to reward a student's philanthropic acts. If that is the case, the application will most likely be focused on descriptions of a student's selfless deeds. On the other hand, a scholarship given by a major corporation may be based on a combination of grades, leadership and character.

If you cannot determine the purpose of the scholarship by reading its description and eligibility requirements, then you need to look for the purpose of the group that sponsors the award. For example, even if the scholarship description does not directly state it, you can be sure that an award given by an organization that is composed of local physicians will probably prefer that the winner have a connection with medicine or an intention to enter the medical field.

The membership of the organization can be a big clue. Just as your friends are a reflection of who you are, most clubs and organizations want to reach students who are similar to their membership. If you don't know much about the organization, contact them to learn background information regarding the history, purpose or contributions of the group. Visit the organization's website. Read their brochures or publications. The more you know about why the organization is giving the award, the better you'll understand how you may or may not fit.

Somewhere on your list of potential scholarships, note in a few words its purpose. You'll be using this information in the next step which is to determine if you can make a case that you are the type of person the scholarship committee is looking for.

Beware of Scholarship Scams

While the great majority of scholarship providers and services have philanthropic intentions, not all do. There are some scholarship services and even scholarships themselves that you need to avoid. According to the Federal Trade Commission, in one year there were more than 175,000 cases reported of scholarship scams, costing consumers $22 million. And this is a low estimate since most scholarship scams go unreported!

While we were fortunate to have not been victims of a scholarship scam, we have to admit that the offers we received were tempting. We both received letters in high school and college from companies that promised to help us find and win "unclaimed" scholarships. The pitch was tempting: There is money out there that no one is claiming. All we needed to do was purchase their service to get a list of these awards. Had we done so, we would have been $400 poorer and certainly none the richer. In this chapter, we will describe some of the common scams that you may encounter. You must avoid these offers, no matter how glamorous they seem.

The key to avoiding a scholarship scam is to understand the motivation of the people behind these scams. Those who operate financial aid rip-offs know that paying for college is something that makes you extremely nervous. They also know that most people don't have extensive experience when it comes to scholarships and may therefore believe that there are such things as "hidden" or "unclaimed" scholarships. These charlatans take advantage of your fears and discomfort by offering an easy answer with a price tag that seems small compared to the promised benefits. Be aware that you are vulnerable to these kinds of inducements. Think about it this way. If you have a weakness for buying clothes, you need to be extra vigilant when you are at the shopping mall. Similarly, because you need money for college, you are more susceptible to tempting scholarship offers. Acknowledging that these fears make you a target of scam artists is the first step to spotting their traps.

Step 2   Think Like a Judge

Once you know the purpose of the scholarship, you need to see if you are a match for the organization that sponsors it. At this point students often make one of two mistakes. Either they 1) overestimate how well they fit the purpose or, more commonly, 2) underestimate their qualifications and don't apply. After working with thousands of students, we have learned that students more often underestimate their abilities than overestimate. Try to be realistic, but also don't sell yourself short. Remember that scholarship judges are not looking for the perfect match. There are a lot of factors that will influence their decision, and many of these things—like personality, character and motivation—are difficult to measure.

Let's look at an example. If you are your school's star journalist, naturally you should apply for journalism scholarships. But if all you have done is write a single letter to the editor, then spend your time applying to scholarships that better match what you have accomplished. You can still apply for a journalism scholarship, especially if you only recently realized that you want to become a journalist, but you will be at a disadvantage compared to the other applicants and therefore should prioritize this award below other awards on your to-do list.

As you go through your list of scholarships, move to the bottom those which are the weakest matches to the goal of the scholarships. Make those awards that fit you best your highest priority. These are the ones that you want to focus on first.

Step 3 | Take a Reality Check

Scholarship deadlines are not like tax deadlines, where there is a single day when all forms are due. The deadlines for scholarships vary. Be aware of these crucial dates. Unless you plan carefully, you may miss out on a scholarship simply because you don't have the time to create a decent application. Sandwiched among studying, sleeping and everything else in your busy life, there is limited time to spend on applying for scholarships. If you find a great scholarship that is due next week but requires a yet to-be-written original composition that would take a month, you should probably pass on the competition. If you know that, given the amount of time available, you won't be able to do an acceptable job, it's better to pass and move on to awards in which you have the time to put together a winning application. Remember too that you may be able to apply for the award next year.

Review Your List Daily

After you prioritize your scholarships with the ones you feel fit you best at the top of the list, push yourself to apply to as many as you can, working from top to bottom. You probably won't get to the end. This is okay since you have the least chance of winning the awards at the bottom anyway. By prioritizing and working methodically down your list, you will have hedged your bets by making sure that your first applications are for the scholarships that you have the best chance of winning while also not limiting yourself to only a handful of awards.

How to Win the Scholarships You Find

Attacking the Scholarship Application

At first glance, scholarship applications look easy—most are only a single page in length. Piece of cake, right? Don't let their diminutive size fool you. The application is a vital part of winning any scholarship. Scholarship judges must sift through hundreds or even thousands of applications, and the application form is what they use to determine which applicants continue to the next stage. It's crucial that you ace your application to make this first cut.

In this chapter, we'll look at strategies you can use to transform an ordinary scholarship application form into a screaming testament of why you deserve to win free cash for college.

Five Steps to Crafting a Winning Application

Step 1   Strategically Choose What to List

Imagine that you need to give a speech to two groups of people. Without knowing who your audience is, you would have a difficult time composing a speech that would appeal to them, right? It would make a huge difference if one were a group of mathematicians and the other a group of fashion designers. To grab the attention of each of these audiences, you'd need to adjust your speech accordingly. References to mathematical theorems would hardly go over well with the designers, just as the mathematicians probably couldn't care less about how black the "new" black really is.

In much the same way, you need to decide what to highlight on your scholarship application based on the purpose of the award. When you know what the scholarship judges are looking for, it makes it easier to decide what to include or omit. As we mentioned earlier, organizations don't give away scholarships and expect nothing in return. Behind their philanthropic motives lies an ulterior motive—to promote their organization's purpose. If you prioritized your list of scholarships correctly, you've already uncovered the purpose for each award. Now look at all your activities, interests, hobbies and achievements. Ask yourself which ones fit the purpose of each award and would make a positive impression on the scholarship judges.

Let's imagine that you are applying for an award given by an organization of professional journalists. In visiting their website, you learn that print and broadcast journalists join this group because they are passionate about the profession of journalism and want to encourage public awareness about the importance of a free press. Immediately, you know that you need to highlight those experiences that demonstrate your zeal for journalism and, if applicable, your belief in the value of a free press.

Among your activities and accomplishments are the following:

- Soccer team captain

- Vice President of the Writers' Club

- Key Club treasurer

- Columnist for your high school newspaper

- English essay contest winner

- Summer job working at a pet store

- Summer internship at a radio station

As you look at this list, you can eliminate some activities outright. Your involvement on the soccer team, with the Key Club, and your job at the pet store are not relevant and don't show how you fit with the purpose of the scholarship.

However, even looking at what's left, you still have to decide which ones to list first. As you think about the purpose of the scholarship, you remember that in the Writers' Club you participated in a workshop that helped a local elementary school start its own newspaper. Since this achievement almost perfectly matches the mission of our hypothetical journalism organization, use your limited space in the application to list it first and to add an explanation.

You might write something like this:

```
Writers' Club, Vice President, organized "Writing Counts"
workshop at Whitman Elementary School, which resulted in the
launch of the school's first student-run newspaper.
```

Think of the impact this would have on the scholarship judges. "Look here, Mark!" one journalist on the judging committee would say. "This student does what we do! Definitely someone we should interview!"

When choosing accomplishments to list, don't be afraid to eliminate any that don't fit—even good ones. You have limited space in which to cram a lot of information. As you fill out the application, you may find that you are trying to squeeze in too many details or simply too many things. You need to be ruthless in trimming down what you submit to the judges. Make sure to include the accomplishments that *best fit* the purpose of the award.

At the same time you are picking which things to include in your application, be sure to also be aware of what might be offensive to the organization's members. Just imagine what would happen if you thoughtlessly mentioned that you were the author of an economics project entitled "How Labor Unions Make the U.S. Unable to Compete and Lower Our Standard of Living" to judges who are members of the International Brotherhood of Teamsters.

Clearly you can't use the same list of activities and accomplishments for every scholarship. You must take the time to craft a unique list that matches what each of the scholarships is intended to reward.

Create a Timeline

Every scholarship has a deadline. Even though you have created a prioritized list of awards, you need also be aware of the deadlines. In fact, the due date for an award may also influence how you prioritize it. It's also helpful to set yourself deadlines and create a schedule for applying. Set deadlines for when you will have the application forms completed, essays written and any required recommendations submitted. Post this schedule where you can see it every day. We also recommend that you share it with your parents. Moms and dads are great at nagging (we mean reminding) you to meet deadlines, so you might as well use their nagging (we mean motivating) skills to your advantage.

Step 2 List Important Accomplishments First

In movies, the most dare-devilish car chase, the most harrowing showdown and the most poignant romantic revelations are usually saved until the end. While this works for Hollywood, it does not for scholarship applications. Since scholarship judges review so many applications and the space on the form is limited, you must learn to highlight your most impressive points first.

If you have listed four extracurricular activities, assume that some judges won't read beyond the first two. This doesn't mean that all judges will be this rushed, but there are always some who are. It's extremely important that you prioritize the information that you present and rank your accomplishments according to the following criteria—which should not come as too much of a surprise.

Fit: The most important factor in ordering your achievements is how they fit with the purpose of the scholarship. This is, after all, why these kind people want to hand you some free dough. Emphasize accomplishments that match the purpose of the scholarship. If you are applying for an award that rewards athleticism, stress how well you've done in a particular sport before listing your volunteer activities.

Scope: Next prioritize your accomplishments by their scope, or how much of an impact they have made. How many people have been affected by your work? To what extent has your accomplishment affected your community? Did your contribution produce measurable results? In simple terms, put the big stuff before the small stuff.

Uniqueness: Since your application will be compared to those of perhaps thousands of others, include accomplishments that are uncommon. Give priority to those that are unique or difficult to win. Being on your school's honor roll is certainly an achievement, but it is an honor that many others have received. Try to select honors that fewer students have received—you want to stand out in order to be selected.

Timeliness: This is the least-important criterion, but if you get stuck and aren't sure how to arrange some of your accomplishments, put the more recent achievements first. Having won an election in the past year is more relevant than having won one three years ago. Some students ask us if they should list junior high or even elementary school achievements. Generally, stick to accomplishments from high school if you're a high school student and to college if you're a college student. An exception is if your accomplishment is extremely impressive and relevant—such as publishing your own book in the eighth grade. Of course, if you run out of recent achievements and there is still space on the form, go ahead and reach back to the past— but try to limit yourself to only one or two items.

You want your application to be as unforgettable as the best Hollywood movies. The only difference between your work and Spielberg's—besides the millions of dollars—is that you need to place the grand finale first.

You Can Recycle Your Applications

The first scholarship for which you apply will take the most time. But with each application you complete, it will get easier. This is because for each successive application, you can draw on the materials you developed for the previous one. To complete your first application, you need to think about your activities and recall achievements that you have forgotten. If there is an essay component, you will need to find a topic and craft an articulate essay. When you work on your second application, you can benefit from the work you've already done for the first. As you're building your timeline, look for scholarships in which you can recycle information from one application to another.

> Recycling will save you time. In addition, you can improve on your work each time that you use it. For example, the second time you answer a question about your plans after graduation, you can craft your response more effectively than the first. As you recycle information, don't just reuse it—improve it!

Step 3   Spin Your Application to Impress the Judges

Politicians are notorious for telling voters what they want to hear. Good politicians never lie, but they do put a flattering "spin" on their words depending on whom they're addressing. While you must never lie on your application forms, you do want to present yourself in the best possible way so that you appeal to your audience. In other words, employ a little spin.

We know that some politicians have a difficult time distinguishing between lying and spinning. You shouldn't. Let's say you are applying for a scholarship that rewards students who are interested in promoting literacy. You have been a volunteer at your local library where, aside from typical page duties each week, you also read stories to a dozen children for story time. Here are three ways you could describe this activity on your application:

Non-spin description:
```
Library volunteer.
```

Lie:
```
Library reading program founder. Started a national program
that reaches thousands of children every day to promote
literacy.
```

Spin:
```
Library volunteer. Promoted literacy among children through
weekly after-school reading program at public library.
```

At one extreme, you can see that a lie exaggerates well beyond the truth. At the other extreme, the non-spin description is not very impressive because it does not explain how the activity relates to the purpose of the scholarship. The spin version is just right. It does not stretch the truth, but it does make clear how this activity fits within the context of the purpose of the scholarship. It focuses on what is important to the judges while at the same time, it ignores other aspects of your job that are not relevant—such as shelving books.

To take this example one step further, let's say that now you are applying for a scholarship that rewards student leaders. One of your other responsibilities as a library volunteer is to maintain the schedule for volunteers and help with the recruitment of new volunteers. Your description for this scholarship might read something like this:

```
Library volunteer. In charge of volunteer schedule and re-
cruitment of new members.
```

Notice how you have "spun" your activity so that it highlights a different aspect of what you did and better shows the judges how you fit their criteria. In the application, you should use the opportunity to spin your accomplishments to match the purpose of the award.

To be able to spin effectively, you need to know your audience. When you prioritized your scholarships earlier, you should have discovered the purpose of each scholarship. Remember that in most cases the scholarship judges want to give their money to students who are the best reflections of themselves. For example, the Future Teachers of America judges will want to fund students who seem the most committed to pursuing a teaching career. The American Congress of Surveying and Mapping judges, on the other hand, want to award their money to students who have the strongest interest in cartography.

Step 4   Write to Impress

The inspiring words of Martin Luther King Jr.'s "I Have a Dream" speech were punctuated with his dramatic, emotion-filled voice, hopeful expression and confident presence. His delivery would not have been as forceful had he spoken in a drab, monotone, with hands stuffed into his pockets and eyes lowered to avoid contact with the audience. Nor would his dramatic presentation have been as effective had his message been unimportant. The lesson? Both content and delivery count. While you don't have the opportunity for person-to-person delivery with your scholarship applications, you can and should present information in a compelling way. Here are some time-tested writing strategies for creating a positive impression through your applications:

Showcase Your Smarts. There's a reason why your parents wanted you to study and do well in school. In addition to the correlation between studying and success in college, almost all scholarship judges (even those of athletic awards) are impressed by academic achievement. College is, after all, about learning (at least that's what you want your parents to believe).

As you are completing your applications, keep in mind that while you may be applying for a public service scholarship, you should also include at least one academic achievement. For example, it does not hurt to list on an athletic scholarship form that you also came in second place at the science fair. This should not be the first thing you list, but it should be included somewhere to show the committee that you have brains in addition to brawn.

Extracurricular Activities and Hobbies Show Your Passion. If your only activity were studying, your life would be severely lacking in excitement. Scholarship organizers recognize this and thus the criteria for many scholarships include extracurricular activities or hobbies. Scholarship committees want evidence that you do more than read textbooks, take exams and watch

Youtube. They want to know that you have other interests. This makes you a more well-rounded person.

As always, when completing your applications, select extracurricular activities and hobbies that fit with the scholarship's mission. If you are applying for a music scholarship, describe how you've been involved in your school's orchestra or how you've taken violin lessons. By showing that you not only have taken classes in music theory but have also been involved with music outside of your studies, the scholarship committee will get a more complete picture of your love for music. Remember to use your activities and hobbies to illustrate your passion for a subject.

Leadership Is Always Better Than Membership. If you've ever tried to motivate a group of peers to do anything (without taking the easy way out—bribery) you know that it takes courage, intelligence and creativity to be a leader. Because of this, many scholarships give extra points to reward leadership. Scholarship judges want to know that the dollars will be awarded to someone who will not only make a difference in the future but who will also be a leader and motivate others to do the same. Think of it this way: If you were a successful businessperson trying to encourage entrepreneurship, wouldn't you want to give your money to a young person who is not only an entrepreneur but who also motivates others to become entrepreneurs?

Describing leadership in your activities or hobbies will also help set you apart from the other applicants. Many students are involved with environmental groups, but what if you are the only one to actually help increase recycling on your campus? Wouldn't that make your application a standout?

To show scholarship judges that you are a leader, list any activities in which you took responsibility for a specific project. Use action verbs when describing your work:

- Organized band fundraiser to purchase new instruments

- Led a weeklong nature tour in Yosemite Valley

- Founded first website to list volunteer activities

- Directed independent musical performance

Remember that you don't need to be an elected officer to be a leader. Many students have organized special projects, led teams or helped run events. Even if you didn't have an official title, you can include these experiences. Here's an example:

`Environmental Action Committee Member. Spearheaded subcommittee on reducing waste and increasing recycling on campus.`

When describing your leadership, include both formal and informal ways you have led groups. This shows the scholarship committee that you are a worthy investment.

Honors and Awards Validate Your Strengths. There's a reason why all trophies are gold and gaudy. They shout to the world in a deafening roar, "Yes, this glittery gold miniature figure means I am the best!" For applications that ask for your honors and awards, impart some of that victorious roar and attitude. In no way are we recommending that you ship your golden statuettes off with your applications. We are saying that you should highlight honors and awards in a way that gets the scholarship committee to pay attention to your application. What makes an award impressive is scope. Not a minty mouthwash, scope in this case is the impact and influence of the award. You worked for the award and earned every golden inch of it. Show the committee that they don't just hand these statuettes out to anybody. One way to do this is to point out how many awards are given:

```
English Achievement Award. Presented to two outstanding ju-
niors each year.
```

By itself, the English Achievement Award does not tell the scholarship committee very much. Maybe half the people in your class were given the award. By revealing the scope of the award (particularly if it was given to only a few) it becomes much more impressive.

In competitions that reach beyond your school, it is important to qualify your awards. For example, while everyone at your school may know that the Left Brain Achievement Award is given to creative art students, the rest of the world does not.

Don't write:
```
Left Brain Achievement Award.
```

Do write:
```
Left Brain Achievement Award. Recognized as an outstanding
creative talent in art as conferred upon by vote of art de-
partment faculty.
```

You've worked hard to earn the honors and awards that you have received, and you should not hesitate to use them in your applications to help you win scholarships.

Know when to leave a space blank. An official mom rule from childhood is this: "If you don't have anything nice to say, don't say it." While this is a good lesson on self-restraint, it does not always hold true for scholarship applications. In general, it is not a good idea to leave any area blank. You don't need to fill the entire space, but you should make an effort to list something in every section. However, before you try to explain how the handmade certificate that your mom presented you for being Offspring of the Year qualifies as an "award," realize that there are limits. If you've never held a job, don't list anything under work experience. If, however, you painted your grandmother's house one summer and got paid for it, you might consider listing it if you don't have any other options.

Perfect every sentence. Succinct and terse, scholarship application forms bear the well-earned reputation for having less space than you need. Often offering only a page or less, scholarship and award forms leave little room for much more than just the facts. As you are completing your applications, remember to abbreviate where appropriate and keep your sentences short. Often judges are scanning the application form. If they want an essay, they will ask for one. However, you do not want to take instructions so literally that you miss their intent. For instance, if the instructions say to list your awards, don't feel like you can't add explanation if you need to. And, as always, be selective in what you list. If you have three great awards, it is better to use your space to list those three with short explanations rather than cram in all 15 awards that you've won in your life. (No argument can be made for the timeliness of your Perfect Attendance Award from kindergarten.) You are trying to present the most relevant information that shows the scholarship judges why you deserve their money. Use the space to explain how each award, job or activity relates to the scholarship.

Also, feel free to interpret some instructions. Work experience does not have to be limited to traditional jobs. Maybe you started your own freelance design business or cut lawns on the weekends—those count! The same goes for leadership positions. Who said that leadership has to be an elected position within an organization? Just be sure to explain the entry if the relationship is not totally clear. Here's an example:

```
Volunteer Wilderness Guide. Led clients through seven-day
trek in Catskills. Responsible for all aspects of the trip
including group safety.
```

Always remember that the application is you. A scholarship application is more than just a form. In the eyes of the scholarship judges, it is *you*. It may not be fair, but in many cases the application is the only thing that the judges will have as a measurement standard. The last thing you want to be is a dry list of academic and extracurricular achievements. You are a living, breathing person. Throughout the application, take every opportunity—no matter how small—to show the judges who you really are. Use descriptions and vocabulary that reveal your passion and commitment. Always remember that the application is a reflection of you.

Step 5 Separate Yourself from the Competition

Think of the scholarship competition as a reverse police lineup where you want to stand out and be picked by the people behind the one-way mirror. You want the judge to say without hesitation, "That's the one!" The only way this will happen is if your application is noticed and doesn't get lost in the stack. One of the best ways to accomplish this is to know what you're up against—in other words, think about who else will be in the lineup with you.

Try to anticipate your competition—even if it's just an educated guess. Depending on to whom the scholarship is offered, you may have a limited or broad pool of competitors. If the award is confined to your school, you may know everyone who will enter on a first-name basis. If it's national, all you may know is that all the applicants have a similar interest in a broad field. For a medical scholarship, for instance, the applicants might be students interested in becoming doctors or nurses. More important than the scope of the competition is the type of students who will apply. One of the biggest challenges in any competition is to break away from the pack. If 500 pre-med students are applying for a $10,000 scholarship from a medical association, you need to make sure that your application stands out from those of the 499 other applicants. If you are lucky, you may have done something that few have done. (Inventing a new vaccine in your spare time would certainly set you apart!) Unfortunately, most of us will have to distinguish ourselves in more subtle ways, such as through the explanation of our activities and accomplishments.

Say you are applying for a scholarship given by a national medical association that seeks to promote the medical sciences. It just so happens that you are considering a pre-med major and you have interned at a local hospital. If you hadn't read this book, you might have listed under activities something like this entry:

`Summer Internship at Beth Israel Children's Hospital.`

But you did read this book! So you know that this is a great activity to elaborate on since it demonstrates your commitment to medicine and shows that you truly are interested in entering the medical field. You also know that you need to stand out from the competition; and as great as this activity is, you know that a lot of other applicants also will have volunteered at hospitals. So instead of simply listing the internship, you add detail to make the experience more unique. You could write it this way:

`Summer Internship at Beth Israel Children's Hospital; assisted with clinical trial of new allergy medication.`

This description is much more unique and memorable. By providing details, you can illustrate to the judges how your volunteer work is different from that of other students. Remember that you can add short descriptions in most applications even if the instructions do not explicitly ask for them.

If you can anticipate who your competition will be and what they might write in their applications, you will be able to find a way to go one step further to distinguish yourself from the crowd. Even the simple act of adding a one-sentence description to an activity can make the difference between standing out or being overlooked.

Now that you know the five steps to insure that your application is a winner, here is our Top Ten list of application form do's and don'ts which will serve as a final reminder of how to create that stunning application!

Be a Neat and Detail Freak

You may have dirty laundry strewn across your room and a pile of papers large enough to be classified as its own life form, but you don't want the scholarship judges to know that. When it comes to applications, neatness and attention to detail do count. We would not ordinarily be neatness zealots—we admit to having our own mountains of life-imbibed papers—but submitting an application with misspellings, missing words or grammatical errors will severely diminish your message. Think how much less impressive the Mona Lisa would be if da Vinci had painted it on a dirty old bed sheet. You may have the most incredible thoughts to convey in your applications, but if your form is filled with errors, none of it will matter. In a sea of hundreds and even thousands of other applications, you don't want yours to be penalized by sloppy presentation.

Top Ten Application Do's and Don'ts

With money on the table, it's much better to learn from others' successes and mistakes before you risk your own fortunes. From interviews with students and scholarship judges and firsthand experience reviewing scholarship applications, we've developed our Top Ten list of scholarship application do's and don'ts. Let's shed the negative energy first and start with the don'ts.

Don'ts

1. DON'T prioritize quantity over quality. It's not the quantity of your accomplishments that is important. It's the quality of your contributions.

2. DON'T stretch the truth. Tall tales are prohibited.

3. DON'T squeeze to the point of illegibility. Scholarship applications afford minimal space. It's impossible to fit in everything that you want to say. Don't try by sacrificing legibility.

4. DON'T write when you have nothing to say. If you don't have something meaningful to present, leave it blank.

5. DON'T forget to edit and proofread.

6. DON'T procrastinate. Don't think you can finish your applications the night before they're due.

7. DON'T settle for less than perfect. You can have imperfections. Just don't let the selection committee know.

8. DON'T miss deadlines. No matter the reason, if you miss the deadline, you won't win the scholarship.

9. DON'T turn in incomplete applications. Make sure your application is finished before sending it.

10. DON'T underestimate what you can convey. Scholarship applications

may appear to be short and simple. Don't undervalue them. In a small space, you can create a powerful story of why you should win.

And now the good stuff.

Do's

1. DO understand the scholarship's mission. Know why they're giving out the dough.

2. DO remember who your audience is. You need to address animal rights activists and retired dentists differently.

3. DO show how you fit with the scholarship's mission. You're not going to win unless you have what the selection committee wants.

4. DO be proud of your accomplishments. Don't be afraid to brag.

5. DO focus on leadership and contributions. Make your contributions known.

6. DO make your application stand out.

7. DO practice to make sure everything fits. Make practice copies of the original form before you begin filling it out. Then use your spare copies for trial and error. If you apply electronically, edit so everything fits.

8. DO get editors. They'll help you create the best, error-free applications you can.

9. DO include a resume. Whether they ask for it or not, make sure you include a tailored scholarship resume. See the next chapter for how to create a great resume.

10. DO take photos of or download your finished applications for reference. Save them for next year when you do this all over again.

Double Check Your App

Once you've completed your applications, check and double-check for accuracy. Look at every line and every question to make sure you've filled out all the information that is requested on the form. Make sure you have someone else take a look at your application. A second set of eyes may catch mistakes that you invariably will miss. Remember that presentation affects how scholarship judges view applications. You want to convey that you are serious about winning the scholarship by submitting an application that is complete and error-free.

Finally, before submitting your application, save or print a copy. If for some reason your application form is lost, you have a copy to resend. Plus, by saving this year's applications, you have recycling possibilities (especially the essays: you'll see what we mean in Chapter 4!) and a great starting place for next year's scholarships.

How to Write a Winning Scholarship Essay

chapter 4

The Essay Can Make or Break Your Chances of Winning

Here's a situation repeated a million times each year. A student receives a scholarship application and quickly glances over the form. It looks pretty straightforward, so it's tossed into the "to do" pile. The day before it's due, the student finally gets around to filling it out. Breezing through the application form, the student is about to celebrate finishing when he or she encounters the final requirement. It reads as follows:

In 1894 Donald VonLudwig came to America with 10 cents in his pocket and within a decade built an empire. Write an 800-word essay on how you would incorporate the lessons of VonLudwig's success into your life.

Uh, oh. Life just got harder. Meet the dreaded scholarship essay. The hypothetical student described above—the one we are poking fun at—was one of us! After a few experiences like this one, (which were usually accompanied by all night writing sessions), we learned to work on the essay first and never underestimate how much time it requires.

For most scholarship competitions, it is the essay that will make or break your chances of winning. Why? Because the essay offers you the best chance to show the scholarship judges why you deserve to win. While your application form will get you to the semifinals, it is the essay that will carry you into the winner's circle.

Since the essay is so important, you must not assume that you can crank out a quality essay the night before it's due. A quality essay will take both time and effort. In this chapter we will take you step by step through the process of crafting a winning essay—don't worry, it's easier than you may have imagined. Plus, you will read examples of essays that won thousands of dollars in scholarships. From these, you can see firsthand how the strategies presented in this chapter are actually put to use in real life.

All Essays Ask the Same Underlying Question

Regardless of the specific wording, the underlying question for almost all essay questions is the same: "Why do you deserve to win?" (Your answer should *not* be, "Because I need the money!")

Think about these questions: The Future Teachers of America scholarship asks you to write about the "future of education". The Veterans of Foreign Wars asks you to define "patriotism". The National Sculpture Society asks you to "describe your extracurricular passions". Believe it or not, all these seemingly different questions are asking for the same answer: Why do you deserve to win our money?

Your answers to each must address this underlying question. When writing the Future Teachers of America essay, you can discuss the general state of education and quote a few facts and figures, but you'd better be sure to include how you personally fit into the future of education. If you are planning to be a teacher, you might elaborate on how you will contribute to shaping students' lives. Similarly use the topic of patriotism to impress the VFW judges with not only what you perceive patriotism to be but also how you have actually acted upon those beliefs. And if you answer the National Sculpture Society question with an essay on how much you love to play the guitar, then you really don't deserve to win!

Six Steps to Writing a Winning Scholarship Essay

By now you should be tired of hearing us repeat our mantra of knowing the purpose of the scholarship. You have used this to guide your selection of those scholarships you are most likely to win and how to complete the application form for them. It shouldn't surprise you that you must also use it to guide your essay. Remember, when you are writing about why you deserve to win, the answer and all the examples that you use should show how you fulfill that mission of the scholarship. With this in mind, let's begin our six steps to writing a winning scholarship essay.

Step 1   Find the Right Topic and Approach

You will encounter two types of essay questions. The first asks you to write about a specific topic. For example, "Why is it important to protect our natural environment?" The second type of question gives you a very broad topic such as, "Tell us about yourself." In the first case you don't need to think about a topic, but you do need to develop an approach to answering the question. In the latter you need to come up with both a topic and an approach. Let's look at how this is done, starting with the more difficult task of finding a topic.

Finding a Topic

Let's imagine that you are applying for a scholarship that presents an essay question so broad that you can essentially choose your own topic. To get the ideas flowing, you should use that idea-generating technique you learned in fifth grade—brainstorming. Take out a notebook or start a new file on your computer and just start listing possible topics and themes. Ask yourself questions like these:

- What was a significant event in my life?

- What teacher, relative or friend has influenced who I am?

- What have I learned from my experiences?

- What are my goals for the future?

- Where will I be ten years from now?

- What motivates me to achieve my goals?

When brainstorming, don't be critical of the topics you unearth—just let the creativity flow. Ask parents and friends for suggestions.

Once you have a list of topics, you can start to eliminate those that don't help you answer the question of why you deserve to win. For example, if you apply to a scholarship that rewards public service, you would not want to write about the time you got lost in the woods for three days and had to survive on a single candy bar and wild roots. While that might make an interesting and exciting essay, it does not show the scholarship judges why you are the epitome of public service. This topic, however, may come in handy when you need to write an essay for a scholarship based on character or leadership or why you love Snickers bars.

After you whittle down your list to a few topics that will help show why you deserve to win this particular scholarship, then choose the topic that is the most interesting to you or that you care about the most. It seems self-evident, but surprisingly many students do not select topics that excite them. Why is it important to pick a topic that you are passionate about? Because if you truly like your topic, you will write a better essay. In fact, your enthusiasm and excitement will naturally permeate your writing, which will make it interesting and memorable. It's so much easier to stay motivated writing about something you enjoy rather than something you find boring.

How to Develop a Unique Approach

Whether you have to think of a topic yourself or one is given to you, the next task is to figure out how you are going to approach it. For any given topic there are probably a hundred ways you could address the subject matter in an essay. Most topics are also way too large to completely cover in an 800- to 1,000-word essay, so you are going to have to narrow it down and only share a small part of the larger story. All this involves coming up with an approach to what you will present in your essay—an approach that must convince the judges that you deserve to win their money.

How to Write
a Winning
Scholarship Essay

Let's take a look at writing about the traumatic experience of being lost in the woods for three days. You choose this topic since the scholarship wants to reward students with strong character and leadership and this is an experience that you believe shows both. But how do you write about it? If you just retell the story of the ordeal, it will not help the judges see why such an experience reveals the quality of your character or leadership. You need to dig deeper and think about how this experience revealed your strengths. To do this, ask yourself questions like these:

- What does this topic reveal about me?

- How has my life been changed by this experience?

- Why did I do what I did?

- What is the lesson that I learned from this experience?

- What aspect of this topic is most important to making my point?

In thinking about your experience alone in the woods, you may realize that on the second day you came close to breaking down and losing all hope of being rescued. This was the critical point where you had to make a decision to give up or push forward. You decide to focus your essay only on this small sliver of time, what went through your mind and how you decided that you were not going to give up. The details of how you got lost and of your eventual rescue would be unimportant and may be mentioned in only a sentence or two. Focusing your essay on just the second day—and more particularly on how you were able to conquer your fears and not lose hope—would clearly demonstrate to the judges that even under extreme pressure, your true character was revealed. Since you also need to address the leadership aspect, you decide to focus on how you took charge of your fears on the second day. To do this, your essay will describe specific actions you took to lead yourself successfully through this ordeal.

Finding the right approach is just as important as finding the right topic. This is especially true if you answer a question that provides a specific topic. With every scholarship applicant writing about the same topic, you need to be sure that your approach persuasively shows the judges why you deserve to win more than anyone else.

Step 2   Share a Slice of Life

Now that you have a topic and an idea for your approach, you need to decide how you are going to convey your message on paper. Keep in mind that scholarship judges are going to read hundreds if not thousands of essays. Often the essays will be on similar topics, particularly if the topic was given in the scholarship application. Therefore, you need to make sure that your writing is original. The best way to do this is to share a "slice of your life" in the essay.

Imagine that you are writing about your summer trip to Europe. Travel is a very common topic. If you decide to write about how your trip made you realize people from around the world are really quite similar, then you run the real risk of sounding just like every other travel essay. The same would be true for writing about sports. If you tell the story of how your team rallied and came from behind to win the game, you can be sure that it will sound like many other essays about sports. To make sure your essay is original, you need to share a "slice of life." Find one incident that happened during your travels or pick one particular moment in the game and use that to make your point. By focusing on a single day, hour or moment, you greatly reduce your chances of having an essay that sounds like everyone else's. Plus, essays that share a slice of life are usually a lot more interesting and memorable.

Let's look at an example. What if you choose to write about how your mom has been your role model? Moms are one of the most popular role models for essays (and they should be, considering the pain of childbirth). How do you make your mom distinct from all the other applicants writing about their moms? Go ahead and take a moment to think about your mom. Be very specific. Can you find one character trait or incident that really influenced you? Let's say your mom has an obsession with collecting porcelain figurines and this passion led to you becoming interested in collecting baseball cards. Because of this, you are now considering a career in sports management. Now we have something! Imagine that first day when you realized how much your mom loved collecting figurines. Maybe you even bought her one as a present and now she cherishes it above all others. Perhaps it was that moment that jump-started your love for baseball cards, which has now developed into a full blown obsession with sports to the point that you intend to make it a career. You've just succeeded in turning a very popular topic—Mom—into an entirely original essay by finding that slice of life. No two people share the exact same slice of life, so by finding one to share, you are almost always guaranteed to have an original essay.

Want another example? Let's set the stage. Imagine that you are applying to a scholarship for students who major in psychology. The question posed on the application is this: "Tell us about an influential person who inspired you to pursue psychology." As you brainstorm, you list the authors of books you've read and some professors whose classes you have enjoyed. But how many students will be writing about these same people? You could even wager money that every other essay will be about Freud!

As you brainstorm, you recall the worst fight you have ever had with your best friend Susan. As you think about this fight that nearly destroyed a 10-year friendship, you realize that it was one of the first times you applied classroom knowledge to a real life experience. In analyzing the fight, you realize that those psychology principles you studied have practical applications beyond the textbook. So for your essay you decide to write about the fight and how it made you even more committed than ever to become a psychology major.

You don't have to look far to find originality. We all have experiences that are unique to us. Even common experiences can be made original, depending on how you approach them. So don't exclude a topic just because it is common. By spending some time thinking about how you will write about it, you may be surprised at how original it could be.

Step 3   Stop Thinking, Start Writing

The most challenging part of writing a scholarship essay is getting started. Our advice: Just start writing. The first words you put down on paper may not be brilliant, but don't worry. You can always return to edit your work. It's easier to edit words you've already written than words that don't exist.

Do you think you have a bad case of writer's block? If so, the cure may surprise you. The best cure for writer's block is to just start writing!

We all have different writing styles, but certain points should be kept in mind as you are writing something that is focused on winning over a scholarship committee. Think about these things as you craft that winning essay:

Write for the Scholarship Judges. Let's pretend you're a stand-up comedian who has two performances booked: one at the trendiest club in town where all cool college students congregate and the other at a retirement home. As a skilled comedian, you would prepare different material aimed at the different audiences. The college crowd would be able to relate to jokes about relationships and dating, while your jokes about dentures and arthritis would probably—and this is a hunch—go over better with the senior citizens. The same goes for writing your essays. Since many are given by specialized organizations or for specific purposes, you need to write an essay that is appropriate for the audience. Think about who is going to read your essay. Is your audience natural science professors, circus performers or used car salesmen? Write your essay so it appeals to that audience. This should guide not only your selection of topics but also your word choice, language and tone.

Be Yourself. While you want to present yourself in a way that attracts the attention of the scholarship judges, you don't want to portray yourself as someone you are not. It's okay to present selected highlights from your life that fit with the award, but it's not ethical to exaggerate or outright lie. If you apply for a scholarship to promote the protection of animals, don't write about your deep compassion for helping animals when you've never ventured closer than 10 feet to one because of your allergies. Feel comfortable about everything you write, and don't go overboard trying to mold yourself into being the student you think the scholarship judges want to read about. If you've done your job of picking scholarships that match you best, you already know that you are a good fit. Your task in the essay is to demonstrate this to the judges.

Personalize Your Essay. Think of the scholarship judges as an audience that has come to see your Broadway show. You are the star. To keep them satisfied, give them what they want. In other words, the scholarship judges want to know about your life and experiences. When you write your essay, write about what has happened to you personally or about how you personally have been affected by something. If you are writing about drug abuse for an essay about a problem that faces college students today, do more than recite the latest national drug use statistics and the benefits of drug rehabilitation programs. Otherwise, your essay may be informative, but it won't be interesting. Instead, write about how a friend nearly overdosed on drugs, how others tried to pressure you into trying drugs or about your volunteer work at a rehabilitation clinic. Instantly, your essay will be more interesting and memorable. Plus, the judges really do want to learn more about you, and the only way for them to do this is if you share something about yourself in your essay.

Make Sure You Have a Point. Try this exercise: See if you can encapsulate the point of your essay into a single sentence. If you can't, you don't have a main point. So, you'd better get one! You may think this is obvious, but many students' essays don't have a main point. Use that most basic lesson from Composition 101: Have a thesis statement that states the main point of your essay. Let's say you are writing about growing up in the country. You might structure your essay around the idea that growing up in the country gave you a strong work ethic. This is the essay's main point. You can describe all the flat land and brush you like, but unless these descriptions help to support your point, you don't have a quality essay.

Support Your Statement. Once you put your main point out there, you can't abandon it. Like a baby learning to walk, you have to support your thesis statement because it can't stand on its own. This means you have to provide reasons why your statement is true. You can do this by giving detailed and vivid examples from your personal experiences and accomplishments.

Use Examples and Illustrations. When a reader can visualize what you are writing, it helps to make an impression. Anecdotes and stories accomplish this very effectively. Examples and illustrations also make your ideas clearer. If you want to be a doctor, explain how you became interested in becoming one. You might describe the impact of getting a stethoscope from your father when you were a child. Or maybe you can write about your first day volunteering at the hospital. Examples help readers picture what you are saying and even relate to your experiences. The scholarship judge may have never volunteered at a hospital; but by reading your example, that judge can easily understand how such an experience could be so influential. The one danger of examples is that you need to be sure to keep them concise. It is often too easy to write a long and detailed example when only a few sentences are sufficient. Remember, in an example you are not retelling an entire story but just pulling out a few highlights to illustrate the point you are trying to make.

Show Activity. If you were forced to sit in an empty room with nothing but a bare wall to stare at, you would probably get bored pretty quickly. The same goes for an essay. Don't force the scholarship judges to read an essay that does nothing. Your essay needs activity and movement to bring it to life. This may consist of dialogue, action, stories and thoughts. The last thing you want to do is bore your readers. With action, you won't have to worry about that!

Highlight Your Growth. You may not have grown an inch since seventh grade, but scholarship judges will look for your growth in other ways. They want to see evidence of emotional and intellectual growth, what your strengths are and how you have developed them. Strengths may include—but certainly aren't limited to—mastery of an academic course, musical talent, a desire to help others, athletic ability, leadership of a group and more. Overcoming adversity or facing a challenge may also demonstrate your growth.

Be Positive. You don't need to break out the pompoms and do a cheer, but you need to convey a positive attitude in your essay. Scholarship committees want to see optimism, excitement and confidence. They prefer not to read essays that are overly pessimistic, antagonistic or critical. This doesn't mean that you have to put a happy spin on every word written or that you can't write about a serious topic or problem. For example, if you were a judge reading the following essays about the very serious topic of teen pregnancy, to which author's education fund would you rather make a contribution?

Thesis 1:
We could reduce the number of pregnant teens if we shifted our efforts away from scare tactics to providing responsible sex education combined with frank discussions regarding the responsibilities of caring for a child.

Thesis 2:
Teen pregnancy is incurable. Teenagers will always act irresponsibly and it would be futile for us to believe that we can control this behavior.

Scholarship committees favor authors who not only recognize problems but also present potential solutions. Leave being pessimistic to adults. You are young, with your entire future ahead of you. Your optimism is what makes you so exciting and why organizations want to give you money to pursue your passion for changing the world. Don't shy away from this opportunity.

Be Concise. The scholarship essay may not have the strict limits of a college admission essay, but that does not give you a license to be verbose. Keep your essay tight, focused and within the recommended length of the scholarship guidelines. If no parameters are given, one or two pages should suffice. You certainly want the readers to get through the entirety of your masterpiece. Remember that most scholarship selection committees are composed of volunteers who are under no obligation to read your entire essay. Make your main points quickly and keep your essay as brief and to the point as possible.

Step 4   Don't Neglect Your Introduction and Conclusion

Studies have found that the most important parts of a speech are the first and last minutes. In between, listeners fade in and out rather than constantly pay attention. It is the introduction and conclusion that leave a lasting impact. This holds true for scholarship essays as well. You need to have a memorable introduction and conclusion. If you don't, the readers may not make it past your introductory paragraph or they may discount your quality essay after reading a lackluster ending. Spend extra time making sure these two parts deliver the message you want. Here are some tips to create knockout introductions and conclusions:

For Introductions

Create action or movement. Think of the introduction as the high-speed car chase at the beginning of a movie that catches the audience's attention.

Pose a question. Questions draw the readers' attention for two reasons. First, they think about how they would answer the query as you have posed it. Second, they are curious to see how you will answer or present solutions to the question in your essay.

Describe. If you can create a vivid image for readers, they will be more likely to want to read on.

For Conclusions

Be thoughtful. Your conclusion should make the second most powerful statement in your essay because this is what your readers will remember. (The most powerful statement should be in your introduction.)

Leave a parting thought. The scholarship committee members have already read your essay (we hope), so you don't need to rehash what you have already said. It's okay to summarize in one sentence, but you want to do more than just "wrap it up". You have one final opportunity to make an impression, so add a parting thought. This should be one last observation or idea that ties into the main point of your essay.

Don't be too quick to end. Too many students tack on a meaningless conclusion or even worse, don't have one at all. Have a decent conclusion that goes with the rest of your essay. Never end your essay with the two words, "The End."

Step 5   Find Editors

Despite what you may think, you're not infallible. Stop gasping—it's true. This means it's important to get someone else to edit your work. Roommates, friends, family members, teachers, professors or advisors make great editors. When you get another person to read your essay, he or she will find errors that eluded you, as well as parts that are unclear to someone reading your essay for the first time. Ask your editors to make sure your ideas are clear, that you answer the question appropriately and that your essay is interesting. Take their suggestions seriously. The more input you get from others and the more times you rewrite your work, the better.

You want your essay to be like silk—smooth and elegant. When you read your work, make sure the connections between ideas are logical and the flow of your writing is understandable. (This is where editors can be extremely helpful.) Also check that you have not included any unnecessary details that might obscure the main point of your essay. Be careful to include any information that is vital to your thesis. Your goal is to produce an essay with clear points and supporting examples that logically flow together.

You also want to make sure that your spelling and grammar are perfect. Again, the best way to do this is to have someone else read your work. If you don't have time to ask someone, then do it yourself—but do it carefully. Read your essay at least once with the sole purpose of looking for spelling and grammatical mistakes. (Your computer's spell check is not 100 percent reliable and won't catch when you accidentally describe how you bake bread with one cup of "flower" instead of "flour.") Try reading your work out loud to listen for grammatical mistakes.

Step 6   Recycle Your Essays

This has no relation to aluminum cans or newspapers. In this case recycling means reusing essays you have written for college applications, classes or even other scholarships. Because colleges and scholarship committees usually ask very broad questions, this is generally doable and saves you a tremendous amount of time. Later in this chapter you will read an example essay. You may be surprised to learn that the author recycled her essay with minimal changes to answer such differing questions as these: "Tell us about one of your dreams," "What is something you believe in strongly?" and "What past experience continues to influence you today?"

However, be careful not to recycle an essay when it just doesn't fit. It's better to spend the extra time to write an appropriate essay than to submit one that doesn't match the scholarship or answer the question.

Seven Sins of the Scholarship Essay

Instead of writing an essay, one student placed the sheet of paper on the floor and tap danced on it. She then wrote that she hoped the scuff marks on the paper were evidence of her enthusiasm. In the judges' eyes, this was a silly stunt and, of course, her application was sent to the rejection pile. While you may not make such an egregious error, there are common mistakes that you need to avoid. Most of these lessons were learned the hard way—through actual experience.

1. DON'T Write a Sob Story

Everyone who applies for a scholarship needs money. Many have overcome obstacles and personal hardships. However, few scholarships are designed to reward students based on the "quantity" of hardships. Scholarship judges are not looking to give their money to those who have suffered the most. On the contrary, they want to give money to students who came up with a plan to succeed despite an obstacle. Therefore, if you are writing about the hardships you have faced, be sure that you spend as much time, if not more, describing how you have overcome or plan to rise above those challenges.

2. DON'T Use the Shotgun Approach

A common mistake is to write one essay and submit it without any changes to dozens of scholarships—hoping that maybe one will be a winner. While we do recommend that you recycle your essays, you should not just copy your essays and blast them out to every scholarship committee. This simply does not work. Unless the scholarships have identical questions, missions and goals, your essay cannot be reused verbatim. Spend the time to craft an essay for each scholarship, and you will win more than if you write just one and blindly send it off to many awards.

3. DON'T Be Afraid to Get Words on Paper

One common cause of writer's block is the fear of beginning. When you sit down to write, don't be afraid to write a draft, or even ideas for a draft, that are not perfect. You will have time to revise your work. What you want to do is get words on paper. They can be wonderfully intelligent words or they can be vague concepts. The point is that you should just write. Too many students wait until the last minute and get stuck at the starting line.

4. DON'T Try to Be Someone Else

Since you want to be the one the scholarship judges are seeking to reward with money, you need to highlight achievements and strengths that match the criteria of the scholarship. But you don't want to lie about yourself or try to be someone you are not. Besides being dishonest, the scholarship judges will probably pick up on your affectation and hold it against you.

5. DON'T Try to Impress with Feats of Literary Gymnastics

You won't get any bonus points for overusing clichés, quotes or words you don't understand. Too many students think that quotes and clichés will impress scholarship judges; but unless they are used sparingly and appropriately, they will win you no favors. (Remember that quotes and clichés are not your words and are therefore not original.) The same goes for overusing the thesaurus.

Do experiment with words that are less familiar to you, but do not make the thesaurus your co-author. It's better to use simple words correctly than to make blunders with complicated ones.

6. DON'T Stray Too Far from the Topic

A mistake that many students make is that they don't actually answer the question. This is especially true with recycled essays. Make sure that your essays, whether written from scratch or recycled from others, address the question asked.

7. DON'T Write Your Stats

A common mistake is to repeat your statistics from your application form. Often these essays begin with "My name is" and go on to list classes, GPAs and extracurricular activities. All this information is found in your application. On top of that, it's boring. If you are going to write about a class or activity, make it interesting by focusing on a specific class or activity.

Example Winning Scholarship Essays

It's one thing to study the theory behind the pheromones of love, but it is entirely a different thing to experience the euphoria, quickened heartbeat and walking-on-clouds feeling that goes with love. In a similar way, you have seen the theory behind writing a powerful scholarship essay. It is now time to see this theory in action.

The following two essays were written by students who won scholarships. In each essay you will see how winning principles are put to use. The results are essays that inspire, provoke and most important, win money. As with any example essay, please remember that this is not necessarily the way your essay should be written. Use these sample essays as illustrations of how a good essay might look. Your essay will naturally be different and unique to your own style and personality.

Winning Essay: My Two Dads

This essay was written by Gregory James Yee, a graduate of Whitney High School in Cerritos, California. Although Gregory is a student at Stanford University, he wrote this essay as part of his application to the University of Southern California. Besides garnering an acceptance to USC, this essay also earned him a $7,500 per year Trustee Scholarship. Remember that many colleges use your college application to automatically consider you for scholarships they offer.

The topic of the essay is Gregory's musical talent, which was discovered early in his life. At the age of two, he could hum *The Star-Spangled Banner* in perfect rhythm and pitch; and at age four, he began piano lessons. Throughout his 15 years of lessons, he won numerous awards, including the Raissa Tselentis Award given to one student nationwide for outstanding performance in the Advanced Bach category of the National Guild Audition. He is also a composer.

My Two Dads

I have two fathers. My first and biological father is the one who taught me how to drive a car, throw a baseball and find the area under a curve using integral calculus, among the innumerable other common duties of a good dad. He has been there for me through the ups of my successful piano career and the downs of my first breakup, and has always offered his insightful hand of guidance. My second father is who I connect with on a different level; he is the only person I know who thinks like I do. My second dad is my music composition teacher, Tony Fox, and he shares the one passion that has been a part of my life since the age of two: music.

Tony is a hardworking professor who can spend hours illustrating the meaning of a particular chord in a famous classical composition or ease an extraordinarily stressful situation with his colorful wit. He may appear intimidating to a new student at USC as the Assistant Band Director, but once someone mentions music, there is no one more adept, more creative or more dedicated to making music for the world to hear than Tony.

Tony has touched my life in a way few people have experienced. At my lessons with him, I bring compositions I am in the progress of perfecting, and with a few words of his guidance, I can almost see the changes needed before he mentions them. Almost instantly after I ask a question — such as which chord progression works best at a certain point in the music or why a certain counter melody sounds so beautiful—we agree on what is best for the music. It is almost as if we know what the other is thinking and merely state aloud our thoughts just in case one or the other is caught off guard. It is truly rare to find two people who agree with each other on what it is exactly that makes compositions aesthetically pleasing. Last year when I was working on a composition, I ran into a discouraging roadblock that could have delayed my progress significantly. No one in my family and none of my friends could help.

However, as soon as I shared the piece with Tony, he made some suggestions and together we made the necessary amendments to the music. The result was a finished project, a beautiful mosaic of our collective design, and it was debuted last year by my high school wind ensemble. When I first heard my music performed, I thought back to the hours I had spent tinkering at my piano and Tony's thoughtful guidance. This is how Tony and I relate. It's a common frequency upon which the most advanced radio cannot even begin to comprehend.

Tony has filled in areas of my life where few people, including my real father, could understand. He is the teacher of lessons big and small, from looking into the eyes of those whose hands I shake to recognizing that time is the most valuable gift one can give or receive. Whereas many of my peers have only one father, I have been fortunate enough to have two of them.

Why This Essay Won

An accomplished musician like Gregory could have written an essay that was simply a retelling of all the musical awards he had won. Instead, Gregory gives insight into what music means to him and takes us into his mind to see the creative and learning process at work. Writing about what he goes through to create a composition allows even those of us who are tone deaf to experience vicariously what it is like to create music.

Notice how Gregory uses powerful imagery to show us how he interacts with his music teacher and overcomes difficulties while composing. Gregory also subtly includes some of his most important musical accomplishments. Although he listed many of his awards in his application, this essay takes us beyond those achievements and really lets us see the wonderful person behind those awards.

Winning Essay: Leadership

Donald H. Matsuda, Jr. is the kind of person who doesn't just act. He inspires others to act as well. In his application for the Truman Scholarship, Donald shared how he directed community leaders and health professionals to start a series of health insurance drives. This is one of the essays that he wrote to become one of 80 Truman Scholars in the country.

From Sacramento and a graduate of Stanford University, Donald also founded the San Mateo Children's Health Insurance Program, directed the United Students for Veterans' Health and founded the Nepal Pediatric Clinical Internship.

Leadership

A few years ago, I saw a shocking headline on the front page of the New York Times that read: "Forty-Four Million Americans Without Health Insurance." Upon reading the article, I was stunned to discover that one-third of these uninsured Americans were children. Such figures made it clear to me that work needed to be done to remedy this problem, and I was ready to take action.

At this time, I was working at the Health for All Clinic as a public health and community outreach intern, and I decided to approach the director about this problem. He clearly agreed that immediate action needed to be taken to control the growing numbers of America's uninsured. However, he admitted that the clinic did not have the time, energy or the funds to invest in such an ambitious endeavor. I was not discouraged by his response. Instead, I saw this challenge as an opportunity to gain firsthand experience as a change agent in the field of public policy.

After completing extensive research, I discovered a unique program called Healthy Families. The ultimate goal of this government program is to provide low-cost insurance coverage to children who do not qualify for traditional insurance plans. I decided to develop my own project from scratch, proposing to launch a sustainable series of Healthy Families insurance drives at the Health for All Clinic. I applied for funding through the Haas Center for Public Service Fellowship program, and the clinic director signed on as my community partner for the project.

During the next six months, I worked very closely with the clinic staff to organize and plan this series of insurance drives. I recruited various ethnic community leaders and healthcare professionals to help generate support for the program and assembled several advertising campaigns in the surrounding communities. The clinic director and I also developed a workshop on immigrant health to attract more diverse populations to our insurance drives. After holding three Healthy Families drives, the clinic managed to sign up over 150 children for this program. The director was elated by this turnout and established an entire Healthy Families division to build upon the success of this project. Upon completion of this project, I started directing other insurance drives with the hope of improving the health and well-being of America's children.

Why This Essay Won

Donald's essay only scratches the surface of his accomplishments, which is exactly how it should be. Instead of listing every leadership role he has ever had, Donald explains how he created a health care program in his community. He begins with his motivation for starting the program and then recounts the initial skepticism that he faced when he first proposed the idea. Donald's essay describes the various difficulties and ultimate success of his project.

Notice that Donald does not describe a typical leadership role, one in which he was elected as a leader. This is an excellent example of how you can take a project in which you played a significant role and show how it demonstrates your leadership abilities. Remember, leadership is not just an elected position.

Where to Find More Winning Scholarship Essays

We believe that reading real essays is the best way for you to really see what works, and these essays are certainly a start. Unfortunately, we could not include more than two examples in this book. If you want more scholarship essay examples, take a look at our book, *How to Write a Winning Scholarship Essay*. In it you will find 30 additional winning essays from students who tested the waters of many topics and wrote in a variety of styles. Also, take a look at our website, SuperCollege (www.supercollege.com), where we post additional example essays. We think you'll be inspired.

The Scholarship Resume

Chapter

5

Write Your Own One-Page Autobiography

If you want to say that your life is a book, then be ready to follow with the analogy that your scholarship resume is the *CliffsNotes* summary. A scholarship resume is your opportunity to tout your greatest achievements and life's accomplishments. The only catch is that you are limited to one page. Some scholarship committees require resumes as a part of the application process so that they can use them to get a quick overview of your achievements. Others don't, but including a resume will always enhance your application.

A scholarship resume is not the same as one that you would use to get a job. It's unlikely that your work experience (if you have any) will be the focus. However, the principles and format are the same. A good resume that scores you a job shows employers that you have the right combination of work experience and skills to be their next hire. Similarly, your scholarship resume should show the committee why you are the most qualified student to win their award.

Think of the scholarship resume as a "cheat sheet" that you give to the judges. By looking at your resume, the judges get a quick overview of your achievements and interests. The resume is not an exhaustive list of everything you have done. It rather highlights and summarizes the most impressive and relevant achievements.

To make sure that it really focuses on the crème de la crème, your resume should fit on a single sheet of paper. This is sometimes harder than it sounds.

Here is the information you need for a scholarship resume:

● **Contact information:** Your vital statistics, including name, address, phone number and email.

- **Education:** Schools you've attended beginning with high school, expected or actual graduation dates.

- **Academic achievements:** Relevant coursework, awards and honors received.

- **Extracurricular experience.** Relevant extracurricular activities, locations and dates of participation, job titles, responsibilities and accomplishments.

- **Work experience:** Where and when you've worked, job titles, responsibilities and accomplishments on the job.

- **Skills and interests:** Additional relevant technical, lingual or other skills or talents that do not fit in the categories above.

Don't worry if your resume presents the same information that's in the application form. Some judges will read only the application or your resume, so it's important your key points are in both. However, in the resume, try to expand on areas that you were not able to cover fully in the application.

Example Resume that Worked

There are many good ways to format a resume. Most important, your resume should be easy to skim and be organized in a logical manner. Here is an example of a well-written scholarship resume. Remember that there are other equally good formats in which to present this information.

Melissa Lee
1000 University Drive
San Francisco, CA 94134
(415) 555-5555
melissa@email.com

Education
University of San Francisco; San Francisco, CA
B.A. candidate in sociology. Expected graduation in 2026.
Honor roll.

Lowell High School; San Francisco, CA
Graduated in 2022 with highest honors. Principal's Honor
Roll, 4 years.

Activities and Awards
SF Educational Project; San Francisco, CA
Program Assistant. Recruited and trained 120 students for
various community service projects in semester-long program.
Managed and evaluated student journals, lesson plans and
program participation. 2020-present.

Lowell High School Newspaper; San Francisco, CA
Editor-In-Chief. Recruited and managed staff of 50. Oversaw
all editorial and business functions. Newspaper was a finalist for the prestigious Examiner Award for excellence in
student journalism. 2018-2022.

Evangelical Church; San Francisco, CA
Teacher. Prepared and taught weekly lessons for third grade
Sunday School class. Received dedication to service award
from congregation. 2018-2022.

Asian Dance Troupe; San Francisco, CA
Member. Performed at community functions and special events.
2020-present.

Employment
Palo Alto Daily News; Palo Alto, CA
Editorial Assistant. Researched and wrote eight feature ar-
ticles on such topics as education reform, teen suicide and
summer fashion. Led series of teen-reader response panels.
Summer 2022.

Russian Hill Public Library; San Francisco, CA
Library Page. Received "Page of the Month" Award for outstanding performance. Summers 2020-2021.

Interests
Fluent in Mandarin and HTML. Interests include journal writing, creative writing, photography, swimming and aerobics.

Some points to note about this resume:

- Notice how this resume is concise and very easy to read. By limiting herself to a single page, Melissa makes sure that even if you just scan her resume, you will pick up her key strengths.

- See how each description includes examples of leadership as well as awards or special recognition.

- Melissa conveys the impact of her work by pointing out concrete results (which you should also do on the application form).

- Notice how her description of summer jobs highlights some of her key accomplishments.

- The final section adds a nice balance by describing some of her other hobbies and interests.

Elements of a Powerful Resume

Your resume should be descriptive enough for the judges to understand each item but not so wordy that they can't find what they need. It should be neatly organized and easy to follow. Having reviewed hundreds of resumes, here are some simple strategies that we've developed to help you:

Include only the important information. Remember to incorporate only the most relevant items and use what you know about the scholarship organization to guide how you prioritize what you share in your resume. Only include things that support your fit with the scholarship's mission. For each piece of information, ask yourself these two questions: Will including this aid the selection committee in seeing that I am a match for the award? Is this information necessary to convince them that I should receive the award?

Focus on responsibilities and achievements. In describing your experiences in work and activities, focus on the responsibilities you held and highlight measurable or unique successes such as starting a project, reaching goals or implementing one of your ideas. For example, if you were the treasurer of the Literary Club, you would want to include that you were responsible for managing a $10,000 annual budget.

Demonstrate in your resume how you showed leadership. Leadership could include leading a project or team, instructing others or mentoring your peers. What's more important than your title or where you worked is the quality of your involvement. Explaining your successes and your role as a leader will provide concrete evidence of your contribution.

Be proud. Your resume is your time to shine. Don't be afraid to draw attention to all that you've accomplished. If you played a key role in a project, say so. If you exceeded your goals, advertise it. No one else is going to do your bragging for you.

Use action verbs. When you are describing your achievements, use action verbs such as these: founded, organized, achieved, created, developed, directed and (our personal favorite) initiated.

Don't tell tall stories. On the flip side of being proud is being untruthful. It's important that you describe yourself in the most glowing way possible, but stay connected with the truth. If you developed a new filing system at your job, don't claim that you single-handedly led a corporate revolution. With your complete scholarship application, selection committees can see through a resume that is exaggerated and doesn't match the rest of the application, essay and recommendations.

Get editors. After the hundredth time reading your resume, you'll probably not notice an error that someone reading it for the first time will catch. Get others to read and edit your resume. Editors can let you know if something doesn't make sense, offer you alternative wording and help correct your boo-boos. Some good choices for editors may be teachers or professors, work supervisors or parents. Work supervisors may be especially helpful since part of their job is to review resumes of job applicants. Your school may also offer resume help in the counseling department or career services office.

Avoid creating an eye test. In trying to squeeze all the information onto a single page, don't make your font size so small that the words are illegible. Try to leave space between paragraphs. The judges may have tired, weary eyes from reading all those applications. Don't strain them even more.

Strive for perfection. It's a given that your resume should be error-free. There's no excuse for mistakes on a one-page document that is meant to exemplify your life's work.

Include Your Resume in Every Application

Once you have a resume, include it with every scholarship application. In addition, you should also give it to your recommenders so that they have a "cheat sheet" that highlights your accomplishments when it comes time to write those letters of recommendations. They will no doubt want to mention some of your successes to make their letters on point and personal. Remember, your resume is *you*!

Getting Great Recommendations

Letters of Recommendation Count

If you need a reason to kiss up to your teachers or professors, here's one: recommendations. Scholarships sometime require that you submit recommendations from teachers, professors, school administrators, employers or others who can vouch for your accomplishments. Scholarship judges use these testaments to get another perspective of your character and accomplishments. Viewed together with your application and essay, the recommendation helps the judges get a more complete picture of who you are. Plus, it's always impressive when someone else extols your virtues.

Many students believe that they have no control over the recommendation part of their application. This isn't true. You actually can have a lot of input regarding the letters that your recommenders write. In this chapter we will explore several ways—all perfectly ethical—to ensure that you get great recommendations.

A recommendation is an important opportunity for someone else to tell scholarship judges why you deserve to win. You may assume that because others do the actual writing, recommendations are completely out of your control. Banish that thought. The secret is to not only pick the right people but to also provide them with all of the information they need to turn out a great letter of recommendation. Many applicants overlook this fact. But not you, right? Armed with superb recommendations, your scholarship application is sure to rise to the top.

Find People to Say Nice Things about You

Your first task is to find recommenders. Unfortunately, Mom, Dad and anyone else related to you is excluded. So, how do you get those recommendations without familial ties to sing your praises?

First, think about all the people in your life who can speak meaningfully about you and your accomplishments. Your list may include teachers, professors, advisors, school administrators, employers, religious leaders, coaches or leaders of organizations and activities in which you are involved. While some scholarships require recommendations from specific people (like a teacher or professor), most are pretty liberal and allow you to select anyone who knows you.

Second, once you have a list of potential recommenders, analyze which of these people could present information about you that best matches the goals of the scholarships.

If you apply for an academic scholarship, you'll want at least one teacher or professor to write a recommendation. If you apply for an athletic scholarship, a coach would be a good choice. Select people who are able to write about the things that are most important to the scholarship judges. A good exercise is to imagine what your potential recommender would write and whether or not this would enhance your case for winning the scholarship.

After considering these two questions, you should be left with only a few people from which to choose. If you can't decide between two equally qualified people, choose the one who knows you the best as a person. For example, if you got A's in three classes and are trying to decide which professor to ask for a recommendation, pick the one who can write *more* than a testament to your academic ability. This is important because a recommendation that contains comments on your character is extremely memorable. Maybe one of the professors knows you well enough to include a few sentences on your drive to succeed or your family background. Ideally, your recommender is able to describe not only your performance in the classroom but also the values and character traits that make you special.

Give Your Recommender the Chance to Say "No"

Once you've selected those you'd like to write your recommendations, ask them to do so—early. A general rule is to allow at least three weeks before the recommendation is due. Explain that you are applying for scholarships and are required to submit recommendations from people who know you and who can comment on some of your achievements.

It's important to ask the person a question like this: "Do you feel comfortable writing a recommendation letter for me?" This allows the person the opportunity to decline your request if he or she doesn't feel comfortable or doesn't have the time. If you get a negative or hesitant response, don't assume that it's because he or she has a low opinion of you. It could simply be that the person doesn't know you well enough or is too busy to write a thoughtful recommendation. It's much better to have the recommender decline to write a letter than to get one that is rushed or not entirely positive. In most cases, however, potential recommenders are flattered and happy to oblige.

Don't Play the Name Game

From being recognized by strangers to getting preferential reservations at the hottest restaurants, there are a lot of perks to being famous. You might think that this special treatment carries over to recommendations, and that scholarship judges will be star-struck by a letter from someone with a fancy title. However, don't assume that just because you ask someone well known to write your recommendations that you are a shoo-in for the scholarship. In fact, you might be surprised to learn that doing so could actually hurt your chances of winning.

So the question is this: "Should I try to find someone famous to write a letter of recommendation for me?" The answer comes down to the principles outlined above. How well does the person know you, and can he or she write about you in a way that presents you as a viable candidate for the scholarship? If the answer is "yes," then by all means ask the person to help you. However, if you don't know the person very well or if what he or she will write could lack a connection to the qualities that the scholarship committee is looking for, it's better to forgo the value of high name recognition and ask someone who can address what's most important in a letter of recommendation.

For example, if you work as a summer intern for your state senator, you may think that a letter from such a political luminary would give your application the star power to set it apart from others with recommendations from mere mortals. However, if you spent more time photocopying or stuffing envelopes than you did developing keen political strategies, and you saw the senator as many times as you have fingers on your left hand, chances are that he or she would have very few meaningful things to say about your performance. "A skilled photocopier" and "brewed a mean cup of coffee" are not compliments you want sent to the scholarship judges.

If you ask someone well known to write your recommendations, make sure that he or she really knows you and can speak about your accomplishments personally and meaningfully. The quality of what is said in the recommendations is much more important than whose signature is at the bottom of the page.

Do the Grunt Work for Your Recommenders

Once you've selected your recommenders, give them everything they need to get the job done. Since they are doing you a favor, make the process as easy as possible for them. This is also where you can most influence what they write and actually direct what accomplishments they highlight. But before we delve into the specifics, here is an overview of what you need to provide each recommender:

Cover letter: This describes the scholarships you are applying for. In the letter, you should list deadlines and give the recommenders direct guidance on what to write. More on this in a bit.

Resume: A resume provides a quick overview of your most important achievements in an easy to follow one-page format. It is also what your recommenders will use as they cite your important achievements.

Recommendation form: Some scholarships provide an actual form that your recommenders need to complete either electronically or on paper. Fill in the parts that you can, such as your name and address.

Pre-addressed, stamped envelopes: Read the application materials to find out if you need to submit your recommendations separately or with the rest of your application. For letters that are to be mailed separately, provide your recommenders with envelopes that are stamped and have the scholarship's mailing address on them. If you are supposed to submit the letters with your application, provide your recommenders with envelopes on which you have written your name. Many recommenders prefer to write letters that are confidential and that you don't get to read. Once you have everything, place it in a folder or envelope and label it with your recommender's name.

Give Your Recommenders a Script

Because you know yourself better than anyone else, you would probably receive the best recommendations if you sat down and wrote them yourself. Unfortunately, this practice is frowned upon by scholarship judges. Short of writing your own recommendations, you can influence how they turn out by providing your recommenders with detailed descriptions of your accomplishments that can help them decide which aspects of you to highlight in their letters. This is best done through the cover letter that you send to the prospective recommender.

Your cover letter provides your recommenders with all the information that they need to write your recommendations, including details about the scholarships and suggestions for what you'd like the recommendations to address. Since the cover letter also includes other essentials like deadlines, mailing or submitting instructions and a thank you, you will not sound as if you are giving orders but rather that you are providing helpful assistance. In fact, your recommenders will appreciate your reminding them what's important and what they should include.

Here are the elements to include in your cover letter:

Details on the scholarships: List the scholarships for which you will use their letters. Give a brief one-paragraph description of the mission of each of the awards and what qualities the scholarship committee seeks. This information will help your recommenders understand which of your qualities are important to convey and who will read the letters.

How you fit the scholarship: This is the most important part of your cover letter because it's your chance to remind your recommenders of your accomplishments and to offer suggestions for what to write. Make sure that you highlight how you match the goals of the scholarships. For example, if you are applying for a scholarship for future teachers, include information about your student teaching experience and the coursework you've taken in education. Leave out the fact that you were on the tennis team.

Deadlines: Inform your recommenders of how long they have to compose the letters. If time permits, ask them to mail the letters a week before the actual deadlines.

What to do with the letters when they're done: Give your recommenders instructions about what to do with the completed letters. You may want to offer to pick them up, or you might explain that you have included addressed, stamped envelopes so that the letters can be mailed. If the letters are to be submitted electronically, provide these details.

Thank you: Recommendations may take several hours to complete, and your recommenders are very busy people. Don't forget to say thank you in advance for writing you a great letter of recommendation.

To illustrate the power of a good cover letter, read the example on the following page as if you were a recommender. Remember that this is only one example and your cover letter will naturally be different. However, regardless of your individual writing style, your cover letter should include the same points as the following example.

Some notes about this cover letter:

- Beth describes each scholarship she is applying for, its goal and deadline, and why she feels she is a match for the award.

- The heart of the cover letter is here, where Beth gives a quick summary of information she suggests her professor include in the letter.

- Beth provides instructions about what to do with the letters when completed.

- This is a well-written cover letter that is brief and easy to understand.

Dear Dr. Louis,

Thank you again for writing my scholarship recommendations. I want to do my best to be competitive for these awards. They are very important for my family as they will help me to pay for my education. Here are the scholarships I am applying for:

SuperCollege.com Scholarship Deadline: July 31
This is a national scholarship based on academic and non-academic achievement, including extracurricular activities and honors. I believe I'm a match for this scholarship because of my commitment to academics (I currently have a 3.85 grade point average) and because of the volunteer work I do with the Youth Literacy Project and the PLUS program.

Quill & Scroll Scholarship Deadline: April 20
This scholarship is for students who want to pursue a career in journalism. As you know, I am an editor for our school newspaper, contributing a column each week on issues that affect our student body. Journalism is the field I want to enter after graduation.

Community Scholarship Deadline: May 5
This scholarship is for students who have given back to their communities through public service. I have always been committed to public service. Outside of class, I not only formed the Youth Literacy Project but have also volunteered with the PLUS program.

To help you with your recommendation, I've enclosed a resume. Also, here are some highlights of specific accomplishments that I was hoping you might comment on in your letter:

* The essay I wrote for your class that won the Young Hemingway competition

* How I formed the Youth Literacy Project with you as the project's advisor

* My three years of volunteer work with the PLUS program

* The weekly column I've written for the newspaper on school issues

After you've finished, please return the recommendations to me in the envelopes I've enclosed. If you have any questions, please feel free to contact me at 555-5555. Again, thank you very much for taking the time to help me.

Sincerely,

Beth

Don't Let Your Recommenders Miss Deadlines

All recommenders have one thing in common: Too much to do and not enough time. It's important that you check with your recommender a couple of weeks before the letters are due. You need to monitor the progress of your recommendations. You may find that they're complete and already in the mail. A more common discovery is that they won't have been touched. Be polite yet diligent when you ask about the progress. It's crucial that you work with your recommenders to get the letters in on time.

The "You Can't Spell Success Without U" Mug

You now have everything you need to receive stellar recommendations. It's important to remember that even if it is a part of their job description, your recommenders are spending their time to help you. Remember this as you ask others to write recommendation letters and be sure to let them know that you appreciate their efforts.

Sometimes, a thank you gift is appropriate. Every time my (Kelly) mother wants to say thank you to a friend or acquaintance, she writes a note and gives a small token gift. My favorite is the "You Can't Spell Success Without U" mug because of its campy play on words.

Whether or not you select an equally campy token of appreciation, it's important that you thank your recommenders. After all, they are dedicating their free time to help you win funds for college.

Ace the Scholarship Interview

The Face-to-Face Encounter

A judge for the Rotary scholarship shared with us the following true story. For the last phase of the scholarship competition for his region, the finalists met with the selection committee for an interview. The interview was very important and was the final step in determining who would win the $25,000 scholarship.

One finalist was an Ivy League student who flew across the country for the interview. Within the first five minutes, it was painfully clear to all the judges that the applicant didn't have the foggiest idea what the Rotary Club stood for. It's as if the applicant thought that his resume and Ivy League pedigree would make him a winner. As you can guess, this applicant had a very disappointing flight back to his college. Lesson number one for the scholarship interview: At the very least, know what the organization stands for.

Many students dread the interview. If your heart beats faster or your palms moisten when you think about the prospect of sitting face to face with the judges, you are not alone. While the other parts of the scholarship application take time and effort, they can be done in the privacy of your home. Interviews, on the other hand, require interaction with—gasp—a real live human.

The good news is that the interview is usually the final step in the scholarship application process and if you make it that far, you're a serious contender. In this chapter, we show you what most scholarship committees are looking for and how you should prepare to deliver a winning interview. We also show you how to make the most of your nervousness and how to turn it into an asset rather than a liability.

There are two secrets for doing well in scholarship interviews. The first is this: Remind yourself over and over again that scholarship interviewers are real people. Repeat it until you believe it. As such, your goal is to have as normal a conversation as possible, despite the fact that thousands of dollars may hang in the balance. It's essential that you treat interviewers as real people, interact with them and ask them questions.

The second secret is just as important: The best way to have successful interviews is to train for them. The more you practice interviewing, the more comfortable you'll be during the real thing. Don't worry—we'll tell you what kinds of questions to expect and how to perfect your answers.

Why Human Interaction Is Necessary

The first step to delivering a knockout interview is to understand why some scholarships require interviews in the first place. With the popularity of technology like e-mail and text messaging, there seems to be less need for human interaction. (Believe it or not, there was a time when telephones were answered by a person instead of a maze of touchtone options.)

For some scholarship committees, a few pieces of paper with scores and autobiographical writing are not enough to get a full picture of who the applicants really are. They are giving away a lot of cash and the judges are responsible for making sure they are giving it to the most deserving students possible.

Scholarship judges use interviews as a way to learn how you compare in person versus on paper. Having been on both sides of the interview table, we can attest to the fact that the person you expect based on the written application is not always the person you meet at the interview. It's important to know that the purpose of interviews is not to interrogate you, but rather for the scholarship committee to get to know you better and probe deeper into the reason that you deserve their money.

Interviewers Are Real People Too

If you've ever met someone famous, you've probably realized that while celebrities' faces may grace the covers of magazines and they have houses big enough to merit their own ZIP code, they eat, drink and sleep and have likes and dislikes just like other people. The same thing holds true for interviewers.

Interviewers can be high-profile professors or high-powered businesspeople, but they are all passionate about some topics and bored with others. They enjoy speaking about themselves and getting to know more about you. Acknowledging this will help keep your nerves under control. Throughout the interview, remind yourself that your interviewer is human, and strive to make the interview a conversation, not an interrogation.

Interview Homework

You'd never walk into a test and expect to do well without studying the material. The same is true for interviews. Don't attempt them without doing your homework. There is basic information you need to know before starting your interviews so that you appear informed and knowledgeable. It's not difficult information to obtain, and it goes a long way in demonstrating that you care enough about winning to have put in some effort. Here are some things you should know before any interview:

Purpose of the scholarship: What is the organization hoping to accomplish by awarding the scholarship? Whether it's promoting students to enter a certain career area, encouraging a hobby or interest or rewarding students for leadership, every scholarship has a mission.

Criteria for selecting the winner: From the scholarship materials, you can get information about what the judges are hoping to find in a winner. From the kinds of information they request in the application to the topic of the essay question, each piece is a clue about what is important to the judges. Scholarships can be based on academic achievement, nonacademic achievement or leadership, to name a few criteria. Understand what kind of student the organization is seeking and stress that side of yourself during the interview.

Background of the awarding organization: Do a little digging on the organization itself. Check out its website or publications. Attend a meeting or speak with someone who's a member. From this detective work, you will get a better idea of who the organization's members are and what they are trying to achieve. It can also be a great topic of conversation during the interview.

Background of your interviewer: If possible, find out as much as you can about who will be interviewing you. In many cases, you may know little more than their names and occupations, but if you can, find out more. You already have one piece of important information about your interviewers: You know that they are passionate about the organization and its mission. They wouldn't be volunteering their time to conduct interviews if they weren't.

Use Your Detective Work to Create an Advantage

Once you've done your detective work on the above topics, it's time to use the information you've uncovered. For example, if you are in front of a group of doctors and they ask you about your activities, you would be better off discussing your work at the local hospital than your success on the baseball diamond. As much as possible, focus the conversation on areas where your activities, goals, interests and achievements match the goal of the awarding organization. By discussing what matters most to the scholarship judges, you will insure that this will be a memorable conversation—one that will set you apart from the other applicants that are interviewed.

By knowing something about your interviewers beforehand, you can think of topics and questions that will be interesting to them. Most interviewers allow some time for you to ask questions. Here again your detective work will come in handy since you can ask them about their background or the history of the organization. By asking intelligent questions (i.e. not the ones that can be answered by simply reading the group's mission statement) you will demonstrate that you've done your homework.

You'll also give interviewers something interesting to talk about—either themselves or their organization. The more information you can get before the interview, the better you will perform. Having this background material will also allow you to answer unexpected questions better and come up with thoughtful questions for the judges if you are put on the spot.

You Are Not the Center of the Universe

Despite what Mom or Dad says, the Earth revolves around the sun, not you. It helps to remember this in your interviews. Your life may be the most interesting ever lived, but this is still no excuse for speaking only about yourself for the duration of the interview.

The secret to successful interviews is simply this: They should be *interactive*. The surest way to bore your interviewers is to spend the entire time speaking only about yourself. You may have had the unfortunate experience of being on the receiving end of a conversation like this if you have a friend who speaks nonstop about herself and who never seems to be interested in your life or what you have to say. Don't you just hate this kind of conversation? So will your scholarship interviewers.

To prevent a self-centered monologue, constantly look for ways to interact with your interviewers. In addition to answering questions, ask some yourself. Ask about their experiences in school or with the organization. Inquire about their thoughts on some of the questions they pose to you. Take time to learn about your interviewers' experiences and perspectives.

Also, speak about topics that interest your interviewers. You can tell which topics intrigue them by their reactions and body language. From the detective work you've done, you also have an idea of what they are passionate about.

Try to make your interviews a two-way conversation instead of a one-way monologue. Engage your interviewers and keep them interested. If you do this, they will remember your interview as a great conversation and you as a wonderful, intelligent person deserving of their award.

Look and Sound the Part

Studies on the effectiveness of speeches have shown that how you sound and how you look when you present your material is more important than what you actually say. From that, we can learn that it is positively essential that you make a good visual presentation. Here are some tips to make sure that you look and sound your best, an important complement to what you actually say to the judges:

Dress appropriately: A backward-turned baseball cap and baggy jeans slung down to your thighs may be standard fare for the mall (at least they were last season), but they are not appropriate for interviews.

You probably don't have to wear a suit unless you find out through your research that the organization is very conservative, but you should dress appropriately. No-no's include the following: hats, bare midriffs, short skirts or shorts and iron-free wrinkles. Think about covering obtrusive tattoos or removing extra ear/nose/tongue/eyebrow rings. Don't dress so formally that you feel uncomfortable, but dress nicely. It may not seem fair, but your dress will affect the impression you make and influence the decision of the judges. Save making a statement of your individuality for a time when money is not in question.

Sit up straight: During interviews, do not slouch. Sitting up straight conveys confidence, leadership and intelligence. It communicates that you are interested in the conversation. Plus, it makes you look taller.

Speak in a positive tone of voice: One thing that keeps interviewers engaged is your tone. Make sure to speak in a positive one. This will not only maintain your interviewers' interest but will also suggest that you have an optimistic outlook. Of course, don't try so hard that you sound fake.

Don't be monotonous: If you've ever had a teacher or professor who speaks at the same rate and tone without variation, you know that this is the surest reason for a nap. Don't give your interviewers heavy eyelids. Record yourself and pay attention to your tone of voice. There should be natural variation in your timbre.

Speak at a natural pace: If you're like most people, the more nervous you are, the faster you speak. Be aware of this so that you don't speed talk through your interview.

Make natural gestures: Let your hands and face convey action and emotions. Use them as tools to illustrate anecdotes and punctuate important points.

Make eye contact: Eye contact engages interviewers and conveys self-assurance and honesty. If it is a group interview, make eye contact with all your interviewers—don't just focus on one. Maintaining good eye contact can be difficult, but just imagine little dollar signs in your interviewers' eyes and you shouldn't have any trouble. Ka-ching!

Smile: There's nothing more depressing than having a conversation with someone who never smiles. Don't smile nonstop, but show some teeth at least once in a while. If you use these tips, you will have a flawless look and sound to match what you're saying. All these attributes together create a powerful portrait of who you are. Unfortunately, not all these things come naturally, and you'll need to practice so that they can become unconscious actions.

The Practice Interview

One of the best ways to prepare for an interview is to do a dress rehearsal. This allows you to run through answering questions you might be asked and to practice honing your interview skills, including demeanor and style. You will feel more comfortable when it comes time for the actual interview. If anything will help you deliver a winning interview, it's practice. It may be difficult, but force yourself to set aside some time to run through a practice session at least once. Here's how:

Find a mock interviewer. Bribe or coerce a friend or family member to be your mock interviewer. Parents or teachers often make the best interviewers because they are closest in age and perspective to most actual scholarship interviewers.

Prep your mock interviewer. Share with your interviewer highlights from this chapter such as the purpose of scholarship interviews, what skills you want to practice and typical interview questions, which are described in the next section. If you're having trouble with eye contact, for example, ask them to take special notice of where you are looking when you speak and to make suggestions for correcting this.

Video yourself. Use your phone to video yourself so that you can review your mock interview afterward. Position it behind your interviewer so you can observe how you appear from their perspective.

Do the dress rehearsal. Grab two chairs and go for it. Answer questions and interact with your mock interviewer as if you were at the real thing. Get feedback. After you are finished, get constructive criticism from your mock interviewer. Find out what you did well and what you need to work on. What were the best parts of the interview? Which of your answers were strong, and which were weak? When did you capture or lose your mock interviewer's attention? Was your conversation one-way or two-way?

Review the video. Evaluate your performance. If you can, watch or listen to the video with your mock interviewer so you can get additional feedback. Listen carefully to how you answer questions so you can improve on them. Pay attention to your tone of voice. Watch your body language to see what you are unconsciously communicating.

Do it again. If you have the time and your mock interviewer has the energy or you can find another mock interviewer, do a second interview. If you can't find anyone, do it solo. Practice your answers, and focus on making some of the weaker ones more interesting. The bottom line is the more you practice, the better you'll do.

How to Answer to the Most Common Interview Questions

The best way to ace an exam would be to know the questions beforehand. The same is true for interview questions. From interviewing dozens of judges and applicants as well as having judged dozens of scholarship competitions ourselves, we've developed a list of commonly asked questions along with suggestions for answering them. This list is by no means comprehensive. There is no way to predict every question you will be asked, and in your actual interviews, the questions may not be worded in exactly the same way. However, the answer that interviewers are seeking is often the same.

Before your interviews, take the time to review this list. Add more questions particular to the specific scholarship to which you are applying. Practice answering these questions to yourself and in your mock interviews with friends and family. You will find that the answers you prepare to these questions will be invaluable during your real interviews. Even though the questions you are asked may be different, the thought that you put in now will help you formulate better answers. To the interviewer, you will sound incredibly articulate and thoughtful. Let's take a look at those questions.

Why did you choose your major?

- For major-based scholarships and even for general scholarships, interviewers want to know what motivated you to select the major, and they want a sense of how dedicated you are to that area of study. Make sure you have reasons for your decision. Keep in mind that an anecdote will provide color to your answer.

- If you are still in high school, you will probably be asked about your intended major. Make sure you have reasons for considering this major.

Why do you want to enter this career field?

- For scholarships that promote a specific career field, interviewers want to know your inspiration for entering the field and how committed you are to it. You will need to articulate the reasons and experiences that prompted your interest in this career and also anything you have done to prepare yourself for associated studies in this area.

- Be prepared to discuss your plans for after graduation, i.e. how will you use your education in the field you have chosen. You may be asked what kind of job you plan to have and why you would like it.

- Know something about the news in the field associated with the scholarship. For example, if you are applying for an information technology award, read up on the trends in the IT industry. There may be some major changes occurring that you will be asked to comment on.

What are your plans after graduation?

- You are not expected to know precisely what you'll do after graduation, but you need to be able to respond to this common question. Speak about what you are thinking about doing once you have that diploma in hand. The more specific you can be, the better.

- Provide reasons for your plans. Explain the process in which you developed your plans and what your motivation is.

- It's okay to discuss a couple of possible paths you may take, but don't bring up six very different options. Even if you are deciding among investment banking, the Peace Corps, banana farming and seminary, don't say so. The interviewer will think that you don't have a clear direction of what you want to do. This may very well be true, but it's not something you want to share. Select the one or two possible paths that you are most likely to take.

Why do you think you should win this scholarship?

- Focus your answer on characteristics and achievements that match the mission of the scholarship. For example, if the scholarship is for biology majors, discuss your accomplishments in the field of biology. Your answer may include personal qualities as well as specific accomplishments.

- Be confident but not arrogant. For this type of question, be careful about balancing pride and modesty in your answer. You want to be confident enough to have reasons why you should win the scholarship, but you don't want to sound overly boastful. To avoid sounding pompous, don't say that you are better than all the other applicants or put down your competition. Instead, focus on your strengths independent of the other people who are applying.

- Have three reasons. Three is the magic number that is not too many or too few. To answer this question just right, offer three explanations for why you fulfill the mission of the scholarship.

Tell me about times when you've been a leader.

- Interviewers ask this type of question (although sometimes worded a little differently) to gauge your leadership ability and your accomplishments as a leader. They want to award scholarships to students who will be leaders in the future. When you answer, try to discuss leadership you've shown that matches what the scholarship is meant to achieve.

- Don't just rattle off the leadership positions you've held. Instead, give qualitative descriptions of what you accomplished as a leader. Did your group meet its goals? Did you start something new? How did you shape the morale of the group you led? For this kind of question, anecdotes and short stories are a good way to illustrate how you've been effective.

- Remember that leadership doesn't have to be a formally elected position. You can describe how you've informally led a special project or group. You could even define how you are a leader among your siblings.

- Be prepared to discuss what kind of leader you are. Your interviewer may ask about your approach to leadership or your philosophy on being a good leader. Have examples ready that show how you like to lead. For example, do you lead by example? Do you focus on motivating others and getting their buy-in?

What are your strengths? Weaknesses?

- As you are applying for jobs, you will answer this question more times than you will shake hands. It is a common job interview question that you may also get asked in scholarship interviews. Be prepared with three strengths and three weaknesses. Be honest about your weaknesses.

- Your strengths should match the mission of the scholarship and should highlight skills and accomplishments that match the characteristics the judges are seeking.

- You should be able to put a positive spin on your weaknesses. (And you'd better say you have some!) For example, your perfectionism could make you frustrated when things don't go the way you plan but could also make you a very motivated person. Your love of sports could detract from your studies but could provide a needed break and be representative of your belief in balance for your life. Just make sure that the spin you put on your weakness is appropriate and that your weakness is really a weakness.

Where do you see yourself ten years from now?

- We know that nobody knows exactly what he or she is going to be doing in ten years. The interviewers don't need specific details. They just want a general idea of what your long-term goals are and what you aspire to become. If you have several possibilities, at least one should be in line with the goals of the scholarship.

- Try to be as specific as possible without sounding unrealistic. For example, you can say that you would like to be working at a high-tech company in marketing, but leave out that you plan to have a daughter Sawyer, son Parker and dog Skip. Too much detail will make your dreams sound too naive.

Tell me about yourself. Or, is there anything you want to add?

- The most difficult questions are often the most open-ended. You have the freedom to say anything. For these kinds of questions, go back to the mission of the scholarship and shape your answer to reflect the characteristics that the judges are seeking in the winner. Practice answering this question several times because it is the one that stumps applicants the most.

- Have three things to say about yourself that match the goal of the scholarship. For example, you could discuss three personal traits you have, such as motivation, leadership skills and interpersonal skills. Or, you could discuss three skills applicable to academics, such as analytical skills, problem-solving skills and your love of a good challenge.

- The alternative, "Is there anything you want to add?" is typically asked at the end of the interview. In this case, make your response brief but meaningful. Highlight the most important thing you want your interviewer to remember.

Other Questions

In addition to these, here are some more common questions:

- What do you think you personally can contribute to this field?

- How do you plan to use what you have studied after graduation?

- Do you plan to continue your studies in graduate school?

- What do you want to specifically focus on within this field of study?

- Do you plan to do a thesis or senior project?

- Who are your role models in the field?

- What do you see as the future of this field?

- How do you see yourself growing in your career?

- What can you add to this field?

- What do you think are the most challenging aspects of this field?

- What is your ideal job after graduating from college?

- Tell me about a time that you overcame adversity.

- What are your opinions about (fill in political or field-related issue)?

- Tell me about your family.

- What do you hope to gain from college?

- Who is a role model for you?

- What is your favorite book? Why?

- What is the most challenging thing you have done?

Remember that with all these questions your goal is to demonstrate that you are the best fit for the scholarship. Be sure to practice these with your mock interviewer. The more comfortable and confident you feel answering these questions, the better you'll do in your interviews.

Questions for the Questioner

There is a huge difference between an interview and an interrogation. In an interview, you also ask questions. Make certain that your interview does not become an interrogation. Ask questions yourself throughout the conversation. Remember that you want to keep the conversation two-way.

Toward the end of your interview, you will probably have the opportunity to ask additional questions. Take this opportunity. If you don't ask any questions, it will appear that you are uninterested in the conversation or haven't put much thought into your interview. Take time before the interview to develop a list of questions you may want to ask. Of course you don't have to ask all your questions, but you need to be prepared to ask a few.

To get you started, we've developed some suggestions. Adapt these questions to the specific scholarship you are applying for and personalize them.

- How did you get involved with this organization?

- How did you enter this field? What was your motivation?

- Who do you see as your mentors in this field?

- What do you think are the most exciting things about your career?

- What advice do you have for someone starting out?

- What do you see as the greatest challenges for this field?

- What do you think will be the greatest advancements in ten years?

- What effect do you think technology will have on this field?

- I read that there is a (insert trend) in this field. What do you think?

The best questions are those that come from your detective work. Let's say that in researching an organization you discover that they recently launched a new program to research a cure for diabetes. Inquiring about this new program would be a perfect question to ask. It not only shows that you have done your homework, but it is also a subject about which the organization is deeply concerned.

Use Time to Your Advantage

The best time to ask Mom or Dad for something is when they're in a good mood. It's all about timing. Timing is also important in interviews. If you have more than one scholarship interview, time them strategically. Schedule less important and less demanding interviews first. This will allow you the opportunity to practice before your more difficult interviews. You will improve your skills as you do more interviews. It makes sense to hone your skills on the less important ones first.

If you are one of a series of applicants who will be interviewed, choose the order that fits you best. If you like to get things over with, try to be interviewed in the beginning. If you need more time to prepare yourself mentally, select a time near the end. We recommend that you don't choose to go first because the judges will use your interview as a benchmark for the rest. They may not recognize you as the best applicant even though it turns out to be true.

The Long-Distance Interview

If you've ever been in a long-distance relationship, you know there's a reason why most don't last. You simply can't communicate over the telephone in the same way you can in person. Scholarship interviews are the same. You may find that an interview will not be face to face but over the telephone instead. If this happens, here are some strategies to help bridge the distance:

Find a quiet place to do the interview where you won't be interrupted. You need to be able to give your full attention to the conversation you are having.

Know who's on the other end of the line. You may interview with a panel of people. Write down each of their names and positions when they first introduce themselves to you. They will be impressed when you are able to respond to them individually and thank each of them by name.

Use notes from your practice interviews. One of the advantages of doing an interview over the telephone is that you can refer to notes without your interviewers knowing. Take advantage of this.

Look and sound like you would in person. Pretend that your interviewers are in the room with you, and use the same gestures and facial expressions that you would if you were meeting in person. It may sound strange, but your interviewers will actually be able to hear through your voice when you are smiling, when you are paying attention and when you are enthusiastic about what you're saying. Don't do your interview lying down in your bed or slouched back in a recliner.

Don't use an unreliable phone. Speaker phones often echo and pick up distracting surrounding noise. If you use a cell phone, make sure you have good reception and a charged battery.

Turn off call waiting. Nothing is more annoying than hearing the call waiting beep while you are trying to focus and deliver an important thought. (And, this may sound obvious, never click over to take a second call.) Use the techniques of regular interviews. You'd be surprised how much is translated over the telephone. Don't neglect good speaking and delivery points just because the interviewers can't see you!

Secrets to the Group Interview

So it's you on one side of the table and a panel of six on the other side. It's certainly not the most natural way to have a conversation. How do you stay calm when you are interviewed by a council of judges?

Think of the group as individuals. Instead of thinking it's you versus the team, think of each of the interviewers as an individual. Try to connect with each person separately.

Try to get everyone's name if you can. Have a piece of paper handy that you can use to jot down everyone's name and role so that you can refer to them in the conversation. You want to be able to target your answers to each of the constituents. If you are interviewing with a panel of employees from a company and you know that Ms. Sweeny works in accounting while Mr. Duff works in human resources, you can speak about your analytical skills to appeal to Ms. Sweeny and your people skills to appeal to Mr. Duff.

Make eye contact. Look into the eyes of each of the panelists. Don't stare, but show them that you are confident. Be careful not to focus on only one member of the group.

Respect the hierarchy. You may find that there is a leader in the group like the scholarship chair or the CEO of the company. Pay a little more attention to stroke the ego of the person or persons in charge. They are used to it, they expect it and a little kissing up never hurt anyone.

Include everyone. In any group situation, there are usually one or two more vocal members who take the lead. Don't focus all your attention only on the loud ones. Spread your attention among the panelists as evenly as possible.

The Disaster Interview

Even if you do your interview homework and diligently practice mock interviewing, you may still find that you and your interviewer(s) just don't connect or that you just don't seem to have the right answers. For students who spend some time preparing, this is a very rare occurrence. Interviewers are not trying to trick you or make you feel bad. They are simply trying to find out more about you and your fit with the award. Still, if you think that you've bombed, here are some things to keep in mind:

Avoid should have, would have, could have. Don't replay the interview in your head again and again, thinking of all the things you should have said. It's too easy to look back and have the best answers. Instead, use what you've learned to avoid making the same mistakes in your next interview.

There are no right answers. Remember that in reality there really are no right answers. Your answers may not have been perfect, but that doesn't mean that they were wrong. There are countless ways to answer the same question.

The toughest judge is you. Realize that you are your own greatest critic. While you may think that you completely bombed an interview, your interviewer will most likely not have as harsh an opinion.

The Post-Interview

After you complete your interviews, follow up with a thank you note. Remember that interviewers are typically volunteers and have made the time to meet with you. If you feel that there is very important information that you forgot to share in your interview, mention it briefly in your thank you note. If not, a simple note will suffice. You will leave a polite, lasting impression on your interviewer(s).

Final Thoughts

Chapter 8

How to Keep the Money You Win

When you learn to skydive, your first lesson does not start with jumping out of an airplane. First you go through training in which you learn techniques and safety measures—on the ground. Only after practicing on the ground can you take to the sky. In your scholarship education, you have just completed the ground training and are ready to take the plunge. As you move from the *strategies* for applying for scholarships to actually *applying* for them, we have a few words of advice on how to keep the dollars you earn and how to stay motivated.

Let's jump ahead to after you win a cache of scholarship dollars. It would be nice once the scholarship checks were written if you could run off for that well-deserved trip to the Bahamas. Alas, there are restrictions on how you can spend the cash and how you must maintain your scholarship. (Besides, everyone knows that Hawaii is the place to go.) Here are some tips to keep in mind:

Get to know your scholarship and financial aid administrators. These people will be able to answer questions about your award and make sure you are spending it in the way that you should.

Give the scholarship committee members proof if they want it. Some awards require that you provide proof of enrollment or transcripts. Send the committee whatever they need.

Be aware of your award's requirements and what happens if something changes. How long does the award last? What happens if you take a leave of absence, study part time, study abroad, transfer schools or quit your studies? College is full of possibilities! Do you have to maintain a minimum grade point average or take courses in a certain field?

Know if there are special requirements for athletic scholarships. If you've won an athletic scholarship, you are most likely required to play the sport. (You didn't get that full ride scholarship for nothing!) Understand the implications of what would happen if you were not able to play because of circumstances such as an injury or not meeting academic requirements.

Find out if the award is a cash cow (renewable). If an award is renewable, you are eligible to get it every year that you are in school. If so, find out what you need to do, and when you need to do it, to renew your scholarship. Some awards just require a copy of your transcript, while others require you to submit an entirely new application.

Understand restrictions for spending the dough. Some awards are limited to tuition. Others can be used for books, travel or even living expenses. Some provide the money directly to your school; others provide a check made out to you. Be aware of what you can spend the money on and what sort of records you need to keep.

Learn the tax implications of your award. Speak with the award administrator or your pals at the IRS (www.irs.gov or 800-829-1040). Be aware of requirements after you graduate. Some awards such as ROTC scholarships require employment after graduation. Because these arrangements can drastically affect your future, learn about the requirements now.

Keep the awarding organization up to date on your progress as a student. Write the organization a thank you note, and keep them updated on your progress at the end of the year. This is not only good manners, but it will also help ensure that the award is around in the future.

Parting Words

I (Gen) remember when I won the Sterling Scholarship, one of the highest honors for students in Hawaii. The awards ceremony was televised live throughout the state. For weeks before submitting my application, I prepared for the competition, compiling a 50-page application book, practicing for the eight hours of interviews and enlisting the help of no less than three teachers from my high school. Even though the scholarship was only $1,000, my parents still keep the trophy on display and share with unwitting visitors the videotape of my triumph. I realize now that I was able to put in such extensive effort because of my outlook on the award. I knew whether I won or lost, I would gain the experience of building a portfolio, becoming a skilled interviewee, working closely with my teachers and meeting some incredible students.

While scholarships are primarily a source of funding for your education, approach them in the same way you do your favorite sport or hobby. I also played for my school's tennis team—and lost just about every match. Yet, I continued because I enjoyed the sport and found the skills a challenge. If you approach your scholarships in this manner, you'll probably win more of them and have fun in the process. Treat them like a chore, and you'll hate every minute, neglecting to put in the effort required to win.

The bottom line is that if you are going to take the time to apply, you should take the time to win. The secrets, tips and strategies in this book will put you within striking distance. Follow them and you'll win more and more often. This book is unique in that it really is two books in one. Now that you know how to win, it's time to begin finding scholarships to put these strategies to use. The second half of this book is a complete listing of scholarships and awards and is indexed by various criteria so you can quickly find those that match your interests and qualifications. And, because we know you just can't get enough of us, we also encourage you to visit our website, SuperCollege. com, for the most up-to-date information on scholarships and financial aid.

We both wish you the best of luck.

A SPECIAL REQUEST

As you jump headlong into the wonderful world of scholarships, we have a special request. We would love to hear about your experiences with scholarships and how this book has helped you. Please send us a note after you've finished raking in your free cash for college.

Gen and Kelly Tanabe
c/o SuperCollege
2713 Newlands Avenue
Belmont, CA 94002

Onward! Flip the page and start finding scholarships. It's time to put all the strategies and tips you've just learned to work for you!

The Ultimate Scholarship Directory

Now it's time to put into action all that you learned in the first half of the book. We've done the hard work of scouring the country to find the best scholarships that you can win. We've made a special effort to select awards with broad eligibility requirements, which means you'll find plenty of scholarships that fit your background, goals and interests.

Before you jump into the directory, spend a few moments to learn how the scholarships are organized so you don't miss out on any awards for which you might be a good fit.

To help find the awards that match you best, we've conveniently organized our directory of scholarships into eight major categories.

Below is the complete list of categories and descriptions of the types of awards you'll find in each one. Remember to also use the various indexes in the back of the book to help you zero in on more scholarships.

General

This section lists scholarships that have the broadest eligibility requirements. Included are awards based on **academics**, **leadership** and **community service** to name a few. While some of the scholarships have GPA requirements, you'll be surprised at how many are not based on grades. Some are even awarded by random drawing.

Humanities / Arts

This section includes awards for students interested in **English** and **writing** as well as **foreign language** and **area studies**. It also includes all of the **visual and performing arts** such as **dancing**, **singing**, **acting**, **music**, **drawing**, **painting**, **sculpture**, **photography** and **graphic art**.

Social Sciences

This section deals with the study of the human aspects of the world. Often called the "soft sciences" it includes:

- Anthropology
- Accounting / Finance
- Archaeology
- Business Management
- Communications
- Criminology
- Economics
- Education / Teaching
- Geography
- History
- Hospitality / Travel
- International Relations
- Journalism / Broadcasting
- Law / Legal Studies
- Marketing / Sales
- Political Science
- Psychology
- Public Administration / Social Work
- Sociology
- Urban Studies

Sciences

Typically known as the "hard sciences," this category includes:

- Aerospace / Aviation
- Agriculture / Horticulture / Animals
- Anatomy
- Architecture
- Astronomy
- Biological Sciences / Life Sciences
- Biochemistry
- Chemistry
- Computer and Information Science
- Dentistry
- Earth and Planetary Sciences
- Ecology
- Engineering
- Forestry / Wildlife
- Geology
- Health Professions / Medicine
- Mathematics
- Neuroscience
- Nursing
- Oceanography
- Paleontology
- Pathology

- Pharmacology
- Physics
- Zoology

State of Residence

Here's your opportunity to get something back from your (or your parents') state tax dollars. Every state offers scholarships and grants for their residents. Some states even offer awards to out-of-state students who study in their states. Be sure to look at both your home state as well as any of the states you are planning to go to college in to find the most awards.

Membership

Many large **companies**, **unions**, **organizations** and **religious organizations** give awards to their members. If you or your parents are members of any of the groups in this category, you may qualify for a scholarship.

Ethnicity /Race/Gender/Family Situation/Sexual Orientation

There are a lot of awards for members of minority and nonminority ethnic groups, women and students with unique family situations.

Disability / Illness

This section has awards for students with physical, hearing, vision, mental and learning disabilities. It also includes awards for students who have been afflicted with certain illnesses.

"Take Off the Blinders" to Find the Most Scholarships

Now that you know the categories, the best way to find scholarships is to jump right in and head to the sections that fit you best.

Do you remember when your elementary school teacher used to say, "Take off the mental blinders"? Ours did to encourage us to think broadly. In the same way, we want to encourage you to "take off the scholarship blinders" and not think about yourself too narrowly. Consider your accomplishments, activities, goals and background as broadly as possible. Look through some of the categories even if you don't immediately see a fit. You might discover that you actually fit one of the leadership scholarships even if you haven't held a formal leadership position. Or you may find an award in the sciences category in a field that you love but never realized was a science.

Don't be afraid to be forward-thinking. Write down any scholarships that fit, even if you have to wait a year to apply. The awards we have selected are from the larger organizations and businesses, so you can be certain that they are going to be around for a long time.

We are really excited that you can now put everything that you learned to good use to help you find and win some free cash for college.

Happy scholarship hunting!

GENERAL

(1) · $1,000 All Star Verified Scholarship

Verified Scholarships
2713 Newlands Avenue, Belmont, CA 94002
Email: admin@verifiedscholarships.com
https://www.verifiedscholarships.com/scholarship-program/
Purpose: This scholarship is to help students pay for college and it may be used to pay for tuition or any related fees such as room and board.
Eligibility: Applicants must be high school, college, graduate or adult students or parents of high school and college students. Applicants must complete the application form and answer in 450 characters or less the question: "What is the best or worst part about finding or applying to scholarships?"
Target applicant(s): Junior high students or younger. High school students. College students. Adult students.
Amount: $1,000.
Number of awards: 3.
Deadline: April 30, August 31, December 31.
How to apply: Applications are available online.
Exclusive: Visit www.UltimateScholarshipBook.com and enter code VE123 for updates on this award.

(2) · $1,000 GK Tanabe Student Scholarship

Gen and Kelly Tanabe Scholarship Program
Phone: 650-395-9655
Email: info@gkscholarship.com
https://www.gkscholarship.com
Purpose: To assist high school, college and graduate school students with educational expenses.
Eligibility: Applicants must be 9th-12th grade high school students, college students or graduate school students who are legal U.S. residents. Students may study any major and attend any college in the U.S.
Target applicant(s): High school students. College students. Adult students.
Amount: $1,000.
Number of awards: 2.
Deadline: July 31, December 31.
How to apply: Applications are available online.
Exclusive: Visit www.UltimateScholarshipBook.com and enter code GE223 for updates on this award.

(3) · $1,000 JumpStart Scholarship

College JumpStart Scholarship Fund
https://www.jumpstart-scholarship.net
Purpose: To recognize students who are committed to using education to better their life and that of their family and/or community.
Eligibility: Applicants must be 10th, 11th or 12th grade high school, college or adult students. Applicants may study any major and attend any college in the U.S. Applicants must be legal residents of the U.S. and complete the online application form including the required personal statement. The award may be used for tuition, room and board, books or any related educational expense.
Target applicant(s): High school students. College students. Adult students.
Amount: $1,000.
Number of awards: 3.
Deadline: April 15, October 17.
How to apply: Applications are available online.

Exclusive: Visit www.UltimateScholarshipBook.com and enter code CO323 for updates on this award.

(4) · $1,000 Moolahspot Scholarship

MoolahSPOT
http://www.moolahspot.com/scholarship/
Purpose: To help students pay for college or graduate school.
Eligibility: Students must be at least 16 years or older and plan to attend or currently attend college or graduate school. Applicants may study any major or plan to enter any career field at any accredited college or graduate school. A short personal statement is required.
Target applicant(s): High school students. College students. Adult students.
Amount: $1,000.
Number of awards: Varies.
Deadline: April 30, August 31, December 31.
How to apply: Applications are only available online.
Exclusive: Visit www.UltimateScholarshipBook.com and enter code MO423 for updates on this award.

(5) · $1,000 Scholarship Detective Launch Scholarship

Scholarship Detective
http://www.scholarshipdetective.com/scholarship/
Purpose: To help college and adult students pay for college or graduate school.
Eligibility: Applicants must be high school, college or graduate students (including adult students) who are U.S. citizens or permanent residents. Students may study any major. The funds may be used to attend an accredited U.S. institution for undergraduate or graduate education.
Target applicant(s): High school students. College students. Adult students.
Amount: $1,000.
Number of awards: 3.
Deadline: May 31, August 31, December 31.
How to apply: Applications are available online.
Exclusive: Visit www.UltimateScholarshipBook.com and enter code SC523 for updates on this award.

(6) · 1 for 2 Education Foundation Scholarship

1 For 2 Education Foundation
4337 East Grand River Road, Suite 198, Howell, MI 48843
Phone: 810-908-6295
Email: 1for2foundation@gmail.com
https://www.1for2edu.com/scholarship/
Purpose: To support highly motivated students who agree to "pay it forward."
Eligibility: Applicants must be enrolling as full-time students at an accredited four-year college or university and maintain a 3.0 GPA. Recipients agree to provide scholarships in the future. The deadline may close earlier than the deadline, once 250 completed applications are received.
Target applicant(s): High school students. College students. Graduate school students. Adult students.
Minimum GPA: 3.7
Amount: Varies.
Number of awards: Up to 2.
Deadline: February 1.
How to apply: Applications are available online.

Exclusive: Visit www.UltimateScholarshipBook.com and enter code 1 623 for updates on this award.

---

(7) · 100th Infantry Battalion Memorial Scholarship Fund

Hawaii Community Foundation - Scholarships
827 Fort Street Mall, Honolulu, HI 96813
Phone: 888-731-3863
Email: scholarships@hcf-hawaii.org
https://www.hawaiicommunityfoundation.org/
Purpose: To support students who promote the legacy of the 100th Infantry Battalion of World War II.
Eligibility: Applicants must be full-time undergraduate or graduate students at a two- or four-year college or university. They must be a direct descendant of a 100th Infantry Battalion World War II veteran and demonstrate excellence in academics and community service. A minimum 3.0 GPA is required. Students do not need to be a Hawaii resident.
Target applicant(s): High school students. College students. Graduate school students. Adult students.
Minimum GPA: 3.0
Amount: Varies.
Number of awards: Varies.
Deadline: January 31.
How to apply: Applications are available online. An application form, transcript and two letters of recommendation are required.
Exclusive: Visit www.UltimateScholarshipBook.com and enter code HA723 for updates on this award.

---

(8) · 1Dental Scholarship

1Dental.com
5535 Airport Freeway, Haltom City, TX 76117
Phone: 800-372-7615
Email: scholarships@1dental.com
http://www.1dental.com/scholarship/
Purpose: To support students in higher education.
Eligibility: Applicants must be currently enrolled high school seniors, college or graduate school students who are also U.S. citizens. Applicants must answer a 30-question survey.
Target applicant(s): High school students. College students. Graduate school students. Adult students.
Amount: $500.
Number of awards: 1.
Deadline: May 31.
How to apply: Apply by submitting the essay by email along with your full name, address, phone number, name of high school or college you are attending, school address, current GPA and grade level.
Exclusive: Visit www.UltimateScholarshipBook.com and enter code 1D823 for updates on this award.

---

(9) · AAU Karate Scholarship

AAU National Headquarters
c/o AAU Karate Scholarship, P.O. Box 22409, Lake Buena Vista, FL 32830
Phone: 407-828-3704
Email: jennifer@aausports.org
https://aaukarate.org/page.php?page_id=105811
Purpose: To reward a young man or woman who participated in AAU Karate for no less than four years.

Eligibility: Applicants must be enrolled in an accredited college or university or plan to attend an accredited college or university in the fall.
Target applicant(s): High school students. College students. Adult students.
Amount: $1,000.
Number of awards: 2.
Deadline: May 21.
How to apply: Applications are available online. An application form, an essay, a letter of recommendation and transcripts are required.
Exclusive: Visit www.UltimateScholarshipBook.com and enter code AA923 for updates on this award.

---

(10) · AAUS Student Scholarships

American Academy of Underwater Sciences
PO Box 9067, Mobile, AL 36691-9067
Phone: 251-591-3775
Email: aausfoundation@gmail.com
https://www.aausfoundation.org/
Purpose: To support students involved in collegiate research in which diving is a principle research tool.
Eligibility: Applicants must be a current member of AAUS and attending an undergraduate or a graduate level program. Selection is based on the project proposal submitted by the applicant. The proposal must describe the benefits of the project and how the funds will be used.
Target applicant(s): College students. Graduate school students. Adult students.
Amount: Up to $3,000.
Number of awards: Varies.
Deadline: June 30.
How to apply: Applications are available online and include a written project proposal and at least one letter of recommendation.
Exclusive: Visit www.UltimateScholarshipBook.com and enter code AM1023 for updates on this award.

---

(11) · Academic Excellence Award

Global Teletherapy
1777 Reisterstown Road, Suite 165R, Baltimore, MD 21208
Phone: 888-511-9395
Email: scholarship@globalteletherapy.com
https://globalteletherapy.com/scholarship/
Purpose: To encourage students to pursue higher education.
Eligibility: Applicants must be currently enrolled in a college or university and in good academic standing. A 3.0 minimum GPA is required. Students must submit a 2,000-word essay on the given topic. Selection is based on clear explanation of ideas and originality. Applications must be emailed.
Target applicant(s): College students. Graduate school students. Adult students.
Minimum GPA: 3.0
Amount: $1,000.
Number of awards: 1.
Deadline: November 12.
How to apply: Applications are via email and must include the essay, name, address, name of school attending and copy of transcript.
Exclusive: Visit www.UltimateScholarshipBook.com and enter code GL1123 for updates on this award.

---

(12) · Achieving Your Goals Scholarship

Atlanta Personal Injury Law Group - Gore LLC
295 West Crossville Road, Suite 200, Roswell, GA 30075

Phone: 404-436-1529
Email: Contact@atlantapersonalinjurylawgroup.com
https://atlinjurylawgroup.com/achieving-your-goals-scholarship/
Purpose: To support students who have unique goals shaped by specific situations or experiences.
Eligibility: Applicants must be enrolled in an undergraduate, graduate or law program within the United States or high school seniors who will be enrolled in college before the application deadline. Students must have a minimum cumulative 3.0 GPA. An essay on a provided topic is required to be submitted.
Target applicant(s): High school students. College students. Graduate school students. Adult students.
Minimum GPA: 3.0
Amount: $1,000.
Number of awards: 1.
Deadline: September 30.
How to apply: Applications are available online.
Exclusive: Visit www.UltimateScholarshipBook.com and enter code AT1223 for updates on this award.

(13) · ACJA/Lambda Alpha Epsilon Scholarship

American Criminal Justice Association
P.O. Box 601047, Sacramento, CA 95860-1047
Phone: 916-484-6553
Email: acjalae@aol.com
https://www.acjalae.org/membership-benefits.html
Purpose: To assist criminal justice students.
Eligibility: Applicants must be undergraduate or graduate students who are studying criminal justice. Students must be ACJA/LAE members, but they may submit a membership form at the time of application. Applicants must have completed at least two semesters or three quarters of their education while earning at least a 3.0 GPA. Applicants must submit transcripts, letters of enrollment and goals statements.
Target applicant(s): High school students. College students. Graduate school students. Adult students.
Minimum GPA: 3.0
Amount: Varies.
Number of awards: Varies.
Deadline: December 31.
How to apply: Applications are available online and by written request.
Exclusive: Visit www.UltimateScholarshipBook.com and enter code AM1323 for updates on this award.

(14) · Adult Skills Education Award

Imagine America Foundation
12001 Sunrise Valley Drive, Suite 203, Reston, VA 20191
Phone: 571-267-3010
Email: Leed@imagine-america.org
https://www.imagine-america.org/students/scholarships-education/
Purpose: To support adult learners with tuition assistance and college scholarships to career colleges.
Eligibility: Applicants must be U.S. citizens or permanent residents enrolling in a participating career college. Applicants must also either have a high school diploma, GED or pass an Ability to Benefit test. The minimum age requirement for application is 19. Applicants must also complete the NCCT Educational Success Potential Assessment. Selection is based on the overall strength of the application.
Target applicant(s): Adult students.
Amount: $1,000.
Number of awards: Varies.
Deadline: June 30.

How to apply: Applications are available online.
Exclusive: Visit www.UltimateScholarshipBook.com and enter code IM1423 for updates on this award.

(15) · AFCEA ROTC Scholarships

Armed Forces Communications and Electronics Association (AFCEA)
4400 Fair Lakes Court, Fairfax, VA 22033
Phone: 703-631-6149
http://www.afcea.org
Purpose: To assist ROTC sophomores or juniors who are majoring in aerospace engineering, electronics, computer science, computer engineering, physics or mathematics.
Eligibility: Applicants must major in electrical or aerospace engineering, electronics, computer science, computer engineering, physics or mathematics at an accredited U.S. four-year college or university. Applicants must also be enrolled full-time as college sophomores or juniors and be nominated by professors of military science, naval science or aerospace studies. Applicants must be U.S. citizens enrolled in ROTC, have good moral character, demonstrate academic excellence and the potential to serve as an officer in the U.S. Armed Forces and have financial need.
Target applicant(s): College students. Adult students.
Minimum GPA: 3.0
Amount: $2,000-$3,000.
Number of awards: Varies.
Deadline: May 31.
How to apply: Applications are available online.
Exclusive: Visit www.UltimateScholarshipBook.com and enter code AR1523 for updates on this award.

(16) · AFSA National Essay Contest

American Foreign Service Association (AFSA)
2101 East Street NW, Washington, DC 20037
Phone: 202-944-5504
Email: dec@afsa.org
http://www.afsa.org/afsa-scholarships
Purpose: To support students interested in writing an essay on foreign service.
Eligibility: Applicants must be U.S. Citizens, high school students and have parents who are not members of the Foreign Service. Students must attend a public, private, parochial school, home school or participate in a high school correspondence program in any of the 50 states, the District of Columbia or U.S. territories or must be U.S. citizens attending schools overseas. The current award is $2,500 to the student and an all expenses paid trip to Washington, DC, for the winner and parents.
Target applicant(s): High school students.
Amount: $2,500.
Number of awards: 1.
Deadline: April 4.
How to apply: The registration form is available online. Applicants must write a no more than 1,250-word essay on the topic provided.
Exclusive: Visit www.UltimateScholarshipBook.com and enter code AM1623 for updates on this award.

(17) · Ag Day Essay Contest

Agriculture Council of America
11020 King Street, Suite 205, Overland Park, KS 66210
Phone: 913-491-1895
Email: jenam@nama.org

https://www.agday.org/essay-contest

Purpose: To support agricultural awareness while encouraging students to pursue higher education.

Eligibility: Applicants must be in 9th to 12th grade during the current school year and be a U.S. citizen. The contest requires an essay or video response to the given prompt on the website.

Target applicant(s): High school students.

Amount: $1,000.

Number of awards: 2.

Deadline: January 31.

How to apply: Applications are available online.

Exclusive: Visit www.UltimateScholarshipBook.com and enter code AG1723 for updates on this award.

(18) · AHHS Foundation Scholarship

American Hackney Horse Society

4059 Iron Works Parkway A-3, Lexington, KY 40511-8462

Phone: 859-255-8694

Email: ahhscsl@qx.net

http://hackneysociety.com/

Purpose: To aid incoming college freshmen who promote the Hackney industry.

Eligibility: The applicant must be a high school senior or recent graduate. Selection is based on academic achievement, financial need, community service, involvement with Hackney Horses and the letters of recommendation.

Target applicant(s): High school students.

Amount: $2,500.

Number of awards: Varies.

Deadline: July 15.

How to apply: Applications are available online and include a personal essay, an official transcript and three letters of recommendation. A personal interview may also be required.

Exclusive: Visit www.UltimateScholarshipBook.com and enter code AM1823 for updates on this award.

(19) · Air Force ROTC ASCP

Air Force Reserve Officer Training Corps

HQ AFROTC/DOR, 60 West Maxwell Boulevard, Maxwell AFB, AL 36112-6501

Phone: 866-423-7682

https://www.afrotc.com/

Purpose: To allow active duty Air Force personnel to earn a commission while completing their bachelor's degree.

Eligibility: Applicants must be active-duty Air Force personnel who are U.S. citizens under the age of 31, with the exception of nurses, who must be under the age of 42. They must also meet all testing and waiver requirements and be recommended by their commanding officer. Applicants must have at least 24 hours of graded college course work with at least a 3.0 cumulative GPA and have a minimum ACT composite score of 26 or an SAT combined Reading and Math score of 1180 or an AFOQT Academic Aptitude score of 55.

Target applicant(s): High school students. College students. Adult students.

Minimum GPA: 3.0

Amount: Up to $18,000 plus textbook allowance and stipend.

Number of awards: Varies.

Scholarship may be renewable.

Deadline: October 15.

How to apply: Application details are available online.

Exclusive: Visit www.UltimateScholarshipBook.com and enter code AI1923 for updates on this award.

(20) · Air Force ROTC High School Scholarship Program

Air Force Reserve Officer Training Corps

HQ AFROTC/DOR, 60 West Maxwell Boulevard, Maxwell AFB, AL 36112-6501

Phone: 866-423-7682

https://www.afrotc.com/

Purpose: To help students with financial need who are also interested in joining the Air Force in order to pay for college.

Eligibility: Applicants must pass the physical fitness assessment and demonstrate academic achievement or outstanding leadership skills. There are three types of award: one that pays full tuition, most fees and a book allowance, one that pays tuition and fees up to $18,000 and a book allowance and one that pays the equivalent of in-state tuition and a book allowance. In return for the scholarship, recipients must serve in the Air Force. Applicants must have minimum ACT score of 24 or minimum SAT score of 1100. GPA minimum requirement is 3.0.

Target applicant(s): High school students.

Minimum GPA: 3.0

Amount: Up to full tuition plus fees, books and stipend.

Number of awards: Varies.

Scholarship may be renewable.

Deadline: January 13.

How to apply: Applications are available online.

Exclusive: Visit www.UltimateScholarshipBook.com and enter code AI2023 for updates on this award.

(21) · Air Force ROTC In-College Program

Air Force Reserve Officer Training Corps

HQ AFROTC/DOR, 60 West Maxwell Boulevard, Maxwell AFB, AL 36112-6501

Phone: 866-423-7682

https://www.afrotc.com/

Purpose: To promote the Air Force ROTC program.

Eligibility: Applicants must be U.S. citizens who have passed the Air Force Officer Qualifying Test, the Air Force ROTC Physical Fitness Test and a Department of Defense medical examination. Students must also be college freshmen or sophomores and have a GPA of 2.5 or higher.

Target applicant(s): College students. Adult students.

Minimum GPA: 2.5

Amount: Varies.

Number of awards: Varies.

Scholarship may be renewable.

Deadline: Varies.

How to apply: Applications are available from your school's Air Force ROTC detachment.

Exclusive: Visit www.UltimateScholarshipBook.com and enter code AI2123 for updates on this award.

(22) · Air Force ROTC Professional Officer Course-Early Release Program

Air Force Reserve Officer Training Corps

HQ AFROTC/DOR, 60 West Maxwell Boulevard, Maxwell AFB, AL 36112-6501

Phone: 866-423-7682

https://www.afrotc.com/

Purpose: To allow active duty Air Force personnel the opportunity for early release in order to complete their bachelor's degrees.

Eligibility: Applicants must be active-duty Air Force personnel who are U.S. citizens under the age of 31, with the exception of nurses, who must be under the age of 42. They must also meet all testing and waiver requirements, be recommended by their commanding officer and not be within one year of receiving their degree.

Target applicant(s): College students. Adult students.

Minimum GPA: 2.5

Amount: Varies.

Number of awards: Varies.

Scholarship may be renewable.

Deadline: Varies.

How to apply: Application details are available online.

Exclusive: Visit www.UltimateScholarshipBook.com and enter code AI2223 for updates on this award.

---

(23) · Air Force ROTC SOAR Program

Air Force Reserve Officer Training Corps
HQ AFROTC/DOR, 60 West Maxwell Boulevard, Maxwell AFB, AL 36112-6501
Phone: 866-423-7682
https://www.afrotc.com/

Purpose: To give active duty Air Force personnel the opportunity to earn their commissions while completing their bachelor's degrees.

Eligibility: Applicants must be active-duty Air Force personnel who are U.S. citizens under the age of 31, with the exception of nurses, who must be under the age of 47. They must also meet all testing and waiver requirements and be recommended by their commanding officer. Students must have at least 24 hours of graded college course work with at least a 3.0 cumulative GPA and have a minimum ACT composite score of 25 or an SAT combined Reading and Math score of 1180 or an AFOQT Academic Aptitude score of 55.

Target applicant(s): College students. Adult students.

Minimum GPA: 3.0

Amount: Up to $18,000 plus textbook allowance and stipend.

Number of awards: Varies.

Scholarship may be renewable.

Deadline: October 15.

How to apply: Application details are available online.

Exclusive: Visit www.UltimateScholarshipBook.com and enter code AI2323 for updates on this award.

---

(24) · Airmen Memorial Foundation Scholarship Program

Air Force Sergeants Association
5211 Auth Road, Suitland, MD 20746
Phone: 301-899-3500
Email: staff@hqafsa.org
http://www.hqafsa.org

Purpose: To assist dependents of Air Force enlisted personnel in obtaining higher education.

Eligibility: Applicants must be dependents of Air Force enlisted personnel who are attending high school or college. They must have a GPA of 3.5 or higher and be accepted to the college of their choice.

Target applicant(s): High school students. College students. Adult students.

Minimum GPA: 3.5

Amount: Up to $2,000.

Number of awards: Varies.

Deadline: April 21.

How to apply: Applications are available online.

Exclusive: Visit www.UltimateScholarshipBook.com and enter code AI2423 for updates on this award.

---

(25) · Akash Kuruvilla Memorial Scholarship

Akash Kuruvilla Memorial Scholarship Fund Inc.
P.O. Box 140900, Gainesville, FL 32614
Email: akmsfinfo@gmail.com
https://www.akmscholarship.com

Purpose: To continue the legacy of Akash Jacob Kuruvilla.

Eligibility: Applicants must be entering or current full-time college students at an accredited U.S. four-year college or university. They must demonstrate academic achievement, leadership, integrity and excellence in diversity. Selection is based on character, financial need and the applicant's potential to impact his or her community.

Target applicant(s): High school students. College students. Adult students.

Amount: $1,000.

Number of awards: 2.

Deadline: June 25.

How to apply: Applications are available online. An application form, essay, personal statement, one recommendation letter and resume are required.

Exclusive: Visit www.UltimateScholarshipBook.com and enter code AK2523 for updates on this award.

---

(26) · All-American Scholars (Cheerleading)

Pop Warner Little Scholars Inc.
586 Middletown Boulevard, Suite C-100, Langhorne, PA 19047
Phone: 215-752-2691
https://www.popwarner.com/Default.aspx?tabid=1404834

Purpose: To recognize Pop Warner participants for their academic accomplishments.

Eligibility: Applicant must be a participant in the Pop Warner program as a cheerleader, be in grade 5 or higher and maintain a 96 percent grade point average or higher. Selection will be based on academic achievement and additional non-sport related activities and achievements.

Target applicant(s): Junior high students or younger. High school students.

Minimum GPA: 3.8

Amount: Varies.

Number of awards: Varies.

Deadline: Varies.

How to apply: Applications are available online.

Exclusive: Visit www.UltimateScholarshipBook.com and enter code PO2623 for updates on this award.

---

(27) · All-American Scholars (Football)

Pop Warner Little Scholars Inc.
586 Middletown Boulevard, Suite C-100, Langhorne, PA 19047
Phone: 215-752-2691
https://www.popwarner.com/Default.aspx?tabid=1404834

Purpose: To recognize Pop Warner participants for their academic accomplishments.

Eligibility: Applicants must be a participant in the Pop Warner program as a football player, be in grade 5 or higher and maintain a 96 percent grade point average or higher. Selection will be based on academic achievement and additional non-sport related activities and achievements.

Target applicant(s): Junior high students or younger. High school students.
Minimum GPA: 3.8
Amount: Varies.
Number of awards: Varies.
Deadline: Varies.
How to apply: Applications are available online.
Exclusive: Visit www.UltimateScholarshipBook.com and enter code PO2723 for updates on this award.

---

(28) · Alpha Kappa Alpha Financial Need Scholars

Alpha Kappa Alpha Educational Advancement Foundation Inc.
5656 S. Stony Island Avenue, Chicago, IL 60637
Phone: 800-653-6528
Email: akaeaf@akaeaf.net
https://akaeaf.org/scholarships
Purpose: To assist undergraduate and graduate students who have overcome hardship to achieve educational goals.
Eligibility: Applicants must be studying full-time at the sophomore level or higher at an accredited institution and have a GPA of 2.5 or higher. Students must also demonstrate leadership, volunteer, civic or academic service. The program is open to students without regard to sex, race, creed, color, ethnicity, religion, sexual orientation or disability. Students do NOT need to be members of Alpha Kappa Alpha. Deadline is April 15 for undergraduate students and August 15 for graduate students.
Target applicant(s): College students. Graduate school students. Adult students.
Minimum GPA: 2.5
Amount: Varies.
Number of awards: Varies.
Deadline: April 15 for undergraduate students; August 15 for graduate students.
How to apply: Applications are available online. An application form, personal statement and three letters of recommendation are required.
Exclusive: Visit www.UltimateScholarshipBook.com and enter code AL2823 for updates on this award.

---

(29) · America's 911 Foundation Scholarship

America's 911 Foundation Inc.
13630 Barnhouse Place, Leesburg, VA 20176
Phone: 703-771-0118
Email: lisa@americas911foundation.org
http://www.americas911foundation.org
Purpose: To support students who are children of a first responder.
Eligibility: Applicants must be a child of an active duty or volunteer first responder. Students must be accepted to a college or university.
Target applicant(s): High school students. College students. Graduate school students. Adult students.
Amount: $2,000.
Number of awards: 15.
Deadline: March.
How to apply: Applications are available online.
Exclusive: Visit www.UltimateScholarshipBook.com and enter code AM2923 for updates on this award.

---

(30) · American Bar Association Law Day Art Contest

American Bar Association (ABA)
321 North Clark Street, Chicago, IL 60654
Phone: 312-988-5000
https://www.americanbar.org/groups/public_education/law-day/
Purpose: To encourage students to learn about the legal system.
Eligibility: Applicants must be high school students in grades 9-12 or the equivalent within the United States. Students must create an art piece representing the theme for Law Day.
Target applicant(s): High school students.
Amount: $750.
Number of awards: 2.
Deadline: March 1.
How to apply: Applications are available online.
Exclusive: Visit www.UltimateScholarshipBook.com and enter code AM3023 for updates on this award.

---

(31) · American Fire Sprinkler Association High School Senior Scholarship Contest

American Fire Sprinkler Association
12750 Merit Drive, Suite 350, Dallas, TX 75251
Phone: 214-349-5965
Email: scholarship@firesprinkler.org
https://www.afsascholarship.org/high-school-contest/
Purpose: To provide financial aid to high school seniors and introduce them to the fire sprinkler industry.
Eligibility: Applicants must be high school seniors who plan to attend a U.S. college, university or certified trade school. Students must read the "Fire Sprinkler Essay" available online and then take an online quiz. Applicants receive one entry in the scholarship drawing for each question answered correctly. Online entries only. No email or U.S. mail submissions.
Target applicant(s): High school students.
Amount: $2,000.
Number of awards: 10.
Deadline: April 1.
How to apply: Applications are available online.
Exclusive: Visit www.UltimateScholarshipBook.com and enter code AM3123 for updates on this award.

---

(32) · American Legion Baseball Scholarship

American Legion Baseball
700 N. Pennsylvania Street, P.O. Box 1055, Indianapolis, IN 46206
Phone: 317-630-1203
Email: baseball@legion.org
https://www.legion.org/scholarships/baseball
Purpose: To award scholarships to members of American Legion-affiliated baseball teams.
Eligibility: Applicants must have graduated high school and be nominated by a head coach or team manager. One player per department (state) will be selected. Nominations should be sent to the local Department Headquarters. Scholarships may be used to further education at any accredited college, university or other institution of higher education.
Target applicant(s): College students. Adult students.
Amount: $2,500-$5,000.
Number of awards: 9.
Deadline: July 15.
How to apply: Applications are available online.
Exclusive: Visit www.UltimateScholarshipBook.com and enter code AM3223 for updates on this award.

(33) · American Legion Legacy Scholarships

American Legion
700 North Pennsylvania Street, P.O. Box 1055, Indianapolis, IN 46206
Phone: 317-630-1202
https://www.legion.org/scholarships
Purpose: To support the children of deceased U.S. military personnel.
Eligibility: Applicants must be the children or adopted children of a parent who was in the U.S. military and died in active duty on or after September 11, 2001. Students must be high school seniors or high school graduates pursuing or planning to pursue undergraduate study in the U.S.
Target applicant(s): High school students. College students. Adult students.
Amount: Up to $20,000.
Number of awards: Varies.
Deadline: April 15.
How to apply: Applications are available online.
Exclusive: Visit www.UltimateScholarshipBook.com and enter code AM3323 for updates on this award.

(34) · American Society of Crime Laboratory Directors Scholarship Program

American Society of Crime Laboratory Directors
139A Technology Drive, Garner, NC 27529
Phone: 919-773-2600
http://www.ascld.org
Purpose: To help students who are enrolled in a forensics-related degree program and who plan to pursue a career in the forensics field.
Eligibility: Applicants must be rising undergraduate juniors, rising undergraduate seniors or graduate students who are enrolled in a degree program in forensic science, forensic chemistry or a related physical or natural science. They must attend an accredited university and must be interested in pursuing a career in the field of forensics. Preference is given to students who are enrolled in degree programs accredited by the Forensic Science Education Program Accreditation Commission (FEPAC). Selection is based on overall academic achievement, achievement in forensics coursework, personal statement, level of interest in forensics careers and recommendation letter.
Target applicant(s): College students. Graduate school students. Adult students.
Amount: $1,000.
Number of awards: Varies.
Deadline: February 15.
How to apply: Applications are available online. An application form, transcripts, personal statement and one recommendation letter are required.
Exclusive: Visit www.UltimateScholarshipBook.com and enter code AM3423 for updates on this award.

(35) · Americanism Essay Contest

Fleet Reserve Association (FRA)
FRA Scholarship Administrator, 125 N. West Street, Alexandria, VA 22314
Phone: 800-372-1924
Email: news-fra@fra.org
https://www.fra.org/fra/Web/Events_and_Programs/7_12th_Grade_Essay_Contest/Web/Content/Essay_Contest.aspx?hkey=707c4b42-2eb8-4992-9d57-31b8bd14c68a
Purpose: To recognize outstanding student essayists.

Eligibility: Applicants must be in grades 7 through 12 and must be sponsored by a Fleet Reserve Association (FRA) branch or Ladies Auxiliary unit. They must submit an essay on a sponsor-determined topic. Selection is based on the overall strength of the essay.
Target applicant(s): Junior high students or younger. High school students.
Amount: $1,000-$5,000.
Number of awards: Varies.
Deadline: December 1.
How to apply: Entry instructions are available online - look under "events and programs" link. An essay and cover sheet are required.
Exclusive: Visit www.UltimateScholarshipBook.com and enter code FL3523 for updates on this award.

(36) · Americorps National Civilian Community Corps

AmeriCorps
1201 New York Avenue NW, Washington, DC 20525
Phone: 202-606-5000
Email: questions@americorps.org
http://www.americorps.gov
Purpose: To strengthen communities and develop leaders through community service.
Eligibility: Applicants must be U.S. citizens who are between 18 and 26 years of age. Recipients must live on one of five AmeriCorps campuses in Denver, Colorado; Sacramento, California; Baltimore, Maryland; Vinton, Iowa or Vicksburg, Mississippi. Applicants must commit to 10 months of service on projects in areas such as education, public safety, the environment and other unmet needs. The projects are located within the region of one of the four campuses.
Target applicant(s): High school students. College students. Graduate school students. Adult students.
Amount: $5,775.
Number of awards: Varies.
Deadline: December 31.
How to apply: Applications are available online.
Exclusive: Visit www.UltimateScholarshipBook.com and enter code AM3623 for updates on this award.

(37) · Americorps Vista

AmeriCorps
1201 New York Avenue NW, Washington, DC 20525
Phone: 202-606-5000
Email: questions@americorps.org
http://www.americorps.gov
Purpose: To provide education assistance in exchange for community service.
Eligibility: Applicants must be United States citizens who are at least 17 years of age. They must be available to serve full-time for one year at a nonprofit organization or local government agency with an objective that may include to fight illiteracy, improve health services, create businesses or strengthen community groups.
Target applicant(s): High school students. College students. Graduate school students. Adult students.
Amount: Varies.
Number of awards: Varies.
Deadline: Rolling.
How to apply: Applications are available online.
Exclusive: Visit www.UltimateScholarshipBook.com and enter code AM3723 for updates on this award.

(38) · AMVETS National Scholarships for Entering College Freshman

AMVETS National Headquarters
4647 Forbes Boulevard, Lanham, MD 20706-4380
Phone: 877-726-8387
Email: thilton@amvets.org
http://www.amvets.org
Purpose: To provide education assistance for graduating JROTC cadets.
Eligibility: Applicants must be high school seniors with a minimum GPA of 3.0 or documented extenuating circumstances. They must be United States citizens and children or grandchildren of U.S. veterans. They must show academic potential and financial need.
Target applicant(s): High school students.
Minimum GPA: 3.0
Amount: $1,000.
Number of awards: 1.
Deadline: April 30.
How to apply: Applications are available online.
Exclusive: Visit www.UltimateScholarshipBook.com and enter code AM3823 for updates on this award.

(39) · AMVETS National Scholarships for Veterans

AMVETS National Headquarters
4647 Forbes Boulevard, Lanham, MD 20706-4380
Phone: 877-726-8387
Email: thilton@amvets.org
http://www.amvets.org
Purpose: To provide financial assistance for veterans.
Eligibility: Applicants must be United States citizens and veterans who demonstrate financial need. They must have been honorably discharged or be on active duty and eligible for release. They must agree to allow AMVET to publicize their award if selected.
Target applicant(s): College students. Adult students.
Amount: $1,000-$12,000.
Number of awards: Varies.
Deadline: April 30.
How to apply: Applications are available online.
Exclusive: Visit www.UltimateScholarshipBook.com and enter code AM3923 for updates on this award.

(40) · Anchor Scholarship Foundation Scholarship

Anchor Scholarship Foundation
138 South Rosemont Road, Suite 10206, Virginia Beach, VA 23452
Phone: 757-671-3200
Email: ScholarshipAdmin@AnchorScholarship.com
http://www.anchorscholarship.com
Purpose: To assist the dependents of current and former members of the Naval Surface Forces, Atlantic and Naval Surface Forces, Pacific.
Eligibility: Applicants must be high school seniors or college students planning to attend or currently attending an accredited, two- or four-year college or university full-time pursuing a first associates, BA or BS degree or Industry Certification in the United States. Applicants must also be dependents of service members who are on active duty or retired and have served a minimum of six years in a unit under the administrative control of Commander, Naval Surface Forces, U.S. Atlantic Fleet or U.S. Pacific Fleet. Applicants must be the dependent child or spouse of a U.S. Navy sailor (active, retired, honorably discharged) now referred to as sponsor. The award is based on academics, extracurricular activities, character, all-around ability and financial need.

Target applicant(s): High school students. College students. Adult students.
Amount: Varies.
Number of awards: Varies.
Deadline: March 1.
How to apply: Applications are available online.
Exclusive: Visit www.UltimateScholarshipBook.com and enter code AN4023 for updates on this award.

(41) · Apartment Guide Scholarship

Apartment Guide/RentPath LLC
950 East Paces Ferry Road, Suite 2600, Atlanta, GA 30326
Phone: 678-421-3000
Email: rgreen@rentpath.com
https://www.apartmentguide.com/students/scholarship/
Purpose: To help offset the cost of higher education.
Eligibility: Applicants must be citizens or legal residents of the U.S. at least 17 years of age. Students must be accepted to or currently enrolled full-time at an accredited U.S. undergraduate program with a minimum GPA of 2.5. A 500-600 word essay on the given topic must be submitted along with the application.
Target applicant(s): High school students. College students. Adult students.
Minimum GPA: 2.5
Amount: $2,500.
Number of awards: 2.
Deadline: April 12.
How to apply: Applications are available online.
Exclusive: Visit www.UltimateScholarshipBook.com and enter code AP4123 for updates on this award.

(42) · Armed Services YMCA Annual Essay Contest

Armed Services YMCA
7405 Alban Station Court, Suite B215, Springfield, VA 22150-2318
Phone: 703-313-9600
Email: essaycontest@asymca.org
http://www.asymca.org
Purpose: To promote reading among children of service members and civilian Department of Defense employees.
Eligibility: Applicants must be K-12 students who are children of active duty or Reserve/Guard military personnel. Entrants up to eighth grade should write an essay of 300 words or less. High school entrants should write an essay of 500 words or less.
Target applicant(s): Junior high students or younger. High school students.
Amount: Varies.
Number of awards: Varies.
Deadline: Varies.
How to apply: Applications are available online.
Exclusive: Visit www.UltimateScholarshipBook.com and enter code AR4223 for updates on this award.

(43) · Army Emergency Relief's MG James Ursano Scholarship Program

Army Emergency Relief (AER)
200 Stovall Street Rm. 5S33, Alexandria, VA 22332
Phone: 703-428-0035
Email: education@aerhq.org
https://www.armyemergencyrelief.org/scholarships/

Purpose: To assist the children of Army families with their undergraduate education, vocational training and service academy education.
Eligibility: Applicants must be dependent children of Army soldiers who are unmarried and under the age of 22. Students must also be registered with the Defense Eligibility Enrollment Reporting System, have a minimum 2.0 GPA and be enrolled and accepted or pending acceptance as full-time students in post-secondary educational institutions. Awards are based primarily on financial need.
Target applicant(s): High school students. College students.
Minimum GPA: 2.0
Amount: Varies.
Number of awards: Varies.
Scholarship may be renewable.
Deadline: April 1.
How to apply: Applications are available online and by mail.
Exclusive: Visit www.UltimateScholarshipBook.com and enter code AR4323 for updates on this award.

(44) · Army Nurse Corps Association Scholarships

Army Nurse Corps Association (ANCA)
Scholarship Program, P.O. Box 458, Lisbon, MD 21765
Phone: 210-650-3534
Email: education@e-anca.org
http://e-anca.org/Scholarships
Purpose: To support nursing and nurse anesthesia students who are or plan to become affiliated with the U.S. Army.
Eligibility: Applicants must be enrolled in a bachelor's or graduate degree program in nursing or nurse anesthesia. They must be in the U.S. Army, planning to enter the U.S. Army or be the parent, spouse or child of a U.S. Army officer. They cannot already be receiving funding from any source that is associated with the U.S. Army. Selection is based on the overall strength of the application.
Target applicant(s): College students. Graduate school students. Adult students.
Amount: Varies.
Number of awards: Varies.
Deadline: Varies.
How to apply: Applications are available online. An application form, personal statement, endorsement from student's academic dean, official transcript and military service documents (if applicable) are required.
Exclusive: Visit www.UltimateScholarshipBook.com and enter code AR4423 for updates on this award.

(45) · Army ROTC Advanced Course

U.S. Army
Human Resources Command, 1600 Spearhead Division Avenue, Department #410, Fort Knox, KY 40122-5401
Phone: 888-276-9472
Email: askhrc.army@us.army.mil
https://www.goarmy.com
Purpose: To prepare ROTC members for service as officers.
Eligibility: Applicants must be rising college juniors who have completed the ROTC Basic Course or Leader's Training Course who have made a commitment to serve as an officer in the Army after they graduate. Students must take an ROTC class or lab each semester of their final two years of school and attend a summer leadership camp.
Target applicant(s): College students. Adult students.
Amount: Varies.
Number of awards: Varies.
Scholarship may be renewable.
Deadline: Varies.

How to apply: Applications are available from your school's military science department.
Exclusive: Visit www.UltimateScholarshipBook.com and enter code U.4523 for updates on this award.

(46) · Army ROTC Four-Year Scholarship Program

Army Headquarters
U.S. Army Cadet Command, 55 Patch Road, Fort Monroe, VA 23651
Email: atccps@monroe.army.mil
https://www.goarmy.com/rotc/scholarships.html
Purpose: To bolster the ranks of the Army, Army Reserve and Army National Guard by providing monetary assistance to eligible student candidates.
Eligibility: Applicants must be U.S. citizens and high school seniors, graduates or college freshmen with at least four years of college remaining who wish to attend one of 600 colleges and earn a commission. Recipients must serve in the Army for four to eight years after graduation.
Target applicant(s): High school students.
Minimum GPA: 2.5
Amount: Up to full tuition.
Number of awards: Varies.
Scholarship may be renewable.
Deadline: February.
How to apply: Applications are available online.
Exclusive: Visit www.UltimateScholarshipBook.com and enter code AR4623 for updates on this award.

(47) · Army ROTC Green To Gold Scholarship Program

Army Headquarters
U.S. Army Cadet Command, 55 Patch Road, Fort Monroe, VA 23651
Email: atccps@monroe.army.mil
https://www.goarmy.com/rotc/scholarships.html
Purpose: To provide scholarship funds for Army enlisted soldiers.
Eligibility: Applicants must be active duty enlisted members of the Army who wish to complete their baccalaureate degree requirements and obtain a commission. Recipients are required to serve in the U.S. Army. Applicants must also meet numerous U.S. Army related requirements, be a high school graduate or equivalent, have a minimum GPA of 2.5 (high school or college) and be a U.S. citizen under age 31.
Target applicant(s): High school students. College students. Adult students.
Minimum GPA: 2.5
Amount: Varies.
Number of awards: Varies.
Deadline: November.
How to apply: Applications are available online.
Exclusive: Visit www.UltimateScholarshipBook.com and enter code AR4723 for updates on this award.

(48) · Arnold Fencing Classic Scholarship

Arnold Schwarzenegger Fencing Classic
5770 Westbourne Avenue, Columbus, OH 43213
Phone: 614-330-2445
Email: arnold@royalarts.org
http://www.arnoldfencingclassic.com
Purpose: To support youth fencers as they pursue higher education.

Eligibility: Applicants must be competing in the Arnold Fencing Classic, be a U.S. citizen and be between the ages of 13 and 18 years old. Selection is based on competitive participation and success in fencing, academic achievement, personal essay and letter of recommendation.
Target applicant(s): Junior high students or younger. High school students. College students.
Amount: $2,500.
Number of awards: 1.
Deadline: February.
How to apply: Applications are available online or may be submitted via email. The application includes a school transcript, personal essay, letter of recommendation, a fencing bio and the completed registration for at least one event at the Arnold Fencing Classic.
Exclusive: Visit www.UltimateScholarshipBook.com and enter code AR4823 for updates on this award.

(49) · Ashley Soule Conroy Foundation Scholarship

Ashley Soule Conroy Foundation
Three Lakeway Center, 3838 North Causeway Boulevard, Suite 3130, Metairie, LA 70002
http://www.ashleysfoundation.org
Purpose: To support undergraduate students in pursuing study abroad.
Eligibility: Applicants must commit to at least one semester of full-time study abroad outside of the U.S. A minimum GPA of 3.0 is required. Students must be currently attending a four-year college and have earned at least 30 credits or completed one year of college. Selection is primarily based on demonstration of financial need, academic achievement and employment history.
Target applicant(s): College students. Adult students.
Minimum GPA: 3.0
Amount: $4,000.
Number of awards: 1-3.
Deadline: October 1, June 1.
How to apply: Applications are available online.
Exclusive: Visit www.UltimateScholarshipBook.com and enter code AS4923 for updates on this award.

(50) · AU Student Essay Contest

Americans United for Separation of Church and State
Attn.: Essay Contest Submission, 1310 L Street NW, Suite 200, Washington, DC 20005
Phone: 202-466-3234 x427
Email: students@au.org
https://www.au.org/essaycontest
Purpose: To emphasize the importance of the separation of church and state.
Eligibility: Applicants must be current high school juniors or seniors in the U.S. Students must submit an essay discussing potential violations of church-state separations as found in the topics listed on the website.
Target applicant(s): High school students.
Amount: $500-$1,500.
Number of awards: 3.
Deadline: April 19.
How to apply: Applications are available online.
Exclusive: Visit www.UltimateScholarshipBook.com and enter code AM5023 for updates on this award.

(51) · Babe Ruth League Scholarships

Babe Ruth League Inc.
1770 Brunswick Avenue, P.O. Box 5000, Trenton, NJ 08638
http://www.baberuthleague.org
Purpose: To provide educational assistance to players in the Babe Ruth Baseball and Softball divisions.
Eligibility: Applicants must be members or former members of the Babe Ruth Baseball or Softball leagues. They must be graduating high school seniors or enrolled college students. A short essay, copy of high school transcript and a letter of recommendation are required.
Target applicant(s): High school students. College students. Adult students.
Amount: Varies.
Number of awards: Varies.
Deadline: June 30.
How to apply: Applications are available online.
Exclusive: Visit www.UltimateScholarshipBook.com and enter code BA5123 for updates on this award.

(52) · BankMobile Financial Empowerment Scholarship

BankMobile
401 Park Avenue South, New York, NY 10016
Phone: 917-543-3254
Email: scholarship@bankmobile.com
https://www.bmtx.com/scholarship
Purpose: To support student financial literacy.
Eligibility: Applicants must be undergraduate or graduate level students, U.S. citizens, and have a minimum 3.0 GPA. Students must submit an essay explaining the importance of financial literacy in both their lives and their career. Special consideration is given to applicants who are actively promoting financial literacy within their community.
Target applicant(s): College students. Graduate school students. Adult students.
Minimum GPA: 3.0
Amount: $1,500.
Number of awards: 1.
Deadline: July 15.
How to apply: Applications are available online and must include an official transcript (high school or college) and the essay.
Exclusive: Visit www.UltimateScholarshipBook.com and enter code BA5223 for updates on this award.

(53) · Barbizon's College Tuition Scholarship

Barbizon International
4950 West Kennedy Boulevard, Suite 200, Tampa, FL 33609
Phone: 888-999-9404
Email: barbizon@barbizonmodeling.com
https://www.barbizonmodeling.com/scholarships/
Purpose: To support students who wish to continue their education.
Eligibility: Applicants must be legal U.S. residents who are planning to attend an accredited college or university. Students must fill out an entry form for the sweepstakes and must be accepted at an accredited college or university within three years of graduation.
Target applicant(s): High school students.
Amount: $100,000.
Number of awards: 1.
Deadline: December 31.
How to apply: Applications are available online.
Exclusive: Visit www.UltimateScholarshipBook.com and enter code BA5323 for updates on this award.

(54) · Be the Boss Scholarship

GoSkills
555 Bryant Street, #901, Palo Alto, CA 94301
Phone: 650-822-7732
Email: support@goskills.com
https://www.goskills.com/Scholarship
Purpose: To encourage women to start their own online business.
Eligibility: Applicants must be female high school or college students interested in starting their own online business. Students must submit their business plan to apply.
Target applicant(s): High school students. College students. Graduate school students. Adult students.
Amount: $2,000.
Number of awards: 2.
Scholarship may be renewable.
Deadline: September 15, March 15.
How to apply: Applications are available online.
Exclusive: Visit www.UltimateScholarshipBook.com and enter code GO5423 for updates on this award.

(55) · Beyond the Boroughs Scholarship

Beyond the Boroughs
30 East 125th Street, Suite 242, New York, NY 10035
Phone: 914-458-2926
Email: ray@beyondtheboroughs.org
http://www.beyondtheboroughs.org
Purpose: To support students with financial need in pursuing a bachelor's degree.
Eligibility: Applicants must be accepted to an accredited four-year college. A minimum GPA of 2.5 is required. Selection is primarily based on demonstration of financial need, academic achievement, work history and extracurricular involvement.
Target applicant(s): High school students. College students. Adult students.
Minimum GPA: 2.5
Amount: $20,000.
Number of awards: Varies.
Scholarship may be renewable.
Deadline: March 15.
How to apply: Applications are available online.
Exclusive: Visit www.UltimateScholarshipBook.com and enter code BE5523 for updates on this award.

(56) · Bob Warnicke Scholarship

Bob Warnicke Memorial Scholarship Fund
USA BMX/BMX Canada, 1645 W. Sunrise Boulevard, Gilbert, AZ 85233
Phone: 480-961-1903
Email: administration@nbl.org
http://www.usabmx.com
Purpose: To help students who have participated in BMX racing events.
Eligibility: Applicants must be members, have a current NBL competition license or official's license and have participated in BMX racing events for at least a year. Students must also be high school graduates and plan to or currently attend a postsecondary institution full- or part-time.
Target applicant(s): High school students. College students. Adult students.
Amount: Varies.
Number of awards: Varies.

Deadline: March.
How to apply: Applications are available online, by mail or by phone.
Exclusive: Visit www.UltimateScholarshipBook.com and enter code BO5623 for updates on this award.

(57) · Bonner Scholars Program

Bonner Foundation
10 Mercer Street, Princeton, NJ 08540
Phone: 609-924-6663
Email: info@bonner.org
http://www.bonner.org/apply
Purpose: To award four-year community service scholarships to students planning to attend one of 75 participating colleges.
Eligibility: Students must complete annual service requirements as stipulated by the organization. Awards are geared toward students demonstrating significant financial need. Scholarship recipients are named Bonner Scholars.
Target applicant(s): High school students.
Amount: Varies.
Number of awards: Varies.
Deadline: Varies.
How to apply: Contact the admission office at each participating school to request an application.
Exclusive: Visit www.UltimateScholarshipBook.com and enter code BO5723 for updates on this award.

(58) · Boomer Benefits Scholarship

Boomer Benefits
5650 N. Riverside Drive #200, Fort Worth, TX 76137
Phone: 855-732-9055
http://boomerbenefits.com
Purpose: To support adult students who are at least 50 years of age in returning to school to complete their degree.
Eligibility: Applicants must be enrolled in an undergraduate or graduate degree program at an accredited educational institution. A minimum GPA of 3.0 is required. Selection is primarily based on demonstration of academic achievement and community service.
Target applicant(s): Adult students.
Minimum GPA: 3.0
Amount: $2,000.
Number of awards: 1.
Deadline: August 27.
How to apply: Applications are available online.
Exclusive: Visit www.UltimateScholarshipBook.com and enter code BO5823 for updates on this award.

(59) · Bridging the Dream Scholarship

Bridging the Dream Scholarship
https://www.salliemae.com/about/scholarship-opportunities/
Purpose: To support students who wish to continue their education into college or graduate school.
Eligibility: Applicants must be citizens or permanent residents of the United States or United States territories. Students must be high school seniors from minority or other historically underserved communities, current college students in the final year of study with financial need or graduate or professional students from minority or other historically underserved communities.
Target applicant(s): High school students. College students. Graduate school students. Adult students.
Minimum GPA: 3.0

Amount: $2,500-$10,000.
Number of awards: 27.
Deadline: March 8.
How to apply: Applications are available online.
Exclusive: Visit www.UltimateScholarshipBook.com and enter code BR5923 for updates on this award.

(60) · Bright!Tax Global Scholar Initiative

Bright!Tax
244 Fifth Avenue, New York, NY 10001
Phone: 212-465-2528
Email: inquiries@brighttax.com
http://www.brighttax.com/scholarships.html
Purpose: To support students wishing to study abroad.
Eligibility: Applicants must be U.S. citizens who want to study abroad for at least one full semester at an accredited institution. Selection is based on academic and extracurricular achievement, community involvement, future ambitions and financial need.
Target applicant(s): High school students. College students. Graduate school students. Adult students.
Amount: $1,000.
Number of awards: Minimum of 2.
Deadline: June 1, November 1.
How to apply: Applications are available online.
Exclusive: Visit www.UltimateScholarshipBook.com and enter code BR6023 for updates on this award.

(61) · Burger King Scholars Program

Burger King Scholars Program
Scholarship America, One Scholarship Way, St. Peter, MN 56082
Phone: 305-378-3000
Email: burgerkingscholars@scholarshipamerica.org
https://burgerking.scholarsapply.org
Purpose: To provide financial assistance for high school seniors who have part-time jobs.
Eligibility: Applicants must be graduating high school seniors (U.S. and Puerto Rico), graduating from grade 12 (Canada) or graduating from home school education in the U.S., Puerto Rico or Canada and must reside in the U.S., Canadian or Puerto Rico. Students must also have a minimum 2.5 GPA and plan to enroll full-time in an accredited two- or four-year college, university or vocational/technical school by the fall term of the graduating year. Applicants do NOT need to work at Burger King, but Burger King employees are eligible. Consideration will be given to each applicant's academic record and participation in school and community activities.
Target applicant(s): High school students.
Minimum GPA: 2.5
Amount: Up to $1,000.
Number of awards: Varies.
Deadline: December 15.
How to apply: Applications are available online and may only be completed online.
Exclusive: Visit www.UltimateScholarshipBook.com and enter code BU6123 for updates on this award.

(62) · C.I.P. Scholarship

College Is Power
1025 Alameda de las Pulgas, No. 215, Belmont, CA 94002
http://collegeispower.com/scholarship.cfm
Purpose: To assist adult students age 17 and over with college expenses.
Eligibility: Applicants must be adult students currently attending or planning to attend a two-year or four-year college or university within the next 12 months. Students must be 17 years or older and U.S. citizens or permanent residents. The award may be used for full- or part-time study at either on-campus or online schools.
Target applicant(s): High school students. College students. Adult students.
Amount: $1,000.
Number of awards: Varies.
Deadline: May 31, August 31, December 31.
How to apply: Applications are available online.
Exclusive: Visit www.UltimateScholarshipBook.com and enter code CO6223 for updates on this award.

(63) · Capt. James J. Regan Scholarship

Explorers Learning for Life
1325 West Walnut Hill Lane, P.O. Box 152225, Irving, TX 75015-2225
Phone: 855-806-9992
Email: exploring@lflmail.org
http://www.exploring.org/scholarships/
Purpose: To support students who are Law Enforcement Explorers.
Eligibility: Students must be at least in their senior year of high school. Applicants must submit three letters of recommendation and an essay.
Target applicant(s): High school students. College students. Adult students.
Amount: $2,500.
Number of awards: 1.
Deadline: May 31.
How to apply: Applications are available online.
Exclusive: Visit www.UltimateScholarshipBook.com and enter code EX6323 for updates on this award.

(64) · Capt. Winifred Quick Collins, USN (Ret) Scholarship

Navy League Foundation
2300 Wilson Boulevard, Suite 200, Arlington, VA 22201-5424
Phone: 800-356-5760
Email: vfrye@navyleague.org
http://www.navyleague.org
Purpose: To support students who are the children or grandchildren of a member of the sea services.
Eligibility: Applicants must be enrolled at an accredited institution of higher education and the children or grandchildren of a member of the sea services to include the following: United States Navy, United States Marine Corps, United States Coast Guard or U.S.-flag Merchant Marine.
Target applicant(s): High school students.
Amount: $10,000.
Number of awards: 1.
Deadline: March 11.
How to apply: Applications are available online.
Exclusive: Visit www.UltimateScholarshipBook.com and enter code NA6423 for updates on this award.

(65) · Captain Caliendo College Assistance Fund

U.S. Coast Guard Chief Petty Officers Association
CCCAF Scholarship Committee, 5520-G Hempstead Way,
Springfield, VA 22151-4009
Phone: 703-941-0395
Email: cgcpoa@aol.com
http://www.uscgcpoa.org
Purpose: To provide financial assistance for children of CPOA/CGEA
members.
Eligibility: Applicants must be dependents of a living or deceased USCG
CPOA/CGEA member who are under the age of 24 as of March 1 of the
award year. The age limit does not apply to disabled children. Proof of
acceptance or enrollment in an institution of higher learning is required.
Target applicant(s): High school students. College students.
Amount: $1,000-$5,000.
Number of awards: 3.
Deadline: April 1.
How to apply: Applications are available online. An essay not exceeding
500 words is required.
Exclusive: Visit www.UltimateScholarshipBook.com and enter code
U.6523 for updates on this award.

(66) · Car Covers $1,000 Scholarship

CarCovers.com
671 Willow Pass Road, Suite 1, Pittsburg, CA 94565
Phone: 800-385-3603
http://www.carcovers.com/resources/scholarship/
Purpose: To support undergraduate and graduate students in funding
their education.
Eligibility: Applicants must submit an essay describing ways to extend
the service life of cars. Selection is based on the overall strength of the
submission.
Target applicant(s): College students. Graduate school students. Adult
students.
Amount: $1,000.
Number of awards: 1.
Deadline: December 15.
How to apply: Applications are available online.
Exclusive: Visit www.UltimateScholarshipBook.com and enter code
CA6623 for updates on this award.

(67) · CareerFitter Scholarship

CareerFitter.com
P.O. Box 124, Pisgah Forest, NC 28768
https://www.careerfitter.com/scholarship
Purpose: To support students in pursuing their college educations.
Eligibility: Applicants must be planning to enroll or already enrolled in
accredited college or graduate school program. Students are encouraged
to take a career test on Career Fitter's website and include the results
on their application. Selection is based on the overall strength of the
application.
Target applicant(s): High school students. College students. Graduate
school students. Adult students.
Minimum GPA: 2.4
Amount: $1,000.
Number of awards: 1.
Scholarship may be renewable.
Deadline: January 31.
How to apply: Applications must be completed online.

Exclusive: Visit www.UltimateScholarshipBook.com and enter code
CA6723 for updates on this award.

(68) · Caring Community Scholarship

Marcus & Mack
57 South 6th Street, Indiana, PA 15701
Phone: 724-349-5602
Email: info@marcusandmack.com
https://marcusandmack.com/#scholarship
Purpose: To support students interested in making their community
a better place.
Eligibility: Applicants must be U.S. citizens currently enrolled or about
to attend an accredited community college, undergraduate or graduate
program within the United States. Students must have a minimum 3.0
GPA. An essay submission is required on a provided topic.
Target applicant(s): High school students. College students. Graduate
school students. Adult students.
Minimum GPA: 3.0
Amount: $2,000.
Number of awards: 1.
Deadline: September 30.
How to apply: Applications are available online.
Exclusive: Visit www.UltimateScholarshipBook.com and enter code
MA6823 for updates on this award.

(69) · Carolyn Hines Memorial Scholarship Program

Civilian Marksmanship Program
P.O. Box 576, Port Clinton, OH 43452
Phone: 419-635-2141
Email: kwilliams@thecmp.org
https://thecmp.org/youth/cmp-scholarship-program/
Purpose: To aid students who have participated in marksmanship
competitions with their higher education costs.
Eligibility: Applicants must be a U.S. Citizen, represent good
moral character, have a 3.0 or higher GPA and participate in rifle or
pistol marksmanship competitions. Selection is based on academic
achievement, a letter of recommendation and a personal letter to the
committee explaining how the scholarship will help you to reach your
goals and marksmanship participation and success.
Target applicant(s): High school students.
Minimum GPA: 3.0
Amount: $1,000.
Number of awards: Varies.
Deadline: March 20.
How to apply: Applications are available online and must include the
letter to the committee, one letter of recommendation, a transcript and
documentation of marksmanship activity.
Exclusive: Visit www.UltimateScholarshipBook.com and enter code
CI6923 for updates on this award.

(70) · Carson Scholars

Carson Scholars Fund
305 W Chesapeake Avenue, Suite 310, Towson, MD 21204
Phone: 877-773-7236
Email: katie@carsonscholars.org
http://carsonscholars.org/scholarships/
Purpose: To recognize students who demonstrate academic excellence
and commitment to the community.
Eligibility: Applicants must be nominated by their school. They must
be in grades 4 through 11 and have a GPA of 3.75 or higher in English,

reading, language arts, math, science, social studies and foreign language. They must have participated in some form of voluntary community service beyond what is required by their school. Scholarship recipients must attend a four-year college or university upon graduation to receive funds.

Target applicant(s): Junior high students or younger. High school students.

Minimum GPA: 3.75

Amount: $1,000.

Number of awards: Varies.

Deadline: January 14.

How to apply: Applications are available from the schools of those nominated. Only one student per school may be nominated.

Exclusive: Visit www.UltimateScholarshipBook.com and enter code CA7023 for updates on this award.

(71) · Cashtelligent Financial Literacy Scholarship

Cashtelligent

https://www.cashtelligent.com/scholarship/

Purpose: This scholarship is designed to encourage students to increase their financial literacy skills and adopt positive habits for managing their personal finances both in college and beyond.

Eligibility: Applicants must be high school or college students, graduate school students, adult students or parents of a student enrolled or planning to enroll in any accredited college in the U.S. There are no requirements for field of study.

Target applicant(s): High school students. College students. Adult students.

Amount: $1,000.

Number of awards: 2.

Deadline: December 31.

How to apply: Applications are available online.

Exclusive: Visit www.UltimateScholarshipBook.com and enter code CA7123 for updates on this award.

(72) · CCA Christian Cheer Nationals

Christian Cheerleaders of America

P.O. Box 49, Bethania, NC 27010

Phone: 877-243-3722

Email: info@cheercca.com

http://www.cheercca.com

Purpose: To support cheerleaders who participate in cheer through Christian Cheerleaders of America.

Eligibility: Applicants must be a junior or senior in high school, participate in Christian Cheerleaders of America and be nominated by the cheer coach. The student should have a 3.0 GPA or higher. Selection is based on academic achievement and Christian service.

Target applicant(s): High school students.

Minimum GPA: 3.0

Amount: Varies.

Number of awards: Varies.

Deadline: February.

How to apply: Nomination forms are available online.

Exclusive: Visit www.UltimateScholarshipBook.com and enter code CH7223 for updates on this award.

(73) · Challenge Scholarship

National Strength and Conditioning Association (NSCA) Foundation

1885 Bob Johnson Drive, Colorado Springs, CO 80906

Phone: 800-815-6826

http://www.nsca.com/foundation/

Purpose: To support NSCA members pursuing studies related to strength and conditioning.

Eligibility: Applicants must be NSCA members for one year before applying and be pursuing careers in strength and conditioning. Students must submit an essay detailing their course of study, career goals and financial need. Applications are evaluated based on grades, courses, experience, honors, recommendations and involvement in the community and with NSCA.

Target applicant(s): High school students. College students. Graduate school students. Adult students.

Amount: $2,000.

Number of awards: Varies.

Deadline: October 15.

How to apply: Applications are available with membership.

Exclusive: Visit www.UltimateScholarshipBook.com and enter code NA7323 for updates on this award.

(74) · Charles T. Stoner Law Scholarship

Women's Basketball Coaches Association

4646 Lawrenceville Highway, Lilburn, GA 30047

Phone: 770-279-8027

Email: dtrujillo@wbca.org

https://wbca.org/recognize/player-awards

Purpose: To aid a female collegiate basketball player in her pursuit of a career in law.

Eligibility: Applicants must be a senior, collegiate women's basketball player who plans on pursuing a career in law and must be nominated by their collegiate head coach.

Target applicant(s): College students. Adult students.

Amount: $1,000.

Number of awards: 1.

Deadline: October.

How to apply: Applicants must be nominated by their collegiate head coach who are WBCA members. Nomination forms are available online. The nomination form, a letter of recommendation, academic major and GPA and present season statistics will all be considered.

Exclusive: Visit www.UltimateScholarshipBook.com and enter code WO7423 for updates on this award.

(75) · Chief Master Sergeants of the Air Force Scholarships

Air Force Sergeants Association

5211 Auth Road, Suitland, MD 20746

Phone: 301-899-3500

Email: staff@hqafsa.org

http://www.hqafsa.org

Purpose: To provide financial assistance to the families of Air Force enlistees.

Eligibility: Applicants must be dependents of enlisted Air Force members, either on active duty or retired. They must meet the eligibility requirements and participate in the Airmen Memorial Foundation Scholarship Program. An unweighted GPA of 3.5 or higher is required. Extenuating circumstances are considered.

Target applicant(s): High school students. College students. Adult students.

Minimum GPA: 3.5

Amount: Varies.

Number of awards: Varies.

Deadline: April 21.

How to apply: Applications are available online.
Exclusive: Visit www.UltimateScholarshipBook.com and enter code AI7523 for updates on this award.

(76) · Chief Petty Officer Scholarship Fund

Chief Petty Officer Scholarship Fund
328 Office Square Lane, Suite 101A, Virginia Beach, VA 23462
Phone: 757-233-9136
Email: cposfboard@cposf.org
http://www.cposf.org
Purpose: To aid the families of Chief Petty Officers of the U.S. Navy.
Eligibility: Applicants must be spouses or children of active, retired, honorably discharged or deceased or reserve Chief, Senior Chief or Master Chief Petty Officers of the U.S. Navy. They must be high school graduates or have earned a GED and plan to attend a college, university or post-secondary vocational institution to earn an AA, BA or BS degree. Current college students may also apply. Selection criteria include scholastic proficiency, character and all-around ability.
Target applicant(s): High school students. College students. Adult students.
Amount: Varies.
Number of awards: Varies.
Deadline: April 1.
How to apply: Applications are available online. An application form, three letters of recommendation, a copy of your dependents ID card and a personal statement are required.
Exclusive: Visit www.UltimateScholarshipBook.com and enter code CH7623 for updates on this award.

(77) · Children of Warriors National Presidents' Scholarship

American Legion Auxiliary
3450 Founders Road, Indianapolis, IN 46268
Phone: 317-569-4500
Email: alahq@alaforveterans.org
https://www.legion-aux.org/scholarships
Purpose: To award scholarships to children, grandchildren and great-grandchildren of veterans who served in the Armed Forces.
Eligibility: Applicants must be the children, grandchildren or great-grandchildren of veterans who served in the Armed Forces for membership in The American Legion, be high school seniors and complete 50 hours of community service. Selection is based on character, application/essay, scholastic achievement, leadership and financial need.
Target applicant(s): High school students.
Amount: $5,000.
Number of awards: 15.
Deadline: March 1.
How to apply: Applications are available online. Applicants should submit applications, four recommendation letters, essays, proof of volunteering, transcripts, ACT or SAT scores and parent's or grandparent's military service description.
Exclusive: Visit www.UltimateScholarshipBook.com and enter code AM7723 for updates on this award.

(78) · Chinese American Citizens Alliance Essay Contest

Chinese American Citizens Alliance
1044 Stockton Street, San Francisco, CA 94108
Phone: 415-829-9332
Email: info@cacanational.org
http://www.cacanational.org
Purpose: To provide a forum for expression for future leaders of the United States.
Eligibility: Applicants must be high school students in grades 9 through 12. Students do NOT need to be Chinese Americans. They must write a 500-word essay on a topic chosen by the Chinese American Citizens Alliance. The essay must be written on a given date at the student's local lodge or other designated location.
Target applicant(s): High school students.
Amount: Up to $1,000.
Number of awards: 13.
Deadline: March 1.
How to apply: Applications are available online. An application form and essay are required.
Exclusive: Visit www.UltimateScholarshipBook.com and enter code CH7823 for updates on this award.

(79) · Christophers Video Contest for College Students

Christophers
5 Hanover Square, 22nd Floor, New York, NY 10004
Phone: 212-759-4050
Email: youth@christophers.org
https://www.christophers.org/video-contest-for-college-students
Purpose: To support college students who believe in The Christophers' mission that any one person can make a difference.
Eligibility: Applicants must be current undergraduate or graduate level college students and U.S. citizens. Selection is based on the video submitted and how well it depicts the theme of "One Person Can Make a Difference."
Target applicant(s): College students. Graduate school students. Adult students.
Amount: $500-$2,000.
Number of awards: 3.
Deadline: January 16.
How to apply: Applications are available online. Students must also submit a video of five minutes or less communicating the theme.
Exclusive: Visit www.UltimateScholarshipBook.com and enter code CH7923 for updates on this award.

(80) · CIA Undergraduate Scholarship Program

Central Intelligence Agency
Office of Public Affairs, Washington, DC 20505
Phone: 703-482-0623
https://www.cia.gov/careers/jobs/undergraduate-scholarship-program/
Purpose: To encourage students to pursue careers with the CIA.
Eligibility: Applicants must be high school seniors or college freshmen or sophomores. High school students must have an SAT score of 1000 or higher or an ACT score of 21 or higher, while all applicants must have a GPA of at least 3.0. Applicants must demonstrate financial need, defined as a gross annual household income ceiling up to $120,000. They must meet all criteria for regular CIA employees, including security checks and medical examinations. Applicants must commit to a work experience each summer during college and agree to CIA employment for 1.5 times the length of their CIA-sponsored scholarship.
Target applicant(s): High school students. College students. Adult students.
Minimum GPA: 3.0
Amount: Varies.
Number of awards: Varies.

Scholarship may be renewable.
Deadline: August 31.
How to apply: Applications are available online. A resume, SAT/ACT scores, family income information, copy of FAFSA or Student Aid Report, transcript and two letters of recommendation are required.
Exclusive: Visit www.UltimateScholarshipBook.com and enter code CE8023 for updates on this award.

(81) · Civic Expression Award
Scholastic Art & Writing Awards
557 Broadway, New York, NY 10012
Email: info@artandwriting.org
http://www.artandwriting.org/scholarships/
Purpose: To support students who explore political or social issues.
Eligibility: Applicants must be in grades 7-12 (ages 13 and up) and enter art or writing works that explore political or social issues. Students may enter work in any of the 28 listed art and writing categories and must include a personal statement of 50 words or more on their work.
Target applicant(s): Junior high students or younger. High school students.
Amount: $1,000.
Number of awards: 6.
Deadline: December 1.
How to apply: Applications are available online.
Exclusive: Visit www.UltimateScholarshipBook.com and enter code SC8123 for updates on this award.

(82) · CJ Pony Parts Scholarship Video Contest
CJ Pony Parts
7461 Allentown Boulevard, Harrisburg, PA 17112
Phone: 800-888-6473
http://www.cjponyparts.com
Purpose: To support graduating seniors and undergraduate students in pursuing post-secondary education.
Eligibility: Applicants must be U.S. residents who will be enrolling in classes for the upcoming semester. Students must submit a video addressing an automotive related topic. Selection is based on the overall strength of the submission.
Target applicant(s): High school students. College students. Adult students.
Amount: $500.
Number of awards: 2.
Deadline: April 15, October 15.
How to apply: Applications are available online.
Exclusive: Visit www.UltimateScholarshipBook.com and enter code CJ8223 for updates on this award.

(83) · Clubs of America Scholarship Award for Career Success
Clubs of America
484 Wegner Road, Lakemoor, IL 60051
Phone: 800-258-2872
Email: scholarship@greatclubs.com
https://www.greatclubs.com/scholarship/
Purpose: To support undergraduate students in funding their education.
Eligibility: Applicants must be enrolled at an accredited U.S. educational institution. A minimum GPA of 3.0 is required. Students must submit an essay explaining their career goals. Selection is based on the overall strength of the submission.
Target applicant(s): College students. Adult students.

Minimum GPA: 3.0
Amount: $1,000.
Number of awards: 1.
Deadline: August 31.
How to apply: Applications are available online.
Exclusive: Visit www.UltimateScholarshipBook.com and enter code CL8323 for updates on this award.

(84) · Coast Guard College Student Pre-Commissioning Initiative
U.S. Coast Guard
2703 Martin Luther King Jr. Avenue SE, Washington, DC 20593-7000
Phone: 877-663-8724
http://www.gocoastguard.com
Purpose: To train future Coast Guard officers for success.
Eligibility: Applicants must be between 19 and 27 years of age and be college sophomores or juniors with at least 60 credits completed toward their degrees. They must be enrolled in a four-year degree program at a Coast Guard-approved institution with at least a 25 percent minority population. Students must be U.S. citizens, have a 2.5 or higher GPA and meet all physical requirements of the Coast Guard. Applicants must have a minimum score of 1100 on the SAT, 23 on the ACT or 109 on the ASVAB.
Target applicant(s): College students. Adult students.
Minimum GPA: 2.5
Amount: Tuition plus salary.
Number of awards: Varies.
Scholarship may be renewable.
Deadline: Varies.
How to apply: Applications are available online. An application form, physical exam results, immunization record, copy of Social Security card and driver's license, transcript, test results, proof of enrollment and tuition statement are required.
Exclusive: Visit www.UltimateScholarshipBook.com and enter code U.8423 for updates on this award.

(85) · Coast Guard Foundation Scholarship Fund
Coast Guard Foundation
394 Taugwonk Road, Stonington, CT 06378
Phone: 860-535-0786
Email: info@cgfdn.org
http://www.coastguardfoundation.org
Purpose: To provide financial assistance to children of Coast Guard members.
Eligibility: Applicants must be unmarried dependent children of U.S. Coast Guard members, living, retired or deceased or Coast Guard reservists on extended active duty. They must be high school seniors or full-time undergraduate students in a four-year program or vocational/technical program. They must be under 23 years old.
Target applicant(s): High school students. College students.
Amount: Varies.
Number of awards: Varies.
Scholarship may be renewable.
Deadline: Varies.
How to apply: Applications are available online.
Exclusive: Visit www.UltimateScholarshipBook.com and enter code CO8523 for updates on this award.

(86) · Coca-Cola Community College Academic Team

Coca-Cola Scholars Foundation
P.O. Box 442, Atlanta, GA 30301
Phone: 800-306-2653
Email: Scholars@coca-cola.com
http://www.coca-colascholarsfoundation.org/apply/
Purpose: To assist community college students with college expenses.
Eligibility: Applicants must be enrolled in community college, have a minimum GPA of 3.5 on a four-point scale and be on track to earn an associate's or bachelor's degree. Students attending community college in the U.S. do NOT need to be members of Phi Theta Kappa. Fifty students will win a $1,500 scholarship, fifty students will win a $1,250 scholarship and fifty students will win a $1,000 scholarship.
Target applicant(s): College students. Adult students.
Minimum GPA: 3.5
Amount: $1,000-$1,500.
Number of awards: 150.
Deadline: December 1.
How to apply: Applications are available online. Nomination from the designated nominator at your school is required. A list of nominators is available at http://www.ptk.org.
Exclusive: Visit www.UltimateScholarshipBook.com and enter code CO8623 for updates on this award.

(87) · Coca-Cola Scholars Program

Coca-Cola Scholars Foundation
P.O. Box 442, Atlanta, GA 30301
Phone: 800-306-2653
Email: Scholars@coca-cola.com
http://www.coca-colascholarsfoundation.org/apply/
Purpose: Begun in 1986 to celebrate the Coca-Cola Centennial, the program is designed to contribute to the nation's future and to assist a wide range of students.
Eligibility: Applicants must be high school seniors in the U.S., be U.S. citizens, nationals or permanent residents and must use the awards at an accredited U.S. college or university. Selection is based on the transcript, school profile, school and non-school related clubs and organizations, honors and awards and volunteer service. Application period typically reopens on August 1st of each year.
Target applicant(s): High school students.
Amount: $20,000.
Number of awards: 150.
Scholarship may be renewable.
Deadline: October 31.
How to apply: Applications are available online.
Exclusive: Visit www.UltimateScholarshipBook.com and enter code CO8723 for updates on this award.

(88) · College Prep Scholarship for High School Juniors

QuestBridge
120 Hawthorne Avenue, Suite 103, Palo Alto, CA 94301
Phone: 888-275-2054
Email: questions@questbridge.org
http://www.questbridge.org
Purpose: To equip outstanding low-income high school juniors with the knowledge necessary to compete for admission to leading colleges.
Eligibility: Applicants must be high school juniors who have a strong academic record and an annual household income of less than $60,000.

Many past award recipients have also been part of the first generation in their family to attend college. Scholarships are open to all qualified students, regardless of race or ethnicity.
Target applicant(s): High school students.
Amount: Varies.
Number of awards: Varies.
Deadline: March.
How to apply: Applications are available on the QuestBridge website in February. An application form, transcript and one teacher recommendation are required.
Exclusive: Visit www.UltimateScholarshipBook.com and enter code QU8823 for updates on this award.

(89) · Collegiate Championship Award Program

U.S. Figure Skating
20 First Street, Colorado Springs, CO 80906
Phone: 719-635-5200
Email: info@usfigureskating.org
https://www.usfigureskating.org/skate/scholarships-and-funding
Purpose: To aid eligible collegiate figure skaters with their college tuition.
Eligibility: The award is presented to the senior ladies champion and senior men's champion at the U.S. Collegiate Figure Skating Championships.
Target applicant(s): College students. Adult students.
Amount: $5,000.
Number of awards: 2.
Deadline: Varies.
How to apply: The award is presented at the U.S. Collegiate Figure Skating Championships.
Exclusive: Visit www.UltimateScholarshipBook.com and enter code U.8923 for updates on this award.

(90) · Congress Bundestag Youth Exchange Program

Congress Bundestag Youth Exchange Program
Email: cbyx@culturalvistas.org
http://www.usagermanyscholarship.org
Purpose: To aid high school students who wish to study abroad in Germany.
Eligibility: Applicants must be U.S. citizens or permanent residents and be current high school students who will be between the ages of 15 and 18 at the beginning of the exchange program. They must have a GPA of 3.0 or higher on a four-point scale. Previous knowledge of the German language is not required. Selection is based on academic achievement, written and oral communication skills and temperamental suitability for adjusting to different cultures.
Target applicant(s): High school students.
Minimum GPA: 3.0
Amount: Varies.
Number of awards: Varies.
Deadline: December.
How to apply: Applications are available online. An application form and supporting materials are required.
Exclusive: Visit www.UltimateScholarshipBook.com and enter code CO9023 for updates on this award.

(91) · Congressional Medal of Honor Society Scholarships

Congressional Medal of Honor Society
40 Patriots Point Road, Mount Pleasant, SC 29464
Phone: 843-884-8862
Email: medalhq@earthlink.net
http://www.cmohs.org
Purpose: To provide education assistance to children of Congressional Medal of Honor recipients.
Eligibility: Applicants must be ROTC undergraduate students of the Air Force, Army, Navy or Marine Corps and must demonstrate leadership and a commitment to serve in the United States Armed Forces. Applicants must also be enrolled as sophomores or juniors. Applicants must have a minimum 3.5 GPA.
Target applicant(s): College students. Adult students.
Minimum GPA: 3.5
Amount: Varies.
Number of awards: Varies.
Deadline: February 19.
How to apply: Applications are available from the Congressional Medal of Honor Society.
Exclusive: Visit www.UltimateScholarshipBook.com and enter code CO9123 for updates on this award.

(92) · Connecticut Domestic Violence Information Center's Good Samaritan Scholarship

Connecticut Domestic Violence Information Center/Law Offices of Mark Sherman
29 5th Street, Suite 2, Stamford, CT 06905
Phone: 203-276-9443
Email: info@ctdomesticviolencehelp.com
https://www.ctdomesticviolencehelp.com/
Purpose: To reward students who embody the spirit of a good Samaritan.
Eligibility: Applicants must be enrolled at an accredited United States institution as an undergraduate, graduate or law school student. Students must be in good academic standing with a 3.0 minimum GPA. An essay on a specific topic is required.
Target applicant(s): High school students. College students. Graduate school students. Adult students.
Minimum GPA: 3.0
Amount: $1,000.
Number of awards: 1.
Deadline: December 31.
How to apply: Applications are available online.
Exclusive: Visit www.UltimateScholarshipBook.com and enter code CO9223 for updates on this award.

(93) · Coolidge Scholarship

Calvin Coolidge Memorial Foundation Inc.
P.O. Box 97, Plymouth, VT 05056
Phone: 802-672-3389
Email: coolidgescholars@coolidgefoundation.org
https://coolidgescholars.org/
Purpose: To reward high school juniors who have achieved academic excellence and have an interest in public policy.
Eligibility: Applicants must be U.S. citizens planning on enrolling full-time in an accredited U.S. college or university. Students must apply during their junior year in high school. Selection is based on academic excellence, interest in public policy and appreciation for Coolidge values and demonstrated humility and leadership.
Target applicant(s): High school students.
Amount: Full tuition.
Number of awards: 2.
Deadline: January 19.
How to apply: Applications are available online through the website and include an essay, a transcript, a resume and two letters of recommendation.
Exclusive: Visit www.UltimateScholarshipBook.com and enter code CA9323 for updates on this award.

(94) · Corporate Culture Scholarship

Investor's Podcast
https://www.theinvestorspodcast.com/corporate-culture/
Purpose: To encourage awareness of sustainable profitability.
Eligibility: Applicants must be current undergraduate or graduate students enrolled at any North American university. Students must write an essay relating to corporate culture and their ideal workplace culture.
Target applicant(s): College students. Graduate school students. Adult students.
Amount: $1,000.
Number of awards: 1.
Deadline: October 1.
How to apply: Applications are available online.
Exclusive: Visit www.UltimateScholarshipBook.com and enter code IN9423 for updates on this award.

(95) · Cottage and Bungalow Scholarship

Cottage and Bungalow
P.O. Box 384, Tullahoma, TN 37388
Phone: 844-677-6604
Email: scholarships@cottageandbungalow.com
https://www.cottageandbungalow.com/scholarship.html
Purpose: To support creativity in education.
Eligibility: Applicants must be legal U.S. students or hold a valid student visa and be at least 18 years of age by December 31 of the current year. Students must be currently enrolled or enrolling in an accredited U.S. institution as a full-time undergraduate or graduate student. Applicants must submit an essay on the given topic on the website.
Target applicant(s): High school students. College students. Graduate school students. Adult students.
Amount: $500.
Number of awards: 1.
Deadline: June.
How to apply: Applications are available online.
Exclusive: Visit www.UltimateScholarshipBook.com and enter code CO9523 for updates on this award.

(96) · Countdown to College Scholarship

Potential Magazine
61 Market Place, Montgomery, AL 36117
Phone: 334-518-7810
http://potentialmagazine.com
Purpose: To support high school students in pursuing post-secondary education.
Eligibility: Applicants must be subscribed to the Countdown to College eNewsletter.
Target applicant(s): High school students.

Amount: $1,000.
Number of awards: 1.
Deadline: May 5.
How to apply: Applications are available online.
Exclusive: Visit www.UltimateScholarshipBook.com and enter code PO9623 for updates on this award.

(97) · Courage to Grow Scholarship

Courage to Grow Scholarship
P.O. Box 2507, Chelan, WA 98816
Phone: 509-731-3056
Email: support@couragetogrowscholarship.com
http://www.couragetogrowscholarship.com
Purpose: To assist high school and college students.
Eligibility: Applicants must be high school juniors and seniors or college students with a minimum GPA of 2.5 and must also be U.S. citizens.
Target applicant(s): High school students. College students. Adult students.
Minimum GPA: 2.5
Amount: $500.
Number of awards: 1 per month.
Deadline: Monthly.
How to apply: Applications are available online.
Exclusive: Visit www.UltimateScholarshipBook.com and enter code CO9723 for updates on this award.

(98) · CPI Champion of Service Award

College Preparatory Invitational
P.O. Box 566357, Miami, FL 33256-6357
Phone: 786-369-9040
Email: info@collegeprepinvitational.com
http://www.collegeprepinvitational.com
Purpose: To support young riders and promote higher education as a foundation to future success.
Eligibility: Applicants must be participants in the College Preparatory Invitational, be students in grades 8 through 12, have a 3.0 GPA or higher and have served a minimum of 36 hours of community service within the last 16 months. The scholarship is awarded to the applicant with the highest number of community hours served.
Target applicant(s): Junior high students or younger. High school students.
Minimum GPA: 3.0
Amount: $500.
Number of awards: 1.
Deadline: December 31.
How to apply: To apply, send a letter with the organization's letterhead documenting service hours performed, a copy of the IRS letter of recognition of exemption of the organization and current school transcript via certified mail.
Exclusive: Visit www.UltimateScholarshipBook.com and enter code CO9823 for updates on this award.

(99) · CPI Essay Award

College Preparatory Invitational
P.O. Box 566357, Miami, FL 33256-6357
Phone: 786-369-9040
Email: info@collegeprepinvitational.com
http://www.collegeprepinvitational.com
Purpose: To aid riders as they pursue higher education.

Eligibility: Applicants must participate in the College Preparatory Invitational and be students in grades 8 through 12. Selection is based on the style, grammar, spelling and creativity of a personal essay.
Target applicant(s): Junior high students or younger. High school students.
Amount: $500.
Number of awards: 2.
Deadline: December 31.
How to apply: Applications are available online.
Exclusive: Visit www.UltimateScholarshipBook.com and enter code CO9923 for updates on this award.

(100) · CPI Highest Point Hunt Seat Rider

College Preparatory Invitational
P.O. Box 566357, Miami, FL 33256-6357
Phone: 786-369-9040
Email: info@collegeprepinvitational.com
http://www.collegeprepinvitational.com
Purpose: To support young riders and promote higher education as a foundation to future success.
Eligibility: Applicants must attend the College Preparatory Invitational and be students in grades 8 through 12. The scholarship is awarded to the rider with the highest point score.
Target applicant(s): Junior high students or younger. High school students.
Amount: $500.
Number of awards: 2.
Deadline: January 1, September 1.
How to apply: Applications are available online.
Exclusive: Visit www.UltimateScholarshipBook.com and enter code CO10023 for updates on this award.

(101) · CPI Written Horsemanship Test Award

College Preparatory Invitational
P.O. Box 566357, Miami, FL 33256-6357
Phone: 786-369-9040
Email: info@collegeprepinvitational.com
http://www.collegeprepinvitational.com
Purpose: To support young riders and promote higher education as a foundation to future success.
Eligibility: Applicants must be participants in the College Preparatory Invitational and be students in grades 8 through 12. Students will take an online test on horsemanship, and the top five will be invited to take a written exam during the invitational.
Target applicant(s): Junior high students or younger. High school students.
Amount: $500.
Number of awards: 2.
Deadline: December 31 (FL), August 31 (NJ).
How to apply: Applicants are required to take an online test on a given date. Information is available online regarding a link to the exam.
Exclusive: Visit www.UltimateScholarshipBook.com and enter code CO10123 for updates on this award.

(102) · Create Real Impact Contest

Impact Teen Drivers
Attn.: Create Real Impact Contest, P.O. Box 161209, Sacramento, CA 95816
Phone: 916-733-7432
Email: info@impactteendrivers.org

https://createrealimpact.com/
Purpose: To raise awareness of the dangers of distracted driving and poor decision making.
Eligibility: Applicants must be legal U.S. residents who are between the ages of 14 and 22. They must be enrolled full-time at an accredited secondary or post-secondary school. They must submit an original, videotaped creative project that offers a solution to the problem of distracted driving. Selection is based on project concept, message effectiveness and creativity.
Target applicant(s): High school students. College students. Graduate school students.
Amount: $500 and $1,500.
Number of awards: 13.
Deadline: November 3.
How to apply: Contest entry instructions are available online. A videotaped creative project is required.
Exclusive: Visit www.UltimateScholarshipBook.com and enter code IM10223 for updates on this award.

(103) · Create-a-Greeting-Card Scholarship

Gallery Collection
Prudent Publishing, 65 Challenger Road, P.O. Box 150, Ridgefield Park, NJ 07660
Phone: 800-950-7064
Email: service@gallerycollection.com
https://www.gallerycollection.com/greeting-cards-scholarship.htm
Purpose: To reward high school, college, university and homeschooled students who enter a contest to create a Christmas card, holiday card, birthday card or all-occasion greeting card.
Eligibility: Applicants must be U.S. citizens or legal residents who are at least 14 years old. The submission must include original artwork or photographs. Selection is based on the overall quality of the submission including creativity, uniqueness and suitability.
Target applicant(s): High school students. College students. Adult students.
Amount: $10,000.
Number of awards: 1.
Deadline: March 2.
How to apply: Applications and submissions may be made online or mailed directly to the scholarship administrator at the Gallery Collection. Entry form and greeting card submission are required. Online submissions are preferred.
Exclusive: Visit www.UltimateScholarshipBook.com and enter code GA10323 for updates on this award.

(104) · Crossword Hobbyist Crossword Scholarship

Crossword Hobbyist
Email: scholarship@crosswordhobbyist.com
https://blog.crosswordhobbyist.com/crossword-hobbyist-crossword-scholarship/
Purpose: To support students who are pursuing a higher education.
Eligibility: Applicants must be current or incoming undergraduate students who will be enrolled for the upcoming fall semester. Students must create a newspaper-style crossword puzzle on a topic they are passionate about. Friends or family members of committee members are not allowed to apply for this scholarship.
Target applicant(s): High school students. College students. Adult students.
Amount: $1,000.
Number of awards: 1.
Deadline: April 30.

How to apply: Applications are available online.
Exclusive: Visit www.UltimateScholarshipBook.com and enter code CR10423 for updates on this award.

(105) · Curt Greene Memorial Scholarship

Harness Horse Youth Foundation
16575 Carey Road, Westfield, IN 46074
Phone: 317-867-5877
Email: ellen@hhyf.org
http://www.hhyf.org
Purpose: To support students who are interested in harness racing.
Eligibility: Students must demonstrate financial need, and must be enrolled or planning to enroll full-time (minimum of 12 credit hours) in an undergraduate program. Applicants must submit an essay and two letters of reference.
Target applicant(s): High school students. College students.
Minimum GPA: 2.5
Amount: $2,500.
Number of awards: Varies.
Deadline: April 30.
How to apply: Applications are available online.
Exclusive: Visit www.UltimateScholarshipBook.com and enter code HA10523 for updates on this award.

(106) · Curwen-Guidry-Blackburn Scholarship Fund

Southern Bowling Congress
9817 Miller Road, Sherwood, AR 72120
Phone: 501-425-2299
Email: dclements858@sbcglobal.net
http://www.southernbowlingcongress.org/scholarship.html
Purpose: To aid any senior youth bowler in Southern Bowling Congress member states in their education.
Eligibility: Students must be high school seniors and currently bowling in a USBC Certified Youth League. Students must reside in a Southern Bowling Congress member state which includes Alabama, Arkansas, Florida, Georgia, Kentucky, Louisiana, Mississippi, Tennessee and Texas. Applicants must have bowled in a USBC Certified Youth League three of four years in high school and have bowled 75 percent of the league schedule. Students must have a minimum grade point average of 2.5 on a 4.0 scale and achieved an ACT composite score of 20 or SAT composite score of 1410.
Target applicant(s): High school students.
Minimum GPA: 2.5
Amount: $750.
Number of awards: 1.
Deadline: March 15.
How to apply: Applications are available online. An application form, official high school grade and credits transcript with a minimum of six semesters of information that includes ACT and/or SAT scores and a personal letter of recommendation from high school principal or counselor are required.
Exclusive: Visit www.UltimateScholarshipBook.com and enter code SO10623 for updates on this award.

(107) · Daedalian Foundation Scholarship Program

Daedalian Foundation
P.O. Box 249, Randolph AFB, TX 78148
Phone: 210-945-2111
Email: info@daedalians.org
http://daedalians.org/programs/scholarships/

Purpose: To aid undergraduates who are studying to become military pilots.
Eligibility: Applicants must be rising or current undergraduates attending a four-year institution and must have a demonstrated interest in pursuing a career in military aviation. Selection is based on the overall strength of the application.
Target applicant(s): High school students. College students. Adult students.
Amount: Varies.
Number of awards: Varies.
Scholarship may be renewable.
Deadline: Varies.
How to apply: Applications are available online. An application form and applicant photo are required.
Exclusive: Visit www.UltimateScholarshipBook.com and enter code DA10723 for updates on this award.

(108) · Daughters of the Cincinnati Scholarship
Daughters of the Cincinnati
National Headquarters, 20 West 44th Street #508, New York, NY 10036
Phone: 212-991-9945
Email: scholarships@daughters1894.org
http://daughters1894.org/
Purpose: To support daughters of Armed Services commissioned officers.
Eligibility: Applicants must be daughters of career officers in the United States Army, Navy, Air Force, Coast Guard or Marine Corps (active, retired or deceased). Daughters of reserve officers or enlisted personnel cannot apply. Applicants must also be high school seniors.
Target applicant(s): High school students.
Amount: $16,000-$20,000 paid over 4 years.
Number of awards: Varies.
Scholarship may be renewable.
Deadline: February 15.
How to apply: More details are available by contacting the organization. An essay, a secondary school report, a letter of recommendation and a Student Aid Report are required.
Exclusive: Visit www.UltimateScholarshipBook.com and enter code DA10823 for updates on this award.

(109) · Davidson Fellows Scholarships
Davidson Institute for Talent Development
9665 Gateway Drive, Suite B, Reno, NV 89521
Phone: 775-852-3483
Email: DavidsonFellows@davidsongifted.org
http://www.davidsongifted.org/
Purpose: To reward young people for their works in mathematics, science, technology, music, literature, philosophy or "outside the box."
Eligibility: Applicants must be 18 or younger and be able to attend the awards reception in Washington, DC. In addition to the monetary award, the institute will pay for travel and lodging expenses. Three nominator forms, three copies of a 15-minute DVD and additional materials are required.
Target applicant(s): Junior high students or younger. High school students.
Amount: $10,000-$50,000.
Number of awards: Varies.
Deadline: February 9.
How to apply: Applications are available online.

Exclusive: Visit www.UltimateScholarshipBook.com and enter code DA10923 for updates on this award.

(110) · Davis-Putter Scholarship Fund
Davis-Putter Scholarship Fund
P.O. Box 7307, New York, NY 10116
Email: information@davisputter.org
http://www.davisputter.org
Purpose: To assist students who are both academically capable and who aid the progressive movement for peace and justice both on campus and in their communities.
Eligibility: Applicants must be undergraduate or graduate students who participate in the progressive movement, acting in the interests of issues such as expansion of civil rights and international solidarity, among others. Applicants must also have demonstrated financial need as well as a solid academic record.
Target applicant(s): College students. Graduate school students. Adult students.
Amount: Up to $15,000.
Number of awards: Varies.
Deadline: April 1.
How to apply: Applications are available online.
Exclusive: Visit www.UltimateScholarshipBook.com and enter code DA11023 for updates on this award.

(111) · Delete Cyberbullying Scholarship Award
Delete Cyberbullying
2261 Market Street #291, San Francisco, CA 94114
Email: help@endcyberbullying.net
http://www.deletecyberbullying.org
Purpose: To get students committed to the cause of deleting cyberbullying.
Eligibility: Applicants must be a U.S. citizen or permanent resident and attending or planning to attend an accredited U.S. college or university for undergraduate or graduate studies. Applicants must also be a high school, college or graduate student or a student planning to enter college.
Target applicant(s): High school students. College students. Graduate school students. Adult students.
Amount: $1,000.
Number of awards: 2.
Deadline: June 30, December 31.
How to apply: Applications are available online. An application form and an essay are required.
Exclusive: Visit www.UltimateScholarshipBook.com and enter code DE11123 for updates on this award.

(112) · Dell Scholars Program
Michael and Susan Dell Foundation
P.O. Box 163867, Austin, TX 78716
Phone: 512-329-0799
Email: apply@dellscholars.org
http://www.dellscholars.org
Purpose: To support underprivileged high school seniors.
Eligibility: Students must be participants in an approved college readiness program, and they must have at least a 2.4 GPA. Applicants must be pursuing a bachelor's degree in the fall directly after graduation. Students must also be U.S. citizens or permanent residents and demonstrate financial need. Selection is based on "individual determination to succeed," future goals, hardships that have been overcome, self motivation and financial need.

Target applicant(s): High school students.
Minimum GPA: 2.4
Amount: $20,000.
Number of awards: 500.
Scholarship may be renewable.
Deadline: December 1.
How to apply: Applications are available online. An online application is required.
Exclusive: Visit www.UltimateScholarshipBook.com and enter code MI11223 for updates on this award.

(113) · Delta Theta Chi Sorority National Memorial Scholarship
Delta Theta Chi Sorority
Attn: Cindi Cook, 2614 S. Lulu, Wichita, KS 67216
https://www.deltathetachi.org/scholarships
Purpose: To support the pursuit of higher education.
Eligibility: Applicants must provide transcripts for the past four years. Students graduating high school or current undergraduate freshmen must provide official documentation of grade point average, SAT and/or ACT scores. Applicants must complete application in full, including the essay, and provide at least one letter of reference.
Target applicant(s): High school students. College students. Graduate school students. Adult students.
Amount: $1,600.
Number of awards: 3.
Deadline: February 1.
How to apply: Applications are available online.
Exclusive: Visit www.UltimateScholarshipBook.com and enter code DE11323 for updates on this award.

(114) · Digital Privacy Scholarship
Digital Responsibility
3561 Homestead Road #113, Santa Clara, CA 95051-5161
Email: mjefferson@digitalresponsibility.org
http://www.digitalresponsibility.org/scholarships/
Purpose: To help students understand why it's important to be cautious about what they post on the Internet.
Eligibility: Applicants must be a high school freshman, sophomore, junior or senior or a current or entering college or graduate school student of any level. Home-schooled students are also eligible. There is no age limit. Students must also be a U.S. citizen or legal resident.
Target applicant(s): High school students. College students. Graduate school students. Adult students.
Amount: $1,000.
Number of awards: 1.
Deadline: June 30.
How to apply: Applications are available online.
Exclusive: Visit www.UltimateScholarshipBook.com and enter code DI11423 for updates on this award.

(115) · Dinah Shore Scholarship
Ladies Professional Golf Association
100 International Golf Drive, Daytona Beach, FL 32124-1092
Phone: 386-274-6200
Email: info@lpgafoundation.org
http://www.lpga.com/lpga-foundation/scholarships
Purpose: To honor the late Dinah Shore.

Eligibility: Applicants must be female high school seniors who have been accepted into a full-time course of study at an accredited U.S. institution of higher learning. They must have played golf regularly for the past two years but not played on a competitive collegiate golf team. A minimum GPA of 3.2 is required.
Target applicant(s): High school students.
Minimum GPA: 3.2
Amount: $5,000.
Number of awards: 1.
Deadline: February.
How to apply: Applications are available online.
Exclusive: Visit www.UltimateScholarshipBook.com and enter code LA11523 for updates on this award.

(116) · Divorce Stigma Scholarship
Atlanta Divorce Law Group
3510 Old Milton Parkway, Alpharetta, GA 30005
Phone: 678-203-9893
Email: contact@atldivorcegroup.com
https://atlantadivorcelawgroup.com/the-divorce-stigma-scholarship/
Purpose: To help dispel the stigma of divorce.
Eligibility: Applicants must be currently enrolled or accepted to an accredited U.S. community college, undergraduate or graduate program and have a minimum GPA of 3.0. Students must write an essay explaining how a divorce produced a positive outcome for those involved.
Target applicant(s): High school students. College students. Graduate school students. Adult students.
Minimum GPA: 3.0
Amount: $1,000.
Number of awards: 1.
Deadline: February 28.
How to apply: Applications are available online.
Exclusive: Visit www.UltimateScholarshipBook.com and enter code AT11623 for updates on this award.

(117) · Dixie Boys Baseball Scholarship Program
Dixie Boys Baseball
P.O. Box 8263, Dothan, AL 36304
Phone: 334-793-3331
Email: jjones29@sw.rr.com
http://baseball.dixie.org
Purpose: To help high school seniors who have participated in a franchised Dixie Boys Baseball Inc. program.
Eligibility: Applicants must plan to pursue undergraduate studies at a college or university. An application, financial statement, two recommendation letters, proof of baseball participation, transcript and essay are required. Selection is based on class rankings, strong school and community leadership and financial need. Programs are located in Alabama, Arkansas, Florida, Georgia, Louisiana, Mississippi, North Carolina, South Carolina, Tennessee, Texas and Virginia.
Target applicant(s): High school students.
Amount: $1,250.
Number of awards: 11.
Deadline: April 1.
How to apply: Applications are available online.
Exclusive: Visit www.UltimateScholarshipBook.com and enter code DI11723 for updates on this award.

(118) · Dixie Softball Scholarships

Dixie Softball Inc.
Doug Garrett, Chairman, Dixie Softball Scholarship Committee, 106 Woodlake Drive, Pineville, LA 71360
Phone: 318-451-4344
Email: dayprodoug@suddenlink.net
https://www.dixiegirlsoftball.com/dixiesoftball
Purpose: To support Dixie softball participants as they seek to further their education beyond high school.
Eligibility: Applicants must be female Dixie Softball participants, be high school seniors and have played softball for at least two seasons. Selection is based on financial need, academic achievement and future goals.
Target applicant(s): High school students.
Amount: $1,500.
Number of awards: 8.
Deadline: February 1.
How to apply: Applications are available online and must include the following: copy of most recent tax return, letter from parent or guardian explaining financial need, verification letter from Dixie Softball league official, photo and personal letter describing goals, activities and achievements.
Exclusive: Visit www.UltimateScholarshipBook.com and enter code DI11823 for updates on this award.

(119) · Dixie Youth Scholarship Program

Dixie Youth Baseball Inc.
Johnny Berthelot, Chairman Scholarship Committee, 110 South Bolivar Street, Suite 207, Marshall, TX 75670
Phone: 903-927-2255
Email: dyb@dixie.org
http://youth.dixie.org
Purpose: To help high school seniors who have participated in a franchised Dixie Youth Baseball league.
Eligibility: Applicants must have been registered on a Dixie Youth Baseball team participating in a franchised Dixie Youth Baseball Inc. league prior to reaching age thirteen. Selection is based on financial need, scholastic record and citizenship. Programs are located in Alabama, Arkansas, Florida, Georgia, Louisiana, Mississippi, North Carolina, South Carolina, Tennessee, Texas and Virginia.
Target applicant(s): High school students.
Amount: $2,000.
Number of awards: Varies.
Deadline: April 1.
How to apply: Contact your local league officials or a district, state or national director for an application, and applications are also available online.
Exclusive: Visit www.UltimateScholarshipBook.com and enter code DI11923 for updates on this award.

(120) · Dizzy Dean Scholarship

Dizzy Dean Baseball Inc.
2470 Highway 51 South, Hernando, MS 38632
Phone: 662-429-7790
Email: dphil10513@aol.com
http://dizzydeanbbinc.org/
Purpose: To aid members of the Dizzy Dean Baseball/Softball program in pursuing their college education.
Eligibility: Applicants must have played on a Dizzy Dean Baseball/ Softball program for four years. Students must also be graduating seniors and be able to provide a high school transcript, copy of diploma and a copy of parent/guardian prior years' federal income tax form.
Target applicant(s): High school students.
Amount: Varies.
Number of awards: Varies.
Scholarship may be renewable.
Deadline: June 15.
How to apply: Applications are available online.
Exclusive: Visit www.UltimateScholarshipBook.com and enter code DI12023 for updates on this award.

(121) · Dollars for Scholars Scholarship

Citizens' Scholarship Foundation of America
One Scholarship Way, St. Peter, MN 56082
Phone: 800-537-4180
Email: dollarsforscholars@scholarshipamerica.org
http://www.scholarshipamerica.org
Purpose: To encourage students to aim for and achieve loftier educational goals.
Eligibility: Applicants must be members of a local Dollars for Scholars chapter. There are more than 1,200 Dollars for Scholars chapters that award more than $29 million in awards each year.
Target applicant(s): High school students.
Amount: Varies.
Number of awards: Varies.
Deadline: Varies.
How to apply: Contact your local Dollars for Scholars chapter for more information. A list of chapters is available online.
Exclusive: Visit www.UltimateScholarshipBook.com and enter code CI12123 for updates on this award.

(122) · Dolphin Scholarships

Dolphin Scholarship Foundation
4966 Euclid Road, Suite 109, Virginia Beach, VA 23462
Phone: 757-671-3200
Email: scholars@dolphinscholarship.org
http://www.dolphinscholarship.org
Purpose: To assist the children of members of the Navy Submarine Force and other Navy submarine support personnel.
Eligibility: Applicants must be the unmarried children or stepchildren of navy submariners or navy members who have served in submarine support activities and must be under 24 years old at the time of the application deadline. The parents must have been part of the Submarine Force for at least eight years, have served in submarine support activities for at least 10 years or died on active duty while in the Submarine Force. The children of submariners who served less than the required number of years due to injury or illness occurring in the line of duty may also be eligible. Applicants must also be high school seniors or college students planning to attend or currently attending an accredited four-year college, working for a bachelor's degree.
Target applicant(s): High school students. College students.
Amount: $2,000-$3,400 per year.
Number of awards: 25-30.
Scholarship may be renewable.
Deadline: March 15.
How to apply: Applications are available online.
Exclusive: Visit www.UltimateScholarshipBook.com and enter code DO12223 for updates on this award.

(123) · Don't Text and Drive Scholarship

Digital Responsibility
3561 Homestead Road #113, Santa Clara, CA 95051-5161
Email: mjefferson@digitalresponsibility.org
http://www.digitalresponsibility.org/scholarships/
Purpose: To help students understand the risks of texting while driving.
Eligibility: Applicants must be a high school freshman, sophomore, junior or senior or a current or entering college or graduate school student of any level. Home-schooled students are also eligible. There is no age limit. Students must also be a U.S. citizen or legal resident.
Target applicant(s): High school students. College students. Graduate school students. Adult students.
Amount: $1,000.
Number of awards: 1.
Deadline: September 30.
How to apply: Applications are available online.
Exclusive: Visit www.UltimateScholarshipBook.com and enter code DI12323 for updates on this award.

(124) · DoSomething.org Monthly Scholarships

Do Something (Scholarships)
19 West 21st Street, Floor 8, New York, NY 10010
Phone: 212-254-2390
Email: scholarships@dosomething.org
https://www.dosomething.org/us/about/easy-scholarships
Purpose: To assist students who participate in a social issue campaign.
Eligibility: Applicants must be age 25 or younger and be U.S. or Canadian citizens. There is a new scholarship each month. Selection is based on a random drawing of all students who participate in the campaign.
Target applicant(s): Junior high students or younger. High school students. College students. Graduate school students.
Amount: Varies.
Number of awards: Varies.
Deadline: Varies.
How to apply: Applications are available online.
Exclusive: Visit www.UltimateScholarshipBook.com and enter code DO12423 for updates on this award.

(125) · Dr. Aileen W. Tobin Scholarship

U.S. Army Ordnance Corps Association
P.O. Box 5251, Ft. Lee, VA 23801
Phone: 410-272-8540
Email: usaoca@usaocaweb.org
http://usaoca.org/index.php/scholarship-information/
Purpose: To honor the memory of LTG Joseph M. Heiser.
Eligibility: Applicants must be active or reserve Ordnance soldiers or OCA members or members or their immediate family. They must write a 300- to 500- word essay about the reasons they are seeking the grant and why they feel they deserve it and a 1,000- to 1,500-word essay on the missions, heritage or history of the U.S. Army Ordnance Corps.
Target applicant(s): High school students. College students. Adult students.
Amount: Varies.
Number of awards: Varies.
Deadline: June 30.
How to apply: Applications are available online.
Exclusive: Visit www.UltimateScholarshipBook.com and enter code U.12523 for updates on this award.

(126) · Dr. James Earl Kennamer Scholarship

National Wild Turkey Federation (NWTF)
770 Augusta Road, Edgefield, SC 29824-0530
Phone: 800-843-6983
Email: scholarshipinfo@nwtf.net
https://www.nwtf.org/
Purpose: To support those students committed to conservation and preserving our hunting heritage.
Eligibility: Applicants must be a senior, have a 3.0 or higher GPA, plan to attend a institution of higher education after high school, be a member of National Wild Turkey Federation and actively participate in hunting sports. Selection is based on scholastic achievement, leadership abilities, community service and commitment to conservation.
Target applicant(s): High school students.
Minimum GPA: 3.0
Amount: $250-$10,000.
Number of awards: Varies.
Deadline: January.
How to apply: Applications are available online and require a personal essay and three letters of reference.
Exclusive: Visit www.UltimateScholarshipBook.com and enter code NA12623 for updates on this award.

(127) · Dwight F. Davis Memorial Scholarship

United States Tennis Association Foundation
70 W. Red Oak Lane, White Plains, NY 10604
Phone: 914-696-7223
Email: foundation@usta.com
http://www.ustafoundation.com/
Purpose: To support youth tennis players who represent the sport with distinction.
Eligibility: Applicants must be high school seniors who have participated in an organized youth tennis program. Students must excel in academics, have participated in extracurricular activities and have participated in various community service projects.
Target applicant(s): High school students.
Amount: $10,000.
Number of awards: 2.
Scholarship may be renewable.
Deadline: March.
How to apply: Applications are available online.
Exclusive: Visit www.UltimateScholarshipBook.com and enter code UN12723 for updates on this award.

(128) · Dwight Mosley Scholarship Award

United States Tennis Association Foundation
70 W. Red Oak Lane, White Plains, NY 10604
Phone: 914-696-7223
Email: foundation@usta.com
http://www.ustafoundation.com/
Purpose: To support youth tennis players of ethnically diverse backgrounds who have excelled both on and off the court.
Eligibility: Applicants must be USTA ranked high school seniors who are of an ethnically diverse background and who have participated extensively in an organized youth community tennis program. Selection is based on academic excellence and exemplary sportsmanship on and off the court.
Target applicant(s): High school students.
Amount: $10,000.
Number of awards: 2.

Scholarship may be renewable.
Deadline: March.
How to apply: Applications are available online.
Exclusive: Visit www.UltimateScholarshipBook.com and enter code UN12823 for updates on this award.

---

(129) · E-waste Scholarship

Digital Responsibility
3561 Homestead Road #113, Santa Clara, CA 95051-5161
Email: mjefferson@digitalresponsibility.org
http://www.digitalresponsibility.org/scholarships/
Purpose: To help students understand the impact of e-waste and what can be done to reduce e-waste.
Eligibility: Applicants must be high school, college, graduate or home-schooled students. There is no age limit. Students must also be U.S. citizens or legal residents. A 140-character message about e-waste is required to apply. The top 10 applications will be selected as finalists; finalists will be asked to write a full length 500- to 1,000-word essay about e-waste. Only online applications are accepted.
Target applicant(s): High school students. College students. Graduate school students. Adult students.
Amount: $1,000.
Number of awards: 1.
Deadline: April 30.
How to apply: Applications are available online.
Exclusive: Visit www.UltimateScholarshipBook.com and enter code DI12923 for updates on this award.

---

(130) · Earl Anthony Memorial Scholarships

United States Bowling Congress
Attn.: Alberta E. Crowe Star of Tomorrow, 621 Six Flags Drive, Arlington, TX 76011
Phone: 800-514-2695
Email: contactus@ibcyouth.com
https://www.bowl.com/scholarships/
Purpose: To recognize USBC members for community involvement and academic achievement.
Eligibility: Applicants must be USBC members in good standing who are high school seniors or current college students. They must have a GPA of 3.0 or higher. Community involvement, academic achievement and financial need are considered.
Target applicant(s): High school students. College students. Adult students.
Minimum GPA: 3.0
Amount: $5,000.
Number of awards: 5.
Deadline: December 1.
How to apply: Applications are available online.
Exclusive: Visit www.UltimateScholarshipBook.com and enter code UN13023 for updates on this award.

---

(131) · Easton/NFAA Scholarship Program

National Field Archery Association
800 Archery Lane, Yankton, SD 57078
Phone: 605-260-9279
Email: info@nfaausa.com
https://www.nfaausa.com
Purpose: To help those students who have participated in National Field Archery Association events continue their education beyond high school.
Eligibility: Applicants must be high school students or a student enrolled in a two-year or four-year college or university. High school students applying to be full time students at a technical training college are also eligible to apply. Applicants must also be current members of NFAA or the NAA/USA Archery. The student must have a minimum GPA of 2.0 in high school or 2.5 in college. Selection is based on academic achievements, level of participation in NFAA and USAT rankings.
Target applicant(s): High school students. College students. Graduate school students. Adult students.
Minimum GPA: 2.0 for high school students; 2.5 for college students
Amount: Varies.
Number of awards: Varies.
Deadline: December 31.
How to apply: Applications are available online.
Exclusive: Visit www.UltimateScholarshipBook.com and enter code NA13123 for updates on this award.

---

(132) · eCampus Tours Scholarship Giveaway

Edsouth
eCampusTours, P.O. Box 36014, Knoxville, TN 37930
Phone: 865-342-0670
Email: info@ecampustours.com
http://www.ecampustours.com
Purpose: To assist students in paying for college.
Eligibility: Eligible students include U.S. citizens, U.S. nationals and permanent residents or students enrolled in a U.S. institution of higher education. Winners must be enrolled in an eligible institution of higher education, as stipulated in the eligibility requirements, within one year of winning the award. Scholarship awards will be paid directly to the college.
Target applicant(s): High school students. College students. Graduate school students. Adult students.
Amount: $1,000.
Number of awards: 2.
Deadline: March 31.
How to apply: Applications are available online or by mail. Registration with eCampusTours is required.
Exclusive: Visit www.UltimateScholarshipBook.com and enter code ED13223 for updates on this award.

---

(133) · Education Accessibility Scholarship

Connecticut Trial Firm LLC
437 Naubuc Avenue, Suite 107, Glastonbury, CT 06033
Phone: 860-471-8333
Email: info@cttrialfirm.com
https://cttrialfirm.com/education-accessibility-scholarship/
Purpose: To encourage students who are the first in their family to attend college.
Eligibility: Applicants must be currently enrolled with the intent to complete either a two-year, four-year or graduate program at any junior college, community college, paralegal program, college or university in the United States. Students must be the first in their family to attend a four-year college or university and have a minimum 3.0 GPA. An essay submission on a provided topic is required.
Target applicant(s): High school students. College students. Graduate school students. Adult students.
Minimum GPA: 3.0
Amount: $1,000.
Number of awards: 1.
Deadline: December 31.
How to apply: Applications are available online.

Exclusive: Visit www.UltimateScholarshipBook.com and enter code CO13323 for updates on this award.

---

(134) · Educational Advancement Foundation Merit Scholarship

Alpha Kappa Alpha Educational Advancement Foundation Inc.
5656 S. Stony Island Avenue, Chicago, IL 60637
Phone: 800-653-6528
Email: akaeaf@akaeaf.net
https://akaeaf.org/scholarships
Purpose: To support academically talented students.
Eligibility: Applicants must be full-time college students at the sophomore level or higher, including graduate students, at an accredited school. They must have a GPA of at least 3.0 and demonstrate community involvement and service. The program is open to students without regard to sex, race, creed, color, ethnicity, religion, sexual orientation or disability. Students do NOT need to be members of Alpha Kappa Alpha.
Target applicant(s): College students. Graduate school students. Adult students.
Minimum GPA: 3.0
Amount: Varies.
Number of awards: Varies.
Deadline: April 15 (undergraduates) and August 15 (graduates).
How to apply: Applications are available online. An application form, personal statement and three letters of recommendation are required.
Exclusive: Visit www.UltimateScholarshipBook.com and enter code AL13423 for updates on this award.

---

(135) · Educational Scholarship Award / George and Rosemary Murray Scholarship Award

25th Infantry Division Association (TIDA)
P.O. Box 7, Flourtown, PA 19031-0007
http://www.25thida.org
Purpose: To aid in the education of the members of the 25th Infantry Division Association or the children and grandchildren of active and former members of the association.
Eligibility: Applicants must be high school seniors who are the child or grandchild of an active association member, the child of a former member who died during combat with the Division or an active member who will be discharged before the end of the award year. Applicants must be entering a four-year college or university as a freshman. Selection is based on future plans, school activities, interests, financial status and academic achievement.
Target applicant(s): High school students.
Amount: Up to $1,500.
Number of awards: Varies.
Deadline: February 28.
How to apply: Applications are available throughout the year in Tropic Lightning Flashes, the quarterly newsletter of the 25th Infantry Division Association.
Exclusive: Visit www.UltimateScholarshipBook.com and enter code 2513523 for updates on this award.

---

(136) · EOD Warrior Foundation Scholarship

EOD Warrior Foundation
716 Crestview Avenue, Niceville, FL 32578
Phone: 850-729-2401
Email: admin@eodmemorial.org
http://www.eodmemorial.org
Purpose: To support those connected to Explosive Ordnance Disposal (EOD) technicians.
Eligibility: Applicants must be accepted or enrolled as full-time undergraduates in a U.S. accredited two-year, four-year or vocational school. Students must also be the family member of an active duty, guard/reserve, retired or deceased EOD technician. The award is based on academic achievement, community involvement and financial need. Applicants should submit the Free Application for Federal Student Aid form.
Target applicant(s): High school students. College students. Adult students.
Amount: Varies.
Number of awards: Varies.
Deadline: February 26.
How to apply: Applications are available online.
Exclusive: Visit www.UltimateScholarshipBook.com and enter code EO13623 for updates on this award.

---

(137) · Equitable Excellence Scholarship

Equitable Holdings Inc.
1290 Avenue of the Americas, New York, NY 10104
https://equitable.com/foundation/equitable-excellence-scholarship
Purpose: To provide financial assistance to ambitious students.
Eligibility: Applicants must be U.S. citizens or legal residents who are current high school seniors and are planning to enroll full-time in an accredited college or university in the fall following their graduation. They must show ambition and drive evidenced by outstanding achievement in school, community or workplace activities. A recommendation from an unrelated adult who can vouch for the student's achievement is required.
Target applicant(s): High school students.
Amount: Up to $20,000.
Number of awards: 200.
Deadline: December 17.
How to apply: Applications are available online.
Exclusive: Visit www.UltimateScholarshipBook.com and enter code EQ13723 for updates on this award.

---

(138) · Ethnic Minority and Women's Enhancement Scholarship

National Collegiate Athletic Association
700 W. Washington Street, P.O. Box 6222, Indianapolis, IN 46206
Phone: 317-917-6222
Email: lthomas@ncaa.org
http://www.ncaa.org/about/resources/ncaa-scholarships-and-grants
Purpose: To assist minority and female students in intercollegiate athletics with graduate scholarships.
Eligibility: Applicants must be seeking admission or have been accepted into a sports administration or program that will help the applicant obtain a career in intercollegiate athletics.
Target applicant(s): College students. Adult students.
Minimum GPA: 3.2
Amount: $10,000.
Number of awards: 26.
Deadline: February 4.
How to apply: Application details are available online.
Exclusive: Visit www.UltimateScholarshipBook.com and enter code NA13823 for updates on this award.

(139) · Eve Kraft Education and College Scholarship

United States Tennis Association Foundation
70 W. Red Oak Lane, White Plains, NY 10604
Phone: 914-696-7223
Email: foundation@usta.com
http://www.ustafoundation.com/
Purpose: To support youth tennis participants who have come from an economically disadvantaged community.
Eligibility: Applicants must be high school seniors who have participated in an organized youth tennis program and who reside in an economically disadvantaged community. Selection is based on academic excellence and community service.
Target applicant(s): High school students.
Amount: $2,500.
Number of awards: 2.
Deadline: March.
How to apply: Applications are available online.
Exclusive: Visit www.UltimateScholarshipBook.com and enter code UN13923 for updates on this award.

(140) · Explore America Travel Scholarship

Hostelling International USA
8401 Colesville Road, Suite 600, Silver Spring, MD 20910
http://www.hiusa.org/travel-scholarships
Purpose: To help students launch their travel careers.
Eligibility: Applicants must be 18 to 30 years old and a U.S. citizen, permanent resident or DACA recipient. Students must demonstrate financial need and have a strong desire and motivation to experience other people and cultures through hostelling.
Target applicant(s): College students. Adult students.
Amount: $1,000.
Number of awards: 10.
Deadline: Varies.
How to apply: Applications are available online.
Exclusive: Visit www.UltimateScholarshipBook.com and enter code HO14023 for updates on this award.

(141) · Explore the World Scholarship

Hostelling International USA
8401 Colesville Road, Suite 600, Silver Spring, MD 20910
http://www.hiusa.org/travel-scholarships
Purpose: To support students who wish to study abroad or participate in service abroad.
Eligibility: Applicants must be between 18 and 30 years of age and a U.S. citizen or permanent resident. Students should be able to prove financial need, live in one of the metropolitan areas listed on the website and plan to travel abroad on an education, volunteer or service learning trip.
Target applicant(s): High school students. College students. Adult students.
Amount: $2,000.
Number of awards: Varies.
Deadline: March.
How to apply: Applications are available online.
Exclusive: Visit www.UltimateScholarshipBook.com and enter code HO14123 for updates on this award.

(142) · Families of Freedom Scholarship Fund

Families of Freedom c/o Scholarship America
One Scholarship Way, P.O. Box 297, St. Peter, MN 56082
Phone: 877-862-0136
Email: familiesoffreedom@scholarshipamerica.org
https://www.familiesoffreedom.org/students-families/families-of-freedom-fund/
Purpose: To support dependents of victims of the 9/11 attacks.
Eligibility: Applicants must be dependent children, spouses or domestic partners of 9/11 victims. Children of victims must enroll in a postsecondary program by age 24 and must continue studies uninterrupted after their 24th birthday to continue to receive assistance. Financial need is required.
Target applicant(s): High school students. College students. Graduate school students. Adult students.
Amount: Varies.
Number of awards: Varies.
Scholarship may be renewable.
Deadline: October 1.
How to apply: Applications are available online. An application form, copy of most recent tax return, transcript and copy of school billing statement are required.
Exclusive: Visit www.UltimateScholarshipBook.com and enter code FA14223 for updates on this award.

(143) · First Cavalry Division Association Scholarship

Foundation of the First Cavalry Division Association
Alumni Of The First Team, 302 North Main Street, Copperas Cove, TX 76522
Phone: 254-547-6537
Email: firstcav@1cda.org
http://www.1cda.org
Purpose: To assist the children of First Cavalry troopers who have become disabled or who died while serving in the Division.
Eligibility: Applicants must be First Cavalry Division troopers who have become totally disabled while serving in the division or active duty members, their spouses or children. Applicants may also be the spouses or children of First Cavalry Division troopers who have died while serving in the division.
Target applicant(s): High school students. College students. Adult students.
Amount: $1,200 per year.
Number of awards: Varies.
Deadline: Varies.
How to apply: Applications are available by request.
Exclusive: Visit www.UltimateScholarshipBook.com and enter code FO14323 for updates on this award.

(144) · FMAA Scholarship Program

Flag Manufacturers Association of America
Hope Silverman, 994 Old Eagle School Road, Suite 1019, Wayne, PA 19087-1866
Phone: 610-971-4850
Email: hope@mmco1.com
https://fmaa-usa.com/Scholarship.php
Purpose: To support students who create a video on the United States flag.
Eligibility: Applicants must create a video essay discussing what the United States flag means to them as a young American in today's world. Students must post their one and a half to two minute video online.
Target applicant(s): High school students. College students. Graduate school students. Adult students.
Amount: Up to $2,000.
Number of awards: Varies.

Deadline: May 30.
How to apply: Applications are available online.
Exclusive: Visit www.UltimateScholarshipBook.com and enter code FL14423 for updates on this award.

---

(145) · FMC Skaters Scholarship

Facility Management Corporation (FMC) Ice Sports
100 Schoosett Street, Building 3, Pembroke, MA 02359
Phone: 888-747-5283
Email: customercare@fmcicesports.com
http://www.fmcicesports.com
Purpose: To support ice sport participants and recreational ice skaters seeking to further their education beyond high school.
Eligibility: Applicants must be a New England resident, a senior in high school and skate at an FMC arena. Selection is based on academic achievement, extracurricular activities, community service and accomplishments and leadership on the ice.
Target applicant(s): High school students.
Amount: Varies.
Number of awards: Varies.
Deadline: May 1.
How to apply: Applications are available online. Along with the application form, students must submit a high school transcript, one letter of recommendation, a student resume and a personal essay.
Exclusive: Visit www.UltimateScholarshipBook.com and enter code FA14523 for updates on this award.

---

(146) · Folds of Honor Higher Education Scholarship

Folds of Honor
5800 N. Patriot Drive, Owasso, OK 74055
Email: scholarships@foldsofhonor.org
https://www.foldsofhonor.org/resources/scholarships/
Purpose: To support spouses and children of American military service members pursuing higher education.
Eligibility: Applicants must be spouses or children of U.S. service members who were killed in action, lost a limb, died while on active duty or who has at least a 10 percent combined service-connected evaluation. Students must be currently attending or recently accepted into an accredited degree program or vocation program.
Target applicant(s): High school students. College students. Adult students.
Amount: $5,000.
Number of awards: Varies.
Deadline: March 31.
How to apply: Applications are available online.
Exclusive: Visit www.UltimateScholarshipBook.com and enter code FO14623 for updates on this award.

---

(147) · Foot Locker Scholar Athletes

Foot Locker Foundation
c/o Do Something Strategic, 1202 Lexington Avenue, Suite 305, New York, NY 10028
Phone: 212-254-2390 ext. 245
Email: footlocker@dosomething.org
https://www.footlockerscholarathletes.com/
Purpose: To honor high school athletes who demonstrate good sportsmanship and contribute to their community.
Eligibility: Applicants must be high school seniors who plan to enter a four-year college in the upcoming fall semester. Students must demonstrate leadership, academic excellence, good sportsmanship and strong moral character. Applicants must also have a minimum 3.0 GPA, be U.S. citizens or permanent legal residents and currently be involved in high school, intramural or community-based sports.
Target applicant(s): High school students.
Minimum GPA: 3.0
Amount: Up to $20,000.
Number of awards: 20.
Scholarship may be renewable.
Deadline: December 17.
How to apply: Applications are available online.
Exclusive: Visit www.UltimateScholarshipBook.com and enter code FO14723 for updates on this award.

---

(148) · Foreclosure.com Scholarship Program

Foreclosure.com
1825 NW Corporate Boulevard, Suite 110, Boca Raton, FL 33431
Phone: 561-988-9669 x 7387
Email: scholarship@foreclosure.com
http://www.foreclosure.com/scholarship/
Purpose: To support current undergraduate college students who are interested in addressing critical issues facing the nation, namely issues involving real estate/housing.
Eligibility: Applicants must be U.S. citizens 13 years of age or older who are currently enrolled as undergraduate college students. They must write an essay between 800 and 2,000 words providing creative solutions to a given topic involving critical issues facing the nation centered around real estate/housing. Selection is based upon the overall strength of the essay and application.
Target applicant(s): College students. Adult students.
Amount: $500-$2,500.
Number of awards: 3.
Deadline: December 15.
How to apply: Applications are available online. An application form and essay are required.
Exclusive: Visit www.UltimateScholarshipBook.com and enter code FO14823 for updates on this award.

---

(149) · Fraternal Order of Eagles Memorial Foundation

Fraternal Order of Eagles
1623 Gateway Circle S., Grove City, OH 43123
Phone: 614-883-2200
Email: help@foe.com
http://www.foe.com
Purpose: To provide financial support for post-secondary education to the children of Eagles.
Eligibility: Applicants must be the children of Eagles who lost their lives while serving in the military or in the commission of their daily employment. Applicants must have a 2.0 minimum GPA, be under the age of 25, unmarried and non-self supporting.
Target applicant(s): High school students. College students. Graduate school students.
Minimum GPA: 2.0
Amount: Varies.
Number of awards: Varies.
Scholarship may be renewable.
Deadline: Varies.
How to apply: Eligible juniors in high school will be sent a form requesting post high school plans, and eligible seniors will be mailed the scholarship application form.

Exclusive: Visit www.UltimateScholarshipBook.com and enter code FR14923 for updates on this award.

(150) · Free Speech Essay Contest

Foundation for Individual Rights in Education
510 Walnut Street, Suite 1250, Philadelphia, PA 19106
Phone: 215-717-3473
Email: essaycontest@thefire.org
https://www.thefire.org/resources/high-school-network/essay-contest/
Purpose: To encourage students to promote the freedom of speech.
Eligibility: Applicants must be juniors or seniors in U.S. high schools including home-schools or U.S. citizens attending overseas schools. Students must submit an essay pertaining to the topic of free speech and censorship.
Target applicant(s): High school students.
Amount: Up to $10,000.
Number of awards: 9.
Deadline: December 31.
How to apply: Applications are available online.
Exclusive: Visit www.UltimateScholarshipBook.com and enter code FO15023 for updates on this award.

(151) · Fulbright Grants

U.S. Department of State
Office of Academic Exchange Programs, Bureau of Educational and Cultural Affairs, U.S. Department of State, SA-44, 301 4th Street SW, Room 234, Washington, DC 20547
Phone: 202-632-3238
Email: fulbright@state.gov
https://us.fulbrightonline.org/
Purpose: To increase the understanding between the people of the United States and the people of other countries.
Eligibility: Applicants must be graduating college seniors, graduate students, young professionals and artists. Funds are generally used to support students in university teaching, advanced research, graduate study or teaching in elementary and secondary schools.
Target applicant(s): Graduate school students. Adult students.
Amount: Varies.
Number of awards: Varies.
Deadline: October 12.
How to apply: Applications are available online.
Exclusive: Visit www.UltimateScholarshipBook.com and enter code U.15123 for updates on this award.

(152) · Future Community Leaders Scholarship

B3 Foundation
P.O. Box 3577, Manhattan Beach, CA 90266
Email: scholarship@b3foundation.org
https://b3foundation.org/scholarships/
Purpose: To support students who are committed to further developing as local community leaders in their chosen field in college and beyond.
Eligibility: Applicants must be graduating high school seniors attending high school in the U.S. Students must have a minimum 3.0 GPA and demonstrate community involvement and a commitment to academic achievement. An application, letters of recommendation, transcript and an essay on a provided prompt are required to be submitted.
Target applicant(s): High school students.
Minimum GPA: 3.0
Amount: $10,000.
Number of awards: 1.

Deadline: March 15.
How to apply: Applications are available online.
Exclusive: Visit www.UltimateScholarshipBook.com and enter code B315223 for updates on this award.

(153) · Future of School Scholarship Program

Future of School Scholarship Program
Scholarship America, One Scholarship Way, Saint Peter, MN 56082
Phone: 507-931-1682
Email: fos-scholarship@scholarshipamerica.org
https://learnmore.scholarsapply.org/fos-scholarship/
Purpose: To support students interested in continuing their education through post-secondary education.
Eligibility: Applicants must be high school seniors who have completed a minimum of five blended or online courses during their last two years of high school and plan to enroll in full-time undergraduate study at an accredited two- or four-year college, university or vocational-technical school. Students must demonstrate academic achievement or personal improvement as a direct result of their enrollment in the blended/online learning. A recommendation form and transcript are required to be submitted.
Target applicant(s): High school students.
Amount: Up to $10,000.
Number of awards: 30.
Scholarship may be renewable.
Deadline: March 16.
How to apply: Applications are available online.
Exclusive: Visit www.UltimateScholarshipBook.com and enter code FU15323 for updates on this award.

(154) · GE-Reagan Foundation Scholarship Program

Ronald Reagan Presidential Foundation
40 Presidential Drive, Simi Valley, CA 93065
Phone: 844-402-0354
Email: ge-reagan@scholarshipamerica.org
https://www.scholarsapply.org/ge-reagan/
Purpose: To reward students who demonstrate leadership, drive, integrity and citizenship.
Eligibility: Applicants must be high school seniors and pursue a bachelor's degree at an accredited U.S. college or university the following fall. Students must demonstrate strong academic performance (3.0 or greater GPA or equivalent), demonstrate financial need and be a U.S. citizen. Funds may be used for student tuition and room and board.
Target applicant(s): High school students.
Minimum GPA: 3.0
Amount: $10,000.
Number of awards: Varies.
Scholarship may be renewable.
Deadline: January 6.
How to apply: Applications are available online. The competition will close earlier than the deadline once 25,000 applications are received.
Exclusive: Visit www.UltimateScholarshipBook.com and enter code RO15423 for updates on this award.

(155) · Gene Carte Student Paper Competition

American Society of Criminology Gene Carte Student Paper Competition
Daniel Ragan, Department of Sociology, University of New Mexico, 1915 Roma N.E., Suite 1103, MSCO5 3080, Albuquerque, NM 87131

Phone: 602-543-6601
Email: dragan@unm.edu
http://www.asc41.com
Purpose: To recognize outstanding student works in criminology.
Eligibility: Applicants must be full-time undergraduate or graduate students. The writing competition requires applicants to write on a topic directly related to criminology and must be accompanied by a letter signed by the dean or department chair. Other paper formatting requirements are listed on the website. The first place winner also receives a travel award.
Target applicant(s): College students. Graduate school students. Adult students.
Amount: $200-$500.
Number of awards: Up to 3.
Deadline: April 15.
How to apply: There is no application form. Paper must be mailed in. The paper specifications are on the website.
Exclusive: Visit www.UltimateScholarshipBook.com and enter code AM15523 for updates on this award.

(156) · General Henry H. Arnold Education Grant Program

Air Force Aid Society
Education Assistance Department, 241 18th Street S, Suite 202, Arlington, VA 22202
Phone: 703-972-2647
Email: ed@afas-hq.org
https://www.afas.org/how-we-help/education-support/
Purpose: To help Air Force family members realize their academic goals.
Eligibility: Applicants must be the dependent sons and daughters of Air Force members, spouses of active duty members or surviving spouses of Air Force members who died while on active duty or in retired status. They must also be high school seniors or college students enrolled or accepted as full-time undergraduates for the following school year and maintain a minimum 2.0 GPA.
Target applicant(s): High school students. College students.
Minimum GPA: 2.0
Amount: $500-$4,000.
Number of awards: Varies.
Scholarship may be renewable.
Deadline: April 30.
How to apply: Applications are available online.
Exclusive: Visit www.UltimateScholarshipBook.com and enter code AI15623 for updates on this award.

(157) · George Blair Ambassador Scholarship

USA Water Ski and Wake Sports Foundation
6039 Cypress Gardens Boulevard, Suite 481, Winter Haven, FL 33884
Phone: 863-324-2472
Email: Scholarships@Waterskihalloffame.com
https://www.usa-wwf.org/scholarships
Purpose: To aid young water skiers with their college expenses so that they can not only pursue a college education but continue with water skiing.
Eligibility: Applicants must be incoming freshmen through senior level college students who are current active members of USA Water Ski & Wake Sports. Students do not have to be collegiate water ski competitors. Selection is based on the number of years as an active member, academic success, financial need, school and community activities and individual contributions to the sport. A short essay is required.

Target applicant(s): High school students. College students. Adult students.
Amount: $2,200.
Number of awards: 1.
Deadline: March 15.
How to apply: Applications are available online and must include two letters of recommendation.
Exclusive: Visit www.UltimateScholarshipBook.com and enter code US15723 for updates on this award.

(158) · George Montgomery/NRA Youth Wildlife Art Contest

National Rifle Association
11250 Waples Mill Road, Fairfax, VA 22030
Phone: 800-672-3888
Email: grantprogram@nrahq.org
https://awards.nra.org/scholarships/
Purpose: To support young artists and encourage awareness of local game birds and animals.
Eligibility: Applicants must be in grades 1 through 12 and submit an original artwork depicting any North American game bird or animal that may be legally hunted or trapped. NRA membership is not required. Art is divided into categories based on grade level and is judged on effort, creativity, anatomical accuracy and composition.
Target applicant(s): Junior high students or younger. High school students.
Amount: Up to $1,000.
Number of awards: Varies.
Deadline: October 31.
How to apply: Application information is available online. A statement of authenticity signed by a parent, guardian or teacher must be submitted along with the artwork.
Exclusive: Visit www.UltimateScholarshipBook.com and enter code NA15823 for updates on this award.

(159) · George S. and Stella M. Knight Essay Contest

National Society, Sons of the American Revolution
1000 South Fourth Street, Louisville, KY 40203
Phone: 502-589-1776
Email: sdelong1@san.rr.com
https://www.sar.org/education/
Purpose: To reward students who have written outstanding essays on the American Revolution, the U.S. Constitution or the Declaration of Independence.
Eligibility: Applicants must be U.S. citizens or legal residents. Students must be high school sophomores, juniors or seniors. Applicants must submit an 800- to 1,200-word essay on some topic that is related to the Declaration of Independence, the American Revolution or the U.S. Constitution. Selection is based on the overall strength of the essay.
Target applicant(s): High school students.
Amount: $1,000-$5,000.
Number of awards: 3.
Deadline: December 31.
How to apply: Applications are available online.
Exclusive: Visit www.UltimateScholarshipBook.com and enter code NA15923 for updates on this award.

(160) · Gift for Life Scholarships

United States Bowling Congress
Attn.: Alberta E. Crowe Star of Tomorrow, 621 Six Flags Drive,
Arlington, TX 76011
Phone: 800-514-2695
Email: contactus@ibcyouth.com
https://www.bowl.com/scholarships/
Purpose: To provide financial assistance to high school students with financial need.
Eligibility: Applicants must be USBC Youth members who are current high school students in grades 9-12. They must have a GPA of 2.5 or higher and demonstrate financial need. Two awards each year are reserved for children of fire department, emergency rescue or police personnel. Candidates may win once per year up until graduation.
Target applicant(s): High school students.
Minimum GPA: 2.5
Amount: $1,000.
Number of awards: 6.
Deadline: December 1.
How to apply: Applications are available online.
Exclusive: Visit www.UltimateScholarshipBook.com and enter code UN16023 for updates on this award.

(161) · Gladys Ann Smith Greater Los Angeles Women's Council Scholarship

Navy League Foundation
2300 Wilson Boulevard, Suite 200, Arlington, VA 22201-5424
Phone: 800-356-5760
Email: vfrye@navyleague.org
http://www.navyleague.org
Purpose: To support students who are the children or grandchildren of a member of the sea services.
Eligibility: Applicants must be enrolled at an accredited institution of higher education and the children or grandchildren of a member of the sea services to include the following: United States Navy, United States Marine Corps, United States Coast Guard or U.S.-flag Merchant Marine.
Target applicant(s): High school students.
Amount: $10,000.
Number of awards: 1.
Deadline: March 11.
How to apply: Applications are available online.
Exclusive: Visit www.UltimateScholarshipBook.com and enter code NA16123 for updates on this award.

(162) · Global Citizen Scholarship

EF Educational Tours
EF Center Boston, Two Education Circle, Cambridge, MA 02141
Phone: 800-665-5364
Email: EF.Global.Citizen@ef.com
http://www.eftours.com
Purpose: To help students reflect on their place in the world through writing and then have a chance to experience it first-hand.
Eligibility: Applicants must be U.S. residents that are currently enrolled in a tour with EF educational tours and must create a video on a topic related to global citizenship. Up to 100 scholarship recipients will receive $1,000 towards their current EF educational tour.
Target applicant(s): High school students.
Amount: $1,000.
Number of awards: 100.

Deadline: August 15, November 15, February 15, May 15.
How to apply: Applications are available online on the EF Tours Facebook page.
Exclusive: Visit www.UltimateScholarshipBook.com and enter code EF16223 for updates on this award.

(163) · Gloria Barron Prize for Young Heroes

Barron Prize
P.O. Box 1470, Boulder, CO 80306
Email: admin@barronprize.org
http://www.barronprize.org
Purpose: To reward young people who have organized and led extraordinary service projects.
Eligibility: Applicants must be residents of the U.S. or Canada between the ages of 8 and 18. Students must be currently working on a service project or have completed a service project within the past year. Selection is primarily based on demonstration of generosity, tenacity and positive impact on the world.
Target applicant(s): Junior high students or younger. High school students.
Amount: $10,000.
Number of awards: 25.
Deadline: April 15.
How to apply: Applications are available online.
Exclusive: Visit www.UltimateScholarshipBook.com and enter code BA16323 for updates on this award.

(164) · GMR Transcription Academic Scholarship

GMR Transcription Services
2552 Walnut Avenue, Suite 110, Tustin, CA 92780
Phone: 714-202-9653
https://www.gmrtranscription.com/scholarship/scholarshiphome.aspx
Purpose: To help students offset the costs of continuing education.
Eligibility: Applicants must be enrolled as full-time students at an accredited college or university. Students must have a minimum 3.0 grade point average. Applicants must submit essays and complete a qualification quiz.
Target applicant(s): College students. Adult students.
Minimum GPA: 3.0
Amount: $500.
Number of awards: 2.
Deadline: June 15 and December 15.
How to apply: Applications are available online.
Exclusive: Visit www.UltimateScholarshipBook.com and enter code GM16423 for updates on this award.

(165) · GNC Nutritional Research Grant

National Strength and Conditioning Association (NSCA) Foundation
1885 Bob Johnson Drive, Colorado Springs, CO 80906
Phone: 800-815-6826
http://www.nsca.com/foundation/
Purpose: To fund nutrition-based research.
Eligibility: Applicants must be graduate students and be NSCA members for one year before applying and pursuing careers in strength and conditioning. Students must also plan a research project that falls within the mission of the NSCA and submit a proposal describing the rationale, purpose and methods of the planned research. Applications are evaluated based on grades, courses, experience, honors, recommendations and involvement in the community and with NSCA.

Target applicant(s): College students. Graduate school students. Adult students.
Amount: Up to $10,000.
Number of awards: Up to 2.
Deadline: February 15.
How to apply: Applications are available with membership.
Exclusive: Visit www.UltimateScholarshipBook.com and enter code NA16523 for updates on this award.

(166) · Golden Door Scholars
Golden Door Scholars
1423 Red Ventures Drive, Fort Mill, SC 29707
Email: info@goldendoorscholars.org
https://www.goldendoorscholars.org/
Purpose: To assist DACA students pursuing higher education.
Eligibility: Applicants must be approved DACA students with strong academic records who are enrolling in an undergraduate program or who are current high school seniors or undergraduate students. Students pursuing engineering, computer science, technology or math are given preference.
Target applicant(s): High school students. College students. Adult students.
Amount: Varies.
Number of awards: Varies.
Deadline: October 25.
How to apply: Applications are available online.
Exclusive: Visit www.UltimateScholarshipBook.com and enter code GO16623 for updates on this award.

(167) · Google SVA Scholarship
Student Veterans of America
1625 K Street North West, Suite 320, Washington, DC 20006
Phone: 202-223-4710
http://studentveterans.org/programs/scholarships
Purpose: To support students who are veterans and are pursuing a degree in computer science.
Eligibility: Applicants must be veterans who are currently enrolled as a full-time undergraduate or graduate student at a four-year university. Students must exhibit a strong academic performance and be pursuing a degree in either computer science or computer engineering. Applicants must currently be in good standing with their military branch or have an honorable discharge.
Target applicant(s): College students. Graduate school students. Adult students.
Amount: $10,000.
Number of awards: 8.
Deadline: December.
How to apply: Applications are available online.
Exclusive: Visit www.UltimateScholarshipBook.com and enter code ST16723 for updates on this award.

(168) · Graduate Research Grant - Master and Doctoral
National Strength and Conditioning Association (NSCA) Foundation
1885 Bob Johnson Drive, Colorado Springs, CO 80906
Phone: 800-815-6826
http://www.nsca.com/foundation/
Purpose: To support research in strength and conditioning.

Eligibility: Applicants must be master's or doctoral students and submit a proposal for a research project in the field of strength and conditioning that fulfills the mission of the NSCA. Students must be NSCA members for one year before applying and pursuing careers in strength and conditioning. Applications are evaluated based on grades, courses, experience, honors, recommendations and involvement in the community and with NSCA.
Target applicant(s): Graduate school students. Adult students.
Amount: Up to $15,000.
Number of awards: Varies.
Deadline: February 15.
How to apply: Applications are available with membership.
Exclusive: Visit www.UltimateScholarshipBook.com and enter code NA16823 for updates on this award.

(169) · Grungo Colarulo Giving Back to the Community
Grungo Colarulo
1926 Greentree Road, Suite 110, Cherry Hill, NJ 08003
Phone: 856-528-4494
Email: info@gcinjurylaw.com
https://gcinjurylaw.com/2021-grungo-colarulo-giving-back-to-the-community-scholarship/
Purpose: To support students dedicated to serving others.
Eligibility: Applicants must be enrolling in or currently enrolled in an accredited undergraduate or graduate program in the U.S. and have a minimum GPA of 3.0. An essay submission on a provided prompt is required.
Target applicant(s): High school students. College students. Graduate school students. Adult students.
Minimum GPA: 3.0
Amount: $1,000.
Number of awards: 1.
Deadline: November 14.
How to apply: Applications are available online.
Exclusive: Visit www.UltimateScholarshipBook.com and enter code GR16923 for updates on this award.

(170) · H&P Veterans Helping Veterans Scholarship
Hill & Ponton
605 E. Robinson Street, Suite 635, Orlando, FL 32801
https://www.hillandponton.com/veterans-scholarship/
Purpose: To support veterans pursuing post-secondary education.
Eligibility: Applicants must be veterans of the U.S. armed forces. Students must plan to use their education to help fellow veterans. Applicants must complete statement explaining how their education will be used to assist veterans.
Target applicant(s): College students. Adult students.
Amount: $1,000.
Number of awards: 4.
Deadline: May 1 and November 1.
How to apply: Applications are available online.
Exclusive: Visit www.UltimateScholarshipBook.com and enter code HI17023 for updates on this award.

(171) · H. U. Lee Scholarship
H.U. Lee Memorial Foundation
6210 Baseline Road, Little Rock, AR 72209
Phone: 501-568-2821 x2263

Email: hulf@ataonline.com
http://www.huleefoundation.org/scholarship-requirements/
Purpose: To support the advancement of discipline, respect and courtesy through Taekwondo.
Eligibility: Applicants must be current high school seniors graduating from an accredited high school with a minimum 3.0 GPA. Students must have received a letter of acceptance from an accredited U.S. college for full-time study beginning no later than September 30. Applicants must have a minimum combined score of 1100 on the SAT and/or 27 on the ACT, must have registered with Selective Service if required and have no convictions of drug possession or distribution.
Target applicant(s): High school students.
Minimum GPA: 3.0
Amount: Varies.
Number of awards: Varies.
Deadline: February 15.
How to apply: Applications are available through the student's instructor. An application form, a sealed copy of high school transcripts with signature of school's director of admissions across the sealed envelope, two recommendation letters and an essay are required.
Exclusive: Visit www.UltimateScholarshipBook.com and enter code H.17123 for updates on this award.

(172) · Hagan Scholarship

Hagan Scholarship Foundation
P.O. Box 1225, Columbia, MO 65205
Email: scholarships@hsfmo.org
https://haganscholarships.org
Purpose: To help high-achieving, dedicated students who live in smaller counties.
Eligibility: Applicants must be U.S. citizens and be graduating seniors from a public high school located in a county with fewer than 50,000 residents. Students must be enrolling in a four-year college or university the first semester following high school graduation. Applicants must work 240 hours in the year prior to the start of each academic year.
Target applicant(s): High school students.
Minimum GPA: 3.5
Amount: Varies.
Number of awards: 600.
Deadline: December 1.
How to apply: Applications are available online.
Exclusive: Visit www.UltimateScholarshipBook.com and enter code HA17223 for updates on this award.

(173) · Hamilton Award

Alexander Hamilton Scholars
200 1st Avenue West, Suite 201, Seattle, WA 98119
Phone: 206-774-0764
Email: program@hamiltonscholars.org
http://www.hamiltonscholars.org
Purpose: To reward the academic, personal, service and entrepreneurial accomplishments of students.
Eligibility: Applicants must be high-achieving, service-focused high school juniors with grit, perseverance and demonstrated need. Students must be committed to participating in a rigorous five-year curriculum designed to provide a comprehensive network of support and practical guidance to Alexander Hamilton Scholars as they transition from high school to college and college to career.
Target applicant(s): High school students.
Amount: $500.
Number of awards: 35.

Deadline: January 15.
How to apply: Applications are available online.
Exclusive: Visit www.UltimateScholarshipBook.com and enter code AL17323 for updates on this award.

(174) · Hanscom Air Force Base Spouses' Club Scholarship

Hanscom Officers' Spouses' Club
75 Grenier Street, Box 8888, Hanscom AFB, MA 01731
Phone: 781-538-5361
Email: scholarship@hanscomsc.org
https://hanscomsc.org/scholarships.html
Purpose: To aid dependents of past and present members of the military.
Eligibility: Applicants must be children or spouses of retired, deceased or current active duty members of any branch of the military. They must hold a valid military ID card. Children of military members must be high school seniors.
Target applicant(s): High school students. College students. Adult students.
Amount: Varies.
Number of awards: Varies.
Deadline: March 12.
How to apply: Applications are available online. An application form and copy of military ID are required.
Exclusive: Visit www.UltimateScholarshipBook.com and enter code HA17423 for updates on this award.

(175) · Hayek Fund for Scholars

Institute for Humane Studies at George Mason University
3434 Washington Boulevard, MS 1C5, Arlington, VA 22201
Phone: 800-697-8799
Email: ihs@gmu.edu
http://www.theihs.org
Purpose: To make awards to graduate students and untenured faculty members for career-enhancing activities.
Eligibility: Applicants must be graduate students or untenured faculty members and must submit a cover letter explaining how participation will advance their liberty-advancing careers. Applicants must also submit an abstract of the paper they are going to present (if applicable), an itemized expense list and resume. Students may attend any university but must be alumni of IHS programs and events.
Target applicant(s): Graduate school students. Adult students.
Amount: Up to $750.
Number of awards: Varies.
Deadline: Rolling.
How to apply: There is no application form.
Exclusive: Visit www.UltimateScholarshipBook.com and enter code IN17523 for updates on this award.

(176) · HD Hogan Rodeo Scholarship

HD Hogan Memorial Rodeo Scholarship Fund
407 S. X Road, Aurora, NE 68818
Email: beabullfighter@hotmail.com
http://www.circlehdrodeo.org/scholarship
Purpose: To aid students in continuing their education and their rodeo careers in college.
Eligibility: Applicants must be a current high school senior and current rodeo participant. Selection is based solely on the essay about what being an American means to you and also what the sport of rodeo means to you.
Target applicant(s): High school students.

Amount: Varies.
Number of awards: Varies.
Deadline: October 1.
How to apply: Applications are in the form of the essay that must be mailed.
Exclusive: Visit www.UltimateScholarshipBook.com and enter code HD17623 for updates on this award.

---

(177) · Heisman High School Scholarship

Acceptance Insurance Company
111 Broadway, Suite 103A, New York, NY 10006
Phone: 800-205-6367
Email: heismanscholarship@scholarshipamerica.org
https://heismanscholarship.com/
Purpose: To reward high school seniors who are outstanding scholar-athletes.
Eligibility: Applicants must participate or have participated in grades 9, 10 or 11 in at least one of the sports recognized by the International Olympic Committee in the Summer and Winter Olympic Games, the Paralympic Games or the National Federation of State High School Association. Students must have a minimum 3.0 GPA, be a leader in school and their community and serve as a role model for underclassmen.
Target applicant(s): High school students.
Minimum GPA: 3.0
Amount: Up to $10,000.
Number of awards: 100.
Deadline: October 19.
How to apply: Applications are available online.
Exclusive: Visit www.UltimateScholarshipBook.com and enter code AC17723 for updates on this award.

---

(178) · Helen Gee Chin Scholarship Foundation Scholarship

Helen Gee Chin Scholarship Foundation
66 Winchester Street, Newton Highlands, MA 02461
Phone: 617-527-8890
Email: hgc@calvinchin.com
http://www.hgcscholarshipfoundation.org
Purpose: To promote academic achievement and inspire individuals to become students of the Chinese martial arts.
Eligibility: Applicants must be a U.S. citizen, plan to attend an accredited U.S. four year college or university as a full-time student for the entire academic year and have a B GPA. Applicants must have studied for at least five years one or more of the Chinese martial arts including Kung Fu, Wu Shu or Tai Chi. Selection is based on achievement in academics and martial arts, recommendations, work experience, educational and career goals and leadership in school and community activities.
Target applicant(s): High school students. College students. Adult students.
Minimum GPA: 3.0
Amount: $1,000-$3,000.
Number of awards: At least 2.
Deadline: June 1.
How to apply: Applications are available online. An application form, an essay, official transcripts covering the previous two years, a recommendation letter from current or most recent Sifu and a recommendation letter from a teacher, counselor or advisor are required.
Exclusive: Visit www.UltimateScholarshipBook.com and enter code HE17823 for updates on this award.

---

(179) · HelloCampus Scholarship

OnPage Ideas Inc. Scholarship Program
5072 Annunciation Circle, Suite 202, Ave Maria, FL 34142
Email: hello@sayhellocampus.com
https://sayhellocampus.com/scholarship
Purpose: To reward students who are campus tour guides or ambassadors.
Eligibility: Applicants must be enrolled full-time at an accredited college or university and U.S. citizens. Students must be college tour guides or ambassadors and have a minimum 2.5 GPA.
Target applicant(s): College students. Adult students.
Minimum GPA: 2.5
Amount: $5,000.
Number of awards: 2.
Deadline: May 1.
How to apply: Applications are available online.
Exclusive: Visit www.UltimateScholarshipBook.com and enter code ON17923 for updates on this award.

---

(180) · High School Scholarship

National Strength and Conditioning Association (NSCA) Foundation
1885 Bob Johnson Drive, Colorado Springs, CO 80906
Phone: 800-815-6826
http://www.nsca.com/foundation/
Purpose: To support high school students entering the strength and conditioning field.
Eligibility: Applicants must be high school seniors planning to graduate with a degree related to strength and conditioning with a current 3.0 GPA. Students must be NSCA members, although applicants may enroll at the time of application, and pursuing a career in strength and conditioning. Applications are evaluated based on grades, courses, experience, honors, recommendations and involvement in the community and with NSCA.
Target applicant(s): High school students.
Minimum GPA: 3.0
Amount: $1,500.
Number of awards: Varies.
Deadline: October 15.
How to apply: Applications are available by contacting the organization.
Exclusive: Visit www.UltimateScholarshipBook.com and enter code NA18023 for updates on this award.

---

(181) · Horatio Alger National Scholarship Program

Horatio Alger Association
Attn.: Scholarship Department, 99 Canal Center Plaza, Suite 320, Alexandria, VA 22314
Phone: 703-684-9444
Email: association@horatioalger.org
https://scholars.horatioalger.org/
Purpose: To assist students who are committed to pursuing a bachelor's degree and have demonstrated integrity, financial need, academic achievement and community involvement.
Eligibility: Applicants must be a high school junior, have at least a 2.0 GPA, be in need of financial aid ($55,000 or less adjusted gross income per family is preferred) and be involved in extracurricular and community activities. Students applying from Louisiana, Montana and Idaho have additional state specific requirements.
Target applicant(s): High school students.
Minimum GPA: 2.0

Amount: $25,000.
Number of awards: 106.
Deadline: March 15.
How to apply: Applications are available online.
Exclusive: Visit www.UltimateScholarshipBook.com and enter code HO18123 for updates on this award.

(182) · Humane Studies Fellowships

Institute for Humane Studies at George Mason University
3434 Washington Boulevard, MS 1C5, Arlington, VA 22201
Phone: 800-697-8799
Email: ihs@gmu.edu
http://www.theihs.org
Purpose: To award scholarships to students who are interested in the classical liberal/libertarian tradition of individual rights and market economies and wish to apply these principles in their work.
Eligibility: Applicants must be graduate students who are in any field and at any stage before completion of the Ph.D., law students, MBA students or other professional students. The fellowships can be used for study in the U.S. or abroad. Applicants must also be enrolled as full-time students at an accredited degree-granting institution. Students must be alumni of IHS programs and events.
Target applicant(s): Graduate school students. Adult students.
Amount: Up to $15,000.
Number of awards: Varies.
Scholarship may be renewable.
Deadline: April 1, August 1, December 1.
How to apply: Applications are available online. There is a $25 application fee that is waived by applying by January 5.
Exclusive: Visit www.UltimateScholarshipBook.com and enter code IN18223 for updates on this award.

(183) · IAFC Foundation Scholarship

International Association of Fire Chiefs Foundation
4025 Fair Ridge Drive, Suite 300, Fairfax, VA 22033-2868
Phone: 571-344-5410
Email: iafcfoun@msn.com
http://www.iafcf.org
Purpose: To assist students in fire sciences or related academic programs.
Eligibility: Applicants must be active members with a minimum of three years volunteer work, two years paid work or a combination of paid and volunteer work of three years with a state, county, provincial, municipal, community, industrial or federal fire department who will use the scholarship at an accredited institution of higher education. Students must submit application forms, statements, a list of credits and a transcript. Preference is given to those demonstrating need, desire and initiative.
Target applicant(s): College students. Adult students.
Amount: Varies.
Number of awards: Varies.
Deadline: June 25.
How to apply: Applications are available online.
Exclusive: Visit www.UltimateScholarshipBook.com and enter code IN18323 for updates on this award.

(184) · IAPMO Essay Scholarship Contest

International Association of Plumbing and Mechanical Officials (IAPMO)
4755 E. Philadelphia Street, Ontario, CA 91761
Phone: 909-472-4100

Email: essay@iwsh.org
https://www.iwsh.org/hidden/iwsh-essay-scholarship-contest/
Purpose: To share the "importance the plumbing and mechanical industry plays in our everyday lives."
Eligibility: Applicants must be current high school seniors or enrolled or accepted as full-time students in an accredited technical school, community college, trade school, four-year accredited college or university or an apprentice program.
Target applicant(s): High school students. College students. Adult students.
Amount: $500-$1,000.
Number of awards: 3.
Deadline: April 30.
How to apply: Applications are available online. An essay of 800 to 1,600 words on the topic provided is required.
Exclusive: Visit www.UltimateScholarshipBook.com and enter code IN18423 for updates on this award.

(185) · IEA Founders College Scholarship Awards

Interscholastic Equestrian Association
467 Main Street, Melrose, MA 02176
Phone: 877-743-3432
Email: info@rideiea.org
https://www.rideiea.org/opportunities/for-riders/
Purpose: To recognize the top participants in the Interscholastic Equestrian Association's National Final Competitions.
Eligibility: Students must be a high school senior, compete in either the IEA Hunt Seat National Finals or the IEA Western National Finals and place in the top two in their category.
Target applicant(s): High school students.
Amount: Up to $1,100.
Number of awards: Varies.
Deadline: Varies.
How to apply: Participant must qualify during their IEA Zone Final Competition.
Exclusive: Visit www.UltimateScholarshipBook.com and enter code IN18523 for updates on this award.

(186) · IEA Zone Specific Scholarships

Interscholastic Equestrian Association
467 Main Street, Melrose, MA 02176
Phone: 877-743-3432
Email: info@rideiea.org
https://www.rideiea.org/opportunities/for-riders/
Purpose: To support high school seniors in each Interscholastic Equestrian Association zone as they further their education beyond high school.
Eligibility: Students must be active participants in an IEA zone, display outstanding sportsmanship, maintain academic excellence and portray and overall role model to the IEA membership. Each zone has varied selection criteria.
Target applicant(s): High school students.
Amount: Varies.
Number of awards: Varies.
Deadline: Varies.
How to apply: All zone applications are available online. Most zones require letters of recommendation, high school transcript and an essay.
Exclusive: Visit www.UltimateScholarshipBook.com and enter code IN18623 for updates on this award.

(187) · Ike Foundation Scholarship

Ike Foundation
348 Palatine Road, Elmer, NJ 08318
Phone: 856-466-7798
Email: theikefoundation@gmail.com
https://theikefoundation.org/forms-and-applications/scholarship-application/
Purpose: To support students involved in the sport of fishing.
Eligibility: Applicants must be U.S. citizens or permanent residents and high school seniors who are planning to enroll full-time in a two- or four-year institution. Students must have a minimum GPA of 3.2 and demonstrate an interest in fishing and/or conservation. Applicants must submit an original essay along with their application materials.
Target applicant(s): High school students.
Minimum GPA: 3.2
Amount: Up to $3,000.
Number of awards: 5.
Deadline: April 1.
How to apply: Applications are available online.
Exclusive: Visit www.UltimateScholarshipBook.com and enter code IK18723 for updates on this award.

(188) · IMCEA Scholarships

International Military Community Executives' Association (IMCEA)
Headquarters - Scholarships
14080 Nacogdoches Road, #329, San Antonio, TX 78247-1944
Phone: 940-463-5145
Email: imcea@imcea.com
https://imcea.org/imcea-scholarships/
Purpose: To provide scholarships for high school students and military welfare and recreation professionals seeking to further their educations.
Eligibility: High school or college applicants must be children of IMCEA members. Candidates must provide information about their activities, honors and awards and submit an essay on the provided topic.
Target applicant(s): High school students. College students. Graduate school students. Adult students.
Amount: $1,000.
Number of awards: 2.
Deadline: July.
How to apply: Applications are available online and an official transcript must also be submitted.
Exclusive: Visit www.UltimateScholarshipBook.com and enter code IN18823 for updates on this award.

(189) · Indianhead Division Scholarships

Second Indianhead Division Association
P.O. Box 218, Fox Lake, IL 60020-0218
Phone: 512-295-5324
Email: warriorvet@verizon.net
http://www.2ida.org/scholarships/
Purpose: To support the children and grandchildren of veterans from the Second Indianhead Division Association.
Eligibility: Applicants' parents or grandparents must have been members of the association for at least three years, or they must have been killed while serving with the Second Infantry Division.
Target applicant(s): High school students. College students. Adult students.
Amount: Varies.
Number of awards: Varies.
Scholarship may be renewable.

Deadline: June 1.
How to apply: Applications are available by phone.
Exclusive: Visit www.UltimateScholarshipBook.com and enter code SE18923 for updates on this award.

(190) · Individual Scholarship Program

International Surfing Association
5580 La Jolla Boulevard, #145, La Jolla, CA 92037
Phone: 858-551-8580
Email: info@isasurf.org
https://www.isasurf.org/development-programs/isa-scholarship/
Purpose: To aid student surfers who plan to pursue higher education after high school.
Eligibility: Applicants must be U18 junior surfers. Selection is based on financial need and the ability of the applicant to represent themselves as a positive role model both within the sport of surfing and at school.
Target applicant(s): Junior high students or younger. High school students.
Amount: Varies.
Number of awards: Varies.
Deadline: September.
How to apply: Applications are available online and must include the following: a recent report card, one letter of recommendation, a personal essay, a budget plan and four photos (family, school, surfing and headshot).
Exclusive: Visit www.UltimateScholarshipBook.com and enter code IN19023 for updates on this award.

(191) · International Association of Fire Chiefs Foundation Fire Explorer Scholarships

Explorers Learning for Life
1325 West Walnut Hill Lane, P.O. Box 152225, Irving, TX 75015-2225
Phone: 855-806-9992
Email: exploring@lflmail.org
http://www.exploring.org/scholarships/
Purpose: To support students who are pursuing careers in fire sciences.
Eligibility: Students must be graduating high school seniors, active fire service Explorers and members of a fire department. Applicants must submit three letters of recommendation and an essay.
Target applicant(s): High school students.
Amount: $500.
Number of awards: Varies.
Deadline: June 25.
How to apply: Applications are available online.
Exclusive: Visit www.UltimateScholarshipBook.com and enter code EX19123 for updates on this award.

(192) · Iowa Student Loan Midwest Senior Scholarship

Iowa Student Loan Education Lending
6805 Vista Drive, West Des Moines, IA 50266
Phone: 855-811-9849
Email: scholarship@studentloan.org
https://www.iowastudentloan.org/scholarships/
Purpose: To help students with expenses related to their pursuit of post-secondary education.
Eligibility: Applicants must be high school seniors who are at least 13 years of age. Students must be a permanent resident of and enrolled in a high school located in one of the following states: Illinois, Nebraska,

South Dakota, Wisconsin, Missouri or Minnesota and who will attend an eligible U.S. college. Selection is based on a random drawing.
Target applicant(s): High school students.
Amount: $1,000.
Number of awards: 10.
Deadline: April 29.
How to apply: Application information is available online. Two online financial literacy tutorials, an online financial literacy assessment and a short essay are required.
Exclusive: Visit www.UltimateScholarshipBook.com and enter code IO19223 for updates on this award.

(193) · ISIA Education Foundation Scholarship

Ice Skating Institute of America (ISIA) Education Foundation
6000 Custer Road, Building 9, Plano, TX 75023
Phone: 972-735-8800
Email: ISI@skateisi.org
http://www.skateisi.com
Purpose: To encourage skaters to make athletic and educational achievements.
Eligibility: Applicants must have completed at least three years of high school with a minimum 3.0 GPA during the last two years and enroll as full-time undergraduate students. Applicants must also have been members of the Ice Skating Institute (ISI), have participated in the ISI Recreational Skater Program for at least four years and have completed 120 hours of volunteer service. Applicants must also submit two evaluation forms and an essay of 500 words or less explaining why they should receive the award.
Target applicant(s): High school students. College students. Adult students.
Minimum GPA: 3.0
Amount: $4,000.
Number of awards: Varies.
Deadline: February 1.
How to apply: Applications are available online.
Exclusive: Visit www.UltimateScholarshipBook.com and enter code IC19323 for updates on this award.

(194) · Jack Kent Cooke Foundation College Scholarship Program

Jack Kent Cooke Foundation
44325 Woodridge Parkway, Lansdowne, VA 20176
Phone: 800-941-3300
Email: scholarships@jkcf.org
http://www.jkcf.org
Purpose: To assist high school seniors with financial need.
Eligibility: Applicants must plan to graduate from a U.S. high school in the spring and plan to enroll in an accredited four-year college beginning in the fall following application. Students must have a minimum 3.5 GPA and have standardized test scores in the top 15 percent: SAT combined critical reading and math score of 1200 or above and/or ACT composite score of 26 or above. Applicants must also demonstrate significant unmet financial need. Family incomes up to $95,000 are considered. However, the majority of recipients will be eligible to receive a Pell grant.
Target applicant(s): High school students.
Minimum GPA: 3.5
Amount: Up to $55,000 per year for four years.
Number of awards: Up to 40.
Scholarship may be renewable.
Deadline: November 18.

How to apply: Applications are available online.
Exclusive: Visit www.UltimateScholarshipBook.com and enter code JA19423 for updates on this award.

(195) · James M. and Erma T. Freemont Foundation Scholarship Program

James M. and Erma T. Freemont Foundation
P.O. Box 82563, Hapeville, GA 30354
http://www.freemontfoundation.com
Purpose: To support students who demonstrate involvement and leadership.
Eligibility: Applicants must be graduating high school seniors, undergraduate or graduate students. Students must demonstrate outstanding academic achievement, leadership and volunteerism in their community and participation in extracurricular school activities.
Target applicant(s): High school students. College students. Graduate school students. Adult students.
Amount: Varies.
Number of awards: Varies.
Deadline: February 4.
How to apply: Applications are available online.
Exclusive: Visit www.UltimateScholarshipBook.com and enter code JA19523 for updates on this award.

(196) · James M. and Virginia M. Smyth Scholarship

Community Foundation for Greater Atlanta Inc.
50 Hurt Plaza, Suite 449, Atlanta, GA 30303
Phone: 404-688-5525
Email: info@cfgreateratlanta.org
https://cfgreateratlanta.org/scholarships/
Purpose: To support students who are pursuing undergraduate degrees.
Eligibility: Students must have at least a 3.0 GPA, and they must have community service experience. Applicants must plan to obtain a degree in the arts and sciences, music, ministry or human services. Preference will be given to students from the following states: Missouri, Mississippi, Georgia, Illinois, Oklahoma, Texas and Tennessee. Applicants must demonstrate financial need. Adult students may also apply.
Target applicant(s): High school students. College students. Adult students.
Minimum GPA: 3.0
Amount: $2,000.
Number of awards: 12-15.
Scholarship may be renewable.
Deadline: January 22.
How to apply: Applications are available online.
Exclusive: Visit www.UltimateScholarshipBook.com and enter code CO19623 for updates on this award.

(197) · Jean Downes Scholarship

USA Water Ski and Wake Sports Foundation
6039 Cypress Gardens Boulevard, Suite 481, Winter Haven, FL 33884
Phone: 863-324-2472
Email: Scholarships@Waterskihalloffame.com
https://www.usa-wwf.org/scholarships
Purpose: To support current active members of USA Water Ski in pursuit of their educational goals.
Eligibility: Applicants must be U.S. citizens and be studying full-time at a two-year or four-year accredited college as an incoming freshman, sophomore, junior or senior. Applicants must attend their chosen college

for the full year during the year of receipt of the scholarship. Selection is based on applicant's academic achievement, need, work record and school and community activities as well as their contributions to the sport of water skiing.

Target applicant(s): College students. Adult students.
Amount: $1,500.
Number of awards: 1.
Deadline: March 15.
How to apply: Applications are available online. An application form, 500-word essay and two recommendation letters are required.
Exclusive: Visit www.UltimateScholarshipBook.com and enter code US19723 for updates on this award.

(198) · Jeanne E. Bray Memorial Scholarship

National Rifle Association
11250 Waples Mill Road, Fairfax, VA 22030
Phone: 800-672-3888
Email: grantprogram@nrahq.org
https://awards.nra.org/scholarships/
Purpose: To help or aid children of public law enforcement officers in obtaining a college education.
Eligibility: Applicants must be a dependent child of any current, retired or deceased law enforcement officer. The parent should also be a member of the NRA.
Target applicant(s): High school students. College students. Adult students.
Amount: Up to $5,000.
Number of awards: Varies.
Scholarship may be renewable.
Deadline: November 15.
How to apply: Applications are available online.
Exclusive: Visit www.UltimateScholarshipBook.com and enter code NA19823 for updates on this award.

(199) · John F. Duffy Scholarship/Grant Program

California Peace Officers' Memorial Foundation
1700 I Street, Suite 100, Sacramento, CA 95811
Email: cpomf@camemorial.org
http://www.camemorial.org
Purpose: To provide financial assistance to survivors of California peace officers who have died in the line of duty.
Eligibility: Applicants must be spouses, children, stepchildren or adopted children of peace officers who died in the line of duty and are enrolled on the California memorial monument. They must carry no less than six units per quarter or eight units per semester at an accredited college or university, and they must maintain a 2.0 or higher GPA.
Target applicant(s): High school students. College students. Graduate school students. Adult students.
Minimum GPA: 2.0
Amount: Up to $4,000.
Number of awards: Varies.
Deadline: June 1.
How to apply: Applications are available online.
Exclusive: Visit www.UltimateScholarshipBook.com and enter code CA19923 for updates on this award.

(200) · John J. Smith Graduate School Scholarship

National Intercollegiate Rodeo Association
2033 Walla Walla Avenue, Walla Walla, WA 99362
Phone: 509-529-4402
Email: rodeo@collegerodeo.com
http://www.collegerodeo.com/
Purpose: To support students who have participated in the National Intercollegiate Rodeo Association as they continue on into graduate level coursework.
Eligibility: Applicants must be current graduate level college students or be entering into a graduate program and be current NIRA members.
Target applicant(s): College students. Graduate school students. Adult students.
Amount: $2,000.
Number of awards: 1.
Deadline: May 20.
How to apply: Applications are available online. The following are to be included with the application: cover letter, proof of acceptance into a graduate level program, an official college transcript and two letters of recommendation.
Exclusive: Visit www.UltimateScholarshipBook.com and enter code NA20023 for updates on this award.

(201) · Jon C. Ladda Memorial Foundation Scholarship

Jon C. Ladda Memorial Foundation
P.O. Box 55, Unionville, CT 06085
Email: info@jonladda.org
http://www.jonladda.org
Purpose: To provide financial assistance to children of Naval Academy graduates and Navy members who have died or become disabled while on active duty.
Eligibility: Applicants must be children of United States Naval Academy graduates or Navy members who served in the submarine service. The Navy member or Academy graduate must have died on active duty or have 100 percent disability and be medically retired. Applicants must also be accepted and enroll in an accredited institution of higher learning.
Target applicant(s): High school students. College students. Adult students.
Amount: Varies.
Number of awards: Varies.
Scholarship may be renewable.
Deadline: March 15.
How to apply: Applications are available by mail.
Exclusive: Visit www.UltimateScholarshipBook.com and enter code JO20123 for updates on this award.

(202) · Jonathan Jasper Wright Award

National Association of Blacks in Criminal Justice
1801 Fayetteville Street, 106 Whiting Criminal Justice Building, P.O. Box 20011-C, Durham, NC 27707
Phone: 919-683-1801
Email: Office@NABCJ.org
https://nabcj.org/
Purpose: To reward regional and national leadership in the field of criminal justice.
Eligibility: Award recipients will be involved in affecting policy change. Nominator should be a member of NABCJ.
Target applicant(s): College students. Graduate school students. Adult students.
Amount: Varies.
Number of awards: 1.
Deadline: March 15.
How to apply: Nomination applications are available online.

Exclusive: Visit www.UltimateScholarshipBook.com and enter code NA20223 for updates on this award.

---

(203) · Joseph P. and Helen T. Cribbins Scholarship

Association of the United States Army
2425 Wilson Boulevard, Arlington, VA 22201
Phone: 703-841-4300
Email: Membersupport@ausa.org
https://www.ausa.org/resources/scholarships
Purpose: To aid U.S. army soldiers who are studying engineering or a related subject.
Eligibility: Applicants must be active duty or honorably discharged enlisted soldiers in the U.S. Army or one of its affiliate entities (Army Reserve, National Guard, etc.). They must be accepted or enrolled at an accredited college or university and majoring in or planning to major in engineering or a related subject. Selection is based on the overall strength of the application.
Target applicant(s): High school students. College students. Adult students.
Amount: $10,000.
Number of awards: Varies.
Deadline: June.
How to apply: Applications are available online. An application form, two recommendation letters, applicant autobiography, an official transcript, a course of study outline, certificates of completion for other training courses (if applicable) and a copy of form DD-214 (for discharged soldiers) are required.
Exclusive: Visit www.UltimateScholarshipBook.com and enter code AS20323 for updates on this award.

---

(204) · Josephine De Karman Fellowship

Josephine De Karman Fellowship Trust
P.O. Box 3389, San Dimas, CA 91773
Phone: 909-592-0607
Email: info@dekarman.org
http://www.dekarman.org
Purpose: To recognize students who demonstrate academic achievement.
Eligibility: Applicants must be undergraduate students entering their senior year or Ph.D. candidates nearing completion of their degree (all requirements except for the dissertation must be completed by January 31). Applicants may not be post-doctoral students. Special consideration is given to doctoral students in the humanities. The award is open to international students living in the U.S.
Target applicant(s): College students. Adult students.
Amount: $14,000-$22,000.
Number of awards: 8.
Deadline: January 31.
How to apply: Applications are available online.
Exclusive: Visit www.UltimateScholarshipBook.com and enter code JO20423 for updates on this award.

---

(205) · Judith Haupt Member's Child Scholarship

Navy Wives Clubs of America (NWCA)
P.O. Box 54022, NSA Mid-South, Millington, TN 38053-6022
Phone: 866-511-6922
Email: scholarships@navywivesclubsofamerica.org
http://www.navywivesclubsofamerica.org
Purpose: To aid college students who are the adult children of members of the Navy Wives Clubs of America (NWCA).

Eligibility: Applicants must be unmarried college students who are the adult children of NWCA members. They cannot be carrying a military ID card and must have been accepted into a college no later than the application due date. Selection is based on academic merit and financial need.
Target applicant(s): High school students. College students. Adult students.
Amount: Varies.
Number of awards: 1.
Deadline: March 31.
How to apply: Applications are available online. An application form and an official transcript are required.
Exclusive: Visit www.UltimateScholarshipBook.com and enter code NA20523 for updates on this award.

---

(206) · Kathern F. Gruber Scholarship Program

Blinded Veterans Association (BVA)
125 N. West Street, 3rd Floor, Alexandria, VA 22314
Phone: 202-371-8880
Email: bva@bva.org
http://www.bva.org
Purpose: To assist the spouses, children and grandchildren of blinded veterans with their higher-learning goals.
Eligibility: Applicants must be the spouses, children or grandchildren of a blind veteran and be accepted or enrolled at an accredited, higher learning institution.
Target applicant(s): High school students. College students. Graduate school students. Adult students.
Amount: $2,000.
Number of awards: 6.
Deadline: April 16.
How to apply: Contact the BVA for application materials.
Exclusive: Visit www.UltimateScholarshipBook.com and enter code BL20623 for updates on this award.

---

(207) · Kevin Higgins College Scholarship

US Rugby Foundation
2131 Pan American Plaza, San Diego, CA 92101
Phone: 619-233-0765
Email: bvizard@usrugbyfoundation.com
https://usrugbyfoundation.org/programs-grants/
Purpose: To support those high school rugby players who plan on continuing to play rugby at the collegiate level.
Eligibility: Applicants must be a U.S. high school senior rugby player, have a 2.5 or better GPA and plan to continue playing rugby at the collegiate level. Selection is based on character recommendations, community service, rugby potential and the personal statement. Financial need will be considered.
Target applicant(s): High school students.
Minimum GPA: 2.5
Amount: $1,000.
Number of awards: Up to 10.
Deadline: August 31.
How to apply: Applications are available online and should include an official transcript, at least one letter of recommendation, a rugby resume, a copy of the previous year's taxes and the personal statement.
Exclusive: Visit www.UltimateScholarshipBook.com and enter code US20723 for updates on this award.

(208) · La Fra Scholarship

Ladies Auxiliary of the Fleet Reserve Association
Gini Larson PNP, National Scholarship Chairman, 2187 Capeheart
Street, Ingleside, TX 78362-6222
Phone: 361-442-5707
Email: lovedduck@aol.com
http://www.la-fra.org
Purpose: To support the female descendants of sea personnel.
Eligibility: Students must have a father or grandfather who was in the
Marine Corps, Coast Guard, Navy, Fleet Reserve, Coast Guard Reserve
or Fleet Marine Corps Reserve.
Target applicant(s): High school students. College students. Graduate
school students. Adult students.
Amount: Varies.
Number of awards: Varies.
Deadline: April 15.
How to apply: Applications are available online.
Exclusive: Visit www.UltimateScholarshipBook.com and enter code
LA20823 for updates on this award.

(209) · LA Tutors Innovation in Education Scholarship

LA Tutors
9454 Wilshire Boulevard, Suite 600, Beverly Hills, CA 90212
Phone: 424-335-0067
Email: contact@latutors123.com
https://www.latutors123.com/scholarship/
Purpose: To reward innovation.
Eligibility: Applicants must be a high school or college student within
the U.S. or Canada. A minimum 3.0 GPA is required. Students must
be a citizen of, permanent resident of or hold a valid student visa in the
U.S. or Canada. Applicants will have designed an innovative project that
makes the difference in the lives of others. The project can include a
website, series of blogs, an app, fundraising event, etc. An essay describing
the goal of the project and providing supporting documentation is
required. The contest is monthly.
Target applicant(s): High school students. College students. Adult
students.
Minimum GPA: 3.0
Amount: $500.
Number of awards: 12.
Deadline: 20th of each month.
How to apply: Application is available online.
Exclusive: Visit www.UltimateScholarshipBook.com and enter code
LA20923 for updates on this award.

(210) · Leadership Essay Contest

United States Naval Institute (USNI)
291 Wood Road, Annapolis, MD 21402
Phone: 410-268-6110
Email: customer@usni.org
https://www.usni.org/essay-contests
Purpose: To promote awareness of sea services.
Eligibility: Applicants must be junior officers, O-4 and below from
the U.S. Navy, Marine Corps or Coast Guard. Students must write an
essay discussing leadership.
Target applicant(s): Adult students.
Amount: $5,000.
Number of awards: 3.
Deadline: September 30.
How to apply: Applications are available online.

Exclusive: Visit www.UltimateScholarshipBook.com and enter code
UN21023 for updates on this award.

(211) · Leifert & Leifert Right to Privacy Scholarship

Law Offices of Leifert & Leifert
2160 West Atlantic Avenue, 2nd Floor, Delray Beach, FL 33445
Phone: 561-988-8000
Email: info@leifertlaw.com
http://www.leifertlaw.com
Purpose: To support students who write essays on the right to privacy.
Eligibility: Applicants must be enrolled in an accredited junior college,
community college, undergraduate or graduate level program in the
United States. A minimum 3.0 GPA or higher is required. Students
who are high school graduates or GED holders about to start college
may also apply. Applicants will submit a 750-word essay on the given
topic on the website.
Target applicant(s): High school students. College students. Graduate
school students. Adult students.
Minimum GPA: 3.0
Amount: $1,000.
Number of awards: 1.
Deadline: August 31.
How to apply: Applications are available online.
Exclusive: Visit www.UltimateScholarshipBook.com and enter code
LA21123 for updates on this award.

(212) · LenovoEDU Scholarship

LenovoEDU
1009 Think Place, Morrisville, NC 27560
Phone: 855-253-6686
https://education.lenovo.com/us/explore/newsroom/b/articles/posts/
us-scholarship
Purpose: To support students' assistance toward their educational
expenses.
Eligibility: Applicants will be required to become a registered member
of the LenovoEDU community to participate. Students must submit
their inspiring and aspirational story of how (if awarded) the scholarship
money will help them achieve their educational goals. Submissions must
be a video, photo or written essay. Applicants must self-promote their
submission on their social media sites.
Target applicant(s): High school students. College students. Graduate
school students. Adult students.
Amount: $1,500.
Number of awards: 1.
Deadline: October 29.
How to apply: Applications are available online.
Exclusive: Visit www.UltimateScholarshipBook.com and enter code
LE21223 for updates on this award.

(213) · Life Lessons Scholarship Program

Life and Health Insurance Foundation for Education
1655 N. Fort Myer Drive, Suite 610, Arlington, VA 22209
Phone: 202-464-5000
Email: info@lifehappens.org
http://www.lifehappens.org
Purpose: To support students who have been affected financially and
emotionally by the death of a parent.
Eligibility: Applicants must submit either a 500-word essay or a three-
minute video describing the impact of losing a parent at a young age.

The grand prize winner of the video contest is selected by an online public vote.

Target applicant(s): High school students. College students.
Amount: Up to $15,000.
Number of awards: 31.
Deadline: March 1.
How to apply: Applications are available online.
Exclusive: Visit www.UltimateScholarshipBook.com and enter code LI21323 for updates on this award.

(214) · Litner + Deganian College Scholarship

Litner + Deganian, P.C.
1776 Briarcliff Road NE, Atlanta, GA 30306
Phone: 770-658-4790
Email: marketing@litnerlaw.com
https://www.litnerlaw.com/scholarship/
Purpose: To encourage students to achieve their educational and professional goals.
Eligibility: Applicants must be U.S. citizens or permanent residents who are currently enrolled or plan to enroll in an accredited United States college or university during the fall semester of the current application year. Students will submit an original video pertaining to the subject outlined on the website.
Target applicant(s): High school students. College students. Graduate school students. Adult students.
Amount: $2,500.
Number of awards: 1.
Deadline: March 31.
How to apply: Applications are available online.
Exclusive: Visit www.UltimateScholarshipBook.com and enter code LI21423 for updates on this award.

(215) · Live Más Scholarship

Taco Bell Foundation
Email: info@livemasscholarship.com
http://www.livemasscholarship.com
Purpose: The Live Más Scholarship is looking for the next generation of innovators, creators and dreamers.
Eligibility: Applicants must be a legal resident of the 50 United States and the District of Columbia, at least 16 years of age and no older than 26 years of age, and on track to apply for or currently enrolled in an accredited post-high school/post-secondary educational programs (including accredited two-and four-year colleges, universities, vocational-technical and trade schools).
Target applicant(s): High school students. College students. Adult students.
Amount: $5,000-$25,000.
Number of awards: 100.
Deadline: January 11.
How to apply: Submit a video (2 minutes or less in length) that tells us the story of your life's passion. It could be a short film, animation or just a simple testimonial. This is not about how well you can make a film—we just want you to show us your passion and explain why you should be considered for a Live Más Scholarship.
Exclusive: Visit www.UltimateScholarshipBook.com and enter code TA21523 for updates on this award.

(216) · Lou Manzione Scholarship

Atlantic Amateur Hockey Association
Attn.: Tom Koester, President, P.O. Box 213, Lafayette Hill, PA 19444
Email: info@atlantic-district.org
https://www.atlantic-district.org/scholarships
Purpose: To aid hockey students who are planning to continue their education beyond high school.
Eligibility: Applicants must be a high school senior in New Jersey, Pennsylvania or Delaware and registered with USA Hockey. Selection is based on the personal essay, scholastic achievement, the coach and teacher recommendations and extracurricular activities.
Target applicant(s): High school students.
Amount: $1,000.
Number of awards: 2.
Deadline: February 1.
How to apply: Applications are available online.
Exclusive: Visit www.UltimateScholarshipBook.com and enter code AT21623 for updates on this award.

(217) · LULAC National Scholastic Achievement Awards

League of United Latin American Citizens
1133 19th Street NW, Suite 1000, Washington, DC 20036
Phone: 202-835-9646
Email: scholarships@lnesc.org
https://www.lnesc.org
Purpose: To aid students of all ethnic backgrounds attending colleges, universities and graduate schools.
Eligibility: Applicants do not need to be Hispanic or Latino to apply. Applicants must have applied to or be enrolled in a college, university or graduate school and be U.S. citizens or legal residents. Students must also have a minimum 3.5 GPA and if entering freshmen a minimum ACT score of 29 or minimum SAT score of 1350. Eligible candidates cannot be related to scholarship committee members, the Council President or contributors to the Council funds. Since applications must be sent from local LULAC Councils, students without LULAC Councils in their states are ineligible.
Target applicant(s): High school students. College students. Graduate school students. Adult students.
Minimum GPA: 3.5
Amount: $2,000.
Number of awards: Varies.
Deadline: March.
How to apply: Applications are available online.
Exclusive: Visit www.UltimateScholarshipBook.com and enter code LE21723 for updates on this award.

(218) · Marian Wood Baird College Scholarship

United States Tennis Association Foundation
70 W. Red Oak Lane, White Plains, NY 10604
Phone: 914-696-7223
Email: foundation@usta.com
http://www.ustafoundation.com/
Purpose: To support youth tennis players who have excelled both on and off the court.
Eligibility: Applicants must be high school seniors who have participated extensively in an organized community tennis program. Students must also excel academically, demonstrate leadership skills and exemplify good sportsmanship both on and off the court.

Target applicant(s): High school students.
Amount: Up to $15,000.
Number of awards: 1.
Scholarship may be renewable.
Deadline: March.
How to apply: Applications are available online.
Exclusive: Visit www.UltimateScholarshipBook.com and enter code UN21823 for updates on this award.

(219) · Marine Corps League Scholarships

Marine Corps League
P.O. Box 3070, Merrifield, VA 22116
Phone: 800-625-1775
http://www.mclnational.org
Purpose: To provide educational opportunities to spouses and descendants of Marine Corps League members.
Eligibility: Applicants must be Marine Corp League or Auxiliary members in good standing, their spouses or their descendants, children of Marines who died in the line of duty or honorably discharged Marines who need rehabilitation training that is not being subsidized by government programs.
Target applicant(s): High school students. College students. Adult students.
Minimum GPA: 3.0
Amount: Varies.
Number of awards: Varies.
Scholarship may be renewable.
Deadline: July 16.
How to apply: Applications are available online.
Exclusive: Visit www.UltimateScholarshipBook.com and enter code MA21923 for updates on this award.

(220) · Marine Corps Scholarship Foundation Scholarship

Marine Corps Scholarship Foundation
909 North Washington Street, Suite 400, Alexandria, VA 22314
Phone: 703-549-0060
Email: Scholarship@mcsf.org
https://www.mcsf.org
Purpose: To provide financial assistance to sons and daughters of U.S. Marines and children of former Marines in their pursuit of higher education.
Eligibility: Applicants must be children or grandchildren of one of the following: an active duty or reserve U. S. Marine; a U.S. Marine who has received an Honorable Discharge, Medical Discharge or was killed while serving in the U.S. Marine Corps; an active duty or reserve U.S. Navy Corpsman who is serving, or has served, with the U.S. Marine Corps; U.S. Navy Chaplain or Religious Programs Specialist who is/was attached to a U.S. Marine Corps unit or who was killed while serving with a U.S. Marine Corps unit or a U.S. Navy Corpsman who has served with the U.S. Marine Corps and has received an Honorable Discharge, Medical Discharge or was killed while serving in the U.S. Navy. Applicants can also be grandchildren of one of the following: A U.S. Marine who served with the 4th Marine Division during World War II and is/was a member of their association, a U.S. Marine who served with the 6th Marine Division during World War II and is/was a member of their association or a U.S. Marine who served in the 531 Gray Ghost Squadron and is/was a member of their association. Applicants must be either high school graduates or undergraduate students. There is a family income limit.

Target applicant(s): High school students. College students. Adult students.
Minimum GPA: 2.0
Amount: Up to $10,000.
Number of awards: Varies.
Scholarship may be renewable.
Deadline: March 1.
How to apply: Applications are available online.
Exclusive: Visit www.UltimateScholarshipBook.com and enter code MA22023 for updates on this award.

(221) · Markley Scholarship

National Association for Campus Activities
13 Harbison Way, Columbia, SC 29212
Phone: 803-732-6222
Email: info@naca.org
https://www.naca.org/FOUNDATION/Pages/Scholarships.aspx
Purpose: To support undergraduate and graduate students who have made exceptional contributions in the field of student activities. The focus is on involvement with NACA Central, along with contributions to other activities-based organizations.
Eligibility: Applicants must attend a college/university in the former NACA South Central Region (AR, LA, NM, OK, TX); must be enrolled as juniors, seniors or graduate students at a four-year institution or as sophomores at a two-year institution and must have a minimum 2.5 GPA.
Target applicant(s): College students. Graduate school students. Adult students.
Minimum GPA: 2.5
Amount: Varies.
Number of awards: Up to 2.
Deadline: November 30.
How to apply: Applications are available online. Only electronic applications and supporting documents submitted through the online scholarship application will be accepted.
Exclusive: Visit www.UltimateScholarshipBook.com and enter code NA22123 for updates on this award.

(222) · Marsh Scholarship Fund

Eastern Surfing Association
11 Long Point Road, Stony Creek, CT 06405
Phone: 386-672-4905
Email: scholastics@surfesa.org
http://www.surfesa.org
Purpose: To assist Eastern Surfing Association (ESA) student surfers.
Eligibility: Applicants must be current ESA members. Transcripts, a recommendation letter, purpose letters and applications are required. The award is based on academics and citizenship, not athletic ability.
Target applicant(s): High school students. College students. Graduate school students. Adult students.
Amount: Varies.
Number of awards: Varies.
Deadline: July 1.
How to apply: Applications are available online and by email.
Exclusive: Visit www.UltimateScholarshipBook.com and enter code EA22223 for updates on this award.

(223) · Marshall Memorial Fellowship

German Marshall Fund of the United States
1744 R Street NW, Washington, DC 20009

Phone: 202-683-2650
Email: info@gmfus.org
https://www.gmfus.org/leadership-programs
Purpose: To provide fellowships for future community leaders to travel in Europe and to explore its societies, institutions and people.
Eligibility: Applicants must be nominated by a recognized leader in their communities or professional fields. They must be between 28 and 40 years of age and demonstrate achievement within their profession, civic involvement and leadership. They must be U.S. citizens or permanent residents or be permanent citizens of one of the 38 countries listed on the scholarship page. European applicants will visit the United States for their fellowship opportunities. Candidates should have little or no previous experience traveling through Europe. Fellows visit five or six cities and meet with policy makers, business professionals and other community leaders.
Target applicant(s): College students. Graduate school students. Adult students.
Amount: Varies.
Number of awards: 75.
Deadline: November 18.
How to apply: Applications are available online.
Exclusive: Visit www.UltimateScholarshipBook.com and enter code GE22323 for updates on this award.

(224) · Marshall Scholar

Marshall Aid Commemoration Commission
Email: info@marshallscholarship.org
http://www.marshallscholarship.org
Purpose: Established in 1953 and financed by the British government, the scholarships are designed to bring academically distinguished Americans to study in the United Kingdom to increase understanding and appreciation of the British society and academic values.
Eligibility: Applicants must be U.S. citizens who expect to earn a degree from an accredited four-year college or university in the U.S. with a minimum 3.7 GPA. Students may apply in one of eight regions in the U.S.
Target applicant(s): College students. Graduate school students. Adult students.
Minimum GPA: 3.7
Amount: Varies.
Number of awards: Up to 40.
Deadline: September 28.
How to apply: Contact your regional center at the address listed on the website.
Exclusive: Visit www.UltimateScholarshipBook.com and enter code MA22423 for updates on this award.

(225) · Mary Church Terrell Award

National Association of Blacks in Criminal Justice
1801 Fayetteville Street, 106 Whiting Criminal Justice Building,
P.O. Box 20011-C, Durham, NC 27707
Phone: 919-683-1801
Email: Office@NABCJ.org
https://nabcj.org/
Purpose: To reward activism for positive change in criminal justice on city and state levels.
Eligibility: The nominator should be a member of NABCJ. This award is given to an individual who has initiated relationships with churches, courts, councils and assemblies.
Target applicant(s): High school students. College students. Adult students.

Amount: Varies.
Number of awards: Varies.
Deadline: March 15.
How to apply: Nomination applications are available online.
Exclusive: Visit www.UltimateScholarshipBook.com and enter code NA22523 for updates on this award.

(226) · Mary Paolozzi Member's Scholarship

Navy Wives Clubs of America (NWCA)
P.O. Box 54022, NSA Mid-South, Millington, TN 38053-6022
Phone: 866-511-6922
Email: scholarships@navywivesclubsofamerica.org
http://www.navywivesclubsofamerica.org
Purpose: To aid students who are members of the Navy Wives Clubs of America (NWCA).
Eligibility: Applicants must have been accepted into a college no later than the application due date. Selection is based on academic merit and financial need.
Target applicant(s): High school students. College students. Graduate school students. Adult students.
Amount: Varies.
Number of awards: 1.
Deadline: March 31.
How to apply: Applications are available online. An application form, official transcript and tax form copies are required.
Exclusive: Visit www.UltimateScholarshipBook.com and enter code NA22623 for updates on this award.

(227) · Medger Evers Award

National Association of Blacks in Criminal Justice
1801 Fayetteville Street, 106 Whiting Criminal Justice Building,
P.O. Box 20011-C, Durham, NC 27707
Phone: 919-683-1801
Email: Office@NABCJ.org
https://nabcj.org/
Purpose: To reward efforts to ensure that all people, including those in institutions, receive equal justice under the law.
Eligibility: This award honors the slain civil rights leader. Nominator should be a member of NABCJ.
Target applicant(s): College students. Graduate school students. Adult students.
Amount: Varies.
Number of awards: 1.
Deadline: March 15.
How to apply: Nomination applications are available online.
Exclusive: Visit www.UltimateScholarshipBook.com and enter code NA22723 for updates on this award.

(228) · Mediacom World Class Scholarship Program

Mediacom
3737 Westown Parkway, Suite A, West Des Moines, IA 50266
Email: scholarship@mediacomcc.com
http://www.mediacomworldclass.com
Purpose: To aid students in Mediacom service areas.
Eligibility: Applicants must be graduating high school seniors. Those who have earned college credits may apply as long as they have not yet graduated high school. Applicants may not be children of Mediacom employees and must live in areas serviced by Mediacom.
Target applicant(s): High school students.
Amount: $1,000.

Number of awards: Varies.
Deadline: February.
How to apply: Applications are available online. An application form, essay, transcript and two reference forms are required.
Exclusive: Visit www.UltimateScholarshipBook.com and enter code ME22823 for updates on this award.

(229) · Memorial Fund Scholarships

U.S. Figure Skating
20 First Street, Colorado Springs, CO 80906
Phone: 719-635-5200
Email: info@usfigureskating.org
https://www.usfigureskating.org/skate/scholarships-and-funding
Purpose: To support students who have a continuing interest in figure skating.
Eligibility: Applicants must be pursuing a college degree, be a current member of U.S. Figure Skating, have competed at the sectional level, be participating in volunteer work in skating if no longer skating and have a 3.0 or higher GPA. Selection is based on financial need, academic success and continuing participation in competitive figure skating or U.S. Figure Skating.
Target applicant(s): High school students. College students. Adult students.
Minimum GPA: 3.0
Amount: Varies.
Number of awards: Varies.
Deadline: August 31.
How to apply: Applications are available online.
Exclusive: Visit www.UltimateScholarshipBook.com and enter code U.22923 for updates on this award.

(230) · Memorial Scholarship Fund

Third Marine Division Association
Patrick J. Conroy, Secretary MSF, 8935 Darrow Road, #227, Twinsburg, OH 44087-0227
Phone: 352-726-2767
Email: scholarship@caltrap.org
http://www.caltrap.com
Purpose: To assist veterans and their families.
Eligibility: Applicants must be the children of Marines (Corpsman or other) who served with the Third Marine Division or in support of the Division at any time and who have been members of the Third Marine Division Association for at least two years. Applicants must be 16-23 and unmarried dependents. Applicants must attend school in the U.S. or Canada. Applicants must have and maintain a minimum 2.5 GPA.
Target applicant(s): High school students. College students.
Minimum GPA: 2.5
Amount: Varies.
Number of awards: Varies.
Scholarship may be renewable.
Deadline: April 16.
How to apply: Applications are available by written request after September 1.
Exclusive: Visit www.UltimateScholarshipBook.com and enter code TH23023 for updates on this award.

(231) · Mensa Foundation Scholarship Program

Mensa Education and Research Foundation
1315 Brookside Drive, Hurst, TX 76053
Phone: 817-607-5577
Email: info@mensafoundation.org
http://www.mensafoundation.org
Purpose: To support students seeking higher education.
Eligibility: Applicants do not need to be members of Mensa. They must be enrolled in a degree program at an accredited U.S. college or university in the academic year after application. They must write an essay explaining career, academic or vocational goals.
Target applicant(s): High school students. College students. Adult students.
Amount: $2,500.
Number of awards: Varies.
Deadline: January 15.
How to apply: Applications are available online in September.
Exclusive: Visit www.UltimateScholarshipBook.com and enter code ME23123 for updates on this award.

(232) · Metro Youth Football Association Scholarship

Metro Youth Football Association
P.O. Box 2171, Cedar Rapids, IA 52406
Phone: 319-393-8696
Email: info@metroyouthfootball.com
http://www.metroyouthfootball.com/scholarship
Purpose: To aid college-bound Metro Youth Tackle Football participants.
Eligibility: Applicants must be graduating high school seniors. They must be current or former Metro Youth Tackle Football (MYTF) participants. They must be current high school football players who have a GPA of 2.5 or higher and have plans to pursue post-secondary education. Selection is based on good citizenship, character and leadership potential.
Target applicant(s): High school students.
Minimum GPA: 2.5
Amount: $2,000.
Number of awards: 2.
Deadline: August 16.
How to apply: Applications are available online. An application form, essay and one recommendation letter are required.
Exclusive: Visit www.UltimateScholarshipBook.com and enter code ME23223 for updates on this award.

(233) · Mike and Gail Donley Spouse Scholarship

Air Force Association
1501 Lee Highway, Arlington, VA 22209
Phone: 800-727-3337
Email: lcross@afa.org
http://www.afa.org
Purpose: To aid U.S. Air Force spouses who wish to pursue undergraduate and graduate degrees.
Eligibility: Applicants must be the spouses of active duty members of the U.S. Air Force, Air National Guard or Air Force Reserve. They must be accepted or enrolled at an accredited college or university and have a GPA of 3.5 or higher. Applicants who are themselves Air Force members or in ROTC are not eligible. Selection is based on the overall strength of the application.
Target applicant(s): High school students. College students. Graduate school students. Adult students.
Minimum GPA: 3.5
Amount: $2,500.
Number of awards: 12.
Deadline: April 30.

How to apply: Applications are available online. An application form, official transcript, personal essay, applicant photo, proof of college acceptance (rising freshmen only) and two letters of recommendation are required.

Exclusive: Visit www.UltimateScholarshipBook.com and enter code AI23323 for updates on this award.

(234) · Military Award Program (MAP)

Imagine America Foundation
12001 Sunrise Valley Drive, Suite 203, Reston, VA 20191
Phone: 571-267-3010
Email: Leed@imagine-america.org
https://www.imagine-america.org/students/scholarships-education/
Purpose: To help those who have served in the military with their education and make the transition from military to civilian life.
Eligibility: Applicants must be enrolling into a participating college and be active duty, reservist, honorably discharged or retired veterans of the U.S. military. They must be likely to enroll in and successfully complete their postsecondary education and may not be a previous recipient of any other Imagine America Foundation scholarships/awards. Applicants must also have financial need.
Target applicant(s): College students. Adult students.
Amount: $1,000.
Number of awards: Varies.
Deadline: Varies.
How to apply: Applications are available online.
Exclusive: Visit www.UltimateScholarshipBook.com and enter code IM23423 for updates on this award.

(235) · Military Family Scholarship

Berry Law Firm
1414 Harney Street, Suite 400, Omaha, NE 68102
Phone: 402-466-8444
Email: info@jsberrylaw.com
https://jsberrylaw.com/2021-military-family-scholarship/
Purpose: To honor service members and their families for their sacrifices made in support of the military.
Eligibility: Applicants must be a U.S. service member, U.S. military veteran or a family member of U.S. military personnel or veterans. Students must be graduating high school seniors or currently enrolled in an undergraduate, graduate or law program at an accredited college or university in the United States and be in good academic standing with a minimum GPA of 3.0 or higher.
Target applicant(s): High school students. College students. Graduate school students. Adult students.
Minimum GPA: 3.0
Amount: $5,000.
Number of awards: 1.
Deadline: December 31.
How to apply: Applications are available online.
Exclusive: Visit www.UltimateScholarshipBook.com and enter code BE23523 for updates on this award.

(236) · Military Family Support Trust Scholarships

Military Family Support Trust
1010 American Eagle Boulevard, Box 400, Sun City Center, FL 33573
Phone: 813-634-4675
Email: president@mfst.us
http://mfst.us/
Purpose: To provide financial assistance to children and grandchildren of military members E-5 and above and others who have served their country.
Eligibility: Applicants must be children or grandchildren of current or former military members, federal employees of GS-7 or higher equivalent officer grade, foreign services officers (FSO-8 and below) and honorably discharged or retired foreign military officers of Allied Nations living in the U.S. The applicant must be a high school senior who has been recommended by his or her principal, have financial need and demonstrate leadership skills. The minimum GPA required is 3.0. The award is renewable for four years.
Target applicant(s): High school students.
Minimum GPA: 3.0
Amount: $2,000-$12,000.
Number of awards: 15.
Scholarship may be renewable.
Deadline: February 1.
How to apply: Applications are available online.
Exclusive: Visit www.UltimateScholarshipBook.com and enter code MI23623 for updates on this award.

(237) · Mometrix College Scholarship

Mometrix Test Preparation
3827 Phelan #179, Beaumont, TX 77707
Phone: 800-673-8175
https://www.mometrix.com/scholarships/
Purpose: To support graduating seniors or students already enrolled in an accredited college or university.
Eligibility: Applicants must submit a 2,000 character (about 400 words) or less essay based on their test preparation practices. First, second and third place prizes are awarded.
Target applicant(s): High school students. College students. Adult students.
Amount: $1,000.
Number of awards: 3.
Deadline: May 14.
How to apply: Applications are available online.
Exclusive: Visit www.UltimateScholarshipBook.com and enter code MO23723 for updates on this award.

(238) · Montgomery GI Bill - Active Duty

North Dakota Department of Veterans Affairs
4201 38th Street South, Suite 104, Fargo, ND 58104-7535
Phone: 701-239-7165
http://www.nd.gov/veterans/benefit-type/education-training
Purpose: To provide educational benefits to veterans.
Eligibility: Applicants must have an Honorable Discharge and high school diploma and meet other service requirements. The bill provides up to 36 months of educational benefits to veterans for college, technical or vocational courses, correspondence courses, apprenticeship/job training or flight training, high-tech training, licensing and certification tests, entrepreneurship training and certain entrance examinations. In most cases the award must be used within 10 years of being discharged.
Target applicant(s): College students. Graduate school students. Adult students.
Amount: Varies.
Number of awards: Varies.
Deadline: Varies.
How to apply: Applications are available online.
Exclusive: Visit www.UltimateScholarshipBook.com and enter code NO23823 for updates on this award.

(239) · Montgomery GI Bill - Selected Reserve

North Dakota Department of Veterans Affairs
4201 38th Street South, Suite 104, Fargo, ND 58104-7535
Phone: 701-239-7165
http://www.nd.gov/veterans/benefit-type/education-training
Purpose: To support members of the United States military Selected Reserve.
Eligibility: Applicants must have a six-year commitment to the Selected Reserve signed after June 30, 1985. The Selected Reserve includes the Army Reserve, Navy Reserve, Air Force Reserve, Marine Corps Reserve and Coast Guard Reserve and the Army National Guard and the Air National Guard. Applicants must have completed basic military training, meet the requirements to receive a high school diploma or equivalency certificate and may use the funds for degree programs, certificate or correspondence courses, cooperative training, independent study programs, apprenticeship/on-the-job training and vocational flight training programs.
Target applicant(s): High school students. College students. Graduate school students. Adult students.
Amount: Varies.
Number of awards: Varies.
Scholarship may be renewable.
Deadline: Varies.
How to apply: Applications are available online.
Exclusive: Visit www.UltimateScholarshipBook.com and enter code NO23923 for updates on this award.

(240) · Montgomery GI Bill Tuition Assistance Top-Up

North Dakota Department of Veterans Affairs
4201 38th Street South, Suite 104, Fargo, ND 58104-7535
Phone: 701-239-7165
http://www.nd.gov/veterans/benefit-type/education-training
Purpose: To support students who are receiving tuition assistance from the military that doesn't cover the full cost of courses.
Eligibility: Applicants must be eligible for MGIB-Active Duty benefits, and they must have served on active duty in the United States military for at least two years.
Target applicant(s): College students. Graduate school students. Adult students.
Amount: Varies.
Number of awards: Varies.
Scholarship may be renewable.
Deadline: Varies.
How to apply: Applications are available online. Contact your education services officer or education counselor for more information.
Exclusive: Visit www.UltimateScholarshipBook.com and enter code NO24023 for updates on this award.

(241) · Most Valuable Student Scholarships

Elks National Foundation Headquarters
2750 North Lakeview Avenue, Chicago, IL 60614
Phone: 773-755-4732
Email: scholarship@elks.org
https://www.elks.org/scholars/
Purpose: To support high school seniors who have demonstrated scholarship, leadership and financial need.
Eligibility: Applicants must be graduating high school seniors who are U.S. citizens and who plan to pursue a four-year degree on a full-time basis at a U.S. college or university. Male and female students compete separately.

Target applicant(s): High school students.
Amount: $1,000-$12,500.
Number of awards: 500.
Scholarship may be renewable.
Deadline: November 15.
How to apply: Contact the scholarship chairman of your local Lodge or the Elks association of your state.
Exclusive: Visit www.UltimateScholarshipBook.com and enter code EL24123 for updates on this award.

(242) · NABF Scholarship Program

National Amateur Baseball Federation
Awards Committee Chairman, P.O. Box 705, Bowie, MD 20718
Phone: 301-464-5460
Email: nabf1914@aol.com
http://www.nabf.com/scholarships
Purpose: To support students who have been involved with the federation.
Eligibility: Applicants must be enrolled in an accredited college or university, must have participated in a federation event and must be sponsored by a member association. Selection is based on grades, financial need and previous awards.
Target applicant(s): High school students. College students. Adult students.
Amount: Varies.
Number of awards: Varies.
Deadline: Varies.
How to apply: Applications are available online.
Exclusive: Visit www.UltimateScholarshipBook.com and enter code NA24223 for updates on this award.

(243) · NACOP Scholarship

National Association of Chiefs of Police
NACOP Scholarship Program, 6350 Horizon Drive, Titusville, FL 32780
Phone: 321-264-0911
Email: kimc@aphf.org
http://www.nacoponline.org
Purpose: To recognize law enforcement individuals.
Eligibility: Applicants must be disabled officers wishing to retrain through education or the collegebound children of a disabled officer. Students must maintain a 2.0 GPA and be enrolled in a minimum of six credit hours.
Target applicant(s): High school students. College students. Adult students.
Minimum GPA: 2.0
Amount: $500.
Number of awards: Varies.
Deadline: Rolling.
How to apply: Applications are available by written request.
Exclusive: Visit www.UltimateScholarshipBook.com and enter code NA24323 for updates on this award.

(244) · NATA Scholarship

National Athletic Trainers' Association
National Athletic Trainers' Association Research and Education Foundation Inc., 2952 Stemmons Freeway, Dallas, TX 75247
Phone: 214-637-6282
Email: barbaran@nata.org
http://www.nata.org

Purpose: To encourage study among athletic trainers.
Eligibility: Applicants must be at least a junior in college and scholarships are available for undergraduate, master's and doctoral levels. Students must have a minimum 3.2 GPA and be sponsored by a certified athletic trainer and be a member of the NATA. There is an earlier deadline to start the application online.
Target applicant(s): College students. Graduate school students. Adult students.
Minimum GPA: 3.2
Amount: $2,300.
Number of awards: 50-75.
Deadline: January.
How to apply: Applications are available online.
Exclusive: Visit www.UltimateScholarshipBook.com and enter code NA24423 for updates on this award.

(245) · National College Match Program
QuestBridge
120 Hawthorne Avenue, Suite 103, Palo Alto, CA 94301
Phone: 888-275-2054
Email: questions@questbridge.org
http://www.questbridge.org
Purpose: To connect outstanding low-income high school seniors with admission and full four-year scholarships to some of the nation's most selective colleges.
Eligibility: Applicants must have demonstrated academic excellence in the face of economic obstacles. Students of all races and ethnicities are encouraged to apply. Many past award recipients have been among the first generation in their families to attend college.
Target applicant(s): High school students.
Amount: Full tuition plus room and board.
Number of awards: Varies.
Scholarship may be renewable.
Deadline: September 28.
How to apply: Applications are available on the QuestBridge website in August of each year. An application form, two teacher recommendations, one counselor recommendation (Secondary School Report), a transcript and SAT and/or ACT score reports are required.
Exclusive: Visit www.UltimateScholarshipBook.com and enter code QU24523 for updates on this award.

(246) · National Intercollegiate Rodeo Foundation Scholarship
National Intercollegiate Rodeo Association
2033 Walla Walla Avenue, Walla Walla, WA 99362
Phone: 509-529-4402
Email: rodeo@collegerodeo.com
http://www.collegerodeo.com/
Purpose: To support student members of NIRA.
Eligibility: Applicants must be current college students, have at least a 3.0 GPA and be state financial assistance qualified or show evidence of financial need. Selection is based on academic achievement, financial need and the essay.
Target applicant(s): College students. Adult students.
Minimum GPA: 3.0
Amount: $1,500.
Number of awards: 1.
Deadline: May 20.

How to apply: Applications are available online and must be submitted with an official transcript, financial verification and at least one but no more than three letters of recommendation and an essay.
Exclusive: Visit www.UltimateScholarshipBook.com and enter code NA24623 for updates on this award.

(247) · National Marbles Tournament Scholarship
National Marbles Tournament
Matt Corley, 10908 Bornedale Drive, Hyattsville, MD 20783
Phone: 301-801-0795
Email: matt.corley@nationalmarblestournament.org
https://www.nationalmarblestournament.org/
Purpose: To assist "mibsters," or marble shooters.
Eligibility: Applicants must win first place in a local marble tournament and then compete in the National Marbles Tournament held each summer in New Jersey. Students must be between 7 and 14 years old.
Target applicant(s): Junior high students or younger. High school students.
Amount: Varies.
Number of awards: Varies.
Deadline: Varies.
How to apply: Information on the tournament is available online.
Exclusive: Visit www.UltimateScholarshipBook.com and enter code NA24723 for updates on this award.

(248) · National Merit Scholarship Program and National Achievement Scholarship Program
National Merit Scholarship Corporation
1560 Sherman Avenue, Suite 200, Evanston, IL 60201-4897
Phone: 847-866-5100
http://www.nationalmerit.org
Purpose: To provide scholarships through a merit-based academic competition.
Eligibility: Applicants must be enrolled full-time in high school, progressing normally toward completion and planning to enter college no later than the fall following completion of high school, be U.S. citizens or permanent legal residents in the process of becoming U.S. citizens and take the PSAT/NMSQT no later than the 11th grade. Participation in the program is based on performance on the exam.
Target applicant(s): High school students.
Amount: $2,500.
Number of awards: Varies.
Scholarship may be renewable.
Deadline: October PSAT test date.
How to apply: Application is made by taking the PSAT/NMSQT test.
Exclusive: Visit www.UltimateScholarshipBook.com and enter code NA24823 for updates on this award.

(249) · National Oratorical Contest
American Legion
Attn.: Americanism and Children and Youth Division, P.O. Box 1055, Indianapolis, IN 46206
Phone: 317-630-1249
Email: acy@legion.org
http://www.legion.org
Purpose: To reward students for their knowledge of government and oral presentation skills.
Eligibility: Applicants must be high school students under the age of 20 who are U.S. citizens or legal residents. Students first give an oration within their state and winners compete at the national level. The oration

must be related to the Constitution of the United States focusing on the duties and obligations citizens have to the government. It must be in English and be between eight and ten minutes. There is also an assigned topic which is posted on the website, and it should be between three and five minutes.
Target applicant(s): High school students.
Amount: $1,500-$18,000.
Number of awards: Varies.
Deadline: Local American Legion department deadline.
How to apply: Applications are available from your local American Legion post or state headquarters. Deadlines for local competitions are set by the local Posts.
Exclusive: Visit www.UltimateScholarshipBook.com and enter code AM24923 for updates on this award.

(250) · National Scholarship Program
National Scholastic Surfing Association
P.O. Box 495, Huntington Beach, CA 92648
Phone: 714-906-7423
Email: jaragon@nssa.org
http://www.nssa.org
Purpose: To assist NSSA members in their pursuit of post-high school education.
Eligibility: Applicants must be competitive student NSSA members and have a minimum 3.0 GPA in the current school year. Scholastic achievement, leadership, service, career goals and recommendations are considered.
Target applicant(s): High school students. College students. Adult students.
Minimum GPA: 3.0
Amount: Varies.
Number of awards: Varies.
Deadline: Varies.
How to apply: Applications are available with organization membership.
Exclusive: Visit www.UltimateScholarshipBook.com and enter code NA25023 for updates on this award.

(251) · National Sportsmanship Award
Interscholastic Equestrian Association
467 Main Street, Melrose, MA 02176
Phone: 877-743-3432
Email: info@rideiea.org
https://www.rideiea.org/opportunities/for-riders/
Purpose: To help riders pursue a college education.
Eligibility: Students must earn a Sportsmanship Award at a local, regional or zone IEA competition during the school year and maintain a 3.0 GPA. Selection is based on academic achievement, extracurricular involvement, equestrian participation and characteristics that portray good sportsmanship and a role model.
Target applicant(s): Junior high students or younger. High school students.
Minimum GPA: 3.0
Amount: $500-$1,000.
Number of awards: 8.
Deadline: May 3.
How to apply: Riders who have earned a Sportsmanship Award at a lower level will be given an application for the national award. The application includes a 250-word essay, personal resume, copy of official transcript and three letters of recommendation.
Exclusive: Visit www.UltimateScholarshipBook.com and enter code IN25123 for updates on this award.

(252) · National Table Tennis Scholarship
National College Table Tennis Association
154 Mill Run Lane, Saint Peters, MO 63376-7106
Phone: 800-581-6770
Email: info@nctta.org
http://www.nctta.org/
Purpose: To support table tennis athletes by providing financial support for their higher education expenses.
Eligibility: Applicants must be attending or plan on attending an active NCTTA school and plan on being active on the collegiate team. Students must be full time and have at least a 2.0 GPA. Selection is based on table tennis skill, academic achievement, financial need and a personal essay. The essay should explain your involvement and contributions to the sport of table tennis.
Target applicant(s): High school students. College students. Adult students.
Minimum GPA: 2.0
Amount: $500.
Number of awards: Varies.
Deadline: May 15.
How to apply: Applications are available online and must include an official transcript.
Exclusive: Visit www.UltimateScholarshipBook.com and enter code NA25223 for updates on this award.

(253) · National Veterans Stipend
Institute of Scrap Recycling Industries
1250 H Street, NW, Suite 400, Washington, DC 20006
Phone: 202-662-8500
Email: ngrant@isri.org
http://www.isri.org/about-isri/recycling-research-foundation
Purpose: To support veterans who are seeking higher education.
Eligibility: Applicants must be U.S. citizens, a veteran of the military and pursuing an undergraduate degree. The foundation understands that not all expenses may be covered through existing government and scholarship aid, and thus will pay a stipend of up to $8,000 ($2,000 per year, renewable for up to four years). A minimum 2.5 GPA is required.
Target applicant(s): High school students. College students. Adult students.
Minimum GPA: 2,5
Amount: $2,000.
Number of awards: 1.
Scholarship may be renewable.
Deadline: June 1.
How to apply: Applications are available online
Exclusive: Visit www.UltimateScholarshipBook.com and enter code IN25323 for updates on this award.

(254) · Naval Enlisted Reserve Association Scholarships
Naval Enlisted Reserve Association
6703 Farragut Avenue, Falls Church, VA 22042-2189
Phone: 800-776-9020
Email: members@nera.org
http://www.nera.org
Purpose: To recognize the service and sacrifices made by Navy, Marine and Coast Guard members, retirees and their families.
Eligibility: Applicants must be members of the Naval Enlisted Reserve Association in good standing or their spouses, children or grandchildren. Children and grandchildren of members must be single and under

23 years of age on the application deadline. Applicants must be graduating high school seniors or students who are already pursuing an undergraduate degree.
Target applicant(s): High school students. College students. Adult students.
Amount: $2,500-$3,000.
Number of awards: 6.
Deadline: June 18.
How to apply: Applications are available online.
Exclusive: Visit www.UltimateScholarshipBook.com and enter code NA25423 for updates on this award.

(255) · Naval Helicopter Association Scholarship

Naval Helicopter Association
P.O. Box 180578, Coronado, CA 92178-0578
Phone: 619-435-7139
Email: nhascholars@hotmail.com
http://www.nhascholarshipfund.org
Purpose: To assist those who wish to pursue educational goals.
Eligibility: Applicants must be members of or dependents of members of the association or have an affiliation with naval aviation. Students may pursue undergraduate degrees in any field.
Target applicant(s): High school students. College students. Graduate school students. Adult students.
Amount: $2,000-$3,000.
Number of awards: Varies.
Deadline: January 31.
How to apply: Applications are available by mail.
Exclusive: Visit www.UltimateScholarshipBook.com and enter code NA25523 for updates on this award.

(256) · Naval Intelligence Essay Contest

United States Naval Institute (USNI)
291 Wood Road, Annapolis, MD 21402
Phone: 410-268-6110
Email: customer@usni.org
https://www.usni.org/essay-contests
Purpose: To promote sea services.
Eligibility: Applicants must be active duty military, reservists, veterans, government civilian personnel or civilians. Students must write an essay discussing the history of Naval Intelligence and how lessons from the past can be applied to today.
Target applicant(s): College students. Adult students.
Amount: $1,500-$5,000.
Number of awards: 3.
Deadline: July 31.
How to apply: Applications are available online.
Exclusive: Visit www.UltimateScholarshipBook.com and enter code UN25623 for updates on this award.

(257) · Navin Narayan College Scholarship

American Red Cross Youth
2025 E Street NW, Washington, DC 20006
Phone: 202-303-4498
Email: syyin.nyc@gmail.com
http://www.redcrossyouth.org
Purpose: The scholarship is named after Navin Narayan, a former youth volunteer with the Red Cross who died from cancer at the age of 23. In his honor, the Red Cross awards this scholarship to youth volunteers who

have made significant humanitarian contributions to the organization and who have also achieved academic excellence in high school.
Eligibility: Applicants must plan to attend a four-year college or university and have volunteered a minimum of two years with the Red Cross.
Target applicant(s): High school students.
Amount: $1,000.
Number of awards: 1.
Deadline: April 2.
How to apply: Application forms are available online.
Exclusive: Visit www.UltimateScholarshipBook.com and enter code AM25723 for updates on this award.

(258) · Navy College Fund

U.S. Navy Personnel
5720 Integrity Drive, Millington, TN 38055
Phone: 866-827-5672
Email: bupers_webmaster@navy.mil
https://www.navy.com/
Purpose: To encourage entry into the Navy for recruits who have skills and specialties for which there is a critical shortage.
Eligibility: Applicants must be Navy recruits who are qualified for training in selected Navy ratings as non-prior service enlistees and agree to serve on active duty for at least three years. They must have graduated from high school, be 17 to 35 years old, agree to a $1,200 pay reduction and receive an "Honorable" Character of Service.
Target applicant(s): High school students. College students. Adult students.
Amount: Varies.
Number of awards: Varies.
Scholarship may be renewable.
Deadline: Varies.
How to apply: Applications are available from Navy recruiters.
Exclusive: Visit www.UltimateScholarshipBook.com and enter code U.25823 for updates on this award.

(259) · Navy Supply Corps Foundation Scholarship

Navy Supply Corps Foundation Inc.
2061 Experiment Station Road, Suite 301, PMB 423, Watkinsville, GA 30677
Phone: 706-354-4111
Email: foundation@usnscf.com
http://www.usnscf.com
Purpose: To provide financial aid for undergraduate studies to spouses and children of Navy Supply Corps Officers and supply enlisted rating.
Eligibility: Applicants must be a spouse, child or grandchild of a living or deceased regular, retired, reserve or prior service Navy Supply Corps officer or a spouse or child of an Active or Retired (Navy) Enlisted with supply enlisted rating (e.g., AK, SK, MS/CS, SH, DK, LI, PC, LS). Awards are based on character, leadership, academic performance, hardship and financial need.
Target applicant(s): Junior high students or younger. High school students. College students. Adult students.
Amount: Varies.
Number of awards: Varies.
Deadline: March.
How to apply: Applications are available online.
Exclusive: Visit www.UltimateScholarshipBook.com and enter code NA25923 for updates on this award.

(260) · Navy-Marine Corps ROTC College Program

U.S. Navy Naval Reserve Officers Training Corps (NROTC)
Naval Service Training Command Officer Development, NAS
Pensacola, 250 Dallas Street, Pensacola, FL 32508-5220
Phone: 800-628-7682
Email: pnsc_nrotc_cgo@navy.mil
https://www.netc.navy.mil/NSTC/NROTC/
Purpose: To provide education opportunities for NROTC students.
Eligibility: Applicants must be accepted to or attending a college with an
NROTC program. They must complete naval science and other specified
university courses and attend a summer training session. Scholarships
are available for two or four years, depending on time of application.
Target applicant(s): College students. Adult students.
Amount: Up to full tuition plus stipend and allowance.
Number of awards: Varies.
Scholarship may be renewable.
Deadline: End of January.
How to apply: Applications are available online.
Exclusive: Visit www.UltimateScholarshipBook.com and enter code
U.26023 for updates on this award.

(261) · Navy-Marine Corps ROTC Four-Year Scholarships

U.S. Navy Naval Reserve Officers Training Corps (NROTC)
Naval Service Training Command Officer Development, NAS
Pensacola, 250 Dallas Street, Pensacola, FL 32508-5220
Phone: 800-628-7682
Email: pnsc_nrotc_cgo@navy.mil
https://www.netc.navy.mil/NSTC/NROTC/
Purpose: To provide education opportunities for ROTC members.
Eligibility: Applicants must plan to attend an eligible college or
university. They must commit to eight years of military service, four
of which must be on active duty. The scholarship pays full tuition and
fees plus a stipend for textbooks.
Target applicant(s): High school students.
Amount: Tuition plus stipend.
Number of awards: Varies.
Scholarship may be renewable.
Deadline: May 31.
How to apply: Applications are available online.
Exclusive: Visit www.UltimateScholarshipBook.com and enter code
U.26123 for updates on this award.

(262) · Navy-Marine Corps ROTC Two-Year Scholarships

U.S. Navy Naval Reserve Officers Training Corps (NROTC)
Naval Service Training Command Officer Development, NAS
Pensacola, 250 Dallas Street, Pensacola, FL 32508-5220
Phone: 800-628-7682
Email: pnsc_nrotc_cgo@navy.mil
https://www.netc.navy.mil/NSTC/NROTC/
Purpose: To provide education opportunities for NROTC students.
Eligibility: Applicants must be attending a college with an NROTC
program as a freshman or sophomore. They must complete naval science
and other specified university courses and attend a summer training
session. They must also attend a Naval Science Institute program during
the summer between their sophomore and junior year.
Target applicant(s): College students. Adult students.
Amount: Varies.
Number of awards: Varies.

Scholarship may be renewable.
Deadline: May 31.
How to apply: Applications are available online.
Exclusive: Visit www.UltimateScholarshipBook.com and enter code
U.26223 for updates on this award.

(263) · Navy/Marine Corps/Coast Guard (NMCCG) Enlisted Dependent Spouse Scholarship

Navy Wives Clubs of America (NWCA)
P.O. Box 54022, NSA Mid-South, Millington, TN 38053-6022
Phone: 866-511-6922
Email: scholarships@navywivesclubsofamerica.org
http://www.navywivesclubsofamerica.org
Purpose: To provide financial assistance to spouses of certain military
members.
Eligibility: Applicants must be spouses of enlisted Navy, Marine Corps
or Coast Guard personnel. They must be accepted to an institution of
higher learning by May 30 of the year of application.
Target applicant(s): High school students. College students. Graduate
school students. Adult students.
Amount: Varies.
Number of awards: 2.
Deadline: March 31.
How to apply: Applications are available online. Financial information
and a transcript are required.
Exclusive: Visit www.UltimateScholarshipBook.com and enter code
NA26323 for updates on this award.

(264) · NCAA Division II Degree Completion Award Program

National Collegiate Athletic Association
700 W. Washington Street, P.O. Box 6222, Indianapolis, IN 46206
Phone: 317-917-6222
Email: lthomas@ncaa.org
http://www.ncaa.org/about/resources/ncaa-scholarships-and-grants
Purpose: To assist student-athletes who are no longer eligible for
athletics-based aid.
Eligibility: Applicants must have exhausted athletics eligibility at an
NCAA Division II school within the past calendar year. They must be
within their first 10 semesters or 15 quarters of full-time attendance and
must have received athletics-related aid from the institution. Applicants
must be within 32 semester or 48 quarter hours of earning their first
undergraduate degree and have a GPA of 2.5 or higher.
Target applicant(s): High school students. College students. Adult
students.
Minimum GPA: 2.5
Amount: Varies.
Number of awards: Varies.
Deadline: February 15.
How to apply: Applications are available online.
Exclusive: Visit www.UltimateScholarshipBook.com and enter code
NA26423 for updates on this award.

(265) · NCAA Postgraduate Scholarship

National Collegiate Athletic Association
700 W. Washington Street, P.O. Box 6222, Indianapolis, IN 46206
Phone: 317-917-6222
Email: lthomas@ncaa.org
http://www.ncaa.org/about/resources/ncaa-scholarships-and-grants

Purpose: To reward student athletes who excel academically and athletically and are at least in their final year of intercollegiate athletics competition.

Eligibility: Student athletes must show achievement in their last year of varsity-level intercollegiate athletics at an NCAA school. Applicants must be nominated by the faculty athletic representative or athletic director and be enrolling as a full- or part-time graduate student. Students must also have a minimum 3.2 GPA.

Target applicant(s): College students. Adult students.

Minimum GPA: 3.2

Amount: $10,000.

Number of awards: Up to 126.

Deadline: January 14 (fall), April 8 (winter), June 3 (spring).

How to apply: Applications are available online.

Exclusive: Visit www.UltimateScholarshipBook.com and enter code NA26523 for updates on this award.

(266) · Newman Civic Fellow Awards

Campus Compact
89 South Street, Boston, MA 02111
Phone: 617-357-1881
Email: campus@compact.org
http://www.compact.org

Purpose: To provide scholarships and opportunities for civic mentoring to students with financial need.

Eligibility: Emphasis is on students who have demonstrated leadership abilities and significant interest in civic responsibility. Students must attend one of the 1,000 Campus Compact member institutions and be nominated by the Campus Compact member president. Applicants must be sophomores or juniors at four-year colleges or must attend a two-year college.

Target applicant(s): College students. Graduate school students. Adult students.

Amount: Varies.

Number of awards: Varies.

Deadline: February 1.

How to apply: Nominations must be made by the Campus Compact member president.

Exclusive: Visit www.UltimateScholarshipBook.com and enter code CA26623 for updates on this award.

(267) · Next Gen Scholars Award

Navy Exchange
3280 Virginia Beach Boulevard, Virginia Beach, VA 23452-5724
Phone: 800-628-3924
https://www.mynavyexchange.com/

Purpose: To assist children of active-duty Navy members in paying for their college educations.

Eligibility: Applicants must be full-time students in first through 12th grade who are dependents of active-duty military members, reservists or retirees and have a B or higher grade point average.

Target applicant(s): Junior high students or younger. High school students.

Minimum GPA: 3.0

Amount: $500-$2,500.

Number of awards: 4.

Deadline: Quarterly.

How to apply: Applications are available from the Navy Exchange.

Exclusive: Visit www.UltimateScholarshipBook.com and enter code NA26723 for updates on this award.

(268) · Nicholas Virgilio Haiku and Senryu Contest

Haiku Society of America
NVHA Haiku Contest, c/o George Vallianos, 16 Sandringham Terrace, Cherry Hill, NJ 08003
http://www.hsa-haiku.org/hsa-contests.htm

Purpose: To reward students for excellent haiku poetry.

Eligibility: Applicants must be in grades 7 through 12. Students must submit up to three original, previously unpublished haiku. Selection is based on the overall strength of the submission.

Target applicant(s): Junior high students or younger. High school students.

Amount: $50.

Number of awards: 6.

Deadline: March 15.

How to apply: Applications are available online.

Exclusive: Visit www.UltimateScholarshipBook.com and enter code HA26823 for updates on this award.

(269) · Non Commissioned Officers Association Scholarships

Non Commissioned Officers Association
9330 Corporate Drive, Suite 708, Selma, TX 78154
Phone: 800-662-2620
Email: tkish@ncoausa.org
http://www.ncoausa.org

Purpose: The scholarships are given to help the children and spouses of members of the Non-Commissioned Officers Association.

Eligibility: Students must be children or spouses of members of the Non-Commissioned Officers Association. Children must be under 25 to receive the scholarship.

Target applicant(s): High school students. College students. Adult students.

Amount: $900.

Number of awards: Varies.

Scholarship may be renewable.

Deadline: March 31.

How to apply: Applications are available online.

Exclusive: Visit www.UltimateScholarshipBook.com and enter code NO26923 for updates on this award.

(270) · NROTC Nurse Corps Scholarship

U.S. Navy Naval Reserve Officers Training Corps (NROTC)
Naval Service Training Command Officer Development, NAS Pensacola, 250 Dallas Street, Pensacola, FL 32508-5220
Phone: 800-628-7682
Email: pnsc_nrotc_cgo@navy.mil
https://www.netc.navy.mil/NSTC/NROTC/

Purpose: To aid students who are planning to pursue nursing degrees at an NROTC college or university.

Eligibility: Applicants must be in the second semester of their junior year of high school. They must plan to attend an NROTC college or university that offers the bachelor's degree in nursing. They must be in the top 10 percent of their class or have a combined critical reading and math SAT score of 1080 or higher or have a combined English and math ACT score of 43 or higher. Selection is based on the overall strength of the application.

Target applicant(s): High school students.

Amount: Varies.

Number of awards: Varies.

Scholarship may be renewable.

Deadline: January 31.
How to apply: Applications are available online. An application form, official transcript, standardized test scores and three references are required.
Exclusive: Visit www.UltimateScholarshipBook.com and enter code U.27023 for updates on this award.

(271) · NROTC Scholarship Program

Naval Service Training Command Officer Development
NAS Pensacola, 250 Dallas Street, Pensacola, FL 32508-5220
Phone: 800-NAV-ROTC
Email: pnsc_nrotc_cgo@navy.mil
http://www.nrotc.navy.mil
Purpose: To prepare young men and women for leadership roles in the Navy and Marine Corps.
Eligibility: Applicants must be U.S. citizens who are at least 17 years old as of September 1 of their first year of college, no older than 23 on June 30 of that first year and must be younger than 27 at the time of anticipated graduation. Students must attend an NROTC college and have no moral or personal convictions against military service. Those interested in the Navy program, including Nurse-option, must have an SAT critical reading score of 530 and a math score of 520 or an ACT score of 22 in English and 22 in math. For the Marine Corps option, students must have an SAT composite score of 1000 or an ACT composite score of 22. Applicants must also meet all Navy or Marine Corps physical standards.
Target applicant(s): High school students. College students.
Amount: Full tuition and fees, books, uniforms and monthly stipend.
Number of awards: Varies.
Scholarship may be renewable.
Deadline: December 31.
How to apply: Applications are available online. Contact information for regional offices is available online.
Exclusive: Visit www.UltimateScholarshipBook.com and enter code NA27123 for updates on this award.

(272) · NSCA Scholarship

National Sporting Clays Association
5931 Roft Road, San Antonio, TX 78253
Phone: 800-877-5338
http://nssa-nsca.org
Purpose: To aid high school senior sporting clay participants to reach their career goals by helping to fund their college expenses.
Eligibility: Applicants must be a high school senior, have at least a 2.5 GPA, be an NSCA participant and plan to attend a four-year degree program in college. Selection is based on scholarship, citizenship and NSCA participation.
Target applicant(s): High school students.
Minimum GPA: 2.5
Amount: $5,000.
Number of awards: 1.
Scholarship may be renewable.
Deadline: March 15.
How to apply: Applications are available online and must include an essay, one letter of recommendation, a transcript and a copy of shooting history and accomplishments.
Exclusive: Visit www.UltimateScholarshipBook.com and enter code NA27223 for updates on this award.

(273) · NSCC Scholarship Funds

Naval Sea Cadet Corps
2300 Wilson Boulevard, Suite 200, Arlington, VA 22201-3308
Phone: 800-356-5760
Email: scholarships@navyleague.org
http://www.seacadets.org
Purpose: To provide financial assistance for Sea Cadets.
Eligibility: Applicants must have been Sea Cadets for at least two years and be members at the time of application. They must have attained the rate of NSCC E-3 or higher and be recommended by their commanding officers, NSCC Committee Chairmen and principals or counselors. They must have a B+ or higher GPA and present evidence of acceptance to an accredited institution of higher learning. SAT or ACT scores and class rank are considered.
Target applicant(s): High school students.
Minimum GPA: 3.3
Amount: $1,000-$5,000.
Number of awards: 15.
Deadline: May 1.
How to apply: Applications are available online.
Exclusive: Visit www.UltimateScholarshipBook.com and enter code NA27323 for updates on this award.

(274) · Odenza Marketing Group Scholarship

Odenza Vacations
4664 Lougheed Highway, Suite 230, Burnaby, BC V5C5T5
Phone: 877-297-2661
http://www.odenzascholarships.com
Purpose: To aid current and future college students who are between the ages of 16 and 25.
Eligibility: Applicants must be U.S. or Canadian citizens who have at least one full year of college study remaining. They must have a GPA of 2.5 or higher. Selection is based on the overall strength of the essays submitted.
Target applicant(s): High school students. College students. Graduate school students.
Minimum GPA: 2.5
Amount: $500.
Number of awards: Varies.
Deadline: October 30.
How to apply: Applications are available online. An application form and two essays are required.
Exclusive: Visit www.UltimateScholarshipBook.com and enter code OD27423 for updates on this award.

(275) · ODS Youth Interscholastic Merit Scholarship

Oregon Dressage Society
P.O. Box 959, Hillsboro, OR 97123-0959
Phone: 503-681-2337
Email: J-G.McCabe@Juno.com
http://www.oregondressage.com
Purpose: To aid well-rounded Oregon Dressage Society high school youth members as they begin attending the college of their choice.
Eligibility: Applicants must be current ODS High School Dressage team members, have been members for at least two years and have been accepted to a college or university. Selection is based on experience as a leader and role model, community service, academic achievements, a personal essay and the letters of reference.
Target applicant(s): High school students.
Amount: Varies.

Number of awards: Varies.
Deadline: April.
How to apply: Application is available online. Application requirements include an application form, a personal essay, a high school transcript and at least two letters of reference.
Exclusive: Visit www.UltimateScholarshipBook.com and enter code OR27523 for updates on this award.

(276) · Oleg Fastovsky Outstanding Citizenship Scholarship

Maryland Criminal Defense Group
5072 Dorsey Hall Drive, Suite 202b, Ellicott City, MD 21042
Phone: 410-424-7784
Email: info@mdcriminalattorney.net
https://mdcriminalattorney.net/outstanding-citizen-scholarship/
Purpose: To help students pursue higher education.
Eligibility: Applicants must be enrolling in an accredited post-secondary program, including community college, undergraduate and graduate programs. Students must have a minimum GPA of 3.0 and submit an essay pertaining to the given prompt.
Target applicant(s): High school students. College students. Adult students.
Minimum GPA: 3.0
Amount: $1,000.
Number of awards: 1.
Deadline: September 30.
How to apply: Applications are available online.
Exclusive: Visit www.UltimateScholarshipBook.com and enter code MA27623 for updates on this award.

(277) · One Earth Award

Scholastic Art & Writing Awards
557 Broadway, New York, NY 10012
Email: info@artandwriting.org
http://www.artandwriting.org/scholarships/
Purpose: To support students whose art or writing addresses human-caused climate change.
Eligibility: Applicants must be in grades 7-12 (ages 13 and up) and enter art or writing works address the pressing issue of human-caused climate change. Students may enter work in any of the 28 listed art and writing categories and must include a personal statement of 50 words or more on their work.
Target applicant(s): Junior high students or younger. High school students.
Amount: $1,000.
Number of awards: 4.
Deadline: December 1.
How to apply: Applications are available online.
Exclusive: Visit www.UltimateScholarshipBook.com and enter code SC27723 for updates on this award.

(278) · Paul and Daisy Soros Fellowships for New Americans

Paul and Daisy Soros
224 W. 57th Street, New York, NY 10019
Phone: 212-547-6926
Email: pdsoros_fellows@sorosny.org
http://www.pdsoros.org
Purpose: Named after Hungarian immigrants, the Paul and Daisy Soros Fellowships are designed to assist the graduate studies of immigrant children.
Eligibility: Applicants must be immigrants who are resident aliens, have been naturalized or are the children of two parents who have been naturalized. The potential winner of a fellowship must already have a bachelor's degree or be a college senior and must not be over the age of 30 by the application deadline.
Target applicant(s): College students. Graduate school students. Adult students.
Amount: Up to $90,000 over 2 years.
Number of awards: 30.
Scholarship may be renewable.
Deadline: October 28.
How to apply: Applications are available online and should be submitted online.
Exclusive: Visit www.UltimateScholarshipBook.com and enter code PA27823 for updates on this award.

(279) · Pauline Langkamp Memorial Scholarship

Navy Wives Clubs of America (NWCA)
P.O. Box 54022, NSA Mid-South, Millington, TN 38053-6022
Phone: 866-511-6922
Email: scholarships@navywivesclubsofamerica.org
http://www.navywivesclubsofamerica.org
Purpose: To aid college students who are the adult children of members of the Navy Wives Clubs of America (NWCA).
Eligibility: Applicants must be the child of an NWCA member. They must not be carrying a military ID card and must be enrolled or planning to enroll at an accredited postsecondary institution. High school seniors must have been accepted into a college or university no later than the application due date. Selection is based on academic merit and financial need.
Target applicant(s): High school students. College students. Adult students.
Amount: Varies.
Number of awards: 1.
Deadline: March 31.
How to apply: Applications are available online. An application form and an official transcript are required.
Exclusive: Visit www.UltimateScholarshipBook.com and enter code NA27923 for updates on this award.

(280) · Pedro Zamora Young Leaders Scholarship

National AIDS Memorial Grove
870 Market Street, Suite 965, San Francisco, CA 94102
Phone: 415-765-0446
Email: mkennedy@aidsmemorial.org
https://www.aidsmemorial.org/pedro-zamora-scholarship
Purpose: To support students with a commitment to ending HIV/AIDS.
Eligibility: Applicants must complete the application with a personal statement and a written essay describing their service or leadership in the fight against HIV/AIDS. Students must provide a letter of recommendation and transcripts demonstrating a minimum grade point average of 2.5.
Target applicant(s): High school students. College students. Adult students.
Minimum GPA: 2.5
Amount: $5,000.
Number of awards: 10.

Deadline: August 2.
How to apply: Applications are available online.
Exclusive: Visit www.UltimateScholarshipBook.com and enter code NA28023 for updates on this award.

---

(281) · PGA WORKS Golf Management University Scholarship

PGA WORKS Golf Management University Scholarship Program
Scholarship America, One Scholarship Way, Saint Peter, MN 56082
Phone: 507-931-1682
Email: pgaworks@scholarshipamerica.org
https://learnmore.scholarsapply.org/pgaworks/
Purpose: To support students pursuing a PGA Golf Management University Program degree.
Eligibility: Applicants must be high school seniors, have graduated high school or be a current undergraduate level student. Students must attend a PGA Golf Management University listed on the sponsor's website and enroll in full-time undergraduate study. Applicants must be pursuing a PGA Golf Management University Program degree and plan to pursue a PGA of America membership.
Target applicant(s): High school students. College students. Adult students.
Amount: $8,000.
Number of awards: 11.
Deadline: January 28.
How to apply: Applications are available online.
Exclusive: Visit www.UltimateScholarshipBook.com and enter code PG28123 for updates on this award.

---

(282) · Pilot International Scholarship

Pilot International Foundation
102 Preston Court, Macon, GA 31210
Phone: 478-477-1208
Email: piffscholarships@pilothq.org
https://www.pilotinternational.org/grants-and-scholarships/
Purpose: To support students who are preparing for a career that focuses on caring for others.
Eligibility: Applicants must be an undergraduate student and pursuing a career that focuses on helping others.
Target applicant(s): College students. Adult students.
Amount: Up to $1,500.
Number of awards: Varies.
Scholarship may be renewable.
Deadline: March 15.
How to apply: Applications are available online.
Exclusive: Visit www.UltimateScholarshipBook.com and enter code PI28223 for updates on this award.

---

(283) · Pilot Pen G2 Overachievers Student Grant

Pilot Pen
3855 Regent Boulevard, Jacksonville, FL 32224
Phone: 904-645-9999
https://powertothepen.com/g2overachievers/
Purpose: To support students involved in community and public service.
Eligibility: Applicants must be ages 13 to 19 years old. Students must demonstrate exceptional academics and a dedication to serving others and must write an essay describing how they are working to help others outside of the classroom.
Target applicant(s): Junior high students or younger. High school students.

Amount: $15,000.
Number of awards: 1.
Deadline: December 15.
How to apply: Applications are available online.
Exclusive: Visit www.UltimateScholarshipBook.com and enter code PI28323 for updates on this award.

---

(284) · Planning Systems Incorporated and Engineering Scholarship

Navy League Foundation
2300 Wilson Boulevard, Suite 200, Arlington, VA 22201-5424
Phone: 800-356-5760
Email: vfrye@navyleague.org
http://www.navyleague.org
Purpose: To support students who are children or grandchildren of a member of the sea services.
Eligibility: Applicants must be enrolled at an accredited institution of higher education and the children or grandchildren of a member of the sea services including the following: United States Navy, United States Marine Corps, United States Coast Guard and U.S.-flag Merchant Marine. Preference is given to students who will seek a degree in science or engineering.
Target applicant(s): High school students.
Amount: $10,000.
Number of awards: 1.
Deadline: March 11.
How to apply: Applications are available online.
Exclusive: Visit www.UltimateScholarshipBook.com and enter code NA28423 for updates on this award.

---

(285) · Pony Alumni Scholarship

Pony Baseball/Softball
1951 Pony Place, P.O. Box 225, Washington, PA 15301
Phone: 724-225-1060
Email: info@pony.org
http://www.pony.org
Purpose: To support those students who have played on a Pony League, Colt League and/or Palomino League team for at least two years as they continue their education beyond high school.
Eligibility: Applicants must have played on one of the leagues for at least two years prior to submitting the application. Applicants must be a senior in high school and submit the application prior to May 1 of their senior year.
Target applicant(s): High school students.
Amount: Varies.
Number of awards: 8.
Deadline: May 1.
How to apply: Applications are available online. The application consists of the application form as well as sending in a school and community activities form, an essay on the supplied topic, a secondary school transcript, test results from the ACT, SAT or TOEFL, a copy of a letter of acceptance to the college, a notarized letter confirming participation in an affiliated league and two letters of recommendation.
Exclusive: Visit www.UltimateScholarshipBook.com and enter code PO28523 for updates on this award.

---

(286) · Power of Parents Scholarship

Brainly Inc.
161 Bowery 2nd Floor, New York, NY 10002
Email: contact@brainly.com

https://brainly.com/scholarships
Purpose: To support students with home-learning experience.
Eligibility: Students must be at least 14 years old and no older than 21 years of age and legally reside in the U.S. Applicants must be current high school students intending to enroll as full-time students or take online classes at an accredited undergraduate U.S. college or university within the next four years and have home-learning experience. An essay on a provided prompt is required.
Target applicant(s): High school students.
Amount: $2,500.
Number of awards: 1.
Deadline: April 30.
How to apply: Applications are available online.
Exclusive: Visit www.UltimateScholarshipBook.com and enter code BR28623 for updates on this award.

(287) · Private Frontier Essay Contest

Stossel in the Classroom
20 Rope Lane, Levittown, NY 11756
Phone: 516-731-3047
Email: RJSchimenz@stosselintheclassroom.org
https://stosselintheclassroom.org/student-contests/
Purpose: To support students who write about the benefits of hashtags, the betterment of life or liberty.
Eligibility: Applicants must be between the ages of 10-18 and reside in North America or Hawaii. An essay on a provided topic is required to be submitted. Essay submissions may be submitted by students, their parents or teachers.
Target applicant(s): Junior high students or younger. High school students.
Amount: Up to $2,500.
Number of awards: 51.
Deadline: March 11.
How to apply: Applications are available online.
Exclusive: Visit www.UltimateScholarshipBook.com and enter code ST28723 for updates on this award.

(288) · Private Frontier Video Contest

Stossel in the Classroom
20 Rope Lane, Levittown, NY 11756
Phone: 516-731-3047
Email: RJSchimenz@stosselintheclassroom.org
https://stosselintheclassroom.org/student-contests/
Purpose: To reward students who are interested in the benefits of hashtags, the betterment of life or liberty.
Eligibility: Applicants must be between the ages of 10-23 and reside in North America or Hawaii. A video submission on a provided topic is required. The video may be submitted by the students, their parents or teachers.
Target applicant(s): Junior high students or younger. High school students. College students.
Amount: Up to $2,500.
Number of awards: 16.
Deadline: March 11.
How to apply: Applications are available online.
Exclusive: Visit www.UltimateScholarshipBook.com and enter code ST28823 for updates on this award.

(289) · Project Yellow Light/Hunter Garner Scholarship

Project Yellow Light
One Shockoe Plaza, Richmond, VA 23219-4132
Phone: 804-698-8203
http://www.projectyellowlight.com
Purpose: To encourage students interested in safe driving.
Eligibility: Applicants must be high school juniors or seniors between the ages of 14 and 20 or full-time undergraduate college students between the ages of 15 and 25. Students must submit a video ad, design for a billboard ad or radio spot to encourage safe driving.
Target applicant(s): High school students. College students.
Amount: Up to $8,000.
Number of awards: 6.
Deadline: March 1 (billboard) or April 1 (radio and video).
How to apply: Applications are available online.
Exclusive: Visit www.UltimateScholarshipBook.com and enter code PR28923 for updates on this award.

(290) · Prudential Emerging Visionaries

Prudential Financial and Ashoka
Prudential Financial Inc., 751 Broad Street, Newark, NJ 07102
Phone: 973-802-4568
Email: EmergingVisionaries@ashoka.org
https://www.prudential.com/links/about/emergingvisionaries
Purpose: To support young people for their innovative solutions to financial and societal challenges facing their communities.
Eligibility: Applicants must be individuals between the ages of 14-18 and a legal resident of the U.S. or Puerto Rico. Participants must have started a project to solve a financial or societal challenge in their community before June 1, 2021.
Target applicant(s): Junior high students or younger. High school students.
Amount: Up to $15,000.
Number of awards: 25.
Deadline: November 4.
How to apply: Applications are available online.
Exclusive: Visit www.UltimateScholarshipBook.com and enter code PR29023 for updates on this award.

(291) · Pursuing a Positive Impact Scholarship

Commonwealth Law Group
3311 West Broad Street, Richmond, VA 23230
Phone: 804-999-9999
Email: contact@hurtinva.com
https://hurtinva.com/2021-pursuing-a-positive-impact-scholarship/
Purpose: To support students who work to benefit their communities.
Eligibility: Applicants must be enrolled or planning to enroll in community college, undergraduate college or university, graduate programs, business school or law school in the United States. Students must have a minimum 3.0 GPA and be in good overall academic standing. An essay submission on a provided topic is required.
Target applicant(s): High school students. College students. Graduate school students. Adult students.
Minimum GPA: 3.0
Amount: $3,000.
Number of awards: 1.
Deadline: October 31.
How to apply: Applications are available online.

Exclusive: Visit www.UltimateScholarshipBook.com and enter code CO29123 for updates on this award.

(292) · Race Entry Student Scholarship

Race Entry LLC
105 S State Street #617, Orem, UT 84058
Phone: 801-851-5520
https://www.raceentry.com/race-to-inspire-scholarship
Purpose: To support runners in pursuing post-secondary education.
Eligibility: Applicants must be enrolled at an accredited U.S. educational institution in the fall of the year in which the award is granted. Students must submit an essay explaining what inspires them to run. Selection is based on the overall strength of the submission.
Target applicant(s): High school students. College students. Adult students.
Amount: $500.
Number of awards: 1.
Deadline: August 15.
How to apply: Applications are available online.
Exclusive: Visit www.UltimateScholarshipBook.com and enter code RA29223 for updates on this award.

(293) · Rawhide Scholarship

National Intercollegiate Rodeo Association
2033 Walla Walla Avenue, Walla Walla, WA 99362
Phone: 509-529-4402
Email: rodeo@collegerodeo.com
http://www.collegerodeo.com/
Purpose: To aid students who exemplify the Rodeo Athletes on Wellness (Rawhide) principles.
Eligibility: Students must be current NIRA members, be college undergraduates and be academically eligible. Selection is based on the applicant's representation of the principles of positive choices, commitment to personal fitness, balance between rodeo and other commitments and having academic and career goals. Applicants should be involved in community service, have been in leadership roles and have a dedication to rodeo.
Target applicant(s): College students. Adult students.
Amount: $500.
Number of awards: Varies.
Deadline: May 20.
How to apply: Applications are available online.
Exclusive: Visit www.UltimateScholarshipBook.com and enter code NA29323 for updates on this award.

(294) · RealtyHop Scholarship

RealtyHop
355 Madison Avenue, 4th Floor, New York, NY 10017
https://www.realtyhop.com/resources/scholarship
Purpose: To support students who demonstrate ambition, diligence, leadership and an entrepreneurial spirit.
Eligibility: Applicants must be graduating high school seniors or currently enrolled undergraduates seeking a bachelor's or associate's degree. Students must submit their application including an essay via their school email address.
Target applicant(s): High school students. College students. Adult students.
Amount: $1,000.
Number of awards: 2.
Deadline: April 30, August 31.

How to apply: Applications are available online.
Exclusive: Visit www.UltimateScholarshipBook.com and enter code RE29423 for updates on this award.

(295) · RentHop Apartment Scholarship

RentHop
32 West 40th Street, New York, NY 10018
Phone: 913-982-6682
Email: college-scholarship@renthrop.com
https://www.renthop.com/college_scholarship
Purpose: To support undergraduate students who display an entrepreneurial spirit as they pursue their college education.
Eligibility: Applicants must be a graduating high school senior or an undergraduate pursuing a bachelor's or an associate's degree. Students will need to submit a 500-word essay on the topic provided.
Target applicant(s): High school students. College students. Adult students.
Amount: $1,000.
Number of awards: 2.
Deadline: April 30 and August 31.
How to apply: An application consists of the essay being emailed to RentHop via a school email address. If applicant doesn't have a school email address, proof of enrollment will need to be provided.
Exclusive: Visit www.UltimateScholarshipBook.com and enter code RE29523 for updates on this award.

(296) · Return 2 College Scholarship

R2C Scholarship Program
Email: info@return2college.com
http://www.return2college.com/awardprogram.cfm
Purpose: To provide financial assistance for college and adult students with college or graduate school expenses.
Eligibility: Applicants must be college or adult students currently attending or planning to attend a two-year or four-year college or graduate school within the next 12 months. Students must be 17 years or older and U.S. citizens or permanent residents. The award may be used for full- or part-time study at either on-campus or online schools.
Target applicant(s): High school students. College students. Adult students.
Amount: $1,000.
Number of awards: Varies.
Deadline: January 31, April 30, September 30.
How to apply: Applications are available online.
Exclusive: Visit www.UltimateScholarshipBook.com and enter code R229623 for updates on this award.

(297) · Rhodes Scholar

Rhodes Scholarship Trust
Attn.: Elliot F. Gerson, 8229 Boone Boulevard, Suite 240, Vienna, VA 22182
Phone: 703-821-5960
Email: amsec@rhodesscholar.org
http://www.rhodesscholar.org
Purpose: To recognize qualities of young people who will contribute to the "world's fight."
Eligibility: Applicants must be U.S. citizens between the ages of 18 and 24 and have a bachelor's degree at the time of the award. The awards provide for two to three years of study at the University of Oxford including educational costs and other expenses. Selection is extremely

competitive and is based on literary and scholastic achievements, athletic achievement and character.
Target applicant(s): College students.
Amount: Full tuition plus stipend.
Number of awards: 32.
Deadline: October 6.
How to apply: Applications are available online.
Exclusive: Visit www.UltimateScholarshipBook.com and enter code RH29723 for updates on this award.

(298) · RISE Financial Progress Scholarship

Elevate Credit Service LLC
RISE Financial Progress Scholarship Program, Scholarship America, One Scholarship Way, Saint Peter, MN 56082
Phone: 800-537-4180
Email: rise-scholarship@scholarshipamerica.org
https://www.risecredit.com/rise-scholarship
Purpose: To help hardworking students pursue higher education.
Eligibility: Applicants must be U.S. citizens or permanent residents currently enrolled or enrolling in a trade, college or university with a minimum GPA of 2.5. Students must complete online financial courses and discuss how it will help them achieve their financial goals.
Target applicant(s): High school students. College students. Adult students.
Minimum GPA: 2.5
Amount: $3,000.
Number of awards: 5.
Deadline: May 3.
How to apply: Applications are available online.
Exclusive: Visit www.UltimateScholarshipBook.com and enter code EL29823 for updates on this award.

(299) · Roller Skating Foundation Scholarship, High School Student Category

Roller Skating Foundation
6905 Corporate Drive, Indianapolis, IN 46278
Phone: 317-347-2626
Email: foundation@rollerskating.com
https://www.rollerskating.com/pages/scholarships/47
Purpose: To aid college-bound high school seniors.
Eligibility: Applicants must be high school seniors who plan to enroll at an accredited college or university in the fall following high school graduation. They must have a GPA of 3.4 or higher on a four-point scale and must be the child of an owner or employee of a RSA skating center or RSA affiliated member. They must have composite standardized test scores that are in the 85th percentile or higher. Selection is based on the overall strength of the application.
Target applicant(s): High school students.
Minimum GPA: 3.4
Amount: $1,000-$3,000.
Number of awards: 3.
Deadline: March 31.
How to apply: Applications are available online. An application form, transcript, personal essay, three recommendation letters and income tax information are required.
Exclusive: Visit www.UltimateScholarshipBook.com and enter code RO29923 for updates on this award.

(300) · Rosalind P. Walter College Scholarship

United States Tennis Association Foundation
70 W. Red Oak Lane, White Plains, NY 10604
Phone: 914-696-7223
Email: foundation@usta.com
http://www.ustafoundation.com/
Purpose: To support young tennis participants who believe in always putting forth a best effort and giving back to the community.
Eligibility: Applicants must be high school seniors who have participated in an organized youth tennis program. Selection is based on high academic achievement, good character and community involvement.
Target applicant(s): High school students.
Amount: $10,000.
Number of awards: 2.
Scholarship may be renewable.
Deadline: March.
How to apply: Applications are available online.
Exclusive: Visit www.UltimateScholarshipBook.com and enter code UN30023 for updates on this award.

(301) · Rover Sitter Scholarship

A Place for Rover Inc.
2101 4th Avenue #400, Seattle, WA 98121
https://www.rover.com/college-scholarship/
Purpose: To support students who are pet sitters.
Eligibility: Applicants must be residents of the United States at least 18 years of age and be existing pet care providers on Rover.com. Applicants must be graduating high school seniors with a minimum grade point average of 3.0 or current undergraduate or graduate students with a 3.0 or better grade point average.
Target applicant(s): High school students. College students. Graduate school students. Adult students.
Minimum GPA: 3.0
Amount: $2,500.
Number of awards: 1.
Deadline: May 1.
How to apply: Applications are available online.
Exclusive: Visit www.UltimateScholarshipBook.com and enter code A 30123 for updates on this award.

(302) · Sallie Mae No Essay Sweepstakes

Sallie Mae
300 Continental Drive, Newark, DE 19713
https://registration.salliemae.com/college-planning/registration/
Purpose: To help students pay for college, Sallie Mae is awarding this $5,432 Plan for College Sweepstakes.
Eligibility: Enter to win $5,432 when you register for Sallie Mae's free college planning tools, resources and calculators. It's fast, easy, free and no essay required. This award can be used at any college to study any subject.
Target applicant(s): High school students. College students. Adult students.
Amount: $5,432.
Number of awards: 1 per month.
Deadline: Monthly.
How to apply: Applications are available online.
Exclusive: Visit www.UltimateScholarshipBook.com and enter code SA30223 for updates on this award.

(303) · Samuel Huntington Public Service Award

Samuel Huntington Fund
Attn: Amy Stacy, National Grid, 40 Sylvan Road, Waltham, MA 02451
Phone: 508-389-2000
Email: amy.stacy@nationalgrid.com
https://www.samuelhuntingtonaward.org/
Purpose: To assist students who wish to perform one year of humanitarian service immediately upon graduation.
Eligibility: Applicants must be graduating college seniors, and must intend to perform one year of public service in the U.S. or abroad. The service may be individual work or through charitable, religious, educational, governmental or other public service organizations.
Target applicant(s): College students. Adult students.
Amount: $20,000.
Number of awards: Up to 3.
Deadline: January 14.
How to apply: Applications are available online.
Exclusive: Visit www.UltimateScholarshipBook.com and enter code SA30323 for updates on this award.

(304) · Sarah Josephine Langstaff Memorial Scholarship

Daughters of the British Empire in the USA
Email: dbescholarshipcommittee@dbenational.org
https://www.dbenational.org/scholarship
Purpose: To support female students with British or Commonwealth of Nations ancestry.
Eligibility: Applicants must be female students, at least 18 years of age and residents of the United States with British or Commonwealth of Nations ancestry. Students must be currently enrolled full-time at an accredited two- or four-year college or university and have a minimum 3.0 GPA. An essay submission and transcript are required.
Target applicant(s): College students. Adult students.
Minimum GPA: 3.0
Amount: $500-$1,000.
Number of awards: Up to 12.
Deadline: November 1.
How to apply: Applications are available online.
Exclusive: Visit www.UltimateScholarshipBook.com and enter code DA30423 for updates on this award.

(305) · SASS Scholarship Foundation Scholarships

Single Action Shooting Society (SASS)
215 Cowboy Way, Edgewood, NM 87015
Phone: 505-843-1320
Email: misty@sassnet.com
http://www.sassscholarship.org/
Purpose: To support students who have participated in SASS by helping with higher education costs.
Eligibility: Applicants must be a high school senior or college undergraduate, have at least a 2.0 GPA and have been active in SASS for at least one year. Selection is based on academic achievement, leadership, character, extracurricular activities and commitment to cowboy action shooting.
Target applicant(s): High school students. College students. Adult students.
Minimum GPA: 2.0
Amount: $2,000.
Number of awards: Varies.

Scholarship may be renewable.
Deadline: April 1.
How to apply: Applications are available online and must also include an official transcript, an essay on the provided topic, five letters of recommendation, a personal statement of goals and a photo of the applicant in full cowboy attire.
Exclusive: Visit www.UltimateScholarshipBook.com and enter code SI30523 for updates on this award.

(306) · Scholars Helping Collars Scholarship

P.L.A.Y.
246 2nd Street, Unit A, San Francisco, CA 94105
Phone: 855-300-7529
https://www.petplay.com/pages/scholarship
Purpose: To reward graduating seniors with a passion for animal welfare.
Eligibility: Applicants must have a history of volunteer work to help animals in need. Students must submit an essay about how that volunteer work has impacted their lives and the importance of animal welfare. Selection is based on the overall strength of the submission.
Target applicant(s): High school students.
Amount: $1,500.
Number of awards: 1.
Deadline: February 28.
How to apply: Applications are available online.
Exclusive: Visit www.UltimateScholarshipBook.com and enter code P.30623 for updates on this award.

(307) · Scholarship America Dream Award

Scholarship America Dream Award
One Scholarship Way, Saint Peter, MN 56082
Phone: 507-931-1682
Email: dreamaward@scholarshipamerica.org
https://scholarshipamerica.org/students/browse-scholarships/apply-for-the-dream-award/
Purpose: To assist students in their second year or higher of post-secondary education.
Eligibility: Applicants must be U.S. citizens or permanent or legal residents who received a high school diploma from a U.S. school. Students must be planning to complete a minimum of one full year of post-secondary education and be planning to enroll as full-time undergraduates at the sophomore level or higher for the coming academic year. Applicants must have a grade point average of 3.0 or better.
Target applicant(s): College students. Adult students.
Minimum GPA: 3.0
Amount: $5,000-$15,000.
Number of awards: Varies.
Scholarship may be renewable.
Deadline: October 15.
How to apply: Applications are available online.
Exclusive: Visit www.UltimateScholarshipBook.com and enter code SC30723 for updates on this award.

(308) · Scholarship for International Students

Deserve
1010 Doyle Street, Suite 200, Menlo Park, CA 94025
Phone: 800-418-7353
Email: hello@deserve.com
https://www.deserve.com/scholarship/
Purpose: To assist international students in the U.S.

Eligibility: Applicants must be studying in the U.S. on an F1, J1 or M1 visa and must be accepted to study or continue studying at an eligible college or university. Students must score in the top 15 percent on a standardized U.S. college entrance exam and must have a 3.0 GPA or higher.
Target applicant(s): College students. Graduate school students. Adult students.
Minimum GPA: 3.0
Amount: $5,000.
Number of awards: 10.
Deadline: October 31.
How to apply: Applications are available online. Recipients are randomly selected.
Exclusive: Visit www.UltimateScholarshipBook.com and enter code DE30823 for updates on this award.

(309) · Scholarships for Military Children

Defense Commissary Agency (DeCA)
1300 E Avenue, Fort Lee, VA 23801-1800
Phone: 804-734-8000
Email: militaryscholar@scholarshipmanagers.com
http://www.militaryscholar.org
Purpose: To provide educational opportunities for children of military personnel.
Eligibility: Applicants must be unmarried dependents under the age of 21 (23 if full-time students) of active duty, reserve, retired or deceased members of the military. They must be enrolled in the Defense Enrollment Eligibility Reporting System database. Applicants must be enrolled or plan to enroll in a full-time undergraduate degree-seeking program and have a minimum GPA of 3.0. Community or junior college students must be in a program that will allow transfer directly into a four-year program. Applicants also must not be accepted to a U.S. Military Academy or be the recipients of full scholarships at any accredited institution.
Target applicant(s): High school students. College students.
Minimum GPA: 3.0
Amount: $2,000.
Number of awards: Varies.
Deadline: February.
How to apply: Applications are available online or from military commissaries.
Exclusive: Visit www.UltimateScholarshipBook.com and enter code DE30923 for updates on this award.

(310) · Scholarships for Student Leaders

National Association for Campus Activities
13 Harbison Way, Columbia, SC 29212
Phone: 803-732-6222
Email: info@naca.org
https://www.naca.org/FOUNDATION/Pages/Scholarships.aspx
Purpose: The NACA foundation is committed to developing professionals in the field of campus activities.
Eligibility: Applicants must be current undergraduate students who hold a significant campus leadership position, have made significant contributions to their campus communities and have demonstrated leadership skills and abilities.
Target applicant(s): College students. Adult students.
Amount: Varies.
Number of awards: Varies.
Deadline: November 30.
How to apply: Applications are available online.

Exclusive: Visit www.UltimateScholarshipBook.com and enter code NA31023 for updates on this award.

(311) · Scholastic Honors Team

U.S. Figure Skating
20 First Street, Colorado Springs, CO 80906
Phone: 719-635-5200
Email: info@usfigureskating.org
https://www.usfigureskating.org/skate/scholarships-and-funding
Purpose: To support high school U.S. Figure Skating members who are distinguished in both figure skating and high school academics.
Eligibility: Students must be a current member of U.S. Figure Skating, entering the junior or senior year of high school, have at least a 3.4 GPA and have competed in a U.S. Figure Skating qualifying competition. Selection is based on academic performance and honors, community and extracurricular involvement, skating achievements and the essay.
Target applicant(s): High school students.
Minimum GPA: 3.4
Amount: $2,500.
Number of awards: Varies.
Deadline: August 31.
How to apply: Applications are available online and must include a high school transcript, SAT/ACT results, photo and essay.
Exclusive: Visit www.UltimateScholarshipBook.com and enter code U.31123 for updates on this award.

(312) · Scott Hamilton Skaters Education Fund

U.S. Figure Skating
20 First Street, Colorado Springs, CO 80906
Phone: 719-635-5200
Email: info@usfigureskating.org
https://www.usfigureskating.org/skate/scholarships-and-funding
Purpose: To assist amateur and professional skaters seeking a college education.
Eligibility: Applicants must be a high school senior or college undergraduate and have competed in a U.S. Figure Skating qualifying competition. Synchronized skating is not eligible. Selection is based on academic success, honors, demonstrated leadership in extracurricular activities, work experience, goals and the essay.
Target applicant(s): High school students. College students. Adult students.
Amount: $4,000-$8,000.
Number of awards: Varies.
Deadline: February 15.
How to apply: Applications are available online and include an official transcript, competition documentation and an IRS 1040 tax form for the past two years.
Exclusive: Visit www.UltimateScholarshipBook.com and enter code U.31223 for updates on this award.

(313) · Seabee Memorial Scholarship

Seabee Memorial Scholarship Association
P.O. Box 391, Springfield, VA 22150
Phone: 703-690-7672
Email: smsa@seabee.org
http://www.seabee.org
Purpose: To provide scholarships for the children of Seabees, both past and present, active, reserve or retired.
Eligibility: Applicants must be sons, daughters, step-children or grandchildren of Regular, Reserve, Retired or deceased officers or

enlisted members who have served or are now serving with the Naval Construction Force or Naval Civil Engineer Corps, or who have served but have been honorably discharged. Applicants must be a senior in high school or a high school graduate. Selection is based on scholastic record, citizenship, financial need and leadership. Scholarships are for undergraduate degree programs only.

Target applicant(s): High school students. College students. Adult students.

Amount: Varies.

Number of awards: Varies.

Deadline: April 15.

How to apply: Applications are available online or by written request.

Exclusive: Visit www.UltimateScholarshipBook.com and enter code SE31323 for updates on this award.

(314) · SelectBlinds.com College Scholarship

SelectBlinds.com
7420 South Kyrene Road, Suite 119, Tempe, AZ 85204
http://www.selectblinds.com/scholarship.html

Purpose: To help students who enter a submission related to window coverings.

Eligibility: Applicants must submit an original idea in the form of an image, photograph, video or other creativity means that addresses one of the following: what is the most creative thing you can do with window coverings, or invent a new technology for window coverings. Students must also answer a short essay. Applicants must be residents of the United States, currently registered at an accredited high school or college and hold a 2.5 or better grade point average.

Target applicant(s): High school students. College students. Adult students.

Minimum GPA: 2.5

Amount: $1,000.

Number of awards: 1.

Deadline: July 15.

How to apply: Applications are available online.

Exclusive: Visit www.UltimateScholarshipBook.com and enter code SE31423 for updates on this award.

(315) · Shari Simon Greenberg Community Scholarships of the Simon Youth Foundation

Simon Youth Foundation
225 W. Washington Street, Indianapolis, IN 46204
Phone: 800-509-3676
Email: syf@simon.com
http://www.syf.org/scholarships/

Purpose: To assist promising students who live in communities with Simon properties.

Eligibility: Applicants must be high school seniors who plan to attend an accredited two- or four-year college, university or technical/vocational school full-time. Scholarships are awarded without regard to race, color, creed, religion, gender, disability or national origin, and recipients are selected on the basis of financial need, academic record, potential to succeed, participation in school and community activities, honors, work experience, a statement of career and educational goals and an outside appraisal. Awards are given at every Simon mall in the U.S.

Target applicant(s): High school students.

Amount: $1,500.

Number of awards: Varies.

Deadline: February 16.

How to apply: Applications are available online. Only the first 3,000 applications that the organization receives are considered.

Exclusive: Visit www.UltimateScholarshipBook.com and enter code SI31523 for updates on this award.

(316) · Shepherd Scholarship

Ancient and Accepted Scottish Rite of Freemasonry Southern Jurisdiction
1733 16th Street NW, Washington, DC 20009-3103
Phone: 202-232-3579
Email: scholarships@scottishrite.org
https://scottishrite.org/philanthropy/scholarships/

Purpose: To provide financial assistance to students pursuing degrees in fields associated with service to country.

Eligibility: Applicants must have accepted enrollment in a U.S. institution of higher learning. Up to four letters of recommendation will be considered. Selection is based on "dedication, ambition, academic preparation, financial need and promise of outstanding performance at the advanced level." Applicants must have a minimum GPA of 3.0 and a Masonic background which includes one of the following: member of a Masonic youth organization, member of Scottish Rite or son, daughter, granddaughter or grandson of a current or past member of the Southern Jurisdiction of Scottish Rite in good standing.

Target applicant(s): High school students. College students. Adult students.

Minimum GPA: 3.0

Amount: $2,000.

Number of awards: Varies.

Scholarship may be renewable.

Deadline: April 12.

How to apply: Applications are available online. An application form, transcript and up to four letters of recommendation are required.

Exclusive: Visit www.UltimateScholarshipBook.com and enter code AN31623 for updates on this award.

(317) · Sheryl A. Horak Memorial Scholarship

Explorers Learning for Life
1325 West Walnut Hill Lane, P.O. Box 152225, Irving, TX 75015-2225
Phone: 855-806-9992
Email: exploring@lflmail.org
http://www.exploring.org/scholarships/

Purpose: To support students who are pursuing careers in law enforcement.

Eligibility: Students must be in their senior year of high school, and they must be members of a Law Enforcement Explorer post. Applicants must submit three letters of recommendation and an essay.

Target applicant(s): High school students. College students. Adult students.

Amount: $1,000.

Number of awards: 1.

Deadline: March 31.

How to apply: Applications are available online.

Exclusive: Visit www.UltimateScholarshipBook.com and enter code EX31723 for updates on this award.

(318) · Sleeknote Scholarship

Sleeknote
Jens Baggesens Vej 90A, 8200 Aarhus, Denmark,
Email: mail@sleeknote.com
https://sleeknote.com/scholarship

Purpose: To help students who create a video essay.

Eligibility: Applicants must be currently enrolled in a high school, university or college and able to submit their application in English. Students must create a short original video essay discussing their chosen field of study and future plans.

Target applicant(s): High school students. College students. Graduate school students. Adult students.

Amount: $1,000.

Number of awards: 2.

Deadline: September 30.

How to apply: Applications are available online.

Exclusive: Visit www.UltimateScholarshipBook.com and enter code SL31823 for updates on this award.

(319) · Sloane Stephens Doc & Glo Scholarship

Bold.org Sloane Stephens Doc & Glo Scholarship
133 Kearny, Suite 400, San Francisco, CA 94108
Email: contact@bold.org
https://bold.org/scholarships/sloane-stephens/

Purpose: To support students in paying for their education and following their dreams.

Eligibility: Applicants must be current high school seniors or undergraduate students. Students must have a minimum 2.5 GPA. An essay is required on a provided prompt.

Target applicant(s): High school students. College students. Adult students.

Minimum GPA: 2.5

Amount: $20,000.

Number of awards: 20.

Deadline: March 2.

How to apply: Applications are available online.

Exclusive: Visit www.UltimateScholarshipBook.com and enter code BO31923 for updates on this award.

(320) · Sodexo STOP Hunger Scholarship

Sodexo Foundation
9801 Washingtonian Boulevard, Gaithersburg, MD 20878
Phone: 800-763-3946
Email: stophunger@sodexofoundation.org
http://us.stop-hunger.org/home/grants.html

Purpose: To aid students who have been active in the movement to eradicate hunger.

Eligibility: Applicants must be U.S. citizens or permanent residents. They must be students in kindergarten through graduate school who are enrolled at an accredited U.S. institution. They must have been active in at least one unpaid volunteer effort to end hunger during the past 12 months. Sodexo employees and previous recipients of this award are ineligible. Selection is based on the overall strength of the application.

Target applicant(s): Junior high students or younger. High school students. College students. Graduate school students.

Amount: $1,000-$5,000.

Number of awards: Up to 25.

Deadline: December 5.

How to apply: Applications are available online. An application form and supporting materials are required.

Exclusive: Visit www.UltimateScholarshipBook.com and enter code SO32023 for updates on this award.

(321) · Soliant's Sunrise Scholarship

Soliant Consulting
Phone: 800-528-0170

Email: scholarship@soliantconsulting.com
https://www.soliantconsulting.com/philanthropy/sunrise-scholarship/

Purpose: To reward students who understand how businesses can be both philanthropic and profitable.

Eligibility: Applicants must be incoming freshmen or current undergraduate students at an accredited two-year or four-year college or university in the United States. A minimum 3.0 GPA is required. Students will need to submit a 500-word essay on the provided topic.

Target applicant(s): High school students. College students. Adult students.

Minimum GPA: 3.0

Amount: $1,000.

Number of awards: 1.

Deadline: April 29.

How to apply: Applications are available online.

Exclusive: Visit www.UltimateScholarshipBook.com and enter code SO32123 for updates on this award.

(322) · Sons of Union Veterans of the Civil War Scholarships

Sons of Union Veterans of the Civil War
Executive Director David W. Demmy, Sr., 1 Lincoln Circle at Reservoir Park, Suite 240 (National Civil War Museum), Harrisburg, PA 17103-2411
Email: execdir@suvcw.org
http://www.suvcw.org

Purpose: To assist students connected with the Sons of Union Veterans of the Civil War in obtaining higher education.

Eligibility: Male applicants must be members or associates of the Sons of Union Veterans of the Civil War. Female applicants must be daughters or granddaughters of members or associates and must be current members of the Women's Relief Corps, Ladies of the Grand Army of the Republic, Daughters of Union Veterans of the Civil War 1861-1865 or Auxiliary to the Sons of Union Veterans of the Civil War. All applicants must rank in the upper quarter of their graduating class, have a record of school and community service and provide three letters of recommendation.

Target applicant(s): High school students. College students. Adult students.

Amount: $2,500.

Number of awards: 2.

Deadline: March 31.

How to apply: Applications are available online.

Exclusive: Visit www.UltimateScholarshipBook.com and enter code SO32223 for updates on this award.

(323) · Southern Region/Elmer Stailing Scholarship

USA Water Ski and Wake Sports Foundation
6039 Cypress Gardens Boulevard, Suite 481, Winter Haven, FL 33884
Phone: 863-324-2472
Email: Scholarships@Waterskihalloffame.com
https://www.usa-wwf.org/scholarships

Purpose: To support current active members of USA Water Ski in their educational goals.

Eligibility: Applicants must be U.S. citizens and be incoming freshmen, sophomores, juniors or seniors at an accredited two-year or four-year college. Applicants must continue to be enrolled full-time at their college during the year of receipt of the scholarship. Selection is based on the applicant's academic achievement, work record, need and school

and community activities as well as their contributions to the sport of water skiing.
Target applicant(s): College students. Adult students.
Amount: $2,000.
Number of awards: 1.
Deadline: March 15.
How to apply: Applications are available online. An application form, 500-word essay and two recommendation letters are required.
Exclusive: Visit www.UltimateScholarshipBook.com and enter code US32323 for updates on this award.

(324) · Spirit of Anne Frank Awards
Anne Frank Center USA
1325 Avenue of the Americas, 28th Floor, New York, NY 10019
https://www.annefrank.com/scholarships
Purpose: To reward students who lead the way in combating prejudice and injustice in their communities.
Eligibility: Students should be high school seniors, be U.S. citizens and plan on attending a four-year college or university in the fall of the upcoming academic year. Applicants must submit a 1,000-word essay characterizing their efforts and dedication toward achieving lasting change with regards to prejudice and intolerance.
Target applicant(s): High school students.
Amount: $1,000-$5,000.
Number of awards: 3.
Deadline: February 28.
How to apply: Applications are available online and must be submitted along with the essay and two letters of recommendation.
Exclusive: Visit www.UltimateScholarshipBook.com and enter code AN32423 for updates on this award.

(325) · Spirit of Giving Scholarship
Wine Country Gift Baskets
Phone: 800-394-0394
Email: scholarship@winecountrygiftbaskets.com
https://www.winecountrygiftbaskets.com/information/scholarship.asp
Purpose: To encourage acts of kindness, service and giving.
Eligibility: Applicants must be high school seniors or currently enrolled students in an accredited U.S. certificate program, college, trade school or university who will be attending the program in the following year. Students must submit an essay relating to giving and service to others.
Target applicant(s): High school students. College students. Adult students.
Amount: $1,000.
Number of awards: 3.
Deadline: July 31.
How to apply: Applications are available online.
Exclusive: Visit www.UltimateScholarshipBook.com and enter code WI32523 for updates on this award.

(326) · Sports Unlimited Scholarship
Sports Unlimited
346 Godshall Drive, Harleysville, PA 19438
Phone: 610-994-9701
https://www.sportsunlimitedinc.com/scholarship.html
Purpose: To support student athletes in pursuing post-secondary education.
Eligibility: Applicants must be graduating seniors or college freshmen or sophomores. Students must submit an essay explaining how to improve a piece of sports equipment.

Target applicant(s): High school students. College students. Adult students.
Amount: $1,000.
Number of awards: 1.
Deadline: September.
How to apply: Applications are available online.
Exclusive: Visit www.UltimateScholarshipBook.com and enter code SP32623 for updates on this award.

(327) · Stamps Scholars
Stamps Family Charitable Foundation Inc.
P.O. Box 98374, Atlanta, GA 30359-2074
Email: info@stampsfoundation.org
https://www.stampsfoundation.org/
Purpose: To support students pursuing higher education with their related expenses.
Eligibility: Applicants must be currently enrolled high school seniors, undergraduates or graduate students attending an accredited college or university. Selection is based on the overall strength of the application as well as the following: academic achievement, leadership ability, integrity, perseverance, extracurricular activities and community involvement.
Target applicant(s): High school students. College students. Graduate school students. Adult students.
Amount: Varies.
Number of awards: Varies.
Deadline: Varies.
How to apply: Applications are available online. An application form, official transcripts and SAT and/or ACT scores are required.
Exclusive: Visit www.UltimateScholarshipBook.com and enter code ST32723 for updates on this award.

(328) · Steps For Change Scholarship
Wealth By Health Steps For Change Foundation
5419 Hollywood Boulevard, Suite B, Los Angeles, CA 90027
Phone: 888-996-9985
Email: scholarships@wealthbyhealth.org
https://www.wealthbyhealth.org/scholarship-programs
Purpose: To support students who have financial need or are from disadvantaged backgrounds and demonstrate their drive to succeed.
Eligibility: Applicants must be current high school seniors expecting to graduate and in the process of applying to, or having been accepted to, a college or university. Students must have a household income of less than $55,000 and a minimum 3.5 cumulative GPA. A one-minute video submission on a provided topic is required.
Target applicant(s): High school students.
Minimum GPA: 3.5
Amount: $2,000.
Number of awards: 3.
Deadline: April 26.
How to apply: Applications are available online.
Exclusive: Visit www.UltimateScholarshipBook.com and enter code WE32823 for updates on this award.

(329) · Stokes Educational Scholarship Program
National Security Agency (NSA)
Attn: MB3, Stokes Program, 9800 Savage Road, Suite 6272, Ft. George G. Meade, MD 20755-6000
Phone: 410-854-4725
Email: help@IntelligenceCareers.gov
https://www.intelligencecareers.gov/icstudents.html?Agency=NSA

Purpose: To recruit those with skills useful to the NSA, especially minority high school students.
Eligibility: Students must be seniors at the time of application, be U.S. citizens, have a 3.0 GPA, have a minimum ACT score of 25 or a minimum SAT score of 1200 and demonstrate leadership skills. Applicants must be planning to major in computer science or computer/electrical engineering.
Target applicant(s): High school students.
Minimum GPA: 3.0
Amount: Up to $30,000.
Number of awards: Varies.
Scholarship may be renewable.
Deadline: October 31.
How to apply: Applications are available online.
Exclusive: Visit www.UltimateScholarshipBook.com and enter code NA32923 for updates on this award.

(330) · Stop-painting.com Scholarship
InSite Solutions LLC
3660 Rogers Road #298, Wake Forest, NC 27587
Phone: 919-569-6765
Email: lara@stop-painting.com
http://stop-painting.com/post/scholarships.asp
Purpose: To support students in their pursuit of higher education so that they may then pursue successful professional careers.
Eligibility: Applicants must be a senior in high school or a student currently attending an accredited college or university. An essay (800 to 1,000 words) about a provided topic related to the importance of organization is required.
Target applicant(s): High school students. College students. Adult students.
Amount: $1,000.
Number of awards: 2.
Deadline: June 15 (fall) and November 15 (spring).
How to apply: Applications are available online and include short-answer questions as well as an essay.
Exclusive: Visit www.UltimateScholarshipBook.com and enter code IN33023 for updates on this award.

(331) · Stuck at Prom Scholarship
Henkel Consumer Adhesives
32150 Just Imagine Drive, Avon, OH 44011-1355
http://stuckatprom.com/
Purpose: To reward students for their creativity with duct tape.
Eligibility: Applicants must attend a high school prom as a couple in the spring wearing the most original attire that they make from duct tape. Both members of the couple do not have to attend the same school. Photographs of past winners are available on the website.
Target applicant(s): High school students.
Amount: $500-$10,000.
Number of awards: Varies.
Deadline: June 9.
How to apply: Applications are available online. Contact information, release form and prom picture are required.
Exclusive: Visit www.UltimateScholarshipBook.com and enter code HE33123 for updates on this award.

(332) · Student Activist Awards
Freedom from Religion Foundation
P.O. Box 750, Madison, WI 53701
Phone: 608-256-8900
Email: info@ffrf.org
https://ffrf.org/outreach/awards
Purpose: To assist high school and college student activists.
Eligibility: Selection is based on activism for free thought or separation of church and state.
Target applicant(s): High school students. College students. Adult students.
Amount: $1,000.
Number of awards: Varies.
Deadline: Varies.
How to apply: Contact the organization for more information.
Exclusive: Visit www.UltimateScholarshipBook.com and enter code FR33223 for updates on this award.

(333) · Student Paper Competition
American Criminal Justice Association
P.O. Box 601047, Sacramento, CA 95860-1047
Phone: 916-484-6553
Email: acjalae@aol.com
https://www.acjalae.org/membership-benefits.html
Purpose: To encourage scholarship in criminal justice students.
Eligibility: Applicants must be student members (undergraduate or graduate) of the American Criminal Justice Association-Lambda Alpha Epsilon and submit an original paper on criminology, law enforcement, juvenile justice, courts, corrections, prevention, planning and evaluation or career development and education in the field of criminal justice. Students may apply for membership along with their paper submission. Applicants should submit applications and three copies of the paper.
Target applicant(s): College students. Graduate school students. Adult students.
Amount: $50-$150.
Number of awards: 9.
Deadline: December 31.
How to apply: Applications are available by contacting the Executive Secretary.
Exclusive: Visit www.UltimateScholarshipBook.com and enter code AM33323 for updates on this award.

(334) · Student Transportation Video Contest
American Road and Transportation Builders Association
1219 28th Street, NW, Washington, DC 20007
Phone: 202-289-4434
Email: lshair@artba.org
https://www.artba.org/foundation/
Purpose: To support students from elementary through graduate school interested in the transportation industry in the United States.
Eligibility: Applicants must be currently enrolled elementary through graduate school students. They must produce a 2-4 minute video on some aspect of the transportation industry in the United States. Selection is based on creativity and the overall strength of the video.
Target applicant(s): Junior high students or younger. High school students. College students. Graduate school students. Adult students.
Amount: Up to $500.
Number of awards: 2.
Deadline: December 3.

How to apply: Videos must be uploaded to YouTube and a link to the video sent to ARTBA by the submission deadline. Submission forms are available online. A submission form, waiver, link to the video, enrollment verification and photo release form are required.
Exclusive: Visit www.UltimateScholarshipBook.com and enter code AM33423 for updates on this award.

(335) · Student Video Contest

World of 7 Billion
2120 L Street NW, Suite 500, Washington, DC 20037
Phone: 800-767-1956
https://www.worldof7billion.org
Purpose: To support students who are interested in global challenges.
Eligibility: Applicants must be in grades 6-12 and students may be located anywhere in the world. Students must submit a 60-second video about human population growth and how it affects climate change, ocean health or rapid urbanization and at least one sustainable solution must be mentioned.
Target applicant(s): Junior high students or younger. High school students.
Amount: $300-$1,200.
Number of awards: 5.
Deadline: February 22.
How to apply: Applications are available online.
Exclusive: Visit www.UltimateScholarshipBook.com and enter code WO33523 for updates on this award.

(336) · Student View Scholarship

Student Insights
136 Justice Drive, Valencia, PA 16059
Phone: 724-612-3685
Email: jbecker@studentinsights.com
http://studentinsights.com
Purpose: To support graduating high school seniors regardless of academic achievement or need.
Eligibility: Applicants must complete an online survey and then they will be entered into a random drawing for an award.
Target applicant(s): High school students.
Amount: Up to $5,000.
Number of awards: 13.
Deadline: April.
How to apply: Applications are available online.
Exclusive: Visit www.UltimateScholarshipBook.com and enter code ST33623 for updates on this award.

(337) · StudentCam Competition

C-SPAN
Phone: 800-523-7586
Email: educate@c-span.org
http://www.studentcam.org
Purpose: To reward students interested in government and societal issues.
Eligibility: Applicants must be either middle school or high school students in the United States, U.S. territories or the District of Columbia. Students must follow rules for the documentary competition. Applicants' entries must reflect the current theme.
Target applicant(s): Junior high students or younger. High school students.
Amount: Varies.
Number of awards: 150.

Deadline: January 20.
How to apply: Applications are available online.
Exclusive: Visit www.UltimateScholarshipBook.com and enter code C-33723 for updates on this award.

(338) · Study.com Academic Awards

Study.com
100 View Street, Suite 202, Mountain View, CA 94041
https://study.com/pages/Academic_Awards_Home.html
Purpose: To support students who are pursuing a higher education.
Eligibility: Applicants must be citizens of the United States who are either graduating high school seniors or students currently enrolled at an accredited college or university. Students must have a minimum of 30 semester hours or 40 quarter hours remaining in their program until graduation.
Target applicant(s): High school students. College students. Adult students.
Amount: $500-$1,000.
Number of awards: 15.
Deadline: April 1.
How to apply: Applications are available online.
Exclusive: Visit www.UltimateScholarshipBook.com and enter code ST33823 for updates on this award.

(339) · Subic Bay-Cubi Point Scholarship 2

Navy League Foundation
2300 Wilson Boulevard, Suite 200, Arlington, VA 22201-5424
Phone: 800-356-5760
Email: vfrye@navyleague.org
http://www.navyleague.org
Purpose: To support students who are either dependents or direct descendants of a member of the U.S. Marine Corps, U.S. Navy or U.S.-Flag Merchant Marines or who are active members of the U.S. Naval Sea Cadet Corps.
Eligibility: Applicants must be enrolled at an accredited institution of higher education. Only dependents or direct descendants of a member of the U.S. Marine Corps, U.S. Navy or U.S.-Flag Merchant Marines or who are active members of the U.S. Naval Sea Cadet Corps are eligible to apply. Selection is based on the overall strength of the application.
Target applicant(s): High school students.
Amount: $10,000.
Number of awards: 2.
Deadline: March 15.
How to apply: Applications are available online.
Exclusive: Visit www.UltimateScholarshipBook.com and enter code NA33923 for updates on this award.

(340) · Summer Graduate Research Fellowships

Institute for Humane Studies at George Mason University
3434 Washington Boulevard, MS 1C5, Arlington, VA 22201
Phone: 800-697-8799
Email: ihs@gmu.edu
http://www.theihs.org
Purpose: To support graduate students who are interested in scholarly research in the classical liberal tradition.
Eligibility: Applicants must be graduate students in areas related to the classical liberal tradition and should be focusing on a discrete writing project. Selection is by invitation-only for graduate student alumni of the other IHS programs, Humane Studies Fellowship and Summer Seminars.

Target applicant(s): Graduate school students. Adult students.
Amount: $5,000 stipend + travel and housing allowance.
Number of awards: Varies.
Deadline: Varies.
How to apply: Applications are available online.
Exclusive: Visit www.UltimateScholarshipBook.com and enter code IN34023 for updates on this award.

(341) · SuperCollege Scholarship

SuperCollege.com
Scholarship Dept. 673, 2713 Newlands Avenue, Belmont, CA 94002
Email: supercollege@supercollege.com
https://www.supercollege.com/scholarship/
Purpose: SuperCollege donates a percentage of the proceeds from the sales of its books to award scholarships to high school, college, graduate and adult students.
Eligibility: Applicants must be high school students, college undergraduates, graduate students or adult students residing in the U.S. and attending or planning to attend any accredited college or university within the next 12 months. The scholarship may be used to pay for tuition, books, room and board, computers or any education-related expenses.
Target applicant(s): High school students. College students. Adult students.
Amount: $1,000.
Number of awards: 12.
Deadline: Monthly.
How to apply: Applications are available online.
Exclusive: Visit www.UltimateScholarshipBook.com and enter code SU34123 for updates on this award.

(342) · Supplemental Education Grant (SEG)

Coast Guard Mutual Assistance (CGMA)
4200 Wilson Boulevard, Coast Guard Stop 7180, Arlington, VA 20598-7180
Phone: 202-493-6621
Email: CGMA@cgmahq.org
https://www.cgmahq.org/programs/education.html
Purpose: To encourage students who are pursuing education to prepare them for their future career.
Eligibility: Applicants must be Coast Guard members applying for themselves or their dependents. Students must be either enrolled in a college or university undergraduate or graduate program, pursuing a multi-course VoTech program approved by the Department of Veteran Affairs or Department of Education that would prepare them for their career, pursuing a GED or completing a correspondence course for a college, university or VoTech program.
Target applicant(s): College students. Adult students.
Amount: $500 per calendar year.
Number of awards: Varies.
Scholarship may be renewable.
Deadline: Varies.
How to apply: Applications are available online.
Exclusive: Visit www.UltimateScholarshipBook.com and enter code CO34223 for updates on this award.

(343) · Sweet Karen Alumni Scholarship

Harness Horse Youth Foundation
16575 Carey Road, Westfield, IN 46074
Phone: 317-867-5877
Email: ellen@hhyf.org
http://www.hhyf.org
Purpose: To help students interested in harness horses with their higher education expenses.
Eligibility: Applicants must be at least a high school senior and be planning to enroll as a full-time student or enrolled as a full-time undergraduate student at their selected college, university or trade school. Students must have participated in a Harness Horse Youth Foundation program to include the following events: Harness Racing Youth League event, Family Weekend and/or Leadership Program from 1999 to present.
Target applicant(s): High school students. College students.
Amount: Up to $1,500.
Number of awards: Varies.
Deadline: April 30.
How to apply: Applications are available online. An application form, financial information and an essay are required.
Exclusive: Visit www.UltimateScholarshipBook.com and enter code HA34323 for updates on this award.

(344) · Tailhook Educational Foundation Scholarship

Tailhook Association
The Tailhook Educational Foundation, 9696 Businesspark Avenue, San Diego, CA 92131-1643
Phone: 800-269-8267
Email: thookassn@aol.com
https://www.tailhook.net/
Purpose: To assist the members of and the children of the members of the United States Navy carrier aviation.
Eligibility: Applicants must be high school graduates who are accepted at an undergraduate institution and are the natural or adopted children of current or former Naval Aviators, Naval Flight Officers or Naval Aircrewmen. Applicants may also be individuals or children of individuals who are serving or have served on board a U.S. Navy Aircraft Carrier in the ship's company or the air wing. Educational and extracurricular achievements, merit and citizenship will be considered.
Target applicant(s): High school students. College students. Adult students.
Amount: Varies.
Number of awards: Varies.
Deadline: March 1.
How to apply: Applications are available online.
Exclusive: Visit www.UltimateScholarshipBook.com and enter code TA34423 for updates on this award.

(345) · Tampa Bay Buccaneers Foundation Girls in Football Scholarship

Tampa Bay Buccaneers Foundation
Girls in Football Scholarship, Scholarship America, One Scholarship Way, Saint Peter, MN 56082
Phone: 507-931-1682
Email: buccaneersgirlsinfootball@scholarshipamerica.org
https://learnmore.scholarsapply.org/buccaneersgirlsinfootball/
Purpose: To support female high school seniors who participate in a form of football.
Eligibility: Applicants must be female high school seniors participating in a form of football (touch, flag, tackle, etc.) planning to enroll in full-time undergraduate study at an accredited four-year college or university. Students must have a minimum 3.0 GPA and plan to use their college education and experience to make an impact in the sports industry. An essay on a provided prompt is required to be submitted.

Target applicant(s): High school students.
Minimum GPA: 3.0
Amount: $5,000.
Number of awards: 4.
Deadline: April 13.
How to apply: Applications are available online.
Exclusive: Visit www.UltimateScholarshipBook.com and enter code TA34523 for updates on this award.

---

(346) · Team Development Scholarships

National Collegiate Water Ski Association
A Sport Division of US Water Ski, 1251 Holy Cow Road, Polk City, FL 33868-8200
Email: secretary@ncwsa.com
http://www.ncwsa.com/scholarships/
Purpose: To aid student water skiers with the continuing pursuit of their educational goals.
Eligibility: Applicants must be a U.S. citizen and a member of USA Water Ski. Selection varies by region and may be based on applicant's academic achievement, need, work record and community and school activities as well as contributions to the sport of water skiing as a skier or worker at tournaments.
Target applicant(s): College students. Adult students.
Amount: $1,500.
Number of awards: 4.
Deadline: Varies.
How to apply: Applications are available from each regional director.
Exclusive: Visit www.UltimateScholarshipBook.com and enter code NA34623 for updates on this award.

---

(347) · Technology Addiction Awareness Scholarship

Digital Responsibility
3561 Homestead Road #113, Santa Clara, CA 95051-5161
Email: mjefferson@digitalresponsibility.org
http://www.digitalresponsibility.org/scholarships/
Purpose: To help students understand the negative effects of too much screen time.
Eligibility: Applicant must be a high school, college, graduate or home schooled student who is a U.S. citizen or legal resident. A 140-character message about technology addiction is required to apply. The top 10 applications will be selected as finalists; finalists will be asked to write a full length 500- to 1,000-word essay about technology addiction. Only online applications are accepted.
Target applicant(s): High school students. College students. Graduate school students. Adult students.
Amount: $1,000.
Number of awards: 1.
Deadline: January 30.
How to apply: Applications are available online.
Exclusive: Visit www.UltimateScholarshipBook.com and enter code DI34723 for updates on this award.

---

(348) · Telluride Association Summer Programs

Telluride Association
217 West Avenue, Ithaca, NY 14850
Phone: 607-273-5011
Email: tasp-queries@tellurideassociation.org
https://www.tellurideassociation.org/our-programs/high-school-students/
Purpose: Summer program to provide high school students with a college-level, intellectually enriching experience.
Eligibility: Applicants must be high school juniors. The association seeks applicants from a variety of socio-economic backgrounds and provides for their tuition and room and board during summer programs in New York and Michigan. Students are invited to apply either by receiving a score on the PSAT/NMSQT that is usually in the top 1 percent or by nomination by a teacher or counselor.
Target applicant(s): High school students.
Amount: Summer program tuition and fees.
Number of awards: Varies.
Deadline: January.
How to apply: Applications are sent to nominated students.
Exclusive: Visit www.UltimateScholarshipBook.com and enter code TE34823 for updates on this award.

---

(349) · Think For Yourself College Scholarship Essay Contest

Let Grow
228 Park Avenue South, Suite 77212, New York, NY 10003
Email: info@letgrow.org
https://letgrow.org/tfyscholarship/
Purpose: To reward high school students who value free speech.
Eligibility: Applicants must be at least 13 years of age and legal residents of the United States. Students must be currently in middle or high school. An essay submission on a provided prompt is required.
Target applicant(s): Junior high students or younger. High school students.
Amount: Up to $5,000.
Number of awards: 4.
Deadline: February.
How to apply: Applications are available online.
Exclusive: Visit www.UltimateScholarshipBook.com and enter code LE34923 for updates on this award.

---

(350) · Tim Olson Memorial Scholarship

USA Water Ski and Wake Sports Foundation
6039 Cypress Gardens Boulevard, Suite 481, Winter Haven, FL 33884
Phone: 863-324-2472
Email: Scholarships@Waterskihalloffame.com
https://www.usa-wwf.org/scholarships
Purpose: To aid current active members of USA Water Ski with the continuing pursuit of their educational goals.
Eligibility: Applicants must be U.S. citizens and be incoming freshmen, sophomores, juniors or seniors at a two-year or four-year accredited college and enrolled full-time. Students must remain enrolled full-time at their chosen college during the year of receipt of the scholarship. Applicants must be a member of USA Water Ski & Wake Sports. Selection is based on the applicant's academic achievement record, need, community and school activities and work record as well as their contributions to the sport of water skiing.
Target applicant(s): College students. Adult students.
Amount: $1,500.
Number of awards: 1.
Deadline: March 15.
How to apply: Applications are available online. An application form, two letters of recommendation and a 500-word essay are required.
Exclusive: Visit www.UltimateScholarshipBook.com and enter code US35023 for updates on this award.

(351) · Trapshooting Hall of Fame College Scholarships

Trapshooting Hall of Fame
P.O. Box 281, Vandalia, OH 45377
Phone: 937-660-5663
Email: SpartaStaff@TrapHOF.org
http://www.traphof.org/Hall-Info/Scholarship-Information/
Purpose: To support high school seniors who have participated in trapshooting.
Eligibility: Applicants must be high school seniors and members of Amateur Trapshooting Association. Selection is based on an essay explaining the need for the scholarship, prior shooting experience and accomplishments.
Target applicant(s): High school students.
Amount: Up to $5,000.
Number of awards: 7.
Deadline: July 1.
How to apply: Applications are available online and must include the essay, one letter of recommendation and a listing of your shooting history and accomplishments.
Exclusive: Visit www.UltimateScholarshipBook.com and enter code TR35123 for updates on this award.

(352) · Travel Scholarship

Volunteer Forever Inc.
1378 Geneva Avenue, San Francisco, CA 94112
https://www.volunteerforever.com/scholarships/
Purpose: To support students who wish to travel.
Eligibility: Applicants must be residents of the U.S., U.K., E.U., Canada, Australia or New Zealand. Students must have plans to volunteer, study, intern, teach or work abroad. The scholarship is awarded each quarter.
Target applicant(s): College students. Graduate school students. Adult students.
Amount: $500-$1,000.
Number of awards: 4.
Deadline: December 31.
How to apply: Applications are available online.
Exclusive: Visit www.UltimateScholarshipBook.com and enter code VO35223 for updates on this award.

(353) · Travel Video Contest

InternationalStudent.com
224 First Street, Neptune, FL 32266
http://www.internationalstudent.com
Purpose: To support students who wish to pursue an international education or study abroad program.
Eligibility: Applicants must be at least 18 years old, be enrolled or currently enrolling in a college or university abroad. Students must submit a video describing a desired trip if they are currently studying abroad or describing a proposed study abroad if they are currently studying in their home country. Applicants must create a video that does not exceed four minutes, submit a fully completed online entry form and be prepared to document the entire experience in a weekly blog, if selected.
Target applicant(s): High school students. College students. Adult students.
Amount: $4,000.
Number of awards: 1.
Deadline: October 13.

How to apply: Applications are available online.
Exclusive: Visit www.UltimateScholarshipBook.com and enter code IN35323 for updates on this award.

(354) · Triple-Impact Competitor Scholarship

Positive Coaching Alliance
1001 N. Rengstorff Avenue, Suite 100, Mountain View, CA 94043
Phone: 650-210-0815
Email: jennie_wulbrun@positivecoach.org
http://www.positivecoach.org
Purpose: To reward high school juniors who participate in sports and embody the "TIC" model.
Eligibility: Students must have a GPA of 2.5 and provide testimonials from a coach, a school administrator and a fellow teammate or competitor. Applicants must be U.S. citizens and current high school juniors who are participants in a sport sponsored by a school or local club.
Target applicant(s): High school students.
Minimum GPA: 2.5
Amount: $500-$2,000.
Number of awards: 100.
Deadline: May 31.
How to apply: Applications are available online.
Exclusive: Visit www.UltimateScholarshipBook.com and enter code PO35423 for updates on this award.

(355) · Truman Scholar

Truman Scholarship Foundation
712 Jackson Place NW, Washington, DC 20006
Phone: 202-395-4831
Email: office@truman.gov
http://www.truman.gov
Purpose: To provide college junior leaders who plan to pursue careers in government, non-profits, education or other public service with financial support for graduate study and leadership training.
Eligibility: Applicants must be juniors, attending an accredited U.S. college or university and be nominated by the institution. Students may not apply directly. Applicants must be U.S. citizens or U.S. nationals, complete an application and write a policy recommendation.
Target applicant(s): College students. Adult students.
Amount: Up to $30,000.
Number of awards: 55-65.
Deadline: February 2.
How to apply: See your school's Truman Faculty Representative or contact the foundation.
Exclusive: Visit www.UltimateScholarshipBook.com and enter code TR35523 for updates on this award.

(356) · Truth Impact Scholarship

Truth Initiative
900 G Street, NW, Fourth Floor, Washington, DC 20001
Phone: 202-454-5555
Email: vacosta@truthinitiative.org
https://www.thetruth.com/
Purpose: To encourage students advocating for change.
Eligibility: Applicants must be 18 years of age or older and attending a higher education institution or trade school. A brief video is required to be submitted with the application.
Target applicant(s): High school students. College students. Graduate school students. Adult students.
Amount: $3,000.

Number of awards: 5.
Deadline: August 30.
How to apply: Applications are available online.
Exclusive: Visit www.UltimateScholarshipBook.com and enter code TR35623 for updates on this award.

(357) · U.S. Bank Scholarship Program
U.S. Bank
c/o U.S. Bank Office of Corporate Citizenship, 1420 Kettner Boulevard, 7th Floor, San Diego, CA 92101
Phone: 800-242-1200
https://financialiq.usbank.com/index/manage-your-household/student-center/enter-to-win-the-student-union-scholarship.html
Purpose: To support graduating high school seniors who plan to attend college.
Eligibility: Applicants must be high school seniors who plan to attend or current college freshmen, sophomores or juniors attending full-time at an accredited two- or four-year college and be U.S. citizens or permanent residents. Recipients are selected through a random drawing.
Target applicant(s): High school students. College students. Adult students.
Amount: $20,000.
Number of awards: Varies.
Deadline: October.
How to apply: Applications are only available online.
Exclusive: Visit www.UltimateScholarshipBook.com and enter code U.35723 for updates on this award.

(358) · U.S. JCI Senate Scholarship Grants
US JCI Senate Foundation
387 Sunset, Lawton, OK 73507
Email: scholarship@usjcisenate.org
http://www.usjcisenate.org
Purpose: To support high school students who wish to further their education.
Eligibility: Applicants must be high school seniors and U.S. citizens who are graduating from a U.S. accredited high school or state approved home school or GED program. Winners must attend college full-time to receive funds. Applications are judged at the state level.
Target applicant(s): High school students.
Amount: $1,000.
Number of awards: Varies.
Deadline: January 14.
How to apply: Applications are available from your school's guidance office.
Exclusive: Visit www.UltimateScholarshipBook.com and enter code US35823 for updates on this award.

(359) · UDT-SEAL Scholarship
Naval Special Warfare Foundation
1619 D Street, Virginia Beach, VA 23459
Phone: 757-363-7490
Email: info@udtseal.org
https://www.navysealfoundation.org/
Purpose: To assist the dependents of UDT-SEAL Association members.
Eligibility: Students must be single dependents of a UDT-SEAL Association member who has served in or is serving in the U.S. Armed Forces and the Naval Special Warfare community. Members must have paid UDT-SEAL Association dues for last four consecutive years. Selection is based on academic achievement, a written essay and extracurricular involvement.
Target applicant(s): High school students. College students.
Amount: Varies.
Number of awards: Varies.
Deadline: February.
How to apply: Applications are available by contacting the NWSF.
Exclusive: Visit www.UltimateScholarshipBook.com and enter code NA35923 for updates on this award.

(360) · Undergraduate Transfer Scholarship
Jack Kent Cooke Foundation Undergraduate Transfer Scholarship
44325 Woodridge Parkway, Lansdowne, VA 20176
Phone: 800-941-3300
Email: scholarships@jkcf.org
http://www.jkcf.org
Purpose: To help community college students transfer to and attend four-year universities.
Eligibility: Applicants must be a current student at an accredited U.S. community college or two-year institution with sophomore status by December 31 of the application year or a recent graduate. Students must plan to enroll full time in a baccalaureate program at an accredited college or university in the following fall and have a cumulative undergraduate grade point average of 3.5 or better on a 4.0 scale. Applicants must also demonstrate significant unmet financial need. Family income of up to $95,000 will be considered. However, the majority of scholarship recipients will be eligible to receive a Pell grant.
Target applicant(s): College students. Adult students.
Minimum GPA: 3.5
Amount: Up to $55,000.
Number of awards: About 85.
Scholarship may be renewable.
Deadline: January 10.
How to apply: Applications are available online.
Exclusive: Visit www.UltimateScholarshipBook.com and enter code JA36023 for updates on this award.

(361) · United Daughters of the Confederacy Scholarships
United Daughters of the Confederacy
328 North Boulevard, Richmond, VA 23220
Phone: 804-355-1636
Email: hqudc@rcn.com
http://www.hqudc.org
Purpose: To support the descendants of Confederates.
Eligibility: Applicants must be lineal descendants of Confederates or other eligible descendants and have a minimum 3.0 GPA.
Target applicant(s): High school students. College students. Graduate school students. Adult students.
Minimum GPA: 3.0
Amount: Varies.
Number of awards: Varies.
Scholarship may be renewable.
Deadline: Varies.
How to apply: Contact any Division Second Vice President as listed on the website.
Exclusive: Visit www.UltimateScholarshipBook.com and enter code UN36123 for updates on this award.

(362) · United States Hispanic Leadership Institute Denny's Hungry for Education

United States Hispanic Leadership Institute Denny's Hunger for Education
Email: hungryforeducation@dennys.com
https://www.dennyshungryforeducation.com/
Purpose: To support students who have ideas for fighting childhood hunger.
Eligibility: Applicants must be high school seniors or college students, be citizens of the United States or be living in the United States legally and have a 2.5 GPA. Students must write an essay as part of their application and have ideas on ending childhood hunger. Applicants may apply regardless or race or national origin.
Target applicant(s): High school students. College students. Adult students.
Minimum GPA: 2.5
Amount: Varies.
Number of awards: 8.
Deadline: December 10.
How to apply: Applications are available online.
Exclusive: Visit www.UltimateScholarshipBook.com and enter code UN36223 for updates on this award.

(363) · Unpakt College Scholarship

Unpakt
555 W. 25th Street, Floor 3, New York, NY 10001
Phone: 212-677-5333
Email: scholarship@unpakt.com
http://www.unpakt.com/scholarship
Purpose: To support students who write about their future.
Eligibility: Applicants must be currently enrolled college students or recent graduates. Students must submit an application and essay discussing where they plan to move after graduation to start their professional life and why.
Target applicant(s): High school students. College students. Adult students.
Amount: Up to $1,000.
Number of awards: 3.
Deadline: December 31.
How to apply: Applications are available online.
Exclusive: Visit www.UltimateScholarshipBook.com and enter code UN36323 for updates on this award.

(364) · Urban Fellows Program

New York City Department of Personnel
1 Centre Street, Room 2425, New York, NY 10007
Phone: 212-386-0058
https://www1.nyc.gov/site/dcas/employment/urban-fellows.page
Purpose: To support high-achieving students pursue government and public service.
Eligibility: Applicants must have received their bachelor's degree within the last two years. Students must commit full-time to the nine-month Fellowship and suspend any graduate study or outside work. Applicants must be eligible to work in the U.S.
Target applicant(s): Graduate school students. Adult students.
Amount: $30,000.
Number of awards: Varies.
Deadline: January 14.
How to apply: Applications are available online.

Exclusive: Visit www.UltimateScholarshipBook.com and enter code NE36423 for updates on this award.

(365) · USA Roller Sports Scholarship Fund

USA Roller Sports
Educational Scholarship Fund, 4730 South Street, Lincoln, NE 68506
Phone: 402-483-7551
Email: matteberry@usarollersports.org
https://www.teamusa.org/USA-Roller-Sports/Resources/For-Athletes/US-Foundation-For-Amateur-Roller-Skating-Grants
Purpose: To support U.S. Roller Sports athletes in paying for educational costs in preparation for accomplishment of career goals.
Eligibility: Applicants must be U.S. citizens or legal residents as well as current USARS members who have held a membership for a minimum of three years. Applicants must also have participated in USARS Sanctioned National Championships. Students must be at least 17 years of age and in their final year of high school or must be high school graduates. A minimum GPA in the final year of high school of 3.0 is required. Eligible applicants must be currently enrolled or plan to enroll in a college or trade school seeking a degree or certificate and be of good academic standing. Selection is based on membership status, eligibility to compete, academic achievement and financial need.
Target applicant(s): High school students. College students. Adult students.
Minimum GPA: 3.0
Amount: $1,000-$2,000.
Number of awards: 3.
Deadline: October 31.
How to apply: Applications are available online.
Exclusive: Visit www.UltimateScholarshipBook.com and enter code US36523 for updates on this award.

(366) · USA Water Ski and Wake Sports Foundation Scholarships

USA Water Ski and Wake Sports Foundation
6039 Cypress Gardens Boulevard, Suite 481, Winter Haven, FL 33884
Phone: 863-324-2472
Email: Scholarships@Waterskihalloffame.com
https://www.usa-wwf.org/scholarships
Purpose: To support those involved in USA Water Ski.
Eligibility: Applicants must be full-time undergraduates at a two- or four-year college as incoming freshmen to incoming seniors. Applicants must also be active members of a USA Water Ski division: AWSA-ABC-AKA-WSDA-NSSA-NCWSA-NCWSRA-USAWB-HYD. Students should submit an application, two reference letters, an essay and a transcript.
Target applicant(s): High school students. College students. Adult students.
Amount: $1,000-$5,000.
Number of awards: Varies.
Scholarship may be renewable.
Deadline: March 15.
How to apply: Applications are available online.
Exclusive: Visit www.UltimateScholarshipBook.com and enter code US36623 for updates on this award.

(367) · USAR Scholarship

USA Racquetball
2812 West Colorado Avenue, Suite 200, Colorado Springs, CO
80904-2906
Phone: 719-635-5396
Email: Peggine@usra.org
http://www.teamusa.org/USA-Racquetball
Purpose: To support USAR members who are aspiring collegiate athletes.
Eligibility: Applicants must be current USAR members and be graduating high school seniors or college undergraduates.
Target applicant(s): High school students. College students. Adult students.
Amount: Varies.
Number of awards: Varies.
Deadline: December 31.
How to apply: Applications are available online.
Exclusive: Visit www.UltimateScholarshipBook.com and enter code US36723 for updates on this award.

(368) · USBC Alberta E. Crowe Star of Tomorrow

United States Bowling Congress
Attn.: Alberta E. Crowe Star of Tomorrow, 621 Six Flags Drive,
Arlington, TX 76011
Phone: 800-514-2695
Email: contactus@ibcyouth.com
https://www.bowl.com/scholarships/
Purpose: To recognize star qualities in female students in high school or college who are competitive bowlers.
Eligibility: Applicants must be female high school seniors or college students 22 years of age or younger and USBC members who compete in certified events. They must hold an average of 175 or higher and must not have competed in professional tournaments except for Pro-AM's. They must also have a GPA of 2.5 or higher.
Target applicant(s): High school students. College students.
Minimum GPA: 2.5
Amount: $6,000.
Number of awards: 1.
Deadline: December 1.
How to apply: Applications are available online.
Exclusive: Visit www.UltimateScholarshipBook.com and enter code UN36823 for updates on this award.

(369) · USBC Annual Zeb Scholarship

United States Bowling Congress
Attn.: Alberta E. Crowe Star of Tomorrow, 621 Six Flags Drive,
Arlington, TX 76011
Phone: 800-514-2695
Email: contactus@ibcyouth.com
https://www.bowl.com/scholarships/
Purpose: To reward USBC Youth members with high academic achievement who have participated in community service.
Eligibility: Applicants must be high school juniors or seniors who are USBC Youth members in good standing. They must have a GPA of 2.0 or higher and must not have competed in any professional bowling tournament except for Pro-Am's.
Target applicant(s): High school students.
Minimum GPA: 2.0
Amount: $2,500 plus travel.
Number of awards: 1.

Deadline: December 1.
How to apply: Applications are available online.
Exclusive: Visit www.UltimateScholarshipBook.com and enter code UN36923 for updates on this award.

(370) · USBC Chuck Hall Star of Tomorrow

United States Bowling Congress
Attn.: Alberta E. Crowe Star of Tomorrow, 621 Six Flags Drive,
Arlington, TX 76011
Phone: 800-514-2695
Email: contactus@ibcyouth.com
https://www.bowl.com/scholarships/
Purpose: To recognize star qualities in male high school and college students who are competitive bowlers.
Eligibility: Applicants must be United States Bowling Congress members who compete in certified events and are high school seniors or college students with a GPA of 3.0 or higher. They must not have competed in a professional bowling tournament except for Pro-AM's.
Target applicant(s): High school students. College students. Adult students.
Minimum GPA: 3.0
Amount: $6,000.
Number of awards: 1.
Scholarship may be renewable.
Deadline: December 1.
How to apply: Applications are available online.
Exclusive: Visit www.UltimateScholarshipBook.com and enter code UN37023 for updates on this award.

(371) · USBC Youth Ambassador of the Year

United States Bowling Congress
Attn.: Alberta E. Crowe Star of Tomorrow, 621 Six Flags Drive,
Arlington, TX 76011
Phone: 800-514-2695
Email: contactus@ibcyouth.com
https://www.bowl.com/scholarships/
Purpose: To recognize contributions to the sport of bowling, academic achievement and community service.
Eligibility: Students must be USBC Youth members who will be 18 years of age or older by August 1 of the year of their selection. They must also be high school seniors and be nominated by a USBC member. The award is given to one male and one female student each year.
Target applicant(s): High school students.
Amount: $1,500.
Number of awards: 2.
Deadline: December.
How to apply: Applications are available online.
Exclusive: Visit www.UltimateScholarshipBook.com and enter code UN37123 for updates on this award.

(372) · USMA Blake Family Metric Scholarship Award

U.S. Metric Association
P.O. Box 471, Windsor, CO 80550-0471
Phone: 779-537-5611
http://www.us-metric.org/usma-blake-family-foundation-metric-awards
Purpose: To support students who help promote metric awareness and usage.
Eligibility: Applicants must be high school seniors who plan to enter college in the fall after graduation. Selection is based on involvement in

promoting metric awareness and usage in the U.S. An additional award is available to a non-student.
Target applicant(s): High school students.
Amount: $2,500.
Number of awards: 1.
Deadline: March 31.
How to apply: Applications are available online.
Exclusive: Visit www.UltimateScholarshipBook.com and enter code U.37223 for updates on this award.

(373) · VA Essay Scholarship
VA Mortgage Center
2101 Chapel Plaza Court, Suite 107, Columbia, MO 65203
Phone: 800-405-6682
https://www.enhancelives.com/
Purpose: To reward students who are members of the military community as they pursue a college education.
Eligibility: Students must be a surviving spouse or child of a deceased veteran from the U.S. military, and be currently enrolled or planning to enroll in a college or university by the spring semester of the following school year. Students must also be comfortable sharing personal stories and aspirations with the Veteran's United Foundation and willing and able to provide requested documentation in a timely manner.
Target applicant(s): College students. Adult students.
Amount: $20,000.
Number of awards: Up to 5.
Deadline: Varies.
How to apply: Applications are available online.
Exclusive: Visit www.UltimateScholarshipBook.com and enter code VA37323 for updates on this award.

(374) · Veterans Caucus Scholarship
Veterans Caucus of the American Academy of Physician Assistants
P.O. Box 362, Danville, PA 17821-0362
Email: fbrace@veteranscaucus.org
http://www.veteranscaucus.org
Purpose: To aid U.S. military veterans who are enrolled in a physician assistant training program.
Eligibility: Applicants must be U.S. military veterans. They must be enrolled in an accredited physician assistant (PA) training program. Selection is based on the overall strength of the application.
Target applicant(s): College students. Graduate school students. Adult students.
Amount: Varies.
Number of awards: 11.
Deadline: May 1.
How to apply: Applications are available online. An application form and personal statement are required.
Exclusive: Visit www.UltimateScholarshipBook.com and enter code VE37423 for updates on this award.

(375) · Voice of Democracy Audio Essay Contests
Veterans of Foreign Wars
406 W. 34th Street, Kansas City, MO 64111
Phone: 816-968-1117
Email: kharmer@vfw.org
https://www.vfw.org/community/youth-and-education
Purpose: To encourage patriotism with students creating audio essays expressing their opinion on a patriotic theme.

Eligibility: Applicants must submit a three- to five-minute audio essay focused on a yearly theme. Students must be in the 9th to 12th grade in a public, private or parochial high school, home study program or overseas U.S. military school. Foreign exchange students are not eligible for the contest, and students who are age 20 or older also may not enter. Previous first place winners on the state level are ineligible.
Target applicant(s): High school students.
Amount: $1,000-$30,000.
Number of awards: Varies.
Deadline: October 31.
How to apply: Applications are available online but must be submitted to a local VFW post.
Exclusive: Visit www.UltimateScholarshipBook.com and enter code VE37523 for updates on this award.

(376) · W. H. Howie McClennan Scholarship
International Association of Fire Fighters
1750 New York Avenue, NW, Washington, DC 20006
Phone: 202-737-8484
Email: scholarships@iaff.org
http://www.iaff.org
Purpose: To provide scholarships for the children of firefighters who died in the line of duty.
Eligibility: Applicants must be the children (natural or legally-adopted) of firefighters who died in the line of duty. Applicant's parent must have been a member in good standing of the International Association of Fire Fighters, AFL-CIO/CLC at time of death. Selection is based on financial need, academic record and promise.
Target applicant(s): High school students. College students. Adult students.
Amount: $2,500.
Number of awards: 1.
Scholarship may be renewable.
Deadline: February 1.
How to apply: Applications are available by written request.
Exclusive: Visit www.UltimateScholarshipBook.com and enter code IN37623 for updates on this award.

(377) · Wade Trophy
Women's Basketball Coaches Association
4646 Lawrenceville Highway, Lilburn, GA 30047
Phone: 770-279-8027
Email: dtrujillo@wbca.org
https://wbca.org/recognize/player-awards
Purpose: To recognize the best women's college basketball player in the country who exceeds expectations on and off the court.
Eligibility: Applicants must be academically eligible NCAA Division I players and members of the WBCA NCAA Division I Coaches' All-American Team. Eligibility is limited to sophomore, junior and senior players.
Target applicant(s): College students. Adult students.
Amount: Varies.
Number of awards: Varies.
Deadline: Varies.
How to apply: There is no formal application process. Eligible applicants are selected by the Wade Trophy Committee at the beginning of the basketball season.
Exclusive: Visit www.UltimateScholarshipBook.com and enter code WO37723 for updates on this award.

(378) · Walter Byers Graduate Scholarship

National Collegiate Athletic Association
700 W. Washington Street, P.O. Box 6222, Indianapolis, IN 46206
Phone: 317-917-6222
Email: lthomas@ncaa.org
http://www.ncaa.org/about/resources/ncaa-scholarships-and-grants
Purpose: To encourage academic excellence of student athletes by recognizing outstanding academic achievement and success in postgraduate studies.
Eligibility: Applicants must have a cumulative GPA of 3.5 or higher in their undergraduate work and have competed in intercollegiate athletics at a NCAA member institution as a member of a varsity team. Applicants should be a graduating senior or be enrolled in graduate studies. If not already in a graduate program, the applicant should have the intent of pursuing a graduate degree within five years at a properly accredited, nonprofit educational institution. Scholarship funds can also apply to a professional degree program at an accredited law school, medical school or the equivalent. Applicants must be able to demonstrate that athletic participation and community service have guided them to build superior character and leadership as well as helping to influence personal and intellectual growth.
Target applicant(s): College students. Graduate school students. Adult students.
Minimum GPA: 3.5
Amount: $24,000.
Number of awards: 2.
Scholarship may be renewable.
Deadline: January 13.
How to apply: Applicants must be nominated by a faculty athletics representative using the online application form. Applications also include a personal essay detailing future personal and academic goals. Included with the packet is a listing of involvement in activities and honors, as well as four recommendations.
Exclusive: Visit www.UltimateScholarshipBook.com and enter code NA37823 for updates on this award.

(379) · Watson Travel Fellowship

Thomas J. Watson Fellowship
11 Park Place, Suite 1503, New York, NY 10007
Phone: 212-245-8859
Email: tjw@watsonfellowship.org
http://watson.foundation/fellowships/tj
Purpose: To award one-year grants for independent study and travel outside the U.S. to graduating college seniors.
Eligibility: Only graduating seniors from the participating colleges are eligible to apply. A list of these colleges is available online. Applicants must first be nominated by their college or university. An interview with a representative will follow. Recipients must graduate before the fellowship can begin.
Target applicant(s): College students. Adult students.
Amount: Up to $36,000.
Number of awards: Varies.
Deadline: November 1.
How to apply: Interested students should contact their local Watson liaison to begin the application process. Once nominated, applicants must complete an online application form, project proposal and personal statement. A photo, transcripts and letters of recommendation are also required.

Exclusive: Visit www.UltimateScholarshipBook.com and enter code TH37923 for updates on this award.

(380) · WBCA Coaches' All-America

Women's Basketball Coaches Association
4646 Lawrenceville Highway, Lilburn, GA 30047
Phone: 770-279-8027
Email: dtrujillo@wbca.org
https://wbca.org/recognize/player-awards
Purpose: To recognize the 10 best women's or girl's basketball players at the NCAA Division I, NCAA Division II, NCAA Division III, NAIA, Junior/Community College and high school levels.
Eligibility: Applicants at the collegiate level must be eligible college women's basketball players whose coaches are members of the WBCA. Applicants at the high school level must be seniors. Selection at all levels is based on current season statistics and achievements, impact on the team, team success, sportsmanship and academic eligibility.
Target applicant(s): High school students. College students. Adult students.
Amount: Varies.
Number of awards: 10.
Deadline: Varies.
How to apply: Applicants must be nominated using the online nomination form.
Exclusive: Visit www.UltimateScholarshipBook.com and enter code WO38023 for updates on this award.

(381) · We The Future Contest

Constituting America
P.O. Box 1988, Colleyville, TX 76034
Phone: 888-937-0917
Email: constitutingamerica@yahoo.com
https://constitutingamerica.org/enter/
Purpose: To encourage students who are learning about the importance of the U.S. Constitution.
Eligibility: Applicants must be U.S. citizens or legal residents and middle, high school or college students. Students must submit an entry in one of the following categories: essay, song, entrepreneurial plan, short film, PSA, STEM or speech - all with the theme of the U.S. Constitution.
Target applicant(s): Junior high students or younger. High school students. College students. Adult students.
Amount: Up to $2,000.
Number of awards: 8-10.
Deadline: September 17.
How to apply: Applications are available online.
Exclusive: Visit www.UltimateScholarshipBook.com and enter code CO38123 for updates on this award.

(382) · We the Students Essay Contest

Bill of Rights Institute
1310 North Courthouse Road, Suite 620, Arlington, VA 22201
Phone: 703-894-1776
Email: info@billofrightsinstitute.org
http://www.billofrightsinstitute.org
Purpose: To support students who are pursuing a higher education.
Eligibility: Applicants must attend school within the United States, be between the ages of 14 and 18 and write an essay as part of the application process.
Target applicant(s): Junior high students or younger. High school students.

Amount: $500-$7,500.
Number of awards: 16.
Deadline: April 15.
How to apply: Applications are available online.
Exclusive: Visit www.UltimateScholarshipBook.com and enter code BI38223 for updates on this award.

(383) · Wells Fargo Veterans Scholarship Program

Wells Fargo Veterans Scholarship Program, Scholarship America
One Scholarship Way, Saint Peter, MN 56082
Phone: 800-537-4180
Email: wellsfargoveterans@scholarshipamerica.org
https://learnmore.scholarsapply.org/wellsfargoveterans/
Purpose: To reward those who have served in the United States military.
Eligibility: Applicants must be honorably-discharged veterans or spouses of disabled veterans who have graduated high school (or obtained a GED) and who have served in the U.S. military. Students must have at least a 2.0 GPA and plan to enroll full-time in an accredited two- or four-year college, university or vocational school the following fall. Award will increase with renewal to encourage completion of program.
Target applicant(s): High school students. College students. Graduate school students. Adult students.
Minimum GPA: 2.0
Amount: Up to $5,000.
Number of awards: 23.
Scholarship may be renewable.
Deadline: July 8.
How to apply: Applications are available online.
Exclusive: Visit www.UltimateScholarshipBook.com and enter code WE38323 for updates on this award.

(384) · Western Digital Scholarship Program

Western Digital Scholarship Program
c/o International Scholarship and Tuition Services Inc. (ISTS), 1321 Murfreesboro Road, Suite 800, Nashville, TN 37217
Phone: 855-670-ISTS
Email: contactus@applyists.com
https://www.westerndigital.com/company/corporate-philanthropy/scholarship-programs
Purpose: To assist students who have demonstrated leadership or entrepreneurial interests.
Eligibility: Applicants must be a high school senior or college freshman, sophomore or junior and must attend or plan to attend a full-time undergraduate program. Students must also demonstrate financial need. Up to 27 $2,500 renewable awards will given to students from the general public, up to three $2,500 renewable awards will be given to dependents of SanDisk employees and two students will be chosen as SanDisk Scholars and awarded full tuition scholarships for up to four years.
Target applicant(s): High school students. College students. Adult students.
Amount: $2,500 to full tuition.
Number of awards: Varies.
Scholarship may be renewable.
Deadline: March 24.
How to apply: Applications are available online. An application form and an essay are required.
Exclusive: Visit www.UltimateScholarshipBook.com and enter code WE38423 for updates on this award.

(385) · White House Fellows Program

White House
1600 Pennsylvania Avenue NW, Washington, DC 20500
Phone: 202-395-4522
Email: whitehousefellows@who.eop.gov
https://www.whitehouse.gov/get-involved/fellows/apply/
Purpose: To provide motivated students with first-hand experience working at high levels of federal government.
Eligibility: Applicants must be U.S. citizens who have completed their undergraduate education and demonstrate early professional achievement and evidence of leadership skills. Students must demonstrate commitment to public service and the ability to work as part of a team and provide three recommendations along with the application.
Target applicant(s): Graduate school students. Adult students.
Amount: Varies.
Number of awards: Varies.
Deadline: January 7.
How to apply: Applications are available online.
Exclusive: Visit www.UltimateScholarshipBook.com and enter code WH38523 for updates on this award.

(386) · William J. Goaziou Scholarship

US Youth Soccer
9220 World Cup Way, Frisco, TX 75033
Phone: 800-476-2237
Email: jmagleby@usyouthsoccer.org
https://www.usyouthsoccer.org/players/scholarship/
Purpose: To aid high school senior soccer players who plan on continuing their education beyond high school.
Eligibility: Applicants must be high school seniors who have participated in a U.S. Youth Soccer program during the past two years. Students must have at least a 3.0 GPA. Selection is based on community service and the desire to give back to the game of soccer.
Target applicant(s): High school students.
Minimum GPA: 3.0
Amount: $1,000.
Number of awards: 2.
Deadline: April.
How to apply: Applications are available online and must also include an official transcript and two letters of recommendation.
Exclusive: Visit www.UltimateScholarshipBook.com and enter code US38623 for updates on this award.

(387) · William L. Hastie Award

National Association of Blacks in Criminal Justice
1801 Fayetteville Street, 106 Whiting Criminal Justice Building, P.O. Box 20011-C, Durham, NC 27707
Phone: 919-683-1801
Email: Office@NABCJ.org
https://nabcj.org/
Purpose: To reward demonstrations of national leadership in criminal justice and the pursuit of policy change within the field.
Eligibility: The award honors the first African American appointed to the bench in 1937 by President Franklin Roosevelt. Nominator should be a member of NABCJ.
Target applicant(s): High school students. College students. Adult students.
Amount: Varies.
Number of awards: 1.
Deadline: March 15.

How to apply: Nomination applications are available online.
Exclusive: Visit www.UltimateScholarshipBook.com and enter code NA38723 for updates on this award.

(388) · WiseGeek Easy Scholarships

WiseGeek
P.O. Box 2130, Sparks, NV 89432
Email: scholarships@wisegeek.com
https://www.wisegeek.com/easy-scholarships.htm
Purpose: To support students in a variety of fields of study and interests.
Eligibility: Applicants must be U.S. citizens or permanent legal residents and enrolled in a college or university. There are a number of scholarships in the program.
Target applicant(s): College students. Graduate school students. Adult students.
Amount: $500.
Number of awards: 1.
Deadline: December 1.
How to apply: Applications are available online.
Exclusive: Visit www.UltimateScholarshipBook.com and enter code WI38823 for updates on this award.

(389) · Women Divers Hall of Fame Scholarships and Grants

Women Divers Hall of Fame
43 Mackey Avenue, Port Washington, NY 10050
Email: scholarships@wdhof.org
https://www.wdhof.org/scholarships/sponsorship
Purpose: To support those of all ages who are pursuing careers involving diving.
Eligibility: Applicants must be interested in a career that involves diving. Several scholarships and grants are available, and each has various requirements. Not all are for women only.
Target applicant(s): Junior high students or younger. High school students. College students. Graduate school students. Adult students.
Amount: Up to $2,000.
Number of awards: Varies.
Deadline: October 31.
How to apply: All applications are online and all require a resume, essay and two letters of recommendation.
Exclusive: Visit www.UltimateScholarshipBook.com and enter code WO38923 for updates on this award.

(390) · Women Marines Association Scholarship Program

Women Marines Association
Scholarships, Dottie Stover-Kendrick, P.O. Box 134, Stilwell, KS 66085
Phone: 888-525-1943
Email: scholarship@womenmarines.org
https://www.womenmarines.org/scholarships
Purpose: To aid Marines and their families.
Eligibility: Applicants must be sponsored by a Women Marines Association member. They must have served or be serving in the Marine Corps or Reserve, be a direct descendant, sibling or descendant of a sibling of a member of the Marines or have completed two years in a Marine JROTC program. A minimum GPA of 3.0 is required.
Target applicant(s): High school students. College students. Adult students.

Minimum GPA: 3.0
Amount: $1,000-$1,500.
Number of awards: Varies.
Deadline: February 28.
How to apply: Applications are available online. An application form, copy of sponsor's membership card, photo, three letters of recommendation, proof of Marine or ROTC status or relationship to a Marine and proof of draft registration (for males) are required.
Exclusive: Visit www.UltimateScholarshipBook.com and enter code WO39023 for updates on this award.

(391) · Women on Par Scholarship

LPGA Amateur Golf Association
1 Deuce Court, Daytona Beach, FL 32124
Phone: 386-236-5353
Email: womenonpar@LPGAAmateurs.com
https://lpgaamateurs.com/memberships/scholarship/
Purpose: To support non-traditional female students.
Eligibility: Applicants must be female, at least 30 years of age and a U.S. or Canadian citizen or legal resident of the U.S. or Canada. Students must be first-time applicants to school or returning to school after an absence to complete a degree and pursuing a technical/vocational, associate's or bachelor's degree. Deadline will be shortened if 200 applications are received before stated date.
Target applicant(s): High school students. College students. Adult students.
Amount: Up to $2,000.
Number of awards: 2.
Deadline: April.
How to apply: Applications are available online.
Exclusive: Visit www.UltimateScholarshipBook.com and enter code LP39123 for updates on this award.

(392) · Women's Army Corps Veterans Association Scholarship

Women's Army Corps Veterans Association
P.O. Box 5577, Fort McClellan, AL 36205
Email: wacva@cox.net
https://www.armywomen.org/pdf/_10ScholarApp.pdf
Purpose: To support relatives of army service women based upon academic achievement and leadership as revealed by co-curricular activities and community involvement.
Eligibility: Applicants must be the child, grandchild, niece or nephew of an Army Service Woman. Students must have a GPA of 3.5 or higher and show academic promise. Students must be graduating seniors and U.S. citizens.
Target applicant(s): High school students.
Minimum GPA: 3.5
Amount: $1,500.
Number of awards: Varies.
Deadline: February 2.
How to apply: Applications are available online.
Exclusive: Visit www.UltimateScholarshipBook.com and enter code WO39223 for updates on this award.

(393) · Women's Overseas Service League Scholarships for Women

Women's Overseas Service League
Scholarship Committee, P.O. Box 124, Cedar Knoll, NJ 07927-0124

http://www.wosl.org/index.htm

Purpose: To assist women in the military and other public service careers.

Eligibility: Applicants must demonstrate a commitment to advancement in their careers and must have completed at least 12 semester or 18 quarter hours of study at an institution of higher learning and be working toward a degree. Students must agree to enroll for at least six semester or nine quarter hours each academic period. A GPA of 2.5 or higher is required.

Target applicant(s): College students. Adult students.

Minimum GPA: 2.5

Amount: $500-$1,000.

Number of awards: Varies.

Scholarship may be renewable.

Deadline: March 1.

How to apply: Applications are available online. An application form, statement of financial need, resume, three letters of reference, essay and transcript are required.

Exclusive: Visit www.UltimateScholarshipBook.com and enter code WO39323 for updates on this award.

(394) · Women's Western Golf Foundation Scholarship

Women's Western Golf Foundation

Mrs. Richard Willis, Scholarship Selection Director, 393 Ramsay Road, Deerfield, IL 60015

Phone: 608-274-0173

Email: dkdink@aol.com

https://wwgf.esfhost.com/info/

Purpose: To support female students who are involved in golf.

Eligibility: Applicants must be in their senior year of high school. Students must demonstrate academic excellence, good character and financial need. Recipients must maintain a 3.0 GPA for award renewal.

Target applicant(s): High school students.

Amount: $2,500.

Number of awards: Varies.

Scholarship may be renewable.

Deadline: March 5.

How to apply: Applications are available by mail.

Exclusive: Visit www.UltimateScholarshipBook.com and enter code WO39423 for updates on this award.

(395) · Young Scholars Program

Jack Kent Cooke Foundation Young Scholars Program

301 ACT Drive, P.O. Box 4030, Iowa City, IA 52243

Phone: 800-941-3300

Email: scholarships@jkcf.org

http://www.jkcf.org

Purpose: To help high-achieving students with financial need and provide them with educational opportunities throughout high school.

Eligibility: Applicants must have financial need, be in the 7th grade and plan to attend high school in the United States. Academic achievement and intelligence are important, and students must display strong academic records, academic awards and honors and submit a strong letter of recommendation. A GPA of 3.65 is usually required, but exceptions are made for students with unique talents or learning differences. The award is also based on students' will to succeed, leadership and public service, critical thinking ability and participation in the arts and humanities. During two summers, recipients must participate in a Young Scholars Week and Young Scholars Reunion in Washington, DC.

Target applicant(s): Junior high students or younger.

Minimum GPA: 3.65

Amount: Varies.

Number of awards: 60.

Scholarship may be renewable.

Deadline: March 22.

How to apply: Applications are available online and at regional talent centers. An application form, parental release, financial and tax forms, school report, teacher recommendation, personal recommendation and survey form are required.

Exclusive: Visit www.UltimateScholarshipBook.com and enter code JA39523 for updates on this award.

(396) · Zale Parry Scholarship

Academy of Underwater Arts and Sciences

27 West Anapamu Street #317, Santa Barbara, CA 93101

Phone: 919-369-0583

https://www.auas-nogi.org/scholarships

Purpose: To support students pursuing a career in ocean exploration, diving equipment technology, hyperbaric research or marine conservation.

Eligibility: Applicants must be enrolled in undergraduate or graduate level studies and must be a certified diver. Selection is based on merit.

Target applicant(s): College students. Graduate school students. Adult students.

Amount: $6,000.

Number of awards: Varies.

Deadline: August 31.

How to apply: Applications are available online and must include two letters of reference, a resume and an essay.

Exclusive: Visit www.UltimateScholarshipBook.com and enter code AC39623 for updates on this award.

(397) · Zen Bei Butoku Kai Scholarship

Zen Bei Butoku- Kai International

301 McCormick Avenue, Capitola, CA 95010

Email: senseilj@yahoo.com

http://zenbeibutokukai.com/index.php/scholarship/

Purpose: To aid students of the martial arts with college expenses.

Eligibility: Applicants must have studied a martial art for more than two years and currently be practicing. Selection is based on the merit of a required paper between 3,000 and 10,000 words describing how martial arts training has affected the applicant's personal growth.

Target applicant(s): College students. Adult students.

Amount: Varies.

Number of awards: Varies.

Deadline: Varies.

How to apply: Applicants must request scholarship funds via regular mail by providing name, address, purpose of funds and amount of funds requested. Applicants should also provide martial arts training history to include dates of training, instructor, style of martial arts, history of the martial art being studied and any letter of recommendation from instructors.

Exclusive: Visit www.UltimateScholarshipBook.com and enter code ZE39723 for updates on this award.

HUMANITIES / ARTS

(398) · ACES Copy Editing Scholarships

American Copy Editor's Society
Eugene S. Pulliam National Journalism Center, 3909 N. Meridian
Street, Indianapolis, IN 46208
Email: alex@copydesk.org
http://www.copydesk.org
Purpose: To support students who are interested in copy editing.
Eligibility: Applicants must be college juniors, seniors or graduate
students. Graduating students who will take full-time copy editing
jobs or internships are eligible. They must demonstrate interest in and
aptitude for copy editing.
Target applicant(s): College students. Graduate school students. Adult
students.
Amount: $1,500-$3,500.
Number of awards: 6.
Deadline: November 15.
How to apply: Applications are available online. An application form,
list of course work related to copy editing, list of copy editing experience,
two letters of recommendation, copies of 5 to 10 headlines written by
applicant and a copy of a story edited by applicant are required.
Exclusive: Visit www.UltimateScholarshipBook.com and enter code
AM39823 for updates on this award.

(399) · ACES Education Fund Scholarship

American Copy Editor's Society
Eugene S. Pulliam National Journalism Center, 3909 N. Meridian
Street, Indianapolis, IN 46208
Email: alex@copydesk.org
http://www.copydesk.org
Purpose: To support students pursuing a career in editing written
materials.
Eligibility: Applicants must be currently enrolled juniors, seniors or
graduate students seeking a degree at a college or university. Students
must provide an academic resume along with three references. Applicants
must write an original essay as well as sample headlines with the given
prompts.
Target applicant(s): College students. Graduate school students. Adult
students.
Amount: $1,500.
Number of awards: 4.
Deadline: November 15.
How to apply: Applications are available online.
Exclusive: Visit www.UltimateScholarshipBook.com and enter code
AM39923 for updates on this award.

(400) · ACL/NJCL National Greek Examination Scholarship

American Classical League
Scholarship Awards, 860 NW Washington Boulevard, Suite A,
Hamilton, OH 45013
Phone: 513-529-7741
Email: info@aclclassics.org
https://www.aclclassics.org/
Purpose: To support outstanding students of Greek.
Eligibility: Applicants must be high school seniors who have earned
purple or blue ribbons in the upper level National Greek Exam. They
must agree to earn six credits in Greek during their freshman year in
college.
Target applicant(s): High school students.
Amount: $2,000.
Number of awards: 1.
Deadline: Varies.
How to apply: Applications are sent to teachers of eligible students
by mail.
Exclusive: Visit www.UltimateScholarshipBook.com and enter code
AM40023 for updates on this award.

(401) · ACL/NJCL National Latin Examination Scholarships

American Classical League
Scholarship Awards, 860 NW Washington Boulevard, Suite A,
Hamilton, OH 45013
Phone: 513-529-7741
Email: info@aclclassics.org
https://www.aclclassics.org/
Purpose: To support outstanding students of Latin.
Eligibility: Applicants must be Latin students and gold medal winners in
the National Latin Exam Awards. They must also be high school seniors
and must agree to take at least one Latin or classical Greek course each
semester of their first year of college.
Target applicant(s): High school students.
Amount: $2,000.
Number of awards: Varies.
Scholarship may be renewable.
Deadline: Varies.
How to apply: Applications are mailed to NLE gold medal winners
who are high school seniors.
Exclusive: Visit www.UltimateScholarshipBook.com and enter code
AM40123 for updates on this award.

(402) · Actors Fund - Career Transition for Dancers Scholarship Program

Actors Fund - Career Transition for Dancers
729 Seventh Avenue, 10th Floor, New York, NY 10019
Phone: 212-221-7300
Email: pschwadron@actorsfund.org
http://www.actorsfund.org/services-and-programs/career-transition-dancers
Purpose: To provide educational grants for dancers seeking second
careers.
Eligibility: Applicants must provide documentation of 100 weeks or
more of paid employment as a dance performer in the U.S. over at
least seven years. For work not performed under union jurisdiction,
applicants must also provide documentation of total gross earnings of
at least $56,000. Choreographers and dance teachers are not eligible
for this program.
Target applicant(s): College students. Graduate school students. Adult
students.
Amount: $2,000.
Number of awards: Varies.
Deadline: June 15 and October 15.
How to apply: Applicants must call to confirm their eligibility.
Exclusive: Visit www.UltimateScholarshipBook.com and enter code
AC40223 for updates on this award.

(403) · Adobe Creativity Scholarships

Adobe
Institute of International Education, 530 Bush Street, Suite 1000, San Francisco, CA 94108
Phone: 415-362-6520
https://www.adobe.com/
Purpose: To support young people in pursuing a degree in a creative field.
Eligibility: Applicants must be Adobe Youth Voices alumni, Adobe Youth Voices award winners and finalists or Project 1324 Creative Challenge winners. Students must submit high school transcripts, portfolio of creative work and letters of reference. Selection is based on the overall strength of the application.
Target applicant(s): High school students. College students. Adult students.
Amount: Varies.
Number of awards: Varies.
Scholarship may be renewable.
Deadline: March.
How to apply: Applications are available online.
Exclusive: Visit www.UltimateScholarshipBook.com and enter code AD40323 for updates on this award.

(404) · AIGA Worldstudio Scholarships

AIGA, The Professional Association for Design
222 Broadway, 19th Floor, New York, NY 10038
Email: scholarship@aiga.org
https://www.aiga.org/worldstudio-scholarship
Purpose: To support art and design students who need financial assistance.
Eligibility: Applicants must be full-time undergraduate or graduate students in fine arts, graphic design, illustration, interactive design or photography. They must have a GPA of at least 2.0 and demonstrate financial need. Applicants must be U.S. citizens or permanent residents. Minority and economically disadvantaged students will be given special consideration.
Target applicant(s): High school students. College students. Graduate school students. Adult students.
Minimum GPA: 2.0
Amount: $500-$5,000.
Number of awards: 20.
Deadline: April.
How to apply: Applications are available online.
Exclusive: Visit www.UltimateScholarshipBook.com and enter code AI40423 for updates on this award.

(405) · Alexia Foundation Student Grants

Alexia Foundation
P.O. Box 87, Bloomingdale, NJ 07403
Phone: 631-354-4960
Email: grants@alexiafoundation.org
http://www.alexiafoundation.org/
Purpose: To support students in producing photojournalism projects that promote world peace and cultural understanding.
Eligibility: Applicants must be enrolled as full-time undergraduate or graduate students in an accredited college or university in the United States or abroad. Professional photographers are not eligible. Selection is based on photographic skill as well as the strength of the proposal.
Target applicant(s): College students. Graduate school students. Adult students.

Amount: Up to full tuition.
Number of awards: Varies.
Deadline: October.
How to apply: Application submission must be completed online. A synopsis, proposal, resume and digital portfolio are required.
Exclusive: Visit www.UltimateScholarshipBook.com and enter code AL40523 for updates on this award.

(406) · Alliance/ACT-SO Journey Award

Scholastic Art & Writing Awards
557 Broadway, New York, NY 10012
Email: info@artandwriting.org
http://www.artandwriting.org/scholarships/
Purpose: To offer financial support to eligible NAACP ACT-SO scholars to attend a residential summer immersion program for visual art or writing.
Eligibility: Applicants must be of African descent in grades 7-11 (ages 13 and up) who participate in the NAACP's Afro-Academic, Cultural, Technological and Scientific Olympics (ACT-SO). Students may apply in 28 categories of art and writing.
Target applicant(s): Junior high students or younger. High school students.
Amount: Varies.
Number of awards: 10.
Deadline: December 1.
How to apply: Applications are available online.
Exclusive: Visit www.UltimateScholarshipBook.com and enter code SC40623 for updates on this award.

(407) · AMCA Music Scholarship

Associated Male Choruses of America
Weldon Wilson, Scholarship Chair, 5143 S. 40th Street, St. Cloud, MN 56301
Phone: 320-260-1081
Email: scholarships@amcofa-sing.org
http://www.amcofa-sing.org/scholarships.html
Purpose: To promote the study of chorus and music studies in college.
Eligibility: Applicants must be full-time students obtaining their bachelor's degree in a music-related field (with preference given to voice or choral concentrations) and be sponsored by a chorus of the Associated Male Choruses of America. Applicants must submit references and a personal letter.
Target applicant(s): College students. Adult students.
Amount: $1,000-$1,200.
Number of awards: Varies.
Deadline: March 1.
How to apply: Applications are available online or by contacting your local AMCA chorus.
Exclusive: Visit www.UltimateScholarshipBook.com and enter code AS40723 for updates on this award.

(408) · Amy Lowell Poetry Travelling Scholarship

Choate, Hall and Stewart
Two International Place, Boston, MA 02110
Phone: 617-248-5253
Email: amylowell@choate.com
http://www.amylowell.org
Purpose: To support travel abroad for American-born poets.
Eligibility: Applicants should submit applications, curriculum vitae and poetry samples. Recipients should not accept another scholarship

during the scholarship year, must travel outside North America and should have three poems by the end of scholarship year.
Target applicant(s): High school students. College students. Graduate school students. Adult students.
Amount: $54,000.
Number of awards: 1-2.
Deadline: October 15.
How to apply: Applications are available online.
Exclusive: Visit www.UltimateScholarshipBook.com and enter code CH40823 for updates on this award.

(409) · Anthem Essay Contest

Ayn Rand Institute
6 Hutton Centre Drive, Suite 600, Santa Ana, CA 92707
Phone: 949-222-6550
Email: essays@aynrand.org
https://aynrand.org/students/essay-contests/
Purpose: To honor high school students who distinguish themselves in their understanding of Ayn Rand's novel "Anthem".
Eligibility: Applicants must be enrolled as an eighth, ninth, tenth, eleventh or twelfth grade student (ages 13-18) at some point during the year in which the contest is being held. Students are permitted to submit one entry per year. Essays should be written in English only and should be no fewer than 600 and no more than 1,200 words in length, double-spaced. Winning essays must demonstrate an outstanding grasp of the philosophic meaning of "Anthem".
Target applicant(s): Junior high students or younger. High school students.
Amount: Up to $2,000.
Number of awards: 9.
Deadline: April 28.
How to apply: Essay is required for the contest. There is no application.
Exclusive: Visit www.UltimateScholarshipBook.com and enter code AY40923 for updates on this award.

(410) · ASCAP Foundation Morton Gould Young Composer Awards

ASCAP Foundation
One Lincoln Plaza, New York, NY 10023
Phone: 212-621-6219
https://www.ascapfoundation.org/programs-and-grants
Purpose: To encourage young composers early in their careers.
Eligibility: Applicants must be composers who have not turned 30 before January 1 of the current year. They must be U.S. citizens or permanent residents or enrolled students with a student visa. Applicants must submit an original composition.
Target applicant(s): Junior high students or younger. High school students. College students. Graduate school students. Adult students.
Amount: Varies.
Number of awards: Varies.
Deadline: February 1.
How to apply: Applications are available online.
Exclusive: Visit www.UltimateScholarshipBook.com and enter code AS41023 for updates on this award.

(411) · Atlas Shrugged Essay Contest

Ayn Rand Institute
6 Hutton Centre Drive, Suite 600, Santa Ana, CA 92707
Phone: 949-222-6550

Email: essays@aynrand.org
https://aynrand.org/students/essay-contests/
Purpose: To honor students who distinguish themselves in their understanding of Ayn Rand's novel "Atlas Shrugged".
Eligibility: Applicants must be high school seniors, college undergraduates or graduate students who submit an 800-1,600-word essay which will be judged on both style and content with an emphasis on writing that is clear, articulate and logically organized. Winning essays must demonstrate an outstanding grasp of the philosophic meaning of "Atlas Shrugged".
Target applicant(s): High school students. College students. Graduate school students. Adult students.
Amount: Up to $10,000.
Number of awards: 9.
Deadline: September 26.
How to apply: Essay is required for the contest. There is no application.
Exclusive: Visit www.UltimateScholarshipBook.com and enter code AY41123 for updates on this award.

(412) · Babbel Language Scholarship

Babbel Inc.
285 Madison Avenue, 26th Floor, New York, NY 10017
Phone: 615-483-5128
Email: language.scholarship@babbel.com
https://www.babbel.com/language-scholarship
Purpose: To support students pursuing an undergraduate language degree.
Eligibility: Applicants must be students currently enrolled in a two- or four-year college program and are either actively studying or planning to study a Babbel language (Spanish, French, German, Italian, Portuguese, Dutch, Russian, Polish, Danish, Norwegian, Swedish, Turkish and Indonesian) at a college level. An essay submission on a provided prompt is required.
Target applicant(s): High school students. College students. Adult students.
Amount: $2,500.
Number of awards: 1.
Deadline: May 7.
How to apply: Applications are available online.
Exclusive: Visit www.UltimateScholarshipBook.com and enter code BA41223 for updates on this award.

(413) · Bill Gove Scholarship

National Speakers Association
Attn: Scholarship Committee, 1500 S. Priest Drive, Tempe, AZ 85281
Phone: 480-968-2552
Email: Jessica@NSAspeaker.org
http://www.nsaspeaker.org/recognition/
Purpose: To encourage study in the field of professional speaking.
Eligibility: Applicants must be full-time students majoring or minoring in speech. Selection is based on application, essay, recommendation and college transcript.
Target applicant(s): College students. Graduate school students. Adult students.
Amount: $5,000.
Number of awards: 1.
Deadline: April.
How to apply: Applications are available online or by written request.
Exclusive: Visit www.UltimateScholarshipBook.com and enter code NA41323 for updates on this award.

(414) · Bridging Scholarships for Study Abroad in Japan

American Association of Teachers of Japanese
Bridging Project Clearinghouse, Campus Box 366, 1424 Broadway, University of Colorado, Boulder, CO 80309-0366
Phone: 303-492-5487
Email: aatj@aatj.org
http://www.aatj.org/
Purpose: To assist students with travel and living expenses while studying in Japan.
Eligibility: Applicants must be undergraduates, U.S. citizens and be enrolled in a U.S. college. Study in Japan must be for at least three months and take place during the academic year (summer programs are not eligible). Students must submit a letter of recommendation and an essay on their interest in studying in Japan.
Target applicant(s): College students. Adult students.
Amount: $2,500-$4,000.
Number of awards: Varies.
Deadline: April 11, October 11.
How to apply: Applications are available online.
Exclusive: Visit www.UltimateScholarshipBook.com and enter code AM41423 for updates on this award.

(415) · CardsDirect Future Designer Scholarship

CardsDirect
12750 Merit Drove, Suite 900, Dallas, TX 75251
Phone: 866-700-5030
Email: scholarship@cardsdirect.com
https://www.cardsdirect.com/scholarship.aspx
Purpose: To support aspiring card designers.
Eligibility: Applicants must be at least 17 years old and accepted at or already enrolled in any accredited post-secondary institution as a full-time student. Students must submit an original design for a holiday card.
Target applicant(s): High school students. College students. Graduate school students. Adult students.
Amount: $2,000.
Number of awards: 1.
Scholarship may be renewable.
Deadline: November 1.
How to apply: Applications are available online.
Exclusive: Visit www.UltimateScholarshipBook.com and enter code CA41523 for updates on this award.

(416) · Career Center

Actors' Fund of America/The Career Center
729 Seventh Avenue, 10th Floor, New York, NY 10019
Phone: 800-221-7303
Email: info@actorsfund.org
http://www.actorsfund.org
Purpose: To assist members of the entertainment industry with finding sideline work and pursuing new careers.
Eligibility: Applicants must be members in good standing of an entertainment industry union and others who have earned $6,500 in each of three of the last five years or $5,000 in each of five of the last 10 years. Those who do not have earnings can substitute 12 weeks of documented industry work.
Target applicant(s): Junior high students or younger. High school students. College students. Graduate school students. Adult students.
Amount: Varies.
Number of awards: Varies.

Deadline: Varies.
How to apply: Applicants must attend an Actors' Work Program Orientation to learn more about the program.
Exclusive: Visit www.UltimateScholarshipBook.com and enter code AC41623 for updates on this award.

(417) · Carl A. Ross Student Paper Award

Appalachian Studies Association
Carl A. Ross Student Paper Award, Casey LaFrance, Chair of the Selection Committee, One John Marshall Drive, Huntington, WV 25755
Phone: 304-696-2904
Email: TC-Lafrance@wiu.edu
http://appalachianstudies.org/awards/
Purpose: To promote Appalachian studies.
Eligibility: Applicants must submit a 12- to 30-page research paper on an Appalachian studies topic. Selections will be made from two categories: middle/high school and undergraduate/graduate.
Target applicant(s): Junior high students or younger. High school students. College students. Graduate school students. Adult students.
Amount: $100.
Number of awards: 2.
Deadline: January 15.
How to apply: Submission of research paper is the application.
Exclusive: Visit www.UltimateScholarshipBook.com and enter code AP41723 for updates on this award.

(418) · Cavett Robert Scholarship

National Speakers Association
Attn: Scholarship Committee, 1500 S. Priest Drive, Tempe, AZ 85281
Phone: 480-968-2552
Email: Jessica@NSAspeaker.org
http://www.nsaspeaker.org/recognition/
Purpose: To encourage study in the field of professional speaking.
Eligibility: Applicants must be full-time students majoring or minoring in speech. Selection is based on application, essay, recommendation and college transcript.
Target applicant(s): College students. Graduate school students. Adult students.
Amount: Varies.
Number of awards: Varies.
Deadline: April.
How to apply: Applications are available online or by written request.
Exclusive: Visit www.UltimateScholarshipBook.com and enter code NA41823 for updates on this award.

(419) · Christopher L. Hunt Scholarship

Educational Theatre Association
4805 Montgomery Road, Suite 400, Cincinnati, OH 45212
Phone: 513-421-3900
Email: awards@schooltheatre.org
https://www.schooltheatre.org/programs/ags/scholarships
Purpose: To reward student achievement in theatre.
Eligibility: Applicants must be inducted Thespians who plan to use skills learned through theatre in a career focused on business or marketing.
Target applicant(s): College students. Graduate school students. Adult students.
Amount: $1,000.
Number of awards: 1.

Deadline: April 1.
How to apply: Applications are available online.
Exclusive: Visit www.UltimateScholarshipBook.com and enter code ED41923 for updates on this award.

---

(420) · Clauder Competition Prize

Portland Stage Company
Attn.: Literary Manager, P.O. Box 1458, Portland, ME 04104
Phone: 207-774-1043
Email: clauder@portlandstage.org
http://www.portlandstage.com
Purpose: To support playwrights.
Eligibility: Applicants must live or attend school in Connecticut, Maine, Massachusetts, New Hampshire, Rhode Island or Vermont. This requirement may be waived for playwrights who have previously lived in New England and produce material relevant to the area. They must submit a full-length play that is an original work and has not been produced or published.
Target applicant(s): High school students. College students. Graduate school students. Adult students.
Amount: Up to $3,000.
Number of awards: Varies.
Deadline: March 31.
How to apply: No application form is required.
Exclusive: Visit www.UltimateScholarshipBook.com and enter code PO42023 for updates on this award.

---

(421) · College Television Awards

Academy of Television Arts and Sciences Foundation
5220 Lankershim Boulevard, North Hollywood, CA 91601
Phone: 818-754-2800
Email: ctasupport@televisionacademy.com
http://www.emmys.org
Purpose: To reward college student film or video producers.
Eligibility: Applicants must produce an original film or video in one of the following categories: drama, comedy, music, documentary, news, magazine show, traditional or computer-generated animation, children's programming or commercials. Professionals may not be involved in the production of the piece, including producers, directors, camera operators, lighting or sound technicians and production managers. Applicants must also be full-time students who have produced their video for course credit at an American college or university during the current year.
Target applicant(s): College students. Graduate school students. Adult students.
Amount: Varies.
Number of awards: Varies.
Deadline: October 3.
How to apply: Applications are available online and are also sent to college film and television departments.
Exclusive: Visit www.UltimateScholarshipBook.com and enter code AC42123 for updates on this award.

---

(422) · Council on International Educational Exchange (CIEE) Scholarships

Council on International Educational Exchange
7 Custom House Street, 3rd Floor, Portland, ME 04101
Phone: 800-40-STUDY
Email: scholarships@ciee.org
http://www.ciee.org
Purpose: To make the study abroad program available to a wider audience and to provide assistance to CIEE Study Center (CSC) members who have demonstrated academic talent and financial need in order to study abroad.
Eligibility: Applicants must plan to participate in a CIEE study abroad program. Financial need is strongly considered along with other materials from the study abroad application. Other eligibility requirements vary according to the specific scholarship. If awarded a scholarship, applicants are required to submit a one-page essay on their experiences after returning.
Target applicant(s): College students. Adult students.
Amount: Up to $4,000.
Number of awards: Varies.
Deadline: April 1 and October 15.
How to apply: Applications are available online.
Exclusive: Visit www.UltimateScholarshipBook.com and enter code CO42223 for updates on this award.

---

(423) · Creative Arts/Design Scholarship

Foundation for Outdoor Advertising Research and Education (FOARE)
The Family Scholarship Endowment, c/o Thomas M. Smith & Associates, 4601 Tilden Street NW, Washington, DC 20016
Phone: 202-364-7130
Email: tmfsmith@rcn.com
http://oaaa.org/AboutOAAA/FOARE/FOAREScholarshipProgram.aspx
Purpose: To support students who are pursuing a degree in creative arts or design.
Eligibility: Applicants must be accepted for enrollment or enrolled at an accredited educational institution. Students must submit a design portfolio. Selection is primarily based on demonstration of financial need, career goals, academic achievement, community service and extracurricular involvement.
Target applicant(s): High school students. College students. Graduate school students. Adult students.
Amount: $3,000.
Number of awards: 1.
Deadline: June 16.
How to apply: Applications are available online.
Exclusive: Visit www.UltimateScholarshipBook.com and enter code FO42323 for updates on this award.

---

(424) · DAAD/AICGS Research Fellowship Program

American Institute for Contemporary German Studies - (AICGS)
1776 Massachusetts Avenue NW, Suite 600, Washington, DC 20036
Phone: 202-332-9312
Email: sdieper@aicgs.org
http://www.aicgs.org
Purpose: To bring scholars and specialists working on Germany, Europe and/or transatlantic relations to AICGS for research stays.
Eligibility: Applicants must have a Ph.D. or be enrolled in a Ph.D. program, hold German citizenship, be non-Germans who work/live permanently in Germany or work at one of the DAAD Centers around the globe. The grant provides a research stay of two-four months at AICGS.
Target applicant(s): Graduate school students. Adult students.
Amount: Up to $4,725 monthly stipend.
Number of awards: Varies.
Deadline: March 15, October 1.
How to apply: Apply via email to jwindell@aicgs.org.

Exclusive: Visit www.UltimateScholarshipBook.com and enter code AM42423 for updates on this award.

(425) · Disney/ABC Television Writing Program

Disney/ABC Television Group
Talent Development and Diversity, 500 South Buena Vista Street, Burbank, CA 91521-4016
Email: abcwritingfellowship@disney.com
http://www.abctalentdevelopment.com/writing_program.html
Purpose: To help writers develop skills for careers in television writing.
Eligibility: Applicants must be age 21 or older. They must be able to work in the U.S. legally. Professional writing experience is not necessary, but applicants must have strong spec script writing skills. Selection is based on the overall strength of the application.
Target applicant(s): College students. Graduate school students. Adult students.
Amount: $50,000.
Number of awards: Varies.
Deadline: June 30.
How to apply: Applications are available online. An application form and spec script samples are required.
Exclusive: Visit www.UltimateScholarshipBook.com and enter code DI42523 for updates on this award.

(426) · Doodle for Google

Google Doodle for Google
1600 Amphitheatre Parkway, Mountain View, CA 94043
Phone: 650-253-0000
Email: doodle4google-team@google.com
http://www.google.com/doodle4google
Purpose: To encourage creativity in United States school students through a logo contest.
Eligibility: Participants must be elementary or secondary school students in the 50 U.S. states or the District of Columbia who have registered for the contest. They must be U.S. residents who have obtained parental consent to enter. Employees, interns, contractors and office-holders of Google Inc. and their immediate families are not eligible.
Target applicant(s): Junior high students or younger. High school students.
Amount: Up to $30,000.
Number of awards: Varies.
Deadline: March 5.
How to apply: Applications are available from participating schools.
Exclusive: Visit www.UltimateScholarshipBook.com and enter code GO42623 for updates on this award.

(427) · Dr. Kenny D. Hasija Scholarship

Educational Theatre Association
4805 Montgomery Road, Suite 400, Cincinnati, OH 45212
Phone: 513-421-3900
Email: awards@schooltheatre.org
https://www.schooltheatre.org/programs/ags/scholarships
Purpose: To reward student achievement in theatre.
Eligibility: Applicants must be inducted members of the International Thespian Society (Thespians) who are graduating seniors or Thespian alumni who are pursuing undergraduate studies at an accredited college or university. Students must be planning on a career in any area of the theater, from performing to producing. Applicants must be from groups traditionally underrepresented in the theatre industry, such as those who are black, indigenous or people of color.

Target applicant(s): High school students. College students. Adult students.
Amount: $1,000.
Number of awards: 1.
Deadline: April 1.
How to apply: Applications are available online.
Exclusive: Visit www.UltimateScholarshipBook.com and enter code ED42723 for updates on this award.

(428) · Dr. Randy Pausch Scholarship Fund

Academy of Interactive Arts and Sciences (AIAS)
c/o Randy Pausch Scholarship, 9800 S. La Cienega Boulevard, 14th Floor, Inglewood, CA 90301
Phone: 310-484-2560
Email: gabriel@interactive.org
http://www.interactive.org
Purpose: To support students pursuing careers in game design, development and production.
Eligibility: Applicants must be full-time students who are currently enrolled in an accredited college or university at the undergraduate or graduate level. They must plan to enter the video game industry and have a GPA of 3.3 or higher. Selection is based on application, required documentation, service, leadership, character and financial need.
Target applicant(s): College students. Graduate school students. Adult students.
Minimum GPA: 3.3
Amount: $2,500.
Number of awards: 2.
Deadline: May 31.
How to apply: Applications are available online. An application form, verification of enrollment, personal statement, two letters of recommendation and transcript are required.
Exclusive: Visit www.UltimateScholarshipBook.com and enter code AC42823 for updates on this award.

(429) · Dumbarton Oaks Fellowships

Dumbarton Oaks
1703 32nd Street NW, Washington, DC 20007
Phone: 202-339-6413
Email: FellowshipPrograms@doaks.org
https://www.doaks.org/research/fellowships-and-awards
Purpose: To provide fellowships to scholars engaged in Byzantine studies, Pre-Columbian studies and garden and landscape studies.
Eligibility: Applicants must hold a doctorate (or appropriate final degree) or have established themselves in their field and wish to pursue their own research or expect to have the Ph.D. in hand prior to taking up residence at Dumbarton Oaks. The fellowships are in the following areas: Byzantine Studies (including related aspects of late Roman, early Christian, western medieval, Slavic and Near Eastern Studies), Pre-Columbian Studies (of Mexico, Central America and Andean South America) and garden and landscape studies. Fellowships are based on demonstrated scholarly ability and preparation (including knowledge of the required languages), interest and value of the study or project and its relevance to Dumbarton Oaks.
Target applicant(s): Graduate school students. Adult students.
Amount: Up to $35,000 plus allowance and health benefits.
Number of awards: Varies.
Deadline: November 1.
How to apply: Applicants must submit ten complete, collated sets of the application letter, proposal and personal and professional data. Applicants must also submit three recommendation letters.

Exclusive: Visit www.UltimateScholarshipBook.com and enter code DU42923 for updates on this award.

(430) · Educational Theatre Association Board of Directors Scholarship

Educational Theatre Association
4805 Montgomery Road, Suite 400, Cincinnati, OH 45212
Phone: 513-421-3900
Email: awards@schooltheatre.org
https://www.schooltheatre.org/programs/ags/scholarships
Purpose: To support student achievement in theatre.
Eligibility: Applicants must be undergraduate students currently enrolled full-time at an accredited college or university who are upcoming sophomores, juniors or seniors. Students must be alumni of the International Thespian Society and pursuing a career in theatre education.
Target applicant(s): College students. Adult students.
Amount: $1,000.
Number of awards: 1.
Deadline: April 1.
How to apply: Applications are available online.
Exclusive: Visit www.UltimateScholarshipBook.com and enter code ED43023 for updates on this award.

(431) · Educational Theatre Association Presidents' Leadership Scholarship

Educational Theatre Association
4805 Montgomery Road, Suite 400, Cincinnati, OH 45212
Phone: 513-421-3900
Email: awards@schooltheatre.org
https://www.schooltheatre.org/programs/ags/scholarships
Purpose: To reward student achievement in theatre.
Eligibility: Applicants must be inducted Thespians who successfully demonstrate leadership abilities.
Target applicant(s): College students. Graduate school students. Adult students.
Amount: $1,000.
Number of awards: 1.
Deadline: April 1.
How to apply: Applications are available online.
Exclusive: Visit www.UltimateScholarshipBook.com and enter code ED43123 for updates on this award.

(432) · Fashion Scholarship Fund Scholarships

Fashion Scholarship Fund
1501 Broadway, Suite 1810, New York, NY 10036
Phone: 212-278-0008
Email: hharrison@fashionscholarshipfund.org
http://www.ymafsf.org/
Purpose: To support students attending FSF member schools across the United States.
Eligibility: Applicants must attend Fashion Scholarship Fund member schools and universities and have a demonstrated interest in fashion. Applicants must also be enrolled as full-time, current college sophomores, juniors or seniors with an overall GPA of 3.0 or above. Selection is based on merit with consideration given to GPA, the quality of a case study project, job experience, community service, personal essay and interview.
Target applicant(s): College students. Adult students.

Minimum GPA: 3.0
Amount: $5,000.
Number of awards: About 100.
Deadline: October 18.
How to apply: Applications are available online. Application, case study project, transcript, personal essay and interview are required.
Exclusive: Visit www.UltimateScholarshipBook.com and enter code FA43223 for updates on this award.

(433) · Federal Junior Duck Stamp Program and Scholarship Competition

U.S. Fish and Wildlife Service Headquarters
Junior Duck Stamp Program, 5275 Leesburg Pike, MS: MB, Falls Church, VA 22041-3803
Phone: 703-358-1714
Email: Suzanne_Fellows@fws.gov
http://www.fws.gov/juniorduck
Purpose: To encourage students to paint waterfowl and learn about the importance of habitat and wildlife conservation.
Eligibility: Applicants must be in kindergarten to 12th grade and submit their artwork to their state or local department. Students must be U.S. citizens, resident aliens or nationals. The first place national winner has their art made into the next Federal Junior Duck Stamp and travels with a parent to the next First Day of Sale event for their stamp.
Target applicant(s): Junior high students or younger. High school students.
Amount: Varies.
Number of awards: Varies.
Deadline: March 15.
How to apply: Applications are available online.
Exclusive: Visit www.UltimateScholarshipBook.com and enter code U.43323 for updates on this award.

(434) · Feldco Windows, Siding and Doors Scholarship

Feldco
9932 South Western Avenue, Chicago, IL 60643
Phone: 708-437-4133
Email: scholarship@4feldco.com
http://www.4feldco.com/scholarship
Purpose: To support students working towards a college education.
Eligibility: Applicants must be U.S. citizens and current high school seniors or undergraduate college students. Students must write an essay on an assigned topic given on the scholarship webpage.
Target applicant(s): High school students. College students. Adult students.
Amount: $1,000.
Number of awards: 1.
Deadline: December 15.
How to apply: Applications are available online.
Exclusive: Visit www.UltimateScholarshipBook.com and enter code FE43423 for updates on this award.

(435) · Fellowships for Regular Program in Greece

American School of Classical Studies at Athens
321 Wall Street, Princeton, NJ 08540
Phone: 609-683-0800
Email: ascsa@ascsa.org
https://www.ascsa.edu.gr/programs/regular-member-program

Purpose: The institution is devoted to allowing advanced graduate students enrolled in North American colleges and institutions to study the classics and related fields of language, literature, art, history, archaeology and philosophy of Greece and the Greek world.
Eligibility: Applicants must have completed at least one to two years of graduate study and must take exams in ancient Greek language, history and either literature or art and archaeology. Students must be able to read French, German, ancient Greek and Latin with an ability to also read modern Greek and Italian considered helpful. Applicants must be graduate students who are preparing for an advanced degree in classical and ancient Mediterranean studies or a related field. The fellowships provide study in Athens or Greece for nine months and may not be used for costs at the student's home institution.
Target applicant(s): Graduate school students. Adult students.
Amount: $11,500 plus housing, board and fees.
Number of awards: Up to 12.
Deadline: January 15.
How to apply: Applications are available online.
Exclusive: Visit www.UltimateScholarshipBook.com and enter code AM43523 for updates on this award.

(436) · Fellowships/Grants to Study in Scandinavia
American-Scandinavian Foundation
58 Park Avenue, New York, NY 10016
Phone: 212-779-3587
Email: info@amscan.org
http://www.amscan.org
Purpose: To encourage research projects related to Scandinavia.
Eligibility: Applicant must be a United States citizen or permanent resident who has completed their undergraduate education by the start of their project in Scandinavia. Applicant must have a well-defined research or study project that makes a stay in Scandinavia essential and should have some ability in the language of the host country. First priority will be given to an applicant who has not previously received an ASF award.
Target applicant(s): College students. Graduate school students. Adult students.
Amount: $5,000-$23,000.
Number of awards: Varies.
Scholarship may be renewable.
Deadline: November 1.
How to apply: Applications are available online and by written request.
Exclusive: Visit www.UltimateScholarshipBook.com and enter code AM43623 for updates on this award.

(437) · FFTA Scholarship Competition
Flexographic Technical Association
900 Marconi Avenue, Ronkonkoma, NY 11779
Phone: 631-737-6020
Email: education@flexography.org
https://www.flexography.org/honors-awards/scholarships/
Purpose: To advance the state of the flexographic industry.
Eligibility: Applicants must demonstrate interest in a career in flexography and must be high school seniors with plans to attend a post-secondary institution or be presently enrolled at a post-secondary institution offering a course of study in flexography. Applicants must exhibit exemplary performance in their studies, particularly in the area of graphic communications and must have a minimum 3.0 GPA.
Target applicant(s): High school students. College students. Adult students.
Minimum GPA: 3.0
Amount: $3,000.

Number of awards: Varies.
Scholarship may be renewable.
Deadline: March.
How to apply: Applications are available online.
Exclusive: Visit www.UltimateScholarshipBook.com and enter code FL43723 for updates on this award.

(438) · Finlandia Foundation National Student Scholarships Program
Finlandia Foundation
470 W. Walnut Street, Pasadena, CA 91103
Phone: 626-795-2081
Email: ffnoffice@mac.com
https://finlandiafoundation.org/programs/scholarships/
Purpose: To support undergraduate and graduate students in Finland and the United States for conducting studies or research related to Finnish culture and society.
Eligibility: Applicants must be full-time undergraduate or graduate students enrolled in a college or university in the U.S. or Finland and must plan research on Finnish culture in the U.S. They must be studying at the sophomore level or higher and have a minimum GPA of 3.0. Financial need, course of study and citizenship are considered in evaluating applications. Students may not receive funds for two consecutive years.
Target applicant(s): High school students. College students. Graduate school students. Adult students.
Minimum GPA: 3.0
Amount: $1,000-$3,000.
Number of awards: Varies.
Deadline: February 1.
How to apply: Applications are available online. Application form and cover letter are required.
Exclusive: Visit www.UltimateScholarshipBook.com and enter code FI43823 for updates on this award.

(439) · Florida Thespians College Scholarship
Florida Thespians
Lindsay Warfield, Director, Steinbrenner High School, 5575 W Lutz Lake Fern Road, Lutz, FL 33558
https://floridathespians.com/
Purpose: To support young thespians who have actively participated at the district level and are qualified to attend the state competition.
Eligibility: Applicants must be members of the International Thespian Society and seriously plan to pursue theatre as a career. They must be high school juniors or seniors who are declared theatre majors or are registered for theatre classes. Applicants must have a minimum 3.0 GPA. Seniors must have an SAT combined score of 1800 or greater or an ACT score of 26 or greater. Junior applicants must have received an Excellent or Superior in any individual events at the district level. Applicants must audition for the awards. Awards are given in three theatre-related areas including acting, musical theatre and design/technical management. Applicants must be approved by their Thespian Troupe director to apply. An additional bonus is available for those who choose to attend college in Florida. Selection is based on the overall strength of the application and audition.
Target applicant(s): High school students.
Minimum GPA: 3.0
Amount: $750.
Number of awards: 10.
Deadline: March.

How to apply: Applications are available online for troupe directors only. Application and audition are required.

Exclusive: Visit www.UltimateScholarshipBook.com and enter code FL43923 for updates on this award.

(440) · Frame My Future Scholarship Contest

Church Hill Classics
594 Pepper Street, Monroe, CT 06468
Phone: 800-477-9005
Email: info@diplomaframe.com
https://www.diplomaframe.com/contests/frame-my-future-scholarship.aspx

Purpose: To help success-driven students attain their higher education goals.

Eligibility: Applicants must be high school seniors or current college students who plan to enroll full-time for the following academic year. Students must be residents of the United States, including APO/FPO addresses but excluding Puerto Rico. Employees of Church Hill Classics and affiliated companies, their family members and individuals living in the same household are not eligible.

Target applicant(s): High school students. College students. Graduate school students. Adult students.

Amount: $500-$6,000.

Number of awards: 4.

Deadline: April 1.

How to apply: Applications must be submitted online. An entry form and original piece of artwork are required.

Exclusive: Visit www.UltimateScholarshipBook.com and enter code CH44023 for updates on this award.

(441) · Gilman International Scholarship

Institute of International Education Gilman Scholarship Program
1800 West Loop South, Suite 250, Houston, TX 77027
Phone: 832-369-3484
Email: gilman@iie.org
https://www.gilmanscholarship.org/

Purpose: To support students with financial need who are planning to study abroad.

Eligibility: Students must be recipients of a Pell Grant. They must be currently attending a two-year or four-year college in the United States. Recipients must study abroad for at least four weeks in any country excluding Cuba and the countries on the Travel Warning list.

Target applicant(s): High school students. College students. Adult students.

Amount: Up to $5,000.

Number of awards: Over 2,900.

Deadline: April 15, August 1, October 15.

How to apply: Applications are available online.

Exclusive: Visit www.UltimateScholarshipBook.com and enter code IN44123 for updates on this award.

(442) · Girls Impact the World Film Festival

Harvard College Social Innovation Collaborative (SIC)
Connecther, 12301 Zeller Lane, Austin, TX 78753
Email: filmfest@connecther.org
https://connectherfilmfest.org/

Purpose: To support high school and undergraduate college students in bringing awareness to global women's issues through a film contest.

Eligibility: Applicants must be current high school or undergraduate college students 25 years of age or under and must not be a resident of Cuba, Iran, North Korea, Sudan or Syria. Applicants must create three- to five-minute short films that either raise awareness about current global issues affecting women or propose solutions to such challenges. Selection is based upon the overall strength of the film.

Target applicant(s): High school students. College students.

Amount: Varies.

Number of awards: Varies.

Deadline: June 1.

How to apply: Film submissions should be made online. A submission form, short film and proof of enrollment are required.

Exclusive: Visit www.UltimateScholarshipBook.com and enter code HA44223 for updates on this award.

(443) · Glenn Miller Scholarship Competition

Glenn Miller Birthplace Society
107 East Main Street, P.O. Box 61, Clarinda, IA 51632
Phone: 712-542-2461
Email: gmbs@heartland.net
http://glennmiller.org

Purpose: To honor Glenn Miller by recognizing future musical leaders.

Eligibility: Applicants may apply as instrumentalists or vocalists. They must be high school seniors or college freshmen who plan to focus on music in their future lives. Applicants must submit an audition file in addition to an application form. High school seniors may reapply as college freshmen as long as they weren't first-place winners the previous year.

Target applicant(s): High school students. College students. Adult students.

Amount: $1,000-$3,000.

Number of awards: 6.

Deadline: March.

How to apply: Applications are available online.

Exclusive: Visit www.UltimateScholarshipBook.com and enter code GL44323 for updates on this award.

(444) · Heinlein Society Scholarship Program

Heinlein Society
3553 Atlantic Avenue, Suite 341, Long Beach, CA 90807-5606
Email: scholarships@heinleinsociety.org
http://www.heinleinsociety.org/scholarship-program/

Purpose: To reward students who are attending a four-year college.

Eligibility: Applicants must be full-time undergraduate students at an accredited college. One scholarship is awarded to a woman majoring in engineering, math or physical sciences (physics/chemistry). Two scholarships are awarded to male or female students majoring in engineering, math or biological or physical sciences as well as science fiction as literature. Students must submit a 500- to 1,000-word essay on one of the topics listed on the website.

Target applicant(s): High school students. College students. Adult students.

Amount: $3,000.

Number of awards: 3.

Deadline: April 1.

How to apply: Applications are available online and must be submitted with a brief bio including future goals and the required essay.

Exclusive: Visit www.UltimateScholarshipBook.com and enter code HE44423 for updates on this award.

(445) · Henry Luce Foundation/ACLS Dissertation Fellowships in American Art

American Council of Learned Societies (ACLS)
633 Third Avenue, New York, NY 10017-6795
Phone: 212-697-1505
Email: mgoldfeder@acls.org
https://www.acls.org/
Purpose: To support Ph.D. candidates working on art history dissertations.
Eligibility: Applicants must be Ph.D. candidates in an art history department in the U.S. who are working on dissertations about American visual arts history. All the Ph.D. requirements should be met except the dissertation before taking the fellowship. Applicants should submit an application, a proposal, a bibliography, illustrations (optional), a publications list (optional), three reference letters and an official transcript of graduate record. The fellowship lasts for a year.
Target applicant(s): Graduate school students. Adult students.
Amount: $30,000 plus up to $4,000 travel allowance.
Number of awards: Varies.
Deadline: October.
How to apply: Applications are available online.
Exclusive: Visit www.UltimateScholarshipBook.com and enter code AM44523 for updates on this award.

(446) · Herb Alpert Young Jazz Composer Awards

ASCAP Foundation
One Lincoln Plaza, New York, NY 10023
Phone: 212-621-6219
https://www.ascapfoundation.org/programs-and-grants
Purpose: To recognize the talent of young jazz composers.
Eligibility: Applicants must be under the age of 30 and U.S. citizens or permanent residents. They must submit one original composition, including a score and performance, if possible.
Target applicant(s): Junior high students or younger. High school students. College students. Graduate school students. Adult students.
Amount: Varies.
Number of awards: Varies.
Deadline: December 15.
How to apply: Applications are available online.
Exclusive: Visit www.UltimateScholarshipBook.com and enter code AS44623 for updates on this award.

(447) · Herblock Award for Editorial Cartoon

Scholastic Art & Writing Awards
557 Broadway, New York, NY 10012
Email: info@artandwriting.org
http://www.artandwriting.org/scholarships/
Purpose: To support students whose visual art offers commentary or criticism on current events, social events or political topics.
Eligibility: Applicants must be in grades 7-12 (ages 13 and up) and enter visual art offering commentary or criticism on current events, social events or political topics. Submissions can be drawings, illustrations, a series of artworks or animated short films.
Target applicant(s): Junior high students or younger. High school students.
Amount: $1,000.
Number of awards: 3.
Deadline: December 1.
How to apply: Applications are available online.

Exclusive: Visit www.UltimateScholarshipBook.com and enter code SC44723 for updates on this award.

(448) · IACI/NUI Visiting Fellowship in Irish Studies

Irish-American Cultural Institute (IACI)
An Foras Cultuir Gael-Mheircheanach, 1 Lackawanna Place, Morristown, NJ 07960
Phone: 973-605-1991
Email: info@iaci-usa.org
http://www.iaci-usa.org
Purpose: To award fellowships to Irish studies scholars to spend one semester at the University of Ireland-Galway.
Eligibility: Applicants must provide a description of how the fellowship will be used and a curriculum vitae with a list of publications.
Target applicant(s): Graduate school students. Adult students.
Amount: $4,000.
Number of awards: Varies.
Deadline: December 31.
How to apply: Application is available online.
Exclusive: Visit www.UltimateScholarshipBook.com and enter code IR44823 for updates on this award.

(449) · IDSA Undergraduate Scholarships

Industrial Designers Society of America
555 Grove Street, Suite 200, Herndon, VA 20170
Phone: 703-707-6000
Email: idsa@idsa.org
http://www.idsa.org
Purpose: To help industrial design students in their final year of schooling.
Eligibility: Applicants must be full-time students enrolled in an IDSA-listed program in their next-to-last year of the program, have a minimum 3.0 GPA, be members of an IDSA Student Chapter and be U.S. citizens or residents. Applicants must submit a letter of intent, 20 visual examples of their work and a transcript. Awards are based solely on the excellence of the submitted works.
Target applicant(s): College students. Adult students.
Minimum GPA: 3.0
Amount: $1,500.
Number of awards: 1.
Deadline: May.
How to apply: Applications are available online.
Exclusive: Visit www.UltimateScholarshipBook.com and enter code IN44923 for updates on this award.

(450) · IFDA Leaders Commemorative Scholarship

International Furnishings and Design Association (IFDA)
36 Bay View Road, Wellesley, MA 02482
Phone: 781-894-3240
Email: linda@westonstudiodesign.com
https://ifda.com/educational-foundation/
Purpose: To aid interior design students.
Eligibility: Applicants must be full-time undergraduate students at an accredited U.S. postsecondary institution. They must be majoring in interior design or a closely-related design subject and have completed four design courses at the time of application. Preference will be given to students who demonstrate leadership and volunteer experience. Selection is based on the overall strength of the application.
Target applicant(s): College students. Adult students.
Amount: $1,500.

Number of awards: 1.
Deadline: March 30.
How to apply: Applications are available online. An application form, personal essay, one recommendation letter and design work examples are required.
Exclusive: Visit www.UltimateScholarshipBook.com and enter code IN45023 for updates on this award.

---

(451) · IFDA Student Member Scholarship

International Furnishings and Design Association (IFDA)
36 Bay View Road, Wellesley, MA 02482
Phone: 781-894-3240
Email: linda@westonstudiodesign.com
https://ifda.com/educational-foundation/
Purpose: To aid interior design students who are members of the International Furnishings and Design Association (IFDA).
Eligibility: Applicants must be full-time undergraduate students who are attending an accredited U.S. postsecondary institution. They must be majoring in interior design or a closely-related design subject and have completed a minimum of four design courses. Selection is based on the overall strength of the application.
Target applicant(s): College students. Adult students.
Amount: $2,000.
Number of awards: 1.
Deadline: March 30.
How to apply: Applications are available online. An application form, personal statement, two recommendation letters and design work examples are required.
Exclusive: Visit www.UltimateScholarshipBook.com and enter code IN45123 for updates on this award.

---

(452) · ILA Jeanne S. Chall Research Fellowship

International Literacy Association
The Jeanne S. Chall Research Fellowship, Division of Research and Policy, P.O. Box 8139, Newark, DE 19714-8139
Phone: 302-731-1600
Email: research@reading.org
https://www.literacyworldwide.org/about-us/awards-grants
Purpose: To support dissertation research in reading.
Eligibility: Applicants must be doctoral students planning or beginning their dissertation on one of the following topics in the field of reading: beginning reading, readability, reading difficulty, stages of reading development, the relation of vocabulary to reading and diagnosing and teaching adults with limited reading ability. Applicants must also be members of the International Literacy Association.
Target applicant(s): Graduate school students. Adult students.
Amount: $5,000.
Number of awards: 1.
Deadline: March 15.
How to apply: Applications are available online.
Exclusive: Visit www.UltimateScholarshipBook.com and enter code IN45223 for updates on this award.

---

(453) · Illustrators of the Future

L. Ron Hubbard's Writers of the Future Contest
7051 Hollywood Boulevard, Los Angeles, CA 90028
Phone: 323-466-3310
Email: contests@authorservicesinc.com
http://www.writersofthefuture.com
Purpose: To discover deserving amateur aspiring illustrators.

Eligibility: Applicants must not have published more than three black-and-white story illustrations or more than one color painting in national media. Applicants must also submit three original illustrations done in either color or black-and-white medium in three different themes.
Target applicant(s): High school students. College students. Graduate school students. Adult students.
Amount: $1,500-$5,000.
Number of awards: 3 each quarter and a grand prize awarded annually.
Deadline: December 31, March 31, June 30, September 30.
How to apply: There is no application form.
Exclusive: Visit www.UltimateScholarshipBook.com and enter code L.45323 for updates on this award.

---

(454) · International Junior Competition

Gina Bachauer International Piano Foundation
138 W. 300 S, Salt Lake City, UT 84101
Phone: 801-297-4250
Email: info@bachauer.com
https://www.bachauer.com/competitions/
Purpose: To reward top piano prodigies, ages 11 to 18.
Eligibility: Applicants must perform at this competition in Salt Lake City, Utah. Students are provided with housing but must provide own transportation to and from Salt Lake City. Applicants must perform a 20-minute program of solo music and a 30-minute program of solo music. Two competition categories available: ages 11 to 14 and ages 15 to 18.
Target applicant(s): Junior high students or younger. High school students.
Amount: Up to $7,000.
Number of awards: 6.
Deadline: September 15.
How to apply: Applications are available online.
Exclusive: Visit www.UltimateScholarshipBook.com and enter code GI45423 for updates on this award.

---

(455) · International Scholarships

American Institute for Foreign Study
College Division, 1 High Ridge Park, Stamford, CT 06905
Phone: 800-727-2437
Email: studyabroad@aifs.com
https://www.aifsabroad.com/scholarships.asp
Purpose: To promote international understanding through study abroad.
Eligibility: Applicants must be currently enrolled college undergraduates with a minimum 3.0 GPA who show leadership potential and are involved in extra-curricular activities centered on multicultural or international issues. Applicants must submit a 1,000-word essay on how study abroad will change their lives.
Target applicant(s): College students. Adult students.
Minimum GPA: 3.0
Amount: $500-$1,000.
Number of awards: Varies.
Deadline: April 15 for fall semester, October 1 for spring semester and March 1 for summer.
How to apply: Applications are available online.
Exclusive: Visit www.UltimateScholarshipBook.com and enter code AM45523 for updates on this award.

(456) · International Trumpet Guild Conference Scholarship

International Trumpet Guild
P.O. Box 2688, Davenport, IA 52809-2688
Email: confscholarships@trumpetguild.org
http://www.trumpetguild.org
Purpose: To improve the artistic level of trumpet players.
Eligibility: Applicants must be students and record audition songs. There are different age group categories, and each category has its own performance requirements. Applicants must be ITG members.
Target applicant(s): Junior high students or younger. High school students. College students. Graduate school students.
Amount: Varies.
Number of awards: Varies.
Deadline: February 1.
How to apply: Applications are available online.
Exclusive: Visit www.UltimateScholarshipBook.com and enter code IN45623 for updates on this award.

(457) · ItaliaRail Study Abroad in Italy Scholarship

ItaliaRail
201 Somerville Avenue, 2nd Floor, Somerville, MA 02143
Phone: 877-375-7245
https://www.italiarail.com/scholarship
Purpose: To support undergraduate students in studying abroad in Italy.
Eligibility: Applicants must have enrolled in their college or university's study abroad program in Italy. Students must submit college transcripts, FAFSA Student Aid Report, a resume and an essay explaining why they want to study abroad in Italy. Selection is based on the overall strength of the application.
Target applicant(s): College students. Adult students.
Amount: $1,000.
Number of awards: 2.
Deadline: November 15.
How to apply: Applications are available online.
Exclusive: Visit www.UltimateScholarshipBook.com and enter code IT45723 for updates on this award.

(458) · Jack Kent Cooke Young Artist Award

From the Top
295 Huntington Avenue, Suite 201, Boston, MA 02115
Phone: 617-437-0707
https://www.fromthetop.org/apply/
Purpose: To reward classical instrumentalists, vocalists and composers who have not yet entered college for extraordinary musical accomplishment.
Eligibility: Applicants must have interest in performing on NPR's "From the Top". Selection is primarily based on demonstration of strong musical ability, unmet financial need and strength of character.
Target applicant(s): High school students.
Amount: Up to $10,000.
Number of awards: 20.
Deadline: January 4, March 15.
How to apply: Applications are available online.
Exclusive: Visit www.UltimateScholarshipBook.com and enter code FR45823 for updates on this award.

(459) · Jaime Guttenberg Dance Scholarship

Orange Ribbons for Jaime
5944 Coral Ridge Drive, Suite 301, Coral Springs, FL 33076
Phone: 561-750-1500
Email: info@orangeribbonsforjaime.org
https://orangeribbonsforjaime.org/
Purpose: To support students with a focus on a career in dance.
Eligibility: Applicants must be applying to a traditional four-year university or performing arts specialty program with a focus on a career in dance. Students must have a minimum of three years in dance classes during high school and a background in community service/volunteerism during high school with a minimum of 100 hours of service. Applicants must have a minimum 3.5 GPA and submit an essay on a provided topic.
Target applicant(s): High school students.
Minimum GPA: 3.5
Amount: Varies.
Number of awards: Varies.
Deadline: March.
How to apply: Applications are available online.
Exclusive: Visit www.UltimateScholarshipBook.com and enter code OR45923 for updates on this award.

(460) · Joel Polsky Academic Achievement Award

American Society of Interior Designers (ASID) Educational Foundation Inc.
608 Massachusetts Avenue NE, Washington, DC 20002-6006
Phone: 202-546-3480
https://www.asid.org/resources/awards/scholarships-and-grants
Purpose: To recognize an interior design student's project.
Eligibility: Applicants must be undergraduate or graduate students in interior design and should submit entry forms and projects such as research papers or doctoral and master's theses that focus on interior design topics. The projects are judged on content, breadth of material, coverage of the topic, innovative subject matter, bibliography and references. The society may exhibit any entry for two years.
Target applicant(s): High school students. College students. Graduate school students. Adult students.
Amount: $5,000.
Number of awards: 1.
Deadline: April.
How to apply: Applications are available online.
Exclusive: Visit www.UltimateScholarshipBook.com and enter code AM46023 for updates on this award.

(461) · John F. and Anna Lee Stacey Scholarship Fund for Art Education

John F. and Anna Lee Stacey Scholarship Fund
1700 NE 63rd Street, Oklahoma City, OK 73111
Phone: 405-478-2250
Email: scholarship@nationalcowboymuseum.org
http://www.nationalcowboymuseum.org/education/staceyfund/
Purpose: To educate young men and women who aim to enter the art profession.
Eligibility: Applicants must be U.S. citizens between the ages of 18 and 35 who aim to make fine art their profession. The online application process will ask the applicant to outline their ambitions and plans and to upload no more than 6 examples of their paintings/drawings for judging. Letters of recommendation will be requested of finalists.

Target applicant(s): High school students. College students. Graduate school students. Adult students.
Amount: Up to $5,000.
Number of awards: Varies.
Deadline: February 1.
How to apply: Applications are available online.
Exclusive: Visit www.UltimateScholarshipBook.com and enter code JO46123 for updates on this award.

---

(462) · John Lennon Scholarship Competition

BMI Foundation Inc.
7 World Trade Center, 250 Greenwich Street, New York, NY 10007
Phone: 212-586-2000
Email: info@bmifoundation.org
http://www.bmifoundation.org
Purpose: Established in 1997 by Yoko Ono in conjunction with the BMI Foundation, the John Lennon Scholarship recognizes the talent of young songwriters.
Eligibility: Applicants must be age 17 to 24 and write an original song to be reviewed by a prestigious panel of judges. Entries are to be submitted by music schools, universities, youth orchestras and the Music Educators National Conference (MENC).
Target applicant(s): College students. Graduate school students.
Amount: Up to $20,000.
Number of awards: 3.
Deadline: April.
How to apply: Please see the website for a full list of eligible organizations that may submit entries.
Exclusive: Visit www.UltimateScholarshipBook.com and enter code BM46223 for updates on this award.

---

(463) · John O. Crane Memorial Fellowship

Institute of Current World Affairs
1779 Massachusetts Avenue NW, Suite 605, Washington, DC 20036
Phone: 202-364-4068
Email: apply@icwa.org
http://www.icwa.org
Purpose: To promote independent study abroad in Eastern Europe and the Middle East.
Eligibility: Applicants must be under the age of 36 and must have strong, credible ties to American society. They must propose an independent research project that would be conducted in Eastern Europe or the Middle East and be proficient in a native language that is commonly spoken in the proposed research site. Selection is based on the overall strength of the application.
Target applicant(s): Graduate school students. Adult students.
Amount: Full financial support.
Number of awards: Varies.
Deadline: December.
How to apply: Application instructions are available online. A letter of interest and resume are required for the initial phase of the application process by August 1.
Exclusive: Visit www.UltimateScholarshipBook.com and enter code IN46323 for updates on this award.

---

(464) · Julius and Esther Stulberg International String Competition

Julius and Esther Stulberg Competition Inc.
359 South Kalamazoo Mall, Suite 14, Kalamazoo, MI 49007
http://www.stulberg.org

Purpose: To support young instrumentalists.
Eligibility: Applicants must be students of violin, viola, cello or double bass, be 19 years of age or younger as of January 1 of the year of competition and perform a Bach piece and a solo for the competition, which is typically held in May.
Target applicant(s): Junior high students or younger. High school students.
Amount: Up to $6,000.
Number of awards: 5.
Deadline: February 1.
How to apply: Applications are available online. An application form, proof of age and audition CD are required.
Exclusive: Visit www.UltimateScholarshipBook.com and enter code JU46423 for updates on this award.

---

(465) · Junior Fellowships

Dumbarton Oaks
1703 32nd Street NW, Washington, DC 20007
Phone: 202-339-6413
Email: FellowshipPrograms@doaks.org
https://www.doaks.org/research/fellowships-and-awards
Purpose: To provide fellowships to scholars engaged in Byzantine studies, Pre-Columbian studies and garden and landscape studies.
Eligibility: Applicants at the time of application should have fulfilled all preliminary requirements for a Ph.D. and be willing to work on a dissertation or final project at Dumbarton Oaks under the direction of a faculty member at their own university. The fellowships are in the following areas: Byzantine Studies (including related aspects of late Roman, early Christian, western medieval, Slavic and Near Eastern Studies), Pre-Columbian Studies (of Mexico, Central America and Andean South America) and garden and landscape studies. Fellowships are based on demonstrated scholarly ability and preparation of the candidate (including knowledge of the required languages) and value of the study or project and its relevance to Dumbarton Oaks.
Target applicant(s): Graduate school students. Adult students.
Amount: Up to $21,000.
Number of awards: Varies.
Deadline: November 1.
How to apply: Applicants must submit ten complete, collated sets of: application letter, proposal and personal and professional data. They must also submit an official transcript and three recommendation letters, with one from the faculty advisor.
Exclusive: Visit www.UltimateScholarshipBook.com and enter code DU46523 for updates on this award.

---

(466) · Language Grants

Blakemore Foundation
701 Fifth Avenue, Suite 4200, Seattle, WA 98104
Phone: 206-427-4838
Email: contactus@blakemorefoundation.org
http://www.blakemorefoundation.org
Purpose: To support students pursuing a professional, business, technical or academic career that involves the regular use of Chinese, Japanese, Korean, Thai, Vietnamese, Indonesian, Khmer or Burmese.
Eligibility: Applicants must be U.S. citizens or permanent residents of the United States at or near an advanced level in one of the languages listed above, having completed (at minimum) the equivalent of third-year college-level language classes. Students must have received (at minimum) a bachelor's degree.
Target applicant(s): College students. Graduate school students. Adult students.

Amount: Varies.
Number of awards: Varies.
Deadline: December 30.
How to apply: Applications are available online.
Exclusive: Visit www.UltimateScholarshipBook.com and enter code BL46623 for updates on this award.

(467) · Legacy Scholarship for Undergraduates

American Society of Interior Designers (ASID) Educational Foundation Inc.
608 Massachusetts Avenue NE, Washington, DC 20002-6006
Phone: 202-546-3480
https://www.asid.org/resources/awards/scholarships-and-grants
Purpose: To support undergraduate students who are pursuing a degree in interior design.
Eligibility: Applicants must be enrolled in their junior or senior year of undergraduate study. Selection is primarily based on demonstration of academic performance and creative achievement. Students must submit a design portfolio, official transcripts, a letter of recommendation and a personal statement.
Target applicant(s): College students. Adult students.
Amount: $4,000.
Number of awards: 1.
Deadline: April 21.
How to apply: Applications are available online.
Exclusive: Visit www.UltimateScholarshipBook.com and enter code AM46723 for updates on this award.

(468) · Leif and Inger Sjoberg Award

American-Scandinavian Foundation
58 Park Avenue, New York, NY 10016
Phone: 212-779-3587
Email: info@amscan.org
http://www.amscan.org
Purpose: To encourage the English translation of Scandinavian literature.
Eligibility: The award is given to the best English translation of poetry, fiction, drama or literary prose written by a Scandinavian author in Danish, Finnish, Icelandic, Norwegian or Swedish after 1800. Translations may not previously have been published in the English language.
Target applicant(s): Junior high students or younger. High school students. College students. Graduate school students. Adult students.
Amount: $2,000.
Number of awards: 1.
Scholarship may be renewable.
Deadline: September 1.
How to apply: There is no application form. Please see website for submission details.
Exclusive: Visit www.UltimateScholarshipBook.com and enter code AM46823 for updates on this award.

(469) · Lions International Peace Poster Contest

Lions Club International
300 W. 22nd Street, Oak Brook, IL 60523-8842
Phone: 630-571-5466
Email: pr@lionsclubs.org
https://www.lionsclubs.org/en/start-our-approach/youth/peace-poster
Purpose: To award creative youngsters cash prizes for outstanding poster designs.

Eligibility: Students must be 11, 12 or 13 years old as of the deadline and must be sponsored by their local Lions club. Entries will be judged at the local, district, multiple district and international levels. Posters will be evaluated on originality, artistic merit and expression of the assigned theme.
Target applicant(s): Junior high students or younger.
Amount: $500-$5,000.
Number of awards: 24.
Deadline: November 15.
How to apply: Applications are available from your local Lion's Club.
Exclusive: Visit www.UltimateScholarshipBook.com and enter code LI46923 for updates on this award.

(470) · Lotte Lenya Competition

Kurt Weill Foundation for Music
7 East 20th Street, 3rd Floor, New York, NY 10003
Phone: 212-505-5240
Email: kwfinfo@kwf.org
http://www.kwf.org
Purpose: To recognize excellence in music theater performance.
Eligibility: Applicants must be between 19 and 32 years old and attend a regional competition, performing four selections. If contestants are unable to participate in any of the scheduled regional auditions, they may instead submit a DVD, which must contain all four of the required repertoire selections. Finalists will be chosen, based on vocal beauty and technique, interpretation, acting, repertoire variety and presence.
Target applicant(s): High school students. College students. Graduate school students. Adult students.
Amount: $500-$20,000 plus travel stipend.
Number of awards: Varies.
Deadline: February 16.
How to apply: Applications are available online.
Exclusive: Visit www.UltimateScholarshipBook.com and enter code KU47023 for updates on this award.

(471) · Malala Yousafzai Scholarship

Online Logo Maker
Rua das Gaivotas, 849, Florianopolis - SC, Brazil
http://www.onlinelogomaker.com/scholarships-for-women
Purpose: To encourage adult women to pursue education.
Eligibility: Applicants must be women age 30 or older who are starting post-secondary education or returning to school to continue interrupted studies. Students must be pursuing education in the arts and design field.
Target applicant(s): Adult students.
Amount: $1,000.
Number of awards: 1.
Deadline: December 1.
How to apply: Applications are available online.
Exclusive: Visit www.UltimateScholarshipBook.com and enter code ON47123 for updates on this award.

(472) · Marian A. Smith Costume Award

Southeastern Theatre Conference Inc.
1175 Revolution Mill Drive, Studio 14, Greensboro, NC 27405
Phone: 336-272-3645
Email: emilystrickland@sjrstate.edu
https://www.setc.org/scholarships-awards/
Purpose: To support graduate students majoring in costume design and/or technology.

Eligibility: Applicants must be finished with their undergraduate degrees at an SETC region institution by the August prior to application. They must also be first-time as well as full-time attendees of a regionally accredited graduate school specializing in costume design and/or costume technology. Selection is based on the overall strength of the application and interview.
Target applicant(s): College students. Graduate school students. Adult students.
Amount: $1,500.
Number of awards: 1.
Deadline: April 1.
How to apply: Applications are available online. An application, personal letter, resume, ten samples of completed work, five references, transcripts and interview are required.
Exclusive: Visit www.UltimateScholarshipBook.com and enter code SO47223 for updates on this award.

(473) · Melba Day Henning Scholarship

Educational Theatre Association
4805 Montgomery Road, Suite 400, Cincinnati, OH 45212
Phone: 513-421-3900
Email: awards@schooltheatre.org
https://www.schooltheatre.org/programs/ags/scholarships
Purpose: To reward student achievement in theatre.
Eligibility: Applicants must be undergraduate students currently enrolled full-time in theatre education study at an accredited college or university who are upcoming juniors or seniors. Students who are part-time or full-time graduate students are also eligible to apply.
Target applicant(s): College students. Graduate school students. Adult students.
Amount: $3,000.
Number of awards: 1.
Deadline: April 1.
How to apply: Applications are available online.
Exclusive: Visit www.UltimateScholarshipBook.com and enter code ED47323 for updates on this award.

(474) · Michael J. Peitz Leadership Scholarship

Educational Theatre Association
4805 Montgomery Road, Suite 400, Cincinnati, OH 45212
Phone: 513-421-3900
Email: awards@schooltheatre.org
https://www.schooltheatre.org/programs/ags/scholarships
Purpose: To support student achievement in theatre.
Eligibility: Applicants must be an inducted Thespian of the International Thespian Society, the student honorary organization of the Educational Theatre Association, who successfully demonstrates leadership abilities.
Target applicant(s): College students. Graduate school students. Adult students.
Amount: $1,500.
Number of awards: 1.
Deadline: April 1.
How to apply: Applications are available online.
Exclusive: Visit www.UltimateScholarshipBook.com and enter code ED47423 for updates on this award.

(475) · Nadia Christensen Prize

American-Scandinavian Foundation
58 Park Avenue, New York, NY 10016
Phone: 212-779-3587
Email: info@amscan.org
http://www.amscan.org
Purpose: To recognize individuals who translate Scandinavian writings.
Eligibility: Selection is based on the overall strength of the application.
Target applicant(s): Junior high students or younger. High school students. College students. Graduate school students. Adult students.
Amount: $2,500.
Number of awards: 1.
Deadline: September 1.
How to apply: Applications are available online. Applications must include one copy of the work that was translated in its original language, one copy of the English translation of the work, a CV containing contact information for the translator and a letter granting the translation to be entered in the competition and published.
Exclusive: Visit www.UltimateScholarshipBook.com and enter code AM47523 for updates on this award.

(476) · National High School Poetry Contest/ Easterday Poetry Award

Live Poets Society
P.O. Box 8841, Turnersville, NJ 08012
Email: lpsnj@comcast.net
http://www.highschoolpoetrycontest.com
Purpose: To provide a venue for young poets to be recognized.
Eligibility: Applicants must be U.S. high school students. Submitted poems must be 20 lines or less, in English, unpublished and not simultaneously submitted to any other competition. Applicants may only submit one poem during any 90-day span and must include a self-addressed, stamped envelope with each mailed entry, or applicants may submit their poems online. Submissions are accepted year-round.
Target applicant(s): High school students.
Amount: $500.
Number of awards: Varies.
Deadline: March 31, June 30, September 30, December 31.
How to apply: There is no application form.
Exclusive: Visit www.UltimateScholarshipBook.com and enter code LI47623 for updates on this award.

(477) · National Junior Classical League (NJCL) Scholarships

National Junior Classical League
860 NW Washington Blvd Suite A, Hamilton, OH 45013
Email: administrator@njcl.org
http://www.njcl.org
Purpose: To support students studying the classics.
Eligibility: Applicants must be NJCL members in good standing, entering college the upcoming year and studying the classics. Special consideration is given to those planning to teach Latin, Greek or classical humanities. Selection is based on financial need, JCL service, academics and recommendations.
Target applicant(s): High school students.
Amount: Up to $4,000.
Number of awards: Varies.
Deadline: June 15.
How to apply: Applications are available online or by written request.
Exclusive: Visit www.UltimateScholarshipBook.com and enter code NA47723 for updates on this award.

(478) · National Latin Exam Scholarship

National Latin Exam
University of Mary Washington, 1301 College Avenue,
Fredericksburg, VA 22401
Phone: 888-378-7721
Email: nle@umw.edu
http://www.nle.org
Purpose: To reward students for their Latin proficiency.
Eligibility: Applicants must be gold medal winners in Latin III-IV Prose, III-IV Poetry or Latin V-VI on the National Latin Exam. Applicants must be high school seniors who agree to take at least one Latin or classical Greek each semester during their first year of college. A classics in translation course does not count.
Target applicant(s): High school students.
Amount: $2,000.
Number of awards: Varies.
Scholarship may be renewable.
Deadline: Varies.
How to apply: Applications are mailed to eligible students. Renewal applications are available online.
Exclusive: Visit www.UltimateScholarshipBook.com and enter code NA47823 for updates on this award.

(479) · National Peace Essay Contest

United States Institute of Peace
2301 Constitution Avenue NW, Washington, DC 20036
Phone: 202-457-1700
Email: essay_contest@usip.org
https://www.usip.org/public-education/students/AFSAEssayContest
Purpose: To expand educational opportunities for young Americans.
Eligibility: Applicants must be in grades 9 through 12 in the U.S. Home-schooled students or students who are U.S. citizens attending high schools overseas are eligible. Applicants need the sponsorship of any school, school club, youth group, community group or religious organization. Selection is based on the quality of the research, analysis, form, style and mechanics of the essay.
Target applicant(s): High school students.
Amount: $1,250-$2,500.
Number of awards: 2.
Deadline: April 5.
How to apply: Applications are available online.
Exclusive: Visit www.UltimateScholarshipBook.com and enter code UN47923 for updates on this award.

(480) · National Sculpture Society Scholarship

National Sculpture Society
75 Varick Street, 11th Floor, New York, NY 10013
Phone: 212-764-5645
Email: nss1893@aol.com
http://www.nationalsculpture.org
Purpose: To award scholarships to students of figurative or representative sculpture.
Eligibility: Applicants must provide brief biographies and an explanation of their background in sculpture, two recommendation letters and photographs of their sculpture work. Students must also demonstrate financial need.
Target applicant(s): College students. Graduate school students. Adult students.
Amount: $2,000.
Number of awards: 4.

Deadline: March.
How to apply: Follow the application guidelines listed on the website.
Exclusive: Visit www.UltimateScholarshipBook.com and enter code NA48023 for updates on this award.

(481) · National Vocal Competition for Young Opera Singers

Loren L. Zachary Society for the Performing Arts
2250 Gloaming Way, Beverly Hills, CA 90210
Phone: 310-276-2731
Email: infoz@zacharysociety.org
http://www.zacharysociety.org
Purpose: To support students pursuing a professional operatic stage career.
Eligibility: Applicants must be 21-35 years old, reside in the U.S. or Canada and must be available for all phases of the competition.
Target applicant(s): College students. Graduate school students. Adult students.
Amount: Varies.
Number of awards: Varies.
Deadline: January 17 (New York), February 5 (Los Angeles).
How to apply: Applications are available online.
Exclusive: Visit www.UltimateScholarshipBook.com and enter code LO48123 for updates on this award.

(482) · New York Life Award

Scholastic Art & Writing Awards
557 Broadway, New York, NY 10012
Email: info@artandwriting.org
http://www.artandwriting.org/scholarships/
Purpose: To support students whose art or writing explores personal grief, loss and bereavement.
Eligibility: Applicants must be in grades 7-12 (ages 13 and up) and enter art or writing works exploring personal grief, loss and bereavement. Students may enter work in any of the 28 listed art and writing categories and must include a personal statement of 50 words or more on their work. State scholarships are available to two students from each of the following states: Arizona, Louisiana, Michigan, Mississippi, Montana, New Jersey, and New Mexico, Ohio, and Tennessee.
Target applicant(s): Junior high students or younger. High school students.
Amount: $500-$1,000.
Number of awards: 16.
Deadline: December 1.
How to apply: Applications are available online.
Exclusive: Visit www.UltimateScholarshipBook.com and enter code SC48223 for updates on this award.

(483) · NFMC Lynn Freeman Olson Composition Awards

National Federation of Music Clubs Olson Awards
James Schnars, 331 Cleveland Street, Apartment 804, Clearwater, FL 33755
Phone: 317-882-4003
Email: info@nfmc-music.org
http://www.nfmc-music.org/competitions-awards/
Purpose: To support student composers.
Eligibility: Applicants must be at least in grade 7 and no older than age 25. Applicants must be members of the National Federation of Music

Clubs and must submit an original piano composition to be judged. This biennial award is given in odd-numbered years.
Target applicant(s): Junior high students or younger. High school students.
Amount: $500-$1,000.
Number of awards: Varies.
Deadline: March 1 (odd numbered years).
How to apply: Applications are available online.
Exclusive: Visit www.UltimateScholarshipBook.com and enter code NA48323 for updates on this award.

(484) · NFMC Wendell Irish Viola Award
National Federation of Music Clubs (AR)
Dr. George Keck, 2112 Hinson Road, Suite 23, Little Rock, AR 72212
Phone: 317-882-4003
Email: keckg@att.net
http://www.nfmc-music.org
Purpose: To recognize musically talented students.
Eligibility: Applicants must be between the ages of 12 and 18 and must be Individual Junior Special members or Active Junior Club members of the National Federation of Music Clubs. Applicants must enter in their state of residence by submitting a taped performance.
Target applicant(s): Junior high students or younger. High school students.
Amount: $250-$1,000.
Number of awards: 7.
Deadline: March 1.
How to apply: Applications are available online.
Exclusive: Visit www.UltimateScholarshipBook.com and enter code NA48423 for updates on this award.

(485) · Office Supply Scholarship
BulkOfficeSupply.com
1614 Hereford Road, Hewlett, NY 11557
Phone: 800-658-1488
Email: service@bulkofficesupply.com
http://www.bulkofficesupply.com/scholarships-in-new-york
Purpose: To support students pursuing teaching or art or who plan on owning their own business.
Eligibility: Applicants must be high school students or college freshmen or sophomores. Students must be pursing degree programs in teaching or art or must wish to own their own business. Applicants will need to submit a 500- to 600-word essay describing where they plan to or are currently attending school, their desired major, how the student developed an interest in teaching, art or owning their own business and how the scholarship would help them to reach their goals.
Target applicant(s): High school students. College students. Adult students.
Amount: $1,000.
Number of awards: 1.
Deadline: February 1.
How to apply: Applications are available online and must include the essay.
Exclusive: Visit www.UltimateScholarshipBook.com and enter code BU48523 for updates on this award.

(486) · Optimist International Essay Contest
Optimist International
4494 Lindell Boulevard, St. Louis, MO 63108
Phone: 314-371-6000
Email: programs@optimist.org
http://www.optimist.org
Purpose: To reward students based on their essay-writing skills.
Eligibility: Applicants must be under 19 years of age as of December 31 of the current school year and application must be made through a local Optimist Club. The essay topic changes each year. Applicants compete at the club, district and international level. District winners receive a $2,500 scholarship. Scoring is based on organization, vocabulary and style, grammar and punctuation, neatness and adherence to the contest rules. The club-level contests are held in early February but vary by club. The deadline for clubs to submit their winning essay to the district competition is February 28.
Target applicant(s): High school students.
Amount: $2,500.
Number of awards: Varies.
Deadline: Early February.
How to apply: Contact your local Optimist Club.
Exclusive: Visit www.UltimateScholarshipBook.com and enter code OP48623 for updates on this award.

(487) · Part-Time Student Scholarship
International Furnishings and Design Association (IFDA)
36 Bay View Road, Wellesley, MA 02482
Phone: 781-894-3240
Email: linda@westonstudiodesign.com
https://ifda.com/educational-foundation/
Purpose: To aid part-time students who are majoring in interior design.
Eligibility: Applicants must be undergraduate students at an accredited U.S. postsecondary institution. They must be majoring in interior design or a related design subject, have completed four design courses at the time of application and be attending school on a part-time basis. Selection is based on the overall strength of the application.
Target applicant(s): College students. Adult students.
Amount: $1,500.
Number of awards: 1.
Deadline: March 30.
How to apply: Applications are available online. An application form, one letter of recommendation, personal essay and design work examples are required.
Exclusive: Visit www.UltimateScholarshipBook.com and enter code IN48723 for updates on this award.

(488) · Patriot's Pen Youth Essay Contest
Veterans of Foreign Wars
406 W. 34th Street, Kansas City, MO 64111
Phone: 816-968-1117
Email: kharmer@vfw.org
https://www.vfw.org/community/youth-and-education
Purpose: To give students in grades 6 through 8 an opportunity to write essays that express their views on democracy.
Eligibility: Applicants must be enrolled as a 6th, 7th or 8th grader in a public, private or parochial school in the U.S., its territories or possessions. Home-schooled students and dependents of U.S. military or civilian personnel in overseas schools may also apply. Foreign exchange students and former applicants who placed in the national finals are ineligible. Students must submit essays based on an annual theme to their local VFW posts. If an essay is picked to advance, the entry is judged at the District (regional) level, then the Department (state) level and finally at the National level. Essays are judged 30 percent on

knowledge of the theme, 35 percent on development of the theme and 35 percent on clarity.
Target applicant(s): Junior high students or younger.
Amount: Up to $5,000.
Number of awards: 54.
Deadline: October 31.
How to apply: Applications are available online or by contacting the local VFW office. Entries must be turned into the local VFW office. Contact information for these offices can be found online or by calling the VFW National Programs headquarters at 816-968-1117.
Exclusive: Visit www.UltimateScholarshipBook.com and enter code VE48823 for updates on this award.

(489) · Platt Family Scholarship Prize Essay Contest
Lincoln Forum
c/o Don McCue, Curator of the Lincoln Memorial Shrine, 125 West Vine Street, Redlands, CA 92373
Phone: 909-798-7632
Email: archives@akspl.org
https://www.thelincolnforum.org/scholarship-essay-contest
Purpose: To reward students who have written the best essays on a topic related to Abraham Lincoln.
Eligibility: Applicants must be full-time undergraduate students who are enrolled at a U.S. college or university during the spring term of the contest entry year. They must submit an essay on a sponsor-determined topic that is related to Abraham Lincoln. Selection is based on the overall strength of the essay.
Target applicant(s): College students. Adult students.
Amount: $500-$1,500.
Number of awards: 3.
Deadline: July 31.
How to apply: Entry instructions are available online. An essay is required.
Exclusive: Visit www.UltimateScholarshipBook.com and enter code LI48923 for updates on this award.

(490) · Playwright Discovery Award
John F. Kennedy Center for the Performing Arts
2700 F Street NW, Washington, DC 20566
Phone: 800-444-1324
Email: vsainfo@kennedy-center.org
https://www.kennedy-center.org/education/opportunities-for-artists/competitions-and-commissions/
Purpose: To award promising young writers scholarship funds and a chance to have one of their scripts professionally produced at the John F. Kennedy Center for the Performing Arts.
Eligibility: Applicants must be students in grades 6-12. Applicants are to create an original one-act script of less than 40 pages that documents the experience of living with a disability. Applicants must have a disability, or the script can be a collaboration of a group of up to 5 students with one student having a disability. Selected scripts will be performed for middle school, high school and adult audiences. First and second place winners will have their plays performed at the JFK Performing Arts Center.
Target applicant(s): Junior high students or younger. High school students.
Amount: Varies.
Number of awards: Varies.
Deadline: March 10.
How to apply: Applications are available online.
Exclusive: Visit www.UltimateScholarshipBook.com and enter code JO49023 for updates on this award.

(491) · Poster Contest for High School Students
Christophers
5 Hanover Square, 22nd Floor, New York, NY 10004
Phone: 212-759-4050
Email: youth@christophers.org
https://www.christophers.org/video-contest-for-college-students
Purpose: To reward students for interpreting a given theme through poster art.
Eligibility: Entrants must be high school students. Students must work individually to create posters of original content. Posters are judged by a panel based on overall impact, expression of the year's theme, artistic merit and originality.
Target applicant(s): High school students.
Amount: $100-$1,000.
Number of awards: Up to 8.
Deadline: February 17.
How to apply: Applications are available online.
Exclusive: Visit www.UltimateScholarshipBook.com and enter code CH49123 for updates on this award.

(492) · Princess Grace Awards
Princess Grace Awards
150 E. 58th Street, 25th Floor, New York, NY 10155
Phone: 212-317-1470
Email: grants@pgfusa.org
http://www.pgfusa.org/
Purpose: To assist emerging young artists in theater, dance and film to realize their career goals.
Eligibility: Applicants must submit an example of their work in the category in which they apply: theatre, dance, choreography, film or playwriting. Theatre and dance applicants require the sponsorship of a professional company or school, one nominee per institution. Awards are based on the artistic quality of the artist's work, potential for future excellence and activities. Applicants must be U.S. citizens and (except playwrights) must be nominated by a school department chair/dean or company artistic director. Awards must be completed in the United States.
Target applicant(s): High school students. College students. Adult students.
Amount: Up to $30,000.
Number of awards: Varies.
Deadline: Varies.
How to apply: Applications are available online.
Exclusive: Visit www.UltimateScholarshipBook.com and enter code PR49223 for updates on this award.

(493) · Print and Graphics Scholarship
Print and Graphics Scholarship Foundation
301 Brush Creek Rd, Warrendale, PA 15086
Phone: 412-259-1740
Email: pgsf@printing.org
https://pgsf.org/
Purpose: To provide financial assistance for postsecondary education to students interested in graphic communications careers.
Eligibility: Applicants must be high school seniors, high school graduates or college students enrolled in a two- or four-year college printing or graphics program. Applicants must be full-time students, be interested in a career in printing technology, printing management, publishing or graphic communications and able to maintain a 3.0 GPA.

Target applicant(s): High school students. College students. Adult students.
Minimum GPA: 3.0
Amount: $1,000-$5,000.
Number of awards: Varies.
Scholarship may be renewable.
Deadline: May 1.
How to apply: Applications are available online.
Exclusive: Visit www.UltimateScholarshipBook.com and enter code PR49323 for updates on this award.

---

(494) · Prize in Ethics Essay Contest

Elie Wiesel Foundation for Humanity
555 Madison Avenue, 20th Floor, New York, NY 10022
Phone: 212-490-7788
Email: info@eliewieselfoundation.org
https://eliewieselfoundation.org/prize-ethics/
Purpose: To promote the thought and discussion of ethics and their place in education.
Eligibility: Applicants must be registered full-time juniors and seniors at accredited colleges and universities in the U.S. Students must write an essay dealing with ethics and have a faculty sponsor review their essay and sign the entry form.
Target applicant(s): College students. Adult students.
Amount: $500-$5,000.
Number of awards: 5.
Deadline: January 21.
How to apply: Applications are available online.
Exclusive: Visit www.UltimateScholarshipBook.com and enter code EL49423 for updates on this award.

---

(495) · Ruth Clark Furniture Design Scholarship

International Furnishings and Design Association (IFDA)
36 Bay View Road, Wellesley, MA 02482
Phone: 781-894-3240
Email: linda@westonstudiodesign.com
https://ifda.com/educational-foundation/
Purpose: To aid interior design students who have an interest in residential furniture design.
Eligibility: Applicants must be full-time undergraduate or graduate students who are majoring in interior design or a closely related subject. They must have a concentration in residential upholstered and/or wood furniture design. Selection is based on the overall strength of the application.
Target applicant(s): College students. Graduate school students. Adult students.
Amount: $3,000.
Number of awards: 1.
Deadline: March 31.
How to apply: Applications are available online. An application form, transcript, personal essay, five original furniture designs and one recommendation letter are required.
Exclusive: Visit www.UltimateScholarshipBook.com and enter code IN49523 for updates on this award.

---

(496) · Ruth Lilly and Dorothy Sargent Rosenberg Poetry Fellowship Program

Poetry Magazine
444 N. Michigan Avenue, Suite 1850, Chicago, IL 60611-4034

Phone: 312-787-7070
Email: mail@poetryfoundation.org
https://www.poetryfoundation.org/programs/foundation/awards
Purpose: To encourage the study of writing and poetry.
Eligibility: Applicants must be U.S. residents between the ages of 21 and 31. They must be currently enrolled undergraduate or graduate students majoring in English or creative writing.
Target applicant(s): College students. Graduate school students. Adult students.
Amount: $25,800.
Number of awards: 5.
Deadline: April 30.
How to apply: Applications are available online. An essay and a poetry submission are required.
Exclusive: Visit www.UltimateScholarshipBook.com and enter code PO49623 for updates on this award.

---

(497) · Sara Tucker Study Grant

Richard Tucker Music Foundation
1790 Broadway, Suite 715, New York, NY 10019
Phone: 212-757-2218
http://www.richardtucker.org
Purpose: To support students who are transitioning from school to a professional career in music.
Eligibility: Applicants must have recently completed a graduate degree program or work in a young artist or apprentice program at a regional company and be generally under 30 years of age. Students must have had various performing opportunities but not in major roles.
Target applicant(s): College students. Adult students.
Amount: $5,000.
Number of awards: 4.
Deadline: July 1.
How to apply: Applications are available online.
Exclusive: Visit www.UltimateScholarshipBook.com and enter code RI49723 for updates on this award.

---

(498) · Scholastic Art and Writing Portfolio Award

Scholastic Art & Writing Awards
557 Broadway, New York, NY 10012
Email: info@artandwriting.org
http://www.artandwriting.org/scholarships/
Purpose: To reward creative young writers and artists.
Eligibility: Applicants must be high school seniors in U.S. or Canadian schools. Students must submit a total of six art or writing works with accompanying artist and personal statements in one of 28 categories of art and writing.
Target applicant(s): High school students.
Amount: Up to $10,000.
Number of awards: 46.
Deadline: December 1.
How to apply: Applications are available online.
Exclusive: Visit www.UltimateScholarshipBook.com and enter code SC49823 for updates on this award.

---

(499) · Senior Fellowship Program

National Gallery of Art
2000B South Club Drive, Landover, MD 20785
Phone: 202-842-6482
Email: thecenter@nga.gov
https://www.nga.gov/research/casva/fellowships.html

Purpose: To award fellowships to scholars in the visual arts.
Eligibility: Applicants should have held the Ph.D. for five years or more or possess an equivalent record of professional accomplishment at the time of application. They must submit application forms, proposals, copies of publications and three letters of recommendation. Fellowships are for full-time research, and scholars are expected to reside in Washington and to participate in the activities of the Center. One Paul Mellon Fellowship, one Frese Senior Fellowship and four to six Ailsa Mellon Bruce and Samuel H. Kress Senior Fellowships will be awarded for the academic year. The Paul Mellon and Ailsa Mellon Bruce Senior Fellowships support research in the history, theory and criticism of the visual arts of any geographical area and of any period. The Samuel H. Kress Senior Fellowships support research on European art before the early nineteenth century. The Frese Senior Fellowship is for study in the history, theory and criticism of sculpture, prints and drawings or decorative arts of any geographical area and of any period. Applications are also accepted from scholars in other disciplines whose work is related.
Target applicant(s): Graduate school students. Adult students.
Amount: Up to $50,000.
Number of awards: 6-8.
Deadline: October 15.
How to apply: Applications are available online.
Exclusive: Visit www.UltimateScholarshipBook.com and enter code NA49923 for updates on this award.

(500) · Sinfonia Foundation Scholarship

Sinfonia Foundation
Scholarship Committee, 10600 Old State Road, Evansville, IN 47711-1399
Phone: 800-473-2649 x110
Email: sef@sinfonia.org
https://www.sinfonia.org/2021/06/09/2021-2022-sef-scholarship-applications-available/
Purpose: To assist the collegiate members and chapters of Sinfonia.
Eligibility: Applicants must be in college for at least two semesters with good academic standing and submit references and an essay.
Target applicant(s): College students. Adult students.
Amount: $2,500-$7,500.
Number of awards: 3.
Deadline: July 15.
How to apply: Applications are available online.
Exclusive: Visit www.UltimateScholarshipBook.com and enter code SI50023 for updates on this award.

(501) · Stella Blum Research Grant

Costume Society of America (CSA)
Ann Wass, 5903 60th Avenue, Riverdale, MD 20737
Phone: 800-272-9447
Email: national.office@costumesocietyamerica.com
http://www.costumesocietyamerica.com
Purpose: To support a CSA student member working in the field of North American costume.
Eligibility: Applicants must be accepted into an undergraduate or graduate degree program at an accredited university for the time during which the grant would apply, conduct a research project in the area of North American costume and be members of the Costume Society of America (CSA) in good standing. Applications are judged according to significance of topic, feasibility, time frame, methodology, bibliography, budget, applicants' qualifications and how the research might further the field of costumes.

Target applicant(s): High school students. College students. Graduate school students. Adult students.
Amount: $2,000 plus a travel component of up to $500 to attend National Symposium.
Number of awards: 1.
Deadline: June 1.
How to apply: Applications are available by email or phone.
Exclusive: Visit www.UltimateScholarshipBook.com and enter code CO50123 for updates on this award.

(502) · Stillman Kelley National Instrumental Awards

National Federation of Music Clubs Stillman-Kelley Award
Nathalie Steinbach, 15 Mount Vernon Avenue, Fredericksburg, VA 22405
Phone: 512-892-5633
http://www.nfmc-music.org
Purpose: To support young musicians and composers.
Eligibility: Applicants must be instrumentalists, must not reach their 19th birthday by March 1 and be members of the National Federation of Music Clubs. This award rotates by region with the Northeastern and Southeastern regions in even years and Central and Western regions in odd years.
Target applicant(s): High school students.
Amount: $200-$1,000.
Number of awards: 8.
Deadline: March 1.
How to apply: Applications are available online.
Exclusive: Visit www.UltimateScholarshipBook.com and enter code NA50223 for updates on this award.

(503) · Student Academy Awards Competition

Academy of Motion Picture Arts and Sciences
8949 Wilshire Boulevard, Beverly Hills, CA 90211
Phone: 310-247-3031
Email: sguthrie@oscars.org
http://www.oscars.org
Purpose: To support filmmakers with no previous professional experience.
Eligibility: Applicants must be full-time students at an accredited U.S. college, university, film school or art school. Films must be made as a part of a school curriculum in the categories of alternative, animation, documentary or narrative. Selection is based on originality, entertainment, production quality and resourcefulness. A film under 40 minutes is required.
Target applicant(s): College students. Graduate school students. Adult students.
Amount: Varies.
Number of awards: Varies.
Deadline: June 1.
How to apply: Applications are available online.
Exclusive: Visit www.UltimateScholarshipBook.com and enter code AC50323 for updates on this award.

(504) · Student Design Competition

International Housewares Association
6400 Shafer Court, Suite 650, Rosemont, IL 60018
Phone: 847-292-4200
http://www.housewares.org
Purpose: To honor and encourage young, up-and-coming designers to enter careers in the housewares industry.

Eligibility: Applicants must be enrolled as an undergraduate or graduate student at an IDSA-affiliated college or university.
Target applicant(s): College students. Graduate school students. Adult students.
Amount: Varies.
Number of awards: Varies.
Deadline: December.
How to apply: Applications are available online.
Exclusive: Visit www.UltimateScholarshipBook.com and enter code IN50423 for updates on this award.

(505) · Student Translation Award

American Translators Association
225 Reinekers Lane, Suite 590, Alexandria, VA 22314
Phone: 703-683-6100
Email: ata@atanet.org
http://www.atanet.org
Purpose: To encourage translation projects by students.
Eligibility: Applicants must be graduate or undergraduate students or a group of students attending an accredited U.S. college or university. The project should have post-grant results such as a publication, conference presentation or teaching material. Computer-assisted translations, dissertations and theses are not eligible, and students who are already published translators are not eligible. Translations must be from a foreign language into English. Preference is given to students who have been or are currently enrolled in translator training programs. There is a limit of one entry per student. Applicants should submit entry forms, statements of purpose, letter of recommendation, translation sample with corresponding source-language text, proof of permission to publish from copyright holder and sample outline or other material demonstrating the nature of the work (if the project is not a translation).
Target applicant(s): High school students. College students. Graduate school students. Adult students.
Amount: $500 plus $500 for conference.
Number of awards: 1.
Deadline: July 31.
How to apply: Applications are available online.
Exclusive: Visit www.UltimateScholarshipBook.com and enter code AM50523 for updates on this award.

(506) · Study Abroad Europe Scholarship

Study Aboard Europe
111 East Mosholu Parkway Suite 3F, New York, NY 10467
Phone: 718-710-0498
Email: info@studyabroadineurope.com
https://www.studyabroadineurope.com/pages.
aspx?id=20&t=Scholarship
Purpose: To assist students who wish to study abroad in one of Study Abroad Europe's programs.
Eligibility: Applicants must be U.S. college students with a minimum 3.0 GPA.
Target applicant(s): College students. Adult students.
Minimum GPA: 3.0
Amount: $250-$1,000.
Number of awards: 3.
Deadline: April 1, June 10, November 15.
How to apply: Applications are available online. An application form, a one-page essay and a letter of recommendation from a professor or an assistant professor are required.
Exclusive: Visit www.UltimateScholarshipBook.com and enter code ST50623 for updates on this award.

(507) · Taylor/Blakeslee University Fellowships

Council for the Advancement of Science Writing (CASW)
P.O. Box 910, Hedgesville, WV 25427
Phone: 304-754-6786
Email: diane@casw.edu
http://www.casw.org
Purpose: To help graduate students in science writing.
Eligibility: Applicants must be U.S. citizens who are enrolled in U.S. graduate-level science writing programs.
Target applicant(s): Graduate school students. Adult students.
Amount: $5,000.
Number of awards: Varies.
Deadline: March 1.
How to apply: Contact the organization for more information.
Exclusive: Visit www.UltimateScholarshipBook.com and enter code CO50723 for updates on this award.

(508) · The Fountainhead Essay Contest

Ayn Rand Institute
6 Hutton Centre Drive, Suite 600, Santa Ana, CA 92707
Email: essays@aynrand.org
https://www.aynrand.org/students/essay-contests
Purpose: To honor high school students who distinguish themselves in their understanding of Ayn Rand's novel "The Fountainhead".
Eligibility: Applicants must be high school juniors or seniors who submit a 800-1,600 word essay which will be judged on both style and content with an emphasis on writing that is clear, articulate and logically organized. Winning essays must demonstrate an outstanding grasp of the philosophic meaning of "The Fountainhead".
Target applicant(s): High school students.
Amount: Up to $5,000.
Number of awards: 84.
Deadline: April 28.
How to apply: Applications are only accepted online.
Exclusive: Visit www.UltimateScholarshipBook.com and enter code AY50823 for updates on this award.

(509) · Thelma A. Robinson Award in Ballet

National Federation of Music Clubs (Coral Gables, FL)
Gay Dill, National Chairman, 814 South Second Street, Atwood, KS 67730
Phone: 330-638-4003
Email: gaydill@att.net
http://www.nfmc-music.org
Purpose: To support students who are ballet dancers.
Eligibility: Applicants must be between the ages of 13 and 19. There is no entry fee, but applicants must be members of the NFMC. The award is given during even-numbered years.
Target applicant(s): Junior high students or younger. High school students.
Amount: $2,500.
Number of awards: 1.
Deadline: February 1.
How to apply: Applications are available online. Award is only open in even-numbered years.
Exclusive: Visit www.UltimateScholarshipBook.com and enter code NA50923 for updates on this award.

(510) · Tombow's Create Your Best Work Art Scholarship

Tombow
355 Satellite Boulevard NE, Suite 300, Suwanee, GA 30024
Phone: 404-821-6333
Email: bluiz@tombowusa.com
https://www.tombowusa.com/art-scholarship
Purpose: To support students pursuing visual arts degrees.
Eligibility: Applicants must be graduating high school seniors or college freshmen or sophomore students in the U.S. Students must be enrolled or accepted into a U.S. university, college or art school and pursuing a visual arts degree. Applicants must submit a portfolio along with their application materials.
Target applicant(s): High school students. College students. Adult students.
Amount: Up to $5,000.
Number of awards: 2.
Deadline: March 1.
How to apply: Applications are available online.
Exclusive: Visit www.UltimateScholarshipBook.com and enter code TO51023 for updates on this award.

(511) · Tricia LeVangie Green/Sustainable Design Scholarship

International Furnishings and Design Association (IFDA)
36 Bay View Road, Wellesley, MA 02482
Phone: 781-894-3240
Email: linda@westonstudiodesign.com
https://ifda.com/educational-foundation/
Purpose: To aid interior design students who have a demonstrated interest in the green movement.
Eligibility: Applicants must be undergraduate students who are enrolled in an interior design or related furnishings design degree program at a U.S. postsecondary institution and have completed four design courses at the time of application. They must have a demonstrated interest in the green movement as it pertains to eco-friendly design and sustainability. Selection is based on the overall strength of the application.
Target applicant(s): College students. Adult students.
Amount: $1,500.
Number of awards: 1.
Deadline: March 30.
How to apply: Applications are available online. An application form, transcript, personal essay, two design work examples and one recommendation letter are required.
Exclusive: Visit www.UltimateScholarshipBook.com and enter code IN51123 for updates on this award.

(512) · Two Ten Footwear Design Scholarship

Two Ten Footwear Foundation
1466 Main Street, Waltham, MA 02451.
Phone: 800-346-3210
http://www.twoten.org
Purpose: To support students who are completing footwear design studies.
Eligibility: Applicants must be citizens of the United States and accepted or enrolled at accredited colleges or vocational institutions. Students must provide a portfolio that includes three design drawings. Applicants must also include their most recent transcripts and keep a 2.5 grade point average while studying in the field of design. Students must demonstrate an interest and commitment to a career in footwear design. Selection is based on financial need and design talent.
Target applicant(s): High school students. College students. Graduate school students. Adult students.
Minimum GPA: 2.5
Amount: Up to $4,000.
Number of awards: Varies.
Scholarship may be renewable.
Deadline: April 1.
How to apply: Applications are available online.
Exclusive: Visit www.UltimateScholarshipBook.com and enter code TW51223 for updates on this award.

(513) · Ukulele Festival Hawaii's College Scholarship Program

Ukulele Festival Hawaii
c/o Roy Sakuma Productions, Inc., 3555 Harding Avenue, Suite 1, Honolulu, HI 96816
Phone: 808-732-3739
Email: info@ukulelefestivalhawaii.org
http://www.roysakuma.net/
Purpose: To support students who play the ukulele.
Eligibility: Applicants must be Hawaii high school seniors in good standing. They must plan to attend a four-year college or university in the fall following graduation.
Target applicant(s): High school students.
Amount: $2,000.
Number of awards: Varies.
Deadline: April 30.
How to apply: Applications are available from Roy Sakuma Productions. An application form is required.
Exclusive: Visit www.UltimateScholarshipBook.com and enter code UK51323 for updates on this award.

(514) · Undergraduate Scholarships

Sigma Alpha Iota Philanthropies
Director, Undergraduate Scholarships, One Tunnel Road, Asheville, NC 28805
Phone: 828-251-0606
Email: jkpete@cox.net
http://www.sai-national.org
Purpose: To assist members of the Sigma Alpha Iota organization who have demonstrated outstanding leadership abilities, musical talent and scholastic achievement.
Eligibility: Applicants must be active members for at least one year in the Sigma Alpha Iota organization, be in good standing and demonstrate financial need.
Target applicant(s): College students. Adult students.
Amount: $1,000-$2,400.
Number of awards: 13.
Deadline: March 15.
How to apply: Applications are available online.
Exclusive: Visit www.UltimateScholarshipBook.com and enter code SI51423 for updates on this award.

(515) · Vectorworks Design Scholarship

Nemetschek Vectorworks
7150 Riverwood Drive, Columbia, MD 21046
Phone: 410-290-5114

http://www.vectorworks.net

Purpose: To reward students for excellent design work.

Eligibility: Applicants must be pursuing an undergraduate or graduate degree in a design-related field at an accredited educational institution. Students must submit a design project. Submissions may be made by individual students or by groups of up to six students. Selection is primarily based on design quality, technology, originality and explanation of the design.

Target applicant(s): College students. Graduate school students. Adult students.

Amount: $10,000.

Number of awards: 10.

Deadline: March 31.

How to apply: Applications are available online.

Exclusive: Visit www.UltimateScholarshipBook.com and enter code NE51523 for updates on this award.

---

(516) · Vercille Voss IFDA Graduate Student Scholarship

International Furnishings and Design Association (IFDA)
36 Bay View Road, Wellesley, MA 02482
Phone: 781-894-3240
Email: linda@westonstudiodesign.com
https://ifda.com/educational-foundation/

Purpose: To aid interior design graduate students.

Eligibility: Applicants must be graduate students who are majoring in interior design or a closely related subject at a U.S. postsecondary institution. Selection is based on the overall strength of the application.

Target applicant(s): College students. Graduate school students. Adult students.

Amount: $2,000.

Number of awards: 1.

Deadline: March 30.

How to apply: Applications are available online. An application form, transcript, personal essay, two original design work examples, one recommendation letter and proof of graduate school acceptance (for entering students only) are required.

Exclusive: Visit www.UltimateScholarshipBook.com and enter code IN51623 for updates on this award.

---

(517) · Visiting Senior Fellowship Program

National Gallery of Art
2000B South Club Drive, Landover, MD 20785
Phone: 202-842-6482
Email: thecenter@nga.gov
https://www.nga.gov/research/casva/fellowships.html

Purpose: To award fellowships to scholars in visual arts.

Eligibility: Applicants must have held their Ph.D. for five years or possess an equivalent record of professional accomplishment at the time of application. Applications are considered for research in the history, theory and criticism of the visual arts of any geographical area and of any period. Applicants must submit application forms, proposals, copies of a publication and two letters of recommendation. Fellowships are for full-time research, and scholars are expected to reside in Washington and to participate in the activities of the Center. Applications are also accepted from scholars in other disciplines whose work is related. The Center awards up to twelve short-term Paul Mellon and Ailsa Mellon Bruce Visiting Senior Fellowships. The deadlines are March 21 for the fellowship from September to February and September 21 for March through August.

Target applicant(s): Graduate school students. Adult students.

Amount: $6,000-$8,000.

Number of awards: Up to 12.

Scholarship may be renewable.

Deadline: March 21, September 21.

How to apply: Applications are available online.

Exclusive: Visit www.UltimateScholarshipBook.com and enter code NA51723 for updates on this award.

---

(518) · VMSD Scholarship

Planning and Visual Education Partnership (PAVE)
8570 Stirling Road, Suite 102-227, Hollywood, FL 33024
Phone: 954-551-9144
Email: info@paveglobal.org
http://paveglobal.org

Purpose: To support students in educational programs preparing them for careers in the retail environments industry.

Eligibility: Applicants must be a third or fourth year student or equivalent or enrolled in a program working toward a degree in interior design, retail design, hospitality design, visual merchandising, UX design, architecture, engineering or product design. Students must be located and studying in the United States with a minimum 3.0 GPA. An essay on a provided prompt and a project folio are required to be submitted.

Target applicant(s): College students. Adult students.

Amount: $1,000.

Number of awards: 1.

Deadline: July 18.

How to apply: Applications are available online.

Exclusive: Visit www.UltimateScholarshipBook.com and enter code PL51823 for updates on this award.

---

(519) · Women Band Directors International College Scholarships

Women Band Directors International
Karen Williams, WBDI Scholarship Chair, 3994 White Oak Road, Waynesville, NC 28785
Email: agreen@lamar.k12.ga.us
http://www.womenbanddirectors.org

Purpose: To support future female band directors.

Eligibility: Applicants must be studying music education with the intention of becoming a band director.

Target applicant(s): College students. Graduate school students. Adult students.

Amount: Varies.

Number of awards: 11.

Deadline: December 1.

How to apply: Applications are available online.

Exclusive: Visit www.UltimateScholarshipBook.com and enter code WO51923 for updates on this award.

---

(520) · Wyland National Art Challenge

Wyland Foundation
6 Mason, Irvine, CA 92618
Phone: 949-643-7070
Email: artchallenge@wylandfoundation.org
http://www.wylandfoundation.org/artchallenge

Purpose: To encourage students with an interest in conservation and art.

Eligibility: Applicants must be students in grades kindergarten through twelve in a U.S. school. Students must participate in the painting of a 4x8 foot mural that addresses the theme of conservation.

Target applicant(s): Junior high students or younger. High school students.
Amount: $1,500.
Number of awards: 3.
Deadline: December 1.
How to apply: Applications are available online.
Exclusive: Visit www.UltimateScholarshipBook.com and enter code WY52023 for updates on this award.

(521) · Young American Creative Patriotic Art Contest

Ladies Auxiliary VFW
406 West 34th Street, 10th Floor, Kansas City, MO 64111
Phone: 816-561-8655
Email: info@vfwauxiliary.org
https://vfwauxiliary.org/scholarships/
Purpose: To encourage patriotic art.
Eligibility: Applicants must be high school students in the same state as the sponsoring Ladies Auxiliary. They must submit one piece of patriotic art on paper or canvas. Art must have been completed during the current school year and must be accompanied by a teacher's signature. Applicants must participate in a local Auxiliary competition before advancing to the national level.
Target applicant(s): High school students.
Amount: Up to $21,000.
Number of awards: Varies.
Deadline: March 31.
How to apply: Applications are available online.
Exclusive: Visit www.UltimateScholarshipBook.com and enter code LA52123 for updates on this award.

SOCIAL SCIENCES

(522) · A. Harry Passow Classroom Teacher Scholarship

National Association for Gifted Children
1331 H Street NW, Suite 1001, Chair, Awards Committee, Washington, DC 20005
Phone: 202-785-4268
Email: nagc@nagc.org
http://www.nagc.org
Purpose: To reward excellent teachers of gifted students of grades K-12.
Eligibility: Applicants must be teachers of gifted students of grades K-12 and be continuing their education. Applicants must also have been members of NAGC for at least one year. Selection is based on commitment to teaching as shown by reviews from students, parents, principal and peers and admission into a graduate or certification program in gifted education.
Target applicant(s): Graduate school students. Adult students.
Amount: $2,000.
Number of awards: Up to 2.
Deadline: May.
How to apply: Applications are available online.
Exclusive: Visit www.UltimateScholarshipBook.com and enter code NA52223 for updates on this award.

(523) · AALL Educational Scholarships

American Association of Law Libraries
105 W. Adams, Suite 3300, Chicago, IL 60603
Email: scholarships@aall.org
https://www.aallnet.org/education-training/scholarships/
Purpose: To encourage students to pursue careers as law librarians.
Eligibility: There are six levels of awards: 1. Library Degree for Law School Graduates, awarded to a law school graduate with law library experience pursuing a degree at an accredited library school. 2. Library School Graduates Attending Law School, awarded to a library school graduate pursuing a degree at an accredited law school who has law library experience and no more than 36 semester credit hours left before obtaining the law degree. 3. Library Degree for Non-Law School Graduates, awarded to a college graduate with law library experience who is seeking a degree involving law librarianship courses at an accredited library school. 4. Library School Graduates Seeking A Non-Law Degree, awarded to library school graduates who are seeking degrees in fields other than law. 5. Law Librarians in Continuing Education Courses, awarded to law librarians with a degree from an accredited library or law school who are continuing their education. 6. Dual JD/MLIS Degree, awarded to college graduates working toward a dual degree in an accredited law school and library school. Preference is given to AALL members, but a non-member can apply. All applicants must intend to have careers as law librarians. There must be financial need for awards 1-4.
Target applicant(s): Graduate school students. Adult students.
Amount: Varies.
Number of awards: Varies.
Scholarship may be renewable.
Deadline: April 1.
How to apply: Applications are available online, by mail with a self-addressed, stamped envelope, by fax, by phone or by email.
Exclusive: Visit www.UltimateScholarshipBook.com and enter code AM52323 for updates on this award.

(524) · ACLS Fellowships

American Council of Learned Societies (ACLS)
633 Third Avenue, New York, NY 10017-6795
Phone: 212-697-1505
Email: mgoldfeder@acls.org
https://www.acls.org/
Purpose: To support a scholar in the study of humanities.
Eligibility: Applicants must have a Ph.D. degree and at least a three year period since their last supported research. An application, a proposal, bibliography, publications list and two reference letters are required. The award levels are based on the position of the applicant: professor and equivalent, associate professor and equivalent and assistant professor and equivalent. The ACLS fellowships include ACLS/SSRC/NEH International and Area Studies Fellowships and ACLS/New York Public Library Fellowships.
Target applicant(s): Graduate school students. Adult students.
Amount: Up to $70,000.
Number of awards: Varies.
Deadline: September 30.
How to apply: Applications are available online.
Exclusive: Visit www.UltimateScholarshipBook.com and enter code AM52423 for updates on this award.

(525) · ACOR-CAORC Fellowships

American Center of Oriental Research (ACOR)
656 Beacon Street, 5th Floor, Boston, MA 02215-2010
Phone: 617-353-6571
Email: acor@bu.edu
https://acorjordan.org
Purpose: To assist master's and pre-doctoral students conducting research in Jordan.
Eligibility: Applicants must be U.S. citizen graduate students researching topics involving scholarship in Near Eastern studies. Recipients are required to engage in scholarly and cultural activities while residing at the American Center of Oriental Research (ACOR) in Jordan. The fellowships last from two to six months. The award includes room and board at ACOR, transportation, a stipend and research funds.
Target applicant(s): Graduate school students. Adult students.
Amount: Varies.
Number of awards: Varies.
Deadline: February 1.
How to apply: Applications are available online.
Exclusive: Visit www.UltimateScholarshipBook.com and enter code AM52523 for updates on this award.

(526) · Adelle and Erwin Tomash Fellowship in the History of Information Processing

Charles Babbage Institute
Center for the History of Information Processing, 211 Andersen Library, University of Minnesota, 222 - 21st Avenue South, Minneapolis, MN 55455
Phone: 612-624-5050
Email: yostx003@tc.umn.edu
http://www.cbi.umn.edu
Purpose: To support a graduate student who is researching the history of computing.
Eligibility: Applicants must be graduate students who have completed all doctoral degree requirements except the research and writing of the dissertation. Students must submit a curriculum vitae and a five-page

statement and justification of the research program. To be eligible, scholars will reside outside the Twin Cities metropolitan region.
Target applicant(s): Graduate school students. Adult students.
Amount: $14,000.
Number of awards: 1.
Deadline: January 15.
How to apply: Visit the website for more information.
Exclusive: Visit www.UltimateScholarshipBook.com and enter code CH52623 for updates on this award.

(527) · Adult Students in Scholastic Transition (ASIST)

Executive Women International (EWI)
3860 South 2300 East, Suite 211, Salt Lake City, UT 84109
Phone: 801-355-2800
Email: ewi@ewiconnect.com
https://ewiconnect.com
Purpose: To assist adult students who face major life transitions.
Eligibility: Applicants may be single parents, individuals just entering the workforce or displaced workers.
Target applicant(s): College students. Adult students.
Amount: $2,000-$10,000.
Number of awards: 13.
Deadline: Varies by chapter.
How to apply: Contact your local EWI chapter.
Exclusive: Visit www.UltimateScholarshipBook.com and enter code EX52723 for updates on this award.

(528) · AICPA Foundation Scholarship for Future CPAs

American Institute of Certified Public Accountants
220 Leigh Farm Road, Durham, NC 27707-8110
Phone: 919-402-4500
Email: scholarships@aicpa.org
https://www.aicpa.org
Purpose: To encourage accounting majors planning to become CPAs.
Eligibility: Applicants must be enrolled as full-time undergraduate or graduate level students pursuing a degree in accounting or an accounting-related major. Students must have completed at least 30 semester hours of college coursework, including at least six semester hours in accounting while maintaining an overall and major GPA of 3.0. Applicants must be U.S. citizens or permanent residents and planning to pursue CPA licensure.
Target applicant(s): College students. Graduate school students. Adult students.
Minimum GPA: 3.0
Amount: $5,000.
Number of awards: 25.
Deadline: March 1.
How to apply: Applications are available online.
Exclusive: Visit www.UltimateScholarshipBook.com and enter code AM52823 for updates on this award.

(529) · AICPA Foundation Two-year Transfer Scholarship

American Institute of Certified Public Accountants
220 Leigh Farm Road, Durham, NC 27707-8110
Phone: 919-402-4500
Email: scholarships@aicpa.org
https://www.aicpa.org

Purpose: To support students transferring from a two-year college to a four-year institution to complete their degree in accounting or an accounting-related field.

Eligibility: Applicants must be currently completing courses at a two-year college/university planning to transfer with a declared intent to major in accounting or an accounting-related field at a four-year college/university and maintaining an overall and major GPA of 3.0. Students must be U.S. citizens or permanent residents and planning to pursue the CPA licensure.

Target applicant(s): College students. Adult students.

Minimum GPA: 3.0

Amount: $5,000.

Number of awards: Varies.

Deadline: March 1.

How to apply: Applications are available online.

Exclusive: Visit www.UltimateScholarshipBook.com and enter code AM52923 for updates on this award.

---

(530) · AICPA John L. Carey Scholarship

American Institute of Certified Public Accountants
220 Leigh Farm Road, Durham, NC 27707-8110
Phone: 919-402-4500
Email: scholarships@aicpa.org
https://www.aicpa.org

Purpose: To support non-business related degree holders who are pursuing graduate studies in accounting.

Eligibility: Applicants must be full-time students who have obtained a liberal arts or other non-business undergraduate degree and have earned 12 credits or fewer in accounting or business. Applicants must be pursuing their CPA. Two essays are required.

Target applicant(s): Graduate school students. Adult students.

Amount: $5,000.

Number of awards: 5.

Deadline: March 1.

How to apply: Applications are available online.

Exclusive: Visit www.UltimateScholarshipBook.com and enter code AM53023 for updates on this award.

---

(531) · AICPA/Robert Half Student Scholarship

American Institute of Certified Public Accountants
220 Leigh Farm Road, Durham, NC 27707-8110
Phone: 919-402-4500
Email: scholarships@aicpa.org
https://www.aicpa.org

Purpose: To support students who are accounting majors planning to become CPAs.

Eligibility: Applicants must be pursuing an undergraduate or graduate-level degree in accounting or an accounting-related major and planning to pursue the CPA licensure. Students must be attending a public or private, not-for-profit four-year college or university in the U.S. or its territories and have completed at least 30 semester hours of college coursework, including at least six semester hours in accounting. Applicants must maintain an overall and major minimum 3.0 GPA and be enrolled as full-time undergraduate or graduate level students.

Target applicant(s): College students. Graduate school students. Adult students.

Minimum GPA: 3.0

Amount: $10,000.

Number of awards: 4.

Deadline: March 1.

How to apply: Applications are available online.

Exclusive: Visit www.UltimateScholarshipBook.com and enter code AM53123 for updates on this award.

---

(532) · AIERF Graduate Scholarship

Appraisal Institute Education Trust
200 W. Madison, Suite 1500, Chicago, IL 60606
Phone: 312-335-4133
Email: wwoodburn@appraisalinstitute.org
http://www.appraisalinstitute.org

Purpose: To support students who are working on a college degree concentrating on real estate appraisal, land economics, real estate or allied fields.

Eligibility: Applicants must be students majoring in real estate appraisal, land economics, real estate or allied fields. Students must be masters or doctoral candidates. Applicants must be full- or part-time students at a U.S. degree granting college or university with a strong academic record.

Target applicant(s): Graduate school students. Adult students.

Amount: $2,000.

Number of awards: Varies.

Deadline: April 1.

How to apply: Applications are available online.

Exclusive: Visit www.UltimateScholarshipBook.com and enter code AP53223 for updates on this award.

---

(533) · AIERF Undergraduate Scholarship

Appraisal Institute Education Trust
200 W. Madison, Suite 1500, Chicago, IL 60606
Phone: 312-335-4133
Email: wwoodburn@appraisalinstitute.org
http://www.appraisalinstitute.org

Purpose: To support students concentrating in real estate appraisal, land economics, real estate or allied fields.

Eligibility: Applicants must be students majoring in real estate appraisal, land economics, real estate or allied fields. Students must have a strong academic record.

Target applicant(s): College students. Adult students.

Amount: $1,000.

Number of awards: Varies.

Deadline: April 1.

How to apply: Applications are available online.

Exclusive: Visit www.UltimateScholarshipBook.com and enter code AP53323 for updates on this award.

---

(534) · Alice L. Haltom Educational Fund Scholarship

Alice L. Haltom Educational Fund
P.O. Box 70530, Houston, TX 77270
http://www.alhef.org/scholarship/

Purpose: To support students pursuing information and records management.

Eligibility: Applicants must be U.S. or Canadian citizens pursuing an education for a career in information and records management. Students must submit an essay, three letters of recommendation and transcripts along with their application.

Target applicant(s): College students. Graduate school students. Adult students.

Amount: $2,000.

Number of awards: Varies.

Deadline: May 1.

How to apply: Applications are available online.

Exclusive: Visit www.UltimateScholarshipBook.com and enter code AL53423 for updates on this award.

(535) · Allied Van Lines Scholarship

Allied Van Lines
One Parkview Plaza, Oakbrook Terrace, IL 60181
Phone: 800-689-8684
https://www.allied.com/scholarship
Purpose: To support students pursuing logistics and moving-related fields.
Eligibility: Applicants must be U.S. citizens or permanent residents enrolling as full-time students pursuing an undergraduate degree in logistics or related field. Students must provide transcripts, enrollment verification and an essay.
Target applicant(s): College students. Adult students.
Amount: $1,000.
Number of awards: 3.
Deadline: December 15.
How to apply: Applications are available online.
Exclusive: Visit www.UltimateScholarshipBook.com and enter code AL53523 for updates on this award.

(536) · Alpha Kappa Psi Scholarships

Alpha Kappa Psi Foundation
7801 E. 88th Street, Indianapolis, IN 46256
Phone: 317-872-1553
Email: foundation@akpsi.org
https://akpsifoundation.org/grants-and-scholarships/foundationscholarships/
Purpose: To support students who are members of the Alpha Kappa Psi society.
Eligibility: Applicants must be initiated Alpha Kappa Psi students who are currently undergraduate or graduate students with at least a 2.75 GPA. Students must have a strong record of chapter or campus leadership.
Target applicant(s): College students. Graduate school students. Adult students.
Minimum GPA: 2.75
Amount: $500-$1,500.
Number of awards: Varies.
Deadline: March 2.
How to apply: Applications are available online.
Exclusive: Visit www.UltimateScholarshipBook.com and enter code AL53623 for updates on this award.

(537) · American Bar Association Law Student Writing Competition

American Bar Association
321 North Clark Street, Chicago, IL 60654
Phone: 312-988-5624
Email: abalsd@americanbar.org
https://www.americanbar.org/groups/diversity/diversity_pipeline/projects_initiatives/legal_opportunity_scholarship/
Purpose: To support and recognize achievement among law students.
Eligibility: The American Bar Association (ABA) sponsors a variety of essay and writing competitions for ABA student members. Applicants must write an article about antitrust and have it published in an ABA-accredited school's law review or journal. Law students currently enrolled or graduating can write eligible articles of general interest to the antitrust law community, such as Civil and Criminal Antitrust Law, Competition Policy, Consumer Protection and International Competition Law. Selection is based on the strength of the essay.
Target applicant(s): Graduate school students. Adult students.
Amount: Varies.
Number of awards: Varies.
Deadline: Varies.
How to apply: Applications are available online. Application requirements vary by competition.
Exclusive: Visit www.UltimateScholarshipBook.com and enter code AM53723 for updates on this award.

(538) · American Culinary Federation Scholarships

American Culinary Federation
180 Center Place Way, St. Augustine, FL 32095
Phone: 904-824-4468
Email: scholarships@acfchefs.net
http://www.acfchefs.org
Purpose: To support high school and college students looking to further their education or compete in student culinary teams at ACF conferences.
Eligibility: Applicants must have a minimum GPA of 2.5, be graduating high school seniors and be accepted into an accredited college or university or be currently enrolled students in an accredited college or university. Applicants must also be planning to major in culinary or pastry arts or be ACF registered apprentices and have career aspirations of being a chef or pastry chef. Selection is based on GPA, participation in culinary competitions, volunteer activities, involvement in the ACF, essay and references.
Target applicant(s): High school students. College students. Adult students.
Minimum GPA: 2.5
Amount: Varies.
Number of awards: Varies.
Deadline: April 30; October 31.
How to apply: Applications are available online. An application form, essay and references are required.
Exclusive: Visit www.UltimateScholarshipBook.com and enter code AM53823 for updates on this award.

(539) · American Express Scholarship Competition

American Hotel and Lodging Educational Foundation (AHLEF)
1250 I Street NW, Suite 1100, Washington, DC 20005-3931
Phone: 202-289-3180
Email: foundation@ahlef.org
https://www.ahlafoundation.org/academic-scholarships
Purpose: To provide financial assistance to students pursuing a degree in hospitality management.
Eligibility: Applicants must be enrolled in an accredited undergraduate program resulting in a degree in hospitality management. Students or their parents must be employed in the lodging industry by an American Hotel and Lodging Association member facility.
Target applicant(s): College students. Adult students.
Amount: $500-$2,000.
Number of awards: Varies.
Deadline: February.
How to apply: Applications are available online.
Exclusive: Visit www.UltimateScholarshipBook.com and enter code AM53923 for updates on this award.

(540) · APF/COGDOP Graduate Student Scholarships

American Psychological Foundation
750 First Street NE, Washington, DC 20002-4242
Phone: 202-336-5843
Email: foundation@apa.org
https://www.apa.org/apf/funding/grants
Purpose: To assist graduate students of psychology with research costs associated with the master's thesis or doctoral dissertation.
Eligibility: Applicants must be graduate students enrolled in an interim master's program or doctoral program. Students currently enrolled in a terminal master's program must intend to enroll in a PhD program. Applicants at any stage of graduate study are encouraged to apply and must be enrolled in the graduate program at the time grants are awarded.
Target applicant(s): Graduate school students. Adult students.
Amount: $2,000-$5,000.
Number of awards: Varies.
Deadline: June 30.
How to apply: Applicants must be nominated.
Exclusive: Visit www.UltimateScholarshipBook.com and enter code AM54023 for updates on this award.

(541) · ARIT Fellowships for Research in Turkey

American Research Institute in Turkey (ARIT)
3260 South Street, Philadelphia, PA 19104-6324
Phone: 215-898-3474
Email: leinwand@sas.upenn.edu
http://ccat.sas.upenn.edu/ARIT
Purpose: To support scholars in their research in Turkey.
Eligibility: Applicants must be scholars or advanced graduate students involved in research on ancient, medieval or modern times in Turkey, in any field of the humanities and social sciences. Student applicants must have completed all requirements for the doctorate except the dissertation before beginning any ARIT-sponsored research. Non-U.S. applicants must be connected to an educational institution in the U.S. or Canada. Applicants should submit applications, three letters of recommendation and graduate transcripts.
Target applicant(s): Graduate school students. Adult students.
Amount: Varies.
Number of awards: Varies.
Deadline: November 1.
How to apply: Applications are available online.
Exclusive: Visit www.UltimateScholarshipBook.com and enter code AM54123 for updates on this award.

(542) · ARRL Foundation General Fund Scholarship

American Radio Relay League Foundation
225 Main Street, Newington, CT 06111-1494
Phone: 860-594-0348
Email: foundation@arrl.org
http://www.arrl.org/scholarship-program
Purpose: To assist ham radio operators in furthering their educations.
Eligibility: Applicants must have any level of ham radio license.
Target applicant(s): High school students. College students. Graduate school students. Adult students.
Amount: $2,000.
Number of awards: Varies.
Deadline: December 31.
How to apply: Applications are available online. Completed applications must be submitted by mail.

Exclusive: Visit www.UltimateScholarshipBook.com and enter code AM54223 for updates on this award.

(543) · Asparagus Club, Thomas K. Zaucha Scholarship

National Grocers Association
1005 N. Glebe Road, Suite 250, Arlington, VA 22201
Phone: 225-387-6126
https://www.nationalgrocers.org/foundation/nga-foundation-scholarships/
Purpose: To support students pursuing degrees related to the grocery field.
Eligibility: Applicants must be rising sophomores through postgraduate students, have a minimum 2.5 GPA and be enrolled in a two- or four-year degree-granting institution. Students must major in business, food management, IT or another field related to a career in the grocery industry. Experience in the grocery industry is preferred but not required.
Target applicant(s): College students. Graduate school students. Adult students.
Minimum GPA: 2.5
Amount: $1,000-$7,000.
Number of awards: 1.
Deadline: April 1.
How to apply: Applications are available online.
Exclusive: Visit www.UltimateScholarshipBook.com and enter code NA54323 for updates on this award.

(544) · Association William S. Bullinger Scholarship

Federal Circuit Bar Association
1620 I Street NW, Suite 801, Washington, DC 20006
Phone: 202-466-3923
Email: fcbascholarships@fedcirbar.org
http://www.fedcirbar.org
Purpose: To support financially needy but academically promising law students.
Eligibility: Applicants must be undergraduate or graduate law students who demonstrate financial need and academic promise. They must submit a one-page statement describing their financial circumstances, their interest in law and their qualifications for the scholarship along with transcripts and a curriculum vitae.
Target applicant(s): College students. Graduate school students. Adult students.
Amount: $5,000.
Number of awards: 1.
Deadline: April.
How to apply: There is no application form.
Exclusive: Visit www.UltimateScholarshipBook.com and enter code FE54423 for updates on this award.

(545) · AWSCPA Scholarship

American Institute of Certified Public Accountants
220 Leigh Farm Road, Durham, NC 27707-8110
Phone: 919-402-4500
Email: scholarships@aicpa.org
https://www.aicpa.org
Purpose: To support female students majoring in accounting.
Eligibility: Applicants must be women enrolled as full-time undergraduate or graduate level students pursuing a degree in accounting or an accounting-related major. Students must have completed at least 30 semester hours of college coursework, including at least six semester

hours in accounting while maintaining an overall and major GPA of 3.0. Applicants must be U.S. citizens or permanent residents and planning to pursue CPA licensure.

Target applicant(s): College students. Graduate school students. Adult students.

Minimum GPA: 3.0

Amount: $5,000.

Number of awards: 4.

Deadline: March 1.

How to apply: Applications are available online.

Exclusive: Visit www.UltimateScholarshipBook.com and enter code AM54523 for updates on this award.

(546) · BEA National Scholarships in Broadcasting

Broadcast Education Association
1771 N Street NW, Washington, DC 20036
Phone: 888-380-7222
Email: beainfo@beaweb.org
http://www.beaweb.org

Purpose: To honor broadcasters and the broadcast industry.

Eligibility: Applicants must be college juniors or seniors or graduate students at BEA member universities, students pursuing freshman and sophomore instruction only or students who have already completed BEA two-year programs at a four-year college.

Target applicant(s): High school students. College students. Graduate school students. Adult students.

Amount: $1,500 to $4,000.

Number of awards: 10.

Deadline: October 15.

How to apply: Applications are available online.

Exclusive: Visit www.UltimateScholarshipBook.com and enter code BR54623 for updates on this award.

(547) · Beauty Changes Lives Foundation Scholarships

Beauty Changes Lives
P.O. Box 7174, Rancho Santa Fe, CA 92067
Phone: 760-733-8383
Email: info@beautychangeslives.org
http://www.beautychangeslives.org

Purpose: To support licensed hairstylists in attending a member school of the American Association of Cosmetology Schools.

Eligibility: Applicants must be accepted or currently enrolled in a member school of the American Association of Cosmetology Schools. Selection is based on the overall strength of the application.

Target applicant(s): College students. Adult students.

Amount: $500-$15,000.

Number of awards: 15.

Deadline: November 30, February 28, May 31, August 31.

How to apply: Applications are available online.

Exclusive: Visit www.UltimateScholarshipBook.com and enter code BE54723 for updates on this award.

(548) · Begun Scholarship

California Library Association
248 E. Foothill Boulevard, Suite 101, Monrovia, CA 91016
Phone: 916-779-4573
Email: info@cla-net.org
http://www.cla-net.org

Purpose: To assist California library or information sciences graduate students at California schools.

Eligibility: Applicants must be California graduate students attending an American Library Association accredited school and have completed core coursework toward a master's of library and science or information studies degree. Recipients must also plan to become a children's or young adult librarian in a California public library and to join the California Library Association if not already a member.

Target applicant(s): Graduate school students. Adult students.

Minimum GPA: 3.0

Amount: $3,000.

Number of awards: 1.

Deadline: Varies.

How to apply: Applications are available online.

Exclusive: Visit www.UltimateScholarshipBook.com and enter code CA54823 for updates on this award.

(549) · Betsy Plank/PRSSA Scholarship

Public Relations Student Society of America
33 Maiden Lane, 11th Floor, New York, NY 10038
Phone: 212-460-1474
Email: prssa@prsa.org
https://prssa.prsa.org/scholarships-and-awards/

Purpose: To assist public relations students.

Eligibility: Applicants must be PRSSA members enrolled in an undergraduate public relations program and be college juniors or seniors. Eligible students may be nominated from each PRSSA chapter. Selection is based on academic achievement, leadership, experience and commitment to public relations. Applicants need to include a 300-word statement of commitment to public relations.

Target applicant(s): College students. Adult students.

Amount: $1,000-$5,000.

Number of awards: 3.

Deadline: May 31.

How to apply: Applications are available online.

Exclusive: Visit www.UltimateScholarshipBook.com and enter code PU54923 for updates on this award.

(550) · Bill, W2ONV, and Ann Salerno Memorial Scholarship

American Radio Relay League Foundation
225 Main Street, Newington, CT 06111-1494
Phone: 860-594-0348
Email: foundation@arrl.org
http://www.arrl.org/scholarship-program

Purpose: To provide financial assistance to amateur radio operators with high academic achievement.

Eligibility: Applicants must hold an active Amateur Radio License of any class and attend an accredited four-year college or university. They must have a GPA of 3.7 or higher, and their household income may not exceed $100,000 per year. They must not have previously received the Salerno Scholarship.

Target applicant(s): High school students. College students. Adult students.

Minimum GPA: 3.7

Amount: $1,000.

Number of awards: 2.

Deadline: December 31.

How to apply: Applications are available online.

Exclusive: Visit www.UltimateScholarshipBook.com and enter code AM55023 for updates on this award.

(551) · Bob East Scholarship

National Press Photographers Foundation Bob East Scholarship
Chuck Fadely, The Miami Herald, One Herald Plaza, Miami, FL 33132
Phone: 305-376-2015
http://www.nppf.org
Purpose: To encourage newcomers in photojournalism.
Eligibility: Applicants must either be an undergraduate in the first three and one half years of college or be planning to pursue postgraduate work.
Target applicant(s): High school students. College students. Graduate school students. Adult students.
Amount: $2,000.
Number of awards: 1.
Deadline: December 2.
How to apply: Applications are available online.
Exclusive: Visit www.UltimateScholarshipBook.com and enter code NA55123 for updates on this award.

(552) · Bob Richardson Legacy Scholarship

National Grocers Association
1005 N. Glebe Road, Suite 250, Arlington, VA 22201
Phone: 225-387-6126
https://www.nationalgrocers.org/foundation/nga-foundation-scholarships/
Purpose: To support students pursuing a degree related to the grocery field.
Eligibility: Applicants must be rising sophomores through postgraduate students, have a minimum 2.5 GPA and be enrolled in a two- or four-year degree-granting institution. Students must major in business, food management, IT or another field related to a career in the grocery industry. Experience in the grocery industry is preferred but not required.
Target applicant(s): College students. Graduate school students. Adult students.
Minimum GPA: 2.5
Amount: Varies.
Number of awards: 1.
Deadline: April 1.
How to apply: Applications are available online.
Exclusive: Visit www.UltimateScholarshipBook.com and enter code NA55223 for updates on this award.

(553) · Bodie McDowell Scholarship

Outdoor Writers Association of America
121 Hickory Street, Suite 1, Missoula, MT 59801
Phone: 406-728-7434
Email: krhoades@owaa.org
http://www.owaa.org
Purpose: To support students in outdoor communications fields.
Eligibility: Applicants must be students of outdoor communications fields including print, film, art or broadcasting and must be either undergraduate students entering their junior or senior year or graduate students.
Target applicant(s): College students. Graduate school students. Adult students.
Amount: $1,000-$5,000.
Number of awards: 3 or more.
Deadline: March 1.

How to apply: Applicants are available online.
Exclusive: Visit www.UltimateScholarshipBook.com and enter code OU55323 for updates on this award.

(554) · Boren Scholarships

National Security Education Program Initiative, Administered by Institute of International Education
1400 K Street, NW, 7th Floor, Washington, DC 20005
Phone: 800-618-6737
Email: boren@iie.org
https://www.borenawards.org
Purpose: To reward students who desire to study abroad in preparation for a career in U.S. national security.
Eligibility: Applicants must be U.S. citizens and undergraduate matriculated students at an accredited U.S. institution who have chosen a proposed country of study.
Target applicant(s): College students. Adult students.
Amount: $8,000-$25,000.
Number of awards: Varies.
Deadline: February 3.
How to apply: Applications are available online.
Exclusive: Visit www.UltimateScholarshipBook.com and enter code NA55423 for updates on this award.

(555) · Bound to Stay Bound Books Scholarship

Association for Library Service to Children
50 E. Huron Street, Chicago, IL 60611
Phone: 800-545-2433
Email: cjewell@ala.org
http://www.ala.org/alsc/awardsgrants
Purpose: To support students pursuing their MLS degrees.
Eligibility: Applicants must intend to pursue an MLS or advanced degree, plan to work in children's librarianship and be U.S. or Canadian citizens. Selection is based on academic excellence, leadership and a desire to work with children in any type of library.
Target applicant(s): College students. Graduate school students. Adult students.
Amount: $8,000.
Number of awards: 4.
Deadline: March 1.
How to apply: Applications are available online.
Exclusive: Visit www.UltimateScholarshipBook.com and enter code AS55523 for updates on this award.

(556) · BSA Research Fellowship

Bibliographical Society of America
P.O. Box 1537, Lenox Hill Station, New York, NY 10021
Phone: 212-452-2710
Email: bsafellowships@bibsocamer.org
https://bibsocamer.org/awards/fellowships/
Purpose: To provide financial assistance to those pursuing bibliographical studies.
Eligibility: Applicants must submit proposals for studying books as historical evidence or an examination of the history of book trades or publishing history.
Target applicant(s): College students. Graduate school students. Adult students.
Amount: $3,000-$6,000.
Number of awards: Varies.
Deadline: October 1.

How to apply: Applications are available online.
Exclusive: Visit www.UltimateScholarshipBook.com and enter code BI55623 for updates on this award.

(557) · Byron Hanke Fellowship

Foundation for Community Association Research
6402 Arlington Boulevard, Suite 500, Falls Church, VA 22042
Phone: 703-970-9220
http://www.cairf.org
Purpose: To support graduate students who are working on topics related to community associations.
Eligibility: Applicants must be currently enrolled in an accredited master's, doctoral or law program in the U.S. or Canada. Students must submit a research paper on community associations. Selection is primarily based on demonstration of research and writing abilities, academic achievement and faculty recommendations.
Target applicant(s): Graduate school students. Adult students.
Amount: $5,000.
Number of awards: 1.
Deadline: May 1.
How to apply: Applications are available online.
Exclusive: Visit www.UltimateScholarshipBook.com and enter code FO55723 for updates on this award.

(558) · California - Hawaii Elks Association Vocational Grants

California-Hawaii Elks Association
5450 E. Lamona Avenue, Fresno, CA 93727-2224
Phone: 559-255-4531
Email: chea@chea-elks.org
https://chea-elks.org/youth-activities/scholarships
Purpose: To provide assistance to those pursuing vocational/technical education.
Eligibility: Applicants must be U.S. citizens and California or Hawaii residents. They must plan to pursue a vocational or technical course of study above and supplemental to high school or preparatory school. A high school diploma or equivalent is not required. Students planning to transfer into a bachelor's degree program upon completion of vocational studies are not eligible.
Target applicant(s): High school students. College students. Adult students.
Amount: $500-$2,000.
Number of awards: Varies.
Scholarship may be renewable.
Deadline: Varies.
How to apply: Applications are available online.
Exclusive: Visit www.UltimateScholarshipBook.com and enter code CA55823 for updates on this award.

(559) · Caples Student Campaign of the Year Award

ASL Marketing
2 Dubon Court, Farmingdale, NY 11735
Phone: 516-248-6100
http://www.caples.org
Purpose: To support students who are interested in direct marketing.
Eligibility: Applicants can be from anywhere in the world and the award is based on the boldness of the concept, the logic of the execution and the overall strength of the outcome.
Target applicant(s): College students. Adult students.
Amount: Varies.

Number of awards: Varies.
Deadline: April 30.
How to apply: Applications are available online.
Exclusive: Visit www.UltimateScholarshipBook.com and enter code AS55923 for updates on this award.

(560) · CardRates.com Financial Futures Scholarship

CardRates.com
15 SE 1st Avenue, Suite B, Gainesville, FL 32601
http://www.cardrates.com/scholarship/
Purpose: To support students pursuing a career in the personal finance industry.
Eligibility: Applicants must be U.S. residents and current college students or graduating high school seniors enrolling in college. Students must be majoring in a field related to personal finance such as business, accounting, finance, mathematics or management and hold a minimum 3.5 GPA.
Target applicant(s): High school students. College students. Adult students.
Minimum GPA: 3.5
Amount: $1,000.
Number of awards: 1.
Deadline: July 31.
How to apply: Applications are available online.
Exclusive: Visit www.UltimateScholarshipBook.com and enter code CA56023 for updates on this award.

(561) · Carole J. Streeter, KB9JBR, Scholarship

American Radio Relay League Foundation
225 Main Street, Newington, CT 06111-1494
Phone: 860-594-0348
Email: foundation@arrl.org
http://www.arrl.org/scholarship-program
Purpose: To support students who are involved in amateur radio.
Eligibility: Applicants must have an amateur radio license of Technician Class or higher. Preference will be given to applicants with Morse Code proficiency and those studying health and healing arts.
Target applicant(s): High school students. College students. Adult students.
Amount: $1,000.
Number of awards: 1.
Deadline: December 31.
How to apply: Applications are available online.
Exclusive: Visit www.UltimateScholarshipBook.com and enter code AM56123 for updates on this award.

(562) · Carole Simpson Scholarship

Radio Television Digital News Association
529 14th Street NW, Suite 1240, Washington, DC 20045
Phone: 202-659-6510
Email: karenh@rtdna.org
http://www.rtdna.org
Purpose: To honor professional achievements in electronic journalism.
Eligibility: Applicants must be full-time college sophomores or higher with at least one full academic year remaining. Applicants may be enrolled in any major as long as their career intent is television or radio news. Applicants may only apply for one RTNDA scholarship. Preference is given to students of color.
Target applicant(s): College students. Adult students.
Amount: $2,000.

Number of awards: 1.
Deadline: January 15.
How to apply: Applications are available online.
Exclusive: Visit www.UltimateScholarshipBook.com and enter code RA56223 for updates on this award.

(563) · Charles Clarke Cordle Memorial Scholarship

American Radio Relay League Foundation
225 Main Street, Newington, CT 06111-1494
Phone: 860-594-0348
Email: foundation@arrl.org
http://www.arrl.org/scholarship-program
Purpose: To assist ham radio operators in furthering their educations.
Eligibility: Applicants must have any class of ham radio license, have a minimum 2.5 GPA and be residents of and attend school in Georgia or Alabama.
Target applicant(s): High school students. College students. Graduate school students. Adult students.
Minimum GPA: 2.5
Amount: $1,000.
Number of awards: 1.
Deadline: December 31.
How to apply: Applications are available online but may not be completed electronically. All completed applications must be mailed.
Exclusive: Visit www.UltimateScholarshipBook.com and enter code AM56323 for updates on this award.

(564) · Charles N. Fisher Memorial Scholarship

American Radio Relay League Foundation
225 Main Street, Newington, CT 06111-1494
Phone: 860-594-0348
Email: foundation@arrl.org
http://www.arrl.org/scholarship-program
Purpose: To assist ham radio operators in furthering their educations.
Eligibility: Applicants must have any class of ham radio license, be residents of the ARRL Southwestern Division (Arizona, Los Angeles, Orange County, San Diego or Santa Barbara), attend a regionally-accredited college or university and study electronics, communications or a related field.
Target applicant(s): High school students. College students. Graduate school students. Adult students.
Amount: $1,000.
Number of awards: 1.
Deadline: December 31.
How to apply: Applications are available online. Completed applications must be submitted by mail, not electronically.
Exclusive: Visit www.UltimateScholarshipBook.com and enter code AM56423 for updates on this award.

(565) · Charlie and Becky Bray Legacy Scholarship

National Grocers Association
1005 N. Glebe Road, Suite 250, Arlington, VA 22201
Phone: 225-387-6126
https://www.nationalgrocers.org/foundation/nga-foundation-scholarships/
Purpose: To support students pursuing degrees related to the grocery field.
Eligibility: Applicants must be rising sophomores through postgraduate students, have a minimum 2.5 GPA and be enrolled in a two- or four-year degree-granting institution. Students must major in business,

food management, IT or another field related to a career in the grocery industry. Experience in the grocery industry is preferred but not required.
Target applicant(s): College students. Graduate school students. Adult students.
Minimum GPA: 2.5
Amount: Varies.
Number of awards: 1.
Deadline: April 1.
How to apply: Applications are available online.
Exclusive: Visit www.UltimateScholarshipBook.com and enter code NA56523 for updates on this award.

(566) · Chester Burger Scholarship for Excellence in Public Relations

Public Relations Student Society of America
33 Maiden Lane, 11th Floor, New York, NY 10038
Phone: 212-460-1474
Email: prssa@prsa.org
https://prssa.prsa.org/scholarships-and-awards/
Purpose: To encourage public relations and journalism graduate students to pursue careers in corporate public relations.
Eligibility: Applicants must be entering or current graduate students at a U.S. college or university. They must be majoring in journalism, public relations or a related field. They must have an undergraduate GPA of 3.0 or higher on a four-point scale and be interested in pursuing a career in corporate public relations. Selection is based on the overall strength of the application.
Target applicant(s): College students. Graduate school students. Adult students.
Minimum GPA: 3.0
Amount: $1,000.
Number of awards: 1.
Deadline: May 31.
How to apply: Applications are available online. An application form, resume, essay and two recommendation letters are required.
Exclusive: Visit www.UltimateScholarshipBook.com and enter code PU56623 for updates on this award.

(567) · CLA Scholarship for Minority Students in Memory of Edna Yelland

California Library Association
248 E. Foothill Boulevard, Suite 101, Monrovia, CA 91016
Phone: 916-779-4573
Email: info@cla-net.org
http://www.cla-net.org
Purpose: To assist minority California graduate students who are pursuing degrees in library or information science.
Eligibility: Applicants must be California residents, be American Indian, African American, Mexican American, Latino, Asian American, Pacific Islander or Filipino and be accepted into or enrolled in an American Library Association accredited state library school. The award is based on financial need, and an interview is required.
Target applicant(s): College students. Graduate school students. Adult students.
Amount: $2,500.
Number of awards: up to 3.
Deadline: Varies.
How to apply: Applications are available online.
Exclusive: Visit www.UltimateScholarshipBook.com and enter code CA56723 for updates on this award.

(568) · Clifford H. Ted Rees Jr. Scholarship

Air-Conditioning, Heating and Refrigeration Institute
Clifford H., 2111 Wilson Boulevard, Suite 500, Arlington, VA 22201
Phone: 703-524-8800
Email: ReesApplications@ahrinet.org
http://www.ahrinet.org
Purpose: To support students preparing for careers in heating, ventilation, air-conditioning and refrigeration (HVACR) technology.
Eligibility: Applicants must be U.S. citizens, nationals or resident aliens intending to become U.S. citizens. They must be enrolled in an accredited HVACR technician training program and have plans to become entry-level commercial refrigeration technicians, residential air-conditioning and heating technicians or light commercial air-conditioning and heating technicians after graduation. Selection is based on stated career goals and commitment to pursuing entry-level work in the HVACR field.
Target applicant(s): College students. Adult students.
Amount: Up to $2,000.
Number of awards: 15.
Deadline: June 1 (fall), October 1 (spring).
How to apply: Applications are available online. An application form, two recommendation letters, personal statement and copy of alien registration card (if applicable) are required.
Exclusive: Visit www.UltimateScholarshipBook.com and enter code AI56823 for updates on this award.

(569) · College Photographer of the Year

National Press Photographers Foundation College Photographer of the Year
David Rees, CPOY Director, School of Journalism, The University of Missouri, 106 Lee Hills Hall, Columbus, MO 65211
Phone: 573-882-4442
Email: jourdlr@showme.missouri.edu
http://nppf.org/nppf-scholarships-grants-and-awards/
Purpose: To reward outstanding student work in photojournalism and provide a forum for student photographers to gauge their skills.
Eligibility: Applicants must be currently enrolled in a full-time four-year college or university, provide a portfolio and demonstrate financial need. Applicants can apply to as many NPPA scholarships as desired, but only one award will be granted to each winner.
Target applicant(s): High school students. College students. Graduate school students. Adult students.
Amount: Varies.
Number of awards: Varies.
Deadline: September.
How to apply: Applications are available by written or email request.
Exclusive: Visit www.UltimateScholarshipBook.com and enter code NA56923 for updates on this award.

(570) · Costa Rican Vacations Scholarship Program

Costa Rica Vacations
Costa Rican Vacations - Travel Agency, Calle 70, San José Province, San Jose, Costa Rica
Phone: 800-606-1860
Email: scholarships@namutravel.com
http://www.vacationscostarica.com/about-us/scholarships
Purpose: To support students in pursuing post-secondary studies in the fields of tourism, hospitality and sustainable development.
Eligibility: Applicants must be enrolled at a U.S.-based university. A minimum GPA of 2.8 is required. Students must submit an essay explaining their career goals in the areas of tourism, hospitality or sustainable development.
Target applicant(s): College students. Graduate school students. Adult students.
Minimum GPA: 2.8
Amount: $1,000.
Number of awards: 2.
Deadline: February 15.
How to apply: Applications are available online.
Exclusive: Visit www.UltimateScholarshipBook.com and enter code CO57023 for updates on this award.

(571) · Darrel Hess Community College Geography Scholarship

Association of American Geographers (AAG) Hess Scholarship
1710 Sixteenth Street NW, Washington, DC 20009-3198
Phone: 202-234-1450
Email: grantsawards@aag.org
http://www.aag.org/cs/grantsawards
Purpose: To support geography majors.
Eligibility: Applicants must be currently enrolled at a U.S. community college, junior college, city college or similar two-year educational institution, have completed at least two transfer courses in geography and plan to transfer to a four-year institution as a geography major. The award is based on academic excellence and promise. Applications, personal statements, two recommendation letters and transcripts are required.
Target applicant(s): College students. Adult students.
Amount: $1,500.
Number of awards: 2.
Deadline: December 31.
How to apply: Applications are available online.
Exclusive: Visit www.UltimateScholarshipBook.com and enter code AS57123 for updates on this award.

(572) · David H. and Beverly A. Barlow Grant

American Psychological Foundation
750 First Street NE, Washington, DC 20002-4242
Phone: 202-336-5843
Email: foundation@apa.org
https://www.apa.org/apf/funding/grants
Purpose: To support graduate students and early career researchers in innovative basic and clinical research on anxiety and anxiety-related disorders.
Eligibility: Applicants must be graduate students or early career researchers no more than 10 years postdoctoral. Students must be affiliated with nonprofit charitable, educational and scientific institutions or governmental entities operating exclusively for charitable and educational purposes. Applicants must have a demonstrated knowledge of anxiety and anxiety research, either basic or clinical.
Target applicant(s): Graduate school students. Adult students.
Amount: Up to $7,500.
Number of awards: Varies.
Deadline: September 15.
How to apply: Applications are available online.
Exclusive: Visit www.UltimateScholarshipBook.com and enter code AM57223 for updates on this award.

(573) · Dayton Amateur Radio Association Scholarship

American Radio Relay League Foundation
225 Main Street, Newington, CT 06111-1494
Phone: 860-594-0348
Email: foundation@arrl.org
http://www.arrl.org/scholarship-program
Purpose: To provide financial assistance to students who are amateur radio operators.
Eligibility: Applicants must be accepted or enrolled at an accredited four-year institution of higher learning. They must possess an Amateur Radio License of any class.
Target applicant(s): High school students. College students. Adult students.
Amount: $1,500.
Number of awards: Varies.
Deadline: December 31.
How to apply: Applications are available online.
Exclusive: Visit www.UltimateScholarshipBook.com and enter code AM57323 for updates on this award.

(574) · DEWALT Trades Scholarship

Stanley Black and Decker
DEWALT Trades Scholarship, Scholarship America, One Scholarship Way, Saint Peter, MN 56082
Phone: 800-537-4180
Email: DEWALTtrade@scholarshipamerica.org
https://learnmore.scholarsapply.org/DEWALTtrade/
Purpose: To support students pursuing a trade degree or certificate.
Eligibility: Applicants must be current high school seniors or college undergraduate students planning to enroll or enrolled in full-time undergraduate study at an accredited two-year college or vocational-technical school for the entire upcoming academic year. Students must be majoring in a trade construction, industrial, motor/power sector, mechanics or technology degree/certificate with a minimum 2.0 GPA.
Target applicant(s): High school students. College students. Adult students.
Minimum GPA: 2.0
Amount: $10,000.
Number of awards: 20.
Deadline: December.
How to apply: Applications are available online.
Exclusive: Visit www.UltimateScholarshipBook.com and enter code ST57423 for updates on this award.

(575) · Distinguished Service Award for Students

Society for Technical Communication
Manager of the Distinguished Community Awards Committee, 9401 Lee Highway, Suite 300, Fairfax, VA 22031
Phone: 703-522-4114
Email: stc@stc.org
http://www.stc.org
Purpose: To assist students who are pursuing degrees in an area of technical communication.
Eligibility: Applicants must be full-time undergraduate or graduate students who have completed at least one year of post-secondary education and who have at least one full year of academic work remaining to complete their degree programs. Students must also be in the field of communication of information about technical subjects and be student members of the STC. Applicants must be nominated by student chapters.
Target applicant(s): College students. Graduate school students. Adult students.
Amount: Varies.
Number of awards: Varies.
Deadline: November.
How to apply: Applications are available online.
Exclusive: Visit www.UltimateScholarshipBook.com and enter code SO57523 for updates on this award.

(576) · Donald Riebhoff Memorial Scholarship

American Radio Relay League Foundation
225 Main Street, Newington, CT 06111-1494
Phone: 860-594-0348
Email: foundation@arrl.org
http://www.arrl.org/scholarship-program
Purpose: To assist ham radio operators in furthering their educations.
Eligibility: Applicants must have at least a technician ham radio license, be undergraduate or graduate students in international studies at an accredited post-secondary institution and be members of ARRL.
Target applicant(s): High school students. College students. Graduate school students. Adult students.
Amount: $1,000.
Number of awards: 1.
Deadline: December 31.
How to apply: Applications are available online. Completed applications must be mailed in. They cannot be completed electronically.
Exclusive: Visit www.UltimateScholarshipBook.com and enter code AM57623 for updates on this award.

(577) · Dr. James L. Lawson Memorial Scholarship

American Radio Relay League Foundation
225 Main Street, Newington, CT 06111-1494
Phone: 860-594-0348
Email: foundation@arrl.org
http://www.arrl.org/scholarship-program
Purpose: To assist ham radio operators in furthering their educations.
Eligibility: Applicants must have at least a general ham radio license, be residents of and attend post-secondary institutions in the New England states (Connecticut, Maine, Massachusetts, New Hampshire, Rhode Island or Vermont) or New York state and be pursuing a bachelor's or graduate degree in electronics, communications or a related field.
Target applicant(s): High school students. College students. Graduate school students. Adult students.
Amount: $1,000.
Number of awards: 1.
Deadline: December 31.
How to apply: Applications are available online but cannot be completed electronically. All applications must be mailed.
Exclusive: Visit www.UltimateScholarshipBook.com and enter code AM57723 for updates on this award.

(578) · Dr. Robert Hawkins Memorial Scholarship

John Philip Sousa Foundation
196 East 650 North, West Lafayette, IN 47906
Phone: 617-529-9402
Email: treynold@worldpath.net
http://www.sousafoundation.net

Purpose: To support students pursuing a degree in instrumental music education.
Eligibility: Applicants must plan on attending a college or university in the United States and pursue a degree in instrumental music education. Students must complete the application in full including essay statement, three letters of recommendation and current transcript.
Target applicant(s): High school students. College students. Adult students.
Amount: $2,000.
Number of awards: 2.
Scholarship may be renewable.
Deadline: November 5.
How to apply: Applications are available online.
Exclusive: Visit www.UltimateScholarshipBook.com and enter code JO57823 for updates on this award.

(579) · Drs. Rosalee G. and Raymond A. Weiss Research and Program Innovation Grants
American Psychological Foundation
750 First Street NE, Washington, DC 20002-4242
Phone: 202-336-5843
Email: foundation@apa.org
https://www.apa.org/apf/funding/grants
Purpose: To support innovation through supporting research, education, and intervention projects and programs.
Eligibility: Applicants must be graduate students or early career researchers no more than 10 years postdoctoral. Students must be affiliated with a nonprofit charitable, educational or scientific institution or governmental entity operating exclusively for charitable and educational purposes. Applicants must have demonstrated competence and capacity to execute the proposed work.
Target applicant(s): Graduate school students. Adult students.
Amount: $1,000.
Number of awards: Varies.
Deadline: September 15.
How to apply: Applications are available online.
Exclusive: Visit www.UltimateScholarshipBook.com and enter code AM57923 for updates on this award.

(580) · Earl Warren Scholarship
NAACP Legal Defense and Educational Fund
40 Rector Street, 5th Floor, New York, NY 10006
Phone: 212-965-2200
http://www.naacpldf.org/
Purpose: To reward promising law students who have potential for training as civil rights and public interest attorneys.
Eligibility: Applicants must be law students entering their first or second year of full-time legal study at an accredited law school. Students must show a strong commitment to racial justice and civil rights. Applicants must be U.S. citizens. Students must either be college graduates, enrolled in their final year of college or university or be a first-year law student. Applicants must have a strong record of academic achievement.
Target applicant(s): College students. Graduate school students. Adult students.
Amount: $30,000.
Number of awards: Varies.
Scholarship may be renewable.
Deadline: May 1.
How to apply: Applications are available online.

Exclusive: Visit www.UltimateScholarshipBook.com and enter code NA58023 for updates on this award.

(581) · Ecolab Scholarship Competition
American Hotel and Lodging Educational Foundation (AHLEF)
1250 I Street NW, Suite 1100, Washington, DC 20005-3931
Phone: 202-289-3180
Email: foundation@ahlef.org
https://www.ahlafoundation.org/academic-scholarships
Purpose: To provide scholarships for students who intend to earn a degree in hospitality management.
Eligibility: Applicants must be enrolled or intend to enroll full-time in a two- or four-year U.S. college or university.
Target applicant(s): High school students. College students. Adult students.
Amount: $1,000-$2,000.
Number of awards: Varies.
Deadline: February.
How to apply: Applications are available online.
Exclusive: Visit www.UltimateScholarshipBook.com and enter code AM58123 for updates on this award.

(582) · Ed Bradley Scholarship
Radio Television Digital News Association
529 14th Street NW, Suite 1240, Washington, DC 20045
Phone: 202-659-6510
Email: karenh@rtdna.org
http://www.rtdna.org
Purpose: To honor professional achievements in electronic journalism.
Eligibility: Applicants must be full-time college sophomores or higher with at least one full academic year remaining. Applicants may be enrolled in any major as long as their career intent is television or radio news. Applicants may only apply for one RTNDA scholarship.
Target applicant(s): College students. Adult students.
Amount: $10,000.
Number of awards: 1.
Deadline: January 15.
How to apply: Applications are available online.
Exclusive: Visit www.UltimateScholarshipBook.com and enter code RA58223 for updates on this award.

(583) · Edmond A. Metzger Scholarship
American Radio Relay League Foundation
225 Main Street, Newington, CT 06111-1494
Phone: 860-594-0348
Email: foundation@arrl.org
http://www.arrl.org/scholarship-program
Purpose: To assist ham radio operators in furthering their educations.
Eligibility: Applicants must have at least a novice ham radio license, be undergraduate or graduate students in electrical engineering, be residents of and attend schools in the ARRL Central Division (Illinois, Indiana or Wisconsin) and be members of ARRL.
Target applicant(s): College students. Graduate school students. Adult students.
Amount: $500.
Number of awards: 1.
Deadline: December 31.
How to apply: Applications are available online. Completed applications must be mailed in. They cannot be completed electronically.

Exclusive: Visit www.UltimateScholarshipBook.com and enter code AM58323 for updates on this award.

(584) · Educational Foundation Scholarship

International Society of Automation
67 T.W. Alexander Drive, P.O. Box 12277, Research Triangle Park, NC 27709
Phone: 919-549-8411
Email: info@isa.org
https://www.isa.org/students/scholarships/
Purpose: To support students interested in the fields of automation and control.
Eligibility: Applicants must be full-time students in a graduate, undergraduate or two-year degree program. Students must have a minimum GPA of 2.5 and be enrolled in a program in automation and control or another closely related field.
Target applicant(s): College students. Graduate school students. Adult students.
Minimum GPA: 2.5
Amount: Varies.
Number of awards: Varies.
Deadline: February 28.
How to apply: Applications are available online.
Exclusive: Visit www.UltimateScholarshipBook.com and enter code IN58423 for updates on this award.

(585) · EGIA Foundation Scholarship Program

EGIA Foundation
3800 Watt Avenue, Suite 105, Sacramento, CA 95821
Phone: 866-562-9060
Email: chanson@egiafoundation.org
https://egiafoundation.org/what-we-do/scholarship
Purpose: To support students wishing to pursue a career in the HVACR industry.
Eligibility: Applicants must be a high school senior or adult student who is enrolled or planning to enroll at an accredited two-year college, vocational or technical school or other approved technical institute to pursue studies in HVACR. A minimum 2.0 GPA or higher is required.
Target applicant(s): High school students. College students. Graduate school students. Adult students.
Minimum GPA: 2.0
Amount: $2,500.
Number of awards: 20.
Deadline: February 1.
How to apply: Applications are available online.
Exclusive: Visit www.UltimateScholarshipBook.com and enter code EG58523 for updates on this award.

(586) · Executive Women International Scholarship Program

Executive Women International (EWI)
3860 South 2300 East, Suite 211, Salt Lake City, UT 84109
Phone: 801-355-2800
Email: ewi@ewiconnect.com
https://ewiconnect.com
Purpose: To assist high school students in achieving their higher education goals.
Eligibility: Applicants must be high school seniors who plan to pursue four-year degrees at accredited colleges or universities. Selection is based on application materials, communication skills, academic record, extracurricular activities and leadership.
Target applicant(s): High school students.
Amount: $1,000-$5,000.
Number of awards: Varies.
Deadline: April 1.
How to apply: Applications are available by request from the applicant's local Executive Women International chapter. An application form and supporting documents are required.
Exclusive: Visit www.UltimateScholarshipBook.com and enter code EX58623 for updates on this award.

(587) · Florence C. and Robert H. Lister Fellowship

Crow Canyon Archeological Center
23390 Road K, Cortez, CO 81321-9908
Phone: 800-422-8975
Email: schoolprograms@crowcanyon.org
http://www.crowcanyon.org
Purpose: To assist graduate students in the archeology of American Indian cultures of the Southwest.
Eligibility: Applicants must be enrolled in a North American Ph.D. program and have projects based on archaeological, ethnoarchaeological or paleoenvironmental research in the southwestern United States and northern Mexico. The award is offered every other year.
Target applicant(s): Graduate school students. Adult students.
Amount: $7,000.
Number of awards: 1.
Deadline: October 13.
How to apply: Applications are available online.
Exclusive: Visit www.UltimateScholarshipBook.com and enter code CR58723 for updates on this award.

(588) · FMS Solutions Holdings LLC Legacy Scholarship

National Grocers Association
1005 N. Glebe Road, Suite 250, Arlington, VA 22201
Phone: 225-387-6126
https://www.nationalgrocers.org/foundation/nga-foundation-scholarships/
Purpose: To support students pursuing education related to the grocery field.
Eligibility: Applicants must be rising sophomores through postgraduate students, have a minimum 2.5 GPA and be enrolled in a two- or four-year degree-granting institution. Students must major in business, food management, IT or another field related to a career in the grocery industry. Experience in the grocery industry is preferred but not required. Preference given to children of state or local law enforcement officers.
Target applicant(s): College students. Graduate school students. Adult students.
Minimum GPA: 2.5
Amount: Varies.
Number of awards: 1.
Deadline: April 1.
How to apply: Applications are available online.
Exclusive: Visit www.UltimateScholarshipBook.com and enter code NA58823 for updates on this award.

(589) · FOARE Scholarship Program

Foundation for Outdoor Advertising Research and Education (FOARE)
The Family Scholarship Endowment, c/o Thomas M. Smith & Associates, 4601 Tilden Street NW, Washington, DC 20016
Phone: 202-364-7130
Email: tmfsmith@rcn.com
http://oaaa.org/AboutOAAA/FOARE/FOAREScholarshipProgram.aspx
Purpose: To support undergraduate and graduate students in pursuing a career in the outdoor advertising industry.
Eligibility: Applicants must be graduating seniors, undergraduate students or graduate students. Selection is primarily based on demonstration of financial need, career goals, academic achievement, community service and extracurricular involvement.
Target applicant(s): High school students. College students. Graduate school students. Adult students.
Amount: $3,000-$5,000.
Number of awards: 10.
Deadline: June 16.
How to apply: Applications are available online.
Exclusive: Visit www.UltimateScholarshipBook.com and enter code FO58923 for updates on this award.

(590) · FOWA Scholarship for Outdoor Communicators

Florida Outdoor Writers Association
24 NW 33 Court, Suite A, Gainesville, FL 32607
Phone: 352-284-1763
Email: dozimmer@ufl.edu
http://www.fowa.org/fowa-scholarship-program/
Purpose: To aid students who plan to enter the field of outdoor communications.
Eligibility: Applicants must be students at Florida colleges or universities or students from any school whose applications are endorsed by a FOWA member or faculty advisor. They must have a career goal that entails communicating love and appreciation of hunting, fishing and other outdoor activities. Selection is based on essay, faculty advisor or FOWA member endorsement, scholastic merit and extracurricular activities. Preference is given to journalism and communications majors.
Target applicant(s): College students. Adult students.
Amount: $1,000.
Number of awards: Up to 3.
Deadline: June 14.
How to apply: Applications are available online. A cover page, essay, resume and letter of endorsement are required. Other supporting materials will be considered.
Exclusive: Visit www.UltimateScholarshipBook.com and enter code FL59023 for updates on this award.

(591) · Francis X. Crowley Scholarship

New England Water Works Association
125 Hopping Brook Road, Holliston, MA 01746
Phone: 508-893-7979
Email: tmacelhaney@preloadinc.com
http://www.newwa.org
Purpose: To support civil engineering, environmental engineering and business management students.
Eligibility: Applicants must be New England Water Works Association student members. They must be enrolled in a postsecondary degree program in civil engineering, environmental engineering or business management. Selection is based on the overall strength of the application.
Target applicant(s): High school students. College students. Graduate school students. Adult students.
Amount: $3,000.
Number of awards: 1.
Deadline: April 1.
How to apply: Applications are available online. An application form, a personal essay, an official transcript and one recommendation letter are required.
Exclusive: Visit www.UltimateScholarshipBook.com and enter code NE59123 for updates on this award.

(592) · Frank M. Coda Scholarship

American Society of Heating, Refrigerating and Air-Conditioning Engineers (ASHRAE)
1791 Tullie Circle, NE, Atlanta, GA 30329
Phone: 404-636-8400
Email: lbenedict@ashrae.org
https://www.ashrae.org/membership--conferences/student-zone/scholarships-and-grants/scholarship-program
Purpose: To support undergraduate students who are preparing for careers in the heating, ventilation, air-conditioning and refrigeration industry.
Eligibility: Applicants must be current or entering full-time undergraduates enrolled in a bachelor's of science, bachelor's of engineering or pre-engineering degree program in preparation for a career in HVACR. They must attend a school that has an ASHRAE student branch, is accredited by ABET or is accredited by a non-USA agency that has signed a Memorandum of Understanding with ABET or the Washington Accord. They must be in the top 30 percent of their class and must have a GPA of 3.0 or higher on a four-point scale. Selection is based on the overall strength of the application.
Target applicant(s): High school students. College students. Adult students.
Minimum GPA: 3.0
Amount: $5,000.
Number of awards: 1.
Scholarship may be renewable.
Deadline: December 1.
How to apply: Applications are available online. An application form, official college transcript (or proof of enrollment for rising freshmen) and two letters of reference are required.
Exclusive: Visit www.UltimateScholarshipBook.com and enter code AM59223 for updates on this award.

(593) · Fred R. McDaniel Memorial Scholarship

American Radio Relay League Foundation
225 Main Street, Newington, CT 06111-1494
Phone: 860-594-0348
Email: foundation@arrl.org
http://www.arrl.org/scholarship-program
Purpose: To assist ham radio operators in furthering their educations.
Eligibility: Applicants must have at least a general ham radio license, be residents of and attend a post-secondary institution in the FCC Fifth Call District (Texas, Oklahoma, Arkansas, Louisiana, Mississippi or New Mexico) and be studying for a bachelor's or graduate degree in electronics, communications or a related field. Preference is given to applicants with a 3.0 GPA or higher.
Target applicant(s): High school students. College students. Graduate school students. Adult students.

Minimum GPA: 3.0
Amount: $1,000.
Number of awards: 1.
Deadline: December 31.
How to apply: Applications are available online but must be sent in by mail.
Exclusive: Visit www.UltimateScholarshipBook.com and enter code AM59323 for updates on this award.

---

(594) · Frederic G. Melcher Scholarship

Association for Library Service to Children
50 E. Huron Street, Chicago, IL 60611
Phone: 800-545-2433
Email: cjewell@ala.org
http://www.ala.org/alsc/awardsgrants
Purpose: To support students who want to become children's librarians.
Eligibility: Applicants must intend to pursue an MLS degree, plan to work in children's librarianship and be U.S. or Canadian citizens. Selection is based on academic excellence, leadership and desire to work with children in any type of library.
Target applicant(s): College students. Graduate school students. Adult students.
Amount: $8,000.
Number of awards: Up to 2.
Deadline: March 1.
How to apply: Applications are available online.
Exclusive: Visit www.UltimateScholarshipBook.com and enter code AS59423 for updates on this award.

---

(595) · FTEE Scholarship: Undergraduate Major in Technology and Engineering Education

International Technology and Engineering Educators Association
Foundation for Technology and Engineering Educators, 1914 Association Drive, Suite 201, Reston, VA 20191-1539
Phone: 703-860-2100
Email: iteea@iteea.org
https://www.iteea.org/Activities/AwardsScholarships.aspx
Purpose: To support undergraduate students majoring in technology education teacher preparation.
Eligibility: Applicants must be members of ITEEA, be full-time undergraduate students and have a minimum 2.5 GPA.
Target applicant(s): College students. Adult students.
Minimum GPA: 2.5
Amount: $500.
Number of awards: 1.
Deadline: December 1.
How to apply: Application information is available online.
Exclusive: Visit www.UltimateScholarshipBook.com and enter code IN59523 for updates on this award.

---

(596) · Fund for American Studies Internships

Fund for American Studies
1621 New Hampshire Avenue NW, Washington, DC 20009
Phone: 800-741-6964
Email: admissions@tfas.org
https://tfas.org/awards/
Purpose: To provide scholarships for students attending one of the Fund's internship programs.

Eligibility: There are programs in comparative political and economic systems, political journalism, business and government, philanthropy and international institutes. Each program includes classes, an internship and special events. Students live in on-campus housing at George Washington University or in furnished apartments in the Capitol Hill neighborhood. Each student takes 3-9 credit hours in courses at George Mason University in addition to interning 30-35 hours per week. Summer and school-year programs are available.
Target applicant(s): College students. Adult students.
Amount: Varies.
Number of awards: Varies.
Deadline: March 16; June 1; November 15.
How to apply: Applications are available online.
Exclusive: Visit www.UltimateScholarshipBook.com and enter code FU59623 for updates on this award.

---

(597) · Future Counselors of America Scholarship

DatingAdvice.com
c/o Digital Brands Inc., 15 SE 1st Avenue, Suite B, Gainesville, FL 32601
https://www.datingadvice.com/
Purpose: To assist psychology students who are planning careers in relationship counseling or a related field.
Eligibility: Applicants must be U.S. undergraduate or graduate students majoring in psychology and must have a minimum 3.5 GPA. Students must write a 500- to 900-word essay on the topic of "The Psychology of Online Dating."
Target applicant(s): College students. Graduate school students. Adult students.
Minimum GPA: 3.5
Amount: $1,000.
Number of awards: 1.
Deadline: June 30.
How to apply: An official transcript and essay must be submitted by mail.
Exclusive: Visit www.UltimateScholarshipBook.com and enter code DA59723 for updates on this award.

---

(598) · Future Teacher Scholarship

Journalism Education Association Future Teacher Scholarship
828 Mid-Campus Drive South, 105 Kedzie Hall, Manhattan, KS 66506-1505
Phone: 785-532-5532
Email: cbowen@kent.edu
http://jea.org/wp/scholarships/
Purpose: To support education majors who intend to teach scholastic journalism.
Eligibility: Applicants must be a college junior, senior or graduate student in a program designed to prepare him/her for teaching at the secondary level. Current secondary-school journalism teachers who are in a degree program to improve their journalism teaching skills are also eligible.
Target applicant(s): College students. Graduate school students. Adult students.
Amount: $1,000.
Number of awards: 5.
Deadline: July 15.
How to apply: Applications are available online.
Exclusive: Visit www.UltimateScholarshipBook.com and enter code JO59823 for updates on this award.

(599) · Gamma Theta Upsilon-Geographical Honor Society Scholarships

Gamma Theta Upsilon
Dr. Michael Longan, Geography and Meteorology Department, Kallay-Christopher Hall, 201C Valparaiso University, Valparaiso, IN 46383
Phone: 219-464-6874
Email: Mike.Longan@valpo.edu
http://gammathetaupsilon.org/scholarships.html
Purpose: To support geography knowledge and awareness by awarding monetary assistance to college and graduate students.
Eligibility: Applicants must be initiated through a Gamma Theta Upsilon chapter.
Target applicant(s): College students. Graduate school students. Adult students.
Amount: Varies.
Number of awards: 5.
Deadline: June 1.
How to apply: Applications are available online.
Exclusive: Visit www.UltimateScholarshipBook.com and enter code GA59923 for updates on this award.

(600) · Gary Yoshimura Scholarship

Public Relations Student Society of America
33 Maiden Lane, 11th Floor, New York, NY 10038
Phone: 212-460-1474
Email: prssa@prsa.org
https://prssa.prsa.org/scholarships-and-awards/
Purpose: To assist public relations students.
Eligibility: Applicants must be PRSSA members with a minimum 3.0 GPA in the pursuit of higher education in the public relations field. Applicants must submit an essay on personal or professional challenges and a statement on financial need.
Target applicant(s): High school students. College students. Graduate school students. Adult students.
Minimum GPA: 3.0
Amount: $2,400.
Number of awards: 1.
Deadline: May 31.
How to apply: Applications are available online.
Exclusive: Visit www.UltimateScholarshipBook.com and enter code PU60023 for updates on this award.

(601) · George A. Strait Minority Scholarship

American Association of Law Libraries
105 W. Adams, Suite 3300, Chicago, IL 60603
Email: scholarships@aall.org
https://www.aallnet.org/education-training/scholarships/
Purpose: To encourage minorities to enter careers as law librarians.
Eligibility: Applicants must be a member of a minority group as defined by U.S. government rules, degree candidates in an accredited library or law school and intend to pursue a career as law librarians. Law library experience is preferred. Applicants must also have financial need and have at least one quarter or semester left after the scholarship is given.
Target applicant(s): Graduate school students. Adult students.
Amount: Varies.
Number of awards: Varies.
Scholarship may be renewable.
Deadline: April 1.

How to apply: Applications are available online, by mail with a self-addressed, stamped envelope, by fax, by phone or by email.
Exclusive: Visit www.UltimateScholarshipBook.com and enter code AM60123 for updates on this award.

(602) · Giles Sutherland Rich Memorial Scholarship

Federal Circuit Bar Association
1620 I Street NW, Suite 801, Washington, DC 20006
Phone: 202-466-3923
Email: fcbascholarships@fedcirbar.org
http://www.fedcirbar.org
Purpose: To support promising law students who demonstrate financial need.
Eligibility: Applicants must be undergraduate or graduate law students who demonstrate academic ability and financial need. They must submit a one-page statement describing their financial need, their interest in law and their qualifications for the award. Applicants must also submit a transcript and curriculum vitae.
Target applicant(s): College students. Graduate school students. Adult students.
Amount: $10,000.
Number of awards: 1.
Deadline: April.
How to apply: There is no application form.
Exclusive: Visit www.UltimateScholarshipBook.com and enter code FE60223 for updates on this award.

(603) · GoFoodservice Scholarship

GoFoodservice
11206 Ampere Court, Louisville, KY 40299
Phone: 800-550-0706
Email: support@gofoodservice.com
https://www.gofoodservice.com/scholarship
Purpose: To support the next generation of chefs and restaurant managers.
Eligibility: Applicants must be graduating high school seniors enrolling in post-secondary education or students already enrolled in a college or accredited institution. Students must be majoring in culinary arts or hospitality management and must submit an essay along with the application.
Target applicant(s): High school students. College students. Adult students.
Amount: $500.
Number of awards: 1.
Deadline: June 15.
How to apply: Applications are available online.
Exclusive: Visit www.UltimateScholarshipBook.com and enter code GO60323 for updates on this award.

(604) · Goldberg-Miller Public Finance Scholarship

Government Finance Officers Association
203 N. LaSalle Street, Suite 2700, Chicago, IL 60601
Phone: 312-977-9700
https://www.gfoa.org/available-scholarships
Purpose: To support graduate students pursuing a career in state/provincial or local government finance.
Eligibility: Applicants must be permanent residents of the U.S. or Canada. Students may not be previous winners of a Government Finance Officers Association (GFOA) scholarship.
Target applicant(s): Graduate school students. Adult students.

Amount: $15,000.
Number of awards: 1.
Deadline: January 14.
How to apply: Applications available online.
Exclusive: Visit www.UltimateScholarshipBook.com and enter code GO60423 for updates on this award.

(605) · Great Scholarship Program

Great Clips
4400 W. 78th Street, Suite 700, Minneapolis, MN 55435
Phone: 800-999-5959
https://jobs.greatclips.com/scholarship-application
Purpose: To support students who are pursuing a career in cosmetology.
Eligibility: Selection is based on the overall strength of the application.
Target applicant(s): High school students.
Amount: $250-$1,500.
Number of awards: Varies.
Deadline: March 1 (Spring) and September 1 (Fall).
How to apply: Applications are available online.
Exclusive: Visit www.UltimateScholarshipBook.com and enter code GR60523 for updates on this award.

(606) · Harrell Family Fellowship

American Center of Oriental Research (ACOR)
656 Beacon Street, 5th Floor, Boston, MA 02215-2010
Phone: 617-353-6571
Email: acor@bu.edu
https://acorjordan.org
Purpose: To assist a graduate student with expenses on an archaeological project in Jordan.
Eligibility: Applicants must be graduate students in a program approved by a recognized academic review body. The funds must be used for archaeological or related research.
Target applicant(s): Graduate school students. Adult students.
Amount: $2,000.
Number of awards: 1.
Deadline: February 1.
How to apply: Applications are available online.
Exclusive: Visit www.UltimateScholarshipBook.com and enter code AM60623 for updates on this award.

(607) · Harry A. Applegate Scholarship

DECA Inc.
1908 Association Drive, Reston, VA 20191
Phone: 703-860-5000
Email: scholarships@deca.org
http://www.deca.org
Purpose: To reward current active members of DECA, the high school division or the college division of DECA.
Eligibility: Applicants must plan to be full-time students at a two-year or four-year program in marketing, entrepreneurship or management. This award is based on merit, not financial need, but applicants may include financial need statements for review. Applicants should submit transcripts, test scores, a statement of club participation, proof of leadership outside DECA, three recommendation letters and proof of membership.
Target applicant(s): High school students. College students. Adult students.
Amount: Varies.
Number of awards: Varies.

Deadline: January 15.
How to apply: Applications are available online and should be submitted to state/provincial DECA advisors.
Exclusive: Visit www.UltimateScholarshipBook.com and enter code DE60723 for updates on this award.

(608) · Harry S. Truman Research Grant

Harry S. Truman Library Institute for National and International Affairs
Grants Administrator, 500 W. U.S. Highway 24, Independence, MO 64050
Phone: 816-268-8248
Email: sullivan.hstli@gmail.com
http://www.trumanlibraryinstitute.org/research-grants/
Purpose: To promote the Truman Library as a center for research.
Eligibility: Graduate students and post-doctoral scholars are most encouraged to apply, but others completing advanced research will be considered. Preference is given to research that has a high chance of being published or otherwise shared publicly. Applicants can receive up to two research grants in a five-year period. Grant winners must submit a report at the end of their studies.
Target applicant(s): Graduate school students. Adult students.
Amount: Up to $2,500.
Number of awards: Varies.
Deadline: April 1 and October 1.
How to apply: Applications are available online.
Exclusive: Visit www.UltimateScholarshipBook.com and enter code HA60823 for updates on this award.

(609) · Henry Belin du Pont Dissertation Fellowship

Hagley Museum and Library
Center for the History of Business, Technology and Society, 298 Buck Road, Wilmington, DE 19807
Phone: 302-658-2400
Email: clockman@Hagley.org
http://www.hagley.org
Purpose: To provide four-month fellowships for doctoral students performing dissertation research.
Eligibility: Applicants must be doctoral students who have completed all course work and are performing dissertation research. Research topics should involve historical questions and should relate to the collections in the Hagley Library. Fellows will receive housing, office space, a computer and Internet access. A presentation is required at the end of the residence period.
Target applicant(s): Graduate school students. Adult students.
Amount: $6,500 plus housing.
Number of awards: Varies.
Deadline: March 31, June 30, October 31.
How to apply: Applications are available online. For more information contact Dr. Roger Horowitz at rhorowitz@hagley.org.
Exclusive: Visit www.UltimateScholarshipBook.com and enter code HA60923 for updates on this award.

(610) · Herbert Hoover Presidential Library Association Travel Grant Program

Hoover Presidential Foundation
P.O. Box 696, West Branch, IA 52358
Phone: 800-828-0475
Email: info@hooverpf.org
http://www.hooverpresidentialfoundation.org

Purpose: To provide financial aid to individuals to research at the Herbert Hoover Presidential Library in West Branch, Iowa.
Eligibility: Applicants must be current graduate students, post-doctoral scholars or independent researchers. Applicants must also ensure that the library's contents will meet their research needs before applying.
Target applicant(s): Graduate school students. Adult students.
Amount: $500-$1,500.
Number of awards: Varies.
Deadline: March 1.
How to apply: Applications are available online.
Exclusive: Visit www.UltimateScholarshipBook.com and enter code HO61023 for updates on this award.

(611) · Honorable William Conner Writing Competition

New York Intellectual Property Association (NYIPLA)
229 Seventh Street, Suite 202, Garden City, NY 11530
Phone: 201-461-6603
Email: admin@nyipla.org
https://www.nyipla.org/nyipla/ConnerWritingAwards.asp
Purpose: To recognize exceptionally written papers that are submitted by law students.
Eligibility: Applicants must be law school students currently enrolled in a J.D. or LL.M. program (day or evening) in an accredited law school in the United States. Entries must be directed to any of the following subject areas of intellectual property: patents, trademarks, copyrights, trade secrets, unfair trade practices, antitrust and data security/privacy issues. Entries must be submitted by email and will be judged on interest and suitability of topic, organization, legal analysis, writing and professionalism of the work product.
Target applicant(s): Graduate school students. Adult students.
Amount: Up to $1,500.
Number of awards: 2.
Deadline: February 27.
How to apply: Applications are available online.
Exclusive: Visit www.UltimateScholarshipBook.com and enter code NE61123 for updates on this award.

(612) · Horatio Alger Career and Technical Scholarship

Horatio Alger Association
Attn.: Scholarship Department, 99 Canal Center Plaza, Suite 320, Alexandria, VA 22314
Phone: 703-684-9444
Email: association@horatioalger.org
https://scholars.horatioalger.org/
Purpose: To support students who have overcome great obstacles.
Eligibility: Applicants must be U.S. citizens under the age of 30 who are enrolling in a career or technical program at an accredited non-profit institution. Students must demonstrate financial need and perseverance in overcoming adversity.
Target applicant(s): High school students. College students. Adult students.
Amount: $2,500.
Number of awards: 1,020.
Deadline: June 15.
How to apply: Applications are available online.
Exclusive: Visit www.UltimateScholarshipBook.com and enter code HO61223 for updates on this award.

(613) · Huntington Fellowships

Huntington Library, Art Collections and Botanical Gardens
1151 Oxford Road, San Marino, CA 91108
Phone: 626-405-2194
Email: cpowell@huntington.org
http://www.huntington.org
Purpose: To provide fellowships to doctoral students and recipients in British and American history, literature, art history and the history of science and medicine.
Eligibility: Applicants must have a Ph.D. or equivalent or be doctoral candidates at the dissertation stage. Cover sheets, project descriptions, curriculum vitae and three letters of recommendation are required.
Target applicant(s): Graduate school students. Adult students.
Amount: $3,000.
Number of awards: More than 150.
Deadline: November 15.
How to apply: Application materials are described online.
Exclusive: Visit www.UltimateScholarshipBook.com and enter code HU61323 for updates on this award.

(614) · Huntington-British Academy Fellowships for Study in Great Britain

Huntington Library, Art Collections and Botanical Gardens
1151 Oxford Road, San Marino, CA 91108
Phone: 626-405-2194
Email: cpowell@huntington.org
http://www.huntington.org
Purpose: To offer scholars exchange fellowships to research British and American history, literature, art history and the history of science and medicine.
Eligibility: Applicants must have a Ph.D. or equivalent. Applicants must submit cover sheets, project descriptions, curriculum vitae and three letters of recommendation.
Target applicant(s): Graduate school students. Adult students.
Amount: Varies.
Number of awards: Varies.
Deadline: November 15.
How to apply: There is no application form, and application materials are described online.
Exclusive: Visit www.UltimateScholarshipBook.com and enter code HU61423 for updates on this award.

(615) · IEHA Scholarship

International Executive Housekeepers Association (IEHA) Education Foundation
1001 Eastwind Drive, Suite 301, Westerville, OH 43081-3361
Phone: 800-200-6342
Email: excel@ieha.org
http://www.ieha.org
Purpose: To support IEHA members who are pursuing undergraduate or associate's degrees or IEHA certification.
Eligibility: Applicants must submit a 2,000-word manuscript about an issue in the housekeeping industry. The winning manuscript will be selected by a panel of judges and published.
Target applicant(s): High school students. College students. Adult students.
Amount: Varies.
Number of awards: Varies.
Deadline: January 10.
How to apply: Applications are available online.

Exclusive: Visit www.UltimateScholarshipBook.com and enter code IN61523 for updates on this award.

(616) · IFEC Scholarships Award

International Foodservice Editorial Council (IFEC)
P.O. Box 581, Pleasant Valley, NY 12569
Phone: 845-229-6973
Email: ifec@ifeconline.com
http://www.ifeconline.com
Purpose: To assist students interested in foodservice combined with communication arts.
Eligibility: Applicants must be enrolled at a post-secondary, degree-granting educational institution and must demonstrate training, skill and interest in the foodservice industry and communication arts. Eligible majors from foodservice and communications areas include culinary arts, hotel/restaurant/hospitality management, dietetics, nutrition, food science/technology, journalism, public relations, mass communication, English, broadcast journalism, marketing, photography, graphic arts and related studies.
Target applicant(s): College students. Graduate school students. Adult students.
Amount: $1,500-$6,000.
Number of awards: 6.
Deadline: March 15.
How to apply: Applications are available online.
Exclusive: Visit www.UltimateScholarshipBook.com and enter code IN61623 for updates on this award.

(617) · IFSEA Worthy Goal Scholarship

International Food Service Executives Association
4955 Miller Street, Suite 107, Wheat Ridge, CO 80033
Phone: 502-589-3602
https://www.ifsea.org
Purpose: To help students receive food service management training beyond the high school level.
Eligibility: Applicants must be enrolled or accepted at a college as a full-time student in a food service related major. Students must provide a financial statement, personal statement, list of work experience and professional activities, transcripts, recommendations and a statement describing how the scholarship would help them reach their goals.
Target applicant(s): High school students. College students. Graduate school students. Adult students.
Amount: $250-$1,500.
Number of awards: Varies.
Deadline: May 31.
How to apply: Applications are available online.
Exclusive: Visit www.UltimateScholarshipBook.com and enter code IN61723 for updates on this award.

(618) · IMA Memorial Education Fund Scholarship

Institute of Management Accountants (IMA)
10 Paragon Drive, Montvale, NJ 07645-1760
Phone: 800-638-4427
Email: students@imanet.org
http://www.imanet.org
Purpose: To support students in fields related to management accounting.
Eligibility: Applicants must be full- and part-time undergraduate and graduate students, be IMA student members and declare which four- or five-year management accounting, financial management or information

technology-related program they plan to pursue as a career or list a related field. Candidates should submit applications, resumes, transcripts, two recommendations and statements. Advanced degree students must pass one part of the CMA/CFM certification.
Target applicant(s): College students. Graduate school students. Adult students.
Minimum GPA: 3.0
Amount: $1,000-$2,500.
Number of awards: Varies.
Deadline: March 10.
How to apply: Applications are available online.
Exclusive: Visit www.UltimateScholarshipBook.com and enter code IN61823 for updates on this award.

(619) · Imagine America High School Scholarship Program

Imagine America Foundation
12001 Sunrise Valley Drive, Suite 203, Reston, VA 20191
Phone: 571-267-3010
Email: Leed@imagine-america.org
https://www.imagine-america.org/students/scholarships-education/
Purpose: To help high school seniors pursue a postsecondary career education.
Eligibility: Applicants must have a minimum 2.5 high school GPA, demonstrate financial need and have demonstrated community service during their senior year.
Target applicant(s): High school students.
Minimum GPA: 2.5
Amount: $1,000.
Number of awards: 5.
Deadline: December 31.
How to apply: Applications are available online.
Exclusive: Visit www.UltimateScholarshipBook.com and enter code IM61923 for updates on this award.

(620) · Incoming Freshman Scholarship

American Hotel and Lodging Educational Foundation (AHLEF)
1250 I Street NW, Suite 1100, Washington, DC 20005-3931
Phone: 202-289-3180
Email: foundation@ahlef.org
https://www.ahlafoundation.org/academic-scholarships
Purpose: To recognize high school students who are interested in hospitality-related programs.
Eligibility: Applicants must be graduating seniors with preference given to those who have completed the two-year Lodging Management Program (LMP) high school program. Students must be planning to attend a post-secondary institution, be U.S. citizens or permanent residents and have a minimum 2.0 GPA.
Target applicant(s): High school students.
Minimum GPA: 2.0
Amount: $2,000-$4,000.
Number of awards: Varies.
Deadline: February.
How to apply: Applications are available online.
Exclusive: Visit www.UltimateScholarshipBook.com and enter code AM62023 for updates on this award.

(621) · International Facility Management Association Foundation Scholarship Program

International Facility Management Association
800 Gessner Road, Suite 900, Houston, TX 77024-4257
Phone: 713-623-4362
Email: amy.arnold@ifma.org
http://foundation.ifma.org
Purpose: To support students currently enrolled in facility management or facility management-related programs.
Eligibility: Applicants must be college or graduate students and include a letter of professional intent, resume and letter of recommendation with application.
Target applicant(s): College students. Graduate school students. Adult students.
Minimum GPA: 3.2
Amount: Varies.
Number of awards: Varies.
Deadline: May 14.
How to apply: Applications are available online.
Exclusive: Visit www.UltimateScholarshipBook.com and enter code IN62123 for updates on this award.

(622) · International Technology Engineering Educators Association Scholarship - FTEE/ Undergraduate

International Technology and Engineering Educators Association
Foundation for Technology and Engineering Educators, 1914 Association Drive, Suite 201, Reston, VA 20191-1539
Phone: 703-860-2100
Email: iteea@iteea.org
https://www.iteea.org/Activities/AwardsScholarships.aspx
Purpose: To encourage students majoring in technology and engineering education teacher preparation.
Eligibility: Applicants must be members of the International Technology Education Association. Students must not be a senior by the application deadline. Applicants must be full-time undergraduate students majoring in technology and engineering education teacher preparation.
Target applicant(s): College students. Adult students.
Minimum GPA: 2.5
Amount: $500.
Number of awards: 1.
Deadline: December 1.
How to apply: Applications are available online.
Exclusive: Visit www.UltimateScholarshipBook.com and enter code IN62223 for updates on this award.

(623) · IRARC Memorial, Joseph P. Rubino, WA4MMD, Scholarship

American Radio Relay League Foundation
225 Main Street, Newington, CT 06111-1494
Phone: 860-594-0348
Email: foundation@arrl.org
http://www.arrl.org/scholarship-program
Purpose: To provide financial assistance to amateur radio operators who are seeking an undergraduate degree or electronic technician certification.
Eligibility: Applicants must hold an active Amateur Radio License in any class and be studying at an accredited institution. They must have a minimum GPA of 2.5. Preference is given to Florida residents, particularly those from Brevard County and those with need and lower GPAs.
Target applicant(s): High school students. College students. Adult students.
Minimum GPA: 2.5
Amount: $750.
Number of awards: Varies.
Deadline: December 31.
How to apply: Applications are available online.
Exclusive: Visit www.UltimateScholarshipBook.com and enter code AM62323 for updates on this award.

(624) · J. Franklin Jameson Fellowship in American History

American Historical Association
400 A Street SE, Washington, DC 20003
Phone: 202-544-2422
Email: info@historians.org
http://www.historians.org
Purpose: To support one semester of scholarly research in the Library of Congress collections.
Eligibility: Applicants must hold a Ph.D. or equivalent, must have earned the degree within the past seven years and may not have published a book-length historical work. Projects should focus on American history.
Target applicant(s): Graduate school students. Adult students.
Amount: $5,000.
Number of awards: Varies.
Deadline: April 1.
How to apply: Application instructions are available online.
Exclusive: Visit www.UltimateScholarshipBook.com and enter code AM62423 for updates on this award.

(625) · Jack G. Shaheen Mass Communications Scholarship

American-Arab Anti-Discrimination Committee
1705 DeSales Street NW, Suite 500, Washington, DC 20036
Phone: 202-244-2990
http://www.adc.org/adcri/jack-g-shaheen-mass-communications-scholarships/
Purpose: To reward Arab-American students who excel in media studies.
Eligibility: Applicants must be U.S. citizens of Arab heritage currently enrolled in college as an undergraduate junior or senior or as a graduate student. Students must be majoring in journalism, radio television or film. Applicants must have a minimum GPA of 3.0 and provide academic transcripts, a one-page statement, two letters of recommendation and copies of your work.
Target applicant(s): College students. Graduate school students. Adult students.
Minimum GPA: 3.0
Amount: $2,500.
Number of awards: 1.
Deadline: April 12.
How to apply: Applications are available online.
Exclusive: Visit www.UltimateScholarshipBook.com and enter code AM62523 for updates on this award.

(626) · Jaime Guttenberg Helping Hands Scholarship

Orange Ribbons for Jaime
5944 Coral Ridge Drive, Suite 301, Coral Springs, FL 33076

Phone: 561-750-1500
Email: info@orangeribbonsforjaime.org
https://orangeribbonsforjaime.org/
Purpose: To reward students with a focus on a career in helping others which includes but is not limited to physical therapy, occupational therapy, speech therapy, psychology or special education.
Eligibility: Applicants must be applying to a traditional four-year university with a focus on a career in helping others, which includes but is not limited to physical therapy, occupational therapy, speech therapy, psychology or special education. Students must have a minimum 3.5 GPA and a background in community service/volunteerism during high school with a minimum of 100 service hours. An essay on a provided topic is required to be submitted.
Target applicant(s): High school students.
Minimum GPA: 3.5
Amount: Varies.
Number of awards: Varies.
Deadline: March.
How to apply: Applications are available online.
Exclusive: Visit www.UltimateScholarshipBook.com and enter code OR62623 for updates on this award.

(627) · James A. Turner, Jr. Memorial Scholarship

American Welding Society Foundation
550 NW LeJeune Road, Miami, FL 33126
Phone: 800-443-9353
Email: info@aws.org
https://www.aws.org/foundation/page/scholarships
Purpose: To aid those interested in a management career in welding store operations or distributorship.
Eligibility: Applicants must be full-time students pursuing a four-year bachelor's of business degree, plan to enter management careers in welding store operations or distributorship, be high school graduates at least 18 years of age and be employed a minimum of 10 hours per week at a welding distributorship. Preference is given to members of the American Welding Society.
Target applicant(s): High school students. College students. Graduate school students. Adult students.
Amount: $3,500.
Number of awards: 1.
Deadline: March 1.
How to apply: Applications are available online.
Exclusive: Visit www.UltimateScholarshipBook.com and enter code AM62723 for updates on this award.

(628) · James Beard Foundation Scholarship

James Beard Foundation Scholarship Program/ISTS
167 West 12th Street, New York, NY 10011
Phone: 212-627-2308
Email: scholarships@jamesbeard.org
https://www.jamesbeard.org/scholarships
Purpose: To support students pursuing a culinary education.
Eligibility: Applicants must be graduating high school seniors or graduates pursuing a culinary or food-focused program at an accredited institution.
Target applicant(s): High school students. College students. Graduate school students. Adult students.
Amount: Up to $20,000.
Number of awards: Up to 60.
Deadline: April 1.
How to apply: Applications are available online.

Exclusive: Visit www.UltimateScholarshipBook.com and enter code JA62823 for updates on this award.

(629) · Jane M. Klausman Women in Business Scholarship Fund

Zonta International
1211 West 22nd Street, Suite 900, Oak Brook, IL 60523
Phone: 630-928-1400
Email: zontaintl@zonta.org
http://www.zonta.org
Purpose: To help female business management majors overcome gender barriers.
Eligibility: Applicants must be women of any age pursuing a business or business-related program who demonstrate outstanding potential. Applicants must also have an outstanding academic record in their college career, and they must show intent to complete a business program.
Target applicant(s): College students. Graduate school students. Adult students.
Amount: $2,000-$8,000.
Number of awards: 38.
Deadline: Various.
How to apply: Applications are available online or from your local Zonta Club.
Exclusive: Visit www.UltimateScholarshipBook.com and enter code ZO62923 for updates on this award.

(630) · Jennifer C. Groot Fellowship

American Center of Oriental Research (ACOR)
656 Beacon Street, 5th Floor, Boston, MA 02215-2010
Phone: 617-353-6571
Email: acor@bu.edu
https://acorjordan.org
Purpose: To assist students with expenses on an archaeological project.
Eligibility: Applicants must be undergraduate or graduate students with little or no archaeological field experience and be U.S. or Canadian citizens. Recipients will travel to Jordan for the project.
Target applicant(s): High school students. College students. Graduate school students. Adult students.
Amount: $1,500.
Number of awards: Up to 3.
Deadline: February 1.
How to apply: Applications are available online but must be submitted by mail.
Exclusive: Visit www.UltimateScholarshipBook.com and enter code AM63023 for updates on this award.

(631) · JFLF Awards Programs

James F. Lincoln Arc Welding Foundation
Secretary, P.O. Box 17188, Cleveland, OH 44117-9949
http://www.jflf.org
Purpose: To award prizes for arc welding projects made by the applicant or a group of applicants.
Eligibility: Projects may fit into one of the following categories: home, recreational or artistic equipment; shop tool, machine or mechanical device; a structure; agricultural equipment or a repair. Applicants must submit a paper about the creation of the project and be enrolled in a shop class. Applicants must also be enrolled in high school, adult evening classes, two-year/community college, vocational school, apprentice

program, trade school, in-plant training or technical school and may not be college students enrolled in a bachelor's or master's program.
Target applicant(s): High school students. College students. Graduate school students. Adult students.
Amount: Up to $1,000.
Number of awards: 95.
Deadline: July 1.
How to apply: Applications are available online.
Exclusive: Visit www.UltimateScholarshipBook.com and enter code JA63123 for updates on this award.

(632) · Joe Francis Haircare Scholarship Program

Joe Francis Haircare Scholarship Foundation
P.O. Box 50625, Minneapolis, MN 55405
Phone: 651-769-1757
Email: contact@joefrancis.com
http://www.joefrancis.com
Purpose: To provide barber and cosmetology students with financial aid.
Eligibility: Applicants must be sponsored by one of the following: a fully accredited, recognized barber or cosmetology school, a licensed salon owner or manager, a full-service distributor or a member of the International Chain Association, Beauty and Barber Supply Institute, Cosmetology Advancement Foundation or National Cosmetology Association. Applicants must be actively enrolled in cosmetology school or planning to enroll during or after the award month of August. Judging is based on financial need, motivation and character.
Target applicant(s): High school students. College students. Adult students.
Amount: $1,200.
Number of awards: Varies.
Deadline: June 1.
How to apply: Applications are available online.
Exclusive: Visit www.UltimateScholarshipBook.com and enter code JO63223 for updates on this award.

(633) · Joe Perdue Scholarship

Club Foundation
1733 King Street, Alexandria, VA 22314
Phone: 703-739-9500
Email: schaverr@clubfoundation.org
http://www.clubfoundation.org
Purpose: To support students pursuing careers in private club management.
Eligibility: Applicants must be pursuing managerial careers in the private club industry, have completed their freshman year of college, have a minimum 2.5 GPA and be enrolled full-time for the following year. An essay and letters of recommendation are also required.
Target applicant(s): College students. Adult students.
Minimum GPA: 2.5
Amount: $2,500.
Number of awards: Varies.
Deadline: June 1.
How to apply: Applications are available online.
Exclusive: Visit www.UltimateScholarshipBook.com and enter code CL63323 for updates on this award.

(634) · John Bayliss Radio Scholarship

John Bayliss Broadcast Foundation
171 17th Street, Pacific Grove, CA 93950
Phone: 212-424-6410
Email: cbutrum@baylissfoundation.org
http://www.beaweb.org/bayliss/radio.html
Purpose: This scholarship helps students who are pursuing careers in radio.
Eligibility: Applicants must be attending an institution of higher learning in the U.S., be entering their junior or senior year and have a GPA of 3.0 or higher. Students must be working toward a career in the radio industry. Preference is given to students with a history of radio-related activities and those pursuing careers in commercial radio.
Target applicant(s): College students. Adult students.
Minimum GPA: 3.0
Amount: $5,000.
Number of awards: Varies.
Deadline: Varies.
How to apply: Applications are available online. An application form, resume, transcript, essay and three letters of recommendation are required.
Exclusive: Visit www.UltimateScholarshipBook.com and enter code JO63423 for updates on this award.

(635) · John D. Graham Scholarship

Public Relations Student Society of America
33 Maiden Lane, 11th Floor, New York, NY 10038
Phone: 212-460-1474
Email: prssa@prsa.org
https://prssa.prsa.org/scholarships-and-awards/
Purpose: To aid journalism and public relations students.
Eligibility: Applicants must be rising undergraduate seniors who are enrolled in a journalism or public relations degree program. Selection is based on academic merit, leadership, writing ability, relevant work experience and stated career goals.
Target applicant(s): College students. Adult students.
Amount: $1,000-$3,000.
Number of awards: 3.
Deadline: May 31.
How to apply: Applications are available online. An application form, resume and one recommendation letter are required.
Exclusive: Visit www.UltimateScholarshipBook.com and enter code PU63523 for updates on this award.

(636) · John F. Kennedy Profile in Courage Essay Contest

John F. Kennedy Library Foundation
Columbia Point, Boston, MA 02125
Phone: 617-514-1649
Email: profiles@nara.gov
http://www.jfklibrary.org/Education/Profile-in-Courage-Essay-Contest.aspx
Purpose: To encourage students to research and write about politics and John F. Kennedy.
Eligibility: Applicants must be in grades 9 through 12 in public or private schools or be home-schooled and write an essay about the political courage of a U.S. elected official who served during or after 1956. Essays must have source citations. Applicants must register online before sending essays and have a nominating teacher review the essay. The winner and teacher will be invited to the Kennedy Library to accept the award, and the winner's teacher will receive a grant. Essays are judged on content (55 percent) and presentation (45 percent).
Target applicant(s): High school students.
Amount: $100-$10,000.
Number of awards: Up to 25.

Deadline: January 14.
How to apply: Applications are available online. A registration form and essay are required.
Exclusive: Visit www.UltimateScholarshipBook.com and enter code JO63623 for updates on this award.

(637) · Joseph S. Rumbaugh Historical Oration Contest

National Society, Sons of the American Revolution
1000 South Fourth Street, Louisville, KY 40203
Phone: 502-589-1776
Email: sdelong1@san.rr.com
https://www.sar.org/education/
Purpose: To encourage students to learn more about the Revolutionary War and its impact on modern America.
Eligibility: Applicants must prepare a speech of five to six minutes on some aspect of the Revolutionary War. The contest is open to high school students at public, private and parochial high schools, as well as home-schooled students. Eligibility for the national contest is determined by contests on the state and local level.
Target applicant(s): High school students.
Amount: $200-$6,000.
Number of awards: Varies.
Deadline: Varies.
How to apply: Applications are available from local chapters of Sons of the American Revolution.
Exclusive: Visit www.UltimateScholarshipBook.com and enter code NA63723 for updates on this award.

(638) · Jungle Scholar

Jungle Scout
2021 East 5th Street, Suite 190, Austin, TX 78702
Phone: 513-600-3353
Email: scholar@junglescout.com
https://www.junglescout.com/jungle-scholar/
Purpose: To support students pursuing business, entrepreneurship and computer science.
Eligibility: Applicants must be students in a U.S. institution pursuing a degree in business- or computer science-related fields with a passion for entrepreneurship. Students must submit an e-commerce or SaaS concept with their application materials.
Target applicant(s): High school students. College students. Graduate school students. Adult students.
Amount: $2,000.
Number of awards: 1.
Deadline: Rolling.
How to apply: Applications are available online.
Exclusive: Visit www.UltimateScholarshipBook.com and enter code JU63823 for updates on this award.

(639) · Junior Fellowships

American Institute of Indian Studies
1130 E. 59th Street, Chicago, IL 60637
Phone: 773-702-8638
Email: aiis@uchicago.edu
http://www.indiastudies.org
Purpose: To support doctoral candidates at U.S. universities who wish to travel to India to conduct dissertation research on Indian aspects of their academic discipline.

Eligibility: Applicants must be doctoral candidates at a U.S. university. Junior fellows are affiliated with Indian universities and research mentors. Awards may last up to 11 months.
Target applicant(s): Graduate school students. Adult students.
Amount: Varies.
Number of awards: Varies.
Deadline: November 15.
How to apply: Applications are available by mail or email.
Exclusive: Visit www.UltimateScholarshipBook.com and enter code AM63923 for updates on this award.

(640) · K2TEO Martin J. Green, Sr. Memorial Scholarship

American Radio Relay League Foundation
225 Main Street, Newington, CT 06111-1494
Phone: 860-594-0348
Email: foundation@arrl.org
http://www.arrl.org/scholarship-program
Purpose: To provide financial assistance to students who are amateur radio operators.
Eligibility: Applicants must hold a general class or higher amateur radio license. Preference is given to students from ham families.
Target applicant(s): High school students. College students. Graduate school students. Adult students.
Amount: $1,000.
Number of awards: 1.
Deadline: December 31.
How to apply: Applications are available online.
Exclusive: Visit www.UltimateScholarshipBook.com and enter code AM64023 for updates on this award.

(641) · Kimberly-Clark Corporation Legacy Scholarship

National Grocers Association
1005 N. Glebe Road, Suite 250, Arlington, VA 22201
Phone: 225-387-6126
https://www.nationalgrocers.org/foundation/nga-foundation-scholarships/
Purpose: To support students pursuing a degree related to the grocery field.
Eligibility: Applicants must be rising sophomores through postgraduate students, have a minimum 2.5 GPA and be enrolled in a two- or four-year degree-granting institution. Students must major in business, food management, IT or another field related to a career in the grocery industry. Experience in the grocery industry is preferred but not required.
Target applicant(s): College students. Graduate school students. Adult students.
Minimum GPA: 2.5
Amount: Varies.
Number of awards: 1.
Deadline: April 1.
How to apply: Applications are available online.
Exclusive: Visit www.UltimateScholarshipBook.com and enter code NA64123 for updates on this award.

(642) · Kit C. King Graduate Scholarship Fund

National Press Photographers Association Kit C. King Graduate Scholarship Fund
120 Hooper Street, Athens, GA 30602-3018
Phone: 706-542-2506

Email: jwbrown@nppf.org
http://nppf.org/nppf-scholarships-grants-and-awards/
Purpose: To support photojournalism students.
Eligibility: Applicants must provide a portfolio, be pursuing an advanced degree in journalism with an emphasis in photojournalism and demonstrate financial need. Applicants can apply to as many NPPA scholarships as desired, but only one award will be granted per winner.
Target applicant(s): Graduate school students. Adult students.
Amount: $2,000.
Number of awards: 1.
Deadline: December.
How to apply: Applications are available online.
Exclusive: Visit www.UltimateScholarshipBook.com and enter code NA64223 for updates on this award.

(643) · L. Phil and Alice J. Wicker Scholarship

American Radio Relay League Foundation
225 Main Street, Newington, CT 06111-1494
Phone: 860-594-0348
Email: foundation@arrl.org
http://www.arrl.org/scholarship-program
Purpose: To assist ham radio operators in furthering their educations.
Eligibility: Applicants must have at least a general ham radio license, be residents of and attending school in the ARRL Roanoke Division (North Carolina, South Carolina, Virginia, West Virginia) and be undergraduate or graduate students in electronics, communications or another related field.
Target applicant(s): College students. Graduate school students. Adult students.
Amount: $2,000.
Number of awards: 1.
Deadline: December 31.
How to apply: Applications are available online. Completed applications must be submitted by mail.
Exclusive: Visit www.UltimateScholarshipBook.com and enter code AM64323 for updates on this award.

(644) · L.B. Cebik, W4RNL and Jean Cebik, N4TZP Memorial Scholarship

American Radio Relay League Foundation
225 Main Street, Newington, CT 06111-1494
Phone: 860-594-0348
Email: foundation@arrl.org
http://www.arrl.org/scholarship-program
Purpose: To provide scholarship assistance to amateur radio operators.
Eligibility: Applicants must hold a Technician Class Amateur Radio License or higher, and they must be attending a four-year college or university.
Target applicant(s): High school students. College students. Adult students.
Amount: $5,000.
Number of awards: 1.
Deadline: December 31.
How to apply: Applications are available online.
Exclusive: Visit www.UltimateScholarshipBook.com and enter code AM64423 for updates on this award.

(645) · Laurels Fund Scholarship

Educational Foundation for Women in Accounting
136 South Keowee Street, Dayton, OH 45402-2241
Phone: 610-407-9229
Email: info@efwa.org
http://www.efwa.org
Purpose: To provide scholarships to women pursuing advanced degrees in accounting.
Eligibility: This award is available to women pursuing a Ph.D. in accounting. The awardees are selected based on scholarship, service and financial need. Applicants must have completed their comprehensive exams before the previous fall semester.
Target applicant(s): Graduate school students. Adult students.
Amount: Up to $5,000.
Number of awards: Varies.
Deadline: May 15.
How to apply: Applications are available online.
Exclusive: Visit www.UltimateScholarshipBook.com and enter code ED64523 for updates on this award.

(646) · Lawrence G. Foster Award for Excellence in Public Relations

Public Relations Student Society of America
33 Maiden Lane, 11th Floor, New York, NY 10038
Phone: 212-460-1474
Email: prssa@prsa.org
https://prssa.prsa.org/scholarships-and-awards/
Purpose: To assist public relations students.
Eligibility: Applicants must be undergraduate students majoring in public relations who are committed to careers in public relations and must be PRSSA members. Applicants must submit an essay on what excellence in public relations is and how they plan to achieve excellence in their own careers.
Target applicant(s): High school students. College students. Adult students.
Amount: $1,500.
Number of awards: 1.
Deadline: May 31.
How to apply: Applications are available online.
Exclusive: Visit www.UltimateScholarshipBook.com and enter code PU64623 for updates on this award.

(647) · Learning and Leadership Grants

NEA Foundation
1201 16th Street NW, Washington, DC 20036
Phone: 202-822-7840
Email: NEAFoundation@nea.org
http://www.neafoundation.org/pages/grants-to-educators/
Purpose: To support public school teachers, public education support professionals and faculty or staff in public institutions of higher education in professional development experiences such as summer institutes or action research.
Eligibility: Applicants must be current public school teachers in grades K-12, public school education support professionals or faculty and staff at public higher education institutions. The professional development must improve practice, curriculum and student achievement. Funds may be used for fees, travel expenses, books or materials. There is also a grant for groups for $5,000.
Target applicant(s): Graduate school students. Adult students.
Amount: $2,000-$5,000.

Number of awards: Varies.
Deadline: October 22.
How to apply: Applications are available online. Applications may be submitted at any time and are reviewed three times each year on February 1, June 1 and October 15.
Exclusive: Visit www.UltimateScholarshipBook.com and enter code NE64723 for updates on this award.

(648) · Lee Thornton Scholarship

Radio Television Digital News Association
529 14th Street NW, Suite 1240, Washington, DC 20045
Phone: 202-659-6510
Email: karenh@rtdna.org
http://www.rtdna.org
Purpose: To support students pursuing careers in radio, television or digital journalism.
Eligibility: Applicants must be a sophomore, junior or senior at a college or university with preference given to students of the University of Maryland and Howard University. Students should be pursuing a degree in journalism, broadcasting or communications. Applicants must include URL links to three to five work samples.
Target applicant(s): College students. Adult students.
Amount: $2,000.
Number of awards: 1.
Deadline: January.
How to apply: Applications are available online.
Exclusive: Visit www.UltimateScholarshipBook.com and enter code RA64823 for updates on this award.

(649) · Legal Opportunity Scholarship Fund

American Bar Association
321 North Clark Street, Chicago, IL 60654
Phone: 312-988-5624
Email: abalsd@americanbar.org
https://www.americanbar.org/groups/diversity/diversity_pipeline/projects_initiatives/legal_opportunity_scholarship/
Purpose: To assist first-year law school students.
Eligibility: Applicants must be U.S. citizens or permanent residents. They must be entering the first year of law school during the year of application. They must have a cumulative undergraduate GPA of 2.5 or higher. Selection is based on the overall strength of the application.
Target applicant(s): College students. Graduate school students. Adult students.
Minimum GPA: 2.5
Amount: $15,000.
Number of awards: 20.
Scholarship may be renewable.
Deadline: April 17.
How to apply: Applications are available online. An application form, personal statement, two recommendation letters and a transcript are required.
Exclusive: Visit www.UltimateScholarshipBook.com and enter code AM64923 for updates on this award.

(650) · LexisNexis / John R. Johnson Memorial Scholarship Endowment

American Association of Law Libraries
105 W. Adams, Suite 3300, Chicago, IL 60603
Email: scholarships@aall.org
https://www.aallnet.org/education-training/scholarships/

Purpose: To encourage current and future law librarians in memory of John Johnson, a prominent law librarian.
Eligibility: Applicants who apply for any of the AALL Educational Scholarships become automatically eligible to receive this award. No separate application is necessary. Applicants must intend to have careers as law librarians. Preference is given to AALL members, but a non-member may apply.
Target applicant(s): Graduate school students. Adult students.
Amount: Varies.
Number of awards: Varies.
Scholarship may be renewable.
Deadline: April 1.
How to apply: Applications are available online, by mail with a self-addressed, stamped envelope, by fax, by phone or by email.
Exclusive: Visit www.UltimateScholarshipBook.com and enter code AM65023 for updates on this award.

(651) · LimNexus Scholarship

National Asian Pacific American Bar Association Law Foundation
P.O. Box 65081, Washington, DC 20035
https://www.napabalawfoundation.org/scholarships
Purpose: To support students who demonstrate a commitment to serving the Asian Pacific American community.
Eligibility: Applicants must be U.S. citizens or permanent residents who are enrolled in an accredited U.S. law school. Students must demonstrate academic achievement, leadership potential and commitment in serving or contributing to the Asian Pacific American community. Applicants must include an essay emphasizing experiences that illustrate their commitment to the APA community.
Target applicant(s): Graduate school students. Adult students.
Amount: $2,500.
Number of awards: 1.
Deadline: September 7.
How to apply: Applications are available online.
Exclusive: Visit www.UltimateScholarshipBook.com and enter code NA65123 for updates on this award.

(652) · Litherland/FTEE Scholarship

International Technology and Engineering Educators Association
Foundation for Technology and Engineering Educators, 1914 Association Drive, Suite 201, Reston, VA 20191-1539
Phone: 703-860-2100
Email: iteea@iteea.org
https://www.iteea.org/Activities/AwardsScholarships.aspx
Purpose: To provide scholarships for undergraduate students pursuing a career in teaching technology.
Eligibility: Applicants must be members of ITEEA, be full-time undergraduate students majoring in technology and engineering education teacher preparation. Students must also have a minimum 2.5 GPA.
Target applicant(s): College students. Adult students.
Minimum GPA: 2.5
Amount: $500.
Number of awards: 1.
Deadline: December 1.
How to apply: Application information is available online.
Exclusive: Visit www.UltimateScholarshipBook.com and enter code IN65223 for updates on this award.

(653) · Lockheed Martin Vocational Scholarship Program

Lockheed Martin Vocational Scholarship
Scholarship America, One Scholarship Way, Saint Peter, MN 56082
Phone: 507-931-1682
Email: lmvocational@scholarshipamerica.org
https://lockheedmartin.com/en-us/who-we-are/communities/stem-education/lockheed-martin-vocational-scholarship.html
Purpose: To support students pursuing an associate's degree or vocational-technical certification.
Eligibility: Applicants must be high school seniors, high school graduates (or GED equivalent) or current undergraduates with less than a bachelor's degree. Students must be U.S. citizens who are planning to enroll at an accredited vocational technical school, trade school, two-year community or state college. Applicants must be studying one of the following fields or a related field: computer and information sciences, support services, engineering technologies/technicians, mechanic and repair technologies, precision production, transportation and materials moving or security and protective services.
Target applicant(s): High school students. College students. Adult students.
Amount: Up to $6,600.
Number of awards: 150.
Deadline: March 11.
How to apply: Applications are available online.
Exclusive: Visit www.UltimateScholarshipBook.com and enter code LO65323 for updates on this award.

(654) · Lou and Carole Prato Sports Reporting Scholarship

Radio Television Digital News Association
529 14th Street NW, Suite 1240, Washington, DC 20045
Phone: 202-659-6510
Email: karenh@rtdna.org
http://www.rtdna.org
Purpose: To provide monetary assistance to a student pursuing a career as a sports reporter for radio or television.
Eligibility: Applicants must be full-time college sophomores or higher with at least one full academic year remaining. Applicants may be enrolled in any major but must have a career goal of becoming a sports reporter for television or radio. Applicants may only apply for one RTNDA scholarship.
Target applicant(s): College students. Adult students.
Amount: $1,000.
Number of awards: 1.
Deadline: January 15.
How to apply: Applications are available online.
Exclusive: Visit www.UltimateScholarshipBook.com and enter code RA65423 for updates on this award.

(655) · Lou Hochberg Awards

Orgone Biophysical Research Laboratory
P.O. Box 1148, Ashland, OR 97520
Phone: 541-522-0118
Email: info@orgonelab.org
http://www.orgonelab.org/hochberg.htm
Purpose: The Orgone Biophysical Research Lab offers a number of awards to students, scholars and journalists through a program set up by Louis Hochberg, a social worker who was dedicated to the sociological discoveries of Wilhelm Reich.

Eligibility: The Lou Hochberg Awards are given to winning theses and dissertations, university and college essays, high school essays and published articles that focus on Reich's sociological work. There are categories for students, scholars or journalists beginning at high school age through adulthood. A suggested list of topics and a bibliography is available online.
Target applicant(s): High school students. College students. Graduate school students. Adult students.
Amount: $500-$1,500.
Number of awards: Varies.
Deadline: Varies.
How to apply: Each award has a specific set of instructions for submitting a package for consideration. Guidelines are listed online.
Exclusive: Visit www.UltimateScholarshipBook.com and enter code OR65523 for updates on this award.

(656) · Maley/FTEE Teacher Professional Development Scholarship

International Technology and Engineering Educators Association
Foundation for Technology and Engineering Educators, 1914 Association Drive, Suite 201, Reston, VA 20191-1539
Phone: 703-860-2100
Email: iteea@iteea.org
https://www.iteea.org/Activities/AwardsScholarships.aspx
Purpose: To support technology education teachers.
Eligibility: Applicants must be members of ITEEA and plan to pursue or continue graduate study. Candidates must provide their plans for graduate study, description of need, college transcript and three recommendation letters.
Target applicant(s): College students. Graduate school students. Adult students.
Amount: $500.
Number of awards: Varies.
Deadline: December 1.
How to apply: Application information is available online.
Exclusive: Visit www.UltimateScholarshipBook.com and enter code IN65623 for updates on this award.

(657) · Maple Flooring Manufacturers Association Scholarship

Maple Flooring Manufacturers Association
One Parkview Plaza Suite 800, Oakbrook Terrace, IL 60181
Phone: 888-480-9138
Email: mfma@maplefloor.org
http://www.maplefloor.org/Programs-Services/Scholarship-Program.aspx
Purpose: To support students pursuing a higher education at a secondary, advanced or trade school.
Eligibility: Applicants must be legal residents of the U.S. attending college in the United States. Students must write a 500-word essay and be studying in one of the following fields: architecture, athletic administration, athletics, boiler inspection training, biological conservation, bio-mechanical sciences, building construction, civil engineering, coaching, commercial driving schools, construction sciences or management, dance education, forest science, forestry studies, engineering technology, environmental resource management, exercise science, industrial technology schools, kinesiology, LEED training or certification, mechanic schools, mechanical drafting, machine technologies, natural resources / conservation, physical administration, physical education, physical rehabilitation or therapy, recreation and

park administration, small engine repair schools, sports and fitness management, survey schools, trucking schools or wood sciences.
Target applicant(s): High school students. College students. Adult students.
Amount: $1,000.
Number of awards: 5.
Deadline: July 9.
How to apply: Applications are available online.
Exclusive: Visit www.UltimateScholarshipBook.com and enter code MA65723 for updates on this award.

(658) · Mary Lou Brown Scholarship

American Radio Relay League Foundation
225 Main Street, Newington, CT 06111-1494
Phone: 860-594-0348
Email: foundation@arrl.org
http://www.arrl.org/scholarship-program
Purpose: To assist ham radio operators with furthering their educations.
Eligibility: Applicants must have at least a general ham radio license, be residents of the ARRL Northwest Division (Alaska, Idaho, Montana, Oregon or Washington), be working for a bachelor's or graduate degree, have a minimum 3.0 GPA and have demonstrated interest in promoting the Amateur Radio Service.
Target applicant(s): High school students. College students. Graduate school students. Adult students.
Minimum GPA: 3.0
Amount: $2,500.
Number of awards: Varies.
Deadline: December 31.
How to apply: Applications are available online. Completed applications must be submitted by mail.
Exclusive: Visit www.UltimateScholarshipBook.com and enter code AM65823 for updates on this award.

(659) · MBA Fellowship

Goldman Sachs
200 West Street, New York, NY 10282
http://www.goldmansachs.com/careers/students/programs/americas/mba-fellowship.html
Purpose: To recognize outstanding students.
Eligibility: Applicants must be first-year MBA students. Students must be seeking a summer associate position at Goldman Sachs. Applicants must be Black, Hispanic/Latino, Native American or women.
Target applicant(s): Graduate school students. Adult students.
Amount: $35,000.
Number of awards: Varies.
Deadline: March 28.
How to apply: Applications are available online.
Exclusive: Visit www.UltimateScholarshipBook.com and enter code GO65923 for updates on this award.

(660) · Media Fellows Program

Washington Media Scholars Foundation
815 Slaters Lane, Suite 201, Alexandria, VA 22314
Phone: 703-299-4399
Email: info@mediascholars.org
http://www.mediascholars.org
Purpose: To aid students who plan to pursue careers in the field of public policy and advertising.

Eligibility: Applicants must be rising undergraduate juniors and seniors who are attending school full time. They must be degree-seeking students who are majoring in subjects that provide preparation for a career in strategic public policy research, planning, advertising or buying. Eligible majors include but are not limited to political science, mass communication, marketing and journalism. They must have a demonstrated interest in pursuing a career in the field of strategic media planning. They must have a major GPA of 3.0 or higher and must demonstrate financial need. Selection is based on the overall strength of the application.
Target applicant(s): College students. Adult students.
Minimum GPA: 3.0
Amount: $1,000-$2,000.
Number of awards: 50.
Deadline: July 16.
How to apply: Applications are available online. An application form, essay and one recommendation letter are required.
Exclusive: Visit www.UltimateScholarshipBook.com and enter code WA66023 for updates on this award.

(661) · Memorial Classic Golf Tournament Scholarship

Funeral Service Foundation
13625 Bishop's Drive, Brookfield, WI 53005-6607
Phone: 877-402-5900
Email: info@funeralservicefoundation.org
https://www.funeralservicefoundation.org/academicscholarships/
Purpose: To help students continue their education in funeral service and mortuary science education.
Eligibility: Applicants must be enrolled full- or part-time in an American Board of Funeral Service Education accredited program. Selection is based on the overall strength of the application.
Target applicant(s): College students. Graduate school students. Adult students.
Minimum GPA: 2.0
Amount: $1,000.
Number of awards: Varies.
Deadline: April 1, November 1.
How to apply: Applications are available online. An application form, essay, academic transcript and video submissions are required.
Exclusive: Visit www.UltimateScholarshipBook.com and enter code FU66123 for updates on this award.

(662) · Merchants Exchange of Portland Scholarship

Merchants Exchange of Portland Scholarship Fund
200 SW Market Street, Suite 190, Portland, OR 97201
Phone: 503-804-0633
http://www.pdxmex.com/scholarship
Purpose: To support students seeking a maritime field career.
Eligibility: Applicants must be current juniors or seniors at a four-year college or university, freshmen or sophomores in a two-year degree program, students in a U.S. Coast Guard-approved training program or graduate students in Maritime affairs or international trade. Students must have a minimum GPA of 2.5 and provide transcripts, essays and a letter of recommendation.
Target applicant(s): College students. Graduate school students. Adult students.
Minimum GPA: 2.5
Amount: $2,000.
Number of awards: 5.
Deadline: May 31.

How to apply: Applications are available online.
Exclusive: Visit www.UltimateScholarshipBook.com and enter code ME66223 for updates on this award.

---

(663) · Minorities and Women Educational Scholarship

Appraisal Institute Education Trust
200 W. Madison, Suite 1500, Chicago, IL 60606
Phone: 312-335-4133
Email: wwoodburn@appraisalinstitute.org
http://www.appraisalinstitute.org
Purpose: To assist minority and women college students in pursuing degrees in real estate appraisal or related fields.
Eligibility: Applicants must be women or American Indians, Alaska Natives, Asians, African Americans, Hispanics or Latinos, Native Hawaiians or other Pacific Islanders. Applicants must be full- or part-time students enrolled in real estate courses and working toward a degree, have a minimum 2.5 GPA and demonstrate financial need.
Target applicant(s): High school students. College students. Adult students.
Minimum GPA: 2.5
Amount: $1,000.
Number of awards: Varies.
Deadline: April 1.
How to apply: Applications are available online.
Exclusive: Visit www.UltimateScholarshipBook.com and enter code AP66323 for updates on this award.

---

(664) · Minority Fellowship Program

American Sociological Association Minority Fellowship Program
1430 K Street NW, Suite 600, Washington, DC 20005
Phone: 202-383-9005
Email: minority.affairs@asanet.org
http://www.asanet.org/career-center/grants-and-fellowships
Purpose: To provide pre-doctoral graduate education for sociology students.
Eligibility: Applicants must be enrolled in and have completed one full year in a Ph.D. program in Sociology. Students must be members of an underrepresented minority group in the U.S.: African American, Latino, Asian/Pacific Islander or American Indians/Alaska Natives. Applicants must also be U.S. citizens, non-citizen nationals of the U.S. or have been lawfully admitted to the U.S. for permanent residence. The fellowship is awarded for 12 months and typically renewable for up to three years in total. Tuition and fees are arranged with the home department. MFP Fellows are selected each year by the MFP Advisory Panel, a rotating, appointed group of senior scholars in sociology. Fellows can be involved in any area of sociological research, though particular MFP award lines devoted to drug abuse research may be possible contingent on funding.
Target applicant(s): Graduate school students. Adult students.
Amount: $18,000.
Number of awards: Varies.
Deadline: January 31.
How to apply: Applications are available online.
Exclusive: Visit www.UltimateScholarshipBook.com and enter code AM66423 for updates on this award.

---

(665) · MLA Scholarship

Medical Library Association
225 West Wacker Drive, Suite 650, Chicago, IL 60606
Phone: 312-419-9094
Email: lopez@mail.mlahq.org
http://www.mlanet.org
Purpose: To aid a student with finishing their education at an ALA-accredited library school.
Eligibility: Applicants must be either entering or less than half-way through an accredited graduate school program in a field relevant to library science and be U.S. or Canadian citizens or permanent residents.
Target applicant(s): Graduate school students. Adult students.
Amount: Up to $5,000.
Number of awards: 1.
Deadline: December 1.
How to apply: Applications are available online.
Exclusive: Visit www.UltimateScholarshipBook.com and enter code ME66523 for updates on this award.

---

(666) · MLA Scholarship for Minority Students

Medical Library Association
225 West Wacker Drive, Suite 650, Chicago, IL 60606
Phone: 312-419-9094
Email: lopez@mail.mlahq.org
http://www.mlanet.org
Purpose: To aid minority students entering or currently attending graduate library school.
Eligibility: Applicants must be member of an underrepresented group, such as Black/African-American, Latin, Asian, Aboriginal, North American Indian or Alaskan Native, or Native Hawaiian or other Pacific Islander. Students must be entering or currently attending an ALA-accredited library school and be no more than halfway through the program. Applicants must also be citizens or permanent residents of the United States or Canada.
Target applicant(s): Graduate school students. Adult students.
Amount: Up to $5,000.
Number of awards: 1.
Deadline: December 1.
How to apply: Applications are available online.
Exclusive: Visit www.UltimateScholarshipBook.com and enter code ME66623 for updates on this award.

---

(667) · Mondelez International Legacy Scholarship

National Grocers Association
1005 N. Glebe Road, Suite 250, Arlington, VA 22201
Phone: 225-387-6126
https://www.nationalgrocers.org/foundation/nga-foundation-scholarships/
Purpose: To support students pursuing education related to the grocery field.
Eligibility: Applicants must be rising sophomores through postgraduate students, have a minimum 2.5 GPA and be enrolled in a two- or four-year degree-granting institution. Students must major in business, food management, IT or another field related to a career in the grocery industry. Experience in the grocery industry is preferred but not required.
Target applicant(s): College students. Graduate school students. Adult students.
Minimum GPA: 2.5
Amount: Varies.
Number of awards: 1.
Deadline: April 1.
How to apply: Applications are available online.
Exclusive: Visit www.UltimateScholarshipBook.com and enter code NA66723 for updates on this award.

(668) · Moody Research Grant

Lyndon B. Johnson Foundation
2313 Red River Street, Austin, TX 78705
Phone: 512-721-0263
Email: samantha@lbjfoundation.org
http://www.lbjlibrary.org
Purpose: To assist with the travel and room-and-board expenses of those wishing to conduct research at the Lyndon B. Johnson Foundation Library.
Eligibility: Applicants must first contact the library to determine if their topic is appropriate for study at the facility. Applicants must also calculate the estimated amount of the grant before making a request.
Target applicant(s): College students. Adult students.
Amount: $600-$3,000.
Number of awards: Varies.
Deadline: March 15 and September 15.
How to apply: Applications are available online.
Exclusive: Visit www.UltimateScholarshipBook.com and enter code LY66823 for updates on this award.

(669) · My Alarm Center Student Scholarship

My Alarm Center
3803 West Chester Pike, Suite 100, Newtown Square, PA 19073
Phone: 855-334-6562
Email: scholarship@myalarmcenter.com
https://www.myalarmcenter.com
Purpose: To support students in pursuing a degree in law enforcement, law, criminal justice or a related field.
Eligibility: Applicants must be graduating high school seniors or college freshmen/sophomores studying law enforcement, law, criminal justice or a related field. Students must submit an essay on a provided prompt. Selection is based on the overall strength of the submission.
Target applicant(s): High school students. College students. Adult students.
Amount: $1,000.
Number of awards: Varies.
Deadline: July 1.
How to apply: Applications are available online.
Exclusive: Visit www.UltimateScholarshipBook.com and enter code MY66923 for updates on this award.

(670) · NACA Mid Atlantic Graduate Student Scholarship

National Association for Campus Activities
13 Harbison Way, Columbia, SC 29212
Phone: 803-732-6222
Email: info@naca.org
https://www.naca.org/FOUNDATION/Pages/Scholarships.aspx
Purpose: To provide assistance to graduate students who are attending a college or university on the East Coast.
Eligibility: Applicants must be enrolled in master's or doctorate degree programs in student personnel services or a related area. Applicants must be attending a graduate school in Washington, DC, Delaware, Maryland, New Jersey, New York or eastern Pennsylvania, be involved in campus activities and plan to pursue a career in campus activities.
Target applicant(s): Graduate school students. Adult students.
Amount: Varies.
Number of awards: Varies.
Deadline: March 31.
How to apply: Applications are available online.

Exclusive: Visit www.UltimateScholarshipBook.com and enter code NA67023 for updates on this award.

(671) · Nancy Curry Scholarship

School Nutrition Association
120 Waterfront Street, Suite 300, National Harbor, MD 20745
Phone: 301-686-3100
Email: servicecenter@schoolnutrition.org
https://schoolnutrition.org/Membership/AwardsScholarships/
Purpose: To support students wishing to enter the school foodservice industry.
Eligibility: Applicants must be School Nutrition Association members for at least one year and be enrolled in a school foodservice-related program at an educational institution. Children of SNA members are not eligible to apply. Applicants must be currently employed in school food service.
Target applicant(s): High school students. College students. Graduate school students. Adult students.
Amount: $500.
Number of awards: 1.
Deadline: January 31.
How to apply: Applications are available online.
Exclusive: Visit www.UltimateScholarshipBook.com and enter code SC67123 for updates on this award.

(672) · Nancy McManus Washington Internship Scholarships

Pi Sigma Alpha
The Washington Center, 2301 M Street NW, Fifth Floor, Washington, DC 20037-1427
Email: info@twc.edu
http://www.apsanet.org/~psa/
Purpose: To provide Pi Sigma Alpha members with scholarships to participate in summer or fall term internships in Washington, DC.
Eligibility: Applicants must belong to Pi Sigma Alpha and be nominated by their local chapter. The award is for a political science internship is based on academic achievement and service to the organization.
Target applicant(s): College students. Graduate school students. Adult students.
Amount: $2,000.
Number of awards: 4.
Deadline: June 1.
How to apply: Applications are available online.
Exclusive: Visit www.UltimateScholarshipBook.com and enter code PI67223 for updates on this award.

(673) · National Academic Scholarships

Association of Government Accountants (AGA)
2208 Mount Vernon Avenue, Alexandria, VA 22301-1314
Phone: 800-242-7211x309
Email: rortiz@agacgfm.org
http://www.agacgfm.org
Purpose: To support public financial management students.
Eligibility: Applicants for full-time or part-time scholarships must be an AGA member or family member (spouse, child or grandchild), and scholarships must be used for full-time or part-time undergraduate study in a financial management academic area such as accounting, auditing, budgeting, economics, finance, electronic data processing, information resources management or public administration. Essays and transcripts are required. There are two categories for high school students/

graduates and undergraduates/graduates. The Academic Scholarships are based on academic achievement and the student's potential for making a contribution to public financial management. A reference letter from an AGA member and from another professional such as a professor, guidance counselor or employer is required. Applicants to the Community Service Scholarships do not have to be AGA members, must be pursuing a degree in a financial management academic discipline and must be actively involved in community service projects. The awards are based on community service and accomplishments. A letter of recommendation from a community service organization and from another professional are required.

Target applicant(s): High school students. College students. Graduate school students. Adult students.
Minimum GPA: 2.5
Amount: $1,500-$3,000.
Number of awards: Varies.
Deadline: April 17.
How to apply: Applications are available online.
Exclusive: Visit www.UltimateScholarshipBook.com and enter code AS67323 for updates on this award.

(674) · National Foundation Scholarships

Institute of Scrap Recycling Industries
1250 H Street, NW, Suite 400, Washington, DC 20006
Phone: 202-662-8500
Email: ngrant@isri.org
http://www.isri.org/about-isri/recycling-research-foundation
Purpose: To support students seeking a graduate degree in scrap processing or recycling.
Eligibility: Applicants must be pursuing a graduate level degree, be a U.S. citizen and have a minimum 2.5 GPA. The program is open to those seeking a graduate degree in a program that supports the scrap processing and recycling industry as a whole.
Target applicant(s): Graduate school students. Adult students.
Minimum GPA: 2.5
Amount: $5,000.
Number of awards: 1.
Deadline: June 1.
How to apply: Applications are available online.
Exclusive: Visit www.UltimateScholarshipBook.com and enter code IN67423 for updates on this award.

(675) · National History Day Contest

National History Day
4511 Knox Road, Suite 205, College Park, MD 20740
Phone: 301-314-9739
Email: info@nhd.org
http://www.nhd.org
Purpose: To reward students for their scholarship, initiative and cooperation.
Eligibility: Applicants must be in grades 6-12 and prepare throughout the school year history presentations based on an annual theme. Around February or March students compete in district History Day contests. District winners then prepare for the state contests, held usually in April or May. Those winners advance to the national contest held in June at the University of Maryland.
Target applicant(s): Junior high students or younger. High school students.
Amount: Varies.
Number of awards: Varies.
Deadline: May.

How to apply: Applications are available online.
Exclusive: Visit www.UltimateScholarshipBook.com and enter code NA67523 for updates on this award.

(676) · National Press Club Scholarship for Journalism Diversity

National Press Club
529 14th Street NW, 13th Floor, Washington, DC 20045
Phone: 202-662-7500
http://www.press.org
Purpose: To support promising future journalists.
Eligibility: Applicants must be high school seniors, have a GPA of 3.0 or higher and plan to enter college the year after graduation. Students must intend to become a journalist and bring diversity to U.S. journalism.
Target applicant(s): High school students.
Minimum GPA: 3.0
Amount: $2,000 plus $500 book stipend.
Number of awards: 1.
Deadline: April 15.
How to apply: Applications are available online. An application form, essay, transcript, copy of FAFSA, letter of acceptance or proof of college application, three letters of recommendation and up to five work samples are required.
Exclusive: Visit www.UltimateScholarshipBook.com and enter code NA67623 for updates on this award.

(677) · National Scholarship Program

American Board of Funeral Service Education
Scholarship Committee, 3414 Ashland Avenue, Suite G, St. Joseph, MO 64506
Phone: 816-233-3747
http://www.abfse.org
Purpose: To assist students enrolled in funeral service or mortuary science programs.
Eligibility: Applicants must be undergraduate students who have completed at least one semester or quarter of study in funeral service or mortuary science education at an accredited school and have at least one term remaining in their study. Applicants must be U.S. citizens.
Target applicant(s): College students. Adult students.
Amount: $500-$2,500.
Number of awards: Varies.
Deadline: March 1 and September 1.
How to apply: Applications are available online.
Exclusive: Visit www.UltimateScholarshipBook.com and enter code AM67723 for updates on this award.

(678) · National Washington Crossing Foundation Scholarship

Washington Crossing Foundation
P.O. Box 503, Levittown, PA 19058
Phone: 215-949-8841
Email: info@gwcf.org
http://www.gwcf.org
Purpose: To support students who are planning careers in government service.
Eligibility: Students must be in their senior year of high school. Applicants must submit an essay and a letter of recommendation.
Target applicant(s): High school students.
Amount: $500-$5,000.

Number of awards: Varies.
Scholarship may be renewable.
Deadline: January 15.
How to apply: Applications are available online.
Exclusive: Visit www.UltimateScholarshipBook.com and enter code WA67823 for updates on this award.

---

(679) · NCRA A to Z Scholarship

National Court Reporters Association
12030 Sunrise Valley Drive, Suite 400, Reston, VA 20191
Phone: 800-272-6272
Email: schools@ncra.org
https://www.ncra.org/home/get-involved/foundation/foundation-programs/NCRF-scholarships-and-grants
Purpose: To support students who are enrolled in a court reporting program.
Eligibility: Applicants must have completed an NCRA A to Z Intro to Steno Machine Shorthand program and received an NCRA A to Z Certificate of Completion. Students must have attained an exemplary academic record and passed one skills test writing 60 to 100 words per minute.
Target applicant(s): College students. Adult students.
Amount: $500.
Number of awards: 10.
Deadline: March 15.
How to apply: Applications are available online.
Exclusive: Visit www.UltimateScholarshipBook.com and enter code NA67923 for updates on this award.

---

(680) · NCRA CASE Student Scholarship

National Court Reporters Association
12030 Sunrise Valley Drive, Suite 400, Reston, VA 20191
Phone: 800-272-6272
Email: schools@ncra.org
https://www.ncra.org/home/get-involved/foundation/foundation-programs/NCRF-scholarships-and-grants
Purpose: To support students from NCRA-approved reporter education programs.
Eligibility: Applicants must attend an NCRA-approved court reporting program and hold student membership in NCRA. Students must have attained an exemplary academic record and passed one skills test writing 140-180 words per minute.
Target applicant(s): College students. Adult students.
Amount: Up to $1,500.
Number of awards: 5.
Deadline: March 15.
How to apply: Applications are available online.
Exclusive: Visit www.UltimateScholarshipBook.com and enter code NA68023 for updates on this award.

---

(681) · NEA-Retired Jack Kinnaman Memorial Scholarship

National Education Association
Center for Governance, Attn: The NEA-Retired Jack Kinnaman Memorial Scholarship, 1201 16th Street NW, 8th Floor, Washington, DC 20036
Phone: 202-822-7132
http://www.nea.org
Purpose: To honor the memory of NEA-retired vice president and former advisory council member Jack Kinnaman.

Eligibility: Applicants must be NEA student members, major in education and have a minimum 2.5 GPA. An essay describing activities in NEA, a brief paragraph describing financial need, two letters of recommendation and a copy of the most recent transcript are required.
Target applicant(s): College students. Adult students.
Minimum GPA: 2.5
Amount: $2,500.
Number of awards: Varies.
Deadline: April 15.
How to apply: Applications are available online.
Exclusive: Visit www.UltimateScholarshipBook.com and enter code NA68123 for updates on this award.

---

(682) · Nell Bryant Robinson Scholarship

Phi Upsilon Omicron Inc.
National Office, P.O. Box 50970, Bowling Green, KY 42102-4270
Phone: 270-904-1340
Email: national@phiu.org
http://www.phiu.org
Purpose: To aid Phi Upsilon Omicron members who are pursuing bachelor's degrees in family and consumer sciences.
Eligibility: Preference is given to applicants who are majoring in food and nutrition or dietetics. Selection is based on the overall strength of the application.
Target applicant(s): College students. Adult students.
Amount: Varies.
Number of awards: Varies.
Deadline: March 1.
How to apply: Applications are available online. An application form, official transcript, personal statement and three recommendation letters are required.
Exclusive: Visit www.UltimateScholarshipBook.com and enter code PH68223 for updates on this award.

---

(683) · Nettie Dracup Memorial Scholarship

National Society of Professional Surveyors (NSPS/AAGS)
Attn: Scholarships, 5119 Pegasus Court, Suite Q, Frederick, MD 21704
Phone: 240-439-4615x105
Email: trisha.milburn@nsps.us.com
https://www.nsps.us.com/page/Scholarships
Purpose: To aid geodetic surveying students.
Eligibility: Applicants must be U.S. citizens who are undergraduate students enrolled in an accredited degree program in geodetic surveying. They must be members of the National Society of Professional Surveyors (NSPS). Selection is based on the applicant's academic achievement, personal statement, recommendations and professional activities.
Target applicant(s): High school students. College students. Adult students.
Amount: $2,000.
Number of awards: 1.
Deadline: January 22.
How to apply: Applications are available online. An application form, official transcript, personal statement, three recommendation letters and proof of ACSM membership are required.
Exclusive: Visit www.UltimateScholarshipBook.com and enter code NA68323 for updates on this award.

(684) · New England FEMARA Scholarships

American Radio Relay League Foundation
225 Main Street, Newington, CT 06111-1494
Phone: 860-594-0348
Email: foundation@arrl.org
http://www.arrl.org/scholarship-program
Purpose: To assist ham radio operators in furthering their educations.
Eligibility: Applicants must have at least a technician ham radio license and be residents of the New England States (Connecticut, Maine, Massachusetts, New Hampshire, Rhode Island or Vermont).
Target applicant(s): High school students. College students. Graduate school students. Adult students.
Amount: $2,000.
Number of awards: Varies.
Deadline: December 31.
How to apply: Applications are available online. Completed applications must be mailed in. They cannot be completed electronically.
Exclusive: Visit www.UltimateScholarshipBook.com and enter code AM68423 for updates on this award.

(685) · NFMC Gretchen E. Van Roy Music Education Scholarship

National Federation of Music Clubs (FL)
NFMC Gretchen E. Van Roy Music Education Scholarship, Cheryl Schmidt, Chairman, 1100 SW 4th Street, Willmar, MN 56201
Phone: 317-882-4003
Email: cschmidt@en-tel.net
http://www.nfmc-music.org/competitions-awards/
Purpose: To support students majoring in music education.
Eligibility: Applicants must be college juniors majoring in music education and must be affiliated with the National Federation of Music Clubs.
Target applicant(s): College students. Adult students.
Amount: $500-$1,500.
Number of awards: 2.
Deadline: April 1.
How to apply: Applications are available online.
Exclusive: Visit www.UltimateScholarshipBook.com and enter code NA68523 for updates on this award.

(686) · North American Van Lines Logistics Scholarship

North American Van Lines
Phone: 800-369-9115
https://www.northamerican.com/scholarship
Purpose: To support students pursuing a degree in logistics or supply chain management.
Eligibility: Applicants must be U.S. citizens and enrolled full-time as an undergraduate at an eligible educational institution. Funds must be used for qualified educational expenses. Students should be pursuing a degree in logistics or supply chain management. Applicants will need to submit a 400-800 word essay on why they selected a career in logistics/supply chain management. The essay should convey a sincere, personalized tone.
Target applicant(s): High school students. College students. Adult students.
Amount: $1,000.
Number of awards: 3.
Deadline: December 15.

How to apply: Applications are available online and must be submitted along with an official transcript, a verification of enrollment and the essay.
Exclusive: Visit www.UltimateScholarshipBook.com and enter code NO68623 for updates on this award.

(687) · NPPF Still and Multimedia Scholarship

National Press Photographers Association
Still Photographer Scholarship, 120 Hooper Street, Athens, GA 30602-3018
Phone: 706-542-2506
Email: tkenniff@nppa.org
http://www.nppa.org
Purpose: To honor the profession of photojournalism.
Eligibility: Applicants must have completed one year in a full-time four-year college or university with courses in photojournalism, provide a portfolio and demonstrate financial need. Applicants can apply to as many NPPA scholarships as desired, but only one award will be granted per winner.
Target applicant(s): College students. Adult students.
Amount: $2,000.
Number of awards: Varies.
Deadline: December.
How to apply: Applications are available online.
Exclusive: Visit www.UltimateScholarshipBook.com and enter code NA68723 for updates on this award.

(688) · NPPF Television News Scholarship

National Press Photographers Foundation Television News Scholarship
120 Hooper Street, Athens, GA 30602-3018
Phone: 706-542-2506
Email: jwbrown@nppf.org
http://www.nppa.org
Purpose: To support students with television news photojournalism potential but with little opportunity and great need.
Eligibility: Applicants must be full-time juniors or seniors at a four-year college or university, provide a portfolio and demonstrate financial need. Applicants must also have courses in TV news photojournalism and continue in this program towards a bachelor's degree. Applicants can apply to as many NPPA scholarships as desired, but only one award will be granted per winner.
Target applicant(s): College students. Adult students.
Amount: $2,000.
Number of awards: 1.
Deadline: December.
How to apply: Applications are available online.
Exclusive: Visit www.UltimateScholarshipBook.com and enter code NA68823 for updates on this award.

(689) · NSA Scholarship Foundation

National Society of Accountants Scholarship Program
1330 Braddock Place, Suite 540, Alexandria, VA 22314
Phone: 800-966-6679
http://www.nsacct.org
Purpose: To support students entering the accounting profession.
Eligibility: Applicants must be undergraduate students majoring in accounting with a minimum 3.0 GPA and be U.S. or Canadian citizens.
Target applicant(s): High school students. College students. Adult students.

Minimum GPA: 3.0
Amount: $500-$2,200.
Number of awards: 39.
Deadline: April.
How to apply: Applications are available online.
Exclusive: Visit www.UltimateScholarshipBook.com and enter code NA68923 for updates on this award.

---

(690) · Optimist International Oratorical Contest

Optimist International
4494 Lindell Boulevard, St. Louis, MO 63108
Phone: 314-371-6000
Email: programs@optimist.org
http://www.optimist.org
Purpose: To reward students based on their oratorical performance.
Eligibility: Applicants must be students in the U.S., Canada or Caribbean under the age of 16 as of December 31st of the entry year. Selection is based on an oratorical contest.
Target applicant(s): Junior high students or younger. High school students.
Amount: $1,000-$2,500.
Number of awards: 2-3.
Deadline: Varies.
How to apply: Contact your local Optimist Club.
Exclusive: Visit www.UltimateScholarshipBook.com and enter code OP69023 for updates on this award.

---

(691) · Otto M. Stanfield Legal Scholarship

Unitarian Universalist Association
24 Farnsworth Street, Boston, MA 02210
Phone: 617-742-2100
Email: uufp@uua.org
http://www.uua.org/giving/awards
Purpose: To help Unitarian Universalist students entering or attending law school.
Eligibility: Applicants should be planning to attend or currently attending law school at the graduate level. The award is based on activity with Unitarian Universalism and financial need. Applicants should submit transcripts and recommendations.
Target applicant(s): Graduate school students. Adult students.
Amount: Varies.
Number of awards: Varies.
Deadline: February 15.
How to apply: Applications are available online.
Exclusive: Visit www.UltimateScholarshipBook.com and enter code UN69123 for updates on this award.

---

(692) · Overseas Press Club Foundation Scholarships/ Fellowships

Overseas Press Club Foundation
40 West 45 Street, New York, NY 10036
Phone: 201-493-9087
Email: foundation@opcofamerica.org
http://www.overseaspressclubfoundation.org
Purpose: To encourage undergraduate and graduate students attending American colleges and universities to pursue careers as foreign correspondents.
Eligibility: Scholarships are open to undergraduate and graduate students with an interest in a career as a foreign correspondent. Eligible students must be attending American colleges or universities.
Target applicant(s): College students. Graduate school students. Adult students.
Amount: $3,000-$4,000.
Number of awards: 17.
Deadline: December 1.
How to apply: Applications are available online.
Exclusive: Visit www.UltimateScholarshipBook.com and enter code OV69223 for updates on this award.

---

(693) · Paul and Helen L. Grauer Scholarship

American Radio Relay League Foundation
225 Main Street, Newington, CT 06111-1494
Phone: 860-594-0348
Email: foundation@arrl.org
http://www.arrl.org/scholarship-program
Purpose: To assist ham radio operators in furthering their educations.
Eligibility: Applicants must have at least a novice ham radio license, be residents and attend school in the ARRL Midwest Division (Iowa, Kansas, Missouri or Nebraska) and be undergraduate or graduate students in electronics, communications or another related field.
Target applicant(s): High school students. College students. Graduate school students. Adult students.
Amount: $1,000.
Number of awards: 1.
Deadline: December 31.
How to apply: Applications are available online. Completed applications must be submitted by mail.
Exclusive: Visit www.UltimateScholarshipBook.com and enter code AM69323 for updates on this award.

---

(694) · PAVE Student Design Competition

Planning and Visual Education Partnership (PAVE)
8570 Stirling Road, Suite 102-227, Hollywood, FL 33024
Phone: 954-551-9144
Email: info@paveglobal.org
http://paveglobal.org
Purpose: To provide undergraduate students with an opportunity to obtain real-life retail design experience.
Eligibility: Applicants must be undergraduate or graduate students studying in the areas of retail design and planning, visual merchandising, interior design or branding. Students will create a design project based on the given information.
Target applicant(s): College students. Graduate school students. Adult students.
Amount: Varies.
Number of awards: Varies.
Deadline: November 5.
How to apply: Application and project details are available online.
Exclusive: Visit www.UltimateScholarshipBook.com and enter code PL69423 for updates on this award.

---

(695) · Peter and Jody Larkin Legacy Scholarship

National Grocers Association
1005 N. Glebe Road, Suite 250, Arlington, VA 22201
Phone: 225-387-6126
https://www.nationalgrocers.org/foundation/nga-foundation-scholarships/

Purpose: To support students pursuing a degree related to the grocery field.

Eligibility: Applicants must be rising sophomores through postgraduate students, have a minimum 2.5 GPA and be enrolled in a two- or four-year degree-granting institution. Students must major in business, food management, IT or another field related to a career in the grocery industry. Experience in the grocery industry is preferred but not required.

Target applicant(s): College students. Graduate school students. Adult students.

Minimum GPA: 2.5

Amount: Varies.

Number of awards: 1.

Deadline: April 1.

How to apply: Applications are available online.

Exclusive: Visit www.UltimateScholarshipBook.com and enter code NA69523 for updates on this award.

---

(696) · PHD Scholarship

American Radio Relay League Foundation
225 Main Street, Newington, CT 06111-1494
Phone: 860-594-0348
Email: foundation@arrl.org
http://www.arrl.org/scholarship-program

Purpose: To assist ham radio operators in furthering their educations.

Eligibility: Applicants must have any class of ham radio license, be residents of the ARRL Midwest Division (Iowa, Kansas, Missouri, Nebraska) and be studying journalism, computer science or electronic engineering. Applicants may also be the children of deceased amateur radio operators.

Target applicant(s): College students. Graduate school students. Adult students.

Amount: $1,000.

Number of awards: 1.

Deadline: December 31.

How to apply: Applications are available online but may not be completed electronically. All completed applications must be mailed.

Exclusive: Visit www.UltimateScholarshipBook.com and enter code AM69623 for updates on this award.

---

(697) · Phi Delta Kappa Scholarship Grant for Prospective Educators

Phi Delta Kappa International
P.O. Box 7888, Bloomington, IN 47407
Phone: 812-339-1156
Email: scholarships@pdkintl.org
https://pdkintl.org/scholarship-overview/

Purpose: To support prospective educators who have a connection to Phi Delta Kappa or are members of Educators Rising.

Eligibility: Applicants must meet at least one of the following criteria: a high school senior who plans on majoring in education and is a good standing member of Educators Rising, a high school senior who is going to major in education and is the child or grandchild of a Kappan in good standing, a high school senior majoring in education who has obtained at least one reference letter from a Kappan in good standing, an undergraduate member of PDK who is currently enrolled in an education program or an undergraduate member of Educators Rising who is currently enrolled in an education program.

Target applicant(s): High school students. College students. Adult students.

Amount: Varies.

Number of awards: Varies.

Deadline: April 5.

How to apply: Applications are available online.

Exclusive: Visit www.UltimateScholarshipBook.com and enter code PH69723 for updates on this award.

---

(698) · Pierre and Patricia Bikai Fellowship

American Center of Oriental Research (ACOR)
656 Beacon Street, 5th Floor, Boston, MA 02215-2010
Phone: 617-353-6571
Email: acor@bu.edu
https://acorjordan.org

Purpose: To help graduate students in an archaeological project at the American Center of Oriental Research.

Eligibility: Applicants must be graduate students. The fellowship includes room and board at ACOR and $600 a month and may be combined with the Harrell and Groot fellowships. The fellowship does not support field work or travel. Recipients must live at the ACOR center in Jordan from June of one year to May of the next.

Target applicant(s): Graduate school students. Adult students.

Amount: $600 monthly plus room and board.

Number of awards: 2.

Deadline: February.

How to apply: Applications are available online.

Exclusive: Visit www.UltimateScholarshipBook.com and enter code AM69823 for updates on this award.

---

(699) · Porch Skilled Trade and Technology Scholarships

Porch.com
2200 1st Avenue South, Seattle, WA 98134
Phone: 800-604-2454
Email: scholarships@porch.com
https://porch.com/resources/scholarships

Purpose: To support students interested in skilled trades and technology.

Eligibility: Applicants must be at least 18 years of age and currently enrolled or planning to enroll as high school seniors or in a community college, undergraduate, graduate, technical college or vocational program. Students must be pursuing a degree that enables their community to learn a new trade, develop skills and technology and have a minimum 3.4 GPA.

Target applicant(s): High school students. College students. Graduate school students. Adult students.

Minimum GPA: 3.4

Amount: $2,000.

Number of awards: 4.

Deadline: July 17.

How to apply: Applications are available online.

Exclusive: Visit www.UltimateScholarshipBook.com and enter code PO69923 for updates on this award.

---

(700) · Predoctoral Fellowships for Historians of American Art to Travel Abroad

National Gallery of Art
2000B South Club Drive, Landover, MD 20785
Phone: 202-842-6482
Email: thecenter@nga.gov
https://www.nga.gov/research/casva/fellowships.html

Purpose: To award fellowships to doctoral students in art history who are studying aspects of art and architecture of the United States, including native and pre-Revolutionary America.

Eligibility: Applicants must be nominated by the chair of a graduate department of art history or other appropriate department. Each department may support two candidates. Applicants should submit proposals, itineraries, a curriculum vitae, two letters of support from professors and an additional letter of nomination from the chair. The fellowship is for a period of six to eight weeks of continuous travel abroad in areas such as Africa, Asia, South America or Europe to sites of historical and cultural interest. The travel fellowship is intended to encourage art-historical experience beyond the applicant's major field not for the advancement of a dissertation. Preference is given to those who have had little opportunity for professional travel abroad.

Target applicant(s): Graduate school students. Adult students.

Amount: Up to $6,000.

Number of awards: Up to 4.

Deadline: November 15.

How to apply: Application materials are described online.

Exclusive: Visit www.UltimateScholarshipBook.com and enter code NA70023 for updates on this award.

(701) · Presidential Scholarships

National Asian Pacific American Bar Association Law Foundation
P.O. Box 65081, Washington, DC 20035
https://www.napabalawfoundation.org/scholarships

Purpose: To support students who demonstrate a commitment to contribute to the Asian Pacific American community.

Eligibility: Applicants must be U.S. citizens or permanent residents and enrolled in an accredited U.S. law school. Students must demonstrate academic achievement, leadership potential and commitment to serving the Asian Pacific American community. Applicants must provide letters of recommendation along with an essay as part of their application.

Target applicant(s): Graduate school students. Adult students.

Amount: $7,500.

Number of awards: 2.

Deadline: September 7.

How to apply: Applications are available online.

Exclusive: Visit www.UltimateScholarshipBook.com and enter code NA70123 for updates on this award.

(702) · Prize in International Insolvency Studies

International Insolvency Institute
10332 Main Street, PMB 112, Fairfax, VA 22030
Phone: 416-595-2965
Email: ftibando@millerthomson.com
http://www.iiiglobal.org

Purpose: To recognize outstanding international insolvency researchers, commentators and analysts.

Eligibility: Applicants must be undergraduate students, graduate students or practitioners of international insolvency studies who have less than nine years of experience. They must submit original analysis, commentary or legal research on the subject of international insolvency. Selection is based on the overall strength of the submission.

Target applicant(s): College students. Graduate school students. Adult students.

Amount: $2,000-$3,000.

Number of awards: Up to 9.

Deadline: March.

How to apply: Application instructions are available online. A scholarly paper is required.

Exclusive: Visit www.UltimateScholarshipBook.com and enter code IN70223 for updates on this award.

(703) · Project Vote Smart National Internship Program

Project Vote Smart
Internship Coordinator, 1 Common Ground, Philipsburg, MT 59858
Phone: 406-859-8683
Email: intern@votesmart.org
https://justfacts.votesmart.org/internships/

Purpose: To encourage students and recent college graduates to develop an interest in voter education.

Eligibility: Applicants must be current college students in good standing or recent college graduates. They must be able to approach voter education work with a non-partisan attitude and be willing to commit to a ten-week internship. Selection is based on the overall strength of the application.

Target applicant(s): College students. Adult students.

Amount: All living costs (including room and board).

Number of awards: Varies.

Deadline: Rolling.

How to apply: Applications are available online. An application form, resume, cover letter and three references are required.

Exclusive: Visit www.UltimateScholarshipBook.com and enter code PR70323 for updates on this award.

(704) · Prospective Educator Scholarships

Pi Lambda Theta Scholarships
P.O. Box 7888, Bloomington, IN 47407-7888
Phone: 812-339-1156
Email: scholarships@pdkintl.org
https://pilambda.org/#scholarships

Purpose: To recognize education majors with leadership potential and a dedication to education.

Eligibility: Applicants must be members of Educators Rising, PDK International or Pi Lambda Theta and must be current undergraduate students.

Target applicant(s): College students. Adult students.

Minimum GPA: 3.5

Amount: Up to $2,500.

Number of awards: Varies.

Deadline: April 5.

How to apply: Applications are available online. Transcripts, letters of recommendation and essays are required.

Exclusive: Visit www.UltimateScholarshipBook.com and enter code PI70423 for updates on this award.

(705) · Quill and Scroll Student Scholarships

Quill and Scroll Society
University of Iowa School of Journalism and Mass Communications, 100 Adler Journalism Building, Iowa City, IA 52242
Phone: 319-335-3457
Email: quill-scroll@uiowa.edu
http://www.quillandscroll.org

Purpose: To aid high school journalists seeking to improve their skills and techniques.

Eligibility: Applicants must be Quill and Scroll members or national winners of the Yearbook Excellence Contest or the International Writing, Photography and Multimedia Contest or Blogging Competition.

Target applicant(s): High school students.
Amount: $500-$1,500.
Number of awards: 4.
Deadline: May 15.
How to apply: Applications are available online.
Exclusive: Visit www.UltimateScholarshipBook.com and enter code QU70523 for updates on this award.

---

(706) · Ray and Gertrude Marshall Scholarship
American Culinary Federation
180 Center Place Way, St. Augustine, FL 32095
Phone: 904-824-4468
Email: scholarships@acfchefs.net
http://www.acfchefs.org
Purpose: To assist students in culinary programs.
Eligibility: Applicants must be ACF junior members enrolled in a post-secondary culinary arts program or an ACF apprenticeship program and must have completed at least one grading period. Selection is based on financial need, GPA, recommendations and work experience.
Target applicant(s): College students. Adult students.
Amount: Varies.
Number of awards: Varies.
Deadline: April 30 and October 31.
How to apply: Applications are available online or by written request.
Exclusive: Visit www.UltimateScholarshipBook.com and enter code AM70623 for updates on this award.

---

(707) · Ray, NRP and Katie, WKTE Pautz Scholarship
American Radio Relay League Foundation
225 Main Street, Newington, CT 06111-1494
Phone: 860-594-0348
Email: foundation@arrl.org
http://www.arrl.org/scholarship-program
Purpose: To provide financial assistance to amateur radio operators from the ARRL Midwest Division.
Eligibility: Applicants must be ARRL members with a General Class or higher Amateur Radio License. They must be residents of Iowa, Kansas, Missouri or Nebraska and should major in electronics, computer science or a related field at a four-year institution.
Target applicant(s): High school students. College students. Adult students.
Amount: $500-$1,000.
Number of awards: 1.
Deadline: December 31.
How to apply: Applications are available online.
Exclusive: Visit www.UltimateScholarshipBook.com and enter code AM70723 for updates on this award.

---

(708) · Reid Blackburn Scholarship
National Press Photographers Foundation
Blackburn Scholarship, 120 Hooper Street, Athens, GA 30602-3018
Phone: 360-759-8027
Email: fay.blackburn@columbian.com
http://www.nppa.org
Purpose: To support photojournalism students.
Eligibility: Applicants must have completed one year at a full-time four-year college or university, provide a portfolio, demonstrate financial need and must have courses in photojournalism and have at least half a year of undergraduate study left. Applicants can apply to as many NPPA scholarships as desired, but only one award will be granted per winner.

Target applicant(s): College students. Adult students.
Amount: $2,000.
Number of awards: Varies.
Deadline: December.
How to apply: Applications are available online.
Exclusive: Visit www.UltimateScholarshipBook.com and enter code NA70823 for updates on this award.

---

(709) · Reiff Law Firm Legal Scholarship
Reiff Law Firm
1500 John F. Kennedy Boulevard #501, Philadelphia, PA 19102
Phone: 215-246-9000
Email: scholarships@reifflawfirm.com
https://www.reifflawfirm.com/legal-scholarship/
Purpose: To support students who are pursuing a legal career.
Eligibility: Applicants must be United States citizens. Students must plan to enroll or be currently enrolled full-time at an accredited college or university in pursuit of a J.D. A minimum 3.0 GPA or higher is required. Applicants must submit a 650-word essay on their goals for employment in the legal field.
Target applicant(s): College students. Graduate school students. Adult students.
Minimum GPA: 3.0
Amount: $1,000.
Number of awards: 1.
Deadline: July 1.
How to apply: Applications are available online.
Exclusive: Visit www.UltimateScholarshipBook.com and enter code RE70923 for updates on this award.

---

(710) · Richard W. Bendicksen, N7ZL, Memorial Scholarship
American Radio Relay League Foundation
225 Main Street, Newington, CT 06111-1494
Phone: 860-594-0348
Email: foundation@arrl.org
http://www.arrl.org/scholarship-program
Purpose: To provide financial assistance to amateur radio operators.
Eligibility: Applicants must hold an active amateur radio license of any class, and they must be attending a four-year institution of higher learning.
Target applicant(s): High school students. College students. Adult students.
Amount: $1,000.
Number of awards: 1.
Deadline: December 31.
How to apply: Applications are available online.
Exclusive: Visit www.UltimateScholarshipBook.com and enter code AM71023 for updates on this award.

---

(711) · Risk Management Association Foundation Scholarship
Risk Management Association Foundation Scholarship Program
Scholarship America, One Scholarship Way, Saint Peter, MN 56082
Phone: 800-537-4180
Email: rma@scholarshipamerica.org
https://landing.rmahq.org/SRC/scholarships-94UZ-1982TH.html
Purpose: To support students who have already completed two years of college.

Eligibility: Applicants must be a U.S. or Canadian citizen who is a current undergraduate student interested in pursuing a career in the banking industry and has completed a minimum of two years of college majoring in accounting, business, finance, economics, banking or related fields of study. Students must be attending full-time and have a minimum 3.0 GPA.
Target applicant(s): College students. Adult students.
Minimum GPA: 3.0
Amount: $1,500-$8,000.
Number of awards: 75.
Scholarship may be renewable.
Deadline: March 31.
How to apply: Application available online.
Exclusive: Visit www.UltimateScholarshipBook.com and enter code RI71123 for updates on this award.

(712) · Ritchie-Jennings Memorial Scholarship

Association of Certified Fraud Examiners
Scholarships Program Coordinator, The Gregor Building, 716 West Avenue, Austin, TX 78701
Phone: 512-478-9000
Email: memberservices@acfe.com
http://www.acfe.com
Purpose: To support the college education of accounting, business, finance and criminal justice students who may become Certified Fraud Examiners in the future.
Eligibility: Applicants must be full-time undergraduate or graduate students with a declared major or minor in criminal justice, accounting, business or finance. Students must submit three letters of recommendation, with at least one from a Certified Fraud Examiner or local CFE Chapter and must write an essay on why they deserve the scholarship and how fraud awareness will help their career.
Target applicant(s): College students. Graduate school students. Adult students.
Amount: $1,000-$10,000.
Number of awards: Varies.
Deadline: February 4.
How to apply: Applications are available online.
Exclusive: Visit www.UltimateScholarshipBook.com and enter code AS71223 for updates on this award.

(713) · Roger Collins Leadership Scholarship

National Grocers Association
1005 N. Glebe Road, Suite 250, Arlington, VA 22201
Phone: 225-387-6126
https://www.nationalgrocers.org/foundation/nga-foundation-scholarships/
Purpose: To support students pursuing degrees related to the grocery field.
Eligibility: Applicants must be rising sophomores through postgraduate students, have a minimum 2.5 GPA and be enrolled in a two- or four-year degree-granting institution. Students must major in business, food management, IT or another field related to a career in the grocery industry. Experience in the grocery industry is preferred but not required.
Target applicant(s): College students. Graduate school students. Adult students.
Minimum GPA: 2.5
Amount: Varies.
Number of awards: 1.
Deadline: April 1.
How to apply: Applications are available online.

Exclusive: Visit www.UltimateScholarshipBook.com and enter code NA71323 for updates on this award.

(714) · Roller Skating Foundation Scholarship, Current College Student Category

Roller Skating Foundation
6905 Corporate Drive, Indianapolis, IN 46278
Phone: 317-347-2626
Email: foundation@rollerskating.com
https://www.rollerskating.com/pages/scholarships/47
Purpose: To aid sports, hotel and food and beverage management students.
Eligibility: Applicants must be rising undergraduate seniors who are majoring in sports, hotel or food and beverage management. They must have a cumulative GPA of 3.4 or higher on a four-point scale and must demonstrate leadership ability. Selection is based on the overall strength of the application.
Target applicant(s): College students. Adult students.
Minimum GPA: 3.4
Amount: $1,000.
Number of awards: 1.
Deadline: March 31.
How to apply: Applications are available online. An application form, transcript, personal essay, three recommendation letters and income tax information are required.
Exclusive: Visit www.UltimateScholarshipBook.com and enter code RO71423 for updates on this award.

(715) · Ron Culp Scholarship for Mentorship

Public Relations Student Society of America
33 Maiden Lane, 11th Floor, New York, NY 10038
Phone: 212-460-1474
Email: prssa@prsa.org
https://prssa.prsa.org/scholarships-and-awards/
Purpose: To aid public relations and journalism students who have mentored others wishing to pursue careers in public relations.
Eligibility: Applicants must be members of the Public Relations Student Society of America (PRSSA) who are in good standing. They must be rising undergraduate seniors who are majoring in journalism, public relations or a related subject at an accredited, four-year postsecondary institution. They must be preparing for careers in public relations and must have mentored others who intend to pursue careers in the field of public relations. Selection is based on the overall strength of the application.
Target applicant(s): College students. Adult students.
Amount: $1,000.
Number of awards: 1.
Deadline: May.
How to apply: Applications are available online. Nomination from someone who is familiar with the applicant's mentoring activities is required.
Exclusive: Visit www.UltimateScholarshipBook.com and enter code PU71523 for updates on this award.

(716) · RTNDA President's Scholarship

Radio Television Digital News Association
529 14th Street NW, Suite 1240, Washington, DC 20045
Phone: 202-659-6510
Email: karenh@rtdna.org
http://www.rtdna.org

Purpose: To honor students pursuing careers in radio, television or digital journalism.
Eligibility: Applicants must be full-time college sophomores, juniors or seniors with at least one full academic year remaining. Applicants may be enrolled in any major as long as their career intent is to pursue a career in radio, television or digital journalism. Applicants may only apply for one RTNDA scholarship.
Target applicant(s): College students. Adult students.
Amount: $2,500.
Number of awards: 1.
Deadline: January 15.
How to apply: Applications are available online.
Exclusive: Visit www.UltimateScholarshipBook.com and enter code RA71623 for updates on this award.

(717) · Ruth Segal Scholarship

Foundation for Outdoor Advertising Research and Education (FOARE)
The Family Scholarship Endowment, c/o Thomas M. Smith & Associates, 4601 Tilden Street NW, Washington, DC 20016
Phone: 202-364-7130
Email: tmfsmith@rcn.com
http://oaaa.org/AboutOAAA/FOARE/FOAREScholarshipProgram.aspx
Purpose: To support students who are pursuing a degree in government affairs, urban affairs, public affairs, political science or a related discipline.
Eligibility: Applicants must be graduating seniors, undergraduate students or graduate students. Selection is primarily based on demonstration of financial need, academic achievement, employment history, community service and extracurricular involvement.
Target applicant(s): High school students. College students. Graduate school students. Adult students.
Amount: $5,000.
Number of awards: 1.
Deadline: June 16.
How to apply: Applications are available online.
Exclusive: Visit www.UltimateScholarshipBook.com and enter code FO71723 for updates on this award.

(718) · Schwan's Food Service Scholarship

School Nutrition Association
120 Waterfront Street, Suite 300, National Harbor, MD 20745
Phone: 301-686-3100
Email: servicecenter@schoolnutrition.org
https://schoolnutrition.org/Membership/AwardsScholarships/
Purpose: To support those entering the school foodservice industry.
Eligibility: Applicants must be School Nutrition Association members for at least one year and be pursuing a field of study related to school foodservice. Applicants must also be employed in school foodservice.
Target applicant(s): High school students. College students. Graduate school students. Adult students.
Amount: Up to $2,500.
Number of awards: Varies.
Scholarship may be renewable.
Deadline: January 31.
How to apply: Applications are available online.
Exclusive: Visit www.UltimateScholarshipBook.com and enter code SC71823 for updates on this award.

(719) · Scott Alan Turner Personal Finance Scholarship

Turner Solutions LLC
2560 King Arthur Boulevard, Suite 124-107, Lewisville, TX 75056
Phone: 817-719-8040
Email: scholarship@scottalanturner.com
https://scottalanturner.com/personal-finance-scholarship/
Purpose: To encourage students who are interested in learning about personal finance and money management.
Eligibility: Applicants must be U.S. citizens or legal residents of the United States graduating high school students or current undergraduate students in good standing at their college or university. Students must be between 16 and 21 years of age, have a 3.0 GPA and either plan to enroll or already be enrolled part- or full-time at a two or four year college or university.
Target applicant(s): High school students. College students.
Minimum GPA: 3.0
Amount: $1,000.
Number of awards: 2.
Deadline: July 1.
How to apply: Applications are available online.
Exclusive: Visit www.UltimateScholarshipBook.com and enter code TU71923 for updates on this award.

(720) · Sharon Stephens Brehm Undergraduate Psychology Scholarships

American Psychological Foundation
750 First Street NE, Washington, DC 20002-4242
Phone: 202-336-5843
Email: foundation@apa.org
https://www.apa.org/apf/funding/grants
Purpose: To reward outstanding psychology undergraduate students who demonstrate financial need.
Eligibility: Applicants must be undergraduates majoring in psychology at an accredited college or university. Students must be enrolled as declared psychology majors with a minimum 3.5 GPA.
Target applicant(s): College students. Adult students.
Minimum GPA: 3.5
Amount: $5,000.
Number of awards: 6.
Deadline: July 1.
How to apply: Applications are available online.
Exclusive: Visit www.UltimateScholarshipBook.com and enter code AM72023 for updates on this award.

(721) · Shawn Carter Foundation Scholarship

Shawn Carter Foundation
Email: scsfapplicant@shawncartersf.com
http://www.shawncartersf.com
Purpose: To assist students at vocational or trade schools.
Eligibility: Applicants must be high school seniors or college students and be between the ages of 18 and 25. Applicants must also be U.S. citizens and have a minimum 2.5 GPA.
Target applicant(s): High school students. College students.
Minimum GPA: 2.5
Amount: $1,500-$2,500.
Number of awards: Varies.
Deadline: April 30.
How to apply: Applications are available online.

Exclusive: Visit www.UltimateScholarshipBook.com and enter code SH72123 for updates on this award.

(722) · Shell Associate Scholarship Program

Shell
P.O. Box 162, 2501 AN, The Hague, NE
Phone: 713-718-6379
Email: shellscholarships@hccsfoundation.org
https://www.shell.us/
Purpose: To support students who are seeking a degree in a technology field.
Eligibility: Applicants must be U.S. citizens and be taking at least six credit hours in the fall and spring. A minimum 2.5 GPA or higher is required. Students should be pursuing a degree in process/production technology, petroleum technology, compressor technology, electrical technology, industrial maintenance technology, instrumentation technology or machinist technology.
Target applicant(s): College students. Adult students.
Minimum GPA: 2.5
Amount: $2,200.
Number of awards: Varies.
Deadline: March 15.
How to apply: Applications are available online.
Exclusive: Visit www.UltimateScholarshipBook.com and enter code SH72223 for updates on this award.

(723) · Shields-Gillespie Scholarship

American Orff-Schulwerk Association (AOSA)
P.O. Box 391089, Cleveland, OH 44139-8089
Phone: 440-543-5366
Email: info@aosa.org
https://aosa.org/resources/scholarships-and-grants/
Purpose: To assist pre-K and kindergarten teachers with program funding, including instruments and training.
Eligibility: Applicants must be a member of AOSA. Applicants must be U.S. citizens or have lived in the United States for the past five years. Programs should focus on music/movement learning.
Target applicant(s): High school students. College students. Graduate school students. Adult students.
Amount: Varies.
Number of awards: Varies.
Deadline: January.
How to apply: Applications are available online for AOSA members.
Exclusive: Visit www.UltimateScholarshipBook.com and enter code AM72323 for updates on this award.

(724) · Special Education Scholarship

Disability Care Center
2875 South Orange Avenue #500, Orlando, FL 32806
Phone: 888-504-0035
Email: scholarship@disabilitycarecenter.org
http://www.disabilitycarecenter.org/giving-back/scholarships/
Purpose: To assist students who are majoring in a special education field.
Eligibility: Applicants must be majoring in special education and must be taking at least one major-required class in the upcoming fall semester. Applicants must also be U.S. citizens and have a minimum GPA of 2.5 or greater. Students will need to submit an essay describing why they are pursuing career in special education and how they plan to make a difference in the lives of the disabled. Selection is based on the essay.

Target applicant(s): High school students. College students. Adult students.
Minimum GPA: 2.5
Amount: $500.
Number of awards: 1.
Deadline: August 1.
How to apply: Applications are available online and must include proof of college acceptance or college ID, proof of registration for fall classes, a copy of most recent transcript, documentation confirming U.S. citizenship and the essay.
Exclusive: Visit www.UltimateScholarshipBook.com and enter code DI72423 for updates on this award.

(725) · Specialty Equipment Market Association (SEMA) Memorial Scholarship

Specialty Equipment Market Association
1575 S. Valley Vista Drive, Diamond Bar, CA 91765
Phone: 909-396-0289
Email: education@sema.org
http://www.sema.org/scholarships
Purpose: To support the education of students pursuing careers in the automotive aftermarket.
Eligibility: Applicants must show financial need, have a minimum 2.5 GPA and pursue a career in the automotive aftermarket or related field.
Target applicant(s): College students. Graduate school students. Adult students.
Minimum GPA: 2.5
Amount: Up to $5,000.
Number of awards: Varies.
Deadline: March 1.
How to apply: Applications are available online.
Exclusive: Visit www.UltimateScholarshipBook.com and enter code SP72523 for updates on this award.

(726) · SPS Future Teacher Scholarship

Society of Physics Students
One Physics Ellipse, College Park, MD 20740
Phone: 301-209-3007
Email: SPS-Programs@aip.org
https://www.spsnational.org/
Purpose: To provide scholarships to physics majors who are participating in a teacher education program and who intend to pursue a career in physics education.
Eligibility: Applicants must be members of SPS and intend to pursue a career in teaching physics. Students must be undergraduate physics majors at least in their junior year of study at the time of application.
Target applicant(s): College students. Adult students.
Amount: $2,000.
Number of awards: 1.
Deadline: March 15.
How to apply: Applications are available online or from chapter advisors.
Exclusive: Visit www.UltimateScholarshipBook.com and enter code SO72623 for updates on this award.

(727) · SSPI Scholarship Program

Society of Satellite Professionals International (SSPI)
Tamara Bond, 55 Broad Street, 14th Floor, New York, NY 10004
Phone: 212-809-5199

Email: rbell@sspi.org
http://www.sspi.org
Purpose: To help high school and university graduates with undergraduate and post-graduate study in satellite-related disciplines.
Eligibility: Applicants must be high school seniors, undergraduate or graduate students who are members of SSPI (membership is free) studying satellite-related technologies, policies or applications. Some scholarships have requirements such as interests, financial need, residency, gender, race or GPA. The award is based on commitment to education and careers in the satellite fields, academic and leadership achievement, potential for contribution to the satellite communications industry and a scientific, engineering, research, business or creative submission.
Target applicant(s): High school students. College students. Graduate school students. Adult students.
Amount: $1,000-$3,500.
Number of awards: Varies.
Deadline: April.
How to apply: Applications are available online.
Exclusive: Visit www.UltimateScholarshipBook.com and enter code SO72723 for updates on this award.

(728) · Stenograph's Milton H. Wright Memorial Scholarship
National Court Reporters Association
12030 Sunrise Valley Drive, Suite 400, Reston, VA 20191
Phone: 800-272-6272
Email: schools@ncra.org
https://www.ncra.org/home/get-involved/foundation/foundation-programs/NCRF-scholarships-and-grants
Purpose: To support the court reporting profession.
Eligibility: Applicants must attend an NCRA-approved court reporting program, have completed an NCRA A to Z Intro to Steno Machine Shorthand program and received an NCRA A to Z Certificate of Completion. Students must have attained an exemplary academic record with a minimum 3.5 GPA and passed one skills test writing 80-120 words per minute.
Target applicant(s): College students. Adult students.
Minimum GPA: 3.5
Amount: $5,000.
Number of awards: 2.
Deadline: March 1.
How to apply: Applications are available online.
Exclusive: Visit www.UltimateScholarshipBook.com and enter code NA72823 for updates on this award.

(729) · Stephen D. Pisinski Memorial Scholarship
Public Relations Student Society of America
33 Maiden Lane, 11th Floor, New York, NY 10038
Phone: 212-460-1474
Email: prssa@prsa.org
https://prssa.prsa.org/scholarships-and-awards/
Purpose: To aid journalism, public relations and communications students.
Eligibility: Applicants must be members of the Public Relations Student Society of America (PRSSA). They must be rising undergraduate juniors or seniors who are majoring in journalism, public relations or communications. They must have a cumulative GPA of 3.3 or higher on a four-point scale. Selection is based on the overall strength of the application.
Target applicant(s): College students. Adult students.

Minimum GPA: 3.3
Amount: $2,000.
Number of awards: 1.
Deadline: May 31.
How to apply: Applications are available online. An application form, official transcript, resume, two writing samples, an essay and two recommendation letters are required.
Exclusive: Visit www.UltimateScholarshipBook.com and enter code PU72923 for updates on this award.

(730) · Steven J. Finkel Service Excellence Scholarship
House of Blues Music Forward Foundation
7060 Hollywood Boulevard, 2nd Floor, Hollywood, CA 90028
Phone: 323-769-4645
Email: info@hobmusicforward.org
https://hobmusicforward.org/program/scholarships/
Purpose: To encourage students who are passionate about the live music customer experience for fans, artists and employees.
Eligibility: Applicants must be full-time juniors or seniors enrolled at an accredited college or university pursuing a career in live entertainment such as: music business management, customer service, hospitality or other related fields. A minimum 3.0 GPA or higher is required. Students must submit a 500-word essay explaining their career goals within the entertainment industry.
Target applicant(s): College students. Adult students.
Minimum GPA: 3.0
Amount: $10,000.
Number of awards: 1.
Deadline: March 31.
How to apply: Applications are available online.
Exclusive: Visit www.UltimateScholarshipBook.com and enter code HO73023 for updates on this award.

(731) · Stuart Cameron and Margaret McLeod Memorial Scholarship
Institute of Management Accountants (IMA)
10 Paragon Drive, Montvale, NJ 07645-1760
Phone: 800-638-4427
Email: students@imanet.org
http://www.imanet.org
Purpose: To help management accounting students.
Eligibility: Applicants must be full- and part-time undergraduate and graduate students, be IMA student members and declare which four- or five-year management accounting, financial management or information technology related program they plan to pursue as a career or list a related field. Candidates should submit applications, resumes, transcripts, two recommendations and statements. Advanced degree students must pass one part of the CMA/CFM certification.
Target applicant(s): College students. Graduate school students. Adult students.
Minimum GPA: 3.0
Amount: $5,000.
Number of awards: 1.
Deadline: March 10.
How to apply: Applications are available online.
Exclusive: Visit www.UltimateScholarshipBook.com and enter code IN73123 for updates on this award.

(732) · Student Achievement Grants

NEA Foundation
1201 16th Street NW, Washington, DC 20036
Phone: 202-822-7840
Email: NEAFoundation@nea.org
http://www.neafoundation.org/pages/grants-to-educators/
Purpose: To promote the academic achievement of students in U.S. public schools and public higher education institutions by providing funds for teachers.
Eligibility: Applicants must be current public school teachers in PreK-12, public school education support professionals or faculty or staff at public higher education institutions. Preference is given to those who work with economically disadvantaged students and NEA members. The grants may be used for materials, supplies, equipment, transportation, software or scholars-in-residence and in some cases professional development. The work should "engage students in critical thinking and problem solving that deepens their knowledge of standards-based subject matter."
Target applicant(s): Graduate school students. Adult students.
Amount: $2,000-$5,000.
Number of awards: Varies.
Deadline: February 1, June 1, October 15.
How to apply: Applications are available online and may be submitted at any time. Applications are reviewed three times each year on February 1, June 1 and October 15.
Exclusive: Visit www.UltimateScholarshipBook.com and enter code NE73223 for updates on this award.

(733) · Student with a Disability Scholarship

American Speech-Language-Hearing Foundation
2200 Research Boulevard, Rockville, MD 20850
Phone: 301-296-8700
Email: foundation@asha.org
https://www.ashfoundation.org/
Purpose: To support a graduate student with a disability studying communication sciences and disorders.
Eligibility: Master's degree candidates must be in programs accredited by the Council on Academic Accreditation for Audiology and Speech Pathology, but doctoral programs do not have to be accredited. The applicants should submit a transcript, essay, reference form and statement of good standing; be recommended by a faculty or workplace committee and have not received scholarships from the ASHA Foundation. Students must attend their programs full-time.
Target applicant(s): Graduate school students. Adult students.
Amount: $5,000.
Number of awards: 1.
Deadline: May.
How to apply: Applications are available online.
Exclusive: Visit www.UltimateScholarshipBook.com and enter code AM73323 for updates on this award.

(734) · Sutliff & Stout Law School Scholarship

Sutliff & Stout Law School Scholarship
550 Post Oak Boulevard, Suite 530, Houston, TX 77027
Phone: 281-853-8446
Email: community@sutliffstout.com
https://www.sutliffstout.com/about-us/community/law-school-scholarship/
Purpose: To support students pursuing a law degree.

Eligibility: Applicants must be accepted into or currently enrolled in an ABA-accredited law school in the U.S. Students must write an essay explaining why they want to study law.
Target applicant(s): College students. Graduate school students. Adult students.
Amount: $1,500.
Number of awards: 1.
Deadline: July 30.
How to apply: Applications are available online.
Exclusive: Visit www.UltimateScholarshipBook.com and enter code SU73423 for updates on this award.

(735) · TACTYC Accounting Scholarship

Teachers of Accounting at Two-Year Colleges
Lori Hatchell - TACTYC Treasurer, P.O. Box 69, Greeley, CO 80632-0069
Email: scholarship@tactyc.org
http://www.tactyc.org
Purpose: To aid accounting students who either are pursuing a two-year undergraduate degree or who are moving to a four-year institution after having completed a two-year accounting degree.
Eligibility: Applicants must be undergraduate accounting students. They must be pursuing a two-year degree or must be pursuing a bachelor's degree in accounting after having completed a two-year accounting degree program. Selection is based on recommendations, GPA and stated career goals.
Target applicant(s): College students. Adult students.
Amount: $1,000.
Number of awards: Varies.
Deadline: March 1.
How to apply: Applications are available online. An application form and supporting materials are required.
Exclusive: Visit www.UltimateScholarshipBook.com and enter code TE73523 for updates on this award.

(736) · Teacher Education Scholarship Fund

American Montessori Society
Attn.: Abbie Kelly, Director of Teacher Education, Affiliation and Services, 116 East 16th Street, New York, NY 10003
Phone: 212-358-1250
Email: abbie@amshq.org
http://www.amshq.org
Purpose: To support future Montessori teachers.
Eligibility: Applicants must be accepted, are in the process of being accepted or are already enrolled in an AMS-affiliated teacher education program. Financial need, the applicant's personal statement and letters of recommendation are considered.
Target applicant(s): High school students. College students. Adult students.
Amount: Varies.
Number of awards: Varies.
Scholarship may be renewable.
Deadline: April 19.
How to apply: Applications are available online.
Exclusive: Visit www.UltimateScholarshipBook.com and enter code AM73623 for updates on this award.

(737) · Teacher of the Year Award

Veterans of Foreign Wars Teacher of the Year Award
406 W. 34th Street, Kansas City, MO 64111

Phone: 816-968-1117
Email: tbeauchamp@vfw.org
http://www.vfw.org
Purpose: To salute the nation's top elementary, junior high and high school teachers who educate their students about citizenship and American history and traditions.
Eligibility: Applicants must be current certified/licensed teachers in grades K-12. Previous winners from the state or national levels are not eligible. Fellow teachers, supervisors, family members or other interested individuals may send in nominations; self-nominations will be accepted.
Target applicant(s): Graduate school students. Adult students.
Amount: $3,000.
Number of awards: 1.
Deadline: October 31.
How to apply: Applications are available online but initial nominations must be sent to the local VFW office. Visit the website for more information.
Exclusive: Visit www.UltimateScholarshipBook.com and enter code VE73723 for updates on this award.

(738) · TechChecks Business Leadership Scholarship

TechChecks
272 Lanes Mill Road, Howell, NJ 07731
Phone: 866-527 3758
Email: sales@techchecks.net
https://www.techchecks.net/techchecks-business-leadership-scholarship
Purpose: To reward students who have strong academic credentials and are pursuing a degree that emphasizes business or marketing.
Eligibility: Applicants must be high school seniors or current college students pursuing a degree in business administration or another business-related field. A minimum 3.5 GPA is required. Students must be U.S. citizens and preference will be given to those who are female, have a disability or belong to one of the following minority groups: African American, Hispanic/Latino, Asian American/Pacific Islander or Native American/American Indian (must provide proof of membership to a tribe). Students must submit an essay on the topic provided. Essay selection will be based on the quality of research, originality and presentation.
Target applicant(s): High school students. College students. Graduate school students. Adult students.
Minimum GPA: 3.5
Amount: $500-$1,000.
Number of awards: 2.
Deadline: June 15.
How to apply: Applications are available online and must include an official transcript as well as the required essay.
Exclusive: Visit www.UltimateScholarshipBook.com and enter code TE73823 for updates on this award.

(739) · Timothy S.Y. Lam Foundation Education Scholarships

Timothy S.Y. Lam Foundation
P.O. Box 98141, Las Vegas, NV 89193-8141
Phone: 702-900-7584
Email: info@timothysylam.org
https://www.timothysylam.org/education-scholarships
Purpose: To support students pursuing a career in the hospitality industry.
Eligibility: Applicants must be at least 18 years of age and pursuing a degree or certification in the hospitality industry. An essay is required

with the application. There are two deadlines each year: May 15 and November 15.
Target applicant(s): College students. Adult students.
Amount: Up to $2,000.
Number of awards: 7.
Deadline: May 15 and November 15.
How to apply: Applications are available online, and must include a resume, an essay, one letter of reference, a photo and an official transcript.
Exclusive: Visit www.UltimateScholarshipBook.com and enter code TI73923 for updates on this award.

(740) · TLMI Four Year College Degree Scholarship Program

Tag and Label Manufacturers Institute Inc.
TLMI Scholarship Committee, 1 Blackburn Center, Gloucester, MA 01930
Phone: 978-282-1400
Email: office@tlmi.com
https://tlmi.connectedcommunity.org/events-awards/tlmi-scholarship-programs
Purpose: To assist upper-level students planning to pursue a career in tag and label manufacturing.
Eligibility: Applicants must demonstrate an interest in the tag and label manufacturing industry while taking appropriate courses at an accredited four-year college. They must be full-time sophomores or juniors with a GPA of at least 3.0. Applicants must submit a personal statement and three letters of recommendation attesting to their character.
Target applicant(s): College students. Adult students.
Minimum GPA: 3.0
Amount: $5,000.
Number of awards: Up to 6.
Deadline: April 1.
How to apply: Applications are available online and by phone.
Exclusive: Visit www.UltimateScholarshipBook.com and enter code TA74023 for updates on this award.

(741) · TLMI Two-Year College or Technical Degree Program Scholarship

Tag and Label Manufacturers Institute Inc.
TLMI Scholarship Committee, 1 Blackburn Center, Gloucester, MA 01930
Phone: 978-282-1400
Email: office@tlmi.com
https://tlmi.connectedcommunity.org/events-awards/tlmi-scholarship-programs
Purpose: To aid students who are enrolled in a flexographic printing program of study.
Eligibility: Applicants must be enrolled full-time in a flexographic printing program at a two-year college or degree-granting technical school. They must have a GPA of 3.0 or higher and have a demonstrated interest in pursuing a career in the tag and label industry. Selection is based on the overall strength of the application.
Target applicant(s): College students. Adult students.
Minimum GPA: 3.0
Amount: $1,000.
Number of awards: Up to 4.
Deadline: April 1.
How to apply: Applications are available online. An application form, official transcript and personal statement are required.

Exclusive: Visit www.UltimateScholarshipBook.com and enter code TA74123 for updates on this award.

(742) · Tom and Judith Comstock Scholarship

American Radio Relay League Foundation
225 Main Street, Newington, CT 06111-1494
Phone: 860-594-0348
Email: foundation@arrl.org
http://www.arrl.org/scholarship-program
Purpose: To assist ham radio operators in furthering their educations.
Eligibility: Applicants must have any class of ham radio license, be residents of Texas or Oklahoma and be high school seniors accepted at a two- or four-year college or university.
Target applicant(s): High school students.
Amount: $2,000.
Number of awards: 1.
Deadline: December 31.
How to apply: Applications are available online but may not be completed electronically. All completed applications must be mailed.
Exclusive: Visit www.UltimateScholarshipBook.com and enter code AM74223 for updates on this award.

(743) · Tom Steel Post-Graduate Fellowship

Pride Law Fund
P.O. Box 2602, San Francisco, CA 94126-2602
Email: Steel@pridelawfund.org
http://www.pridelawfund.org
Purpose: To support law students with a project that serves the lesbian, gay, bisexual and transgendered community.
Eligibility: Applicants must be students in their last year of law school or lawyers within three years of graduating from law school. The award is based on the quality and scope of the project, proposal, public service activities and relation to the LGBT community. Applicants should submit applications, resumes, project descriptions, two reference letters, budget, timetable and law school transcript.
Target applicant(s): Graduate school students. Adult students.
Amount: $30,000.
Number of awards: 1.
Deadline: February.
How to apply: Applications are available online.
Exclusive: Visit www.UltimateScholarshipBook.com and enter code PR74323 for updates on this award.

(744) · TOPSS Competition for High School Psychology Students

American Psychological Association
750 First Street NE, Washington, DC 20002
Phone: 800-374-2721
https://www.apa.org/apf/funding
Purpose: To assist students who are studying psychology.
Eligibility: Applicants must be high school students who have been or are presently enrolled in a psychology course and must write an essay answering a question from the APA. A Teachers of Psychology in Secondary Schools (TOPSS) member must sponsor all candidates, and each school may submit no more than five papers.
Target applicant(s): High school students.
Amount: $250.
Number of awards: 4.
Deadline: March 8.

How to apply: Submission information is available online.
Exclusive: Visit www.UltimateScholarshipBook.com and enter code AM74423 for updates on this award.

(745) · Tri State Surveying and Photogrammetry Kris M. Kunze Memorial Scholarship

National Society of Professional Surveyors (NSPS/AAGS)
Attn: Scholarships, 5119 Pegasus Court, Suite Q, Frederick, MD 21704
Phone: 240-439-4615x105
Email: trisha.milburn@nsps.us.com
https://www.nsps.us.com/page/Scholarships
Purpose: To aid current and future land surveying professionals who are taking courses in business.
Eligibility: Applicants must be National Society of Professional Surveyors (NSPS) members. They must be licensed professional land surveyors, certified photogrammetrists, land surveying interns or current full-time land surveying students who are taking courses in business administration or management. Selection is based on academic merit, personal statement, recommendations, professional involvement and financial need. Scholarship is offered in odd years only.
Target applicant(s): College students. Adult students.
Amount: $2,000.
Number of awards: 1.
Deadline: January 22.
How to apply: Applications are available online. An application form, official transcript, personal statement, three letters of recommendation and proof of NSPS membership are required.
Exclusive: Visit www.UltimateScholarshipBook.com and enter code NA74523 for updates on this award.

(746) · United Commercial Travelers of America (UCT) Scholarship Program

Order of United Commercial Travelers of America
1801 Watermark Drive, Suite 100, P.O. Box 159019, Columbus, OH 43215-8619
Phone: 614-487-9680
http://www.uct.org/uct-in-action/scholarship-programs/
Purpose: To support students or teachers who work primarily with students who have intellectual disabilities.
Eligibility: Applicants must be a current teacher or current undergraduate student who is pursuing course work to enhance their work with individuals who have intellectual disabilities. Students must work in North America.
Target applicant(s): College students. Adult students.
Amount: Up to $2,500.
Number of awards: 1.
Scholarship may be renewable.
Deadline: November 15.
How to apply: Applications are available online.
Exclusive: Visit www.UltimateScholarshipBook.com and enter code OR74623 for updates on this award.

(747) · United States Senate Youth Program

William Randolph Hearst Foundation
90 New Montgomery Street, Suite 1212, San Francisco, CA 94105
Phone: 800-841-7048 x 4540
Email: ussyp@hearstfdn.org
http://ussenateyouth.org

Purpose: To expose students to their government in action.
Eligibility: Applicants must be high school juniors or seniors in an elected position at school or in civic or educational offices. USSYP brings the highest level officials from each branch of government together with a group of 104 high school student delegates for an intensive week-long educational program held in Washington, DC.
Target applicant(s): High school students.
Amount: $10,000.
Number of awards: 104.
Deadline: Varies by state.
How to apply: To apply, contact your high school principal, counselor or state selection contact. State selection contact information is located on the home page of the website.
Exclusive: Visit www.UltimateScholarshipBook.com and enter code WI74723 for updates on this award.

(748) · University of California Public Policy and International Affairs Law Fellowship

University of California at Berkeley
UCPPIA Summer Institute, Goldman School of Public Policy, 2607 Hearst Avenue, Berkeley, CA 94720-7320
Phone: 510-642-4670
Email: noah.romero@berkeley.edu
https://gspp.berkeley.edu/programs/undergraduate-programs/ppia-junior-summer-institute
Purpose: To encourage prospective graduate students to pursue a joint degree in law and public policy.
Eligibility: Applicants must be U.S. citizens or legal permanent residents. They must be rising undergraduate seniors who have at least one more semester (or two more quarters) of coursework remaining before graduation. They must be interested in law and public service careers, and must have a demonstrated interest in policy issues that affect underserved populations. They must have overcome obstacles in their pursuit of higher education. Selection is based on the overall strength of the application.
Target applicant(s): College students. Adult students.
Amount: At least $5,000.
Number of awards: 10.
Deadline: November.
How to apply: Applications are available online. An application form and personal statement are required.
Exclusive: Visit www.UltimateScholarshipBook.com and enter code UN74823 for updates on this award.

(749) · University of California Public Policy and International Affairs Summer Institute

University of California at Berkeley
UCPPIA Summer Institute, Goldman School of Public Policy, 2607 Hearst Avenue, Berkeley, CA 94720-7320
Phone: 510-642-4670
Email: noah.romero@berkeley.edu
https://gspp.berkeley.edu/programs/undergraduate-programs/ppia-junior-summer-institute
Purpose: To aid students who are interested in pursuing graduate studies in public policy.
Eligibility: Applicants must be U.S. citizens or legal permanent residents who are rising undergraduate seniors who have at least one more semester (or two more quarters) of coursework remaining before graduation. They must be interested in public service careers and must have a demonstrated interest in policy issues that affect underserved populations. They must

have overcome obstacles in their pursuit of higher education. Selection is based on the overall strength of the application.
Target applicant(s): College students. Adult students.
Amount: Varies.
Number of awards: 30.
Deadline: Varies.
How to apply: Applications are available online. An application form and personal statement are required.
Exclusive: Visit www.UltimateScholarshipBook.com and enter code UN74923 for updates on this award.

(750) · University of the Aftermarket Foundation Scholarship

Global Automotive Aftermarket Symposium Inc.
c/o Auto Care Association, 7101 Wisconsin Avenue, Suite 1300, Bethesda, MD 20814
Phone: 312-768-7379
Email: uafscholarships@autocare.org
https://automotivescholarships.com/scholarships
Purpose: To support students who intend to have a career in the automotive industry.
Eligibility: Applicants must have graduated from high school or acquired their GED. Students must be enrolled or planning to enroll as a full-time student in a two- or four- year college or an ASE/NATEF certified post-secondary automotive, collision repair or heavy duty program.
Target applicant(s): High school students. College students. Adult students.
Amount: Varies.
Number of awards: Varies.
Deadline: March 31.
How to apply: Applications are available online.
Exclusive: Visit www.UltimateScholarshipBook.com and enter code GL75023 for updates on this award.

(751) · USGIF Scholarship Program

United States Geospatial Intelligence Foundation (USGIF)
2325 Dulles Corner Boulevard, Suite 450, Herndon, VA 20171
Phone: 888-698-7443
Email: scholarships@usgif.org
http://usgif.org/
Purpose: To assist those who are studying geospatial sciences.
Eligibility: Applicants must be high school seniors or college or graduate students. Selection is based on academic and professional achievement in a field related to geospatial intelligence tradecraft.
Target applicant(s): High school students. College students. Graduate school students. Adult students.
Amount: Varies.
Number of awards: Varies.
Deadline: May 16.
Exclusive: Visit www.UltimateScholarshipBook.com and enter code UN75123 for updates on this award.

(752) · Vern and Elaine Clark Outdoor Advertising Industry

Foundation for Outdoor Advertising Research and Education (FOARE)
The Family Scholarship Endowment, c/o Thomas M. Smith & Associates, 4601 Tilden Street NW, Washington, DC 20016

Phone: 202-364-7130
Email: tmfsmith@rcn.com
http://oaaa.org/AboutOAAA/FOARE/FOAREScholarshipProgram.aspx
Purpose: To support undergraduate and graduate students who are pursuing a career in the outdoor advertising industry.
Eligibility: Selection is primarily based on academic achievement, career goals and community involvement. Applicants must submit a letter of recommendation from someone in the outdoor advertising industry and a letter of recommendation addressing the applicant's community service.
Target applicant(s): High school students. College students. Graduate school students. Adult students.
Amount: $4,000.
Number of awards: 1.
Deadline: June 16.
How to apply: Applications are available online.
Exclusive: Visit www.UltimateScholarshipBook.com and enter code FO75223 for updates on this award.

(753) · Vincent Chin Scholarship

Asian American Journalists Association
1301 K Street, NW, 300W, 3rd Floor, Washington, DC 20005
https://www.aaja.org/news-and-resources/scholarships-internships/
Purpose: To support college students interested in pursuing careers in journalism.
Eligibility: Applicants must be undergraduate students enrolled full-time and must be currently taking or planning to take journalism courses and/or pursuing a career in journalism. Applicants are not required to be Asian Americans but must support the mission of the AAJA and be committed to work within the community. Selection is based on the applicant's promise to support the field of journalism and issues faced by Pacific Islanders and Asian Americans. In addition, selection is based on financial need, academic achievement and demonstrated ability in journalism as well as the applicant's resume, two letters of recommendation, essay and work samples.
Target applicant(s): College students. Adult students.
Amount: $1,500.
Number of awards: 1.
Deadline: April 21.
How to apply: Applications are available online.
Exclusive: Visit www.UltimateScholarshipBook.com and enter code AS75323 for updates on this award.

(754) · Virtual Business Scholarship

Knowledge Matters
1 Roundhouse Plaza, Suite 304, Northampton, MA 01060
Phone: 877-965-3276
http://www.knowledgematters.com
Purpose: To support high school juniors and seniors in pursuing a degree in business, marketing or personal finance.
Eligibility: Applicants must be nominated by a high school teacher. Students must demonstrate excellence in business, marketing or personal finance courses. Selection is based on the overall strength of the application.
Target applicant(s): High school students.
Amount: $2,000.
Number of awards: 1.
Deadline: April 27.
How to apply: Applications are available online.

Exclusive: Visit www.UltimateScholarshipBook.com and enter code KN75423 for updates on this award.

(755) · Wesley-Logan Prize

American Historical Association
400 A Street SE, Washington, DC 20003
Phone: 202-544-2422
Email: info@historians.org
http://www.historians.org
Purpose: To award a prize to a scholarly/literary book focusing on the history of dispersion, relocation, settlement or adjustment of people from Africa or on their return to that continent.
Eligibility: Books must have been published between May 1 of the previous year and April 30 of the entry year. Entries are mailed directly to committee members.
Target applicant(s): Junior high students or younger. High school students. College students. Graduate school students. Adult students.
Amount: Varies.
Number of awards: Varies.
Deadline: May 15.
How to apply: Application information is available on approximately March 30.
Exclusive: Visit www.UltimateScholarshipBook.com and enter code AM75523 for updates on this award.

(756) · WIIT Charitable Trust Scholarship

Women in International Trade Charitable Trust
c/o Affinity Strategies, 100 M Street S.E., Suite 600, Washington, DC 20003
Phone: 202-293-2948
Email: info@wiittrust.org
http://www.wiittrust.org
Purpose: To support female undergraduate and graduate students who are pursuing a degree in international trade.
Eligibility: Applicants must submit an essay on a relevant international trade topic (see suggestions below) and can either be a bespoke essay submission or an appropriately formatted existing academic paper from current class works. Students must show a demonstrated interest in international development, international relations, international trade, international economics or international business. Selection is based on the overall strength of the submission. Students must be enrolled at an accredited U.S. educational institution.
Target applicant(s): College students. Graduate school students. Adult students.
Amount: Up to $1,500.
Number of awards: 2.
Deadline: April 1 and November 1.
How to apply: Applications are available online.
Exclusive: Visit www.UltimateScholarshipBook.com and enter code WO75623 for updates on this award.

(757) · William (Bill) Ezzell Scholarship

American Institute of Certified Public Accountants
220 Leigh Farm Road, Durham, NC 27707-8110
Phone: 919-402-4500
Email: scholarships@aicpa.org
https://www.aicpa.org
Purpose: To support accounting Ph.D. candidates who demonstrate significant potential to become mentors for the next generation of CPAs.

Eligibility: Applicants must have a minimum of three years of professional accounting experience and earned an undergraduate or a master's degree in accounting. Students must be CPAs and U.S. citizens or permanent residents. Applicants must have either applied to a full-time accounting Ph.D. program and are awaiting word on acceptance, received acceptance into a full-time accounting Ph.D. program or matriculated into a full-time accounting doctoral program and pursuing appropriate coursework.
Target applicant(s): Graduate school students. Adult students.
Amount: $10,000.
Number of awards: 5.
Deadline: March 1.
How to apply: Applications are available online.
Exclusive: Visit www.UltimateScholarshipBook.com and enter code AM75723 for updates on this award.

(758) · William B. Ruggles Right to Work Scholarship

National Institute for Labor Relations Research (NILRR)
William B. Ruggles Scholarship Selection Committee, 5211 Port Royal Road, Suite 510, Springfield, VA 22151
Phone: 703-321-9606
Email: research@nilrr.org
http://www.nilrr.org/resources/online-scholarship-application-401/
Purpose: To support students who are dedicated to high journalistic standards.
Eligibility: Applicants must be undergraduate or graduate students majoring in journalism and demonstrate an understanding of the principles of voluntary unionism and the economic and social problems of compulsory unionism.
Target applicant(s): High school students. College students. Graduate school students. Adult students.
Amount: $2,000.
Number of awards: 1.
Deadline: January 31.
How to apply: Applications are available online.
Exclusive: Visit www.UltimateScholarshipBook.com and enter code NA75823 for updates on this award.

(759) · Women Grocers of America (WGA) Mary Macey Scholarship(s)

National Grocers Association
1005 N. Glebe Road, Suite 250, Arlington, VA 22201
Phone: 225-387-6126
https://www.nationalgrocers.org/foundation/nga-foundation-scholarships/
Purpose: To support students pursuing a degree related to the grocery field.
Eligibility: Applicants must be rising sophomores through postgraduate students, have a minimum 2.5 GPA and be enrolled in a two- or four-year degree-granting institution. Students must major in business, food management, IT or another field related to a career in the grocery industry. Experience in the grocery industry is preferred but not required.
Target applicant(s): College students. Graduate school students. Adult students.
Minimum GPA: 2.5
Amount: Varies.
Number of awards: Varies.
Deadline: April 1.
How to apply: Applications are available online.
Exclusive: Visit www.UltimateScholarshipBook.com and enter code NA75923 for updates on this award.

(760) · YASME Foundation Scholarship

American Radio Relay League Foundation
225 Main Street, Newington, CT 06111-1494
Phone: 860-594-0348
Email: foundation@arrl.org
http://www.arrl.org/scholarship-program
Purpose: To support science and engineering students who are involved in amateur radio.
Eligibility: Applicants must have an active amateur radio license. Students must be enrolled in a four-year college or university. Preference will be given to students in the top 10 percent of their class and those who have participated in community service and local amateur radio clubs.
Target applicant(s): High school students. College students. Adult students.
Amount: $5,000.
Number of awards: Varies.
Scholarship may be renewable.
Deadline: December 31.
How to apply: Applications are available online.
Exclusive: Visit www.UltimateScholarshipBook.com and enter code AM76023 for updates on this award.

(761) · Youth Scholarship

Society of Broadcast Engineers
9102 N. Meridian Street, Suite 150, Indianapolis, IN 46260
Phone: 317-846-9000
Email: mclappe@sbe.org
http://www.sbe.org
Purpose: To help students who plan to pursue a career in the technical aspects of broadcasting.
Eligibility: Applicants must be graduating high school seniors who plan to enroll in a technical school, college or university and should pursue studies leading to a career in broadcasting engineering or a related field. Preference is given to members of SBE, but any student may apply. Applicants should submit applications, transcripts, biographies and statements. Recipients must write a paper about broadcast engineering.
Target applicant(s): High school students.
Amount: $2,500.
Number of awards: Up to 3.
Deadline: July 1.
How to apply: Applications are available online.
Exclusive: Visit www.UltimateScholarshipBook.com and enter code SO76123 for updates on this award.

(762) · Zippia's Teacher Dream Job Scholarship

Zippia Inc.
P.O. Box 14340, San Francisco, CA 94114-0340
Phone: 254-294-7742
Email: scholarship@zippia.com
https://www.zippia.com/teacher-jobs/scholarship/
Purpose: To support students whose dream job is teaching.
Eligibility: Applicants must be college, university, associate's program, junior college, vocational school or high school students who are at least 18 years of age. Students must submit an essay on a provided prompt.
Target applicant(s): High school students. College students. Adult students.
Amount: $1,000.
Number of awards: 1.
Deadline: December 31.
How to apply: Applications are available online.

Exclusive: Visit www.UltimateScholarshipBook.com and enter code ZI76223 for updates on this award.

(763) · A.O. Putnam Memorial Scholarship

Institute of Industrial and Systems Engineers
3577 Parkway Lane, Suite 200, Norcross, GA 30092
Phone: 800-494-0460
Email: bcameron@iienet.org
http://www.iise.org/

Purpose: To help undergraduate Institute members who plan to pursue careers in management consulting.

Eligibility: Applicants must be undergraduate students enrolled in a college in the United States, Canada or Mexico with an accredited industrial engineering program, major in industrial engineering and be active members. Preference is given to students who plan to work in management consulting. Students may not apply directly for this scholarship and must be nominated. The award is based on academic ability, character, leadership, potential service to the industrial engineering profession and financial need. Minimum 3.4 GPA required.

Target applicant(s): High school students. College students. Adult students.

Minimum GPA: 3.4

Amount: $1,000.

Number of awards: 2.

Deadline: November 15.

How to apply: Nomination forms are available online.

Exclusive: Visit www.UltimateScholarshipBook.com and enter code IN76323 for updates on this award.

(764) · AAAE Foundation Scholarship

American Association of Airport Executives
601 Madison Street, Ste. 400, Alexandria, VA 22314
Phone: 703-824-0500
Email: member.services@aaae.org
https://www.aaae.org

Purpose: To support students of aviation.

Eligibility: Applicants must be enrolled in an aviation program with at least junior standing and at least a 3.0 GPA. Eligibility is unrelated to membership in AAAE. Winners are selected based on academic records, financial need, participation in school and community activities, work experience and a personal statement. Applicants must recommended by their school.

Target applicant(s): College students. Graduate school students. Adult students.

Minimum GPA: 3.0

Amount: $500-$1,500.

Number of awards: 8.

Deadline: February.

How to apply: To obtain an application, contact the scholarship or financial aid office at the college you attend. Scholarship information is usually mailed to universities and colleges in early January.

Exclusive: Visit www.UltimateScholarshipBook.com and enter code AM76423 for updates on this award.

(765) · AACT National Candy Technologists John Kitt Memorial Scholarship Program

Warrell Corp
Attn: Kevin Silva, 1250 Slate Hill Road, Camp Hill, PA 17011
Phone: 201-652-2655
Email: aactinfo@gomc.com
http://www.aactcandy.org

Purpose: To aid students with a demonstrated interested in confectionery technology.

Eligibility: Applicants must be rising college sophomores, juniors or seniors at an accredited four-year college or university in North America. They must major in food science, chemical science, biological science or a related area. A GPA of 3.0 or higher is required.

Target applicant(s): College students. Adult students.

Minimum GPA: 3.0

Amount: $5,000.

Number of awards: 1.

Deadline: April 30.

How to apply: Applications are available online. An application form, list of academic, work and other activities, list of honors and awards, statement of goals and transcript are required.

Exclusive: Visit www.UltimateScholarshipBook.com and enter code WA76523 for updates on this award.

(766) · AAGS - NSPS Scholarships

National Society of Professional Surveyors (NSPS/AAGS)
Attn: Scholarships, 5119 Pegasus Court, Suite Q, Frederick, MD 21704
Phone: 240-439-4615x105
Email: trisha.milburn@nsps.us.com
https://www.nsps.us.com/page/Scholarships

Purpose: To reward excellent surveying and mapping students.

Eligibility: There are several different types of awards. The first is for students enrolled in two-year degree programs in surveying technology. The second is for students enrolled in or accepted to a graduate program in geodetic surveying or geodesy. The third is for students enrolled in four-year degree programs in surveying (or in related areas such as geomatics or surveying engineering). The last type is for students enrolled in a two-year or four-year surveying (or closely related) degree program, either full or part-time. All awards are based on academic record, statement, recommendation letters and professional activities.

Target applicant(s): High school students. College students. Graduate school students. Adult students.

Amount: $2,000-$3,000.

Number of awards: Varies.

Deadline: January 21.

How to apply: Applications are available online.

Exclusive: Visit www.UltimateScholarshipBook.com and enter code NA76623 for updates on this award.

(767) · AAGS Joseph F. Dracup Scholarship Award

National Society of Professional Surveyors (NSPS/AAGS)
Attn: Scholarships, 5119 Pegasus Court, Suite Q, Frederick, MD 21704
Phone: 240-439-4615x105
Email: trisha.milburn@nsps.us.com
https://www.nsps.us.com/page/Scholarships

Purpose: To aid ACSM members who are enrolled in a four-year degree program in surveying or a closely related subject.

Eligibility: Applicants must be members of AAGS (American Association for Geodetic Surveying). Preference will be given to students whose coursework is significantly focused on geodetic surveying. Students who will be graduating before December of the award disbursement year are ineligible. Selection is based on academic merit, personal statement, recommendations, professional involvement and financial need.

Target applicant(s): High school students. College students. Adult students.

Amount: $2,000.

Number of awards: 1.

Scholarship may be renewable.

Deadline: January 22.

How to apply: Applications are available online. An application form, personal statement, official transcript, three recommendation letters and proof of ACSM membership are required.

Exclusive: Visit www.UltimateScholarshipBook.com and enter code NA76723 for updates on this award.

(768) · AAMA Student Essay Competition

American Association of Medical Assistants
20 North Wacker Drive, Suite 1575, Chicago, IL 60606
Phone: 800-228-2262
Email: info@aama-ntl.org
http://www.aama-ntl.org

Purpose: To reward aspiring medical assistants through an essay competition.

Eligibility: Applicants must be enrolled in and have completed at least one quarter or semester at a college-level medical assisting program accredited by the Commission on Accreditation of Allied Health Education Programs (CAAHEP). Completed entry form and essay (between 400 and 500 words) based on the year's prompt must be submitted by the deadline.

Target applicant(s): High school students. College students. Graduate school students. Adult students.

Amount: $1,000.

Number of awards: 1.

Deadline: July 1.

How to apply: Applications are available online.

Exclusive: Visit www.UltimateScholarshipBook.com and enter code AM76823 for updates on this award.

(769) · Abel Wolman Fellowship

American Water Works Association
6666 W. Quincy Avenue, Denver, CO 80235-3098
Phone: 800-926-7337
Email: scholarships@awwa.org
http://www.awwa.org

Purpose: To support doctoral students pursuing advanced training and research in the field of water supply and treatment.

Eligibility: Applicants must obtain a Ph.D. within two years of the award, must be citizens of the U.S., Canada or Mexico and should submit applications, transcripts, GRE scores, three recommendation letters, course of study and description of the dissertation research study and how it pertains to water supply and treatment. The award is based on academics, the connection between the research and water supply and treatment and the applicant's research skills.

Target applicant(s): Graduate school students. Adult students.

Amount: Varies.

Number of awards: Varies.

Scholarship may be renewable.

Deadline: December 20.

How to apply: Applications are available online.

Exclusive: Visit www.UltimateScholarshipBook.com and enter code AM76923 for updates on this award.

(770) · Academic Achievement Award

American Water Works Association
6666 W. Quincy Avenue, Denver, CO 80235-3098
Phone: 800-926-7337

Email: scholarships@awwa.org

http://www.awwa.org

Purpose: To recognize contributions to the field of public water supply.
Eligibility: Master's theses and doctoral dissertations that are relevant to the water supply industry are eligible. Unbound manuscripts must be the work of a single author and be submitted during the competition year in which they were submitted for the degree. Students may major in any area as long as the research is directly related to the drinking water supply industry. In addition to the application, students must submit a one-page abstract of the manuscript and a letter of endorsement from the major professor or department chair. The doctoral dissertation awards are $3,000 and $1,500. The master's thesis awards are $3,000 and $1,500.
Target applicant(s): Graduate school students. Adult students.
Amount: $1,500-$3,000.
Number of awards: 4.
Deadline: October 1.
How to apply: Applications are available online.
Exclusive: Visit www.UltimateScholarshipBook.com and enter code AM77023 for updates on this award.

(771) · Academic Education Award

American Association of Occupational Health Nurses (AAOHN) Foundation

330 N. Wabash Avenue, Suite 2000, Chicago, IL 60611

Phone: 312-321-5173

Email: info@aaohn.org

http://aaohn.org/page/scholarships

Purpose: To provide further education for occupational and environmental health professionals.
Eligibility: Applicants must be registered nurses enrolled full- or part-time in a nationally accredited school of nursing baccalaureate program with an interest in occupational and environmental health or be registered nurses enrolled full- or part-time in a graduate program that has application to occupational and environmental health. Applicants should submit a narrative and letters of recommendation.
Target applicant(s): College students. Graduate school students. Adult students.
Amount: $2,500.
Number of awards: 4.
Scholarship may be renewable.
Deadline: February 1.
How to apply: Applications are available online.
Exclusive: Visit www.UltimateScholarshipBook.com and enter code AM77123 for updates on this award.

(772) · Academy of Nutrition and Dietetics Foundation Student Scholarship

Academy of Nutrition and Dietetics

120 South Riverside Plaza, Suite 2000, Chicago, IL 60606-6995

Phone: 800-877-1600

Email: scholarship@eatright.org

https://eatrightfoundation.org/

Purpose: To encourage students in a dietetic program.
Eligibility: Applicants should be American Dietetic Association members and enrolled in their junior or senior year of a baccalaureate or coordinated program in dietetics or the second year of study in a dietetic technician program, a dietetic internship program or a graduate program. One application form is used for all ADAF scholarships.
Target applicant(s): College students. Graduate school students. Adult students.
Amount: $500-$10,000.

Number of awards: Varies.
Deadline: April 23.
How to apply: Applications are available online.
Exclusive: Visit www.UltimateScholarshipBook.com and enter code AC77223 for updates on this award.

(773) · ACEC New York Scholarship Program

American Council of Engineering Companies of New York

6 Airline Drive, Albany, NY 12205

Phone: 518-452-8611

Email: amanda@acecny.org

http://www.acecny.org

Purpose: To support students who plan to become consulting engineers.
Eligibility: Applicants must be in their third year of study in a four-year program or their fourth year of study in a five-year program at an engineering school in New York State. They must major in mechanical engineering, electrical engineering, structural engineering, civil engineering, environmental engineering, chemical engineering, engineering technology or surveying. They must plan to make New York State their home and/or career area. Selection is based on work experience (25 percent), college activities and recommendations (15 percent), essay (30 percent) and GPA (30 percent).
Target applicant(s): College students. Adult students.
Amount: $2,500-$10,000.
Number of awards: Varies.
Deadline: January.
How to apply: Applications are available online. An application form, essay, transcript and two recommendations are required.
Exclusive: Visit www.UltimateScholarshipBook.com and enter code AM77323 for updates on this award.

(774) · ACI Scholarship

American Concrete Institute

Attn.: ACI Foundation, Scholarship Coordinator, 38800 Country Club Drive, Farmington Hills, MI 48331

Phone: 248-848-3700

Email: scholarships@concrete.org

https://www.acifoundation.org/scholarships.aspx

Purpose: To support students who are interested in studying concrete.
Eligibility: Applicants must be nominated by a faculty member who is also a member of ACI in order to receive an application. Students must be full-time undergraduate or graduate students during the award year who plan to study in the U.S. or Canada. Applicants must be proficient in the English language. Students should submit applications via email.
Target applicant(s): College students. Graduate school students. Adult students.
Amount: $3,000-$5,000.
Number of awards: Varies.
Deadline: October 1.
How to apply: Applications are available online.
Exclusive: Visit www.UltimateScholarshipBook.com and enter code AM77423 for updates on this award.

(775) · ACI Student Fellowship Program

American Concrete Institute

Attn.: ACI Foundation, Scholarship Coordinator, 38800 Country Club Drive, Farmington Hills, MI 48331

Phone: 248-848-3700

Email: scholarships@concrete.org

https://www.acifoundation.org/scholarships.aspx

Purpose: To encourage careers in the concrete field.

Eligibility: Applicants must be full-time undergraduate or graduate students nominated by a faculty member who is also a member of the ACI. Students must be studying engineering, construction management or another relevant field. Applicants may live anywhere in the world, but actual study must take place in the U.S. or Canada. Finalists for a fellowship must attend an ACI convention for an interview. In addition to the monetary award, the scholarship also includes conference fees, mentoring and a potential internship.

Target applicant(s): College students. Graduate school students. Adult students.

Amount: Up to $15,000.

Number of awards: Varies.

Scholarship may be renewable.

Deadline: October 15.

How to apply: Applicants must be nominated by ACI-member faculty in order to receive an application.

Exclusive: Visit www.UltimateScholarshipBook.com and enter code AM77523 for updates on this award.

---

(776) · ADEA/Crest Oral-B Scholarships for Dental Hygiene Students Pursuing Academic Careers

American Dental Education Association
655 K Street NW, Suite 800, Washington, DC 20001
Phone: 202-289-7201
Email: lunde@adea.org
https://www.adea.org/studentawards/

Purpose: To encourage dental hygiene students who are pursuing education beyond an associate degree and who have an interest in academic careers.

Eligibility: Applicants must be enrolled in a baccalaureate degree program or graduate degree program in dental hygiene at an ADEA member institution. Students must show a commitment to pursuing an academic career in dental hygiene and be an ADEA individual member.

Target applicant(s): College students. Graduate school students. Adult students.

Amount: $3,000.

Number of awards: 2.

Deadline: November 1.

How to apply: Applications are available online.

Exclusive: Visit www.UltimateScholarshipBook.com and enter code AM77623 for updates on this award.

---

(777) · ADEA/GlaxoSmithKline Consumer Healthcare Preventive Dentistry Scholarships

American Dental Education Association
655 K Street NW, Suite 800, Washington, DC 20001
Phone: 202-289-7201
Email: lunde@adea.org
https://www.adea.org/studentawards/

Purpose: To support predoctoral dental students who have demonstrated academic excellence in preventive dentistry.

Eligibility: Applicants must be enrolled at a U.S. or Canadian dental school as a full-time student and possess a superior academic record. Students must demonstrate, through personal activities and achievements, a strong interest in preventive dentistry and be nominated by the dean of their dental school or the dean's designate.

Target applicant(s): Graduate school students. Adult students.

Amount: $2,500.

Number of awards: 12.

Deadline: November 1.

How to apply: Applications are available online.

Exclusive: Visit www.UltimateScholarshipBook.com and enter code AM77723 for updates on this award.

---

(778) · ADEA/Sigma Phi Alpha Linda Devore Scholarship

American Dental Education Association
655 K Street NW, Suite 800, Washington, DC 20001
Phone: 202-289-7201
Email: lunde@adea.org
https://www.adea.org/studentawards/

Purpose: To aid allied dental education students.

Eligibility: Applicants must be members of the American Dental Education Association (ADEA) and be enrolled in a dental hygiene, dental education or public health degree program. They must be in good academic standing and demonstrate leadership in dental education or health care. Selection is based on the overall strength of the application.

Target applicant(s): College students. Graduate school students. Adult students.

Amount: $1,500.

Number of awards: 1.

Deadline: November 1.

How to apply: Applications are available online. An application form, an official transcript, a personal statement and two reference letters are required.

Exclusive: Visit www.UltimateScholarshipBook.com and enter code AM77823 for updates on this award.

---

(779) · ADHA Institute Scholarship Program

American Dental Hygienists' Association (ADHA) Institute for Oral Health
Scholarship Award Program, 444 North Michigan Avenue, Suite 3400, Chicago, IL 60611
Phone: 312-440-8900
Email: institute@adha.net
https://www.adha.org/ioh-scholarships-main

Purpose: To assist students pursuing a career in dental hygiene.

Eligibility: Applicants should be enrolled full-time (unless applying for a part-time scholarship) in an accredited dental hygiene program in the U.S., be finishing their first year and have a minimum 3.0 GPA. Undergraduate students should be active members of the Student American Dental Hygienists' Association or the American Dental Hygienists Association. Graduate students should be active members of the Student American Dental Hygienists' Association or the American Dental Hygienists Association, have a valid dental hygiene license and a bachelor's degree. There should be financial need of at least $1,500, with the exception of the merit-based scholarships.

Target applicant(s): College students. Graduate school students. Adult students.

Minimum GPA: 3.0

Amount: Varies.

Number of awards: Varies.

Deadline: February 2.

How to apply: Applications are available online.

Exclusive: Visit www.UltimateScholarshipBook.com and enter code AM77923 for updates on this award.

(780) · AFCEA Ralph W. Shrader Diversity Scholarships

Armed Forces Communications and Electronics Association (AFCEA)
4400 Fair Lakes Court, Fairfax, VA 22033
Phone: 703-631-6149
http://www.afcea.org
Purpose: Monetary assistance is awarded to graduate students studying electrical, computer, chemical or aerospace engineering, mathematics, physics, computer science, computer technology, electronics, communications technology or engineering or information management systems.
Eligibility: Applicants must be U.S. citizens, full-time postgraduate students working toward a master's degree in electrical, computer, chemical or aerospace engineering, mathematics, physics, computer science, computer technology, electronics, communications technology, communications engineering or information management at an accredited U.S. university. Distance learning or online programs will not qualify. Primary consideration will be given for demonstrated excellence. Applicants do not need to be affiliated with the U.S. military.
Target applicant(s): Graduate school students. Adult students.
Amount: Varies.
Number of awards: Varies.
Deadline: April 30.
How to apply: Applications are available online.
Exclusive: Visit www.UltimateScholarshipBook.com and enter code AR78023 for updates on this award.

(781) · AGC Education and Research Foundation Undergraduate Scholarship

Associated General Contractors (AGC) Education and Research Foundation
2300 Wilson Boulevard, Suite 400, Arlington, VA 22201
Phone: 703-837-5342
Email: info@agc.org
http://www.agcfoundation.org
Purpose: To support rising undergraduate construction and construction-related engineering students pursue their ABET and ACCE-accredited construction and construction-related engineering degrees.
Eligibility: Applicants must be second-year students at a two-year college planning to transfer to a four-year program for the fall, rising college sophomores or juniors in a four-year program or seniors in a five-year program. Juniors and seniors must have one full academic year of study remaining at the time of application submission and be pursuing a B.S. degree in construction or construction-related engineering program.
Target applicant(s): College students. Adult students.
Minimum GPA: 2.0
Amount: $2,500.
Number of awards: 100.
Scholarship may be renewable.
Deadline: November 1.
How to apply: Applications are available online.
Exclusive: Visit www.UltimateScholarshipBook.com and enter code AS78123 for updates on this award.

(782) · AGC Graduate Scholarships

Associated General Contractors of America
2300 Wilson Boulevard, Suite 300, Arlington, VA 22201
Phone: 703-837-5342
Email: patricianm@agc.org
http://www.agc.org
Purpose: Monetary assistance is awarded to college seniors pursuing graduate degrees that will lead to careers in construction or civil engineering.
Eligibility: Applicants must be college seniors enrolled in an undergraduate construction or civil engineering degree program or college graduates with a degree in construction or civil engineering. Applicants must also be enrolled or planning to enroll full-time in a graduate level construction or civil engineering degree program.
Target applicant(s): College students. Graduate school students. Adult students.
Amount: $7,500.
Number of awards: Varies.
Deadline: November 1.
How to apply: Applications are available online.
Exclusive: Visit www.UltimateScholarshipBook.com and enter code AS78223 for updates on this award.

(783) · AGC Undergraduate Scholarships

Associated General Contractors of America
2300 Wilson Boulevard, Suite 300, Arlington, VA 22201
Phone: 703-837-5342
Email: patricianm@agc.org
http://www.agc.org
Purpose: To assist students pursuing studies that lead to a career in construction or civil engineering.
Eligibility: Applicants must be a second-year student at a two-year school planning to transfer to a four-year program, or a rising college sophomore or junior in a four-year program or rising senior in a five-year program enrolled in or planning to enroll in ABET- or ACCE-accredited construction or civil engineering programs pursuing a B.S. degree in construction or construction-related engineering.
Target applicant(s): College students. Adult students.
Amount: $2,500.
Number of awards: Varies.
Scholarship may be renewable.
Deadline: November 1.
How to apply: Applications are available online.
Exclusive: Visit www.UltimateScholarshipBook.com and enter code AS78323 for updates on this award.

(784) · AHIMA Foundation Merit Scholarships

American Health Information Management Association (AHIMA) Foundation
233 N. Michigan Avenue, 21st Floor, Chicago, IL 60601-5809
Phone: 312-233-1131
Email: info@ahimafoundation.org
http://www.ahimafoundation.org
Purpose: To provide merit scholarships to those enrolled in degree programs pursuing health information technology or health information administration.
Eligibility: Applicants must be members of AHIMA, have a minimum 3.0 GPA on a 4.0 scale, have completed 24 credit hours in health information management (HIM) or health information technology (HIT), have at least six credit hours remaining in their course of study and be taking at least six hours per semester in pursuit of the degree. The degrees eligible are AA degrees, BA/BS degrees and those who are credentialed and pursing a master's degree. Scholarships are also available for HIM professionals pursuing graduate degrees in the health information field.

Target applicant(s): College students. Graduate school students. Adult students.
Minimum GPA: 3.0
Amount: $1,000-$2,500.
Number of awards: Varies.
Deadline: September 15.
How to apply: Applications are available online.
Exclusive: Visit www.UltimateScholarshipBook.com and enter code AM78423 for updates on this award.

(785) · AIA/Architects Foundation Diversity Advancement Scholarship

American Institute of Architects
1735 New York Ave NW, Washington, DC 20006-5292
Phone: 800-242-3837
Email: divscholarship@aia.org
https://www.aia.org/pages/2736-scholarships
Purpose: To provide scholarships for students who intend to study architecture and who could not otherwise afford to enter a degree-seeking program.
Eligibility: Applicants must be students from a minority race or ethnicity who intend to study architecture in an NAAB-accredited program. Students who are U.S. residents entering, attending or transferring to an NAAB-accredited program are also eligible.
Target applicant(s): High school students. College students. Adult students.
Amount: $4,000.
Number of awards: Varies.
Scholarship may be renewable.
Deadline: Varies.
How to apply: Applications are available by email. An application form and a recommendation letter are required.
Exclusive: Visit www.UltimateScholarshipBook.com and enter code AM78523 for updates on this award.

(786) · AIAA Foundation Undergraduate Scholarship Program

American Institute of Aeronautics and Astronautics
12700 Sunrise Valley Drive, Suite 200, Reston, VA 20191-5807
Phone: 800-639-AIAA
Email: stephenb@aiaa.org
http://www.aiaa.org
Purpose: AIAA advances the arts, sciences and technology of aeronautics and astronautics.
Eligibility: Applicants must be enrolled in an accredited college or university and have completed at least one semester or quarter of college work with a minimum 3.3 GPA. Applicants must plan to enter a career in science or engineering related to the technical activities of the AIAA. Applicants must be AIAA student members in good standing to apply. Selection is based on scholarship, career goals, recommendations and extracurricular activities.
Target applicant(s): College students. Adult students.
Minimum GPA: 3.3
Amount: $500-$5,000.
Number of awards: Varies.
Scholarship may be renewable.
Deadline: January 31.
How to apply: Applications are available online.
Exclusive: Visit www.UltimateScholarshipBook.com and enter code AM78623 for updates on this award.

(787) · AISI/AIST Foundation Premier Scholarship

Association for Iron and Steel Technology (AIST)
186 Thorn Hill Road, Warrendale, PA 15086-7528
Phone: 724-814-3000
Email: lwharrey@aist.org
https://www.aist.org/students-faculty/scholarships
Purpose: To encourage engineering students to pursue careers in the iron and steel industry.
Eligibility: Applicants must be undergraduate sophomores who are enrolled full-time at an accredited college or university and be majoring in engineering. They must have a GPA of 3.0 or higher on a four-point scale and must have a demonstrated career interest in the iron and steel industry. Selection is based on the overall strength of the application.
Target applicant(s): College students. Adult students.
Minimum GPA: 3.0
Amount: $12,000.
Number of awards: 1.
Scholarship may be renewable.
Deadline: October 31.
How to apply: Applications are available online. An application form, transcript, personal essay and two letters of recommendation are required.
Exclusive: Visit www.UltimateScholarshipBook.com and enter code AS78723 for updates on this award.

(788) · AIST Benjamin F. Fairless Scholarship (AIME)

Association for Iron and Steel Technology (AIST)
186 Thorn Hill Road, Warrendale, PA 15086-7528
Phone: 724-814-3000
Email: lwharrey@aist.org
https://www.aist.org/students-faculty/scholarships
Purpose: To honor the memory of Benjamin F. Fairless, former Chairman of the Board of U.S. Steel Corporation.
Eligibility: Applicants must be enrolled full-time in an accredited university in North America and majoring in engineering, metallurgy or materials science. Applicants must also have a GPA of 2.5 or higher and plan to pursue a career in the iron and steel industry.
Target applicant(s): College students. Adult students.
Minimum GPA: 2.5
Amount: $3,000.
Number of awards: 2.
Deadline: October 31.
How to apply: Applications are available online.
Exclusive: Visit www.UltimateScholarshipBook.com and enter code AS78823 for updates on this award.

(789) · AIST Ronald E. Lincoln Memorial Scholarship

Association for Iron and Steel Technology (AIST)
186 Thorn Hill Road, Warrendale, PA 15086-7528
Phone: 724-814-3000
Email: lwharrey@aist.org
https://www.aist.org/students-faculty/scholarships
Purpose: To honor the memory of Ronald Lincoln and to reward students who demonstrate leadership and innovation.
Eligibility: Applicants must be enrolled full-time in an accredited university in North America and majoring in engineering, metallurgy or materials science. Applicants must also have a GPA of 2.5 or higher and plan to pursue a career in the iron and steel industry.
Target applicant(s): College students. Adult students.
Minimum GPA: 2.5

Amount: $3,000.
Number of awards: 3.
Deadline: October 31.
How to apply: Applications are available online.
Exclusive: Visit www.UltimateScholarshipBook.com and enter code AS78923 for updates on this award.

---

(790) · AIST Smith Graduate Scholarship

Association for Iron and Steel Technology (AIST)
186 Thorn Hill Road, Warrendale, PA 15086-7528
Phone: 724-814-3000
Email: lwharrey@aist.org
https://www.aist.org/students-faculty/scholarships
Purpose: To aid graduate engineering students who are interested in careers in metallurgy.
Eligibility: Applicants must be full-time graduate students who are enrolled in an engineering degree program at an accredited college or university in the U.S. or Canada. They must have a demonstrated interest in pursuing a career in metallurgy within the iron and steel industry. Selection is based on the overall strength of the application.
Target applicant(s): Graduate school students. Adult students.
Amount: Up to $6,000.
Number of awards: Varies.
Deadline: October 31.
How to apply: Applications are available online. An application form and supporting materials are required.
Exclusive: Visit www.UltimateScholarshipBook.com and enter code AS79023 for updates on this award.

---

(791) · AIST William E. Schwabe Memorial Scholarship

Association for Iron and Steel Technology (AIST)
186 Thorn Hill Road, Warrendale, PA 15086-7528
Phone: 724-814-3000
Email: lwharrey@aist.org
https://www.aist.org/students-faculty/scholarships
Purpose: To honor the memory of William E. Schwabe, steelmaking pioneer.
Eligibility: Applicants must be enrolled full-time in an accredited university in North America and majoring in engineering, metallurgy or materials science. Applicants must also have a GPA of 2.5 or higher and plan to pursue a career in the iron and steel industry.
Target applicant(s): College students. Adult students.
Minimum GPA: 2.5
Amount: $3,000.
Number of awards: 1.
Deadline: October 31.
How to apply: Applications are available online.
Exclusive: Visit www.UltimateScholarshipBook.com and enter code AS79123 for updates on this award.

---

(792) · AIST Willy Korf Memorial Fund

Association for Iron and Steel Technology (AIST)
186 Thorn Hill Road, Warrendale, PA 15086-7528
Phone: 724-814-3000
Email: lwharrey@aist.org
https://www.aist.org/students-faculty/scholarships
Purpose: To honor the memory of the late Willy Korf, the founder of the Korf Group, and to assist students who plan to enter the fields of engineering, metallurgy or materials science in the iron and steel industry.

Eligibility: Applicants must be enrolled full-time in an accredited university in North America, and majoring in engineering, metallurgy or materials science. Applicants must also have a GPA of 3.0 or higher and plan to pursue a career in the iron and steel industry.
Target applicant(s): High school students. College students. Adult students.
Minimum GPA: 3.0
Amount: $3,000.
Number of awards: 4.
Deadline: October 31.
How to apply: Applications are available online.
Exclusive: Visit www.UltimateScholarshipBook.com and enter code AS79223 for updates on this award.

---

(793) · Alice T. Schafer Mathematics Prize

Association for Women in Mathematics
P.O. Box 40876, Providence, RI 02940
Phone: 401-455-4042
Email: awm@awm-math.org
http://www.awm-math.org
Purpose: To support female students who are studying mathematics.
Eligibility: Nominees must be female college undergraduates and either be U.S. citizens or have a school address in the U.S. Selection is based on performance in advanced mathematics courses and special programs, interest in mathematics, ability to conduct independent work and performance in mathematical competitions at the local or national level.
Target applicant(s): College students. Adult students.
Amount: Varies.
Number of awards: Varies.
Deadline: October 1.
How to apply: Applicants must be nominated.
Exclusive: Visit www.UltimateScholarshipBook.com and enter code AS79323 for updates on this award.

---

(794) · Alice W. Rooke Scholarship

National Society Daughters of the American Revolution
Committee Services Office, Attn.: Scholarships, 1776 D Street NW, Washington, DC 20006-5303
Phone: 202-628-1776
Email: scholarships@dar.org
https://www.dar.org/national-society/scholarships/general-information
Purpose: To assist students in becoming medical doctors.
Eligibility: Applicants must be accepted into or enrolled in a graduate course of study to become a medical doctor. All applicants must obtain a letter of sponsorship from their local DAR chapter. However, affiliation with DAR is not required.
Target applicant(s): Graduate school students. Adult students.
Amount: Up to $5,000.
Number of awards: 1.
Scholarship may be renewable.
Deadline: January 31.
How to apply: Applications are available by written request with a self-addressed, stamped envelope.
Exclusive: Visit www.UltimateScholarshipBook.com and enter code NA79423 for updates on this award.

(795) · Alpha Mu Tau Fraternity Undergraduate Scholarships

American Society for Clinical Laboratory Science
Alpha Mu Tau Scholarship, Attn: Joe Briden, AMTF Scholarship Coordinator, 7809 S. 21st Drive, Phoenix, AZ 85041-7736
Phone: 571-748-3770
Email: awards@ascls.org
http://www.ascls.org
Purpose: To support new professionals in the clinical laboratory sciences.
Eligibility: Applicants must be undergraduate students entering or in their last year of study in an NAACLS-accredited program in Clinical Laboratory Science/Medical Technology or Clinical Laboratory Technician/Medical Laboratory Technician. Applicants must be a U.S. citizen or a permanent resident of the U.S.
Target applicant(s): College students. Adult students.
Amount: Varies.
Number of awards: Varies.
Deadline: April 1.
How to apply: Applications are available online.
Exclusive: Visit www.UltimateScholarshipBook.com and enter code AM79523 for updates on this award.

(796) · AMBUCS Scholars

AMBUCS
P.O. Box 5127, High Point, NC 27262
Phone: 800-838-1845
Email: ambucs@ambucs.org
http://www.ambucs.org
Purpose: To provide more opportunities for the disabled by encouraging students to become therapists.
Eligibility: Students must be US citizens accepted in a graduate-level program that is accredited by the appropriate therapy profession authority in physical therapy, occupational therapy, speech language pathology or hearing audiology. Assistant or undergraduate programs are not eligible. Awards are based on financial need, commitment to local community, character for compassion and integrity and career objectives.
Target applicant(s): College students. Graduate school students. Adult students.
Amount: $500-$6,000.
Number of awards: Varies.
Deadline: May 1.
How to apply: Applications are available online.
Exclusive: Visit www.UltimateScholarshipBook.com and enter code AM79623 for updates on this award.

(797) · Amelia Earhart Fellowships

Zonta International
1211 West 22nd Street, Suite 900, Oak Brook, IL 60523
Phone: 630-928-1400
Email: zontaintl@zonta.org
http://www.zonta.org
Purpose: To support women in science and engineering.
Eligibility: Applicants must be pursuing graduate PhD/doctoral degrees in aerospace-related sciences and aerospace-related engineering.
Target applicant(s): Graduate school students. Adult students.
Amount: $10,000.
Number of awards: 35.
Deadline: November.

Exclusive: Visit www.UltimateScholarshipBook.com and enter code ZO79723 for updates on this award.

(798) · American Architectural Foundation and Sir John Soane's Museum Foundation Traveling Fellowship

American Institute of Architects
1735 New York Ave NW, Washington, DC 20006-5292
Phone: 800-242-3837
Email: divscholarship@aia.org
https://www.aia.org/pages/2736-scholarships
Purpose: To provide scholarships enabling graduate students to travel to England and to study the work of Sir John Soane (or Sir John Soane's Museum and its collections).
Eligibility: Applicants must be enrolled in graduate programs focusing on the history of art, architecture, decorative arts or interior design.
Target applicant(s): Graduate school students. Adult students.
Amount: $5,000.
Number of awards: 2.
Deadline: March 1.
How to apply: Applications are available online.
Exclusive: Visit www.UltimateScholarshipBook.com and enter code AM79823 for updates on this award.

(799) · American Quarter Horse Foundation (AQHF) Youth Activities Scholarship

American Quarter Horse Foundation
Scholarship Program, 2601 East Interstate 40, Amarillo, TX 79104
Phone: 806-378-5029
Email: foundation@aqha.org
https://www.aqha.com/scholarships1
Purpose: To encourage future Quarter Horse industry professionals.
Eligibility: Applicants must be current members of AQHA and have a minimum 2.5 GPA. Students must be current college students. Selection is based on financial need, academic achievement, equine involvement, references and career plans. A transcript and three references are required for all scholarships.
Target applicant(s): College students. Graduate school students. Adult students.
Minimum GPA: 2.5
Amount: Varies.
Number of awards: Varies.
Scholarship may be renewable.
Deadline: July 1.
How to apply: Applications are available online.
Exclusive: Visit www.UltimateScholarshipBook.com and enter code AM79923 for updates on this award.

(800) · American Water Scholarship

American Water Works Association
6666 W. Quincy Avenue, Denver, CO 80235-3098
Phone: 800-926-7337
Email: scholarships@awwa.org
http://www.awwa.org
Purpose: To support graduate-level students interested in giving service to the water industry.
Eligibility: Applicants must be graduate students working towards a masters or doctoral degree. Students must be planning a career related

to the service of the water industry. Selection is based upon the overall strength of the application.
Target applicant(s): College students. Graduate school students. Adult students.
Amount: $5,000.
Number of awards: Varies.
Deadline: December 20.
How to apply: Applications are available online.
Exclusive: Visit www.UltimateScholarshipBook.com and enter code AM80023 for updates on this award.

(801) · AMS Graduate Fellowship in the History of Science

American Meteorological Society
Fellowship and Scholarship Department, 45 Beacon Street, Boston, MA 02108-3693
Phone: 617-227-2426 x246
Email: dsampson@ametsoc.org
http://www.ametsoc.org/AMS/
Purpose: To support students writing dissertations on the history of atmospheric or related oceanic or hydrologic sciences.
Eligibility: Applicants must be graduate students who plan to write dissertations on the history of atmospheric or related oceanic or hydrologic sciences. Students must submit a cover letter with vitae, official transcripts, a typed description of the dissertation topic and three letters of recommendation.
Target applicant(s): Graduate school students. Adult students.
Amount: $15,000.
Number of awards: Varies.
Deadline: May 1.
How to apply: Submit materials to address listed.
Exclusive: Visit www.UltimateScholarshipBook.com and enter code AM80123 for updates on this award.

(802) · AMS Graduate Fellowships

American Meteorological Society
Fellowship and Scholarship Department, 45 Beacon Street, Boston, MA 02108-3693
Phone: 617-227-2426 x246
Email: dsampson@ametsoc.org
http://www.ametsoc.org/AMS/
Purpose: To attract students to prepare for careers in the meteorological, oceanic and hydrologic fields.
Eligibility: Applicants must be entering their first year of graduate study the following year and plan to pursue advanced degrees in the atmospheric and related oceanic and hydrologic sciences and have a minimum 3.25 GPA. Awards are based on undergraduate performance. References, transcripts and GRE scores may be sent under separate cover. References can be sent to dfernand@ametsoc.org.
Target applicant(s): College students. Adult students.
Minimum GPA: 3.25
Amount: $25,000.
Number of awards: Varies.
Deadline: January 1.
How to apply: Applications are available online.
Exclusive: Visit www.UltimateScholarshipBook.com and enter code AM80223 for updates on this award.

(803) · AMS Minority Scholarship

American Meteorological Society
Fellowship and Scholarship Department, 45 Beacon Street, Boston, MA 02108-3693
Phone: 617-227-2426 x246
Email: dsampson@ametsoc.org
http://www.ametsoc.org/AMS/
Purpose: To support minority students who have been traditionally underrepresented in the sciences, especially Hispanic, Native American and African American students.
Eligibility: Applicants must be minority students who will be entering their freshman year of college in the following fall and must plan to pursue degrees in the atmospheric or related oceanic and hydrologic sciences. Applicants must submit applications, transcripts, recommendation letters and SAT or equivalent scores. Original materials should be mailed to the closest AMS Local Chapter listed at the bottom of the application, and copies should be mailed to headquarters.
Target applicant(s): High school students.
Amount: $6,000.
Number of awards: Varies.
Scholarship may be renewable.
Deadline: February 12.
How to apply: Applications are available online.
Exclusive: Visit www.UltimateScholarshipBook.com and enter code AM80323 for updates on this award.

(804) · AMS Senior Named Scholarships

American Meteorological Society
Fellowship and Scholarship Department, 45 Beacon Street, Boston, MA 02108-3693
Phone: 617-227-2426 x246
Email: dsampson@ametsoc.org
http://www.ametsoc.org/AMS/
Purpose: To encourage undergraduate students to pursue careers in the atmospheric and related oceanic and hydrologic sciences.
Eligibility: Applicants must be full-time students majoring in the atmospheric or related oceanic or hydrologic science and entering their final undergraduate year, show intent to make the atmospheric or related sciences their career and have a minimum 3.25 GPA. For the Schroeder scholarship, applicants must demonstrate financial need. For the Murphy scholarship, applicants must demonstrate interest in weather forecasting through curricular or extracurricular activities and for the Crow scholarship, applicants must demonstrate interest in applied meteorology. The Glahn scholarship will be awarded to a student with a strong interest in statistical meteorology.
Target applicant(s): College students. Adult students.
Minimum GPA: 3.25
Amount: Up to $10,000.
Number of awards: Varies.
Deadline: March 26.
How to apply: Applications are available online.
Exclusive: Visit www.UltimateScholarshipBook.com and enter code AM80423 for updates on this award.

(805) · AMT Student Scholarship

American Medical Technologists
10700 W. Higgins Road, Suite 150, Rosemont, IL 60018
Phone: 800-275-1268
Email: mail@americanmedtech.org
https://www.americanmedtech.org

Purpose: To provide financial assistance to students interested in medical technology careers.

Eligibility: Applicants must be high school graduates or current seniors planning to attend an accredited institution to pursue an American Medical Technologists-certified career, which includes medical laboratory technology, medical assisting, dental assisting, phlebotomy and office laboratory technician. Applicants must provide evidence of financial need.

Target applicant(s): High school students.

Amount: $500.

Number of awards: 5.

Deadline: April 1.

How to apply: Applications are available online.

Exclusive: Visit www.UltimateScholarshipBook.com and enter code AM80523 for updates on this award.

(806) · Analytical Chemistry Scholarship

Jordi Labs
200 Gilbert Street, Mansfield, MA 02048
Phone: 508-966-1301
Email: tperez@jordilabs.com
https://jordilabs.com/blog/analytical-chemistry-scholarship/

Purpose: To support the pursuit of a science degree.

Eligibility: Applicants must be enrolling as or currently enrolled undergraduate or graduate students pursuing a career in analytical chemistry.

Target applicant(s): High school students. College students. Graduate school students. Adult students.

Amount: $1,000.

Number of awards: 5.

Deadline: July 31.

How to apply: Applications are available online.

Exclusive: Visit www.UltimateScholarshipBook.com and enter code JO80623 for updates on this award.

(807) · Angus Foundation Scholarships

American Foundation
3201 Frederick Avenue, St. Joseph, MO 64506
Phone: 816-383-5100
Email: angus@angus.org
http://www.angus.org/Foundation/WhatWeDo/Youth/Default.aspx

Purpose: To provide scholarships to youth active with the Angus breed.

Eligibility: Applicants must have been members of the National Junior Angus Association and must be junior, regular or life members of the American Angus Association at the time of application. Applicants must be high school seniors or enrolled in a junior college, four-year college or other accredited institution of post-secondary education in an undergraduate program and have a minimum 2.0 GPA. Students may not have reached their 25th birthday by January 1 of the year of application.

Target applicant(s): High school students. College students.

Minimum GPA: 2.0

Amount: $1,000-$5,000.

Number of awards: Varies.

Deadline: May 1.

How to apply: Applications are available online or by written request.

Exclusive: Visit www.UltimateScholarshipBook.com and enter code AM80723 for updates on this award.

(808) · Annual NBNA Scholarships

National Black Nurses Association
8630 Fenton Street, Suite 330, Silver Spring, MD 20910-3803
Phone: 301-589-3200
Email: Info@nbna.org
http://www.nbna.org

Purpose: To promote excellence in education and in continuing education programs for African American nurses and allied health professionals.

Eligibility: Applicants must be African Americans currently enrolled in a nursing program and be in good academic standing, be members of the NBNA, be members of a local chapter and have at least a full year of school remaining. Applicants must submit with their application an essay, references, an official transcript and evidence of participation in student nurse activities and involvement in the African American community.

Target applicant(s): College students. Adult students.

Amount: $1,000-$6,000.

Number of awards: Varies.

Deadline: May 1.

How to apply: Applications are available online.

Exclusive: Visit www.UltimateScholarshipBook.com and enter code NA80823 for updates on this award.

(809) · Annual University Scholarship

Antibodies-online Inc.
P.O. Box 5201, Limerick, PA 19468
Phone: 877-302-8632
Email: scholarship@antibodies-online.com
https://www.antibodies-online.com/scholarship/

Purpose: To support students who are pursuing degrees in the life sciences.

Eligibility: Applicants must be high school seniors, undergraduates or graduate students enrolled in an accredited college or university for the upcoming fall or spring semester. Students must be majoring in life sciences or related fields. Applicants must submit a 250-word essay on why they decided to pursue a degree in life science and how they plan to further advance this field, as well as a 150-word essay on what their favorite scientific discovery is and why.

Target applicant(s): High school students. College students. Graduate school students. Adult students.

Amount: $1,000.

Number of awards: 2.

Deadline: January 20 and July 20.

How to apply: Applications are available online.

Exclusive: Visit www.UltimateScholarshipBook.com and enter code AN80923 for updates on this award.

(810) · ANS Graduate Scholarship

American Nuclear Society
555 North Kensington Avenue, La Grange Park, IL 60526
Phone: 800-323-3044
Email: hr@ans.org
http://www.ans.org

Purpose: To assist full-time graduate students who are pursuing advanced degrees in a nuclear-related field.

Eligibility: Applicants must be full-time students at an accredited graduate school in a program leading to an advanced degree in nuclear science, nuclear engineering or a nuclear-related field. There are also

individual graduate scholarships. Applicants should submit applications, transcripts, recommendation letter and three reference forms.
Target applicant(s): Graduate school students. Adult students.
Amount: Varies.
Number of awards: Up to 29.
Deadline: February 1.
How to apply: Applications are available online.
Exclusive: Visit www.UltimateScholarshipBook.com and enter code AM81023 for updates on this award.

(811) · ANS Incoming Freshman Scholarships

American Nuclear Society
555 North Kensington Avenue, La Grange Park, IL 60526
Phone: 800-323-3044
Email: hr@ans.org
http://www.ans.org
Purpose: To aid high school seniors who are planning to major in nuclear engineering at the undergraduate level.
Eligibility: Applicants must be graduating high school seniors who have been accepted at an accredited postsecondary institution. They must have plans to major in nuclear engineering. Selection is based on academic merit, personal essay and recommendations.
Target applicant(s): High school students.
Amount: $1,000.
Number of awards: Up to 4.
Deadline: April 1.
How to apply: Applications are available online. An application form, personal essay, two letters of recommendation and an official transcript are required.
Exclusive: Visit www.UltimateScholarshipBook.com and enter code AM81123 for updates on this award.

(812) · ANS Undergraduate Scholarship

American Nuclear Society
555 North Kensington Avenue, La Grange Park, IL 60526
Phone: 800-323-3044
Email: hr@ans.org
http://www.ans.org
Purpose: To assist undergraduate students who are pursuing careers in the field of nuclear science.
Eligibility: Applicants must be at least sophomores or students who have completed two or more years and will be entering as juniors or seniors in an accredited university and must be enrolled in a program leading to a degree in nuclear science, nuclear engineering or a nuclear-related field. Applicants should submit applications, transcripts, recommendation letter and three reference forms. There are individual undergraduate scholarships for students who have completed two or more years in a course of study leading to a degree in nuclear science, nuclear engineering or a nuclear-related field.
Target applicant(s): College students. Adult students.
Amount: Varies.
Number of awards: Up to 38.
Deadline: February 1.
How to apply: Applications are available online.
Exclusive: Visit www.UltimateScholarshipBook.com and enter code AM81223 for updates on this award.

(813) · AOC Scholarships

Association of Old Crows
1000 N. Payne Street, Suite 200, Alexandria, VA 22314-1652
Phone: 703-549-1600
Email: stourangeau@warriorss.com
https://www.crows.org
Purpose: To encourage students interested in strong defense capability emphasizing electronic warfare and information operations.
Eligibility: Applicants must be U.S. citizens enrolled full-time at an accredited college or university in an undergraduate degree program as a junior or senior. Students should be studying engineering or technology with a minimum cumulative GPA of 3.0. Selection is based on interest and potential future contribution to national defense and academic excellence in the STEM area of study.
Target applicant(s): College students. Adult students.
Minimum GPA: 3.0
Amount: $12,500.
Number of awards: 2.
Deadline: April 30.
How to apply: Applications are available online.
Exclusive: Visit www.UltimateScholarshipBook.com and enter code AS81323 for updates on this award.

(814) · AORN Foundation Scholarship Program

Association of Perioperative Registered Nurses
2170 S. Parker Road, Suite 400, Denver, CO 80231
Phone: 800-755-2676
Email: sstokes@aorn.org
https://www.aorn.org/aorn-foundation/foundation-scholarships
Purpose: To encourage the education of nurses and future nurses.
Eligibility: Applicants must be current nursing students or AORN members accepted to an accredited program and have a minimum 3.0 GPA. Applicants must also demonstrate financial need.
Target applicant(s): College students. Graduate school students. Adult students.
Minimum GPA: 3.0
Amount: Varies.
Number of awards: Varies.
Deadline: June.
How to apply: Applications are available online.
Exclusive: Visit www.UltimateScholarshipBook.com and enter code AS81423 for updates on this award.

(815) · AOS Student and Postdoctoral Research Awards

American Ornithologists' Union
Avian Ecology Lab, Archbold Biological Station, 123 Main Drive, Venus, FL 33960
Phone: 863-465-2571
Email: rbowman@archbold-station.org
http://www.aou.org
Purpose: To provide research funding for members of the American Ornithologists Union.
Eligibility: Applicants must be members of the AOU and must submit proposals for research projects on avian biology, avian systematics, paleo-ornithology, biogeography, neotropical biology or ornithology.
Target applicant(s): High school students. College students. Graduate school students. Adult students.
Amount: Up to $2,500.
Number of awards: Varies.
Deadline: February 5.
How to apply: The submission procedure and tips for writing a proposal are described on the website.

Exclusive: Visit www.UltimateScholarshipBook.com and enter code AM81523 for updates on this award.

(816) · Appaloosa Youth Association Art Contest

Appaloosa Horse Club
Appaloosa Youth Association, 2720 West Pullman Road, Moscow, ID 83843
Phone: 208-882-5578
Email: youth@appaloosa.com
https://www.appaloosa.com/appaloosa-youth-association
Purpose: To allow students to showcase their artistic talents with Appaloosa-themed projects.
Eligibility: Applicants age 18 and under should submit drawings, paintings and hand-built ceramics or sculptures with the Appaloosa theme. There are three age divisions: 10 and under and 11 to 13 and 14 to 18. Awards are based on originality, creativity and the theme.
Target applicant(s): Junior high students or younger. High school students.
Amount: $50-$100.
Number of awards: 9.
Deadline: May 1.
How to apply: Applications are available online.
Exclusive: Visit www.UltimateScholarshipBook.com and enter code AP81623 for updates on this award.

(817) · Appaloosa Youth Association Essay Contest

Appaloosa Horse Club
Appaloosa Youth Association, 2720 West Pullman Road, Moscow, ID 83843
Phone: 208-882-5578
Email: youth@appaloosa.com
https://www.appaloosa.com/appaloosa-youth-association
Purpose: To reward students for essays that demonstrate their love of the Appaloosa breed.
Eligibility: Applicants must be 18 and under and should submit entry forms and essays on the provided themes. There are two age divisions: 13 and under and 14 to 18. Awards are based on originality and accuracy.
Target applicant(s): Junior high students or younger. High school students.
Amount: $50-$100.
Number of awards: 6.
Deadline: May 1.
How to apply: Applications are available online.
Exclusive: Visit www.UltimateScholarshipBook.com and enter code AP81723 for updates on this award.

(818) · Apprentice Ecologist Initiative Youth Scholarship Program

Nicodemus Wilderness Project
P.O. Box 40712, Albuquerque, NM 87196-0712
Email: mail@wildernessproject.org
http://www.wildernessproject.org/volunteer_apprentice_ecologist.php
Purpose: To aid ecologically-minded youth.
Eligibility: Applicants must be students who are between the ages of 13 and 21. They must devise and complete an environmental conservation project then write an essay describing the experience. Selection is based on the quality of the project and essay.
Target applicant(s): Junior high students or younger. High school students. College students.

Amount: $1,750.
Number of awards: 3.
Deadline: December 31.
How to apply: Application instructions are available online. An essay and a project photo are required.
Exclusive: Visit www.UltimateScholarshipBook.com and enter code NI81823 for updates on this award.

(819) · ASABE Foundation Engineering Scholarship

American Society of Agricultural and Biological Engineers Foundation
Administrator, Scholarship Fund, 2950 Niles Road, St. Joseph, MI 49085
Phone: 269-429-0300
Email: hq@asabe.org
http://www.asabe.org
Purpose: To assist student members of ASABE.
Eligibility: Applicants must have completed at least one year of undergraduate study and have at least one year of undergraduate study remaining, major in agricultural or biological engineering at an eligible accredited degree program in the U.S. or Canada, have a minimum 2.5 GPA and demonstrate financial need. Students must also be members of ASABE.
Target applicant(s): College students. Adult students.
Minimum GPA: 2.5
Amount: $1,200.
Number of awards: 1.
Deadline: March 15.
How to apply: Application is available online.
Exclusive: Visit www.UltimateScholarshipBook.com and enter code AM81923 for updates on this award.

(820) · ASCA/AISC Student Design Competition

Association of Collegiate Schools of Architecture
1735 New York Avenue NW, Washington, DC 20006
Phone: 202-785-2324
Email: eellis@acsa-arch.org
http://www.acsa-arch.org
Purpose: To encourage innovation in architecture.
Eligibility: Applicants must be architecture students at ACSA member schools in the United States, Canada or Mexico and be college juniors, seniors or graduate students. Students must submit a design project on one of the association's featured themes, and they must work under the direction of a faculty sponsor.
Target applicant(s): College students. Graduate school students. Adult students.
Amount: $300-$2,000.
Number of awards: 6.
Deadline: January 13.
How to apply: Applications are available online.
Exclusive: Visit www.UltimateScholarshipBook.com and enter code AS82023 for updates on this award.

(821) · ASCO Numatics Industrial Automation Engineering Scholarship

ASCO Numatics
160 Park Avenue, Florham Park, NJ 07932
Phone: 973-966-2000
https://www.asco.com/en-us

Purpose: To support students pursuing careers in industrial automation and related disciplines.
Eligibility: Applicants must have completed their sophomore year in a bachelor's degree program or be enrolled in a graduate program. ASCO employees and their relatives are not eligible. Winners are not eligible to apply for future scholarships.
Target applicant(s): College students. Graduate school students. Adult students.
Amount: $5,000.
Number of awards: 2.
Deadline: June 30.
How to apply: Applications are available online.
Exclusive: Visit www.UltimateScholarshipBook.com and enter code AS82123 for updates on this award.

(822) · ASDSO Senior Undergraduate Scholarship
Association of State Dam Safety Officials
239 South Limestone Street, Lexington, KY 40508
Phone: 859-550-2788 x 6
Email: info@damsafety.org
https://damsafety.org/apply-scholarship
Purpose: To increase awareness of careers in dam safety.
Eligibility: Applicants must be U.S. citizens who will be full-time seniors in the following school year in an accredited civil engineering program or a related field and show an interest in a career related to dam design, construction or operation. Students must have a minimum 2.5 GPA for the first three years of college, be recommended by their academic advisor and write an essay on what ASDSO is and why dam safety is important. Selection is based on academic achievement, financial need, work experience and activities and essay.
Target applicant(s): College students. Adult students.
Minimum GPA: 2.5
Amount: $5,000-$10,000.
Number of awards: Varies.
Deadline: March 31.
How to apply: Applications are available online.
Exclusive: Visit www.UltimateScholarshipBook.com and enter code AS82223 for updates on this award.

(823) · ASEV Scholarships
American Society for Enology and Viticulture
P.O. Box 1855, Davis, CA 95617-1855
Phone: 530-753-3142
Email: society@asev.org
http://www.asev.org
Purpose: To support those seeking a degree in enology, viticulture or in a curriculum focusing on a science basic to the wine and grape industry.
Eligibility: Applicants must be undergraduate or graduate students enrolled in or accepted into a full-time accredited four-year university program and must reside in North America (Canada, Mexico or the U.S.). Undergraduate students must be at least juniors for the upcoming academic year and have a minimum 3.0 GPA. Graduate students must have a minimum 3.2 GPA. Applicants must be enrolled in a major or in a graduate group concentrating on enology or viticulture or in a curriculum with a focus on a science basic to the wine and grape industry. The application, transcripts and two letters of recommendation are required.
Target applicant(s): College students. Graduate school students. Adult students.
Minimum GPA: 3.0 for undergraduate students, 3.2 for graduate students

Amount: Varies.
Number of awards: Varies.
Deadline: March 1.
How to apply: Applications are available online, by phone or by email.
Exclusive: Visit www.UltimateScholarshipBook.com and enter code AM82323 for updates on this award.

(824) · ASF Olin Fellowships
Atlantic Salmon Federation
P.O. Box 807, Calais, ME 04619-0807
Phone: 506-529-1033
Email: asfweb@nbnet.nb.ca
http://www.asf.ca
Purpose: To help fund projects that focus on solving problems in Atlantic salmon biology, management and conservation.
Eligibility: Applicants must be studying or actively engaged in salmon management or research. The award is open to U.S. and Canadian applicants.
Target applicant(s): College students. Adult students.
Amount: $1,000-$3,000.
Number of awards: Varies.
Deadline: March 15.
How to apply: Applications are available by mail.
Exclusive: Visit www.UltimateScholarshipBook.com and enter code AT82423 for updates on this award.

(825) · ASHA Youth Scholarships
American Saddlebred Horse Association Foundation
4083 Iron Works Parkway, Lexington, KY 40511
Phone: 859-259-2742
Email: b.newell@asha.net
https://www.asha.net/clubs/youthscholarships/
Purpose: To help youths involved with Saddlebreds.
Eligibility: This award is based on academic excellence, financial need, extracurricular activities, community service, involvement with American Saddlebred horses and personal references. An interview may be part of the selection process. Applicants should write an essay about school experiences, special interests, hobbies and American Saddlebred Horse Association activities. Scholarships are given only to high school seniors or recent graduates.
Target applicant(s): High school students.
Amount: Varies.
Number of awards: Varies.
Deadline: June 1.
How to apply: Applications are available online.
Exclusive: Visit www.UltimateScholarshipBook.com and enter code AM82523 for updates on this award.

(826) · ASHRAE Engineering Technology Scholarships
American Society of Heating, Refrigerating and Air-Conditioning Engineers (ASHRAE)
1791 Tullie Circle, NE, Atlanta, GA 30329
Phone: 404-636-8400
Email: lbenedict@ashrae.org
https://www.ashrae.org/membership--conferences/student-zone/scholarships-and-grants/scholarship-program
Purpose: To support students who are interested in pursuing a career in engineering or technology.
Eligibility: Applicants must be full-time undergraduate students pursuing a bachelor's or associate's degree in an engineering or

engineering technology program, have a cumulative GPA of 3.0 and be a student member of ASHRAE. Selection is based on the overall strength of the application.
Target applicant(s): College students. Adult students.
Minimum GPA: 3.0
Amount: $5,000.
Number of awards: 5.
Scholarship may be renewable.
Deadline: December 1.
How to apply: Applications are available online.
Exclusive: Visit www.UltimateScholarshipBook.com and enter code AM82623 for updates on this award.

(827) · ASHRAE Memorial Scholarship
American Society of Heating, Refrigerating and Air-Conditioning Engineers (ASHRAE)
1791 Tullie Circle, NE, Atlanta, GA 30329
Phone: 404-636-8400
Email: lbenedict@ashrae.org
https://www.ashrae.org/membership--conferences/student-zone/scholarships-and-grants/scholarship-program
Purpose: To support undergraduate students enrolled in an engineering or engineering technology program recognized by ASHRAE.
Eligibility: Applicants must be enrolled full-time in an accredited undergraduate engineering or engineering technology program recognized by ASHRAE. Students must maintain a GPA of no less than 3.0, demonstrate financial need and show a potential service to the HVAC&R profession. Applicants must also meet at least one of three criteria: undergraduate institution hosts a recognized ASHRAE student branch, program of study is accredited by the Accreditation Board for Engineering and Technology (ABET), program of study is accredited by an agency outside the USA that is a signatory of the Washington Accord or has a signed Memorandum of Understanding with ABET.
Target applicant(s): High school students. College students. Adult students.
Minimum GPA: 3.0
Amount: $5,000.
Number of awards: 1.
Scholarship may be renewable.
Deadline: December 1.
How to apply: Applications are available online.
Exclusive: Visit www.UltimateScholarshipBook.com and enter code AM82723 for updates on this award.

(828) · ASLA Council of Fellows Scholarships
Landscape Architecture Foundation
1129 20th Street NW, Suite 202, Washington, DC 20036
Phone: 202-331-7070
Email: scholarships@lafoundation.org
https://www.lafoundation.org/what-we-do/scholarships
Purpose: To encourage students who are financially needy or who are from underrepresented groups to pursue careers in landscape architecture.
Eligibility: Applicants must be U.S. citizens or permanent residents. They must be in the third, fourth or fifth year of a Landscape Architecture Accreditation Board (LAAB)-accredited undergraduate degree program in landscape architecture. Selection is based on the overall strength of the application.
Target applicant(s): College students. Adult students.
Amount: $5,000-$10,000.
Number of awards: Up to 4.

Deadline: February 1.
How to apply: Applications are available online. An application form, personal essay, two recommendation letters, financial aid information and an applicant photo are required.
Exclusive: Visit www.UltimateScholarshipBook.com and enter code LA82823 for updates on this award.

(829) · ASME Auxiliary Lucy and Charles W. E. Clarke Scholarship
American Society of Mechanical Engineers (ASME)
Two Park Avenue, New York, NY 10016-5990
Phone: 800-843-2763
Email: lefeverb@asme.org
https://www.asmefoundation.org/programs/stemeducation/asme-scholarships/
Purpose: To help FIRST Robotics team members who are interested in pursuing a career in mechanical engineering or mechanical engineering technology.
Eligibility: Applicants must be high school seniors who are FIRST Robotics team members. They must be nominated for the award by an ASME member, an ASME Auxiliary member or a student ASME member who is also involved with FIRST. Students must plan to enroll in an ABET-accredited or similarly accredited mechanical engineering or mechanical engineering technology degree program. They must be able to begin undergraduate studies no later than the fall following graduation from high school. Selection is based on the overall strength of the application.
Target applicant(s): High school students.
Amount: $5,000.
Number of awards: Varies.
Deadline: March 23.
How to apply: Applications are available online. An application form, nomination letter, resume or transcript and financial data worksheet are required.
Exclusive: Visit www.UltimateScholarshipBook.com and enter code AM82923 for updates on this award.

(830) · ASME Foundation Scholarships
American Society of Mechanical Engineers (ASME)
Two Park Avenue, New York, NY 10016-5990
Phone: 800-843-2763
Email: lefeverb@asme.org
https://www.asmefoundation.org/programs/stemeducation/asme-scholarships/
Purpose: To aid ASME student members who are enrolled in an undergraduate mechanical engineering, mechanical engineering technology or related degree program.
Eligibility: Applicants must be current ASME student members who are currently enrolled in (or have been accepted into) an ABET-accredited (or similarly accredited) undergraduate degree program in mechanical engineering, mechanical engineering technology or a subject related to one of these. They must be rising or current sophomores, juniors or seniors with a minimum 3.5 GPA. Selection is based on academic achievement and professional potential in engineering.
Target applicant(s): College students. Adult students.
Minimum GPA: 3.5
Amount: $11,000.
Number of awards: 1.
Deadline: March.
How to apply: Applications are available online through an electronic application system. Current ASME membership, submittal of

application through the online system, a transcript and recommendation letters are required.
Exclusive: Visit www.UltimateScholarshipBook.com and enter code AM83023 for updates on this award.

(831) · ASNE Scholarship Program

American Society of Naval Engineers
1423 Powhatan Street, Suite 1, Alexandria, VA 22314
Phone: 703-836-6727
Email: Scholarships@navalengineers.org
http://www.navalengineers.org/Education
Purpose: To encourage college students to enter the field of naval engineering and to provide support to naval engineers pursuing advanced education.
Eligibility: Applications must be for the last year of a full-time or co-op undergraduate program or for one year of full-time graduate study for a designated engineering or physical science degree at an accredited school. Applicants must be U.S. citizens pursuing careers in naval engineering. Graduate student applicants must be members of ASNE. An applicant's academic record, work history, professional promise and interest, extracurricular activities and recommendations are considered. Financial need may be considered.
Target applicant(s): College students. Graduate school students. Adult students.
Amount: $4,000.
Number of awards: Varies.
Deadline: February 7.
How to apply: Applications are available online or by written request.
Exclusive: Visit www.UltimateScholarshipBook.com and enter code AM83123 for updates on this award.

(832) · ASNT Fellowship

American Society for Nondestructive Testing
Awards and Honors Program, 1711 Arlingate Lane, P.O. Box 28518, Columbus, OH 43228-0518
Phone: 614-274-6003 x 233
Email: awards@asnt.org
http://www.asnt.org
Purpose: To fund research in nondestructive testing.
Eligibility: The award is given to an educational institution to fund research in nondestructive testing (NDT) at the postgraduate level. One proposal per faculty member will be considered annually. Applicants should submit a research proposal, a program of study, description of facilities, budget, background on faculty advisor, and background on a graduate student.
Target applicant(s): Graduate school students. Adult students.
Amount: $20,000.
Number of awards: Up to 5.
Deadline: October 15.
How to apply: Applications are available online.
Exclusive: Visit www.UltimateScholarshipBook.com and enter code AM83223 for updates on this award.

(833) · Association of Federal Communications Consulting Engineers Scholarships

Association of Federal Communications Consulting Engineers
P.O. Box 19333, Washington, DC 20036-0333
Phone: 703-780-4824
Email: scholarships@afcce.org
https://afcce.org/scholarships/

Purpose: To aid full-time undergraduate students attending an accredited college or university in pursuit of a degree in a telecommunications-related subject.
Eligibility: Applicants must be full-time (12+ units per semester) undergraduate or graduate students at an accredited postsecondary institution. They must be rising juniors or above and must be enrolled in a subject that is related to the radio communications consulting engineering field. They are encouraged to acquire an AFCCE member who will act as a sponsor. Selection is based on the overall strength of the application.
Target applicant(s): College students. Graduate school students. Adult students.
Amount: Up to $2,500.
Number of awards: Varies.
Deadline: October 31 (spring), May 31 (fall).
How to apply: Applications are available online. An application form, transcript, personal statement and sponsorship by an AFCCE member are required.
Exclusive: Visit www.UltimateScholarshipBook.com and enter code AS83323 for updates on this award.

(834) · Association of Food and Drug Officials Scholarship Award

Association of Food and Drug Officials
2550 Kingston Road, Suite 311, York, PA 17402
Phone: 717-757-2888
Email: afdo@afdo.org
http://www.afdo.org
Purpose: To support college students who are studying food, drug or consumer product safety.
Eligibility: Applicants must be in their third or fourth year of college at an accredited institution and demonstrate a desire to work in a career of research, regulatory work, quality control or teaching in an area related to food, drug or consumer product safety. Applicants must also have demonstrated leadership capabilities, a minimum 3.0 GPA and submit two letters of recommendation from faculty.
Target applicant(s): College students. Adult students.
Minimum GPA: 3.0
Amount: $1,500.
Number of awards: 3.
Deadline: March 1.
How to apply: Applications are available online.
Exclusive: Visit www.UltimateScholarshipBook.com and enter code AS83423 for updates on this award.

(835) · Association of Information Technology Professionals (AITP) Scholarships

Association of Information Technology Professionals (AITP) Scholarships
P.O. Box 583, Omaha, NE 68101
Email: omahaAITP@gmail.com
http://www.aitpomaha.com/scholarship-information.html
Purpose: To support students pursuing information systems and technology education.
Eligibility: Applicants must be enrolling in or currently enrolled in an accredited two- or four-year program in Nebraska, Iowa, Missouri, Kansas, North Dakota or South Dakota with the intent of earning a degree in information systems, computer science or related field.
Target applicant(s): High school students. College students. Adult students.
Amount: $1,000.

Number of awards: Varies.
Deadline: June 30.
How to apply: Applications are available online.
Exclusive: Visit www.UltimateScholarshipBook.com and enter code AS83523 for updates on this award.

(836) · ASTM International Katherine and Bryant Mather Scholarship

ASTM International
100 Barr Harbor Drive, P.O. Box C700, West Conshohocken, PA 19428-2959
Phone: 610-832-9585
Email: awards@astm.org
https://www.astm.org/memstudent23.html
Purpose: To aid students who are enrolled in degree programs that are related to the cement and concrete technology industry.
Eligibility: Applicants must be full-time undergraduate sophomores, undergraduate juniors, undergraduate seniors or graduate students. They must be enrolled in a degree program that is related to cement construction or concrete materials technology at an accredited institution of higher learning. Selection is based on the overall strength of the application.
Target applicant(s): College students. Graduate school students. Adult students.
Amount: Up to $7,500.
Number of awards: Varies.
Scholarship may be renewable.
Deadline: April.
How to apply: Applications are available online. An application form, one reference letter, an official transcript and a personal statement are required.
Exclusive: Visit www.UltimateScholarshipBook.com and enter code AS83623 for updates on this award.

(837) · Astronaut Scholarship

Astronaut Scholarship Foundation
Kennedy Space Center, SR 405, Titusville, FL 32899
Phone: 321-449-4876
Email: info@astronautscholarship.org
http://www.astronautscholarship.org
Purpose: To ensure the United States' continued leadership in science by assisting promising physical science and engineering students.
Eligibility: Applicants must be sophomore, junior or senior undergraduate or graduate students in natural or applied science, engineering or mathematics at Brown University, Colorado School of Mines, Clemson University, Florida Institute of Technology, Georgia Institute of Technology, Harvey Mudd College, Johns Hopkins University, Louisiana State University, Massachusetts Institute of Technology, Miami University, North Carolina State University, North Dakota State University, Ohio State, Pennsylvania State University, Purdue University, Syracuse University, Texas A&M University, Tufts University, University of Arizona, University of Central Florida, University of Chicago, University of Colorado, University of Kansas, University of Kentucky, University of Minnesota, University of Michigan, University of Oklahoma, University of Rochester, University of Southern California, University of Texas at Austin, University of Virginia, University of Washington, University of Wisconsin or Washington University and must be nominated by faculty or staff. Applicants may not directly apply for the scholarship. Students must have excellent grades and performed research or lab work in their field.

Target applicant(s): College students. Graduate school students. Adult students.
Amount: $10,000.
Number of awards: 32.
Deadline: Varies.
How to apply: Applicants must be nominated.
Exclusive: Visit www.UltimateScholarshipBook.com and enter code AS83723 for updates on this award.

(838) · ATLANT Women in Fintech

Atlant Women in Fintech
https://www.f6s.com/atlantmentorshipprogram/apply
Purpose: To support female students in the fields of computer science and technology.
Eligibility: Applicants must be female graduate students in the fields of computer science, computer engineering, informatics or a related technical field. Students must have a strong desire for professional and personal development and a commitment to the program for the entire duration.
Target applicant(s): Graduate school students. Adult students.
Amount: $5,600.
Number of awards: Up to 10.
Deadline: July.
How to apply: Applications are available online.
Exclusive: Visit www.UltimateScholarshipBook.com and enter code AT83823 for updates on this award.

(839) · AUA Foundation Research Scholars Program

American Foundation for Urologic Disease Inc.
1000 Corporate Boulevard, Linthicum, MD 21090
Phone: 410-689-3750
Email: grants@auafoundation.org
https://www.urologyhealth.org/research/for-researchers
Purpose: To help young men and women who intend to pursue careers in urologic research.
Eligibility: Applicants must be researchers who conduct their research in the U.S. or Canada. Funding is provided for post-doctoral research only.
Target applicant(s): Graduate school students. Adult students.
Amount: Varies.
Number of awards: Varies.
Deadline: November.
How to apply: Applications are available online.
Exclusive: Visit www.UltimateScholarshipBook.com and enter code AM83923 for updates on this award.

(840) · Automotive Hall of Fame Scholarships

Automotive Hall of Fame
Award and Scholarship Programs, 21400 Oakwood Boulevard, Dearborn, MI 48124
Phone: 313-240-4000
http://www.automotivehalloffame.org/scholarships/
Purpose: To assist students interested in automotive careers.
Eligibility: Applicants must be interested in automotive careers. Other requirements vary depending on the specific scholarship. Minimum GPA of 3.0 required.
Target applicant(s): High school students. College students. Adult students.
Minimum GPA: 3.0
Amount: Varies.

Number of awards: Varies.
Deadline: June 30.
How to apply: Applications are available online or by sending a self-addressed, stamped envelope.
Exclusive: Visit www.UltimateScholarshipBook.com and enter code AU84023 for updates on this award.

---

(841) · Auxiliary Legacy Scholarship

National Society of Professional Engineers
1420 King Street, Alexandria, VA 22314-2794
Phone: 703-684-2885
Email: students@nspe.org
https://www.nspe.org/resources/students/scholarships
Purpose: To aid female students who want to major in engineering.
Eligibility: Applicants must be female college sophomores majoring in engineering. Applicants must be U.S. citizens. Selection is based only on achievement.
Target applicant(s): College students. Adult students.
Amount: $2,500.
Number of awards: 1.
Scholarship may be renewable.
Deadline: April 1.
How to apply: Applications are available online.
Exclusive: Visit www.UltimateScholarshipBook.com and enter code NA84123 for updates on this award.

---

(842) · Avacare Medical Scholarship

Avacare Medical
1665 Corporate Road West, Lakewood, NJ 08701
Phone: 877-813-7799
Email: scholarships@avacaremedical.com
https://avacaremedical.com/scholarship
Purpose: To reward students who participate in inspiring acts of kindness.
Eligibility: Applicants must be at least 13 years of age, have a minimum 3.0 GPA and be a U.S. citizen. Students must be studying or planning on studying a medicine-related field. Students must be at least a high school senior. Selection is based on judge scores as well as public votes. Submissions may be a blog post, an image or a short video clip and should tell about an inspiring act of kindness. Finalists are selected based on content, creativity and quality of work.
Target applicant(s): High school students. College students. Graduate school students. Adult students.
Minimum GPA: 3.0
Amount: $1,000.
Number of awards: 1.
Deadline: December 15.
How to apply: A completed project must be mailed or emailed along with a transcript, full name, email address, phone number and which medical field pursuing.
Exclusive: Visit www.UltimateScholarshipBook.com and enter code AV84223 for updates on this award.

---

(843) · Aviation Distributors and Manufacturers Association Scholarship Program

Aviation Distributors and Manufacturers Association
100 North 20th Street, Suite 400, Philadelphia, PA 19103-1462
Phone: 215-320-3872
Email: adma@fernley.com
https://www.adma.org/

Purpose: To help students who are planning to pursue careers in aviation.
Eligibility: Applicants must be third- or fourth-year students enrolled at an accredited four-year institution of higher learning and working towards the Bachelor of Science (BS) in aviation management or professional piloting, or must be second-year A&P mechanic students enrolled in an accredited two-year program. They must have a minimum GPA of 3.0. Selection is based on academic achievement, recommendation letters, extracurricular activities, leadership skills and financial need.
Target applicant(s): College students. Adult students.
Minimum GPA: 3.0
Amount: Varies.
Number of awards: Varies.
Deadline: May 21.
How to apply: Applications are available online. An application form, two recommendation letters, a transcript and a personal statement are required.
Exclusive: Visit www.UltimateScholarshipBook.com and enter code AV84323 for updates on this award.

---

(844) · Aviation Insurance Association Education Foundation Scholarship

Aviation Insurance Association
7200 W. 75th Street, Overland Park, KS 66204
Phone: 913-627-9632
Email: mandie@aiaweb.org
http://www.aiaweb.org/Scholarships.aspx
Purpose: To help upper division undergraduate aviation students and graduate aviation students.
Eligibility: Applicants must be enrolled in an undergraduate or graduate program in aviation at a school that is a member of the University Aviation Association (UAA). They must have completed at least 45 units of coursework in their degree program, 15 or more of which must be for aviation courses. They must have a GPA of 2.5 or higher. Students must also currently be an intern or recently have completed an internship program within the aviation insurance industry in one of the following areas: agent/broker, underwriter, claims professional or attorney. Awards are given in the spring and fall.
Target applicant(s): College students. Graduate school students. Adult students.
Minimum GPA: 2.5
Amount: $2,500.
Number of awards: 4.
Deadline: Varies.
How to apply: Applications are available online. Five sets of the following items are required: application form, personal statement, transcript, one letter of recommendation and any FAA certificates (if applicable).
Exclusive: Visit www.UltimateScholarshipBook.com and enter code AV84423 for updates on this award.

---

(845) · Baroid Scholarship

American Ground Water Trust
50 Pleasant Street, Concord, NH 03301
Phone: 603-228-5444
https://agwt.org/content/scholarship-opportunities
Purpose: To support high school seniors intending to pursue a career in a groundwater-related field.

Eligibility: Applicants must be high school seniors entering an accredited four-year college or university and intending to pursue a career in a ground water-related field.
Target applicant(s): High school students.
Minimum GPA: 3.0
Amount: $2,000.
Number of awards: Varies.
Deadline: July 30.
How to apply: Applications are available online.
Exclusive: Visit www.UltimateScholarshipBook.com and enter code AM84523 for updates on this award.

(846) · Barry M. Goldwater Scholarship and Excellence in Education Program

Barry M. Goldwater Scholarship and Excellence in Education Foundation
6225 Brandon Avenue, Suite 315, Springfield, VA 22150
Phone: 703-756-6012
Email: goldwater@act.org
http://goldwater.scholarsapply.org
Purpose: To assist college students who pursue studies that lead to careers as scientists, mathematicians and engineers.
Eligibility: Applicants must be full-time college sophomores or juniors, U.S. citizens or resident aliens, have a minimum "B" GPA and be in the upper fourth of their class. Award must be used during the junior or senior year of college. Selection is based on potential and intent to pursue careers in mathematics, the natural sciences or engineering.
Target applicant(s): College students. Adult students.
Minimum GPA: 3.0
Amount: Up to $7,500.
Number of awards: Up to 300.
Deadline: January (last Friday).
How to apply: Institutions nominate college sophomores or juniors. Applicants may not apply directly to the foundation.
Exclusive: Visit www.UltimateScholarshipBook.com and enter code BA84623 for updates on this award.

(847) · Bart Kamen Memorial FIRST Scholarship

FIRST
200 Bedford Street, Manchester, NH 03101
Email: scholarships@firstinspires.org
https://www.firstinspires.org/bart-kamen-scholarship
Purpose: To support undergraduate students pursuing medical education.
Eligibility: Applicants must be a high school senior or graduate enrolling in an undergraduate program as a full-time student at a college or university in the U.S. Students must be applying for or accepted to a program in biomedical engineering or pre-med studies. Applicants must have participated for a minimum of one year as a team member on a FIRST LEGO league, FIRST Tech Challenge or FIRST Robotics competition team.
Target applicant(s): High school students.
Amount: $10,000.
Number of awards: 4.
Scholarship may be renewable.
Deadline: February.
How to apply: Applications are available online.
Exclusive: Visit www.UltimateScholarshipBook.com and enter code FI84723 for updates on this award.

(848) · Battery Division Student Research Award

Electrochemical Society
65 South Main Street, Building D, Pennington, NJ 08534-2839
Phone: 609-737-1902
Email: awards@electrochem.org
https://www.electrochem.org/student-awards
Purpose: To recognize young engineers and scientists in the field of electrochemical power sources.
Eligibility: Applicants must be accepted or enrolled in a college or university and must submit transcripts, an outline of the proposed research project, a description of how the project is related to the field of electrochemical power sources, a record of achievements in industrial work and a letter of recommendation from the research supervisor. Awards are based on academic performance, past research, proposed research and the recommendation.
Target applicant(s): High school students. College students. Graduate school students. Adult students.
Amount: $1,000.
Number of awards: Varies.
Deadline: March 15.
How to apply: Application materials are described online.
Exclusive: Visit www.UltimateScholarshipBook.com and enter code EL84823 for updates on this award.

(849) · Beef Industry Scholarship

National Cattlemen's Foundation
9110 East Nichols Avenue, Suite 300, Centennial, CO 80112
Phone: 303-694-0305
Email: ncf@beef.org
https://www.nationalcattlemensfoundation.org/scholarships
Purpose: To aid students who are preparing for careers in the beef industry.
Eligibility: Applicants must be graduating high school seniors or college undergraduates, and they must have plans to be enrolled full-time in a two-year or four-year undergraduate program during the upcoming academic year. They must be enrolled in a beef industry-related program of study and have a demonstrated interest in pursuing a career in the beef industry through previous coursework taken, internships completed or other life experiences. They or their families must be members of the National Cattlemen's Beef Association. Selection is based on the strength of the essay, letter of intent and reference letters.
Target applicant(s): High school students. College students. Adult students.
Amount: $1,500.
Number of awards: 10.
Scholarship may be renewable.
Deadline: December.
How to apply: Applications are available online. An application form, letter of intent, personal essay and two reference letters are required.
Exclusive: Visit www.UltimateScholarshipBook.com and enter code NA84923 for updates on this award.

(850) · Benjamin J. Keiser Memorial Coastal Engineering Scholarship

Surfers' Environmental Alliance
P.O. Box 3154, Long Branch, NJ 07740-3154
Email: rlee@seasurfer.org
https://www.seasurfer.org/sea-scholarships

Purpose: To support students who have a passion for environmental awareness and marine conservation.
Eligibility: Applicants must be in high school through graduate level studies, have at least a 3.2 GPA, be a U.S. citizen and be pursuing or plan on pursuing a degree in coastal engineering. Selection is based on goals, community service and involvement and academic excellence.
Target applicant(s): High school students. College students. Graduate school students. Adult students.
Minimum GPA: 3.2
Amount: Up to $3,500.
Number of awards: Varies.
Deadline: May.
How to apply: Applications are available online and include an essay.
Exclusive: Visit www.UltimateScholarshipBook.com and enter code SU85023 for updates on this award.

---

(851) · Benton-Meier Scholarships

American Psychological Association
750 First Street NE, Washington, DC 20002
Phone: 800-374-2721
https://www.apa.org/apf/funding
Purpose: To assist neuropsychology graduate students.
Eligibility: Applicants must demonstrate need and potential for a promising career in the field of neuropsychology. Applicants should also submit a letter that documents their scholarly and research accomplishments, financial need and how the award will be used.
Target applicant(s): Graduate school students. Adult students.
Amount: $2,000.
Number of awards: 1.
Deadline: June 1.
How to apply: A request for proposal form is available online.
Exclusive: Visit www.UltimateScholarshipBook.com and enter code AM85123 for updates on this award.

---

(852) · Berna Lou Cartwright Scholarship

American Society of Mechanical Engineers (ASME)
Two Park Avenue, New York, NY 10016-5990
Phone: 800-843-2763
Email: lefeverb@asme.org
https://www.asmefoundation.org/programs/stemeducation/asme-scholarships/
Purpose: To aid U.S. mechanical engineering majors.
Eligibility: Applicants must be U.S. citizens who are entering the final year of an ABET-accredited undergraduate degree program in mechanical engineering. Selection is based on academic achievement, character, participation in the American Society of Mechanical Engineers (if applicable) and financial need.
Target applicant(s): College students. Adult students.
Amount: $3,000.
Number of awards: Up to 2.
Deadline: February 18.
How to apply: Applications are available online. An application form, official transcript and three recommendation letters are required.
Exclusive: Visit www.UltimateScholarshipBook.com and enter code AM85223 for updates on this award.

---

(853) · Bili Kane Scholarship, Undergraduate

Shape America
1900 Association Drive, Reston, VA 20191
Phone: 800-213-7193

http://www.shapeamerica.org
Purpose: To support health education students.
Eligibility: Applicants must be full-time undergraduate health majors in their sophomore, junior or senior years. They must have a GPA of at least 3.25 and write an essay about what they hope to accomplish as a health educator.
Target applicant(s): College students. Adult students.
Minimum GPA: 3.25
Amount: $1,000.
Number of awards: 1.
Deadline: October 15.
How to apply: Applications are available online.
Exclusive: Visit www.UltimateScholarshipBook.com and enter code SH85323 for updates on this award.

---

(854) · Biographies of Contemporary Women in Mathematics Essay Contest

Association for Women in Mathematics
P.O. Box 40876, Providence, RI 02940
Phone: 401-455-4042
Email: awm@awm-math.org
http://www.awm-math.org
Purpose: To increase awareness of women's contributions to the mathematical sciences.
Eligibility: Applicants must interview a woman working in a mathematical career and write an essay based on the interview. Applicants may be from the sixth grade to graduate school students.
Target applicant(s): Junior high students or younger. High school students. College students. Adult students.
Amount: Varies.
Number of awards: At least 3.
Deadline: February 1.
How to apply: Applications are available online and must be submitted online.
Exclusive: Visit www.UltimateScholarshipBook.com and enter code AS85423 for updates on this award.

---

(855) · BMW/SAE Engineering Scholarship

Society of Automotive Engineers International
Scholarships Program, 400 Commonwealth Drive, Warrendale, PA 15096
Phone: 724-776-4841
Email: scholarships@sae.org
https://www.sae.org/participate/scholarships
Purpose: To support engineering students with high potential.
Eligibility: Applicants must be U.S. citizens with a GPA of 3.75 or higher. They must rank in the 90th percentile in math and critical reading on the SAT or ACT and must pursue an engineering or related degree through an ABET-accredited program.
Target applicant(s): College students. Adult students.
Minimum GPA: 3.75
Amount: $1,500.
Number of awards: 1.
Scholarship may be renewable.
Deadline: March 15.
How to apply: Applications are available online. An application form, transcript and SAT/ACT scores are required.
Exclusive: Visit www.UltimateScholarshipBook.com and enter code SO85523 for updates on this award.

(856) · BrightLife Direct Physical Therapy Scholarship

BrightLife Direct
1110 Bonifant Street, Suite 200, Silver Spring, MD 20910
Phone: 877-545-8585
Email: scholarship@brightlifedirect.com
http://www.brightlifedirect.com/brightlife-physical-therapist-scholarship.asp
Purpose: To assist students who are seeking to become certified occupational and physical therapists.
Eligibility: Applicants must be U.S. citizens, in good academic standing with a minimum 3.0 GPA, currently enrolled in a CAPTE or ACOTE accredited program and have completed at least one year of their program. Students will need to complete a short essay on why they decided to pursue a career in physical/occupational therapy.
Target applicant(s): College students. Adult students.
Minimum GPA: 3.0
Amount: $1,000.
Number of awards: 1.
Deadline: July 10.
How to apply: Applications are available online.
Exclusive: Visit www.UltimateScholarshipBook.com and enter code BR85623 for updates on this award.

(857) · Brill Family Scholarship

Society of Women Engineers
130 East Randolph Street, Suite 3500, Chicago, IL 60601
Phone: 877-793-4636
Email: scholarships@swe.org
https://swe.org/scholarships/
Purpose: To encourage women advancing in the field of engineering through a college education.
Eligibility: Applicants must have a minimum 3.0 GPA and be a full time student. Students must be U.S. citizens and must be planning to study at an ABET-accredited program in aeronautical/aerospace engineering or biomedical engineering.
Target applicant(s): College students. Adult students.
Minimum GPA: 3.0
Amount: $2,000.
Number of awards: 1.
Deadline: February 15.
How to apply: Applications are available online.
Exclusive: Visit www.UltimateScholarshipBook.com and enter code SO85723 for updates on this award.

(858) · Bryant L. Bench Carollo Engineers Inc. Scholarship

American Water Works Association
6666 W. Quincy Avenue, Denver, CO 80235-3098
Phone: 800-926-7337
Email: scholarships@awwa.org
http://www.awwa.org
Purpose: To support masters-level students interested in water-energy nexus within the water industry.
Eligibility: Applicants must be pursuing a masters degree. They must also have an interest in water-energy nexus issues in relation to water, water reuse or wastewater. This is a one-time award. Selection is based upon the overall strength of the application.
Target applicant(s): College students. Graduate school students. Adult students.
Amount: $10,000.

Number of awards: 1.
Deadline: December 20.
How to apply: Applications are available online.
Exclusive: Visit www.UltimateScholarshipBook.com and enter code AM85823 for updates on this award.

(859) · BSN Scholarship

Association of Rehabilitation Nurses
8735 W. Higgins Road, Suite 300, Chicago, IL 60631-2738
Phone: 800-229-7530
Email: info@rehabnurse.org
https://rehabnurse.org/membership/recognition/scholarship-opportunities
Purpose: To help nurses pursuing a bachelor's of science in nursing.
Eligibility: Applicants must be members of and involved in ARN, enrolled in a bachelor's of science in nursing (BSN) program, have completed at least one course, be currently practicing rehabilitation nursing and have a minimum of two years' experience in rehabilitation nursing. Applications, transcripts, a summary of professional and educational goals and achievements and two recommendation letters are required. Applications should be submitted by fax or email.
Target applicant(s): College students. Adult students.
Amount: $1,500.
Number of awards: Varies.
Deadline: July 1.
How to apply: Applications are available online.
Exclusive: Visit www.UltimateScholarshipBook.com and enter code AS85923 for updates on this award.

(860) · Bunge North America FFA Scholarship

National FFA Organization
P.O. Box 68960, 6060 FFA Drive, Indianapolis, IN 46268-0960
Phone: 888-332-2668
Email: scholarships@ffa.org
https://www.ffa.org/participate/grants-and-scholarships/
Purpose: To support FFA members working toward undergraduate degrees in select areas.
Eligibility: Applicants must be current FFA members under 23 years of age working toward two-year or four-year degrees at U.S. institutions in the areas of agricultural production, communication, education, management, finance, sales, marketing, science, engineering or public service in agriculture. Applicants must live in one of the 48 continental states and must possess a minimum 2.5 GPA. Selection is based on leadership ability and the overall strength of the application.
Target applicant(s): High school students. College students.
Minimum GPA: 2.5
Amount: $1,000.
Number of awards: 8.
Deadline: January 14.
How to apply: Applications are available online.
Exclusive: Visit www.UltimateScholarshipBook.com and enter code NA86023 for updates on this award.

(861) · C.B. Gambrell Undergraduate Scholarship

Institute of Industrial and Systems Engineers
3577 Parkway Lane, Suite 200, Norcross, GA 30092
Phone: 800-494-0460
Email: bcameron@iienet.org
http://www.iise.org/

Purpose: To help undergraduate industrial engineering students from the U.S.

Eligibility: Applicants must be full-time undergraduate students who have completed their freshman year in an accredited industrial engineering program, have a minimum 3.4 GPA, major in industrial engineering and be active members. Students may not apply directly for this scholarship and must be nominated. The award is based on academic ability, character, leadership, potential service to the industrial engineering profession and financial need.

Target applicant(s): College students. Adult students.

Minimum GPA: 3.4

Amount: $1,000.

Number of awards: 2.

Deadline: November 15.

How to apply: Nomination forms are available online.

Exclusive: Visit www.UltimateScholarshipBook.com and enter code IN86123 for updates on this award.

---

(862) · Campus Safety Health and Environmental Management Association Scholarship

Campus Safety Health, and Environmental Management Association (CSHEMA)

Scholarship Committee, 7044 South 13th Street, Oak Creek, WI 53154

Phone: 703-234-4141

Email: info@cshema.org

https://www.cshema.org

Purpose: To encourage the study of safety.

Eligibility: Applicants must be full-time undergraduate or graduate students with at least one year left in their degree program. Applicants must also write an essay about health, safety or environmental issues relevant to the university or college campus.

Target applicant(s): High school students. College students. Adult students.

Amount: $3,000.

Number of awards: 1.

Deadline: April 15.

How to apply: Applications are available online.

Exclusive: Visit www.UltimateScholarshipBook.com and enter code CA86223 for updates on this award.

---

(863) · Careers in Agriculture Scholarship Program

Winfield Solutions LLC

Careers in Agriculture - MS 5735, P.O. Box 64281, St. Paul, MN 55164-0281

Phone: 855-494-6343

Email: info@winfieldsolutionsllc.com

https://www.winfieldunited.com

Purpose: To aid high school seniors and college freshmen and sophomores who are interested in pursuing a career in agriculture.

Eligibility: Applicants must be high school seniors who plan to enroll in a two-year or four-year degree program related to agriculture in the fall following graduation or first- or second-year college students pursuing degrees in agronomy, crop production or related fields. Dependents of employees of Winfield Solutions LLC or Land O' Lakes Inc. are ineligible. Selection is based on academic achievement, proven leadership in agriculture and professional interest in the field of agriculture.

Target applicant(s): High school students. College students. Adult students.

Amount: $5,000.

Number of awards: 4.

Deadline: May 22.

How to apply: Applications are available online. An application form, two character evaluations, a transcript and a personal essay are required.

Exclusive: Visit www.UltimateScholarshipBook.com and enter code WI86323 for updates on this award.

---

(864) · Carville M. Akehurst Memorial Scholarship

Horticultural Research Institute

525 9th Street NW, Suite 800, Washington, DC 20004

Phone: 202-789-2900

http://www.hriresearch.org

Purpose: To provide scholarships for undergraduate and graduate students who plan to pursue careers in horticulture.

Eligibility: Applicants must be enrolled full-time in a landscaping or horticultural program at a two- or four-year accredited institution and be residents of Maryland, Virginia or West Virginia.

Target applicant(s): College students. Graduate school students. Adult students.

Minimum GPA: 2.7

Amount: Up to $3,000.

Number of awards: 1.

Scholarship may be renewable.

Deadline: September 10.

How to apply: Applications are available online.

Exclusive: Visit www.UltimateScholarshipBook.com and enter code HO86423 for updates on this award.

---

(865) · Cedarcrest Farms Scholarship

American Jersey Cattle Association

6486 East Main Street, Reynoldsburg, OH 43068-2362

Phone: 614-861-3636

Email: info@usjersey.com

http://www.usjersey.com

Purpose: To aid American Jersey Cattle Association members studying dairy product marketing, large animal veterinary practice, dairy manufacturing or dairy production.

Eligibility: Applicants must be AJCA members studying dairy manufacturing, dairy product marketing, dairy production or large animal veterinary practice at the undergraduate or graduate level. They must have a GPA of 2.5 or above and must plan to pursue a career in agriculture. Selection is based on the overall strength of the application.

Target applicant(s): College students. Graduate school students. Adult students.

Minimum GPA: 2.5

Amount: $1,250.

Number of awards: Varies.

Deadline: July 1.

How to apply: Applications are available online. An application form, transcript and up to two letters of recommendation are required.

Exclusive: Visit www.UltimateScholarshipBook.com and enter code AM86523 for updates on this award.

---

(866) · Chairish Design Your Future Scholarship

Chairish

465 California Street, Suite 1250, San Francisco, CA 94104

https://www.chairish.com/pages/scholarship

Purpose: To support students pursuing design-related fields.

Eligibility: Applicants must be currently enrolled or enrolling at an accredited two-year, four-year or technical institution in the United States and pursuing a degree in the design and engineering-related

fields. Students must be from an underrepresented or disadvantaged background such as a racial minority or have a disability, have a minimum 3.0 GPA and must submit an essay along with the application.
Target applicant(s): High school students. College students. Graduate school students. Adult students.
Minimum GPA: 3.0
Amount: $2,500.
Number of awards: 2.
Deadline: January 1 and June 30.
How to apply: Applications are available online.
Exclusive: Visit www.UltimateScholarshipBook.com and enter code CH86623 for updates on this award.

(867) · Charles H. Bussmann Undergraduate Scholarship

Marine Technology Society
1100 H Street NW, Suite LL-100, Washington, DC 20005
Phone: 202-717-8705
https://www.mtsociety.org/scholarships
Purpose: To support Marine Technology Society members who are pursuing an undergraduate degree in a marine-related field.
Eligibility: Applicants must be MTS student members who are accepted for enrollment or enrolled full-time at an educational institution. Selection is based on the overall strength of the application.
Target applicant(s): High school students. College students. Adult students.
Amount: $2,500.
Number of awards: 1.
Deadline: April 15.
How to apply: Applications are available online.
Exclusive: Visit www.UltimateScholarshipBook.com and enter code MA86723 for updates on this award.

(868) · Charlotte McGuire Scholarship

American Holistic Nurses Association
AHNA Office Manager, 2900 SW Plass Court, Topeka, KS 66611-1980
Phone: 800-278-2462 x10
Email: info@ahna.org
http://www.ahna.org
Purpose: To provide scholarships to nurses in undergraduate or graduate nursing programs or other graduate programs related to holistic nursing.
Eligibility: Applicants must be pursuing an education in holistic nursing and be members of the AHNA. Applicants must have a minimum 3.0 GPA.
Target applicant(s): College students. Graduate school students. Adult students.
Minimum GPA: 3.0
Amount: $1,000.
Number of awards: 2.
Deadline: April 15.
How to apply: Applications are available online or from AHNA Headquarters.
Exclusive: Visit www.UltimateScholarshipBook.com and enter code AM86823 for updates on this award.

(869) · ChiroHealthUSA Foxworth Family Scholarship

ChiroHealthUSA
120 Stone Creek Boulevard, Suite 100, Flowood, MS 39232
https://www.chirohealthusa.com/students/foxworth-family-scholarship/
Purpose: To support students studying chiropractic health.
Eligibility: Applicants must be full-time students enrolled in a doctorate of chiropractic program at an accredited U.S. institution and hold a minimum 2.7 GPA. Students must provide two recommendations along with their application.
Target applicant(s): Graduate school students. Adult students.
Minimum GPA: 2.7
Amount: $15,000.
Number of awards: 1.
Deadline: April 30.
How to apply: Applications are available online.
Exclusive: Visit www.UltimateScholarshipBook.com and enter code CH86923 for updates on this award.

(870) · Chuck Reville, K3FT Memorial Scholarship

Foundation for Amateur Radio Inc.
FAR Scholarships, P.O. Box 911, Columbia, MD 21044
Phone: 410-552-2652
Email: farscholarships@gmail.com
http://www.farweb.org
Purpose: To support licensed amateur radio enthusiasts who are pursuing bachelor's degrees in engineering or any of the physical sciences.
Eligibility: Applicants must be licensed amateur radio enthusiasts who are enrolled full-time in a bachelor's degree program in engineering or physical science. Selection is based on the overall strength of the application.
Target applicant(s): College students. Adult students.
Amount: $1,000.
Number of awards: 1.
Deadline: April 30.
How to apply: Applications are available online. An application form is required.
Exclusive: Visit www.UltimateScholarshipBook.com and enter code FO87023 for updates on this award.

(871) · Colgate Bright Smiles, Bright Futures Minority Scholarships

American Dental Hygienists' Association (ADHA) Institute for Oral Health
Scholarship Award Program, 444 North Michigan Avenue, Suite 3400, Chicago, IL 60611
Phone: 312-440-8900
Email: institute@adha.net
https://www.adha.org/ioh-scholarships-main
Purpose: To support members of groups underrepresented in dental hygiene programs.
Eligibility: Applicants must have completed one year of an accredited dental hygiene curriculum and be a member of a group that is underrepresented in the field of dental hygiene. Examples of eligible groups include African-American, Hispanic, Asian, Native American and male students. Applicants must also demonstrate financial need of at least $1,500, be active members of SADHA or ADHA and submit a goals statement.
Target applicant(s): College students. Adult students.
Amount: $1,250.
Number of awards: 2.
Deadline: February 2.
How to apply: Applications are available online.

Exclusive: Visit www.UltimateScholarshipBook.com and enter code AM87123 for updates on this award.

(872) · Collegiate Inventors Competition

National Inventors Hall of Fame
3701 Highland Park NW, North Canton, OH 44720
Phone: 330-849-6887
Email: collegiate@invent.org
http://www.invent.org
Purpose: To encourage college students in science, engineering, mathematics, technology and creative invention and to stimulate interest in technology and economic leadership.
Eligibility: Applicants must have been full-time college or university students during part of the 12-month period prior to the entry date. Up to four students may work as a team, and at least one student must meet the full-time criteria. Judging is based on originality and inventiveness, as well as the invention's potential value to society.
Target applicant(s): College students. Graduate school students. Adult students.
Amount: Varies.
Number of awards: Varies.
Deadline: June.
How to apply: Applications are available online.
Exclusive: Visit www.UltimateScholarshipBook.com and enter code NA87223 for updates on this award.

(873) · Complete Water Solutions Scholarship

Complete Water Solutions
851 West Main Street, Twin Lakes, WI 53181
Phone: 855-787-4200
Email: scholarships@complete-water.com
https://www.complete-water.com/complete-water-solutions-scholarship
Purpose: To support students who are interested in trades (plumbing, HVAC, boiler operators, electrical), reverse osmosis or water quality.
Eligibility: Applicants must be current or prospective students enrolled in a trade school, water treatment certified training course or an accredited institution in the United States. Students must submit a two- to three-minute video or an essay on a specific subject matter.
Target applicant(s): High school students. College students. Adult students.
Amount: $2,500.
Number of awards: 1.
Deadline: June 1.
How to apply: Applications are available online.
Exclusive: Visit www.UltimateScholarshipBook.com and enter code CO87323 for updates on this award.

(874) · Composites Division/Harold Giles Scholarship

Society of Plastics Engineers
6 Berkshire Boulevard, Suite 306, Bethel, CT 06801
Phone: 203-775-0471
Email: info@4spe.org
http://www.4spe.org/spe-foundation
Purpose: To aid undergraduate and graduate students who have an interest in the plastics industry.
Eligibility: Applicants must have an interest in the plastics industry, major in or take courses leading to a career in the plastics industry and be in good academic standing. Financial need is considered.

Target applicant(s): College students. Graduate school students. Adult students.
Amount: Varies.
Number of awards: 2.
Deadline: April 1.
How to apply: Applications are available online.
Exclusive: Visit www.UltimateScholarshipBook.com and enter code SO87423 for updates on this award.

(875) · Computational Science Graduate Fellowship

Department of Energy
Krell Institute, 1609 Golden Aspen Drive, Suite 101, Ames, IA 50010
Phone: 515-956-3696
https://www.krellinst.org/csgf/
Purpose: To support students pursuing a Ph.D. in engineering and the physical, computer, mathematical or life sciences.
Eligibility: Applicants must be enrolled at an accredited U.S. college or university during the fellowship period.
Target applicant(s): College students. Adult students.
Amount: Varies.
Number of awards: Varies.
Scholarship may be renewable.
Deadline: January 12.
How to apply: Applications are available online.
Exclusive: Visit www.UltimateScholarshipBook.com and enter code DE87523 for updates on this award.

(876) · Corrosion Division Morris Cohen Graduate Student Award

Electrochemical Society
65 South Main Street, Building D, Pennington, NJ 08534-2839
Phone: 609-737-1902
Email: awards@electrochem.org
https://www.electrochem.org/student-awards
Purpose: To recognize graduate research in corrosion science and/or engineering.
Eligibility: Applicants must be graduate students who have completed all the requirements for their degrees within two years prior to the nomination deadline. Nomination may be made by the applicant's research supervisor or someone familiar with the applicant's research work. A summary of the applicant's master's or Ph.D. research work, reports, memberships and involvement with scientific societies, awards, an academic record and reprints of publications are required.
Target applicant(s): College students. Graduate school students. Adult students.
Amount: $1,000 plus travel expenses.
Number of awards: 1.
Deadline: December 15.
How to apply: Application materials are listed online.
Exclusive: Visit www.UltimateScholarshipBook.com and enter code EL87623 for updates on this award.

(877) · Creative Biolabs

Creative Biolabs
45 Ramsey Road, Shirley, NY 11967
Phone: 631-871-5806
Email: marketing@creative-biolabs.com
https://www.creative-biolabs.com/scholarship-program.html

Purpose: To support students pursuing medical and science-related education.
Eligibility: Applicants must be enrolled as a freshman, undergraduate, graduate or doctoral student at an accredited college or university. Students must be pursuing a major in a science-related field. Applicants must have a cumulative grade point average of 3.0 or higher. Students must submit, application, transcripts and essay. Selection criteria includes GPA, learning plan, leadership ability and social concerns.
Target applicant(s): College students. Graduate school students. Adult students.
Minimum GPA: 3.0
Amount: $1,000.
Number of awards: 1.
Deadline: September 30.
How to apply: Applications are available online.
Exclusive: Visit www.UltimateScholarshipBook.com and enter code CR87723 for updates on this award.

(878) · Crest Oral-B Laboratories Dental Hygiene Scholarships

American Dental Hygienists' Association (ADHA) Institute for Oral Health
Scholarship Award Program, 444 North Michigan Avenue, Suite 3400, Chicago, IL 60611
Phone: 312-440-8900
Email: institute@adha.net
https://www.adha.org/ioh-scholarships-main
Purpose: To support students pursuing a baccalaureate degree with an interest in research in dental hygiene as well as private and public dental hygiene education.
Eligibility: Applicants must be full-time students at an accredited college or university in the United States pursuing a baccalaureate degree in dental hygiene or a related field and must have completed at least one year of a dental hygiene curriculum. Applicants must also have a strong interest in pursuing research in dental hygiene and promoting private and public dental hygiene education, be active members of the ADHA, have a minimum dental hygiene GPA of 3.5 and have a minimum demonstrated financial need of $1,500. Selection is based upon professional and academic excellence and the overall strength of the application.
Target applicant(s): College students. Adult students.
Minimum GPA: 3.5
Amount: $3,000.
Number of awards: 2.
Deadline: November 2.
How to apply: Applications are available online after October 1.
Exclusive: Visit www.UltimateScholarshipBook.com and enter code AM87823 for updates on this award.

(879) · Cummin's Inc. Scholarship

Society of Women Engineers
130 East Randolph Street, Suite 3500, Chicago, IL 60601
Phone: 877-793-4636
Email: scholarships@swe.org
https://swe.org/scholarships/
Purpose: To support African-American female college engineering students.
Eligibility: Applicants must be U.S. citizens with a 3.0 GPA, be from an under-represented group and be willing to intern. Students must major in automotive engineering, chemical engineering, computer engineering, computer science, electrical engineering, industrial engineering, mechanical engineering, manufacturing engineering, materials science and engineering, industrial systems, metrology or metallurgy.
Target applicant(s): College students. Adult students.
Minimum GPA: 3.0
Amount: $2,500.
Number of awards: 2.
Deadline: February 15.
How to apply: Applications are available online.
Exclusive: Visit www.UltimateScholarshipBook.com and enter code SO87923 for updates on this award.

(880) · Curtis E. Huntington Memorial Scholarship

Actuarial Foundation
475 North Martingale Road, Suite 600, Schaumburg, IL 60173
Phone: 847-706-3535
Email: scholarships@actfnd.org
http://www.actuarialfoundation.org
Purpose: To assist students who plan to become actuaries.
Eligibility: Students must be enrolled as a full-time senior student at a U.S. accredited educational institution, have successfully completed at least one actuarial examination, have a minimum cumulative GPA of 3.0 (on 4.0 scale) and must be nominated by a professor at their school. Only two applicants per school permitted.
Target applicant(s): College students. Adult students.
Minimum GPA: 3.0
Amount: $3,000.
Number of awards: Varies.
Deadline: March 31.
How to apply: Applications are available online.
Exclusive: Visit www.UltimateScholarshipBook.com and enter code AC88023 for updates on this award.

(881) · Dairy Student Recognition Program

National Dairy Shrine
P.O. Box 725, Denmark, WI 54208
Phone: 920-863-6333
Email: info@dairyshrine.org
http://www.dairyshrine.org
Purpose: To recognize graduating college seniors planning careers related to dairy.
Eligibility: Applicants must be U.S. citizens planning to enter the fields such as dairy production agriculture, marketing, agricultural law, business, veterinary medicine or environmental science. Selection is based on leadership skills, academic achievement and interest in dairy cattle.
Target applicant(s): High school students. College students. Adult students.
Amount: Varies.
Number of awards: Varies.
Deadline: April 15.
How to apply: Applications are available online, and two applicants per college or university are accepted each year.
Exclusive: Visit www.UltimateScholarshipBook.com and enter code NA88123 for updates on this award.

(882) · Dan L. Meisinger Sr. Memorial Learn to Fly Scholarship

National Air Transportation Foundation Meisinger Scholarship
818 Connecticut Avenue NW, Suite 900, Washington, DC 20006

Phone: 202-774-1535
Email: safety1st@nata.aero
http://www.nata.aero
Purpose: To provide an annual flight training scholarship.
Eligibility: Applicants must be college students enrolled in an aviation program with a B or better GPA and residents of Kansas, Missouri or Illinois will be given preference. Students should be recommended by an aviation professional; independent applications are also considered.
Target applicant(s): College students. Graduate school students. Adult students.
Minimum GPA: 3.0
Amount: $2,500.
Number of awards: Varies.
Deadline: Last Friday in November.
How to apply: Applications are available online.
Exclusive: Visit www.UltimateScholarshipBook.com and enter code NA88223 for updates on this award.

(883) · David A. O'Neil Scholarship
Society of Naval Architects and Marine Engineers (SNAME)
99 Canal Center Plaza, Suite 310, Alexandria, VA 22314
Phone: 703-997-6701
Email: scholarships@sname.org
https://www.sname.org/scholarships
Purpose: To aid students who are pursuing a master's degree in a subject that is related to the marine industry.
Eligibility: Applicants must be members of the Society of Naval Architects and Marine Engineers (SNAME). They must be working towards a master's degree in ocean engineering, marine engineering, naval architecture or another marine-related subject. Students who will be receiving their degree before October 1 of the application year are ineligible. Selection is based on the overall strength of the application.
Target applicant(s): College students. Graduate school students. Adult students.
Amount: Up to $20,000.
Number of awards: Varies.
Deadline: February 1.
How to apply: Applications are available online. An application form, transcript, standardized test scores and three recommendation letters are required.
Exclusive: Visit www.UltimateScholarshipBook.com and enter code SO88323 for updates on this award.

(884) · David Alan Quick Scholarship
EAA Aviation Center
3000 Poberezny Road, Oshkosh, WI 54902
Phone: 920-426-4800
Email: scholarships@eaa.org
http://www.eaa.org/en/eaa
Purpose: To support students in aerospace or aeronautical engineering.
Eligibility: Applicants must be in their junior or senior year at an accredited college or university pursuing a degree in aerospace or aeronautical engineering. Applicants must be involved in school and community activities as well as aviation and be EAA members or be recommended by an EAA member.
Target applicant(s): College students. Adult students.
Amount: $500.
Number of awards: 1.
Scholarship may be renewable.
Deadline: January 31.
How to apply: Applications are available online.

Exclusive: Visit www.UltimateScholarshipBook.com and enter code EA88423 for updates on this award.

(885) · David Arver Memorial Scholarship
Aircraft Electronics Association
3570 NE Ralph Powell Road, Lee's Summit, MO 64064
Phone: 816-347-8400
Email: info@aea.net
https://aea.net/educationalfoundation/scholarships.asp
Purpose: To support students who wish to pursue a career in avionics or aircraft repair.
Eligibility: Applicants must be high school seniors or college students who plan to or are attending an accredited school in an avionics or aircraft repair program.
Target applicant(s): High school students. College students. Adult students.
Amount: $1,000.
Number of awards: 1.
Deadline: April 1.
How to apply: Applications are available by contacting the organization for more information.
Exclusive: Visit www.UltimateScholarshipBook.com and enter code AI88523 for updates on this award.

(886) · David R. Jones IV Scholarship
Association of Modified Asphalt Producers
AMAP Headquarters, P.O. Box 305, Avon, OH 44011
Phone: 314-843-2627
http://modifiedasphalt.org
Purpose: To support graduate and undergraduate students in asphalt technology.
Eligibility: Applicants must be college graduate or undergraduate students who are currently enrolled at an accredited college and have completed their sophomore year. Students must be majoring in a field that is related to asphalt technology such as chemical engineering, civil engineering, chemistry or any related major. Applicants with experience and interest in the field of asphalt technology will be given preference.
Target applicant(s): College students. Graduate school students. Adult students.
Amount: $2,000.
Number of awards: 3.
Deadline: January.
How to apply: Applications are available online.
Exclusive: Visit www.UltimateScholarshipBook.com and enter code AS88623 for updates on this award.

(887) · DEED Funding Opportunities
Demonstration of Energy and Efficiency Developments (DEED)
1875 Connecticut Avenue, NW, Suite 1200, Washington, DC 20009
Phone: 202-467-2960
Email: DEED@publicpower.org
http://www.publicpower.org
Purpose: To support engineering students interested in technical careers.
Eligibility: Applicants must be U.S. citizens attending an accredited college, university or vocational institution full-time and must not be graduating within a year of the application deadline. Selection is based on the overall strength of the application.
Target applicant(s): College students. Graduate school students. Adult students.

Amount: $5,000.
Number of awards: Varies.
Deadline: February 15, October 15.
How to apply: Applications are available online.
Exclusive: Visit www.UltimateScholarshipBook.com and enter code DE88723 for updates on this award.

(888) · Delta Faucet Company Scholarships

PHCC Educational Foundation
180 South Washington Street, Suite 100, Falls Church, VA 22046
Phone: 800-533-7694
Email: scholarships@naphcc.org
http://www.phccweb.org
Purpose: To elevate the technical and business competence of the plumbing-heating-cooling (p-h-c) industry by awarding scholarships to students who are enrolled in a p-h-c-related major.
Eligibility: Applicants must be students who are currently enrolled or plan to be enrolled in a PHCC-approved plumbing or HVACR apprentice program at an accredited four-year college or university or two-year technical college, community college or trade school. Apprentice program students must also be working full-time for a licensed plumbing or HVAC contractor who is a member of the Plumbing-Heating-Cooling Contractors-National Association. Students must be enrolled in a full-time certificate or degree program at an accredited two-year community college, technical college, or trade school, with a major directly related to the plumbing-heating-cooling (p-h-c) profession such as the following: business management; mechanical CAD design; construction management with a specialty in mechanical construction and plumbing or HVACR installation, service and repair. Applicants can also be enrolled in a full-time undergraduate degree program at an accredited four-year college or university in the following majors: business management; construction management with a specialization in mechanical construction and mechanical engineering.
Target applicant(s): High school students. College students. Adult students.
Amount: $2,500.
Number of awards: 6.
Deadline: May 1.
How to apply: Applications are available online, by email or by phone.
Exclusive: Visit www.UltimateScholarshipBook.com and enter code PH88823 for updates on this award.

(889) · Desk and Derrick Educational Trust

Desk and Derrick Educational Trust
c/o Natalie Bright, 1415 23rd Street, Canyon, TX 79015
Phone: 281-392-7181
Email: info@theeducationaltrust.org
http://theeducationaltrust.org/
Purpose: To promote studies in the energy industry.
Eligibility: Applicants must be U.S. or Canadian citizens, have completed two years of undergraduate study, have a minimum 3.2 GPA and demonstrate financial need. Students must be pursuing a degree in a field related to the petroleum, energy or allied industries and plan to work full-time in the petroleum, energy or allied industry or research alternative fuels such as coal, electric, solar, wind hydroelectric, nuclear or ethanol.
Target applicant(s): College students. Adult students.
Minimum GPA: 3.2
Amount: Varies.
Number of awards: Varies.
Deadline: April 1.

How to apply: Applications are available online.
Exclusive: Visit www.UltimateScholarshipBook.com and enter code DE88923 for updates on this award.

(890) · DMI Milk Marketing Scholarship

National Dairy Shrine
P.O. Box 725, Denmark, WI 54208
Phone: 920-863-6333
Email: info@dairyshrine.org
http://www.dairyshrine.org
Purpose: To encourage students to pursue careers in the marketing of dairy foods.
Eligibility: Applicants must be second, third or fourth year college students at two- or four-year universities, have a minimum 2.5 GPA and major in dairy science, animal science, agricultural communications, agricultural education, general agriculture or food and nutrition.
Target applicant(s): College students. Adult students.
Minimum GPA: 2.5
Amount: $1,000-$1,500.
Number of awards: Up to 5.
Deadline: April 15.
How to apply: Applications are available online.
Exclusive: Visit www.UltimateScholarshipBook.com and enter code NA89023 for updates on this award.

(891) · DNA Day Essay Contest

American Society of Human Genetics
6120 Executive Boulevard, Suite 500, Rockville, MD 20852
Phone: 301-634-7300
http://www.ashg.org
Purpose: To support high school students who are interested in genetics.
Eligibility: Applicants must be in grades 9-12 and submit an essay in which they discuss the application of gene therapy in curing or repairing a particular disease or condition. Selection favors presentations that offer well-reasoned arguments, thus exemplifying a student's deep understanding of all concepts related to the essay question.
Target applicant(s): High school students.
Amount: Up to $1,000.
Number of awards: 13.
Deadline: March 1.
How to apply: Applications are available online.
Exclusive: Visit www.UltimateScholarshipBook.com and enter code AM89123 for updates on this award.

(892) · Donald F. and Mildred Topp Othmer Scholarships

American Institute of Chemical Engineers - (AIChE)
120 Wall Street, Floor 23, New York, NY 10005-4020
Phone: 800-242-4363
Email: awards@aiche.org
https://www.aiche.org/community/awards
Purpose: To support AIChE student members.
Eligibility: Applicants must be members of an AIChE Student Chapter or Chemical Engineering Club. Applicants must be nominated by their student chapter advisors. Awards are presented on the basis of academic achievement and involvement in student chapter activities.
Target applicant(s): College students. Graduate school students. Adult students.
Amount: $1,000.

Number of awards: 15.
Deadline: June 15.
How to apply: Applications are available online.
Exclusive: Visit www.UltimateScholarshipBook.com and enter code AM89223 for updates on this award.

(893) · Dorothy Budnek Memorial Scholarship

Association for Radiologic and Imaging Nursing
2201 Cooperative Way, Suite 600, Herndon, VA 20171
Phone: 866-486-2762
Email: info@arinursing.org
https://www.arinursing.org/about/awards-scholarships/
Purpose: To help ARNA members continue their nursing education.
Eligibility: Applicants must be active members of the American Radiological Nurses Association for three years, have a current nursing license and be enrolled in an approved academic program. Students should submit the application, a statement of purpose, two recommendation letters, a transcript which shows a minimum 2.5 GPA, a statement of financial support and a copy of the nursing license.
Target applicant(s): Graduate school students. Adult students.
Minimum GPA: 2.5
Amount: $600.
Number of awards: 1.
Deadline: October 30.
How to apply: Applications are available online.
Exclusive: Visit www.UltimateScholarshipBook.com and enter code AS89323 for updates on this award.

(894) · Dorothy M. and Earl S. Hoffman Award

American Vacuum Society
125 Maiden Lane, 15th Floor, New York, NY 10038
Phone: 212-248-0200
Email: angela@avs.org
http://www.avs.org
Purpose: To recognize excellence in continuing graduate studies in the sciences and technologies related to AVS.
Eligibility: Applicants must be graduate students in an accredited academic institution. An application, summary of research, letters of recommendation and transcript are required. The award is based on achievement in research and academic record. The top five student nominees are invited to present talks on their research to the trustees at the international symposium. The trustees then select one recipient for the Dorothy M. and Earl S. Hoffman Award. The award covers travel expenses to the symposium.
Target applicant(s): Graduate school students. Adult students.
Amount: Varies.
Number of awards: 1.
Deadline: May 1.
How to apply: Applications are available online.
Exclusive: Visit www.UltimateScholarshipBook.com and enter code AM89423 for updates on this award.

(895) · Douglas Dockery Thomas Fellowship in Garden History and Design

Landscape Architecture Foundation
1129 20th Street NW, Suite 202, Washington, DC 20036
Phone: 202-331-7070
Email: scholarships@lafoundation.org
https://www.lafoundation.org/what-we-do/scholarships
Purpose: To aid graduate students who are working on research projects related to garden design.
Eligibility: Applicants must be graduate students who are enrolled at a U.S. college or university. They must be researching some aspect of garden design. Selection is based on academic merit and applicability of proposed research to the aims of the Garden Club of America.
Target applicant(s): Graduate school students. Adult students.
Amount: $4,000.
Number of awards: 1.
Deadline: February 1.
How to apply: Application instructions are available online. A cover letter, research proposal, budget proposal, resume and three recommendation letters are required.
Exclusive: Visit www.UltimateScholarshipBook.com and enter code LA89523 for updates on this award.

(896) · Dr. Esther Wilkins Scholarship

American Dental Hygienists' Association (ADHA) Institute for Oral Health
Scholarship Award Program, 444 North Michigan Avenue, Suite 3400, Chicago, IL 60611
Phone: 312-440-8900
Email: institute@adha.net
https://www.adha.org/ioh-scholarships-main
Purpose: To support students who have completed an entry-level program in dental hygiene and are pursuing additional degrees in order to obtain a career in dental hygiene education.
Eligibility: Applicants must be full-time students at an accredited college or university in the United States pursuing a degree in dental hygiene education or a related field and must have completed at least one year of a dental hygiene curriculum. Applicants must also have completed an entry-level program in dental hygiene and be active members of the ADHA. They must have a minimum 3.0 GPA and have a minimum demonstrated financial need of $1,500. Selection is based upon the overall strength of the application.
Target applicant(s): College students. Graduate school students. Adult students.
Minimum GPA: 3.0
Amount: $1,000.
Number of awards: Varies.
Deadline: February 1.
How to apply: Applications are available online after October 1. An application form and essay are required.
Exclusive: Visit www.UltimateScholarshipBook.com and enter code AM89623 for updates on this award.

(897) · Duane M. Hanson Scholarship

American Society of Heating, Refrigerating and Air-Conditioning Engineers (ASHRAE)
1791 Tullie Circle, NE, Atlanta, GA 30329
Phone: 404-636-8400
Email: lbenedict@ashrae.org
https://www.ashrae.org/membership--conferences/student-zone/scholarships-and-grants/scholarship-program
Purpose: To support engineering students pursuing a degree that will prepare them for an HVAC&R profession.
Eligibility: Applicants must be enrolled in a full-time undergraduate engineering program of study traditionally designed to prepare students for a career in HVAC&R professions. Students must have GPA of at least 3.0. Applicants must also meet at least one of three criteria: undergraduate institution hosts a recognized ASHRAE student

branch, program of study is accredited by the Accreditation Board for Engineering and Technology (ABET), program of study is accredited by an agency outside the U.S. that is a signatory of the Washington Accord or has a signed Memorandum of Understanding with ABET.

Target applicant(s): High school students. College students. Adult students.

Minimum GPA: 3.0

Amount: $5,000.

Number of awards: 1.

Scholarship may be renewable.

Deadline: December 1.

How to apply: Applications are available online.

Exclusive: Visit www.UltimateScholarshipBook.com and enter code AM89723 for updates on this award.

(898) · Dutch and Ginger Arver Scholarship

Aircraft Electronics Association

3570 NE Ralph Powell Road, Lee's Summit, MO 64064

Phone: 816-347-8400

Email: info@aea.net

https://aea.net/educationalfoundation/scholarships.asp

Purpose: To support students who wish to pursue a career in avionics or aircraft repair.

Eligibility: Applicants must be high school seniors or college students who plan to or are attending an accredited school in avionics or aircraft repair.

Target applicant(s): High school students. College students. Adult students.

Amount: $1,000.

Number of awards: 1.

Deadline: April 1.

How to apply: Applications are available by contacting the organization for more information.

Exclusive: Visit www.UltimateScholarshipBook.com and enter code AI89823 for updates on this award.

(899) · Dwight D. Gardner Scholarship

Institute of Industrial and Systems Engineers

3577 Parkway Lane, Suite 200, Norcross, GA 30092

Phone: 800-494-0460

Email: bcameron@iienet.org

http://www.iise.org/

Purpose: To reward undergraduate members.

Eligibility: Applicants must be undergraduate students enrolled in a college in the United States, Canada or Mexico with an accredited industrial engineering program, major in industrial engineering and be active members. Students may not apply directly for this scholarship and must be nominated. The award is based on academic ability, character, leadership, potential service to the industrial engineering profession and financial need.

Target applicant(s): High school students. College students. Adult students.

Minimum GPA: 3.4

Amount: $2,500-$3,500.

Number of awards: 3.

Deadline: November 15.

How to apply: Nomination forms are available online.

Exclusive: Visit www.UltimateScholarshipBook.com and enter code IN89923 for updates on this award.

(900) · E. Noel Luddy Scholarship

Association of Federal Communications Consulting Engineers

P.O. Box 19333, Washington, DC 20036-0333

Phone: 703-780-4824

Email: scholarships@afcce.org

https://afcce.org/scholarships/

Purpose: To support students majoring in engineering, broadcasting, telecommunications or related fields.

Eligibility: Applicants must be full-time students working towards an undergraduate degree at an accredited four-year educational institution or a graduate degree through an accredited program in engineering or a field related to broadcasting or telecommunications. Selection is based on the overall strength of the application.

Target applicant(s): College students. Graduate school students. Adult students.

Amount: Up to $2,500.

Number of awards: Varies.

Deadline: October 31, May 31.

How to apply: Applications are available online. An application form, AFCCE sponsor, personal statement and transcript are required.

Exclusive: Visit www.UltimateScholarshipBook.com and enter code AS90023 for updates on this award.

(901) · E.J. Sierieja Memorial Fellowship

Institute of Industrial and Systems Engineers

3577 Parkway Lane, Suite 200, Norcross, GA 30092

Phone: 800-494-0460

Email: bcameron@iienet.org

http://www.iise.org/

Purpose: To reward graduate students pursuing advanced studies in the area of transportation.

Eligibility: Applicants must be full-time graduate students, majoring in transportation and active members. Students may not apply directly for this scholarship and must be nominated. The award is based on academic ability, character, leadership, potential service to the industrial engineering profession and financial need. Preference is given to students focusing on rail transportation.

Target applicant(s): Graduate school students. Adult students.

Minimum GPA: 3.4

Amount: $2,000.

Number of awards: 1.

Deadline: November 15.

How to apply: Nomination forms are available online.

Exclusive: Visit www.UltimateScholarshipBook.com and enter code IN90123 for updates on this award.

(902) · East Asia and Pacific Summer Institutes

National Science Foundation East Asia and Pacific Summer Institutes

4201 Wilson Boulevard, Arlington, VA 22230

Phone: 703-292-5111

Email: eapsi@nsf.gov

https://www.nsf.gov/

Purpose: To develop globally-engaged U.S. scientists and engineers knowledgeable about the Asian and Pacific regions.

Eligibility: Applicants must be U.S. graduate students enrolled in a research-oriented master's or Ph.D. program or college graduates enrolled in a joint bachelor's/master's program at a U.S. institution. Students must pursue studies in science, engineering and education research. The award provides summer research experience in Australia, China,

Japan, Korea, New Zealand, Singapore or Taiwan, a $5,000 stipend, round-trip airfare, living expenses and orientation in Washington, DC.
Target applicant(s): Graduate school students. Adult students.
Amount: $5,000 stipend plus airfare and living expenses.
Number of awards: Varies.
Deadline: November.
How to apply: Applications are available online. A cover sheet, application form, project summary, project description, biographical sketch, two letters of recommendation and supplementary documents listed on the website are required.
Exclusive: Visit www.UltimateScholarshipBook.com and enter code NA90223 for updates on this award.

(903) · Edward D. Hendrickson/SAE Engineering Scholarship

Society of Automotive Engineers International
Scholarships Program, 400 Commonwealth Drive, Warrendale, PA 15096
Phone: 724-776-4841
Email: scholarships@sae.org
https://www.sae.org/participate/scholarships
Purpose: To reward students pursuing an engineering or related science degree.
Eligibility: Students must maintain a 3.75 GPA. Applicants must rank in the 90th percentile in both math and critical reading on either the SAT or the ACT. Scholarship may be renewed for an additional three years. Students must be pursuing their degree through an ABET accredited program.
Target applicant(s): High school students. College students. Adult students.
Minimum GPA: 3.75
Amount: $5,000.
Number of awards: 1.
Scholarship may be renewable.
Deadline: March 15.
How to apply: Applications are available online.
Exclusive: Visit www.UltimateScholarshipBook.com and enter code SO90323 for updates on this award.

(904) · Eight and Forty Lung and Respiratory Nursing Scholarship Fund

American Legion
Attn.: Americanism and Children and Youth Division, P.O. Box 1055, Indianapolis, IN 46206
Phone: 317-630-1249
Email: acy@legion.org
http://www.legion.org
Purpose: To assist registered nurses.
Eligibility: Applicants must plan to be employed full-time in hospitals, clinics or health departments in a position related to lung and respiratory control.
Target applicant(s): College students. Graduate school students. Adult students.
Minimum GPA: 3.0
Amount: $3,000.
Number of awards: Varies.
Deadline: May 15.
How to apply: Applications are available by written request.
Exclusive: Visit www.UltimateScholarshipBook.com and enter code AM90423 for updates on this award.

(905) · Elekta Radiation Therapy Scholarship

American Society of Radiologic Technologists Foundation (ASRT)
ASRT Foundation, 15000 Central Avenue South East, Albuquerque, NM 87123
Phone: 800-444-2778
Email: foundation@asrt.org
https://foundation.asrt.org/what-we-do/scholarships
Purpose: To encourage the best radiation therapy students to pursue a higher education.
Eligibility: Applicants must be members of the American Society of Radiologic Technologists (ASRT) and must be U.S. citizens, national or permanent residents. Students must finish their certificate or program degree by September 1 of the year in which scholarship applications are due. Applicants must be enrolled in an accredited radiologic science programs with at least one semester of radiologic studies completed with a 3.0 GPA and be in good standing with ASRT.
Target applicant(s): College students. Adult students.
Minimum GPA: 3.0
Amount: $5,000.
Number of awards: 4.
Scholarship may be renewable.
Deadline: Varies.
How to apply: Applications are available online.
Exclusive: Visit www.UltimateScholarshipBook.com and enter code AM90523 for updates on this award.

(906) · Elizabeth McLean Memorial Scholarship

Society of Women Engineers
130 East Randolph Street, Suite 3500, Chicago, IL 60601
Phone: 877-793-4636
Email: scholarships@swe.org
https://swe.org/scholarships/
Purpose: To support female students working towards a career in civil engineering.
Eligibility: Applicants must be women majoring in civil engineering with a 3.0 GPA. Students must be in school full-time.
Target applicant(s): College students. Adult students.
Minimum GPA: 3.0
Amount: $1,500.
Number of awards: 1.
Deadline: February 15.
How to apply: Applications are available online.
Exclusive: Visit www.UltimateScholarshipBook.com and enter code SO90623 for updates on this award.

(907) · Elmer J. and Hester Jane Johnson Memorial FFA Scholarship

National FFA Organization
P.O. Box 68960, 6060 FFA Drive, Indianapolis, IN 46268-0960
Phone: 888-332-2668
Email: scholarships@ffa.org
https://www.ffa.org/participate/grants-and-scholarships/
Purpose: To support FFA members working toward a four-year degree in agricultural education.
Eligibility: Applicants must complete the financial portion of the application and be pursuing a four-year degree in agricultural education. Selection is based upon financial need, leadership ability and academic ability.
Target applicant(s): High school students. College students.
Amount: $1,000.

Number of awards: 1.
Deadline: January 14.
How to apply: Applications are available online.
Exclusive: Visit www.UltimateScholarshipBook.com and enter code NA90723 for updates on this award.

(908) · Elson T. Killam Memorial Scholarship

New England Water Works Association
125 Hopping Brook Road, Holliston, MA 01746
Phone: 508-893-7979
Email: tmacelhaney@preloadinc.com
http://www.newwa.org
Purpose: To support civil and environmental engineering students who are members of the New England Water Works Association.
Eligibility: Applicants must be enrolled in a civil or environmental engineering degree program and must be members of NEWWA. Students must reside in New England or attend a college/university in New England. Selection is based on the overall strength of the application.
Target applicant(s): High school students. College students. Graduate school students. Adult students.
Amount: $1,500.
Number of awards: 1.
Deadline: April 1.
How to apply: Applications are available online. An application form, official transcript and one recommendation letter are required.
Exclusive: Visit www.UltimateScholarshipBook.com and enter code NE90823 for updates on this award.

(909) · ENA Foundation Undergraduate Scholarship

Emergency Nurses Association
915 Lee Street, Des Plaines, IL 60016
Phone: 847-460-4100
Email: foundation@ena.org
http://www.ena.org
Purpose: To promote research and education in emergency care.
Eligibility: Applicants must be nurses pursuing baccalaureate degrees in nursing and must have been ENA members for at least 12 months before applying. Selection is based on application, statement of goals, references and transcript.
Target applicant(s): College students. Adult students.
Amount: $2,500.
Number of awards: 1.
Deadline: April 30.
How to apply: Applications are available online.
Exclusive: Visit www.UltimateScholarshipBook.com and enter code EM90923 for updates on this award.

(910) · EngineerGirl Essay Contest

National Academy of Engineering
500 Fifth Street NW, Room 1047, Washington, DC 20001
http://www.engineergirl.org
Purpose: To support engineering-minded elementary, middle and high school students.
Eligibility: Applicants must be a student in the third through twelfth grades who submit an essay positing how engineering might positively impact a vulnerable species' life. One submission only; also, employees or those related to or living with employees of the National Academies of Sciences, Engineering and Medicine are prohibited from applying, as are prior winners who wish to reapply within the same category.

Target applicant(s): Junior high students or younger. High school students.
Amount: $500.
Number of awards: 1.
Deadline: February 1.
How to apply: Applications are available online.
Exclusive: Visit www.UltimateScholarshipBook.com and enter code NA91023 for updates on this award.

(911) · Engineering Undergraduate Scholarship

American Society for Nondestructive Testing
Awards and Honors Program, 1711 Arlingate Lane, P.O. Box 28518, Columbus, OH 43228-0518
Phone: 614-274-6003 x 233
Email: awards@asnt.org
http://www.asnt.org
Purpose: To support students studying nondestructive testing.
Eligibility: Applicants must be undergraduate students enrolled in an engineering program and specialize in nondestructive testing (NDT). A nominating letter, transcript, three letters of recommendation and an essay describing the role of NDT/NDE in their career are required.
Target applicant(s): College students. Adult students.
Amount: $3,000.
Number of awards: Up to 3.
Deadline: December 15.
How to apply: Applications are available online.
Exclusive: Visit www.UltimateScholarshipBook.com and enter code AM91123 for updates on this award.

(912) · Eugene S. Kropf Scholarship

University Aviation Association - Eugene S. Kropf Scholarship
Kevin R. Kuhlmann, Professor of Aviation and Aerospace Science, Metropolitan State College of Denver, Campus Box 30, P.O. Box 173362, Denver, CO 80217-3362
Phone: 334-844-2434
Email: uaamail@uaa.aero
http://www.uaa.aero/
Purpose: To support students studying an aviation-related curriculum.
Eligibility: Applicants must be U.S. citizens enrolled in an aviation-related curriculum of a two-year or a four-year degree at a UAA member college or university. Students must have a 3.0 GPA and write a 250-word paper on how they can improve aviation education.
Target applicant(s): College students. Adult students.
Minimum GPA: 3.0
Amount: $500.
Number of awards: 1.
Deadline: June 30.
How to apply: Applications are available online.
Exclusive: Visit www.UltimateScholarshipBook.com and enter code UN91223 for updates on this award.

(913) · Evolve IP Scholarship

Evolve IP
989 Old Eagle School Road, Suite 815, Wayne, PA 19087
Phone: 610-964 8000
Email: social@evolveip.net
http://www.evolveip.net/about/careers#scholarship
Purpose: To support students who are pursuing a degree in technology or computer sciences.

Eligibility: Applicants must be a high school or college student who plans on a career in technology or computer sciences. Scholarships will be awarded based on need in addition to the strength of the student's academic background and demonstrated leadership.
Target applicant(s): High school students. College students. Graduate school students. Adult students.
Amount: $1,500.
Number of awards: 2.
Deadline: June 30.
How to apply: Applications are available online
Exclusive: Visit www.UltimateScholarshipBook.com and enter code EV91323 for updates on this award.

(914) · ExploraVision Science Competition

ExploraVision
Toshiba/NSTA ExploraVision Awards, 1840 Wilson Boulevard, Arlington, VA 22201
Phone: 800-397-5679
http://www.exploravision.org
Purpose: To encourage students to contemplate the technology of the future through working together and researching the technology and science of today.
Eligibility: Applicants must be citizens or legal residents of the United States or Canada who are no older than 21. Students must enter in teams of two to four. Teams must submit an entry form, an abstract, a description of their project, a bibliography and five sample web pages. Twenty-four teams will be selected as winners based on scientific accuracy, communication, feasibility of vision and creativity of their projects.
Target applicant(s): Junior high students or younger. High school students.
Amount: $10,000.
Number of awards: 48-96.
Deadline: February 8.
How to apply: Applications are available online.
Exclusive: Visit www.UltimateScholarshipBook.com and enter code EX91423 for updates on this award.

(915) · Ezoe Memorial Foundation Academic Scholarship

Ezoe Memorial Foundation
208, Toranomon Hoso Building, I-20-3, Nishi-Shinbashi, Minato-ku, Tokyo Japan, 105-0003
Email: info@ezoe-mf.or.jp
https://www.recruit-foundation.org/en/
Purpose: To support students interested in being globally active in their field.
Eligibility: Applicants must be under 24 years old on April 1 and be currently enrolled or planning to enroll in a college outside of Japan that meets the criteria of being in the top 30 schools, being a top 30 school for the applicant's field of study or ranking as a number one school. Students must be pursuing a science-related program and be interested in becoming globally active. The application process and interviews will be held in Japanese.
Target applicant(s): High school students. College students. Adult students.
Amount: Varies.
Number of awards: 10.
Deadline: October 4.
How to apply: Applications are available online.

Exclusive: Visit www.UltimateScholarshipBook.com and enter code EZ91523 for updates on this award.

(916) · F.W. Beich Beichley Scholarship

American Society of Mechanical Engineers (ASME)
Two Park Avenue, New York, NY 10016-5990
Phone: 800-843-2763
Email: lefeverb@asme.org
https://www.asmefoundation.org/programs/stemeducation/asme-scholarships/
Purpose: To support mechanical engineering students.
Eligibility: Applicants must be ASME student members enrolled in an eligible accredited mechanical engineering baccalaureate program. Selection is based on leadership, scholastic ability, potential contribution to the mechanical engineering profession and financial need. The scholarship is only applicable for study in the junior or senior year.
Target applicant(s): College students. Adult students.
Amount: $3,000.
Number of awards: 1.
Deadline: February 17.
How to apply: Applications are available online.
Exclusive: Visit www.UltimateScholarshipBook.com and enter code AM91623 for updates on this award.

(917) · FarmAid FFA Scholarship

National FFA Organization
P.O. Box 68960, 6060 FFA Drive, Indianapolis, IN 46268-0960
Phone: 888-332-2668
Email: scholarships@ffa.org
https://www.ffa.org/participate/grants-and-scholarships/
Purpose: To support students who are FFA members, come from family farms and are pursuing four-year degrees in agriculture.
Eligibility: Applicants must complete the financial analysis part of the application. A minimum GPA of 2.0 is required. Selection is based on the overall strength of the application.
Target applicant(s): High school students. College students.
Minimum GPA: 2.0
Amount: $3,000 over three years.
Number of awards: 4.
Deadline: January 14.
How to apply: A complete application form is required.
Exclusive: Visit www.UltimateScholarshipBook.com and enter code NA91723 for updates on this award.

(918) · Father James B. Macelwane Annual Award in Meteorology

American Meteorological Society
Fellowship and Scholarship Department, 45 Beacon Street, Boston, MA 02108-3693
Phone: 617-227-2426 x246
Email: dsampson@ametsoc.org
http://www.ametsoc.org/AMS/
Purpose: To encourage interest in meteorology among college students.
Eligibility: Applicants must be enrolled as undergraduates and submit an original student paper on an aspect of atmospheric science. No more than two students from any one institution may enter papers in any one contest, and there is no application form needed.
Target applicant(s): College students. Adult students.
Amount: $1,000.
Number of awards: 1.

Deadline: June 4.
How to apply: Submit materials to address listed.
Exclusive: Visit www.UltimateScholarshipBook.com and enter code AM91823 for updates on this award.

(919) · Feeding Tomorrow General Education Scholarships/Freshman Scholarships

Institute of Food Technologists (IFT)
525 W. Van Buren, Suite 1000, Chicago, IL 60607
Phone: 312-782-8424
Email: ejplummer@ift.org
https://www.ift.org/community/students
Purpose: To help young food scientists who plan to work in industry, government and academia.
Eligibility: Applicants for the freshman scholarships must be academically outstanding high school graduates or seniors who will enter college for the first time in an approved program in food science/technology and must have a minimum 3.0 GPA. All candidates must submit applications, transcripts and a recommendation.
Target applicant(s): High school students.
Minimum GPA: 3.0
Amount: Varies.
Number of awards: Varies.
Deadline: June 15.
How to apply: Applications are available online.
Exclusive: Visit www.UltimateScholarshipBook.com and enter code IN91923 for updates on this award.

(920) · Fellowship Award

Damon Runyon Cancer Research Foundation
One Exchange Plaza, 55 Broadway, Suite 302, New York, NY 10006
Phone: 212-455-0520
Email: awards@damonrunyon.org
http://www.damonrunyon.org
Purpose: To support the training of postdoctoral scientists as they start their research careers.
Eligibility: Applicants must have completed one or more of the following degrees or its equivalent: M.D., Ph.D., M.D./Ph.D., D.D.S. or D.V.M. Applicants should submit an application cover sheet, sponsor's biographical sketch, CV, degree certificate, letter, research proposal, summary of research form, up to three reprints of work and four letters of reference. This is a three-year award with various deadlines and funding. The research must be conducted at a university, hospital or research institution. International candidates may apply to do their research only in the United States.
Target applicant(s): Graduate school students. Adult students.
Amount: $52,000-$60,000 plus expenses.
Number of awards: Varies.
Deadline: March 15 and August 16.
How to apply: Applications are available online.
Exclusive: Visit www.UltimateScholarshipBook.com and enter code DA92023 for updates on this award.

(921) · Fellowship in Aerospace History

American Historical Association
400 A Street SE, Washington, DC 20003
Phone: 202-544-2422
Email: info@historians.org
http://www.historians.org
Purpose: To provide funding for an academic research project related to aerospace history.
Eligibility: Applicants must possess a doctorate degree in history or a related field or be enrolled in a doctorate program (all coursework completed). One fellow will be appointed for one academic year. The fellow will be expected to write a report and present a paper or lecture on the research at the end of the term.
Target applicant(s): Graduate school students. Adult students.
Amount: $21,250.
Number of awards: At least 1.
Deadline: April 1.
How to apply: Applications are available online.
Exclusive: Visit www.UltimateScholarshipBook.com and enter code AM92123 for updates on this award.

(922) · Foundation for Neonatal Research and Education Scholarships

Foundation for Neonatal Research and Education
c/o Anthony J. Jannetti Inc., East Holly Avenue, Box 56, Pitman, NJ 08071-0056
Phone: 856-256-2343
Email: contact@fnre.com
https://www2.ajj.com/client-partners/associations-conferences-and-publications/foundation-neonatal-research-and-education
Purpose: To aid practicing neonatal nurses who are pursuing additional education through an undergraduate or graduate degree program in nursing.
Eligibility: Applicants must be accepted into a Bachelor of Science in Nursing (BSN) program (current Registered Nurses), a Master of Science in Nursing (MSN) program for advanced practice in neonatal nursing, a doctoral degree program in nursing or a Master's or post-Master's nursing degree program in Business Management or Nursing Administration. They must have a GPA of 3.0 or higher and must be actively involved in neonatal nursing at the professional level. They cannot have received a grant or scholarship from the FNRE within the past five years, and they cannot be current members of the FNRE Scholarship Committee or Board. Selection is based on the overall strength of the application.
Target applicant(s): College students. Graduate school students. Adult students.
Minimum GPA: 3.0
Amount: Varies.
Number of awards: Varies.
Deadline: May 1.
How to apply: Applications are available online. An application form, resume, enrollment verification letter, personal statement, three evaluation letters and a transcript are required.
Exclusive: Visit www.UltimateScholarshipBook.com and enter code FO92223 for updates on this award.

(923) · Foundation for Surgical Technology Medical Mission Scholarship

Association of Surgical Technologists
6 W. Dry Creek Circle, Littleton, CO 80120
Phone: 800-637-7433
Email: scholarships@ast.org
http://ffst.org/
Purpose: To help practitioners with continuing education or medical missionary work.

Eligibility: Applicants must be active AST members, document the educational program or mission program and provide two recommendation letters.
Target applicant(s): Adult students.
Amount: Varies.
Number of awards: Varies.
Deadline: December 31.
How to apply: Applications are available online.
Exclusive: Visit www.UltimateScholarshipBook.com and enter code AS92323 for updates on this award.

(924) · Foundation for Surgical Technology Scholarships

Association of Surgical Technologists
6 W. Dry Creek Circle, Littleton, CO 80120
Phone: 800-637-7433
Email: scholarships@ast.org
http://ffst.org/
Purpose: To support the continuing education of surgical technology students.
Eligibility: Applicants should be enrolled in accredited surgical technology programs and be eligible to sit for the Certified Surgical Technologist examination sponsored by the National Board of Surgical Technology and Surgical Assisting. Applications, transcripts, a minimum 3.0 GPA, essays and recommendation letters are required.
Target applicant(s): College students. Adult students.
Minimum GPA: 3.0
Amount: Varies.
Number of awards: Varies.
Deadline: March 1.
How to apply: Applications are available online.
Exclusive: Visit www.UltimateScholarshipBook.com and enter code AS92423 for updates on this award.

(925) · Frank and Brennie Morgan Prize for Outstanding Research in Mathematics by an Undergraduate Student

American Mathematical Society and Mathematical Association of America
Professor Carla Savage, MAA Secretary, Computer Science Department, North Carolina State University, Box 8206, Raleigh, NC 27695
Phone: 410-704-2980
Email: siegel@towson.edu
http://www.ams.org
Purpose: Awarded to an undergraduate student (or students who have collaborated) for research in the field of mathematics.
Eligibility: Applicants must be undergraduate students at colleges or universities in the United States or its possessions, Canada and Mexico. Students must be nominated.
Target applicant(s): High school students. College students. Adult students.
Amount: $1,200.
Number of awards: 1.
Deadline: June 30.
How to apply: Nomination information is available by email. Questions should be directed to Dr. Martha J. Siegel at the address above. Nominations and submissions should be sent to: Morgan Prize Committee, c/o Robert J. Daverman, American Mathematical Society, 312D Ayres Hall, University of Tennessee, Knoxville, TN 37996.

Exclusive: Visit www.UltimateScholarshipBook.com and enter code AM92523 for updates on this award.

(926) · Frank and Dorothy Miller ASME Auxiliary Scholarships

American Society of Mechanical Engineers (ASME)
Two Park Avenue, New York, NY 10016-5990
Phone: 800-843-2763
Email: lefeverb@asme.org
https://www.asmefoundation.org/programs/stemeducation/asme-scholarships/
Purpose: To support U.S. mechanical engineering and mechanical engineering technology undergraduates.
Eligibility: Applicants must be U.S. citizens and residents of North America. They must be rising undergraduate sophomores, juniors or seniors who are enrolled in an ABET-accredited (or equivalent) mechanical engineering, mechanical engineering technology or related program at a U.S. postsecondary institution. They must be ASME student members who are in good standing. Selection is based on leadership, integrity and potential contribution to the field of mechanical engineering.
Target applicant(s): College students. Adult students.
Amount: $2,000.
Number of awards: 2.
Deadline: February 18.
How to apply: The application form is available through ASME's online scholarship application system. This form, an official transcript, a personal statement and up to two recommendation letters are required.
Exclusive: Visit www.UltimateScholarshipBook.com and enter code AM92623 for updates on this award.

(927) · Fred M. Young, Sr./SAE Engineering Scholarship

Society of Automotive Engineers International
Scholarships Program, 400 Commonwealth Drive, Warrendale, PA 15096
Phone: 724-776-4841
Email: scholarships@sae.org
https://www.sae.org/participate/scholarships
Purpose: To support high school seniors who are planning to study engineering at the undergraduate level.
Eligibility: Applicants must be U.S. citizens and must be high school seniors. They must have SAT or ACT scores that rank in the 90th percentile and must have a GPA of 3.75 or higher on a four-point scale. They must plan to enroll in an ABET-accredited undergraduate engineering program. Selection is based on the overall strength of the application.
Target applicant(s): High school students.
Minimum GPA: 3.75
Amount: $1,000.
Number of awards: 1.
Scholarship may be renewable.
Deadline: March 15.
How to apply: Applications are available online. An application form, official transcript and standardized test scores are required.
Exclusive: Visit www.UltimateScholarshipBook.com and enter code SO92723 for updates on this award.

(928) · Freshman Undergraduate Scholarship

American Meteorological Society
Fellowship and Scholarship Department, 45 Beacon Street, Boston, MA 02108-3693
Phone: 617-227-2426 x246
Email: dsampson@ametsoc.org
http://www.ametsoc.org/AMS/
Purpose: To encourage high school students to pursue careers in the atmospheric and related oceanic and hydrologic sciences.
Eligibility: Applicants must enter as full-time freshmen the following fall and major in the atmospheric or related oceanic and hydrologic sciences. Applicants should submit applications, transcripts, recommendation letter and SAT or equivalent scores.
Target applicant(s): High school students.
Amount: $5,000.
Number of awards: Varies.
Scholarship may be renewable.
Deadline: February 5.
How to apply: Applications are available online.
Exclusive: Visit www.UltimateScholarshipBook.com and enter code AM92823 for updates on this award.

(929) · Full-Time Employee Student Scholarship

Air Traffic Control Association
225 Reinekers Lane, Suite 400, Alexandria, VA 22314
Phone: 703-299-2430
Email: info@atca.org
http://www.atca.org
Purpose: To help students in advanced study programs in air traffic control and other aviation disciplines.
Eligibility: Applicants must be full-time employees enrolled in advanced study programs to improve their skills in air traffic control or an aviation discipline.
Target applicant(s): College students. Graduate school students. Adult students.
Amount: Varies.
Number of awards: Varies.
Deadline: May 15.
How to apply: Applications are available online. An application form, two letters of reference, academic transcripts, an essay and answers to career and leadership questions are required.
Exclusive: Visit www.UltimateScholarshipBook.com and enter code AI92923 for updates on this award.

(930) · Future Leaders in Tech Scholarship

Perlego
138 Holborn, London, England EC1N 2SW
https://www.perlego.com/mission-scholarship-bursary-programme
Purpose: To support students who are underprivileged, persons of color and/or females interested in studying technology, computer science and select engineering courses.
Eligibility: Applicants must be current high school and college students who are at least 16 years of age or older and are underprivileged, persons of color and/or females. Students must attend or plan to attend a two-year or four-year college, university, vocational or technical school or certificate program and be U.S. citizens or permanent legal residents. Applicants must be interested in studying technology, computer science and select engineering courses and have a minimum 3.0 GPA. An essay on a provided prompt is required to be submitted.
Target applicant(s): High school students. College students. Adult students.
Minimum GPA: 3.0
Amount: $20,000.
Number of awards: 1.
Deadline: August 20.
How to apply: Applications are available online.
Exclusive: Visit www.UltimateScholarshipBook.com and enter code PE93023 for updates on this award.

(931) · Gabriel A. Hartl Scholarship

Air Traffic Control Association
225 Reinekers Lane, Suite 400, Alexandria, VA 22314
Phone: 703-299-2430
Email: info@atca.org
http://www.atca.org
Purpose: To support air traffic control students.
Eligibility: Applicants must be enrolled half- to full-time in a two- to four-year air traffic control program at an institution approved and/or licensed by the Federal Aviation Administration as directly supporting the FAA's college and training initiative.
Target applicant(s): High school students. College students. Adult students.
Amount: Varies.
Number of awards: Varies.
Deadline: May 15.
How to apply: Applications are available online.
Exclusive: Visit www.UltimateScholarshipBook.com and enter code AI93123 for updates on this award.

(932) · Gaige Fund Award

American Society of Ichthyologists and Herpetologists
P.O. Box 1897, Lawrence, KS 66044-8897
Phone: 785-843-1235
Email: asih@allenpress.com
https://asih.org/student-awards
Purpose: To support young herpetologists.
Eligibility: Applicants must be members of ASIH and studying for an advanced degree. The award may be used for museum or laboratory study, travel, fieldwork or other activities that will enhance their careers and their contributions to the science of herpetology. Both merit and need will be considered.
Target applicant(s): College students. Graduate school students. Adult students.
Amount: $400-$1,000.
Number of awards: Varies.
Deadline: March 1.
How to apply: Applications are available by email or written request.
Exclusive: Visit www.UltimateScholarshipBook.com and enter code AM93223 for updates on this award.

(933) · Garland Duncan Scholarships

American Society of Mechanical Engineers (ASME)
Two Park Avenue, New York, NY 10016-5990
Phone: 800-843-2763
Email: lefeverb@asme.org
https://www.asmefoundation.org/programs/stemeducation/asme-scholarships/
Purpose: To support mechanical engineering students.

Eligibility: Applicants must be ASME student members, be enrolled in an eligible accredited mechanical engineering baccalaureate program, have strong academic performance and be college sophomores, juniors or seniors. Selection is based on character, integrity, leadership, scholastic ability, potential contribution to the mechanical engineering profession and financial need.

Target applicant(s): College students. Adult students.

Amount: $5,000.

Number of awards: 2.

Deadline: February 18.

How to apply: Applications are available online.

Exclusive: Visit www.UltimateScholarshipBook.com and enter code AM93323 for updates on this award.

(934) · Garmin Scholarship

Aircraft Electronics Association
3570 NE Ralph Powell Road, Lee's Summit, MO 64064
Phone: 816-347-8400
Email: info@aea.net
https://aea.net/educationalfoundation/scholarships.asp

Purpose: To support students who wish to pursue a career in avionics and aircraft repair.

Eligibility: Applicants must be high school seniors or college students who plan to or are attending an accredited school in an avionics or aircraft repair program.

Target applicant(s): High school students. College students. Adult students.

Amount: $2,000.

Number of awards: Varies.

Deadline: April 1.

How to apply: Applications are available online.

Exclusive: Visit www.UltimateScholarshipBook.com and enter code AI93423 for updates on this award.

(935) · Gary Wagner, K3OMI, Scholarship

American Radio Relay League Foundation
225 Main Street, Newington, CT 06111-1494
Phone: 860-594-0348
Email: foundation@arrl.org
http://www.arrl.org/scholarship-program

Purpose: To support engineering students who are involved in amateur radio.

Eligibility: Applicants must have an amateur radio license of Novice Class or higher. Students may be pursuing a bachelor's degree in any field of engineering. They must be residents of one of the following states: North Carolina, Virginia, West Virginia, Maryland or Tennessee. Preference will be given to students with financial need.

Target applicant(s): High school students. College students. Adult students.

Amount: $1,000.

Number of awards: 1.

Deadline: December 31.

How to apply: Applications are available online.

Exclusive: Visit www.UltimateScholarshipBook.com and enter code AM93523 for updates on this award.

(936) · GBT Student Support Program

National Radio Astronomy Observatory (NRAO)
NRAO Headquarters, 520 Edgemont Road, Charlottesville, VA 22903
Phone: 434-296-0211
Email: info@nrao.edu
https://science.nrao.edu/opportunities/student-programs/summerstudents

Purpose: To support student research at the Robert C. Byrd Green Bank Telescope (GBT).

Eligibility: GBT is the largest fully steerable single aperture antenna. Students begin the application process by completing a preliminary funding proposal form. If the proposal is accepted, they will be informed of further requirements.

Target applicant(s): College students. Graduate school students. Adult students.

Amount: Up to $35,000.

Number of awards: Varies.

Deadline: February 1.

How to apply: Applications are available online.

Exclusive: Visit www.UltimateScholarshipBook.com and enter code NA93623 for updates on this award.

(937) · GCSAA Scholars Competition

Golf Course Superintendents Association of America
1421 Research Park Drive, Lawrence, KS 66049
Phone: 800-472-7878
Email: mwright@gcsaa.org
https://www.gcsaa.org/education/scholarships

Purpose: To support students preparing for careers in golf course management.

Eligibility: Applicants must be GCSAA members who are undergraduate students enrolled in an accredited degree program in turf management or a closely related subject. They must have completed at least 24 semester credits or one year of full-time study in their degree program. Selection is based on academic excellence, career potential, recommendations, work history and extracurricular activities.

Target applicant(s): College students. Adult students.

Amount: $500-$6,000.

Number of awards: Varies.

Deadline: June 1.

How to apply: Applications are available online. An application form, personal essay, transcripts and reports from the applicant's academic advisor and golf course superintendent are required.

Exclusive: Visit www.UltimateScholarshipBook.com and enter code GO93723 for updates on this award.

(938) · General James H. Doolittle Scholarship

Communities Foundation of Texas
5500 Caruth Haven Lane, Dallas, TX 75225
Phone: 214-750-4222
Email: info@cftexas.org
https://www.cftexas.org/cft-scholarships

Purpose: To support aeronautical engineering and aerospace science students.

Eligibility: Applicants must be undergraduate juniors, undergraduate seniors or graduate students enrolled in a degree program in aerospace science or aeronautical engineering. Students do not need to be Texas residents. Selection is based on the overall strength of the application.

Target applicant(s): College students. Graduate school students. Adult students.
Minimum GPA: 2.75
Amount: Up to $5,000.
Number of awards: Varies.
Deadline: May 1.
How to apply: Applications are available online. An application form and supporting documents are required.
Exclusive: Visit www.UltimateScholarshipBook.com and enter code CO93823 for updates on this award.

(939) · GeneTex Scholarship Program

GeneTex Inc.
2456 Alton Parkway, Irvine, CA 92606
Phone: 949-553-1900
Email: scholarship@genetex.com
http://www.genetex.com/scholarship
Purpose: To support students pursuing STEM degrees.
Eligibility: Applicants must be enrolled at an accredited college or university and be in good standing. Students must be majoring in a STEM (science, technology, engineering or math) area.
Target applicant(s): High school students. College students. Adult students.
Amount: $2,000.
Number of awards: 1.
Deadline: December 17.
How to apply: Applications are available online.
Exclusive: Visit www.UltimateScholarshipBook.com and enter code GE93923 for updates on this award.

(940) · Geneva Rock Scholarship

Geneva Rock
302 West 5400 South, Suite 200, Murray, UT 84107
https://genevarock.com/scholarship/
Purpose: To support students dedicated to building the future.
Eligibility: Applicants must be currently enrolled or enrolling in an accredited university, college, trade or vocational school pursuing a career in a construction-related field. Students must include a written essay along with their application.
Target applicant(s): College students. Adult students.
Amount: $2,000.
Number of awards: 2.
Deadline: July 1, November 15.
How to apply: Applications are available online.
Exclusive: Visit www.UltimateScholarshipBook.com and enter code GE94023 for updates on this award.

(941) · George A. Hall / Harold F. Mayfield Grant

Wilson Ornithological Society
Department of Biology and Biomedical Science, Dr. James Chace, Associate Professor, 100 Ochre Point Avenue, Newport, RI 02840-4192
Email: rbpayne@umich.edu
http://www.wilsonsociety.org
Purpose: To assist those who are conducting avian research.
Eligibility: Applicants must be independent researchers without access to funds available at colleges, universities or government agencies and must be non-professionals currently conducting avian research. Applicants must also be willing to present their research results at an annual meeting of the Wilson Ornithological Society.

Target applicant(s): Graduate school students. Adult students.
Amount: $1,000.
Number of awards: 1.
Deadline: February 1.
How to apply: Applications are available online.
Exclusive: Visit www.UltimateScholarshipBook.com and enter code WI94123 for updates on this award.

(942) · Gertrude Cox Scholarship For Women In Statistics

American Statistical Association
Attn: Awards Nominations, 732 N. Washington Street, Alexandria, VA 22314
Phone: 703-684-1221
Email: awards@amstat.org
http://www.amstat.org
Purpose: To encourage women to pursue education for careers in statistics.
Eligibility: Applicants must be women who are full-time students in a graduate-level statistics programs.
Target applicant(s): Graduate school students. Adult students.
Amount: $1,000.
Number of awards: 2.
Deadline: February 23.
How to apply: Applications are available online.
Exclusive: Visit www.UltimateScholarshipBook.com and enter code AM94223 for updates on this award.

(943) · Gilbreth Memorial Fellowship

Institute of Industrial and Systems Engineers
3577 Parkway Lane, Suite 200, Norcross, GA 30092
Phone: 800-494-0460
Email: bcameron@iienet.org
http://www.iise.org/
Purpose: To support graduate student Institute members.
Eligibility: Applicants must be graduate students at an institution in the United States, Canada or Mexico, majoring in industrial engineering or its equivalent and active members. Students may not apply directly for this scholarship and must be nominated. The award is based on academic ability, character, leadership, potential service to the industrial engineering profession and financial need.
Target applicant(s): Graduate school students. Adult students.
Minimum GPA: 3.4
Amount: $1,250-$2,000.
Number of awards: 4.
Deadline: November 15.
How to apply: Nomination forms are available online.
Exclusive: Visit www.UltimateScholarshipBook.com and enter code IN94323 for updates on this award.

(944) · Giuliano Mazzetti Scholarship

Society of Manufacturing Engineers Education Foundation
One SME Drive, P.O. Box 930, Dearborn, MI 48121
Phone: 313-425-3300
Email: foundation@sme.org
https://www.smeef.org/scholarships
Purpose: To support undergraduate students of manufacturing engineering and technology.

Eligibility: Applicants must be full-time undergraduate students who have completed 30 or more credit hours at a postsecondary institution located in the United States or Canada. They must be studying manufacturing engineering, technology or a related subject and must have plans to pursue a career in one of these same fields. Students must have a GPA of 3.0 or more on a four-point scale. Selection is based on the overall strength of the application.

Target applicant(s): College students. Adult students.

Minimum GPA: 3.0

Amount: Varies.

Number of awards: Varies.

Deadline: February 1.

How to apply: Applications are available online. An application form, personal statement, resume, transcript and two recommendation letters are required.

Exclusive: Visit www.UltimateScholarshipBook.com and enter code SO94423 for updates on this award.

---

(945) · Gladys Anderson Emerson Scholarship

Iota Sigma Pi (ISP) ND

Professor Kathryn A. Thomasson, Iota Sigma Pi Director for Student Awards, University of North Dakota, Department of Chemistry, P.O. Box 9024, Grand Forks, ND 58202-9024

Phone: 701-777-3199

Email: kthomasson@chem.und.edu

https://www.iotasigmapi.org/

Purpose: To reward achievement in the fields of chemistry and biochemistry by women.

Eligibility: Applicants must have attained junior status at an accredited college or university, be female and be nominated by a member of Iota Sigma Pi.

Target applicant(s): College students. Adult students.

Amount: $2,000.

Number of awards: Up to 2.

Deadline: February 15.

How to apply: Applications are available online.

Exclusive: Visit www.UltimateScholarshipBook.com and enter code IO94523 for updates on this award.

---

(946) · Gloria Barron Wilderness Society Scholarship

Wilderness Society

1615 M Street NW, Washington, DC 20036

Phone: 800-843-9453

Email: https://wilderness.org

https://wilderness.org

Purpose: To support graduate students pursuing a career in long-term protection of wilderness in the U.S.

Eligibility: Applicants must provide a cover letter, proposal, current resume and letters of recommendation along with the application.

Target applicant(s): Graduate school students. Adult students.

Amount: Varies.

Number of awards: Varies.

Deadline: April 15.

How to apply: Applications are available online.

Exclusive: Visit www.UltimateScholarshipBook.com and enter code WI94623 for updates on this award.

---

(947) · GoodRx Pharmacy Innovation Scholarship

GoodRx

Scholarship America, One Scholarship Way, Saint Peter, MN 56082

Phone: 800-537-4180

Email: goodrx@scholarshipamerica.org

https://www.goodrx.com/scholarship

Purpose: To support students interested in becoming pharmacists and pharmacy technicians.

Eligibility: Applicants must either currently be undergraduates or graduate-level students pursuing pharmacy or pharmacy technician studies at an accredited two- or four-year college, university or vocational-technical school or currently studying towards or have recently received a pharmacy technician certification. Students must have a minimum 3.0 GPA.

Target applicant(s): College students. Graduate school students. Adult students.

Minimum GPA: 3.0

Amount: $1,000.

Number of awards: 10.

Deadline: May 5.

How to apply: Applications are available online.

Exclusive: Visit www.UltimateScholarshipBook.com and enter code GO94723 for updates on this award.

---

(948) · Gordon Rankin Corrosion Engineering Scholarship

National Association of Corrosion Engineers (NACE) International Foundation

15835 Park Ten Place, Houston, TX 77084-5145

Phone: 281-228-6205

Email: nace.foundation@nace.org

http://nace-foundation.org/programs/students/scholarships/

Purpose: To aid students in their continued studies in corrosion.

Eligibility: Applicants must be U.S. citizens enrolled full-time as an undergraduate at an accredited two or four-year U.S. college or university. Applicants must be enrolled in the study of corrosion or corrosion control and must have a GPA of 3.0 or higher.

Target applicant(s): College students. Adult students.

Minimum GPA: 3.0

Amount: $1,000.

Number of awards: Up to 2.

Deadline: January 1.

How to apply: Applications are available online. An application form, two recommendation forms, an academic transcript and scholarship essay questions are required.

Exclusive: Visit www.UltimateScholarshipBook.com and enter code NA94823 for updates on this award.

---

(949) · Graduate Research Award (GRA)

American Vacuum Society

125 Maiden Lane, 15th Floor, New York, NY 10038

Phone: 212-248-0200

Email: angela@avs.org

http://www.avs.org

Purpose: To support graduate studies in the sciences and technologies related to the AVS.

Eligibility: Applicants must be graduate students in an accredited academic institution. Awards are based on research and academic record. The awards cover travel expenses to the international symposium. Applicants should submit applications, recommendation letters, research summaries and transcripts.

Target applicant(s): Graduate school students. Adult students.

Amount: Varies.

Number of awards: 10.

Deadline: May 1.
How to apply: Applications are available online.
Exclusive: Visit www.UltimateScholarshipBook.com and enter code AM94923 for updates on this award.

(950) · Graduate Research Fellowship Program

National Science Foundation
GRF Operations Center, 1818 N Street NW, Suite 600,
Washington, DC 20036
Phone: 866-NSF-GRFP
Email: info@nsfgrfp.org
https://www.fastlane.nsf.gov/
Purpose: To assist science and engineering graduate students.
Eligibility: Applicants must be full-time students who have completed no more than 12 months of graduate study and be U.S. citizens, U.S. nationals or permanent residents. The fields of study are interdisciplinary, computer and information science and engineering, mathematical sciences, geosciences, psychology, social sciences, life sciences, chemistry, physics and astronomy and engineering.
Target applicant(s): Graduate school students. Adult students.
Amount: Up to $44,000.
Number of awards: 2,700.
Deadline: October.
How to apply: Applications are available online. An online application form, official transcript and three letters of reference submitted electronically are required.
Exclusive: Visit www.UltimateScholarshipBook.com and enter code NA95023 for updates on this award.

(951) · Graduate Scholarships

Institute of Food Technologists (IFT)
525 W. Van Buren, Suite 1000, Chicago, IL 60607
Phone: 312-782-8424
Email: ejplummer@ift.org
https://www.ift.org/community/students
Purpose: To reward graduate students researching food science or technology.
Eligibility: Applicants should be graduate students pursuing an M.S. and/or Ph.D. at the time the fellowship becomes effective and should research an area of food science or technology. Applications, transcripts and three recommendation letters are required.
Target applicant(s): Graduate school students. Adult students.
Amount: $1,000-$5,000.
Number of awards: Varies.
Deadline: March 2.
How to apply: Applications are available online.
Exclusive: Visit www.UltimateScholarshipBook.com and enter code IN95123 for updates on this award.

(952) · Graduate Student Research Grants

Geological Society of America Graduate Student Research Grants
Matt Dawson, P.O. Box 9140, Boulder, CO 80301-9140
Phone: 303-357-1018
Email: mdawson@geosociety.org
https://www.geosociety.org
Purpose: To support thesis and dissertation research for graduate students in geological science.
Eligibility: Applicants must currently be enrolled in a geological science graduate program at an institution in the United States, Canada, Mexico or Central America. Applicants must also be members of the Geological Society of America (GSA).
Target applicant(s): Graduate school students. Adult students.
Amount: Varies.
Number of awards: Varies.
Deadline: February 2.
How to apply: Applications are available online.
Exclusive: Visit www.UltimateScholarshipBook.com and enter code GE95223 for updates on this award.

(953) · Graduate Student Scholarship

American Speech-Language-Hearing Foundation
2200 Research Boulevard, Rockville, MD 20850
Phone: 301-296-8700
Email: foundation@asha.org
https://www.ashfoundation.org/
Purpose: To support graduate students in communication sciences and disorders.
Eligibility: Applicants must be full-time graduate students in U.S. communication sciences and disorders programs. Master's degree candidates must be in programs accredited by the Council on Academic Accreditation for Audiology and Speech Pathology, but doctoral programs do not have to be accredited. Transcripts, an essay, a reference form and a statement of good standing are required.
Target applicant(s): College students. Graduate school students. Adult students.
Amount: $5,000.
Number of awards: Up to 21.
Deadline: May.
How to apply: Applications are available online.
Exclusive: Visit www.UltimateScholarshipBook.com and enter code AM95323 for updates on this award.

(954) · Graduate Summer Student Research Assistantship

National Radio Astronomy Observatory (NRAO)
NRAO Headquarters, 520 Edgemont Road, Charlottesville, VA 22903
Phone: 434-296-0211
Email: info@nrao.edu
https://science.nrao.edu/opportunities/student-programs/summerstudents
Purpose: To allow graduate students to perform astronomical research at National Radio Astronomy Observatory (NRAO) sites.
Eligibility: Applicants must be first- or second-year graduate students interested in astronomical research. Recipients work on-site for 10 to 12 weeks, beginning in late May or early June.
Target applicant(s): Graduate school students. Adult students.
Amount: Varies.
Number of awards: Varies.
Deadline: February 1.
How to apply: Applications are available online.
Exclusive: Visit www.UltimateScholarshipBook.com and enter code NA95423 for updates on this award.

(955) · H.P. Bud Milligan Aviation Scholarship

EAA Aviation Center
3000 Poberezny Road, Oshkosh, WI 54902
Phone: 920-426-4800
Email: scholarships@eaa.org

http://www.eaa.org/en/eaa
Purpose: To support excellence among individuals studying aviation.
Eligibility: Applicants must be enrolled in an accredited college, aviation academy or technical school pursuing a course of study focusing on aviation. Applicants must also be involved in school and community activities as well as aviation and be an EAA member or be recommended by an EAA member.
Target applicant(s): High school students. College students. Adult students.
Amount: $500.
Number of awards: 1.
Scholarship may be renewable.
Deadline: January 31.
How to apply: Applications are available online.
Exclusive: Visit www.UltimateScholarshipBook.com and enter code EA95523 for updates on this award.

(956) · Harold and Inge Marcus Scholarship

Institute of Industrial and Systems Engineers
3577 Parkway Lane, Suite 200, Norcross, GA 30092
Phone: 800-494-0460
Email: bcameron@iienet.org
http://www.iise.org/
Purpose: To aid industrial engineering students who are members of the Institute of Industrial Engineers (IIE).
Eligibility: Applicants must be undergraduate industrial engineering students who have been formally nominated for the award by their industrial engineering department heads. They must be full-time students who are active IIE members in good standing and must have an undergraduate GPA of 3.4 or higher on a four-point scale. Selection is based on academic achievement, integrity, financial need and potential contribution to the industrial engineering field.
Target applicant(s): College students. Adult students.
Minimum GPA: 3.4
Amount: $1,000.
Number of awards: 5.
Deadline: November 15.
How to apply: Applications will be mailed to those who have been formally nominated by their department heads. A formal nomination, an application packet and supporting documents are required.
Exclusive: Visit www.UltimateScholarshipBook.com and enter code IN95623 for updates on this award.

(957) · Harold Bettinger Scholarship

American Floral Endowment
1001 North Fairfax Street, Suite 201, Alexandria, VA 22314
Phone: 703-838-5211
Email: dchedester@afeendowment.org
http://endowment.org/scholarships/
Purpose: To aid current horticulture students who are planning to pursue careers in a horticulture-related business.
Eligibility: Applicants must be U.S. or Canadian citizens or residents. They must be graduate students or rising undergraduate sophomores, juniors or seniors. They must have a GPA of 2.0 or higher. They must be horticulture students who are pursuing a major or minor in business or marketing, and must have plans to pursue a career in the horticulture business field. Selection is based on the overall strength of the application.
Target applicant(s): College students. Graduate school students. Adult students.
Minimum GPA: 2.0
Amount: Varies.

Number of awards: Varies.
Deadline: May 1.
How to apply: Applications are available online. An application form, two letters of recommendation, a personal statement and a transcript are required.
Exclusive: Visit www.UltimateScholarshipBook.com and enter code AM95723 for updates on this award.

(958) · Harry J. Harwick Scholarship

Medical Group Management Association
104 Inverness Terrace East, Englewood, CO 80112
Phone: 877-275-6462
Email: acmpe@mgma.com
https://mgma.com/career-pathways/career-advancement/career-resources/scholarships
Purpose: To aid undergraduate and graduate students of public health, health care management, health care administration and related areas of medical practice management.
Eligibility: Applicants must be enrolled in an undergraduate or graduate degree program in public health, health care management, health care administration or a related medical practice management subject. Undergraduates must be enrolled in a program that is a member of the Association of University Programs in Health Administration (AUPHA), and graduate students must be enrolled in a program that has been accredited by the Commission on Accreditation of Healthcare Management Education (CAHME). Selection is based on the overall strength of the application.
Target applicant(s): High school students. College students. Graduate school students. Adult students.
Amount: $3,000.
Number of awards: Varies.
Deadline: May.
How to apply: Applications are available online. An application form and supporting documents are required.
Exclusive: Visit www.UltimateScholarshipBook.com and enter code ME95823 for updates on this award.

(959) · Health Careers Scholarship

International Order of the King's Daughters and Sons
Director, P.O. Box 1040, Chautauqua, NY 14722
Email: headquarters@iokds.org
https://iokds.org/scholarships/
Purpose: To assist students interested in pursuing health careers.
Eligibility: Applicants must be full-time students pursuing a career in medicine, dentistry, nursing, pharmacy, physical or occupational therapy or medical technologies. R.N. students and those pursuing an M.D. or D.D.S must have completed at least one year of schooling at an accredited institution. All others must be entering at least their third year of school. Pre-med students are not eligible. Applicants must be U.S. or Canadian citizens.
Target applicant(s): College students. Graduate school students. Adult students.
Amount: Varies.
Number of awards: Varies.
Deadline: April 1.
How to apply: Applications are available by sending a self-addressed, stamped legal size envelope.
Exclusive: Visit www.UltimateScholarshipBook.com and enter code IN95923 for updates on this award.

(960) · Healthline and Prevention Institute Stronger Scholarship

Healthline
660 Third Street, San Francisco, CA 94107
Phone: 415-281-3100
http://www.healthline.com/health/scholarship-program
Purpose: To support emerging future health leaders.
Eligibility: Applicants must be current juniors or seniors in pursuit of an undergraduate degree. Students must be a person of color who identifies as Black, Indigenous, Hispanic, Latino/Latina and/or Pacific Islander. Applicants must demonstrate the advancement of the mental health profession, either through research, patient advocacy, raising awareness or community building.
Target applicant(s): College students. Adult students.
Amount: $7,000.
Number of awards: 3.
Deadline: April 20.
How to apply: Applications are available online.
Exclusive: Visit www.UltimateScholarshipBook.com and enter code HE96023 for updates on this award.

(961) · Helen C. Evans Scholarship

Armenian General Benevolent Union (AGBU)
55 East 59th Street, 7th Floor, New York, NY 10022-1112
Phone: 212-319-6383
Email: scholarship@agbu.org
http://www.agbu.org
Purpose: To support graduate students pursuing studies in the areas of Armenian art, art history, architecture or early Christianity.
Eligibility: Applicants must be enrolled in full-time graduate degree programs pursuing studies in the areas of Armenian art, art history, architecture or early Christianity. Students must demonstrate a strong interest in pursuing world-leading research, teaching, dissemination of future work that will help develop the areas of Armenian art, art history, architecture or early Christianity and related fields. This scholarship is open to students of both Armenian and non-Armenian descent. Applicants must complete and submit a pre-screening form before being invited to apply.
Target applicant(s): Graduate school students. Adult students.
Amount: Up to $5,000.
Number of awards: Varies.
Deadline: May 1.
How to apply: Applications are available online.
Exclusive: Visit www.UltimateScholarshipBook.com and enter code AR96123 for updates on this award.

(962) · Henry Adams Scholarship

American Society of Heating, Refrigerating and Air-Conditioning Engineers (ASHRAE)
1791 Tullie Circle, NE, Atlanta, GA 30329
Phone: 404-636-8400
Email: lbenedict@ashrae.org
https://www.ashrae.org/membership--conferences/student-zone/scholarships-and-grants/scholarship-program
Purpose: To aid undergraduate engineering students who are preparing for careers in the heating, ventilation, air-conditioning and refrigeration (HVACR) industry.
Eligibility: Applicants must be undergraduate engineering or pre-engineering students. They must be enrolled in or accepted into an ABET-accredited school, a school that is accredited by a non-U.S. agency that has entered into a Memorandum of Understanding agreement with ABET or a school that hosts a recognized student branch of the American Society of Heating, Refrigerating and Air-Conditioning Engineers (ASHRAE). The applicant's program of study must offer adequate preparation for a career in the HVACR industry. Applicants must have a GPA of 3.0 or higher and must be ranked in the top 30 percent of their class. Selection is based on the overall strength of the application.
Target applicant(s): High school students. College students. Adult students.
Minimum GPA: 3.0
Amount: $3,000.
Number of awards: 1.
Scholarship may be renewable.
Deadline: December 1.
How to apply: Applications are available online. An application form, official transcript and one recommendation letter are required.
Exclusive: Visit www.UltimateScholarshipBook.com and enter code AM96223 for updates on this award.

(963) · Herbert Levy Memorial Scholarship

Society of Physics Students
One Physics Ellipse, College Park, MD 20740
Phone: 301-209-3007
Email: SPS-Programs@aip.org
https://www.spsnational.org/
Purpose: To provide financial assistance for physics students in any year of undergraduate study.
Eligibility: Applicants must be physics majors, be members of SPS and demonstrate scholarly achievement and financial need.
Target applicant(s): College students. Adult students.
Amount: $2,000.
Number of awards: 1.
Deadline: March 15.
How to apply: Applications are available online or from SPS Chapter Advisors.
Exclusive: Visit www.UltimateScholarshipBook.com and enter code SO96323 for updates on this award.

(964) · Hertz Foundation's Graduate Fellowship Award

Fannie and John Hertz Foundation
Attn: Applications, 2300 First Street, Suite 250, Livermore, CA 94550
Phone: 925-373-1642
Email: askhertz@hertzfoundation.org
http://www.hertzfoundation.org
Purpose: To help graduate students in the applied physical and engineering sciences.
Eligibility: Applicants must be college seniors planning to pursue or graduate students currently pursuing a Ph.D. in the applied physical and engineering sciences or modern biology which applies the physical sciences. Successful applicants must attend one of the foundation's approved schools. The award is based on merit, creativity and potential for research.
Target applicant(s): College students. Graduate school students. Adult students.
Amount: Up to full tuition plus stipend.
Number of awards: Varies.
Scholarship may be renewable.
Deadline: October 1.

How to apply: Applications are available online, by phone or by email.
Exclusive: Visit www.UltimateScholarshipBook.com and enter code FA96423 for updates on this award.

(965) · HIMSS Foundation Scholarship

Healthcare Information and Management Systems Society
230 E. Ohio Street, Suite 500, Chicago, IL 60611-3269
Phone: 312-664-4467
Email: scholarships@himss.org
http://www.himss.org
Purpose: To provide scholarships based on academic achievement and leadership in the field of healthcare information and management systems.
Eligibility: Applicants must be members of HIMSS and study healthcare information and management systems. Scholarships are also available from individual chapters listed on the HIMSS website.
Target applicant(s): College students. Graduate school students. Adult students.
Amount: $5,000.
Number of awards: 4.
Deadline: October 15.
How to apply: Application details are available online.
Exclusive: Visit www.UltimateScholarshipBook.com and enter code HE96523 for updates on this award.

(966) · Holly Cornell Scholarship

American Water Works Association
6666 W. Quincy Avenue, Denver, CO 80235-3098
Phone: 800-926-7337
Email: scholarships@awwa.org
http://www.awwa.org
Purpose: To support female and/or minority master's students pursuing advanced training in the field of water supply and treatment.
Eligibility: Applicants must be females and/or minorities who have been accepted to or are current master's degree students in engineering. Applications, transcripts, GRE scores, three recommendation letters, statements and course of study are required. The award is based on academics and leadership.
Target applicant(s): Graduate school students. Adult students.
Amount: $7,500.
Number of awards: 1.
Deadline: December 20.
How to apply: Applications are available online.
Exclusive: Visit www.UltimateScholarshipBook.com and enter code AM96623 for updates on this award.

(967) · Horkheimer/Smith Youth Service Award

Astronomical League
9201 Ward Parkway, Suite 100, Kansas City, MO 64114
Phone: 816-333-7759
Email: horkheimerservice@astroleague.org
https://www.astroleague.org/al/awards/awards.html
Purpose: To assist young Astronomical League members.
Eligibility: Applicants must be Astronomical League members under the age of 19 on the date of the application. The award is based on astronomical service and service to the league.
Target applicant(s): Junior high students or younger. High school students.
Amount: $1,750 plus travel expenses.
Number of awards: 3.

Deadline: March 31.
How to apply: Applications are available online.
Exclusive: Visit www.UltimateScholarshipBook.com and enter code AS96723 for updates on this award.

(968) · Houzz Women in Architecture

Houzz Inc.
285 Hamilton Avenue, Palo Alto, CA 94301
Email: scholarships@houzz.com
http://houzz.com/scholarships
Purpose: To support women architecture students.
Eligibility: Applicants must be female students enrolled at an U.S. university as an undergraduate or graduate student. Students must be majoring in architecture.
Target applicant(s): College students. Graduate school students. Adult students.
Amount: $2,500.
Number of awards: 1.
Deadline: March 31.
How to apply: Applications are available online.
Exclusive: Visit www.UltimateScholarshipBook.com and enter code HO96823 for updates on this award.

(969) · HSA Research Grants

Herb Society of America
Attn.: Research Grant, 9019 Kirtland Chardon Road, Kirtland, OH 44094
Phone: 440-256-0514
Email: herbs@herbsociety.org
http://www.herbsociety.org
Purpose: To educate about herbs and contribute to the fields of horticulture, science, literature, history, art and/or economics.
Eligibility: Applicants must have a proposed program of scientific, academic or artistic investigation of herbal plants. Applicants must describe their research needs in 500 words or less and include a proposed budget with specific budget items listed. This grant may not be used in combination with funding from another source and may not be used to pay for salaries, tuition or private garden development.
Target applicant(s): High school students. College students. Adult students.
Amount: Up to $5,000.
Number of awards: Varies by year.
Deadline: January 31.
How to apply: Applications are available online or by written request.
Exclusive: Visit www.UltimateScholarshipBook.com and enter code HE96923 for updates on this award.

(970) · Hutton Junior Fisheries Biology Program

American Fisheries Society (AFS)
425 Barlow Place, Suite 110, Bethesda, MD 20814
Phone: 301-897-8616
Email: Hutton@fisheries.org
https://hutton.fisheries.org/
Purpose: To stimulate interest in pursuing fisheries science and aquatic resources among high school students.
Eligibility: Applicants must be a junior or senior in high school. Students must provide official copies of student transcripts. Preference will be given to qualified women and minority applicants.
Target applicant(s): High school students.
Amount: $4,000.

Number of awards: Varies.
Deadline: February 15.
How to apply: Applications are available online.
Exclusive: Visit www.UltimateScholarshipBook.com and enter code AM97023 for updates on this award.

(971) · IBTTA Scholarship Program

International Bridge, Tunnel and Turnpike Association Foundation
IBTTA Scholarship Program, Scholarship America, One Scholarship Way, Saint Peter, MN 56082
Phone: 507-931-1682
Email: ibtta@scholarshipamerica.org
https://learnmore.scholarsapply.org/ibtta
Purpose: To support students who are working towards a transportation-related degree.
Eligibility: Applicants must be current undergraduate college students who have completed at least two full semesters of undergraduate coursework or graduate students. Students must be planning to enroll full-time and have a minimum 2.5 GPA. Applicants must be pursuing a degree in one of the following fields: civil engineering, city and regional planning, construction management, public policy or public administration, structural engineering, finance, accounting, information technology, business management, marketing, communications, operations management or other transportation-related degrees.
Target applicant(s): College students. Graduate school students. Adult students.
Minimum GPA: 2.5
Amount: $5,000.
Number of awards: 6.
Deadline: April 19.
How to apply: Applications are available online.
Exclusive: Visit www.UltimateScholarshipBook.com and enter code IN97123 for updates on this award.

(972) · IIE Council of Fellows Undergraduate Scholarship

Institute of Industrial and Systems Engineers
3577 Parkway Lane, Suite 200, Norcross, GA 30092
Phone: 800-494-0460
Email: bcameron@iienet.org
http://www.iise.org/
Purpose: To support undergraduate student members.
Eligibility: Applicants must be full-time undergraduate students enrolled in a college in the United States, Canada or Mexico with an accredited industrial engineering program, major in industrial engineering and be active members. Students may not apply directly for this scholarship and must be nominated. The award is based on academic ability, character, leadership, potential service to the industrial engineering profession and financial need. Applicant must have a minimum 3.4 GPA.
Target applicant(s): College students. Adult students.
Minimum GPA: 3.4
Amount: $1,500.
Number of awards: 2.
Deadline: November 15.
How to apply: Nomination forms are available online.
Exclusive: Visit www.UltimateScholarshipBook.com and enter code IN97223 for updates on this award.

(973) · Industrial Electrolysis and Electrochemical Engineering Division H.H. Dow Memorial Student Award

Electrochemical Society
65 South Main Street, Building D, Pennington, NJ 08534-2839
Phone: 609-737-1902
Email: awards@electrochem.org
https://www.electrochem.org/student-awards
Purpose: To recognize young engineers and scientists in the fields of electrochemical engineering and applied electrochemistry.
Eligibility: Applicants must be accepted to or enrolled in a graduate program. The application requires transcripts, a description of the research project, a description of how the project relates to electrochemical engineering or applied electrochemistry, a biography, a resume or curriculum vitae and a letter of recommendation from the research supervisor. The award is based on academic performance, research and the recommendation.
Target applicant(s): Graduate school students. Adult students.
Amount: $1,000.
Number of awards: Varies.
Deadline: September 1.
How to apply: Application materials are described online.
Exclusive: Visit www.UltimateScholarshipBook.com and enter code EL97323 for updates on this award.

(974) · Industrial Electrolysis and Electrochemical Engineering Division Student Achievement Awards

Electrochemical Society
65 South Main Street, Building D, Pennington, NJ 08534-2839
Phone: 609-737-1902
Email: awards@electrochem.org
https://www.electrochem.org/student-awards
Purpose: To recognize young engineers and scientists in electrochemical engineering and to encourage the recipients to enter careers in the field.
Eligibility: Applicants must be accepted by or enrolled in a college or university and propose a research project. The application must include transcripts, research outline, statement describing how the project relates to electrochemical engineering, record of industrial work and letter of recommendation from the research supervisor. The award is based on academic performance, research and the recommendation.
Target applicant(s): High school students. College students. Graduate school students. Adult students.
Amount: $1,000.
Number of awards: Varies.
Deadline: September 1.
How to apply: Application materials are described online.
Exclusive: Visit www.UltimateScholarshipBook.com and enter code EL97423 for updates on this award.

(975) · Injection Molding Division Scholarship

Society of Plastics Engineers
6 Berkshire Boulevard, Suite 306, Bethel, CT 06801
Phone: 203-775-0471
Email: info@4spe.org
http://www.4spe.org/spe-foundation
Purpose: To aid students who have employment or academic experience in injection molding.
Eligibility: Applicants must be full-time undergraduate or graduate students who are in good academic standing. They must have experience in injection molding through courses taken, research conducted or

formal employment. They must have an interest in the plastics/polymer industry and must have taken courses that would prepare them for a career in this field. Selection is based on academic merit and financial need.

Target applicant(s): High school students. College students. Graduate school students. Adult students.
Amount: $3,000.
Number of awards: 1.
Deadline: April 1.
How to apply: Applications are available online. An application form, three recommendation letters, transcripts, a personal statement, a list of extracurricular activities and honors and employment history are required.
Exclusive: Visit www.UltimateScholarshipBook.com and enter code SO97523 for updates on this award.

(976) · Institute of Electrical and Electronics Engineers Life Members' Fellowship in Electrical History

Institute of Electrical and Electronics Engineers (IEEE)
445 Hoes Lane, Piscataway, NJ 08854
Phone: 732-562-3860
Email: supportieee@ieee.org
http://www.ieee.org/scholarships
Purpose: To support students in engineering and technology-related fields.
Eligibility: Applicants must be studying engineering, computer science and information technology, physical sciences, biological and medical sciences, mathematics, technical communications, education, management or law and policy. The award may be used during one year of full-time graduate work or one year of post-doctoral research. Students must provide a detailed 15-page description of the proposed research, along with three letters of recommendation.
Target applicant(s): Graduate school students. Adult students.
Amount: Varies.
Number of awards: 1.
Deadline: February 1.
How to apply: Applications are available online.
Exclusive: Visit www.UltimateScholarshipBook.com and enter code IN97623 for updates on this award.

(977) · International Gas Turbine Institute Scholarship

American Society of Mechanical Engineers (ASME)
Two Park Avenue, New York, NY 10016-5990
Phone: 800-843-2763
Email: lefeverb@asme.org
https://www.asmefoundation.org/programs/stemeducation/asme-scholarships/
Purpose: To aid American Society of Mechanical Engineers (ASME) student members who are interested in the gas turbine industry.
Eligibility: Applicants must be student members of ASME who are in good standing. They must be enrolled in an accredited undergraduate or graduate degree program in mechanical engineering or aerospace engineering. They must be interested in the turbomachinery, gas turbine or propulsion industry. Preference will be given to those who have employment or research experience in one of the aforementioned industries. Selection is based on academic achievement and demonstrated interest in the gas turbine industry.
Target applicant(s): High school students. College students. Graduate school students. Adult students.
Amount: $2,000.
Number of awards: 20.

Deadline: March 4.
How to apply: Applications may be completed online. An electronic application form, official transcript, personal statement and one to two recommendation letters are required.
Exclusive: Visit www.UltimateScholarshipBook.com and enter code AM97723 for updates on this award.

(978) · International Student Scholarship

American Speech-Language-Hearing Foundation
2200 Research Boulevard, Rockville, MD 20850
Phone: 301-296-8700
Email: foundation@asha.org
https://www.ashfoundation.org/
Purpose: To support an international graduate student in communication sciences and disorders.
Eligibility: Applicants must be full-time students in the U.S. Master's degree candidates must be in programs accredited by the Council on Academic Accreditation for Audiology and Speech Pathology, but doctoral programs do not have to be accredited. The applicants should submit transcripts, an essay and a reference form.
Target applicant(s): College students. Graduate school students. Adult students.
Amount: $5,000.
Number of awards: Up to 2.
Deadline: May.
How to apply: Applications are available online.
Exclusive: Visit www.UltimateScholarshipBook.com and enter code AM97823 for updates on this award.

(979) · International Women's Fishing Association Scholarship

International Women's Fishing Association
P.O. Box 530816, Miami Shores, FL 33153
Email: kelleykeys@aol.com
https://iwfa.memberclicks.net/criteria
Purpose: To help students in graduate programs in the marine sciences.
Eligibility: Applicants must have graduated or have been approved for graduation from an accredited college or university and plan on pursuing a graduate degree in the marine sciences. Selection is based on academic success, personal character, aptitude in the student's area of study and financial need.
Target applicant(s): Graduate school students. Adult students.
Amount: Up to $3,000.
Number of awards: Varies.
Deadline: March 1.
How to apply: Applications are available online. Students must include an official transcript, a photo, a letter describing career goals and a list of three people who will be sending letters of recommendation.
Exclusive: Visit www.UltimateScholarshipBook.com and enter code IN97923 for updates on this award.

(980) · Intertech Foundation STEM Scholarship

Intertech Foundation
1575 Thomas Center Drive, Eagan, MN 55122
Phone: 651-288-7000
Email: info@intertech.com
https://www.intertech.com/stem-scholarships/
Purpose: To assist college-bound students who have excelled at math and science.

Eligibility: Applicants must be college-bound high school seniors or current college students who are U.S. citizens and have at least a 3.3 GPA. Students must plan to major in computer science in college.
Target applicant(s): High school students. College students. Adult students.
Minimum GPA: 3.3
Amount: $2,500.
Number of awards: 1.
Deadline: April 15.
How to apply: There is no application form. A high school transcript, a resume, two letters of recommendation, a copy of a college acceptance letter and a one-page essay about how the student plans to participate in the professional software development industry are required.
Exclusive: Visit www.UltimateScholarshipBook.com and enter code IN98023 for updates on this award.

(981) · Irene and Daisy MacGregor Memorial Scholarship
National Society Daughters of the American Revolution
Committee Services Office, Attn.: Scholarships, 1776 D Street NW, Washington, DC 20006-5303
Phone: 202-628-1776
Email: scholarships@dar.org
https://www.dar.org/national-society/scholarships/general-information
Purpose: To assist students in becoming medical doctors.
Eligibility: Applicants must be accepted into or enrolled in a graduate course of study to become a medical doctor. Those pursuing study in psychiatric nursing at the graduate level at a medical school may also apply, and preference is given to females. All applicants must obtain a letter of sponsorship from their local DAR chapter. However, affiliation with DAR is not required.
Target applicant(s): Graduate school students. Adult students.
Amount: Up to $5,000.
Number of awards: Varies.
Scholarship may be renewable.
Deadline: January 31.
How to apply: Applications are available by written request with a self-addressed, stamped envelope.
Exclusive: Visit www.UltimateScholarshipBook.com and enter code NA98123 for updates on this award.

(982) · Irene Woodall Graduate Scholarship
American Dental Hygienists' Association (ADHA) Institute for Oral Health
Scholarship Award Program, 444 North Michigan Avenue, Suite 3400, Chicago, IL 60611
Phone: 312-440-8900
Email: institute@adha.net
https://www.adha.org/ioh-scholarships-main
Purpose: To support students pursuing a master's degree in dental hygiene.
Eligibility: Applicants must be full-time students at an accredited college or university in the United States pursuing a master's degree in dental hygiene or a related field and must have completed at least one year of a dental hygiene curriculum. Applicants must also be active members of the ADHA, have a minimum 3.5 GPA and have a minimum demonstrated financial need of $1,500. Selection is based upon the overall strength of the application.
Target applicant(s): College students. Graduate school students. Adult students.

Minimum GPA: 3.5
Amount: $1,000.
Number of awards: 1.
Deadline: February 1.
How to apply: Applications are available online after October 1.
Exclusive: Visit www.UltimateScholarshipBook.com and enter code AM98223 for updates on this award.

(983) · IRF Fellowship Program
International Road Federation
Madison Place, 500 Montgomery Street, 5th Floor, Alexandria, VA 22314
Phone: 703-535-1001
Email: info@irfnews.org
http://www.irfnet.org
Purpose: To provide fellowships in support of graduate study in a transportation-related field.
Eligibility: Applicants must demonstrate potential leadership in the highway industry in financing, administration, planning, design, construction, operations or maintenance. They must also have two years of work experience in transportation, a bachelor's of science degree (or equivalent) in a transportation-related discipline and a commitment to full-time study for a minimum of one year.
Target applicant(s): Graduate school students. Adult students.
Amount: Varies.
Number of awards: Varies.
Deadline: October 15.
How to apply: More information is available online.
Exclusive: Visit www.UltimateScholarshipBook.com and enter code IN98323 for updates on this award.

(984) · Jack Horkheimer Service Award/Parker Award
Astronomical League
9201 Ward Parkway, Suite 100, Kansas City, MO 64114
Phone: 816-333-7759
Email: horkheimerservice@astroleague.org
https://www.astroleague.org/al/awards/awards.html
Purpose: To recognize exceptional service by high school League astronomers.
Eligibility: Applicants must be a League member under 19 years of age. Selection is based upon service to the League.
Target applicant(s): High school students.
Amount: $1,000.
Number of awards: 1.
Deadline: March 31.
How to apply: Applications are available online. An application form, photo, details of public service, documentation of Astronomy Club duties or officer positions held, documentation of League Observing Awards earned, documentation of general observing achievements and documentation of other Astronomical Service are required.
Exclusive: Visit www.UltimateScholarshipBook.com and enter code AS98423 for updates on this award.

(985) · Jackson Laboratory Scholarship
Jackson Laboratory
Training and Education Office, 600 Main Street, Bar Harbor, ME 04609
Phone: 207-288-6250
Email: scholarship@jax.org

https://www.jax.org/scholarship

Purpose: To reward students pursuing a college education in research or medical fields.

Eligibility: Applicants must reside in Connecticut, Maine or in Sacramento County, California and must be pursuing a degree in biomedicine. Students must receive a nomination from a teacher and have financial need or be first-generation college students. Students must also have a 3.5 GPA and be graduating high school seniors.

Target applicant(s): High school students.

Minimum GPA: 3.5

Amount: $10,000.

Number of awards: 3.

Deadline: February 15.

How to apply: Applications are available online.

Exclusive: Visit www.UltimateScholarshipBook.com and enter code JA98523 for updates on this award.

---

(986) · Jane Delano Student Nurse Scholarship

American Red Cross

National Headquarters, 431 18th Street NW, Washington, DC 20006

Phone: 202-303-5000

Email: NationalAwards@redcross.org

http://www.redcross.org

Purpose: To aid Red Cross volunteers who are attending nursing school.

Eligibility: Applicants must be enrolled in an accredited nursing school and be in good academic standing. They must have volunteered with a Red Cross unit at least once within the past five years and have completed at least one academic year of college at the time of application. Selection is based on the overall strength of the application.

Target applicant(s): College students. Graduate school students. Adult students.

Amount: Varies.

Number of awards: Varies.

Deadline: May 1.

How to apply: Applications are available online. An application form, a personal essay, an endorsement from a Red Cross unit and an endorsement from the student's nursing school dean or chair are required.

Exclusive: Visit www.UltimateScholarshipBook.com and enter code AM98623 for updates on this award.

---

(987) · Jean Theodore Lacordaire Prize

Coleopterists Society

Dr. Darren A. Pollock, Chair, Department of Biology, Eastern New Mexico University, Portales, NM 88130

Phone: 575-562-2862

Email: Darren.Pollock@enmu.edu

http://www.coleopsoc.org/

Purpose: To recognize the work of coleopterists.

Eligibility: Applicants must be graduate students whose papers are nominated for the competition. The papers must be based on the applicant's dissertation research about coleoptera (beetle) systematics or biology published in the preceding calendar year. Self-nominations are not accepted.

Target applicant(s): Graduate school students. Adult students.

Amount: $300.

Number of awards: 1.

Deadline: March 1.

How to apply: Application materials are described online.

Exclusive: Visit www.UltimateScholarshipBook.com and enter code CO98723 for updates on this award.

---

(988) · Jill S. Tietjen P.E. Scholarship

Society of Women Engineers

130 East Randolph Street, Suite 3500, Chicago, IL 60601

Phone: 877-793-4636

Email: scholarships@swe.org

https://swe.org/scholarships/

Purpose: To support female engineering students pursuing a higher education.

Eligibility: Applicants must be currently enrolled in an accredited engineering or engineering technology program with a minimum of a 3.0 GPA. The award is to be used during the sophomore, junior or senior year of college.

Target applicant(s): College students. Adult students.

Minimum GPA: 3.0

Amount: $2,000.

Number of awards: 1.

Deadline: February 15.

How to apply: Applications are available online.

Exclusive: Visit www.UltimateScholarshipBook.com and enter code SO98823 for updates on this award.

---

(989) · Jimmy A. Young Memorial Education Recognition Award

American Association for Respiratory Care

9425 North MacArthur Boulevard, Suite 100, Irving, TX 75063-4706

Phone: 972-243-2272

Email: info@aarc.org

http://www.aarc.org/education/educator-resources/scholarships/

Purpose: To recognize outstanding minority students in respiratory care education programs.

Eligibility: Applicants must be enrolled in an accredited respiratory care education program and have a minimum 3.0 GPA. Students must submit an original paper on respiratory care. Preference is given to minority students.

Target applicant(s): College students. Graduate school students. Adult students.

Minimum GPA: 3.0

Amount: Up to $1,000.

Number of awards: 1.

Deadline: June 1.

How to apply: Applications are available online.

Exclusive: Visit www.UltimateScholarshipBook.com and enter code AM98923 for updates on this award.

---

(990) · John and Elsa Gracik Scholarships

American Society of Mechanical Engineers (ASME)

Two Park Avenue, New York, NY 10016-5990

Phone: 800-843-2763

Email: lefeverb@asme.org

https://www.asmefoundation.org/programs/stemeducation/asme-scholarships/

Purpose: To support mechanical engineering students.

Eligibility: Applicants must be ASME student members, enrolled in an eligible accredited mechanical engineering baccalaureate program and be U.S. citizens. Selection is based on scholastic ability, financial

need, character, leadership and potential contribution to the mechanical engineering profession.
Target applicant(s): College students. Adult students.
Amount: $2,500.
Number of awards: 10.
Deadline: February 18.
How to apply: Applications are available online.
Exclusive: Visit www.UltimateScholarshipBook.com and enter code AM99023 for updates on this award.

(991) · John and Muriel Landis Scholarship

American Nuclear Society
555 North Kensington Avenue, La Grange Park, IL 60526
Phone: 800-323-3044
Email: hr@ans.org
http://www.ans.org
Purpose: To assist disadvantaged students to seek careers in a nuclear-related field.
Eligibility: Applicants must be undergraduate or graduate students enrolled or planning to enroll in a U.S. college or university who are also planning a career in nuclear science, nuclear engineering or another nuclear-related field. High school seniors may apply. Students must have greater than average financial need. Applicants must submit applications, transcripts, sponsor forms and three reference forms.
Target applicant(s): High school students. College students. Graduate school students. Adult students.
Amount: $5,000.
Number of awards: Up to 9.
Deadline: February 1.
How to apply: Applications are available online.
Exclusive: Visit www.UltimateScholarshipBook.com and enter code AM99123 for updates on this award.

(992) · John C. Bajus Scholarship

Marine Technology Society
1100 H Street NW, Suite LL-100, Washington, DC 20005
Phone: 202-717-8705
https://www.mtsociety.org/scholarships
Purpose: To support Marine Technology Society members who are pursuing a degree in a marine-related field.
Eligibility: Applicants must be MTS student members who are accepted for enrollment or enrolled full-time in an undergraduate or graduate program. Selection is primarily based on demonstration of commitment to community service and volunteer work.
Target applicant(s): College students. Graduate school students. Adult students.
Amount: $1,000.
Number of awards: 1.
Deadline: April 15.
How to apply: Applications are available online.
Exclusive: Visit www.UltimateScholarshipBook.com and enter code MA99223 for updates on this award.

(993) · John Henry Comstock Graduate Student Awards

Entomological Society of America
3 Park Place, Suite 307, Annapolis, MD 21401-3722
Phone: 301-731-4535
Email: esa@entsoc.org
http://www.entsoc.org
Purpose: To encourage graduate students interested in entomology to attend the Annual Meeting of the Entomological Society of America.
Eligibility: Applicants must be graduate students and members of the ESA. Each ESA branch has its own eligibility requirements, so an interested student must contact their Branch Secretary-Treasurer for more information.
Target applicant(s): Graduate school students. Adult students.
Amount: Travel expenses plus $100.
Number of awards: 6.
Deadline: Varies.
How to apply: Applications are available online.
Exclusive: Visit www.UltimateScholarshipBook.com and enter code EN99323 for updates on this award.

(994) · John J. McKetta Scholarship

American Institute of Chemical Engineers - (AIChE)
120 Wall Street, Floor 23, New York, NY 10005-4020
Phone: 800-242-4363
Email: awards@aiche.org
https://www.aiche.org/community/awards
Purpose: To support chemical engineering students.
Eligibility: Applicants must be chemical engineering incoming undergraduate juniors or seniors and be planning a career in the chemical engineering process industries. Applicants must also have a minimum 3.0 GPA and be attending an ABET accredited school in the U.S., Canada or Mexico. Selection is based on an essay outlining career goals, leadership in an AIChE student chapter or other university sponsored activity and letters of recommendation. Preference is given to members of AIChE.
Target applicant(s): College students. Adult students.
Minimum GPA: 3.0
Amount: $5,000.
Number of awards: 1.
Deadline: June 15.
How to apply: Applications are available online.
Exclusive: Visit www.UltimateScholarshipBook.com and enter code AM99423 for updates on this award.

(995) · John L. Imhoff Scholarship

Institute of Industrial and Systems Engineers
3577 Parkway Lane, Suite 200, Norcross, GA 30092
Phone: 800-494-0460
Email: bcameron@iienet.org
http://www.iise.org/
Purpose: To reward a student who has contributed to the development of the industrial engineering profession through international understanding.
Eligibility: Applicants must be pursuing a B.S., master's or doctorate degree in an accredited IE program, have a minimum 3.4 GPA and have at least two years of school remaining. Students may not apply directly for this scholarship and must be nominated. An essay describing the candidate's international contributions to industrial engineering and three references are required. IIE membership is not required.
Target applicant(s): High school students. College students. Adult students.
Minimum GPA: 3.4
Amount: $1,000.
Number of awards: At least 1.
Deadline: November 15.
How to apply: More information is available online.

(996) · John Mabry Forestry Scholarship

Railway Tie Association
115 Commerce Drive, Suite C, Fayetteville, GA 30214
Phone: 770-460-5553
Email: ties@rta.org
http://www.rta.org
Purpose: To aid forestry school students.
Eligibility: Applicants must be enrolled in an accredited forestry program at an postsecondary institution. They must be in the second year of a two-year technical school program or in the third or fourth year of a four-year college or university program. Students who are in the final year of their program must remain enrolled for the entirety of the academic year. Selection is based on academic merit, leadership ability, stated career goals and financial need.
Target applicant(s): College students. Adult students.
Amount: $2,000.
Number of awards: 2.
Deadline: June 30.
How to apply: Applications are available online. An application form and supporting documents are required.
Exclusive: Visit www.UltimateScholarshipBook.com and enter code RA99623 for updates on this award.

(997) · John S. Marshall Memorial Scholarship

American Institute of Mining, Metallurgical and Petroleum Engineers (AIME)
12999 East Adam Aircraft Circle, Englewood, CO 80112
Phone: 303-325-5185
Email: aime@aimehq.org
http://www.aimehq.org/programs/scholarships
Purpose: To aid mining engineering students.
Eligibility: Applicants must be rising undergraduate juniors or seniors who are enrolled in an ABET-accredited mining engineering degree program on a full-time basis. They must be student members of the Society for Mining, Metallurgy and Exploration (SME). They must have plans to pursue a career in the mining industry and must demonstrate financial need. Selection is based on the overall strength of the application.
Target applicant(s): College students. Adult students.
Amount: Varies.
Number of awards: Varies.
Deadline: October.
How to apply: Applications are available online. An application form and two letters of recommendation are required.
Exclusive: Visit www.UltimateScholarshipBook.com and enter code AM99723 for updates on this award.

(998) · John S.W. Fargher, Jr. Scholarship

Institute of Industrial and Systems Engineers
3577 Parkway Lane, Suite 200, Norcross, GA 30092
Phone: 800-494-0460
Email: bcameron@iienet.org
http://www.iise.org/
Purpose: To reward graduate students in industrial engineering who have demonstrated leadership.
Eligibility: Applicants must be full-time graduate students with at least one full year left who are enrolled in a college in the United States with an accredited industrial engineering program. Candidates must also major in industrial engineering or engineering management and be active members who have demonstrated leadership in industrial engineering-related activities. Students may not apply directly for this scholarship and must be nominated.
Target applicant(s): Graduate school students. Adult students.
Minimum GPA: 3.0
Amount: Varies.
Number of awards: 1.
Deadline: February 1.
How to apply: More information is available online.
Exclusive: Visit www.UltimateScholarshipBook.com and enter code IN99823 for updates on this award.

(999) · John V. Wehausen Graduate Scholarship

Society of Naval Architects and Marine Engineers (SNAME)
99 Canal Center Plaza, Suite 310, Alexandria, VA 22314
Phone: 703-997-6701
Email: scholarships@sname.org
https://www.sname.org/scholarships
Purpose: To aid students who are seeking a master's degree in a marine-related subject.
Eligibility: Applicants must be members of the Society of Naval Architects and Marine Engineers (SNAME) or another respected marine society. They must be pursuing a master's degree in naval architecture, ocean engineering, marine engineering or another marine-related subject. Students who will be completing their degree before April 15 of the award disbursement year are ineligible. Selection is based on the overall strength of the application.
Target applicant(s): College students. Graduate school students. Adult students.
Amount: Up to $20,000.
Number of awards: 1.
Deadline: February 1.
How to apply: Applications are available online. An application form, transcript and three reference letters are required.
Exclusive: Visit www.UltimateScholarshipBook.com and enter code SO99923 for updates on this award.

(1000) · John Wright Memorial Scholarship

Tree Research and Education Endowment Fund
552 S. Washington Street, Suite 109, Naperville, IL 60540
Phone: 630-369-8300
Email: treefund@treefund.org
http://www.treefund.org
Purpose: To help undergraduate and technical college students pursuing careers in commercial arboriculture.
Eligibility: Applicants must be high school seniors entering college or community college or returning college students seeking a first bachelor's degree or associate's degree while attending an accredited U.S. college or university. All applicants must plan to enter the arboriculture industry and have a minimum 3.0 GPA. Consideration will be given for honorably discharged veterans and present members of the U.S. Armed Forces, Reserves and National Guard.
Target applicant(s): High school students. College students. Adult students.
Minimum GPA: 3.0
Amount: $2,000.
Number of awards: 1.
Deadline: March 15.

How to apply: Applications are available online.
Exclusive: Visit www.UltimateScholarshipBook.com and enter code TR100023 for updates on this award.

(1001) · Johnny Davis Memorial Scholarship

Aircraft Electronics Association
3570 NE Ralph Powell Road, Lee's Summit, MO 64064
Phone: 816-347-8400
Email: info@aea.net
https://aea.net/educationalfoundation/scholarships.asp
Purpose: To support students of avionics and aircraft repair.
Eligibility: Applicants must be high school seniors or college students who plan to or are attending an accredited school in an avionics or aircraft repair program.
Target applicant(s): High school students. College students. Adult students.
Amount: $1,000.
Number of awards: 1.
Deadline: April 1.
How to apply: Applications are available by contacting the organization for more information.
Exclusive: Visit www.UltimateScholarshipBook.com and enter code AI100123 for updates on this award.

(1002) · Joseph Frasca Excellence in Aviation Scholarship

University Aviation Association (UAA)
Dr. David NewMyer, College of Applied Sciences and Arts, Southern Illinois University Carbondale, 1365 Douglas Drive, MC 6623, Carbondale, IL 62901-6623
Phone: 618-453-8898
Email: newmyer@siu.edu
https://www.uaa.aero/uaa_scholarships.php
Purpose: To encourage students to reach the highest level of achievement in their aviation studies.
Eligibility: Applicants must be juniors or seniors enrolled at a UAA member college or university with at least a 3.0 GPA. Students must demonstrate excellence in all areas related to aviation and have FAA certification in either aviation maintenance or flight. Applicants must be a member of at least one aviation organization and be involved in aviation activities that demonstrate interest in and enthusiasm for aviation.
Target applicant(s): College students. Adult students.
Minimum GPA: 3.0
Amount: $2,000.
Number of awards: 2.
Deadline: June 30.
How to apply: Applications are available online.
Exclusive: Visit www.UltimateScholarshipBook.com and enter code UN100223 for updates on this award.

(1003) · Junior Showmanship Scholarship Program

American Kennel Club
260 Madison Avenue, New York, NY 10016
Phone: 212-696-8200
http://www.akc.org
Purpose: To assist students who are involved with AKC purebred dogs.
Eligibility: Applicants must be under age 18 with an AKC registered purebred dog. Selection is based on involvement with AKC registered dogs, academic achievement and financial need. The scholarship program awards a total of $150,000 annually.

Target applicant(s): Junior high students or younger. High school students.
Amount: Varies.
Number of awards: Varies.
Deadline: March 1.
How to apply: Applications are available online.
Exclusive: Visit www.UltimateScholarshipBook.com and enter code AM100323 for updates on this award.

(1004) · Kappa Delta Phi

American Occupational Therapy Foundation
Attn: Jeanne Cooper, 4720 Montgomery Lane, Suite 202, Bethesda, MD 20814
Phone: 240-292-1034
Email: jcooper@aotf.org
https://www.aotf.org/Scholarships
Purpose: To encourage students who are pursuing post-baccalaureate degrees in occupational therapy.
Eligibility: Applicants must be currently enrolled full-time in an AOTA accredited occupational therapy program. Students must have completed at least one year of occupational therapy specific course work. Priority is given to students of Arizona, California, Florida, Iowa, Indiana, Kentucky, Missouri and Ohio.
Target applicant(s): College students. Graduate school students. Adult students.
Amount: $2,000.
Number of awards: Varies.
Deadline: October 1.
How to apply: Applications are available online.
Exclusive: Visit www.UltimateScholarshipBook.com and enter code AM100423 for updates on this award.

(1005) · Karen O'Neil Memorial Scholarship

Emergency Nurses Association
915 Lee Street, Des Plaines, IL 60016
Phone: 847-460-4100
Email: foundation@ena.org
http://www.ena.org
Purpose: To promote advanced degrees in emergency nursing.
Eligibility: Applicants must be nurses pursuing an advanced degree and must have been ENA members for at least 12 months before applying.
Target applicant(s): Graduate school students. Adult students.
Amount: $3,000.
Number of awards: 1.
Deadline: April 30.
How to apply: Applications are available online.
Exclusive: Visit www.UltimateScholarshipBook.com and enter code EM100523 for updates on this award.

(1006) · Karla Girts Memorial Community Outreach Scholarship

American Dental Hygienists' Association (ADHA) Institute for Oral Health
Scholarship Award Program, 444 North Michigan Avenue, Suite 3400, Chicago, IL 60611
Phone: 312-440-8900
Email: institute@adha.net
https://www.adha.org/ioh-scholarships-main
Purpose: To support undergraduate students and those working towards degree completion within the dental hygiene arena who are

also committed to work within the geriatric population in an effort to improve the oral health of this population.

Eligibility: Applicants must be full-time students at an accredited college or university in the United States pursuing an associate, baccalaureate or degree completion program in dental hygiene or a related field and must commit to working towards improvement of oral health within the geriatric population. Applicants must have completed at least one year of a dental hygiene curriculum, be active members of the ADHA, have a minimum 3.0 GPA and have a minimum demonstrated financial need of $1,500. Selection is based upon the overall strength of the application.

Target applicant(s): College students. Graduate school students. Adult students.

Minimum GPA: 3.0

Amount: $2,000.

Number of awards: 2.

Deadline: February 1.

How to apply: Applications are available online after October 1. An application form and essay are required.

Exclusive: Visit www.UltimateScholarshipBook.com and enter code AM100623 for updates on this award.

(1007) · Kenneth Andrew Roe Scholarship

American Society of Mechanical Engineers (ASME)
Two Park Avenue, New York, NY 10016-5990
Phone: 800-843-2763
Email: lefeverb@asme.org
https://www.asmefoundation.org/programs/stemeducation/asme-scholarships/
Purpose: To support students who are studying mechanical engineering.
Eligibility: Applicants must be ASME student members, be enrolled in an ABET accredited mechanical engineering baccalaureate program, be North American residents and be U.S. citizens. Applicants must also have strong academic performance, character and integrity. The award is to be used during the junior or senior undergraduate years.
Target applicant(s): College students. Adult students.
Amount: $13,000.
Number of awards: 1.
Deadline: February 17.
How to apply: Applications are available online.
Exclusive: Visit www.UltimateScholarshipBook.com and enter code AM100723 for updates on this award.

(1008) · LabRoots Scholarship

Labroots
18340 Yorba Linda Boulevard, Suite 107 PMB 427, Yorba Linda, CA 92886
https://www.labroots.com/scholarships
Purpose: To support students in STEM studies.
Eligibility: Applicants must be enrolled in or accepted for an undergraduate or graduate degree at a recognized university. Students must be seeking a degree in a STEM field.
Target applicant(s): High school students. College students. Graduate school students. Adult students.
Amount: $3,000.
Number of awards: 2.
Deadline: January 29; September 3.
How to apply: Applications are available online.
Exclusive: Visit www.UltimateScholarshipBook.com and enter code LA100823 for updates on this award.

(1009) · Landscape Forms Scholarship in Memory of Peter Lindsay Schaudt, FASLA

Landscape Architecture Foundation
1129 20th Street NW, Suite 202, Washington, DC 20036
Phone: 202-331-7070
Email: scholarships@lafoundation.org
https://www.lafoundation.org/what-we-do/scholarships
Purpose: To aid landscape architecture students.
Eligibility: Applicants must be full-time undergraduate students who are enrolled in a landscape architecture degree program at a school that has been accredited by the Landscape Architectural Accreditation Board (LAAB). They must be in the final year of their degree program. Selection is based on academic merit and creativity.
Target applicant(s): College students. Adult students.
Amount: $5,000.
Number of awards: 1.
Deadline: February 1.
How to apply: Applications are available online. An application form, essay, work samples and two recommendation letters are required.
Exclusive: Visit www.UltimateScholarshipBook.com and enter code LA100923 for updates on this award.

(1010) · Larry Williams Photography and AYA Photo Contest

Appaloosa Horse Club
Appaloosa Youth Association, 2720 West Pullman Road, Moscow, ID 83843
Phone: 208-882-5578
Email: youth@appaloosa.com
https://www.appaloosa.com/appaloosa-youth-association
Purpose: To support students who express their love of the Appaloosa through photography.
Eligibility: Applicants must submit multiple photographs in two divisions: 13 and under and 14 to 18.
Target applicant(s): Junior high students or younger. High school students.
Amount: Up to $100.
Number of awards: 6.
Deadline: May 1.
How to apply: Applications are available online.
Exclusive: Visit www.UltimateScholarshipBook.com and enter code AP101023 for updates on this award.

(1011) · Larson Aquatic Research Support (LARS)

American Water Works Association
6666 W. Quincy Avenue, Denver, CO 80235-3098
Phone: 800-926-7337
Email: scholarships@awwa.org
http://www.awwa.org
Purpose: To support doctoral and master's students interested in careers in the fields of corrosion control, treatment and distribution of domestic and industrial water supplies, aquatic chemistry and/or environmental chemistry.
Eligibility: Applicants must pursue an advanced (master's or doctoral) degree at an institution of higher education located in Canada, Guam, Puerto Rico, Mexico or the U.S. Applications, resumes, transcripts, GRE scores, three recommendation letters and a course of study are required. Master's students also must submit a statement of educational plans and career objectives or a research plan. Ph.D. students must submit research

plans. The master's grant is $5,000, and the doctoral grant is $7,000. The award is based on academics and leadership.
Target applicant(s): Graduate school students. Adult students.
Amount: $5,000-$7,000.
Number of awards: 2.
Deadline: December.
How to apply: Applications are available online.
Exclusive: Visit www.UltimateScholarshipBook.com and enter code AM101123 for updates on this award.

(1012) · Lawrence C. Fortier Memorial Scholarship

Air Traffic Control Association
225 Reinekers Lane, Suite 400, Alexandria, VA 22314
Phone: 703-299-2430
Email: info@atca.org
http://www.atca.org
Purpose: To help students seeking higher education in air traffic control and other aviation disciplines.
Eligibility: Applicants must be enrolled half- to full-time in a program leading to a bachelor's degree or higher in an aviation-related course of study.
Target applicant(s): High school students. College students. Graduate school students. Adult students.
Amount: Varies.
Number of awards: Varies.
Deadline: May 15.
How to apply: Applications are available online. An application form, two letters of reference, academic transcripts, an essay and answers to leadership and career questions are required.
Exclusive: Visit www.UltimateScholarshipBook.com and enter code AI101223 for updates on this award.

(1013) · Leaders Scholarship

Medical Group Management Association
104 Inverness Terrace East, Englewood, CO 80112
Phone: 877-275-6462
Email: acmpe@mgma.com
https://mgma.com/career-pathways/career-advancement/career-resources/scholarships
Purpose: To support students pursuing advanced degrees in the medical field.
Eligibility: Applicants must be enrolled in a graduate degree program pertaining to medical practice management at a university located in the U.S. Students must include transcripts, two letters of reference, curriculum and resume along with the application.
Target applicant(s): Graduate school students. Adult students.
Amount: $5,000.
Number of awards: 1.
Deadline: May.
How to apply: Applications are available online.
Exclusive: Visit www.UltimateScholarshipBook.com and enter code ME101323 for updates on this award.

(1014) · Learner Education Women in Mathematics Scholarship

Learner
204 Sandy Bank Road, Media, PA 19063
Phone: 800-654-7390
Email: chris@learnerscholarship.com
https://www.learner.com/scholarship
Purpose: To support female students interested in careers in math-related fields.
Eligibility: Applicants must be females who are current high school seniors planning to study or current undergraduate students studying mathematics. An essay on a provided prompt is required to be submitted.
Target applicant(s): High school students. College students. Adult students.
Amount: $1,000.
Number of awards: 1.
Deadline: August 1.
How to apply: Applications are available online.
Exclusive: Visit www.UltimateScholarshipBook.com and enter code LE101423 for updates on this award.

(1015) · Lee Magnon Memorial Scholarship

National Association of Corrosion Engineers (NACE) International Foundation
15835 Park Ten Place, Houston, TX 77084-5145
Phone: 281-228-6205
Email: nace.foundation@nace.org
http://nace-foundation.org/programs/students/scholarships/
Purpose: To help outstanding students pursue a career in the field of engineering and/or science.
Eligibility: Applicants must be enrolled full-time as an undergraduate at an accredited two- or four-year college or university. Applicants must be studying engineering and/or science at their chosen school. Applicants must have permanent residence in the NACE Central Area which includes the following states: Arkansas, Colorado, Illinois, Iowa, Kansas, Louisiana, Minnesota, Missouri, Montana, Nebraska, New Mexico, North Dakota, Oklahoma, South Dakota, Texas, Wisconsin and Wyoming.
Target applicant(s): College students. Adult students.
Amount: $2,500.
Number of awards: 1.
Deadline: January 1.
How to apply: Applications are available online. An application form, two recommendation forms, an academic transcript and scholarship essay questions are required.
Exclusive: Visit www.UltimateScholarshipBook.com and enter code NA101523 for updates on this award.

(1016) · Lee S. Evans Scholarship

National Housing Endowment
1201 15th Street NW, Washington, DC 20005
Phone: 202-266-8069
Email: Scholarships@nahb.org
http://www.nationalhousingendowment.org/page.aspx/generic/sectionID=3267
Purpose: To aid students who are preparing for careers in residential construction management.
Eligibility: Applicants must be full-time undergraduate or graduate students. They must have completed at least one semester of college coursework at the time of applying for the scholarship and must have at least one year remaining in their programs of study at the time of award disbursement; fifth-year seniors are ineligible. Applicants must have a demonstrated interest in pursuing a career in the residential construction industry. Preference will be given to current student members of the National Association of Home Builders (NAHB) and to applicants who are enrolled in a four-year degree program that focuses on construction

management. Selection is based on academic merit, recommendations, extracurricular activities, work experience and financial need.
Target applicant(s): College students. Graduate school students. Adult students.
Amount: Varies.
Number of awards: Varies.
Scholarship may be renewable.
Deadline: March.
How to apply: Applications are available online. An application form, an official transcript, a degree program outline and two letters of recommendation are required.
Exclusive: Visit www.UltimateScholarshipBook.com and enter code NA101623 for updates on this award.

(1017) · Lee Tarbox Memorial Scholarship

Aircraft Electronics Association
3570 NE Ralph Powell Road, Lee's Summit, MO 64064
Phone: 816-347-8400
Email: info@aea.net
https://aea.net/educationalfoundation/scholarships.asp
Purpose: To support students of avionics and aircraft repair.
Eligibility: Applicants must be high school seniors or college students who plan to or are attending an accredited school in an avionics or aircraft repair program.
Target applicant(s): High school students. College students. Adult students.
Amount: $2,500.
Number of awards: 1.
Deadline: April 1.
How to apply: Applications are available by contacting the organization for more information.
Exclusive: Visit www.UltimateScholarshipBook.com and enter code AI101723 for updates on this award.

(1018) · Len Assante Scholarship Fund

National Ground Water Association
601 Dempsey Road, Westerville, OH 43081-8978
Phone: 800-551-7379
Email: ngwa@ngwa.org
https://www.groundwater.org/kids/scholarships.html
Purpose: To support students in fields related to the ground water industry.
Eligibility: Applicants must be high school graduates or college students with a minimum 2.5 GPA who are studying fields related to the ground water industry including geology, hydrology, hydrogeology, environmental sciences or microbiology or well drilling two-year associate degree programs.
Target applicant(s): High school students. College students. Adult students.
Minimum GPA: 2.5
Amount: Varies.
Number of awards: Varies.
Deadline: May 15.
How to apply: Applications are available by mail or e-mail.
Exclusive: Visit www.UltimateScholarshipBook.com and enter code NA101823 for updates on this award.

(1019) · Lewis C. Hoffman Scholarship

American Ceramic Society
600 North Cleveland Avenue, Suite 210, Westerville, OH 43082

Phone: 866-721-3322
Email: mstout@ceramics.org
http://www.ceramics.org
Purpose: To support undergraduate ceramics and materials science and engineering students.
Eligibility: Applicants must be full-time undergraduates who will have completed 70 or more semester credits (or quarter credit equivalent) at the time of award disbursement. Selection is based on essay response, GPA, recommendation letter, extracurricular involvements and standardized test scores (if available).
Target applicant(s): College students. Adult students.
Amount: $2,000.
Number of awards: 1.
Deadline: June 15.
How to apply: This scholarship does not require an application form. The applicant's essay response, a recommendation letter and a list of extracurricular activities is required.
Exclusive: Visit www.UltimateScholarshipBook.com and enter code AM101923 for updates on this award.

(1020) · Libbie H. Hyman Memorial Scholarship

Society for Integrative and Comparative Biology
1313 Dolley Madison Boulevard, Suite 402, McLean, VA 22101
Phone: 703-790-1745
http://www.sicb.org/grants/hyman/
Purpose: To support students seeking field station experience to study invertebrates.
Eligibility: Applicants must be first- or second-year graduate students or advanced undergraduates seeking to carry on invertebrate research at a marine, freshwater or terrestrial field station. Students must complete the application including a proposal, two letters of reference and transcripts.
Target applicant(s): College students. Graduate school students. Adult students.
Amount: Varies.
Number of awards: Varies.
Deadline: February 4.
How to apply: Applications are available online.
Exclusive: Visit www.UltimateScholarshipBook.com and enter code SO102023 for updates on this award.

(1021) · Light Metals Division Scholarship

Minerals, Metals and Materials Society
184 Thorn Hill Road, Warrendale, PA 15086
Phone: 724-776-9000
Email: students@tms.org
http://www.tms.org
Purpose: To aid undergraduate students who are majoring in metallurgical engineering or materials science and engineering.
Eligibility: Applicants must be full-time undergraduate sophomores or juniors who are enrolled in a degree program in metallurgical engineering or materials science and engineering. They must be student members of TMS, The Minerals, Metals and Materials Society. Selection is based on academic merit, extracurricular activities, recommendations and personal statement.
Target applicant(s): College students. Adult students.
Amount: $4,000.
Number of awards: 3.
Deadline: March 15.
How to apply: Applications are available online. An application form, transcript, personal statement and three recommendation letters are required.

Exclusive: Visit www.UltimateScholarshipBook.com and enter code MI102123 for updates on this award.

(1022) · Lisa Zaken Award For Excellence

Institute of Industrial and Systems Engineers
3577 Parkway Lane, Suite 200, Norcross, GA 30092
Phone: 800-494-0460
Email: bcameron@iienet.org
http://www.iise.org/
Purpose: To reward excellence in scholarly activities and leadership related to the industrial engineering profession on campus.
Eligibility: Applicants must be undergraduate or graduate students with at least one year remaining, have a 3.0 or higher GPA, major in industrial engineering and be active members who have been leaders in IIE. Students may not apply directly for this scholarship and must be nominated. The award is based on academic ability and leadership related to industrial engineering.
Target applicant(s): College students. Graduate school students. Adult students.
Minimum GPA: 3.0
Amount: $1,500.
Number of awards: 1.
Deadline: February 1.
How to apply: Nomination forms are available online.
Exclusive: Visit www.UltimateScholarshipBook.com and enter code IN102223 for updates on this award.

(1023) · Lockheed Martin STEM Scholarship Program

Lockheed Martin STEM Scholarship Program
Scholarship America, One Scholarship Way, Saint Peter, MN 56082
Phone: 800-537-4180
Email: lockheedmartin@scholarshipamerica.org
https://lockheedmartin.com/en-us/who-we-are/communities/stem-education/lm-scholarship-program.html
Purpose: To encourage the study of STEM fields.
Eligibility: Applicants must be U.S. citizens who are high school seniors with a GPA of 2.5 or better or current college freshmen or sophomores with a minimum 2.5 GPA. Students must be enrolling full-time at an accredited four-year institution majoring in an engineering field, math, physics, information systems or information assurance.
Target applicant(s): High school students. College students. Adult students.
Minimum GPA: 2.5
Amount: $10,000.
Number of awards: 200.
Deadline: April 1.
How to apply: Applications are available online.
Exclusive: Visit www.UltimateScholarshipBook.com and enter code LO102323 for updates on this award.

(1024) · Lois Britt Pork Industry Memorial Scholarship Program

National Pork Producers Council
122 C Street, NW, Suite 875, Washington, DC 20001
Phone: 202-347-3600
Email: Boellingc@nppc.org
http://nppc.org/programs/scholarships/
Purpose: To support students who are preparing for careers in the pork industry.

Eligibility: Applicants must be undergraduates enrolled in either a two-year swine program or a four-year college of agriculture. They must be interested in pursuing a career in the pork industry. Selection is based on the strength of the personal essay.
Target applicant(s): College students. Adult students.
Amount: $2,500.
Number of awards: 10.
Deadline: January 4.
How to apply: Applications are available online. An information sheet, cover letter, personal essay and two reference letters are required.
Exclusive: Visit www.UltimateScholarshipBook.com and enter code NA102423 for updates on this award.

(1025) · Long-Term Member Sponsored Scholarship

Society of Automotive Engineers International
Scholarships Program, 400 Commonwealth Drive, Warrendale, PA 15096
Phone: 724-776-4841
Email: scholarships@sae.org
https://www.sae.org/participate/scholarships
Purpose: This scholarship recognizes outstanding SAE student members who actively support SAE and its activities.
Eligibility: Applicants must be college juniors and student members of SAE, major in engineering and actively support SAE and its programs. The scholarship will be awarded purely on the basis of the student's support for SAE and its programs.
Target applicant(s): College students. Adult students.
Amount: $1,000.
Number of awards: Varies.
Deadline: March 15.
How to apply: Applications are available online.
Exclusive: Visit www.UltimateScholarshipBook.com and enter code SO102523 for updates on this award.

(1026) · Louis Agassiz Fuertes Award

Wilson Ornithological Society
Department of Biology and Biomedical Science, Dr. James Chace, Associate Professor, 100 Ochre Point Avenue, Newport, RI 02840-4192
Email: rbpayne@umich.edu
http://www.wilsonsociety.org
Purpose: To support ornithologists' research.
Eligibility: Applicants must be students or young professionals doing avian research. Applicants must be willing to report their research results at an annual meeting of the Wilson Ornithological Society.
Target applicant(s): High school students. College students. Graduate school students. Adult students.
Amount: $2,500.
Number of awards: Up to 2.
Deadline: February 1.
How to apply: Applications are available online.
Exclusive: Visit www.UltimateScholarshipBook.com and enter code WI102623 for updates on this award.

(1027) · Lowell H. and Dorothy Loving Undergraduate Scholarship

National Society of Professional Surveyors (NSPS/AAGS)
Attn: Scholarships, 5119 Pegasus Court, Suite Q, Frederick, MD 21704

Phone: 240-439-4615x105
Email: trisha.milburn@nsps.us.com
https://www.nsps.us.com/page/Scholarships
Purpose: To aid undergraduate surveying and mapping students.
Eligibility: Applicants must be members of the National Society of Professional Surveyors (NSPS). They must be undergraduate juniors or seniors who are enrolled in a surveying and mapping degree program at a four-year institution located in the U.S. They must have a plan of study that includes coursework in two or more of the following areas: spatial measurement system analysis and design, land surveying, photogrammetry and remote sensing or geometric geodesy. Selection is based on academic merit, personal statement, recommendation letters, professional involvement and financial need.
Target applicant(s): College students. Adult students.
Amount: $2,000.
Number of awards: 1.
Scholarship may be renewable.
Deadline: January 22.
How to apply: Applications are available online. An application form, personal statement, proof of ACSM membership, three letters of recommendation and an official transcript are required.
Exclusive: Visit www.UltimateScholarshipBook.com and enter code NA102723 for updates on this award.

(1028) · Loy McCandless Marks Scholarship in Tropical Horticulture

Garden Club of America
14 East 60th Street, New York, NY 10022
Phone: 212-753-8287
Email: scholarshipapplications@gcamerica.org
https://www.gcamerica.org/index.cfm/scholarships/details/id/19
Purpose: To promote the study of tropical plants in horticulture and landscape architecture.
Eligibility: Applicants must be U.S. citizens or permanent residents enrolled in a U.S. institution as a graduate or advanced undergraduate. Students must use the award to study abroad within one year.
Target applicant(s): College students. Graduate school students. Adult students.
Amount: $5,000.
Number of awards: 1.
Deadline: February 1.
How to apply: Applications are available online.
Exclusive: Visit www.UltimateScholarshipBook.com and enter code GA102823 for updates on this award.

(1029) · Ludo Frevel Crystallography Scholarships

International Centre for Diffraction Data
12 Campus Boulevard, Newtown Square, PA 19073
http://www.icdd.com
Purpose: To support graduate students in crystallography-related fields.
Eligibility: Applicants must be graduate students enrolled in a degree program relating to crystallography. Students must submit a proposed research project along with their application.
Target applicant(s): Graduate school students. Adult students.
Amount: $2,500.
Number of awards: Varies.
Deadline: October 14.
How to apply: Applications are available online.
Exclusive: Visit www.UltimateScholarshipBook.com and enter code IN102923 for updates on this award.

(1030) · Mandell and Lester Rosenblatt Undergraduate Scholarship

Society of Naval Architects and Marine Engineers (SNAME)
99 Canal Center Plaza, Suite 310, Alexandria, VA 22314
Phone: 703-997-6701
Email: scholarships@sname.org
https://www.sname.org/scholarships
Purpose: To assist college undergraduates who are studying marine industry fields.
Eligibility: Applicants must be U.S., Canadian or international college students who are members of the SNAME and are working towards degrees in naval architecture, marine engineering, ocean engineering or marine industry related areas fields. An application form, three recommendation letters and an essay are required.
Target applicant(s): High school students. College students. Adult students.
Amount: Up to $6,000.
Number of awards: 1.
Scholarship may be renewable.
Deadline: June 1.
How to apply: Applications are available online.
Exclusive: Visit www.UltimateScholarshipBook.com and enter code SO103023 for updates on this award.

(1031) · Marliave Fund

Association of Engineering Geologists Foundation Marliave Fund
P.O. Box 161683, Boiling Springs, SC 29316
Email: staff@aegfoundation.org
http://www.aegfoundation.org
Purpose: To reward outstanding students in engineering geology and geological engineering.
Eligibility: Applicants must be seniors or graduate students in a college or university program directly applicable to geological engineering and be members of the Association of Engineering Geologists.
Target applicant(s): College students. Graduate school students. Adult students.
Amount: Varies.
Number of awards: 1.
Deadline: February 1.
How to apply: Applications are available online or by written request.
Exclusive: Visit www.UltimateScholarshipBook.com and enter code AS103123 for updates on this award.

(1032) · Marshall E. McCullough Scholarship

National Dairy Shrine
P.O. Box 725, Denmark, WI 54208
Phone: 920-863-6333
Email: info@dairyshrine.org
http://www.dairyshrine.org
Purpose: To support students who plan careers in agricultural-related communications.
Eligibility: Applicants must be high school seniors planning to enter a four-year university with intent to major in the dairy or animal sciences with a communications emphasis or agricultural journalism with a dairy or animal science emphasis, and they must intend to work in the dairy industry following graduation.
Target applicant(s): High school students.
Amount: $1,500-$2,000.
Number of awards: 2.

Deadline: April 15.
How to apply: Applications are available online.
Exclusive: Visit www.UltimateScholarshipBook.com and enter code NA103223 for updates on this award.

(1033) · Marvin Mundel Memorial Scholarship

Institute of Industrial and Systems Engineers
3577 Parkway Lane, Suite 200, Norcross, GA 30092
Phone: 800-494-0460
Email: bcameron@iienet.org
http://www.iise.org/
Purpose: To assist undergraduate engineering students with an interest in work measurement and methods engineering.
Eligibility: Applicants must be full-time undergraduate students enrolled in a college in the United States, Canada or Mexico with an accredited industrial engineering program, major in industrial engineering and be active members. Students may not apply directly for this scholarship and must be nominated. The award is based on academic ability, character, leadership, potential service to the industrial engineering profession and financial need. Preference is given to students with a demonstrated interest in work measurement and methods engineering.
Target applicant(s): High school students. College students. Adult students.
Minimum GPA: 3.4
Amount: $1,250.
Number of awards: 2.
Deadline: November 15.
How to apply: Nomination forms are available online.
Exclusive: Visit www.UltimateScholarshipBook.com and enter code IN103323 for updates on this award.

(1034) · Mary Rhein Memorial Scholarship

Mu Alpha Theta Scholarship Committee
c/o University of Oklahoma, 3200 Marshall Avenue, Suite 150, Norman, OK 73019
Phone: 405-325-4489
Email: matheta@ou.edu
https://mualphatheta.org/muat_scholarships
Purpose: To aid graduating high school seniors who are active Mu Alpha Theta members.
Eligibility: Applicants must be graduating high school seniors who are outstanding mathematics students. They must be active Mu Alpha Theta members who have been of service in the area of mathematics and who have participated in local, regional or national mathematics competitions. Applicants must have plans to pursue a mathematics-related career. Selection is based on the overall strength of the application.
Target applicant(s): High school students. College students. Adult students.
Amount: $5,000.
Number of awards: 1.
Deadline: February 1.
How to apply: Applications are available online. An application form, student essay, official transcript and three recommendation letters are required.
Exclusive: Visit www.UltimateScholarshipBook.com and enter code MU103423 for updates on this award.

(1035) · Mary V. Munger Scholarship

Society of Women Engineers
130 East Randolph Street, Suite 3500, Chicago, IL 60601
Phone: 877-793-4636
Email: scholarships@swe.org
https://swe.org/scholarships/
Purpose: To support female students working towards a major in engineering.
Eligibility: Applicants must be planning to study at an ABET-accredited program in engineering, technology or computing and have a minimum 3.0 GPA. The award may be used during the junior or senior year of college and is open to re-entry and adult students.
Target applicant(s): College students. Adult students.
Minimum GPA: 3.0
Amount: $2,750.
Number of awards: 2.
Deadline: February 14.
How to apply: Applications are available online.
Exclusive: Visit www.UltimateScholarshipBook.com and enter code SO103523 for updates on this award.

(1036) · Masonic-Range Science Scholarship

Society for Range Management (SRM)
10030 W. 27th Avenue, Wheat Ridge, CO 80215-6601
Phone: 303-986-3309
Email: vtrujillo@rangelands.org
https://rangelands.org/students/masonic-scholarship/
Purpose: To help a high school senior, college freshman or college sophomore majoring in range science or a closely related field.
Eligibility: Applicants must be sponsored by a member of the Society for Range Management (SRM), the National Association of Conservation Districts (NACD) or the Soil and Water Conservation Society (SWCS). Applicants must also submit an application form, transcript, SAT or ACT scores and two letters of reference.
Target applicant(s): High school students. College students. Adult students.
Amount: Varies.
Number of awards: Varies.
Deadline: March 1.
How to apply: Applications are available online.
Exclusive: Visit www.UltimateScholarshipBook.com and enter code SO103623 for updates on this award.

(1037) · Materials Processing and Manufacturing Division Scholarship

Minerals, Metals and Materials Society
184 Thorn Hill Road, Warrendale, PA 15086
Phone: 724-776-9000
Email: students@tms.org
http://www.tms.org
Purpose: To aid undergraduate student members of TMS who are majoring in metallurgical engineering or materials science and engineering.
Eligibility: Applicants must be full-time undergraduate sophomores or juniors whose studies must be focused on the integration of process control technology into manufacturing, materials technology research or the manufacturing process. Selection is based on academic merit, personal statement, recommendations, leadership skills, extracurricular activities and coursework relevance.
Target applicant(s): College students. Adult students.
Amount: $2,500.
Number of awards: 2.
Deadline: March 15.

How to apply: Applications are available online. An application form, personal statement, three recommendation letters and a transcript are required.
Exclusive: Visit www.UltimateScholarshipBook.com and enter code MI103723 for updates on this award.

(1038) · Medical Scrubs Collection
Medical Scrubs Collection
1665 Corporate Road West, Lakewood, NJ 08701
Phone: 888-567-2782
Email: scholarships@medicalscrubscollection.com
https://medicalscrubscollection.com/scholarship-program
Purpose: To reward students pursuing medical education.
Eligibility: Applicants must be U.S. citizens or registered aliens. Students must be high school seniors or currently enrolled in an accredited U.S. post-secondary institution. Applicants must have a minimum grade point average of 3.0 and intend to pursue a degree in a medical field.
Target applicant(s): High school students. College students. Adult students.
Minimum GPA: 3.0
Amount: $1,000.
Number of awards: 1.
Deadline: December 15.
How to apply: Applications are available online.
Exclusive: Visit www.UltimateScholarshipBook.com and enter code ME103823 for updates on this award.

(1039) · Medical Student Research Scholarship
American Academy of Neurology
201 Chicago Avenue, Minneapolis, MN 55415
Phone: 800-879-1960
Email: ggates@aan.com
http://www.aan.com
Purpose: To support medical students with limited research experience.
Eligibility: Applicants must be medical students with limited research experience relevant to clinical or neuroscience fields who have a supporting preceptor and a project with clearly defined goals. Students must conduct their project through a U.S. or Canadian institution of the student's choice and jointly designed by the student and sponsoring institution.
Target applicant(s): Graduate school students. Adult students.
Amount: Varies.
Number of awards: Varies.
Deadline: March 8.
How to apply: Applications are available online.
Exclusive: Visit www.UltimateScholarshipBook.com and enter code AM103923 for updates on this award.

(1040) · Medical Student Training in Aging Research (MSTAR) Program
American Federation for Aging Research (AFAR)
55 West 39th Street, 16th Floor, New York, NY 10018
Phone: 212-703-9977
Email: grants@afar.org
http://www.afar.org
Purpose: To support early medical students who demonstrate an interest in geriatric medicine or age-related research with an opportunity to serve under top experts in the field.
Eligibility: Applicants must be osteopathic or allopathic students who have completed at least one year of medical school at a U.S. institution.

Students must have a faculty sponsor from their home institution. The program lasts 8 to 12 weeks, and monthly stipends are provided.
Target applicant(s): Graduate school students. Adult students.
Amount: $1,980 per month.
Number of awards: Up to 100.
Deadline: January.
How to apply: Applications are available online.
Exclusive: Visit www.UltimateScholarshipBook.com and enter code AM104023 for updates on this award.

(1041) · Melvin J. Schiff Fellowship Fund
National Association of Corrosion Engineers (NACE) International Foundation
15835 Park Ten Place, Houston, TX 77084-5145
Phone: 281-228-6205
Email: nace.foundation@nace.org
http://nace-foundation.org/programs/students/scholarships/
Purpose: To help an outstanding student, professional or technician interested in furthering their knowledge of corrosion and corrosion control.
Eligibility: Applicants must be a permanent resident of the U.S. and be professionals, technicians or full- or part-time students enrolled in an accredited U.S. college or university. Selection is based on the overall strength of the application.
Target applicant(s): College students. Graduate school students. Adult students.
Amount: $1,000.
Number of awards: 1.
Deadline: January 1.
How to apply: Applications are available online. An application form, two recommendation forms, an academic transcript and essay scholarship questions are required.
Exclusive: Visit www.UltimateScholarshipBook.com and enter code NA104123 for updates on this award.

(1042) · Melvin R. Green Scholarships
American Society of Mechanical Engineers (ASME)
Two Park Avenue, New York, NY 10016-5990
Phone: 800-843-2763
Email: lefeverb@asme.org
https://www.asmefoundation.org/programs/stemeducation/asme-scholarships/
Purpose: To support mechanical engineering students.
Eligibility: Applicants must have outstanding character and integrity, be ASME student members, be enrolled in an eligible accredited mechanical engineering baccalaureate program, be college sophomores, juniors, seniors or graduate students and have strong academic performance. Selection is based on scholastic ability, leadership, financial need and potential contribution to mechanical engineering profession.
Target applicant(s): College students. Graduate school students. Adult students.
Amount: $4,000.
Number of awards: Up to 2.
Deadline: March 4.
How to apply: Applications are available online.
Exclusive: Visit www.UltimateScholarshipBook.com and enter code AM104223 for updates on this award.

(1043) · Meredith Thoms Memorial Scholarship

Society of Women Engineers
130 East Randolph Street, Suite 3500, Chicago, IL 60601
Phone: 877-793-4636
Email: scholarships@swe.org
https://swe.org/scholarships/
Purpose: To support female students pursuing a college degree in engineering.
Eligibility: Applicants must be enrolled in an accredited engineering or engineering technology program with a 3.0 GPA. The award may be used during the sophomore, junior or senior year of college.
Target applicant(s): College students. Adult students.
Minimum GPA: 3.0
Amount: $4,000.
Number of awards: 4.
Deadline: February 15.
How to apply: Applications are available online.
Exclusive: Visit www.UltimateScholarshipBook.com and enter code SO104323 for updates on this award.

(1044) · MGMA Midwest Section Scholarship

Medical Group Management Association
104 Inverness Terrace East, Englewood, CO 80112
Phone: 877-275-6462
Email: acmpe@mgma.com
https://mgma.com/career-pathways/career-advancement/career-resources/scholarships
Purpose: To aid MGMA Midwest Section members who are pursuing higher education in a subject that is related to medical practice management.
Eligibility: Applicants must be members of the Medical Group Management Association (MGMA). They must be residents of one of the MGMA Midwest Section states, namely Illinois, Indiana, Iowa, Michigan, Minnesota, Nebraska, North Dakota, Ohio, South Dakota or Wisconsin. They must be undergraduate or graduate students who are enrolled in a degree program that is related to medical practice management (such as public health, business administration or health care administration). Selection is based on the overall strength of the application.
Target applicant(s): High school students. College students. Graduate school students. Adult students.
Amount: $2,500.
Number of awards: Varies.
Deadline: May.
How to apply: Applications are available online. An application form and supporting materials are required.
Exclusive: Visit www.UltimateScholarshipBook.com and enter code ME104423 for updates on this award.

(1045) · MGMA Western Section Scholarship

Medical Group Management Association
104 Inverness Terrace East, Englewood, CO 80112
Phone: 877-275-6462
Email: acmpe@mgma.com
https://mgma.com/career-pathways/career-advancement/career-resources/scholarships
Purpose: To aid MGMA Western Section members who are pursuing higher education in subjects that are related to medical practice management.
Eligibility: Applicants must be residents of one of the MGMA Western Section states, namely Alaska, Arizona, California, Colorado, Hawaii, Idaho, Montana, Nevada, New Mexico, Oregon, Utah, Washington or Wyoming. They must be undergraduate or graduate students who are enrolled in a degree program relating to medical practice management (such as public health, business administration or health care administration). Selection is based on the overall strength of the application.
Target applicant(s): High school students. College students. Graduate school students. Adult students.
Amount: $2,500.
Number of awards: Varies.
Deadline: May.
How to apply: Applications are available online. An application form and supporting materials are required.
Exclusive: Visit www.UltimateScholarshipBook.com and enter code ME104523 for updates on this award.

(1046) · Michael Kidger Memorial Scholarship

Kidger Optics Associates
http://www.kidger.com/mkms_home.html
Purpose: To support students in the optical design field.
Eligibility: Applicants must be in the optical design field and must have one year remaining of their studies. Students must submit a summary of their academic background and interest in optical design and two letters of recommendation.
Target applicant(s): College students. Adult students.
Amount: $5,000.
Number of awards: 1.
Deadline: March 31.
How to apply: Applications are available online.
Exclusive: Visit www.UltimateScholarshipBook.com and enter code KI104623 for updates on this award.

(1047) · Michael Moody Fitness Scholarship

Michael Moody Fitness
38 E 5th Avenue, Denver, CO 80203
Phone: 773-484-8094
Email: michael@michaelmoodyfitness.com
http://www.michaelmoodyfitness.com/student-scholarship-chicago/
Purpose: To support students seeking a career in health and fitness related fields.
Eligibility: Applicants must be U.S. citizens or legal residents and be a current high school senior, undergraduate or graduate level student planning on enrolling in an accredited college or university full-time in the upcoming school year. Students should be able to demonstrate that they have outstanding achievement in school, as well as participation and leadership in school activities and work experience. Applicants should be pursuing a degree in one of the following: athletic training, personal training, physical education teaching and coaching, health and physical fitness, exercise science, sports and recreation management, health sciences or another related field.
Target applicant(s): High school students. College students. Graduate school students. Adult students.
Amount: $1,500.
Number of awards: 1.
Deadline: August 1.
How to apply: Applications are available online.
Exclusive: Visit www.UltimateScholarshipBook.com and enter code MI104723 for updates on this award.

(1048) · Mid-Continent Instruments and Avionics Scholarship

Aircraft Electronics Association

3570 NE Ralph Powell Road, Lee's Summit, MO 64064

Phone: 816-347-8400

Email: info@aea.net

https://aea.net/educationalfoundation/scholarships.asp

Purpose: To support students who wish to pursue a career in avionics or aircraft repair.

Eligibility: Applicants must be high school seniors or college students who plan to or are attending an accredited school in an avionics or aircraft repair program.

Target applicant(s): High school students. College students. Adult students.

Amount: $1,000.

Number of awards: 1.

Deadline: April.

How to apply: Applications are available by contacting the organization for more information.

Exclusive: Visit www.UltimateScholarshipBook.com and enter code AI104823 for updates on this award.

(1049) · MIE Solutions

MIE Solutions

13252 Garden Grove Boulevard, Suite 215, Garden Grove, CA 92843

Phone: 714-786-6230

Email: support@mie-solutions.com

https://www.mie-solutions.com/scholarship-opportunity/

Purpose: To support students pursuing computer science and engineering studies.

Eligibility: Applicants must be legal U.S. residents currently attending an accredited U.S. college or university or a graduating senior enrolling in an accredited post-secondary institution. Students must provide an essay or presentation regarding their interest in computer science.

Target applicant(s): High school students. College students. Adult students.

Amount: $500.

Number of awards: 1.

Deadline: November 30.

How to apply: Applications are available online.

Exclusive: Visit www.UltimateScholarshipBook.com and enter code MI104923 for updates on this award.

(1050) · Migrant Health Scholarships

National Center for Farmworker Health Inc.

Migrant Health Scholarship, 1770 FM 967, Buda, TX 78610

Phone: 512-312-2700

Email: favre@ncfh.org

http://www.ncfh.org/scholarships.html

Purpose: To aid migrant health center staff who wish to pursue higher education in health care.

Eligibility: Applicants must be employees at a migrant/community health center. They must be interested in seeking further training in health care. Special consideration will be given to applicants who have a family background in farm working. Selection is based on demonstrated professional commitment to migrant health, stated career goals and personal experiences.

Target applicant(s): High school students. College students. Graduate school students. Adult students.

Amount: Varies.

Number of awards: Varies.

Deadline: Varies.

How to apply: Applications are available online. An application form and supporting materials are required.

Exclusive: Visit www.UltimateScholarshipBook.com and enter code NA105023 for updates on this award.

(1051) · Minority Fellowship Program

American Nurses Association (ANA)

8515 Georgia Avenue, Suite 400, Silver Spring, MD 20910-3492

Phone: 301-628-5247

Email: mfp@ana.org

http://www.nursingworld.org

Purpose: To provide stipends and tuition assistance to nurses studying minority psychiatric-mental health and substance abuse.

Eligibility: Applicants must be members of the ANA, have their master's degree and plan to pursue doctoral degrees. Eligible applicants must be registered nurses and members of a ethnic/racial minority group.

Target applicant(s): Graduate school students. Adult students.

Amount: Varies.

Number of awards: Varies.

Deadline: April 30.

How to apply: Applications available online.

Exclusive: Visit www.UltimateScholarshipBook.com and enter code AM105123 for updates on this award.

(1052) · Minority Student Scholarship

American Speech-Language-Hearing Foundation

2200 Research Boulevard, Rockville, MD 20850

Phone: 301-296-8700

Email: foundation@asha.org

https://www.ashfoundation.org/

Purpose: To support a minority graduate student in communication sciences and disorders.

Eligibility: Applicants should be full-time minority graduate students. Master's degree candidates must be in programs accredited by the Council on Academic Accreditation for Audiology and Speech Pathology, but doctoral programs do not have to be accredited. Transcripts, an essay and a reference form are required.

Target applicant(s): College students. Graduate school students. Adult students.

Amount: $5,000.

Number of awards: Up to 2.

Deadline: May.

How to apply: Applications are available online.

Exclusive: Visit www.UltimateScholarshipBook.com and enter code AM105223 for updates on this award.

(1053) · MIT THINK Scholarship Program

MIT Tech Fair

Email: think@mit.edu

https://think.mit.edu/#guidelines

Purpose: To support high school students interested in science, technology, engineering and math.

Eligibility: Applicants must be full-time high school students and must be a U.S. resident during the academic year. U.S. citizenship is not required and U.S. citizens living outside the country are not eligible. Students must submit a proposal following the provided guidelines and instructions.

Target applicant(s): High school students.
Amount: Up to $7,000.
Number of awards: Varies.
Deadline: January 1.
How to apply: Applications are available online.
Exclusive: Visit www.UltimateScholarshipBook.com and enter code MI105323 for updates on this award.

(1054) · Mollie Butler Memorial Scholarship

Welsh Pony and Cob Society
720 Green Street, Stephens City, VA 22655
Phone: 540-868-7669
Email: info@welshpony.org
https://wpcsa.org/youth/scholarship-application/
Purpose: To support students pursuing education and research in equine-related fields.
Eligibility: Applicants must be graduating high school or attending college, graduate school or professional training in equine fields of study.
Target applicant(s): College students. Graduate school students. Adult students.
Amount: $500-$1,000.
Number of awards: 2.
Deadline: July 1.
How to apply: Applications are available online.
Exclusive: Visit www.UltimateScholarshipBook.com and enter code WE105423 for updates on this award.

(1055) · Moody's Mega Math Challenge

Society for Industrial and Applied Mathematics/SIAM
3600 Market Street, 6th Floor, Philadelphia, PA 19104
Phone: 215-382-9800
https://www.siam.org/
Purpose: To support students who complete a math challenge.
Eligibility: Applicants must be from high schools in the United States. Students on the team must be juniors and seniors from the same high school.
Target applicant(s): High school students.
Amount: $5,000-$20,000.
Number of awards: Varies.
Deadline: February 19.
How to apply: Applications are available online.
Exclusive: Visit www.UltimateScholarshipBook.com and enter code SO105523 for updates on this award.

(1056) · MTI Bert Krisher Memorial Scholarship

National Association of Corrosion Engineers (NACE) International Foundation
15835 Park Ten Place, Houston, TX 77084-5145
Phone: 281-228-6205
Email: nace.foundation@nace.org
http://nace-foundation.org/programs/students/scholarships/
Purpose: To help students pursue careers in materials engineering in the process industries.
Eligibility: Applicants must be enrolled full-time as an undergraduate at an accredited college or university in North America, Europe or Asia. Selection is based on experience, academic achievement, personal and professional activities and overall strength of the application.
Target applicant(s): College students. Adult students.
Amount: $5,000.

Number of awards: Up to 2.
Deadline: January 1.
How to apply: Applications are available online. An application form, three recommendation forms, an academic transcript, a work experience form and essay scholarship questions are required.
Exclusive: Visit www.UltimateScholarshipBook.com and enter code NA105623 for updates on this award.

(1057) · MTS Student Scholarship for Two-Year, Technical, Engineering and Community College Students

Marine Technology Society
1100 H Street NW, Suite LL-100, Washington, DC 20005
Phone: 202-717-8705
https://www.mtsociety.org/scholarships
Purpose: To support students who are enrolled at a two-year, technical, engineering or community college in a marine-related field
Eligibility: Applicants must be MTS student members who are accepted for enrollment or enrolled full-time at an educational institution.
Target applicant(s): High school students. College students. Adult students.
Amount: $3,000.
Number of awards: 1.
Deadline: April 15.
How to apply: Applications are available online.
Exclusive: Visit www.UltimateScholarshipBook.com and enter code MA105723 for updates on this award.

(1058) · MTS Student Scholarship for Undergraduate Students

Marine Technology Society
1100 H Street NW, Suite LL-100, Washington, DC 20005
Phone: 202-717-8705
https://www.mtsociety.org/scholarships
Purpose: To support Marine Technology Society members who are pursuing an undergraduate degree in a marine-related field.
Eligibility: Applicants must be MTS student members who are accepted for enrollment or enrolled full-time at an educational institution.
Target applicant(s): College students. Graduate school students. Adult students.
Amount: $3,000.
Number of awards: 1.
Deadline: April 15.
How to apply: Applications are available online.
Exclusive: Visit www.UltimateScholarshipBook.com and enter code MA105823 for updates on this award.

(1059) · Murse World Scholarship

Murse World
1665 Corporate Road West, Lakewood, NJ 08701
Phone: 732-719-8600
Email: scholarships@murseworld.com
https://www.murseworld.com/scholarship
Purpose: To assist students pursuing medical education.
Eligibility: Applicants must be graduating high school seniors or currently enrolled in an accredited U.S. college or university with the intent of pursuing a degree in a medical field including therapy, nursing, dentistry and nutrition. Students must be U.S. citizens or legal residents with a minimum GPA of 3.0 and must write an original essay.

Target applicant(s): High school students. College students. Graduate school students. Adult students.
Minimum GPA: 3.0
Amount: $1,000.
Number of awards: 1.
Deadline: January 15.
How to apply: Applications are available online.
Exclusive: Visit www.UltimateScholarshipBook.com and enter code MU105923 for updates on this award.

(1060) · Myrtle and Earl Walker Scholarship

Society of Manufacturing Engineers Education Foundation
One SME Drive, P.O. Box 930, Dearborn, MI 48121
Phone: 313-425-3300
Email: foundation@sme.org
https://www.smeef.org/scholarships
Purpose: To help manufacturing engineering and technology undergraduates.
Eligibility: Applicants must be full-time undergraduate students who are studying manufacturing engineering or technology at an accredited postsecondary institution located in the U.S. or Canada. They must have a GPA of 3.0 or higher on a four-point scale and must have completed 15 or more credit hours. They must have plans to pursue a career in manufacturing engineering or technology. Selection is based on the overall strength of the application.
Target applicant(s): College students. Adult students.
Minimum GPA: 3.0
Amount: Varies.
Number of awards: Varies.
Deadline: February 1.
How to apply: Applications are available online. An application form, personal statement, resume, transcript and two recommendation letters are required.
Exclusive: Visit www.UltimateScholarshipBook.com and enter code SO106023 for updates on this award.

(1061) · N.G. Kaul Memorial Scholarship

New York Water Environment Association Inc.
525 Plum Street, Suite 102, Syracuse, NY 13204
Phone: 877-556-9932
Email: theresa@nywea.org
http://www.nywea.org
Purpose: To support students pursuing advanced degrees in environmental engineering and science.
Eligibility: Applicants must be graduate students pursuing degrees in environmental or civil engineering or environmental science with a concentration on water quality. Students must provide two letters of recommendations, a transcript, a resume and two essays along with their application.
Target applicant(s): Graduate school students. Adult students.
Amount: Up to $5,000.
Number of awards: Varies.
Deadline: February 26.
How to apply: Applications are available online.
Exclusive: Visit www.UltimateScholarshipBook.com and enter code NE106123 for updates on this award.

(1062) · NACE Eastern Area Scholarship

National Association of Corrosion Engineers (NACE) International Foundation
15835 Park Ten Place, Houston, TX 77084-5145
Phone: 281-228-6205
Email: nace.foundation@nace.org
http://nace-foundation.org/programs/students/scholarships/
Purpose: To help students interested in their pursuit of a career in the field of engineering and/or science.
Eligibility: Applicants must be a permanent resident of the United States and be enrolled full-time as an undergraduate in an accredited engineering or physical science degree program at a two or four-year college or university. Students must have a GPA of 3.0 or higher and have a permanent address within the NACE Eastern Area which includes the following states and/or U.S. Territories: Alabama, Connecticut, Delaware, Florida, Georgia, Indiana (excluding Lake, Porter La Porte, Newton and Jasper counties), Kentucky, Maine, Maryland, Massachusetts, Michigan, Mississippi, New Hampshire, New Jersey, New York, North Carolina, Ohio, Pennsylvania, Puerto Rico, Rhode Island, South Carolina, Tennessee, Vermont, Virginia and West Virginia.
Target applicant(s): College students. Adult students.
Minimum GPA: 3.0
Amount: $3,000.
Number of awards: 1.
Deadline: January 1.
How to apply: Applications are available online. An application form, two recommendation forms, an academic transcript and essay scholarship questions are required.
Exclusive: Visit www.UltimateScholarshipBook.com and enter code NA106223 for updates on this award.

(1063) · NACE Foundation Academic Scholarship

National Association of Corrosion Engineers (NACE) International Foundation
15835 Park Ten Place, Houston, TX 77084-5145
Phone: 281-228-6205
Email: nace.foundation@nace.org
http://nace-foundation.org/programs/students/scholarships/
Purpose: To aid students in the study of corrosion or corrosion control.
Eligibility: Applicants must be enrolled full-time as an undergraduate student at a two or four-year accredited college or university. Applicants must be pursuing a science or engineering degree. Selection is based on the overall strength of the application.
Target applicant(s): College students. Adult students.
Amount: $5,000.
Number of awards: Up to 5.
Deadline: January 1.
How to apply: Applications are available online. An application form, two recommendation forms, an academic transcript and essay scholarship questions are required.
Exclusive: Visit www.UltimateScholarshipBook.com and enter code NA106323 for updates on this award.

(1064) · NACE Past Presidents Scholarship

National Association of Corrosion Engineers (NACE) International Foundation
15835 Park Ten Place, Houston, TX 77084-5145
Phone: 281-228-6205
Email: nace.foundation@nace.org

http://nace-foundation.org/programs/students/scholarships/
Purpose: To aid students in their pursuit of study in science or engineering related to corrosion or corrosion control.
Eligibility: Applicants must be enrolled full-time as an undergraduate at a two- or four-year accredited college or university and must be pursuing a degree in the field of science and/or engineering. Selection is based on the overall strength of the application.
Target applicant(s): College students. Adult students.
Amount: $2,500.
Number of awards: 2.
Deadline: January 1.
How to apply: Applications are available online. An application form, two recommendation forms, an academic transcript and essay scholarship questions are required.
Exclusive: Visit www.UltimateScholarshipBook.com and enter code NA106423 for updates on this award.

(1065) · Naomi Brack Student Scholarship

Organization for Associate Degree Nursing National Office
7794 Grow Drive, Pensacola, FL 32514-7072
Phone: 877-966-6236
Email: harriet.mcclung@oadn.org
http://www.oadn.org
Purpose: To aid associate's degree nursing (ADN) students.
Eligibility: Applicants must be currently enrolled in an associate's degree program in nursing at a state-approved institution. They must have a GPA of 3.0 or more on a four-point scale and must be active in their school's student nursing association. Selection is based on the overall strength of the application.
Target applicant(s): College students. Adult students.
Minimum GPA: 3.0
Amount: $1,000.
Number of awards: Varies.
Deadline: June 15.
How to apply: Applications are available online. An application form, personal statement, transcript, nomination form and two letters of recommendation are required.
Exclusive: Visit www.UltimateScholarshipBook.com and enter code OR106523 for updates on this award.

(1066) · NAPA Research and Education Foundation Scholarship

National Asphalt Pavement Association
5100 Forbes Boulevard, Lanham, MD 20706-4407
Phone: 888-468-6499
http://www.asphaltpavement.org/
Purpose: To aid engineering and construction students who are interested in hot mix asphalt technology.
Eligibility: Applicants must be U.S. citizens who are enrolled full-time at an accredited postsecondary institution. They must be majoring in construction management, civil engineering or construction engineering. The applicant's school must offer at least one course on hot mix asphalt (HMA) technology. Selection is based on academic achievement, leadership potential, extracurricular involvements and stated career goals.
Target applicant(s): College students. Graduate school students. Adult students.
Amount: Varies.
Number of awards: Varies.
Scholarship may be renewable.
Deadline: Varies.

How to apply: Applications may be requested from the student's state National Asphalt Pavement Association representative. An application form and supporting materials are required.
Exclusive: Visit www.UltimateScholarshipBook.com and enter code NA106623 for updates on this award.

(1067) · National Association for Surface Finishing Scholarships

National Association for Surface Finishing
1155 Fifteenth Street NW, Washington, DC 20005
Phone: 202-457-8401
http://www.nasf.org
Purpose: To support students pursuing the study of surface science.
Eligibility: Applicants must be undergraduate juniors or seniors or graduate students studying chemical engineering, material science, mechanical, metallurgical or environmental engineering or chemistry. Students must have a minimum 3.0 GPA if an undergraduate or 3.3 if a graduate-level student.
Target applicant(s): College students. Graduate school students. Adult students.
Minimum GPA: 3.0 for undergraduate students, 3.3 for graduate students
Amount: $1,500.
Number of awards: 1.
Deadline: February 1.
How to apply: Applications are available online.
Exclusive: Visit www.UltimateScholarshipBook.com and enter code NA106723 for updates on this award.

(1068) · National Aviation Explorer Scholarships

Explorers Learning for Life
1325 West Walnut Hill Lane, P.O. Box 152225, Irving, TX 75015-2225
Phone: 855-806-9992
Email: exploring@lflmail.org
http://www.exploring.org/scholarships/
Purpose: To support students who are pursuing careers in the aviation industry.
Eligibility: Students must be active members of an Aviation Explorer post. Applicants must submit an essay and three letters of recommendation.
Target applicant(s): Junior high students or younger. High school students. College students. Adult students.
Amount: $3,000-$10,000.
Number of awards: Varies.
Deadline: May 31.
How to apply: Applications are available online.
Exclusive: Visit www.UltimateScholarshipBook.com and enter code EX106823 for updates on this award.

(1069) · National Dairy Shrine/Iager Dairy Scholarship

National Dairy Shrine
P.O. Box 725, Denmark, WI 54208
Phone: 920-863-6333
Email: info@dairyshrine.org
http://www.dairyshrine.org
Purpose: To aid dairy and animal science students who are planning for careers in the dairy industry.
Eligibility: Applicants must be entering the second year of a two-year agricultural college program in dairy or animal science. They must

have a GPA of 2.5 or higher on a four-point scale. Selection is based on academic merit, leadership skills and professional commitment to the dairy industry.
Target applicant(s): College students. Adult students.
Minimum GPA: 2.5
Amount: $1,000.
Number of awards: Up to 2.
Deadline: April 15.
How to apply: Applications are available online. An application form, official transcript, personal essay and two recommendation letters are required.
Exclusive: Visit www.UltimateScholarshipBook.com and enter code NA106923 for updates on this award.

(1070) · National Environmental Health Association Graduate Scholarship

National Environmental Health Association and the American Academy of Sanitarians
NEHA/AAS Scholarship, 720 South Colorado Boulevard, Suite 1000-N, Denver, CO 80246-1926
Phone: 303-756-9090
Email: cdimmitt@neha.org
http://www.neha.org
Purpose: To encourage commitment to environmental health studies.
Eligibility: Applicants must be enrolled in a graduate program at an accredited institution with a declared curriculum in environmental health sciences and have at least one semester of coursework remaining.
Target applicant(s): Graduate school students. Adult students.
Amount: $2,500.
Number of awards: 1.
Deadline: March 31.
How to apply: Applications are available online.
Exclusive: Visit www.UltimateScholarshipBook.com and enter code NA107023 for updates on this award.

(1071) · National Foliage Foundation General Scholarships

National Foliage Foundation
1533 Park Center Drive, Orlando, FL 32835
Phone: 800-375-3642
Email: info@nationalfoliagefoundation.org
https://www.nationalhorticulturefoundation.org/
Purpose: To aid horticulture students who are interested in pursuing careers in foliage growing and marketing.
Eligibility: Applicants must be graduating high school seniors or full-time undergraduate or graduate students. They must be enrolled in or planning to enroll in a horticulture or related degree program and must have a GPA of 2.5 or higher. They must be interested in pursuing a career in foliage marketing or growing. Selection is based on the overall strength of the application.
Target applicant(s): High school students. College students. Graduate school students. Adult students.
Minimum GPA: 2.5
Amount: Varies.
Number of awards: Varies.
Scholarship may be renewable.
Deadline: January 15.
How to apply: Applications are available online. An application form, transcript, two recommendation letters and a personal essay are required.

Exclusive: Visit www.UltimateScholarshipBook.com and enter code NA107123 for updates on this award.

(1072) · National Garden Clubs Scholarship

National Garden Clubs Inc.
4401 Magnolia Avenue, St. Louis, MO 63110
Phone: 314-776-7574
Email: headquarters@gardenclub.org
http://www.gardenclub.org
Purpose: To promote the study of horticulture and related fields.
Eligibility: Applicants must be full-time juniors, seniors, graduate students or sophomores applying for their junior year and major in one of the following fields: agriculture education, horticulture, floriculture, landscape design, botany, biology, plant pathology/science, forestry, agronomy, environmental concerns, economics, environmental conservation, city planning, wildlife science, habitat or forest/systems ecology, land management or related areas. Students must have a minimum 3.25 cumulative GPA and be a U.S. citizen.
Target applicant(s): College students. Graduate school students. Adult students.
Minimum GPA: 3.25
Amount: $4,000.
Number of awards: Up to 41.
Deadline: February 1.
How to apply: Applications are available online and must be mailed to the applicants' state Garden Club scholarship chairman.
Exclusive: Visit www.UltimateScholarshipBook.com and enter code NA107223 for updates on this award.

(1073) · National Potato Council Scholarship

National Potato Council
1300 L Street NW #910, Washington, DC 20005
Phone: 202-682-9456
Email: info@pleaf.org
http://www.nationalpotatocouncil.org
Purpose: To aid students pursuing studies that support the potato industry.
Eligibility: Applicants must be graduate agribusiness students. Selection is based on academic achievement, leadership abilities and potato-related areas of graduate study (such as agricultural engineering, agronomy, crop and soil sciences, entomology, food sciences, horticulture and plant pathology).
Target applicant(s): Graduate school students. Adult students.
Amount: $10,000.
Number of awards: 1.
Deadline: June 18.
How to apply: Applications are available online. An application form, essay, transcripts, list of activities and two references are required.
Exclusive: Visit www.UltimateScholarshipBook.com and enter code NA107323 for updates on this award.

(1074) · National Space Club Keynote Scholar

National Space Club
204 E Street NE, Washington, DC 20002
Phone: 202-547-0060
Email: info@spaceclub.org
http://www.spaceclub.org/youth-education.html
Purpose: To aid STEM students.
Eligibility: Applicants must be U.S. citizens and must be high school seniors, undergraduates or graduate students planning to attend or

attending an accredited college or university with the intention to follow a course of study related to a career in a science, technology, engineering or math field with a preference for space-related interests. Selection is based on the overall strength of the application.

Target applicant(s): High school students. College students. Graduate school students. Adult students.

Amount: $10,000.

Number of awards: 1.

Deadline: December 3.

How to apply: Applications are available online. An application form, transcripts, two letters of recommendation, statement of intent and video audition are required.

Exclusive: Visit www.UltimateScholarshipBook.com and enter code NA107423 for updates on this award.

(1075) · National Student Nurses' Association Scholarship

National Student Nurses' Association
45 Main Street, Suite 606, Brooklyn, NY 11201
Phone: 718-210-0705
Email: nsna@nsna.org
http://www.nsna.org

Purpose: To promote interest in the nursing field.

Eligibility: Applicants must be currently enrolled in a state-approved school of nursing or pre-nursing in associate degree, baccalaureate, diploma, doctorate or master's programs.

Target applicant(s): College students. Graduate school students. Adult students.

Amount: $1,000-$5,000.

Number of awards: Varies.

Deadline: February 11.

How to apply: Applications are available online.

Exclusive: Visit www.UltimateScholarshipBook.com and enter code NA107523 for updates on this award.

(1076) · National Young Astronomer Award

Astronomical League
9201 Ward Parkway, Suite 100, Kansas City, MO 64114
Phone: 816-333-7759
Email: horkheimerservice@astroleague.org
https://www.astroleague.org/al/awards/awards.html

Purpose: To support young astronomers.

Eligibility: Applicants must be 14 to 19 years old, not yet enrolled in college at the award deadline and do not have to be members of an astronomy club or of the Astronomical League. International students of the same age are eligible if they are enrolled in a U.S. secondary school on the application deadline. The application consists of the application form, summary of astronomy-related activities and optional exhibits.

Target applicant(s): Junior high students or younger. High school students.

Amount: Varies.

Number of awards: 3.

Deadline: March 31.

How to apply: Applications are available online.

Exclusive: Visit www.UltimateScholarshipBook.com and enter code AS107623 for updates on this award.

(1077) · NAWIC Founders' Undergraduate Scholarship

National Association of Women in Construction
327 South Adams Street, Fort Worth, TX 76104
Phone: 800-552-3506
Email: nawic@nawic.org
http://www.nawic.org

Purpose: To aid undergraduates who are preparing for careers in construction.

Eligibility: Applicants must be full-time, degree-seeking undergraduates who are studying a construction-related subject at a postsecondary institution located in the U.S. or Canada. Students do not need to be female. They must have a cumulative GPA of 3.0 or higher and have plans to pursue a career in a construction-related field. Selection is based on stated career goals, extracurricular activities, work experience, academic achievement and financial need.

Target applicant(s): College students. Adult students.

Minimum GPA: 3.0

Amount: Varies.

Number of awards: Varies.

Scholarship may be renewable.

Deadline: February 28.

How to apply: Applications are available online. An application form, transcript, employment history, extracurricular activities list and personal statement are required.

Exclusive: Visit www.UltimateScholarshipBook.com and enter code NA107723 for updates on this award.

(1078) · NBRC/AMP Gareth B. Gish, MS, RRT Memorial and William F. Miller, MD Postgraduate Education Recognition Awards

American Association for Respiratory Care
9425 North MacArthur Boulevard, Suite 100, Irving, TX 75063-4706
Phone: 972-243-2272
Email: info@aarc.org
http://www.aarc.org/education/educator-resources/scholarships/

Purpose: To aid qualified respiratory therapists in pursuing advanced degrees.

Eligibility: Applicants must be respiratory therapists who have been accepted into an advanced degree program of a fully accredited school. Application must be accompanied by an original essay describing how the award will aid in achieving an advanced degree and future goals in health care. A minimum 3.0 GPA is required.

Target applicant(s): College students. Graduate school students. Adult students.

Minimum GPA: 3.0

Amount: $2,500.

Number of awards: 2.

Deadline: June 1.

How to apply: Applications are available online.

Exclusive: Visit www.UltimateScholarshipBook.com and enter code AM107823 for updates on this award.

(1079) · NBRC/AMP William W. Burgin, Jr. MD and Robert M. Lawrence, MD Education Recognition Award

American Association for Respiratory Care
9425 North MacArthur Boulevard, Suite 100, Irving, TX 75063-4706

Phone: 972-243-2272
Email: info@aarc.org
http://www.aarc.org/education/educator-resources/scholarships/
Purpose: To recognize outstanding students in respiratory care education programs.
Eligibility: Applicants must be third or fourth-year students enrolled in an accredited respiratory therapy program leading to a bachelor's degree and must have a minimum 3.0 GPA. In addition to an original paper dealing with respiratory care, applicants must submit an original essay describing how this award will help them reach their degrees and their future goals in the field of health care.
Target applicant(s): College students. Adult students.
Minimum GPA: 3.0
Amount: Up to $7,500.
Number of awards: 1.
Deadline: June 1.
How to apply: Applications are available online.
Exclusive: Visit www.UltimateScholarshipBook.com and enter code AM107923 for updates on this award.

(1080) · NCAPA Endowment Annual Student Grants

North Carolina Academy of Physician Assistants
Attn: Kat Nicholas, 1121 Slater Road, Durham, NC 27703
Phone: 800-352-2271
Email: ncapa@ncapa.org
http://ncapa.org/students/scholarships/
Purpose: To aid physician assistant school students.
Eligibility: Applicants must be current student members of the North Carolina Academy of Physician Assistants (NCAPA). They must be rising second- or third-year students in an accredited physician assistant degree program. Selection is based on the overall strength of the application.
Target applicant(s): College students. Graduate school students. Adult students.
Amount: Varies.
Number of awards: Varies.
Deadline: June.
How to apply: Applications are available online. An application form, financial aid statement, personal essay and official transcript are required.
Exclusive: Visit www.UltimateScholarshipBook.com and enter code NO108023 for updates on this award.

(1081) · NCGA William C. Berg Academic Excellence in Agriculture Scholarship

National Corn Growers Association
632 Cepi Drive, Chesterfield, MO 63005
Phone: 636-733-9004
Email: corninfo@ncga.com
https://www.ncga.com/key-issues/other-topics/scholarship-programs
Purpose: To support students pursuing degrees in agriculture-related fields.
Eligibility: Applicants must be pursuing an undergraduate or graduate degree in an agricultural field and be a member or child of a member of the NCGA.
Target applicant(s): College students. Graduate school students. Adult students.
Amount: $1,000.
Number of awards: 5.
Deadline: January 31.
How to apply: Applications are available online.

Exclusive: Visit www.UltimateScholarshipBook.com and enter code NA108123 for updates on this award.

(1082) · NCPA Foundation Presidential Scholarship

National Community Pharmacists Association
NCPA Foundation, 100 Daingerfield Road, Alexandria, VA 22314
Phone: 703-683-8200
Email: info@ncpanet.org
http://www.ncpanet.org
Purpose: To support students who plan to enter the pharmaceutical field.
Eligibility: Applicants must be student members of NCPA and enrolled in a U.S. school or college of pharmacy full-time. Selection is based on academic achievement and leadership.
Target applicant(s): College students. Graduate school students. Adult students.
Amount: $2,000.
Number of awards: Varies.
Deadline: March.
How to apply: Applications are available online.
Exclusive: Visit www.UltimateScholarshipBook.com and enter code NA108223 for updates on this award.

(1083) · NDPRB Undergraduate Scholarship Program

National Dairy Promotion and Research Board
c/o Nate Janssen, Dairy Management Inc., 10255 West Higgins Road, Suite 900, Rosemont, IL 60018-5615
Phone: 847-627-3335
Email: nate.janssen@rosedmi.com
http://www.dairy.org
Purpose: To aid undergraduates who are studying a dairy-related subject.
Eligibility: Applicants must be rising undergraduate sophomores, juniors or seniors. They must be majoring in a subject that emphasizes dairy (such as agriculture education, business, communications, economics, food science, journalism, marketing or public relations). Applicants must plan to pursue a career in the dairy industry. Selection is based on stated career goals, academic excellence, dairy-related coursework completed, leadership and integrity.
Target applicant(s): College students. Adult students.
Amount: $3,500.
Number of awards: Up to 11.
Scholarship may be renewable.
Deadline: May 7.
How to apply: Applications are available online. An application form, personal statement, one recommendation letter and an official transcript are required.
Exclusive: Visit www.UltimateScholarshipBook.com and enter code NA108323 for updates on this award.

(1084) · NDS / Klussendorf / McKown Scholarships

National Dairy Shrine
P.O. Box 725, Denmark, WI 54208
Phone: 920-863-6333
Email: info@dairyshrine.org
http://www.dairyshrine.org
Purpose: To honor students in dairy husbandry fields.
Eligibility: Applicants must be first, second or third year college students at two- or four-year universities, must major in a dairy husbandry field and plan to enter the dairy field.
Target applicant(s): College students. Adult students.

Amount: $1,500.
Number of awards: 7.
Deadline: April 15.
How to apply: Applications are available online.
Exclusive: Visit www.UltimateScholarshipBook.com and enter code NA108423 for updates on this award.

(1085) · NDSEG Fellowship Program

Department of Defense, American Society for Engineering Education
1818 N Street NW, Suite 600, Washington, DC 20036
Phone: 202-331-3546
Email: ndseg@asee.org
https://ndseg.sysplus.com/
Purpose: To award fellowships to those in science and engineering.
Eligibility: Applicants must pursue a doctoral degree in an area of Department of Defense interest: aeronautical and astronautical engineering, biosciences, chemical engineering, chemistry, civil engineering, cognitive, neural and behavioral sciences, computer and computational sciences, electrical engineering, geosciences, materials science and engineering, mathematics, mechanical engineering, naval architecture and ocean engineering, oceanography and physics. Applicants must have completed no more than one academic year of graduate study as a part-time or full-time student or be in their final year of undergraduate studies. The award is based on academic achievement, personal statements, recommendations and Graduate Record Examination scores. Fellowships may be used only at U.S. institutions of higher education offering doctoral degrees.
Target applicant(s): College students. Graduate school students. Adult students.
Amount: Full tuition plus fees, stipend and medical insurance.
Number of awards: Varies.
Scholarship may be renewable.
Deadline: November 30.
How to apply: Applications are available online.
Exclusive: Visit www.UltimateScholarshipBook.com and enter code DE108523 for updates on this award.

(1086) · NEHA/AAS/APU Scholarship Awards

National Environmental Health Association and the American Academy of Sanitarians
NEHA/AAS Scholarship, 720 South Colorado Boulevard, Suite 1000-N, Denver, CO 80246-1926
Phone: 303-756-9090
Email: cdimmitt@neha.org
http://www.neha.org
Purpose: To support students planning careers in environmental health.
Eligibility: Applicants must be either undergraduate or graduate students. The undergraduate scholarships are to be used during the junior or senior year at an Environmental Health Accreditation Council (EHAC) or NEHA member school. The graduate scholarship is available to applicants who are enrolled in a graduate program of study in environmental health sciences and/or public health and have at least one semester of coursework remaining.
Target applicant(s): College students. Graduate school students. Adult students.
Amount: $1,000-$2,000.
Number of awards: 4.
Scholarship may be renewable.
Deadline: March 1.
How to apply: Applications are available online.

Exclusive: Visit www.UltimateScholarshipBook.com and enter code NA108623 for updates on this award.

(1087) · Nellie Yeoh Whetten Award

American Vacuum Society
125 Maiden Lane, 15th Floor, New York, NY 10038
Phone: 212-248-0200
Email: angela@avs.org
http://www.avs.org
Purpose: To support women in graduate studies in the sciences and technologies related to AVS.
Eligibility: Applicants must be female graduate students in an accredited academic institution and must send an application, report on candidate form, two letters of recommendation and college and graduate school transcripts.
Target applicant(s): Graduate school students. Adult students.
Amount: Varies.
Number of awards: Varies.
Deadline: May 1.
How to apply: Applications are available online.
Exclusive: Visit www.UltimateScholarshipBook.com and enter code AM108723 for updates on this award.

(1088) · New Century Scholars Doctoral Scholarship

American Speech-Language-Hearing Foundation
2200 Research Boulevard, Rockville, MD 20850
Phone: 301-296-8700
Email: foundation@asha.org
https://www.ashfoundation.org/
Purpose: To support graduate students and researchers who are studying communication sciences and disorders.
Eligibility: Students applying for the scholarship must be enrolled in a research or teaching doctoral program to obtain a Ph.D. or its equivalent. Researchers applying for the grant must have teacher-investigator careers, either in an academic environment or in external research institutions.
Target applicant(s): Graduate school students. Adult students.
Amount: $10,000.
Number of awards: Up to 15.
Deadline: May.
How to apply: Applications are available online.
Exclusive: Visit www.UltimateScholarshipBook.com and enter code AM108823 for updates on this award.

(1089) · New Face of Tech Scholarship Program

1,000 Dreams Fund
1875 K Street NW, 4th Floor, Washington, DC 20006
Email: programs@1000dreamsfund.org
https://1000dreamsfund.org/programs/new-face-of-tech-scholarship-program/
Purpose: To support women students studying science, technology, engineering, arts or math (STEAM).
Eligibility: Applicants must be women students studying science, technology, engineering, arts or math (STEAM). Scholarship award can be used at any accredited college or university.
Target applicant(s): High school students. College students. Adult students.
Amount: $2,000.
Number of awards: Varies.
Deadline: April.
How to apply: Applications are available online.

Exclusive: Visit www.UltimateScholarshipBook.com and enter code 1,108923 for updates on this award.

(1090) · NFMC Dorothy Dann Bullock Music Therapy Award and the NFMC Ruth B. Robertson Music Therapy Award

National Federation of Music Clubs Bullock and Robertson Awards
Margaret Smith, 2501 Maple Ridge Drive, Tuscaloosa, AL 35406
Phone: 317-882-4003
Email: Margbill1956@att.net
http://www.nfmc-music.org/competitions-awards/
Purpose: To assist students who plan to enter careers in music therapy.
Eligibility: Applicants must be college students majoring in music therapy in schools approved by the National Association of Music Therapists and AMTA. Selection is based on musical talent, skills and training with an emphasis on piano ability in accompanying and sight reading. Other selection criteria are self-reliance, leadership, ability to work with groups and dedication to music therapy as a career. Applicants must be members of the National Federation of Music Clubs.
Target applicant(s): College students. Adult students.
Amount: $650-$1,500.
Number of awards: Varies.
Deadline: March 1.
How to apply: Applications are available online.
Exclusive: Visit www.UltimateScholarshipBook.com and enter code NA109023 for updates on this award.

(1091) · NHSC Scholarship

U.S. Department of Health and Human Services
Health Resources and Services Administration, Bureau of Health Workforce, 5600 Fishers Lane, Rockville, MD 20857
Phone: 800-221-9393
Email: callcenter@hrsa.gov
http://nhsc.hrsa.gov/scholarships
Purpose: To aid students committed to providing health care in communities of great need.
Eligibility: Applicants must be enrolled or accepted into allopathic or osteopathic medical schools, family nurse practitioner programs, nurse-midwifery programs, physician assistant programs or dental school. Upon completion of training, scholars must choose practice sites in federally designated health professional shortage areas for one year for each year of support received.
Target applicant(s): College students. Graduate school students. Adult students.
Amount: Full tuition and fees plus stipend.
Number of awards: Varies.
Scholarship may be renewable.
Deadline: April.
How to apply: Applications are available by telephone request.
Exclusive: Visit www.UltimateScholarshipBook.com and enter code U.109123 for updates on this award.

(1092) · NIH Undergraduate Scholarship Program

Office of Intramural Training and Education
National Institute of Health - DHHS, 2 Center Drive, Building 2, Room 2E24, Bethesda, MD 20892-0230
Phone: 800-528-7689
Email: ugsp@nih.gov
http://www.training.nih.gov/programs/ugsp
Purpose: To offer competitive scholarships to students who are committed to careers in biomedical, behavioral and social science health-related research.
Eligibility: Applicants must be enrolled or accepted for enrollment as full-time students at an accredited undergraduate institution, have an underprivileged background and have a minimum 3.3 GPA or be within the top 5 percent of their class. Applicants must also show a commitment to pursuing careers in biomedical, behavioral and social science research at the NIH.
Target applicant(s): College students. Adult students.
Minimum GPA: 3.3
Amount: Up to $20,000.
Number of awards: Varies.
Scholarship may be renewable.
Deadline: March 17.
How to apply: Applications are available online.
Exclusive: Visit www.UltimateScholarshipBook.com and enter code OF109223 for updates on this award.

(1093) · Novus Biologicals Scholarship Program

Novus Biologicals
8100 Southpark Way, A-8, Littleton, CO 80120
Phone: 303-730-1950
Email: scholarship@novusbio.com
http://www.novusbio.com/scholarship-program.html
Purpose: To reward students who plan to pursue a career in science.
Eligibility: Students must provide a personal statement and a character statement. Applicants must be accepted to or enrolled in a science-related program. Scholarship awarded twice each year.
Target applicant(s): High school students. College students. Graduate school students. Adult students.
Amount: $1,500.
Number of awards: 2.
Deadline: July 20, December 8.
How to apply: Applications are available online.
Exclusive: Visit www.UltimateScholarshipBook.com and enter code NO109323 for updates on this award.

(1094) · NPCA Educational Foundation Scholarships

National Precast Concrete Association (NPCA)
1320 City Center Drive, Suite 200, Carmel, IN 46032
Phone: 800-366-7731
Email: mharrell@precast.org
http://precast.org/foundation/scholarships/
Purpose: To aid students who are preparing for careers in the precast concrete industry.
Eligibility: Applicants must be high school seniors or undergraduate students who are enrolled in or planning to enroll in a program of study that is related to the building, construction or precast concrete industries. Selection is based on the overall strength of the application.
Target applicant(s): High school students. College students. Adult students.
Amount: Up to $2,500.
Number of awards: Varies.
Scholarship may be renewable.
Deadline: March 11.
How to apply: Applications are available online. An application form, transcript and two letters of recommendation are required.
Exclusive: Visit www.UltimateScholarshipBook.com and enter code NA109423 for updates on this award.

(1095) · NPFDA Scholarships

National Poultry and Food Distributors Association
2014 Osborne Road, St. Marys, GA 31558
Phone: 770-535-9901
Email: info@npfda.org
http://www.npfda.org/npfda-scholarships
Purpose: To aid NPFDA member children and/or employees with their college tuition.
Eligibility: Applicants must be an employee or child of an employee of a NPFDA Member Company and be a rising undergraduate junior or senior who are full-time students at a U.S. post-secondary institution. Applicants should be pursuing a poultry- or agriculture-related program of study. Selection is based on the overall strength of the application.
Target applicant(s): College students. Adult students.
Amount: $2,500.
Number of awards: 5.
Deadline: April 30.
How to apply: Applications are available online. An application form, official transcript, personal statement and one letter of recommendation are required.
Exclusive: Visit www.UltimateScholarshipBook.com and enter code NA109523 for updates on this award.

(1096) · Nurse Candidate Program

Navy Medicine Professional Development Center
8955 Wood Road, Bethesda, MD 20889-5611
Phone: 301-295-2333
Email: usn.ohstudent@mail.mil
https://www.navy.com/what-to-expect/education-opportunities/undergraduate-degree-opportunities
Purpose: To aid students who are pursuing the bachelor of science in nursing (BSN).
Eligibility: Applicants must be U.S. citizens and be full-time students who have completed two or more years of a four-year bachelor of science in nursing (BSN) degree program at an accredited college or university. They must meet the Navy's physical fitness requirements. Recipients of this award will be required to fulfill an active duty service obligation of up to five years as an officer in the Navy Nurse Corps. Selection is based on the overall strength of the application.
Target applicant(s): College students. Adult students.
Amount: Up to $34,000.
Number of awards: Varies.
Scholarship may be renewable.
Deadline: Varies.
How to apply: Applications may be obtained by contacting a Navy recruiting officer. An application form and supporting materials are required.
Exclusive: Visit www.UltimateScholarshipBook.com and enter code NA109623 for updates on this award.

(1097) · Nurse Corps Scholarship Program

Health Resources and Services Administration (HRSA)
5600 Fishers Lane, Rockville, MD 20857
Phone: 800-221-9393
Email: gethelp@hrsa.org
http://www.hrsa.gov
Purpose: To aid needy students in obtaining nursing training and education in order to specifically decrease the major shortage of nurses in given health care facilities.
Eligibility: Applicants must be U.S. citizens accepted by or enrolled in a nursing program at an accredited nursing school within the U.S. leading to an associate, baccalaureate or graduate nursing degree or diploma. Applicants must have no federal judgment liens and not be delinquent on a federal debt or have current service commitments. They must begin their nursing program no later than September 30. Selection is based on financial need, academic success, essay answers, resume and letters of recommendation. Preference is given to applicants enrolled full-time in undergraduate or master's nurse practitioner programs. Financial support is provided in exchange for a commitment to serve at least 2 years in a qualifying Nurse Corps site.
Target applicant(s): High school students. College students. Graduate school students. Adult students.
Amount: Full tuition, fees and monthly stipend.
Number of awards: Varies.
Deadline: April 30.
How to apply: Applications are available online. An application form, proof of U.S. citizenship, verification of acceptance report, student aid report, essay answers, resume/curriculum vitae, transcripts and two letters of recommendation are required.
Exclusive: Visit www.UltimateScholarshipBook.com and enter code HE109723 for updates on this award.

(1098) · Nurseries Foundation Award

Oregon Association of Nurseries
29751 SW Town Center Loop West, Wilsonville, OR 97070
Phone: 503-682-5089
Email: onf@oan.org
http://www.oan.org
Purpose: To aid horticulture students.
Eligibility: Applicants must be majoring in horticulture. Selection is based on the overall strength of the application.
Target applicant(s): College students. Adult students.
Amount: $1,000.
Number of awards: 1.
Deadline: March.
How to apply: Applications are available online. An application form, official transcript and three recommendation letters are required.
Exclusive: Visit www.UltimateScholarshipBook.com and enter code OR109823 for updates on this award.

(1099) · Old Guard Oral Presentation Competition

American Society of Mechanical Engineers (ASME)
Two Park Avenue, New York, NY 10016-5990
Phone: 800-843-2763
Email: lefeverb@asme.org
https://www.asmefoundation.org/programs/stemeducation/asme-scholarships/
Purpose: To support the professional development of student members of the American Society of Mechanical Engineers (ASME).
Eligibility: Applicants must be certified as ASME student members in good standing. They must be undergraduate engineering students who have been chosen by their student section or academic department head to participate. Applicants must do a 20-minute oral presentation on a relevant engineering topic. Selection is based on presentation content, organization, delivery, effectiveness and discussion.
Target applicant(s): College students. Adult students.
Amount: Varies.
Number of awards: Varies.
Deadline: Varies.

How to apply: Entry forms are available online. An entry form and oral presentation are required.
Exclusive: Visit www.UltimateScholarshipBook.com and enter code AM109923 for updates on this award.

(1100) · Olin E. Teague Scholarship

National Space Club
204 E Street NE, Washington, DC 20002
Phone: 202-547-0060
Email: info@spaceclub.org
http://www.spaceclub.org/youth-education.html
Purpose: To aid students pursuing a degree in the aerospace fields.
Eligibility: Applicants must be a high school senior attending an accredited U.S. high school and also be a U.S. citizen. Students should plan on pursuing a degree that will lead to a career in an aerospace field.
Target applicant(s): High school students.
Amount: $4,000.
Number of awards: 1.
Deadline: October 15.
How to apply: Applications are available online.
Exclusive: Visit www.UltimateScholarshipBook.com and enter code NA110023 for updates on this award.

(1101) · Operations and Power Division Scholarship

American Nuclear Society
555 North Kensington Avenue, La Grange Park, IL 60526
Phone: 800-323-3044
Email: hr@ans.org
http://www.ans.org
Purpose: To aid nuclear science and nuclear engineering students.
Eligibility: Applicants must be U.S. citizens or permanent residents and be student members of the American Nuclear Society (ANS). They must be undergraduate or graduate students who have completed two or more years of study toward a four-year degree in nuclear science or nuclear engineering. Students must be enrolled at an accredited U.S. postsecondary institution. Selection is based on academic merit.
Target applicant(s): College students. Adult students.
Amount: Varies.
Number of awards: Varies.
Deadline: February 1.
How to apply: Applications are available online. An application form, transcript and three references are required.
Exclusive: Visit www.UltimateScholarshipBook.com and enter code AM110123 for updates on this award.

(1102) · Osmosis Raise the Line Scholarship

Osmosis
Email: support@osmosis.org
https://www.osmosis.org/scholarship
Purpose: To encourage students in health professions programs.
Eligibility: Applicants must be enrolled in or accepted into a health professions program and be working toward one of the following degrees: incoming premed, MD, DO, PA1, BSN, RN or NP. Students must have at least one academic year remaining in their studies. A short questionnaire and a video submission are required.
Target applicant(s): High school students. College students. Graduate school students. Adult students.
Amount: Up to $5,000.
Number of awards: 6.
Deadline: August 17.

How to apply: Applications are available online.
Exclusive: Visit www.UltimateScholarshipBook.com and enter code OS110223 for updates on this award.

(1103) · Outstanding Undergraduate Researchers Award Program

Computing Research Association
1828 L Street NW, Suite 800, Washington, DC 20036-4632
Phone: 202-234-2111
Email: info@cra.org
https://cra.org/about/awards/
Purpose: To support undergraduates who have completed outstanding research in the field of computing.
Eligibility: Applicants must be undergraduates at a North American college or university and must have conducted some type of computing research. Nominations from two faculty members and a recommendation from the chair of the applicant's home department are also required. Preference is given to undergraduate seniors. Selection is based on the quality of computing research, academic achievement and community involvement.
Target applicant(s): College students. Adult students.
Amount: Up to $1,500.
Number of awards: 4.
Deadline: October 15.
How to apply: The nomination form is available online. A recommendation from the chair of the applicant's home department and nominations from two faculty members are required.
Exclusive: Visit www.UltimateScholarshipBook.com and enter code CO110323 for updates on this award.

(1104) · Paradigm Challenge

Project Paradigm
P.O. Box 27729, Los Angeles, CA 90027
http://www.projectparadigm.org
Purpose: To encourage youth to use STEM plus kindness, creativity and collaboration to make a difference in the world.
Eligibility: Applicants must be 18 years of age or younger. Students will need to submit a description of 140 characters or less of their idea to reduce waste in their homes, schools, community or around the world.
Target applicant(s): Junior high students or younger. High school students.
Amount: $200-$100,000.
Number of awards: 100.
Deadline: May 1.
How to apply: Applications available online.
Exclusive: Visit www.UltimateScholarshipBook.com and enter code PR110423 for updates on this award.

(1105) · Paros-Digiquartz Scholarship

Marine Technology Society
1100 H Street NW, Suite LL-100, Washington, DC 20005
Phone: 202-717-8705
https://www.mtsociety.org/scholarships
Purpose: To support Marine Technology Society members with an interest in marine instrumentation in pursuing post-secondary education.
Eligibility: Applicants must be MTS student members who are accepted for enrollment or enrolled full-time in an undergraduate or graduate program.

Target applicant(s): College students. Graduate school students. Adult students.
Amount: $2,000.
Number of awards: 1.
Deadline: April 15.
How to apply: Applications are available online.
Exclusive: Visit www.UltimateScholarshipBook.com and enter code MA110523 for updates on this award.

(1106) · Path to Pro Scholarship

Home Depot Foundation
https://www.myscholarship.app/home-depot-foundation
Purpose: To support students focused on carpentry, electrical, HVAC, plumbing or construction management studies.
Eligibility: Applicants must be high school seniors, high school graduates or have a GED equivalent. Students must plan to enroll, or be enrolled, in an approved trade-related program at an accredited two-year school in the United States focused on carpentry, electrical, HVAC, plumbing or construction management programs.
Target applicant(s): High school students. College students. Adult students.
Amount: $2,000.
Number of awards: Up to 15.
Deadline: June 30, September 30, December 31.
How to apply: Applications are available online.
Exclusive: Visit www.UltimateScholarshipBook.com and enter code HO110623 for updates on this award.

(1107) · Paul A. Stewart Grants

Wilson Ornithological Society
Department of Biology and Biomedical Science, Dr. James Chace, Associate Professor, 100 Ochre Point Avenue, Newport, RI 02840-4192
Email: rbpayne@umich.edu
http://www.wilsonsociety.org
Purpose: To promote bird research.
Eligibility: Applicants' proposals should, but are not required to, cover the area of the study of bird movements based on banding, using the analysis and recovery of banded birds, with an emphasis on economic ornithology. Applicants must be willing to present their research results at an annual meeting of the Wilson Ornithological Society.
Target applicant(s): Junior high students or younger. High school students. College students. Graduate school students. Adult students.
Amount: $1,000.
Number of awards: Up to 4.
Deadline: February 15.
How to apply: Applications are available online.
Exclusive: Visit www.UltimateScholarshipBook.com and enter code WI110723 for updates on this award.

(1108) · Payette Sho-Ping Chin Memorial Academic Scholarship

American Institute of Architects
740 15th Street NW, Washington, DC 20005
Phone: 202-787-1001
Email: scholarships@architectsfoundation.org
https://architectsfoundation.org
Purpose: To support women seeking an architectural degree.

Eligibility: Applicants must be female students in their third year of undergraduate or any level of graduate study in an accredited architecture program. Students must have a grade point average of 3.0 or better and be a U.S. citizen.
Target applicant(s): College students. Graduate school students. Adult students.
Minimum GPA: 3.0
Amount: $10,000.
Number of awards: 1.
Deadline: January 14.
How to apply: Applications are available online
Exclusive: Visit www.UltimateScholarshipBook.com and enter code AM110823 for updates on this award.

(1109) · Payzer Scholarship

EAA Aviation Center
3000 Poberezny Road, Oshkosh, WI 54902
Phone: 920-426-4800
Email: scholarships@eaa.org
http://www.eaa.org/en/eaa
Purpose: To support students interested in technical careers.
Eligibility: Applicants must be accepted or enrolled in an accredited college or university with an emphasis on technical information and must intend to pursue a career in engineering, mathematics or the physical or biological sciences. Applicants must also be involved in school and community activities as well as aviation and be members of EAA.
Target applicant(s): High school students. College students. Graduate school students. Adult students.
Amount: $5,000.
Number of awards: 1.
Deadline: January 31.
How to apply: Applications are available online.
Exclusive: Visit www.UltimateScholarshipBook.com and enter code EA110923 for updates on this award.

(1110) · Peggy Dixon Two-Year Scholarship

Society of Physics Students
One Physics Ellipse, College Park, MD 20740
Phone: 301-209-3007
Email: SPS-Programs@aip.org
https://www.spsnational.org/
Purpose: To help students seeking a bachelor's degree in physics to transition from a two-year to a four-year program.
Eligibility: Applicants must be members of SPS. Students must have finished at least one semester or quarter of the introductory physics sequence and must be registered in the appropriate subsequent physics classes.
Target applicant(s): College students. Adult students.
Amount: $2,000.
Number of awards: 1.
Deadline: March 15.
How to apply: Applications are available online or from chapter advisors.
Exclusive: Visit www.UltimateScholarshipBook.com and enter code SO111023 for updates on this award.

(1111) · Perennial Plant Association Scholarship

Perennial Plant Association
3383 Schirtzinger Road, Hilliard, OH 43026
Phone: 614-771-8431

Email: ppa@perennialplant.org
http://www.perennialplant.org
Purpose: To aid undergraduates who are studying horticulture or a related subject.
Eligibility: Applicants must be enrolled in a two- or four-year degree program while majoring or minoring in horticulture or a related subject. They must have a GPA of 3.0 or higher on a four-point scale. Previous recipients of this scholarship are not eligible. Preference will be given to applicants who are planning to pursue careers in perennials. Selection is based on the overall strength of the application.
Target applicant(s): College students. Adult students.
Minimum GPA: 3.0
Amount: $1,000.
Number of awards: Varies.
Deadline: April 19.
How to apply: Applications are available online. An application form, official transcript, personal statement and three recommendation letters are required.
Exclusive: Visit www.UltimateScholarshipBook.com and enter code PE111123 for updates on this award.

(1112) · Perfect Plants Nursery Scholarship

Perfect Plants
P.O. Box 442, Lloyd, FL 32337
Phone: 850-997-3008
Email: Scholars@myperfectplants.com
https://myperfectplants.com/scholarship-application/
Purpose: To support students pursuing horticultural education.
Eligibility: Applicants must be current or enrolling undergraduate students with a minimum GPA of 3.0 who are pursuing a course of study leading to a career in the horticultural industry. Students must submit an essay and letters of recommendation along with their application and transcripts.
Target applicant(s): High school students. College students. Adult students.
Minimum GPA: 3.0
Amount: $1,000.
Number of awards: 1.
Deadline: August 20.
How to apply: Applications are available online.
Exclusive: Visit www.UltimateScholarshipBook.com and enter code PE111223 for updates on this award.

(1113) · Petroleum Division College Scholarships

ASME International Petroleum Technology Institute
Collegiate Council, 11757 Katy Freeway, Houston, TX 77079
Phone: 281-493-3491
http://www.asme-ipti-cc.org/
Purpose: To aid undergraduate engineering students who are members of the American Society of Mechanical Engineers (ASME).
Eligibility: Applicants must be ASME student members who are enrolled in an ABET-accredited undergraduate degree program in engineering. They must have an overall GPA of 2.5 or higher on a four-point scale. Selection is based on the overall strength of the application.
Target applicant(s): High school students. College students. Adult students.
Minimum GPA: 2.5
Amount: $2,000.
Number of awards: 20.
Deadline: September 17.

How to apply: Applications are available online. An application form, official transcript, personal statement and one recommendation letter are required.
Exclusive: Visit www.UltimateScholarshipBook.com and enter code AS111323 for updates on this award.

(1114) · PHCC Educational Foundation Scholarship

PHCC Educational Foundation
180 South Washington Street, Suite 100, Falls Church, VA 22046
Phone: 800-533-7694
Email: scholarships@naphcc.org
http://www.phccweb.org
Purpose: To elevate the technical and business competence of the plumbing-heating-cooling (p-h-c) industry by awarding scholarships to students who are enrolled in a p-h-c-related major.
Eligibility: Applicants must be currently enrolled or plan to enroll in a p-h-c-related major at an accredited four-year college or university or two-year technical college, community college or trade school. Students enrolled in an approved apprentice program must also be working full-time for a licensed plumbing or HVACR contractor who is a member of the PHCC. Two scholarships will be awarded to students who are enrolled in either a PHCC-approved apprentice program or a full-time certificate or degree program at an accredited two-year community college, technical college or trade school. Three scholarships are awarded to students who are enrolled in an undergraduate degree program at an accredited four-year college or university.
Target applicant(s): High school students. College students. Adult students.
Amount: $1,000-$5,000.
Number of awards: Up to 39.
Deadline: May 1.
How to apply: Applications are available online or by email.
Exclusive: Visit www.UltimateScholarshipBook.com and enter code PH111423 for updates on this award.

(1115) · Phoebe Pember Memorial Scholarship

United Daughters of the Confederacy
328 North Boulevard, Richmond, VA 23220
Phone: 804-355-1636
Email: hqudc@rcn.com
http://www.hqudc.org
Purpose: To aid Confederate descendants who are undergraduate nursing students.
Eligibility: Applicants must be the direct descendant of an eligible Confederate. They must be enrolled in an undergraduate degree program in nursing at an accredited U.S. college or university and have a GPA of 3.0 or higher on a four-point scale. Selection is based on the overall strength of the application.
Target applicant(s): College students. Adult students.
Minimum GPA: 3.0
Amount: Varies.
Number of awards: Varies.
Scholarship may be renewable.
Deadline: Varies.
How to apply: Applications are available online. An application form, personal statement, official transcript, one letter of recommendation, endorsement from sponsoring UDC Chapter, applicant photo and proof of Confederate ancestry are required.
Exclusive: Visit www.UltimateScholarshipBook.com and enter code UN111523 for updates on this award.

(1116) · Physician Assistant Foundation Scholarship

Physician Assistant Foundation
PA Foundation Scholarship Committee, 950 North Washington Street, Alexandria, VA 22314-1552
Phone: 703-519-5686
Email: cshedlock@aapa.org
http://www.aapa.org
Purpose: To support physician assistants.
Eligibility: Applicants must be American Academy of Physician Assistants (AAPA) members and currently enrolled in the professional phase of a PA training program at an ARC-PA-accredited physician assistant program. Students are judged on the basis of financial need, community and professional involvement, goals and academic performance.
Target applicant(s): College students. Adult students.
Amount: $1,000.
Number of awards: 26.
Deadline: August 13.
How to apply: Applications are available online.
Exclusive: Visit www.UltimateScholarshipBook.com and enter code PH111623 for updates on this award.

(1117) · Pioneers of Flight

National Air Transportation Foundation
Pioneers of Flight Scholarship Program, Attn.: Professor Gregory Schwab, Chair, Department of Aerospace Technology, TC 216, Indiana State University, Terre Haute, IN 47809
Email: aeschwab@isugw.indstate.edu
https://www.nata.aero/scholarships/pioneers-of-flight-scholarship
Purpose: To assist students pursuing general aviation as a career.
Eligibility: Applicants must be full-time students at an accredited four-year institution, be sophomores or juniors at the time of application and plan to pursue a career in aviation. Students must have a minimum 3.0 GPA.
Target applicant(s): College students. Adult students.
Minimum GPA: 3.0
Amount: $1,000.
Number of awards: 2.
Deadline: Last Friday in December.
How to apply: Applications are available online.
Exclusive: Visit www.UltimateScholarshipBook.com and enter code NA111723 for updates on this award.

(1118) · PixelPlex Bi-Annual STEM Scholarship

PixelPlex
520 West 28th Street, Suite 31, New York, NY 10001
Phone: 646-490-0772
Email: scholarship@pixelplex.io
https://pixelplex.io/scholarship/
Purpose: To encourage students pursuing education in STEM fields as well as economics and business.
Eligibility: Applicants must be U.S. citizens or permanent residents. Students must be enrolled or accepted into a college or university in the United States. The applicants' field of study must be related to STEM fields, economics or business. An essay is required on a provided prompt.
Target applicant(s): High school students. College students. Graduate school students. Adult students.
Amount: $2,000.
Number of awards: 1.
Deadline: December 5.

How to apply: Applications are available online.
Exclusive: Visit www.UltimateScholarshipBook.com and enter code PI111823 for updates on this award.

(1119) · Plastics Pioneers Association Scholarships

Society of Plastics Engineers
6 Berkshire Boulevard, Suite 306, Bethel, CT 06801
Phone: 203-775-0471
Email: info@4spe.org
http://www.4spe.org/spe-foundation
Purpose: To aid students who are planning for careers in plastics technology and engineering.
Eligibility: Applicants must be full-time undergraduate students who intend to pursue careers as plastics technicians or engineers. Selection is based on the overall strength of the application.
Target applicant(s): High school students. College students. Adult students.
Amount: $3,000.
Number of awards: Varies.
Deadline: March 15.
How to apply: Applications are available online. An application form, three recommendation letters, a transcript and personal statement are required.
Exclusive: Visit www.UltimateScholarshipBook.com and enter code SO111923 for updates on this award.

(1120) · Polymer Modifiers and Additives Division Scholarships

Society of Plastics Engineers
6 Berkshire Boulevard, Suite 306, Bethel, CT 06801
Phone: 203-775-0471
Email: info@4spe.org
http://www.4spe.org/spe-foundation
Purpose: To aid students who have an interest in the plastics industry.
Eligibility: Applicants must have an interest in the plastics industry, major in or take courses leading to a career in the plastics industry and be in good academic standing. Financial need is considered.
Target applicant(s): High school students. College students. Adult students.
Amount: Varies.
Number of awards: Varies.
Deadline: April 1.
How to apply: Applications are available online.
Exclusive: Visit www.UltimateScholarshipBook.com and enter code SO112023 for updates on this award.

(1121) · PPG Protective and Marine Coatings Academic Scholarship

National Association of Corrosion Engineers (NACE) International Foundation
15835 Park Ten Place, Houston, TX 77084-5145
Phone: 281-228-6205
Email: nace.foundation@nace.org
http://nace-foundation.org/programs/students/scholarships/
Purpose: To help students interested in pursuing science and/or engineering degrees.
Eligibility: Applicants must be an undergraduate enrolled full-time at an accredited two- or four-year college or university and must be pursuing

a degree with an emphasis on corrosion or coatings. Applicants must have a GPA of 3.0 or higher in their chosen field of study.
Target applicant(s): College students. Adult students.
Minimum GPA: 3.0
Amount: $5,000.
Number of awards: Up to 2.
Deadline: January 1.
How to apply: Applications are available online. An application form, three recommendation forms, an academic transcript and essay scholarship questions are required.
Exclusive: Visit www.UltimateScholarshipBook.com and enter code NA112123 for updates on this award.

(1122) · Predoctoral Fellowship Program

National Gallery of Art
2000B South Club Drive, Landover, MD 20785
Phone: 202-842-6482
Email: thecenter@nga.gov
https://www.nga.gov/research/casva/fellowships.html
Purpose: To support advanced graduate research in the history, theory and criticism of art, architecture and urbanism.
Eligibility: Applicants for predoctoral fellowships must be nominated by the chair of the graduate department of art history or other appropriate departments. Applicants must have completed all departmental requirements, including course work, residency and general and preliminary examinations. Certification in two languages other than English is required. Applicants should submit nomination forms, supporting letters from two individuals and writing samples. There are various fellowships. The David E. Finley Fellowship requires applicants have a significant interest in curatorial work. The Paul Mellon Fellowship is for the completion of a doctoral dissertation in Western art. The Samuel H. Kress Fellowship is for the completion of a doctoral dissertation in European art on a topic before the early nineteenth century. The Wyeth Fellowship is for the completion of a doctoral dissertation that concerns aspects of art of the United States, including native and pre-Revolutionary America. The Ittleson Fellowship is for the completion of a doctoral dissertation in the visual arts in a field other than Western art. The Andrew W. Mellon Fellowship is for the completion of a doctoral dissertation in cross-cultural studies or in a field other than Western art through the twentieth century. The Robert H. and Clarice Smith Fellowship is for research on Northern European art between 1400 and 1700, intended for the advancement or completion of either a doctoral dissertation or a resulting publication. The Chester Dale Fellowships are for the advancement or completion of a doctoral dissertation in any area of Western art, with a preference for modern and contemporary topics. The Center offers a Paul Mellon Postdoctoral Fellowship for recipients of the David E. Finley, Paul Mellon, Samuel H. Kress, Wyeth, Ittleson, Andrew W. Mellon and two-year Chester Dale fellowships if the dissertation has been accepted by June 1 of the residence year. Several candidates for each fellowship will be invited to Washington for interviews.
Target applicant(s): Graduate school students. Adult students.
Amount: $30,000 plus allowances.
Number of awards: 9.
Deadline: November 15.
How to apply: Application materials are described online. Contact your dissertation advisor and departmental chair to obtain nomination forms.
Exclusive: Visit www.UltimateScholarshipBook.com and enter code NA112223 for updates on this award.

(1123) · Predoctoral Research Training Fellowship

American Epilepsy Society
135 South LaSalle Street, Suite 2850, Chicago, IL 60603
Email: info@aesnet.org
https://www.aesnet.org/research-funding/funding/early-career/predoctoral-research-fellowships
Purpose: To support pre-doctoral students with dissertation research relating to epilepsy.
Eligibility: Applicants must be full-time graduate students pursuing a Ph.D. degree in neuroscience, physiology, pharmacology, psychology, biochemistry, genetics, nursing, pharmacy or other related areas; have a dissertation research project; have a qualified mentor who can supervise the project and have access to resources to conduct the project. The project must be in the U.S. and its territories. The award is based on the quality of the dissertation project, relevance to epilepsy, the applicant's qualifications, the mentor's qualifications and the quality of the proposed environment.
Target applicant(s): Graduate school students. Adult students.
Amount: Varies.
Number of awards: Varies.
Deadline: January 14.
How to apply: Applicants must submit three recommendation letters including one from the mentor, a statement of intent, a biographical sketch, a cover sheet form, a lay summary, transcripts and a research plan.
Exclusive: Visit www.UltimateScholarshipBook.com and enter code AM112323 for updates on this award.

(1124) · Presidents Scholarship of the Institute of Industrial Engineers

Institute of Industrial and Systems Engineers
3577 Parkway Lane, Suite 200, Norcross, GA 30092
Phone: 800-494-0460
Email: bcameron@iienet.org
http://www.iise.org/
Purpose: To support undergraduate industrial engineering students.
Eligibility: Applicants must be active student members of the Institute of Industrial Engineers (IIE). They must be full-time undergraduates enrolled in an industrial engineering degree program and have a GPA of 3.4 or higher on a four-point scale. They must have demonstrated leadership skills. Applicants must be nominated by their academic department heads. Selection is based on professional leadership potential, character, financial need and academic merit.
Target applicant(s): College students. Adult students.
Minimum GPA: 3.4
Amount: $1,000.
Number of awards: 1.
Deadline: November 15.
How to apply: Nomination forms are available online. A nomination form completed by the applicant's academic department head is required.
Exclusive: Visit www.UltimateScholarshipBook.com and enter code IN112423 for updates on this award.

(1125) · Pretty Photoshop Actions Bi-annual Scholarship

Pretty Photoshop Actions
Email: scholarship@photoshopactions.com
https://www.photoshopactions.com/pages/pretty-photoshop-actions-scholarship-program
Purpose: To help offset the cost of higher education.

Eligibility: Applicants must be graduating high school seniors or enrolled at a college or university in the U.S. or Canada. Students must create an Adobe Photoshop tutorial essay.
Target applicant(s): High school students. College students. Adult students.
Amount: $500.
Number of awards: 1.
Deadline: October 15.
How to apply: Applications are available online.
Exclusive: Visit www.UltimateScholarshipBook.com and enter code PR112523 for updates on this award.

(1126) · Pulte Group Build Your Future Scholarship Program
National Housing Endowment
1201 15th Street NW, Washington, DC 20005
Phone: 202-266-8069
Email: Scholarships@nahb.org
http://www.nationalhousingendowment.org/page.aspx/generic/sectionID=3267
Purpose: To aid U.S. students who plan to pursue careers in the building industry.
Eligibility: Applicants must be U.S. undergraduate freshmen, sophomores or juniors who are enrolled full-time in a housing-related degree program (construction, civil engineering, architecture, building trades or management, etc.). They must have at least one full academic year remaining in their course of study and maintain an overall GPA of at least 2.5 and major GPA of at least 3.0. Preference will be given to applicants who demonstrate financial need or who are members of a building industry-related service or professional organization, especially the National Association of Home Builders. Selection is based on financial need, academic achievement, GPA, work experience, extracurricular activities and professional goals.
Target applicant(s): College students. Adult students.
Minimum GPA: 2.5
Amount: Varies.
Number of awards: Varies.
Scholarship may be renewable.
Deadline: March.
How to apply: Applications are available online. An application form, a transcript, two recommendation letters, a list of degree requirements, a personal essay and a statement of financial status are required.
Exclusive: Visit www.UltimateScholarshipBook.com and enter code NA112623 for updates on this award.

(1127) · R&D Systems Scholarship Program
R&D Systems Inc.
614 McKinley Place NE, Minneapolis, MN 55413
Phone: 800-343-7475
Email: scholarship@novusbio.com
https://www.rndsystems.com/grants-scholarships/scholarship-application
Purpose: To support students who are pursuing a degree in a science-related field.
Eligibility: Applicants must be enrolled, or plan to be enrolled, in a undergraduate or graduate level science program.
Target applicant(s): High school students. College students. Graduate school students. Adult students.
Amount: $1,500.
Number of awards: 2.
Deadline: June 16 and December 8.

How to apply: Applications are available online.
Exclusive: Visit www.UltimateScholarshipBook.com and enter code R&112723 for updates on this award.

(1128) · Rain Bird Intelligent Use of Water Scholarship
Landscape Architecture Foundation
1129 20th Street NW, Suite 202, Washington, DC 20036
Phone: 202-331-7070
Email: scholarships@lafoundation.org
https://www.lafoundation.org/what-we-do/scholarships
Purpose: To recognize outstanding landscape architecture students.
Eligibility: Applicants must be college juniors or fourth- or fifth-year seniors who are landscape architecture, horticulture or irrigation science students who have a demonstrated commitment to the landscape architecture profession and exhibit financial need. Applications can only be sent by email.
Target applicant(s): College students. Adult students.
Amount: $2,500.
Number of awards: 1.
Deadline: February 1.
How to apply: Applicants should follow the guidelines.
Exclusive: Visit www.UltimateScholarshipBook.com and enter code LA112823 for updates on this award.

(1129) · Ralph K. Hillquist Honorary SAE Scholarship
Society of Automotive Engineers International
Scholarships Program, 400 Commonwealth Drive, Warrendale, PA 15096
Phone: 724-776-4841
Email: scholarships@sae.org
https://www.sae.org/participate/scholarships
Purpose: To aid mechanical and automotive engineering students.
Eligibility: Applicants must be U.S. citizens and full-time undergraduate juniors who are enrolled in an ABET-accredited mechanical or automotive engineering degree program at a U.S. college or university. They must have a GPA of 3.0 or higher. Preference will be given to applicants who have completed coursework in noise and vibration (e.g. physics, statics, vibration or dynamics). Selection is based on academic merit, leadership and special studies in noise and vibration.
Target applicant(s): College students. Adult students.
Minimum GPA: 3.0
Amount: $1,000.
Number of awards: 1.
Deadline: March 15.
How to apply: Applications are available online. An application form, official transcript and standardized test scores are required.
Exclusive: Visit www.UltimateScholarshipBook.com and enter code SO112923 for updates on this award.

(1130) · Raney Fund Award
American Society of Ichthyologists and Herpetologists
P.O. Box 1897, Lawrence, KS 66044-8897
Phone: 785-843-1235
Email: asih@allenpress.com
https://asih.org/student-awards
Purpose: To support young ichthyologists.
Eligibility: Applicants should be members of ASIH and should be enrolled for an advanced degree, although those with developing careers may receive the award under exceptional circumstances. Awards may be used for museums or laboratory study, travel, fieldwork or other activities

that will enhance their professional careers and their contributions to the science of ichthyology. Scholarships are awarded on the basis of merit and need.

Target applicant(s): Graduate school students. Adult students.
Amount: $400-$1,000.
Number of awards: Varies.
Deadline: March 1.
How to apply: Applications are available by email or written request.
Exclusive: Visit www.UltimateScholarshipBook.com and enter code AM113023 for updates on this award.

(1131) · Raymond Davis Scholarship

Society for Imaging Science and Technology
7003 Kilworth Lane, Springfield, VA 22151
Phone: 703-642-9090
Email: info@imaging.org
http://www.imaging.org
Purpose: To support students who are studying imaging science and technology.
Eligibility: Applicants must be full-time graduate or undergraduate students studying photographic or imaging engineering or science who have completed or will complete two academic years of college before the term of the scholarship.
Target applicant(s): College students. Graduate school students. Adult students.
Amount: At least $1,000.
Number of awards: Varies.
Deadline: October 1.
How to apply: Applications are available online.
Exclusive: Visit www.UltimateScholarshipBook.com and enter code SO113123 for updates on this award.

(1132) · Regeneron Science Talent Search

Regeneron Science Talent Search
Society for Science and the Public, 1719 N Street NW, Washington, DC 20036
Phone: 202-785-2255
Email: sts@societyforscience.org
https://student.societyforscience.org/regeneron-sts
Purpose: To recognize excellence in science among the nation's youth and encourage the exploration of science.
Eligibility: Applicants must be high school seniors in the U.S., Puerto Rico, Guam, Virgin Islands, American Samoa, Wake or Midway Islands or the Marianas. U.S. citizens attending foreign schools are also eligible. Applicants must complete college entrance exams and complete individual research projects and provide a report on the research.
Target applicant(s): High school students.
Amount: Up to $250,000.
Number of awards: 40.
Deadline: November 10.
How to apply: Applications are available by request.
Exclusive: Visit www.UltimateScholarshipBook.com and enter code RE113223 for updates on this award.

(1133) · Resident Research Scholarship

American Academy of Neurology
201 Chicago Avenue, Minneapolis, MN 55415
Phone: 800-879-1960
Email: ggates@aan.com
http://www.aan.com

Purpose: To support neurology residents who are interested in a career in research in neuroscience.
Eligibility: Applicants must be neurology residents who are interested in a career in research in neuroscience. The award is intended to be a springboard into the AAN's Research Program or other programs focused on early-career investigators.
Target applicant(s): Graduate school students. Adult students.
Amount: Varies.
Number of awards: Varies.
Deadline: October 28.
How to apply: Applications are available online.
Exclusive: Visit www.UltimateScholarshipBook.com and enter code AM113323 for updates on this award.

(1134) · Reuben Trane Scholarship

American Society of Heating, Refrigerating and Air-Conditioning Engineers (ASHRAE)
1791 Tullie Circle, NE, Atlanta, GA 30329
Phone: 404-636-8400
Email: lbenedict@ashrae.org
https://www.ashrae.org/membership--conferences/student-zone/scholarships-and-grants/scholarship-program
Purpose: To support engineering undergraduates who are preparing for careers in the heating, ventilation, air-conditioning and refrigeration (HVACR) industry.
Eligibility: Applicants must be attending a school that houses a student branch of the American Society of Heating, Refrigerating and Air-Conditioning Engineers (ASHRAE), is ABET-accredited (U.S. institutions) or is ABET-affiliated (international institutions). Applicants must be undergraduate students who are enrolled in an engineering or pre-engineering curriculum that provides adequate preparation for a career in the HVACR industry. They must have a GPA of 3.0 or higher on a four-point scale or must be in the top 30 percent of their class. Selection is based on the overall strength of the application.
Target applicant(s): High school students. College students. Adult students.
Minimum GPA: 3.0
Amount: $10,000.
Number of awards: 3.
Scholarship may be renewable.
Deadline: December 1.
How to apply: Applications are available online. The application form, official transcript, one letter of recommendation and the evaluation form from an ASHRAE student branch interview (if applicable) are required.
Exclusive: Visit www.UltimateScholarshipBook.com and enter code AM113423 for updates on this award.

(1135) · RevPart STEM Scholarship

RevPart
129 Bethea Road, Suite 402, Fayetteville, GA 30214
Phone: 844-738-7278
Email: info@revpart.com
https://revpart.com/scholarship/
Purpose: To encourage students pursuing a higher education in their chosen study of area of study in a STEM-related field.
Eligibility: Applicants must be a current undergraduate or graduate student majoring in a STEM-related field at an accredited college or institution.
Target applicant(s): High school students. College students. Graduate school students. Adult students.
Amount: $250-$1,000.

Number of awards: 3.
Deadline: December 31.
How to apply: Applications are available online.
Exclusive: Visit www.UltimateScholarshipBook.com and enter code RE113523 for updates on this award.

(1136) · Richard J. Stull Student Essay Competition in Healthcare Management

American College of Healthcare Executives
One North Franklin Street, Suite 1700, Chicago, IL 60606
Phone: 312-424-9316
Email: sbrown@ache.org
https://www.ache.org/membership/student-resources
Purpose: To support future healthcare executives.
Eligibility: Applicants must be undergraduate or graduate students enrolled in a healthcare administration degree program at a U.S. or Canadian postsecondary institution that is an American College of Healthcare Executives (ACHE) Higher Education network participant. They must be ACHE student associates or active affiliates. Submitted essays cannot have been published before and must be the sole creation of the applicant. Residents and other postgraduate students are ineligible. Selection is based on relevance of subject matter, creativity, practical applicability of subject matter and clarity.
Target applicant(s): High school students. College students. Graduate school students. Adult students.
Amount: Up to $3,000.
Number of awards: 6.
Deadline: December 6.
How to apply: Essay submission guidelines are available online. An essay is required.
Exclusive: Visit www.UltimateScholarshipBook.com and enter code AM113623 for updates on this award.

(1137) · Richard Jensen Scholarship

National Alliance of Independent Crop Consultants
P.O. Box 209, Vonore, TN 37885
Phone: 901-861-0511
Email: AllisonJones@NAICC.org
http://thefeae.org/jensen-scholarship/
Purpose: To aid undergraduate students of crop production.
Eligibility: Applicants must be undergraduate juniors who are majoring in an agricultural subject that is related to crop production (such as agronomy, horticulture, weed science, soil sciences, entomology or plant pathology). Selection is based on the overall strength of the application.
Target applicant(s): College students. Adult students.
Amount: $3,000.
Number of awards: 1.
Deadline: December 1.
How to apply: Applications are available online. An application form, transcript, proof of enrollment and two reference letters are required.
Exclusive: Visit www.UltimateScholarshipBook.com and enter code NA113723 for updates on this award.

(1138) · Richard L. Davis, FACMPE - Managers Scholarship

Medical Group Management Association
104 Inverness Terrace East, Englewood, CO 80112
Phone: 877-275-6462
Email: acmpe@mgma.com
https://mgma.com/career-pathways/career-advancement/career-resources/scholarships
Purpose: To aid medical practice management professionals who are college students.
Eligibility: Applicants must be current medical practice management professionals who are enrolled in an undergraduate or graduate degree program that is related to medical practice management. Selection is based on the overall strength of the application.
Target applicant(s): College students. Graduate school students. Adult students.
Amount: $2,500.
Number of awards: Varies.
Deadline: May.
How to apply: Applications are available online. An application form and supporting materials are required.
Exclusive: Visit www.UltimateScholarshipBook.com and enter code ME113823 for updates on this award.

(1139) · Richard L. Davis, FACMPE/Barbara B. Watson, FACMPE - National Scholarship

Medical Group Management Association
104 Inverness Terrace East, Englewood, CO 80112
Phone: 877-275-6462
Email: acmpe@mgma.com
https://mgma.com/career-pathways/career-advancement/career-resources/scholarships
Purpose: To aid medical practice management students.
Eligibility: Applicants must be undergraduate or graduate students who are enrolled in a degree program that is related to medical practice management (such as healthcare administration, public health or business administration). Selection is based on the overall strength of the application.
Target applicant(s): High school students. College students. Graduate school students. Adult students.
Amount: $2,500.
Number of awards: Varies.
Deadline: May.
How to apply: Applications are available online. An application form and supporting materials are required.
Exclusive: Visit www.UltimateScholarshipBook.com and enter code ME113923 for updates on this award.

(1140) · Richard Lee Vernon Aviation Scholarship

EAA Aviation Center
3000 Poberezny Road, Oshkosh, WI 54902
Phone: 920-426-4800
Email: scholarships@eaa.org
http://www.eaa.org/en/eaa
Purpose: To support students pursuing training leading to a professional aviation occupations.
Eligibility: Applicants must be accepted to an accredited college, university or aviation technical school pursuing a course of study focusing on aviation. Applicants must also be involved in school and community activities as well as aviation. Recipient must show need for financial support.
Target applicant(s): High school students. College students. Adult students.
Amount: $500.
Number of awards: 1.
Deadline: January 31.
How to apply: Applications are available online.

Exclusive: Visit www.UltimateScholarshipBook.com and enter code EA114023 for updates on this award.

(1141) · Ridgeline International Community Scholarship

Ridgeline International
8255 Greensboro Drive, Suite 500, McLean, VA 22102
Phone: 703-544-2424
Email: atavares@ridgelineintl.com
https://www.ridgelineintl.com/about#scholarship
Purpose: To reward students who show grit, resilience and agility and take an active role in their community.
Eligibility: Applicants must be graduating high school seniors and current undergraduate students. Students must be pursuing higher education in the science, technology, engineering and math fields. Applicants who are awarded a scholarship may also be considered for future internship and full-time opportunities.
Target applicant(s): High school students. College students. Adult students.
Amount: $5,000.
Number of awards: 3.
Deadline: June 30.
How to apply: Applications are available online.
Exclusive: Visit www.UltimateScholarshipBook.com and enter code RI114123 for updates on this award.

(1142) · RMEL Foundation Scholarships

Rocky Mountain Electrical League
6855 South Havana Street, Suite 430, Centennial, CO 80112
Phone: 303-865-5544
Email: jamessakamoto@rmel.org
http://www.rmel.org
Purpose: To support students pursuing certificate or degree-seeking programs related to the electric energy industry.
Eligibility: Applicants must be U.S. citizens and full-time students pursuing either a certificate, associate or baccalaureate degree in the electric energy arena including: power plant technology, electric line working, power line technology, electrical power technology, electrical line worker technology, electrical distribution systems, utility line technician and traditional or alternative power generation technology. Selection is based on future goals in the electric energy arena, motivation, service and academic performance.
Target applicant(s): High school students. College students. Graduate school students. Adult students.
Amount: Up to $3,000.
Number of awards: Varies.
Deadline: February 27.
How to apply: Applications are available online. An application form and transcripts are required.
Exclusive: Visit www.UltimateScholarshipBook.com and enter code RO114223 for updates on this award.

(1143) · Robert B. Oliver ASNT Scholarship

American Society for Nondestructive Testing
Awards and Honors Program, 1711 Arlingate Lane, P.O. Box 28518, Columbus, OH 43228-0518
Phone: 614-274-6003 x 233
Email: awards@asnt.org
http://www.asnt.org
Purpose: To support students in nondestructive testing.

Eligibility: Applicants must be undergraduate students enrolled in an engineering program and specialize in nondestructive testing (NDT). A nominating letter, transcript and an essay describing the role of NDT/NDE in their career are required. The award is based on creativity, content, format and readability and the student's involvement in a research project.
Target applicant(s): College students. Adult students.
Amount: $2,500.
Number of awards: Up to 3.
Deadline: February 15.
How to apply: Applications are available online.
Exclusive: Visit www.UltimateScholarshipBook.com and enter code AM114323 for updates on this award.

(1144) · Robert E. Dougherty Educational Foundation Scholarship Award

Composite Panel Association
Robert E. Dougherty Educational Foundation, 19465 Deerfield Avenue, Suite 306, Leesburg, VA 20176
Phone: 703-724-1128
Email: gheroux@cpamail.org
https://www.compositepanel.org/about-cpa/red-education-foundation.html
Purpose: To aid students who have interned in the composite panel industry.
Eligibility: Applicants must be nominated by a CPA member company or North American company that meets the eligibility requirements of CPA membership and must have interned for a company within the previous 24 months. Students must be North American citizens and be graduate or undergraduate students who are studying industrial engineering, mechanical engineering, chemical engineering, chemistry, biology, physics, forest products, wood science or wood technology. Selection is based on the overall strength of the application.
Target applicant(s): College students. Graduate school students. Adult students.
Amount: Up to $4,000.
Number of awards: 3.
Scholarship may be renewable.
Deadline: March 16.
How to apply: Applications are available online. An application form, official transcript and academic adviser appraisal are required.
Exclusive: Visit www.UltimateScholarshipBook.com and enter code CO114423 for updates on this award.

(1145) · Robert E. Thunen Memorial Scholarships

Thunen Scholarship Committee
IES San Francisco Section, Mary-Jane Lawless, 1201 Park Avenue, Suite 100, Emeryville, CA 94608
Phone: 510-864-0204
Email: mrcatisbac@aol.com
https://www.ies.org/membership/society-awards/
Purpose: To help students who plan to pursue illumination as a career.
Eligibility: Applicants must be full-time junior, senior or graduate students in an accredited four-year college in Northern California, Nevada, Oregon or Washington who plan to pursue illumination as a career. The application, statement of purpose and at least three letters of recommendation are required. Students should review the IES Lighting Handbook to see the available fields of study.
Target applicant(s): College students. Graduate school students. Adult students.
Amount: $2,500.

Number of awards: At least 2.
Deadline: April 1.
How to apply: Applications are available by mail and email.
Exclusive: Visit www.UltimateScholarshipBook.com and enter code TH114523 for updates on this award.

(1146) · Robert N. and Helen H. Herbert Undergraduate Scholarship

Society of Naval Architects and Marine Engineers (SNAME)
99 Canal Center Plaza, Suite 310, Alexandria, VA 22314
Phone: 703-997-6701
Email: scholarships@sname.org
https://www.sname.org/scholarships
Purpose: To assist college undergraduates who are studying marine industry fields.
Eligibility: Applicants must be U.S., Canadian or international college students who are members of the SNAME and are working towards degrees in naval architecture, marine engineering, ocean engineering or marine industry related areas fields. An application form, three recommendation letters and an essay are required.
Target applicant(s): College students. Adult students.
Amount: Up to $6,000.
Number of awards: 1.
Deadline: June 1.
How to apply: Applications are available online.
Exclusive: Visit www.UltimateScholarshipBook.com and enter code SO114623 for updates on this award.

(1147) · Roofing Industry Scholarship - Melvin Kruger Endowed Scholarship

National Roofing Foundation (NRF)
10255 West Higgins Road, Suite 600, Rosemont, IL 60018
Phone: 847-299-9070
http://www.nrca.net
Purpose: To support members of the National Roofing Contractors Association (NRCA).
Eligibility: Applicants must be full-time employees of NRCA member companies or their immediate family members. Students must be high school seniors or graduates or full-time undergraduate students at an accredited two- or four-year post-secondary institution. Applicants must major in a roofing or building construction course of study for a full academic year.
Target applicant(s): High school students. College students. Adult students.
Amount: $5,000.
Number of awards: 3.
Scholarship may be renewable.
Deadline: February 1.
How to apply: Applications are available online.
Exclusive: Visit www.UltimateScholarshipBook.com and enter code NA114723 for updates on this award.

(1148) · Roy J. Shlemon Awards

Geological Society of America Foundation (GSAF)
P.O. Box 9140, Boulder, CO 80301
Phone: 800-472-1988 x1054
Email: info@gsafweb.org
https://www.geosociety.org/gsa
Purpose: To assist graduate students in conducting research in environmental and engineering geology.
Eligibility: Applicants must be members of the Geological Society of America's Engineering Geology Division, and they must be conducting research at the master's or doctoral level.
Target applicant(s): Graduate school students. Adult students.
Amount: Up to $3,000.
Number of awards: At least 2.
Deadline: February 2.
How to apply: Applications are available online.
Exclusive: Visit www.UltimateScholarshipBook.com and enter code GE114823 for updates on this award.

(1149) · Rubber Division Undergraduate Scholarship

American Chemical Society
Christie Robinson, Training and Development Director, Rubber Division, ACS, 411 Wolf Ledges Parkway, Suite 201, Akron, OH 44311
Phone: 800-227-5558
Email: crobinson@rubber.org
http://www.acs.org
Purpose: To aid undergraduate students who are majoring in subjects related to the rubber industry.
Eligibility: Applicants must be rising undergraduate juniors or seniors. They must be majoring in chemistry, chemical engineering, polymer science, mechanical engineering, physics or any other subject that is related to the rubber industry. Selection is based on the overall strength of the application.
Target applicant(s): College students. Adult students.
Amount: $5,000.
Number of awards: 2.
Deadline: March 1.
How to apply: Applications are available online. An application form and supporting materials are required.
Exclusive: Visit www.UltimateScholarshipBook.com and enter code AM114923 for updates on this award.

(1150) · Russell and Sigurd Varian Award

American Vacuum Society
125 Maiden Lane, 15th Floor, New York, NY 10038
Phone: 212-248-0200
Email: angela@avs.org
http://www.avs.org
Purpose: To support continuing graduate studies in the sciences and technologies related to AVS.
Eligibility: Applicants must be graduate students in an accredited academic institution. Five finalists are invited to present talks on their research to the trustees at the international symposium. The trustees then select one student to receive the award, which also covers travel expenses. Applicants should submit applications, research summaries, letters of recommendations and transcripts.
Target applicant(s): Graduate school students. Adult students.
Amount: Varies.
Number of awards: 1.
Deadline: May 1.
How to apply: Applications are available online.
Exclusive: Visit www.UltimateScholarshipBook.com and enter code AM115023 for updates on this award.

(1151) · Ruth Abernathy Presidential Scholarship

Shape America
1900 Association Drive, Reston, VA 20191
Phone: 800-213-7193
http://www.shapeamerica.org
Purpose: To honor deserving students in the areas of health, physical education, recreation and dance.
Eligibility: Applicants must be members of the American Alliance for Health, Physical Education, Recreation and Dance (AAHPERD), but they may join when applying and must major in health, physical education, recreation or dance. Undergraduate applicants must have a minimum 3.5 GPA and have junior or senior status when applying. Graduate applicants must have a minimum 3.5 GPA and have completed one semester of full-time study. Selection is based on scholastic achievement, leadership, community service and character.
Target applicant(s): College students. Graduate school students. Adult students.
Minimum GPA: 3.5
Amount: $1,250-$1,750.
Number of awards: 5.
Deadline: October 15.
How to apply: Applications are available online.
Exclusive: Visit www.UltimateScholarshipBook.com and enter code SH115123 for updates on this award.

(1152) · Salvatore J. Monte Thermoplastic Materials and Foams Division Scholarship

Society of Plastics Engineers
6 Berkshire Boulevard, Suite 306, Bethel, CT 06801
Phone: 203-775-0471
Email: info@4spe.org
http://www.4spe.org/spe-foundation
Purpose: To aid undergraduate students who have a demonstrated interest in thermoplastic materials and foams.
Eligibility: Applicants must be full-time undergraduate students who are interested in thermoplastic materials and foams. This interest must be shown by relevant internship experiences, jobs held, coursework completed or research undertaken. Selection is based on the overall strength of the application.
Target applicant(s): High school students. College students. Adult students.
Amount: $2,500.
Number of awards: 1.
Deadline: April 1.
How to apply: Applications are available online. An application form, three references, transcript and personal statement are required.
Exclusive: Visit www.UltimateScholarshipBook.com and enter code SO115223 for updates on this award.

(1153) · Samuel Fletcher Tapman ASCE Student Chapter/Club Scholarship

American Society of Civil Engineers (ASCE)
Attn.: Honors and Awards Program, 1801 Alexander Bell Drive, Reston, VA 20191-4400
Phone: 800-548-2723
Email: awards@asce.org
http://www.asce.org
Purpose: To support worthy civil engineering undergraduate students in furthering their education.

Eligibility: Applicants must be enrolled in an ABET-accredited civil engineering program or related field. Students must be members in good standing of their local ASCE Student Chapters at the time of application submission and award acceptance. Scholarships must be used by sophomore, junior or senior engineering students.
Target applicant(s): College students. Adult students.
Amount: $3,000.
Number of awards: 12.
Scholarship may be renewable.
Deadline: February 10.
How to apply: Applications are available online.
Exclusive: Visit www.UltimateScholarshipBook.com and enter code AM115323 for updates on this award.

(1154) · Sandra Imprescia Essay Scholarship

International Water, Sanitation and Hygiene Foundation
4755 East Philadelphia Street, Ontario, CA 91761
Phone: 909-472-4100
Email: essay@iwsh.org
https://www.iapmo.org/iwsh
Purpose: To encourage students who have an awareness of the importance of the plumbing industry.
Eligibility: Applicants must be a high school senior or enrolled in an accredited technical school, community college, trade school or four-year accredited college/university. Students must submit an essay between 800- to 1,600-words on the topic listed on the website.
Target applicant(s): High school students. College students. Adult students.
Amount: $500-$1,000.
Number of awards: 3.
Deadline: April 30.
How to apply: Applications are available online.
Exclusive: Visit www.UltimateScholarshipBook.com and enter code IN115423 for updates on this award.

(1155) · Scholarships for Disadvantaged Students

Department of Health and Human Services
Health Resources and Services Administration, Bureau of Health Workforce, 5600 Fishers Lane, Rockville, MD 20857
Phone: 800-221-9393
Email: kross@hrsa.gov
https://bhw.hrsa.gov/loansscholarships
Purpose: To support students from disadvantaged backgrounds who are pursuing health-related careers.
Eligibility: Applicants must be full-time students, be from a disadvantaged background, demonstrate financial need and be studying in a health field, including medicine, nursing, veterinary medicine, dentistry, pharmacy and others. They must be U.S. citizens, nationals or permanent residents. All other criteria are set by individual schools.
Target applicant(s): High school students. College students. Graduate school students. Adult students.
Amount: Up to $30,000.
Number of awards: Varies.
Deadline: March.
How to apply: Applications are available from participating schools.
Exclusive: Visit www.UltimateScholarshipBook.com and enter code DE115523 for updates on this award.

(1156) · Schonstedt Scholarship in Surveying

National Society of Professional Surveyors (NSPS/AAGS)
Attn: Scholarships, 5119 Pegasus Court, Suite Q, Frederick, MD 21704
Phone: 240-439-4615x105
Email: trisha.milburn@nsps.us.com
https://www.nsps.us.com/page/Scholarships
Purpose: To aid surveying students.
Eligibility: Applicants must be members of the American Congress on Surveying and Mapping (ACSM). They must be enrolled in a four-year surveying degree program. Preference will be given to applicants with junior or senior standing. Selection is based on academic merit, personal statement, references and extracurricular activities.
Target applicant(s): College students. Adult students.
Amount: $2,000.
Number of awards: 1.
Scholarship may be renewable.
Deadline: January 22.
How to apply: Applications are available online. An application form, proof of ASCM membership, official transcript, personal statement and three reference letters are required.
Exclusive: Visit www.UltimateScholarshipBook.com and enter code NA115623 for updates on this award.

(1157) · Science Ambassador Scholarship

Cards Against Humanity
1917 North Elston Avenue, Chicago, IL 60642-1219
Phone: 224-623-9009
Email: saraheckhaus@cardsagainsthumanity.com
https://www.scienceambassadorscholarship.org
Purpose: To support women pursuing STEM education.
Eligibility: Applicants must self-identify as female and be graduating high school seniors or currently enrolled full-time undergraduate students. Students must be majoring in a STEM-related field. Applicants must create a video for their application submission.
Target applicant(s): High school students. College students. Adult students.
Amount: Varies.
Number of awards: 1.
Deadline: December.
How to apply: Applications are available online.
Exclusive: Visit www.UltimateScholarshipBook.com and enter code CA115723 for updates on this award.

(1158) · SEA Environmental Studies Scholarship

Surfers' Environmental Alliance
P.O. Box 3154, Long Branch, NJ 07740-3154
Email: rlee@seasurfer.org
https://www.seasurfer.org/sea-scholarships
Purpose: To aid students who seek to promote environmental awareness and marine conservation.
Eligibility: Students must be in high school through graduate level studies, have at least a 3.2 GPA, be a U.S. citizen and be pursuing environmental studies/sciences. Selection is based on goals, community service and involvement and academic excellence.
Target applicant(s): High school students. College students. Graduate school students. Adult students.
Minimum GPA: 3.2
Amount: Up to $3,500.
Number of awards: Varies.

Deadline: May 15.
How to apply: Applications are available online and include an essay.
Exclusive: Visit www.UltimateScholarshipBook.com and enter code SU115823 for updates on this award.

(1159) · SEE Education Foundation Scholarships

International Society of Explosives Engineers
30325 Bainbridge Road, Cleveland, OH 44139
Phone: 440-349-4400
Email: isee@isee.org
https://www.isee.org/students
Purpose: To aid students who are preparing for careers in the commercial explosives industry.
Eligibility: Applicants must be pursuing a degree from a technical, undergraduate, graduate or doctoral program in fields of education related to the commercial explosives industry. Students should demonstrate financial need. Selection is based on the overall strength of the application.
Target applicant(s): College students. Graduate school students. Adult students.
Amount: Varies.
Number of awards: Varies.
Deadline: May 7.
How to apply: Applications are available online. An application form, goal statement, income information, two letters of reference and an official transcript are required.
Exclusive: Visit www.UltimateScholarshipBook.com and enter code IN115923 for updates on this award.

(1160) · Sertoma Communicative Disorders Scholarship

Sertoma Inc.
1912 E. Meyer Boulevard, Kansas City, MO 64132
Phone: 816-333-8300
Email: infosertoma@sertomahq.org
http://www.sertoma.org
Purpose: To fund graduate students of audiology and speech-language pathology.
Eligibility: Applicants must be citizens of the U.S. Applicants must also be accepted into a graduate level program in speech language pathology and/or audiology at a college in the U.S. recognized by ASHA's Council and have a minimum 3.5 overall GPA in all undergraduate and graduate-level courses.
Target applicant(s): College students. Graduate school students. Adult students.
Minimum GPA: 3.5
Amount: $1,000.
Number of awards: Varies.
Deadline: March 30.
How to apply: Applications are available online.
Exclusive: Visit www.UltimateScholarshipBook.com and enter code SE116023 for updates on this award.

(1161) · Sharps Scholarship Program

Sharps Compliance Inc.
9220 Kirby Drive, Suite 500, Houston, TX 77054
Phone: 800-772-5657
Email: scholarship@sharpsinc.com
http://www.sharpsinc.com

Purpose: To reward health care students who have written the best essays on the topic of accidental needle-stick injuries.

Eligibility: Applicants must be U.S. or Canadian citizens. They must be enrolled or planning to enroll at an accredited college or university during the fall or spring term following the application deadline. They must be studying or planning to study a health care-related subject and must submit a 1,250- to 1,500-word essay on the topic provided. Selection is based on the overall strength of the essay.

Target applicant(s): High school students. College students. Adult students.

Amount: $750-$1,500.

Number of awards: 3.

Deadline: May 31.

How to apply: Application instructions are available online. An entry form and essay are required.

Exclusive: Visit www.UltimateScholarshipBook.com and enter code SH116123 for updates on this award.

(1162) · Sigma Phi Alpha Undergraduate Scholarship

American Dental Hygienists' Association (ADHA) Institute for Oral Health
Scholarship Award Program, 444 North Michigan Avenue, Suite 3400, Chicago, IL 60611
Phone: 312-440-8900
Email: institute@adha.net
https://www.adha.org/ioh-scholarships-main

Purpose: To aid outstanding Sigma Phi Alpha Dental Hygiene Honor Society students.

Eligibility: Applicants must be members of the Sigma Phi Alpha Dental Hygiene Honor Society who are enrolled in a certificate, associate's degree or bachelor's degree program in dental hygiene at a school that has an active chapter of Sigma Phi Alpha. They must have a major GPA of 3.5 or higher. Selection is based on the overall strength of the application.

Target applicant(s): High school students. College students. Adult students.

Minimum GPA: 3.5

Amount: $1,000.

Number of awards: 1.

Deadline: February 2.

How to apply: Applications are available online. An application form and supporting materials are required.

Exclusive: Visit www.UltimateScholarshipBook.com and enter code AM116223 for updates on this award.

(1163) · SMART Scholarship

American Society for Engineering Education
1818 N. Street, NW, Suite 600, Washington, DC 20036-2479
Phone: 202-331-3500
Email: smart@asee.org
https://www.smartscholarship.org/smart

Purpose: To support undergraduate and graduate students pursuing degrees in Science, Technology, Engineering and Mathematics (STEM) fields.

Eligibility: Applicants must be a U.S. citizen, 18 or older, have a minimum GPA of 3.0, be able to participate in summer internships at the Department of Defense (DoD) and be willing to accept post-graduate work at the DoD. The award includes payment of full tuition, a stipend, a book allowance and room and board.

Target applicant(s): College students. Graduate school students. Adult students.

Minimum GPA: 3.0

Amount: Varies.

Number of awards: Varies.

Scholarship may be renewable.

Deadline: December 1.

How to apply: Applications are available online.

Exclusive: Visit www.UltimateScholarshipBook.com and enter code AM116323 for updates on this award.

(1164) · SNMTS Paul Cole Scholarship

Society of Nuclear Medicine and Molecular Imaging
Development Office, 1850 Samuel Morse Drive, Reston, VA 20190
Phone: 703-708-9000
Email: tellmer@snmmi.org
http://www.snmmi.org/

Purpose: To promote excellence in healthcare through the support of education and research in nuclear medicine technology.

Eligibility: Applicants must have a minimum 2.5 GPA and be high school seniors or college undergraduates enrolled in or accepted by accredited institutions and be in the nuclear medicine technology field. Applicant must prove financial need.

Target applicant(s): High school students. College students. Graduate school students. Adult students.

Minimum GPA: 2.5

Amount: $500-$1,000.

Number of awards: 18.

Deadline: February 17.

How to apply: Applications are available online.

Exclusive: Visit www.UltimateScholarshipBook.com and enter code SO116423 for updates on this award.

(1165) · Society of Exploration Geophysicists (SEG) Scholarship

Society of Exploration Geophysicists
Scholarship Committee, SEG Foundation, P.O. Box 702740, Tulsa, OK 74170-2740
Phone: 918-497-5500
Email: scholarships@seg.org
http://www.seg.org

Purpose: To fund individuals who are involved or interested in the field of geophysics.

Eligibility: Applicants must intend to pursue a career in exploration geophysics. Applicants must also be one of the following: A high school student with above average grades planning to enter college the next fall term, an undergraduate whose grades are above average or a graduate student pursuing a career in exploration geophysics in operations, teaching or research.

Target applicant(s): High school students. College students. Graduate school students. Adult students.

Amount: $500-$10,000.

Number of awards: Varies.

Scholarship may be renewable.

Deadline: March 1.

How to apply: Applications are available online or by written request.

Exclusive: Visit www.UltimateScholarshipBook.com and enter code SO116523 for updates on this award.

(1166) · Society of Manufacturing Engineers Directors Scholarship

Society of Manufacturing Engineers Education Foundation
One SME Drive, P.O. Box 930, Dearborn, MI 48121
Phone: 313-425-3300
Email: foundation@sme.org
https://www.smeef.org/scholarships
Purpose: To aid undergraduate manufacturing engineering students.
Eligibility: Applicants must be full-time undergraduates who are enrolled at an accredited U.S. or Canadian postsecondary institution. They must be majoring in manufacturing engineering or a related subject and have completed at least 30 college credit hours. They must have a GPA of 3.5 or higher on a four-point scale and must have plans to pursue a career in manufacturing. Preference will be given to those with proven leadership skills. Selection is based on the overall strength of the application.
Target applicant(s): College students. Adult students.
Minimum GPA: 3.5
Amount: Varies.
Number of awards: Varies.
Deadline: February 1.
How to apply: Applications are available online. An application form and supporting materials are required.
Exclusive: Visit www.UltimateScholarshipBook.com and enter code SO116623 for updates on this award.

(1167) · Society of Plastics Engineers (SPE) Foundation Scholarships

Society of Plastics Engineers
6 Berkshire Boulevard, Suite 306, Bethel, CT 06801
Phone: 203-775-0471
Email: info@4spe.org
http://www.4spe.org/spe-foundation
Purpose: To aid students who have demonstrated or expressed an interest in the plastics industry.
Eligibility: Applicants must have a demonstrated or expressed interest in the plastics industry and be majoring in or taking courses that would lead to a career in the plastics industry. Applicants must be in good academic standing. Financial need is considered for most scholarships.
Target applicant(s): College students. Graduate school students. Adult students.
Amount: Varies.
Number of awards: Varies.
Scholarship may be renewable.
Deadline: April 1.
How to apply: Applications are available online.
Exclusive: Visit www.UltimateScholarshipBook.com and enter code SO116723 for updates on this award.

(1168) · Society of Vacuum Coaters Foundation Scholarship

Society of Vacuum Coaters Foundation
Attn.: Nicol Campana, 9639 Kinsman Road, Materials Park, OH 44073-0002
Email: svcfoundation@svc.org
http://www.svcfoundation.org
Purpose: To promote the study of vacuum coating technology.
Eligibility: Applicants must be entering or currently enrolled in studies related to vacuum coating technology at an accredited technical, vocational, two-year, undergraduate or graduate program. Preference is given to those majoring in engineering, physics, materials science or other fields related to vacuum coating. Selection is based on the applicant's field of study, academic achievement, personal qualities and financial need.
Target applicant(s): High school students. College students. Graduate school students. Adult students.
Amount: Varies.
Number of awards: Varies.
Deadline: October 8.
How to apply: Applications are available online. Two copies of scholarship materials must be submitted including the application form, transcript and two recommendation forms.
Exclusive: Visit www.UltimateScholarshipBook.com and enter code SO116823 for updates on this award.

(1169) · SPIE Optics and Photonics Education Scholarship

SPIE, The International Society for Optical Engineering
P.O. Box 10, Bellingham, WA 98227-0010
Phone: 360-676-3290
Email: scholarships@spie.org
https://www.spie.org/membership/student-services/scholarships
Purpose: To promote students who have the potential to contribute to the field of optics.
Eligibility: Applicants must be high school, undergraduate or graduate students enrolled full-time in programs in the field of optics, photonics or related discipline (e.g., physics or electrical engineering). Students must be members of SPIE, although they may submit a membership application along with the scholarship application, and high school applicants receive a one-year complimentary membership.
Target applicant(s): High school students. College students. Graduate school students. Adult students.
Amount: Up to $11,000.
Number of awards: Varies.
Deadline: February 15.
How to apply: Applications are available online.
Exclusive: Visit www.UltimateScholarshipBook.com and enter code SP116923 for updates on this award.

(1170) · Spring Meadow Nursery Scholarship

Horticultural Research Institute
525 9th Street NW, Suite 800, Washington, DC 20004
Phone: 202-789-2900
http://www.hriresearch.org
Purpose: To help students obtain a degree in horticulture.
Eligibility: Applicants must be enrolled full-time in an undergraduate or graduate landscape horticultural or related program at a two- or four-year accredited institution. Preference is given to those who plan to pursue a career in horticulture. Students must have a 2.25 overall GPA and a 2.7 GPA in their major.
Target applicant(s): College students. Graduate school students. Adult students.
Minimum GPA: 2.25
Amount: Up to $4,000.
Number of awards: 3.
Scholarship may be renewable.
Deadline: September 10.
How to apply: Applications are available online.
Exclusive: Visit www.UltimateScholarshipBook.com and enter code HO117023 for updates on this award.

(1171) · SPS Leadership Scholarships

Society of Physics Students
One Physics Ellipse, College Park, MD 20740
Phone: 301-209-3007
Email: SPS-Programs@aip.org
https://www.spsnational.org/
Purpose: To further the study of physics.
Eligibility: Applicants must be undergraduates at least in their junior year, physics majors and active members of SPS.
Target applicant(s): College students. Adult students.
Amount: $2,000-$5,000.
Number of awards: Varies.
Deadline: March 15.
How to apply: Applications are available online and from SPS Chapter Advisors.
Exclusive: Visit www.UltimateScholarshipBook.com and enter code SO117123 for updates on this award.

(1172) · STANLEY Technology Scholarship Program

Stanley Technology Scholarship Program
Scholarship America, One Scholarship Way, Saint Peter, MN 56082
Phone: 800-537-4180
Email: stanley-scholarship@scholarshipamerica.org
https://apply.scholarsapply.org/stanley-scholarship
Purpose: To support students interested in security technology.
Eligibility: Applicants must be in their final year of high school, high school graduates or current college or university undergraduates planning to enroll in full-time undergraduate study at an accredited college, university or vocational-technical school. Students must be pursuing an eligible degree in a security, information science, technology or computer science related field of study.
Target applicant(s): High school students. College students. Adult students.
Amount: Up to $5,000.
Number of awards: 21.
Deadline: April 15.
How to apply: Applications are available online.
Exclusive: Visit www.UltimateScholarshipBook.com and enter code ST117223 for updates on this award.

(1173) · STEEL Engineering Education Link Initiative

Association for Iron and Steel Technology (AIST)
186 Thorn Hill Road, Warrendale, PA 15086-7528
Phone: 724-814-3000
Email: lwharrey@aist.org
https://www.aist.org/students-faculty/scholarships
Purpose: To increase the number of students studying engineering and pursuing careers in the iron and steel industry.
Eligibility: Applicants must commit to a paid summer internship at a North American steel company or industry supplier and must be a citizen of the United States, Canada or Mexico. Students must be enrolled full-time in a four-year undergraduate program at an accredited North American university. Applicants must maintain a minimum GPA of 2.5 and demonstrate interest in the iron and steel industry.
Target applicant(s): College students. Adult students.
Minimum GPA: 2.5
Amount: $6,000.
Number of awards: Up to 20.
Scholarship may be renewable.
Deadline: October 31.

How to apply: Applications are available online. Questions about this specific scholarship may be directed to blakshmi@steel.org or 202-452-7143.
Exclusive: Visit www.UltimateScholarshipBook.com and enter code AS117323 for updates on this award.

(1174) · Steel Intern Scholarships

Association for Iron and Steel Technology (AIST)
186 Thorn Hill Road, Warrendale, PA 15086-7528
Phone: 724-814-3000
Email: lwharrey@aist.org
https://www.aist.org/students-faculty/scholarships
Purpose: To reward students who commit to a paid summer internship at a North American or steel-related company.
Eligibility: Applicants must citizens of a NAFTA country (USA, Canada, Mexico) and express a strong interest in the iron and steel industry. Students in the following engineering/engineering technology majors may apply: metallurgy, materials science, electrical, mechanical, chemical, industrial, environmental, computer science, data science and safety. Applicants must be freshmen, sophomores, juniors or seniors planning to attend graduate school. Students must be enrolled full-time in a four-year undergraduate or graduate program at an accredited North American university with a minimum 2.5 GPA.
Target applicant(s): College students. Adult students.
Minimum GPA: 2.5
Amount: $6,000.
Number of awards: Up to 30.
Deadline: October 31.
How to apply: Applications are available online.
Exclusive: Visit www.UltimateScholarshipBook.com and enter code AS117423 for updates on this award.

(1175) · Steinman Scholarship

National Society of Professional Engineers
1420 King Street, Alexandria, VA 22314-2794
Phone: 703-684-2885
Email: students@nspe.org
https://www.nspe.org/resources/students/scholarships
Purpose: To aid talented students studying engineering.
Eligibility: Applicants must be undergraduate engineering majors who will enter the junior year and be U.S. citizens. Selection is based on GPA, internship experience, recommendations and ethics essay.
Target applicant(s): College students. Adult students.
Amount: $10,000.
Number of awards: 1.
Deadline: April 1.
How to apply: Applications are available online.
Exclusive: Visit www.UltimateScholarshipBook.com and enter code NA117523 for updates on this award.

(1176) · Stephanie Carroll Memorial Scholarship

NADONA/LTC
1329 E. Kemper Road, Suite 4100A, Springdale, OH 45246
Phone: 800-222-0539
http://www.nadona.org
Purpose: To support students who are interested in pursuing studies in long-term care or geriatrics.
Eligibility: Applicants must be undergraduate or graduate students enrolled in an accredited nursing program who will make a commitment to practice in long-term care or geriatrics for two years following

graduation. Students may submit applications electronically at info@nadona.org. Selection is based on the overall strength of the application.
Target applicant(s): College students. Graduate school students. Adult students.
Amount: Varies.
Number of awards: 1.
Deadline: April 1.
How to apply: Applications are available online.
Exclusive: Visit www.UltimateScholarshipBook.com and enter code NA117623 for updates on this award.

(1177) · Steven G. King Play Environments Scholarship

Landscape Architecture Foundation
1129 20th Street NW, Suite 202, Washington, DC 20036
Phone: 202-331-7070
Email: scholarships@lafoundation.org
https://www.lafoundation.org/what-we-do/scholarships
Purpose: To aid landscape architecture students who are interested in designing play environments.
Eligibility: Applicants must be landscape architecture graduate students or upperclass undergraduate students. They must be enrolled at a college or university that has been accredited by the Landscape Architectural Accreditation Board (LAAB). They must have a demonstrated interest in designing play environments. Selection is based on the overall strength of the application.
Target applicant(s): College students. Graduate school students. Adult students.
Amount: $5,000.
Number of awards: 1.
Deadline: February 1.
How to apply: Applications are available online. An application form, essay, play environment plan and two recommendation letters are required.
Exclusive: Visit www.UltimateScholarshipBook.com and enter code LA117723 for updates on this award.

(1178) · Structural Materials Division Scholarship

Minerals, Metals and Materials Society
184 Thorn Hill Road, Warrendale, PA 15086
Phone: 724-776-9000
Email: students@tms.org
http://www.tms.org
Purpose: To aid metallurgical and materials science engineering students.
Eligibility: Applicants must be student members of The Minerals, Metals and Materials Society (TMS), be full-time undergraduate sophomores or juniors and be majoring in metallurgical or materials science engineering. Their studies must concentrate on the science and engineering of load-bearing materials. Selection is based on the overall strength of the application.
Target applicant(s): College students. Adult students.
Amount: $2,500.
Number of awards: 1.
Deadline: March 15.
How to apply: Applications are available online. An application form, personal statement, transcript and three recommendation letters are required.
Exclusive: Visit www.UltimateScholarshipBook.com and enter code MI117823 for updates on this award.

(1179) · Student Cash Grant Program

American Society of Certified Engineering Technicians (ASCET)
15621 West 87th Street Parkway, Suite 205, Lenexa, KS 66219
Phone: 773-242-7238
Email: office@ascet.org
https://ascet.org/page/FinancialAid
Purpose: To help engineering technology students.
Eligibility: Applicants must be a student, certified, regular, registered or associate member of the American Society of Certified Engineering Technicians (ASCET) or be high school seniors in the last five months of the academic year who will be enrolled in an engineering technology curriculum no later than six months following the selection for the award. Students must have passing grades in their present curriculum and submit transcripts and a recommendation letter.
Target applicant(s): High school students. College students. Adult students.
Amount: $400.
Number of awards: Varies.
Deadline: January 30.
How to apply: Applications are available online.
Exclusive: Visit www.UltimateScholarshipBook.com and enter code AM117923 for updates on this award.

(1180) · Student Poster Session Awards

Electrochemical Society
65 South Main Street, Building D, Pennington, NJ 08534-2839
Phone: 609-737-1902
Email: awards@electrochem.org
https://www.electrochem.org/student-awards
Purpose: To reward students for work related to fields of interest to ECS.
Eligibility: Applicants must be pursuing degrees at any college or university and prepare an abstract on work performed. The applicants must also prepare a poster to present at the society meeting where they will be judged. Two awards are in the categories of electrochemical science and technology and solid-state science and technology.
Target applicant(s): College students. Graduate school students. Adult students.
Amount: Varies.
Number of awards: Varies.
Deadline: Varies.
How to apply: Application materials are described online.
Exclusive: Visit www.UltimateScholarshipBook.com and enter code EL118023 for updates on this award.

(1181) · Student Research Awards

Crohn's and Colitis Foundation of America Inc.
733 Third Avenue, Suite 510, New York, NY 10017
Phone: 800-932-2423
Email: info@ccfa.org
https://www.crohnscolitisfoundation.org/research/grants-fellowships/student-research-awards
Purpose: To stimulate interest in research careers in inflammatory bowel disease by providing salary support for research projects.
Eligibility: Applicants must be undergraduate, graduate or medical students not yet engaged in thesis research. Students must attend an accredited North American school and conduct their research with a mentor. The planned research project must last at least 10 weeks and must be relevant to IBD.
Target applicant(s): College students. Graduate school students. Adult students.

Amount: Up to $2,500.
Number of awards: Up to 16.
Deadline: March 31.
How to apply: Applications are available online.
Exclusive: Visit www.UltimateScholarshipBook.com and enter code CR118123 for updates on this award.

(1182) · Student Research Scholarships

Bat Conservation International
Phone: 512-327-9721
Email: scholarships@batcon.org
http://www.batcon.org
Purpose: To support students who will contribute to our knowledge about bats.
Eligibility: Applicants must be graduate students and submit a research proposal that addresses a specific area of bat conservation. The application form provides several potential research topics.
Target applicant(s): College students. Graduate school students. Adult students.
Amount: $3,000.
Number of awards: Varies.
Deadline: October 31.
How to apply: Applications are available online.
Exclusive: Visit www.UltimateScholarshipBook.com and enter code BA118223 for updates on this award.

(1183) · Susan Miszkowicz Memorial Scholarship

Society of Women Engineers
130 East Randolph Street, Suite 3500, Chicago, IL 60601
Phone: 877-793-4636
Email: scholarships@swe.org
https://swe.org/scholarships/
Purpose: To support female students working towards a college degree in engineering.
Eligibility: Applicants must be currently enrolled in an accredited engineering, technology or computing program with a minimum of a 3.0 GPA. The award is to be used during the sophomore, junior or senior year of college.
Target applicant(s): College students. Adult students.
Minimum GPA: 3.0
Amount: $1,500.
Number of awards: 1.
Deadline: February 15.
How to apply: Applications are available online.
Exclusive: Visit www.UltimateScholarshipBook.com and enter code SO118323 for updates on this award.

(1184) · Tau Beta Pi/Society of Automotive Engineers Engineering Scholarship

Society of Automotive Engineers International
Scholarships Program, 400 Commonwealth Drive, Warrendale, PA 15096
Phone: 724-776-4841
Email: scholarships@sae.org
https://www.sae.org/participate/scholarships
Purpose: To aid future college students who are planning to major in engineering.
Eligibility: Applicants must be U.S. citizens, be graduating high school seniors and have plans to major in engineering at an ABET-accredited

institution. They must have a GPA of 3.75 or higher and must have SAT or ACT scores that rank in the 90th percentile. Selection is based on the overall strength of the application.
Target applicant(s): High school students.
Minimum GPA: 3.75
Amount: $1,000.
Number of awards: 6.
Deadline: March 15.
How to apply: Applications are available online. An application form, official transcript and standardized test scores are required.
Exclusive: Visit www.UltimateScholarshipBook.com and enter code SO118423 for updates on this award.

(1185) · Ted and Ruth Neward Scholarship

Society of Plastics Engineers
6 Berkshire Boulevard, Suite 306, Bethel, CT 06801
Phone: 203-775-0471
Email: info@4spe.org
http://www.4spe.org/spe-foundation
Purpose: To aid students who have an interest in the plastics industry.
Eligibility: Applicants must be U.S. citizens, have an interest in the plastics industry, major in or take courses leading to a career in the plastics industry and be in good academic standing. Financial need is considered.
Target applicant(s): College students. Graduate school students. Adult students.
Amount: Varies.
Number of awards: Varies.
Deadline: April 1.
How to apply: Applications are available online.
Exclusive: Visit www.UltimateScholarshipBook.com and enter code SO118523 for updates on this award.

(1186) · Ted Rollins ECO Scholarship

Ted Rollins
1001 Morehead Square Drive, Suite 320, Charlotte, NC 28203
Email: caroline@tedrollinsecoscholars.com
http://www.tedrollinsecoscholars.com
Purpose: To support students pursuing a major related to sustainability.
Eligibility: Applicants must be either high school seniors or current undergraduate students planning to major in a field related to business, marketing or sustainability. Students must plan to take at least 10 credit hours during the upcoming fall semester. Applicants must write an essay on a topic assigned on the website.
Target applicant(s): High school students. College students. Adult students.
Amount: $1,000.
Number of awards: 1.
Deadline: December 1.
How to apply: Applications are available online.
Exclusive: Visit www.UltimateScholarshipBook.com and enter code TE118623 for updates on this award.

(1187) · Theodore D. Harrington Scholarship

National Association of Corrosion Engineers (NACE) International Foundation
15835 Park Ten Place, Houston, TX 77084-5145
Phone: 281-228-6205
Email: nace.foundation@nace.org
http://nace-foundation.org/programs/students/scholarships/

Purpose: To support an individual with an interest in furthering their knowledge of corrosion control.
Eligibility: Applicants must have a permanent residence in the NACE Western Area which includes the following states: Arizona, California, Idaho, Nevada, Oregon, Utah and Washington. Applicants must take courses offered by an accredited college or university or programs approved by the area upon application. Selection is based on the overall strength of information provided by the applicant.
Target applicant(s): College students. Graduate school students. Adult students.
Amount: $1,200.
Number of awards: 1.
Deadline: January 1.
How to apply: Applications are available online. An academic transcript, two nomination forms, one recommendation form and essay scholarship questions are required.
Exclusive: Visit www.UltimateScholarshipBook.com and enter code NA118723 for updates on this award.

(1188) · Thermo Fisher Scientific Antibody Scholarship
Thermo Fisher Scientific
3747 North Meridian Road, Rockford, IL 61105
Phone: 815-968-0747
Email: antibodyscholarship@thermofisher.com
https://www.thermofisher.com/us/en/home/life-science/antibodies/thermo-fisher-scientific-antibody-scholarship-program.html
Purpose: To help students with the expenses related to their pursuit of higher education.
Eligibility: Applicants must be enrolled or accepted for enrollment as an undergraduate or graduate student at an accredited college or university. Students must have a cumulative grade point average of 3.0 and declared a major of one of the following: chemistry, biology, biochemistry or a related life science field. Applicants must be United States citizens or students possessing the appropriate visa status to study in the U.S. Selection is based on the overall strength of the application and any submitted materials.
Target applicant(s): High school students. College students. Graduate school students. Adult students.
Minimum GPA: 3.0
Amount: $5,000-$10,000.
Number of awards: 6.
Deadline: May 5.
How to apply: Applications are available online.
Exclusive: Visit www.UltimateScholarshipBook.com and enter code TH118823 for updates on this award.

(1189) · Thermoforming Division Memorial Scholarships
Society of Plastics Engineers
6 Berkshire Boulevard, Suite 306, Bethel, CT 06801
Phone: 203-775-0471
Email: info@4spe.org
http://www.4spe.org/spe-foundation
Purpose: To aid students who have an interest in the plastics industry.
Eligibility: Applicants must have an interest in the plastics industry, major in or take courses leading to a career in the plastics industry and be in good academic standing. Applicants must have experience in the thermoforming industry, such as courses taken, research conducted or jobs held.
Target applicant(s): College students. Graduate school students. Adult students.

Amount: Varies.
Number of awards: Varies.
Deadline: April 1.
How to apply: Applications are available online.
Exclusive: Visit www.UltimateScholarshipBook.com and enter code SO118923 for updates on this award.

(1190) · Thermoplastic Elastomers Special Interest Group Scholarship
Society of Plastics Engineers
6 Berkshire Boulevard, Suite 306, Bethel, CT 06801
Phone: 203-775-0471
Email: info@4spe.org
http://www.4spe.org/spe-foundation
Purpose: To aid students who have a demonstrated interest in thermoplastic elastomers.
Eligibility: Applicants must be full-time undergraduate or graduate students who have a proven interest in thermoplastic elastomers. This interest must be shown by relevant jobs held, internships completed, coursework completed or research undertaken. Selection is based on the overall strength of the application.
Target applicant(s): College students. Graduate school students. Adult students.
Amount: $2,500.
Number of awards: 1.
Deadline: April 1.
How to apply: Applications are available online. An application form, official transcript, three references and a personal statement are required.
Exclusive: Visit www.UltimateScholarshipBook.com and enter code SO119023 for updates on this award.

(1191) · Thomas E. Powers/Detroit Section Scholarship
Society of Plastics Engineers
6 Berkshire Boulevard, Suite 306, Bethel, CT 06801
Phone: 203-775-0471
Email: info@4spe.org
http://www.4spe.org/spe-foundation
Purpose: To aid undergraduate students who are interested in the plastics industry.
Eligibility: Applicants must be full-time undergraduate students in good academic standing who have completed coursework in or are majoring in a subject that relates to the plastics industry (such as engineering, polymer science, physics or chemistry). Selection is based on the overall strength of the application.
Target applicant(s): College students. Adult students.
Amount: $4,000.
Number of awards: 1.
Deadline: August 6.
How to apply: Applications are available online. An application form, personal statement, transcript and three recommendation letters are required.
Exclusive: Visit www.UltimateScholarshipBook.com and enter code SO119123 for updates on this award.

(1192) · Thomas M. Stetson Scholarship
American Ground Water Trust
50 Pleasant Street, Concord, NH 03301
Phone: 603-228-5444
https://agwt.org/content/scholarship-opportunities

Purpose: To provide scholarships for high school seniors pursuing careers in a ground water-related field.
Eligibility: Applicants must be high school seniors with intentions to pursue a career in ground water-related field. Applicants must attend a college or university located west of the Mississippi River. A minimum GPA of 3.0 is required.
Target applicant(s): High school students.
Minimum GPA: 3.0
Amount: $2,000.
Number of awards: 1.
Deadline: June 30.
How to apply: Applications are available online.
Exclusive: Visit www.UltimateScholarshipBook.com and enter code AM119223 for updates on this award.

(1193) · Thomas R. Camp Scholarship

American Water Works Association
6666 W. Quincy Avenue, Denver, CO 80235-3098
Phone: 800-926-7337
Email: scholarships@awwa.org
http://www.awwa.org
Purpose: To support students conducting applied research in the drinking water field.
Eligibility: Applicants must pursue graduate degrees at an institution of higher education in Canada, Guam, Puerto Rico, Mexico or the U.S. This is awarded to doctoral students in even years and master's students in odd years. Applicants must submit applications, resumes, transcripts, GRE scores, three recommendation letters, statements and research plans. The award is based on academics and leadership.
Target applicant(s): Graduate school students. Adult students.
Amount: $5,000.
Number of awards: 1.
Deadline: December 20.
How to apply: Applications are available online.
Exclusive: Visit www.UltimateScholarshipBook.com and enter code AM119323 for updates on this award.

(1194) · Tilford Fund

Association of Engineering Geologists Foundation
Tilford Fund, 4123 Broadway, Suite 817, Oakland, CA 94611
Phone: 510-990-0059
Email: staff@aegfoundation.org
https://www.aegfoundation.org
Purpose: To provide financial assistance for field studies in engineering geology.
Eligibility: Applicants must be members of the Association of Engineering Geologists who are college or graduate students. Applicants are chosen on the basis of scholarship, ability, participation and potential for contributions to the profession.
Target applicant(s): College students. Graduate school students. Adult students.
Amount: Varies.
Number of awards: Varies.
Deadline: February 1.
How to apply: Applications are available online.
Exclusive: Visit www.UltimateScholarshipBook.com and enter code AS119423 for updates on this award.

(1195) · Timothy S. and Palmer W. Bigelow, Jr. Scholarship

Horticultural Research Institute
525 9th Street NW, Suite 800, Washington, DC 20004
Phone: 202-789-2900
http://www.hriresearch.org
Purpose: To help students from New England who want to pursue a career in horticulture.
Eligibility: Applicants must be seniors in a two-year course and have finished the first year, juniors in a four-year course and have finished the first two years or be graduate students. Undergraduates must have a minimum 2.25 GPA and graduate students a minimum 3.0 GPA. Students must be from Connecticut, Maine, Massachusetts, New Hampshire, Rhode Island or Vermont. Preference will be given to applicants who have financial need and who plan to work in the nursery industry after graduation, including starting a business.
Target applicant(s): College students. Graduate school students. Adult students.
Minimum GPA: 2.25 for undergraduate students, 3.0 for graduate students
Amount: $3,000.
Number of awards: 1.
Deadline: September 10.
How to apply: Applications are available online or by mail.
Exclusive: Visit www.UltimateScholarshipBook.com and enter code HO119523 for updates on this award.

(1196) · TMC/SAE Donald D. Dawson Technical Scholarship

Society of Automotive Engineers International
Scholarships Program, 400 Commonwealth Drive, Warrendale, PA 15096
Phone: 724-776-4841
Email: scholarships@sae.org
https://www.sae.org/participate/scholarships
Purpose: To aid current and future engineering students.
Eligibility: Applicants must be U.S. citizens, be high school seniors or current undergraduate students and be enrolled in or planning to enroll in an ABET-accredited engineering degree program. They must have a GPA of 3.25 or higher and an SAT math score of 600 or higher and a critical reading score of 550 or higher or must have an ACT composite score of 27 or higher. Selection is based on the overall strength of the application.
Target applicant(s): High school students. College students. Adult students.
Minimum GPA: 3.25
Amount: $1,500.
Number of awards: 1.
Scholarship may be renewable.
Deadline: March 15.
How to apply: Applications are available online. An application form, personal essay, official transcript and standardized test scores are required.
Exclusive: Visit www.UltimateScholarshipBook.com and enter code SO119623 for updates on this award.

(1197) · TMS Best Paper Contest

Minerals, Metals and Materials Society
184 Thorn Hill Road, Warrendale, PA 15086
Phone: 724-776-9000

Email: students@tms.org
http://www.tms.org
Purpose: To support the professional development of metallurgy and materials science students.
Eligibility: Applicants must be student members of The Minerals, Metals and Materials Society (TMS). They must prepare and submit a technical essay on a topic that is related to metallurgy or materials science. Selection is based on originality and the quality of research.
Target applicant(s): High school students. College students. Graduate school students. Adult students.
Amount: $250.
Number of awards: 4.
Deadline: May 1.
How to apply: Submission guidelines are available online. A technical essay, cover sheet and faculty endorsement are required.
Exclusive: Visit www.UltimateScholarshipBook.com and enter code MI119723 for updates on this award.

(1198) · TMS Technical Division Student Poster Contest

Minerals, Metals and Materials Society
184 Thorn Hill Road, Warrendale, PA 15086
Phone: 724-776-9000
Email: students@tms.org
http://www.tms.org
Purpose: To aid student members of the Minerals, Metals and Materials Society.
Eligibility: Applicants must be student members of the Minerals, Metals and Materials Society (TMS), be full-time undergraduate or graduate students and create a poster that addresses a topic that would be of interest for one of the five technical divisions of TMS. Selection is based on the overall strength of the poster.
Target applicant(s): College students. Graduate school students. Adult students.
Amount: Up to $1,000.
Number of awards: 10.
Deadline: Varies.
How to apply: Applications are available online. An application form and poster are required.
Exclusive: Visit www.UltimateScholarshipBook.com and enter code MI119823 for updates on this award.

(1199) · TMS/International Symposium of Superalloys Scholarships

Minerals, Metals and Materials Society
184 Thorn Hill Road, Warrendale, PA 15086
Phone: 724-776-9000
Email: students@tms.org
http://www.tms.org
Purpose: To aid metallurgical engineering and materials science and engineering students.
Eligibility: Applicants must be student members of the Minerals, Metals and Materials Society (TMS) and be full-time undergraduate or graduate students majoring in metallurgical engineering or materials science and engineering. They must have a demonstrated interest in the high-temperature, high-performance materials used in the gas turbine industry. Selection is based on academic merit, extracurricular activities, relevant coursework completed and recommendation letters.
Target applicant(s): College students. Graduate school students. Adult students.
Amount: $2,000.

Number of awards: 2.
Deadline: March 15.
How to apply: Applications are available online. An application form, transcript, personal essay and three recommendation letters are required.
Exclusive: Visit www.UltimateScholarshipBook.com and enter code MI119923 for updates on this award.

(1200) · Tocris Scholarship

Tocris Bioscience
10730 E. Briarwood Avenue, Centennial, CO 80112
Phone: 303-730-1950
Email: scholarship@biotechne.com
https://www.tocris.com/scholarship
Purpose: To support students who plan to pursue a science-related degree in life science, medical science or health science.
Eligibility: Applicants must be residents of the United States, United Kingdom or Canada who are accepted or enrolled in a college or university and plan to pursue a science-related degree in life science, medical science or health science. Students may apply at any level of education including diploma, associate degree, baccalaureate, graduate or PhD.
Target applicant(s): High school students. College students. Graduate school students. Adult students.
Amount: $1,500.
Number of awards: 1.
Deadline: December 8.
How to apply: Applications are available online and must include a transcript and two short answer essays.
Exclusive: Visit www.UltimateScholarshipBook.com and enter code TO120023 for updates on this award.

(1201) · Trent R. Dames and William W. Moore Fellowship

American Society of Civil Engineers (ASCE)
Attn.: Honors and Awards Program, 1801 Alexander Bell Drive, Reston, VA 20191-4400
Phone: 800-548-2723
Email: awards@asce.org
http://www.asce.org
Purpose: To support engineers, earth scientists, professors and graduate students pursuing graduate studies researching new applications and advancements in geotechnical engineering or earth sciences in relation to social, economic, environmental and political issues.
Eligibility: Applicants must be members of ASCE at the time of application submission. Prior fellowship recipients can apply for any additional fellowships provided they meet the current fellowship's eligibility requirements. Completed applications and all supporting material as outlined in the application process must be submitted.
Target applicant(s): Graduate school students. Adult students.
Amount: $6,000.
Number of awards: 2.
Deadline: February 10.
How to apply: Applications are available online.
Exclusive: Visit www.UltimateScholarshipBook.com and enter code AM120123 for updates on this award.

(1202) · Tuskegee Airmen Scholarship Foundation Scholarships

Tuskegee Airmen Scholarship Foundation
1816 S. Figueroa Street, Suite #L5, Los Angeles, CA 90015

Phone: 213-742-9541
Email: info@taisf.org
http://www.taisf.org
Purpose: To aid students who intend to pursue careers in aviation, aerospace engineering, aerospace research or engineering technology.
Eligibility: Applicants must be high school seniors who have a GPA of 3.0 or higher on a four-point scale. They must have a demonstrated interest in pursuing a career in aerospace research, aerospace engineering, aviation or engineering technology. Selection is based on academic merit, extracurricular activities, character and financial need.
Target applicant(s): High school students.
Minimum GPA: 3.0
Amount: $1,500.
Number of awards: 40.
Scholarship may be renewable.
Deadline: January.
How to apply: Applications are available by request from the student's local Tuskegee Airmen chapter. An application form, two essays and family income verification are required.
Exclusive: Visit www.UltimateScholarshipBook.com and enter code TU120223 for updates on this award.

(1203) · Tutor the People Pre-Med Scholarship

Tutor the People LLC
87 Lafayette Street, New York, NY 10013
Phone: 800-277-5508
http://tutorthepeople.com
Purpose: To support undergraduate students in pursuing a pre-medical education.
Eligibility: Applicants must submit an essay explaining their professional and educational goals in the field of medicine. Selection is based on the overall strength of the submission.
Target applicant(s): High school students. College students. Adult students.
Amount: $1,000.
Number of awards: 1.
Deadline: December 31.
How to apply: Applications are available online.
Exclusive: Visit www.UltimateScholarshipBook.com and enter code TU120323 for updates on this award.

(1204) · UAA Janice K. Barden Aviation Scholarship

UAA/Barden Aviation Scholarship
1200 G Street NW, Suite 1100, Washington, DC 20005
Phone: 202-783-9250
Email: info@nbaa.org
https://nbaa.org/professional-development/scholarships/
Purpose: To aid aviation students attending a University Aviation Association (UAA) or National Business Aviation Association (NBAA) member school.
Eligibility: Applicants must be U.S. citizens who are studying a subject that is related to aviation. Selection is based on the overall strength of the application. Applicants must have a minimum 3.0 GPA.
Target applicant(s): College students. Adult students.
Minimum GPA: 3.0
Amount: $1,000.
Number of awards: 5.
Deadline: January.
How to apply: Applications are available online. An application form, personal essay, transcript, resume and one recommendation letter are required.

Exclusive: Visit www.UltimateScholarshipBook.com and enter code UA120423 for updates on this award.

(1205) · Undergraduate Award for Excellence in Chemistry

Iota Sigma Pi (ISP) ND
Professor Kathryn A. Thomasson, Iota Sigma Pi Director for Student Awards, University of North Dakota, Department of Chemistry, P.O. Box 9024, Grand Forks, ND 58202-9024
Phone: 701-777-3199
Email: kthomasson@chem.und.edu
https://www.iotasigmapi.org/
Purpose: To reward female undergraduate students for excellence in the field of chemistry study.
Eligibility: Applicants must be female senior chemistry students at an accredited four-year college or university and be nominated by a member of the faculty.
Target applicant(s): College students. Adult students.
Amount: $500.
Number of awards: 1.
Deadline: February 15.
How to apply: Applications are available online.
Exclusive: Visit www.UltimateScholarshipBook.com and enter code IO120523 for updates on this award.

(1206) · Undergraduate Engineering Scholarships

American Society of Heating, Refrigerating and Air-Conditioning Engineers (ASHRAE)
1791 Tullie Circle, NE, Atlanta, GA 30329
Phone: 404-636-8400
Email: lbenedict@ashrae.org
https://www.ashrae.org/membership--conferences/student-zone/scholarships-and-grants/scholarship-program
Purpose: To encourage heating, ventilating, air conditioning and refrigeration education.
Eligibility: Applicants must be full-time undergraduates majoring in engineering or pre-engineering in a related course of study approved by the Accreditation Board for Engineering and Technology (ABET) or another accrediting agency recognized by ASHRAE with a minimum 3.0 GPA. Selection is based on leadership, character and potential contribution to the heating, ventilating, air conditioning or refrigeration profession. Applicants must also submit three recommendations from instructors and an official transcript.
Target applicant(s): High school students. College students. Adult students.
Minimum GPA: 3.0
Amount: $5,000.
Number of awards: Varies.
Deadline: December 1.
How to apply: Applications are available online.
Exclusive: Visit www.UltimateScholarshipBook.com and enter code AM120623 for updates on this award.

(1207) · Undergraduate Scholarship and Construction Trades Scholarship

National Association of Women in Construction
327 South Adams Street, Fort Worth, TX 76104
Phone: 800-552-3506
Email: nawic@nawic.org
http://www.nawic.org

Purpose: To offer financial aid to students pursuing construction-related degrees.
Eligibility: Applicants must be currently enrolled in a construction-related degree program as full-time students, have at least one term of study remaining in a course of study leading to a degree or an associate degree in a construction-related field, desire a career in a construction-related field and have a minimum 3.0 GPA. Awards are given to male and female students.
Target applicant(s): College students. Adult students.
Minimum GPA: 3.0
Amount: $500-$2,500.
Number of awards: Varies.
Deadline: February 28.
How to apply: Applications are available online.
Exclusive: Visit www.UltimateScholarshipBook.com and enter code NA120723 for updates on this award.

(1208) · Undergraduate Scholarships

Institute of Food Technologists (IFT)
525 W. Van Buren, Suite 1000, Chicago, IL 60607
Phone: 312-782-8424
Email: ejplummer@ift.org
https://www.ift.org/community/students
Purpose: To encourage undergraduate students in food science or technology.
Eligibility: Applicants must be college sophomores, juniors or seniors pursuing an approved program in food science or food technology. Applications, transcripts and a recommendation letter are required.
Target applicant(s): College students. Adult students.
Amount: $1,000-$3,000.
Number of awards: 9.
Deadline: March 2.
How to apply: Applications are available online.
Exclusive: Visit www.UltimateScholarshipBook.com and enter code IN120823 for updates on this award.

(1209) · Undergraduate Student Research Grants: South-Central Section

Geological Society of America South-Central Section
Wm. Jay Sims, Earth Science Department, University of Arkansas at Little Rock, 2801 S. University, Little Rock, AR 72204-1099
Phone: 303-357-1000
Email: programs@geosociety.org
http://www.geosociety.org
Purpose: To provide research grants to undergraduate students studying geology who are members of GSA.
Eligibility: Applicants must be members of GSA, attend school in the South-Central section and present research at a section meeting or the GSA annual meeting.
Target applicant(s): High school students. College students. Adult students.
Amount: $500.
Number of awards: Varies.
Deadline: April 1.
How to apply: Applications are available online.
Exclusive: Visit www.UltimateScholarshipBook.com and enter code GE120923 for updates on this award.

(1210) · Undergraduate Student Summer Research Fellowships

American Physiological Society
Education Office, 9650 Rockville Pike, Bethesda, MD 20814-3991
Phone: 301-634-7787
Email: education@the-aps.org
https://www.physiology.org/?SSO=Y
Purpose: To support full-time summer study for undergraduate students in the laboratory of an established researcher.
Eligibility: Applicants must be enrolled in an undergraduate program, and faculty sponsor must be an active member of APS. Students must have a minimum 3.0 GPA. Fellowships are awarded to students pursuing a career as a basic research scientist.
Target applicant(s): High school students. College students. Adult students.
Minimum GPA: 3.0
Amount: $4,000 stipend plus up to $1,300 travel expenses.
Number of awards: Varies.
Deadline: February 1.
How to apply: Applications are available online.
Exclusive: Visit www.UltimateScholarshipBook.com and enter code AM121023 for updates on this award.

(1211) · Undergraduate Summer Student Research Assistantship

National Radio Astronomy Observatory (NRAO)
NRAO Headquarters, 520 Edgemont Road, Charlottesville, VA 22903
Phone: 434-296-0211
Email: info@nrao.edu
https://science.nrao.edu/opportunities/student-programs/summerstudents
Purpose: To allow students to perform astronomical research at National Radio Astronomy Observatory (NRAO) sites.
Eligibility: Depending on the specific program, applicants must be either undergraduates or graduating college seniors. Recipients work on-site for 10 to 12 weeks, beginning in late May or early June.
Target applicant(s): College students. Adult students.
Amount: Varies.
Number of awards: Varies.
Deadline: February 1.
How to apply: Applications are available online.
Exclusive: Visit www.UltimateScholarshipBook.com and enter code NA121123 for updates on this award.

(1212) · United Parcel Service Scholarship for Female Students

Institute of Industrial and Systems Engineers
3577 Parkway Lane, Suite 200, Norcross, GA 30092
Phone: 800-494-0460
Email: bcameron@iienet.org
http://www.iise.org/
Purpose: To help female undergraduate engineering students.
Eligibility: Applicants must be full-time female students at an institution in the United States, Canada or Mexico with an accredited industrial engineering program, majoring in industrial engineering or its equivalent and active members. Students may not apply directly for this scholarship and must be nominated. The award is based on academic ability, character, leadership, potential service to the industrial

engineering profession and financial need. Applicants must have a minimum 3.4 GPA.
Target applicant(s): College students. Adult students.
Minimum GPA: 3.4
Amount: $4,000.
Number of awards: 1.
Deadline: November 15.
How to apply: Nomination forms are available online.
Exclusive: Visit www.UltimateScholarshipBook.com and enter code IN121223 for updates on this award.

(1213) · USDA/1890 National Scholars Program
U.S. Department of Agriculture
c/o Juanita Whiting, 1400 Independence Avenue SW, Washington, DC 20250
Phone: 301-851-2062
Email: Juanita.L.Whiting@aphis.usda.gov
https://www.usda.gov/youth/scholarships
Purpose: To aid students who are planning to study agriculture or a related subject in college.
Eligibility: Applicants must be U.S. citizens and be rising undergraduate freshmen, sophomores or juniors who have a high school diploma or a GED. They must have a GPA of 3.0 or higher. They must plan to enroll or be enrolled at an 1890 Land Grant institution and have plans to major in agriculture; agriculture business/management; agriculture economics; agricultural engineering/mechanics; agricultural productions and technology; agronomy or crop science; animal science; botany; farm and range management; fish, game or wildlife management; food services/technology; forestry and related services; home economics/nutrition/human development; horticulture; natural resources management; soil conservation/soil science or other related disciplines (e.g., biological sciences, pre-veterinary medicine or computer science). They must also have proven leadership skills and must have experience with community service. Selection is based on the overall strength of the application.
Target applicant(s): High school students. College students. Adult students.
Minimum GPA: 3.0
Amount: Varies.
Number of awards: Varies.
Deadline: January 31.
How to apply: Applications are available by request from the Civil Rights Enforcement and Compliance section of the Animal and Plant Health Inspection Service branch of the USDA. An application form and supporting materials are required.
Exclusive: Visit www.UltimateScholarshipBook.com and enter code U.121323 for updates on this award.

(1214) · Usrey Family Scholarship
Horticultural Research Institute
525 9th Street NW, Suite 800, Washington, DC 20004
Phone: 202-789-2900
http://www.hriresearch.org
Purpose: To help students who are seeking careers in horticulture.
Eligibility: Applicants must be in an undergraduate or graduate landscape horticulture program or related field at a two or four-year California state university or college. Applicants must also be current, full-time students, academically competitive and have a minimum 2.25 GPA and a minimum 2.7 GPA in the major. Preference is given to applicants who plan to work in the nursery industry after graduation. Applicants must submit applications, cover letters, resumes, transcripts and two recommendation letters.

Target applicant(s): College students. Graduate school students. Adult students.
Minimum GPA: 2.25
Amount: $1,000.
Number of awards: 1.
Deadline: September 10.
How to apply: Applications are available online.
Exclusive: Visit www.UltimateScholarshipBook.com and enter code HO121423 for updates on this award.

(1215) · Vertical Flight Foundation Technical Scholarships
Vertical Flight Foundation
217 N. Washington Street, Alexandria, VA 22314
Phone: 703-684-6777
Email: staff@vtol.org
http://www.vtol.org
Purpose: The Vertical Flight Foundation was founded to support the education in rotorcraft and vertical-takeoff-and-landing aircraft engineering.
Eligibility: Applicants must be full-time students at accredited schools of engineering and submit a transcript with an academic endorsement from a professor or dean. Applicants need not be members of AHS.
Target applicant(s): High school students. College students. Graduate school students. Adult students.
Amount: Up to $6,000.
Number of awards: Varies.
Deadline: February 1.
How to apply: Applications are available online.
Exclusive: Visit www.UltimateScholarshipBook.com and enter code VE121523 for updates on this award.

(1216) · VIP Women in Technology Scholarship
Visionary Integration Professionals
80 Iron Point Circle, Suite 100, Folsom, CA 95630
Phone: 916-985-9625
Email: wits@trustvip.com
https://trustvip.com/company/vip-cares/
Purpose: To aid female students who are preparing for careers in information technology or a related subject.
Eligibility: Applicants must be attending or accepted at a two- or four-year postsecondary institution located in the U.S. They must be planning to pursue a career in information technology or a related field. Selection is based on academic merit, a personal essay and extracurricular activities.
Target applicant(s): High school students. College students. Adult students.
Minimum GPA: 3.0
Amount: Up to $2,500.
Number of awards: Varies.
Deadline: March 31.
How to apply: Applications are available online. An application form, official transcript, personal essay and list of extracurricular activities are required.
Exclusive: Visit www.UltimateScholarshipBook.com and enter code VI121623 for updates on this award.

(1217) · Visiting Medical Student Scholar
American Academy of Neurology
201 Chicago Avenue, Minneapolis, MN 55415

Phone: 800-879-1960
Email: ggates@aan.com
http://www.aan.com
Purpose: To support U.S. medical students who plan to pursue a neurology visiting student rotation.
Eligibility: Applicants must be third or fourth-year AAN member U.S. medical students who plan to pursue a neurology visiting student rotation. Students must plan on completing their rotation at an LCME/AOA approved U.S. medical school.
Target applicant(s): Graduate school students. Adult students.
Amount: Varies.
Number of awards: Varies.
Deadline: Varies.
How to apply: Applications are available online.
Exclusive: Visit www.UltimateScholarshipBook.com and enter code AM121723 for updates on this award.

(1218) · Walter B. Sinnott Scholarship

American Water Works Association - New York Section
Submit To: Jenny Ingrao, Executive Director, New York Section
American Water Works Association, 614 Seventh North Street, Liverpool, NY 13088
Phone: 315-455-2614
Email: jenny@nysawwa.org
https://nysawwa.org/
Purpose: To reward students who are enrolled in a program to study in the water supply field.
Eligibility: Students must be at least a freshman enrolled full-time at an accredited college or university in the United States.
Target applicant(s): College students. Adult students.
Amount: $2,500.
Number of awards: 1.
Deadline: February.
How to apply: Applications are available online.
Exclusive: Visit www.UltimateScholarshipBook.com and enter code AM121823 for updates on this award.

(1219) · Way Scholarship

Way.com
47627 Lakeview Boulevard, Fremont, CA 94538
Phone: 408-598-3338
Email: waycare@way.com
https://www.way.com/care/scholarship
Purpose: To support students who write about artificial intelligence.
Eligibility: Applicants must be high school seniors or undergraduate freshmen or sophomores between the ages of 16 and 25. An essay submission on a provided topic is required.
Target applicant(s): High school students. College students.
Amount: $1,000.
Number of awards: 1.
Deadline: November 1.
How to apply: Applications are available online.
Exclusive: Visit www.UltimateScholarshipBook.com and enter code WA121923 for updates on this award.

(1220) · Welch Scholars Grant

American Osteopathic Foundation (AOF)
142 East Ontario Street, Suite 1450, Chicago, IL 60611
Phone: 312-202-8234
Email: info@aof.org

https://aof.org/grants-awards
Purpose: To support osteopathic medical students.
Eligibility: Applicants must be osteopathic medical students who have successfully completed their first year of studies. Students must be in good academic standing at an accredited College of Osteopathic Medicine. Applicants are chosen based on academic achievement, participation in extracurricular activities and financial need.
Target applicant(s): Graduate school students. Adult students.
Amount: $1,500.
Number of awards: Varies.
Deadline: September 30.
How to apply: Applications are available online.
Exclusive: Visit www.UltimateScholarshipBook.com and enter code AM122023 for updates on this award.

(1221) · William F. Helms Internship Program

U.S. Department of Agriculture
c/o Juanita Whiting, 1400 Independence Avenue SW, Washington, DC 20250
Phone: 301-851-2062
Email: Juanita.L.Whiting@aphis.usda.gov
https://www.usda.gov/youth/scholarships
Purpose: To support students who are pursuing higher education studies in agriculture or the biological sciences.
Eligibility: Applicants must be U.S. citizens who are undergraduate sophomores or juniors at an accredited U.S. college or university. They must be studying a subject in agriculture or the biological sciences and have a GPA of 2.5 or higher. Applicants must agree to work for the Agency during school breaks (both summer and holiday breaks) a minimum of 640 hours prior to completion of studies. Selection is based on the overall strength of the application.
Target applicant(s): College students. Adult students.
Minimum GPA: 2.5
Amount: Up to $5,000.
Number of awards: Varies.
Scholarship may be renewable.
Deadline: Varies.
How to apply: Applications are available by request from the U.S. Department of Agriculture. An application form, personal statement, transcript, three recommendation letters and documentation of U.S. military service (if applicable) are required.
Exclusive: Visit www.UltimateScholarshipBook.com and enter code U.122123 for updates on this award.

(1222) · William J. Adams, Jr. and Marijane E. Adams Scholarship

American Society of Agricultural and Biological Engineers Foundation
Administrator, Scholarship Fund, 2950 Niles Road, St. Joseph, MI 49085
Phone: 269-429-0300
Email: hq@asabe.org
http://www.asabe.org
Purpose: To aid undergraduate students with an interest in agricultural machinery product design and development.
Eligibility: Applicants must be biological or agricultural engineering majors in eligible accredited programs in the U.S. or Canada. Applicants must also have completed at least one year of undergraduate study and have at least one year of undergraduate study remaining, have a minimum 2.5 GPA, have an interest in agricultural machinery product design and development and demonstrate financial need.

Target applicant(s): College students. Adult students.
Minimum GPA: 2.5
Amount: $1,200.
Number of awards: 1.
Deadline: March 15.
How to apply: Application is by formal letter.
Exclusive: Visit www.UltimateScholarshipBook.com and enter code AM122223 for updates on this award.

(1223) · Women in STEM Scholarship/BHW Scholarship
BHW Group
6011 W. Courtyard Drive, Suite 410, Austin, TX 78730
Phone: 512-220-0035
https://thebhwgroup.com/scholarship
Purpose: To support female students pursuing a degree in a science or mathematics field.
Eligibility: Applicants must be incoming freshman or currently enrolled female students pursuing an undergraduate or master's degree. Students must be majoring in science, technology, engineering or mathematics. Applicants must be enrolled in a U.S. school and submit an essay along with their completed application.
Target applicant(s): High school students. College students. Graduate school students. Adult students.
Amount: $3,000.
Number of awards: 1.
Deadline: April 15.
How to apply: Applications are available online.
Exclusive: Visit www.UltimateScholarshipBook.com and enter code BH122323 for updates on this award.

(1224) · Women's Scholarship
National Strength and Conditioning Association (NSCA) Foundation
1885 Bob Johnson Drive, Colorado Springs, CO 80906
Phone: 800-815-6826
http://www.nsca.com/foundation/
Purpose: To encourage women to enter the field of strength and conditioning.
Eligibility: Applicants should be women age 17 and older who have been accepted by an accredited institution for and undergraduate or a graduate degree in strength and conditioning. Applicants must be NSCA members and plan to pursue careers in strength and conditioning. A cover letter of application, application form, resume, transcript, three letters of recommendation and essay are required. The award is based on grades, strength and conditioning experience, NSCA involvement, awards, community involvement, essay and recommendations.
Target applicant(s): High school students. College students. Graduate school students. Adult students.
Amount: $1,500.
Number of awards: Varies.
Deadline: October 15.
How to apply: Application materials are described online.
Exclusive: Visit www.UltimateScholarshipBook.com and enter code NA122423 for updates on this award.

(1225) · Yanmar/SAE Scholarship
Society of Automotive Engineers International
Scholarships Program, 400 Commonwealth Drive, Warrendale, PA 15096
Phone: 724-776-4841
Email: scholarships@sae.org
https://www.sae.org/participate/scholarships
Purpose: This scholarship is sponsored by the SAE Foundation and the Yanmar Diesel America Corporation.
Eligibility: Applicants must be full-time college juniors pursuing an engineering or related science degree or enrolled in a postgraduate engineering or related science program. Applicants must also pursue a course of study or research related to the conservation of energy in transportation, agriculture and construction and power generation.
Target applicant(s): College students. Graduate school students. Adult students.
Amount: $1,000.
Number of awards: 1.
Scholarship may be renewable.
Deadline: March 15.
How to apply: Applications are available online.
Exclusive: Visit www.UltimateScholarshipBook.com and enter code SO122523 for updates on this award.

(1226) · Youth Incentive Award
Coleopterists Society
Dr. David G. Furth, Entomology, NHB, MRC 165, P.O. Box 37012, Smithsonian institution, Washington, DC 20013-7012
Phone: 202-633-0990
Email: furthd@si.edu
http://www.coleopsoc.org
Purpose: To recognize young people studying beetles.
Eligibility: Applicants should be coleopterists in grades 7-12 and submit individual proposals such as field collecting trips to conduct beetle species inventories or diversity studies, attending workshops or visiting entomology or natural history museums for training and projects on beetles, studying beetle biology, etc. Students are strongly encouraged to find an adult advisor (i.e., teacher, youth group leader, parent) to provide guidance in the proposal development, but the proposal must be written by the applicant. The Coleopterists Society can help establish contacts between applicants and professional coleopterists. The award is based on creativity, educational benefit to the applicant, scientific merit, feasibility and budget. There are two winners: one for grades 7-9 and one for grades 10-12.
Target applicant(s): Junior high students or younger. High school students.
Amount: $200-$400.
Number of awards: 2.
Deadline: November 1.
How to apply: Applications are available online.
Exclusive: Visit www.UltimateScholarshipBook.com and enter code CO122623 for updates on this award.

(1227) · Youth Program
Appaloosa Horse Club
Appaloosa Youth Association, 2720 West Pullman Road, Moscow, ID 83843
Phone: 208-882-5578
Email: youth@appaloosa.com
https://www.appaloosa.com/appaloosa-youth-association
Purpose: To reward student members of the Appaloosa Youth Association or the Appaloosa Horse Club who are pursuing higher education.
Eligibility: Applicants must be members of the Appaloosa Youth Association or the Appaloosa Horse Club and must attend or plan to

attend an institute of higher learning. Students may also be the son or daughter of Appaloosa Horse Club members.

Target applicant(s): High school students. College students. Graduate school students. Adult students.

Minimum GPA: 2.5

Amount: $1,000-$2,000.

Number of awards: Up to 9.

Scholarship may be renewable.

Deadline: April.

How to apply: Applications are available online.

Exclusive: Visit www.UltimateScholarshipBook.com and enter code AP122723 for updates on this award.

STATE OF RESIDENCE

(1228) · A.D. Osherman Scholarship Fund

Greater Houston Community Foundation

515 Post Oak Boulevard, Suite 1000, Houston, TX 77027

Phone: 713-333-2200

Email: scholarships@ghcf.org

https://ghcf.org/

Purpose: To support students of Texas in pursuing post-secondary education.

Eligibility: Applicants must demonstrate financial need. A minimum GPA of 2.75 is required. Students must take a minimum of 12 credits in both the fall and spring semesters. Preference is given to minority students, veterans and/or first-generation college students.

Target applicant(s): High school students. College students. Adult students.

Minimum GPA: 2.75

Amount: $3,000.

Number of awards: 3.

Deadline: April.

How to apply: Applications are available online.

Exclusive: Visit www.UltimateScholarshipBook.com and enter code GR122823 for updates on this award.

(1229) · Academic Challenge Scholarship

Arkansas Department of Higher Education

423 Main Street, Suite 400, Little Rock, AR 72201

Phone: 501-371-2050

Email: finaid@adhe.arknet.edu

http://scholarships.adhe.edu/scholarships-and-programs/a-z/

Purpose: To encourage Arkansas high school graduates to enroll in Arkansas colleges and universities.

Eligibility: Applicants must be graduating Arkansas high school seniors who meet academic minimum standards and income requirements. Must submit FAFSA.

Target applicant(s): High school students.

Minimum GPA: 2.25

Amount: $2,000-$5,000.

Number of awards: Varies.

Scholarship may be renewable.

Deadline: July 1.

How to apply: Applications are available through your high school counselor. FAFSA required.

Exclusive: Visit www.UltimateScholarshipBook.com and enter code AR122923 for updates on this award.

(1230) · Academic Excellence Scholarship

State of Wisconsin Higher Educational Aids Board

P.O. Box 7885, Madison, WI 53707

Phone: 608-267-2206

Email: heabmail@wisconsin.gov

http://heab.state.wi.us

Purpose: To assist outstanding Wisconsin students who are planning to attend college in Wisconsin.

Eligibility: Applicants must be high school seniors who plan to enroll full-time at an eligible Wisconsin college or university. The award is given to the student with the highest GPA in each public and private Wisconsin high school.

Target applicant(s): High school students.

Amount: Up to $2,250.
Number of awards: Varies.
Deadline: March 1.
How to apply: No application is required. Each high school designates the student who has the highest GPA of the graduating high school class.
Exclusive: Visit www.UltimateScholarshipBook.com and enter code ST123023 for updates on this award.

(1231) · Academic Scholars Program

Oklahoma State Regents for Higher Education/Academic Scholars Program
655 Research Parkway, Suite 200, Oklahoma City, OK 73104
Phone: 800-858-1840
Email: studentinfo@osrhe.edu
https://secure.okcollegestart.org/Financial_Aid_Planning/Scholarships/Academic_Scholarships/Academic_Scholars_Program.aspx
Purpose: To assist students in attending Oklahoma colleges and universities.
Eligibility: Applicants can qualify for the program by being Oklahoma or out-of-state students who are named National Merit Scholars, National Merit Finalists or U.S. Presidential Scholars; by being Oklahoma residents who score above the 99.5 percentile on the SAT or ACT or by being nominated by an Oklahoma public college or institution. Applicants must attend an Oklahoma college or university. Selection is based on academic merit.
Target applicant(s): High school students.
Amount: Up to $5,500.
Number of awards: Varies.
Scholarship may be renewable.
Deadline: Varies.
How to apply: Applications are available from the applicant's high school guidance counselor, by telephone request and online. An application form and supporting documents are required.
Exclusive: Visit www.UltimateScholarshipBook.com and enter code OK123123 for updates on this award.

(1232) · Access College Early Scholarship

Nebraska Coordinating Commission for Postsecondary Education
P.O. Box 95005, Lincoln, NE 68509-5005
Phone: 402-471-2847
Email: ritchie.morrow@nebraska.gov
https://ccpe.nebraska.gov/
Purpose: To support Nebraska high school students who are enrolled in early college courses.
Eligibility: Applicants must demonstrate financial need through proof of participation in government aid programs or documentation of recent family hardships. They may be in any year of high school.
Target applicant(s): High school students.
Amount: Full tuition and fees.
Number of awards: Varies.
Scholarship may be renewable.
Deadline: September 15, December 15, March 31, May 15, June 15.
How to apply: Applications are available online.
Exclusive: Visit www.UltimateScholarshipBook.com and enter code NE123223 for updates on this award.

(1233) · Access to Better Learning and Education Grant Program

Florida Department of Education
Office of Student Financial Assistance, State Scholarship and Grant Programs, 325 West Gaines Street, Suite 1314, Tallahassee, FL 32399-0400
Phone: 888-827-2004
Email: osfa@fldoe.org
http://www.floridastudentfinancialaid.org
Purpose: To help undergraduate students from Florida who want to attend Florida private colleges or universities.
Eligibility: Applicants must be Florida residents for at least a year and first-time undergraduate students enrolled in degree programs (except theology or divinity degrees). Applicants must meet Florida's general state aid eligibility requirements and enroll in at least 12 credit hours per semester. Award renewable for up to nine semesters. Participating institutions determine application procedures, deadlines and student eligibility. Award amount determined by the Legislature in the General Appropriation Act each year.
Target applicant(s): High school students. College students. Adult students.
Amount: Varies.
Number of awards: Varies.
Scholarship may be renewable.
Deadline: Varies.
How to apply: Contact the financial aid office at eligible Florida colleges and universities.
Exclusive: Visit www.UltimateScholarshipBook.com and enter code FL123323 for updates on this award.

(1234) · ACEC Colorado Scholarship Program

American Council of Engineering Companies of Colorado
800 Grant Street, Suite 100, Denver, CO 80203
Phone: 303-832-2200
Email: acec@acec-co.org
http://www.acec-co.org
Purpose: To support engineering students.
Eligibility: Applicants must be full-time students pursuing a bachelor's degree in engineering or surveying at an accredited college or university in Colorado. They must be entering their junior, senior or fifth year. Selection is based on GPA (24 points), essay (25 points), work experience (24 points), recommendation (17 points) and extracurricular activities (10 points).
Target applicant(s): College students. Adult students.
Amount: Varies.
Number of awards: Varies.
Deadline: January.
How to apply: Applications are available online. An application form, transcript, essay and recommendation are required.
Exclusive: Visit www.UltimateScholarshipBook.com and enter code AM123423 for updates on this award.

(1235) · ACEC Scholarship

American Council of Engineering Companies California (ACEC)
1303 J Street, Suite 450, Sacramento, CA 95814
Phone: 916-441-7991
Email: staff@acec-ca.org
https://www.acec-ca.org/page/ScholarshipApp
Purpose: To support students interested in pursuing a degree in engineering or land surveying.

Eligibility: Applicants must be U.S. citizens, undergraduate students enrolled full-time in an engineering or land surveying program or graduate students enrolled at least half-time. Students must have a minimum GPA of 3.5 in completed engineering/land surveying courses and a minimum overall GPA of 3.2. Selection is made based on the overall strength of the application.
Target applicant(s): College students. Graduate school students. Adult students.
Minimum GPA: 3.2
Amount: $7,500.
Number of awards: Varies.
Deadline: January 29.
How to apply: Applications are available online.
Exclusive: Visit www.UltimateScholarshipBook.com and enter code AM123523 for updates on this award.

(1236) · ACLU of Utah Youth Activist Scholarship
American Civil Liberties Union of Utah
355 North 300 West, Salt Lake City, UT 84102
Phone: 801-521-9862
Email: scholarship@acluutah.org
https://www.acluutah.org/resources/itemlist/category/68-youth-activist-scholarship
Purpose: To support Utah students who have demonstrated a strong commitment to civil liberties.
Eligibility: Applicants must be high school seniors who plan to attend college full-time. Applicants must have demonstrated their commitment to civil liberties through activism. Previous winners have been involved in programs related to racial diversity, rights of disabled students, women's equality, freedom of religion, freedom of expression and equality for all. Students with GPAs of less than 3.0 must submit an explanation of their grades.
Target applicant(s): High school students.
Amount: $3,500.
Number of awards: 4.
Deadline: March 22.
How to apply: Applications are available online.
Exclusive: Visit www.UltimateScholarshipBook.com and enter code AM123623 for updates on this award.

(1237) · Adult Student Grant
State Student Assistance Commission of Indiana
W462 Indiana Government Center South, 402 West Washington Street, Indianapolis, IN 46204
Phone: 888-528-4719
Email: grants@ssaci.state.in.us
http://www.in.gov/che/
Purpose: To help part-time Indiana students pursue higher education.
Eligibility: Applicants must be Indiana residents and a U.S. citizen or eligible non-citizen. Students must be undergraduates taking at least six but not more than 12 credit hours per term at eligible institutions. This is a need-based award.
Target applicant(s): College students. Adult students.
Amount: $2,000.
Number of awards: Varies.
Scholarship may be renewable.
Deadline: July 1.
How to apply: Applications are available online.
Exclusive: Visit www.UltimateScholarshipBook.com and enter code ST123723 for updates on this award.

(1238) · Advanced Practice Healthcare Scholarship Program
Office of Statewide Health Planning and Development
Health Professions Education Foundation, 400 R Street, Suite 460, Sacramento, CA 95811-6213
Phone: 916-326-3640
Email: hpef-email@oshpd.ca.gov
https://oshpd.ca.gov/loans-scholarships-grants/scholarships/
Purpose: To increase medical care to underserved areas of California by assisting residents who are studying to become dentists, dental hygienists, nurse practitioners, certified midwives and physician assistants.
Eligibility: Applicants must be California residents who have been accepted by or are enrolled in an accredited California program. Financial need, work experience and career goals are considered, and preference is given to applicants who plan to remain in a medically underserved area past the service time. Those selected must sign a two-year service agreement to work in a medically underserved area of California.
Target applicant(s): College students. Graduate school students. Adult students.
Amount: Up to $50,000.
Number of awards: Varies.
Scholarship may be renewable.
Deadline: February 23.
How to apply: Applications are available online.
Exclusive: Visit www.UltimateScholarshipBook.com and enter code OF123823 for updates on this award.

(1239) · AFS Twin City Memorial Scholarship
Foundry Educational Foundation
1695 North Penny Lane, Schaumburg, IL 60173
Phone: 847-490-9200
Email: info@fefinc.org
http://www.fefinc.org/scholarships.html
Purpose: To aid students from Minnesota, western Wisconsin and northern Iowa who are attending a Foundry Education Foundation (FEF) member school.
Eligibility: Applicants must be residents of Minnesota, western Wisconsin or northern Iowa. Preference will be given to students who are completing coursework in a foundry-related subject. Selection is based on the overall strength of the application.
Target applicant(s): College students. Adult students.
Amount: Varies.
Number of awards: Varies.
Deadline: October 4.
How to apply: Applications are available online. An application form and supporting materials are required.
Exclusive: Visit www.UltimateScholarshipBook.com and enter code FO123923 for updates on this award.

(1240) · AFS Wisconsin Past President Scholarship
Foundry Educational Foundation
1695 North Penny Lane, Schaumburg, IL 60173
Phone: 847-490-9200
Email: info@fefinc.org
http://www.fefinc.org/scholarships.html
Purpose: To aid Wisconsin-area students who wish to pursue careers in the cast metal industry.
Eligibility: Students must be enrolled at an Foundry Educational Foundation (FEF) member school, a school located in Wisconsin or a

school located in a state that is adjacent to Wisconsin. They also must have previous work experience, preferably in the cast metal industry. Selection is based on the student's academic record, his or her residential proximity to the AFS Wisconsin Chapter area, the proximity of the student's school to the AFS Wisconsin Chapter area, relevance of the student's degree program to the cast metal industry and relevant work experience.

Target applicant(s): High school students. College students. Adult students.
Amount: Varies.
Number of awards: Varies.
Deadline: December 15.
How to apply: Applications are available online. A completed FEF profile and supporting documents are required.
Exclusive: Visit www.UltimateScholarshipBook.com and enter code FO124023 for updates on this award.

(1241) · AGC of Massachusetts Scholarships

Associated General Contractors of Massachusetts
888 Worcester Street, Suite 40, Wellesley, MA 02482
Phone: 781-786-8917
Email: canoni@agcmass.org
http://www.agcmass.org/scholarships
Purpose: To aid Massachusetts residents who are college sophomores, juniors or seniors and who are enrolled in degree programs related to construction or civil engineering.
Eligibility: Applicants must be undergraduate sophomores or above at an accredited college or university. They must be legal residents of Massachusetts (though they may attend school outside of the state) and must be enrolled in a degree program related to construction or civil engineering. Selection is based on financial need and the overall strength of the application.
Target applicant(s): College students. Adult students.
Amount: Varies.
Number of awards: Varies.
Scholarship may be renewable.
Deadline: July 15.
How to apply: Applications are available online. An application form and an official transcript are required.
Exclusive: Visit www.UltimateScholarshipBook.com and enter code AS124123 for updates on this award.

(1242) · AGC of Ohio Scholarships

Associated General Contractors of Ohio
1755 Northwest Boulevard, Columbus, OH 43212
Phone: 614-486-6446
Email: parker@agcohio.com
https://agcohio.com/workforce-development/agc-scholarships/
Purpose: To support undergraduate students who are residents of Ohio and interested in pursuing careers in construction-related fields.
Eligibility: Applicants must be a U.S. citizens and undergraduate students in at least the second year of a two-year, four-year or five-year degree seeking program. The minimum GPA requirement is 2.5. Selection is based on the overall strength of the application.
Target applicant(s): College students. Adult students.
Minimum GPA: 2.5
Amount: $1,000.
Number of awards: 7.
Deadline: March 5.
How to apply: Applications are available online. An application form, official college transcripts and essay are required and must be mailed.

Exclusive: Visit www.UltimateScholarshipBook.com and enter code AS124223 for updates on this award.

(1243) · Agnes M. Lindsay Scholarship

Massachusetts Department of Higher Education
Office of Student Financial Assistance, 454 Broadway, Suite 200, Revere, MA 02151
Phone: 617-727-9420
Email: osfa@osfa.mass.edu
https://www.mass.edu/osfa/programs/programs.asp
Purpose: To provide assistance to Massachusetts students who are from rural parts of the state, demonstrate financial need and attend a Massachusetts public institution of higher education.
Eligibility: Applicants must be permanent Massachusetts residents for at least one year before the beginning of the academic year. Applicants must also be enrolled full-time in an undergraduate program and maintain satisfactory academic progress.
Target applicant(s): High school students. College students. Adult students.
Amount: Varies.
Number of awards: Varies.
Deadline: Varies.
How to apply: Applications are available by phone.
Exclusive: Visit www.UltimateScholarshipBook.com and enter code MA124323 for updates on this award.

(1244) · Aid for Part-Time Study

New York State Higher Education Services Corporation (HESC)
99 Washington Avenue, Albany, NY 12255
Phone: 888-697-4372
Email: scholarships@hesc.ny.gov
http://www.hesc.ny.gov
Purpose: To assist part-time undergraduate students at New York State institutions.
Eligibility: Applicants must meet income eligibility requirements, be enrolled for at least 3 but less than 12 semester hours per semester or at least 4 but less than 8 semester hours per quarter in an eligible undergraduate program, be New York State residents and be U.S. citizens or eligible noncitizens. Tuition charges must exceed $100 per year, and once payments begin, students must maintain a C average.
Target applicant(s): High school students. College students. Adult students.
Amount: Up to $2,000.
Number of awards: Varies.
Scholarship may be renewable.
Deadline: Varies.
How to apply: Contact the financial aid office to receive an APTS application.
Exclusive: Visit www.UltimateScholarshipBook.com and enter code NE124423 for updates on this award.

(1245) · Alabama Concrete Industries Association Scholarships

Alabama Concrete Industries Association
1745 Platt Place, Montgomery, AL 36117
Phone: 334-265-0501
Email: rlindsay@alconcrete.org
http://alconcrete.org/scholarships/
Purpose: To support students studying fields related to the concrete industry.

Eligibility: Applicants must be college seniors majoring in architecture, engineering or building sciences at universities in Alabama. They must be Alabama residents with a 2.5 or higher GPA.

Target applicant(s): High school students. College students. Adult students.

Minimum GPA: 2.5

Amount: $8,000.

Number of awards: 2.

Scholarship may be renewable.

Deadline: November 30.

How to apply: Applications are available from your school's guidance office. An application form, letter of recommendation and essay are required.

Exclusive: Visit www.UltimateScholarshipBook.com and enter code AL124523 for updates on this award.

(1246) · Albert E. and Florence W. Newton Nursing Scholarship

Rhode Island Foundation
One Union Station, Providence, RI 02903
Phone: 401-274-4564
Email: rbogert@rifoundation.org
https://rifoundation.org/grants-scholarships/browse-scholarships

Purpose: To aid undergraduate nursing students.

Eligibility: Applicants must be undergraduate students seeking a diploma or degree in nursing. They must demonstrate financial need. Preference will be given to Rhode Island residents. Selection is based on academic merit and financial need.

Target applicant(s): High school students. College students. Adult students.

Amount: $500-$5,000.

Number of awards: Varies.

Scholarship may be renewable.

Deadline: April 19.

How to apply: Applications are available online. An application form and supporting materials are required.

Exclusive: Visit www.UltimateScholarshipBook.com and enter code RH124623 for updates on this award.

(1247) · Albert M. Lappin Scholarship

American Legion, Department of Kansas
1314 SW Topeka Boulevard, Topeka, KS 66612
Phone: 785-232-9315
https://ksamlegion.org/

Purpose: To assist the education of needy and worthy children of American Legion and American Legion Auxiliary members.

Eligibility: Applicants must be high school seniors or college freshmen or sophomores who are average or better students. They must be the son or daughter of a veteran and enrolling or enrolled in a post-secondary school in Kansas. A parent must have been a member of the Kansas American Legion or American Legion Auxiliary for the previous three years. In addition, the children of deceased parents are eligible if the parent was a paid member at the time of death. Applicants must submit a 1040 income statement, documentation of parent's veteran status, three letters of recommendation with only one from a teacher, an essay on the topic of "Why I Want to Go to College" and a high school transcript. Applicants must maintain a C average in college and verify enrollment at the start of each semester.

Target applicant(s): High school students. College students. Adult students.

Amount: $1,000.

Number of awards: 1.

Scholarship may be renewable.

Deadline: February 15.

How to apply: Applications are available online.

Exclusive: Visit www.UltimateScholarshipBook.com and enter code AM124723 for updates on this award.

(1248) · Alisa's Angels Scholarship

Alisa's Angels Foundation
3404 N. Soldier Trail, Tucson, AZ 85749
http://alisasangels.org

Purpose: To support graduating seniors of Arizona in pursuing post-secondary education.

Eligibility: A minimum GPA of 2.75 is required. Selection is primarily based on demonstration of service to others. Students must submit high school transcripts, an essay describing their service work and a letter of recommendation from a teacher, counselor or faith leader.

Target applicant(s): High school students.

Minimum GPA: 2.75

Amount: $5,000.

Number of awards: Varies.

Scholarship may be renewable.

Deadline: February.

How to apply: Applications are available online.

Exclusive: Visit www.UltimateScholarshipBook.com and enter code AL124823 for updates on this award.

(1249) · All Iowa Opportunity Scholarship

Iowa College Student Aid Commission
475 SW Fifth Street, Suite D, Des Moines, IA 50309
Phone: 515-725-3400
Email: info@iowacollegeaid.gov
https://www.iowacollegeaid.gov/ScholarshipsAndGrants

Purpose: To recognize Iowa's top students.

Eligibility: Applicants must be Iowa residents who graduated high school in the last two years. Students must demonstrate financial need. Awards may only be used at eligible Iowa institutions. Submit both a FAFSA and an Iowa Financial Aid Application by the deadline to be considered.

Target applicant(s): High school students.

Amount: Up to $4,644.

Number of awards: Varies.

Scholarship may be renewable.

Deadline: March 1.

How to apply: Applications are available online.

Exclusive: Visit www.UltimateScholarshipBook.com and enter code IO124923 for updates on this award.

(1250) · Allan Eldin and Agnes Sutorik Geiger Scholarship Fund

Hawaii Community Foundation - Scholarships
827 Fort Street Mall, Honolulu, HI 96813
Phone: 888-731-3863
Email: scholarships@hcf-hawaii.org
https://www.hawaiicommunityfoundation.org/

Purpose: To support Hawaii students who are pursuing degrees in veterinary science.

Eligibility: Students must have at least a 3.0 GPA, be full-time students and demonstrate financial need.

Target applicant(s): College students. Graduate school students. Adult students.
Minimum GPA: 3.0
Amount: Varies.
Number of awards: Varies.
Deadline: January 31.
How to apply: To apply, register online, complete the online application and select the scholarships to which you wish to apply. In addition, mail the supporting materials: printed confirmation page from the online application, personal statement, copy of Student Aid Report (SAR) available at www.fafsa.ed.gov and official transcript.
Exclusive: Visit www.UltimateScholarshipBook.com and enter code HA125023 for updates on this award.

(1251) · Allan Johnston Memorial Scholarship

Los Alamos National Laboratory Foundation
1112 Plaza del Norte, Espanola, NM 87532
Phone: 505-753-8890
Email: tony@lanlfoundation.org
http://www.lanlfoundation.org
Purpose: To support undergraduate students from northern New Mexico.
Eligibility: Students must have at least a 3.25 cumulative unweighted GPA, and they must have either an SAT score (combined Math plus Critical Reading only) of at least 930 or an ACT score of at least 19. Applicants must submit an essay and two letters of recommendation.
Target applicant(s): High school students. College students. Adult students.
Minimum GPA: 3.25
Amount: $1,000.
Number of awards: Varies.
Deadline: January 18.
How to apply: Applications are available online.
Exclusive: Visit www.UltimateScholarshipBook.com and enter code LO125123 for updates on this award.

(1252) · Allied Healthcare Scholarship Program

Office of Statewide Health Planning and Development
Health Professions Education Foundation, 400 R Street, Suite 460, Sacramento, CA 95811-6213
Phone: 916-326-3640
Email: hpef-email@oshpd.ca.gov
https://oshpd.ca.gov/loans-scholarships-grants/scholarships/
Purpose: To increase the number of allied healthcare professionals working in medically underserved areas of California.
Eligibility: Applicants must be enrolled in a California community college or university and be studying one of the following programs: medical imaging, occupational therapy, physical therapy, respiratory care, social work, pharmacy and diagnostic medical sonography, pharmacy technician, medical laboratory technologist, surgical technician or ultrasound technician. Those selected will complete a one-year service contract or work volunteer hours in a medically underserved area of California. Financial need, work experience, academic achievement and community involvement are considered. Preference is given to those who expect to graduate within two years of application.
Target applicant(s): High school students. College students. Graduate school students. Adult students.
Minimum GPA: 2.0
Amount: Up to $8,000.
Number of awards: Varies.
Scholarship may be renewable.

Deadline: February 22.
How to apply: Applications are available online.
Exclusive: Visit www.UltimateScholarshipBook.com and enter code OF125223 for updates on this award.

(1253) · Alma White - Delta Kappa Gamma Scholarship

Hawaii Community Foundation - Scholarships
827 Fort Street Mall, Honolulu, HI 96813
Phone: 888-731-3863
Email: scholarships@hcf-hawaii.org
https://www.hawaiicommunityfoundation.org/
Purpose: To support students in Hawaii who are planning careers in teaching.
Eligibility: Applicants must be majoring in education. Students must be a college junior, college senior or graduate student. Minimum 2.7 GPA required.
Target applicant(s): College students. Graduate school students. Adult students.
Minimum GPA: 2.7
Amount: Varies.
Number of awards: Varies.
Deadline: January 31.
How to apply: To apply, register online, complete the online application and select the scholarships to which you wish to apply. In addition, mail the supporting materials: printed confirmation page from the online application, personal statement, copy of Student Aid Report (SAR) available at www.fafsa.ed.gov and official transcript.
Exclusive: Visit www.UltimateScholarshipBook.com and enter code HA125323 for updates on this award.

(1254) · Alyssa McCroskey Memorial Scholarship

California Association on Postsecondary Education and Disability (CAPED)
10073 Valley View Street, #242, Cypress, CA 90630
Phone: 562-397-2810
Email: capedscholarships2018@gmail.com
http://www.caped.co/scholarships/
Purpose: To support students with a learning disability who are pursuing higher education.
Eligibility: Applicants must have a verifiable learning disability and be making a positive difference in the lives of other students who are struggling to maintain or regain their mental health. Students must be currently enrolled as a student at a four-year California college or university with a GPA of 2.5 for undergraduates or 3.0 for graduate students. Applicants must have completed at least six semester or eight quarter units as an undergraduate student or three semester or four quarter units as a graduate student.
Target applicant(s): College students. Graduate school students. Adult students.
Minimum GPA: 2.5 for undergraduate students, 3.0 for graduate students
Amount: $1,000.
Number of awards: 1.
Deadline: August 31.
How to apply: Applications are available online.
Exclusive: Visit www.UltimateScholarshipBook.com and enter code CA125423 for updates on this award.

(1255) · Ambassador Minerva Jean Falcon Hawaii Scholarship

Hawaii Community Foundation - Scholarships
827 Fort Street Mall, Honolulu, HI 96813
Phone: 888-731-3863
Email: scholarships@hcf-hawaii.org
https://www.hawaiicommunityfoundation.org/
Purpose: To support students of Filipino ancestry.
Eligibility: Students must be starting their freshman year of college, must attend school in Hawaii and must have a minimum 2.7 GPA.
Target applicant(s): High school students. College students. Adult students.
Minimum GPA: 2.7
Amount: Varies.
Number of awards: Varies.
Deadline: January 31.
How to apply: To apply, register online, complete the online application and select the scholarships to which you wish to apply. In addition, mail the supporting materials: printed confirmation page from the online application, personal statement, copy of Student Aid Report (SAR) available at www.fafsa.ed.gov and official transcript.
Exclusive: Visit www.UltimateScholarshipBook.com and enter code HA125523 for updates on this award.

(1256) · American Association of Japanese University Women Scholarship Program

American Association of Japanese University Women
Scholarship Committee, 3543 West Boulevard, Los Angeles, CA 90016
Phone: 310-230-7860
Email: aajuwscholar@gmail.com
http://www.aajuw.org
Purpose: To support female students who demonstrate leadership and facilitate cultural relationships.
Eligibility: Applicants must be starting their junior or senior year in college or be in graduate school at a California school. They must be able to attend the awards ceremony in Los Angeles at their own expense. Applicants must demonstrate a desire to fulfill a leadership role in their chosen field of study and be a contributor to U.S.-Japan relations and cultural exchanges. Students must also submit an essay showing how their studies will contribute to leadership or to the relationship between the United States and Japan.
Target applicant(s): College students. Graduate school students. Adult students.
Amount: $2,000.
Number of awards: Varies.
Deadline: February.
How to apply: Applications are available online. Application form, transcripts, resume, an essay and two letters of recommendation are required.
Exclusive: Visit www.UltimateScholarshipBook.com and enter code AM125623 for updates on this award.

(1257) · American Council of Engineering Companies of New Jersey Member Organization Scholarship

American Council of Engineering Companies of New Jersey
310 West State Street, Trenton, NJ 08618
Phone: 609-571-9958
Email: info@acecnj.org
http://www.acecnj.org/scholarship.php
Purpose: To help students who are enrolled in engineering or accredited land surveying degree programs.
Eligibility: Applicants must be rising undergraduate juniors or above enrolled in an ABET-accredited bachelor's degree program in engineering, a master's degree program in engineering, a doctoral degree program in engineering or an accredited land surveying program. Master's students must either be enrolled in an ABET-accredited program or must hold a bachelor's degree in engineering from an ABET-accredited school. Doctoral students must hold either an ABET-accredited bachelor's degree or an ABET-accredited master's degree in engineering. They must be U.S. citizens. Selection is based on GPA, personal essay, recommendation letter, work experience and extracurricular involvement.
Target applicant(s): College students. Graduate school students. Adult students.
Amount: Up to $5,000.
Number of awards: Up to 6.
Deadline: February 5.
How to apply: Applications are available online. An application form, a personal essay, an official transcript and one recommendation form are required.
Exclusive: Visit www.UltimateScholarshipBook.com and enter code AM125723 for updates on this award.

(1258) · American Indian Endowed Scholarship

Washington Student Achievement Council
P. O. Box 43430, Olympia, WA 98504-3430
Phone: 360-753-7850
Email: aies@wsac.wa.gov
https://wsac.wa.gov/
Purpose: To help students who have ties to the Native American community and have financial need pay for higher education.
Eligibility: Applicants must have financial need according to a completed Free Application for Federal Student Aid (FAFSA), be residents of Washington state and enroll full-time as an undergraduate or graduate student at an eligible in-state institution.
Target applicant(s): High school students. College students. Graduate school students. Adult students.
Amount: $500-$2,000.
Number of awards: Varies.
Scholarship may be renewable.
Deadline: March 1.
How to apply: Applications are available online.
Exclusive: Visit www.UltimateScholarshipBook.com and enter code WA125823 for updates on this award.

(1259) · American Institute of Graphic Arts (AIGA) Honolulu Chapter Scholarship Fund

Hawaii Community Foundation - Scholarships
827 Fort Street Mall, Honolulu, HI 96813
Phone: 888-731-3863
Email: scholarships@hcf-hawaii.org
https://www.hawaiicommunityfoundation.org/
Purpose: To support students who are majoring in graphic design, visual communication or commercial arts.
Eligibility: Students must be residents of Hawaii.
Target applicant(s): High school students. College students. Adult students.
Minimum GPA: 2.7
Amount: Varies.

Number of awards: Varies.
Deadline: January 31.
How to apply: To apply, register online, complete the online application and select the scholarships to which you wish to apply. In addition, mail the supporting materials: printed confirmation page from the online application, personal statement, copy of Student Aid Report (SAR) available at www.fafsa.ed.gov and official transcript.
Exclusive: Visit www.UltimateScholarshipBook.com and enter code HA125923 for updates on this award.

(1260) · American Legion - Connecticut Oratorical Contest

American Legion - Connecticut
287 West Street, Rocky Hill, CT 06067
Phone: 860-436-9986
http://www.ctlegion.org
Purpose: Scholarship awards are given to high school students who win an oratorical contest on the understanding of the U.S. Constitution.
Eligibility: Applicants must prepare an oration on an assigned topic with specific time constraints. Students will explore the substance and meaning of the Constitution.
Target applicant(s): High school students.
Amount: Varies.
Number of awards: Varies.
Deadline: March 1.
How to apply: Applications are available online.
Exclusive: Visit www.UltimateScholarshipBook.com and enter code AM126023 for updates on this award.

(1261) · American Legion Auxiliary, Department of California $1,000 Scholarships

American Legion Auxiliary, Department of California
401 Van Ness Avenue, Suite 319, San Francisco, CA 94102-4570
Phone: 415-861-5092
Email: calegionaux@calegionaux.org
https://calegionauxiliary.com/resources/scholarships/
Purpose: To provide support to the children of U.S. Armed Forces members.
Eligibility: One of the applicant's parents must have served in the U.S. Armed Forces during an eligible period. Applicants must be California resident high school seniors or graduates who have had to postpone school due to health or financial reasons and plan to attend a California college or university. Applicants must also demonstrate financial need.
Target applicant(s): High school students.
Amount: $1,000.
Number of awards: 4.
Deadline: March.
How to apply: Applications are available online.
Exclusive: Visit www.UltimateScholarshipBook.com and enter code AM126123 for updates on this award.

(1262) · American Legion Auxiliary, Department of California $2,000 Scholarships

American Legion Auxiliary, Department of California
401 Van Ness Avenue, Suite 319, San Francisco, CA 94102-4570
Phone: 415-861-5092
Email: calegionaux@calegionaux.org
https://calegionauxiliary.com/resources/scholarships/
Purpose: To provide support to children of U.S. Armed Forces members.
Eligibility: One of the applicant's parents must have served in the U.S. Armed Forces during an eligible period. Applicants must attend a California college or university, be California resident high school seniors or graduates who have not begun college because of illness or need and demonstrate need.
Target applicant(s): High school students.
Amount: $2,000.
Number of awards: 1.
Deadline: March.
How to apply: Applications are available online.
Exclusive: Visit www.UltimateScholarshipBook.com and enter code AM126223 for updates on this award.

(1263) · American Legion Auxiliary, Department of California $500 Scholarships

American Legion Auxiliary, Department of California
401 Van Ness Avenue, Suite 319, San Francisco, CA 94102-4570
Phone: 415-861-5092
Email: calegionaux@calegionaux.org
https://calegionauxiliary.com/resources/scholarships/
Purpose: To provide support to the children of U.S. Armed Forces members.
Eligibility: One of applicant's parents must have served in the U.S. Armed Forces during an eligible period. Applicants must be California resident high school seniors or graduates who have had to postpone school due to health or financial reasons and plan to attend a California college or university. Applicants must also demonstrate financial need.
Target applicant(s): High school students. College students. Adult students.
Amount: $500.
Number of awards: 3.
Deadline: March 15.
How to apply: Applications are available online.
Exclusive: Visit www.UltimateScholarshipBook.com and enter code AM126323 for updates on this award.

(1264) · American Legion Department of Arkansas High School Oratorical Scholarship Program

American Legion, Department of Arkansas
Department Oratorical Chairman, Roger Lacy, P.O. Box 3280, Little Rock, AR 72203
Phone: 501-375-1104
Email: alegion@swbell.net
http://www.arlegion.org
Purpose: To enhance high school students' experience with and understanding of the U.S. Constitution. The contest will help develop students' leadership skills and civic appreciation, as well as the ability to deliver thoughtful, insightful orations regarding U.S. citizenship and its inherent responsibilities.
Eligibility: Applicants must be high school students under the age of 20 who are U.S. citizens or legal residents and residents of the state. Students first give an oration within their state and winners compete at the national level. The oration must be related to the Constitution of the United States focusing on the duties and obligations citizens have to the government. It must be in English and be between eight and ten minutes. There is also an assigned topic which is posted on the website, and it should be between three and five minutes.
Target applicant(s): High school students.
Amount: $1,000-$2,000.

Number of awards: 3.
Deadline: December 31.
How to apply: Applications are available online.
Exclusive: Visit www.UltimateScholarshipBook.com and enter code AM126423 for updates on this award.

(1265) · American Legion Department of Florida General Scholarship

American Legion, Department of Florida
Elizabeth Douglas, Programs Director, 1912A Lee Road, Orlando, FL 32810
Phone: 800-393-3378
Email: mail@floridalegion.org
https://www.floridalegion.org/programs-services/scholarships/
Purpose: To support descendants of American Legion members and deceased veterans.
Eligibility: Applicants must be direct descendants of American Legion members in good standing or deceased U.S. veterans who would have been eligible for membership. They must be seniors at accredited Florida high schools who plan to pursue undergraduate study upon graduation. Funds must be used within four years of graduation, excluding active military service.
Target applicant(s): High school students.
Amount: $500-$2,500.
Number of awards: 7.
Deadline: March 1.
How to apply: Applications are available online. An application form and copy of documentation of veteran's service are required.
Exclusive: Visit www.UltimateScholarshipBook.com and enter code AM126523 for updates on this award.

(1266) · American Legion Scholarship Award

American Legion - Department of Illinois
2720 East Lincoln Street, Bloomington, IL 61704
Phone: 309-663-0361
Email: hdqs@illegion.org
http://www.illegion.org/scholarships/
Purpose: To award scholarships to graduating students enrolled in Illinois high schools.
Eligibility: Applicants must be children or grandchildren of American Legion Illinois members and must be in their senior year of high school. Awards may be used to further education at an accredited college, university or technical school.
Target applicant(s): High school students.
Amount: Varies.
Number of awards: Varies.
Deadline: March 15.
How to apply: Application information is available by contacting the American Legion, Department of Illinois.
Exclusive: Visit www.UltimateScholarshipBook.com and enter code AM126623 for updates on this award.

(1267) · Americanism and Government Scholarship Program

American Legion, Department of Wisconsin
2930 American Legion Drive, P.O. Box 388, Portage, WI 53901-0388
Phone: 608-745-1090
Email: info@wilegion.org
https://wilegion.org/oratorical-scholarships/
Purpose: To reward outstanding performance on the Americanism and Government Test, a 50-question examination based on state and federal government and history.
Eligibility: Participants must be enrolled in a Wisconsin high school and in their sophomore, junior or senior year.
Target applicant(s): High school students.
Amount: $250-$500.
Number of awards: 45.
Deadline: March 8.
How to apply: Application information is available by contacting your local principal, teacher or guidance counselor.
Exclusive: Visit www.UltimateScholarshipBook.com and enter code AM126723 for updates on this award.

(1268) · Americanism Essay Scholarship

American Legion - Department of Illinois
2720 East Lincoln Street, Bloomington, IL 61704
Phone: 309-663-0361
Email: hdqs@illegion.org
http://www.illegion.org/scholarships/
Purpose: To reward outstanding 500-word essays written on assigned topics.
Eligibility: Applicants must be enrolled in an Illinois school in grades seven to twelve.
Target applicant(s): Junior high students or younger. High school students.
Amount: $100-$1,200.
Number of awards: 15.
Deadline: February 4.
How to apply: Application information is available by contacting the local American Legion Unit or Auxiliary.
Exclusive: Visit www.UltimateScholarshipBook.com and enter code AM126823 for updates on this award.

(1269) · Ann Griffel Scholarship

Iowa Golf Association
Attn: Ann Griffel Scholarship Committee, 1605 North Ankeny Boulevard, Suite 210, Ankeny, IA 50023
Phone: 888-388-4442
Email: info@iowagolf.org
https://iowagolf.org/scholarships/
Purpose: To support girls who have played golf in the state of Iowa.
Eligibility: Applicants must plan to attend an Iowa college, university or trade school. Selection is based on academic performance, extracurricular activities and leadership qualities.
Target applicant(s): High school students.
Amount: $2,000.
Number of awards: Varies.
Deadline: April 1.
How to apply: Applications are sent to all high school girls golf coaches in the state of Iowa at the beginning of the year. The application should be mailed in, along with two letters of recommendation, a high school transcript, a photo and a personal essay.
Exclusive: Visit www.UltimateScholarshipBook.com and enter code IO126923 for updates on this award.

(1270) · Anthony Muñoz Scholarship Fund

Anthony Muñoz Foundation
8919 Rossash Road, Cincinnati, OH 45236

Phone: 513-772-4900
Email: cwillis@munozfoundation.org
https://www.munozfoundation.org/scholarship-fund/
Purpose: To assist Kentucky, Indiana and Ohio students.
Eligibility: Applicants must be high school seniors who reside in the counties specified by the foundation and plan to attend college in Kentucky, Indiana or Ohio. Students must have a minimum ACT composite score of 18 or at least a 2.5 GPA and must demonstrate academic achievement, leadership and financial need.
Target applicant(s): High school students.
Minimum GPA: 2.5
Amount: $20,000.
Number of awards: Up to 7.
Deadline: May.
How to apply: Applications are available online and must be mailed or faxed.
Exclusive: Visit www.UltimateScholarshipBook.com and enter code AN127023 for updates on this award.

(1271) · Antonio Cirino Memorial Award

Rhode Island Foundation
One Union Station, Providence, RI 02903
Phone: 401-274-4564
Email: rbogert@rifoundation.org
https://rifoundation.org/grants-scholarships/browse-scholarships
Purpose: To support Rhode Island students who are pursuing careers in art education.
Eligibility: Applicants must demonstrate an interest in learning about and practicing art. Preference will be given to visual artists. Students must be enrolled or planning to enroll in a master's or doctoral program that will lead to a career in art education.
Target applicant(s): College students. Graduate school students. Adult students.
Amount: $2,000-$12,000.
Number of awards: Varies.
Scholarship may be renewable.
Deadline: April.
How to apply: Applications are available online.
Exclusive: Visit www.UltimateScholarshipBook.com and enter code RH127123 for updates on this award.

(1272) · Arc of Washington State Trust Fund Stipend Award

Arc of Washington State
Attn: Diana Stadden, 2638 State Avenue NE, Olympia, WA 98506
Phone: 360-357-5596
Email: info@arctrustfund.org
http://www.arcwa.org
Purpose: To help students attending school in Alaska, Idaho, Oregon and Washington state who wish to pursue careers working with the developmentally disabled.
Eligibility: Applicants must be undergraduate juniors or above (including graduate-level students) and must be enrolled in a college or university located in Idaho, Washington state, Alaska or Oregon. They must be interested in working with the developmentally disabled. Selection is based on the overall strength of the application.
Target applicant(s): College students. Graduate school students. Adult students.
Amount: Varies.
Number of awards: Varies.

Deadline: March 15.
How to apply: Applications are available online. An application form, official transcripts, personal statement and two letters of recommendation are required.
Exclusive: Visit www.UltimateScholarshipBook.com and enter code AR127223 for updates on this award.

(1273) · Archibald Rutledge Scholarship Program

South Carolina State Department of Education
1429 Senate Street, Columbia, SC 29201
Phone: 803-734-0323
Email: cpower@ed.sc.gov
http://ed.sc.gov
Purpose: To support students who exhibit academic and artistic excellence.
Eligibility: Applicants must be high school seniors in South Carolina public schools, have attended South Carolina public schools for the past two consecutive years and be U.S. citizens. There are five categories: creative writing, dance, music, theater and visual arts. For the creative writing category, a sonnet, lyric or narrative poem no longer than one page must be submitted. For the dance category, an original, short dance composition of three to ten minutes. For the music category, an original composition of three to ten minutes must be submitted. For the theater category, an original one-act play with a performing time of eight to fifteen minutes. For the visual arts category, an original visual composition must be submitted. Compositions are judged on creativity, originality and quality of expression and content.
Target applicant(s): High school students.
Amount: $2,000.
Number of awards: 5.
Deadline: February 22.
How to apply: Applications are available online. An application form, composition and process folio are required.
Exclusive: Visit www.UltimateScholarshipBook.com and enter code SO127323 for updates on this award.

(1274) · Arizona BPW Foundation Annual Scholarships

Arizona Business and Professional Women's Foundation
P.O. Box 32596, Phoenix, AZ 85064
Email: azbpwfoundation@gmail.com
http://www.arizonabpwfoundation.org/
Purpose: To provide education assistance to women.
Eligibility: Applicants must be women who are returning to school to broaden their job prospects at a community college or trade school in Arizona. They must provide a career goal statement, financial need statement, most recent transcript, most recent income tax return and two letters of recommendation.
Target applicant(s): High school students. College students. Adult students.
Amount: Varies.
Number of awards: Varies.
Deadline: June 18.
How to apply: Applications are available online.
Exclusive: Visit www.UltimateScholarshipBook.com and enter code AR127423 for updates on this award.

(1275) · Arizona National Livestock Show Scholarship

Arizona National Livestock Show
1826 W. McDowell Road, Phoenix, AZ 85007
Phone: 602-258-8568

Email: information@anls.org
https://anls.org/
Purpose: To assist students who participate in the Arizona National Livestock Show.
Eligibility: Applicants must be currently taking at least 12 hours and have completed at least 12 semester hours at a college or university and have a minimum 2.5 GPA.
Target applicant(s): College students. Adult students.
Minimum GPA: 2.5
Amount: $40,000 total for all awards.
Number of awards: Up to 20.
Deadline: March 15.
How to apply: Applications are available online.
Exclusive: Visit www.UltimateScholarshipBook.com and enter code AR127523 for updates on this award.

(1276) · Arkansas Cheer Coaches Association Cheer Classics Team of Excellence

Arkansas Cheer Coaches Association
Attn.: Connie Moody, P.O. Box 1654, Heber Springs, AR 72543
http://www.arkansascheercoaches.com
Purpose: To support Arkansas senior cheerleaders who promote a high level of school spirit in the community as they further their education beyond high school.
Eligibility: Applicants must be senior cheerleaders who will be competing in the Cheer Classics put on by the Arkansas Cheer Coaches Association. Selection is based on the two-page essay, community service and three letters of recommendation.
Target applicant(s): High school students.
Amount: Varies.
Number of awards: Varies.
Deadline: March.
How to apply: Applications are available online. In addition to the online form, applicants must submit a two-page essay and three letters of recommendation.
Exclusive: Visit www.UltimateScholarshipBook.com and enter code AR127623 for updates on this award.

(1277) · Arkansas Game and Fish Commission Conservation Scholarship

Arkansas Game and Fish Commission
2 Natural Resources Drive, Little Rock, AR 72205
Phone: 800-364-4263
Email: Shawna.Hitchcock@agfc.ar.gov
http://www.agfc.com
Purpose: To aid Arkansas students preparing for careers in natural resources conservation.
Eligibility: Applicants must be Arkansas residents who are high school seniors or undergraduate or graduate-level college students. They must have a GPA of 2.5 or above and must be planning to pursue a career in natural resources conservation. They cannot have received full scholarship or grant funding from another source. Selection is based on the standardized scoring of each application as a whole.
Target applicant(s): High school students. College students. Graduate school students. Adult students.
Minimum GPA: 2.5
Amount: Up to $2,000 per semester.
Number of awards: Varies.
Scholarship may be renewable.
Deadline: January 15.

How to apply: Applications are available online. An application form, personal statement, essay, official transcript, three personal references, one recommendation letter, photograph and statement of intent to pursue a four-year degree (for those currently attending a two-year institution) are required.
Exclusive: Visit www.UltimateScholarshipBook.com and enter code AR127723 for updates on this award.

(1278) · Arkansas Service Memorial Scholarship Endowment

Arkansas Community Foundation
1400 W. Markham, Suite 206, Little Rock, AR 72201
Phone: 888-220-2723
Email: arcf@arcf.org
http://www.arcf.org
Purpose: To provide financial assistance for students with a parent who died in service to his or her community, state or nation.
Eligibility: Applicants must be Arkansas residents who plan to attend an institution of higher learning in the state. Scholarships are awarded by local Arkansas Community Foundation chapters.
Target applicant(s): High school students. College students. Graduate school students. Adult students.
Amount: $2,500.
Number of awards: Varies.
Scholarship may be renewable.
Deadline: April 1.
How to apply: Applications are available online.
Exclusive: Visit www.UltimateScholarshipBook.com and enter code AR127823 for updates on this award.

(1279) · Art Scholarship

Liberty Graphics
P.O. Box 5, 44 Main Street, Liberty, ME 04949
Phone: 207-589-4596
Email: sales@lgtees.com
http://www.lgtees.com
Purpose: To encourage exploration and expression through traditional visual mediums.
Eligibility: Applicants must be seniors at a Maine high school and be legal residents of Maine. Students must submit artwork, usually with a theme of Maine and the outdoors.
Target applicant(s): High school students.
Amount: $1,000.
Number of awards: 1.
Deadline: April 16.
How to apply: Applications are available from your high school guidance counselor or on the Liberty Graphics website beginning in late February or early March of each year.
Exclusive: Visit www.UltimateScholarshipBook.com and enter code LI127923 for updates on this award.

(1280) · Aspire Award

Tennessee Student Assistance Corporation
404 James Robertson Parkway, Suite 1510, Parkway Towers, Nashville, TN 37243
Phone: 800-342-1663
Email: tsac.aidinfo@tn.gov
https://www.tn.gov/collegepays/financial-aid.html
Purpose: To provide supplemental support to recipients of the Tennessee HOPE Scholarship.

Eligibility: Applicants must be entering freshmen with a minimum ACT score of 21, minimum SAT score of 980 or minimum 3.0 GPA. Home-schooled applicants must have a minimum ACT score of 21 or SAT score of 980. GED applicants must have a minimum GED score of 525 and minimum ACT score of 21 or SAT score of 980. Independent students or the parents of dependent students must have an adjusted gross income under $36,000.

Target applicant(s): High school students.
Minimum GPA: 3.0
Amount: Up to $750 per semester.
Number of awards: Varies.
Deadline: Varies.
How to apply: Applications are available through completion of the FAFSA.
Exclusive: Visit www.UltimateScholarshipBook.com and enter code TE128023 for updates on this award.

(1281) · Associate Degree Nursing Scholarship Program

Office of Statewide Health Planning and Development
Health Professions Education Foundation, 400 R Street, Suite 460, Sacramento, CA 95811-6213
Phone: 916-326-3640
Email: hpef-email@oshpd.ca.gov
https://oshpd.ca.gov/loans-scholarships-grants/scholarships/
Purpose: To increase the number of registered nurses working in medically underserved areas of California.
Eligibility: Applicants must be California residents enrolled in an associate degree nursing program at a California school, have a minimum 2.0 GPA and be fluent in a language other than English. Financial need, work experience, community involvement and academic achievement are considered. Preference is given to those who will graduate within two years and to those who plan to remain in a medically underserved area past the service time required. Recipients must sign a two-year service contract to work in a medically underserved area as an RN.
Target applicant(s): High school students. College students. Adult students.
Minimum GPA: 2.0
Amount: Up to $10,000.
Number of awards: Varies.
Scholarship may be renewable.
Deadline: February 22.
How to apply: Applications are available online.
Exclusive: Visit www.UltimateScholarshipBook.com and enter code OF128123 for updates on this award.

(1282) · Associated General Contractors of Connecticut Scholarships

Connecticut Construction Industries Association
912 Silas Deane Highway, Suite 112, Wethersfield, CT 06109
Phone: 860-529-6855
Email: ccia-info@ctconstruction.org
https://www.ctconstruction.org/i4a/pages/index.cfm?pageid=3559
Purpose: To aid students planning to pursue careers in civil engineering or building and construction technology.
Eligibility: Applicants must be high school seniors who intend to enroll in a four-year civil engineering or construction technology program or who plan to complete a construction program at a two-year institution before entering a four-year institution. They must be U.S. citizens or legal residents and must be interested in a career in construction. Selection is based on academic achievement, level of interest in a construction career, work experience, evaluation forms, extracurricular activities and financial need. The award is for two years.
Target applicant(s): High school students. College students. Adult students.
Amount: $2,500.
Number of awards: Varies.
Deadline: February 28.
How to apply: Applications are available online. An application form, two personal evaluation forms, one faculty evaluation form and an official transcript are required.
Exclusive: Visit www.UltimateScholarshipBook.com and enter code CO128223 for updates on this award.

(1283) · Associated General Contractors of Minnesota Scholarships

Associated General Contractors of Minnesota
Capitol Office Building, 525 Park Street, Suite 110, St. Paul, MN 55103-2186
Phone: 651-632-8929
Email: mbeckmann@agcmn.org
http://www.agcmn.org
Purpose: To support outstanding students in Minnesota.
Eligibility: Applicants must attend a Minnesota institution of higher learning with a concentration in construction or construction-related courses. Applications are judged equally on academic performance, career objectives, financial need, personal information and application clarity.
Target applicant(s): College students. Adult students.
Amount: $500-$2,500.
Number of awards: 5-8.
Deadline: May 21.
How to apply: Applications are available online. An application form, personal statement, academic core plan, career objectives and recent color photo are required.
Exclusive: Visit www.UltimateScholarshipBook.com and enter code AS128323 for updates on this award.

(1284) · ASWA Seattle Chapter Scholarship

American Society of Women Accountants - Seattle Chapter
800 Fifth Avenue, Suite 101, PMB 237, Seattle, WA 98104-3191
Phone: 206-467-8645
Email: scholarship@aswaseattle.org
http://seattleafwa.org/scholarships/
Purpose: To aid accounting students in Washington state.
Eligibility: Applicants must be part-time or full-time accounting students at an accredited postsecondary institution located in Washington state. Students must have finished at least 30 semester hours (or 45 quarter hours) within four weeks of the application deadline. They must have an overall GPA of 2.0 or higher. The scholarship is open to both male and female students. Selection is based on GPA, stated career goals and financial need.
Target applicant(s): College students. Graduate school students. Adult students.
Minimum GPA: 2.0
Amount: Varies.
Number of awards: Varies.
Deadline: April 30.
How to apply: Applications are available online. An application form, an official transcript, two recommendation letters and financial aid transcripts are required.
Exclusive: Visit www.UltimateScholarshipBook.com and enter code AM128423 for updates on this award.

(1285) · Atsuhiko Tateuchi Memorial Scholarship

Seattle Foundation
1200 Fifth Avenue, Suite 1300, Seattle, WA 98101-3151
Phone: 206-515-2119
Email: scholarships@seattlefoundation.org
http://www.seattlefoundation.org
Purpose: To provide financial assistance for hard-working students from the Pacific Rim states.
Eligibility: Applicants must be high school seniors or undergraduate students from Washington, Oregon, California, Hawaii or Alaska with demonstrated financial need. They must have a GPA of 3.0 or higher. Preference is given to students with Japanese or other Asian ancestry.
Target applicant(s): High school students. College students. Adult students.
Minimum GPA: 3.0
Amount: $5,000.
Number of awards: 10.
Scholarship may be renewable.
Deadline: March 1.
How to apply: Applications are available online.
Exclusive: Visit www.UltimateScholarshipBook.com and enter code SE128523 for updates on this award.

(1286) · AWAF Scholarships

Association for Women in Architecture Foundation
1315 Storm Parkway, Torrance
Phone: 310-534-8466
Email: scholarships@awaplus
https://www.awaplusd.org/a
Purpose: To support wome
Eligibility: Applicants mus
a California school and mu
architecture, landscape a
interior design or enviro
completed a minimum
due date. The award is
need, recommendation
Target applicant(s): C
students.
Amount: Varies.
Number of awards:
Deadline: March 1
How to apply: Ap
Exclusive: Visit w
AS128623 for up

(1287) · Bac
Program

Office of State
Health Profes
Sacramento,
Phone: 916-
Email: hpef
https://osh
Purpose:
medically
attending
Eligibili
nursing
Financi

involvement are considered. A two-year service agreement to work in a medically underserved area of California is required. Preference is given to those who expect to graduate within two years and to those who plan to remain in a medically underserved area after the service agreement has expired. Applicant must have minimum 2.0 GPA.
Target applicant(s): College students. Adult students.
Minimum GPA: 2.0
Amount: Up to $13,000.
Number of awards: Varies.
Scholarship may be renewable.
Deadline: February 23.
How to apply: Applications are available online.
Exclusive: Visit www.UltimateScholarshipBook.com and enter code OF128723 for updates on this award.

(1288) · BAFTX Graduate Scholarship

British American Foundation of Texas
Email: info@baftx.org
http://www.baftx.org
Purpose: To support graduate students from Texas or the UK pursuing STEM education.
Eligibility: Applicants must be residents of Texas enrolled as full-time graduate students within the Texas or U.K. education system with demonstrated financial need. Students must be 21 years or older majoring in STEM or business with a GPA of 3.25 or higher.
Target applicant(s): College students. Graduate school students. Adult students.
Minimum GPA: 3.25
Amount: Varies.
Number of awards: 1.
Deadline: March 31.
How to apply: Applications are available online.
Exclusive: Visit www.UltimateScholarshipBook.com and enter code ... for updates on this award.

(1289) · BAFTX Undergraduate Award

British American Foundation of Texas
Email: info@baftx.org
http://www.baftx.org
Purpose: To help offset the cost of higher education for Texas or United Kingdom residents.
Eligibility: Applicants must be residents of Texas or the United Kingdom enrolled as full-time students within Texas or the U.K. and demonstrate financial need. Students must be pursuing a major in science, technology, engineering, math or business and have a minimum GPA of 3.25. Applicants must be able to interview and attend an awards
Target applicant(s): High school students. College students. Adult students.
Minimum GPA: 3.25
Amount: Varies.
Number of awards: 1.
Deadline: March 31.
How to apply: Applications are available online.
Exclusive: Visit www.UltimateScholarshipBook.com and enter code AR128923 for updates on this award.

(1290) · Beginning Teacher Scholarships

Texas Retired Teachers Foundation
Attn: Scholarship Committee, 313 E. 12th Street, Suite 220, Austin, TX 78701
Phone: 512-476-1622
Email: info@trtf.org
https://trtf.org/TRTF/TRTF_INITIATIVES/TRTF/Initiatives/Initiatives.aspx
Purpose: To assist Texas students whose relatives are members of the Texas Retired Teachers Association.
Eligibility: Applicants must be relatives of an active member of the Texas Retired Teachers Association (TRTA), earning or earned a bachelor's or master's degree in education and pursuing or have pursued their teaching certification exam.
Target applicant(s): High school students. College students. Graduate school students. Adult students.
Amount: $750.
Number of awards: 10.
Deadline: February 25.
How to apply: Applications are available online.
Exclusive: Visit www.UltimateScholarshipBook.com and enter code TE129023 for updates on this award.

(1291) · Ben and Vicky Cayetano Scholarship Fund

Hawaii Community Foundation - Scholarships
827 Fort Street Mall, Honolulu, HI 96813
Phone: 888-731-3863
Email: scholarships@hcf-hawaii.org
https://www.hawaiicommunityfoundation.org/
Purpose: To support exceptional Hawaii students.
Eligibility: Applicants must be upcoming high school graduates in Hawaii. They must have a GPA of 3.5 or higher. Preference is given to students who have overcome financial and social obstacles and to the students with the greatest financial need.
Target applicant(s): High school students.
Minimum GPA: 3.5
Amount: Varies.
Number of awards: Varies.
Deadline: January 31.
How to apply: Applications are available online. An application form, personal statement, copy of FAFSA Student Aid Report, transcript, two letters of recommendation and an essay are required.
Exclusive: Visit www.UltimateScholarshipBook.com and enter code HA129123 for updates on this award.

(1292) · Ben W. Fortson, Jr., Scholarship

Surveying and Mapping Society of Georgia
P.O. Box 113, LaGrange, GA 30241
Phone: 770-947-1767
Email: ginger_samsog@att.net
https://www.samsog.org
Purpose: To help Georgia undergraduate land surveying students.
Eligibility: Applicants must be Georgia residents enrolled in an undergraduate land surveying program of study at an accredited institution of higher learning. They must have completed at least 20 percent of their program requirements before receiving any scholarship monies awarded. Students must also maintain a 2.4 overall GPA and 2.7 GPA in surveying courses. Preference is given to full-time students seeking a bachelor's degree. Selection is based on the overall strength of the application.

Target applicant(s): College students. Adult students.
Minimum GPA: 2.4
Amount: $3,000.
Number of awards: 1.
Deadline: June 30.
How to apply: Applications are available online. An application form and transcript are required.
Exclusive: Visit www.UltimateScholarshipBook.com and enter code SU129223 for updates on this award.

(1293) · Better Business Bureau of Delaware Foundation Student Ethics Scholarship

Better Business Bureau (BBB) of Delaware Education Foundation
Attn.: Scholarship Committee, 60 Reads Way, New Castle, DE 19720
Phone: 302-221-5259
Email: csauers@delaware.bbb.org
http://www.bbb.org/delaware/
Purpose: To assist Delaware high school seniors who exemplify high ethics.
Eligibility: Applicants must demonstrate leadership, community service, personal integrity and academic strength and must plan to attend an accredited college or university. A minimum GPA of 3.0 is required of applicants.
Target applicant(s): High school students.
Minimum GPA: 3.0
Amount: $2,500.
Number of awards: 2.
Deadline: January 12.
How to apply: Applicants must be nominated by an employee or owner of a company that is accredited by the BBB. An application form, two letters of recommendation, an essay, supporting documentation, a copy of the transcript and certification by sponsor to the BBB are required.
Exclusive: Visit www.UltimateScholarshipBook.com and enter code BE129323 for updates on this award.

(1294) · Betty Bacon Memorial Scholarship

California Association on Postsecondary Education and Disability (CAPED)
10073 Valley View Street, #242, Cypress, CA 90630
Phone: 562-397-2810
Email: caped.scholarship.committee@gmail.com
http://www.caped.co/scholarships/
Purpose: To support students with a learning disability who are pursuing higher education.
Eligibility: Applicants must have a verifiable learning disability and be currently enrolled as a student at a four-year California college or university with a GPA of 2.5 for undergraduates or 3.0 for graduate students. Students must have completed at least six semester or eight quarter units as an undergraduate student or three semester or four quarter units as an graduate student.
Target applicant(s): College students. Graduate school students. Adult students.
Minimum GPA: 2.5 for undergraduate students, 3.0 for graduate students
Amount: $1,000.
Number of awards: 1.
Deadline: August 31.
How to apply: Applications are available online.

Exclusive: Visit www.UltimateScholarshipBook.com and enter code CA129423 for updates on this award.

(1295) · Bick Bickson Scholarship Fund

Hawaii Community Foundation - Scholarships
827 Fort Street Mall, Honolulu, HI 96813
Phone: 888-731-3863
Email: scholarships@hcf-hawaii.org
https://www.hawaiicommunityfoundation.org/
Purpose: To support students pursuing studies in marketing, law or travel.
Eligibility: Applicants must be residents of Hawaii who have need of financial assistance and plan to attend an accredited college or university full-time within the United States as an undergraduate or graduate student. Students must have a 3.0 GPA and plan to major in one of the following areas: marketing, law or travel industry management.
Target applicant(s): High school students. College students. Graduate school students. Adult students.
Minimum GPA: 3.0
Amount: Varies.
Number of awards: Varies.
Deadline: January 31.
How to apply: Applications are available online.
Exclusive: Visit www.UltimateScholarshipBook.com and enter code HA129523 for updates on this award.

(1296) · Big Y Scholarship Programs

Big Y
Scholarship Committee, P.O. Box 7840, Springfield, MA 01102-7840
Phone: 413-504-4047
Email: scholarship@bigy.com
http://www.bigy.com
Purpose: To reward students in the Big Y market area and those affiliated with Big Y.
Eligibility: Applicants must either be Big Y employees or their dependents or must reside or attend school in western or central Massachusetts, Norfolk County, Massachusetts or Connecticut. The scholarships are available to high school seniors, undergraduates, graduates, community college students and adult students. Applicants should submit transcripts, college entrance exams scores and two recommendation letters. Big Y employees must submit one recommendation from their supervisor. Selection is based on achievements, awards, community involvement, leadership positions and class rank. Eight scholarships are available specifically for dependents of law enforcement officers and firefighters.
Target applicant(s): High school students. College students. Graduate school students. Adult students.
Amount: Varies.
Number of awards: 300.
Deadline: February 1.
How to apply: Applications are available at any Big Y location from October through January each year. Applications are also available at guidance offices of schools within Big Y's market area.
Exclusive: Visit www.UltimateScholarshipBook.com and enter code BI129623 for updates on this award.

(1297) · Bill Teegins Memorial Scholarship

Oklahoma Association of Broadcasters
6520 N. Western, Suite 104, Oklahoma City, OK 73116
Phone: 405-848-0771
Email: struby@oabok.org
https://oabok.org/careerseducation/scholarships/
Purpose: To support students majoring in broadcasting at Oklahoma colleges and universities.
Eligibility: Applicants must be enrolled in an Oklahoma college or university broadcasting program, be majoring in broadcasting and have an intent to enter the broadcasting career upon graduation. Students must be a junior or senior for the upcoming school year and must maintain a "B" average.
Target applicant(s): College students. Adult students.
Minimum GPA: 3.0
Amount: $2,000.
Number of awards: 1.
Deadline: February 4.
How to apply: Applications are available online.
Exclusive: Visit www.UltimateScholarshipBook.com and enter code OK129723 for updates on this award.

(1298) · Blossom Kalama Evans Memorial Scholarship Fund

Hawaii Community Foundation - Scholarships
827 Fort Street Mall, Honolulu, HI 96813
Phone: 888-731-3863
Email: scholarships@hcf-hawaii.org
https://www.hawaiicommunityfoundation.org/
Purpose: To support students who are dedicated to serving the native Hawaiian community.
Eligibility: Applicants must be of Hawaiian ancestry, have at least a 2.7 GPA and must be a college junior, college senior or graduate student.
Target applicant(s): College students. Graduate school students. Adult students.
Minimum GPA: 2.7
Amount: Varies.
Number of awards: Varies.
Deadline: January 31.
How to apply: To apply, register online, complete the online application and select the scholarships to which you wish to apply. In addition, mail the supporting materials: printed confirmation page from the online application, personal statement, copy of Student Aid Report (SAR) available at www.fafsa.ed.gov and official transcript.
Exclusive: Visit www.UltimateScholarshipBook.com and enter code HA129823 for updates on this award.

(1299) · Bob C. Powers Scholarship

North Texas Fair and Rodeo
2217 N. Carroll Boulevard, Denton, TX 76201
Phone: 940-387-2632
Email: nkimmey@ntfair.com
http://www.ntfair.com/p/get-involved/195
Purpose: To support graduating high school seniors by investing in their future.
Eligibility: Applicants must be a high school senior and involved in school, their community and FFA, FHA or 4-H activities. Selection is based on academic achievement, extracurricular activities and financial need.
Target applicant(s): High school students.
Amount: $2,000.
Number of awards: 1.
Deadline: June 1.

How to apply: Applications are available online and must include two letters of recommendation and two photos.

Exclusive: Visit www.UltimateScholarshipBook.com and enter code NO129923 for updates on this award.

(1300) · Bob Eddy Scholarship Program

Connecticut Society of Professional Journalists
Attn: Paul Singley, P.O. Box 5071, Woodbridge, CT 06525
Phone: 212-683-5700 x364
Email: psingley@ctspj.org
http://connecticutspj.org/
Purpose: To support students interested in journalism careers.
Eligibility: Applicants must be rising college juniors or seniors at a four-year college and Connecticut residents or students of Connecticut schools. They should be able to submit samples of work that shows interest and competency in journalism.
Target applicant(s): College students. Adult students.
Amount: $1,000-$2,500.
Number of awards: 4.
Deadline: April 25.
How to apply: Applications are available online. An application form, transcript, essay and writing samples, tapes or related work in any media are required.
Exclusive: Visit www.UltimateScholarshipBook.com and enter code CO130023 for updates on this award.

(1301) · Bob Stevens Memorial Scholarship

Garden State Scholastic Press Foundation
New Jersey Press Foundation, 840 Bear Tavern Road, Suite 305, West Trenton, NJ 08628-1019
Email: scholarship@gsspa.org
http://www.gsspa.org
Purpose: To support high school journalism students.
Eligibility: Applicants must be graduating New Jersey high school seniors who are nominated by a GSSPA member, have a GPA of 3.0 or higher and have participated in high school journalism for at least two years.
Target applicant(s): High school students.
Minimum GPA: 3.0
Amount: $1,500.
Number of awards: 1.
Deadline: February 7.
How to apply: Applications are available online. An application form, transcript, three or four letters of recommendation and portfolio with work samples are required.
Exclusive: Visit www.UltimateScholarshipBook.com and enter code GA130123 for updates on this award.

(1302) · Boeing Company STEM Scholarship

Independent Colleges of Washington
600 Stewart Street, Suite 600, Seattle, WA 98101
Phone: 206-623-4494
Email: info@icwashington.org
https://icwashington.org/page/scholarships
Purpose: To assist students attending independent Washington colleges.
Eligibility: Applicants must be a junior or senior enrolled at an ICW member institution at the time of the award and be involved with community service. A GPA of 3.25 is required and applicants must be majoring in science, technology, engineering, mathematics, a health care field or be preparing to teach in a STEM field.

Target applicant(s): College students. Adult students.
Minimum GPA: 3.25
Amount: $2,500.
Number of awards: 1.
Deadline: March.
How to apply: Applications are available online. An application form, resume, essay, letter of recommendation and transcript are required.
Exclusive: Visit www.UltimateScholarshipBook.com and enter code IN130223 for updates on this award.

(1303) · Boettcher Foundation Scholarship

Boettcher Foundation
600 Seventeenth Street, Suite 2210 South, Denver, CO 80202-5422
Phone: 800-323-9640
Email: scholarships@boettcherfoundation.org
http://boettcherfoundation.org/
Purpose: To recognize dynamic thinkers, doers, and difference makers and encourage them to stay in Colorado for their education so they can positively impact their communities across our state.
Eligibility: Applicants must be graduating Colorado high school seniors who have lived in Colorado for their full junior and senior years of high school, graduates from a Colorado high school and be citizens, legal permanent residents or lawfully present in the United States or meet the requirements and have applied or started the process of applying for citizenship, legal status or lawful presence. They should submit applications, essays, transcripts and standardized test scores. Selection is based on academic merit, intellectual curiosity, demonstration of leadership skills, community service and character.
Target applicant(s): High school students.
Amount: Full tuition.
Number of awards: 50.
Scholarship may be renewable.
Deadline: November 1.
How to apply: Contact high school counselors for more information.
Exclusive: Visit www.UltimateScholarshipBook.com and enter code BO130323 for updates on this award.

(1304) · Bohdan Kolinsky Memorial Sports Journalism Scholarship

Connecticut Sports Writers Alliance
P.O. Box 70, Unionville, CT 06085-0070
Phone: 860-677-0087
Email: rbrtbarton@aol.com
http://www.ctsportswriters.com/
Purpose: To aid aspiring sports journalists.
Eligibility: Applicants must be Connecticut high school seniors, be admitted to an accredited four-year college and plan to pursue studies leading to a career in sports journalism. Students who meet academic standards can receive additional aid.
Target applicant(s): High school students.
Amount: $2,000.
Number of awards: 1.
Scholarship may be renewable.
Deadline: February 19.
How to apply: Applications are available online. An application form, essay, summary of academic and employment history, evidence of good academic standing, letter of recommendation and three samples of published work are required.
Exclusive: Visit www.UltimateScholarshipBook.com and enter code CO130423 for updates on this award.

(1305) · Booz Allen Hawaii Scholarship Fund

Hawaii Community Foundation - Scholarships
827 Fort Street Mall, Honolulu, HI 96813
Phone: 888-731-3863
Email: scholarships@hcf-hawaii.org
https://www.hawaiicommunityfoundation.org/
Purpose: To support undergraduate students in Hawaii.
Eligibility: Students must be residents of Hawaii or dependents of military members stationed there. Applicants must be attending or planning to attend a four-year college or university. Students must have at least a 3.0 GPA.
Target applicant(s): High school students. College students. Adult students.
Minimum GPA: 3.0
Amount: Varies.
Number of awards: Varies.
Deadline: January 31.
How to apply: To apply, register online, complete the online application and select the scholarships to which you wish to apply. In addition, mail the supporting materials: printed confirmation page from the online application, personal statement, copy of Student Aid Report (SAR) available at www.fafsa.ed.gov and official transcript.
Exclusive: Visit www.UltimateScholarshipBook.com and enter code HA130523 for updates on this award.

(1306) · Boy Scout and Eagle Scout Scholarship

American Legion, Department of Illinois
P.O. Box 2910, Bloomington, IL 61702-2910
Phone: 309-663-0361
Email: hdqs@illegion.org
http://www.illegion.org/scholarships/
Purpose: To reward a member of the Boy Scouts with a one-year scholarship.
Eligibility: Applicants must be graduating seniors in high school, Senior Boy Scouts or Explorers and residents of Illinois. Students must write an essay on Americanism and/or Boy Scout programs.
Target applicant(s): High school students.
Amount: $1,000.
Number of awards: 3.
Deadline: April 15.
How to apply: Application information is available by contacting your local Boy Scout office or American Legion Scout Chairman.
Exclusive: Visit www.UltimateScholarshipBook.com and enter code AM130623 for updates on this award.

(1307) · BPW/Maine Career Advancement Scholarship

Futurama Foundation
c/o Marilyn Ladd, Office Manager, 103 County Road, Oakland, ME 04963
Email: mvladd@colby.edu
http://bpwmefoundation.org/scholarship-program/
Purpose: To provide financial assistance for women who want to advance their careers.
Eligibility: Applicants must be female Maine residents who are age 30 or older. They must need financial assistance to improve their skills or complete education for career advancement. They must have a definite plan to use their training to improve their chances of advancement, train for a new career or to enter or reenter the job market. Applicants must be officially accepted into their course of study or program.

Target applicant(s): College students. Adult students.
Amount: $1,200.
Number of awards: 1.
Deadline: April 13.
How to apply: Applications are available from your local BPW chapter or your financial aid office.
Exclusive: Visit www.UltimateScholarshipBook.com and enter code FU130723 for updates on this award.

(1308) · Business and Professional Women of Kentucky Foundation Grant

Kentucky Federation of Business and Professional Women
c/o Joanne Story, BPW/KY Foundation Scholarship Chair, 380 Beauchamp Boulevard, Somerset, KY 42503
Phone: 606-875-3200
Email: joanne.story@kctcs.edu
http://bpw-ky.org/
Purpose: To promote economic self-sufficiency for Kentucky women.
Eligibility: Applicants must be Kentucky residents who are at least 18 years of age. They must be employed or planning a career in the Kentucky workforce and attending an institution of higher learning. Individuals may receive a grant no more than once every 24 months.
Target applicant(s): High school students. College students. Adult students.
Amount: Varies.
Number of awards: Varies.
Deadline: April 30 and October 15.
How to apply: Applications are available online.
Exclusive: Visit www.UltimateScholarshipBook.com and enter code KE130823 for updates on this award.

(1309) · Business and Professional Women/Maine Continuing Education Scholarship

Futurama Foundation
c/o Marilyn Ladd, Office Manager, 103 County Road, Oakland, ME 04963
Email: mvladd@colby.edu
http://bpwmefoundation.org/scholarship-program/
Purpose: To provide financial assistance to female students.
Eligibility: Applicants must be Maine residents who have completed at least one year of college or will have done so by the end of the spring semester following application. They must be in good standing or on an approved leave of absence of one year or less at their educational institution. Financial need is required, and the student must have a definite plan to complete the program in which she is enrolled.
Target applicant(s): College students. Adult students.
Amount: $1,500.
Number of awards: 1.
Deadline: April 13.
How to apply: Applications are available online.
Exclusive: Visit www.UltimateScholarshipBook.com and enter code FU130923 for updates on this award.

(1310) · Byers Scholarship

Keep Iowa Beautiful
300 E. Locust Street, Suite 100, Des Moines, IA 50309
Phone: 515-323-6507
https://keepiowabeautiful.org/grants-scholarships/
Purpose: To support Iowa high school seniors.

Eligibility: Applicants must be graduating high school seniors in Iowa who plan to enroll in an Iowa college or university to study environmental science, community development, landscape architecture, architecture, community planning or marketing and communications.
Target applicant(s): High school students.
Amount: $1,000.
Number of awards: 5.
Deadline: February 11.
How to apply: Applications are available online.
Exclusive: Visit www.UltimateScholarshipBook.com and enter code KE131023 for updates on this award.

(1311) · C. Bertrand and Marian Othmer Schultz Collegiate Scholarship

Nebraska Academy of Sciences Inc.
P.O. Box 22988, Lincoln, NE 68542-2988
Phone: 402-472-2644
Email: nebacad@unl.edu
https://nebraskaacademyofsciences.wildapricot.org/Scholarships
Purpose: To assist Nebraska college students who are majoring in a natural science.
Eligibility: Applicants must be sophomores or juniors who attend a four-year, accredited college or university in Nebraska and major in a natural science including chemistry, physics, biology or geology. Students must plan to enter a career in a science-related industry, science teaching or scientific research.
Target applicant(s): College students. Adult students.
Amount: $1,500.
Number of awards: 2.
Deadline: February 1.
How to apply: Applications are available online. A letter of nomination, transcript and letter describing the applicant's career plans are available.
Exclusive: Visit www.UltimateScholarshipBook.com and enter code NE131123 for updates on this award.

(1312) · Cal Grant A

California Student Aid Commission
Specialized Programs Operations Branch - Chafee, P.O. Box 419029, Rancho Cordova, CA 95741-9029
Phone: 888-224-7268
Email: studentsupport@csac.ca.gov
http://www.csac.ca.gov/
Purpose: To assist California students in obtaining higher education.
Eligibility: Applicants must be California residents who are attending or plan to attend an eligible California college or university pursuing at least two years of coursework. They must enroll for no less than half time and meet program income requirements. They may not have already earned a bachelor's degree or higher, and they must not be in default on a student loan or owe a grant repayment without having made satisfactory arrangements for repayment. Students with a GPA of 3.0 or higher who meet all requirements will receive an entitlement award, and students with a GPA of at least 2.4 may apply for a competitive award.
Target applicant(s): High school students. College students. Adult students.
Minimum GPA: 2.4
Amount: Varies.
Number of awards: Varies.
Scholarship may be renewable.
Deadline: March 2.
How to apply: Application materials are available online. A FAFSA and a GPA verification form are required.

346

Exclusive: Visit www.UltimateScholarshipBook.com and enter code CA131223 for updates on this award.

(1313) · Cal Grant B

California Student Aid Commission
Specialized Programs Operations Branch - Chafee, P.O. Box 419029, Rancho Cordova, CA 95741-9029
Phone: 888-224-7268
Email: studentsupport@csac.ca.gov
http://www.csac.ca.gov/
Purpose: To provide living expense, tuition and fee assistance for low-income students.
Eligibility: Applicants must be California residents with financial need for attendance at an eligible California college or university. They must enroll for at least half time. A minimum GPA of 2.0 is required. Students who meet financial and eligibility requirements will receive a Cal Grant B entitlement award. Other eligible students can apply for a Cal Grant B competitive award. Competitive award selection is based on family income, education level of parents, GPA, time out of high school and special considerations.
Target applicant(s): High school students. College students. Adult students.
Minimum GPA: 2.0
Amount: Varies.
Number of awards: Varies.
Scholarship may be renewable.
Deadline: March 2.
How to apply: Application materials are available online. A FAFSA and a GPA verification form are required.
Exclusive: Visit www.UltimateScholarshipBook.com and enter code CA131323 for updates on this award.

(1314) · Cal Grant C

California Student Aid Commission
Specialized Programs Operations Branch - Chafee, P.O. Box 419029, Rancho Cordova, CA 95741-9029
Phone: 888-224-7268
Email: studentsupport@csac.ca.gov
http://www.csac.ca.gov/
Purpose: To aid students participating in occupational and vocational programs.
Eligibility: Applicants must be California residents. They must enroll in a vocational program at a California community college, independent college or vocational school that is at least four months long. Funds may be received for up to two years. Eligible students will receive an application by mail from the California Student Aid Commission.
Target applicant(s): High school students. College students. Adult students.
Amount: Varies.
Number of awards: Varies.
Scholarship may be renewable.
Deadline: March 2.
How to apply: Applications are available by mail. A FAFSA and an application form are required.
Exclusive: Visit www.UltimateScholarshipBook.com and enter code CA131423 for updates on this award.

(1315) · Cal Grant Entitlement Award

California Student Aid Commission
Specialized Programs Operations Branch - Chafee, P.O. Box 419029, Rancho Cordova, CA 95741-9029
Phone: 888-224-7268
Email: studentsupport@csac.ca.gov
http://www.csac.ca.gov/
Purpose: To support California resident students.
Eligibility: Applicants must complete the Free Application for Federal Student Aid (FAFSA) and file a verified grade point average with the California Student Aid Commission. Students must be California residents, be U.S. citizens or eligible noncitizens, meet U.S. Selective Service requirements, attend an eligible California postsecondary institution, be enrolled at least half-time, maintain satisfactory academic progress and not be in default on any student loan. Cal Grant A Entitlement Awards are for undergraduate institutions of not less than two academic years. Cal Grant B Entitlement Awards are for low-income students for living and transportation expenses, supplies and books at institutions of not less than one year. Cal Grant C Awards are for occupational or vocational programs. Cal Grant T Awards are for teacher credential candidates.
Target applicant(s): High school students. College students. Adult students.
Amount: Varies.
Number of awards: Varies.
Deadline: March 2.
How to apply: Applications are available by request.
Exclusive: Visit www.UltimateScholarshipBook.com and enter code CA131523 for updates on this award.

(1316) · California - Hawaii Elks Major Project Undergraduate Scholarship Program for Students with Disabilities

California-Hawaii Elks Association
5450 E. Lamona Avenue, Fresno, CA 93727-2224
Phone: 559-255-4531
Email: chea@chea-elks.org
https://chea-elks.org/youth-activities/scholarships
Purpose: To provide education assistance for students with disabilities.
Eligibility: Applicants must be U.S. citizens and California or Hawaii residents who have a physical, neurological, visual or hearing impairment or a speech/language disorder. They must be high school seniors or graduates or have passed the GED or California High School Proficiency Examination.
Target applicant(s): High school students.
Amount: $1,000-$3,000.
Number of awards: 20-30.
Scholarship may be renewable.
Deadline: March 15.
How to apply: Applications are available online.
Exclusive: Visit www.UltimateScholarshipBook.com and enter code CA131623 for updates on this award.

(1317) · California Council of the Blind Scholarships

California Council of the Blind
2143 Hurley Way, Suite 250, Sacramento, CA 95825
Phone: 510-537-7877
Email: ccotb@ccbnet.org
http://ccbnet.org/drupal7/
Purpose: To assist blind California residents for college, graduate or vocational studies.
Eligibility: Applicants must be legally blind residents of California attending an accredited college, university or vocational school full-time or with at least 12 units per term. The school does not have to be in California. Proof of blindness is required. A letter from the local chapter's president or member recommending the applicant is helpful. Award money can't be spent on food, clothing or shelter.
Target applicant(s): College students. Graduate school students. Adult students.
Amount: Varies.
Number of awards: Varies.
Scholarship may be renewable.
Deadline: July 15.
How to apply: Applications are available online.
Exclusive: Visit www.UltimateScholarshipBook.com and enter code CA131723 for updates on this award.

(1318) · California Fee Waiver Program for Children of Veterans

California Department of Veterans Affairs
1227 O Street, Sacramento, CA 95814
Phone: 800-952-5626
https://www.calvet.ca.gov
Purpose: To provide educational assistance for dependents of veterans.
Eligibility: Applicants must be the children, spouses, unmarried surviving spouses or registered domestic partners of veterans who are deceased or totally disabled due to service-related causes. The veteran must have served during a qualifying war period, and the child must be under 27 years of age (30 if the child is a veteran). There is no age limit for spouses or domestic partners. Children of veterans who have a service-connected disability, had one at the time of death or died of service-related causes may qualify if their income is at or below the national poverty level. In this case, there is no age limit.
Target applicant(s): High school students. College students. Adult students.
Amount: Full tuition.
Number of awards: Varies.
Scholarship may be renewable.
Deadline: Varies.
How to apply: Applications are available online.
Exclusive: Visit www.UltimateScholarshipBook.com and enter code CA131823 for updates on this award.

(1319) · California Fee Waiver Program for Dependents of Deceased or Disabled National Guard Members

California Department of Veterans Affairs
1227 O Street, Sacramento, CA 95814
Phone: 800-952-5626
https://www.calvet.ca.gov
Purpose: To provide education assistance to dependents of deceased or disabled National Guard members.
Eligibility: Applicants must be dependents or surviving spouses or domestic partners of California National Guard members who were killed or permanently disabled during active duty in service to the state. Spouses or domestic partners must not have remarried or terminated the relationship.
Target applicant(s): High school students. College students. Adult students.

Amount: Full tuition.
Number of awards: Varies.
Scholarship may be renewable.
Deadline: Varies.
How to apply: Applications are available online.
Exclusive: Visit www.UltimateScholarshipBook.com and enter code CA131923 for updates on this award.

(1320) · California Fee Waiver Program for Recipients of the Medal of Honor and Their Children

California Department of Veterans Affairs
1227 O Street, Sacramento, CA 95814
Phone: 800-952-5626
https://www.calvet.ca.gov
Purpose: To provide financial assistance for Medal of Honor recipients and their families.
Eligibility: Applicants must be Medal of Honor recipients, their children or dependents of a Registered Domestic Partner. Children must meet age, income and residency requirements. This award is only applicable toward undergraduate studies.
Target applicant(s): High school students. College students. Adult students.
Amount: Full tuition.
Number of awards: Varies.
Scholarship may be renewable.
Deadline: Varies.
How to apply: Applications are available online.
Exclusive: Visit www.UltimateScholarshipBook.com and enter code CA132023 for updates on this award.

(1321) · California Freethought Day High School Essay Scholarship

California Freethought Day
P.O. Box 15464, Sacramento, CA 95851
Phone: 209-610-0651
Email: chair@freethoughtday.org
http://freethoughtday.org/essay.html
Purpose: To encourage California students to pursue reason.
Eligibility: Applicants must be California high school students in grades 9 -12 who plan to pursue post-secondary education. Students must demonstrate involvement in community organizations and school clubs and have an interest in free speech, science and the separation of church and state. Applicants must write an essay pertaining to fake news.
Target applicant(s): High school students.
Amount: $1,000.
Number of awards: 1.
Deadline: September 16.
How to apply: Applications are available online.
Exclusive: Visit www.UltimateScholarshipBook.com and enter code CA132123 for updates on this award.

(1322) · California Law Enforcement Personnel Dependents Grant Program

California Student Aid Commission
Specialized Programs Operations Branch - Chafee, P.O. Box 419029, Rancho Cordova, CA 95741-9029
Phone: 888-224-7268
Email: studentsupport@csac.ca.gov
http://www.csac.ca.gov/

Purpose: To provide assistance for the families of deceased or disabled law enforcement personnel.
Eligibility: Applicants must be spouses or children of California peace officers, Department of Corrections or Youth Authority employees or full-time firefighters who were killed or totally disabled due to accident or injury in the line of duty. They must enroll at an accredited California community college, college or university for a minimum of six units. Financial need is required. Awards match the amount of a Cal Grant award.
Target applicant(s): High school students. College students. Adult students.
Amount: $100-$12,192.
Number of awards: Varies.
Scholarship may be renewable.
Deadline: Rolling.
How to apply: Applications are available by mail or phone. An application form, copy of FAFSA Student Aid Report and documentation of the law enforcement personnel's death or injury are required.
Exclusive: Visit www.UltimateScholarshipBook.com and enter code CA132223 for updates on this award.

(1323) · California Masonic Foundation Scholarship

California Masonic Foundation
1111 California Street, San Francisco, CA 94108-2284
Phone: 415-776-7000
Email: foundation@californiamasons.org
https://freemason.org/masonic-charities/scholarships/
Purpose: To aid students in pursuit of a higher education.
Eligibility: Applicants must be U.S. citizens, be California residents for at least one year, be current high school seniors with a minimum 3.0 GPA, plan to attend an accredited two- or four-year college or university full-time and demonstrate financial need. There are a number of awards based on residence, career goals and general selection criteria.
Target applicant(s): High school students.
Minimum GPA: 3.0
Amount: Varies.
Number of awards: Varies.
Scholarship may be renewable.
Deadline: Varies.
How to apply: Applications are available online.
Exclusive: Visit www.UltimateScholarshipBook.com and enter code CA132323 for updates on this award.

(1324) · California Oratorical Contest

American Legion, Department of California
1601 7th Street, Sanger, CA 93657
Phone: 415-431-2400
Email: calegion@pacific.net
http://www.calegion.org
Purpose: To enhance high school students' experience with and understanding of the U.S. Constitution. The contest will help develop students' leadership skills and civic appreciation, as well as the ability to deliver thoughtful, insightful orations regarding U.S. citizenship and its inherent responsibilities.
Eligibility: Applicants must be high school students under the age of 20 who are U.S. citizens or legal residents and residents of the state. Students first give an oration within their state and winners compete at the national level. The oration must be related to the Constitution of the United States focusing on the duties and obligations citizens have to the government. It must be in English and be between eight and ten

minutes. There is also an assigned topic which is posted on the website, and it should be between three and five minutes.
Target applicant(s): Junior high students or younger. High school students.
Amount: $1,500-$18,000.
Number of awards: Varies.
Deadline: January 15.
How to apply: Applications are available by email.
Exclusive: Visit www.UltimateScholarshipBook.com and enter code AM132423 for updates on this award.

(1325) · California Restaurant Association Educational Foundation Scholarship for High School Seniors

California Restaurant Association
621 Capitol Mall, Suite 2000, Sacramento, CA 95814
Phone: 800-765-4842
Email: craef@calrest.org
https://calrestfoundation.org/scholarships/
Purpose: To aid students with restaurant work experience.
Eligibility: Applicants must be high school seniors who are California residents and U.S. citizens or permanent residents and be enrolled in at least nine credit hours at an accredited institution of higher learning and have a GPA of 2.5 or higher. Students must plan to enroll in two consecutive semesters and have at least 250 hours of work experience in the restaurant industry.
Target applicant(s): High school students.
Minimum GPA: 2.5
Amount: Varies.
Number of awards: Varies.
Deadline: May.
How to apply: Applications are available online. An application form, essay, copy of curriculum, transcript, proof of work experience and one to three letters of recommendation are required.
Exclusive: Visit www.UltimateScholarshipBook.com and enter code CA132523 for updates on this award.

(1326) · California Restaurant Association Educational Foundation Scholarships for Undergraduate Students

California Restaurant Association
621 Capitol Mall, Suite 2000, Sacramento, CA 95814
Phone: 800-765-4842
Email: craef@calrest.org
https://calrestfoundation.org/scholarships/
Purpose: To support students with restaurant work experience.
Eligibility: Applicants must be California residents, U.S. citizens or permanent residents and undergraduate students who are enrolled in at least nine credit hours at an accredited institution of higher learning. A GPA of 2.5 or higher is required. Applicants must enroll in two consecutive semesters and have completed at least one grading term of a postsecondary program. High school students going into their freshman year must have 250 hours of restaurant work experience, rising sophomores must have 400 hours and those beyond the sophomore year must have 550 hours of experience.
Target applicant(s): High school students. College students. Adult students.
Minimum GPA: 2.5
Amount: Varies.
Number of awards: Varies.

Deadline: May 1.
How to apply: Applications are available online. An application form, essay, copy of curriculum, transcript, proof of work experience and one to three letters of recommendation are required.
Exclusive: Visit www.UltimateScholarshipBook.com and enter code CA132623 for updates on this award.

(1327) · California State PTA Volunteer Service Scholarship

California State PTA
2327 L Street, Sacramento, CA 95816-5014
Phone: 916-440-1985
Email: grants@capta.org
http://capta.org/programs-events/scholarships/
Purpose: To support high school seniors who have contributed to the community.
Eligibility: Applicants must attend a public California high school, be high school seniors who have served their school and community and be members of the PTA.
Target applicant(s): High school students.
Amount: $500.
Number of awards: 60.
Deadline: October 1.
How to apply: Applications are available online.
Exclusive: Visit www.UltimateScholarshipBook.com and enter code CA132723 for updates on this award.

(1328) · Candon, Todd and Seabolt Scholarship Fund

Hawaii Community Foundation - Scholarships
827 Fort Street Mall, Honolulu, HI 96813
Phone: 888-731-3863
Email: scholarships@hcf-hawaii.org
https://www.hawaiicommunityfoundation.org/
Purpose: To support Hawaii students who are majoring in accounting or finance.
Eligibility: Students must be in their junior or senior year of college with at least a 3.2 GPA.
Target applicant(s): College students. Adult students.
Minimum GPA: 3.2
Amount: Varies.
Number of awards: Varies.
Deadline: January 31.
How to apply: To apply, register online, complete the online application and select the scholarships to which you wish to apply. In addition, mail the supporting materials: printed confirmation page from the online application, personal statement, copy of Student Aid Report (SAR) available at www.fafsa.ed.gov and official transcript.
Exclusive: Visit www.UltimateScholarshipBook.com and enter code HA132823 for updates on this award.

(1329) · CAPED Excellence Scholarship

California Association for Postsecondary Education and Disability
Disabled Student Programs and Services, San Bernardino Valley College, 701 South Mt. Vernon Avenue, San Bernardino, CA 92410
Phone: 909-384-8663
Email: capedscholarships@gmail.com
http://www.caped.co/scholarships/
Purpose: To provide financial assistance to high achievers in academics, community and campus life.

Eligibility: Applicants must have a verifiable disability and demonstrate financial need. A minimum GPA of 2.5 is required for undergraduates and a minimum GPA of 3.0 for graduate students. Applicants must be taking at least six semester units or four quarter units at a public or private California institution of higher learning.

Target applicant(s): High school students. College students. Graduate school students. Adult students.

Minimum GPA: 2.5 for undergraduate students, 3.0 for graduate students

Amount: $1,500.

Number of awards: 1.

Deadline: August 31.

How to apply: Applications are available online.

Exclusive: Visit www.UltimateScholarshipBook.com and enter code CA132923 for updates on this award.

(1330) · CAPPS Scholarship Program

California Association of Private Postsecondary Schools
2520 Venture Oaks Way, Suite 170, Sacramento, CA 95833
Phone: 916-447-5500
Email: info@cappsonline.org
http://www.cappsonline.org

Purpose: To allow private postsecondary schools to offer tuition scholarships to students.

Eligibility: Applicants must be legal California residents who have fulfilled the admission requirements for the school that is pledging their CAPPS scholarship. Application is restricted to high school and adult students only. Recipients are chosen on the basis of application date and each individual school's judging standards.

Target applicant(s): High school students. College students. Adult students.

Amount: Varies.

Number of awards: 5.

Deadline: August.

How to apply: Applications are available online.

Exclusive: Visit www.UltimateScholarshipBook.com and enter code CA133023 for updates on this award.

(1331) · Car Career Scholarship

California New Car Dealers Association (CNCDA)
1517 L Street, Sacramento, CA 95814
Phone: 916-403-7942
Email: scholarship@cncda.org
https://learnmore.scholarsapply.org/cncda/

Purpose: To support students interested in the auto technician industry.

Eligibility: Applicants must be residents in California and high school seniors or graduates or current college undergraduates who plan to enroll in part-time or full-time undergraduate study at an accredited two-year college or vocational-technical school. Students must be pursuing an automotive technology degree and have a minimum 2.5 GPA.

Target applicant(s): High school students. College students. Adult students.

Minimum GPA: 2.5

Amount: Up to $10,000.

Number of awards: 20.

Deadline: June 15.

How to apply: Applications are available online.

Exclusive: Visit www.UltimateScholarshipBook.com and enter code CA133123 for updates on this award.

(1332) · Career Colleges and Schools of Texas Scholarship Program

Career Colleges and Schools of Texas
Lisa Tomsio, 823 Congress Avenue, Suite 230, Austin, TX 78701
Phone: 512-402-7797
Email: scholars@careerscholarships.org
http://ccst.org/

Purpose: To help Texas high school seniors who want to attend trade or technical schools in the state.

Eligibility: Participating institutions, which are listed on the website, provide scholarships to students who choose to enroll at their schools. Since each school has its own guidelines, applicants should contact a particular school for more information.

Target applicant(s): High school students.

Amount: $1,000.

Number of awards: Varies.

Deadline: Varies.

How to apply: Applicants should contact their high school counselors or participating schools.

Exclusive: Visit www.UltimateScholarshipBook.com and enter code CA133223 for updates on this award.

(1333) · Carl C. Smith Memorial Scholarship

Oklahoma Association of Broadcasters
6520 N. Western, Suite 104, Oklahoma City, OK 73116
Phone: 405-848-0771
Email: struby@oabok.org
https://oabok.org/careerseducation/scholarships/

Purpose: To support students majoring in broadcasting at Oklahoma colleges and universities.

Eligibility: Applicants must be enrolled in an Oklahoma college or university broadcasting program, be majoring in broadcasting and have an intent to enter the broadcasting career upon graduation. Students must be a junior or senior for the upcoming school year and must maintain a "B" average.

Target applicant(s): College students. Adult students.

Minimum GPA: 3.0

Amount: $2,000.

Number of awards: 1.

Deadline: February 4.

How to apply: Applications are available online.

Exclusive: Visit www.UltimateScholarshipBook.com and enter code OK133323 for updates on this award.

(1334) · Cash Grant Program

Massachusetts Department of Higher Education
Office of Student Financial Assistance, 454 Broadway, Suite 200, Revere, MA 02151
Phone: 617-727-9420
Email: osfa@osfa.mass.edu
https://www.mass.edu/osfa/programs/programs.asp

Purpose: To help needy students pay college or university fees and non-state-supported tuition.

Eligibility: Students must be permanent residents of Massachusetts for at least one year before the academic year for which the grant is awarded. Students must also demonstrate financial need, be enrolled in at least three credits per semester in an eligible undergraduate program and not have previously earned a bachelor's degree or higher.

Target applicant(s): High school students. College students. Adult students.

Amount: Up to full tuition.
Number of awards: Varies.
Scholarship may be renewable.
Deadline: Varies.
How to apply: Applications are available from your financial aid office.
Exclusive: Visit www.UltimateScholarshipBook.com and enter code MA133423 for updates on this award.

(1335) · Categorical Tuition Waiver

Massachusetts Department of Higher Education
Office of Student Financial Assistance, 454 Broadway, Suite 200, Revere, MA 02151
Phone: 617-727-9420
Email: osfa@osfa.mass.edu
https://www.mass.edu/osfa/programs/programs.asp
Purpose: To provide financial support to Massachusetts students who would otherwise not be able to afford higher education.
Eligibility: Applicants must be residents of the state of Massachusetts for at least one year prior to the beginning of the academic year in which the scholarship is used. They also must be members of one of the following groups of people: veterans or active members of the armed forces, Native Americans, senior citizens or clients of either the Massachusetts Rehabilitation Commission or Commission for the Blind. Students must be enrolled in at least three credits per semester in a state undergraduate or certificate program, and they must remain in satisfactory academic standing.
Target applicant(s): High school students. College students. Adult students.
Amount: Up to full tuition.
Number of awards: Varies.
Deadline: Varies.
How to apply: Applications are available at college financial aid offices.
Exclusive: Visit www.UltimateScholarshipBook.com and enter code MA133523 for updates on this award.

(1336) · Cathay Bank Foundation Scholarship

Asian Pacific Community Fund
1145 Wilshire Boulevard, Suite 105, Los Angeles, CA 90017
Phone: 213-624-6400
Email: scholarships@apcf.org
https://www.apcf.org/scholarships
Purpose: To assist low-income students to pursue higher education.
Eligibility: Applicants must be high school seniors residing in California, Illinois, Maryland, Massachusetts, Nevada, New Jersey, New York, Texas or Washington who are enrolling as first-year students in an accredited four-year college in one of the listed states of residency. Students must have a minimum GPA of 3.0 and have a household income that falls at or below the low-income level. There is no ethnicity requirement.
Target applicant(s): High school students.
Minimum GPA: 3.0
Amount: $1,000.
Number of awards: Up to 20.
Deadline: April 1.
How to apply: Applications are available online.
Exclusive: Visit www.UltimateScholarshipBook.com and enter code AS133623 for updates on this award.

(1337) · CCCAM Scholarships

Competitive Cheer Coaches Association of Michigan
5675 N. Division, Comstock Park, MI 49321

Email: scholarship@cccam.org
https://www.cccam.org/scholarship/
Purpose: To support the pursuit of higher education by competitive cheer athletes.
Eligibility: Applicants must be a graduating senior, be a current member of a Michigan High School Athletic Association (MHSAA) competitive cheer team and have a minimum GPA of 3.5 through their junior year. The applicant's cheer team must compete in the annual Scholarship Invitational and the team coach must be a current CCCAM member.
Target applicant(s): High school students.
Minimum GPA: 3.5
Amount: Varies.
Number of awards: Varies.
Deadline: February 26.
How to apply: Applications are available online and must be completed and mailed in with the applicant's short essay, a sealed copy of the high school transcript and two letters of recommendation.
Exclusive: Visit www.UltimateScholarshipBook.com and enter code CO133723 for updates on this award.

(1338) · CCNMA Scholarships

CCNMA: Latino Journalists of California
ASU Cronkite School of Journalism, 725 Arizona Avenue, Suite 404, Santa Monica, CA 90401-1734
Phone: 424-229-9482
Email: ccnmainfo@ccnma.org
https://www.ccnma.org/general-1
Purpose: To support Latino students with career goals in journalism.
Eligibility: Applicants must be Latino and either California residents or be attending California schools. While the student's degree does not have to be in journalism, they must demonstrate plans to pursue a career in journalism. An interview and autobiographical essay are required. Awards are based also on financial need, academic achievement and civic responsibility.
Target applicant(s): High school students. College students. Graduate school students. Adult students.
Amount: $500-$1,000.
Number of awards: Varies.
Deadline: April 30.
How to apply: Applications are available online.
Exclusive: Visit www.UltimateScholarshipBook.com and enter code CC133823 for updates on this award.

(1339) · Central Arizona DX Association Scholarship

American Radio Relay League Foundation
225 Main Street, Newington, CT 06111-1494
Phone: 860-594-0348
Email: foundation@arrl.org
http://www.arrl.org/scholarship-program
Purpose: To provide scholarship assistance to amateur radio operators from Arizona.
Eligibility: Applicants must be Arizona residents with a Technician Class or higher Amateur Radio License. They must have a GPA of 3.2 or higher. Graduating high school seniors receive preference over current college students.
Target applicant(s): High school students. College students. Adult students.
Minimum GPA: 3.2
Amount: $1,000.
Number of awards: 1.
Deadline: December 31.

How to apply: Applications are available online.
Exclusive: Visit www.UltimateScholarshipBook.com and enter code AM133923 for updates on this award.

(1340) · Certificate, License or Other Industry-Recognized Credential

New Hampshire Charitable Foundation
37 Pleasant Street, Concord, NH 03301-4005
Phone: 603-225-6641
Email: info@nhcf.org
https://www.nhcf.org/how-can-we-help-you/
Purpose: To support students who are pursuing short-term vocational or technical studies.
Eligibility: Applicants must be residents of New Hampshire and be pursuing a certificate, license or other credential in vocational or technical fields such as: automotive technology, plumbing, construction, heating, advanced manufacturing, computer repair, licensed nursing, etc. Preference is given to students whose fields are in the traditional manufacturing trade sector, who have a clear vision of how their education will improve their career goals and who have had little or no other educational training opportunities.
Target applicant(s): College students. Adult students.
Amount: Varies.
Number of awards: Varies.
Deadline: December 15.
How to apply: Applications are available online.
Exclusive: Visit www.UltimateScholarshipBook.com and enter code NE134023 for updates on this award.

(1341) · CESDA Diversity Scholarship

Colorado Educational Services and Development Association
P.O. Box 40214, Denver, CO 80204
Phone: 303-352-3231
Email: melissa.quinteros@ccd.edu
http://www.cesda.org
Purpose: To provide financial assistance for disadvantaged students.
Eligibility: Applicants must be either first generation college students, members of underrepresented ethnic or racial minorities or show financial need. They must be Colorado residents who are high school seniors at the time of application. Students must have a GPA of 2.8 or higher and enroll in a two- or four-year Colorado college or university in the fall following graduation. They must take at least six credit hours to qualify.
Target applicant(s): High school students.
Minimum GPA: 2.8
Amount: $1,000.
Number of awards: 6.
Deadline: April 5.
How to apply: Applications are available online.
Exclusive: Visit www.UltimateScholarshipBook.com and enter code CO134123 for updates on this award.

(1342) · CEW Scholarships

Center for the Education of Women
330 E. Liberty, Ann Arbor, MI 48104-2274
Phone: 734-998-7080
Email: contactcew@umich.edu
http://www.umich.edu/~cew
Purpose: To support women who are returning to college after an interruption.

Eligibility: Applicants must be women who are returning to school. For undergraduates, a minimum 2 year (24 month) consecutive interruption in education anytime since high school. For graduate students, a minimum 5 year (60 month) consecutive interruption in education anytime since high school. Candidates must be working toward a clear educational goal at any University of Michigan campus. Preference is given to women wishing to study in non-traditional fields such as mathematics, physical sciences and engineering.
Target applicant(s): Graduate school students. Adult students.
Amount: $1,000-$10,000.
Number of awards: Approximately 40.
Deadline: April 1.
How to apply: Applications are available online.
Exclusive: Visit www.UltimateScholarshipBook.com and enter code CE134223 for updates on this award.

(1343) · CHAHRM Scholarship

Colorado Healthcare Association for Human Resource Management
c/o Michelle Pollart, Scholarship Chair, Prowers Medical Center, 401 Kendall Drive, Lamar, CO 81052
Phone: 719-336-7119
Email: chahrm@hotmail.com
http://www.chahrm.org
Purpose: To aid students enrolled in a healthcare or human resources degree program.
Eligibility: Applicants must be in the final year of study for a degree in a healthcare- or human resources-related subject at an accredited technical college or university. They must have a GPA of 3.0 or higher. Selection is based on academic merit, stated career goals, work history, extracurricular activities and references.
Target applicant(s): College students. Adult students.
Minimum GPA: 3.0
Amount: $1,000.
Number of awards: 2.
Deadline: September.
How to apply: Applications are available online. An application form, a transcript, a personal essay and a faculty advisor reference are required.
Exclusive: Visit www.UltimateScholarshipBook.com and enter code CO134323 for updates on this award.

(1344) · Charles Dubose Scholarship

Connecticut Architecture Foundation
370 James Street, Suite 402, New Haven, CT 06513
Phone: 203-865-2195
Email: ctarchfoundation@gmail.com
https://cafct.org/
Purpose: To assist architecture students.
Eligibility: Applicants must have completed two years of an NAAB accredited architecture program leading to a bachelor's degree as of June 30 of the year of application. Students enrolled in non-accredited programs who have been accepted to an NAAB accredited master's degree program, as well as those currently enrolled in such a program, are also eligible. Applicants must be full-time students. Preference is given to students at the University of Pennsylvania, Georgia Institute of Technology and Fontainebleau summer program and to Connecticut residents.
Target applicant(s): College students. Graduate school students. Adult students.
Amount: $1,200-$5,000.
Number of awards: Varies.
Deadline: April 20.

How to apply: Applications are available online. An application form, statement of goals, resume, financial aid information sheet, two letters of reference and submission of a favorite project are required.
Exclusive: Visit www.UltimateScholarshipBook.com and enter code CO134423 for updates on this award.

(1345) · Charles W. and Annette Hill Scholarship

American Legion, Department of Kansas
1314 SW Topeka Boulevard, Topeka, KS 66612
Phone: 785-232-9315
https://ksamlegion.org/
Purpose: To provide financial assistance to needy and worthy children of members of the American Legion.
Eligibility: Applicants must be descendants of an American Legion member with a GPA of at least 3.0. Special consideration will be given to students studying science, engineering or business administration. Applicants must submit three letters of recommendation with only one from a teacher, an essay on "Why I Want to Go to College," a high school transcript, documentation of parent's veteran status and a 1040 income statement. Applicants must maintain a 3.0 GPA in college and verify enrollment at the start of each semester.
Target applicant(s): High school students. College students. Adult students.
Minimum GPA: 3.0
Amount: $1,000.
Number of awards: 1.
Scholarship may be renewable.
Deadline: February 15.
How to apply: Applications are available online.
Exclusive: Visit www.UltimateScholarshipBook.com and enter code AM134523 for updates on this award.

(1346) · Charles W. Riley Fire and Emergency Medical Services Scholarship Program

Maryland Higher Education Commission
Office of Student Financial Assistance, 6 North Liberty Street, Baltimore, MD 21201
Phone: 800-974-1024
Email: osfamail@mhec.state.md.us
https://mhec.maryland.gov
Purpose: To support Maryland students who are majoring and working in firefighting or emergency medical services fields.
Eligibility: Applicants must be active firefighters, ambulance or rescue squad members living and serving in the state of Maryland. Students must attend a Maryland college majoring in fire service technology or emergency medical technology. They must continue to serve throughout college and for one year after graduating.
Target applicant(s): College students. Adult students.
Minimum GPA: 2.5
Amount: At least 1/2 tuition and fees.
Number of awards: Varies.
Scholarship may be renewable.
Deadline: May 1.
How to apply: Applications are available online.
Exclusive: Visit www.UltimateScholarshipBook.com and enter code MA134623 for updates on this award.

(1347) · Chick and Sophie Major Memorial Duck Calling Contest

Stuttgart Arkansas Chamber of Commerce
P.O. Box 1500, 507 S. Main, Stuttgart, AR 72160
Phone: 870-673-1602
Email: stuttgartchamber@centurytel.net
http://www.stuttgartarkansas.org/scholarship-contest.html
Purpose: To assist students who win the duck calling contest.
Eligibility: Applicants must be graduating high school seniors and participate in the annual competition that occurs in Stuttgart, Arkansas.
Target applicant(s): High school students.
Amount: $500-$2,000.
Number of awards: 4.
Deadline: November.
How to apply: Details on the competition are available online.
Exclusive: Visit www.UltimateScholarshipBook.com and enter code ST134723 for updates on this award.

(1348) · Children and Youth Scholarships

American Legion, Department of Maine
5 Verti Drive, Winslow, ME 04901-0727
Phone: 207-873-3229
Email: legionme@mainelegion.org
http://www.mainelegion.org/pages/programs/scholarships.php
Purpose: To provide financial support to Maine students.
Eligibility: Applicants must be high school seniors or college students attending or planning to attend an accredited college or vocational school. Applicants must also demonstrate financial need and include two letters of recommendation and a personal statement.
Target applicant(s): High school students. College students. Adult students.
Amount: $500.
Number of awards: 7.
Deadline: May 1.
How to apply: Applications are available online.
Exclusive: Visit www.UltimateScholarshipBook.com and enter code AM134823 for updates on this award.

(1349) · Chiropractic Education Assistance Scholarship

Oklahoma State Regents for Higher Education/Chiropractic Education Assistance Scholarship
655 Research Parkway, Suite 200, Oklahoma City, OK 73104
Phone: 800-858-1840
Email: studentinfo@osrhe.edu
https://secure.okcollegestart.org/Financial_Aid_Planning/Scholarships/Career_Scholarships/Chiropractic_Education_Assistance_Scholarship.aspx
Purpose: To support Oklahoma state residents pursuing chiropractic studies at accredited out-of-state schools.
Eligibility: Applicants must be residents of the state of Oklahoma who have lived in Oklahoma for at least the past five years who are either enrolled or accepted at an accredited school for chiropractic study. Students must have a 3.0 GPA.
Target applicant(s): High school students. College students. Adult students.
Minimum GPA: 3.0
Amount: Up to $6,000.
Number of awards: Varies.
Scholarship may be renewable.

Deadline: July 30.
How to apply: Applications are available online.
Exclusive: Visit www.UltimateScholarshipBook.com and enter code OK134923 for updates on this award.

(1350) · Christa McAuliffe Scholarship

Tennessee Student Assistance Corporation
404 James Robertson Parkway, Suite 1510, Parkway Towers, Nashville, TN 37243
Phone: 800-342-1663
Email: tsac.aidinfo@tn.gov
https://www.tn.gov/collegepays/financial-aid.html
Purpose: To support Tennessee students who are pursuing careers in teaching.
Eligibility: Applicants must be in the second semester of their junior year in a teaching program at a Tennessee college, and they must be enrolled full-time. Students must have at least a 3.5 GPA and an SAT or ACT score that is at least as high as the national average. They must not have any defaulted state or federal student loans. Recipients must agree to teach in a Tennessee elementary or secondary school for a period of time upon graduation.
Target applicant(s): College students. Adult students.
Minimum GPA: 3.5
Amount: $500.
Number of awards: 1.
Deadline: April.
How to apply: Applications are available online.
Exclusive: Visit www.UltimateScholarshipBook.com and enter code TE135023 for updates on this award.

(1351) · Christian A. Herter Memorial Scholarship Program

Massachusetts Department of Higher Education
Office of Student Financial Assistance, 454 Broadway, Suite 200, Revere, MA 02151
Phone: 617-727-9420
Email: osfa@osfa.mass.edu
https://www.mass.edu/osfa/programs/programs.asp
Purpose: To provide educational opportunities to Massachusetts students who demonstrate academic promise and a desire to attend post-secondary institutions.
Eligibility: Applicants must be enrolled in a public or private secondary school in the Commonwealth of Massachusetts and be legal residents of the state. Applicants must have a cumulative grade point average of 2.5 and exhibit difficult personal circumstances, high financial need and strong academic promise to continue education beyond the secondary level.
Target applicant(s): High school students.
Minimum GPA: 2.5
Amount: Varies.
Number of awards: Varies.
Scholarship may be renewable.
Deadline: February.
How to apply: Applications are available online.
Exclusive: Visit www.UltimateScholarshipBook.com and enter code MA135123 for updates on this award.

(1352) · CIF Scholar-Athlete of the Year

California Interscholastic Federation (CIF)
CIF State Office, Attn.: CIF Scholar-Athlete of the Year, 4658 Duckhorn Drive, Sacramento, CA 95834
Phone: 916-239-4477
Email: info@cifstate.org
http://www.cifstate.org/parents-students/awards_and_scholarships/index
Purpose: To recognize high school student-athletes with exemplary academic and athletic careers and personal standards.
Eligibility: Applicants must be high school seniors with a minimum 3.5 GPA, demonstrate outstanding athletic performance in a minimum of two years of varsity play in California and exhibit character, trustworthiness, respect, responsibility, fairness, caring and citizenship.
Target applicant(s): High school students.
Minimum GPA: 3.5
Amount: $5,000.
Number of awards: 2.
Deadline: February.
How to apply: Applications are available by request.
Exclusive: Visit www.UltimateScholarshipBook.com and enter code CA135223 for updates on this award.

(1353) · Cindy Luberto Scholarship for Women Athletes

CT RollerGirls Inc.
P.O. Box 1774, Naugatuck, CT 06770
Email: scholarship@ctrollerderby.com
https://www.ctrollerderby.com/copy-of-2020-scholarship-for-women-
Purpose: To support Connecticut women athletes who participate in recreational, community or school athletics.
Eligibility: Applicants must be female high school seniors and participate in a sport that is organized, recreational or intramural. Selection is based on a 250-word essay describing the passion for the sport that is played and how that sport or your participation is unique.
Target applicant(s): High school students.
Amount: $500.
Number of awards: 1.
Deadline: April 1.
How to apply: Applications are available online and include an essay and a photo of the applicant playing the sport.
Exclusive: Visit www.UltimateScholarshipBook.com and enter code CT135323 for updates on this award.

(1354) · Clair A. Hill Scholarship

Association of California Water Agencies
980 9th Street, Suite 1000, Sacramento, CA 95814
Phone: 916-441-4545
Email: awards@acwa.com
http://www.acwa.com
Purpose: To support California undergraduates pursuing degrees in a water resources-related subject.
Eligibility: Applicants must be California residents who are rising juniors or seniors at a participating postsecondary institution located in California. They must be pursuing an undergraduate degree in a water resources-related subject and be full-time students enrolled for the entirety of the upcoming school year. Selection is based on professional commitment to the water resources field, academic achievement and financial need.

Target applicant(s): College students. Adult students.
Amount: $5,000.
Number of awards: 1.
Deadline: March 1.
How to apply: Applications are available online. An application form, personal essay, transcript and two to three letters of recommendation are required.
Exclusive: Visit www.UltimateScholarshipBook.com and enter code AS135423 for updates on this award.

(1355) · Clanseer and Anna Johnson Scholarships

Community Foundation of New Jersey
P.O. Box 338, Morristown, NJ 07963-0338
Phone: 973-267-5533
Email: csmith@cfnj.org
http://cfnj.org/current-funds/student-scholarships/
Purpose: To provide education assistance for disadvantaged African American students.
Eligibility: Applicants must have been born in the United States and be New Jersey residents. They must have an A or B average in science and math-related subjects and maintain above average grades overall. Financial need and merit are considered. Scholarship winners are asked to perform at least ten hours of community service each week for a year following graduation.
Target applicant(s): High school students.
Amount: $6,000.
Number of awards: 4.
Deadline: June.
How to apply: Applications are available online.
Exclusive: Visit www.UltimateScholarshipBook.com and enter code CO135523 for updates on this award.

(1356) · Clem Judd, Jr., Memorial Scholarship

Hawaii Lodging and Tourism Association
2270 Kalakaua Avenue, Suite 1702, Honolulu, HI 96815
Phone: 808-923-0407
Email: info@hawaiilodging.org
http://www.hawaiilodging.org/scholarships.html
Purpose: To help Hawaiian residents majoring in hotel management.
Eligibility: Applicants must have a minimum 3.0 GPA, be a resident of Hawaii, be able to prove Hawaiian ancestry and be a junior or senior enrolled full-time at a U.S. university or college.
Target applicant(s): College students. Adult students.
Minimum GPA: 3.0
Amount: $1,000-$2,500.
Number of awards: Up to 2.
Deadline: May 12.
How to apply: Applications are available by written request beginning February 1.
Exclusive: Visit www.UltimateScholarshipBook.com and enter code HA135623 for updates on this award.

(1357) · Collaborative Teachers Tuition Waiver

Massachusetts Department of Higher Education
Office of Student Financial Assistance, 454 Broadway, Suite 200, Revere, MA 02151
Phone: 617-727-9420
Email: osfa@osfa.mass.edu
https://www.mass.edu/osfa/programs/programs.asp

Purpose: To provide graduate school tuition waivers for Massachusetts teachers who become student teacher mentors.
Eligibility: Applicants must be public school teachers living and working in the state of Massachusetts. They must also agree to mentor a student teacher from a state college or university in their own classroom, and they must be planning to attend graduate school at one of the nine campuses of Massachusetts State College or the University of Massachusetts.
Target applicant(s): Graduate school students. Adult students.
Amount: Varies.
Number of awards: Varies.
Scholarship may be renewable.
Deadline: Varies.
How to apply: Applications are available at college financial aid offices.
Exclusive: Visit www.UltimateScholarshipBook.com and enter code MA135723 for updates on this award.

(1358) · College Access Program

Kentucky Higher Education Assistance Authority
P.O. Box 798, Frankfort, KY 40602
Phone: 800-928-8926
Email: blane@kheaa.com
http://www.kheaa.com
Purpose: To aid Kentucky students with financial need.
Eligibility: Applicants must be Kentucky residents, be enrolled at least half-time in undergraduate academic programs and have an Expected Family Contribution (EFC) based on the FAFSA of lower than approximately $3,850.
Target applicant(s): High school students. College students. Adult students.
Amount: Up to $1,900.
Number of awards: Varies.
Deadline: Varies.
How to apply: Complete the Free Application for Federal Student Aid (FAFSA).
Exclusive: Visit www.UltimateScholarshipBook.com and enter code KE135823 for updates on this award.

(1359) · College Affordability Grant

New Mexico Higher Education Department
2044 Galisteo Street, Suite 4, Santa Fe, NM 87505-2100
Phone: 505-476-8400
Email: cesaria.tapia1@state.nm.us
https://hed.state.nm.us/financial-aid
Purpose: To support New Mexico residents who are attending public colleges in the state.
Eligibility: Applicants must demonstrate financial need, and they cannot have any other state grants or scholarships. Students must be enrolled in at least six credit hours per semester.
Target applicant(s): High school students. College students. Adult students.
Amount: Up to $1,500.
Number of awards: Varies.
Scholarship may be renewable.
Deadline: Varies.
How to apply: Applications are available at college financial aid offices.
Exclusive: Visit www.UltimateScholarshipBook.com and enter code NE135923 for updates on this award.

(1360) · Collegiate Scholarship

Texas 4-H Youth Development Foundation
4180 Highway 6, College Station, TX 77845
Phone: 979-845-1211
Email: texas4h@ag.tamu.edu
https://texas4-h.tamu.edu/
Purpose: To support undergraduate students in Texas.
Eligibility: Applicants must have actively participated in a 4-H program during their high school years. They must be currently enrolled full-time with at least a 2.7 GPA. Recipients must have completed at least 30 credit hours by the time scholarship payments begin. Awards are based on financial need, academic achievement and 4-H experience.
Target applicant(s): College students. Adult students.
Minimum GPA: 2.7
Amount: Varies.
Number of awards: Varies.
Deadline: February 15.
How to apply: Applications are available online.
Exclusive: Visit www.UltimateScholarshipBook.com and enter code TE136023 for updates on this award.

(1361) · Collegiate Shooting Scholarship Program

National Rifle Association
11250 Waples Mill Road, Fairfax, VA 22030
Phone: 800-672-3888
Email: grantprogram@nrahq.org
https://awards.nra.org/scholarships/
Purpose: To support students who have a strong interest in shooting sports as they continue their education beyond high school.
Eligibility: Applicants must live in Pennsylvania or Virginia, be a high school senior, have at least a 3.0 GPA and have a strong interest in shooting sports and the Second Amendment. Selection is based on the application, essay and letter of reference.
Target applicant(s): High school students.
Minimum GPA: 3.0
Amount: $5,000.
Number of awards: Varies.
Deadline: June 1.
How to apply: Applications are available online. A copy of a letter of acceptance to the college or university of choice must be sent with the application.
Exclusive: Visit www.UltimateScholarshipBook.com and enter code NA136123 for updates on this award.

(1362) · Colorado Council Volunteerism and Community Service Scholarship

Colorado Council Volunteerism and Community Service
P.O. Box 3383, Pagosa Springs, CO 81147
Phone: 970-264-2231
Email: mthompson@pagosa.k12.co.us
http://www.coloradocouncil.org/scholarship
Purpose: To support Colorado students interested in community service who are pursuing higher education.
Eligibility: Applicants must be graduating high school seniors who have been residents of Colorado for their final two years of high school. Students must be accepted at a Colorado Council Member Institution and be enrolled as a full-time student within six months after graduation from high school.
Target applicant(s): High school students.
Minimum GPA: 2.5

Amount: $1,500.
Number of awards: 16.
Deadline: February 15.
How to apply: Applications are available online.
Exclusive: Visit www.UltimateScholarshipBook.com and enter code CO136223 for updates on this award.

(1363) · Colorado Masons Benevolent Fund Scholarships

Colorado Masons Benevolent Fund Association
P.O. Box 703, Westminster, CO 80036-0703
Phone: 719-623-5349
Email: education@cmbfa.org
https://grandlodgeofcolorado.org/philanthropy/scholarships
Purpose: To help Colorado students.
Eligibility: Applicants must be graduating seniors from a Colorado public high school planning to attend a Colorado postsecondary institution. Selection is based on leadership, maturity, need and scholastic ability without reference to race, creed, color, sex or Masonic relationship.
Target applicant(s): High school students.
Amount: Up to $7,000.
Number of awards: Varies.
Scholarship may be renewable.
Deadline: March 15.
How to apply: Applications are available online.
Exclusive: Visit www.UltimateScholarshipBook.com and enter code CO136323 for updates on this award.

(1364) · Colorado Oratorical Contest

American Legion, Department of Colorado
7465 E. 1st Avenue, Suite D, Denver, CO 80230
Phone: 303-366-5201
Email: drivercoach69@yahoo.com
http://www.coloradolegion.org
Purpose: To enhance high school students' experience with and understanding of the U.S. Constitution. The contest will help develop students' leadership skills and civic appreciation, as well as the ability to deliver thoughtful, insightful orations regarding U.S. citizenship and its inherent responsibilities.
Eligibility: Applicants must be high school students under the age of 20 who are U.S. citizens or legal residents and residents of the state. Students first give an oration within their state and winners compete at the national level. The oration must be related to the Constitution of the United States focusing on the duties and obligations citizens have to the government. It must be in English and be between eight and ten minutes. There is also an assigned topic which is posted on the website, and it should be between three and five minutes.
Target applicant(s): Junior high students or younger. High school students.
Amount: $1,000-$18,000.
Number of awards: Varies.
Deadline: January 31.
How to apply: Applications are available online.
Exclusive: Visit www.UltimateScholarshipBook.com and enter code AM136423 for updates on this award.

(1365) · Colorado Student Grant

Colorado Department of Higher Education
1560 Broadway, Suite 1600, Denver, CO 80202

Phone: 303-862-3001
http://highered.colorado.gov/
Purpose: To assist Colorado student residents.
Eligibility: Applicants must be Colorado residents who plan to enroll or are enrolled in eligible programs at eligible Colorado postsecondary institutions. Applicants must make satisfactory academic progress and have not defaulted in educational loans or grants. Awards are need-based and merit-based and are made by institutions to students.
Target applicant(s): High school students. College students. Adult students.
Amount: Varies.
Number of awards: Varies.
Deadline: Varies.
How to apply: Contact your financial aid office.
Exclusive: Visit www.UltimateScholarshipBook.com and enter code CO136523 for updates on this award.

(1366) · Colorado Women's Education Foundation
Colorado Women's Education Foundation
P.O. Box 1189, Boulder, CO 80306-1189
Phone: 303-443-2573
Email: office@cwef.org
http://cwef.org/scholarships/
Purpose: To provide education assistance for adult women.
Eligibility: Applicants must be women who are 25 years of age or older, United States citizens and Colorado residents for at least 12 months prior to the application deadline. They must be enrolled in or attending an accredited college, university or vocational training institution and reside in Colorado while completing their program.
Target applicant(s): College students. Adult students.
Amount: At least $1,000.
Number of awards: At least 20.
Scholarship may be renewable.
Deadline: May 31.
How to apply: Applications are available online.
Exclusive: Visit www.UltimateScholarshipBook.com and enter code CO136623 for updates on this award.

(1367) · Community Banker Association of Illinois Annual Essay Scholarship Program
Community Banker Association of Illinois
901 Community Drive, Springfield, IL 62703-5184
Phone: 800-736-2224
Email: bobbiw@cbai.com
http://www.cbai.com
Purpose: To assist Illinois high school seniors.
Eligibility: Applicants must write essays and be sponsored by a participating CBAI member bank. There is an essay topic related to community banking, and the short essays are judged on understanding of community banking philosophy, accurate information, clear and concise sentences, logical organization, proper grammar, correct punctuation and spelling and conclusion/summary.
Target applicant(s): High school students.
Amount: Up to $4,000.
Number of awards: 24.
Deadline: March 2.
How to apply: A list of participating banks and more information is available by email.
Exclusive: Visit www.UltimateScholarshipBook.com and enter code CO136723 for updates on this award.

(1368) · Community Scholarship Fund
Hawaii Community Foundation - Scholarships
827 Fort Street Mall, Honolulu, HI 96813
Phone: 888-731-3863
Email: scholarships@hcf-hawaii.org
https://www.hawaiicommunityfoundation.org/
Purpose: To assist college and graduate students majoring in arts, education, humanities or social science.
Eligibility: Applicants must demonstrate accomplishment, motivation, initiative, vision and intention to work in Hawaii and major in the arts, architecture, education, humanities or social science.
Target applicant(s): High school students. College students. Graduate school students. Adult students.
Minimum GPA: 3.3
Amount: Varies.
Number of awards: Varies.
Deadline: January 31.
How to apply: To apply, register online, complete the online application and select the scholarships to which you wish to apply. In addition, mail the supporting materials: printed confirmation page from the online application, personal statement, copy of Student Aid Report (SAR) available at www.fafsa.ed.gov and official transcript.
Exclusive: Visit www.UltimateScholarshipBook.com and enter code HA136823 for updates on this award.

(1369) · Competitive Scholarships
New Mexico Higher Education Department
2044 Galisteo Street, Suite 4, Santa Fe, NM 87505-2100
Phone: 505-476-8400
Email: cesaria.tapia1@state.nm.us
https://hed.state.nm.us/financial-aid
Purpose: To provide a financial incentive for exceptional out-of-state students to attend college in New Mexico.
Eligibility: Applicants must be non-residents of the state of New Mexico, and they must be willing to enroll full-time in a public four-year university in New Mexico. Students applying to Eastern New Mexico University, New Mexico Highlands University, New Mexico Institute of Mining and Technology or Western New Mexico University must have one of the following combinations: a GPA of at least 3.0 and an ACT score of at least 23, or a GPA of at least 3.5 and an ACT of at least 20. Students applying to the University of New Mexico or New Mexico State University must have either an ACT score of 26 and a GPA of 3.0 or an ACT score of 23 and a GPA of 3.5.
Target applicant(s): High school students. College students. Adult students.
Minimum GPA: 3.0
Amount: $100.
Number of awards: Varies.
Scholarship may be renewable.
Deadline: Varies.
How to apply: Applications are available at college financial aid offices.
Exclusive: Visit www.UltimateScholarshipBook.com and enter code NE136923 for updates on this award.

(1370) · Confederation of Oregon School Administrators Scholarships
Coalition of Oregon School Administrators
707 13th Street SE, Suite 100, Salem, OR 97301
Phone: 503-581-3141
Email: sara@oasc.org

https://www.cosa.k12.or.us/
Purpose: To provide financial assistance to Oregon students who plan to attend Oregon colleges or universities.
Eligibility: Applicants must be graduating seniors at an Oregon public high school who plan to attend a public or private institution of higher learning in the state. They must have a 3.5 or higher GPA, be active in school and community activities and be endorsed by a COSA member.
Target applicant(s): High school students.
Minimum GPA: 3.5
Amount: $1,000.
Number of awards: 10.
Deadline: March 1.
How to apply: Applications are available online.
Exclusive: Visit www.UltimateScholarshipBook.com and enter code CO137023 for updates on this award.

(1371) · Connecticut Association of Land Surveyors Memorial Scholarship Fund

Connecticut Association of Land Surveyors Inc.
78 Beaver Road, Wethersfield, CT 06109
Phone: 860-563-1990
Email: kathy@ctsurveyors.com
http://ctsurveyors.org
Purpose: To support Connecticut students who are preparing for careers in land surveying.
Eligibility: Applicants must be Connecticut residents who are enrolled in or who have been accepted into a postsecondary academic program in surveying or a related subject (geography, engineering or science). They must have plans to pursue a career in land surveying and must demonstrate interest in the field through previous work experience or other activities. Selection is based on the overall strength of the application.
Target applicant(s): College students. Adult students.
Amount: Varies.
Number of awards: Varies.
Deadline: June 1.
How to apply: Applications are available online. A resume, transcript and statement of qualifications are required.
Exclusive: Visit www.UltimateScholarshipBook.com and enter code CO137123 for updates on this award.

(1372) · Connecticut Building Congress Scholarships

Connecticut Building Congress Scholarship Fund Inc.
c/o DiBlasi Associates P.C., 500 Purdy Hill Road, Monroe, CT 06468
Phone: 203-452-1331
Email: tomd@diblasi-engrs.com
http://www.cbc-ct.org/CBC_Scholarship
Purpose: To aid students pursuing degrees in construction fields.
Eligibility: Applicants must be graduating seniors at Connecticut high schools and Connecticut residents. Students must be entering associate, bachelor's or master's degree programs in architecture, engineering, construction management, surveying, planning or another construction-related course of study.
Target applicant(s): High school students.
Amount: $500-$2,000.
Number of awards: Varies.
Scholarship may be renewable.
Deadline: March 5.

How to apply: Applications are available online. An application form, essay, transcript and FAFSA Student Aid Report are required.
Exclusive: Visit www.UltimateScholarshipBook.com and enter code CO137223 for updates on this award.

(1373) · Continuing/Re-entry Students Scholarship

American Legion Auxiliary, Department of California
401 Van Ness Avenue, Suite 319, San Francisco, CA 94102-4570
Phone: 415-861-5092
Email: calegionaux@calegionaux.org
https://calegionauxiliary.com/resources/scholarships/
Purpose: To provide support to children of U.S. Armed Forces members.
Eligibility: One of the applicant's parents must have served in the U.S. Armed Forces during an eligible period. Applicants must be California residents planning to attend a California college or university and must be continuing or re-entry college students.
Target applicant(s): College students. Adult students.
Amount: $500-$1,000.
Number of awards: 5.
Deadline: March 16, September 1.
How to apply: Applications are available online.
Exclusive: Visit www.UltimateScholarshipBook.com and enter code AM137323 for updates on this award.

(1374) · Cora Aguda Manayan Fund

Hawaii Community Foundation - Scholarships
827 Fort Street Mall, Honolulu, HI 96813
Phone: 888-731-3863
Email: scholarships@hcf-hawaii.org
https://www.hawaiicommunityfoundation.org/
Purpose: To support Hawaii students of Filipino ancestry who are dedicated to helping others.
Eligibility: Students must be majoring in a health-related field. Preference may be given to students who are attending school in Hawaii. Applicants must have a minimum 3.0 GPA and have financial need.
Target applicant(s): High school students. College students. Adult students.
Minimum GPA: 3.0
Amount: Varies.
Number of awards: Varies.
Deadline: January 31.
How to apply: To apply, register online, complete the online application and select the scholarships to which you wish to apply. In addition, mail the supporting materials: printed confirmation page from the online application, personal statement, copy of Student Aid Report (SAR) available at www.fafsa.ed.gov and official transcript.
Exclusive: Visit www.UltimateScholarshipBook.com and enter code HA137423 for updates on this award.

(1375) · COSA Youth Development Program Scholarships

Coalition of Oregon School Administrators
707 13th Street SE, Suite 100, Salem, OR 97301
Phone: 503-581-3141
Email: sara@oasc.org
https://www.cosa.k12.or.us/
Purpose: To provide financial assistance for Oregon students.
Eligibility: Applicants must be students at an Oregon public high school who are active in their communities and schools. They must

have a GPA of 3.5 or higher and plan to attend an Oregon college or university. A field of study must be chosen. An endorsement from a COSA member is required, and the student must enroll in college the fall after high school graduation.
Target applicant(s): High school students.
Minimum GPA: 3.5
Amount: $1,000.
Number of awards: 10.
Deadline: March 1.
How to apply: Applications are available online, from your high school guidance counselor and the COSA office. An application form, one-page autobiography, letter of recommendation from a COSA member and transcript are required.
Exclusive: Visit www.UltimateScholarshipBook.com and enter code CO137523 for updates on this award.

(1376) · Courageous Heart Scholarship
Texas 4-H Youth Development Foundation
4180 Highway 6, College Station, TX 77845
Phone: 979-845-1211
Email: texas4h@ag.tamu.edu
https://texas4-h.tamu.edu/
Purpose: To support Texas high school students who have overcome serious obstacles related to health, family or education.
Eligibility: Applicants must be current active members and have actively participated in a 4-H program for two of the past three years. They must have formally applied to a Texas college or university, and they must meet all requirements for admission. Students must provide documentation of the obstacles they have faced.
Target applicant(s): High school students.
Amount: $5,000.
Number of awards: Varies.
Deadline: February 15.
How to apply: Applications are available online.
Exclusive: Visit www.UltimateScholarshipBook.com and enter code TE137623 for updates on this award.

(1377) · Critical Care Scholarship Program
Critical Care Training Center
6426 Bellingham Avenue, North Hollywood, CA 91606
Phone: 818-766-1111
Email: scholarship@acls123.com
http://www.acls123.com/interactive-scholarship-program/
Purpose: To assist future healthcare providers throughout California.
Eligibility: Applicants must be California residents pursuing a degree in healthcare/nursing. Students are required to submit an essay on the designated topic found on the website. After applicants are narrowed down, the essays will then need to be shared on Facebook, Twitter, LinkedIn or other social networking pages and receive votes. The contest runs quarterly.
Target applicant(s): College students. Adult students.
Amount: $2,500.
Number of awards: 4.
Deadline: Quarterly.
How to apply: Applications are available online.
Exclusive: Visit www.UltimateScholarshipBook.com and enter code CR137723 for updates on this award.

(1378) · Crumley Roberts Next Step Scholarship
Crumley Roberts, Attorneys at Law
2400 Freeman Mill Road, Greensboro, NC 27455
https://www.crumleyroberts.com/the-roberts-center/leadership-advancement-and-scholarships/chairmans-scholarship/
Purpose: To support North Carolina, South Carolina and Alabama community college students who plan to transfer to accredited four-year institutions of higher learning.
Eligibility: Applicants must be a minimum of 18 years of age and have a minimum GPA of 3.2.
Target applicant(s): College students. Adult students.
Minimum GPA: 3.2
Amount: $2,500.
Number of awards: 1.
Deadline: January 31.
How to apply: Applications are available to be printed online but must then be mailed. An application form, two letters of recommendation, a transcript and an essay are required.
Exclusive: Visit www.UltimateScholarshipBook.com and enter code CR137823 for updates on this award.

(1379) · CTA César E. Chávez and Dolores Huerta Education Award Program
California Teachers Association (CTA)
CTA Human Rights Department, P.O. Box 921, Burlingame, CA 94011-0921
Phone: 650-697-1400
https://www.cta.org/for-educators/scholarships-awards
Purpose: To honor César Chávez by rewarding students and teachers who follow his vision and guiding principles.
Eligibility: A student or group of up to five students must submit an essay or visual piece under the supervision of a teacher or professor who is a member of the CTA. Students may be in kindergarten through high school or in community college. All works must focus on topics such as non-violence and their relationship to Chávez's legacy. Visit the website for a complete list of topics and specific essay and visual arts submission requirements.
Target applicant(s): Junior high students or younger. High school students. College students. Adult students.
Amount: Up to $550.
Number of awards: Varies.
Deadline: March 5.
How to apply: Applications are available online.
Exclusive: Visit www.UltimateScholarshipBook.com and enter code CA137923 for updates on this award.

(1380) · CTAHPERD Gibson-Laemel Scholarship
Connecticut Association of Health, Physical Education, Recreation and Dance
c/o Janice Skene, CTAHPERD Scholarship Chair, Buttonball Lane School, 376 Buttonball Lane, Glastonbury, CT 06033
Phone: 860-652-7276
Email: skenej@glastonburyus.org
http://www.ctahperd.org
Purpose: To support students majoring in areas related to physical education.
Eligibility: Applicants must be Connecticut students who have declared a major in health, physical education, recreation or dance. Students must be college juniors or seniors, maintain a GPA of 2.7 or higher and be CTAHPERD members.

Target applicant(s): College students. Adult students.
Minimum GPA: 2.7
Amount: $1,000.
Number of awards: Varies.
Deadline: June 15.
How to apply: Applications are available online. An application form, personal statement, transcript and two letters of recommendation are required.
Exclusive: Visit www.UltimateScholarshipBook.com and enter code CO138023 for updates on this award.

(1381) · Cynthia and Alan Baran Fine Arts and Music Scholarship Fund

Community Foundation of Middle Tennessee
3833 Cleghorn Avenue, Suite 400, Nashville, TN 37215-2519
Phone: 888-540-5200
Email: pcole@cfmt.org
https://www.cfmt.org/grants-scholarships/
Purpose: To aid students in pursuing careers in visual arts and music.
Eligibility: Applicants must be current students at an accredited college or university, take at least six credit hours and be enrolled in a bachelor's of fine art, bachelor's of studio art, master's of fine art or bachelor's or master's in music program. Art students must major in painting, drawing, sculpture, ceramics, photography or printmaking. Preference for music scholarships is given to those studying acoustic mandolin or acoustic guitar. A minimum GPA of 3.0 is required.
Target applicant(s): College students. Graduate school students. Adult students.
Minimum GPA: 3.0
Amount: Varies.
Number of awards: Varies.
Deadline: March 15.
How to apply: Applications are available online. An application form, transcript, essay, Student Aid Report and two appraisal forms are required.
Exclusive: Visit www.UltimateScholarshipBook.com and enter code CO138123 for updates on this award.

(1382) · Daniel E. Lambert Memorial Scholarship

American Legion, Department of Maine
5 Verti Drive, Winslow, ME 04901-0727
Phone: 207-873-3229
Email: legionme@mainelegion.org
http://www.mainelegion.org/pages/programs/scholarships.php
Purpose: To support the descendants of veterans who demonstrate financial need and who are residents of Maine.
Eligibility: Applicants must be enrolled in an accredited college or vocational technical school and be U.S. citizens. A parent or grandparent must be a veteran, verified by a copy of military discharge papers with the application. Applicants must have good character and believe in the American way of life.
Target applicant(s): College students. Adult students.
Amount: $1,000.
Number of awards: Up to 2.
Deadline: May 1.
How to apply: Applications are available online.
Exclusive: Visit www.UltimateScholarshipBook.com and enter code AM138223 for updates on this award.

(1383) · Daniels Scholarship Program

Daniels Fund
101 Monroe Street, Denver, CO 80206
Phone: 303-393-7220
http://www.danielsfund.org
Purpose: To support students who have a proven record of character strength, leadership and a commitment to their communities in accomplishing their goal of obtaining a post-secondary education.
Eligibility: Applicants must be graduating high school seniors enrolling in any nonprofit accredited college or university and be a resident of Colorado, New Mexico, Utah or Wyoming. Students must submit a FAFSA to demonstrate financial need, have a minimum 2.0 GPA and earn an ACT score of 17 and minimum SAT Math score of 470 along with a minimum SAT Critical Reading score of 450.
Target applicant(s): High school students.
Minimum GPA: 2.0
Amount: Varies.
Number of awards: Varies.
Scholarship may be renewable.
Deadline: November 15.
How to apply: Applications are available online.
Exclusive: Visit www.UltimateScholarshipBook.com and enter code DA138323 for updates on this award.

(1384) · David E. Simon Scholarship

Indiana Golf Association
P.O. Box 516, Franklin, IN 46131
Phone: 317-738-9696
Email: astrong@indianagolf.org
https://www.indianagolf.org/scholarships/
Purpose: To aid those students who have worked at an Indiana golf facility in their pursuit of a college education.
Eligibility: Applicants must be a senior in high school, have worked in an Indiana golf facility in the previous 12 months, have a 3.0 GPA, display strong character and prove financial need. Selection is based on financial need, personal essay and academic achievement.
Target applicant(s): High school students.
Minimum GPA: 3.0
Amount: $5,000.
Number of awards: Varies.
Deadline: February 26.
How to apply: Applications are available online and must include an IRS 1040 form, high school transcript, personal essay and at least one letter of reference. In addition to the main application form, students should submit the academic evaluation form and employment evaluation form.
Exclusive: Visit www.UltimateScholarshipBook.com and enter code IN138423 for updates on this award.

(1385) · DC Tuition Assistance Grant Program

Government of the District of Columbia
DC Tuition Assistance Grant Program, 810 First Street NE, Third Floor, Washington, DC 20002
Phone: 877-485-6751
Email: osse@dc.gov
http://osse.dc.gov
Purpose: To provide financial assistance to students in the District of Columbia who wish to attend either a public university in a different state or a historically black college or university.
Eligibility: Applicants must be residents who have lived in the District of Columbia for at least 12 months prior to the beginning of their freshman

year of college. Applicants must also either plan to or be currently enrolled at least half-time in an undergraduate or certificate program.
Target applicant(s): High school students. College students.
Amount: Up to $10,000.
Number of awards: Varies.
Scholarship may be renewable.
Deadline: July.
How to apply: Applications are available online.
Exclusive: Visit www.UltimateScholarshipBook.com and enter code GO138523 for updates on this award.

(1386) · Delaware Diamond State Scholarship

Department of Education - School Supports
The Townsend Building, 401 Federal Street, Suite 2, Dover, DE 19901-3639
Phone: 800-292-7935
Email: dhec@doe.k12.de.us
https://www.doe.k12.de.us/page/316
Purpose: To support academically-talented Delaware student residents.
Eligibility: Applicants must be residents of Delaware, U.S. citizens or eligible non-citizens, high school seniors who rank in the upper quarter of their class and score a minimum of 1200 on the SAT and enroll as full-time students in a degree program at a regionally accredited college.
Target applicant(s): High school students.
Amount: $1,250.
Number of awards: 50.
Scholarship may be renewable.
Deadline: February 26.
How to apply: Applications are available online.
Exclusive: Visit www.UltimateScholarshipBook.com and enter code DE138623 for updates on this award.

(1387) · Delaware Educational Benefits for Children of Deceased Veterans and Others

Department of Education - School Supports
The Townsend Building, 401 Federal Street, Suite 2, Dover, DE 19901-3639
Phone: 800-292-7935
Email: dhec@doe.k12.de.us
https://www.doe.k12.de.us/page/316
Purpose: To assist children of deceased veterans.
Eligibility: Applicants must be U.S. citizens or eligible non-citizens who have been Delaware residents for at least three years prior to application. They must be the child of an armed forces member who died from a service-related cause, is/was a prisoner of war or has been declared missing in action; a state police officer whose death was service-related or a Department of Transportation employee who worked on the state highway system whose death was job-related. Applicants must be 16 to 24 years of age. Priority is given to students attending a Delaware public college, followed by students attending Delaware private colleges and those attending out-of-state institutions. Those attending private or out-of-state colleges must pursue majors that are not offered by Delaware public colleges.
Target applicant(s): High school students. College students.
Amount: Full tuition and fees.
Number of awards: Varies.
Scholarship may be renewable.
Deadline: 6-8 weeks prior to the start of classes.
How to apply: Applications are available online. An application form is required.

Exclusive: Visit www.UltimateScholarshipBook.com and enter code DE138723 for updates on this award.

(1388) · Delaware Scholarship Incentive Program

Department of Education - School Supports
The Townsend Building, 401 Federal Street, Suite 2, Dover, DE 19901-3639
Phone: 800-292-7935
Email: dhec@doe.k12.de.us
https://www.doe.k12.de.us/page/316
Purpose: To assist Delaware student residents.
Eligibility: Applicants must be legal residents of Delaware and U.S. citizens or eligible non-citizens who are enrolled full-time at a regionally-accredited undergraduate institution in Delaware or Pennsylvania. Other undergraduate and graduate students will be considered if their major is not available at a public college in Delaware. Students must demonstrate substantial financial need and have a minimum 2.5 GPA. Applicants must also submit the Free Application for Federal Student Aid (FAFSA).
Target applicant(s): High school students. College students. Graduate school students. Adult students.
Minimum GPA: 2.5
Amount: $1,000 a year.
Number of awards: Varies.
Scholarship may be renewable.
Deadline: April 15.
How to apply: Delaware residents are automatically considered for the scholarship when their FAFSA form is received.
Exclusive: Visit www.UltimateScholarshipBook.com and enter code DE138823 for updates on this award.

(1389) · Delaware Solid Waste Authority John P. "Pat" Healy Scholarship

Department of Education - School Supports
The Townsend Building, 401 Federal Street, Suite 2, Dover, DE 19901-3639
Phone: 800-292-7935
Email: dhec@doe.k12.de.us
https://www.doe.k12.de.us/page/316
Purpose: To aid Delaware students who are preparing for careers in environmental engineering or environmental science.
Eligibility: Applicants must be Delaware residents, U.S. citizens or eligible non-citizens and full-time students. They must be high school seniors, undergraduate freshmen or undergraduate sophomores majoring in or planning to major in environmental sciences or environmental engineering at a Delaware college or university. They also must complete a Free Application for Federal Student Aid (FAFSA) form for the upcoming school year. Selection is based on academic achievement, leadership skills, extracurricular involvement and financial need.
Target applicant(s): High school students. College students. Adult students.
Amount: $1,500-$2,500.
Number of awards: Varies.
Scholarship may be renewable.
Deadline: March.
How to apply: Applications are available online. An application form, personal essay, transcript and FAFSA are required.
Exclusive: Visit www.UltimateScholarshipBook.com and enter code DE138923 for updates on this award.

(1390) · Delegate Scholarship

Maryland Higher Education Commission
Office of Student Financial Assistance, 6 North Liberty Street,
Baltimore, MD 21201
Phone: 800-974-1024
Email: osfamail@mhec.state.md.us
https://mhec.maryland.gov
Purpose: To assist Maryland undergraduate and graduate students who can demonstrate financial need.
Eligibility: Applicants must be legal residents of the state of Maryland and complete the Free Application for Federal Student Aid (FAFSA). They must show financial need if the Office of Student Financial Assistance (OFSA) makes the award for the applicant's delegate. Applicants must be or must plan to be degree-seeking students at a Maryland institution. Selection is based on the overall strength of the application.
Target applicant(s): High school students. College students. Graduate school students. Adult students.
Amount: Up to $19,000.
Number of awards: Varies.
Scholarship may be renewable.
Deadline: March 1.
How to apply: Complete and file the Free Application for Federal Student Aid (FAFSA). Contact delegate's office for specific application forms. The Office of Student Financial Assistance (OSFA) can provide a list of all state legislators. An application form and supporting documents are required.
Exclusive: Visit www.UltimateScholarshipBook.com and enter code MA139023 for updates on this award.

(1391) · Dennis Schoepp Memorial Scholarship

Funeral Service Foundation
13625 Bishop's Drive, Brookfield, WI 53005-6607
Phone: 877-402-5900
Email: info@funeralservicefoundation.org
https://www.funeralservicefoundation.org/academicscholarships/
Purpose: To aid students with tuition costs associated with mortuary science education.
Eligibility: Applicants must be a student of funeral service from Montana and be enrolled full- or part-time in an American Board of Funeral Service Education accredited program. Selection is based on the overall strength of the application.
Target applicant(s): College students. Graduate school students. Adult students.
Minimum GPA: 2.0
Amount: Varies.
Number of awards: Varies.
Deadline: April 1, November 1.
How to apply: Applications are available online. An application form, essay, academic transcript and video submissions are required.
Exclusive: Visit www.UltimateScholarshipBook.com and enter code FU139123 for updates on this award.

(1392) · Department of Children and Families (DCF) Foster Child Tuition Waiver and Fee Assistance Program

Massachusetts Department of Higher Education
Office of Student Financial Assistance, 454 Broadway, Suite 200, Revere, MA 02151
Phone: 617-727-9420
Email: osfa@osfa.mass.edu
https://www.mass.edu/osfa/programs/programs.asp
Purpose: To provide financial support to Massachusetts foster children who are pursuing higher education.
Eligibility: Applicants must be current or former foster children who were placed in Massachusetts state custody for at least 12 months due to a Care and Protection Petition. They must not have been adopted or returned home, and they must be 24 years old or younger. Students must be enrolled as full-time undergraduates at a state-supported school.
Target applicant(s): High school students. College students. Adult students.
Amount: Full tuition.
Number of awards: Varies.
Deadline: Varies.
How to apply: Applications are available at college financial aid offices.
Exclusive: Visit www.UltimateScholarshipBook.com and enter code MA139223 for updates on this award.

(1393) · Dick Griffiths Memorial Scholarship

California Association on Postsecondary Education and Disability (CAPED)
10073 Valley View Street, #242, Cypress, CA 90630
Phone: 562-397-2810
Email: capedscholarships2018@gmail.com
http://www.caped.co/scholarships/
Purpose: To support students with a learning disability in math who are pursuing higher education.
Eligibility: Applicants must have a verifiable learning disability in math and be currently enrolled as a student at a California college or university with a GPA of 2.5 for undergraduates or 3.0 for graduate students. Students must have completed at least six semester or eight quarter units as an undergraduate student or three semester or four quarter units as a graduate student.
Target applicant(s): College students. Graduate school students. Adult students.
Minimum GPA: 2.5 for undergraduate students, 3.0 for graduate students
Amount: $1,000.
Number of awards: 1.
Deadline: August 31.
How to apply: Applications are available online.
Exclusive: Visit www.UltimateScholarshipBook.com and enter code CA139323 for updates on this award.

(1394) · District of Columbia Tuition Assistance Grant

DC Tuition Assistance Grant Office
1050 1st Street NE, Fifth Floor, Washington, DC 20002
Phone: 202-727-2824
Email: osse@dc.gov
https://osse.dc.gov/
Purpose: To make attending out-of-state, private and Historically Black schools more affordable for DC residents.
Eligibility: Applicants must be residents of Washington, DC for at least 12 months before the start of their freshman year of college, high school graduates or GED recipients, enrolled at least half-time at an eligible institution and be 24 years of age or younger. Applicants must maintain satisfactory academic progress, not have defaulted on student loans, have registered with the Selective Service, be U.S. citizens or permanent residents, have not already received a B.A. or B.S. and have not been incarcerated. The award provides up to $10,000 a year for the difference between in-state and out-of-state tuition at public four year

institutions in the U.S. and up to $2,500 per year for private colleges in DC, private Historically Black Colleges and Universities or two-year colleges nationwide.
Target applicant(s): High school students. College students.
Amount: $2,500-$10,000.
Number of awards: Varies.
Scholarship may be renewable.
Deadline: September 17.
How to apply: Applications are available online.
Exclusive: Visit www.UltimateScholarshipBook.com and enter code DC139423 for updates on this award.

(1395) · Don't Mess with Texas Scholarship

Don't Mess with Texas
Sherry Matthews Advocacy, 200 South Congress Avenue, Austin, TX 78704
Phone: 512-476-4368
Email: scholarship@dontmesswithtexas.org
http://www.dontmesswithtexas.org/education-overview/
Purpose: To support students concerned about litter.
Eligibility: Student must be a Texas high school senior who wants to attend a two- or four-year college or university in Texas. To apply for the scholarship, students must complete the application and one or two essays and submit two letters of recommendation (one from a school-related source and the other from a non-school related source).
Target applicant(s): High school students.
Amount: Varies.
Number of awards: Varies.
Deadline: March.
How to apply: Applications are available online.
Exclusive: Visit www.UltimateScholarshipBook.com and enter code DO139523 for updates on this award.

(1396) · Don't Wait to Reach Your Potential Scholarship for Alabama Teens

Potential Magazine
61 Market Place, Montgomery, AL 36117
Phone: 334-518-7810
http://potentialmagazine.com
Purpose: To help Alabama students pursue post-secondary education.
Eligibility: Applicants must be Alabama residents in grades 9-12. Students are required to sign up for the weekly eNewsletter.
Target applicant(s): High school students.
Amount: $500.
Number of awards: 1.
Deadline: January 4.
How to apply: Applications are available online.
Exclusive: Visit www.UltimateScholarshipBook.com and enter code PO139623 for updates on this award.

(1397) · Dorian De Long Arts and Music Scholarship

Jefferson County Education Association
12650 W 64th Ave, Unit E195, Arvada, CO 80004
Email: educate@ddamscholarship.com
https://www.ddamscholarship.com
Purpose: To support students who are pursuing a degree in the arts.
Eligibility: Applicants must be graduating Colorado high school seniors who are pursuing the study of arts.
Target applicant(s): High school students.

Amount: $1,500.
Number of awards: 1.
Scholarship may be renewable.
Deadline: March 1.
How to apply: Applications are available online.
Exclusive: Visit www.UltimateScholarshipBook.com and enter code JE139723 for updates on this award.

(1398) · Doris and Clarence Glick Classical Music Scholarship

Hawaii Community Foundation - Scholarships
827 Fort Street Mall, Honolulu, HI 96813
Phone: 888-731-3863
Email: scholarships@hcf-hawaii.org
https://www.hawaiicommunityfoundation.org/
Purpose: To provide financial assistance for Hawaii students of classical music.
Eligibility: Applicants must be majoring in music with an emphasis on classical music. They must have a GPA of 2.7 or higher, and they must describe their program of study as it relates to classical music in their personal statement.
Target applicant(s): High school students. College students. Graduate school students. Adult students.
Minimum GPA: 2.7
Amount: Varies.
Number of awards: Varies.
Deadline: January 31.
How to apply: To apply, register online, complete the online application and select the scholarships to which you wish to apply. In addition, mail the supporting materials: printed confirmation page from the online application, personal statement, copy of Student Aid Report (SAR) available at www.fafsa.ed.gov and official transcript.
Exclusive: Visit www.UltimateScholarshipBook.com and enter code HA139823 for updates on this award.

(1399) · Dorothy D. Greer Journalist of the Year Scholarship Competition

Colorado Student Media Association
Jack Kennedy, CSMA Executive Director, 9253 Sori Lane, Highlands Ranch, CO 80126
Phone: 303-550-4755
Email: jpkjournalism@gmail.com
http://colostudentmedia.com/
Purpose: To support outstanding young journalists.
Eligibility: Applicants must be Colorado high school seniors whose schools are members of the Colorado Student Media Association. Students must have worked on their yearbook or newspaper for at least two years. A GPA of 3.0 or higher is required. Selection criteria include neatness (10 percent), quality of work (40 percent), personal statement (20 percent), letters of recommendation (20 percent) and grades (10 percent).
Target applicant(s): High school students.
Minimum GPA: 3.0
Amount: Up to $3,000.
Number of awards: 1.
Deadline: February 15.
How to apply: Applications are available online. An application form, personal statement, transcript, three to four letters of recommendation, samples of published work and action photo are required.

Exclusive: Visit www.UltimateScholarshipBook.com and enter code CO139923 for updates on this award.

(1400) · Douvas Memorial Scholarship

Wyoming Department of Education
2300 Capitol Avenue, Hathaway Building, 2nd Floor, Cheyenne, WY 82002-0050
Phone: 307-777-3469
Email: laurie.hernandez@wyo.gov
http://edu.wyoming.gov
Purpose: To assist first generation Americans in obtaining higher education.
Eligibility: Applicants must have been born in the United States but have parents who were born outside the country. They must be high school seniors or between the ages of 18 and 22, and they must be Wyoming residents. They must attend a Wyoming community college or the University of Wyoming.
Target applicant(s): High school students. College students.
Amount: $500.
Number of awards: 1.
Deadline: April 30.
How to apply: Applications are available online.
Exclusive: Visit www.UltimateScholarshipBook.com and enter code WY140023 for updates on this award.

(1401) · Dr. and Mrs. Arthur F. Sullivan Fund

Connecticut Community Foundation Center for Philanthropy
43 Field Street, Waterbury, CT 06702
Phone: 203-753-1315
Email: scholarships@conncf.org
http://www.conncf.org
Purpose: To provide financial assistance to students who are entering or enrolled in medical school.
Eligibility: Applicants must be accepted to or enrolled in medical school. They must reside in the Connecticut Community Foundation's service area and demonstrate exemplary academic achievement. Scholarship awarded in even years.
Target applicant(s): College students. Graduate school students. Adult students.
Amount: Varies.
Number of awards: Varies.
Deadline: March 15.
How to apply: Applications are available online.
Exclusive: Visit www.UltimateScholarshipBook.com and enter code CO140123 for updates on this award.

(1402) · Dr. Edison and Sallie Miyawaki Scholarship Fund

Hawaii Community Foundation - Scholarships
827 Fort Street Mall, Honolulu, HI 96813
Phone: 888-731-3863
Email: scholarships@hcf-hawaii.org
https://www.hawaiicommunityfoundation.org/
Purpose: To reward students with outstanding achievement in extracurricular activities.
Eligibility: Applicants must be Hawaii residents who plan to attend an accredited institution of higher learning. They must have a GPA between 2.5 and 3.0, demonstrate financial need and participate in an extracurricular sports program.

Target applicant(s): High school students. College students. Graduate school students. Adult students.
Minimum GPA: 2.5
Amount: Varies.
Number of awards: Varies.
Deadline: January 31.
How to apply: To apply, register online, complete the online application and select the scholarships to which you wish to apply. In addition, mail the supporting materials: printed confirmation page from the online application, personal statement, copy of Student Aid Report (SAR) available at www.fafsa.ed.gov and official transcript.
Exclusive: Visit www.UltimateScholarshipBook.com and enter code HA140223 for updates on this award.

(1403) · Dr. Hans and Clara Zimmerman Foundation Education Scholarship

Hawaii Community Foundation - Scholarships
827 Fort Street Mall, Honolulu, HI 96813
Phone: 888-731-3863
Email: scholarships@hcf-hawaii.org
https://www.hawaiicommunityfoundation.org/
Purpose: To provide financial assistance to Hawaii students who want to study education.
Eligibility: Applicants major in education with an emphasis in teaching. They must have a GPA of 2.8 or higher, demonstrate good character and be full-time students. Preference is given to students of Hawaiian ethnicity and to students with at least two years of teaching experience. Applicants must discuss their teaching philosophies in their personal statement.
Target applicant(s): High school students. College students. Graduate school students. Adult students.
Minimum GPA: 2.8
Amount: Varies.
Number of awards: Varies.
Deadline: January 31.
How to apply: To apply, register online, complete the online application and select the scholarships to which you wish to apply. In addition, mail the supporting materials: printed confirmation page from the online application, personal statement, copy of Student Aid Report (SAR) available at www.fafsa.ed.gov and official transcript.
Exclusive: Visit www.UltimateScholarshipBook.com and enter code HA140323 for updates on this award.

(1404) · Dr. Hans and Clara Zimmerman Foundation Health Scholarships

Hawaii Community Foundation - Scholarships
827 Fort Street Mall, Honolulu, HI 96813
Phone: 888-731-3863
Email: scholarships@hcf-hawaii.org
https://www.hawaiicommunityfoundation.org/
Purpose: To provide financial assistance to Hawaii students who want to study in health fields.
Eligibility: Applicants must plan to major in a health-related field other than sports medicine, non-clinical psychology or social work at a U.S. college or university. They must be full-time college juniors, college seniors or graduate students, and they must have a GPA of 3.0 or higher.
Target applicant(s): College students. Graduate school students. Adult students.
Minimum GPA: 3.0
Amount: Varies.

Number of awards: Varies.

Deadline: January 31.

How to apply: To apply, register online, complete the online application and select the scholarships to which you wish to apply. In addition, mail the supporting materials: printed confirmation page from the online application, personal statement, copy of Student Aid Report (SAR) available at www.fafsa.ed.gov and official transcript.

Exclusive: Visit www.UltimateScholarshipBook.com and enter code HA140423 for updates on this award.

(1405) · Dr. Ralph E. White Graduating Senior Scholarship

California State PTA

2327 L Street, Sacramento, CA 95816-5014

Phone: 916-440-1985

Email: grants@capta.org

http://capta.org/programs-events/scholarships/

Purpose: To support students who intend to pursue a career in a medical field.

Eligibility: Applicants must be California residents and high school seniors graduating from a California high school. Students must be a member of their school PTA/PTSA in good standing, or if the high school does not have a PTA/PTSA, a member of a PTA/PTSA in good standing and a council, district or state PTA board member. An essay is required to be submitted on a provided prompt.

Target applicant(s): High school students.

Amount: $500.

Number of awards: 2.

Deadline: February 1.

How to apply: Applications are available online.

Exclusive: Visit www.UltimateScholarshipBook.com and enter code CA140523 for updates on this award.

(1406) · Dr. William S. Boyd Scholarship

Chiropractic Association of Louisiana

10636 Timberlake Drive, Baton Rouge, LA 70810

http://www.cal-online.org

Purpose: To aid Louisiana chiropractic students.

Eligibility: Applicants must be Louisiana residents who are juniors or seniors at a CCE-accredited chiropractic college located in Louisiana. They must have a GPA of 2.75 or higher and must intend to work in Louisiana after graduation. Selection is based on the overall strength of the application.

Target applicant(s): College students. Adult students.

Minimum GPA: 2.75

Amount: Varies.

Number of awards: At least 1.

Deadline: June 30.

How to apply: Applications are available by request from the CAL. An application form, three letters of recommendation and an endorsement from a current member of the CAL are required.

Exclusive: Visit www.UltimateScholarshipBook.com and enter code CH140623 for updates on this award.

(1407) · Dunkin' Donuts Connecticut Scholarship

Dunkin' Donuts Connecticut Scholarship

Email: dunkindonuts@scholarshipamerica.org

https://learnmore.scholarsapply.org/dunkinct/

Purpose: To provide financial assistance for well-rounded students.

Eligibility: Applicants must be high school seniors and Connecticut residents who excel in academics, demonstrate leadership and participate in school and community activities. They must plan to enroll at least half-time in a bachelor's degree, associate degree or certificate program at an accredited institution of higher learning.

Target applicant(s): High school students.

Amount: $1,000.

Number of awards: Up to 10.

Deadline: March.

How to apply: Applications are available from Dunkin' Donuts stores and high school guidance offices beginning March 1 of each year.

Exclusive: Visit www.UltimateScholarshipBook.com and enter code DU140723 for updates on this award.

(1408) · E.H. Marth Food Protection and Food Science Scholarship

WAFP Scholarship Committee

c/o Tera Montgomery, 1 University Plaza, Platteville, WI 53818

Phone: 608-342-6027

Email: montgomeryt@uwplatt.edu

http://www.wifoodprotection.org/scholarships.php

Purpose: To support students who are preparing for careers that are related to food or environmental sanitation.

Eligibility: Applicants must be Wisconsin residents who are enrolled at or have been accepted into a postsecondary institution that is either located in the state of Wisconsin or that has a reciprocal enrollment agreement with Wisconsin. They must be or plan to be enrolled full-time in an undergraduate academic program that is related to food science, environmental sanitation or dairy science. Selection is based on the overall strength of the application.

Target applicant(s): College students. Adult students.

Amount: $3,000.

Number of awards: 1.

Scholarship may be renewable.

Deadline: June 25.

How to apply: Applications are available online. An application form, official transcript and letter of recommendation are required.

Exclusive: Visit www.UltimateScholarshipBook.com and enter code WA140823 for updates on this award.

(1409) · Eagle Scout of the Year

American Legion, Department of Wisconsin

2930 American Legion Drive, P.O. Box 388, Portage, WI 53901-0388

Phone: 608-745-1090

Email: info@wilegion.org

https://wilegion.org/oratorical-scholarships/

Purpose: To reward outstanding service as an Eagle Scout at the state level.

Eligibility: Applicants must demonstrate outstanding service in community, church and school and must be at least 15 years of age, in high school and either members of a troop chartered by the American Legion/Auxiliary or sons or grandsons of members of the American Legion/Auxiliary. Students must have received the Eagle Scout Award as well as the Boy Scout religious emblem. Scholarships may be used to attend a state-accredited college, university or other school above the high school level.

Target applicant(s): High school students.

Amount: $2,500-$10,000.

Number of awards: 4.

Deadline: March 1.

How to apply: Applications are available from the local Legion Post or from the Wisconsin American Legion Headquarters.
Exclusive: Visit www.UltimateScholarshipBook.com and enter code AM140923 for updates on this award.

(1410) · Early Childhood Educators Scholarship

Massachusetts Department of Higher Education
Office of Student Financial Assistance, 454 Broadway, Suite 200, Revere, MA 02151
Phone: 617-727-9420
Email: osfa@osfa.mass.edu
https://www.mass.edu/osfa/programs/programs.asp
Purpose: To support the education of Massachusetts teachers employed in early childhood settings.
Eligibility: Applicants must be legal residents of Massachusetts who have worked as early childhood educators in the state for at least one year prior to receiving the scholarship. They must continue working in the profession while enrolled in school and upon completion of the degree. Students must be enrolled in Early Childhood Education or a related undergraduate program, and they cannot have any previously earned bachelor's degrees.
Target applicant(s): College students. Graduate school students. Adult students.
Amount: Varies.
Number of awards: Varies.
Scholarship may be renewable.
Deadline: October 1.
How to apply: Applications are available online.
Exclusive: Visit www.UltimateScholarshipBook.com and enter code MA141023 for updates on this award.

(1411) · Early College for ME

Early College for ME
Maine Community College System, 323 State Street, Augusta, ME 04330-7131
Phone: 207-629-4000
Email: mpour@mccs.me.edu
https://www.mccs.me.edu/
Purpose: To help high school students who are undecided about college.
Eligibility: Applicants must be in their junior year at one of the 74 Maine high schools participating in the program. The list of schools is online at http://www.earlycollege.me.edu/participating.html. Students must be Maine residents for at least one year prior to entering the first year of college and must have not yet made plans for college and yet be capable of succeeding at a community college. High schools may also take financial need into consideration when selecting students for the program as well as whether or not the student is the first one to attend college in their family. The program provides community college courses in the senior year of high school, as available, as well as financial aid for a one-year or two-year degree program at a Maine community college.
Target applicant(s): High school students.
Amount: Up to $2,000.
Number of awards: Varies.
Deadline: Varies, set by each school.
How to apply: Speak with your guidance counselor at your high school about entering the program.
Exclusive: Visit www.UltimateScholarshipBook.com and enter code EA141123 for updates on this award.

(1412) · Early Starters Award

British American Foundation of Texas
Email: info@baftx.org
http://www.baftx.org
Purpose: To set Texas students on the track of saving for college.
Eligibility: Applicants must be residents of Texas and attend middle school within the Texas education system. Students must have an "A" grade average and demonstrate financial need.
Target applicant(s): Junior high students or younger.
Minimum GPA: 3.4
Amount: $1,000.
Number of awards: 1.
Deadline: January 31.
How to apply: Applications are available online.
Exclusive: Visit www.UltimateScholarshipBook.com and enter code BR141223 for updates on this award.

(1413) · Ed and Charlotte Rodgers Scholarships

Alabama Road Builders Association Inc.
630 Adams Avenue, Montgomery, AL 36104
Phone: 334-832-4331
Email: hayley@alrba.org
http://www.alrba.org
Purpose: To support financially needy civil engineering students.
Eligibility: Applicants must be full-time civil engineering students who have completed their sophomore year of college. They must be in good standing academically, have a good GPA and demonstrate financial need. Selection is based on leadership skills, awards received and extracurricular involvements.
Target applicant(s): College students. Adult students.
Amount: Varies.
Number of awards: Varies.
Deadline: August 1.
How to apply: Applications are available online. An application form, a recent photo and a personal essay are required.
Exclusive: Visit www.UltimateScholarshipBook.com and enter code AL141323 for updates on this award.

(1414) · Edmund F. Maxwell Foundation Scholarship

Edmund F. Maxwell Foundation
P.O. Box 55548, Seattle, WA 98155-0548
Email: admin@maxwell.org
http://www.maxwell.org
Purpose: To assist high-achieving students who follow the ideals of Edmund F. Maxwell: ability, aptitude and citizenship.
Eligibility: Applicants must be from western Washington, plan to attend an accredited independent school that is primarily not tax-funded and have a minimum SAT score of 1200. Students must submit a FAFSA form and demonstrate financial need.
Target applicant(s): High school students.
Amount: Up to $5,000.
Number of awards: Varies.
Scholarship may be renewable.
Deadline: April 30.
How to apply: Applications are available online.
Exclusive: Visit www.UltimateScholarshipBook.com and enter code ED141423 for updates on this award.

(1415) · Educational Award/Graduating High School Female

New York State Women's 600 Club
Connie Canfield, Chairman, 1288 Scribner Hollow Road, East Jewett, NY 12424-5538
Phone: 518-589-5319
Email: cmc600ed@gmail.com
http://www.bowlny.com/
Purpose: To support New York graduating high school senior female bowlers as they embark on their college careers.
Eligibility: Applicant must be a member of a league or high school bowling team certified by USBC. Applicants must also have bowled at least 39 games in the current season or 18 games during the current high school season. Each applicant must also be sponsored by a current member of the New York State Women's 600 Bowling Club.
Target applicant(s): High school students.
Amount: Varies.
Number of awards: Varies.
Deadline: March 1.
How to apply: Applications are available online and consist of forms to be completed by the applicant, a league official, a school official and the NYSW 600 member sponsor.
Exclusive: Visit www.UltimateScholarshipBook.com and enter code NE141523 for updates on this award.

(1416) · Educational Excellence Scholarship

Kentucky Higher Education Assistance Authority
P.O. Box 798, Frankfort, KY 40602
Phone: 800-928-8926
Email: blane@kheaa.com
http://www.kheaa.com
Purpose: To reward outstanding Kentucky high school students.
Eligibility: Applicants must have a minimum 2.5 GPA, be graduating from eligible Kentucky high schools and meet high school graduation requirements. The scholarship amount is based on high school GPA and ACT composite score.
Target applicant(s): High school students.
Minimum GPA: 2.5
Amount: Up to $500.
Number of awards: Varies.
Scholarship may be renewable.
Deadline: Varies.
How to apply: High schools send eligible students' GPAs to the Kentucky Department of Education. There is no application for this award.
Exclusive: Visit www.UltimateScholarshipBook.com and enter code KE141623 for updates on this award.

(1417) · Educational Opportunity Fund (EOF) Grant

New Jersey Commission on Higher Education
P.O. Box 542, Trenton, NJ 08625
Phone: 609-292-4310
Email: meverett@che.state.nj.us
http://www.state.nj.us/highereducation
Purpose: To support underprivileged students in New Jersey.
Eligibility: Applicants must be able to show financial need and a background of family poverty, and they cannot exceed the established maximum income. They must be enrolled full-time in one of the participating public or private colleges in New Jersey, and they must have been residents of the state for at least 12 months prior to enrollment. Students pursuing a bachelor's degree cannot have any prior baccalaureate degrees, and students pursuing a two-year degree cannot have any previous associate's degrees. Applicants must not major in theology or divinity.
Target applicant(s): High school students. College students. Graduate school students. Adult students.
Amount: $200-$2,500.
Number of awards: Varies.
Scholarship may be renewable.
Deadline: Varies.
How to apply: Applications are available from campus EOF directors.
Exclusive: Visit www.UltimateScholarshipBook.com and enter code NE141723 for updates on this award.

(1418) · Educational Training Voucher Programs for Foster Youth

Foster Care to Success
21351 Gentry Drive, Suite 130, Sterling, VA 20166
Phone: 800-585-6188
Email: support@statevoucher.org
http://www.fc2success.org/programs/scholarships-and-grants/
Purpose: To support foster care students pursuing a higher education.
Eligibility: Applicants must have been in foster care for their 18th birthday and have aged out at that time, been adopted from foster care with the adoption finalized after their 16th birthday, or have their foster care case closed between the ages of 18 and 21. Students must be residents of Alabama, Arizona, Colorado, Maryland, Missouri, New York, North Carolina, Ohio or the District of Columbia. Students must be a U.S. citizen with assets worth less than $10,000. Applicants must be at least 17 but younger than 21 to apply for the first time. Students must have been accepted into a degree, certificate or other accredited program at a college, university, technical or vocational school.
Target applicant(s): High school students. College students. Adult students.
Amount: $5,000.
Number of awards: Varies.
Scholarship may be renewable.
Deadline: January.
How to apply: Applications are available online.
Exclusive: Visit www.UltimateScholarshipBook.com and enter code FO141823 for updates on this award.

(1419) · Edward L. Simeth Scholarships

Tool, Die and Machining Association of Wisconsin
W175 N11117 Stonewood Drive, Suite 204, Germantown, WI 53022
Phone: 262-532-2440
Email: toolmaker@TDMAW.org
https://tdmaw.org/Scholarships-Available%21
Purpose: To support Wisconsin students who are enrolled in a machine tool operations or tool and die training program at an accredited technical school.
Eligibility: Applicants must be Wisconsin residents, and they must have a high school diploma or GED. They must have completed at least one semester at an accredited technical school located in Wisconsin or pursuing a state apprenticeship and be enrolled in a machine tool operations or tool and die program. Selection is based on the overall strength of the application.
Target applicant(s): College students. Adult students.
Minimum GPA: 3.0
Amount: Up to $500 per semester.

Number of awards: Varies.
Scholarship may be renewable.
Deadline: July 15 (Fall), December 1 (Spring).
How to apply: Applications are available online. An application form, an official transcript and two references are required.
Exclusive: Visit www.UltimateScholarshipBook.com and enter code TO141923 for updates on this award.

(1420) · Edward Payson and Bernice Piilani Irwin Scholarship

Hawaii Community Foundation - Scholarships
827 Fort Street Mall, Honolulu, HI 96813
Phone: 888-731-3863
Email: scholarships@hcf-hawaii.org
https://www.hawaiicommunityfoundation.org/
Purpose: To provide financial assistance to Hawaii students who are pursuing careers in journalism.
Eligibility: Applicants must be college juniors, college seniors or graduate students majoring in journalism or communications. They must have a GPA of 2.75 or higher.
Target applicant(s): College students. Graduate school students. Adult students.
Minimum GPA: 2.75
Amount: Varies.
Number of awards: Varies.
Deadline: January 31.
How to apply: To apply, register online, complete the online application and select the scholarships to which you wish to apply. In addition, mail the supporting materials: printed confirmation page from the online application, personal statement, copy of Student Aid Report (SAR) available at www.fafsa.ed.gov and official transcript.
Exclusive: Visit www.UltimateScholarshipBook.com and enter code HA142023 for updates on this award.

(1421) · Eizo and Toyo Sakumoto Trust Scholarship

Hawaii Community Foundation - Scholarships
827 Fort Street Mall, Honolulu, HI 96813
Phone: 888-731-3863
Email: scholarships@hcf-hawaii.org
https://www.hawaiicommunityfoundation.org/
Purpose: To assist Hawaiian students of Japanese ancestry.
Eligibility: Applicants must be Hawaii residents of primarily Japanese ancestry who were born in the state and who are a graduate level student at a college or university in Hawaii. They must have a GPA of 3.5 or higher and prove financial need.
Target applicant(s): Graduate school students. Adult students.
Minimum GPA: 3.5
Amount: Varies.
Number of awards: Varies.
Deadline: January 31.
How to apply: To apply, register online, complete the online application and select the scholarships to which you wish to apply. In addition, mail the supporting materials: printed confirmation page from the online application, personal statement, copy of Student Aid Report (SAR) available at www.fafsa.ed.gov and official transcript.
Exclusive: Visit www.UltimateScholarshipBook.com and enter code HA142123 for updates on this award.

(1422) · Ellison Onizuka Memorial Scholarship Fund

Hawaii Community Foundation - Scholarships
827 Fort Street Mall, Honolulu, HI 96813
Phone: 888-731-3863
Email: scholarships@hcf-hawaii.org
https://www.hawaiicommunityfoundation.org/
Purpose: To provide financial assistance to Hawaii students who plan to major in aerospace engineering.
Eligibility: Applicants must be graduating high school in the year of application and plan to pursue a degree in aerospace engineering or a related field. Students must have a GPA of 3.0, and their transcripts must list their SAT scores.
Target applicant(s): High school students.
Minimum GPA: 3.0
Amount: Varies.
Number of awards: Varies.
Deadline: January 31.
How to apply: To apply, register online, complete the online application and select the scholarships to which you wish to apply. In addition, mail the supporting materials: printed confirmation page from the online application, two letters of recommendation, personal statement, copy of Student Aid Report (SAR) available at www.fafsa.ed.gov and official transcript. The personal statement must describe participation in extracurricular activities, clubs and community service.
Exclusive: Visit www.UltimateScholarshipBook.com and enter code HA142223 for updates on this award.

(1423) · Emily M. Hewitt and Stephen K. Stocking Memorial Scholarship

Calaveras Big Trees Association
P.O. Box 1196, Arnold, CA 95223
Phone: 209-795-3840
Email: info@bigtrees.org
http://www.bigtrees.org
Purpose: To support students who are committed to communicate a love of nature and an understanding of need to practice conservation.
Eligibility: Applicants must be enrolled full-time in an accredited California post-secondary educational institution and must have career goals that are related to communicating and interpreting nature's wonder. Students pursuing degrees in environmental protection, forestry, wildlife and fisheries biology, parks and recreation, park management, environmental law and public policy, environmental art and California history are encouraged to apply. Selection is based on dedication to the ideals of the scholarship and financial need.
Target applicant(s): High school students. College students. Graduate school students. Adult students.
Amount: $3,000.
Number of awards: 2.
Deadline: April 15.
How to apply: Student must submit a statement of personal and career goals, a resume (and portfolio if applicable) and transcripts of all college work completed to date. On the cover page, include your name, address, phone number and college major.
Exclusive: Visit www.UltimateScholarshipBook.com and enter code CA142323 for updates on this award.

(1424) · Engineering Foundation of Wisconsin Scholarship

Wisconsin Society of Professional Engineers
7044 South 13th Street, Oak Creek, WI 53154

Phone: 414-908-4950
Email: customercare@wspe.org
http://www.wspe.org
Purpose: To aid Wisconsin high school seniors who are planning to pursue education and careers in engineering.
Eligibility: Applicants must be current high school seniors who are U.S. citizens and Wisconsin residents. They must plan to enroll in an undergraduate engineering program at an ABET-accredited school and must intend to pursue careers in engineering after graduating. They must have a GPA of 3.0 or more and an ACT composite score of at least 24. Selection is based on GPA, ACT score, class rank, extracurricular involvement, honors, personal essay and any AP or college-level courses taken.
Target applicant(s): High school students.
Minimum GPA: 3.0
Amount: $2,000.
Number of awards: 2.
Deadline: December.
How to apply: Applications are available online. An application form, transcript and personal essay are required.
Exclusive: Visit www.UltimateScholarshipBook.com and enter code WI142423 for updates on this award.

(1425) · Engineers Foundation of Ohio General Fund Scholarship

Engineers Foundation of Ohio
400 South Fifth Street, Suite 300, Columbus, OH 43215-5430
Phone: 614-223-1177
Email: efo@ohioengineer.com
http://www.ohioengineer.com
Purpose: To aid Ohio engineering students.
Eligibility: Applicants must be U.S. citizens and residents of Ohio. They must be rising juniors or seniors enrolled full-time in an ABET-accredited engineering program that leads to the bachelor of science or its equivalent. They must have a GPA of 3.0 or higher on a 4-point scale. Selection is based on academic achievement, extracurricular involvements and financial need.
Target applicant(s): College students. Adult students.
Minimum GPA: 3.0
Amount: $1,000.
Number of awards: 1.
Deadline: January 15.
How to apply: Applications are available online. An application form, personal essay, faculty evaluation and transcript are required.
Exclusive: Visit www.UltimateScholarshipBook.com and enter code EN142523 for updates on this award.

(1426) · Epsilon Sigma Alpha

North Carolina Division of Vocational Rehabilitation Services
2601 Mail Service Center, Raleigh, NC 27699-2801
Phone: 888-234-6400
Email: jterrell@ncbar.org
https://www.cfnc.org/pay-for-college/apply-for-financial-aid/
Purpose: To provide financial assistance to students who want to work with exceptional children.
Eligibility: Applicants must be enrolled in an accredited college or university, either at the undergraduate level or as a North Carolina teacher seeking training, and must be training to work with special needs children up to the age of 21 in an educational setting. They must agree to teach at a North Carolina public school for at least one year after graduation.

Target applicant(s): College students. Graduate school students. Adult students.
Amount: $500-$2,500.
Number of awards: Varies.
Deadline: February 1.
How to apply: Applications are available online.
Exclusive: Visit www.UltimateScholarshipBook.com and enter code NO142623 for updates on this award.

(1427) · ERC Eco Scholarship Fund

Environmental Research Center
3111 Camino Del Rio North, Suite 400, San Diego, CA 92108
Phone: 619-500-3090
Email: ERCprograms@gmail.com
http://www.erc501c3.org
Purpose: To support graduating high school seniors residing in California who intend to major in an environmental studies program.
Eligibility: Applicants must be U.S. citizens and residents of California who are graduating high school seniors. Students must be accepted to a California college or university and intend to pursue a degree in environmental studies. A minimum high school GPA of 3.25 is required and applicants must have completed at least one high school science class in addition to the minimum amount required for graduation.
Target applicant(s): High school students.
Minimum GPA: 3.25
Amount: $1,000.
Number of awards: Varies.
Deadline: Ongoing.
How to apply: Applications are available online.
Exclusive: Visit www.UltimateScholarshipBook.com and enter code EN142723 for updates on this award.

(1428) · Eskridge Auto Group Free Ride

Eskridge Auto Group
5307 South Division, Guthrie, OK 73044
https://www.eskridgelexus.com/eskridge-free-ride/
Purpose: To reward hard working Oklahoma students.
Eligibility: Applicants must be nominated for the award. Students must be high school seniors with a minimum 3.25 grade point average. Applicants must complete an interview if chosen as a finalist.
Target applicant(s): High school students.
Minimum GPA: 3.25
Amount: $25,000.
Number of awards: Varies.
Deadline: January.
How to apply: Applications are available online.
Exclusive: Visit www.UltimateScholarshipBook.com and enter code ES142823 for updates on this award.

(1429) · Esther Kanagawa Memorial Art Scholarship

Hawaii Community Foundation - Scholarships
827 Fort Street Mall, Honolulu, HI 96813
Phone: 888-731-3863
Email: scholarships@hcf-hawaii.org
https://www.hawaiicommunityfoundation.org/
Purpose: To provide financial assistance to Hawaii students who are majoring in fine arts.
Eligibility: Applicants must be current high schools seniors who plan to major in fine arts at an accredited college or university. They must have a GPA of 2.7 or higher and demonstrate financial need and good character.

Target applicant(s): High school students.
Minimum GPA: 2.7
Amount: Varies.
Number of awards: Varies.
Deadline: January 31.
How to apply: To apply, register online, complete the online application and select the scholarships to which you wish to apply. In addition, mail the supporting materials: printed confirmation page from the online application, personal statement, copy of Student Aid Report (SAR) available at www.fafsa.ed.gov and official transcript.
Exclusive: Visit www.UltimateScholarshipBook.com and enter code HA142923 for updates on this award.

(1430) · Excellence in Service Award

Florida's Office of Campus Volunteers
Florida Campus Compact, 1801 Miccosukee Commons Drive, Suite 200, Tallahassee, FL 32308
Phone: 850-488-7782
Email: info@floridacompact.org
https://midatlantic.compact.org
Purpose: To reward students who perform outstanding acts of service in their communities.
Eligibility: Applicants must be full-time undergraduate students at an accredited public or private institution of higher education within the state of Florida.
Target applicant(s): College students. Adult students.
Amount: Varies.
Number of awards: Varies.
Deadline: June.
How to apply: Applications are available online.
Exclusive: Visit www.UltimateScholarshipBook.com and enter code FL143023 for updates on this award.

(1431) · Exemption for Highest Ranking High School Graduate

Texas Higher Education Coordinating Board
1200 East Anderson Lane, Austin, TX 78752
Phone: 512-427-6101
Email: pamela.harris@thecb.state.tx.us
http://www.collegeforalltexans.com
Purpose: To support students who are the top graduate of their high school class.
Eligibility: Applicant must be a resident, nonresident or foreign student of Texas and intending on attending a Texas public college or university. Students must provide documentation of their high school ranking. Applicants will receive full tuition for their first year of college.
Target applicant(s): High school students.
Amount: Varies.
Number of awards: Varies.
Deadline: Varies.
How to apply: Applications are available online.
Exclusive: Visit www.UltimateScholarshipBook.com and enter code TE143123 for updates on this award.

(1432) · Exemption for Texas Veterans (Hazelwood Exemption)

Texas Higher Education Coordinating Board
1200 East Anderson Lane, Austin, TX 78752
Phone: 512-427-6101

Email: pamela.harris@thecb.state.tx.us
http://www.collegeforalltexans.com
Purpose: To support qualified veterans with educational benefits at public institutions of higher education in Texas.
Eligibility: Applicants must be a qualified veteran, spouse or dependent child to qualify for this exemption. Students must have been accepted to a Texas public college or university. Applicants must provide proof of GI Bill benefits. Students must enroll in the Hazlewood On-Line database as part of the exemption process.
Target applicant(s): College students. Adult students.
Amount: Up to 150 semester hours.
Number of awards: 1.
Scholarship may be renewable.
Deadline: Varies.
How to apply: Applications are available online.
Exclusive: Visit www.UltimateScholarshipBook.com and enter code TE143223 for updates on this award.

(1433) · Exemption from Tuition Fees for Dependents of Kentucky Veterans

Kentucky Department of Veterans Affairs
Attn.: Tuition Waiver Coordinator, 321 West Main Street, Suite 390, Louisville, KY 40202
Phone: 502-595-4447
Email: barbaraa.hale@ky.gov
https://veterans.ky.gov/Benefits/Pages/education.aspx
Purpose: To support the families of Kentucky veterans.
Eligibility: Applicants must be children, stepchildren, adopted children, spouses or unremarried widows or widowers of qualifying Kentucky veterans. The veteran must have died on active duty or as a result of a service-connected disability, be 100 percent disabled from service, be totally disabled with wartime service or be deceased and have served during wartime. Children of veterans must be 26 years of age or younger.
Target applicant(s): High school students. College students. Adult students.
Amount: Full tuition.
Number of awards: Varies.
Deadline: Varies.
How to apply: Applications are available online. An application form, birth or marriage certificate, veteran's discharge certificate, death certificate or disability award letter and evidence of Kentucky residency are required.
Exclusive: Visit www.UltimateScholarshipBook.com and enter code KE143323 for updates on this award.

(1434) · F. Koehnen Ltd. Scholarship Fund

Hawaii Community Foundation - Scholarships
827 Fort Street Mall, Honolulu, HI 96813
Phone: 888-731-3863
Email: scholarships@hcf-hawaii.org
https://www.hawaiicommunityfoundation.org/
Purpose: To provide financial assistance to students whose parents or grandparents are employed in Hawaiian retail establishments.
Eligibility: Applicants must be Hawaii high school graduates with a GPA of 2.0 or higher. They must be children or grandchildren of retail employees on the island of Hawaii.
Target applicant(s): High school students. College students. Graduate school students. Adult students.
Minimum GPA: 2.0
Amount: Varies.
Number of awards: Varies.

Deadline: January 31.

How to apply: To apply, register online, complete the online application and select the scholarships to which you wish to apply. In addition, mail the supporting materials: printed confirmation page from the online application, personal statement, copy of Student Aid Report (SAR) available at www.fafsa.ed.gov and official transcript.

Exclusive: Visit www.UltimateScholarshipBook.com and enter code HA143423 for updates on this award.

(1435) · Family District 1 Scholarships

American Hellenic Education Progressive Association
1909 Q Street NW, Suite 500, Washington, DC 20009
Phone: 202-232-6300
Email: ahepa@ahepa.org
https://ahepa.org/education/

Purpose: To provide financial assistance for those pursuing higher education.

Eligibility: Applicants must be graduating seniors, high school graduates or current undergraduate or graduate students who plan to attend a college or university full-time during the calendar year of application. They must be residents of Alabama, Georgia, Mississippi, South Carolina, Tennessee or Florida.

Target applicant(s): High school students. College students. Graduate school students. Adult students.

Amount: Varies.

Number of awards: Varies.

Deadline: April.

How to apply: Applications are available online. The current application must be used and must be sent by certified mail and return receipt requested.

Exclusive: Visit www.UltimateScholarshipBook.com and enter code AM143523 for updates on this award.

(1436) · Fellowship on Women and Public Policy

Center for Women in Government and Civil Society
University at Albany, SUNY, 135 Western Avenue, Draper Hall 302, Albany, NY 12222
Phone: 518-442-3900
http://www.cwig.albany.edu

Purpose: To encourage New York state graduate students to pursue jobs in public policy.

Eligibility: Students must be enrolled in a graduate program at an accredited college or university in New York and have completed at least 12 credits before applying but not be scheduled to graduate before the internship, and must have minimum 3-5 years work/internship experience and minimum 3.0 GPA. Applicants must demonstrate an interest in improving the status of women and underrepresented populations.

Target applicant(s): Graduate school students. Adult students.

Minimum GPA: 3.0

Amount: $10,000 stipend and tuition assistance.

Number of awards: Varies.

Deadline: Varies.

How to apply: Applications are available online.

Exclusive: Visit www.UltimateScholarshipBook.com and enter code CE143623 for updates on this award.

(1437) · Fields of Learning Scholarship

Fields of Learning
9357 Sperry Road, Kirtland Hills, OH 44060

Phone: 440-256-3757
http://www.fieldsoflearning.org

Purpose: To encourage students who wish to pursue education following high school and have an interest in high school football.

Eligibility: Applicants must write an essay of 700 to 1,500 words based on a true story about what the student has learned related to high school football. Students must intend to use the funds for post high school education within one year of graduating high school. Applicants can be in grades nine through twelve. Students do not have to be on the football team to apply.

Target applicant(s): High school students.

Amount: Varies.

Number of awards: Varies.

Deadline: March 31.

How to apply: Applications are available online.

Exclusive: Visit www.UltimateScholarshipBook.com and enter code FI143723 for updates on this award.

(1438) · First Generation Matching Grant Program

Florida Department of Education
Office of Student Financial Assistance, State Scholarship and Grant Programs, 325 West Gaines Street, Suite 1314, Tallahassee, FL 32399-0400
Phone: 888-827-2004
Email: osfa@fldoe.org
http://www.floridastudentfinancialaid.org

Purpose: To help Florida undergraduate students with financial need who are enrolled in state universities and whose parents have not earned bachelor's degrees.

Eligibility: Applicants must submit applications and the Free Application for Federal Student Aid (FAFSA). Each university determines its own deadline.

Target applicant(s): High school students. College students. Adult students.

Amount: Varies.

Number of awards: Varies.

Deadline: Varies.

How to apply: Applications are at the financial aid offices of state universities.

Exclusive: Visit www.UltimateScholarshipBook.com and enter code FL143823 for updates on this award.

(1439) · First State Manufactured Housing Association Scholarship

Department of Education - School Supports
The Townsend Building, 401 Federal Street, Suite 2, Dover, DE 19901-3639
Phone: 800-292-7935
Email: dhec@doe.k12.de.us
https://www.doe.k12.de.us/page/316

Purpose: To provide assistance to residents of manufactured homes.

Eligibility: Applicants must be legal residents of Delaware. They may be high school seniors or former graduates seeking higher education. They must have lived in a manufactured home for at least one year prior to application. They may enroll in any accredited program full- or part-time. Selection criteria include scholastic achievement, financial need, essay and recommendations.

Target applicant(s): High school students. College students. Adult students.

Amount: Up to $1,000.

Number of awards: Up to 4.

Deadline: March 4.

How to apply: Applications are available online. An application form, essay, FAFSA and transcript are required.

Exclusive: Visit www.UltimateScholarshipBook.com and enter code DE143923 for updates on this award.

(1440) · Florida Bright Futures Scholarship Program

Florida Department of Education

Office of Student Financial Assistance, State Scholarship and Grant Programs, 325 West Gaines Street, Suite 1314, Tallahassee, FL 32399-0400

Phone: 888-827-2004

Email: osfa@fldoe.org

http://www.floridastudentfinancialaid.org

Purpose: Lottery-funded scholarships are awarded to Florida high school seniors as reward for academic achievements and to assist with postsecondary education.

Eligibility: Applicants must earn a Florida high school diploma or equivalent, have not been found guilty or pled no contest to a felony charge and meet the award's academic requirements. Applicants must also be Florida residents, U.S. citizens or eligible noncitizens and be accepted by and enrolled in an eligible Florida public or private college or vocational school at least quarter time. Application must be completed during the senior year of high school.

Target applicant(s): High school students.

Amount: Varies.

Number of awards: Varies.

Deadline: August 31.

How to apply: Apply by completing the Florida Financial Aid Application. The application is available online at www.floridastudentfinancialaid.org or from your high school guidance counselor.

Exclusive: Visit www.UltimateScholarshipBook.com and enter code FL144023 for updates on this award.

(1441) · Florida Engineers in Construction Scholarship

Florida Engineering Society

125 South Gadsden Street, Tallahassee, FL 32302-0750

Phone: 850-224-7121

Email: allen@fleng.org

https://www.fleng.org

Purpose: To aid Florida engineering majors who are interested in careers in construction.

Eligibility: Applicants must be undergraduate juniors or seniors enrolled or accepted in an accredited degree program in engineering at a Florida university. They must have a GPA of at least 3.0 on a 4.0 scale and must have plans to pursue a career in construction. Please include a recommendation by an engineering faculty members. Selection is based on the overall strength of the application.

Target applicant(s): College students. Adult students.

Minimum GPA: 3.0

Amount: $1,000.

Number of awards: 1.

Deadline: April 19.

How to apply: Applications are available online. An application form, a transcript and one letter of recommendation are required.

Exclusive: Visit www.UltimateScholarshipBook.com and enter code FL144123 for updates on this award.

(1442) · Florida Governor's Black History Month Essay Contest

Volunteer Florida

Black History Month Committee, 3800 Esplanade Way, Suite 180, Tallahassee, FL 32311

Phone: 850-414-7400

Email: info@volunteerflorida.org

http://www.floridablackhistory.com

Purpose: To promote Black History Month.

Eligibility: Applicants must be Florida students in grades 4-12 and compose an essay on the given topic. Winners receive a four-year full scholarship to a Florida state college or university and a trip to the Governor's Black History Month celebration.

Target applicant(s): Junior high students or younger. High school students.

Amount: Full tuition.

Number of awards: 3.

Scholarship may be renewable.

Deadline: February 26.

How to apply: Applications are available online. A parental waiver, essay and student's contact information are required.

Exclusive: Visit www.UltimateScholarshipBook.com and enter code VO144223 for updates on this award.

(1443) · Florida Oratorical Contest

American Legion, Department of Florida

Elizabeth Douglas, Programs Director, 1912A Lee Road, Orlando, FL 32810

Phone: 800-393-3378

Email: mail@floridalegion.org

https://www.floridalegion.org/programs-services/scholarships/

Purpose: To enhance high school students' experience with and understanding of the U.S. Constitution. The contest will help develop students' leadership skills and civic appreciation, as well as the ability to deliver thoughtful, insightful orations regarding U.S. citizenship and its inherent responsibilities.

Eligibility: Applicants must be high school students under the age of 20 who are U.S. citizens or legal residents and residents of the state. Students first give an oration within their state and winners compete at the national level. The oration must be related to the Constitution of the United States focusing on the duties and obligations citizens have to the government. It must be in English and be between eight and ten minutes. There is also an assigned topic which is posted on the website, and it should be between three and five minutes.

Target applicant(s): Junior high students or younger. High school students.

Amount: $500-$18,000.

Number of awards: Varies.

Deadline: December 1.

How to apply: Applications are available by contacting the local American Legion Post.

Exclusive: Visit www.UltimateScholarshipBook.com and enter code AM144323 for updates on this award.

(1444) · Florida Student Assistance Grant Program

Florida Department of Education

Office of Student Financial Assistance, State Scholarship and Grant Programs, 325 West Gaines Street, Suite 1314, Tallahassee, FL 32399-0400

Phone: 888-827-2004

Email: osfa@fldoe.org
http://www.floridastudentfinancialaid.org
Purpose: To help degree-seeking, Florida resident, undergraduate students who have financial need and who are enrolled in participating postsecondary institutions.
Eligibility: There are three student financial aid programs: The Florida Public Student Assistance Grant is for students who attend state universities and public community colleges. The Florida Private Student Assistance Grant is for students who attend eligible private, non-profit, four-year colleges and universities. The Florida Postsecondary Student Assistance Grant is for students who attend eligible degree-granting private colleges and universities that are ineligible under the Florida Private Student Assistance Grant. High school students in the top 20 percent of their classes receive priority funding.
Target applicant(s): High school students. College students. Adult students.
Amount: At least $200.
Number of awards: Varies.
Scholarship may be renewable.
Deadline: Varies.
How to apply: Applicants must submit the Free Application for Federal Student Aid (FAFSA).
Exclusive: Visit www.UltimateScholarshipBook.com and enter code FL144423 for updates on this award.

(1445) · Foster Child Grant Program
Massachusetts Department of Higher Education
Office of Student Financial Assistance, 454 Broadway, Suite 200, Revere, MA 02151
Phone: 617-727-9420
Email: osfa@osfa.mass.edu
https://www.mass.edu/osfa/programs/programs.asp
Purpose: To assist children who have lived in foster homes in obtaining higher education.
Eligibility: Applicants must be placed in the custody of the Department of Social Services and be permanent residents of the state of Massachusetts. Students must be younger than 25 years of age at the start of the academic year and apply for financial aid.
Target applicant(s): High school students. College students. Graduate school students.
Amount: Up to $6,000.
Number of awards: Varies.
Scholarship may be renewable.
Deadline: Varies.
How to apply: Applications are available by phone from the Massachusetts Office of Student Financial Assistance or from your social worker.
Exclusive: Visit www.UltimateScholarshipBook.com and enter code MA144523 for updates on this award.

(1446) · Four-year or Bachelor's Degree Program
New Hampshire Charitable Foundation
37 Pleasant Street, Concord, NH 03301-4005
Phone: 603-225-6641
Email: info@nhcf.org
https://www.nhcf.org/how-can-we-help-you/
Purpose: To support New Hampshire students who are seeking a four-year degree program.
Eligibility: Applicants must be New Hampshire residents who are enrolling in a four-year degree program. Students must prove financial

need. Selection is based on need, academic merit, community service, extracurricular activities and work experience.
Target applicant(s): College students. Adult students.
Amount: $250-$7,500.
Number of awards: Varies.
Deadline: April 16.
How to apply: Applications are available online.
Exclusive: Visit www.UltimateScholarshipBook.com and enter code NE144623 for updates on this award.

(1447) · Four-Year Undergraduate Scholarships
Los Alamos National Laboratory Foundation
1112 Plaza del Norte, Espanola, NM 87532
Phone: 505-753-8890
Email: tony@lanlfoundation.org
http://www.lanlfoundation.org
Purpose: To support students from northern New Mexico who have demonstrated leadership skills in their homes, schools and communities.
Eligibility: Students must have at least a 3.25 cumulative unweighted GPA, and they must have either an SAT score (combined Math plus Critical Reading only) of at least 930 or an ACT score of at least 19. Applicants must submit an essay and two letters of recommendation.
Target applicant(s): High school students. College students. Adult students.
Minimum GPA: 3.25
Amount: Varies.
Number of awards: Varies.
Scholarship may be renewable.
Deadline: January.
How to apply: Applications are available online.
Exclusive: Visit www.UltimateScholarshipBook.com and enter code LO144723 for updates on this award.

(1448) · Frances A. Mays Scholarship Award
Virginia Association for Health, Physical Education, Recreation and Dance
7812 Falling Hill Terrace, Chesterfield, VA 23832
http://www.vahperd.org
Purpose: To aid students majoring in fields related to physical education.
Eligibility: Applicants must be seniors at Virginia colleges or universities pursuing a degree in health, physical education, recreation or dance and be members of VAHPERD and AAHPERD. Students must demonstrate high ideals, good scholarship and professional ethics. Applicants must be nominated by their schools.
Target applicant(s): College students. Adult students.
Minimum GPA: 2.8
Amount: Varies.
Number of awards: 1.
Deadline: October 1.
How to apply: Applications are available from your university's VAHPERD representative. An application form and letter of reference are required.
Exclusive: Visit www.UltimateScholarshipBook.com and enter code VI144823 for updates on this award.

(1449) · Frances Lansbury Memorial Award/Adult Female Learner

New York State Women's 600 Club
Connie Canfield, Chairman, 1288 Scribner Hollow Road, East Jewett, NY 12424-5538
Phone: 518-589-5319
Email: cmc600ed@gmail.com
http://www.bowlny.com/
Purpose: To promote the continuing education of a New York woman.
Eligibility: Applicant must be 20 years old by March 1 and be continuing her education in a school of higher education. She must also be sponsored by a current New York State Women's 600 Bowling Club member.
Target applicant(s): College students. Graduate school students. Adult students.
Amount: Varies.
Number of awards: 1.
Deadline: March 1.
How to apply: Applications are available online and consist of forms to be completed by the applicant, the sponsor and the employer or school official.
Exclusive: Visit www.UltimateScholarshipBook.com and enter code NE144923 for updates on this award.

(1450) · Frank O'Bannon Grant Program

State Student Assistance Commission of Indiana
W462 Indiana Government Center South, 402 West Washington Street, Indianapolis, IN 46204
Phone: 888-528-4719
Email: grants@ssaci.state.in.us
http://www.in.gov/che/
Purpose: To aid Indiana students in attending eligible postsecondary schools.
Eligibility: Applicants must be high school graduates and attend or plan to attend eligible Indiana colleges or universities full-time.
Target applicant(s): High school students. College students. Adult students.
Amount: Varies.
Number of awards: Varies.
Deadline: April 15.
How to apply: Complete the Free Application for Federal Student Aid (FAFSA).
Exclusive: Visit www.UltimateScholarshipBook.com and enter code ST145023 for updates on this award.

(1451) · Fresh Start Scholarship

Fresh Start Scholarship Foundation Inc.
P.O. Box 7784, Wilmington, DE 19803
Phone: 302-397-3440
Email: fssf@freshstartscholarship.org
http://www.freshstartscholarship.org
Purpose: To help women who are returning to school.
Eligibility: Applicants should be women at least 20 years old with financial need who have a high school diploma or G.E.D., have had at least a two year break in education either after finishing high school or during college studies and are enrolled in a Delaware college in a two- or four-year degree program at the undergraduate level. Applicants should have at least a C average if already in college.
Target applicant(s): College students. Adult students.
Minimum GPA: 2.0

Amount: Varies.
Number of awards: Varies.
Scholarship may be renewable.
Deadline: May 15.
How to apply: Applications are available online or by mail and include a personal statement. A social service agency or college representative should recommend applicants.
Exclusive: Visit www.UltimateScholarshipBook.com and enter code FR145123 for updates on this award.

(1452) · Friends of the California State Fair Scholarship Program

California State Fair
1600 Exposition Boulevard, Sacramento, CA 95815
Phone: 916-263-3247
Email: scholarship@calexpo.com
https://www.castatefair.org/scholarship/
Purpose: To reward and motivate well-rounded, high-achieving California students.
Eligibility: Applicants must be enrolled or plan to enroll in a four-year accredited California institution of higher learning. They must have a GPA of 3.0 or higher and have a valid California ID.
Target applicant(s): High school students. College students. Adult students.
Minimum GPA: 3.0
Amount: Up to $2,500.
Number of awards: Varies.
Deadline: March 2.
How to apply: Applications are available online.
Exclusive: Visit www.UltimateScholarshipBook.com and enter code CA145223 for updates on this award.

(1453) · Future Ready Iowa Grant

Iowa College Student Aid Commission
475 SW Fifth Street, Suite D, Des Moines, IA 50309
Phone: 515-725-3400
Email: info@iowacollegeaid.gov
https://www.iowacollegeaid.gov/ScholarshipsAndGrants
Purpose: To support Iowa students who have previously earned at least half the credits necessary for an eligible bachelor's degree that leads to a high-demand job.
Eligibility: Applicants must have applied for all other available financial aid and have not been enrolled in post-secondary education for two or more years. Eligible institutions are accredited Iowa colleges or universities that offer bachelor's degree programs aligned with high-demand jobs.
Target applicant(s): College students. Adult students.
Amount: Varies.
Number of awards: Varies.
Deadline: July 1.
How to apply: Applications are available online.
Exclusive: Visit www.UltimateScholarshipBook.com and enter code IO145323 for updates on this award.

(1454) · Future Ready Iowa Last-Dollar Scholarship

Iowa College Student Aid Commission
475 SW Fifth Street, Suite D, Des Moines, IA 50309
Phone: 515-725-3400
Email: info@iowacollegeaid.gov

https://www.iowacollegeaid.gov/ScholarshipsAndGrants
Purpose: To support Iowa students with higher education expenses.
Eligibility: Applicants must be recent high school graduates enrolling in an eligible program full-time, recent high school graduates who are enrolling in an eligible program part-time and are employed in an approved work-based learning program or adult learners 20 years of age or older starting an eligible program at least part-time. Students must have applied for all other available financial aid and plan to earn a credential for a high-demand job. Eligible institutions are Iowa community colleges or accredited private colleges in Iowa that offer qualified programs of study.
Target applicant(s): High school students. College students. Adult students.
Amount: Varies.
Number of awards: Varies.
Deadline: August 1.
How to apply: Applications are available online.
Exclusive: Visit www.UltimateScholarshipBook.com and enter code IO145423 for updates on this award.

(1455) · Future Teachers Scholarship

Oklahoma State Regents for Higher Education/Future Teachers Scholarship
655 Research Parkway, Suite 200, Oklahoma City, OK 73104
Phone: 800-858-1840
Email: studentinfo@osrhe.edu
https://secure.okcollegestart.org/Financial_Aid_Planning/Scholarships/Career_Scholarships/Future_Teachers_Scholarship_Program.aspx
Purpose: To encourage students to become teachers in critical teacher shortage areas in Oklahoma public schools.
Eligibility: Applicants must be residents of Oklahoma who have been nominated by their institution on the basis of rank in the top 15 percent of high school class, rank in the top 15 percent of students in SAT or ACT scores, admission to an education program at an accredited Oklahoma institution or high academic achievement in undergraduate coursework. Applicants must maintain a GPA of 2.5 or higher and agree to teach in a shortage area in an Oklahoma public school for at least three years after graduation and licensure.
Target applicant(s): High school students. College students. Adult students.
Minimum GPA: 2.5
Amount: Up to $1,500.
Number of awards: 125.
Deadline: Varies.
How to apply: Applications are submitted by the nominating institution.
Exclusive: Visit www.UltimateScholarshipBook.com and enter code OK145523 for updates on this award.

(1456) · GEAR UP Idaho Scholarship 2

Idaho State Board of Education
P.O. Box 83720, Boise, ID 83720-0037
Phone: 208-334-2270
Email: Joy.Miller@osbe.idaho.gov
https://boardofed.idaho.gov/scholarships/
Purpose: Monetary assistance is provided to Idaho resident high school students for freshman expenses at Idaho colleges or universities.
Eligibility: Applicants must have graduated from an Idaho high school, be entering freshmen at an eligible Idaho college or university, be residents of Idaho and have a minimum 3.0 GPA or minimum ACT

score of 20. Applicants must also be younger than 22 years old and complete at least 12 credits per semester with a minimum 2.5 GPA to remain eligible for renewal.
Target applicant(s): High school students.
Minimum GPA: 3.0
Amount: Varies.
Number of awards: Varies.
Scholarship may be renewable.
Deadline: June 1.
How to apply: Contact eligible college or university financial aid office.
Exclusive: Visit www.UltimateScholarshipBook.com and enter code ID145623 for updates on this award.

(1457) · General Assembly Merit Scholarship

Tennessee Student Assistance Corporation
404 James Robertson Parkway, Suite 1510, Parkway Towers, Nashville, TN 37243
Phone: 800-342-1663
Email: tsac.aidinfo@tn.gov
https://www.tn.gov/collegepays/financial-aid.html
Purpose: To provide supplemental support to recipients of the Tennessee HOPE Scholarship.
Eligibility: Students graduating from public schools or category 1, 2 and 3 private schools must have at least a 3.75 GPA and either a 29 on the ACT or a 1280 on the SAT. Home-schooled or non-category 1, 2 or 3 private school students must complete at least 12 college credit hours while in high school, and they must have at least a 3.0 GPA in those courses. Recipients of the Aspire Award are not eligible.
Target applicant(s): High school students. College students. Adult students.
Minimum GPA: 3.75
Amount: Up to $1,500.
Number of awards: Varies.
Deadline: Varies.
How to apply: Applications are available through completion of the FAFSA.
Exclusive: Visit www.UltimateScholarshipBook.com and enter code TE145723 for updates on this award.

(1458) · George and Donna Nigh Public Service Scholarship

Oklahoma State Regents for Higher Education/George and Donna Nigh Public Service Scholarship
655 Research Parkway, Suite 200, Oklahoma City, OK 73104
Phone: 800-858-1840
Email: studentinfo@osrhe.edu
https://secure.okcollegestart.org/Financial_Aid_Planning/Scholarships/Career_Scholarships/Nigh_Public_Service_Scholarship.aspx
Purpose: To support Oklahoma students who are pursuing a career in public service.
Eligibility: Applicants must be residents of the state of Oklahoma who are enrolled full-time in an undergraduate program at an Oklahoma college or university. Students must be enrolled in a program leading to a career in public service and must demonstrate exceptional academic achievement.
Target applicant(s): College students. Adult students.
Amount: $1,000.
Number of awards: Varies.
Deadline: Varies.

How to apply: Applications are available online.
Exclusive: Visit www.UltimateScholarshipBook.com and enter code OK145823 for updates on this award.

(1459) · George Mason Business Scholarship Fund

Hawaii Community Foundation - Scholarships
827 Fort Street Mall, Honolulu, HI 96813
Phone: 888-731-3863
Email: scholarships@hcf-hawaii.org
https://www.hawaiicommunityfoundation.org/
Purpose: To assist Hawaii students who are majoring in business administration.
Eligibility: Applicants must be seniors at a Hawaiian college or university and have a GPA of 3.0 or higher. They must discuss why they have chosen to pursue a business career and how they expect to make a difference in the business world in their personal statement.
Target applicant(s): College students. Adult students.
Minimum GPA: 3.0
Amount: Varies.
Number of awards: Varies.
Deadline: January 31.
How to apply: To apply, register online, complete the online application and select the scholarships to which you wish to apply. In addition, mail the supporting materials: printed confirmation page from the online application, personal statement, copy of Student Aid Report (SAR) available at www.fafsa.ed.gov and official transcript.
Exclusive: Visit www.UltimateScholarshipBook.com and enter code HA145923 for updates on this award.

(1460) · Georgia Oratorical Contest

American Legion, Department of Georgia
3035 Mt. Zion Road, Stockbridge, GA 30281
Phone: 678-289-8883
Email: amerlegga@bellsouth.net
http://departmentofgeorgiaoratorical.weebly.com/
Purpose: To enhance high school students' experience with and understanding of the U.S. Constitution. The contest will help develop students' leadership skills and civic appreciation, as well as the ability to deliver thoughtful, insightful orations regarding U.S. citizenship and its inherent responsibilities.
Eligibility: Applicants must be high school students under the age of 20 who are U.S. citizens or legal residents and residents of the state. Students first give an oration within their state and winners compete at the national level. The oration must be related to the Constitution of the United States focusing on the duties and obligations citizens have to the government. It must be in English and be between eight and ten minutes. There is also an assigned topic which is posted on the website, and it should be between three and five minutes.
Target applicant(s): Junior high students or younger. High school students.
Amount: Up to $1,300.
Number of awards: Varies.
Deadline: December 1.
How to apply: Applications are available by contacting the local American Legion Post.
Exclusive: Visit www.UltimateScholarshipBook.com and enter code AM146023 for updates on this award.

(1461) · Georgia Press Educational Foundation Scholarships

Georgia Press Educational Foundation Inc.
Georgia Press Building, 30266 Mercer University Drive, Suite 200, Atlanta, GA 30343-4137
Phone: 770-454-6776
Email: mail@gapress.org
http://gapress.org/scholarships-internships/
Purpose: To aid students interested in newspaper journalism.
Eligibility: Applicants must be high school seniors or undergraduate students who have been Georgia residents for three years, or their parents must have been Georgia residents for two years. Students must attend a Georgia college or university, demonstrate financial need and be recommended by a counselor, principal, professor or Georgia Press Association member.
Target applicant(s): High school students. College students. Adult students.
Amount: $1,500-$2,000.
Number of awards: Varies.
Deadline: March 1.
How to apply: Applications are available online. An application form, transcript, copy of SAT scores, copy of tax return, anticipated budget, school photograph and letter of recommendation are required.
Exclusive: Visit www.UltimateScholarshipBook.com and enter code GE146123 for updates on this award.

(1462) · Georgia Thespians Achievement Scholarships

Georgia Thespians
2897 North Druid Hills Road, Box 225, Atlanta, GA 30329
Phone: 678-910-4487
Email: gathespiansscholarships@gmail.com
https://gathespians.org/conference/scholarships/
Purpose: To support outstanding thespians.
Eligibility: Applicants must be Georgia high school juniors or seniors and perform an audition in one of the following categories: acting, technical theatre, singing or theatre education.
Target applicant(s): High school students.
Amount: $2,000.
Number of awards: 5.
Deadline: December 8.
How to apply: Applications are available online. An application form and resume of thespian troupe experience are required.
Exclusive: Visit www.UltimateScholarshipBook.com and enter code GE146223 for updates on this award.

(1463) · Georgia Tuition Equalization Grant

Georgia Student Finance Commission
2082 East Exchange Place, Tucker, GA 30084
Phone: 800-505-4732
Email: gsfcinfo@gsfc.org
https://www.gafutures.org/
Purpose: To support Georgia resident students.
Eligibility: Applicants must be full-time students at eligible private colleges or universities in Georgia and be U.S. citizens and legal residents of the state of Georgia.
Target applicant(s): College students. Adult students.
Amount: $300 per quarter or $450 per semester.
Number of awards: Varies.
Scholarship may be renewable.

Deadline: Varies.
How to apply: Applications are available online.
Exclusive: Visit www.UltimateScholarshipBook.com and enter code GE146323 for updates on this award.

(1464) · Gilbert Matching Student Grant

Massachusetts Department of Higher Education
Office of Student Financial Assistance, 454 Broadway, Suite 200, Revere, MA 02151
Phone: 617-727-9420
Email: osfa@osfa.mass.edu
https://www.mass.edu/osfa/programs/programs.asp
Purpose: To assist needy students in attending private institutions of higher education or nursing schools.
Eligibility: Students must be permanent residents of Massachusetts, demonstrate financial need, maintain satisfactory academic progress and attend an eligible Massachusetts institution. Applicants must not have earned a bachelor's or professional degree, nor a first diploma from a hospital or professional nursing program.
Target applicant(s): High school students. College students. Adult students.
Amount: $200-$2,500.
Number of awards: Varies.
Scholarship may be renewable.
Deadline: Varies.
How to apply: Applications are available from your school's financial aid office.
Exclusive: Visit www.UltimateScholarshipBook.com and enter code MA146423 for updates on this award.

(1465) · Golden Apple Scholars of Illinois (Illinois Scholars Program)

Golden Apple Foundation
8 South Michigan Avenue, Chicago, IL 60603
Phone: 312-407-0006
http://www.goldenapple.org
Purpose: To offer scholarships to promising students pursuing teaching degrees.
Eligibility: Applicants must be Illinois high school seniors or college sophomores at one of the 53 partner universities in Illinois who are interested in teaching. There are a limited number of spots for college sophomores, and all college students must be nominated by a university liaison. A minimum GPA of 2.5 is required. Students must commit to teaching in an Illinois school of need for five years after graduation.
Target applicant(s): High school students. College students. Adult students.
Minimum GPA: 2.5
Amount: Up to $23,000.
Number of awards: Varies.
Scholarship may be renewable.
Deadline: February.
How to apply: Applications are available by calling 312-407-0433, extension 105.
Exclusive: Visit www.UltimateScholarshipBook.com and enter code GO146523 for updates on this award.

(1466) · Golden LEAF Scholars Program - Two-Year Colleges

North Carolina Division of Vocational Rehabilitation Services
2601 Mail Service Center, Raleigh, NC 27699-2801
Phone: 888-234-6400
Email: jterrell@ncbar.org
https://www.cfnc.org/pay-for-college/apply-for-financial-aid/
Purpose: To provide need-based financial assistance to North Carolina community college students.
Eligibility: Applicants must be residents of one of the 73 eligible counties and meet specific income requirements as evidenced by FAFSA information (for curriculum students) or the federal TRIO formula (for occupational education students). Degree-seeking students must be enrolled at least half-time.
Target applicant(s): High school students. College students. Adult students.
Amount: Up to $2,250 per year.
Number of awards: Varies.
Scholarship may be renewable.
Deadline: Varies.
How to apply: Applications are available online.
Exclusive: Visit www.UltimateScholarshipBook.com and enter code NO146623 for updates on this award.

(1467) · Good Eats Scholarship Fund

Hawaii Community Foundation - Scholarships
827 Fort Street Mall, Honolulu, HI 96813
Phone: 888-731-3863
Email: scholarships@hcf-hawaii.org
https://www.hawaiicommunityfoundation.org/
Purpose: To provide financial assistance to Hawaii students pursuing degrees in agriculture and culinary arts, and to encourage them to return to Hawaii upon graduation.
Eligibility: Applicants must be Hawaii residents who plan to study culinary arts or agriculture at a college or university in the continental United States. They must have a GPA of 2.7 or higher and demonstrate interest in food production and preparation through their school or community activities.
Target applicant(s): High school students. College students. Adult students.
Minimum GPA: 2.7
Amount: Varies.
Number of awards: Varies.
Deadline: January 31.
How to apply: To apply, register online, complete the online application and select the scholarships to which you wish to apply. In addition, mail the supporting materials: printed confirmation page from the online application, personal statement, copy of Student Aid Report (SAR) available at www.fafsa.ed.gov and official transcript.
Exclusive: Visit www.UltimateScholarshipBook.com and enter code HA146723 for updates on this award.

(1468) · Gorgas Scholarship Competition

Alabama Junior Academy of Science
c/o Dr. Ellen Buckner, CHS 1506, Samford University, 800 Lakeshore Drive, Birmingham, AL 35229
Phone: 251-445-9449
Email: ebbuckner@gmail.com
http://alabamajunioracademyofscience.org/

Purpose: To aid Alabama residents who are planning to pursue higher education in science.

Eligibility: Applicants must be Alabama residents who are high school seniors and have completed a scientific research project and an accompanying report of no more than 20 pages. They must have completed all college entrance requirements by October 1 of the year of application submission. Selection is based on the quality of the scientific research paper that is submitted as part of the application.

Target applicant(s): High school students.

Amount: Up to $10,000.

Number of awards: Varies.

Deadline: January 18.

How to apply: Applications are available online. An entry form, research paper, official transcript, one letter of recommendation and additional research-related documentation are required.

Exclusive: Visit www.UltimateScholarshipBook.com and enter code AL146823 for updates on this award.

(1469) · Governor Guinn Millennium Scholarship Program

Nevada Office of the State Treasurer
101 N. Carson Street, Suite 4, Carson City, NV 89701
Phone: 702-486-3383
Email: MillenniumScholars@nevadatreasurer.gov
http://www.nevadatreasurer.gov/Programs/Programs/
Purpose: To assist students who have attained high academic achievement in a Nevada high school.

Eligibility: Applicants must graduate from a Nevada public or private high school with a GPA of 3.25 or higher, pass all areas of the Nevada High School Proficiency Exam and have been a resident of Nevada for at least two years in high school.

Target applicant(s): College students. Adult students.

Minimum GPA: 3.25

Amount: Varies.

Number of awards: 2.

Scholarship may be renewable.

Deadline: April.

How to apply: Applications are not required. Your school district will submit your name to the State Treasurer's office if you are eligible.

Exclusive: Visit www.UltimateScholarshipBook.com and enter code NE146923 for updates on this award.

(1470) · Governor's Cup Scholarship

Idaho State Board of Education
P.O. Box 83720, Boise, ID 83720-0037
Phone: 208-334-2270
Email: Joy.Miller@osbe.idaho.gov
https://boardofed.idaho.gov/scholarships/
Purpose: Monetary assistance is provided to Idaho resident high school seniors planning to attend state colleges.

Eligibility: Applicants must be Idaho high school seniors planning to attend Idaho colleges or universities full-time and have a minimum 2.8 GPA. Public service is a significant factor.

Target applicant(s): High school students.

Minimum GPA: 2.8

Amount: $3,000.

Number of awards: 25.

Scholarship may be renewable.

Deadline: February 15.

How to apply: Applications are available online.

Exclusive: Visit www.UltimateScholarshipBook.com and enter code ID147023 for updates on this award.

(1471) · Governor's Distinguished Scholarship

Arkansas Department of Higher Education
423 Main Street, Suite 400, Little Rock, AR 72201
Phone: 501-371-2050
Email: finaid@adhe.arknet.edu
http://scholarships.adhe.edu/scholarships-and-programs/a-z/
Purpose: To assist outstanding Arkansas high school graduates to encourage them to attend postsecondary schools in Arkansas.

Eligibility: Applicants must be Arkansas graduating high school seniors who will attend an Arkansas college or university. Selection is based on academic achievement, test scores and leadership. A minimum ACT score of 32, SAT score of 1410 or 3.5 GPA in academic courses is required.

Target applicant(s): High school students.

Minimum GPA: 3.5

Amount: $4,000.

Number of awards: Varies.

Scholarship may be renewable.

Deadline: February 1.

How to apply: Applications are available through your high school counselor and online.

Exclusive: Visit www.UltimateScholarshipBook.com and enter code AR147123 for updates on this award.

(1472) · GPB Art Harris Scholarship

Great Plains Bank
5909 NW Expressway, Suite 400, Oklahoma City, OK 73132
Phone: 405-720-4813
Email: lhopkins@gpbankok.net
https://www.gpbankok.com/about
Purpose: To support students pursuing a higher education who live in the Great Plains Bank service area.

Eligibility: Applicants must be graduating high school seniors within the Great Plains Bank service area who have at least a 2.0 GPA. Students must have need of financial assistance and be residents of Oklahoma state and citizens of the United States. An essay is required as part of the application process.

Target applicant(s): High school students.

Minimum GPA: 2.0

Amount: $5,000.

Number of awards: 1.

Deadline: April 30.

How to apply: Applications are available online.

Exclusive: Visit www.UltimateScholarshipBook.com and enter code GR147223 for updates on this award.

(1473) · Graduate Tuition Waiver

Massachusetts Department of Higher Education
Office of Student Financial Assistance, 454 Broadway, Suite 200, Revere, MA 02151
Phone: 617-727-9420
Email: osfa@osfa.mass.edu
https://www.mass.edu/osfa/programs/programs.asp
Purpose: To provide financial support to Massachusetts graduate students.

Eligibility: Students must be enrolled in graduate level courses at a Massachusetts public school that is not a community college. Applicants

must not owe any refunds on previously received financial aid, and they must not have defaulted on any government loans.
Target applicant(s): Graduate school students. Adult students.
Amount: Varies.
Number of awards: Varies.
Deadline: Varies.
How to apply: Applications are available at college financial aid offices.
Exclusive: Visit www.UltimateScholarshipBook.com and enter code MA147323 for updates on this award.

(1474) · Granville P. Meade Scholarship

Virginia Department of Education
P.O. Box 2120, Richmond, VA 23218
Phone: 804-225-3349
Email: joseph.wharff@doe.virginia.gov
http://www.doe.virginia.gov/
Purpose: To support graduating high school seniors in Virginia.
Eligibility: Students must have been born in Virginia, and they must plan to attend a public or private Virginia school. They must demonstrate financial need, academic achievement, extracurricular activities and good character. Recipients must maintain a 2.5 GPA.
Target applicant(s): High school students.
Minimum GPA: 2.5
Amount: $2,000.
Number of awards: Varies.
Scholarship may be renewable.
Deadline: March 5.
How to apply: Applications are available online.
Exclusive: Visit www.UltimateScholarshipBook.com and enter code VI147423 for updates on this award.

(1475) · Greater Kanawha Valley Foundation Scholarship Program

Greater Kanawha Valley Foundation
1600 Huntington Square, 900 Lee Street, East, Charleston, WV 25301
Phone: 304-346-3620
Email: shoover@tgkvf.org
https://tgkvf.org/scholarships/available-scholarships/
Purpose: To provide financial assistance to prospective college students from the state of West Virginia.
Eligibility: Applicants must be residents of West Virginia, be full-time students (12 hours) and demonstrate good moral character. Many awards are available, and each individual award may have additional eligibility requirements. Applicants must have a minimum 2.5 GPA and an ACT score of at least 20.
Target applicant(s): High school students. College students. Adult students.
Minimum GPA: 2.5
Amount: Varies.
Number of awards: Varies.
Scholarship may be renewable.
Deadline: February 15.
How to apply: Applications are available online.
Exclusive: Visit www.UltimateScholarshipBook.com and enter code GR147523 for updates on this award.

(1476) · Greenhouse Scholars Scholarship

Greenhouse Scholars
1820 Folsom Street, Boulder, CO 80302
Phone: 303-459-5482
Email: scholars@greenhousescholars.org
http://www.greenhousescholars.org
Purpose: To provide personal, professional and financial support to high-performing, under-resourced students who are leaders and contributors to their communities.
Eligibility: Applicants must be high school seniors who plan to attend a four-year college or university. They must be U.S. citizens or permanent residents who reside and attend school in Colorado, Georgia, Illinois, New York or North Carolina. They must have an unweighted GPA of 3.5 or higher, and they must demonstrate leadership, perseverance and financial need. Their household income must be $70,000 a year or less. Winners participate in the Whole Person Program which includes Summer Symposium, Mentorship, Professional Networking, Impact and Internship programming and more!
Target applicant(s): High school students.
Minimum GPA: 3.5
Amount: Up to $5,000.
Number of awards: Varies.
Scholarship may be renewable.
Deadline: November 19.
How to apply: Applications are available online.
Exclusive: Visit www.UltimateScholarshipBook.com and enter code GR147623 for updates on this award.

(1477) · Grossman Scholarship

Volunteers for Outdoor Colorado
600 South Marion Parkway, Denver, CO 80209
Phone: 303-715-1010
Email: scholarships@voc.org
https://www.voc.org/grossman-scholarship
Purpose: To support students committed to caring for our environment's natural resources.
Eligibility: Applicants must be Colorado residents and graduating high school seniors, graduate students or non-traditional students. Students must be pursuing a degree program with an environmental, natural resource, climate or outdoor industry emphasis at an accredited four-year college or university, two-year community college or a certificate program offered by an accredited college or university within the state of Colorado. Applicants must demonstrate a commitment to caring for our environment's natural resources within their personal, educational and/or professional time.
Target applicant(s): High school students. College students. Graduate school students. Adult students.
Amount: $5,000.
Number of awards: 4.
Deadline: March 31.
How to apply: Applications are available online.
Exclusive: Visit www.UltimateScholarshipBook.com and enter code VO147723 for updates on this award.

(1478) · Guy M. Wilson Scholarship

American Legion, Department of Michigan
212 N. Verlinden Avenue, Ste. A, Lansing, MI 48915
Phone: 517-371-4720 x11
Email: programs@michiganlegion.org
http://www.michiganlegion.org

Purpose: To aid students who are the sons or daughters or grandchildren of veterans who plan to attend a Michigan college.

Eligibility: Applicants must be residents of Michigan who are planning to attend a Michigan college or university and who are the sons or daughters or grandchildren of veterans. Students must have a minimum GPA of 2.5 and must have demonstrated financial need. Applicants must provide proof of a parent's military service record and an indication of their abilities to fulfill their goals and intentions. They should send scholarship information to their county district committee person.

Target applicant(s): High school students.

Minimum GPA: 2.5

Amount: $500.

Number of awards: Varies.

Deadline: January 4.

How to apply: Applications are available online.

Exclusive: Visit www.UltimateScholarshipBook.com and enter code AM147823 for updates on this award.

(1479) · H-E-B Scholarships for UIL Participants

Sports in Action
405 State Highway 121, Suite A-200, Lewisville, TX 75067
Phone: 972-898-8585
Email: uil@registermyathlete.com
http://www.sportsinaction.com/scholarship/

Purpose: To reward students for their community service and involvement.

Eligibility: Applicants must be current Texas high school seniors with a minimum 3.3 GPA. Students must have participated in a UIL competition as high school students and have been active in community service programs. Awards are distributed as follows: five students who competed in athletics, five students who competed in music and five students who competed in academic events.

Target applicant(s): High school students.

Minimum GPA: 3.3

Amount: $2,000.

Number of awards: 15.

Deadline: January 28.

How to apply: Applications are available online.

Exclusive: Visit www.UltimateScholarshipBook.com and enter code SP147923 for updates on this award.

(1480) · H.L. Taylor Scholarship Program

Iowa PTA
P.O. Box 10634, Cedar Rapids, IA 52410
Phone: 319-573-0049
Email: execdir@iowapta.org
http://iowapta.org/index.php/programs/scholarships

Purpose: To support Iowa students pursuing post-secondary education.

Eligibility: Applicants must be graduating high school seniors in Iowa whose school district has an active PTA at any level of education. Students must be residents of Iowa and plan to enroll at an accredited Iowa post-secondary institution.

Target applicant(s): High school students.

Amount: $500.

Number of awards: Varies.

Deadline: February 1.

How to apply: Applications are available online.

Exclusive: Visit www.UltimateScholarshipBook.com and enter code IO148023 for updates on this award.

(1481) · H.M. Muffly Memorial Scholarship

Colorado Nurses Foundation
2851 S. Parker Road, Suite 1210, Aurora, CO 80014
Phone: 720-457-1191
Email: sonja.hix-cortina@civicamanagement.com
https://www.coloradonursesfoundation.com/

Purpose: To aid nursing students working towards bachelor's, master's or doctoral degrees.

Eligibility: Applicants must be Colorado residents who are planning to practice nursing in Colorado. They must be juniors or seniors working towards the Bachelor of Science in Nursing (BSN); Registered Nurses (RNs) pursuing the bachelor's degree or higher in a school of nursing; practicing RNs pursuing a doctoral degree in nursing or second- or third-year Doctor of Nursing Practice (DNP) students. Undergraduates must have a GPA of 3.25 or higher, and graduate students must have a GPA of 3.5 or higher. Selection is based on GPA, financial need, recommendations, community involvement and commitment to professional practice in Colorado.

Target applicant(s): College students. Graduate school students. Adult students.

Minimum GPA: 3.25 for undergraduate students, 3.5 for graduate students

Amount: $2,500.

Number of awards: 2.

Deadline: October 31.

How to apply: Applications are available online. An application form, schedule of classes, two recommendation letters, financial need statement, transcript and personal essay are required.

Exclusive: Visit www.UltimateScholarshipBook.com and enter code CO148123 for updates on this award.

(1482) · Hal W. Almen/West OKC Rotary Scholarship

Oklahoma City Community Foundation
1000 North Broadway, Oklahoma City, OK 73102
Phone: 405-235-5603
Email: scholarships@occf.org
https://occf.org/

Purpose: To support students from the state of Oklahoma with furthering their education.

Eligibility: Applicants must be a graduating senior from a Oklahoma high school. Students must have a 2.75 GPA or higher to be considered for this award. Financial need is considered and applicant's family income cannot exceed $100,000. Students must provide a written statement that focuses on how their local Rotary club supports their local community.

Target applicant(s): High school students.

Minimum GPA: 2.75

Amount: $4,000.

Number of awards: 3.

Deadline: February 28.

How to apply: Applications are available online.

Exclusive: Visit www.UltimateScholarshipBook.com and enter code OK148223 for updates on this award.

(1483) · Harold C. and Frances L. Stuart Scholarship

Oklahoma Association of Broadcasters
6520 N. Western, Suite 104, Oklahoma City, OK 73116
Phone: 405-848-0771
Email: struby@oabok.org
https://oabok.org/careerseducation/scholarships/

Purpose: To support students majoring in broadcasting at Oklahoma colleges and universities.

Eligibility: Applicants must be enrolled in an Oklahoma college or university broadcasting program, be majoring in broadcasting and have an intent to enter the broadcasting career upon graduation. Students must be a junior or senior for the upcoming school year and must maintain a "B" average.

Target applicant(s): College students. Adult students.

Minimum GPA: 3.0

Amount: $2,000.

Number of awards: 1.

Deadline: February 4.

How to apply: Applications are available online.

Exclusive: Visit www.UltimateScholarshipBook.com and enter code OK148323 for updates on this award.

(1484) · Harold K. Douthit Scholarship

Ohio News Media Foundation
1335 Dublin Road, Suite 216-B, Columbus, OH 43215
Phone: 614-486-6677
Email: ariggs@ohionews.org
https://www.ohionews.org/aws/ONA/pt/sp/foundation

Purpose: To support students pursuing a major in a journalism-related field at an Ohio college or university.

Eligibility: Applicants must be enrolled in an Ohio college or university and be majoring in a journalism-related field such as journalism, advertising or marketing. Students must have at least a 3.0 GPA and write an essay as part of their application showcasing their writing skill along with including work samples related to degree.

Target applicant(s): College students. Adult students.

Minimum GPA: 3.0

Amount: $750.

Number of awards: 1.

Deadline: May 24.

How to apply: Applications are available online.

Exclusive: Visit www.UltimateScholarshipBook.com and enter code OH148423 for updates on this award.

(1485) · Harriet Hayes Austin Memorial Scholarship for Nursing

Topeka Community Foundation
5431 SW 29th Street, Suite 300, Topeka, KS 66614
Phone: 785-272-4804
Email: matalone@topekacommunityfoundation.org
http://www.topekacommunityfoundation.org

Purpose: To aid students who are pursuing the Bachelor of Science in Nursing (BSN) degree at an accredited postsecondary institution located in Kansas.

Eligibility: Applicants must be U.S. citizens who are enrolled in or who plan to enroll in a BSN program at an accredited school located in Kansas. They must demonstrate financial need. Preference is given to Kansas residents. Selection is based on the overall strength of the application.

Target applicant(s): High school students. College students. Adult students.

Amount: $1,000.

Number of awards: 5.

Deadline: February.

How to apply: Applications are available online. An application form, official transcript, one letter of recommendation, personal statements, financial analysis form and proof of U.S. citizenship are required.

Exclusive: Visit www.UltimateScholarshipBook.com and enter code TO148523 for updates on this award.

(1486) · Harry Alan Gregg Foundation Grants

Harry Alan Gregg Foundation Grants
1 Verney Drive, Greenfield, NH 03047
Phone: 603-547-3311
Email: hgf@crotchedmountain.org
http://www.crotchedmountain.org

Purpose: To provide financial assistance for the disabled.

Eligibility: Applicants must be New Hampshire residents with physical, intellectual or emotional disabilities or their families. Funds may be used for a variety of purposes but must benefit the person with a disability. Selection is based on need. Applications are reviewed four times a year, with deadlines in March, June, September and December.

Target applicant(s): High school students. College students. Graduate school students. Adult students.

Amount: Up to $1,200.

Number of awards: Varies.

Deadline: June 10, September 9, December 9, March 10.

How to apply: Applications are available online. Documentation of the expense must be provided before payment will be made.

Exclusive: Visit www.UltimateScholarshipBook.com and enter code HA148623 for updates on this award.

(1487) · Harry Barfield KBA Scholarship Program

Kentucky Broadcasters Association
101 Enterprise Drive, Frankfort, KY 40601
Phone: 888-843-5221
Email: kba@kba.org
http://www.kba.org

Purpose: To aid aspiring young broadcasters.

Eligibility: Applicants must be attending a college or university in Kentucky and major or plan to major in broadcasting or telecommunications. Preference is given to second semester sophomores, and funds are awarded in the junior year and renewable for the senior year. Applicants should have a minimum 3.0 GPA, although some consideration will be given to those with lower GPAs who have exceptional credentials otherwise.

Target applicant(s): College students. Adult students.

Minimum GPA: 3.0

Amount: $2,500.

Number of awards: Varies.

Scholarship may be renewable.

Deadline: May 1.

How to apply: Applications are available online. An application form, transcript, essay, list of extracurricular activities and letter of recommendation are required.

Exclusive: Visit www.UltimateScholarshipBook.com and enter code KE148723 for updates on this award.

(1488) · Hattie Tedrow Memorial Fund Scholarship

American Legion, Department of North Dakota
405 W. Maine Avenue, Suite 4A, P.O. Box 5057, West Fargo, ND 58078
Phone: 701-293-3120
Email: LegionEd@legion.org

https://www.ndlegion.org/scholarships/
Purpose: To support descendants of veterans.
Eligibility: Applicants must be high school seniors, North Dakota residents and U.S. citizens. They must be direct descendants of veterans with honorable service in the U.S. military.
Target applicant(s): High school students.
Amount: Up to $2,000.
Number of awards: Varies.
Deadline: April 1.
How to apply: Applications are available by mail. An application form, essay and proof of veteran's military service are required.
Exclusive: Visit www.UltimateScholarshipBook.com and enter code AM148823 for updates on this award.

(1489) · Hawaii Community Foundation Scholarships

Hawaii Community Foundation - Scholarships
827 Fort Street Mall, Honolulu, HI 96813
Phone: 888-731-3863
Email: scholarships@hcf-hawaii.org
https://www.hawaiicommunityfoundation.org/
Purpose: To help Hawaii residents who show financial need.
Eligibility: The Hawaii Community Foundation Scholarship Program has over 200 different scholarship funds covering areas such as vocational education, those in foster care, ethnicity, religion and major. Applicants must be Hawaii residents who plan to attend nonprofit two- or four-year colleges as either full-time undergraduate or graduate students. Applicants must also have academic achievement and good moral character. A personal statement, Student Aid Report, transcript, recommendation letter and essay may be required depending on the specific scholarship.
Target applicant(s): High school students. College students. Graduate school students. Adult students.
Amount: Varies.
Number of awards: Varies.
Deadline: January 31.
How to apply: Applications are available online.
Exclusive: Visit www.UltimateScholarshipBook.com and enter code HA148923 for updates on this award.

(1490) · Hawaii High School Athletic Association Hall of Honor

Hawaii High School Athletic Association
P.O. Box 62029, Honolulu, HI 96839
Phone: 808-800-4092
Email: info@hhsaa.org
http://www.sportshigh.com
Purpose: To support Hawaii high school seniors who are athletes.
Eligibility: Applicants must be graduating high school seniors and athletes in any organized sport in Hawaii. Selection is based primarily on sports achievements. Factors considered include contributions to the team, sportsmanship, character, participation in school activities and community involvement.
Target applicant(s): High school students.
Amount: $2,000.
Number of awards: 12.
Deadline: May 20.
How to apply: Applications are available by written request.
Exclusive: Visit www.UltimateScholarshipBook.com and enter code HA149023 for updates on this award.

(1491) · Hawaii Pizza Hut Scholarship Fund

Hawaii Community Foundation - Scholarships
827 Fort Street Mall, Honolulu, HI 96813
Phone: 888-731-3863
Email: scholarships@hcf-hawaii.org
https://www.hawaiicommunityfoundation.org/
Purpose: To support students in Hawaii with financial need.
Eligibility: Applicants must be Hawaii residents, attend a two- or four-year college or university and have a GPA between 3.0 and 3.5.
Target applicant(s): High school students. College students. Adult students.
Minimum GPA: 3.0
Amount: Varies.
Number of awards: Varies.
Deadline: January 31.
How to apply: To apply, register online, complete the online application and select the scholarships to which you wish to apply. In addition, mail the supporting materials: printed confirmation page from the online application, personal statement, copy of Student Aid Report (SAR) available at www.fafsa.ed.gov and official transcript.
Exclusive: Visit www.UltimateScholarshipBook.com and enter code HA149123 for updates on this award.

(1492) · Hawaii Rotary Youth Foundation Scholarship

Hawaii Rotary Youth Foundation
3536 Harding Avenue, Honolulu, HI 96816
Phone: 808-735-1073
Email: office@hawaiirotaryyouthfoundation.org
http://www.hawaiirotaryyouthfoundation.org
Purpose: To encourage graduating high school seniors from Hawaii to pursue a higher education.
Eligibility: Applicants must be graduating high school seniors sponsored by a District 5000 Rotary Club in the state of Hawaii. Students must plan to enroll full-time at a four-year college or university in the United States. Applicants must be U.S. citizens and residents of Hawaii.
Target applicant(s): High school students.
Amount: $5,000.
Number of awards: Varies.
Deadline: February 1.
How to apply: Applications are available online.
Exclusive: Visit www.UltimateScholarshipBook.com and enter code HA149223 for updates on this award.

(1493) · Hawaii Society of Certified Public Accountants Scholarship Fund

Hawaii Community Foundation - Scholarships
827 Fort Street Mall, Honolulu, HI 96813
Phone: 888-731-3863
Email: scholarships@hcf-hawaii.org
https://www.hawaiicommunityfoundation.org/
Purpose: To provide financial assistance for those pursuing degrees in accounting.
Eligibility: Applicants must be college juniors, college seniors or graduate students attending an accredited four-year Hawaii institution of higher learning with a major or concentration in accounting. They must have a minimum GPA of 3.0.
Target applicant(s): College students. Graduate school students. Adult students.
Minimum GPA: 3.0
Amount: Varies.

Number of awards: Varies.
Deadline: January 31.
How to apply: To apply, register online, complete the online application and select the scholarships to which you wish to apply. In addition, mail the supporting materials: printed confirmation page from the online application, personal statement, copy of Student Aid Report (SAR) available at www.fafsa.ed.gov and official transcript.
Exclusive: Visit www.UltimateScholarshipBook.com and enter code HA149323 for updates on this award.

(1494) · Health Research and Educational Trust Pathway Scholarship

New Jersey Hospital Association
760 Alexander Road, P.O. Box 1, Princeton, NJ 08543-0001
Phone: 609-275-4000
Email: jhritz@njha.com
http://www.njha.com
Purpose: To aid New Jersey students enrolled in certain healthcare-related degree programs.
Eligibility: Applicants must be New Jersey residents. They must be undergraduate juniors, undergraduate seniors or graduate students enrolled in a nursing, allied health professions, healthcare administration or hospital administration degree program. Applicants must have a GPA of 3.0 or higher and must demonstrate financial need. Selection is based on the quality of the personal essay submitted as part of the application.
Target applicant(s): College students. Graduate school students. Adult students.
Minimum GPA: 3.0
Amount: At least $2,000.
Number of awards: Varies.
Deadline: October 4.
How to apply: Application instructions are available online. Applicant contact information, a personal essay, an official transcript and proof of financial need are required.
Exclusive: Visit www.UltimateScholarshipBook.com and enter code NE149423 for updates on this award.

(1495) · Henry A. Zuberano Scholarship

Hawaii Community Foundation - Scholarships
827 Fort Street Mall, Honolulu, HI 96813
Phone: 888-731-3863
Email: scholarships@hcf-hawaii.org
https://www.hawaiicommunityfoundation.org/
Purpose: To assist Hawaii students who are majoring in political science, international relations, international business or public administration.
Eligibility: Applicants must have a GPA of 2.7 or higher.
Target applicant(s): High school students. College students. Adult students.
Minimum GPA: 2.7
Amount: Varies.
Number of awards: Varies.
Deadline: January 31.
How to apply: To apply, register online, complete the online application and select the scholarships to which you wish to apply. In addition, mail the supporting materials: printed confirmation page from the online application, personal statement, copy of Student Aid Report (SAR) available at www.fafsa.ed.gov and official transcript.
Exclusive: Visit www.UltimateScholarshipBook.com and enter code HA149523 for updates on this award.

(1496) · Henry Sachs Foundation Scholarship

Henry Sachs Foundation
90 S. Cascade Avenue, Suite 1410, Colorado Springs, CO 80903
Phone: 719-633-2353
Email: info@sachsfoundation.org
http://www.sachsfoundation.org/scholarships
Purpose: To aid African-American high school students in Colorado to obtain a college education.
Eligibility: Applicants must be African-American residents of Colorado for at least five years. Applicants must be either seniors in high school or have graduated in the last three years but are not currently attending college. Awards are based on high school grade point average and financial need. If selected, applicants must attend a personal interview in order to receive the grant money.
Target applicant(s): High school students.
Minimum GPA: 3.0
Amount: $6,000.
Number of awards: Varies.
Scholarship may be renewable.
Deadline: March 15.
How to apply: Applications are available online.
Exclusive: Visit www.UltimateScholarshipBook.com and enter code HE149623 for updates on this award.

(1497) · Herbert Hoover Uncommon Student Award

Hoover Presidential Foundation
P.O. Box 696, West Branch, IA 52358
Phone: 800-828-0475
Email: info@hooverpf.org
http://www.hooverpresidentialfoundation.org
Purpose: To honor Herbert Hoover by rewarding students who live up to his ideal of the "uncommon man."
Eligibility: Applicants must be juniors in an Iowa high school or be homeschooled. Students must submit a project proposal and two letters of recommendation. Recipients must attend a weekend program during the summer and are expected to complete the proposed project. Grades, essays and test scores are not considered.
Target applicant(s): High school students.
Amount: $1,500.
Number of awards: Up to 15.
Deadline: March 15.
How to apply: Applications are available online.
Exclusive: Visit www.UltimateScholarshipBook.com and enter code HO149723 for updates on this award.

(1498) · Herman J. Smith Scholarship

National Housing Endowment
1201 15th Street NW, Washington, DC 20005
Phone: 202-266-8069
Email: Scholarships@nahb.org
http://www.nationalhousingendowment.org/page.aspx/generic/sectionID=3267
Purpose: To aid students who are planning for careers in mortgage finance or the construction industry.
Eligibility: Applicants must be full-time undergraduate or graduate students attending an accredited four-year institution. They must have at least one more year of study to complete after the date of award disbursement; fifth-year seniors are ineligible for this award. They must be majoring in and planning to pursue a career in mortgage finance, construction management or another construction-related subject.

Preference is given to Texas residents, students who attend school in Texas and current members of their school's National Association of Home Builders student chapter. Selection is based on academic merit, recommendations, work experience, extracurricular activities, career goals and financial need.
Target applicant(s): College students. Graduate school students. Adult students.
Amount: Varies.
Number of awards: Varies.
Scholarship may be renewable.
Deadline: March.
How to apply: Applications are available online. An application form, course schedule, official transcripts and three recommendation letters are required.
Exclusive: Visit www.UltimateScholarshipBook.com and enter code NA149823 for updates on this award.

(1499) · Herman Sani Scholarship

Iowa Golf Association
Attn: Ann Griffel Scholarship Committee, 1605 North Ankeny Boulevard, Suite 210, Ankeny, IA 50023
Phone: 888-388-4442
Email: info@iowagolf.org
https://iowagolf.org/scholarships/
Purpose: To assist Iowa college-bound students as they further their education.
Eligibility: Applicant must be a high school senior with a background in golf. Selection is based on academic achievement, extracurricular activities and leadership qualities. Selection is not based on golf accomplishments or abilities.
Target applicant(s): High school students.
Amount: $2,000.
Number of awards: Varies.
Scholarship may be renewable.
Deadline: April 1.
How to apply: Applications are available online and include a personal essay, two letters of recommendation and an official transcript.
Exclusive: Visit www.UltimateScholarshipBook.com and enter code IO149923 for updates on this award.

(1500) · Hermine Solt Student Scholarship

Pennsylvania Association of Educational Office Professionals (PAEOP)
Lenore Filipovic, Phoenixville Area School District, 386 City Line Avenue, Phoenixville, PA 19460
Email: herminsoltstudentscholarship@gmail.com
https://www.paeop.com/page/71
Purpose: To support students in Pennsylvania who are pursuing a higher education in a business-related field.
Eligibility: Applicants must be graduating high school seniors from either a Pennsylvania high school or Pennsylvania cyber charter school who have a 3.0 GPA. Students must attending an approved post-secondary institution, college or university majoring in the business field.
Target applicant(s): High school students.
Minimum GPA: 3.0
Amount: $500.
Number of awards: Varies.
Deadline: March 1.
How to apply: Applications are available online.
Exclusive: Visit www.UltimateScholarshipBook.com and enter code PE150023 for updates on this award.

(1501) · Hideko and Zenzo Matsuyama Scholarship Fund

Hawaii Community Foundation - Scholarships
827 Fort Street Mall, Honolulu, HI 96813
Phone: 888-731-3863
Email: scholarships@hcf-hawaii.org
https://www.hawaiicommunityfoundation.org/
Purpose: To provide financial assistance for high school graduates who are seeking higher education.
Eligibility: Applicants must be graduates of Hawaiian high schools or GED recipients who plan to attend a college or university in Hawaii or the continental U.S. full-time. They must have a GPA of 3.0 or higher. Applicants must be of Japanese ancestry.
Target applicant(s): High school students. College students. Adult students.
Minimum GPA: 3.0
Amount: Varies.
Number of awards: Varies.
Deadline: January 31.
How to apply: To apply, register online, complete the online application and select the scholarships to which you wish to apply. In addition, mail the supporting materials: printed confirmation page from the online application, personal statement, copy of Student Aid Report (SAR) available at www.fafsa.ed.gov and official transcript.
Exclusive: Visit www.UltimateScholarshipBook.com and enter code HA150123 for updates on this award.

(1502) · High School Senior Essay Contest

Masonic Charity Foundation of Oklahoma
P.O. Box 2406, Edmond, OK 73083
Phone: 405-348-7500
Email: information@mcfok.org
https://www.mcfok.org/programs/
Purpose: To support high school seniors attending Oklahoma public schools.
Eligibility: Applicants must be high school seniors attending an Oklahoma public school. An original essay submission of 1,000-1,250 words is required on a provided topic. Selection based on adherence to the prescribed topic, organization of material, interest, originality, spelling, grammar, punctuation and neatness.
Target applicant(s): High school students.
Amount: Up to $2,000.
Number of awards: 10.
Deadline: October 31.
How to apply: Applications are available online.
Exclusive: Visit www.UltimateScholarshipBook.com and enter code MA150223 for updates on this award.

(1503) · High Technology Scholar/Intern Tuition Waiver

Massachusetts Department of Higher Education
Office of Student Financial Assistance, 454 Broadway, Suite 200, Revere, MA 02151
Phone: 617-727-9420
Email: osfa@osfa.mass.edu
https://www.mass.edu/osfa/programs/programs.asp
Purpose: To provide financial aid and internship connections to computer technology and engineering students in Massachusetts.
Eligibility: Students must be enrolled in an undergraduate program at a Massachusetts public college and must not have previously earned

a bachelor's degree. Applicants must have approval from the company or organization that is funding the scholarship. Students must not owe refunds on any previous financial aid or have any defaulted government loans.

Target applicant(s): High school students. College students. Adult students.

Amount: Up to full tuition.

Number of awards: Varies.

Deadline: Varies.

How to apply: Applications are available at college financial aid offices.

Exclusive: Visit www.UltimateScholarshipBook.com and enter code MA150323 for updates on this award.

(1504) · Higher Education Academic Scholarship Program (Bright Flight)

Missouri Student Assistance Resource Services (MOSTARS)
Missouri Department of Higher Education, Attn: Bright Flight, P.O. Box 1469, Jefferson City, MO 65102
Phone: 800-473-6757
Email: info@dhe.mo.gov
http://dhe.mo.gov/ppc/grants/
Purpose: This merit-based program encourages top-ranked high school seniors to attend approved Missouri postsecondary schools.
Eligibility: Applicants must be U.S. citizens or eligible noncitizens, Missouri residents and have an ACT or SAT score within the top 3 percent of all Missouri students taking those tests. Applicants must be high school seniors who enroll as first-time, full-time students at an approved Missouri postsecondary school.
Target applicant(s): High school students.
Amount: Up to $3,000.
Number of awards: Varies.
Scholarship may be renewable.
Deadline: Varies.
How to apply: For an application contact your high school counselor or MOSTARS.
Exclusive: Visit www.UltimateScholarshipBook.com and enter code MI150423 for updates on this award.

(1505) · Higher Education Adult Part-Time Student (HEAPS) Grant Program

West Virginia Higher Education Policy Commission
1018 Kanawha Boulevard, East, Suite 700, Charleston, WV 25301
Phone: 304-558-2101
Email: jacob.abrams@wvhepc.edu
http://www.wvhepc.edu/
Purpose: To assist adult West Virginia students.
Eligibility: Applicants must be West Virginia residents, be U.S. citizens or permanent residents, be enrolled or accepted for enrollment in an undergraduate institution on a part-time basis and demonstrate financial need.
Target applicant(s): High school students. College students. Adult students.
Amount: $2,000.
Number of awards: Varies.
Scholarship may be renewable.
Deadline: Varies.
How to apply: Complete the Free Application for Federal Student Aid (FAFSA).
Exclusive: Visit www.UltimateScholarshipBook.com and enter code WE150523 for updates on this award.

(1506) · Higher Education Legislative Plan (HELP)

Mississippi Office of Student Financial Aid
3825 Ridgewood Road, Jackson, MS 39211
Phone: 800-327-2980
Email: sfa@ihl.state.ms.us
https://www.msfinancialaid.org/
Purpose: To assist financially needy Mississippi students to afford tuition.
Eligibility: Applicants must be U.S. citizens or eligible noncitizens, Mississippi residents and have a minimum college GPA of 2.5 and have graduated from high school within the past two years. Applicants must be attending an eligible Mississippi institution, must have a minimum ACT score of 20 and must document an average gross income of $39,500 or less over the prior two years, and must have the results of a processed Student Aid Report (SAR). Students who file the Free Application for Federal Student Aid (FAFSA) will receive a SAR report.
Target applicant(s): High school students. College students. Adult students.
Minimum GPA: 2.5
Amount: Full tuition.
Number of awards: Varies.
Scholarship may be renewable.
Deadline: March 31.
How to apply: Contact the Mississippi Office of Student Financial Aid for an application.
Exclusive: Visit www.UltimateScholarshipBook.com and enter code MI150623 for updates on this award.

(1507) · Ho'omaka Hou - A New Beginning Fund

Hawaii Community Foundation - Scholarships
827 Fort Street Mall, Honolulu, HI 96813
Phone: 888-731-3863
Email: scholarships@hcf-hawaii.org
https://www.hawaiicommunityfoundation.org/
Purpose: To support students who have overcome substance abuse or other difficulties in their lives.
Eligibility: Applicants must show financial need. Students must attend college or technical school in Hawaii. Minimum 2.7 GPA required.
Target applicant(s): High school students. College students. Adult students.
Minimum GPA: 2.7
Amount: Varies.
Number of awards: Varies.
Deadline: January 31.
How to apply: Applications are available online. In addition, mail the supporting materials: personal statement, one letter of recommendation, copy of Student Aid Report (SAR) available at www.fafsa.ed.gov and official transcript.
Exclusive: Visit www.UltimateScholarshipBook.com and enter code HA150723 for updates on this award.

(1508) · Honors Award

Louisiana Office of Student Financial Assistance
605 N. Fifth Street, Baton Rouge, LA 70802
Phone: 800-259-5626 x1012
Email: custserv@la.gov
https://mylosfa.la.gov/students-parents/scholarships-grants/tops/
Purpose: To aid Louisiana student residents.
Eligibility: Applicants must be Louisiana residents and U.S. citizens, apply during their senior year in high school, use the award at a Louisiana

college or university, have a minimum 3.0 GPA and have a minimum ACT score of 27 or equivalent SAT score.
Target applicant(s): High school students.
Minimum GPA: 3.0
Amount: Full tuition plus $800 stipend.
Number of awards: Varies.
Scholarship may be renewable.
Deadline: July 1.
How to apply: The application is the Free Application for Federal Student Aid (FAFSA). ACT or SAT scores must also be reported.
Exclusive: Visit www.UltimateScholarshipBook.com and enter code LO150823 for updates on this award.

(1509) · HOPE Scholarship Program
Georgia Student Finance Commission
2082 East Exchange Place, Tucker, GA 30084
Phone: 800-505-4732
Email: gsfcinfo@gsfc.org
https://www.gafutures.org/
Purpose: To support students attending Georgia institutions.
Eligibility: Applicants must have graduated from high school and be attending or planning to attend college in Georgia. Students must be U.S. citizens or eligible non-citizens, be a legal resident of the state of Georgia and have a minimum 3.0 GPA. Students should submit applications as early as possible.
Target applicant(s): High school students. College students. Adult students.
Minimum GPA: 3.0
Amount: Varies.
Number of awards: Varies.
Scholarship may be renewable.
Deadline: Last day of classes.
How to apply: Applications are available online.
Exclusive: Visit www.UltimateScholarshipBook.com and enter code GE150923 for updates on this award.

(1510) · HospitalityMaine Scholarship
HospitalityMaine
45 Melville Street, Augusta, ME 04330
Phone: 207-213-2060
https://www.hospitalitymaine.com/page/Resources
Purpose: To support students enrolled in hospitality-related programs.
Eligibility: Applicants must be Maine residents and accepted to an accredited institution of higher learning with specialties in hotel administration or culinary sciences. Students must plan to begin a career in hospitality upon completion of their degrees.
Target applicant(s): High school students. College students. Adult students.
Amount: Varies.
Number of awards: Varies.
Deadline: May 1.
How to apply: Applications are available from the Maine Innkeepers Association.
Exclusive: Visit www.UltimateScholarshipBook.com and enter code HO151023 for updates on this award.

(1511) · Houston Livestock Show and Rodeo Scholarships
Houston Livestock Show and Rodeo
Educational Programs Department, P.O. Box 20070, Houston, TX 77225-0070
Phone: 832-667-1285
Email: scholarship@rodeohouston.com
https://www.rodeohouston.com/Educational-Support/Scholarships
Purpose: To support graduating high school students who are Texas residents.
Eligibility: Applicants must be U.S. citizens and be graduating high school seniors from public schools who have completed a current FAFSA. Applicants must also plan to attend and have applied to an accredited, not-for-profit university in Texas after graduation. SAT or ACT scores are required. Selection is based on financial need, academic performance and demonstrated leadership. Multiple types of scholarship are available. Specific eligibility criteria and deadlines differ for each scholarship.
Target applicant(s): High school students.
Amount: Varies.
Number of awards: Varies.
Deadline: February.
How to apply: Applications are available online. A copy of the application and other required documentation (varies for each scholarship) must be mailed to the Office of Educational Programs.
Exclusive: Visit www.UltimateScholarshipBook.com and enter code HO151123 for updates on this award.

(1512) · Howard P. Rawlings Educational Assistance (EA) Grant
Maryland Higher Education Commission
Office of Student Financial Assistance, 6 North Liberty Street, Baltimore, MD 21201
Phone: 800-974-1024
Email: osfamail@mhec.state.md.us
https://mhec.maryland.gov
Purpose: To help Maryland students who demonstrate financial need.
Eligibility: Applicants (and their parents, if applicants are dependents) must be residents of the state of Maryland. They must be high school seniors or undergraduate students and must be or plan to become full-time, degree-seeking students. They must complete the Free Application for Federal Student Aid (FAFSA) and must demonstrate financial need. Selection is based on financial need.
Target applicant(s): High school students. College students. Adult students.
Amount: $400-$3,000.
Number of awards: Varies.
Scholarship may be renewable.
Deadline: March 1.
How to apply: To apply, applicants must fill out and submit the FAFSA.
Exclusive: Visit www.UltimateScholarshipBook.com and enter code MA151223 for updates on this award.

(1513) · Howard P. Rawlings Guaranteed Access (GA) Grant
Maryland Higher Education Commission
Office of Student Financial Assistance, 6 North Liberty Street, Baltimore, MD 21201
Phone: 800-974-1024
Email: osfamail@mhec.state.md.us
https://mhec.maryland.gov

Purpose: To help Maryland students with financial need afford college.
Eligibility: Applicants and their parents must both be legal residents of the state of Maryland. Applicants must be U.S. citizens or eligible noncitizens, complete the Free Application for Federal Student Aid (FAFSA) and the Guaranteed Access (GA) Grant application. Applicants and families must also meet the established income limits to qualify.
Target applicant(s): High school students.
Amount: Up to $18,400.
Number of awards: Varies.
Scholarship may be renewable.
Deadline: March 1.
How to apply: Complete the FAFSA.
Exclusive: Visit www.UltimateScholarshipBook.com and enter code MA151323 for updates on this award.

(1514) · Hugh A. Smith Scholarship Fund

American Legion, Department of Kansas
1314 SW Topeka Boulevard, Topeka, KS 66612
Phone: 785-232-9315
https://ksamlegion.org/
Purpose: To provide assistance to needy and worthy children of American Legion and American Legion Auxiliary members.
Eligibility: Applicants must be average or better students who are high school seniors or college freshmen or sophomores enrolling or enrolled in a post-secondary school in Kansas. They must be the son or daughter of a veteran, and a parent must have been a member of the Kansas American Legion or American Legion Auxiliary for the past three years. The children of deceased parents are also eligible if the parent was a paid member at the time of death. Applicants must submit three letters of recommendation, including one from a teacher, an essay on "Why I Want to Go to College," high school transcript, a 1040 income statement and documentation of parent's veteran status.
Target applicant(s): High school students. College students. Adult students.
Amount: $500.
Number of awards: 1.
Deadline: February 15.
How to apply: Applications are available online.
Exclusive: Visit www.UltimateScholarshipBook.com and enter code AM151423 for updates on this award.

(1515) · IAD Foundation Scholarships

Iowa Automobile Dealers Foundation for Education
1111 Office Park Road, West Des Moines, IA 50265
Phone: 515-440-7625
Email: mcason@iada.com
https://iada.com/about/iad-foundation-for-education/
Purpose: To support Iowa students pursuing automotive-related studies.
Eligibility: Applicants must be Iowa high school graduates enrolling in a two- or four-year post-secondary institution to pursue automotive-related studies.
Target applicant(s): High school students.
Amount: Varies.
Number of awards: 9.
Deadline: March 1.
How to apply: Applications are available online.
Exclusive: Visit www.UltimateScholarshipBook.com and enter code IO151523 for updates on this award.

(1516) · ICCA Scholarships

Iowa Cheerleading Coaches' Association
Attn.: JoEllen Wesselmann, P.O. Box 207, Huxley, IA 50124
Phone: 515-494-3541
Email: iccajo@hotmail.com
http://iowacheercoaches.org/
Purpose: To aid graduating Iowa cheerleaders who display outstanding scholastic achievement in their pursuit of higher education.
Eligibility: Applicants must be a high school senior and have a coach who is a current member of the Iowa Cheerleading Coaches' Association. Students must also have a 3.5 GPA or higher. Selection is based on academic achievement, leadership and community involvement.
Target applicant(s): High school students.
Minimum GPA: 3.5
Amount: $500.
Number of awards: Varies.
Deadline: February 15.
How to apply: Applications are available online and include the basic application, the one page essay, activity listing, cheerleading coach letter of recommendation, additional letter of recommendation and letter from high school counselor verifying grade point average.
Exclusive: Visit www.UltimateScholarshipBook.com and enter code IO151623 for updates on this award.

(1517) · Idaho State Broadcasters Association Scholarships

Idaho State Broadcasters Association
1674 Hill Road, Suite 3, Boise, ID 83702
Phone: 208-345-3072
Email: isba@qwestoffice.net
http://www.idahobroadcasters.org
Purpose: To aid students planning careers in broadcasting.
Eligibility: Applicants must be enrolled full-time in an Idaho college or university, have exhibited superior potential in activities or courses related to broadcasting and be respected among their peer groups. Students must have a GPA of 2.0 or higher in the first two years of college and a GPA of 2.5 in the last two years.
Target applicant(s): College students. Adult students.
Minimum GPA: 2.0
Amount: $1,000.
Number of awards: At least 2.
Deadline: March 15.
How to apply: Applications are available online. An application form, letter of recommendation, transcript and essay are required.
Exclusive: Visit www.UltimateScholarshipBook.com and enter code ID151723 for updates on this award.

(1518) · Illinois AMVETS Ladies Auxiliary Memorial Scholarship

Illinois AMVETS Service Foundation
AMVETS Department of Illinois, 2200 South Sixth Street, Springfield, IL 62703
Phone: 217-528-4713
Email: crystal@ilamvets.org
http://www.ilamvets.org
Purpose: To provide financial assistance to children and grandchildren of U.S. veterans and members of the military.
Eligibility: Applicants must be Illinois high school seniors who have taken the SAT or ACT, and they must be the children or grandchildren

of veterans who were honorably discharged after September 15, 1940 or who are currently serving in the military.

Target applicant(s): High school students.
Amount: Varies.
Number of awards: Varies.
Deadline: March 1.
How to apply: Applications are available online.
Exclusive: Visit www.UltimateScholarshipBook.com and enter code IL151823 for updates on this award.

(1519) · Illinois AMVETS Ladies Auxiliary Worchid Scholarship

Illinois AMVETS Service Foundation
AMVETS Department of Illinois, 2200 South Sixth Street, Springfield, IL 62703
Phone: 217-528-4713
Email: crystal@ilamvets.org
http://www.ilamvets.org
Purpose: To provide financial assistance for students whose parents are U.S. veterans.
Eligibility: Applicants must be Illinois high school seniors whose mother or father is now deceased but had served after September 15, 1940, and was Honorably Discharged. Death of the parent does not have to be from military action or as a result of a service-related disability. Applicants must also have taken the SAT or ACT.
Target applicant(s): High school students.
Amount: Varies.
Number of awards: Varies.
Deadline: March 1.
How to apply: Applications are available online.
Exclusive: Visit www.UltimateScholarshipBook.com and enter code IL151923 for updates on this award.

(1520) · Illinois AMVETS Sad Sacks Nursing Scholarship

Illinois AMVETS Service Foundation
AMVETS Department of Illinois, 2200 South Sixth Street, Springfield, IL 62703
Phone: 217-528-4713
Email: crystal@ilamvets.org
http://www.ilamvets.org
Purpose: To assist Illinois students who are pursuing a career in nursing.
Eligibility: Applicants must be Illinois high school seniors who have been accepted into a nursing program or students who are already attending nursing school in Illinois. They must have financial need and a satisfactory academic record, character and activity record. Dependents of deceased or disabled veterans receive priority.
Target applicant(s): High school students. College students. Adult students.
Amount: Varies.
Number of awards: Varies.
Deadline: March 1.
How to apply: Applications are available online.
Exclusive: Visit www.UltimateScholarshipBook.com and enter code IL152023 for updates on this award.

(1521) · Illinois AMVETS Service Foundation Scholarship

Illinois AMVETS Service Foundation
AMVETS Department of Illinois, 2200 South Sixth Street, Springfield, IL 62703
Phone: 217-528-4713
Email: crystal@ilamvets.org
http://www.ilamvets.org
Purpose: To help Illinois students pay for college.
Eligibility: Applicants musts be Illinois high school seniors who have taken the SAT or ACT. Preference is given to students who are the children or grandchildren of Illinois veterans.
Target applicant(s): High school students.
Amount: $1,000.
Number of awards: Varies.
Deadline: March 1.
How to apply: Applications are available online.
Exclusive: Visit www.UltimateScholarshipBook.com and enter code IL152123 for updates on this award.

(1522) · Illinois Association for Health, Physical Education, Recreation and Dance Scholarships

Illinois Association for Health, Physical Education, Recreation and Dance
P.O. Box 1326, Jacksonville, IL 62651
Phone: 217-245-6413
Email: iahperd@gmail.com
http://www.iahperd.org/grants/scholarships
Purpose: To support physical education students.
Eligibility: Applicants must be full-time junior or senior level undergraduate students at colleges or universities in Illinois and must major in health, physical education, recreation or dance. Students must have been members of IAHPERD since December 1 of the previous year and may receive this award no more than twice.
Target applicant(s): College students. Adult students.
Amount: $1,500-$2,000.
Number of awards: 6.
Scholarship may be renewable.
Deadline: June 1.
How to apply: Applications are available online. An application form, cover letter, resume, essay, transcript and two letters of recommendation are required.
Exclusive: Visit www.UltimateScholarshipBook.com and enter code IL152223 for updates on this award.

(1523) · Illinois Department of Children and Family Services Scholarship Program

Illinois Department of Children and Family Services
406 E. Monroe Street, Springfield, IL 62701
Phone: 217-557-5805
https://www2.illinois.gov/dcfs/
Purpose: To support students who have been under the guardianship of the Department of Children and Family Services.
Eligibility: Applicants must be between 16 and 21 years of age as of the application deadline and have a diploma from an accredited high school or a GED by the end of the current school year. Students must be in the Subsidized Guardianship Program, or the department must have court-ordered legal guardianship or have had legal guardianship for the applicant before adoption was finalized. Recipients must attend an Illinois state community college or university.

Target applicant(s): High school students. College students.
Amount: Up to full tuition plus $511 monthly stipend.
Number of awards: 53.
Scholarship may be renewable.
Deadline: March.
How to apply: Applications are available online. An application form, transcript or copy of GED, SAT or ACT scores, three letters of recommendation and a college transcript (if applicable) are required.
Exclusive: Visit www.UltimateScholarshipBook.com and enter code IL152323 for updates on this award.

(1524) · Illinois Engineering Initiative Scholarship

Illinois Society of Professional Engineers
100 East Washington Street, Springfield, IL 62701
Phone: 217-544-7424
Email: emily@frontlineco.com
https://ilengineeringinitiative.org/
Purpose: To support students enrolled in an engineering program accredited by the Accreditation Board of Engineering and Technology (ABET) at an Illinois university.
Eligibility: Applicants must attend an Illinois university and be enrolled in an engineering program accredited by the Accreditation Board of Engineering and Technology (ABET) and be of at least junior standing having earned not less than 60 semester hours credit by the application deadline. Students must have a B average or better in those courses which are accredited toward the engineering degree and show evidence of financial need.
Target applicant(s): College students. Adult students.
Minimum GPA: 3.0
Amount: $2,000.
Number of awards: 1.
Deadline: May 15.
How to apply: Applications are available online.
Exclusive: Visit www.UltimateScholarshipBook.com and enter code IL152423 for updates on this award.

(1525) · Illinois Oratorical Program Scholarships

American Legion - Department of Illinois
2720 East Lincoln Street, Bloomington, IL 61704
Phone: 309-663-0361
Email: hdqs@illegion.org
http://www.illegion.org/scholarships/
Purpose: To enhance high school students' experience with and understanding of the U.S. Constitution. The contest will help develop students' leadership skills and civic appreciation, as well as the ability to deliver thoughtful, insightful orations regarding U.S. citizenship and its inherent responsibilities.
Eligibility: Applicants must be high school students under the age of 20 who are U.S. citizens or legal residents and residents of the state. Students first give an oration within their state and winners compete at the national level. The oration must be related to the Constitution of the United States focusing on the duties and obligations citizens have to the government. It must be in English and be between eight and ten minutes. There is also an assigned topic which is posted on the website, and it should be between three and five minutes.
Target applicant(s): High school students.
Amount: $100-$2,000.
Number of awards: 11.
Deadline: January.
How to apply: Application information is available by contacting the local American Legion Post or Illinois Department Headquarters.

Exclusive: Visit www.UltimateScholarshipBook.com and enter code AM152523 for updates on this award.

(1526) · Incentive Program for Aspiring Teachers

Massachusetts Department of Higher Education
Office of Student Financial Assistance, 454 Broadway, Suite 200, Revere, MA 02151
Phone: 617-727-9420
Email: osfa@osfa.mass.edu
https://www.mass.edu/osfa/programs/programs.asp
Purpose: To provide financial support for Massachusetts college students who are studying to become teachers.
Eligibility: Applicants must be in their third or fourth year at a public college in the state of Massachusetts, and they must be enrolled in a field with teacher shortages. They must have a 3.0 GPA in general education courses, and they must remain in satisfactory academic standing while receiving the scholarship. Students must agree to work in a public school in Massachusetts for two years after earning a bachelor's degree.
Target applicant(s): College students. Adult students.
Minimum GPA: 3.0
Amount: Full tuition.
Number of awards: Varies.
Scholarship may be renewable.
Deadline: Varies.
How to apply: Applications are available at college financial aid offices.
Exclusive: Visit www.UltimateScholarshipBook.com and enter code MA152623 for updates on this award.

(1527) · Independence Excavating, A DiGeronimo Company Scholarship

Associated General Contractors of Ohio
1755 Northwest Boulevard, Columbus, OH 43212
Phone: 614-486-6446
Email: parker@agcohio.com
https://agcohio.com/workforce-development/agc-scholarships/
Purpose: To aid students who are preparing for construction-related careers at postsecondary institutions located in Ohio, Pennsylvania and West Virginia.
Eligibility: Applicants must be U.S. citizens. They must be in at least the second year of study in a two-year, four-year or five-year undergraduate degree program that is related to construction. They must be enrolled at a postsecondary institution located in West Virginia, Pennsylvania or Ohio and have a GPA of 2.5 or higher. Applicants must have plans to work in the construction industry. Selection is based on the overall strength of the application.
Target applicant(s): College students. Adult students.
Minimum GPA: 2.5
Amount: Varies.
Number of awards: Varies.
Deadline: March 5.
How to apply: Applications are available online. An application form, transcript and personal essay are required.
Exclusive: Visit www.UltimateScholarshipBook.com and enter code AS152723 for updates on this award.

(1528) · Indiana Broadcasters Association College Scholarships

Indiana Broadcasters Association
P.O. Box 902, Carmel, IN 46082

Phone: 317-770-0970
Email: sam@indianabroadcasters.org
https://www.indianabroadcasters.org/scholarships/
Purpose: To support student broadcasters.
Eligibility: Applicants must be Indiana residents and current college students with a 3.0 or higher GPA. Students must be actively participating in a college broadcast facility or working for a commercial broadcast facility and be attending an IBA member institution that has a radio/TV facility on campus and/or offers majors in telecommunications or broadcast journalism.
Target applicant(s): College students. Adult students.
Minimum GPA: 3.0
Amount: Varies.
Number of awards: 6.
Deadline: February.
How to apply: Applications are available online. An application form, essay and transcript request form are required.
Exclusive: Visit www.UltimateScholarshipBook.com and enter code IN152823 for updates on this award.

(1529) · Indiana Golf Foundation Scholarship

Indiana Golf Association
P.O. Box 516, Franklin, IN 46131
Phone: 317-738-9696
Email: astrong@indianagolf.org
https://www.indianagolf.org/scholarships/
Purpose: To support youth who have participated in the Indiana Junior Golf Program.
Eligibility: Applicants must be high school seniors who have participated in the Indiana Junior Golf Program for at least two years, have a 3.0 GPA or higher, display strong character and have financial need. Selection is based on these criteria as well as a personal essay.
Target applicant(s): High school students.
Minimum GPA: 3.0
Amount: $2,500.
Number of awards: 4.
Deadline: February 26.
How to apply: Applications are available online and must also include the personal essay, high school transcript, IRS Form 1040 and at least one letter of recommendation.
Exclusive: Visit www.UltimateScholarshipBook.com and enter code IN152923 for updates on this award.

(1530) · Indiana Oratorical Contest

American Legion, Department of Indiana
5440 Herbert Lord Road, Indianapolis, IN 46216
Phone: 317-630-1300
Email: programs@indlegion.org
http://www.indianalegion.org
Purpose: To enhance high school students' experience with and understanding of the U.S. Constitution. The contest will help develop students' leadership skills and civic appreciation, as well as the ability to deliver thoughtful, insightful orations regarding U.S. citizenship and its inherent responsibilities.
Eligibility: Applicants must be high school students under the age of 20 who are U.S. citizens or legal residents and residents of the state. Students first give an oration within their state and winners compete at the national level. The oration must be related to the Constitution of the United States focusing on the duties and obligations citizens have to the government. It must be in English and be between eight and ten

minutes. There is also an assigned topic which is posted on the website, and it should be between three and five minutes.
Target applicant(s): High school students.
Amount: $200-$3,400.
Number of awards: Varies.
Deadline: February 1.
How to apply: Application information is available from the local American Legion Post and online.
Exclusive: Visit www.UltimateScholarshipBook.com and enter code AM153023 for updates on this award.

(1531) · Iowa 4-H and FFA Livestock Show Competition

Iowa Foundation for Agricultural Advancement
Winner's Circle Scholarships, c/o SGI, 30805 595th Avenue, Cambridge, IA 50046
Phone: 515-291-3941
Email: linda@slweldon.net
http://www.iowastatefair.org/participate/competition/
Purpose: To aid Iowa students who have been active in 4-H or FFA.
Eligibility: Applicants must be Iowa residents, be incoming freshmen at an Iowa college or university and have experience in 4-H and/or FFA livestock projects. They must have plans to major in animal science, agriculture or a related subject. Preference will be given to applicants from Polk County. Selection is based on the overall strength of the application.
Target applicant(s): High school students.
Amount: $3,000.
Number of awards: 1.
Deadline: April 1.
How to apply: Applications are available online. An application form and supporting materials are required.
Exclusive: Visit www.UltimateScholarshipBook.com and enter code IO153123 for updates on this award.

(1532) · Iowa 4-H College Scholarships

Iowa 4-H Foundation
Extension 4-H Youth Building, 1259 Stange Road, Ames, IA 50011-1002
Phone: 515-294-4443
https://www.iowa4hfoundation.org
Purpose: To assist Iowa 4-H participants to pursue higher education.
Eligibility: Applicants must be Iowa residents and 4-H members who are enrolling in or currently enrolled in an Iowa post-secondary institution. Students must submit two letters of recommendation along with their materials.
Target applicant(s): High school students. College students. Adult students.
Amount: Varies.
Number of awards: Varies.
Deadline: February 1.
How to apply: Applications are available online.
Exclusive: Visit www.UltimateScholarshipBook.com and enter code IO153223 for updates on this award.

(1533) · Iowa Financial Know-How Challenge: Senior Scholarship

Iowa Student Loan Education Lending
6805 Vista Drive, West Des Moines, IA 50266

Phone: 855-811-9849
Email: scholarship@studentloan.org
https://www.iowastudentloan.org/scholarships/
Purpose: To reward Iowa students interested in financial literacy.
Eligibility: Applicants must be legal U.S. residents who reside in Iowa. Students must be graduating seniors at an Iowa high school and plan to attend college. Applicants must complete online financial literacy tutorials and assessments as well as write an essay.
Target applicant(s): High school students.
Amount: $2,000.
Number of awards: 25.
Deadline: March 11.
How to apply: Applications are available online.
Exclusive: Visit www.UltimateScholarshipBook.com and enter code IO153323 for updates on this award.

(1534) · Iowa Newspaper Association Scholarships

Iowa Newspaper Association
319 E 5th Street, Des Moines, IA 50309
Phone: 515-244-2145
Email: ina@inanews.com
http://www.inanews.com
Purpose: To support students preparing for careers in the newspaper industry.
Eligibility: Applicants must be Iowa residents who are high school seniors or current college students and must attend an in-state college or university. Students must plan to work in the newspaper industry in Iowa upon completion of their degrees.
Target applicant(s): High school students. College students. Adult students.
Amount: $500-$1,000.
Number of awards: Varies.
Deadline: February 12.
How to apply: Applications are available online. An application form, two letters of reference, personal statement and two writing samples are required.
Exclusive: Visit www.UltimateScholarshipBook.com and enter code IO153423 for updates on this award.

(1535) · Iowa Oratorical Contest

American Legion, Department of Iowa
720 Lyon Street, Des Moines, IA 50309
Phone: 800-365-8387
Email: programs@ialegion.org
https://www.ialegion.org/oratorical/
Purpose: To enhance high school students' experience with and understanding of the U.S. Constitution. The contest will help develop students' leadership skills and civic appreciation, as well as the ability to deliver thoughtful, insightful orations regarding U.S. citizenship and its inherent responsibilities.
Eligibility: Applicants must be high school students under the age of 20 who are U.S. citizens or legal residents and residents of the state. Students first give an oration within their state and winners compete at the national level. The oration must be related to the Constitution of the United States focusing on the duties and obligations citizens have to the government. It must be in English and be between eight and ten minutes. There is also an assigned topic which is posted on the website, and it should be between three and five minutes.
Target applicant(s): High school students.
Amount: Up to $18,000.
Number of awards: Varies.

Deadline: Varies.
How to apply: Applications are available online.
Exclusive: Visit www.UltimateScholarshipBook.com and enter code AM153523 for updates on this award.

(1536) · Iowa PGA Foundation Charlie Burkart Scholarship

Iowa PGA Foundation
3184 HWY 22 Riverside, Riverside, IA 52327
https://www.iowapgajuniorgolf.com/charlie-burkart/
Purpose: To assist Iowa student golf athletes to pursue post-secondary education.
Eligibility: Applicants must reside within the boundaries of the Iowa PGA section, including the cities of Monmouth, Macomb, Galesburg, Moline, Rock Island, Kewanee and Galena. Students must demonstrate an interest in golf, community involvement and financial need.
Target applicant(s): High school students. College students. Adult students.
Amount: $1,500.
Number of awards: 1.
Scholarship may be renewable.
Deadline: June 18.
How to apply: Applications are available online.
Exclusive: Visit www.UltimateScholarshipBook.com and enter code IO153623 for updates on this award.

(1537) · Iowa Physician Assistant Society Scholarship

Iowa Physician Assistant Society
6919 Vista Drive, West Des Moines, IA 50266
Phone: 515-282-8192
Email: info@iapasociety.org
https://www.iapasociety.org/index.php/students/scholarship-information
Purpose: To aid Iowa students who are enrolled in a physician assistant degree program.
Eligibility: Applicants must be enrolled in an approved Physician Assistant (PA) degree program at a postsecondary institution located in Iowa. They must have had an outstanding undergraduate academic record, strong leadership skills and a well-developed knowledge of the role of the professional physician assistant. Selection is based on academic merit, demonstrated leadership ability, commitment to the field of physician assisting, extracurricular activities and professional awareness.
Target applicant(s): College students. Adult students.
Amount: $1,000.
Number of awards: 3.
Deadline: September 5.
How to apply: Applications are available online. An application form, transcript and personal statement are required.
Exclusive: Visit www.UltimateScholarshipBook.com and enter code IO153723 for updates on this award.

(1538) · Iowa Pork Foundation Scholarship

Iowa Pork Producers Association
1636 NW 114th Street, P.O. Box 71009, Clive, IA 50325
Phone: 800-372-7675
Email: info@iowapork.org
http://www.iowapork.org
Purpose: To aid Iowa agriculture students who are interested in the pork industry.

Eligibility: Applicants must be Iowa residents who are enrolled at or who plan to enroll at a two-year or four-year postsecondary institution located in Iowa. They must be majoring in or have plans to major in an agriculture-related undergraduate program that focuses on swine production. They must maintain a GPA of 2.5 or higher. Selection is based on the overall strength of the application.
Target applicant(s): High school students. College students. Adult students.
Minimum GPA: 2.5
Amount: $1,000-$2,000.
Number of awards: 18.
Scholarship may be renewable.
Deadline: April 1.
How to apply: Applications are available online. An application form, two recommendation letters and a transcript are required.
Exclusive: Visit www.UltimateScholarshipBook.com and enter code IO153823 for updates on this award.

(1539) · Iowa Scholarship for the Arts
Iowa Arts Council
600 E. Locust, Des Moines, IA 50319-0290
Phone: 515-281-6412
https://iowaculture.gov/arts/grants
Purpose: To aid outstanding young artists.
Eligibility: Applicants must be Iowa residents and graduating high school seniors and show proven artistic ability in dance, literature, music, theatre, traditional arts or visual arts. Students must be accepted full-time to an accredited Iowa college or university and must major in one of the aforementioned areas.
Target applicant(s): High school students.
Amount: $1,500.
Number of awards: Varies.
Deadline: April 1.
How to apply: Applications are available online. An application form, two letters of recommendation and an essay are required.
Exclusive: Visit www.UltimateScholarshipBook.com and enter code IO153923 for updates on this award.

(1540) · Iowa Thespian Chapter Board Senior Scholarships
Iowa Thespian Chapter
Leslie LaCorte, Iowa Thespian Treasurer, Davenport North High School, 626 West 53rd Street, Davenport, IA 52806
Phone: 563-332-5151
Email: myattw@pleasval.k12.ia.us
http://www.iowathespians.org
Purpose: To aid promising young thespians.
Eligibility: Applicants must be Iowa high school seniors and have an overall GPA of 2.0 or higher with a GPA of 3.0 or higher in arts-related classes. Students must be members of the International Thespian Society in good standing. Applicants must plan to major or minor in theatre, film, radio and television, broadcasting, music or dance. Applicants must also perform an audition at the Iowa Thespian Festival in the performance, technical or theatre educator category.
Target applicant(s): High school students.
Minimum GPA: 2.0
Amount: $1,000.
Number of awards: Varies.
Deadline: October 15.

How to apply: Applications are available from the Iowa Thespian Society. An application form and resume are required.
Exclusive: Visit www.UltimateScholarshipBook.com and enter code IO154023 for updates on this award.

(1541) · Iowa Tuition Grants
Iowa College Student Aid Commission
475 SW Fifth Street, Suite D, Des Moines, IA 50309
Phone: 515-725-3400
Email: info@iowacollegeaid.gov
https://www.iowacollegeaid.gov/ScholarshipsAndGrants
Purpose: To help students attend Iowa's independent colleges and universities.
Eligibility: Applicants must be enrolled in or planning to enroll at least part-time in an eligible Iowa college or university and demonstrate financial need. Priority is given to the neediest applicants.
Target applicant(s): High school students. College students. Adult students.
Amount: Up to $6,800.
Number of awards: Varies.
Scholarship may be renewable.
Deadline: July 1.
How to apply: Complete the Free Application for Federal Student Aid (FAFSA).
Exclusive: Visit www.UltimateScholarshipBook.com and enter code IO154123 for updates on this award.

(1542) · Iowa Vocational-Technical Tuition Grants
Iowa College Student Aid Commission
475 SW Fifth Street, Suite D, Des Moines, IA 50309
Phone: 515-725-3400
Email: info@iowacollegeaid.gov
https://www.iowacollegeaid.gov/ScholarshipsAndGrants
Purpose: To aid those Iowa residents enrolled in vocational-technical programs at community colleges.
Eligibility: Applicants must be enrolled in or planning to enroll in a career education or option course for 3 credit hours consisting of at least 15 weeks duration at an Iowa area community college and be U.S. citizens or permanent residents. Applicants must prove financial need.
Target applicant(s): High school students. College students. Adult students.
Amount: Up to $1,000.
Number of awards: Varies.
Scholarship may be renewable.
Deadline: July 1.
How to apply: Complete the Free Application for Federal Student Aid (FAFSA).
Exclusive: Visit www.UltimateScholarshipBook.com and enter code IO154223 for updates on this award.

(1543) · Irving W. Cook, WA0CGS, Scholarship
American Radio Relay League Foundation
225 Main Street, Newington, CT 06111-1494
Phone: 860-594-0348
Email: foundation@arrl.org
http://www.arrl.org/scholarship-program
Purpose: To provide scholarship assistance to Kansas residents who are amateur radio operators.
Eligibility: Applicants must be residents of Kansas and holders of an active amateur radio license of any class. Preference is given to students

who are studying electronics, communications or a related subject at the baccalaureate level or higher.
Target applicant(s): College students. Graduate school students. Adult students.
Amount: $1,000.
Number of awards: 1.
Deadline: December 31.
How to apply: Applications are available online.
Exclusive: Visit www.UltimateScholarshipBook.com and enter code AM154323 for updates on this award.

(1544) · ISAA Scholarship Program

Iowa State Archery Association
ISAA Scholarship Program, Jan Kostka, Chair, 1425 Plymouth Road, Mason City, IA 50401
Email: jankostka@mac.com
http://www.isaaproam.com
Purpose: To aid students who have participated in the Iowa State Archery Association as they continue their education beyond high school.
Eligibility: Applicants must be a high school senior, have obtained a GED or be a full-time college student. The student must have been an active member of ISAA for at least two years. Selection is based on participation in ISAA activities, academic achievement, financial need, community involvement and the reference letters.
Target applicant(s): High school students. College students. Graduate school students. Adult students.
Amount: Up to $1,000.
Number of awards: Varies.
Deadline: February 8.
How to apply: Applications are available online.
Exclusive: Visit www.UltimateScholarshipBook.com and enter code IO154423 for updates on this award.

(1545) · ISPE/M.E. Amstutz Memorial Award

Illinois Society of Professional Engineers
100 East Washington Street, Springfield, IL 62701
Phone: 217-544-7424
Email: emily@frontlineco.com
https://ilengineeringinitiative.org/
Purpose: To aid Illinois undergraduate engineering students.
Eligibility: Applicants must be undergraduate juniors or seniors who are enrolled in an ABET-accredited engineering degree program at an Illinois college or university. They must have a B average or better in engineering coursework and must demonstrate financial need. Selection is based on academic merit, financial need, extracurricular activities and a personal essay.
Target applicant(s): College students. Adult students.
Minimum GPA: 3.0
Amount: $1,000.
Number of awards: 1.
Deadline: September 10.
How to apply: Applications are available online.
Exclusive: Visit www.UltimateScholarshipBook.com and enter code IL154523 for updates on this award.

(1546) · Ivomec Generations of Excellence Internship and Scholarship Program

Texas CattleWomen
Erin Worrell, 657 Blue Oak Trail, Harper, TX 78631

Phone: 512-413-1616
Email: worrellerin@gmail.com
https://txcattlewomen.org/tcw-chapters/
Purpose: To aid Texas students who are preparing for careers in the beef industry.
Eligibility: Applicants must be permanent residents of Texas and be graduate students or rising undergraduate juniors or seniors who are enrolled at a Texas college or university. They must be majoring in agriculture or a related subject, must have a background in beef cattle and have a GPA of 2.5 or higher. Selection is based on the overall strength of the application.
Target applicant(s): College students. Graduate school students. Adult students.
Minimum GPA: 2.5
Amount: $1,000.
Number of awards: 1.
Deadline: May 31.
How to apply: Applications are available online. An application form and supporting materials are required.
Exclusive: Visit www.UltimateScholarshipBook.com and enter code TE154623 for updates on this award.

(1547) · J.R. Popalisky Scholarship

American Water Works Association - Missouri Section
https://awwa-mo.org
Purpose: To aid Missouri students whose coursework is related to the water supply industry.
Eligibility: Applicants must be U.S. citizens who are enrolled at an accredited college or university located in Missouri. They must have completed coursework in subjects relating to the water supply industry (such as environmental engineering, civil engineering or environmental science). Students who are receiving funding from an employer are ineligible. Selection is based on coursework relevance, GPA, financial need, recommendations, personal essay and extracurricular activities.
Target applicant(s): College students. Adult students.
Amount: $1,000.
Number of awards: At least 1.
Deadline: March 25.
How to apply: Applications are available online. An application form, personal essay and a financial analysis form are required.
Exclusive: Visit www.UltimateScholarshipBook.com and enter code AM154723 for updates on this award.

(1548) · Jack E. Barger, Sr. Memorial Nursing Scholarship

Nursing Foundation of Pennsylvania
3605 Vartan Way, Suite 204, Harrisburg, PA 17110
Phone: 717-827-4369
Email: info@thenfp.org
http://www.thenfp.org/scholarships/
Purpose: To aid Pennsylvania nursing undergraduates who are serving in the military, are veterans, are military spouses, are veterans' spouses or who are the children of active duty military or veterans.
Eligibility: Candidates must be residents of Pennsylvania and must be enrolled in an undergraduate nursing program at an institution located in Pennsylvania. They must be active duty military, veterans, military spouses, veterans' spouses or the children of active duty military or veterans. Candidates are nominated for this award by the deans and department heads in the school of nursing at their institutions. Selection of award recipients will be determined by lottery.

Target applicant(s): High school students. College students. Adult students.
Amount: $1,000.
Number of awards: 6.
Deadline: March 30.
How to apply: Candidates are not required to submit an application for this award. Instead, the dean or department head of the candidate's school must submit a formal nomination to the scholarship committee.
Exclusive: Visit www.UltimateScholarshipBook.com and enter code NU154823 for updates on this award.

(1549) · Jack F. Tolbert Memorial Student Grant Program

Maryland Higher Education Commission
Office of Student Financial Assistance, 6 North Liberty Street, Baltimore, MD 21201
Phone: 800-974-1024
Email: osfamail@mhec.state.md.us
https://mhec.maryland.gov
Purpose: To assist students who are attending or planning to attend a private career school.
Eligibility: Students and their parents if they are dependents must be residents of Maryland. Applicants must also enroll at an approved private career school in the state for at least 18 hours per week.
Target applicant(s): High school students. College students. Adult students.
Amount: Up to $500.
Number of awards: Varies.
Scholarship may be renewable.
Deadline: Rolling.
How to apply: Students apply by completing the Free Application for Federal Student Aid (FAFSA) and turning it in to the financial aid office of the career school they will attend.
Exclusive: Visit www.UltimateScholarshipBook.com and enter code MA154923 for updates on this award.

(1550) · Jack Hughes Education Scholarship

California Nevada Racquetball Association
Terry Rogers, CNRA Scholarship Chairperson, 8317 Divernon Avenue, Las Vegas, NV 89149
Email: info@californianevadaracquetball.org
http://www.californiaracquetball.org
Purpose: To help graduating seniors and college undergraduates who are USA Racquetball (USAR) members expand racquetball.
Eligibility: Applicants must be high school seniors who will be graduating or college undergraduates. Students must reside in California or Nevada and demonstrate a desire to expand racquetball. Applicants must also be current USAR members.
Target applicant(s): High school students. College students. Adult students.
Amount: Varies.
Number of awards: Varies.
Deadline: August 15.
How to apply: Applications are available online.
Exclusive: Visit www.UltimateScholarshipBook.com and enter code CA155023 for updates on this award.

(1551) · James B. Morris Scholarship

James B. Morris Scholarship Fund
P.O. Box 12145, Des Moines, IA 50312
http://www.morrisscholarship.org
Purpose: To support Iowa minority students pursuing post-secondary education.
Eligibility: Applicants must be U.S. citizens of a minority ethnic status who are either Iowa high school graduates attending any U.S. college or university or non-Iowa residents who are attending an Iowa college or university. Students must have a minimum GPA of 2.5.
Target applicant(s): High school students. College students. Graduate school students. Adult students.
Minimum GPA: 2.5
Amount: Varies.
Number of awards: Varies.
Deadline: February 28.
How to apply: Applications are available online.
Exclusive: Visit www.UltimateScholarshipBook.com and enter code JA155123 for updates on this award.

(1552) · James F. Davis Memorial Scholarship

National Foliage Foundation
1533 Park Center Drive, Orlando, FL 32835
Phone: 800-375-3642
Email: info@nationalfoliagefoundation.org
https://www.nationalhorticulturefoundation.org/
Purpose: To aid students pursuing higher education in horticulture or a related discipline in Florida.
Eligibility: Applicants must be rising freshmen or undergraduates at an accredited postsecondary institution located in Florida. They must be full-time students who are enrolled in or who are planning to enroll in a degree program in horticulture or a related subject. They must have a GPA of 2.0 or higher. Selection is based on the overall strength of the application.
Target applicant(s): High school students. College students. Adult students.
Minimum GPA: 2.0
Amount: Varies.
Number of awards: Varies.
Scholarship may be renewable.
Deadline: January 15.
How to apply: Applications are available online. An application form, transcript, personal essay and two letters of recommendation are required.
Exclusive: Visit www.UltimateScholarshipBook.com and enter code NA155223 for updates on this award.

(1553) · James H. Dunn, Jr. Memorial Fellowship

Governor's Office of the State of Illinois
Dunn Fellowship Program, 207 State House, Springfield, IL 62706
Phone: 217-782-0244
Email: GOV.DunnFellowshipApp@illinois.gov
https://www2.illinois.gov/sites/gov/Pages/default.aspx
Purpose: To provide college graduates with an opportunity to experience daily operations in state government for one year.
Eligibility: Fellows must possess a bachelor's degree. Fellows will be assigned to various posts in the Governor's office or in an office under the Governor's jurisdiction.
Target applicant(s): College students. Adult students.
Amount: $31,332 plus benefits.

Number of awards: Varies.
Deadline: March 17.
How to apply: Applications are available online or by mail.
Exclusive: Visit www.UltimateScholarshipBook.com and enter code GO155323 for updates on this award.

(1554) · James J. Burns and C.A. Haynes Textile Scholarship

Rhode Island Foundation
One Union Station, Providence, RI 02903
Phone: 401-274-4564
Email: rbogert@rifoundation.org
https://rifoundation.org/grants-scholarships/browse-scholarships
Purpose: To support students who are planning to work in the textile industry.
Eligibility: Students must be currently enrolled in a textile program. They must demonstrate financial need or academic excellence. Preference will be given to students whose parents are members of the National Association of Textile Supervisors.
Target applicant(s): High school students. College students. Graduate school students. Adult students.
Amount: $1,000.
Number of awards: Varies.
Deadline: May.
How to apply: Applications are available online.
Exclusive: Visit www.UltimateScholarshipBook.com and enter code RH155423 for updates on this award.

(1555) · James V. Day Scholarship

American Legion, Department of Maine
5 Verti Drive, Winslow, ME 04901-0727
Phone: 207-873-3229
Email: legionme@mainelegion.org
http://www.mainelegion.org/pages/programs/scholarships.php
Purpose: To provide financial assistance to the children or grandchildren of American Legion, Department of Maine members.
Eligibility: Applicants must be U.S. citizens, residents of Maine and graduating high school seniors. They must be enrolled in an accredited college or vocational technical school and provide evidence of financial need. Applicants must demonstrate good character and a belief in the American way of life.
Target applicant(s): High school students.
Amount: $500.
Number of awards: Up to 2.
Deadline: May 1.
How to apply: Applications are available online.
Exclusive: Visit www.UltimateScholarshipBook.com and enter code AM155523 for updates on this award.

(1556) · Jean Lee/Jeff Marvin Collegiate Scholarships

Indiana Association for Health, Physical Education, Recreation and Dance
2007 Wilno Drive, Marion, IN 46952
Phone: 765-664-8319
Email: hatch@cometck.com
http://www.indianashape.org/scholarships.html
Purpose: To aid students pursuing degrees in physical education-related fields.

Eligibility: Applicants must be attending an Indiana college or university and be upcoming juniors or seniors who are majoring in health education, physical education, recreation, dance education or allied areas.
Target applicant(s): College students. Adult students.
Amount: $1,000.
Number of awards: 6.
Deadline: January 15.
How to apply: Applications are available online. An application form, goals statement, statement of need, list of activities during college attendance, philosophy statement and two letters of recommendation are required.
Exclusive: Visit www.UltimateScholarshipBook.com and enter code IN155623 for updates on this award.

(1557) · Jimmie L. Dean Scholarship

Jimmie L. Dean Scholarship Foundation Inc.
20 East 5th Street, Suite 1200G, Tulsa, OK 74103
Email: info@jimmiedeanfoundation.org
https://jimmiedeanfoundation.org
Purpose: To encourage Oklahoma students to pursue education.
Eligibility: Applicants must be legal residents and have lived in Oklahoma for the past six years. Students must be graduating from an Oklahoma high school or have completed graduation requirements through homeschooling. Applicants must be attending an Oklahoma college, university or technical school as a full-time, first-time student.
Target applicant(s): High school students.
Amount: Up to $10,000.
Number of awards: Varies.
Scholarship may be renewable.
Deadline: April 15.
How to apply: Applications are available online.
Exclusive: Visit www.UltimateScholarshipBook.com and enter code JI155723 for updates on this award.

(1558) · Jimmy Rane Foundation Scholarships

Jimmy Rane Foundation
P.O. Box 40, Abbeville, AL 36310
Phone: 800-310-4053
Email: contactus@applyists.com
http://www.jimmyranefoundation.org
Purpose: To support students who are planning to pursue undergraduate degrees.
Eligibility: Applicants must be high school seniors or college freshmen or sophomores who are residents of Alabama, Arkansas, Delaware, Florida, Georgia, Iowa, Kansas, Kentucky, Louisiana, Maryland, Mississippi, Missouri, Nebraska, New Jersey, New York, North Carolina, Ohio, Oklahoma, Pennsylvania, South Carolina, Tennessee, Texas, Virginia, West Virginia or the District of Columbia. Students must have a minimum GPA of 3.0 for high school seniors or 2.75 for college students. Selection is based on academic excellence, community involvement, leadership skills, awards and honors and financial need.
Target applicant(s): High school students. College students.
Minimum GPA: 3.0 for high school seniors, 2.75 for college students
Amount: $500-$5,000.
Number of awards: Varies.
Deadline: February 7.
How to apply: Applications are available online.
Exclusive: Visit www.UltimateScholarshipBook.com and enter code JI155823 for updates on this award.

(1559) · Joe Foss, An American Hero Scholarship

Sioux Falls Area Community Foundation
The Depot at Cherapa Place, 200 N. Cherapa Place, Sioux Falls, SD 57103-2205
Phone: 605-336-7055
Email: pgale@sfacf.org
https://www.sfacf.org/grants-scholarships/scholarships
Purpose: To support high school seniors who have strong values, courage and patriotism.
Eligibility: Applicants must have at least a 3.5 GPA and an ACT score of 21 or above. Students must reside in South Dakota.
Target applicant(s): High school students.
Minimum GPA: 3.5
Amount: $1,000.
Number of awards: 6.
Deadline: March 15.
How to apply: Applications are available online.
Exclusive: Visit www.UltimateScholarshipBook.com and enter code SI155923 for updates on this award.

(1560) · Johanna Drew Cluney Fund

Hawaii Community Foundation - Scholarships
827 Fort Street Mall, Honolulu, HI 96813
Phone: 888-731-3863
Email: scholarships@hcf-hawaii.org
https://www.hawaiicommunityfoundation.org/
Purpose: To aid students pursuing vocational education.
Eligibility: Applicants must be Hawaii residents who are enrolled full-time in vocational degree programs at a University of Hawaii school and who have a minimum 2.0 GPA. They must be first-time degree seekers who plan to enter the workforce upon graduation.
Target applicant(s): College students. Adult students.
Minimum GPA: 2.0
Amount: Varies.
Number of awards: Varies.
Deadline: January 31.
How to apply: Applications are available online. An application form, personal statement and letter of recommendation are required.
Exclusive: Visit www.UltimateScholarshipBook.com and enter code HA156023 for updates on this award.

(1561) · John and Abigail Adams Scholarship

Massachusetts Department of Higher Education
Office of Student Financial Assistance, 454 Broadway, Suite 200, Revere, MA 02151
Phone: 617-727-9420
Email: osfa@osfa.mass.edu
https://www.mass.edu/osfa/programs/programs.asp
Purpose: To attract high-performing high school seniors to Massachusetts public institutions of higher education and to reward previous achievements.
Eligibility: Applicants must be permanent residents of Massachusetts, score in the Advanced category in one category of the 10th grade MCAS test and in the Proficient or Advanced category in the other and have a combined MCAS score in the top 25 percent of their school district. Scholarship winners must maintain a 3.0 or higher GPA for continued eligibility.
Target applicant(s): High school students.
Minimum GPA: 3.0
Amount: Up to full tuition.

Number of awards: Varies.
Scholarship may be renewable.
Deadline: Varies.
How to apply: No application is necessary, but students must complete the Free Application for Federal Student Aid.
Exclusive: Visit www.UltimateScholarshipBook.com and enter code MA156123 for updates on this award.

(1562) · John and Anne Clifton Scholarship

Hawaii Community Foundation - Scholarships
827 Fort Street Mall, Honolulu, HI 96813
Phone: 888-731-3863
Email: scholarships@hcf-hawaii.org
https://www.hawaiicommunityfoundation.org/
Purpose: To assist students pursuing vocational degrees.
Eligibility: Applicants must be enrolled in a vocational program at a University of Hawaii school and have at least a 2.0 GPA.
Target applicant(s): High school students. College students. Adult students.
Minimum GPA: 2.0
Amount: Varies.
Number of awards: Varies.
Deadline: January 31.
How to apply: Applications are available online.
Exclusive: Visit www.UltimateScholarshipBook.com and enter code HA156223 for updates on this award.

(1563) · John D. and Virginia Riesch Scholarship

Wisconsin Medical Society Foundation
330 East Lakeside Street, Madison, WI 53715
Phone: 866-442-3800
Email: elizabeth.ringle@wismed.org
http://www.wisconsinmedicalsociety.org
Purpose: To aid students who are training to become physicians or nurses.
Eligibility: Applicants must be U.S. citizens. They must be full-time students enrolled in a medical school or nursing degree program at an accredited Wisconsin college or university. Rising undergraduate freshmen, undergraduate medical students and nursing students enrolled in a less than two-year program are ineligible. Preference will be given to Wisconsin residents and to applicants who are planning to practice in Wisconsin. Selection is based on academic merit, personal qualities, recommendations and financial need.
Target applicant(s): College students. Graduate school students. Adult students.
Amount: Varies.
Number of awards: 2.
Deadline: February 1.
How to apply: Applications are available online. An application form, personal statement, transcript and two recommendation letters are required.
Exclusive: Visit www.UltimateScholarshipBook.com and enter code WI156323 for updates on this award.

(1564) · John Dawe Dental Education Fund

Hawaii Community Foundation - Scholarships
827 Fort Street Mall, Honolulu, HI 96813
Phone: 888-731-3863
Email: scholarships@hcf-hawaii.org
https://www.hawaiicommunityfoundation.org/

Purpose: To provide financial assistance to Hawaii students pursuing careers in dental professions.

Eligibility: Applicants must be enrolled full-time in a school of dentistry, dental hygiene or dental assisting. They must have a GPA of 2.7 or higher. Two letters of recommendation and a letter from the applicant's school confirming enrollment in the dentistry or dental hygiene program are required.

Target applicant(s): High school students. College students. Adult students.

Minimum GPA: 2.7

Amount: Varies.

Number of awards: Varies.

Deadline: January 31.

How to apply: To apply, register online, complete the online application and select the scholarships to which you wish to apply. In addition, mail the supporting materials: printed confirmation page from the online application, personal statement, copy of Student Aid Report (SAR) available at www.fafsa.ed.gov and official transcript.

Exclusive: Visit www.UltimateScholarshipBook.com and enter code HA156423 for updates on this award.

(1565) · John R. Lillard VAOC Scholarship

Virginia Department of Aviation
VAOC Scholarship, Attn: Betty Wilson, 5702 Gulfstream Road, Richmond, VA 23250-2422
Phone: 804-236-3624
Email: director@doav.virginia.gov
https://doav.virginia.gov/

Purpose: To aid Virginia high school seniors who are planning for careers in aviation.

Eligibility: Applicants must be Virginia high school seniors who have an unweighted GPA of 3.5 or higher. They must be accepted into or enrolled in an aviation-related program at an accredited postsecondary institution and must have plans to pursue a career in aviation. Selection is based on academic merit, personal essay, leadership skills and financial need.

Target applicant(s): High school students.

Minimum GPA: 3.5

Amount: $3,000.

Number of awards: Varies.

Deadline: March 5.

How to apply: Applications are available online. An application form, personal essay, official transcript, verification of college acceptance or enrollment, list of extracurricular activities and up to three recommendation letters are required.

Exclusive: Visit www.UltimateScholarshipBook.com and enter code VI156523 for updates on this award.

(1566) · John Schwartz Scholarship

American Institute of Wine and Food - Pacific Northwest Chapter
213-37 39th Avenue, Box 216, Bayside, NY 11361
Phone: 800-274-2493
Email: bsteinmetz100@hotmail.com
http://www.aiwf.org

Purpose: To aid students pursuing culinary degrees.

Eligibility: Applicants must have been Washington State residents for at least two years, be enrolled in a Washington State accredited culinary or winemaking arts program and have a GPA of 3.0 or higher.

Target applicant(s): College students. Adult students.

Minimum GPA: 3.0

Amount: $2,000.

Number of awards: 4.

Deadline: Varies.

How to apply: Applications are available from your school's culinary or winemaking arts department. An application form, resume and references are required.

Exclusive: Visit www.UltimateScholarshipBook.com and enter code AM156623 for updates on this award.

(1567) · John W. Rogers Memorial Scholarship

Missouri Bankers Foundation
P.O. Box 57, 207 East Capitol Avenue, Jefferson City, MO 65101
Phone: 573-636-8151
Email: rpreston@mobankers.com
https://www.mobankers.com/

Purpose: To aid high school seniors who are planning to pursue higher education in agriculture or a banking-related subject.

Eligibility: Applicants must be graduating high school seniors who have plans to major in agriculture or a banking-related subject at the postsecondary level. Preference will be given to applicants who are planning to attend the University of Missouri-Columbia. Selection is based on the overall strength of the application.

Target applicant(s): High school students.

Amount: $1,000.

Number of awards: 2.

Deadline: March 5.

How to apply: Applications are available online. An application form, official transcript, ACT scores, a list of extracurricular activities and two recommendation letters are required.

Exclusive: Visit www.UltimateScholarshipBook.com and enter code MI156723 for updates on this award.

(1568) · Jose Marti Scholarship Challenge Grant

Florida Department of Education
Office of Student Financial Assistance, State Scholarship and Grant Programs, 325 West Gaines Street, Suite 1314, Tallahassee, FL 32399-0400
Phone: 888-827-2004
Email: osfa@fldoe.org
http://www.floridastudentfinancialaid.org

Purpose: To help Florida students in need who are of Hispanic origin.

Eligibility: Applicants must have been born in or have a natural parent who was born in either Mexico or Spain, or a Hispanic country of the Caribbean, Central or South America, regardless of race. Students must plan to attend Florida public or eligible private institutions as undergraduate or graduate students, but graduating high school seniors get preference.

Target applicant(s): High school students. College students. Graduate school students. Adult students.

Minimum GPA: 3.0

Amount: $2,000.

Number of awards: Varies.

Scholarship may be renewable.

Deadline: April 1.

How to apply: Applicants must submit the initial student Florida Financial Aid Application by April 1 and the Free Application for Federal Student Aid (FAFSA) by May 15.

Exclusive: Visit www.UltimateScholarshipBook.com and enter code FL156823 for updates on this award.

(1569) · Joseph Shinoda Memorial Scholarship

Joseph Shinoda Memorial Scholarship Foundation Inc.
c/o Barbara A. McCaleb, Executive Secretary, 234 Via La Paz, San Luis Obispo, CA 93401
http://www.shinodascholarship.org
Purpose: To aid students who are preparing for careers in commercial floriculture.
Eligibility: Applicants must be enrolled at an accredited four-year institution in the U.S. or at a community college located in California and be rising undergraduate sophomores, juniors or seniors. They must be majoring in a floriculture-related subject and be planning to pursue a career in domestic floriculture in the U.S. after graduation. Selection is based on academic merit, character, work experience and financial need.
Target applicant(s): College students. Adult students.
Amount: $1,000-$5,000.
Number of awards: Varies.
Deadline: March 30.
How to apply: Applications are available online. An application form, an official transcript and two letters of recommendation are required.
Exclusive: Visit www.UltimateScholarshipBook.com and enter code JO156923 for updates on this award.

(1570) · Judge William F. Cooper Scholarship

Center for Scholarship Administration
4320 Wade Hampton Boulevard, Suite G, Taylors, SC 29687-0031
Phone: 864-268-3363
Email: allisonleewagoner@bellsouth.net
https://www.csascholars.org/index.php
Purpose: To provide financial assistance to female students from Georgia who plan to attend college.
Eligibility: Applicants must be high school seniors who have financial need. Students must have an acceptable GPA and plan to study in any field except law, theology or medicine. Nursing is acceptable.
Target applicant(s): High school students.
Amount: Varies.
Number of awards: Varies.
Scholarship may be renewable.
Deadline: March 2.
How to apply: Applications are available online.
Exclusive: Visit www.UltimateScholarshipBook.com and enter code CE157023 for updates on this award.

(1571) · KAB Broadcast Scholarship Program

Kansas Association of Broadcasters
Scholarship Committee, 214 SW 6th Avenue, Suite 300, Topeka, KS 66603
Phone: 785-235-1307
Email: kent@kab.net
https://kab.net/resources/scholarships/
Purpose: To support future broadcasters.
Eligibility: Applicants must be Kansas residents and be attending a Kansas college or university the fall semester after application. Those attending four-year institutions must be entering the junior or senior year, and those attending two-year institutions must be entering their sophomore year. Students must enroll in a broadcast or related curriculum for at least 12 hours. A GPA of 2.5 or greater is required.
Target applicant(s): College students. Adult students.
Minimum GPA: 2.5
Amount: Up to $16,000.
Number of awards: Varies.

Deadline: May 1.
How to apply: Applications are available online. An application form, essay and up to three letters of recommendation are required.
Exclusive: Visit www.UltimateScholarshipBook.com and enter code KA157123 for updates on this award.

(1572) · Kaiser Permanente Health Care Career Scholarship

Kaiser Permanente
Phone: 503-813-3992
Email: kpnw-scholarsihps@kp.org
http://www.kp.org/communitybenefit/scholarship/nw
Purpose: To empower students to enter the healthcare profession.
Eligibility: Applicants must be from Oregon or southwest Washington and be graduating high school seniors from approved schools in the Kaiser Permanente Northwest service area, which spans from north of Longview, Washington to Eugene, Oregon. Applicants must have a 2.5 GPA and plan to enroll full-time at a college or university for the upcoming fall semester.
Target applicant(s): High school students.
Minimum GPA: 2.5
Amount: $5,000-$10,000.
Number of awards: 139.
Deadline: December.
How to apply: Applications are available online.
Exclusive: Visit www.UltimateScholarshipBook.com and enter code KA157223 for updates on this award.

(1573) · Kansas Agricultural Aviation Association Scholarship

Kansas Agricultural Aviation Association
P.O. Box 585, Colwich, KS 67030
Phone: 316-796-1180
Email: grossflying@hotmail.com
http://www.ksagaviation.org
Purpose: To aid Kansas students who are pursuing higher education in Kansas.
Eligibility: Applicants must be Kansas residents and high school graduates who are planning to enroll at a Kansas postsecondary institution. They must be recommended for the award by a member of the Kansas Agricultural Aviation Association (KAAA) and must demonstrate financial need. Preference will be given to students who are majoring in or planning to major in agriculture, agricultural business, aviation or engineering. Selection is based on academic merit and financial need.
Target applicant(s): High school students.
Amount: $2,500.
Number of awards: 1.
Deadline: March 15.
How to apply: Applications are available online. An application form, transcript, financial need statement and two recommendation letters are required.
Exclusive: Visit www.UltimateScholarshipBook.com and enter code KA157323 for updates on this award.

(1574) · Kansas Career Technical Workforce Grant

Kansas Board of Regents
Curtis State Office Building, Suite 520, 1000 SW Jackson Street, Topeka, KS 66612

Phone: 785-430-4255
Email: dlindeman@ksbor.org
http://www.kansasregents.org/students/student_financial_aid
Purpose: To assist Kansas students to attend vocational colleges.
Eligibility: Applicants must be enrolled in approved vocational programs and take the vocational exam. Selection is based on exam scores. Students must register for the vocational exam by the scholarship deadline.
Target applicant(s): High school students. College students. Adult students.
Amount: Up to $1,000.
Number of awards: Varies.
Scholarship may be renewable.
Deadline: May 1.
How to apply: Applications are available online.
Exclusive: Visit www.UltimateScholarshipBook.com and enter code KA157423 for updates on this award.

(1575) · Kansas Comprehensive Grants

Kansas Board of Regents
Curtis State Office Building, Suite 520, 1000 SW Jackson Street, Topeka, KS 66612
Phone: 785-430-4255
Email: dlindeman@ksbor.org
http://www.kansasregents.org/students/student_financial_aid
Purpose: To help needy Kansas students attend Kansas colleges and universities.
Eligibility: Applicants must be enrolled full-time at an eligible Kansas institution. Selection is based on financial need.
Target applicant(s): College students. Adult students.
Amount: $100-$3,500.
Number of awards: Varies.
Deadline: April 1.
How to apply: Complete the Free Application for Federal Student Aid (FAFSA).
Exclusive: Visit www.UltimateScholarshipBook.com and enter code KA157523 for updates on this award.

(1576) · Kansas Ethnic Minority Scholarship

Kansas Board of Regents
Curtis State Office Building, Suite 520, 1000 SW Jackson Street, Topeka, KS 66612
Phone: 785-430-4255
Email: dlindeman@ksbor.org
http://www.kansasregents.org/students/student_financial_aid
Purpose: To aid outstanding Kansas minority students with financial need.
Eligibility: Applicants must be African American, Native Indian or Alaskan Native, Asian or Pacific Islander or Hispanic. Priority is given to graduating high school seniors. Applicants must have one of the following: a minimum ACT score of 21 or SAT score of 990, a minimum 3.0 GPA, a top 33 percent ranking in their high school class, completion of Kansas Scholars Curriculum, selection by National Merit Corporation or selection by College Board as a Hispanic Scholar.
Target applicant(s): High school students.
Minimum GPA: 3.0
Amount: Up to $1,850.
Number of awards: Varies.
Scholarship may be renewable.
Deadline: May 1.
How to apply: Applications are available online.

Exclusive: Visit www.UltimateScholarshipBook.com and enter code KA157623 for updates on this award.

(1577) · Kansas Oratorical Contest

American Legion, Department of Kansas
1314 SW Topeka Boulevard, Topeka, KS 66612
Phone: 785-232-9315
https://ksamlegion.org/
Purpose: To enhance high school students' experience with and understanding of the U.S. Constitution. The contest will help develop students' leadership skills and civic appreciation, as well as the ability to deliver thoughtful, insightful orations regarding U.S. citizenship and its inherent responsibilities.
Eligibility: Applicants must be high school students under the age of 20 who are U.S. citizens or legal residents and residents of the state. Students first give an oration within their state and winners compete at the national level. The oration must be related to the Constitution of the United States focusing on the duties and obligations citizens have to the government. It must be in English and be between eight and ten minutes. There is also an assigned topic which is posted on the website, and it should be between three and five minutes.
Target applicant(s): High school students.
Amount: $150-$750.
Number of awards: Varies.
Deadline: February 1.
How to apply: Applications are available from schools and local American Legion Posts.
Exclusive: Visit www.UltimateScholarshipBook.com and enter code AM157723 for updates on this award.

(1578) · Kansas State Scholarship

Kansas Board of Regents
Curtis State Office Building, Suite 520, 1000 SW Jackson Street, Topeka, KS 66612
Phone: 785-430-4255
Email: dlindeman@ksbor.org
http://www.kansasregents.org/students/student_financial_aid
Purpose: To aid needy Kansas students designated as state scholars.
Eligibility: Applicants must have taken the ACT, completed the Regents Scholars Curriculum and be graduating seniors. Applicants are ranked by an index combining ACT score and GPA. The top students are chosen.
Target applicant(s): High school students.
Amount: Varies.
Number of awards: Varies.
Scholarship may be renewable.
Deadline: July 1.
How to apply: Complete the Free Application for Federal Student Aid (FAFSA).
Exclusive: Visit www.UltimateScholarshipBook.com and enter code KA157823 for updates on this award.

(1579) · Karen Ann Shopis-Fox Memorial Scholarship

American Society of Landscape Architects
370 James Street, 4th Floor, New Haven, CT 06513
Phone: 800-878-1474
Email: executivedirector@ctasla.org
http://www.ctasla.org
Purpose: To support students who are studying landscape architecture or environmental education.

Eligibility: Applicants must be Connecticut residents and be enrolled in an accredited post-secondary landscape architecture or environmental education program. Both undergraduate and graduate students may apply.

Target applicant(s): College students. Graduate school students. Adult students.

Amount: $1,500-$2,500.

Number of awards: Varies.

Deadline: April 16.

How to apply: Applications are available online. An application form, transcript, personal statement and letter of recommendation are required.

Exclusive: Visit www.UltimateScholarshipBook.com and enter code AM157923 for updates on this award.

(1580) · Kathryn D. Sullivan Earth and Marine Science Fellowship

South Carolina Space Grant Consortium
Department of Geology and Environmental Sciences, College of Charleston, 66 George Street, Charleston, SC 29424
Phone: 843-953-5463
Email: scozzarot@cofc.edu
https://scspacegrant.cofc.edu/scholarshipsandfellowships
Purpose: To aid graduate students who are studying the natural sciences, technology or engineering.

Eligibility: Applicants must be U.S. citizens and be either full-time graduate students enrolled in an accredited consortium member institution or a successful applicant for full time admission to a Masters or Doctorate program in an accredited consortium member institution. Selection is based on recommendation letters, academic merit, faculty sponsorship and stated academic goals and interests in science, technology and engineering.

Target applicant(s): Graduate school students. Adult students.

Amount: $14,000.

Number of awards: 1.

Deadline: January 29.

How to apply: Applications are available online. An application form, personal essay, two recommendation letters, a transcript and a resume are required.

Exclusive: Visit www.UltimateScholarshipBook.com and enter code SO158023 for updates on this award.

(1581) · Kentucky Tuition Grant

Kentucky Higher Education Assistance Authority
P.O. Box 798, Frankfort, KY 40602
Phone: 800-928-8926
Email: blane@kheaa.com
http://www.kheaa.com
Purpose: To provide grants to Kentucky residents to attend the Commonwealth's independent colleges.

Eligibility: Applicants must be full-time students enrolled at eligible private institutions. Students must not be enrolled in divinity, theology or religious education degree programs. This is a need-based program.

Target applicant(s): High school students. College students. Adult students.

Amount: Up to $2,920.

Number of awards: Varies.

Deadline: Varies.

How to apply: Complete the Free Application for Federal Student Aid (FAFSA).

Exclusive: Visit www.UltimateScholarshipBook.com and enter code KE158123 for updates on this award.

(1582) · Kentucky Veterans Tuition Waiver Program

Kentucky Department of Veterans Affairs
Attn.: Tuition Waiver Coordinator, 321 West Main Street, Suite 390, Louisville, KY 40202
Phone: 502-595-4447
Email: barbaraa.hale@ky.gov
https://veterans.ky.gov/Benefits/Pages/education.aspx
Purpose: To assist the families of Kentucky veterans in obtaining higher education.

Eligibility: Applicants must be Kentucky residents and be children, stepchildren, adopted children, spouses or unremarried widows/widowers of Kentucky veterans and must be age 26 or younger. The veteran must have died in active duty or as a result of a service-connected disability, have a service-connected 100 percent disability, have served during wartime and be totally disabled or have died for any reason.

Target applicant(s): High school students. College students. Adult students.

Amount: Full tuition waiver.

Number of awards: Varies.

Scholarship may be renewable.

Deadline: Varies.

How to apply: Applications are available online.

Exclusive: Visit www.UltimateScholarshipBook.com and enter code KE158223 for updates on this award.

(1583) · Kibbie Grant (Iowa Skilled Workforce Shortage Tuition Grant)

Iowa College Student Aid Commission
475 SW Fifth Street, Suite D, Des Moines, IA 50309
Phone: 515-725-3400
Email: info@iowacollegeaid.gov
https://www.iowacollegeaid.gov/ScholarshipsAndGrants
Purpose: To support Iowa students enrolled in community college.

Eligibility: Applicants must be Iowa residents enrolled in an Iowa community college. Students must be enrolled in at least three credit hours in a qualified program of study and demonstrate financial need.

Target applicant(s): High school students. College students. Adult students.

Amount: Varies.

Number of awards: Varies.

Deadline: July 1.

How to apply: Applications are available online.

Exclusive: Visit www.UltimateScholarshipBook.com and enter code IO158323 for updates on this award.

(1584) · Kilbourn-Sawyer Memorial Scholarship

Vermont Student Assistance Corporation
Scholarships, P.O. Box 2000, Winooski, VT 05404
Phone: 888-253-4819
http://www.vsac.org/pay/student-aid-options/scholarships/vsac-assisted-scholarships
Purpose: To aid Vermont students who are planning to pursue higher education in a construction-related field.

Eligibility: Applicants must be Vermont residents, U.S. citizens or eligible non-citizens and graduating high school seniors. They must demonstrate academic achievement and financial need and plan to pursue higher education in construction or engineering at an institution approved for federal Title IV funding. Selection is based on personal essays, academic merit, recommendation letter and financial need.

Target applicant(s): High school students.
Amount: $2,500.
Number of awards: 1.
Deadline: February 11.
How to apply: Applications are available online. An application form, official transcript, academic certification form, two personal essays and one recommendation letter are required.
Exclusive: Visit www.UltimateScholarshipBook.com and enter code VE158423 for updates on this award.

(1585) · Kittie M. Fairey Educational Fund Scholarships

Center for Scholarship Administration Inc.
Kittie M. Fairey Educational Fund Scholarship Program, 4320 Wade Hampton Boulevard, Suite G, Taylors, SC 29687-0031
Phone: 864-268-3363
Email: allisonleewagoner@bellsouth.net
https://www.csascholars.org/index.php
Purpose: To help South Carolina high school seniors who want to attend colleges or universities in the state.
Eligibility: Applicants must be South Carolina high school seniors with a combined SAT score of 1800 or composite ACT score of 26 who plan to be full-time students at an accredited college or university in South Carolina. Selection is based on academic merit and financial need, and the applicant's parents' adjusted gross income must not exceed $40,000. A transcript, recommendation letter, essay and parents' tax documents are required.
Target applicant(s): High school students.
Minimum GPA: 3.0
Amount: Varies.
Number of awards: Varies.
Scholarship may be renewable.
Deadline: December.
How to apply: Applications are available online.
Exclusive: Visit www.UltimateScholarshipBook.com and enter code CE158523 for updates on this award.

(1586) · Kohl Excellence Scholarships

Herb Kohl Educational Foundation Inc.
Kim Marggraf, P.O. Box 877, Sheboygan, WI 53082-0877
Phone: 920-457-1727
Email: marggraf@excel.net
http://www.kohleducation.org
Purpose: To assist Wisconsin students in obtaining higher education.
Eligibility: Applicants must be Wisconsin residents who are graduating high school in the year of application. They must be in good standing with their schools and demonstrate the potential for success in postsecondary education. The submission deadline is usually in early November.
Target applicant(s): High school students.
Amount: $10,000.
Number of awards: 100.
Deadline: November.
How to apply: Applications are available online starting in October of each year and from Wisconsin high schools in mid-September. Three letters of recommendation are required.
Exclusive: Visit www.UltimateScholarshipBook.com and enter code HE158623 for updates on this award.

(1587) · Kokosing Construction Co. Scholarship

Associated General Contractors of Ohio
1755 Northwest Boulevard, Columbus, OH 43212
Phone: 614-486-6446
Email: parker@agcohio.com
https://agcohio.com/workforce-development/agc-scholarships/
Purpose: To support undergraduate students who are residents of Ohio and interested in pursuing careers in construction-related fields.
Eligibility: Applicants must be a U.S. citizens and undergraduate students in at least the second year of a two-year, four-year or five-year degree seeking program. The minimum GPA requirement is 2.5. Selection is based on the overall strength of the application.
Target applicant(s): College students. Adult students.
Minimum GPA: 2.5
Amount: $1,000.
Number of awards: 1.
Deadline: February.
How to apply: Applications are available online. An application form, official college transcripts and essay are required and must be mailed.
Exclusive: Visit www.UltimateScholarshipBook.com and enter code AS158723 for updates on this award.

(1588) · Lambeth Family Scholarship

Seattle Foundation
1200 Fifth Avenue, Suite 1300, Seattle, WA 98101-3151
Phone: 206-515-2119
Email: scholarships@seattlefoundation.org
http://www.seattlefoundation.org
Purpose: To aid students who are pursuing higher education in computer science, the natural sciences, business, mathematics or engineering.
Eligibility: Applicants must be enrolled in a degree-granting program in business, computer science, engineering, mathematics or the natural sciences. Selection is based on the overall strength of the application.
Target applicant(s): High school students. College students. Adult students.
Amount: $3,000.
Number of awards: 8.
Deadline: March 1.
How to apply: Applications are available online. An application form and supporting documents are required.
Exclusive: Visit www.UltimateScholarshipBook.com and enter code SE158823 for updates on this award.

(1589) · Laura N. Dowsett Fund

Hawaii Community Foundation - Scholarships
827 Fort Street Mall, Honolulu, HI 96813
Phone: 888-731-3863
Email: scholarships@hcf-hawaii.org
https://www.hawaiicommunityfoundation.org/
Purpose: To support Hawaii students who are majoring in occupational therapy.
Eligibility: Applicants must be college juniors, college seniors or graduate students. Minimum 2.7 GPA required.
Target applicant(s): College students. Graduate school students. Adult students.
Minimum GPA: 2.7
Amount: Varies.
Number of awards: Varies.
Deadline: January 31.

How to apply: To apply, register online, complete the online application and select the scholarships to which you wish to apply. In addition, mail the supporting materials: printed confirmation page from the online application, personal statement, copy of Student Aid Report (SAR) available at www.fafsa.ed.gov and official transcript.
Exclusive: Visit www.UltimateScholarshipBook.com and enter code HA158923 for updates on this award.

(1590) · Leaders Advancing & Helping Communities Scholarship

Leaders Advancing & Helping Communities
5275 Kenilworth Street, Dearborn, MI 48126-3197
Phone: 888-315-5242
Email: assistant@lahc.org
https://lahc.org/scholarship-program/
Purpose: To encourage all high school seniors to get a higher education.
Eligibility: Applicants must be U.S. citizens, Michigan residents, be high school seniors and have a GPA of 3.5 or higher. Students do not need to be Lebanese Americans to apply. Applicants must demonstrate financial need.
Target applicant(s): High school students.
Minimum GPA: 3.5
Amount: Varies.
Number of awards: Varies.
Deadline: September.
How to apply: Applications are available online.
Exclusive: Visit www.UltimateScholarshipBook.com and enter code LE159023 for updates on this award.

(1591) · Leadership for Diversity Scholarship

California School Library Association
6444 E. Spring Street #247, Long Beach, CA 90815-1553
Phone: 888-655-8480
Email: info@csla.net
http://csla.net/awards/
Purpose: To encourage diversity in the library media teacher profession.
Eligibility: Applicants must be members of a traditionally underrepresented group attending or planning to attend an accredited library media teacher credential program and plan to work in California for three years after completing the program. Applicants must provide a 250-word statement about their qualifications, career goals, financial situation and commitment to supporting multicultural students and two letters of reference.
Target applicant(s): High school students. College students. Graduate school students. Adult students.
Amount: $1,500.
Number of awards: 1.
Deadline: October 1.
How to apply: Applications are available online.
Exclusive: Visit www.UltimateScholarshipBook.com and enter code CA159123 for updates on this award.

(1592) · LEAF Scholarships

California Landscape Contractors Association
1491 River Park Drive, Suite 100, Sacramento, CA 95815
Phone: 916-830-2780
Email: leaf@clca.org
http://www.clca.org
Purpose: To support ornamental horticulture students.

Eligibility: Applicants must attend an accredited California community college or state university and take a minimum of six credits.
Target applicant(s): College students. Adult students.
Amount: Varies.
Number of awards: Varies.
Deadline: April 15.
How to apply: Applications are available online. An application form, transcript and three letters of reference are required.
Exclusive: Visit www.UltimateScholarshipBook.com and enter code CA159223 for updates on this award.

(1593) · Legislative for Future Excellence (LIFE) Scholarship Program

South Carolina Commission on Higher Education
1122 Lady Street, Suite 300, Columbia, SC 29201
Phone: 803-737-2262
Email: cbrown@che.sc.gov
http://www.che.sc.gov
Purpose: Monetary assistance is provided to South Carolina resident students pursuing higher education.
Eligibility: Applicants must graduate from a high school in South Carolina or outside of South Carolina if parent is a legal resident of South Carolina, attend an eligible South Carolina public or private college full-time and be a resident of South Carolina. Entering freshmen must meet two of the following: have a minimum 3.0 GPA, a minimum SAT score of 1100 or ACT score of 24 or graduate in the top 30 percent of their class.
Target applicant(s): High school students. College students. Adult students.
Minimum GPA: 3.0
Amount: Up to full tuition.
Number of awards: Varies.
Scholarship may be renewable.
Deadline: Varies.
How to apply: Your college will determine your eligibility based on your high school transcript. There is no application form.
Exclusive: Visit www.UltimateScholarshipBook.com and enter code SO159323 for updates on this award.

(1594) · Legislative Lottery Scholarships

New Mexico Higher Education Department
2044 Galisteo Street, Suite 4, Santa Fe, NM 87505-2100
Phone: 505-476-8400
Email: cesaria.tapia1@state.nm.us
https://hed.state.nm.us/financial-aid
Purpose: To support graduating New Mexico high school seniors with financial need.
Eligibility: Applicants must be graduating high school seniors in New Mexico, enroll full-time at an eligible New Mexico public college or university and maintain a minimum 2.5 GPA during the first college semester.
Target applicant(s): High school students.
Amount: Varies.
Number of awards: Varies.
Scholarship may be renewable.
Deadline: Varies.
How to apply: Contact your financial aid office.
Exclusive: Visit www.UltimateScholarshipBook.com and enter code NE159423 for updates on this award.

(1595) · Lemieux-Lovejoy Youth Scholarship

Futurama Foundation
c/o Marilyn Ladd, Office Manager, 103 County Road, Oakland, ME 04963
Email: mvladd@colby.edu
http://bpwmefoundation.org/scholarship-program/
Purpose: To honor the memory of Rachel E. Lemieux and to provide financial assistance to Maine high school seniors and recent graduates.
Eligibility: Applicants must be female Maine residents who are high school seniors or who have recently graduated from high school.
Target applicant(s): High school students.
Amount: $1,500.
Number of awards: 1.
Deadline: April 13.
How to apply: Applications are available from your local BPW chapter.
Exclusive: Visit www.UltimateScholarshipBook.com and enter code FU159523 for updates on this award.

(1596) · Leo Bourassa Scholarship

Virginia Lakes and Watersheds Association
VLWA Scholarship Committee, CH2M HILL, 5701 Cleveland Street, Suite 200, Virginia Beach, VA 23462
Phone: 757-671-6222
Email: scholarship@vlwa.org
http://www.vlwa.org
Purpose: To acknowledge students for their accomplishments in the field of water resources.
Eligibility: Applicants must be Virginia residents and students in good standing at an accredited college or university in the state. They must complete at least two semesters of undergraduate study by the award date. They must also be full-time undergraduate or full- or part-time graduate students enrolled in curriculum related to water resources.
Target applicant(s): College students. Graduate school students. Adult students.
Amount: $500-$3,000.
Number of awards: Varies.
Deadline: April 1.
How to apply: Applications are available online.
Exclusive: Visit www.UltimateScholarshipBook.com and enter code VI159623 for updates on this award.

(1597) · Leo H. Grether Memorial Scholarship

Iowa High School Music Association
P.O. Box 10, Boone, IA 50036
http://www.ihsma.org
Purpose: To support Iowa students pursuing vocal music education.
Eligibility: Applicants must be Iowa residents and graduating high school seniors enrolling in college to pursue a vocal music education major. Students must submit a recording of two selections and essay along with their application materials.
Target applicant(s): High school students.
Amount: $2,500.
Number of awards: 1.
Deadline: April 15.
How to apply: Applications are available online.
Exclusive: Visit www.UltimateScholarshipBook.com and enter code IO159723 for updates on this award.

(1598) · Licensed Vocational Nurse to Associate Degree Nursing Scholarship

Health Professions Education Foundation
400 R Street, Suite 460, Sacramento, CA 95811
Phone: 916-326-3640
Email: stran@oshpd.ca.gov
https://oshpd.ca.gov/loans-scholarships-grants/scholarships/
Purpose: To aid licensed vocational nurses in California who are pursuing an associate's degree in nursing.
Eligibility: Applicants must be licensed vocational nurses (LVNs) who are enrolled in or have been accepted into an accredited associate's degree in nursing (ADN) program in the state of California. They must be attending or planning to attend school at least part-time (six or more credits per semester) and must commit to two years of nursing practice in an underserved area of California after graduation. Selection is based on the overall strength of the application.
Target applicant(s): College students. Adult students.
Amount: Up to $8,000.
Number of awards: Varies.
Deadline: February 22.
How to apply: Applications are available online. An application form, official transcript, personal statement, financial information, two recommendation letters and proof of vocational nurse licensure are required.
Exclusive: Visit www.UltimateScholarshipBook.com and enter code HE159823 for updates on this award.

(1599) · Lila M. Van Sweringen Student Scholarship

Educational Office Professionals of Ohio
Mrs. Carla Huntsinger, Scholarship Chairperson, 100 Scarlet Oaks Drive, Cincinnati, OH 45241
https://eopo-oh.org/Student_Scholarship
Purpose: To support high school seniors and college students from Ohio who are pursuing a higher education in an office-related career.
Eligibility: Applicants must be residents of Ohio who are either current college students or high school seniors who will be attending a post-secondary institution in the fall of the next school year. Students must be pursuing an office-related career.
Target applicant(s): High school students. College students. Adult students.
Amount: $1,000.
Number of awards: Varies.
Deadline: January 7.
How to apply: Applications are available online.
Exclusive: Visit www.UltimateScholarshipBook.com and enter code ED159923 for updates on this award.

(1600) · Lilly Endowment Community Scholarship Program

Independent Colleges of Indiana
30 South Meridian Street, Suite 800, Indianapolis, IN 46204
Phone: 317-236-6090
Email: smartchoice@icindiana.org
http://www.icindiana.org
Purpose: To raise the level of education in Indiana.
Eligibility: Applicants must be Indiana high school seniors who have been accepted into a full-time bachelor's degree program at an accredited public or private institution of higher learning in Indiana.
Target applicant(s): High school students.
Amount: Full tuition plus fees and $900 book stipend.

Number of awards: 142.
Scholarship may be renewable.
Deadline: Varies.
How to apply: Applications are available online and from local Indiana Community Foundations.
Exclusive: Visit www.UltimateScholarshipBook.com and enter code IN160023 for updates on this award.

(1601) · Lily and Catello Sorrentino Memorial Scholarship

Rhode Island Foundation
One Union Station, Providence, RI 02903
Phone: 401-274-4564
Email: rbogert@rifoundation.org
https://rifoundation.org/grants-scholarships/browse-scholarships
Purpose: To assist adult students who are continuing their undergraduate studies at colleges or universities in Rhode Island.
Eligibility: Applicants must be residents of Rhode Island, be over 25 years of age and attend a non-parochial college or university in the state.
Target applicant(s): College students. Adult students.
Amount: Varies.
Number of awards: Varies.
Deadline: April.
How to apply: Applications are available online.
Exclusive: Visit www.UltimateScholarshipBook.com and enter code RH160123 for updates on this award.

(1602) · Linda Craig Memorial Scholarship Presented by St. Vincent Sports Performance

Pacers Foundation
Linda Craig Memorial Scholarship Committee, 125 S. Pennsylvania Street, Indianapolis, IN 46204
Phone: 317-917-2500
Email: bill.benner@pacers.com
http://www.pacersfoundation.org/
Purpose: To support Indiana students interested in sports medicine, physical therapy and related fields.
Eligibility: Applicants must U.S. citizens who have completed at least one full year of an undergraduate program majoring in medicine, sports medicine, physical therapy or a related area. They must have a GPA of at least 3.0 and demonstrate outstanding character, integrity and leadership. Applicants may not have received a full scholarship from any other organization.
Target applicant(s): College students. Adult students.
Minimum GPA: 3.0
Amount: $2,500.
Number of awards: 3.
Deadline: April 15.
How to apply: Applications are available online.
Exclusive: Visit www.UltimateScholarshipBook.com and enter code PA160223 for updates on this award.

(1603) · Lloyd F. Hutt Scholarship

Lake Michigan Credit Union
Phone: 616-242-9790
https://www.lmcu.org/about/community-relations/hutt-scholarship/
Purpose: To support Michigan or Florida students or members or children of members of the credit union.

Eligibility: Applicants must be residents of Michigan or Florida or members of Lake Michigan Credit Union or the children of members. Students must be high school seniors who plan to enter a trade school, college or university.
Target applicant(s): High school students.
Amount: $2,000.
Number of awards: 20.
Deadline: January 31.
How to apply: Applications are available online.
Exclusive: Visit www.UltimateScholarshipBook.com and enter code LA160323 for updates on this award.

(1604) · Loan Assistance Repayment Program Primary Care Services

Maryland Higher Education Commission
Office of Student Financial Assistance, 6 North Liberty Street, Baltimore, MD 21201
Phone: 800-974-1024
Email: osfamail@mhec.state.md.us
https://mhec.maryland.gov
Purpose: To support primary care physicians and medical residents.
Eligibility: Medical resident applicants must be graduates of a Maryland college, and they must have at least one year remaining in a primary care residency program. Physician applicants must have a valid primary care license and currently work in an underserved area of Maryland. All applicants must have outstanding loans on which they have not defaulted. Specialization in one of the following fields is required: general internal medicine, family practice medicine, general pediatrics, obstetrics/gynecology or gynecology. Applicants must agree to work in an underserved area of Maryland for two to four years after winning the scholarship and completing their residency.
Target applicant(s): Graduate school students. Adult students.
Amount: Up to $25,000.
Number of awards: Varies.
Scholarship may be renewable.
Deadline: April 15.
How to apply: Applications are available from the Department of Health and Mental Hygiene.
Exclusive: Visit www.UltimateScholarshipBook.com and enter code MA160423 for updates on this award.

(1605) · Lois Livingston McMillen Memorial Fund

Connecticut Community Foundation Center for Philanthropy
43 Field Street, Waterbury, CT 06702
Phone: 203-753-1315
Email: scholarships@conncf.org
http://www.conncf.org
Purpose: To provide financial assistance to women who are studying or plan to study art, especially painting or design.
Eligibility: Applicants must be women who plan to study art at an accredited college or university, or in an artist-in-residence program. They must also live in the Connecticut Community Foundation's service area.
Target applicant(s): High school students. College students. Adult students.
Amount: Varies.
Number of awards: Varies.
Scholarship may be renewable.
Deadline: March 15.
How to apply: Applications are available online.

Exclusive: Visit www.UltimateScholarshipBook.com and enter code CO160523 for updates on this award.

(1606) · Lori Rhett Memorial Scholarship

National Association for Campus Activities
13 Harbison Way, Columbia, SC 29212
Phone: 803-732-6222
Email: info@naca.org
https://www.naca.org/FOUNDATION/Pages/Scholarships.aspx
Purpose: The scholarship recognizes the achievements of student leaders who are undergraduate or graduate students.
Eligibility: Applicants must be U.S. citizens and have a minimum GPA of 2.5. Students must hold a significant campus leadership position and demonstrate significant leadership skills and abilities. Applicants must also be making significant contributions through on- or off-campus volunteering and must attend school in Alaska, Idaho, Montana, Oregon or Washington.
Target applicant(s): College students. Graduate school students. Adult students.
Minimum GPA: 2.5
Amount: Varies.
Number of awards: 1.
Deadline: November 30.
How to apply: Applications are available online.
Exclusive: Visit www.UltimateScholarshipBook.com and enter code NA160623 for updates on this award.

(1607) · Los Alamos Employees' Scholarship

Los Alamos National Laboratory Foundation
1112 Plaza del Norte, Espanola, NM 87532
Phone: 505-753-8890
Email: tony@lanlfoundation.org
http://www.lanlfoundation.org
Purpose: To provide financial assistance for students in northern New Mexico who plan to pursue undergraduate degrees in fields of study that will benefit the community.
Eligibility: Selection is based on academic performance, including the pursuit in high school of a rigorous course of study, GPA and standardized test scores, varied extracurricular and community service activities, strong critical thinking skills and career goals that are relevant to the needs of the northern New Mexico community. Some consideration is also given to financial need, ethnic diversity and equally representing all the regions of northern New Mexico. Applicants must have a minimum 3.25 GPA and either minimum score of 19 on the ACT or 930 on the SAT (Math and Critical Reading).
Target applicant(s): College students. Adult students.
Minimum GPA: 3.25
Amount: Varies.
Number of awards: Varies.
Scholarship may be renewable.
Deadline: January 18.
How to apply: Applications are available online.
Exclusive: Visit www.UltimateScholarshipBook.com and enter code LO160723 for updates on this award.

(1608) · Lottery Tuition Assistance Program

South Carolina Commission on Higher Education
Mr. Gerrick Hampton, Lottery Tuition Assistance Program Manager, 1122 Lady Street, Suite 300, Columbia, SC 29201
Phone: 803-734-4397
Email: ghampton@che.sc.gov
http://www.che.sc.gov
Purpose: To assist South Carolina residents attending a two-year public or independent institution of higher learning.
Eligibility: Applicants must complete the Free Application for Federal Student Aid (FAFSA), be residents of South Carolina and be enrolled as a degree-seeking student in a minimum of six credit hours at an eligible two-year technical institution, a USC two-year regional campus or Spartanburg Methodist College.
Target applicant(s): High school students. College students. Adult students.
Amount: Up to $1,200 per term.
Number of awards: Varies.
Deadline: Varies.
How to apply: Applications are available by telephone request.
Exclusive: Visit www.UltimateScholarshipBook.com and enter code SO160823 for updates on this award.

(1609) · Louis B. Russell Scholarship

Indiana State Teachers Association
150 W. Market Street, Suite 900, Indianapolis, IN 46204
Phone: 844-275-4782
Email: ccherry@ista-in.org
https://www.ista-in.org/our-profession/scholarships-awards
Purpose: To provide financial assistance to ethnic minorities who are seeking vocational or technical education.
Eligibility: Applicants must be ethnic minority high school seniors who plan to pursue education in the area of industrial arts, vocational education or technical education at an accredited college or university.
Target applicant(s): High school students.
Amount: $1,000.
Number of awards: 1.
Scholarship may be renewable.
Deadline: March 1.
How to apply: Applications are available online.
Exclusive: Visit www.UltimateScholarshipBook.com and enter code IN160923 for updates on this award.

(1610) · Louisiana Go Grant

Louisiana Office of Student Financial Assistance
605 N. Fifth Street, Baton Rouge, LA 70802
Phone: 800-259-5626 x1012
Email: custserv@la.gov
https://mylosfa.la.gov/students-parents/scholarships-grants/tops/
Purpose: To help students from moderate and low income families afford a college education.
Eligibility: Applicants must be Louisiana residents who have been admitted and enrolled in an undergraduate program at a Louisiana public or private college or university. They must be first-time freshmen or adult students who have not been enrolled in credit-bearing courses for at least one academic year. Financial need is required.
Target applicant(s): High school students. College students. Adult students.
Amount: Up to $3,000.
Number of awards: Varies.
Deadline: Varies.
How to apply: All eligible students who have filed a Free Application for Federal Student Aid are considered for this grant.
Exclusive: Visit www.UltimateScholarshipBook.com and enter code LO161023 for updates on this award.

(1611) · Louisiana Memorial Scholarship

American Radio Relay League Foundation
225 Main Street, Newington, CT 06111-1494
Phone: 860-594-0348
Email: foundation@arrl.org
http://www.arrl.org/scholarship-program
Purpose: To provide financial assistance to Louisiana students who are amateur radio operators.
Eligibility: Applicants must hold a Technician Class or higher Amateur Radio License and either be Louisiana residents or attend school in Louisiana. They must have a GPA of 3.0 or higher. Only students who are accepted to or enrolled in a four-year college or university are eligible.
Target applicant(s): High school students. College students. Adult students.
Minimum GPA: 3.0
Amount: $750.
Number of awards: 1.
Deadline: December 31.
How to apply: Applications are available online.
Exclusive: Visit www.UltimateScholarshipBook.com and enter code AM161123 for updates on this award.

(1612) · Luso-American Education Foundation General Youth Scholarship

Luso-American Education Foundation
P.O. Box 2967, Dublin, CA 94568
Phone: 925-828-3883
Email: odom@luso-american.org
https://www.luso-american.org/laef
Purpose: To provide educational opportunities for Portuguese students.
Eligibility: Applicants must be residents of California and high school students who are of Portuguese descent with a GPA of 3.5 or higher, or who are taking classes in the Portuguese language with a GPA of 3.0 or higher. They must be enrolled in a college, university, trade or business school and have taken the SAT or ACT. Two letters of recommendation are required.
Target applicant(s): High school students.
Minimum GPA: 3.0
Amount: $500-$1,500.
Number of awards: Varies.
Deadline: March 1.
How to apply: Applications are available by phone, fax, mail or email.
Exclusive: Visit www.UltimateScholarshipBook.com and enter code LU161223 for updates on this award.

(1613) · M. Josephine O'Neil Arts Award

Delta Kappa Gamma Society International Lambda State Organization
c/o Athena Columbus, 8127 North Oketo Avenue, Niles, IL 60714-2941
Phone: 847-983-8326
Email: athenac13@comcast.net
http://www.deltakappagamma.org/IL
Purpose: To support outstanding female artists.
Eligibility: Applicants must be Illinois residents and be sophomores at an accredited community college or current or upcoming juniors at an accredited four-year college or university. Students must demonstrate outstanding accomplishment in music, visual arts, dance, theater or the literary arts.
Target applicant(s): College students. Adult students.

Amount: Up to $6,000.
Number of awards: Varies.
Deadline: January 9.
How to apply: Applications are available online. An application form, transcript, evidence of accomplishment in the arts (such as reviews, awards, etc.) and an artwork sample are required.
Exclusive: Visit www.UltimateScholarshipBook.com and enter code DE161323 for updates on this award.

(1614) · Mabel Mayforth Scholarship

Federated Garden Clubs of Vermont Inc.
c/o Marybeth Tevis, Scholarship Chair, 973 Stock Farm Road, Randolph, VT 05060
Phone: 802-728-6083
Email: marybeth@eravt.com
http://www.vermontfgcv.com
Purpose: To support students who are studying in fields related to plants.
Eligibility: Applicants must be Vermont residents who are college juniors, seniors or graduate students and must major horticulture, landscape, design, conservation, forestry, agronomy, plant pathology or biology with a special interest in plants, ecology and allied subjects. They must be full-time students at an accredited institution with a GPA of 3.0 or higher. Previous winners may reapply.
Target applicant(s): College students. Graduate school students. Adult students.
Minimum GPA: 3.0
Amount: Varies.
Number of awards: 1.
Deadline: May 15.
How to apply: Applications are available online. An application form, list of extracurricular activities, letter of application, transcript and three letters of recommendation are required.
Exclusive: Visit www.UltimateScholarshipBook.com and enter code FE161423 for updates on this award.

(1615) · Mackinac Scholarship

American Society of Civil Engineers-Michigan Section
ASCE Scholarships, 215 N. Walnut Street, Lansing, MI 48933
Phone: 517-332-2066
Email: cschmitz@acecmi.org
http://sections.asce.org/michigan
Purpose: To aid Michigan civil engineering students.
Eligibility: Applicants must be U.S. citizens and Michigan residents. They must be rising undergraduate juniors or seniors who are enrolled full-time in an ABET-accredited civil engineering degree program. They must have a GPA of 2.5 or higher on a four-point scale. Selection is based on academic achievement, personal qualities and financial need.
Target applicant(s): College students. Adult students.
Minimum GPA: 2.5
Amount: $10,000.
Number of awards: 1.
Deadline: May (Memorial Day).
How to apply: Applications are available online. An application form and an official transcript are required.
Exclusive: Visit www.UltimateScholarshipBook.com and enter code AM161523 for updates on this award.

(1616) · Maine BPW Continuing Education Scholarship

Futurama Foundation
c/o Marilyn Ladd, Office Manager, 103 County Road, Oakland, ME 04963
Email: mvladd@colby.edu
http://bpwmefoundation.org/scholarship-program/
Purpose: To provide financial assistance to Maine women who are already attending an institution of higher learning.
Eligibility: Applicants must be female Maine residents who are currently attending a college or training program.
Target applicant(s): College students. Graduate school students. Adult students.
Amount: $1,500.
Number of awards: Varies.
Deadline: April 13.
How to apply: Applications are available from your local BPW chapter.
Exclusive: Visit www.UltimateScholarshipBook.com and enter code FU161623 for updates on this award.

(1617) · Maine Community Foundation Scholarship Program

Maine Community Foundation
245 Main Street, Ellsworth, ME 04605
Phone: 207-667-9735
Email: jwarren@mainecf.org
http://www.mainecf.org
Purpose: To provide financial assistance to Maine students.
Eligibility: There are a number of scholarships in this program for Maine traditional and adult students to attend private high schools, undergraduate colleges or graduate schools. Many are limited to residents of a specific county or graduates of a certain high school.
Target applicant(s): High school students. College students. Graduate school students. Adult students.
Amount: Varies.
Number of awards: Varies.
Deadline: Varies.
How to apply: Applications are available online.
Exclusive: Visit www.UltimateScholarshipBook.com and enter code MA161723 for updates on this award.

(1618) · Maine Demolay and Pine Tree Youth Foundation Scholarships

Maine Demolay and Pine Tree Youth Foundation
Benjamin Weisner, 288 Rowe Station Road, New Gloucester, ME 04402
Phone: 207-773-5184
Email: grandlodge@mainemason.org
http://www.pinetreeyouth.org
Purpose: To support Maine high school seniors.
Eligibility: Applicants must submit a short essay. Students must demonstrate educational and civic achievement.
Target applicant(s): High school students.
Amount: Varies.
Number of awards: Varies.
Deadline: March 26.
How to apply: Applications are available online.
Exclusive: Visit www.UltimateScholarshipBook.com and enter code MA161823 for updates on this award.

(1619) · Maine State Society Foundation Scholarship

Maine State Society Foundation of Washington, DC
6508 Bowie Drive, Springfield, VA 22150
Email: mssfscholarship@gmail.com
https://mainestatesociety.org/foundation/
Purpose: To provide financial assistance to Maine students.
Eligibility: Applicants or their parent must have been born in or have been a legal resident of the state of Maine for at least four years. Applicants must be full-time students who are at least sophomores and must attend an accredited, non-profit college or university located in Maine.
Target applicant(s): College students.
Minimum GPA: 3.0
Amount: At least $1,000.
Number of awards: Varies.
Deadline: March 15.
How to apply: Applications are available by mail and online.
Exclusive: Visit www.UltimateScholarshipBook.com and enter code MA161923 for updates on this award.

(1620) · Maine Veterans Dependents Educational Benefits

Bureau of Veterans' Services
117 State House Station, Augusta, ME 04333-0117
Phone: 207-430-6035
Email: mainebvs@maine.gov
http://www.maine.gov/veterans/
Purpose: To provide the opportunity for dependents of veterans to obtain higher education.
Eligibility: Applicants must be spouses or children of a veteran in the state of Maine. They must be at least 16 years old, be high school graduates and be residents of the state of Maine for the last 5 years. They must be pursuing a college degree. Benefits must be awarded prior to the dependent's 22nd birthday, unless he is serving in the U.S. Armed Forces, in which case they may be awarded until his 26th birthday.
Target applicant(s): High school students. College students. Adult students.
Amount: Varies.
Number of awards: Varies.
Scholarship may be renewable.
Deadline: Varies.
How to apply: Applications are available online.
Exclusive: Visit www.UltimateScholarshipBook.com and enter code BU162023 for updates on this award.

(1621) · Mamoru and Aiko Takitani Foundation Scholarship

Mamoru and Aiko Takitani Foundation
P.O. Box 10687, Honolulu, HI 96816-0687
Phone: 808-228-0209
Email: info@takitanifoundation.org
http://www.takitani.org
Purpose: To assist Hawaii resident students with business school, technical school, community college or four-year college expenses.
Eligibility: Applicants must be graduating high school seniors and Hawaii residents. Applicants must also demonstrate scholastic achievement, participation in activities and have been accepted into an accredited institution. Community service and financial need are also considered.
Target applicant(s): High school students.

Amount: $1,000-$10,000.
Number of awards: Varies.
Deadline: February 5.
How to apply: Contact your high school guidance counselor.
Exclusive: Visit www.UltimateScholarshipBook.com and enter code MA162123 for updates on this award.

(1622) · Margaret A. Pemberton Scholarship

Black Nurses Association of Greater Washington, DC Area Inc.
P.O. Box 55285, Washington, DC 20040
Phone: 202-291-8866
Email: contactus@bnaofgwdca.org
http://www.bnaofgwdca.org
Purpose: To aid Washington, DC students who are planning to pursue higher education in nursing.
Eligibility: Applicants must be U.S. citizens, be graduating seniors who are students at a Washington, DC high school and be accepted into a National League for Nursing bachelor's degree program at a U.S. postsecondary institution. They must have a GPA of 2.8 or higher and must demonstrate financial need. Selection is based on the overall strength of the application.
Target applicant(s): High school students.
Minimum GPA: 2.8
Amount: Varies.
Number of awards: 1.
Deadline: April 15.
How to apply: Applications are available online. An application form, personal statement, official transcript, copy of college acceptance letter and two recommendation letters are required.
Exclusive: Visit www.UltimateScholarshipBook.com and enter code BL162223 for updates on this award.

(1623) · Margaret A. Stafford Nursing Scholarship

Delaware Community Foundation
P.O. Box 1636, Wilmington, DE 19899
Phone: 302-571-8004
Email: rgentsch@delcf.org
http://www.delcf.org
Purpose: To aid Delaware students who are pursuing higher education in nursing.
Eligibility: Applicants must be Delaware residents who are enrolled in or who have been accepted into a nursing degree program at an accredited college or university. Selection is based on the overall strength of the application.
Target applicant(s): High school students. College students. Adult students.
Amount: Varies.
Number of awards: Varies.
Deadline: March 15.
How to apply: Applications are available online. An application form, transcript, personal statement and two recommendation letters are required.
Exclusive: Visit www.UltimateScholarshipBook.com and enter code DE162323 for updates on this award.

(1624) · MARILN Professional Scholarship Award

Massachusetts/Rhode Island League for Nursing
Award Committee, P.O. Box 407, Westwood, MA 02090
Phone: 781-366-0722
Email: nursing.mariln@gmail.com
http://www.nln.org
Purpose: To aid Massachusetts and Rhode Island practical nursing students.
Eligibility: Applicants must be Massachusetts or Rhode Island residents and have lived in Massachusetts or Rhode Island for at least four years before having entered that practical nursing program. They must be full-time students who have completed two consecutive semesters of their program of study. Selection is based on stated career goals and professional potential.
Target applicant(s): College students. Adult students.
Amount: Varies.
Number of awards: Varies.
Deadline: August 15.
How to apply: Applications are available online. An application form, official transcript, personal essay and two recommendation letters are required.
Exclusive: Visit www.UltimateScholarshipBook.com and enter code MA162423 for updates on this award.

(1625) · Marion Maccarrell Scott Scholarship

Hawaii Community Foundation - Scholarships
827 Fort Street Mall, Honolulu, HI 96813
Phone: 888-731-3863
Email: scholarships@hcf-hawaii.org
https://www.hawaiicommunityfoundation.org/
Purpose: To support graduating high school students in Hawaii who are committed to world peace.
Eligibility: Applicants must have attended a public high school in Hawaii, and they must plan to attend college on the U.S. mainland. Students must have at least a 2.8 GPA.
Target applicant(s): High school students.
Minimum GPA: 2.8
Amount: Varies.
Number of awards: Varies.
Deadline: January 31.
How to apply: To apply, register online, complete the online application and select the scholarships to which you wish to apply. In addition, mail the supporting materials: printed confirmation page from the online application, personal statement, essay, copy of Student Aid Report (SAR) available at www.fafsa.ed.gov and official transcript.
Exclusive: Visit www.UltimateScholarshipBook.com and enter code HA162523 for updates on this award.

(1626) · Marlin R. Scarborough Memorial Scholarship

South Dakota Board of Regents
306 East Capitol Ave, Suite 200, Pierre, SD 57501-2545
Phone: 605-773-3455
Email: info@sdbor.edu
http://www.sdbor.edu
Purpose: To support undergraduate students in South Dakota.
Eligibility: Applicants must submit an essay detailing their leadership qualities, academic achievements and community service. Students must attend a public South Dakota university with at least a 3.5 GPA, and they must be in their junior year at the time they receive the scholarship funding.
Target applicant(s): College students. Adult students.
Minimum GPA: 3.5
Amount: Varies.
Number of awards: 1.
Deadline: Varies.
How to apply: Applications are available online.

Exclusive: Visit www.UltimateScholarshipBook.com and enter code SO162623 for updates on this award.

(1627) · Martin Devlin Scholarship

Physician Assistant Academy of Vermont
45 Lyme Road, Suite 304, Hanover, NH 03755
Phone: 603-643-2325
Email: paav@conmx.net
http://www.paav.org
Purpose: To aid current and recent Vermont physician assistant students.
Eligibility: Applicants must be Vermont residents and must be currently enrolled in a physician assistant program in Vermont or must be recent graduates of such a program who have outstanding student loans and are working or intending to work in Vermont. Previous winners of this scholarship are ineligible. Selection is based on the overall strength of the application.
Target applicant(s): College students. Graduate school students. Adult students.
Amount: $1,000.
Number of awards: 1.
Deadline: June 30.
How to apply: Applications are available online. An application form, personal statement, school enrollment verification (if applicable) and employment verification (if applicable) are required.
Exclusive: Visit www.UltimateScholarshipBook.com and enter code PH162723 for updates on this award.

(1628) · Marvin L. Zuidema Scholarship Award

American Society of Civil Engineers-Michigan Section
ASCE Scholarships, 215 N. Walnut Street, Lansing, MI 48933
Phone: 517-332-2066
Email: cschmitz@acecmi.org
http://sections.asce.org/michigan
Purpose: To aid American Society of Civil Engineers (ASCE) student members in Michigan who have contributed meaningfully to student civil engineering activities.
Eligibility: Applicants must be U.S. citizens, Michigan residents and rising juniors or seniors who are enrolled full-time in an ABET-accredited civil engineering degree program. They must have a GPA of 2.5 or higher on a four-point scale and have made a notable contribution to civil engineering student activities. Selection is based on academic merit.
Target applicant(s): College students. Adult students.
Minimum GPA: 2.5
Amount: $1,500.
Number of awards: 1.
Deadline: May, Memorial Day.
How to apply: Applications are available online. An application form and an official transcript are required.
Exclusive: Visit www.UltimateScholarshipBook.com and enter code AM162823 for updates on this award.

(1629) · Mary Ann K. Murtha Memorial Scholarship

American Legion Auxiliary, Department of New York
112 State Street, Suite 1310, Albany, NY 12207
Phone: 518-463-1162
Email: nyalaeducation@gmail.com
http://www.deptny.org/?page_id=2128
Purpose: To provide financial assistance to students whose parents, grandparents or great-grandparents served in the Armed Forces during wartime.
Eligibility: Applicants must be children, grandchildren or great-grandchildren of Armed Forces veterans who served during World War I, World War II, the Korean Conflict, the Vietnam War, Grenada/Lebanon, Panama, the Persian Gulf and War on Terrorism. Students must be high school seniors, U.S. citizens and New York State residents.
Target applicant(s): High school students.
Amount: $1,000.
Number of awards: 1.
Deadline: March 1.
How to apply: Applications are available online.
Exclusive: Visit www.UltimateScholarshipBook.com and enter code AM162923 for updates on this award.

(1630) · Mary Benevento/CTAHPERD Scholarship

Connecticut Association of Health, Physical Education, Recreation and Dance
c/o Janice Skene, CTAHPERD Scholarship Chair, Buttonball Lane School, 376 Buttonball Lane, Glastonbury, CT 06033
Phone: 860-652-7276
Email: skenej@glastonburyus.org
http://www.ctahperd.org
Purpose: To aid Connecticut students who are planning to pursue higher education in school health teaching, physical education, recreation or dance.
Eligibility: Applicants must be U.S. citizens and Connecticut residents. They must be high school seniors who are planning to pursue a bachelor's degree in school health teaching, physical education, recreation or dance at an accredited Connecticut postsecondary institution. Selection is based on academic merit, professional potential and character.
Target applicant(s): High school students.
Amount: $1,000.
Number of awards: Varies.
Deadline: June 15.
How to apply: Applications are available online. An application form, transcript, personal statement and one letter of recommendation are required.
Exclusive: Visit www.UltimateScholarshipBook.com and enter code CO163023 for updates on this award.

(1631) · Mary Eileen Dixey Scholarship

American Occupational Therapy Foundation
Attn: Jeanne Cooper, 4720 Montgomery Lane, Suite 202, Bethesda, MD 20814
Phone: 240-292-1034
Email: jcooper@aotf.org
https://www.aotf.org/Scholarships
Purpose: To aid New Hampshire occupational therapy students.
Eligibility: Applicants must be New Hampshire residents who are members of the American Occupational Therapy Association (AOTA). They must be enrolled full-time in an accredited occupational therapy program at the associate's or master's degree level in the state of New Hampshire. Master's level students must be enrolled in a first professional degree program and must have completed at least one year of study to be eligible. Selection is based on the overall strength of the application.
Target applicant(s): College students. Graduate school students. Adult students.
Amount: Varies.
Number of awards: Varies.

Deadline: October 1.
How to apply: Applications are available online. An application form, two personal references and a program director statement are required.
Exclusive: Visit www.UltimateScholarshipBook.com and enter code AM163123 for updates on this award.

(1632) · Mary Keith Duff Memorial Scholarship

Travis Credit Union
P.O. Box 2069, Vacaville, CA 95696
Phone: 707-449-4000
https://www.traviscu.org/community/events-seminars-community-education/scholarships/
Purpose: To assist members of the Travis Credit Union.
Eligibility: Applicants must be graduating high school seniors and have a minimum 3.0 GPA. Selection is based on GPA, honors and awards, employment and community service, leadership and extracurricular activities, essay and financial need. Students must plan to enroll in a two-year or four-year college or university full-time or with 12 or more credits or units.
Target applicant(s): High school students.
Minimum GPA: 3.0
Amount: $2,000.
Number of awards: 22.
Deadline: March 5.
How to apply: Applications are available online between January 1 and March 5 of each year.
Exclusive: Visit www.UltimateScholarshipBook.com and enter code TR163223 for updates on this award.

(1633) · Mary Macon McGuire Scholarship

General Federation of Women's Clubs of Virginia
P.O. Box 8750, Richmond, VA 23226
Phone: 804-288-3724
Email: scholarships@gfwcvirginia.org
https://gfwcvirginia.org/
Purpose: To support Virginia women who are returning to school in order to better support their families.
Eligibility: Applicants must be a female head of household and a resident of Virginia. Students must be currently enrolled in a course of study at an accredited Virginia school. Students must submit an essay and three letters of recommendation. Applicants must show financial need.
Target applicant(s): College students. Adult students.
Amount: $2,500.
Number of awards: 2.
Deadline: March 15.
How to apply: Applications are available online.
Exclusive: Visit www.UltimateScholarshipBook.com and enter code GE163323 for updates on this award.

(1634) · Masonic Scholarship Program

Grand Lodge of Iowa, A.F. and A.M.
Scholarship Selection Committee, P.O. Box 279, Cedar Rapids, IA 52406-0279
Phone: 319-365-1438
Email: scholarships@gl-iowa.org
https://grandlodgeofiowa.org/grand-lodge/awards/
Purpose: To reward high school seniors from Iowa public high schools for academics and leadership skills.
Eligibility: Applicants must be pursuing a post-secondary education in any state at an institution which provides a two-year or four-year college program or vocational training. They do not need to have a Masonic connection. Selection is based on academic record, communication skills and financial need, but the most important is service to school and community with an emphasis on leadership roles. Finalists will be asked to appear before the committee for personal interviews.
Target applicant(s): High school students.
Amount: $2,000.
Number of awards: 60.
Deadline: February 1.
How to apply: Applications are available online or from guidance departments at Iowa public high schools.
Exclusive: Visit www.UltimateScholarshipBook.com and enter code GR163423 for updates on this award.

(1635) · Masonry Institute of Iowa Foundation Scholarship Program

Masonry Institute of Iowa
6919 Vista Drive, West Des Moines, IA 50266
Email: admin@masonryinstituteofiowa.org
https://masonryinstituteofiowa.wildapricot.org/Scholarships
Purpose: To support students pursuing construction, architecture and engineering.
Eligibility: Applicants must be current Iowa high school or college students attending an Iowa institution and pursuing a program related to construction, engineering, masonry or architecture.
Target applicant(s): High school students. College students. Adult students.
Amount: Varies.
Number of awards: Varies.
Deadline: February 28.
How to apply: Applications are available online.
Exclusive: Visit www.UltimateScholarshipBook.com and enter code MA163523 for updates on this award.

(1636) · Massachusetts Community Colleges Access Grant

Massachusetts Community Colleges
85 Devonshire Street, 7th Floor, Boston, MA 02109
Phone: 617-542-2911
Email: info@masscc.org
http://www.masscc.org/student-resources/financial-aid-resources
Purpose: To make a Massachusetts community college education accessible for all.
Eligibility: Applicants must be pursuing an associate degree at a Massachusetts community college. Students whose household income is $36,000 per year or less are eligible to receive funds to cover full tuition and fees.
Target applicant(s): High school students. College students. Adult students.
Amount: Up to full tuition.
Number of awards: Varies.
Deadline: Varies.
How to apply: Applications are available from Massachusetts community college financial aid offices.
Exclusive: Visit www.UltimateScholarshipBook.com and enter code MA163623 for updates on this award.

(1637) · Massachusetts Part-Time Grant

Massachusetts Department of Higher Education
Office of Student Financial Assistance, 454 Broadway, Suite 200, Revere, MA 02151
Phone: 617-727-9420
Email: osfa@osfa.mass.edu
https://www.mass.edu/osfa/programs/programs.asp
Purpose: To aid Massachusetts part-time undergraduate students.
Eligibility: Applicants must U.S. citizens or eligible non-citizens who have been Massachusetts residents for at least one year. They must be enrolled in an undergraduate degree or certificate program on a part-time basis (6 to 11 credits per semester) at a Massachusetts postsecondary institution. They must not owe refund money on an educational grant or have any defaulted student loans. Applicants who have earned a bachelor's or professional degree previously are ineligible.
Target applicant(s): High school students. College students. Adult students.
Amount: At least $200.
Number of awards: Varies.
Scholarship may be renewable.
Deadline: Varies.
How to apply: Application is made by completing the FAFSA and then contacting your financial aid office.
Exclusive: Visit www.UltimateScholarshipBook.com and enter code MA163723 for updates on this award.

(1638) · Massachusetts Student Broadcaster Scholarship

Massachusetts Broadcasters Association
43 Riverside Avenue, PMB 401, Medford, MA 02155
Phone: 800-471-1875
Email: jordan@massbroadcasters.org
http://www.massbroadcasters.org
Purpose: To support student broadcasters.
Eligibility: Applicants must be Massachusetts residents who are enrolled or plan to enroll in an accredited institution of higher learning that offers degrees in television and radio broadcasting. Students must meet their school's definition of a full-time student. Selection is based on financial need, academic merit, community service, extracurricular activities and work experience.
Target applicant(s): High school students. College students. Adult students.
Amount: $2,000-$3,000.
Number of awards: 11.
Deadline: April 16.
How to apply: Applications are available online. An application form, transcript and financial statement are required.
Exclusive: Visit www.UltimateScholarshipBook.com and enter code MA163823 for updates on this award.

(1639) · MASSGrant

Massachusetts Department of Higher Education
Office of Student Financial Assistance, 454 Broadway, Suite 200, Revere, MA 02151
Phone: 617-727-9420
Email: osfa@osfa.mass.edu
https://www.mass.edu/osfa/programs/programs.asp
Purpose: To provide need-based financial assistance to undergraduate students who reside in Massachusetts and who are enrolled in and pursuing a program of higher education.

Eligibility: Applicants must be permanent legal residents of Massachusetts and have an Expected Family Contribution (EFC) between $0 and $5,198. Applicants must be enrolled as full-time students in a certificate, associate or bachelor's degree program and not have received a prior bachelor's degree or its equivalent.
Target applicant(s): High school students. College students. Adult students.
Amount: Varies.
Number of awards: Varies.
Scholarship may be renewable.
Deadline: July 1.
How to apply: Complete and submit the Free Application for Federal Student Aid (FAFSA).
Exclusive: Visit www.UltimateScholarshipBook.com and enter code MA163923 for updates on this award.

(1640) · Master's, Ph.D. or Other Advanced Degree Program

New Hampshire Charitable Foundation
37 Pleasant Street, Concord, NH 03301-4005
Phone: 603-225-6641
Email: info@nhcf.org
https://www.nhcf.org/how-can-we-help-you/
Purpose: To support New Hampshire students who are seeking graduate level studies.
Eligibility: Applicants must be New Hampshire residents who are enrolling in graduate level studies, including master's, Ph.D. or another advanced degree program. Selection is based on financial need, academic merit, community service, school activities and work experience. Students must file a FAFSA and submit a copy of the SAR with the application.
Target applicant(s): Graduate school students. Adult students.
Amount: Varies.
Number of awards: Varies.
Deadline: April 16.
How to apply: Applications are available online.
Exclusive: Visit www.UltimateScholarshipBook.com and enter code NE164023 for updates on this award.

(1641) · Math and Science Teaching Incentive Scholarships

New York State Higher Education Services Corporation (HESC)
99 Washington Avenue, Albany, NY 12255
Phone: 888-697-4372
Email: scholarships@hesc.ny.gov
http://www.hesc.ny.gov
Purpose: To support students in New York who are planning careers in math or science secondary education.
Eligibility: Applicants must have at least a 2.5 GPA. Recipients must agree to work for at least five years after graduation as a secondary school science or math teacher in the state of New York.
Target applicant(s): College students. Graduate school students. Adult students.
Minimum GPA: 2.5
Amount: Up to full tuition.
Number of awards: Varies.
Scholarship may be renewable.
Deadline: Varies.
How to apply: Applications are available online.

Exclusive: Visit www.UltimateScholarshipBook.com and enter code NE164123 for updates on this award.

(1642) · May T. Henry Scholarship Fund

Stride Bank
Wealth Management Division, P.O. Box 3448, Enid, OK 73702-3448
Phone: 580-233-3535
Email: customerservice@stridebank.com
https://stridebank.com/scholarships.html
Purpose: To support students who plan to attend post-secondary education institutions in Oklahoma.
Eligibility: Applicants must be high school seniors who plan to attend a college, university or technical school supported by the state of Oklahoma. Students must have graduated from an accredited high school or equivalent institution and not be related to any member of the selection committee.
Target applicant(s): High school students.
Amount: $1,000.
Number of awards: Varies.
Deadline: April 1.
How to apply: Applications are available online.
Exclusive: Visit www.UltimateScholarshipBook.com and enter code ST164223 for updates on this award.

(1643) · MCEC Technical Scholarship

Grand Lodge of Iowa, A.F. and A.M.
Scholarship Selection Committee, P.O. Box 279, Cedar Rapids, IA 52406-0279
Phone: 319-365-1438
Email: scholarships@gl-iowa.org
https://grandlodgeofiowa.org/grand-lodge/awards/
Purpose: To support Iowa students pursuing trade education.
Eligibility: Applicants must be graduating high school seniors in Iowa who plan to enroll in a mechanical or trade course of study at an accredited Iowa community college.
Target applicant(s): High school students.
Amount: Varies.
Number of awards: Varies.
Deadline: March 1.
How to apply: Applications are available online.
Exclusive: Visit www.UltimateScholarshipBook.com and enter code GR164323 for updates on this award.

(1644) · McLean Scholarship for Nursing and Physician Assistant Majors

Association of Independent Colleges and Universities of Pennsylvania
101 North Front Street, Harrisburg, PA 17101-1404
Phone: 717-232-8649
Email: klinger@aicup.org
https://www.aicup.org/philanthropy/aicup-scholarships/
Purpose: To aid undergraduates who are studying to become nurses and physician assistants.
Eligibility: Applicants must be full-time undergraduates who are majoring in nursing or physician assisting at an Association of Independent Colleges and Universities of Pennsylvania (AICUP) member school. They must have a GPA of 3.0 or higher and must have proven leadership skills. Selection is based on the overall strength of the application.
Target applicant(s): College students. Adult students.

Minimum GPA: 3.0
Amount: $4,000.
Number of awards: 7.
Deadline: April 15.
How to apply: Applications are available online. An application form and personal essay are required.
Exclusive: Visit www.UltimateScholarshipBook.com and enter code AS164423 for updates on this award.

(1645) · Medallion Fund

New Hampshire Charitable Foundation
37 Pleasant Street, Concord, NH 03301-4005
Phone: 603-225-6641
Email: info@nhcf.org
https://www.nhcf.org/how-can-we-help-you/
Purpose: To improve the skilled workforce in areas of need in New Hampshire.
Eligibility: Applicants must be enrolling in an accredited vocational or technical program that does not lead to a bachelor's or advanced degree. They must be legal residents of New Hampshire and intend to work in a vocational or technical career when their schooling is complete. Preference is given to those who plan to go into the manufacturing trade sector or have little or no other opportunities for training or education.
Target applicant(s): High school students. College students. Adult students.
Amount: Varies.
Number of awards: Varies.
Deadline: December 15.
How to apply: Applications are available online.
Exclusive: Visit www.UltimateScholarshipBook.com and enter code NE164523 for updates on this award.

(1646) · MEFA UPlan Prepaid Tuition Waiver Program

Massachusetts Educational Financing Authority
160 Federal Street, 4th Floor, Boston, MA 02110
Phone: 800-449-6332
Email: info@mefa.org
http://www.mefa.org
Purpose: To provide financial aid in the form of tuition waivers to Massachusetts students who prepay their tuition at lower rates.
Eligibility: Applicants must be planning to attend a school in the state of Massachusetts which participates in the UPlan program.
Target applicant(s): Junior high students or younger. High school students. College students. Adult students.
Amount: Varies.
Number of awards: Varies.
Scholarship may be renewable.
Deadline: Varies.
How to apply: Applications are available online.
Exclusive: Visit www.UltimateScholarshipBook.com and enter code MA164623 for updates on this award.

(1647) · Mellinger Scholarships

Edward Arthur Mellinger Educational Foundation Inc.
1025 E. Broadway, P.O. Box 770, Monmouth, IL 61462
Phone: 309-734-2419
Email: info@mellinger.org
http://www.mellinger.org
Purpose: The E. A. Mellinger Foundation supports education as a memorial to its namesake.

Eligibility: Applicants must live in western Illinois or eastern Iowa, submit the FAFSA form and demonstrate financial need and attend an accredited university. Awards are based on academic achievement. Part-time students are also eligible for scholarships, and loans are also available to graduate students.

Target applicant(s): High school students. College students. Adult students.

Amount: Varies.

Number of awards: Varies.

Scholarship may be renewable.

Deadline: May 1.

How to apply: Applications are available by mail or online. Application forms are only available from February 1 to May 1 each year.

Exclusive: Visit www.UltimateScholarshipBook.com and enter code ED164723 for updates on this award.

(1648) · Mexican Scholarship Fund

Central Indiana Community Foundation
615 North Alabama Street, Suite 119, Indianapolis, IN 46204-1498
Phone: 317-634-2423
Email: scholarships@cicf.org
http://www.cicf.org
Purpose: To provide financial assistance to Indiana residents of Mexican descent.

Eligibility: Applicants must have a minimum GPA of 3.0, demonstrate academic promise and demonstrate financial need. Preference is given to students of Mexican descent. Awards may be used for tuition, required fees or room and board.

Target applicant(s): High school students.

Minimum GPA: 3.0

Amount: Varies.

Number of awards: Varies.

Deadline: February 1.

How to apply: Applications are available online.

Exclusive: Visit www.UltimateScholarshipBook.com and enter code CE164823 for updates on this award.

(1649) · MFA Foundation Scholarships

MFA Incorporated
201 Ray Young Drive, Columbia, MO 65201
Phone: 573-874-5111
https://www.mfa-inc.com/About/Youth
Purpose: To aid Midwest college-bound high school seniors.

Eligibility: Applicants must be high school seniors who live in an area where a sponsoring MFA agency is located. They must have plans to enroll full-time at an accredited college or university no later than September 1 of the application year. Selection is based on character, extracurricular activities and financial need.

Target applicant(s): High school students.

Amount: $2,000.

Number of awards: About 300.

Deadline: February 15.

How to apply: Applications are available by request from the applicant's high school counselor. An application form and supporting materials are required.

Exclusive: Visit www.UltimateScholarshipBook.com and enter code MF164923 for updates on this award.

(1650) · Michael Curry Summer Internship Program

Governor's Office of the State of Illinois Michael Curry Summer Internship Program
207 State House, Springfield, IL 62706
https://www2.illinois.gov/sites/gov/Pages/default.aspx
Purpose: To provide internships for college juniors, seniors or graduate students.

Eligibility: Applicants must be Illinois residents. Recipients work full-time in an agency under the jurisdiction of the Governor for 10 weeks during the summer.

Target applicant(s): College students. Graduate school students. Adult students.

Amount: $1,346 stipend.

Number of awards: Varies.

Deadline: April 30.

How to apply: Applications are available online or by mail.

Exclusive: Visit www.UltimateScholarshipBook.com and enter code GO165023 for updates on this award.

(1651) · Michigan Competitive Scholarship

Michigan Student Aid
Student Scholarships and Grants, P.O. Box 30462, Lansing, MI 48909-7962
Phone: 888-447-2687
Email: ssg@michigan.gov
http://www.michigan.gov/mistudentaid/
Purpose: To assist students who plan to attend a Michigan public or private college.

Eligibility: Applicants must be Michigan residents since July 1 of the previous calendar year and have received a qualifying score on the ACT and a minimum 2.0 GPA. Applicants must also demonstrate financial need and be enrolled in an approved Michigan college or university. Applicants cannot be pursuing a degree in theology, divinity or religious education. This award is based on both financial need and academic merit.

Target applicant(s): High school students. College students. Adult students.

Minimum GPA: 2.0

Amount: Varies.

Number of awards: Varies.

Scholarship may be renewable.

Deadline: March 1.

How to apply: File a Free Application for Federal Student Aid (FAFSA).

Exclusive: Visit www.UltimateScholarshipBook.com and enter code MI165123 for updates on this award.

(1652) · Michigan Council of Women in Technology University Scholarship

Michigan Council of Women in Technology Foundation
Attn.: Scholarship Committee, One Towne Square, Suite 690, Southfield, MI 48076
Phone: 248-218-2578
Email: scholarships@mcwt.org
https://mcwt.org/programs/list/University-Initiatives/Scholarship-Program
Purpose: To support female information technology students.

Eligibility: Applicants must be high school seniors or undergraduate or graduate students who are Michigan residents and U.S. citizens with a GPA of 3.0 or higher. Students must be enrolled in a full-time undergraduate or graduate degree program in a major such

as information systems, computer science, computer engineering, software engineering, computer information systems, digital forensics or software engineering. (Note: This is not a complete list.) Applicants must maintain program requirements and will be subject to verification.
Target applicant(s): High school students. College students. Graduate school students. Adult students.
Minimum GPA: 3.0
Amount: Varies.
Number of awards: Varies.
Scholarship may be renewable.
Deadline: January 31.
How to apply: Applications are available online. An application form, transcript, two letters of recommendation and research project description (for research grant applicants only) are required.
Exclusive: Visit www.UltimateScholarshipBook.com and enter code MI165223 for updates on this award.

(1653) · Michigan Engineering Scholarships
Michigan Society of Professional Engineers
P.O. Box 15276, Lansing, MI 48901-5276
Phone: 517-487-9388
Email: Scholarship@MichiganSPE.org
https://www.michiganspe.org/scholarships/
Purpose: To aid Michigan students who are planning to pursue an undergraduate degree in engineering.
Eligibility: Applicants must be U.S. citizens, residents of Michigan and high school seniors. They must be accepted at an ABET-accredited college or university in Michigan and must have plans to pursue a degree in engineering. Students must have a GPA of 3.0 or higher for both the 10th and 11th grade years and a minimum composite ACT score of 26 or higher. Selection is based on GPA, ACT score, personal essay, extracurricular activities, any college-level coursework completed and honors received.
Target applicant(s): High school students.
Minimum GPA: 3.0
Amount: Varies.
Number of awards: Varies.
Deadline: February 19.
How to apply: Applications are available online. An application form, personal essay and official transcript are required.
Exclusive: Visit www.UltimateScholarshipBook.com and enter code MI165323 for updates on this award.

(1654) · Michigan Oratorical Contest
American Legion, Department of Michigan
212 N. Verlinden Avenue, Ste. A, Lansing, MI 48915
Phone: 517-371-4720 x11
Email: programs@michiganlegion.org
http://www.michiganlegion.org
Purpose: To enhance high school students' experience with and understanding of the U.S. Constitution. The contest will help develop students' leadership skills and civic appreciation, as well as the ability to deliver thoughtful, insightful orations regarding U.S. citizenship and its inherent responsibilities.
Eligibility: Applicants must be high school students under the age of 20 who are U.S. citizens or legal residents and residents of the state. Students first give an oration within their state and winners compete at the national level. The oration must be related to the Constitution of the United States focusing on the duties and obligations citizens have to the government. It must be in English and be between eight and ten

minutes. There is also an assigned topic which is posted on the website, and it should be between three and five minutes.
Target applicant(s): High school students.
Amount: Up to $1,500.
Number of awards: Varies.
Deadline: November 12.
How to apply: Application information is available online under the link "Forms and Applications."
Exclusive: Visit www.UltimateScholarshipBook.com and enter code AM165423 for updates on this award.

(1655) · Michigan Tuition Grant
Michigan Student Aid
Student Scholarships and Grants, P.O. Box 30462, Lansing, MI 48909-7962
Phone: 888-447-2687
Email: ssg@michigan.gov
http://www.michigan.gov/mistudentaid/
Purpose: To assist Michigan students who are pursuing higher education in Michigan.
Eligibility: Applicants must be U.S. citizens, permanent residents or approved refugees. They must be Michigan residents who have lived there since at least July 1 of the previous calendar year and must be undergraduate students who are attending an approved Michigan college or university at least part-time. They must demonstrate financial need and not be in default on a federal student loan. Applicants who are pursuing degrees in divinity, theology or religious education are ineligible. Selection is based on financial need.
Target applicant(s): College students. Adult students.
Amount: Up to full tuition.
Number of awards: Varies.
Scholarship may be renewable.
Deadline: March 1.
How to apply: Application is made by filing the FAFSA.
Exclusive: Visit www.UltimateScholarshipBook.com and enter code MI165523 for updates on this award.

(1656) · Michigan Tuition Incentive Program
Michigan Department of Treasury
P.O. Box 30462, Lansing, MI 48909
Phone: 888-447-2687
Email: osg@michigan.gov
http://www.michigan.gov/
Purpose: To encourage Michigan students to complete high school and seek higher education.
Eligibility: Applicants must be upcoming high school graduates or GED recipients under the age of 20 and also must have received Medicaid for 24 months in a 36 month period after their 12th birthday. Qualifying students will receive an acceptance form, which must be returned to the Office of Scholarships and Grants to become eligible. The program covers tuition and mandatory fees for students pursuing an associate degree and up to $2,000 for studies in pursuit of a four-year degree.
Target applicant(s): High school students.
Amount: Up to full tuition.
Number of awards: Varies.
Scholarship may be renewable.
Deadline: Varies.
How to apply: Applications are available from the Michigan Department of Human Services.
Exclusive: Visit www.UltimateScholarshipBook.com and enter code MI165623 for updates on this award.

(1657) · Middle School Essay Contest

American Legion, Department of Virginia
1708 Commonwealth Avenue, Richmond, VA 23230
Phone: 804-353-6606
http://www.valegion.org
Purpose: To promote citizenship in young Virginia students.
Eligibility: Applicants must be middle school students and write an essay on an assigned topic. The essay should be written at the student's desk during school time and will be evaluated based on originality, sincerity and the student's ability to communicate meaning.
Target applicant(s): Junior high students or younger.
Amount: Up to $500.
Number of awards: Varies.
Deadline: December 18.
How to apply: Applications are available online and from sponsoring Posts.
Exclusive: Visit www.UltimateScholarshipBook.com and enter code AM165723 for updates on this award.

(1658) · Midwest Student Exchange Program

Midwestern Higher Education Compact
105 Fifth Avenue South, Suite 450, Minneapolis, MN 55401
Phone: 612-677-2777
Email: msep@mhec.org
http://msep.mhec.org
Purpose: The program aims to increase higher education options for Midwestern students and families within the region.
Eligibility: Applicants must currently live in Illinois, Indiana, Kansas, Minnesota, Missouri, Nebraska, North Dakota, Ohio or Wisconsin and wish to attend a participating school in one of these states outside their own. Other eligibility requirements vary depending on the state and school. Awards are tuition reduction for out-of-state schools in the participating region.
Target applicant(s): High school students. College students. Graduate school students. Adult students.
Amount: Varies.
Number of awards: Varies.
Scholarship may be renewable.
Deadline: Varies.
How to apply: Students must clearly mark that they are an MSEP student when applying to the school of their choice.
Exclusive: Visit www.UltimateScholarshipBook.com and enter code MI165823 for updates on this award.

(1659) · Mikkelson Foundation Scholarship

Mikkelson Foundation
P.O. Box 768, Monument, CO 80132
http://mikkelsonfoundation.org
Purpose: To support graduating seniors of Colorado in pursuing a degree in engineering, physical or biological sciences or mathematics.
Eligibility: Applicants must have a minimum GPA of 3.7 and a minimum SAT score of 1200 or a minimum ACT score of 28. Students must submit three letters of recommendation, official transcripts and a personal essay.
Target applicant(s): High school students.
Minimum GPA: 3.7
Amount: $3,000.
Number of awards: 2.
Deadline: April 16.
How to apply: Applications are available online.

Exclusive: Visit www.UltimateScholarshipBook.com and enter code MI165923 for updates on this award.

(1660) · Mildred Towle Scholarship - Study Abroad

Hawaii Community Foundation - Scholarships
827 Fort Street Mall, Honolulu, HI 96813
Phone: 888-731-3863
Email: scholarships@hcf-hawaii.org
https://www.hawaiicommunityfoundation.org/
Purpose: To support Hawaii students who plan to study abroad.
Eligibility: Applicants must study abroad as a junior, senior or graduate student. Students must have at least a 3.0 GPA. Preference will be given to applicants pursuing studies in the social sciences regarding international understanding and interracial fellowship. Applicants must prove financial need.
Target applicant(s): College students. Graduate school students. Adult students.
Minimum GPA: 3.0
Amount: Varies.
Number of awards: Varies.
Deadline: January 31.
How to apply: To apply, register online, complete the online application and select the scholarships to which you wish to apply. In addition, mail the supporting materials: printed confirmation page from the online application, personal statement, copy of Student Aid Report (SAR) available at www.fafsa.ed.gov and official transcript.
Exclusive: Visit www.UltimateScholarshipBook.com and enter code HA166023 for updates on this award.

(1661) · Mildred Towle Scholarship for African-Americans

Hawaii Community Foundation - Scholarships
827 Fort Street Mall, Honolulu, HI 96813
Phone: 888-731-3863
Email: scholarships@hcf-hawaii.org
https://www.hawaiicommunityfoundation.org/
Purpose: To support African American students who are attending colleges in Hawaii.
Eligibility: Students must have at least a 3.0 GPA.
Target applicant(s): High school students. College students. Adult students.
Minimum GPA: 3.0
Amount: Varies.
Number of awards: Varies.
Deadline: January 31.
How to apply: To apply, register online, complete the online application and select the scholarships to which you wish to apply. In addition, mail the supporting materials: printed confirmation page from the online application, personal statement, copy of Student Aid Report (SAR) available at www.fafsa.ed.gov and official transcript.
Exclusive: Visit www.UltimateScholarshipBook.com and enter code HA166123 for updates on this award.

(1662) · Milton Fisher Scholarship for Innovation and Creativity

Milton Fisher Scholarship for Innovation and Creativity
Renee B. Fisher Foundation, c/o Community Foundation for Greater New Haven, 70 Audubon Street, 5th Floor, New Haven, CT 06510
Phone: 203-777-2386
Email: info@mfscholarship.org

http://mfscholarship.org/

Purpose: To reward and encourage innovative problem solving.

Eligibility: Applicants must be high school juniors or seniors or must be entering or in the first year of an undergraduate degree program. Students must be Connecticut or New York City residents who attend or plan to attend an institution in the U.S. or students who attend or plan to attend a Connecticut or New York City institution of higher learning. Students must have come up with a solution to a problem faced by their school, community or family; solve an artistic, scientific or technical problem or develop a new group that serves an important need.

Target applicant(s): High school students. College students. Adult students.

Amount: Up to $20,000.

Number of awards: 8-10.

Scholarship may be renewable.

Deadline: May 3.

How to apply: Applications are available online.

Exclusive: Visit www.UltimateScholarshipBook.com and enter code MI166223 for updates on this award.

(1663) · Minnesota Academic Excellence Scholarship

Minnesota Office of Higher Education Services
1450 Energy Park Drive, Suite 350, Saint Paul, MN 55108-5227
Phone: 651-642-0567
Email: meghan.flores@state.mn.us
http://www.ohe.state.mn.us/

Purpose: To help students who have demonstrated outstanding ability, achievement and potential in selected areas of study.

Eligibility: Applicants must be Minnesota residents who have been admitted to a full-time program in an approved Minnesota college or university. Applicants must have demonstrated achievement in one of the following subjects: English or creative writing, fine arts, foreign language, math, science or social science.

Target applicant(s): High school students. College students. Adult students.

Amount: Up to full tuition.

Number of awards: Varies.

Scholarship may be renewable.

Deadline: Varies.

How to apply: For information about the status of this program, applicants should contact the schools they wish to attend.

Exclusive: Visit www.UltimateScholarshipBook.com and enter code MI166323 for updates on this award.

(1664) · Minnesota Division Izaak Walton League Scholarship

Izaak Walton League of America-Minnesota Division
2233 University Avenue West, Suite 339, St. Paul, MN 55114
Phone: 651-221-0215
Email: ikes@minnesotaikes.org
http://www.minnesotaikes.org

Purpose: To aid Minnesota residents who are studying environmental or conservation subjects in college.

Eligibility: Applicants must be U.S. citizens and Minnesota residents. They must be in the second year or higher of a college degree program in environmental science, environmental education, conservation, environmental law, wildlife management or a related subject. Selection is based on academic merit and financial need.

Target applicant(s): College students. Adult students.

Amount: Up to $1,000.

Number of awards: Varies.

Deadline: May 1.

How to apply: Applications are available online. An application form, transcript, personal essay, resume and two letters of recommendation are required.

Exclusive: Visit www.UltimateScholarshipBook.com and enter code IZ166423 for updates on this award.

(1665) · Minnesota Hockey Scholarship

Minnesota Hockey
Executive Director, Minnesota Hockey Scholarship Committee, 317 Washington Street, St. Paul, MN 55102
Phone: 651-602-5727
Email: info@minnesotahockey.org
http://www.minnesotahockey.org

Purpose: To support hockey students who wish to further their education beyond high school.

Eligibility: Applicants must be a resident of Minnesota, a high school senior, participate on a youth Junior Gold team or a girl's 19 and under team of an affiliate association of Minnesota Hockey and have a minimum GPA of 2.0. Selection is based on academic achievement, a personal essay and the letters of recommendation.

Target applicant(s): High school students.

Minimum GPA: 2.0

Amount: $1,000.

Number of awards: Varies.

Deadline: March 26.

How to apply: Applications are available online.

Exclusive: Visit www.UltimateScholarshipBook.com and enter code MI166523 for updates on this award.

(1666) · Minnesota Indian Scholarship Program

Minnesota Office of Higher Education Services
1450 Energy Park Drive, Suite 350, Saint Paul, MN 55108-5227
Phone: 651-642-0567
Email: meghan.flores@state.mn.us
http://www.ohe.state.mn.us/

Purpose: To provide money to help Native American students pay for higher education.

Eligibility: Applicants must be at least one-fourth Native American, Minnesota residents and members of a federally recognized Indian tribe. Applicants must be a high school graduate or possess a GED and have been accepted by an approved college, university or vocational school in Minnesota.

Target applicant(s): High school students. College students. Graduate school students. Adult students.

Amount: Up to $6,000.

Number of awards: Varies.

Scholarship may be renewable.

Deadline: July 1.

How to apply: This award is administered by the Minnesota Department of Children, Families, and Learning (CFL), and must be approved by the Minnesota Indian Scholarship Committee. To receive an application, contact your local tribal education office.

Exclusive: Visit www.UltimateScholarshipBook.com and enter code MI166623 for updates on this award.

(1667) · Minnesota Oratorical Contest

American Legion, Department of Minnesota
Third Floor, Veterans Service Building, 20 W. 12th Street, Room 300A, St. Paul, MN 55155
Phone: 651-291-1800
Email: department@mnlegion.org
http://www.mnlegion.org
Purpose: To enhance high school students' experience with and understanding of the U.S. Constitution. The contest will help develop students' leadership skills and civic appreciation, as well as the ability to deliver thoughtful, insightful orations regarding U.S. citizenship and its inherent responsibilities.
Eligibility: Applicants must be high school students under the age of 20 who are U.S. citizens or legal residents and residents of the state. Students first give an oration within their state and winners compete at the national level. The oration must be related to the Constitution of the United States focusing on the duties and obligations citizens have to the government. It must be in English and be between eight and ten minutes. There is also an assigned topic which is posted on the website, and it should be between three and five minutes.
Target applicant(s): High school students.
Amount: Up to $1,500.
Number of awards: 4.
Deadline: February.
How to apply: Application information is available by email.
Exclusive: Visit www.UltimateScholarshipBook.com and enter code AM166723 for updates on this award.

(1668) · Minnesota State Grant

Minnesota Office of Higher Education Services
1450 Energy Park Drive, Suite 350, Saint Paul, MN 55108-5227
Phone: 651-642-0567
Email: meghan.flores@state.mn.us
http://www.ohe.state.mn.us/
Purpose: To aid Minnesota students who are pursuing higher education in Minnesota.
Eligibility: Applicants must be U.S. citizens or permanent residents who are Minnesota residents. They must be high school graduates, GED recipients or at least 17 years old by the end of the academic year. They must be enrolled in a diploma, certificate or degree program for at least three credits at an eligible Minnesota school. Applicants who are in default of a federal or state SELF student loan are ineligible, as are those who owe the Office of Higher Education for the overpayment of a state grant. They cannot have earned a baccalaureate degree previously or be more than 30 days past due on child support payments. Selection is based on financial need.
Target applicant(s): High school students. College students. Adult students.
Amount: Up to $11,753.
Number of awards: Varies.
Scholarship may be renewable.
Deadline: Varies.
How to apply: Application is made by filing the FAFSA.
Exclusive: Visit www.UltimateScholarshipBook.com and enter code MI166823 for updates on this award.

(1669) · Minority Scholarship

Ohio News Media Foundation
1335 Dublin Road, Suite 216-B, Columbus, OH 43215
Phone: 614-486-6677
Email: ariggs@ohionews.org
https://www.ohionews.org/aws/ONA/pt/sp/foundation
Purpose: To support minority graduating high school seniors from Ohio who are pursuing a degree in a journalism-related field at an Ohio college or university.
Eligibility: Applicants must be African American, Hispanic, Asian American or American Indian high school students graduating from an Ohio high school and must be enrolled at an Ohio college or university for the upcoming fall. Students must have at least a 2.5 GPA and be majoring in a journalism-related field such as journalism, advertising or marketing. Applicants must write an autobiography as part of their essay, must get recommendations and may submit work samples.
Target applicant(s): High school students.
Minimum GPA: 2.5
Amount: $750.
Number of awards: 1.
Deadline: May 24.
How to apply: Applications are available online.
Exclusive: Visit www.UltimateScholarshipBook.com and enter code OH166923 for updates on this award.

(1670) · Mississippi Association of Broadcasters Scholarship Program

Mississippi Association of Broadcasters
Scholarship Committee, 855 S Pear Orchard Road, Suite 403, Ridgeland, MS 39157
Phone: 601-957-9121
Email: info@msbroadcasters.org
http://www.msbroadcasters.org/about-us/scholarships
Purpose: To support students involved in broadcasting.
Eligibility: Applicants must be Mississippi residents and be enrolled in an accredited broadcast curriculum at a Mississippi two- or four-year college.
Target applicant(s): College students. Adult students.
Amount: Varies.
Number of awards: Varies.
Deadline: March 1.
How to apply: Applications are available online. An application form, essay and up to three letters of recommendation are required.
Exclusive: Visit www.UltimateScholarshipBook.com and enter code MI167023 for updates on this award.

(1671) · Mississippi Eminent Scholars Grant (MESG)

Mississippi Office of Student Financial Aid
3825 Ridgewood Road, Jackson, MS 39211
Phone: 800-327-2980
Email: sfa@ihl.state.ms.us
https://www.msfinancialaid.org/
Purpose: To recognize academically high performing Mississippi students.
Eligibility: Applicants must be U.S. citizens or eligible noncitizens and current legal residents of Mississippi who are enrolled as full-time, first-time-in-college undergraduates. Applicants must have a high school GPA of 3.5 and a minimum ACT of 29. National Merit/National Achievement semifinalists with a 3.5 grade point average qualify without the test score.
Target applicant(s): High school students.
Minimum GPA: 3.5
Amount: $2,500.
Number of awards: Varies.

Scholarship may be renewable.
Deadline: September 15.
How to apply: Applicants must complete an MTAG/MESG application and either a FAFSA or a Statement of Certification (a waiver for completing the FAFSA).
Exclusive: Visit www.UltimateScholarshipBook.com and enter code MI167123 for updates on this award.

(1672) · Mississippi Scholarship

American Radio Relay League Foundation
225 Main Street, Newington, CT 06111-1494
Phone: 860-594-0348
Email: foundation@arrl.org
http://www.arrl.org/scholarship-program
Purpose: To provide financial assistance to Mississippi students who are amateur radio operators and are studying electronics or communications.
Eligibility: Applicants must be licensed amateur radio operators and residents of Mississippi who attend an institution of higher learning in Mississippi. They must be seeking a bachelor's degree or higher in electronics, communication or a related field, and they must be under 30 years old.
Target applicant(s): High school students. College students. Graduate school students. Adult students.
Amount: $500.
Number of awards: 1.
Deadline: December 31.
How to apply: Applications are available online.
Exclusive: Visit www.UltimateScholarshipBook.com and enter code AM167223 for updates on this award.

(1673) · Mississippi Tuition Assistance Grant (MTAG)

Mississippi Office of Student Financial Aid
3825 Ridgewood Road, Jackson, MS 39211
Phone: 800-327-2980
Email: sfa@ihl.state.ms.us
https://www.msfinancialaid.org/
Purpose: To assist financially needy Mississippi students to afford tuition.
Eligibility: Applicants must be current legal residents of Mississippi who are enrolled as full-time undergraduates. Applicants must have a high school grade-point average of 2.5 and a minimum ACT of 15.
Target applicant(s): High school students. College students. Adult students.
Minimum GPA: 2.5
Amount: $500-$1,000.
Number of awards: Varies.
Scholarship may be renewable.
Deadline: September 15.
How to apply: Applicants must complete an MTAG/MESG application and either a FAFSA or a Statement of Certification (a waiver for completing the FAFSA).
Exclusive: Visit www.UltimateScholarshipBook.com and enter code MI167323 for updates on this award.

(1674) · Missouri 4-H Foundation Scholarships

Missouri 4-H Foundation
109 Whitten Hall, Columbia, MO 65211
Phone: 573-882-2680
Email: 4hfoundation@missouri.edu
https://extension.missouri.edu/programs/missouri-4-h-foundation/scholarships
Purpose: To aid present and former Missouri 4-H members who are preparing for careers in veterinary medicine and animal science.
Eligibility: Applicants must be Missouri residents who are present or former members of 4-H and who are rising undergraduate freshmen. They must have a GPA of 2.5 or higher on a four-point scale. Selection is based on 4-H achievements, stated career goals and financial need.
Target applicant(s): High school students.
Minimum GPA: 2.5
Amount: $500-$2,500.
Number of awards: 6.
Deadline: March.
How to apply: Applications are available online. An application form, transcript, financial information and essay are required.
Exclusive: Visit www.UltimateScholarshipBook.com and enter code MI167423 for updates on this award.

(1675) · Missouri Oratorical Contest

American Legion, Department of Missouri
P.O. Box 179, Jefferson City, MO 65102
Phone: 800-846-9023
Email: bmayberry@missourilegion.org
http://www.missourilegion.org/
Purpose: To enhance high school students' experience with and understanding of the U.S. Constitution. The contest will help develop students' leadership skills and civic appreciation, as well as the ability to deliver thoughtful, insightful orations regarding U.S. citizenship and its inherent responsibilities.
Eligibility: Applicants must be high school students under the age of 20 who are U.S. citizens or legal residents and residents of the state. Students first give an oration within their state and winners compete at the national level. The oration must be related to the Constitution of the United States focusing on the duties and obligations citizens have to the government. It must be in English and be between eight and ten minutes. There is also an assigned topic which is posted on the website, and it should be between three and five minutes.
Target applicant(s): High school students.
Amount: $1,400-$18,000.
Number of awards: Varies.
Deadline: November 30.
How to apply: Application information is available by email.
Exclusive: Visit www.UltimateScholarshipBook.com and enter code AM167523 for updates on this award.

(1676) · Missouri State Thespian Scholarships

Missouri State Thespians
Attn.: Jennifer Forrest-James, 419 Sorrento Drive, Ballwin, MO 63021
Email: mstscholarships@gmail.com
http://missourithespians.org/
Purpose: To support young Missouri thespians.
Eligibility: Applicants must be high school seniors, International Thespians members and delegates to the conference. Students must have a GPA of 2.5 or higher and audition in the category of performance, technical or theatre education.
Target applicant(s): High school students.
Minimum GPA: 2.5
Amount: Varies.
Number of awards: Varies.
Deadline: November.

How to apply: Applications are available online. An application form is required.
Exclusive: Visit www.UltimateScholarshipBook.com and enter code MI167623 for updates on this award.

(1677) · Mitcheli Scholarship

Mitchell Institute
75 Washington Avenue, Suite 2E, Portland, ME 04101
Phone: 207-773-7700
Email: info@mitchellinstitute.org
http://mitchellinstitute.org/scholarship/
Purpose: To provide educational opportunities to students in Maine.
Eligibility: Applicants must be legal residents of Maine graduating from a public high school in Maine and attending a two- or four-year program at an accredited college. Scholarships are based on academic performance, community service and financial need. One scholarship is given out at every Maine public high school, with one extra scholarship per county intended for first-generation college students. While the deadline for the application is April 1, supporting materials have a deadline of May 1.
Target applicant(s): High school students.
Amount: $2,500-$10,000.
Number of awards: 135.
Scholarship may be renewable.
Deadline: April 1.
How to apply: Applications are available online.
Exclusive: Visit www.UltimateScholarshipBook.com and enter code MI167723 for updates on this award.

(1678) · Monetary Award Program (MAP)

Illinois Department of Public Health
Center for Rural Health, 535 West Jefferson Street, Springfield, IL 62761
Phone: 217-782-1624
Email: dph.nesp@illinois.gov
http://www.dph.illinois.gov
Purpose: To provide grants to eligible Illinois undergraduate students.
Eligibility: Applicants must be residents of Illinois, enrolled at a MAP-approved Illinois institution and carry a minimum of three hours per term. Applicants must also demonstrate financial need and maintain satisfactory academic progress.
Target applicant(s): High school students. College students. Adult students.
Amount: Varies.
Number of awards: Varies.
Scholarship may be renewable.
Deadline: October 1.
How to apply: Complete the Free Application for Federal Student Aid (FAFSA).
Exclusive: Visit www.UltimateScholarshipBook.com and enter code IL167823 for updates on this award.

(1679) · Montana CattleWomen Scholarship

Montana CattleWomen Inc.
420 N. California, Helena, MT 59601
Phone: 406-442-3420
Email: lorrie@mtbeef.org
https://montanacattlewomen.org/resources
Purpose: To support a Montana university or college student whose major field of study benefits the livestock industry.

Eligibility: Applicants must be from Montana and currently enrolled as a sophomore or higher in an accredited university or college in Montana. Students must have a cumulative grade point average of 2.7 or more and demonstrate a need for financial assistance. Selection is based on demonstrated need and student's potential to benefit the livestock industry. Preference is given to students from an agriculture background and/or members or children of members of Montana CattleWomen.
Target applicant(s): College students. Adult students.
Minimum GPA: 2.7
Amount: $1,000.
Number of awards: 1.
Deadline: May 14.
How to apply: Application instructions are available online. A personal resume, academic resume, high school and college transcripts, essay, applicant photo, photo of family living situation and three recommendation letters are required.
Exclusive: Visit www.UltimateScholarshipBook.com and enter code MO167923 for updates on this award.

(1680) · Montana University System Honor Scholarship

Montana University System
Student Financial Services (SFS), Scholarship Department, P.O. Box 203101, Helena, MT 59620-3201
Phone: 800-537-7508
https://mus.edu/Prepare/Pay/Scholarships/
Purpose: To reward Montana high school seniors with outstanding academic achievement.
Eligibility: Applicants must have a 3.4 or higher GPA, meet specific college preparatory requirements and have been enrolled in an accredited Montana high school for at least three years prior to graduation, including their senior year. Applicants must also be accepted to and attend a Montana public university or community college.
Target applicant(s): High school students.
Minimum GPA: 3.4
Amount: Up to full tuition.
Number of awards: Up to 200.
Scholarship may be renewable.
Deadline: March 15.
How to apply: Applications are available from your high school guidance counselor.
Exclusive: Visit www.UltimateScholarshipBook.com and enter code MO168023 for updates on this award.

(1681) · Moody Scholar Program

Moody Foundation
600 North Pearl Street, Suite 2165, Dallas, TX 75201
https://moodyf.org/moody-scholars/
Purpose: To support students enrolled in a Texas college.
Eligibility: Applicants must be ranked in the top 25 percent of their graduating class. Award is renewable for up to four years of undergraduate work. Evidence of financial need is required.
Target applicant(s): High school students. College students. Adult students.
Minimum GPA: 3.0
Amount: $4,000.
Number of awards: 50.
Scholarship may be renewable.
Deadline: December.
How to apply: Applications are available online.

Exclusive: Visit www.UltimateScholarshipBook.com and enter code MO168123 for updates on this award.

(1682) · MSAA Scholarship Program

Minnesota State Archery Association
c/o Cheri Irlbeck, MSAA Secretary, 33266 County Hwy 4, Sanborn, MN 56083
Phone: 507-640-1683
Email: secretary.msaa@mnarchery.org
http://www.mnarchery.org
Purpose: To promote the sport of archery and encourage outstanding students to attend the college of their choice.
Eligibility: Students must apply as a senior in high school or within the first three years of college. The applicant must be a Minnesota State Archery Association member in good standing.
Target applicant(s): High school students. College students. Adult students.
Amount: $500.
Number of awards: 2.
Deadline: June 15.
How to apply: Applications are available online.
Exclusive: Visit www.UltimateScholarshipBook.com and enter code MI168223 for updates on this award.

(1683) · MSPE Kenneth B. Fishbeck, P.E., Memorial Grant

Michigan Society of Professional Engineers
P.O. Box 15276, Lansing, MI 48901-5276
Phone: 517-487-9388
Email: Scholarship@MichiganSPE.org
https://www.michiganspe.org/scholarships/
Purpose: To aid Michigan students who are planning to pursue higher education in engineering.
Eligibility: Applicants must be high school seniors who are Michigan residents and U.S. citizens. They must have a GPA of 3.0 or higher for the sophomore and junior years of high school and a composite ACT score of 26 or higher. Students must be accepted into a Michigan institution of higher learning that has an ABET-accredited engineering degree program. Selection is based on personal essay, awards and recognitions, GPA, ACT scores and any college-level coursework that has been completed.
Target applicant(s): High school students.
Minimum GPA: 3.0
Amount: Varies.
Number of awards: Varies.
Deadline: February.
How to apply: Applications are available online. An application form, transcript, personal essay and ACT score report are required.
Exclusive: Visit www.UltimateScholarshipBook.com and enter code MI168323 for updates on this award.

(1684) · Music Committee Scholarship

American Legion, Department of Kansas
1314 SW Topeka Boulevard, Topeka, KS 66612
Phone: 785-232-9315
https://ksamlegion.org/
Purpose: To support Kansas students who have distinguished themselves in the field of music.
Eligibility: Applicants must be Kansas residents who are currently high school seniors or college freshmen or sophomores. They must have a

proven talent and background in music and be planning to major or minor in music at an approved Kansas post-secondary institution. Applicants must also be average or better students. Three letters of recommendation with only one from a music teacher, a 1040 income statement, a high school transcript and a statement describing why they are applying for the scholarship are required. The scholarship will be awarded in two installments; recipients must maintain a C average to receive the second installment.
Target applicant(s): High school students. College students. Adult students.
Amount: $1,000.
Number of awards: 1.
Deadline: February 15.
How to apply: Applications are available online.
Exclusive: Visit www.UltimateScholarshipBook.com and enter code AM168423 for updates on this award.

(1685) · My Action Plan for College Young Scholars Initiative

My Action Plan for College
P.O. Box 121, Hull, MA 02045
Phone: 508-631-0936
Email: ernest@mapforcollege.com
http://www.mapforcollege.com/scholarships.html
Purpose: To support 8th graders who plan to attend college.
Eligibility: Students must be current eighth graders with a goal to attend college one day. Applicants must submit a 250-300 word hand-written essay including the topics of academic and extra-curricular plans for college. Selection is based on the overall strength of the application.
Target applicant(s): Junior high students or younger.
Amount: $125-$750.
Number of awards: 6.
Deadline: August 31.
How to apply: Essays should be submitted by mail.
Exclusive: Visit www.UltimateScholarshipBook.com and enter code MY168523 for updates on this award.

(1686) · NACA Mid Atlantic Undergraduate Scholarship for Student Leaders

National Association for Campus Activities
13 Harbison Way, Columbia, SC 29212
Phone: 803-732-6222
Email: info@naca.org
https://www.naca.org/FOUNDATION/Pages/Scholarships.aspx
Purpose: To provide financial assistance to East Coast student leaders.
Eligibility: Students must hold a significant campus leadership position, demonstrate significant leadership skills and abilities and make significant contributions through on- or off-campus volunteering. Students must attend school in Delaware, New Jersey, Maryland, New York, eastern Pennsylvania or Washington, DC.
Target applicant(s): College students. Adult students.
Minimum GPA: 2.5
Amount: Varies.
Number of awards: 2.
Deadline: November 30.
How to apply: Applications are available online. Only the first 75 applicants are considered.
Exclusive: Visit www.UltimateScholarshipBook.com and enter code NA168623 for updates on this award.

(1687) · NACA Northern Plains Regional Student Leadership Scholarship

National Association for Campus Activities
13 Harbison Way, Columbia, SC 29212
Phone: 803-732-6222
Email: info@naca.org
https://www.naca.org/FOUNDATION/Pages/Scholarships.aspx
Purpose: To help students who are working toward undergraduate or graduate degrees that lead to careers in student activities or services.
Eligibility: Applicants must be undergraduate or graduate students taking at least six credits per semester and be enrolled in or have previously earned a degree from a college or university in Wisconsin or the Upper Peninsula of Michigan. Applicants must also have demonstrated leadership and service to their campus community.
Target applicant(s): College students. Graduate school students. Adult students.
Amount: Varies.
Number of awards: Varies.
Deadline: November 30.
How to apply: Applications are available online.
Exclusive: Visit www.UltimateScholarshipBook.com and enter code NA168723 for updates on this award.

(1688) · NACA South Student Leadership Scholarships

National Association for Campus Activities
13 Harbison Way, Columbia, SC 29212
Phone: 803-732-6222
Email: info@naca.org
https://www.naca.org/FOUNDATION/Pages/Scholarships.aspx
Purpose: To provide financial assistance to Southeast student leaders.
Eligibility: Students must hold a significant campus leadership position, demonstrate significant leadership skills and abilities and make significant contributions through on- or off-campus volunteering. Students must attend school in Alabama, Florida, Georgia, Mississippi, North Carolina, South Carolina, Tennessee, Virginia or Puerto Rico.
Target applicant(s): College students. Adult students.
Amount: Varies.
Number of awards: Up to 4.
Deadline: November 30.
How to apply: Applications are available online.
Exclusive: Visit www.UltimateScholarshipBook.com and enter code NA168823 for updates on this award.

(1689) · NACE Sandia Mountain Section Scholarship

National Association of Corrosion Engineers (NACE) International Foundation
15835 Park Ten Place, Houston, TX 77084-5145
Phone: 281-228-6205
Email: nace.foundation@nace.org
http://nace-foundation.org/programs/students/scholarships/
Purpose: To aid students interested in the careers of corrosion and engineering.
Eligibility: Applicants must an undergraduate enrolled full-time at an accredited college or university located in one of two states in the San Juan Basin which include Colorado and New Mexico. Applicants must have a serious interest in pursuing full-time employment in the corrosion industry. Selection is based on the overall strength of the application.
Target applicant(s): College students. Adult students.
Amount: $2,500.
Number of awards: 1.

Deadline: January 1.
How to apply: Applications are available online. An application form, two recommendation forms, academic transcripts and essay scholarship questions are required.
Exclusive: Visit www.UltimateScholarshipBook.com and enter code NA168923 for updates on this award.

(1690) · NADCA Indiana Chapter 25 Scholarship

Foundry Educational Foundation
1695 North Penny Lane, Schaumburg, IL 60173
Phone: 847-490-9200
Email: info@fefinc.org
http://www.fefinc.org/scholarships.html
Purpose: To aid Indiana region students who have a demonstrated interest in the die cast and cast metal industries.
Eligibility: Applicants must be residents of Indiana or of a state that is adjacent to Indiana. They must be enrolled at an Indiana school or at a Foundry Educational Foundation (FEF) member school located in a state adjacent to Indiana. They must have prior work experience in manufacturing, the die casting industry or the cast metal industry. Preference will be given to applicants who are studying a subject related to the die casting industry. Selection is based on the overall strength of the application.
Target applicant(s): High school students. College students. Adult students.
Amount: Varies.
Number of awards: Varies.
Deadline: October 1.
How to apply: Applications are available online. An application form and supporting documents are required.
Exclusive: Visit www.UltimateScholarshipBook.com and enter code FO169023 for updates on this award.

(1691) · Nancy Penn Lyons Scholarship Fund

Community Foundation for Greater Atlanta Inc.
50 Hurt Plaza, Suite 449, Atlanta, GA 30303
Phone: 404-688-5525
Email: info@cfgreateratlanta.org
https://cfgreateratlanta.org/scholarships/
Purpose: To provide assistance to needy students who have been accepted to prestigious or out-of-state universities.
Eligibility: Applicants must be graduating high school seniors who have been Georgia residents for at least one year. They must have an ACT score of 22 or higher or an SAT composite score of 1000 or higher and a GPA of 3.0 or greater. They must have participated in community service and have financial need, and they must not be attending a public institution in the state of Georgia.
Target applicant(s): High school students.
Minimum GPA: 3.0
Amount: $5,000.
Number of awards: 5.
Scholarship may be renewable.
Deadline: January 22.
How to apply: Applications are available online.
Exclusive: Visit www.UltimateScholarshipBook.com and enter code CO169123 for updates on this award.

(1692) · Nathaniel A. Murray Scholarship

Alpha Phi Alpha Fraternity Inc.
Omicron Eta Lambda Chapter, P.O. Box 1844, Washington, DC 20013
http://www.ohlalpha1906.com
Purpose: To support graduating seniors of Washington, DC in pursuing post-secondary education.
Eligibility: A minimum GPA of 2.5 is required. Selection is primarily based on demonstration of leadership potential, excellent character and academic achievement.
Target applicant(s): High school students.
Minimum GPA: 2.5
Amount: Varies.
Number of awards: Varies.
Deadline: April 15.
How to apply: Applications are available online.
Exclusive: Visit www.UltimateScholarshipBook.com and enter code AL169223 for updates on this award.

(1693) · Nathaniel Alston Student Achievement Award

Pennsylvania Society of Physician Assistants
P.O. Box 128, Greensburg, PA 15601
Phone: 724-836-6411
Email: hohpac@windstream.net
https://pspa.net/
Purpose: To aid outstanding physician assistant students attending school in Pennsylvania.
Eligibility: Applicants must be current students in good standing who are enrolled in an accredited physician assistant program in the state of Pennsylvania. They must be current Pennsylvania Society of Physician Assistants (PSPA) members who demonstrate outstanding leadership and participation in their schools and communities. Selection is based on the overall strength of the application.
Target applicant(s): College students. Graduate school students. Adult students.
Amount: $2,000.
Number of awards: Varies.
Deadline: June 30.
How to apply: Applications are available online. An application form and personal essay are required.
Exclusive: Visit www.UltimateScholarshipBook.com and enter code PE169323 for updates on this award.

(1694) · NAWIC Granite State Chapter Scholarships

National Association of Women in Construction-Granite State Chapter #218
Attn: Peggy DeWever, 46 Heron Cove Road, Eliot, ME 03903
Phone: 603-659-4442
Email: nawic@nawic.org
https://www.nawic.org/nawic/NFSFScholarships.asp
Purpose: To aid New Hampshire students who are preparing for careers in the field of construction.
Eligibility: Applicants must be New Hampshire residents who are entering the second, third or fourth year of an undergraduate program in a construction-related subject. They must have a GPA of 2.0 or higher. Selection is based on the overall strength of the application.
Target applicant(s): College students. Adult students.
Minimum GPA: 2.0
Amount: Varies.

Number of awards: Varies.
Deadline: February 28.
How to apply: Instructions for how to apply are available online. A personal essay and transcript are required.
Exclusive: Visit www.UltimateScholarshipBook.com and enter code NA169423 for updates on this award.

(1695) · NCRA Scholarship

North Carolina Racquetball Association (NCRA)
195 Hill Lane, Sneads Ferry, NC 28460
Phone: 910-327-4441
Email: ncra@ncracquetball.com
http://www.ncracquetball.com
Purpose: To support those NCRA junior racquetball participants who wish to pursue higher education after high school.
Eligibility: Applicants must be NCRA members in good standing, be a senior in high school or a college undergraduate and have a "B" overall grade point average.
Target applicant(s): High school students. College students. Adult students.
Minimum GPA: 3.0
Amount: $500.
Number of awards: 4.
Deadline: June 15.
How to apply: Applications are available online or by calling the NCRA office. The application includes a release form, at least one letter of reference, the teacher report form, a personal essay, an official transcript and a photo.
Exclusive: Visit www.UltimateScholarshipBook.com and enter code NO169523 for updates on this award.

(1696) · NDVA Waiver of Tuition

Nebraska Department of Veterans' Affairs
State Service Office, 3800 Village Drive, P.O. Box 85816, Lincoln, NE 68501-5816
Phone: 402-420-4021
Email: ndva@nebraska.gov
https://veterans.nebraska.gov/
Purpose: To provide assistance to children and spouses of Nebraska veterans.
Eligibility: Applicants must be the children, stepchildren, spouses or widows of veterans who died of a service-connected injury or illness, became totally and permanently disabled as a result of military service or was classified as MIA or POW during armed conflict after August 4th, 1964. They must be Nebraska residents and attend a state college, university or community college.
Target applicant(s): High school students. College students. Adult students.
Amount: Full tuition.
Number of awards: Varies.
Scholarship may be renewable.
Deadline: Prior to the start of any term.
How to apply: Applications are available from your County Veterans Service Officer.
Exclusive: Visit www.UltimateScholarshipBook.com and enter code NE169623 for updates on this award.

(1697) · Nebraska Academy of Sciences High School Scholarships

Nebraska Academy of Sciences Inc.
P.O. Box 22988, Lincoln, NE 68542-2988
Phone: 402-472-2644
Email: nebacad@unl.edu
https://nebraskaacademyofsciences.wildapricot.org/Scholarships
Purpose: To assist Nebraska high school students.
Eligibility: There are six scholarships given to Nebraska high school seniors including those who plan to study geology, earth sciences, prairie and soil conservation, climate and environmental change and business and the environment.
Target applicant(s): High school students.
Amount: $300-$1,500.
Number of awards: Varies.
Deadline: March 1.
How to apply: Applications are available online. Requirements vary by the individual award.
Exclusive: Visit www.UltimateScholarshipBook.com and enter code NE169723 for updates on this award.

(1698) · Nebraska Actuaries Club Scholarship

Nebraska Actuaries Club
c/o Laura Huscroft, Enterprise Risk Management, Mutual of Omaha, 3301 Dodge Street, Omaha, NE 68131
Email: Laura.Huscroft@MutualofOmaha.com
http://n-a-c.org/
Purpose: To aid Nebraska students who plan to major in actuarial science or a related subject.
Eligibility: Applicants must be U.S. high school seniors who are planning to attend an accredited college or university located in the state of Nebraska. They must be planning to major in actuarial science, economics, mathematics or statistics and must intend to pursue an actuarial career. Applicants must have demonstrated mathematical ability. Selection is based on the overall strength of the application.
Target applicant(s): High school students.
Amount: $2,000-$4,000.
Number of awards: 4.
Deadline: March 31.
How to apply: Applications are available online. An application form, recommendation letter and standardized test scores are required.
Exclusive: Visit www.UltimateScholarshipBook.com and enter code NE169823 for updates on this award.

(1699) · Ned McWherter Scholars Program

Tennessee Student Assistance Corporation
404 James Robertson Parkway, Suite 1510, Parkway Towers, Nashville, TN 37243
Phone: 800-342-1663
Email: tsac.aidinfo@tn.gov
https://www.tn.gov/collegepays/financial-aid.html
Purpose: To assist outstanding Tennessee students who are planning to attend a Tennessee college or university.
Eligibility: Applicants must be U.S. citizens or legal residents and Tennessee residents who are graduating high school seniors. They must have plans to attend an eligible Tennessee undergraduate institution full-time and have a GPA of 3.5 or higher. Applicants must have a combined math and reading SAT score of at least 1280 or an ACT composite score of 29 or higher. Selection is based on the overall strength of the application.

Target applicant(s): High school students.
Minimum GPA: 3.5
Amount: $6,000.
Number of awards: Varies.
Scholarship may be renewable.
Deadline: February 15.
How to apply: Applications are available online. An application form, official transcripts and standardized test scores are required.
Exclusive: Visit www.UltimateScholarshipBook.com and enter code TE169923 for updates on this award.

(1700) · Need Based Tuition Waiver Program

Massachusetts Department of Higher Education
Office of Student Financial Assistance, 454 Broadway, Suite 200, Revere, MA 02151
Phone: 617-727-9420
Email: osfa@osfa.mass.edu
https://www.mass.edu/osfa/programs/programs.asp
Purpose: To support Massachusetts students who are in need of supplemental financial aid.
Eligibility: Applicants must live in the state of Massachusetts for at least one year prior to the beginning of the school year, and they must be enrolled in a state-funded college. They must be in an undergraduate program with at least three credits per semester. Students must not owe any refunds on prior scholarships and cannot have any defaulted government loans. They must also be able to show proof of financial need.
Target applicant(s): High school students. College students. Adult students.
Amount: Up to full tuition.
Number of awards: Varies.
Deadline: Varies.
How to apply: Applications are available at college financial aid offices.
Exclusive: Visit www.UltimateScholarshipBook.com and enter code MA170023 for updates on this award.

(1701) · Nevada Women's Fund Scholarships

Nevada Women's Fund
770 Smithridge Drive, Suite 300, Reno, NV 89502
Phone: 775-786-2335
Email: info@nevadawomensfund.org
http://www.nevadawomensfund.org
Purpose: To improve the lives of women and children in northern Nevada.
Eligibility: Northern Nevada residents and those attending northern Nevada schools receive preference. Applicants must be enrolled in an accredited two or four year degree or certifying program, will take a minimum of 6 to 8 credits per semester and have a cumulative GPA of 3.0.
Target applicant(s): High school students. College students. Graduate school students. Adult students.
Minimum GPA: 3.0
Amount: $500-$5,000.
Number of awards: Varies.
Deadline: February 28.
How to apply: Applications are available online or from several offices listed on the website.
Exclusive: Visit www.UltimateScholarshipBook.com and enter code NE170123 for updates on this award.

(1702) · New Century Scholarship

Utah System of Higher Education
New Century Scholarship, P.O. Box 145116, Salt Lake City, UT 84114-5116
Phone: 801-321-7221
Email: newcentury@ushe.edu
https://ushe.edu/
Purpose: To assist Utah high school students.
Eligibility: Applicants must be high school students who have completed the equivalent of an associate's degree at a Utah state institution of higher education or completed a specific math and science curriculum by September 1 of their high school graduation year. The award provides assistance for the bachelor's degree at a state college.
Target applicant(s): High school students.
Amount: Up to $1,250.
Number of awards: Varies.
Scholarship may be renewable.
Deadline: February 1.
How to apply: Applications are available online.
Exclusive: Visit www.UltimateScholarshipBook.com and enter code UT170223 for updates on this award.

(1703) · New England Regional Student Program

New England Board of Higher Education
45 Temple Place, Boston, MA 02111
Phone: 617-357-9620
Email: rsp@nebhe.org
http://www.nebhe.org
Purpose: The program lowers tuition rates for New England students who must travel out of state for their desired major.
Eligibility: Students must be residents of Connecticut, Maine, Massachusetts, New Hampshire, Rhode Island or Vermont and attend a school in another of those states that offers an RSP program in their major. The major must not be available at an in-school state.
Target applicant(s): High school students. College students. Graduate school students. Adult students.
Amount: Varies.
Number of awards: Varies.
Scholarship may be renewable.
Deadline: Varies.
How to apply: Students should note that they are interested in the RSP program on their regular college application.
Exclusive: Visit www.UltimateScholarshipBook.com and enter code NE170323 for updates on this award.

(1704) · New Hampshire Charitable Foundation Statewide Student Aid Program

New Hampshire Charitable Foundation
37 Pleasant Street, Concord, NH 03301-4005
Phone: 603-225-6641
Email: info@nhcf.org
https://www.nhcf.org/how-can-we-help-you/
Purpose: To allow New Hampshire students to access over 50 scholarship and loan opportunities through a single application.
Eligibility: Applicants must be New Hampshire residents who plan to pursue a bachelor's degree or graduate students of any age. They must enroll at least half-time to qualify.
Target applicant(s): High school students. College students. Graduate school students. Adult students.
Amount: $100-$7,500.

Number of awards: Varies.
Deadline: April 16 (under 24); For those over 24: December 15.
How to apply: Applications are available online.
Exclusive: Visit www.UltimateScholarshipBook.com and enter code NE170423 for updates on this award.

(1705) · New Jersey Oratorical Contest

American Legion, Department of New Jersey
135 W. Hanover Street, Trenton, NJ 08618
Phone: 609-695-5418
Email: adjudant@njamericanlegion.org
http://www.njamericanlegion.org
Purpose: To enhance high school students' experience with and understanding of the U.S. Constitution. The contest will help develop students' leadership skills and civic appreciation, as well as the ability to deliver thoughtful, insightful orations regarding U.S. citizenship and its inherent responsibilities.
Eligibility: Applicants must be high school students under the age of 20 who are U.S. citizens or legal residents and residents of the state. Students first give an oration within their state and winners compete at the national level. The oration must be related to the Constitution of the United States focusing on the duties and obligations citizens have to the government. It must be in English and be between eight and ten minutes. There is also an assigned topic which is posted on the website, and it should be between three and five minutes.
Target applicant(s): High school students.
Amount: Up to $4,000.
Number of awards: 5.
Deadline: February 1.
How to apply: Application information is available by email: ray@njamericanlegion.org.
Exclusive: Visit www.UltimateScholarshipBook.com and enter code AM170523 for updates on this award.

(1706) · New Jersey State Elks Special Children's Committee Scholarship

New Jersey State Elks
665 Rahway Avenue, P.O. Box 1596, Woodbridge, NJ 07095
Phone: 732-326-1300
Email: ndame788@aol.com
http://www.njelks.org/index.php/our-programs/scholarship-information
Purpose: To assist students with physical handicaps in obtaining higher education.
Eligibility: Applicants must be New Jersey residents and high school seniors with physical handicaps. They must demonstrate financial need and excellent academic standing.
Target applicant(s): High school students.
Amount: Up to $2,500.
Number of awards: 2.
Scholarship may be renewable.
Deadline: April 23.
How to apply: Applications are available online or by phone.
Exclusive: Visit www.UltimateScholarshipBook.com and enter code NE170623 for updates on this award.

(1707) · New Jersey World Trade Center Scholarship

New Jersey Higher Education Student Assistance Authority
P.O. Box 540, Trenton, NJ 08625
Phone: 800-792-8670

Email: clientservices@hesaa.org

http://www.hesaa.org

Purpose: To support the children and spouses of those who died as a result of the World Trade Center attack.

Eligibility: Applicants must be a dependent child or spouse of a New Jersey resident who was killed in the September 11, 2001 attack, died from resulting injuries or exposure to the attack site or are missing and presumed dead as a result of the attack. Students must be full-time undergraduates, and they may attend any eligible school in the U.S.

Target applicant(s): High school students. College students. Adult students.

Amount: Full tuition.

Number of awards: Varies.

Scholarship may be renewable.

Deadline: October 1 and March 1.

How to apply: Applications are available online.

Exclusive: Visit www.UltimateScholarshipBook.com and enter code NE170723 for updates on this award.

(1708) · New Mexico Scholars

New Mexico Higher Education Department

2044 Galisteo Street, Suite 4, Santa Fe, NM 87505-2100

Phone: 505-476-8400

Email: cesaria.tapia1@state.nm.us

https://hed.state.nm.us/financial-aid

Purpose: To support New Mexico undergraduate students with financial need attend postsecondary institutions in New Mexico.

Eligibility: Applicants must be undergraduate students attending selected New Mexico public institutions or designated private non-profit colleges, meet family income requirements, be under the age of 22 and have graduated in the top 5 percent of their high school class, have a minimum ACT score of 25 or a minimum 1140 SAT score. Students must be enrolled full time.

Target applicant(s): College students.

Amount: Up to full tuition.

Number of awards: Varies.

Scholarship may be renewable.

Deadline: Varies.

How to apply: Contact your financial aid office. Must complete a FAFSA.

Exclusive: Visit www.UltimateScholarshipBook.com and enter code NE170823 for updates on this award.

(1709) · New York Legion Auxiliary Department Scholarship

American Legion Auxiliary, Department of New York

112 State Street, Suite 1310, Albany, NY 12207

Phone: 518-463-1162

Email: nyalaeducation@gmail.com

http://www.deptny.org/?page_id=2128

Purpose: To assist students whose parents, grandparents or great-grandparents served in the Armed Forces during wartime.

Eligibility: Applicants must be children, grandchildren or great-grandchildren of veterans who served in the Armed Forces during World War I, World War II, the Korean Conflict, the Vietnam War, Grenada/Lebanon, Panama, the Persian Gulf or War on Terrorism. Students must be high school seniors or graduates and be New York State residents and U.S. citizens.

Target applicant(s): High school students.

Amount: $1,000.

Number of awards: 1.

Deadline: March 1.

How to apply: Applications are available online.

Exclusive: Visit www.UltimateScholarshipBook.com and enter code AM170923 for updates on this award.

(1710) · New York Legion Auxiliary District Scholarships

American Legion Auxiliary, Department of New York

112 State Street, Suite 1310, Albany, NY 12207

Phone: 518-463-1162

Email: nyalaeducation@gmail.com

http://www.deptny.org/?page_id=2128

Purpose: To provide financial assistance to children, grandchildren and great-grandchildren of war veterans.

Eligibility: Applicants must be children, grandchildren or great-grandchildren of Armed Forces veterans of World War I, World War II, the Korean Conflict, the Vietnam War, Grenada/Lebanon, Panama, the Persian Gulf or War on Terrorism. Students must be high school seniors and must be U.S. citizens and New York State residents.

Target applicant(s): High school students.

Amount: $1,000.

Number of awards: 1.

Deadline: March 1.

How to apply: Applications are available online.

Exclusive: Visit www.UltimateScholarshipBook.com and enter code AM171023 for updates on this award.

(1711) · New York Oratorical Contest

American Legion, Department of New York

1304 Park Boulevard, Troy, NY 12180

Phone: 518-463-2215

Email: info@nylegion.org

https://nylegion.net/programs-services/#h36

Purpose: To enhance high school students' experience with and understanding of the U.S. Constitution. The contest will help develop students' leadership skills and civic appreciation, as well as the ability to deliver thoughtful, insightful orations regarding U.S. citizenship and its inherent responsibilities.

Eligibility: Applicants must be high school students under the age of 20 who are U.S. citizens or legal residents and residents of the state. Students first give an oration within their state and winners compete at the national level. The oration must be related to the Constitution of the United States focusing on the duties and obligations citizens have to the government. It must be in English and be between eight and ten minutes. There is also an assigned topic which is posted on the website, and it should be between three and five minutes.

Target applicant(s): High school students.

Amount: $2,000-$6,000.

Number of awards: 5.

Deadline: November 19.

How to apply: Application information is available by contacting the local American Legion Post.

Exclusive: Visit www.UltimateScholarshipBook.com and enter code AM171123 for updates on this award.

(1712) · New York State Association of Agricultural Fairs/New York State Showpeople's Association Scholarships

New York State Association of Agricultural Fairs
Norma W. Hamilton, Executive Secretary, 67 Verbeck Avenue, Schaghticoke, NY 12154
Phone: 518-753-4956
Email: carousels4@aol.com
http://nyfairs.org/scholarships.htm
Purpose: To aid New York students who are preparing for careers in agriculture, fair management or the outdoor amusement business.
Eligibility: Applicants must be New York state residents or must attend school in the state of New York and must be high school seniors or current undergraduate students. They can be enrolled in or planning to enroll in any degree program but additional consideration may be given to those pursuing degrees in agriculture, fair management or the outdoor amusement business. They must be attending or planning to attend an accredited postsecondary institution and must be active in local fairs. Selection is based on fair participation, leadership, citizenship and essay.
Target applicant(s): High school students. College students. Adult students.
Amount: $1,000.
Number of awards: 10.
Deadline: Second Friday in April.
How to apply: Applications are available online. An application form, personal essay, two recommendation letters and a transcript are required.
Exclusive: Visit www.UltimateScholarshipBook.com and enter code NE171223 for updates on this award.

(1713) · New York State Society of Physician Assistants Scholarship

New York State Society of Physician Assistants
N83 W13410 Leon Road, Menomonee Falls, WI 53051
Email: info@nysspa.org
http://www.nysspa.org
Purpose: To aid New York State Society of Physician Assistants (NYSSPA) student members.
Eligibility: Applicants must be NYSSPA members who are currently enrolled in an ARC-PA accredited physician assistant degree program in the state of New York. They must be in the professional phase of their degree program. Previous NYSSPA Scholarship winners, NYSSPA board members and NYSSPA committee chairs are ineligible. Selection is based on academic achievement, financial need and professional activities.
Target applicant(s): College students. Graduate school students. Adult students.
Amount: Varies.
Number of awards: Varies.
Deadline: August 31.
How to apply: Applications are available online. An application form, one reference letter, a personal essay and a financial aid award letter are required.
Exclusive: Visit www.UltimateScholarshipBook.com and enter code NE171323 for updates on this award.

(1714) · New York State USBC Scholarships

New York State USBC
55 Edgewood Drive, Batavia, NY 14020
Phone: 585-343-3736
Email: bowlny300@yahoo.com
https://www.bowlny.com/youth_scholarships.php
Purpose: To assist bowlers in New York.
Eligibility: Applicants must be members of a New York State USBC Youth certified league and be high school seniors. Selection includes academic and extracurricular achievement.
Target applicant(s): High school students.
Amount: $1,000-$5,000.
Number of awards: Varies.
Scholarship may be renewable.
Deadline: March 1.
How to apply: Applications are available online.
Exclusive: Visit www.UltimateScholarshipBook.com and enter code NE171423 for updates on this award.

(1715) · New York State USBC Spirit Awards

New York State USBC
55 Edgewood Drive, Batavia, NY 14020
Phone: 585-343-3736
Email: bowlny300@yahoo.com
https://www.bowlny.com/youth_scholarships.php
Purpose: To assist bowlers in grades 8-11 in New York.
Eligibility: Applicants must demonstrate sportsmanship, commitment and leadership.
Target applicant(s): Junior high students or younger. High school students.
Amount: $250-$750.
Number of awards: 3.
Deadline: March 1.
How to apply: Bowlers are nominated by their bowling coach.
Exclusive: Visit www.UltimateScholarshipBook.com and enter code NE171523 for updates on this award.

(1716) · New York Women in Communications Foundation Scholarships

New York Women in Communications Foundation
355 Lexington Avenue, 15th Floor, New York, NY 10017
Phone: 212-297-2133
http://www.nywici.org/students/scholarships
Purpose: To support high school, college and graduate students currently residing in New York, New Jersey, Connecticut or Pennsylvania with the pursuit of a degree in a communications-related field.
Eligibility: Applicants are required to have a minimum GPA of 3.2 and must be majoring, declaring a major or pursuing an advanced degree in a communications-related field at an accredited college or university in the United States. Graduate students must already be members of New York Women in Communications.
Target applicant(s): High school students. College students. Graduate school students. Adult students.
Minimum GPA: 3.2
Amount: $10,000.
Number of awards: 18-20.
Deadline: January.
How to apply: Applications are available online.
Exclusive: Visit www.UltimateScholarshipBook.com and enter code NE171623 for updates on this award.

(1717) · Nightingale Awards of Pennsylvania Scholarship

Nightingale Awards of Pennsylvania
2400 Ardmore Boulevard, Suite 302, Pittsburgh, PA 15221

Phone: 412-871-3353
Email: info@nightingaleawards.org
http://www.nightingaleawards.org/scholarships/
Purpose: To support Pennsylvania nursing students.
Eligibility: Applicants must be Pennsylvania residents who are enrolled in or have been accepted into a Pennsylvania nursing program in licensed practical nursing, registered nursing or graduate-level nursing practice. They must have completed at least one course in nursing and must have a B average or better. Previous recipients of this scholarship are ineligible. Selection is based on academic achievement, leadership ability, extracurricular activities and professional dedication to nursing.
Target applicant(s): College students. Graduate school students. Adult students.
Minimum GPA: 3.0
Amount: Varies.
Number of awards: Varies.
Deadline: March 31.
How to apply: Applications are available online. An application form, official transcript, two recommendation letters, a copy of the applicant's nursing program acceptance letter, a personal statement and a research proposal abstract (Ph.D. applicants only) are required.
Exclusive: Visit www.UltimateScholarshipBook.com and enter code NI171723 for updates on this award.

(1718) · Nissan Scholarship

Nissan North America
P.O. Box 685003, Franklin, TN 37068
Phone: 800-647-7261
Email: webmaster@nissanusa.com
http://www.nissanusa.com
Purpose: To assist Mississippi high school seniors in attending public two-year or four-year colleges.
Eligibility: Applicants must have a minimum GPA of 2.5 and a minimum ACT score of 20 or SAT score of 820, have demonstrated financial need and be accepted as a full-time student at a Mississippi public college or university.
Target applicant(s): High school students.
Minimum GPA: 2.5
Amount: Full tuition.
Number of awards: Varies.
Deadline: March 1.
How to apply: No application is necessary. However, students must mail an essay, resume, high school transcript with ACT or SAT score and FAFSA results to Mississippi Office of Student Financial Aid, 3825 Ridgewood Road, Jackson, MS 39211-6453.
Exclusive: Visit www.UltimateScholarshipBook.com and enter code NI171823 for updates on this award.

(1719) · NJ Student Tuition Assistance Reward Scholarship

New Jersey Higher Education Student Assistance Authority
P.O. Box 540, Trenton, NJ 08625
Phone: 800-792-8670
Email: clientservices@hesaa.org
http://www.hesaa.org
Purpose: To support community college students in New Jersey who graduated from high school with excellent academic standing.
Eligibility: Applicants must have graduated from a New Jersey high school in the top 20 percent of their class, and they must have been state residents for at least 12 months prior to graduation. Students must

enroll full-time in their home county college by the fifth semester after graduating from high school.
Target applicant(s): High school students. College students. Adult students.
Minimum GPA: 3.0
Amount: Up to full tuition.
Number of awards: Varies.
Scholarship may be renewable.
Deadline: September 15.
How to apply: Applications are available at college financial aid offices.
Exclusive: Visit www.UltimateScholarshipBook.com and enter code NE171923 for updates on this award.

(1720) · NJ Student Tuition Assistance Reward Scholarship II

New Jersey Higher Education Student Assistance Authority
P.O. Box 540, Trenton, NJ 08625
Phone: 800-792-8670
Email: clientservices@hesaa.org
http://www.hesaa.org
Purpose: To support NJ STARS students who are transferring to four-year colleges.
Eligibility: Applicants must be county college graduates with an associate's degree, and they must have a GPA of at least 3.0. They must either be NJ STARS recipients or have other full state or federal aid during the semester in which they graduate. Students must be enrolled full-time at a New Jersey four-year college within two semesters of graduation.
Target applicant(s): College students. Adult students.
Minimum GPA: 3.0
Amount: Up to $2,500 a year.
Number of awards: Varies.
Scholarship may be renewable.
Deadline: October 1.
How to apply: Applications are available at college financial aid offices.
Exclusive: Visit www.UltimateScholarshipBook.com and enter code NE172023 for updates on this award.

(1721) · NJCDCA Scholarship

New Jersey Cheerleading and Dance Coaches Association
Doug Linden, 276 Stamets Road, Milford, NJ 08848
Phone: 908-797-6262
Email: doug.linden@njcdca.com
http://www.njcheerleading.com/index.htm
Purpose: To recognize New Jersey senior cheerleaders and dancers for their academic achievements and athletic excellence.
Eligibility: Applicants must be a high school senior and member of a cheer or dance team that is a New Jersey Cheerleading and Dance Coaches Association member. Selection is based on academic and athletic achievement, community involvement, personal essay and coach recommendation.
Target applicant(s): High school students.
Amount: Varies.
Number of awards: Varies.
Deadline: March 15.
How to apply: Applications are available online and include the application form, a personal essay, an official high school transcript and a coach recommendation form.
Exclusive: Visit www.UltimateScholarshipBook.com and enter code NE172123 for updates on this award.

(1722) · NJSCA High School Scholarship

New Jersey School Counselor Association Inc.
Sheila Brewer, NJSCA High School Awards Chair, 5 Split Rock
Place, Moorestown, NJ 08057
Phone: 609-893-8141
Email: sbrewer@pemb.org
http://www.njsca.org
Purpose: To spread awareness of the importance of the role of school counselors.
Eligibility: Applicants must be New Jersey residents who will be graduating high school in the year of application. They must have been accepted to and plan to enroll in an institution of higher learning. A 300-500 word essay is required.
Target applicant(s): High school students.
Amount: Varies.
Number of awards: Varies.
Deadline: March 15.
How to apply: Applications are available online.
Exclusive: Visit www.UltimateScholarshipBook.com and enter code NE172223 for updates on this award.

(1723) · NMASBO Scholarship

New Mexico Association of School Business Officials
P.O. Box 7535, Albuquerque, NM 87194-7535
Phone: 505-923-3283
Email: info@nmasbo.org
https://nmasbo.org
Purpose: To support graduating high school seniors in New Mexico.
Eligibility: Students must have at least a 3.0 GPA. Applicants must submit an essay and two letters of recommendation. Students must plan to attend a New Mexico college or university on a full-time basis.
Target applicant(s): High school students.
Minimum GPA: 3.0
Amount: $1,500.
Number of awards: 6-10.
Deadline: February 8.
How to apply: Applications are available online.
Exclusive: Visit www.UltimateScholarshipBook.com and enter code NE172323 for updates on this award.

(1724) · NNM American Society of Mechanical Engineers Scholarship

Los Alamos National Laboratory Foundation
1112 Plaza del Norte, Espanola, NM 87532
Phone: 505-753-8890
Email: tony@lanlfoundation.org
http://www.lanlfoundation.org
Purpose: To support undergraduate students from northern New Mexico who are majoring in mechanical engineering.
Eligibility: Students must have at least a 3.25 GPA, and they must have either an SAT score (combined Math plus Critical Reading only) of at least 930 or an ACT score of at least 19. Applicants must submit an essay and two letters of recommendation.
Target applicant(s): High school students. College students. Adult students.
Minimum GPA: 3.25
Amount: $1,000.
Number of awards: Varies.
Deadline: January 18.
How to apply: Applications are available online.

Exclusive: Visit www.UltimateScholarshipBook.com and enter code LO172423 for updates on this award.

(1725) · Norman and Ruth Good Educational Endowment

Lincoln Community Foundation
215 Centennial Mall South, Suite 100, Lincoln, NE 68508
Phone: 402-474-2345
Email: robertm@lcf.org
http://www.lcf.org
Purpose: To assist Nebraska students.
Eligibility: Applicants must be attending a private college in Nebraska and must be in their junior or senior year. Applicants may not apply if the scholarship money is to be used for summer programs or schools that are not valid degree-granting institutions.
Target applicant(s): College students. Adult students.
Minimum GPA: 3.5
Amount: $2,500.
Number of awards: Varies.
Scholarship may be renewable.
Deadline: March 15.
How to apply: Applications are available online.
Exclusive: Visit www.UltimateScholarshipBook.com and enter code LI172523 for updates on this award.

(1726) · Norman S. and Betty M. Fitzhugh Fund

Greater Kanawha Valley Foundation
1600 Huntington Square, 900 Lee Street, East, Charleston, WV 25301
Phone: 304-346-3620
Email: shoover@tgkvf.org
https://tgkvf.org/scholarships/available-scholarships/
Purpose: To provide financial assistance to West Virginia residents wishing to earn a college degree.
Eligibility: Applicants must be full-time students (12 hours) and demonstrate good moral character and academic excellence. Students must have a minimum 2.5 GPA and minimum ACT score of 20.
Target applicant(s): High school students. College students. Adult students.
Minimum GPA: 2.5
Amount: $750.
Number of awards: 1.
Scholarship may be renewable.
Deadline: February 15.
How to apply: Applications are available online or by email.
Exclusive: Visit www.UltimateScholarshipBook.com and enter code GR172623 for updates on this award.

(1727) · North Carolina 4-H Development Fund Scholarships

North Carolina 4-H Youth Development
Shannon McCollum, Extension 4-H Associate, NCCES 4-H/FCS
Team, NCSU Campus Box 7655, Raleigh, NC 27695
Phone: 919-515-8486
Email: shannon_mccollum@ncsu.edu
https://nc4h.ces.ncsu.edu/
Purpose: To help North Carolina students who have been involved with the 4-H Club who want to go to college in the state.

Eligibility: Applicants must be enrolling as undergraduates at a four-year North Carolina college or university or a junior or community college in the state, provided the program of study is transferable to a four-year college. Students must also have a strong record of 4-H Club participation, have an excellent high school academic record and show an aptitude for college work through SAT scores. An application form, transcript, photo page and two recommendation letters are required. For some of the awards, financial need is necessary. Some awards have geographic restrictions to regions of the state while others are for a degree program or a specific college or university. Some scholarships are renewable.
Target applicant(s): High school students.
Amount: Varies.
Number of awards: Varies.
Scholarship may be renewable.
Deadline: February 1.
How to apply: Applications are available through each county cooperative extension office in North Carolina by phone or online.
Exclusive: Visit www.UltimateScholarshipBook.com and enter code NO172723 for updates on this award.

(1728) · North Carolina Community College Grant

North Carolina Division of Vocational Rehabilitation Services
2601 Mail Service Center, Raleigh, NC 27699-2801
Phone: 888-234-6400
Email: jterrell@ncbar.org
https://www.cfnc.org/pay-for-college/apply-for-financial-aid/
Purpose: To assist North Carolina community college students.
Eligibility: Applicants must be North Carolina residents, demonstrate financial need and attend a North Carolina community college for at least six credit hours per semester. Selection is based on financial need.
Target applicant(s): College students. Adult students.
Amount: Up to $2,400.
Number of awards: Varies.
Deadline: Varies.
How to apply: Application is made by completing the FAFSA.
Exclusive: Visit www.UltimateScholarshipBook.com and enter code NO172823 for updates on this award.

(1729) · North Carolina Education Lottery Scholarship

North Carolina Division of Vocational Rehabilitation Services
2601 Mail Service Center, Raleigh, NC 27699-2801
Phone: 888-234-6400
Email: jterrell@ncbar.org
https://www.cfnc.org/pay-for-college/apply-for-financial-aid/
Purpose: To provide financial assistance to North Carolina residents with financial need who are attending North Carolina colleges and universities.
Eligibility: Applicants must be enrolled for at least six credit hours per semester in an undergraduate degree-seeking program at an eligible North Carolina institution and meet satisfactory academic progress requirements. Students who meet the same criteria as the Federal Pell Grant and those with an Estimated Family Contribution of $5,000 or less are eligible for the scholarship.
Target applicant(s): College students. Adult students.
Amount: $100-$3,000.
Number of awards: Varies.
Deadline: October 1.
How to apply: Qualified students who submit the Free Application for Federal Student Aid (FAFSA) will be considered.

Exclusive: Visit www.UltimateScholarshipBook.com and enter code NO172923 for updates on this award.

(1730) · North Carolina Oratorical Contest

American Legion, Department of North Carolina
4 N. Blount Street, P.O. Box 26657, Raleigh, NC 27611-6657
Phone: 919-832-7506
Email: nclegion@nc.rr.com
http://nclegion.org/
Purpose: To enhance high school students' experience with and understanding of the U.S. Constitution. The contest will help develop students' leadership skills and civic appreciation, as well as the ability to deliver thoughtful, insightful orations regarding U.S. citizenship and its inherent responsibilities.
Eligibility: Applicants must be high school students under the age of 20 who are U.S. citizens or legal residents and residents of the state. Students first give an oration within their state and winners compete at the national level. The oration must be related to the Constitution of the United States focusing on the duties and obligations citizens have to the government. It must be in English and be between eight and ten minutes. There is also an assigned topic which is posted on the website, and it should be between three and five minutes.
Target applicant(s): High school students.
Amount: $1,500-$18,000.
Number of awards: Varies.
Deadline: March 15.
How to apply: Application information is available by contacting the local post by email.
Exclusive: Visit www.UltimateScholarshipBook.com and enter code AM173023 for updates on this award.

(1731) · North Dakota Academic Scholarship

North Dakota Department of Public Instruction
600 E. Boulevard Avenue, Bismarck, ND 58505
Phone: 701-328-2260
Email: cte@nd.gov
https://www.nd.gov/dpi/education-programs
Purpose: To assist North Dakota high school seniors pursuing post-secondary education at a North Dakota college or university.
Eligibility: Applicants must plan to enroll full-time at an accredited North Dakota postsecondary institution and maintain a minimum 2.75 college GPA. The scholarship may not exceed $6,000 nor extend beyond six years. For additional scholarship criteria, see the information at the website listed below.
Target applicant(s): High school students.
Minimum GPA: 2.75
Amount: Up to $6,000.
Number of awards: Varies.
Scholarship may be renewable.
Deadline: June 3.
How to apply: Application instructions are available from your counselor.
Exclusive: Visit www.UltimateScholarshipBook.com and enter code NO173123 for updates on this award.

(1732) · North Dakota Career and Technical Education Scholarship

North Dakota Department of Public Instruction
600 E. Boulevard Avenue, Bismarck, ND 58505
Phone: 701-328-2260

Email: cte@nd.gov

https://www.nd.gov/dpi/education-programs

Purpose: To assist North Dakota high school seniors pursuing post-secondary education at a North Dakota college or university.

Eligibility: Applicants must plan to enroll full-time at an accredited North Dakota postsecondary institution and maintain a minimum 2.75 college GPA. The total scholarship value is $6,000 paid by semester or quarter but may not extend beyond six years. For additional scholarship criteria, see the information at the website listed below.

Target applicant(s): High school students.

Minimum GPA: 2.75

Amount: $6,000.

Number of awards: Varies.

Scholarship may be renewable.

Deadline: June 3.

How to apply: Application instructions are available from your counselor.

Exclusive: Visit www.UltimateScholarshipBook.com and enter code NO173223 for updates on this award.

(1733) · North Dakota Career Builders Scholarship

North Dakota University System Career Builders Scholarship

North Dakota University System, 10th Floor, State Capitol, 600 East Boulevard Avenue, Dept. 215, Bismarck, ND 58505-0230

Phone: 701-328-2960

Email: ndfinaid@ndus.edu

https://ndus.edu/career-builders/

Purpose: To support students interested in high-need and emerging occupations in North Dakota.

Eligibility: Applicants must be enrolled in programs at the associate's level and below or other programs, up to and including bachelor programs, that are four semesters or six quarters in length. Students must be enrolled in a qualifying certificate or degree program at a North Dakota institution that directly relates to high-need occupations. Applicants must live in North Dakota and work within North Dakota for three years following program completion to retain the scholarship.

Target applicant(s): College students. Adult students.

Minimum GPA: 2.5

Amount: Varies.

Number of awards: Varies.

Deadline: Varies.

How to apply: Applications are available online.

Exclusive: Visit www.UltimateScholarshipBook.com and enter code NO173323 for updates on this award.

(1734) · North Dakota Dollars for Scholars

North Dakota Dollars for Scholars

P.O. Box 5509, Bismarck, ND 58506-5509

Phone: 701-328-5702

Email: statedirector@nddfs.org

https://northdakota.dollarsforscholars.org/index.php?section=chapter Website&action=main&fwID=788

Purpose: To support North Dakota students with their post-secondary education expenses.

Eligibility: Applicants must have graduated from a North Dakota high school or were home educated in North Dakota.

Target applicant(s): High school students. College students. Graduate school students. Adult students.

Amount: Up to $2,500.

Number of awards: Varies.

Deadline: April 1.

How to apply: Applications are available online.

Exclusive: Visit www.UltimateScholarshipBook.com and enter code NO173423 for updates on this award.

(1735) · North Dakota Scholars Program

North Dakota University System

10th Floor, State Capitol, 600 East Boulevard Avenue, Dept. 215, Bismarck, ND 58505-0230

Phone: 701-328-2960

Email: ndus.office@ndus.edu

http://www.ndus.edu

Purpose: To assist outstanding North Dakota high school students.

Eligibility: Applicants must be North Dakota high school seniors who have scored in the top 5 percent of all students in North Dakota who have taken the ACT by July 1 in the calendar year preceding college enrollment. They must have plans to attend a North Dakota postsecondary institution. Selection is based on academic merit.

Target applicant(s): High school students.

Amount: Full tuition.

Number of awards: Varies.

Scholarship may be renewable.

Deadline: Varies.

How to apply: Applications are available by written request. An application form and supporting documents are required.

Exclusive: Visit www.UltimateScholarshipBook.com and enter code NO173523 for updates on this award.

(1736) · North Dakota School Counseling Association

North Dakota School Counselor Association

1601 College Drive, Devils Lake, ND 58301

http://www.ndsca.us/awards.html

Purpose: To support North Dakota students pursuing post-secondary education.

Eligibility: Applicants must be graduating seniors from a North Dakota high school. Students must submit an application signed by their school counselor, write an essay and provide a letter of recommendation.

Target applicant(s): High school students.

Amount: $1,000.

Number of awards: Varies.

Deadline: December.

How to apply: Applications are available online.

Exclusive: Visit www.UltimateScholarshipBook.com and enter code NO173623 for updates on this award.

(1737) · North Dakota State Student Incentive Grant

North Dakota University System

10th Floor, State Capitol, 600 East Boulevard Avenue, Dept. 215, Bismarck, ND 58505-0230

Phone: 701-328-2960

Email: ndus.office@ndus.edu

http://www.ndus.edu

Purpose: To assist North Dakota students who have financial need.

Eligibility: Applicants must be U.S. citizens or permanent residents. They must be North Dakota residents who are high school graduates or GED recipients and enrolled as full-time students in a North Dakota undergraduate program that lasts for at least one academic year. They must be first-time undergraduate students who have no defaulted student loans and who owe no Title IV grant or loan refunds. Selection is based on financial need.

Target applicant(s): High school students. College students. Adult students.
Amount: Varies.
Number of awards: Varies.
Scholarship may be renewable.
Deadline: March 1.
How to apply: Application is made by completing the Free Application for Federal Student Aid (FAFSA).
Exclusive: Visit www.UltimateScholarshipBook.com and enter code NO173723 for updates on this award.

(1738) · North Texas State Fair Association Scholarship

North Texas Fair and Rodeo
2217 N. Carroll Boulevard, Denton, TX 76201
Phone: 940-387-2632
Email: nkimmey@ntfair.com
http://www.ntfair.com/p/get-involved/195
Purpose: To support high school senior students by investing in their future.
Eligibility: Applicants must be a high school senior who has actively participated in school, community, FFA, FHA or 4-H activities. Selection is based on academic success, extracurricular involvement and financial need.
Target applicant(s): High school students.
Amount: $2,000.
Number of awards: Varies.
Deadline: June 1.
How to apply: Applications are available online and should include two letters of recommendation and two photos.
Exclusive: Visit www.UltimateScholarshipBook.com and enter code NO173823 for updates on this award.

(1739) · Northrop Grumman Scholarship

Society of Women Engineers
130 East Randolph Street, Suite 3500, Chicago, IL 60601
Phone: 877-793-4636
Email: scholarships@swe.org
https://swe.org/scholarships/
Purpose: To support high school seniors who reside in a community where Northrop Grumman has a major presence and who intend to pursue a career in engineering, computer science, mathematics or physics.
Eligibility: Scholarships are available for students living in each of Maryland's 23 counties, one scholarship for a student living in the city of Baltimore and two scholarships for applicants living in specific counties/communities from the following states: Alabama, California, Colorado, Florida, Illinois, New York, Ohio, Utah or Virginia. Applicants must have a minimum composite SAT score of 1150 or ACT score of 27 and a minimum GPA of 3.5.
Target applicant(s): College students. Adult students.
Minimum GPA: 3.5
Amount: $5,000.
Number of awards: 5.
Scholarship may be renewable.
Deadline: February 15.
How to apply: Applications are available online.
Exclusive: Visit www.UltimateScholarshipBook.com and enter code SO173923 for updates on this award.

(1740) · Northwest Danish Association Scholarships

Northwest Danish Association
Meridian Office Building, 1833 North 105th Street, Suite 101, Seattle, WA 98133-8973
Phone: 206-523-3263
Email: seattle@nwdanish.org
http://www.northwestdanish.org
Purpose: To support students who are residents of Oregon or Washington.
Eligibility: Applicants must be residents of or enrolled full-time in accredited schools in Oregon or Washington. Applicants must also be NWDA members (or have a family membership if under 18 years of age). Through travel, field of study, study abroad, heritage or life experience, applicants must clearly be able to illustrate their connection to Denmark. The NWDA scholarship must be used in seeking an academic degree, vocational degree, re-training for employment or training. Those who have participated in NWDA activities or programs will be given preference.
Target applicant(s): High school students. College students. Graduate school students. Adult students.
Amount: Varies.
Number of awards: Varies.
Deadline: May 1.
How to apply: Applications are available online. An application form, essay, two references, official transcript and completed FAFSA form are required.
Exclusive: Visit www.UltimateScholarshipBook.com and enter code NO174023 for updates on this award.

(1741) · Nursing Education Scholarship Program

Illinois Department of Public Health
Center for Rural Health, 535 West Jefferson Street, Springfield, IL 62761
Phone: 217-782-1624
Email: dph.nesp@illinois.gov
http://www.dph.illinois.gov
Purpose: To increase the number of nurses in Illinois.
Eligibility: Applicants must be Illinois residents, having lived in the state for one year prior to applying and be U.S. citizens or permanent residents. Applicants must be accepted to or enrolled in an approved nursing program and demonstrate financial need. Scholarship recipients must agree to work as a nurse in Illinois after graduation.
Target applicant(s): High school students. College students. Graduate school students. Adult students.
Amount: Up to full tuition.
Number of awards: Varies.
Scholarship may be renewable.
Deadline: April 30.
How to apply: Applications are available online.
Exclusive: Visit www.UltimateScholarshipBook.com and enter code IL174123 for updates on this award.

(1742) · Nursing Incentive Scholarship Fund

Kentucky Board of Nursing
312 Whittington Parkway, Suite 300, Louisville, KY 40222
Phone: 800-305-2042
https://kbn.ky.gov/Education/Pages/nursing.aspx
Purpose: To support Kentucky students pursuing nursing education.
Eligibility: Applicants must be Kentucky residents accepted to a nursing program who are completing core nursing courses. Students in

prelicensure and BSN completion programs must complete a minimum of 15 credit hours and nine credit hours if in a graduate nursing program. Applicants must maintain a high enough GPA to allow continuation in the program. Recipients must work as a full-time nurse in Kentucky for one year for each academic year funded.

Target applicant(s): College students. Graduate school students. Adult students.

Amount: $3,000.

Number of awards: Varies.

Deadline: June 8.

How to apply: Applications are available online.

Exclusive: Visit www.UltimateScholarshipBook.com and enter code KE174223 for updates on this award.

(1743) · NYWEA Major Environmental Career Scholarship

New York Water Environment Association Inc.
525 Plum Street, Suite 102, Syracuse, NY 13204
Phone: 877-556-9932
Email: theresa@nywea.org
http://www.nywea.org

Purpose: To support New York students who are planning to pursue a bachelor's degree in an environment-related subject.

Eligibility: Applicants must be residents of the state of New York and must be high school seniors who plan to enroll full-time in an environment-related bachelor's degree program no later than the fall following graduation. The programs could include but are not limited to environmental engineering, civil engineering with an environmental minor, chemical engineering with an environmental minor, hydrogeology with an environmental emphasis or biology or microbiology with an environmental emphasis. Selection is based on the overall strength of the application.

Target applicant(s): High school students.

Amount: $12,000.

Number of awards: 1.

Deadline: February 26.

How to apply: Applications are available online. An application form, official transcript, two recommendation letters and two personal essays are required.

Exclusive: Visit www.UltimateScholarshipBook.com and enter code NE174323 for updates on this award.

(1744) · Ohio Classical Conference Scholarship for Prospective Latin Teachers

Ohio Classical Conference
c/o Kelly Kusch, Covington Latin School, 21 East Eleventh Street, Covington, KY 41011
Phone: 513-227-6847
Email: kelly.kusch@covingtonlatin.org
https://ohioclassicalconference.org/occ-scholarships-4/

Purpose: To aid Ohio students who are planning for careers as Latin teachers.

Eligibility: Applicants must be undergraduate students who are residents of Ohio or who are enrolled at an accredited Ohio postsecondary institution, or can be graduates of Ohio high schools pursuing study at accredited colleges or universities elsewhere in the U.S. They must have sophomore standing or above and be taking courses that provide preparation for a career as a K-12 Latin teacher. Selection is based on the overall strength of the application.

Target applicant(s): College students. Adult students.

Amount: $1,500.

Number of awards: 1.

Deadline: April 1.

How to apply: Applications are available online. An application form, official transcript, two recommendation letters, course schedule and personal statement are required.

Exclusive: Visit www.UltimateScholarshipBook.com and enter code OH174423 for updates on this award.

(1745) · Ohio Newspaper Women's Association (ONWA) Annual Scholarship

Ohio News Media Foundation
1335 Dublin Road, Suite 216-B, Columbus, OH 43215
Phone: 614-486-6677
Email: ariggs@ohionews.org
https://www.ohionews.org/aws/ONA/pt/sp/foundation

Purpose: To support male or female junior or senior students pursuing a journalism-related degree at an Ohio college or university.

Eligibility: Applicants must be enrolled in an Ohio college or university as a junior or senior and be majoring in a journalism-related field such as journalism, advertising or marketing. Students must have two professor recommendations and submit three or four newspaper clippings or work samples demonstrating their skills along with answers to questions given on the application.

Target applicant(s): College students. Adult students.

Amount: $2,000.

Number of awards: 1.

Deadline: May 15.

How to apply: Applications are available online.

Exclusive: Visit www.UltimateScholarshipBook.com and enter code OH174523 for updates on this award.

(1746) · Ohio Section Scholarships

Institute of Transportation Engineers - Ohio Section
1391 West 5th Avenue, PMB 157, Columbus, OH 43212
Phone: 614-898-7100
Email: gburch@hntb.com
http://ohioite.org/Scholarship

Purpose: To aid students who are enrolled in a degree program that is related to transportation engineering.

Eligibility: Applicants must be full-time students who are attending an ABET-accredited college or university located in the state of Ohio. They must be enrolled in a civil engineering or other transportation-related degree program and have a GPA of 2.5 or higher. Selection is based on academic achievement, stated career goals and extracurricular activities.

Target applicant(s): College students. Graduate school students. Adult students.

Minimum GPA: 2.5

Amount: $1,000.

Number of awards: 1.

Deadline: October.

How to apply: Applications are available online. An application form, personal statement, official transcript and one recommendation letter are required.

Exclusive: Visit www.UltimateScholarshipBook.com and enter code IN174623 for updates on this award.

(1747) · Ohio State Association/AOTF Scholarships

American Occupational Therapy Foundation
Attn: Jeanne Cooper, 4720 Montgomery Lane, Suite 202, Bethesda, MD 20814

Phone: 240-292-1034
Email: jcooper@aotf.org
https://www.aotf.org/Scholarships
Purpose: To aid Ohio occupational therapy students who are members of the American Occupational Therapy Foundation.
Eligibility: Applicants must be Ohio residents who are enrolled in an accredited occupational therapy associate's or first professional degree program at a school located in Ohio. Selection is based on the overall strength of the application.
Target applicant(s): College students. Graduate school students. Adult students.
Amount: Varies.
Number of awards: 3.
Deadline: October 1.
How to apply: Applications are available online. An application form, two personal references and a letter from the student's academic program director are required.
Exclusive: Visit www.UltimateScholarshipBook.com and enter code AM174723 for updates on this award.

(1748) · Ohio Turfgrass Foundation Scholarships

Ohio Turfgrass Foundation
Scholarships Committee, 2710 North Star Road, Columbus, OH 43221
Phone: 614-285-4683
Email: info@ohioturfgrass.org
http://www.ohioturfgrass.org
Purpose: To aid Ohio students who are pursuing higher education in subjects related to the turfgrass industry.
Eligibility: Applicants must be Ohio undergraduate or graduate students who are enrolled in a degree program that is related to turfgrass science. They must have a cumulative GPA of 2.5 or higher and a major GPA of 2.75 or higher. Selection is based on academic merit, professional commitment to the turfgrass industry and financial need.
Target applicant(s): College students. Graduate school students. Adult students.
Minimum GPA: 2.5
Amount: Varies.
Number of awards: Varies.
Deadline: November 15.
How to apply: Applications are available online. An application form, transcript and two recommendation letters are required.
Exclusive: Visit www.UltimateScholarshipBook.com and enter code OH174823 for updates on this award.

(1749) · OK-AHEAD Scholarship

Oklahoma Association on Higher Education and Disability
3000 West Memorial Road, Suite 123-105, Oklahoma City, OK 73120-6108
Email: jenifer.randle@okdhas.org
https://www.ahead-ok.org
Purpose: To support Oklahoma students with disabilities.
Eligibility: Applicants must be high school seniors or current post-secondary students with plans to pursue a degree or certification from an Oklahoma technology center or Oklahoma two-year or four-year college or university. Students must be enrolled in at least 6 hours of college classes or a full-time Career Tech program attending 15 hours a week or more with a minimum 2.0 GPA. Applicants must provide documentation regarding their disability.
Target applicant(s): High school students. College students. Adult students.

Minimum GPA: 2.0
Amount: Up to $300.
Number of awards: 3.
Deadline: March 1.
How to apply: Applications are available online.
Exclusive: Visit www.UltimateScholarshipBook.com and enter code OK174923 for updates on this award.

(1750) · Oklahoma Foundation for Excellence Academic All-State Scholarships

Oklahoma Foundation for Excellence
101 Park Avenue, Suite 420, Oklahoma City, OK 73102-7201
Phone: 405-236-0006
Email: info@ofe.org
http://www.ofe.org
Purpose: To reward Oklahoma students who have high academic achievement.
Eligibility: Applicants must be high school seniors who are nominated by their school principals or superintendents. They must have an ACT score of 30 or higher or an SAT score of 1340 or higher or be a semi-finalist for a National Merit, National Achievement or National Hispanic Scholarship. An essay is required.
Target applicant(s): High school students.
Amount: $1,000.
Number of awards: 100.
Deadline: December 2.
How to apply: Applications are available from your school.
Exclusive: Visit www.UltimateScholarshipBook.com and enter code OK175023 for updates on this award.

(1751) · Oklahoma Hall of Fame Scholarship

Oklahoma Hall of Fame
1400 Classen Drive, Oklahoma City, OK 73106
Phone: 405-235-4458
Email: gmc@oklahomahof.com
https://oklahomahof.com/scholarships
Purpose: To support Oklahoma high school seniors committed to attending an Oklahoma college or university.
Eligibility: Applicants must be Oklahoma high school seniors committed to attending an Oklahoma college or university. Students must be nominated for this scholarship by teachers, administrators or any adult not related to the student. Selection is based on the student's leadership roles, civic or community involvement, academic achievement and knowledge of and pride for Oklahoma.
Target applicant(s): High school students.
Amount: $6,000.
Number of awards: 1.
Deadline: September 1.
How to apply: Applications are available online.
Exclusive: Visit www.UltimateScholarshipBook.com and enter code OK175123 for updates on this award.

(1752) · Oklahoma Rural Rehabilitation Corporation Scholarships

Oklahoma Rural Rehabilitation Corporation
401 South Lewis Street, Stillwater, OK 74074-3518
Phone: 405-377-2010
Email: orrcjudy@att.net
http://www.orrcinc.com/scholarships.html

Purpose: To support rural high school graduates entering any private or public college or technical school in Oklahoma.
Eligibility: Applicants must be a rural Oklahoma resident and meet the state of Oklahoma requirements to graduate high school. Students must be entering any private or public college or technical school in Oklahoma during the following term.
Target applicant(s): High school students.
Amount: $500-$700.
Number of awards: Varies.
Deadline: April 15.
How to apply: Applications are available online.
Exclusive: Visit www.UltimateScholarshipBook.com and enter code OK175223 for updates on this award.

(1753) · Oklahoma Schools Insurance Group (OSIG) Scholarship

Oklahoma Schools Insurance Group (OSIG)
Scholarship Committee, P.O. Box 3068, Tulsa, OK 74101
https://www.osig.org/s/osig/scholarship.htm
Purpose: To support graduating high school seniors from each quadrant in the state of Oklahoma.
Eligibility: Applicants must be graduating high school seniors enrolled in an OSIG member school in good standing. An essay submission on a provided topic, transcripts, letters of recommendation and ACT/SAT scores are required.
Target applicant(s): High school students.
Amount: $1,000-$2,000.
Number of awards: 12.
Deadline: March 2.
How to apply: Applications are available online.
Exclusive: Visit www.UltimateScholarshipBook.com and enter code OK175323 for updates on this award.

(1754) · Oklahoma Society of Land Surveyors Scholarships

Oklahoma Society of Land Surveyors
13905 Twin Ridge Road, Edmond, OK 73034
Phone: 405-202-5792
Email: osls@osls.org
http://www.osls.org
Purpose: To aid those who are preparing for careers in land surveying.
Eligibility: Applicants must be high school seniors who are planning to study land surveying in college, or they must be working toward licensure under the direct supervision of a professional land surveyor. High school seniors must be Oklahoma residents who have a GPA of 2.5 or higher. Applicants who are already working in the field must be associate members of the Oklahoma Society of Land Surveyors (OSLS) and must be recommended by a registered professional land surveyor. Selection is based on citizenship, leadership and commitment to professional land surveying.
Target applicant(s): High school students. College students. Adult students.
Minimum GPA: 2.5
Amount: Varies.
Number of awards: Varies.
Deadline: May 15.
How to apply: Applications are available online. An application form, official transcript, ACT scores and one recommendation letter are required.

Exclusive: Visit www.UltimateScholarshipBook.com and enter code OK175423 for updates on this award.

(1755) · Oklahoma State Fair Inc. Scholarship Program

Oklahoma State Fair
Email: kkelly@okstatefair.com
http://www.okstatefair.com
Purpose: To encourage Oklahoma students to continue their education.
Eligibility: Applicants must be graduating seniors from an accredited high school or homeschool in Oklahoma. Students must attend a college, university, vocation or technical school in Oklahoma. Applicants must be U.S. citizens and legal residents of Oklahoma.
Target applicant(s): High school students.
Amount: $2,500.
Number of awards: 10.
Deadline: March 26.
How to apply: Applications are available online.
Exclusive: Visit www.UltimateScholarshipBook.com and enter code OK175523 for updates on this award.

(1756) · Oklahoma Tuition Aid Grant Program (OTAG)

Oklahoma State Regents for Higher Education/Oklahoma Tuition Aid Grant Program (OTAG)
655 Research Parkway, Suite 200, Oklahoma City, OK 73104
Phone: 800-858-1840
Email: studentinfo@osrhe.edu
https://secure.okcollegestart.org/Financial_Aid_Planning/Oklahoma_Grants/Oklahoma_Tuition_Aid_Grant.aspx
Purpose: To assist Oklahoma undergraduates who are pursuing higher education in Oklahoma.
Eligibility: Applicants must be Oklahoma residents who are attending eligible undergraduate institutions in Oklahoma. They must be graduates of Oklahoma high schools and must have resided with their parents in Oklahoma while attending high school for at least two years before graduating. They must demonstrate financial need. Qualified undocumented immigrants are eligible for this award. Selection is based on financial need.
Target applicant(s): High school students. College students. Adult students.
Amount: Up to $1,300.
Number of awards: Varies.
Deadline: Varies.
How to apply: Application is made by completing the FAFSA.
Exclusive: Visit www.UltimateScholarshipBook.com and enter code OK175623 for updates on this award.

(1757) · Oklahoma Tuition Equalization Grant Program (OTEG)

Oklahoma State Regents for Higher Education (OTEG)
655 Research Parkway, Suite 200, Oklahoma City, OK 73104
Phone: 800-858-1840
Email: studentinfo@osrhe.edu
https://secure.okcollegestart.org/Financial_Aid_Planning/Oklahoma_Grants/Oklahoma_Tuition_Equalization_Grant.aspx
Purpose: To provide financial assistance for Oklahoma residents who are attending private institutions in the state.
Eligibility: Applicants must be enrolled in an undergraduate program at a private institution of higher learning full-time. They must have a

family income of no more than $50,000, make satisfactory academic progress and not have already earned a bachelor's degree.

Target applicant(s): High school students. College students. Adult students.

Amount: $2,000.

Number of awards: Varies.

Deadline: Varies.

How to apply: Eligible students who file a Free Application for Federal Student Aid (FAFSA) will be considered.

Exclusive: Visit www.UltimateScholarshipBook.com and enter code OK175723 for updates on this award.

(1758) · Oklahoma Youth with Promise Scholarship Fund

Oklahoma City Community Foundation
1000 North Broadway, Oklahoma City, OK 73102
Phone: 405-235-5603
Email: scholarships@occf.org
https://occf.org/

Purpose: To provide educational assistance to students who graduated while in foster care.

Eligibility: Applicants must be graduates of Oklahoma high schools who were in the custody of the Oklahoma Department of Human Services at the time of graduation. They must have a minimum GPA of 2.0. Financial need is considered.

Target applicant(s): High school students. College students. Adult students.

Minimum GPA: 2.0

Amount: $2,000.

Number of awards: Varies.

Deadline: June 1.

How to apply: Applications are available online.

Exclusive: Visit www.UltimateScholarshipBook.com and enter code OK175823 for updates on this award.

(1759) · Oklahoma's Promise

Oklahoma State Regents for Higher Education/Oklahoma's Promise
655 Research Parkway, Suite 200, Oklahoma City, OK 73104
Phone: 800-858-1840
Email: studentinfo@osrhe.edu
https://www.okhighered.org/okpromise

Purpose: To assist children of families with income below $60,000 in preparing for and paying for college.

Eligibility: Applicants must be Oklahoma residents who are enrolled in the eighth, ninth, tenth or eleventh grade at an Oklahoma high school (or are homeschool students between the ages of 13 and 16) and whose parents' income is less than $60,000 per year. They must take certain college preparatory courses in high school, maintain a GPA of 2.5 or higher and "stay out of trouble" such as criminal acts, drugs or alcohol.

Target applicant(s): Junior high students or younger. High school students.

Minimum GPA: 2.5

Amount: Full tuition.

Number of awards: Varies.

Scholarship may be renewable.

Deadline: June 30.

How to apply: Applications are available online.

Exclusive: Visit www.UltimateScholarshipBook.com and enter code OK175923 for updates on this award.

(1760) · Oliver Joel and Ellen Pell Denny Healthcare Scholarship Fund

Winston-Salem Foundation
751 West Fourth Street, Suite 200, Winston-Salem, NC 27101-2702
Phone: 336-725-2382
Email: StudentAid@wsfoundation.org
http://www.wsfoundation.org

Purpose: To aid North Carolina allied health students.

Eligibility: Applicants must be residents of North Carolina. They must be studying a subject in the field of allied health at an accredited postsecondary institution and have a GPA of 2.5 or higher. They must be seeking a first-time certificate, diploma, associate's degree or bachelor's degree. Master's degree holders are ineligible. Applicants must demonstrate financial need. Preference will be given to residents of Davidson, Davie, Forsyth, Stokes, Surry, Wilkes and Yadkin counties. Selection is based on the overall strength of the application.

Target applicant(s): High school students. College students. Adult students.

Minimum GPA: 2.5

Amount: Up to $3,000.

Number of awards: Varies.

Deadline: July 1.

How to apply: Applications are available online. An application form, official transcript, tax forms and financial aid award letter are required.

Exclusive: Visit www.UltimateScholarshipBook.com and enter code WI176023 for updates on this award.

(1761) · One Family Scholars Program

One Family Inc.
423 West Broadway, Suite 402, Boston, MA 02127
Phone: 617-423-0504
Email: scholars@onefamilyinc.org
http://www.onefamilyinc.org

Purpose: To provide financial support, mentoring, leadership development and other resources for Massachusetts low income single parents who are returning to school.

Eligibility: Applicants must be a single parent with a child under the age of 18 and have family earnings which fall 200 percent or more below the poverty level. They should have clear and obtainable career goals as well as the proven desire and ability to complete the chosen academic program. Students must continue to remain residents of the state of Massachusetts throughout the program, and they must remain active in attendance at required meetings, workshops and retreats. Applicants must be referred by two organizations that they are currently involved with or be endorsed by a partnering organization from One Family's network.

Target applicant(s): College students. Adult students.

Amount: Varies.

Number of awards: Varies.

Scholarship may be renewable.

Deadline: July 2 and October 29.

How to apply: Applications are available by phone.

Exclusive: Visit www.UltimateScholarshipBook.com and enter code ON176123 for updates on this award.

(1762) · Opportunity Award

Louisiana Office of Student Financial Assistance
605 N. Fifth Street, Baton Rouge, LA 70802
Phone: 800-259-5626 x1012
Email: custserv@la.gov

https://mylosfa.la.gov/students-parents/scholarships-grants/tops/
Purpose: To aid Louisiana student residents.
Eligibility: Applicants must be Louisiana residents, U.S. citizens, have a minimum 2.5 GPA, have a minimum ACT score of 20 or equivalent SAT score and apply during their senior year in high school. Applicants must use the award at a Louisiana college or university.
Target applicant(s): High school students.
Minimum GPA: 2.5
Amount: Up to full tuition.
Number of awards: Varies.
Scholarship may be renewable.
Deadline: July 1.
How to apply: The application is the Free Application for Federal Student Aid (FAFSA). ACT or SAT scores must also be reported.
Exclusive: Visit www.UltimateScholarshipBook.com and enter code LO176223 for updates on this award.

(1763) · Opportunity Grant

Washington State Board for Community and Technical Colleges
P.O. Box 42495, 1300 Quince Street SE, Olympia, WA 98504-2495
Phone: 360-704-4400
Email: kwheeler@sbctc.edu
http://www.sbctc.edu/
Purpose: To assist Washington adult students.
Eligibility: Applicants must be adult students with financial need who are attending a community or technical college and who have a minimum 2.0 GPA. The grant provides funding for up to 45 credits over a maximum of three years and up to $1,000 for books and supplies per year. In addition, there are support services such as tutoring, career advising, emergency transportation and emergency child care.
Target applicant(s): College students. Adult students.
Minimum GPA: 2.0
Amount: Full tuition.
Number of awards: Varies.
Scholarship may be renewable.
Deadline: Varies.
How to apply: Applicants must complete the Free Application for Federal Student Aid (FAFSA). Contact your college for more information.
Exclusive: Visit www.UltimateScholarshipBook.com and enter code WA176323 for updates on this award.

(1764) · Oratorical Contest Scholarship

American Legion - Nebraska
Department Headquarters, P.O. Box 5205, Lincoln, NE 68505
Phone: 402-464-6338
Email: actsecylegion@windstream.net
http://www.nebraskalegion.net
Purpose: To encourage students to work hard to gain a comprehensive understanding of the Constitution of the United States of America. This contest also seeks to encourage high school students to become leaders, build effective communication skills and learn of and accept any and all responsibilities associated with being an American citizen.
Eligibility: Students, current and under age twenty, must be current attendees or residents of the state where they are to participate in the contest. Students must compete at the local American Legion Post level. The winner will then move on to the district contest, with the winners advancing to the area competition. Four winners will move forward to the state finals each January. Winners will be awarded for each of these competitions, however the national scholarship awards will be awarded to the top three students in the final round of the national contest.

Target applicant(s): Junior high students or younger. High school students.
Amount: $1,500-$18,000.
Number of awards: Varies.
Deadline: Varies.
How to apply: There is no application for this program.
Exclusive: Visit www.UltimateScholarshipBook.com and enter code AM176423 for updates on this award.

(1765) · Oregon Army National Guard

Oregon Army National Guard
Oregon Military Department, 1776 Militia Way SE, Salem, OR 97301
Phone: 800-452-7500
http://www.oregonarmyguard.com
Purpose: To support students from Oregon who are in the National Guard.
Eligibility: Students must serve in the Oregon Army National Guard. The educational program provides tuition and expenses for vocational school, distance learning, alternative credit programs or college. The Student Loan Repayment Program helps students in repaying up to $50,000. Students must take the Armed Services Vocational Aptitude Battery (ASVAB).
Target applicant(s): High school students. College students. Graduate school students. Adult students.
Amount: Varies.
Number of awards: Varies.
Scholarship may be renewable.
Deadline: Varies.
How to apply: Applications are available online.
Exclusive: Visit www.UltimateScholarshipBook.com and enter code OR176523 for updates on this award.

(1766) · Oregon Farm Bureau Memorial Scholarships

Oregon Farm Bureau
1320 Capitol Street NE, Suite 200, Salem, OR 97301
Phone: 800-334-6323
Email: andrea@oregonfb.org
http://www.oregonfb.org
Purpose: To aid Oregon high school graduates who are preparing for careers in agriculture or forestry.
Eligibility: Applicants must be Oregon high school or home school graduates with a full year of completed college coursework. Students must be enrolled in a degree program that is related to agriculture or forestry. Selection is based on the overall strength of the application.
Target applicant(s): College students. Adult students.
Amount: Varies.
Number of awards: 10-16.
Deadline: March 1.
How to apply: Applications are available online. An application form, transcript and three letters of recommendation are required.
Exclusive: Visit www.UltimateScholarshipBook.com and enter code OR176623 for updates on this award.

(1767) · OROS Scholarship

Organization of Rural Oklahoma Schools
P.O. Box 199, Dewar, OK 74431
Phone: 918-694-1572
http://www.orosok.org/vnews/display.v/SEC/Scholarship
Purpose: To support students in rural Oklahoma schools.

Eligibility: Applicants must be graduating high school seniors whose school is a registered member of Organization of Rural Oklahoma Schools. Scholarship will be awarded to one student from each quadrant of the state of Oklahoma.
Target applicant(s): High school students.
Amount: $500-$1,000.
Number of awards: 5.
Deadline: March 1.
How to apply: Applications are available online and must be submitted through the high school.
Exclusive: Visit www.UltimateScholarshipBook.com and enter code OR176723 for updates on this award.

(1768) · Osher Scholarship

Maine Community College System
323 State Street, Augusta, ME 04330-7131
Phone: 207-629-4000
Email: info@mccs.me.edu
http://www.mccs.me.edu
Purpose: To aid liberal arts students at Maine community colleges.
Eligibility: Students must be Maine residents who are not currently enrolled in any college or university program and who have completed no more than 24 college credits. They must also qualify for and be accepted into the associate of arts degree program in liberal/general studies at a Maine community college.
Target applicant(s): High school students. College students. Adult students.
Amount: Varies.
Number of awards: Varies.
Deadline: Varies.
How to apply: Applications are available from community colleges.
Exclusive: Visit www.UltimateScholarshipBook.com and enter code MA176823 for updates on this award.

(1769) · Our First Amendment Freedoms Art and Essay Contest

Anti-Defamation League Midwest
120 South LaSalle, Suite 1150, Chicago, IL 60603
Phone: 312-533-3939
Email: midwest@adl.org
https://chicago.adl.org/fivefreedoms/
Purpose: To support students interested in the First Amendment.
Eligibility: Applicants must be 6th to 12th grade students in Illinois, Wisconsin, Indiana, Minnesota, North Dakota or South Dakota. Students must submit an essay or artwork related to the First Amendment. Selection is based on the overall strength of the submission.
Target applicant(s): Junior high students or younger. High school students.
Amount: Up to $5,000.
Number of awards: Up to 14.
Deadline: December 31.
How to apply: Applications are available online.
Exclusive: Visit www.UltimateScholarshipBook.com and enter code AN176923 for updates on this award.

(1770) · Outrigger Duke Kahanamoku Scholarship

Outrigger Duke Kahanamoku Foundation
P.O. Box 160924, 4354 Pahoa Avenue, Honolulu, HI 96816
Phone: 808-545-4880
Email: info@dukefoundation.org
https://www.dukefoundation.org/
Purpose: To support Hawaii students who are involved in water sports.
Eligibility: Applicants for the Duke Award must be nominated by a school or athletic official. Each school may nominate up to 3 candidates to be considered for the Duke Award.
Target applicant(s): High school students. College students. Adult students.
Minimum GPA: 3.0
Amount: Up to $15,000.
Number of awards: 1.
Deadline: January 31.
How to apply: Applications are available online.
Exclusive: Visit www.UltimateScholarshipBook.com and enter code OU177023 for updates on this award.

(1771) · Page Education Foundation Grants

Page Education Foundation
901 North 3rd Street, Suite 355, Minneapolis, MN 55458
Phone: 612-332-0406
https://www.page-ed.org/scholar-applicants/
Purpose: To support students of color in Minnesota.
Eligibility: Applicants must be students of color who graduated from a Minnesota high school. Students must be enrolling full-time at an accredited Minnesota post-secondary institution and be willing to complete a minimum of 50 hours of volunteer tutoring for children.
Target applicant(s): High school students. College students. Graduate school students. Adult students.
Amount: Up to $2,500.
Number of awards: Varies.
Deadline: April 1.
How to apply: Applications are available online.
Exclusive: Visit www.UltimateScholarshipBook.com and enter code PA177123 for updates on this award.

(1772) · Palmetto Fellows Scholarship Program

South Carolina Commission on Higher Education
1122 Lady Street, Suite 300, Columbia, SC 29201
Phone: 803-737-2262
Email: cbrown@che.sc.gov
http://www.che.sc.gov
Purpose: Monetary assistance is awarded to academically talented South Carolina high school seniors in an effort to encourage them to go to South Carolina colleges.
Eligibility: Applicants must have a minimum SAT score of 1200 or ACT score of 27, have a minimum 3.5 GPA, rank in the top 6 percent of their class, be residents of South Carolina, be enrolled in a public or private high school, be U.S. citizens or permanent residents and plan to attend a college in South Carolina.
Target applicant(s): High school students.
Minimum GPA: 3.5
Amount: Up to $10,000.
Number of awards: Varies.
Scholarship may be renewable.
Deadline: Varies.
How to apply: Applications are available through your high school guidance office.
Exclusive: Visit www.UltimateScholarshipBook.com and enter code SO177223 for updates on this award.

(1773) · Paraprofessional Scholarship

California School Library Association
6444 E. Spring Street #247, Long Beach, CA 90815-1553
Phone: 888-655-8480
Email: info@csla.net
http://csla.net/awards/
Purpose: To increase the number of trained and qualified library technicians in Southern California.
Eligibility: Applicants must be classified library media workers currently enrolled in a two-year paraprofessional program to become a certified library technician. Students must be Southern California residents planning to work in California as library media technicians after completing the program and be members of the California School Library Association. Three letters of recommendation are required.
Target applicant(s): College students. Graduate school students. Adult students.
Amount: Up to $500.
Number of awards: 1.
Deadline: October 15.
How to apply: Applications are available online.
Exclusive: Visit www.UltimateScholarshipBook.com and enter code CA177323 for updates on this award.

(1774) · Paraprofessional Teacher Preparation Grant

Massachusetts Department of Higher Education
Office of Student Financial Assistance, 454 Broadway, Suite 200, Revere, MA 02151
Phone: 617-727-9420
Email: osfa@osfa.mass.edu
https://www.mass.edu/osfa/programs/programs.asp
Purpose: To assist Massachusetts public school paraprofessionals who wish to become certified as full-time teachers.
Eligibility: Applicants must be employed for at least two years as a paraprofessional in a Massachusetts public school and enroll in an undergraduate program leading to teacher certification, or be employed as a paraprofessional for less than two years and enroll in an undergraduate course of study leading to teacher certification in a high need discipline. Applicants must not have previously earned a bachelor's degree.
Target applicant(s): High school students. College students. Adult students.
Amount: Up to $7,500.
Number of awards: Varies.
Scholarship may be renewable.
Deadline: August 1.
How to apply: Applications are available online.
Exclusive: Visit www.UltimateScholarshipBook.com and enter code MA177423 for updates on this award.

(1775) · Part-Time Grant

Maryland Higher Education Commission
Office of Student Financial Assistance, 6 North Liberty Street, Baltimore, MD 21201
Phone: 800-974-1024
Email: osfamail@mhec.state.md.us
https://mhec.maryland.gov
Purpose: To assist part-time, degree-seeking undergraduates.
Eligibility: All applicants and their parents (if applicants are dependents of their parents) must be Maryland residents. Part-time applicants must complete the Free Application for Federal Student Aid (FAFSA) and contact the financial aid office of the college attending and request to be considered for the Part-Time Grant. Selection is based on financial need. Recommended to apply as soon after January 1 as possible.
Target applicant(s): High school students. College students. Adult students.
Amount: $200-$2,000.
Number of awards: Varies.
Scholarship may be renewable.
Deadline: Varies.
How to apply: Applications are available by request from the applicant's financial aid office. An application form and a completed FAFSA are required.
Exclusive: Visit www.UltimateScholarshipBook.com and enter code MA177523 for updates on this award.

(1776) · Part-Time Grants

Vermont Student Assistance Corporation
Scholarships, P.O. Box 2000, Winooski, VT 05404
Phone: 888-253-4819
http://www.vsac.org/pay/student-aid-options/scholarships/vsac-assisted-scholarships
Purpose: To assist Vermont part-time undergraduate students.
Eligibility: Applicants must be Vermont residents enrolled in or planning to enroll in an undergraduate degree or certificate program part-time (for less than 12 credits per semester). Those who have earned a bachelor's degree previously are ineligible. Selection is based on financial need.
Target applicant(s): High school students. College students. Adult students.
Amount: Varies.
Number of awards: Varies.
Deadline: Varies.
How to apply: Applications are available online. An application form, a completed FAFSA and supporting documents are required.
Exclusive: Visit www.UltimateScholarshipBook.com and enter code VE177623 for updates on this award.

(1777) · Part-Time TAP Program

New York State Higher Education Services Corporation (HESC)
99 Washington Avenue, Albany, NY 12255
Phone: 888-697-4372
Email: scholarships@hesc.ny.gov
http://www.hesc.ny.gov
Purpose: To support undergraduate students in the state of New York.
Eligibility: Applicants may attend the State University of New York, the City University of New York or any other public New York school. Students must be enrolled in 6-12 credits per semester, and they must have at least a 2.0 GPA. Applicants must have earned 12 credits per semester in at least two consecutive prior semesters. Students must demonstrate financial need through the FAFSA.
Target applicant(s): College students. Adult students.
Minimum GPA: 2.0
Amount: Varies.
Number of awards: Varies.
Scholarship may be renewable.
Deadline: Varies.
How to apply: Applications are available online.
Exclusive: Visit www.UltimateScholarshipBook.com and enter code NE177723 for updates on this award.

(1778) · Part-Time Tuition Aid Grant

New Jersey Higher Education Student Assistance Authority
P.O. Box 540, Trenton, NJ 08625
Phone: 800-792-8670
Email: clientservices@hesaa.org
http://www.hesaa.org
Purpose: To support part-time students who are attending county colleges in New Jersey.
Eligibility: Applicants must be residents of New Jersey for at least 12 months prior to college enrollment. They cannot have any previous degrees or defaulted student loans. Students must be enrolled in 6-11 credits per semester at an approved New Jersey county college, and they cannot be majoring in theology or divinity.
Target applicant(s): High school students. College students. Adult students.
Amount: Up to full tuition.
Number of awards: Varies.
Scholarship may be renewable.
Deadline: September 15 (fall and full-year) and February 15 (spring).
How to apply: Applications are available through completion of the FAFSA.
Exclusive: Visit www.UltimateScholarshipBook.com and enter code NE177823 for updates on this award.

(1779) · Past Department Presidents' Junior Scholarship Award

American Legion Auxiliary, Department of California
401 Van Ness Avenue, Suite 319, San Francisco, CA 94102-4570
Phone: 415-861-5092
Email: calegionaux@calegionaux.org
https://calegionauxiliary.com/resources/scholarships/
Purpose: To reward American Legion Auxiliary Juniors.
Eligibility: Applicants must be California resident high school students planning to attend a California college or university, be American Legion Auxiliary members with three years as a Junior and be the children, grandchildren or great grandchildren of a veteran.
Target applicant(s): High school students.
Amount: Varies.
Number of awards: 1.
Deadline: Varies.
How to apply: Applications are available online.
Exclusive: Visit www.UltimateScholarshipBook.com and enter code AM177923 for updates on this award.

(1780) · Past Presidents' Parley Nursing Scholarships

American Legion Auxiliary, Department of California
401 Van Ness Avenue, Suite 319, San Francisco, CA 94102-4570
Phone: 415-861-5092
Email: calegionaux@calegionaux.org
https://calegionauxiliary.com/resources/scholarships/
Purpose: To provide support to the U.S. Armed Forces members and their spouses and children.
Eligibility: Applicants must be residents of California, enrolled or planning to enroll in a nursing program and be the wife, husband, widow, widower or child of a veteran or be veterans themselves.
Target applicant(s): High school students. College students. Graduate school students. Adult students.
Amount: $2,000.
Number of awards: 1.
Deadline: April - 1st Friday.

How to apply: Applications are available online.
Exclusive: Visit www.UltimateScholarshipBook.com and enter code AM178023 for updates on this award.

(1781) · Patty and Melvin Alperin First Generation Scholarship

Rhode Island Foundation
One Union Station, Providence, RI 02903
Phone: 401-274-4564
Email: rbogert@rifoundation.org
https://rifoundation.org/grants-scholarships/browse-scholarships
Purpose: To provide opportunities for students whose parents did not graduate from college.
Eligibility: Applicants must be Rhode Island high school seniors and first-generation college students. They must be enrolled in an accredited institution of higher learning that offers either two-year or four-year degrees.
Target applicant(s): High school students.
Amount: $1,000-$1,500.
Number of awards: Varies.
Scholarship may be renewable.
Deadline: April.
How to apply: Applications are available online.
Exclusive: Visit www.UltimateScholarshipBook.com and enter code RH178123 for updates on this award.

(1782) · Paul Flaherty Athletic Scholarship

American Legion, Department of Kansas
1314 SW Topeka Boulevard, Topeka, KS 66612
Phone: 785-232-9315
https://ksamlegion.org/
Purpose: To support student athletes.
Eligibility: Applicants must be high school seniors or college freshmen or sophomores and have participated in high school athletics. Students must be average or better students and submit three letters of recommendation, one of which must be from a coach, a high school transcript, a 1040 income statement and an essay on the topic, "Why I Want to Go to College."
Target applicant(s): High school students. College students. Adult students.
Amount: $250.
Number of awards: 1.
Deadline: July 15.
How to apply: Applications are available online.
Exclusive: Visit www.UltimateScholarshipBook.com and enter code AM178223 for updates on this award.

(1783) · Paulina L. Sorg Scholarship

Hawaii Community Foundation - Scholarships
827 Fort Street Mall, Honolulu, HI 96813
Phone: 888-731-3863
Email: scholarships@hcf-hawaii.org
https://www.hawaiicommunityfoundation.org/
Purpose: To support nursing or physical therapy students in Hawaii.
Eligibility: Applicants must be college juniors, college seniors or graduate students attending full-time in a physical therapy degree program with a minimum 2.7 GPA.
Target applicant(s): College students. Graduate school students. Adult students.
Minimum GPA: 2.7

Amount: Varies.
Number of awards: Varies.
Deadline: January 31.
How to apply: To apply, register online, complete the online application and select the scholarships to which you wish to apply. In addition, mail the supporting materials: printed confirmation page from the online application, personal statement, copy of Student Aid Report (SAR) available at www.fafsa.ed.gov and official transcript.
Exclusive: Visit www.UltimateScholarshipBook.com and enter code HA178323 for updates on this award.

(1784) · Pennsylvania American Legion Essay Contest

American Legion, Department of Pennsylvania
P.O. Box 2324, Harrisburg, PA 17105
Phone: 717-730-9100
Email: hq@pa-legion.com
http://www.pa-legion.com
Purpose: To encourage Pennsylvania high school students to develop research and writing skills.
Eligibility: Applicants must be Pennsylvania students who are in grades 9 through 12. They must submit an essay of 500 to 1,000 words on a topic that is determined by the scholarship committee. Selection is based on essay grammar, spelling, originality and factual accuracy.
Target applicant(s): High school students.
Amount: $2,500-$3,500.
Number of awards: Varies.
Deadline: January 9.
How to apply: Entry instructions are available online. An essay and cover page are required.
Exclusive: Visit www.UltimateScholarshipBook.com and enter code AM178423 for updates on this award.

(1785) · Pennsylvania Business Education Association Scholarship

Pennsylvania Business Education Association
c/o Renee Hughes, PBEA Scholarship Chair, 506 Pine Hill Drive, Pine Grove, PA 17963
Email: rhughes@pgasd.com
http://www.pbea.info
Purpose: To aid Pennsylvania business teacher education students.
Eligibility: Applicants must be enrolled in a business teacher education program at a postsecondary institution located in Pennsylvania. They must be pursuing an undergraduate degree, master's degree or teaching certificate in the subject. They must have a GPA of 3.0 or higher. Selection is based on the overall strength of the application.
Target applicant(s): College students. Graduate school students. Adult students.
Minimum GPA: 3.0
Amount: Up to $1,000.
Number of awards: 1.
Deadline: October 1.
How to apply: Applications are available online. An application form, official transcript, personal statement and three recommendation letters are required.
Exclusive: Visit www.UltimateScholarshipBook.com and enter code PE178523 for updates on this award.

(1786) · Pennsylvania Educational Gratuity Program

Pennsylvania Department of Military and Veterans Affairs
Building P-0-47, Fort Indiantown Gap, Annville, PA 17003-5002
Phone: 717-861-8910
Email: Ra-eg@pa.gov
http://www.dmva.pa.gov
Purpose: To provide financial assistance to children of veterans.
Eligibility: Applicants must be dependents of honorably discharged veterans who served during wartime or armed conflict and have service-connected disabilities or who died in service during war or armed conflict. They must be 16 to 23 years of age and have lived in and attended school in Pennsylvania for five years prior to application, and they must demonstrate financial need.
Target applicant(s): High school students. College students.
Amount: Up to $500.
Number of awards: Varies.
Scholarship may be renewable.
Deadline: Varies.
How to apply: Applications are available from your local Department of Military and Veterans Affairs.
Exclusive: Visit www.UltimateScholarshipBook.com and enter code PE178623 for updates on this award.

(1787) · Pennsylvania Knights Templar Educational Foundation Scholarships

Pennsylvania Masonic Youth Foundation
Masonic Conference Center, Patton Hall, 1244 Bainbridge Road, Elizabethtown, PA 17022-9423
Phone: 800-266-8424
Email: pmyf@pagrandlodge.com
https://pmyf.org/
Purpose: To assist students in pursuing higher education.
Eligibility: Applicants must be working toward a two- or four-year college degree, graduate degree or trade school education. This award is open to students regardless of Masonic ties, age, race or religion.
Target applicant(s): High school students. College students. Adult students.
Amount: Varies.
Number of awards: Varies.
Deadline: March 15.
How to apply: Applications are available by mail.
Exclusive: Visit www.UltimateScholarshipBook.com and enter code PE178723 for updates on this award.

(1788) · Pennsylvania Land Surveyors' Foundation Scholarship

Pennsylvania Society of Land Surveyors
908 North Second Street, Harrisburg, PA 17102
Phone: 717-540-6811
Email: psls@psls.org
http://www.psls.org/scholarship
Purpose: To aid Pennsylvania students who are planning for careers as land surveyors.
Eligibility: Applicants must be U.S. citizens and residents of Pennsylvania. They must be accepted into or enrolled in a two- or four-year degree program in land surveying. Selection is based on academic merit, statement of purpose, extracurricular activities and recommendations.
Target applicant(s): High school students. College students. Adult students.

Amount: Varies.
Number of awards: Varies.
Deadline: May 1.
How to apply: Applications are available online. An application form, transcript, standardized test scores (high school applicants only) and a guidance counselor evaluation form are required.
Exclusive: Visit www.UltimateScholarshipBook.com and enter code PE178823 for updates on this award.

(1789) · Pennsylvania Oratorical Contest

American Legion, Department of Pennsylvania
P.O. Box 2324, Harrisburg, PA 17105
Phone: 717-730-9100
Email: hq@pa-legion.com
http://www.pa-legion.com
Purpose: To enhance high school students' experience with and understanding of the U.S. Constitution. The contest will help develop students' leadership skills and civic appreciation, as well as the ability to deliver thoughtful, insightful orations regarding U.S. citizenship and its inherent responsibilities.
Eligibility: Applicants must be high school students under the age of 20 who are U.S. citizens or legal residents and residents of the state. Students first give an oration within their state and winners compete at the national level. The oration must be related to the Constitution of the United States focusing on the duties and obligations citizens have to the government. It must be in English and be between eight and ten minutes. There is also an assigned topic which is posted on the website, and it should be between three and five minutes.
Target applicant(s): High school students.
Amount: $4,000-$7,500.
Number of awards: 3.
Deadline: December.
How to apply: Applications are available from school coordinators and online.
Exclusive: Visit www.UltimateScholarshipBook.com and enter code AM178923 for updates on this award.

(1790) · Pennsylvania Society of Tax and Accounting Professionals Scholarships

Pennsylvania Society of Tax and Accounting Professionals
20 Erford Road, Suite 200A, Lemoyne, PA 17043
Phone: 800-270-3352
Email: info@pstap.org
http://www.pstap.org/
Purpose: To aid Pennsylvania accounting students.
Eligibility: Applicants must be full-time undergraduate students who are enrolled at a college or university located in Pennsylvania. They must be majoring in accounting, must have completed 60 credits or more of their degree program and must have a GPA of 3.0. Selection is based on academic achievement, leadership, extracurricular activities and financial need.
Target applicant(s): College students. Adult students.
Minimum GPA: 3.0
Amount: $1,000-$2,000.
Number of awards: 3.
Deadline: September 1.
How to apply: Applications are available online. An application form and an official transcript are required.
Exclusive: Visit www.UltimateScholarshipBook.com and enter code PE179023 for updates on this award.

(1791) · Pennsylvania State Bowling Association Scholarship Program

Pennsylvania State Bowling Association
100 Dutch Hill Road, Bloomsburg, PA 17815
Phone: 570-784-9142
Email: psbasect@ptd.net
https://bowlpa.com
Purpose: To support those students who have participated in the USBC Youth or USBC league in Pennsylvania as they pursue a college education.
Eligibility: Students must be a graduating senior or have recently graduated with the intent to begin collegiate studies. Applicants must have a minimum GPA of 2.0. Selection is based on academic achievements, involvement in bowling and non-bowling activities and financial need.
Target applicant(s): High school students.
Minimum GPA: 2.0
Amount: $1,500.
Number of awards: 4.
Scholarship may be renewable.
Deadline: March.
How to apply: Applications are available online. In addition to the form, applicants must submit an official high school transcript and a brief autobiography detailing academic as well as extracurricular achievements.
Exclusive: Visit www.UltimateScholarshipBook.com and enter code PE179123 for updates on this award.

(1792) · Pennsylvania State Grant Program

Pennsylvania Higher Education Assistance Agency (PHEAA)
Pennsylvania State Grant Program, P.O. Box 8157, Harrisburg, PA 17105
Phone: 800-692-7392
Email: granthelp@pheaa.org
http://www.pheaa.org
Purpose: To assist Pennsylvania undergraduates who demonstrate financial need.
Eligibility: Applicants must be current Pennsylvania residents who have lived in the state for at least 12 consecutive months. They must be graduates of an approved high school or GED recipients and be enrolled in or plan to enroll in a two-year or longer degree program at an approved college or university. They must be enrolled for at least six credit hours per academic term and must meet financial need criteria. Applicants who have earned a bachelor's degree previously or who have a defaulted student loan are ineligible. Selection is based on financial need.
Target applicant(s): High school students. College students. Adult students.
Amount: Varies.
Number of awards: Varies.
Deadline: May 1, August 1, August 15.
How to apply: Applications are available online. An application form, a completed FAFSA and supporting documents are required.
Exclusive: Visit www.UltimateScholarshipBook.com and enter code PE179223 for updates on this award.

(1793) · PenSPRA Scholarship

Pennsylvania School Public Relations Association
Shelly Belcher, Communications Coordinator, Peters Township School District, 631 East McMurray Road, McMurray, PA 15317
Phone: 724-941-6251 x7205
Email: belchers@pt-sd.org

https://penspra.com/

Purpose: To support Pennsylvania students pursuing a career in the communications field.

Eligibility: Applicants must be Pennsylvania public high school students with a 3.0 GPA who are pursuing a degree in communications or a related field such as public relations, journalism, English, advertising or graphic arts. Students must have been accepted to or applied to a college, university, technical school or other institution of higher learning. Applicants must live within one of PenSPRA's three regions (Eastern, Central and Western).

Target applicant(s): High school students.

Minimum GPA: 3.0

Amount: $1,000.

Number of awards: 2.

Deadline: April 23.

How to apply: Applications are available online.

Exclusive: Visit www.UltimateScholarshipBook.com and enter code PE179323 for updates on this award.

(1794) · PG&E Better Together STEM Scholarship Program

PG&E Better Together STEM Scholarship Program, Scholarship America
One Scholarship Way, Saint Peter, MN 56082
Phone: 800-537-4180
Email: pge@scholarshipamerica.org
https://pge.com/scholarships

Purpose: To encourage students from California to further their studies in STEM-related fields.

Eligibility: Applicants must be PG&E customers who are either high school seniors, current college students, veterans or adults returning to school studying one of the following STEM related careers: Engineering (electrical, mechanical, computer, industrial or environmental), computer science/information systems, cyber security or environmental sciences. Students must intend to be full-time undergraduate students for the entire upcoming school year working toward their first degree at a PG&E Partner School in California.

Target applicant(s): High school students. College students. Adult students.

Amount: Up to $10,000.

Number of awards: 40.

Scholarship may be renewable.

Deadline: June 1.

How to apply: Applications are available online.

Exclusive: Visit www.UltimateScholarshipBook.com and enter code PG179423 for updates on this award.

(1795) · Phyllis V. Roberts Scholarship

General Federation of Women's Clubs of Virginia
P.O. Box 8750, Richmond, VA 23226
Phone: 804-288-3724
Email: scholarships@gfwcvirginia.org
https://gfwcvirginia.org/

Purpose: To support undergraduate and graduate students in the field of food and nutritional sciences.

Eligibility: Applicants must be Virginia residents and have a minimum 3.0 GPA. Students will need to submit a short essay explaining why they have chosen a degree in food science/nutritional science. Applicants should have a goal of helping to address food insecurity in our communities.

Target applicant(s): College students. Graduate school students. Adult students.

Minimum GPA: 3.0

Amount: $1,000.

Number of awards: 3.

Deadline: March 15.

How to apply: Application is available online and must include three letters of reference, a college verification of GPA, a resume and the short essay.

Exclusive: Visit www.UltimateScholarshipBook.com and enter code GE179523 for updates on this award.

(1796) · Pinnacol Foundation Scholarship Program

Pinnacol Foundation
7501 E. Lowry Boulevard, Denver, CO 80230
Phone: 303-361-4775
Email: pinnacolfoundation@pinnacol.com
https://www.pinnacolfoundation.org/

Purpose: To provide assistance for students whose parent was killed or injured in a work-related accident.

Eligibility: Applicants must be dependents of workers killed or permanently injured in compensable work-related accidents during employment with Colorado-based employers. They must be between the ages of 16 and 25 and have a diploma or GED or be high school seniors in good standing with a minimum GPA of 2.0. Letter of recommendation, essay, transcripts and documentation of the parent's injury or death are required.

Target applicant(s): High school students. College students.

Minimum GPA: 2.0

Amount: Varies.

Number of awards: Varies.

Scholarship may be renewable.

Deadline: February 15.

How to apply: Applications are available online.

Exclusive: Visit www.UltimateScholarshipBook.com and enter code PI179623 for updates on this award.

(1797) · Plan NH Scholarship and Fellowship Program

Plan New Hampshire
P.O. Box 1105, Portsmouth, NH 03802
Phone: 603-452-7526
Email: info@plannh.org
https://plannh.org/programs/scholarship-and-fellowship

Purpose: To support students who foster excellence in the planning and design of New Hampshire's development.

Eligibility: Applicants must be residents of New Hampshire and be pursuing a degree in or related to: architecture, landscape architecture, studio art, engineering, interior design, construction-related field or trade, environmental science, land or community planning or historic preservation. Students must be current college undergraduate or graduate level students with a superior grade point average. Applicants must also prove leadership experience, work excellence and dedication to life's work in their field with a focus on the New England area.

Target applicant(s): College students. Graduate school students. Adult students.

Amount: Varies.

Number of awards: Varies.

Deadline: April.

How to apply: Applications are available online.

Exclusive: Visit www.UltimateScholarshipBook.com and enter code PL179723 for updates on this award.

(1798) · PRSA-Hawaii/Roy Leffingwell Public Relations Scholarship

Hawaii Community Foundation - Scholarships
827 Fort Street Mall, Honolulu, HI 96813
Phone: 888-731-3863
Email: scholarships@hcf-hawaii.org
https://www.hawaiicommunityfoundation.org/
Purpose: To support Hawaii students who are pursuing careers in public relations.
Eligibility: Applicants must be college juniors, college seniors or graduate students. They must be majoring in public relations, journalism or communications. A minimum GPA of 2.7 is required.
Target applicant(s): College students. Graduate school students. Adult students.
Minimum GPA: 2.7
Amount: Varies.
Number of awards: Varies.
Deadline: January 31.
How to apply: To apply, register online, complete the online application and select the scholarships to which you wish to apply. In addition, mail the supporting materials: printed confirmation page from the online application, personal statement, copy of Student Aid Report (SAR) available at www.fafsa.ed.gov and official transcript.
Exclusive: Visit www.UltimateScholarshipBook.com and enter code HA179823 for updates on this award.

(1799) · R. Flake Shaw Scholarship

North Carolina Farm Bureau
Attn: R. Flake Shaw Scholarship, P.O. Box 27766, Raleigh, NC 27611
Phone: 919-782-1705
Email: ncfbscholarship@ncfb.org
http://www.ncfb.org
Purpose: To aid North Carolina students who are preparing for careers in agriculture.
Eligibility: Applicants must be North Carolina students who are pursuing an associate's or bachelor's degree in an agriculture-related subject. They must be planning to pursue a career in agriculture and demonstrate leadership ability and financial need. Preference will be given to applicants who are the family members of Farm Bureau members. Selection is based on academic merit, character, stated career goals and financial need.
Target applicant(s): High school students. College students. Adult students.
Amount: $1,000-$4,000.
Number of awards: 8.
Scholarship may be renewable.
Deadline: March 8.
How to apply: Applications are available online. An application form, transcript, personal statement and financial information are required.
Exclusive: Visit www.UltimateScholarshipBook.com and enter code NO179923 for updates on this award.

(1800) · R. Preston Woodruff, Jr. Scholarships

Arkansas Student Loan Authority
3801 Woodland Heights, Suite 200, Little Rock, AR 72212
Phone: 800-443-6030
Email: info@asla.info
https://www.asla.info/scholarships
Purpose: To support students who live in Arkansas or are planning to attend school there.
Eligibility: Students must be a resident of Arkansas and be enrolled or planning to enroll in an undergraduate program at a postsecondary education institution in Arkansas with at least a half-time schedule. Applicants must be a high school senior or current college student.
Target applicant(s): High school students. College students. Adult students.
Amount: $1,000.
Number of awards: Varies.
Scholarship may be renewable.
Deadline: April 1.
How to apply: Applications are available online.
Exclusive: Visit www.UltimateScholarshipBook.com and enter code AR180023 for updates on this award.

(1801) · R.W. Bob Holden Scholarship

Hawaii Hotel Industry Foundation
Attn: Scholarship Committee, 2270 Kalakaua Avenue, Suite 1506, Honolulu, HI 96815
Phone: 808-923-0407
http://www.hawaiilodging.org/scholarships.html
Purpose: To reward students enrolled in a college or university majoring in hotel or lodging management program.
Eligibility: Applicants must be Hawaii residents. Students must be enrolled as full-time juniors or seniors attending an accredited university or college in the United States.
Target applicant(s): College students. Adult students.
Minimum GPA: 3.0
Amount: $2,000.
Number of awards: 1.
Deadline: May 12.
How to apply: Applications are available online.
Exclusive: Visit www.UltimateScholarshipBook.com and enter code HA180123 for updates on this award.

(1802) · Rae Lee Siporin Award

Los Alamos National Laboratory Foundation
1112 Plaza del Norte, Espanola, NM 87532
Phone: 505-753-8890
Email: tony@lanlfoundation.org
http://www.lanlfoundation.org
Purpose: To support undergraduate students from northern New Mexico.
Eligibility: Students must have at least a 3.25 GPA, and they must have either an SAT score (combined Math plus Critical Reading only) of at least 930 or an ACT score of at least 19. Applicants must submit an essay and two letters of recommendation.
Target applicant(s): High school students. College students. Adult students.
Minimum GPA: 3.25
Amount: $1,000.
Number of awards: Varies.
Deadline: January 18.
How to apply: Applications are available online.
Exclusive: Visit www.UltimateScholarshipBook.com and enter code LO180223 for updates on this award.

(1803) · Ranelius Scholarship Program

Minnesota Turkey Growers Association
Scholarship Selection Committee, 108 Marty Drive, Buffalo, MN 55313-9338
Phone: 763-682-2171
Email: info@minnesotaturkey.com
https://minnesotaturkey.com/
Purpose: To aid Minnesota students who are preparing for careers in the poultry industry.
Eligibility: Applicants must be Minnesota residents. They must be enrolled in or planning to enroll in a postsecondary educational program that provides adequate preparation for a career in the turkey or poultry industry. Preference will be given to applicants who have not won the award previously, members of the Minnesota Turkey Growers Association (MTGA), family members of MTGA members and employees of MTGA members. Selection is based on academic merit, extracurricular activities and demonstrated interest in the poultry industry.
Target applicant(s): High school students. College students. Adult students.
Amount: Varies.
Number of awards: Varies.
Scholarship may be renewable.
Deadline: January 15.
How to apply: Applications are available online. An application form, personal essay and one recommendation letter are required.
Exclusive: Visit www.UltimateScholarshipBook.com and enter code MI180323 for updates on this award.

(1804) · Ray Anthony Peacock Scholarship

Ray A. Peacock Foundation
3874 Blodgett Street, Houston, TX 77004
Phone: 281-793-7358
http://www.rapscholarship.com
Purpose: To support graduating seniors of Texas in pursuing post-secondary education.
Eligibility: Applicants must demonstrate excellent writing skills, a history of community or public service and have unmet financial need. A minimum GPA of 3.0 is required. Students must submit an essay about their goals and accomplishments, transcripts and two letters of recommendation.
Target applicant(s): High school students.
Minimum GPA: 3.0
Amount: Varies.
Number of awards: Varies.
Deadline: March 1.
How to apply: Applications are available online.
Exclusive: Visit www.UltimateScholarshipBook.com and enter code RA180423 for updates on this award.

(1805) · Raymond F. Cain Scholarship Fund

Hawaii Community Foundation - Scholarships
827 Fort Street Mall, Honolulu, HI 96813
Phone: 888-731-3863
Email: scholarships@hcf-hawaii.org
https://www.hawaiicommunityfoundation.org/
Purpose: To support students in Hawaii who are majoring in fields related to landscape architecture.
Eligibility: Applicants must have at least a 2.7 GPA, and they must have financial need.

Target applicant(s): High school students. College students. Graduate school students. Adult students.
Minimum GPA: 2.7
Amount: Varies.
Number of awards: Varies.
Deadline: January 31.
How to apply: To apply, register online, complete the online application and select the scholarships to which you wish to apply. In addition, mail the supporting materials: printed confirmation page from the online application, personal statement, copy of Student Aid Report (SAR) available at www.fafsa.ed.gov and official transcript.
Exclusive: Visit www.UltimateScholarshipBook.com and enter code HA180523 for updates on this award.

(1806) · Raymond J. Faust Scholarship

American Water Works Association - Michigan Section
Attn.: Faust Scholarship Committee, P.O. Box 150469, Grand Rapids, MI 49515
Phone: 517-292-2912
Email: feedback@mi-water.org
http://www.mi-water.org/?page=Scholarships
Purpose: To aid Michigan Section American Water Works Association members who are preparing for careers in the water utility industry.
Eligibility: Applicants must be members of the Michigan Section of the American Water Works Association (AWWA). They must be current water utility employees, the dependents of current water utility employees or prospective water utility professionals. They must be pursuing or planning to pursue a college degree in a subject that relates to the drinking water field. Selection is based on commitment to the water supply industry.
Target applicant(s): High school students. College students. Adult students.
Amount: Varies.
Number of awards: Varies.
Deadline: July 1.
How to apply: Applications are available online. An application form is required.
Exclusive: Visit www.UltimateScholarshipBook.com and enter code AM180623 for updates on this award.

(1807) · Raymond T. Wellington, Jr. Memorial Scholarship

American Legion Auxiliary, Department of New York
112 State Street, Suite 1310, Albany, NY 12207
Phone: 518-463-1162
Email: nyalaeducation@gmail.com
http://www.deptny.org/?page_id=2128
Purpose: To provide financial assistance to students who are children, grandchildren and great-grandchildren of war veterans.
Eligibility: Applicants must be children, grandchildren or great grand-children of Armed Forces veterans who served in World War II, the Korean Conflict, the Vietnam War, Grenada/Lebanon, Panama, the Persian Gulf or War on Terrorism. Students must be high school seniors or high school graduates and must be U.S. citizens and New York State residents.
Target applicant(s): High school students.
Amount: $1,000.
Number of awards: 1.
Deadline: March 1.
How to apply: Applications are available online.

Exclusive: Visit www.UltimateScholarshipBook.com and enter code AM180723 for updates on this award.

(1808) · RBC Wealth Management Colorado Scholarship

Denver Foundation
55 Madison, 8th Floor, Denver, CO 80206
Phone: 303-300-1790
Email: information@denverfoundation.org
https://denverfoundation.org/scholarships/scholarship-opportunities/
Purpose: To provide assistance to outstanding Colorado high school seniors who plan to pursue degrees in science, engineering or math.
Eligibility: Applicants must be graduating seniors at a Colorado high school who have a 3.75 or higher GPA and have completed college preparatory coursework.
Target applicant(s): High school students.
Minimum GPA: 3.75
Amount: $3,000.
Number of awards: 5.
Deadline: March 15.
How to apply: Applications are available online.
Exclusive: Visit www.UltimateScholarshipBook.com and enter code DE180823 for updates on this award.

(1809) · Reach Higher Montana Scholarships

Reach Higher Montana
40 West 6th Avenue, Helena, MT 59601
Phone: 406-422-1275
http://www.reachhighermontana.org/scholarships/
Purpose: To support students from Montana who are pursuing a higher education.
Eligibility: Applicants must be graduating high school seniors from Montana or residents of Montana who graduated from a Montana high school and are currently attending a college or university in Montana. Students must be attending at least half-time with a 2.5 GPA.
Target applicant(s): High school students. College students. Adult students.
Minimum GPA: 2.5
Amount: $1,000.
Number of awards: Varies.
Deadline: January 15.
How to apply: Applications are available online.
Exclusive: Visit www.UltimateScholarshipBook.com and enter code RE180923 for updates on this award.

(1810) · Red Boucher Scholarship

Alaska Community Foundation
3201 C Street, Suite 110, Anchorage, AK 99503
Phone: 907-334-6700
Email: scholarships@alaskacf.org
https://alaskacf.org/
Purpose: To support graduating seniors and graduates of Alaskan high schools in pursuing a degree in technology education and/or training.
Eligibility: Applicants must be enrolled full-time in a technology related program by the beginning of the semester in which the award is granted. A minimum GPA of 3.0 is required. Preference is given to students with demonstrated financial need.
Target applicant(s): High school students. College students. Adult students.
Minimum GPA: 3.0

Amount: $1,000.
Number of awards: Varies.
Deadline: January 20.
How to apply: Applications are available online.
Exclusive: Visit www.UltimateScholarshipBook.com and enter code AL181023 for updates on this award.

(1811) · Regional University Baccalaureate Scholarship

Oklahoma State Regents for Higher Education/Regional University Baccalaureate Scholarship
655 Research Parkway, Suite 200, Oklahoma City, OK 73104
Phone: 800-858-1840
Email: studentinfo@osrhe.edu
https://secure.okcollegestart.org/Financial_Aid_Planning/Scholarships/Academic_Scholarships/Regional_University_Baccalaureate_Scholarship.aspx
Purpose: To provide financial assistance to students of regional universities.
Eligibility: Applicants must be Oklahoma residents who are enrolled in a bachelor's degree program at one of the following schools: Cameron University, East Central University, Langston University, Northeastern State University, Northwestern Oklahoma State University, Oklahoma Panhandle State University, Rogers State University, Southeastern Oklahoma State University, Southwestern Oklahoma State University, University of Central Oklahoma or the University of Science and Arts of Oklahoma. They must also either have an ACT score of 30 or higher or be a National Merit Semifinalist or Commended Student.
Target applicant(s): High school students.
Amount: $3,000.
Number of awards: Varies.
Scholarship may be renewable.
Deadline: Varies.
How to apply: Applications are available from your university.
Exclusive: Visit www.UltimateScholarshipBook.com and enter code OK181123 for updates on this award.

(1812) · Regions Riding Forward Scholarship Essay Contest

Regions Bank
1900 Fifth Avenue North, Birmingham, AL 35203
https://www.regions.com/ridingforward
Purpose: To encourage retelling stories like those of Black individuals, leaders and activists.
Eligibility: Applicants must be high school seniors or college freshmen, sophomores or juniors who live or attend an accredited college in states with Regions branches. Students must write an essay about a Black American individual who has been an inspiration.
Target applicant(s): High school students. College students. Adult students.
Amount: $3,500-$5,000.
Number of awards: 30.
Deadline: March 31.
How to apply: Applications are available online.
Exclusive: Visit www.UltimateScholarshipBook.com and enter code RE181223 for updates on this award.

(1813) · Retail Chapter Awards

Oregon Association of Nurseries
29751 SW Town Center Loop West, Wilsonville, OR 97070
Phone: 503-682-5089
Email: onf@oan.org
http://www.oan.org
Purpose: To aid students who are majoring in ornamental horticulture or a related subject.
Eligibility: Applicants must be majoring in ornamental horticulture or a related subject. Selection is based on the overall strength of the application.
Target applicant(s): College students. Adult students.
Amount: $1,000.
Number of awards: 3.
Deadline: March.
How to apply: Applications are available online. An application form, official transcript and three references letters are required.
Exclusive: Visit www.UltimateScholarshipBook.com and enter code OR181323 for updates on this award.

(1814) · Rhode Island Foundation Association of Former Legislators Scholarship

Rhode Island Foundation
One Union Station, Providence, RI 02903
Phone: 401-274-4564
Email: rbogert@rifoundation.org
https://rifoundation.org/grants-scholarships/browse-scholarships
Purpose: To assist Rhode Island high school seniors with an excellent track record of community service.
Eligibility: Applicants must be Rhode Island high school seniors who have been accepted into college, have demonstrated need and have a substantial amount of community service.
Target applicant(s): High school students.
Amount: $1,000-$1,500.
Number of awards: Varies.
Deadline: April.
How to apply: Applications are available online.
Exclusive: Visit www.UltimateScholarshipBook.com and enter code RH181423 for updates on this award.

(1815) · RI Promise

Rhode Island Office of the Postsecondary Commissioner
560 Jefferson Boulevard, Suite 100, Warwick, RI 02886
Phone: 401-736-1100
https://www.riopc.edu
Purpose: To assist outstanding Rhode Island high school students.
Eligibility: Applicants must be graduating Rhode Island high school seniors who plan to attend a postsecondary institution full-time and demonstrate academic achievement and financial need.
Target applicant(s): High school students.
Amount: Varies.
Number of awards: Varies.
Scholarship may be renewable.
Deadline: March 1.
How to apply: Complete the Free Application for Federal Student Aid (FAFSA).
Exclusive: Visit www.UltimateScholarshipBook.com and enter code RH181523 for updates on this award.

(1816) · Richard A. Brown Memorial Scholarship for Students

Texas Computer Education Association
P.O. Box 18507, Austin, TX 78760
Phone: 800-282-8232
Email: tceaoffice@tcea.org
https://tcea.org/membership/scholarships/
Purpose: To aid students who are preparing for careers in education.
Eligibility: Applicants must be full-time undergraduates who are attending an accredited college or university and must be preparing for a career in education. They must have completed 24 credits or more of their degree program and must have a GPA of 2.75 or higher on a four-point scale. Selection is based on the overall strength of the application.
Target applicant(s): College students. Adult students.
Minimum GPA: 2.75
Amount: $1,000.
Number of awards: Varies.
Deadline: October.
How to apply: Applications are available online. An application form, transcript, three recommendation letters and two personal statements are required.
Exclusive: Visit www.UltimateScholarshipBook.com and enter code TE181623 for updates on this award.

(1817) · Richard D. Johnson Memorial Post-Secondary Scholarship

American Legion - Alaska
1550 Charter Circle, Anchorage, AK 99508
Phone: 907-278-8598
Email: office@alaskalegion.org
http://www.alaskalegion.org
Purpose: To support graduating high school seniors with their post-secondary education to prepare for the future.
Eligibility: Applicants must be average students involved in school, church and community activities with strong beliefs in the importance of patriotic organizations such as the American Legion. They must have a GPA between 2.0 and 3.0 with an improving outlook on life. Students must show need and have set goals upon graduating from high school. A minimum 500-word essay is required.
Target applicant(s): High school students. College students. Adult students.
Minimum GPA: 2.0
Amount: $1,000.
Number of awards: 1.
Deadline: March 30.
How to apply: Applications are available online.
Exclusive: Visit www.UltimateScholarshipBook.com and enter code AM181723 for updates on this award.

(1818) · Richard D. Wiegers Scholarship

Illinois Real Estate Educational Foundation
P.O. Box 2607, Springfield, IL 62708
Phone: 866-854-7333
Email: ssundquist@ilreef.org
http://www.ilreef.org
Purpose: To aid Illinois students who are preparing for careers in business, law and finance.
Eligibility: Applicants must be Illinois residents who are attending an Illinois college or university. They must be graduate students who are majoring in business or undergraduate students who are majoring

in business, finance or pre-law studies. Selection is based on academic merit, stated career goals, references and financial need.

Target applicant(s): College students. Graduate school students. Adult students.

Amount: Up to $1,000.

Number of awards: Varies.

Deadline: April 1.

How to apply: Applications are available online. An application form, official transcript, two reference letters, a personal statement and course of study outline are required.

Exclusive: Visit www.UltimateScholarshipBook.com and enter code IL181823 for updates on this award.

(1819) · Richard E. Bangert Business Award

Independent Colleges of Washington

600 Stewart Street, Suite 600, Seattle, WA 98101

Phone: 206-623-4494

Email: info@icwashington.org

https://icwashington.org/page/scholarships

Purpose: To aid business students who are attending one of the Independent Colleges of Washington (ICW) member institutions.

Eligibility: Applicants must be attending an Independent Colleges of Washington (ICW) member institution, namely Whitworth University, St. Martin's University, Gonzaga University, Pacific Lutheran University, Whitman College, University of Puget Sound, Walla Walla University, Heritage University, Seattle University or Seattle Pacific University. They must be rising undergraduate juniors or seniors who are majoring in business or a related subject and must demonstrate financial need. Selection is based on the overall strength of the application.

Target applicant(s): College students. Adult students.

Amount: $2,125.

Number of awards: 4.

Deadline: March.

How to apply: Applications are available online. An application form, resume, one recommendation letter, transcript and personal essay are required.

Exclusive: Visit www.UltimateScholarshipBook.com and enter code IN181923 for updates on this award.

(1820) · Richard Goolsby Scholarship Fund

Foundation for the Carolinas

220 North Tryon Street, Charlotte, NC 28202

Phone: 704-973-4500

Email: mmccrorey@fftc.org

https://www.fftc.org/scholarships

Purpose: To support students who are interested in the plastics industry.

Eligibility: Applicants must be full-time graduate students or rising undergraduate sophomores, juniors or seniors. They must have completed science, business or engineering coursework related to plastics and must be interested in the plastics industry. Selection is based on the overall strength of the application.

Target applicant(s): College students. Graduate school students. Adult students.

Amount: Varies.

Number of awards: Varies.

Deadline: March 31.

How to apply: Applications are available online. An application form and supporting materials are required.

Exclusive: Visit www.UltimateScholarshipBook.com and enter code FO182023 for updates on this award.

(1821) · Ritchie M. Gregory Fund

Hawaii Community Foundation - Scholarships

827 Fort Street Mall, Honolulu, HI 96813

Phone: 888-731-3863

Email: scholarships@hcf-hawaii.org

https://www.hawaiicommunityfoundation.org/

Purpose: To support students who are majoring in art.

Eligibility: Applicants must be residents of Hawaii, demonstrate financial need and have a minimum 2.7 GPA. Students must also plan to attend an accredited two- or four-year college or university full-time as an undergraduate or graduate student.

Target applicant(s): High school students. College students. Graduate school students. Adult students.

Minimum GPA: 2.7

Amount: Varies.

Number of awards: Varies.

Deadline: January 31.

How to apply: To apply, register online, complete the online application and select the scholarships to which you wish to apply. In addition, mail the supporting materials: printed confirmation page from the online application, personal statement, copy of Student Aid Report (SAR) available at www.fafsa.ed.gov and official transcript.

Exclusive: Visit www.UltimateScholarshipBook.com and enter code HA182123 for updates on this award.

(1822) · Road to Safety Scholarship Contest

Metzger Wickersham Injury Lawyers

Attn: Road to Safety Scholarship Contest, 2321 Paxton Church Road, Harrisburg, PA 17110

Phone: 717-268-4288

Email: road2safety@mwke.com

https://www.mwke.com

Purpose: To encourage students to take a stand against dangerous driving.

Eligibility: Applicants must be graduating, college-bound high school seniors in Pennsylvania. Students must submit a project sending a message about the dangers of drunk driving and/or distracted driving.

Target applicant(s): High school students.

Amount: $500-$1,000.

Number of awards: 3.

Deadline: April.

How to apply: Applications are available online.

Exclusive: Visit www.UltimateScholarshipBook.com and enter code ME182223 for updates on this award.

(1823) · Rob Branham Scholarship

Advertising Club of Connecticut

P.O. Box 549, Wallingford, CT 06492

Phone: 860-295-8929

Email: admin@adclubct.org

http://adclubct.org/scholarship/

Purpose: To help students planning careers in advertising, marketing and supporting industries.

Eligibility: Applicants must attend or be accepted to an accredited university or technical or trade school. They must major in advertising, marketing, broadcast media or print production. They must be sponsored by a member of the Advertising Club of Connecticut. Selection is based on GPA (20 percent), essay (30 percent), work experience and activities (30 percent) and SAT/ACT scores (20 percent).

Target applicant(s): High school students. College students. Adult students.
Amount: Varies.
Number of awards: Varies.
Deadline: September 15.
How to apply: Applications are available online. An application form, referral letter, two letters of recommendation, essay, transcript and SAT/ACT scores are required.
Exclusive: Visit www.UltimateScholarshipBook.com and enter code AD182323 for updates on this award.

(1824) · Robanna Fund

Hawaii Community Foundation - Scholarships
827 Fort Street Mall, Honolulu, HI 96813
Phone: 888-731-3863
Email: scholarships@hcf-hawaii.org
https://www.hawaiicommunityfoundation.org/
Purpose: To support Hawaii students who plan to work in health care.
Eligibility: Applicants must be in an undergraduate health-related program and have a minimum GPA of 2.7. Students must also demonstrate financial need and plan to attend an accredited two- or four-year college full-time.
Target applicant(s): High school students. College students. Graduate school students. Adult students.
Minimum GPA: 2.7
Amount: Varies.
Number of awards: Varies.
Deadline: January 31.
How to apply: To apply, register online, complete the online application and select the scholarships to which you wish to apply. In addition, mail the supporting materials: printed confirmation page from the online application, personal statement, copy of Student Aid Report (SAR) available at www.fafsa.ed.gov and official transcript.
Exclusive: Visit www.UltimateScholarshipBook.com and enter code HA182423 for updates on this award.

(1825) · Robert D. Blue Scholarship

Robert D. Blue Scholarship
Michael L. Fitzgerald, Treasurer of State, State Capitol Building, Des Moines, IA 50319
Phone: 515-281-7003
Email: rdbluescholarship@iowa.gov
http://www.rdblue.org/scholarship/
Purpose: To provide financial assistance to deserving Iowa students.
Eligibility: Applicants must be Iowa residents who plan to attend an Iowa institution of higher learning the following school year. They may be high school seniors or current college students. An essay and two references are required.
Target applicant(s): High school students. College students. Adult students.
Amount: $500-$1,000.
Number of awards: Varies.
Deadline: May 10.
How to apply: Applications are available online.
Exclusive: Visit www.UltimateScholarshipBook.com and enter code RO182523 for updates on this award.

(1826) · Robert R. Robinson Memorial Scholarship

Michigan Townships Association
512 Westshire Drive, Lansing, MI 48917

Phone: 517-321-6467
http://www.michigantownships.org
Purpose: To aid Michigan students who are planning for careers in public administration.
Eligibility: Applicants must be undergraduate juniors, undergraduate seniors or graduate students who are attending a Michigan college or university. They must be majoring in public administration and must have plans to pursue a career in that field. Selection is based on academic merit, extracurricular activities and stated career goals.
Target applicant(s): College students. Graduate school students. Adult students.
Amount: Varies.
Number of awards: Varies.
Deadline: July 30.
How to apply: Applications are available online. An application form, one letter of recommendation, a personal essay and a resolution of support from a Michigan township board are required.
Exclusive: Visit www.UltimateScholarshipBook.com and enter code MI182623 for updates on this award.

(1827) · Roberta B. Willis Scholarship - Need and Merit-Based Award

Connecticut Office of Higher Education
39 Woodland Street, Hartford, CT 06105-2326
Phone: 860-947-1855
Email: sfa@ctohe.org
http://www.ctohe.org
Purpose: To aid Connecticut residents with higher education expenses.
Eligibility: Applicants must be a high school senior or high school graduate with a high school junior year class rank of 20 percent or better. Students must have a minimum SAT score of 1800 or ACT score of 27 and plan to attend a Connecticut public or non-profit private college. Selection is based on financial need and academic merit.
Target applicant(s): High school students.
Amount: $4,650-$5,250.
Number of awards: Varies.
Deadline: February 15.
How to apply: Applications are available through high school guidance offices. An application form and Free Application for Federal Student Aid are required.
Exclusive: Visit www.UltimateScholarshipBook.com and enter code CO182723 for updates on this award.

(1828) · Roberta B. Willis Scholarship - Need-Based Award

Connecticut Office of Higher Education
39 Woodland Street, Hartford, CT 06105-2326
Phone: 860-947-1855
Email: sfa@ctohe.org
http://www.ctohe.org
Purpose: To aid Connecticut residents with higher education expenses.
Eligibility: Applicants must be attending a public or non-profit private Connecticut college or university and be enrolled in full-time study in a two- or four-year program. Students must have a federal Expected Family Contribution within the allowable range. Selection is based on need.
Target applicant(s): College students. Adult students.
Amount: Up to $4,500.
Number of awards: Varies.
Deadline: February 15.
How to apply: A Free Application for Federal Student Aid is required.

Exclusive: Visit www.UltimateScholarshipBook.com and enter code CO182823 for updates on this award.

(1829) · Rockefeller State Wildlife Scholarship

Louisiana Office of Student Financial Assistance
605 N. Fifth Street, Baton Rouge, LA 70802
Phone: 800-259-5626 x1012
Email: custserv@la.gov
https://mylosfa.la.gov/students-parents/scholarships-grants/tops/
Purpose: To assist Louisiana students in wildlife, forestry or marine science.
Eligibility: Applicants must be Louisiana residents for at least one year, be enrolled as full-time undergraduate or graduate students in a Louisiana public college or university, earn a degree in wildlife, forestry or marine science and have a minimum 2.5 GPA (3.0 if a graduate level student). Applicants must also submit the Free Application for Federal Student Aid (FAFSA) and be U.S. citizens.
Target applicant(s): College students. Graduate school students. Adult students.
Minimum GPA: 2.5 for undergraduate students, 3.0 for graduate students
Amount: $2,000-$3,000.
Number of awards: Varies.
Scholarship may be renewable.
Deadline: July 1.
How to apply: Applications are available online or by written request.
Exclusive: Visit www.UltimateScholarshipBook.com and enter code LO182923 for updates on this award.

(1830) · Rollie Hopgood Future Teachers Scholarship

American Federation of Teachers (AFT) Michigan
2661 East Jefferson, Detroit, MI 48207
Phone: 313-393-2200
Email: tftlindamoore@gmail.com
https://aftmichigan.org/
Purpose: To aid students who are affiliated with AFT Michigan and who are planning to become teachers.
Eligibility: Applicants must be planning to become teachers. They must be affiliated with AFT Michigan through a parent or other member. Selection is based on the overall strength of the application.
Target applicant(s): High school students. College students. Adult students.
Amount: $1,000.
Number of awards: Varies.
Deadline: June 30.
How to apply: Applications are available online. An application form and supporting materials are required.
Exclusive: Visit www.UltimateScholarshipBook.com and enter code AM183023 for updates on this award.

(1831) · Rosa L. Parks Scholarships

Rosa L. Parks Scholarship Foundation
160 W. Fort Street, Detroit, MI 48226
Phone: 313-222-2538
Email: info@rosaparksscholarship.org
http://www.rosaparksscholarshipfoundation.org/
Purpose: To provide education funds for students who hold ideals close to those of Rosa Parks.

Eligibility: Applicants must be Michigan high school seniors who will graduate by August of the application year. They must have a GPA of 2.5 or higher and have taken the SAT or ACT. An essay is required.
Target applicant(s): High school students.
Minimum GPA: 2.5
Amount: $2,000.
Number of awards: 40.
Deadline: Varies.
How to apply: Applications are available online.
Exclusive: Visit www.UltimateScholarshipBook.com and enter code RO183123 for updates on this award.

(1832) · Rosedale Post 346 Scholarship

American Legion, Department of Kansas
1314 SW Topeka Boulevard, Topeka, KS 66612
Phone: 785-232-9315
https://ksamlegion.org/
Purpose: To assist the children of members of the Kansas American Legion or American Legion Auxiliary.
Eligibility: Applicants must be high school seniors or college freshmen or sophomores who are enrolling or enrolled in an approved post-secondary school. They also must be average or better students who are the children of veterans. The children of deceased parents are also eligible if the parent was a paid member at the time of death. Applicants must submit three letters of recommendation with at least one from a teacher, an essay on "Why I Want to Go to College," a 1040 income statement, documentation of parent's veteran status and a certified high school transcript.
Target applicant(s): High school students. College students. Adult students.
Amount: $1,500.
Number of awards: 2.
Deadline: February 15.
How to apply: Applications are available online.
Exclusive: Visit www.UltimateScholarshipBook.com and enter code AM183223 for updates on this award.

(1833) · Rosemary and Nellie Ebrie Fund

Hawaii Community Foundation - Scholarships
827 Fort Street Mall, Honolulu, HI 96813
Phone: 888-731-3863
Email: scholarships@hcf-hawaii.org
https://www.hawaiicommunityfoundation.org/
Purpose: To assist college and graduate students who have Hawaiian ancestry or were born or have been a long-time residents of the Island.
Eligibility: Applicants must be residents of the Island of Hawaii and be of Hawaiian or part-Hawaiian ancestry. Applicants must also submit a four-sheet application and financial form, personal statement, recommendations and transcript.
Target applicant(s): High school students. College students. Graduate school students. Adult students.
Minimum GPA: 2.7
Amount: Varies.
Number of awards: Varies.
Deadline: January 31.
How to apply: Applications are available by written request.
Exclusive: Visit www.UltimateScholarshipBook.com and enter code HA183323 for updates on this award.

(1834) · Rosewood Family Scholarship Program

Florida Department of Education
Office of Student Financial Assistance, State Scholarship and Grant Programs, 325 West Gaines Street, Suite 1314, Tallahassee, FL 32399-0400
Phone: 888-827-2004
Email: osfa@fldoe.org
http://www.floridastudentfinancialaid.org
Purpose: To help Florida minority students especially direct descendants of Rosewood families.
Eligibility: Applicants must be full-time, undergraduate students who attend state universities, public community colleges or public postsecondary vocational-technical schools. Direct descendants of Rosewood families affected by the incidents of January 1923 receive preference. The descendants must provide family information on the Florida Financial Aid Application.
Target applicant(s): High school students. College students. Adult students.
Amount: Up to $6,100.
Number of awards: Up to 50.
Scholarship may be renewable.
Deadline: April 1.
How to apply: Applicants must submit the Initial Student Florida Financial Aid Applications online by April 1. Florida residents must submit the Free Application for Federal Student Aid (FAFSA) online by May 15. Non-residents must submit the FAFSA in time to receive the Student Aid Report (SAR) from the processor and send a copy of the SAR to the Office of Student Financial Assistance by May 15.
Exclusive: Visit www.UltimateScholarshipBook.com and enter code FL183423 for updates on this award.

(1835) · Roy W. Likins Scholarship

American Water Works Association - Florida Section
1300 Ninth Street, Suite B-124, St. Cloud, FL 34769
Phone: 407-957-8448
Email: marjoriecraig@polk-county.net
http://www.fsawwa.org
Purpose: To aid Florida students who are preparing for careers in the drinking water industry.
Eligibility: Applicants must be undergraduate upperclassmen or graduate students who are enrolled at an accredited postsecondary institution located in Florida. They must be majoring in a subject that is related to the drinking water industry and have a GPA of 3.0 or higher on a four-point scale. Previous recipients of this award are ineligible. Selection is based on academic achievement, extracurricular activities, character and stated career goals.
Target applicant(s): College students. Graduate school students. Adult students.
Minimum GPA: 3.0
Amount: $2,500-$25,000.
Number of awards: Varies.
Scholarship may be renewable.
Deadline: July 31.
How to apply: Applications are available online. An application form, personal statement, official transcript and two recommendation letters are required.
Exclusive: Visit www.UltimateScholarshipBook.com and enter code AM183523 for updates on this award.

(1836) · Russ Brannen/KENT FEEDS Memorial Beef Scholarship

Iowa Foundation for Agricultural Advancement
Winner's Circle Scholarships, c/o SGI, 30805 595th Avenue, Cambridge, IA 50046
Phone: 515-291-3941
Email: linda@slweldon.net
http://www.iowastatefair.org/participate/competition/
Purpose: To aid incoming freshmen at Iowa four-year colleges and universities.
Eligibility: Applicants must be incoming freshmen at an Iowa four-year college or university. They must have been actively involved in FFA beef cattle projects. Preference will be given to applicants who have experience in cattle showmanship contest and expositions. Selection is based on livestock project participation, academic merit and leadership.
Target applicant(s): High school students.
Amount: $1,500.
Number of awards: 1.
Deadline: April 1.
How to apply: Applications are available online. An application form, extracurricular activities list and personal essay are required.
Exclusive: Visit www.UltimateScholarshipBook.com and enter code IO183623 for updates on this award.

(1837) · Ruth Lutes Bachmann Scholarship

Grand Lodge of Missouri: Ancient, Free and Accepted Masons
6033 Masonic Drive, Suite B, Columbia, MO 65202-6568
Phone: 573-474-8561
Email: grlodge@momason.org
http://momason.org/scholarships/
Purpose: To aid Missouri high school seniors who are planning to become nurses or school teachers.
Eligibility: Applicants must have plans to pursue higher education in nursing or school teaching. Selection is based on academic merit and promise.
Target applicant(s): High school students.
Minimum GPA: 3.0
Amount: $1,000.
Number of awards: 1.
Scholarship may be renewable.
Deadline: March 15.
How to apply: Applications are available online. An application form, personal statement, transcript and standardized test scores are required.
Exclusive: Visit www.UltimateScholarshipBook.com and enter code GR183723 for updates on this award.

(1838) · Safety Essay Contest

American Legion, Department of New Jersey
135 W. Hanover Street, Trenton, NJ 08618
Phone: 609-695-5418
Email: adjutant@njamericanlegion.org
http://www.njamericanlegion.org
Purpose: To reward students for exceptional essays regarding safety.
Eligibility: Applicants must be in the 6th, 7th or 8th grade and enrolled in a New Jersey school.
Target applicant(s): Junior high students or younger.
Amount: Up to $250.
Number of awards: 4.
Deadline: January 20.

How to apply: Application information is available from the local Department.

Exclusive: Visit www.UltimateScholarshipBook.com and enter code AM183823 for updates on this award.

(1839) · Schlutz Family Beef Breeding Scholarship

Iowa Foundation for Agricultural Advancement
Winner's Circle Scholarships, c/o SGI, 30805 595th Avenue, Cambridge, IA 50046
Phone: 515-291-3941
Email: linda@slweldon.net
http://www.iowastatefair.org/participate/competition/
Purpose: To aid Iowa entering undergraduate freshmen who have experience in beef projects.
Eligibility: Applicants must be rising undergraduate freshmen at an Iowa postsecondary institution. They must have experience in beef projects and activities. Preference will be given to applicants who demonstrate an interest in continuing an involvement in the beef cattle industry after graduation from college. Selection is based on the overall strength of the application.
Target applicant(s): High school students.
Amount: $2,000.
Number of awards: 1.
Deadline: April 1.
How to apply: Applications are available online. An application form and supporting materials are required.
Exclusive: Visit www.UltimateScholarshipBook.com and enter code IO183923 for updates on this award.

(1840) · Schneider-Emanuel American Legion Scholarship

American Legion, Department of Wisconsin
2930 American Legion Drive, P.O. Box 388, Portage, WI 53901-0388
Phone: 608-745-1090
Email: info@wilegion.org
https://wilegion.org/oratorical-scholarships/
Purpose: To award scholarships to American Legion members and their children or grandchildren and members of the Sons of the American Legion or Auxiliary.
Eligibility: Applicants must have graduated from an accredited Wisconsin high school and plan to earn an undergraduate degree at a U.S. college or university. Applicants must also have participated in one or more American Legion-sponsored activities listed in the eligibility requirements.
Target applicant(s): High school students. College students. Adult students.
Minimum GPA: 3.0
Amount: $1,000.
Number of awards: 3.
Deadline: March 1.
How to apply: Applications are available online.
Exclusive: Visit www.UltimateScholarshipBook.com and enter code AM184023 for updates on this award.

(1841) · Scholars for Excellence in Child Care

Oklahoma State Regents for Higher Education/Scholars for Excellence in Child Care
655 Research Parkway, Suite 200, Oklahoma City, OK 73104
Phone: 866-343-3881
Email: gmcpherson@osrhe.edu
https://www.okhighered.org/scholars/
Purpose: To aid child care professionals in Oklahoma who wish to pursue credentials in child development and early childhood education.
Eligibility: Applicants must be child care professionals in Oklahoma. They must be pursuing or planning to pursue additional education or credentials in early childhood education or child development. Selection is based on the overall strength of the application.
Target applicant(s): College students. Adult students.
Amount: Varies.
Number of awards: Varies.
Deadline: Varies.
How to apply: Applications are available online. An application form and supporting materials are required.
Exclusive: Visit www.UltimateScholarshipBook.com and enter code OK184123 for updates on this award.

(1842) · Scholarships for Academic Excellence

New York State Higher Education Services Corporation (HESC)
99 Washington Avenue, Albany, NY 12255
Phone: 888-697-4372
Email: scholarships@hesc.ny.gov
http://www.hesc.ny.gov
Purpose: To assist outstanding New York State high school graduates.
Eligibility: Applicants must be New York residents who are high school graduates, enrolled full-time in an eligible undergraduate program in New York State and are U.S. citizens or eligible noncitizens. Selection is based on grades in Regents exams.
Target applicant(s): College students. Adult students.
Amount: $500-$1,500.
Number of awards: 8,000.
Scholarship may be renewable.
Deadline: Varies.
How to apply: Students are nominated by their high schools.
Exclusive: Visit www.UltimateScholarshipBook.com and enter code NE184223 for updates on this award.

(1843) · Scholarships in Mathematics Education

Illinois Council of Teachers of Mathematics
ICTM Scholarship, c/o Sue and Randy Pippen, 24807 Winterberry Lane, Plainfield, IL 60585
Email: scholarships@ictm.org
http://www.ictm.org/
Purpose: To aid Illinois mathematics education students.
Eligibility: Applicants must be enrolled at an accredited Illinois postsecondary institution in an undergraduate mathematics education curriculum that provides preparation for becoming a teacher. They must be rising juniors or seniors who have a GPA of 3.0 or higher on a four-point scale. Applicants must be pursuing a first bachelor's degree. Selection is based on the overall strength of the application.
Target applicant(s): College students. Adult students.
Minimum GPA: 3.0
Amount: $1,500.
Number of awards: 2-5.
Deadline: May 9.
How to apply: Applications are available online. An application form, lesson planning form, personal essay, two recommendation letters and a transcript are required.
Exclusive: Visit www.UltimateScholarshipBook.com and enter code IL184323 for updates on this award.

(1844) · Senator Patricia K. McGee Nursing Faculty Scholarship

New York State Higher Education Services Corporation (HESC)
99 Washington Avenue, Albany, NY 12255
Phone: 888-697-4372
Email: scholarships@hesc.ny.gov
http://www.hesc.ny.gov
Purpose: To increase the number of nursing educators and clinical faculty members in the State of New York.
Eligibility: Applicants must be U.S. citizens or eligible non-citizens and residents of New York for one year or more. They must be registered nurses who are licensed in New York, and they must be accepted into a graduate nursing program at an approved college or university in New York. Students must also agree to four years of service as nursing faculty in the state.
Target applicant(s): Graduate school students. Adult students.
Amount: Up to $20,000.
Number of awards: Varies.
Scholarship may be renewable.
Deadline: Varies.
How to apply: Applications are available online after June of each year.
Exclusive: Visit www.UltimateScholarshipBook.com and enter code NE184423 for updates on this award.

(1845) · Senatorial Scholarship

Maryland Higher Education Commission
Office of Student Financial Assistance, 6 North Liberty Street, Baltimore, MD 21201
Phone: 800-974-1024
Email: osfamail@mhec.state.md.us
https://mhec.maryland.gov
Purpose: To assist Maryland undergraduate and graduate students who can demonstrate financial need.
Eligibility: Applicants must be U.S. citizens or eligible noncitizens, legal residents of the state of Maryland and complete the Free Application for Federal Student Aid (FAFSA). Some senators have supplementary forms. Contact your area's senator's office for complete details. All applicants must enroll at a two- or four-year Maryland college or university as degree-seeking undergraduate or graduate student, or attend certain private career schools. Applicants must show financial need. High school applicants must also take the SAT or the ACT.
Target applicant(s): High school students. College students. Graduate school students. Adult students.
Amount: $400-$11,250.
Number of awards: Varies.
Scholarship may be renewable.
Deadline: March 1.
How to apply: Complete and file the Free Application for Federal Student Aid (FAFSA). Contact senator for specific application forms. The Office of Student Financial Assistance (OSFA) can provide a list of all State legislators.
Exclusive: Visit www.UltimateScholarshipBook.com and enter code MA184523 for updates on this award.

(1846) · SGT Felix M. Del Greco, Jr. Scholarship

Connecticut National Guard Foundation Inc.
State Armory, 360 Broad Street, Hartford, CT 06105-3795
Phone: 860-241-1550
Email: scholarship.committee@ctngfoundation.org
https://ctngfi.org/
Purpose: To provide financial assistance to children of Connecticut National Guard members.
Eligibility: Applicants must be sons or daughters of a member of the Connecticut Army National Guard. They must be enrolled in or plan to attend an accredited degree or technical program.
Target applicant(s): High school students. College students. Adult students.
Amount: $4,000.
Number of awards: 2.
Deadline: March 15.
How to apply: Applications are available online.
Exclusive: Visit www.UltimateScholarshipBook.com and enter code CO184623 for updates on this award.

(1847) · Shipley Rose Buckner Memorial Scholarship

Funeral Service Foundation
13625 Bishop's Drive, Brookfield, WI 53005-6607
Phone: 877-402-5900
Email: info@funeralservicefoundation.org
https://www.funeralservicefoundation.org/academicscholarships/
Purpose: To aid female Tennessee students with tuition costs of mortuary science education programs.
Eligibility: Applicants must be enrolled as a funeral service student full- or part-time in an American Board of Funeral Service Education accredited program. Selection is based on the overall strength of the application.
Target applicant(s): College students. Graduate school students. Adult students.
Minimum GPA: 2.0
Amount: $5,000.
Number of awards: Varies.
Deadline: April 1, November 1.
How to apply: Applications are available online. An application form, essay, academic transcript and video submissions are required.
Exclusive: Visit www.UltimateScholarshipBook.com and enter code FU184723 for updates on this award.

(1848) · Shirley McKown Scholarship Fund

Hawaii Community Foundation - Scholarships
827 Fort Street Mall, Honolulu, HI 96813
Phone: 888-731-3863
Email: scholarships@hcf-hawaii.org
https://www.hawaiicommunityfoundation.org/
Purpose: To support Hawaii students who are majoring in journalism, advertising or public relations.
Eligibility: Applicants must be attending a four-year college or university with at least a 3.0 GPA. They must be college juniors, college seniors or graduate students.
Target applicant(s): College students. Graduate school students. Adult students.
Minimum GPA: 3.0
Amount: Varies.
Number of awards: Varies.
Deadline: January 31.
How to apply: To apply, register online, complete the online application and select the scholarships to which you wish to apply. In addition, mail the supporting materials: printed confirmation page from the online application, personal statement, copy of Student Aid Report (SAR) available at www.fafsa.ed.gov and official transcript.
Exclusive: Visit www.UltimateScholarshipBook.com and enter code HA184823 for updates on this award.

(1849) · Shook Construction Harry F. Gaeke Memorial Scholarship

Associated General Contractors of Ohio
1755 Northwest Boulevard, Columbus, OH 43212
Phone: 614-486-6446
Email: parker@agcohio.com
https://agcohio.com/workforce-development/agc-scholarships/
Purpose: To aid students preparing for careers in the construction industry.
Eligibility: Applicants must be U.S. citizens either living in or attending school in Ohio, Kentucky or Indiana. They must be in at least the second year of an undergraduate degree program that is related to construction and have a GPA of 2.5 or higher. Selection is based on the overall strength of the application.
Target applicant(s): College students. Adult students.
Minimum GPA: 2.5
Amount: $1,000.
Number of awards: 1.
Deadline: March 5.
How to apply: Applications are available online. An application form, transcript and personal essay are required.
Exclusive: Visit www.UltimateScholarshipBook.com and enter code AS184923 for updates on this award.

(1850) · Shuichi, Katsu and Itsuyo Suga Scholarship

Hawaii Community Foundation - Scholarships
827 Fort Street Mall, Honolulu, HI 96813
Phone: 888-731-3863
Email: scholarships@hcf-hawaii.org
https://www.hawaiicommunityfoundation.org/
Purpose: To support Hawaii students who are majoring in math, physics or science and technology.
Eligibility: Applicants must have at least a 3.0 GPA.
Target applicant(s): High school students. College students. Graduate school students. Adult students.
Minimum GPA: 3.0
Amount: Varies.
Number of awards: Varies.
Deadline: January 31.
How to apply: To apply, register online, complete the online application and select the scholarships to which you wish to apply. In addition, mail the supporting materials: printed confirmation page from the online application, personal statement, copy of Student Aid Report (SAR) available at www.fafsa.ed.gov and official transcript.
Exclusive: Visit www.UltimateScholarshipBook.com and enter code HA185023 for updates on this award.

(1851) · Sioux Falls Area Retired Teachers Scholarship

Sioux Falls Area Community Foundation
The Depot at Cherapa Place, 200 N. Cherapa Place, Sioux Falls, SD 57103-2205
Phone: 605-336-7055
Email: pgale@sfacf.org
https://www.sfacf.org/grants-scholarships/scholarships
Purpose: To aid South Dakota students who are majoring in education.
Eligibility: Applicants must be rising undergraduate juniors or seniors who are majoring in education at an accredited South Dakota college or university. They must have a GPA of 2.5 or better, demonstrate financial need, participate in extracurricular activities and display a commitment to the teaching profession. Selection is based on the overall strength of the application.
Target applicant(s): College students. Adult students.
Minimum GPA: 2.5
Amount: $1,500.
Number of awards: 1.
Deadline: March 15.
How to apply: Applications are available from the applicant's financial aid office or guidance counselor. An application form and supporting materials are required.
Exclusive: Visit www.UltimateScholarshipBook.com and enter code SI185123 for updates on this award.

(1852) · Sister Helen Marie Pellicer Scholarship

Florida Academy of Nutrition and Dietetics Foundation
Scholarship Chair, P.O. Box 12608, Tallahassee, FL 32317-2608
Phone: 850-386-8850
Email: cstapell@eatrightflorida.org
http://www.eatrightflorida.org
Purpose: To aid Florida dietetics students.
Eligibility: Applicants must be U.S. citizens or permanent residents, Florida residents and undergraduate upperclassmen who are majoring in dietetics. They must have a GPA of 2.5 or higher on a four-point scale. Selection is based on the overall strength of the application.
Target applicant(s): College students. Adult students.
Minimum GPA: 2.5
Amount: $1,000.
Number of awards: 1.
Deadline: December.
How to apply: Applications are available online. An application form, official transcript and two recommendation letters are required.
Exclusive: Visit www.UltimateScholarshipBook.com and enter code FL185223 for updates on this award.

(1853) · Sister Mary Petronia Van Straten and Ethel A. Neijahr Scholarships

Wisconsin Mathematics Council Inc.
W175 N11117 Stonewood Drive, Suite 204, Germantown, WI 53022
Phone: 262-437-0174
Email: wismath@teamwi.com
http://www.wismath.org
Purpose: To aid Wisconsin teacher education students.
Eligibility: Applicants must be Wisconsin legal residents, be enrolled in a teacher education program and have completed or be in the process of completing a course in mathematics teaching methods. They must have a GPA of 3.0 or higher. Selection is based on the overall strength of the application.
Target applicant(s): College students. Adult students.
Minimum GPA: 3.0
Amount: $2,000.
Number of awards: 2.
Deadline: July 1.
How to apply: Applications are available online. An application form, official transcript, two letters of recommendation, a plan of study and a personal essay are required.
Exclusive: Visit www.UltimateScholarshipBook.com and enter code WI185323 for updates on this award.

(1854) · Six Meter Club of Chicago Scholarship

American Radio Relay League Foundation
225 Main Street, Newington, CT 06111-1494
Phone: 860-594-0348
Email: foundation@arrl.org
http://www.arrl.org/scholarship-program
Purpose: To support Illinois residents who are involved in amateur radio.
Eligibility: Applicants must have an active amateur radio license in any class. Students must be enrolled in an Illinois university or technical school for undergraduate study. A minimum GPA of 2.5 is preferred.
Target applicant(s): High school students. College students. Adult students.
Minimum GPA: 2.5
Amount: $500.
Number of awards: 1.
Deadline: December 31.
How to apply: Applications are available online.
Exclusive: Visit www.UltimateScholarshipBook.com and enter code AM185423 for updates on this award.

(1855) · Smart Choices Scholarship Program

Washington Interscholastic Activities Association (WIAA)
435 Main Avenue South, Renton, WA 98057
Phone: 425-687-8585
Email: smartchoices@wiaa.com
http://www.wiaa.com/
Purpose: To support graduating seniors who have proven excellence in activities, academics, leadership and community service.
Eligibility: Applicants must be high school seniors, have a minimum GPA of 3.2 and participate in a WIAA high school sport or activity during the current school year. Applicants must also be dairy consumers. Selection will be based on academic achievement, leadership and community service.
Target applicant(s): High school students.
Minimum GPA: 3.2
Amount: $1,000-$5,000.
Number of awards: 10.
Deadline: April 1.
How to apply: Applications are available online.
Exclusive: Visit www.UltimateScholarshipBook.com and enter code WA185523 for updates on this award.

(1856) · Smith Diversity Scholarship

Lutheran Family Services of Nebraska
124 South 24th Street, Omaha, NE 56102
Phone: 402-681-7024
Email: mmcdowell@lfs.neb.org
https://www.lfsneb.org/smith-diversity-scholarship/
Purpose: To support graduating high school seniors from low-income, minority families who are residents of Nebraska.
Eligibility: Applicants must be a resident of Nebraska at time of graduation. Students must show financial need. Preference will be given to applicants from disadvantaged ethnic backgrounds that do not identify as Caucasian.
Target applicant(s): High school students.
Amount: $25,000.
Number of awards: 5-6.
Scholarship may be renewable.
Deadline: January.

How to apply: Applications are available online.
Exclusive: Visit www.UltimateScholarshipBook.com and enter code LU185623 for updates on this award.

(1857) · Smith Scholarship Program

Smith Scholarship Foundation
400 Caldwell Trace, Birmingham, AL 35242
Phone: 205-202-4076
Email: appsupport@smithscholarships.com
http://www.smithscholarships.com
Purpose: To provide assistance for students who face financial, physical or emotional challenges and who have participated in volunteer work or assisted their families.
Eligibility: Applicants must be seniors at an Alabama high school and plan to attend an Alabama four-year college the following fall. Students must also write two essays about their future plans and their community service or family assistance endeavors and provide three letters of recommendation. A minimum C+ GPA is required.
Target applicant(s): High school students.
Minimum GPA: 2.33
Amount: Varies.
Number of awards: Varies.
Deadline: January 1.
How to apply: Applications are available online or by mail.
Exclusive: Visit www.UltimateScholarshipBook.com and enter code SM185723 for updates on this award.

(1858) · Society of American Military Engineers, Albuquerque Post Scholarship

New Mexico Engineering Foundation
P.O. Box 3828, Albuquerque, NM 87190-3828
Email: scholarship@nmef.net
http://www.nmef.net
Purpose: To support New Mexico students who plan to pursue college degrees in science, engineering or mathematics.
Eligibility: Applicants must be high school seniors and residents of New Mexico. They must plan to enroll in a math, science or engineering undergraduate degree program. Selection is based on academic achievement, leadership experiences at school, involvement in the community and financial need.
Target applicant(s): High school students.
Amount: $2,000.
Number of awards: 2.
Deadline: June 1.
How to apply: Applications are available online. An application form, a transcript and one letter of recommendation are required.
Exclusive: Visit www.UltimateScholarshipBook.com and enter code NE185823 for updates on this award.

(1859) · Sons of Italy Grand Lodge of California College Scholarship

Order Sons of Italy in America, Grand Lodge of California
Attention: Scholarship Commission, 5051 Mission Street, San Francisco, CA 94112-3473
Phone: 415-586-1316
http://www.osiaca.org/Scholarships/How-To-Apply
Purpose: To support students of Italian ancestry graduating from public or private high schools in California, Nevada and Klamath Falls, Oregon.

Eligibility: Applicants must be of at least partial Italian ancestry and be enrolled at a college or trade school for the upcoming fall semester. Selection is based upon academic performance, leadership activities, financial need, essay detailing Italian ancestry, a personal statement and letters of recommendation.
Target applicant(s): High school students.
Amount: $500-$5,000.
Number of awards: Varies.
Deadline: March 1.
How to apply: Applications are available online. An application, personal statement, SAT/PSAT/ACT scores, GPA, record of activities, transcript and two letters of recommendation are required.
Exclusive: Visit www.UltimateScholarshipBook.com and enter code OR185923 for updates on this award.

(1860) · Sons of Italy Grand Lodge of California Italian Language Study Grant

Order Sons of Italy in America, Grand Lodge of California
Attention: Scholarship Commission, 5051 Mission Street, San Francisco, CA 94112-3473
Phone: 415-586-1316
http://www.osiaca.org/Scholarships/How-To-Apply
Purpose: To support students of Italian ancestry graduating from public or private high schools in California, Nevada and Klamath Falls, Oregon with a 30-day summer study abroad program in Italy.
Eligibility: Applicants must be of at least partial Italian ancestry and be enrolled at a college or trade school for the upcoming fall semester. Applicants must also have finished a foreign language course in high school. Selection is based upon academic performance, leadership activities, financial need, essay detailing Italian ancestry, a personal statement and letters of recommendation.
Target applicant(s): High school students.
Amount: Varies.
Number of awards: Varies.
Deadline: March 1.
How to apply: Applications are available online. An application, personal statement, SAT/PSAT/ACT scores, GPA, record of activities, transcript and two letters of recommendation are required.
Exclusive: Visit www.UltimateScholarshipBook.com and enter code OR186023 for updates on this award.

(1861) · South Carolina Farm Bureau Foundation Scholarships

South Carolina Farm Bureau Foundation
P.O. Box 754, Columbia, SC 29202-0754
Email: sanderson@scfb.org
http://www.scfb.org
Purpose: To aid agriculture students from South Carolina Farm Bureau member families.
Eligibility: Applicants must be from a South Carolina Farm Bureau member family. They must be rising undergraduate sophomores, juniors or seniors. They must be majoring in agriculture or a related subject. Selection is based on commitment to the field of agriculture, character and demonstrated leadership ability.
Target applicant(s): College students. Adult students.
Amount: $3,000.
Number of awards: 6.
Deadline: April 30.

How to apply: Applications are available by request from the South Carolina Farm Bureau. An application form and supporting materials are required.
Exclusive: Visit www.UltimateScholarshipBook.com and enter code SO186123 for updates on this award.

(1862) · South Carolina Hope Scholarship

South Carolina Commission on Higher Education
1122 Lady Street, Suite 300, Columbia, SC 29201
Phone: 803-737-2262
Email: cbrown@che.sc.gov
http://www.che.sc.gov
Purpose: Monetary assistance is provided to those freshmen who do not qualify for LIFE or Palmetto Fellows Scholarships.
Eligibility: Applicants must attend an eligible South Carolina public or private college full-time, be South Carolina residents and have a minimum 3.0 GPA. The award is only applicable to the first year of college.
Target applicant(s): High school students.
Minimum GPA: 3.0
Amount: Up to $2,800.
Number of awards: Varies.
Deadline: Varies.
How to apply: Your college will determine your eligibility based on your high school transcript. There is no application form.
Exclusive: Visit www.UltimateScholarshipBook.com and enter code SO186223 for updates on this award.

(1863) · South Carolina Nurses Foundation Nurses Care Scholarship

South Carolina Nurses Foundation Inc.
Chairperson, SCNF Awards Committee, 1821 Gadsden Street, Columbia, SC 29201
Email: scnursesfoundation@gmail.com
http://www.scnursesfoundation.org
Purpose: To aid South Carolina nursing students.
Eligibility: Applicants must be South Carolina residents and be enrolled in an undergraduate registered nurse (RN) degree program or a graduate degree program in nursing. They must be in good academic standing, have plans to practice nursing in South Carolina after graduation and must demonstrate financial need. Selection is based on the overall strength of the application.
Target applicant(s): College students. Graduate school students. Adult students.
Amount: Varies.
Number of awards: Varies.
Deadline: June.
How to apply: Applications are available online. An application form, personal statement, transcript and two recommendation letters are required.
Exclusive: Visit www.UltimateScholarshipBook.com and enter code SO186323 for updates on this award.

(1864) · South Carolina Tuition Grants Program

South Carolina Tuition Grants Commission
115 Atrium Way, Suite 102, Columbia, SC 29223
Phone: 803-896-1120
Email: info@sctuitiongrants.org
https://sctuitiongrants.org/

Purpose: To assist students who wish to attend independent South Carolina colleges.

Eligibility: Students must be legal residents of South Carolina with financial need. High school seniors must graduate in the top 75 percent of their class or score a minimum of 900 on the SAT or 19 on the ACT. College applicants must complete and pass a minimum of 24 semester hours each year.

Target applicant(s): High school students. College students. Adult students.

Amount: Up to $3,200.

Number of awards: Varies.

Scholarship may be renewable.

Deadline: June 30.

How to apply: Fill out the FAFSA, which is available online.

Exclusive: Visit www.UltimateScholarshipBook.com and enter code SO186423 for updates on this award.

(1865) · South Dakota Free Tuition for Veterans and Others Who Performed War Service

South Dakota Board of Regents
306 East Capitol Ave, Suite 200, Pierre, SD 57501-2545
Phone: 605-773-3455
Email: info@sdbor.edu
http://www.sdbor.edu

Purpose: To allow veterans and others who served in war the opportunity to receive higher education.

Eligibility: Applicants must be veterans or others who performed active war service. They must South Dakota residents who qualify for resident tuition and not be entitled to have their tuition or expenses paid by the United States.

Target applicant(s): College students. Adult students.

Amount: Full tuition.

Number of awards: Varies.

Scholarship may be renewable.

Deadline: Varies.

How to apply: Applications are available from your financial aid office.

Exclusive: Visit www.UltimateScholarshipBook.com and enter code SO186523 for updates on this award.

(1866) · Southern Scholarship Foundation Scholarship

Southern Scholarship Foundation
322 Stadium Drive, Tallahassee, FL 32304
Phone: 850-222-3833
Email: elee@southernscholarship.org
http://www.southernscholarship.org

Purpose: To provide rent-free housing scholarships to students attending specific Florida institutions.

Eligibility: Applicants must have financial need, have a minimum 3.0 GPA, demonstrate high character and attend or plan to attend Florida A&M University, Florida Gulf Coast University, Florida State University, the University of Florida, Tallahassee Community College or Santa Fe Community College.

Target applicant(s): High school students. College students. Adult students.

Minimum GPA: 3.0

Amount: Room and board.

Number of awards: Varies.

Scholarship may be renewable.

Deadline: November 1 (Spring), April 1 (Fall).

How to apply: Applications are available online.

Exclusive: Visit www.UltimateScholarshipBook.com and enter code SO186623 for updates on this award.

(1867) · Stan Forrer Scholarship

Oklahoma Association of Broadcasters
6520 N. Western, Suite 104, Oklahoma City, OK 73116
Phone: 405-848-0771
Email: struby@oabok.org
https://oabok.org/careerseducation/scholarships/

Purpose: To support students majoring in broadcasting at Oklahoma colleges and universities.

Eligibility: Applicants must be enrolled in an Oklahoma college or university broadcasting program, be majoring in broadcasting and have an intent to enter the broadcasting career upon graduation. Students must be a junior or senior for the upcoming school year and must maintain a "B" average.

Target applicant(s): College students. Adult students.

Minimum GPA: 3.0

Amount: $2,000.

Number of awards: 1.

Deadline: February 4.

How to apply: Applications are available online.

Exclusive: Visit www.UltimateScholarshipBook.com and enter code OK186723 for updates on this award.

(1868) · Stanley O. McNaughton Community Service Award

Independent Colleges of Washington
600 Stewart Street, Suite 600, Seattle, WA 98101
Phone: 206-623-4494
Email: info@icwashington.org
https://icwashington.org/page/scholarships

Purpose: To reward students who are committed to community service and who attend an independent college of Washington.

Eligibility: Applicants must be juniors or seniors who have participated in community service in high school and college. Students attending Gonzaga University, Heritage University, Pacific Lutheran University, Saint Martin's University, Seattle Pacific University, Seattle University, University of Puget Sound, Walla Walla University, Whitman College or Whitworth University are eligible.

Target applicant(s): College students. Adult students.

Amount: $2,000.

Number of awards: 1.

Deadline: March.

How to apply: Applications are available online or from your school's financial aid office.

Exclusive: Visit www.UltimateScholarshipBook.com and enter code IN186823 for updates on this award.

(1869) · Stanley Z. Koplik Certificate of Mastery Tuition Waiver Program

Massachusetts Department of Higher Education
Office of Student Financial Assistance, 454 Broadway, Suite 200, Revere, MA 02151
Phone: 617-727-9420
Email: osfa@osfa.mass.edu
https://www.mass.edu/osfa/programs/programs.asp

Purpose: To support Massachusetts students who have demonstrated academic merit.

Eligibility: Applicants must be currently enrolled in a public high school in the state of Massachusetts. Students must receive an "Advanced" score on at least one part of the 10th grade MCAS test, and they must score "Proficient" on all of the other sections. They must also have good scores on at least two AP exams, two SAT II exams or combinations of one of those tests and other achievements determined by the Koplik program. Students must maintain a 3.3 GPA while participating in the scholarship.
Target applicant(s): High school students.
Minimum GPA: 3.3
Amount: Up to full tuition.
Number of awards: Varies.
Scholarship may be renewable.
Deadline: Varies.
How to apply: Applications are available from high schools.
Exclusive: Visit www.UltimateScholarshipBook.com and enter code MA186923 for updates on this award.

(1870) · State Employees Association of North Carolina (SEANC) Scholarships
SEANC Scholarship Foundation
1621 Midtown Place, Raleigh, NC 27609
Phone: 919-833-6436
Email: cwilson@seanc.org
https://www.seanc.org/scholarship
Purpose: To provide financial assistance to SEANC members, their spouses and their children who plan to attend college.
Eligibility: Applicants must be the spouses or children of members and demonstrate either financial need or merit, or applicants must be members working full-time and enrolled in six or more semester hours of undergraduate work or three or more hours of graduate work. Students who are spouses or children must be enrolled full-time.
Target applicant(s): High school students. College students. Graduate school students. Adult students.
Amount: Varies.
Number of awards: Varies.
Deadline: April 15.
How to apply: Applications are available online or from your guidance counselor or financial aid office.
Exclusive: Visit www.UltimateScholarshipBook.com and enter code SE187023 for updates on this award.

(1871) · State Need-based Grants
South Carolina Commission on Higher Education
1122 Lady Street, Suite 300, Columbia, SC 29201
Phone: 803-737-2262
Email: cbrown@che.sc.gov
http://www.che.sc.gov
Purpose: Monetary assistance for higher education is provided to South Carolina resident students.
Eligibility: Applicants must be obtaining their first baccalaureate or professional degree, complete the Free Application for Federal Student Aid (FAFSA) and be residents of South Carolina. Students must have a minimum 2.0 GPA and be enrolled in their first one-year program, first associate's degree, first program leading to a baccalaureate degree, first baccalaureate degree or first professional degree to be eligible.
Target applicant(s): High school students. College students. Adult students.
Minimum GPA: 2.0
Amount: Up to $2,500.
Number of awards: Varies.
Scholarship may be renewable.

Deadline: Varies.
How to apply: Complete the FAFSA and contact your college's financial aid office if you plan to attend a public college or the South Carolina Commission on Higher Education if you plan to attend a private college.
Exclusive: Visit www.UltimateScholarshipBook.com and enter code SO187123 for updates on this award.

(1872) · State of Maine Grant Program
Maine Education Assistance Division
Finance Authority of Maine (FAME), 5 Community Drive, P.O. Box 949, Augusta, ME 04332
Phone: 800-228-3734
Email: education@famemaine.com
http://www.famemaine.com
Purpose: To support Maine undergraduate students who have financial need.
Eligibility: Applicants must be U.S. citizens or eligible non-citizens, be Maine residents and submit the Free Application for Federal Student Aid (FAFSA) by May 1. They must have an Expected Family Contribution (EFC) of $5,000 or less. Selection is based on financial need.
Target applicant(s): High school students. College students. Adult students.
Amount: $1,700.
Number of awards: Varies.
Scholarship may be renewable.
Deadline: May 1.
How to apply: Application is made by completing the FAFSA.
Exclusive: Visit www.UltimateScholarshipBook.com and enter code MA187223 for updates on this award.

(1873) · State Work Study
Washington Student Achievement Council
P. O. Box 43430, Olympia, WA 98504-3430
Phone: 360-753-7850
Email: aies@wsac.wa.gov
https://wsac.wa.gov/
Purpose: To help low and middle income students earn money for college while gaining work experience.
Eligibility: Applicants must have demonstrated financial need according to the FAFSA or WASFA, enroll at least half-time in an eligible undergraduate or graduate program, be authorized to work in the United States and not be seeking a degree in theology.
Target applicant(s): High school students. College students. Graduate school students. Adult students.
Amount: $2,000-$5,000 per year.
Number of awards: Varies.
Scholarship may be renewable.
Deadline: Varies.
How to apply: Eligible students who have filed a Free Application for Federal Student Aid (FAFSA) will be considered.
Exclusive: Visit www.UltimateScholarshipBook.com and enter code WA187323 for updates on this award.

(1874) · Stephen Phillips Memorial Scholarship Fund
Stephen Phillips Memorial Scholarship Fund
P.O. Box 870, Salem, MA 01970
Phone: 978-744-2111
Email: staff@spscholars.org
http://phillips-scholarship.org/
Purpose: To aid New England residents pursuing higher education.

Eligibility: Applicants must be U.S. residents or resident aliens who are permanent residents of Connecticut, Massachusetts, Maine, New Hampshire, Rhode Island or Vermont. They must be enrolled in a demanding undergraduate course of study pursuing their first degrees. A GPA of 3.0 or higher is required. Applicants must demonstrate citizenship, character, serious-mindedness and financial need.

Target applicant(s): High school students. College students. Adult students.

Minimum GPA: 3.0

Amount: $3,000-$18,000.

Number of awards: Varies.

Deadline: May 2.

How to apply: Applications are available online. An application form, essay, transcript, counselor or professor recommendation, additional letter of recommendation, FAFSA Student Aid Report, financial aid award letter, documentation of college costs and student's and parents' tax forms are required.

Exclusive: Visit www.UltimateScholarshipBook.com and enter code ST187423 for updates on this award.

(1875) · Sterling Scholar Awards of Utah

Deseret News-KSL Broadcast Group Sterling Scholar
55 North 300 West, Suite 800, Salt Lake City, UT 84145
Phone: 801-323-4223
Email: michaelsonj@deseretmgt.com
http://www.sterlingscholar.org

Purpose: To aid outstanding Utah students.

Eligibility: Applicants must be Utah public high school seniors. They must be nominated by their schools in one of 14 categories. Selection is based on scholarship (50 percent), leadership (25 percent) and community service/citizenship (25 percent).

Target applicant(s): High school students.

Amount: Varies.

Number of awards: Varies.

Deadline: January.

How to apply: Applications are available from your school's Sterling Awards organizer. An ID page, application form, transcript, proof of ACT scores, principal's report, standardized test data sheet and letter of recommendation are required.

Exclusive: Visit www.UltimateScholarshipBook.com and enter code DE187523 for updates on this award.

(1876) · Steve Dearduff Scholarship Fund

Community Foundation for Greater Atlanta Inc.
50 Hurt Plaza, Suite 449, Atlanta, GA 30303
Phone: 404-688-5525
Email: info@cfgreateratlanta.org
https://cfgreateratlanta.org/scholarships/

Purpose: To aid students who are preparing for careers in the fields of medicine and social work.

Eligibility: Applicants must be legal residents of Georgia and be enrolled at or accepted into an accredited postsecondary institution. They must be majoring in medicine or social work, have a GPA of 2.0 or higher and have a demonstrated commitment to community service. They must demonstrate financial need. Selection is based on academic merit, career potential, community service involvement and financial need.

Target applicant(s): High school students. College students. Graduate school students. Adult students.

Minimum GPA: 2.0

Amount: Up to $2,500.

Number of awards: Up to 3.

Scholarship may be renewable.

Deadline: January 22.

How to apply: Applications are available online. An application form and supporting materials are required.

Exclusive: Visit www.UltimateScholarshipBook.com and enter code CO187623 for updates on this award.

(1877) · Steve Fasteau Past Presidents' Scholarship

California Association for Postsecondary Education and Disability
Disabled Student Programs and Services, San Bernardino Valley College, 701 South Mt. Vernon Avenue, San Bernardino, CA 92410
Phone: 909-384-8663
Email: capedscholarships@gmail.com
http://www.caped.co/scholarships/

Purpose: To support disabled students.

Eligibility: Applicants must be college students with high academic achievement. They must demonstrate leadership and dedication to the advancement of students with disabilities in higher education. Undergraduate students must have a minimum GPA of 2.5 and at least six semester units, and graduate students must have a minimum GPA of 3.0 and at least three semester units from a public or private California college or university.

Target applicant(s): High school students. College students. Graduate school students. Adult students.

Minimum GPA: 2.5 for undergraduate students, 3.0 for graduate students

Amount: $1,000.

Number of awards: 1.

Deadline: August 31.

How to apply: Applications are available online. An application form, letter of application, letter of recommendation, verification of disability, transcript and proof of enrollment are required.

Exclusive: Visit www.UltimateScholarshipBook.com and enter code CA187723 for updates on this award.

(1878) · Student Incentive Grants

New Mexico Higher Education Department
2044 Galisteo Street, Suite 4, Santa Fe, NM 87505-2100
Phone: 505-476-8400
Email: cesaria.tapia1@state.nm.us
https://hed.state.nm.us/financial-aid

Purpose: To support New Mexico undergraduate students with financial need to attend postsecondary institutions in New Mexico.

Eligibility: Applicants must be New Mexico resident undergraduate students and attend public and selected private nonprofit postsecondary institutions in New Mexico at least half-time. Students must also be U.S. citizens.

Target applicant(s): College students. Adult students.

Amount: $200-$2,500.

Number of awards: Varies.

Deadline: Varies.

How to apply: Submit the FAFSA and contact your financial aid office. Deadlines are set by individual institutions.

Exclusive: Visit www.UltimateScholarshipBook.com and enter code NE187823 for updates on this award.

(1879) · Students With Injuries Scholarship

Maison Law Personal Injury Lawyer
525 West Main Street, Suite B-1033, Visalia, CA 93291
Phone: 559-396-3889

Email: maisonlawscholarshipprogram@gmail.com
https://maisonlaw.com/community/injury-scholarship/
Purpose: To support students who have suffered a serious injury.
Eligibility: Applicants must be graduating, college-bound high school seniors or be currently enrolled in an accredited college or university with a minimum 3.0 GPA. Students are required to submit an essay on a provided prompt.
Target applicant(s): High school students. College students. Graduate school students. Adult students.
Minimum GPA: 3.0
Amount: $1,000.
Number of awards: 1.
Deadline: May 1.
How to apply: Applications are available online.
Exclusive: Visit www.UltimateScholarshipBook.com and enter code MA187923 for updates on this award.

(1880) · Susan Bunch Memorial Scholarship

California Association on Postsecondary Education and Disability (CAPED)
10073 Valley View Street, #242, Cypress, CA 90630
Phone: 562-397-2810
Email: capedscholarships2018@gmail.com
http://www.caped.co/scholarships/
Purpose: To support students with a learning disability who are pursuing a higher education.
Eligibility: Applicants must have a verifiable learning disability and be currently enrolled as a student at a California college or university with a GPA of 2.5 for undergraduates or 3.0 for graduate students. Students must have completed at least six semester or eight quarter units as an undergraduate student or three semester or four quarter units as a graduate student.
Target applicant(s): College students. Graduate school students. Adult students.
Minimum GPA: 2.5 for undergraduate students, 3.0 for graduate students
Amount: $1,000.
Number of awards: 1.
Deadline: August 31.
How to apply: Applications are available online.
Exclusive: Visit www.UltimateScholarshipBook.com and enter code CA188023 for updates on this award.

(1881) · Susan Howard Community Service Award

British American Foundation of Texas
Email: info@baftx.org
http://www.baftx.org
Purpose: To support Texas students with a passion for community service.
Eligibility: Applicants must be residents of Texas or the U.K. enrolled as full-time students within the Texas or U.K. education systems. Students must demonstrate financial need, be 11 to 21 years old and be currently working on an inspiring community service project.
Target applicant(s): Junior high students or younger. High school students. College students.
Amount: $5,000.
Number of awards: 1.
Deadline: March 31.
How to apply: Applications are available online.
Exclusive: Visit www.UltimateScholarshipBook.com and enter code BR188123 for updates on this award.

(1882) · Susan Thompson Buffett Foundation Scholarship Program

Susan Thompson Buffett Foundation
808 Conagra Drive, Omaha, NE 68102
Phone: 402-943-1383
Email: Scholarships_App@stbfoundation.org
http://www.buffettscholarships.org
Purpose: To support Nebraska students with financial need attend college.
Eligibility: Applicants must live in Nebraska, meet in-state residency requirements and be Nebraska high school or GED graduates. Students must have a minimum 2.0 GPA in high school, be in need of financial assistance and be a first-time freshman planning to attend a Nebraska public college.
Target applicant(s): High school students. College students. Adult students.
Minimum GPA: 2.0
Amount: Varies.
Number of awards: Varies.
Scholarship may be renewable.
Deadline: February 1.
How to apply: Applications are available online.
Exclusive: Visit www.UltimateScholarshipBook.com and enter code SU188223 for updates on this award.

(1883) · Sussman-Miller Educational Assistance Award

Albuquerque Community Foundation (ACF)
P.O. Box 25266, Albuquerque, NM 87125-5266
Phone: 505-883-6240
Email: foundation@albuquerquefoundation.org
https://abqcf.org/student-aid/
Purpose: To assist New Mexico high school graduates and college undergraduates.
Eligibility: Students must be New Mexico residents for a minimum of one year, have been awarded a financial package that does not satisfy demonstrated need and be accepted by and have chosen to attend a U.S. post-secondary, accredited, nonprofit educational institution full-time. High school applicants need to graduate from an accredited public or private high school and have a 3.0 minimum GPA. Undergraduate applicants must have completed a minimum of one semester of undergraduate study with a 2.5 minimum GPA and cannot be applying for residency in another state.
Target applicant(s): High school students. College students. Adult students.
Minimum GPA: 3.0 for high school students, 2.5 for undergraduate students
Amount: $500-$2,000.
Number of awards: Varies.
Deadline: April 24 and June 14.
How to apply: Applications are available online.
Exclusive: Visit www.UltimateScholarshipBook.com and enter code AL188323 for updates on this award.

(1884) · Talent Incentive Program Grant

State of Wisconsin Higher Educational Aids Board
P.O. Box 7885, Madison, WI 53707
Phone: 608-267-2206
Email: heabmail@wisconsin.gov
http://heab.state.wi.us

Purpose: To assist Wisconsin students who have financial need.
Eligibility: Applicants must be Wisconsin residents who are first-time college freshmen at a Wisconsin postsecondary institution. They must be enrolled at least part-time and must demonstrate financial need. Selection is based on financial need.
Target applicant(s): High school students. College students. Adult students.
Amount: $600 to $1,800.
Number of awards: Varies.
Scholarship may be renewable.
Deadline: Varies.
How to apply: Applicants must complete the FAFSA and must be nominated for this award by their financial aid office or by a Wisconsin Educational Opportunities Program (WEOP) counselor.
Exclusive: Visit www.UltimateScholarshipBook.com and enter code ST188423 for updates on this award.

(1885) · Teacher Shortage Employment Incentive Program

Oklahoma State Regents for Higher Education
655 Research Parkway, Suite 200, Oklahoma City, OK 73104
Phone: 800-858-1840
Email: studentinfo@osrhe.edu
http://www.okhighered.org
Purpose: To encourage students who major in mathematics or science to serve as teachers of mathematics and science in Oklahoma public secondary schools.
Eligibility: Applicants must be willing to teach mathematics or science at an Oklahoma public secondary school for at least five years. Students must complete an approved professional teacher education program from an Oklahoma accredited teacher education unit which must include a student teaching requirement. Applicants must also hold a valid certificate to teach mathematics or science at the secondary level.
Target applicant(s): College students. Adult students.
Amount: Varies.
Number of awards: Varies.
Deadline: Varies.
How to apply: Applications are available online.
Exclusive: Visit www.UltimateScholarshipBook.com and enter code OK188523 for updates on this award.

(1886) · Tech High School Alumni Association/W.O. Cheney Merit Scholarship

Community Foundation for Greater Atlanta Inc.
50 Hurt Plaza, Suite 449, Atlanta, GA 30303
Phone: 404-688-5525
Email: info@cfgreateratlanta.org
https://cfgreateratlanta.org/scholarships/
Purpose: To aid future college students who are planning to major in engineering, mathematics or one of the physical sciences.
Eligibility: Applicants must be U.S. citizens, Georgia residents and high school seniors who have been accepted at an accredited four-year postsecondary institution. They must be planning to major in mathematics, one of the physical sciences or engineering and must be full-time students who have a proven interest in community service. They must have an SAT composite (math and critical reading) score of 1300 or higher and must either be in the top 10 percent of their class or have a GPA of 3.0 or higher. Selection is based on the overall strength of the application.
Target applicant(s): High school students.
Minimum GPA: 3.0

Amount: $5,000.
Number of awards: Up to 4.
Scholarship may be renewable.
Deadline: February 15.
How to apply: Applications are available online. An application form and supporting materials are required.
Exclusive: Visit www.UltimateScholarshipBook.com and enter code CO188623 for updates on this award.

(1887) · Technical Certification Scholarship

Texas 4-H Youth Development Foundation
4180 Highway 6, College Station, TX 77845
Phone: 979-845-1211
Email: texas4h@ag.tamu.edu
https://texas4-h.tamu.edu/
Purpose: To support Texas high school seniors who plan to pursue a technical program.
Eligibility: Applicants must be current active members and have actively participated in a 4-H program for at least two of the past three years. They must have formally applied to a Texas college or university, and they must meet all requirements for admission. Students must not have any plans to continue their college education after completion of a technical program.
Target applicant(s): High school students.
Amount: Varies.
Number of awards: Varies.
Deadline: February 15.
How to apply: Applications are available online.
Exclusive: Visit www.UltimateScholarshipBook.com and enter code TE188723 for updates on this award.

(1888) · Ted and Nora Anderson Scholarships

American Legion, Department of Kansas
1314 SW Topeka Boulevard, Topeka, KS 66612
Phone: 785-232-9315
https://ksamlegion.org/
Purpose: To support worthy and needy children of American Legion and American Legion Auxiliary members as they pursue their educations.
Eligibility: Applicants must be high school seniors or college freshmen or sophomores who are average or better students. They must be enrolling or enrolled in a post-secondary school in Kansas and the son or daughter of a veteran. At least one parent must have been a member of the Kansas American Legion or American Legion Auxiliary for the past three years. The children of deceased parents are also eligible as long as the parent was a paid member at the time of death. Applicants must submit three letters of recommendation with only one from a teacher, a 1040 income statement, documentation of parent's veteran status, an essay on "Why I Want to Go to College" and a high school transcript.
Target applicant(s): High school students. College students. Adult students.
Amount: $500.
Number of awards: 4.
Deadline: February 15.
How to apply: Applications are available online.
Exclusive: Visit www.UltimateScholarshipBook.com and enter code AM188823 for updates on this award.

(1889) · Ted Brickley/Bernice Shickora Scholarship

New Jersey Chapter of the American Society of Safety Engineers
Liberty Mutual Insurance Company, Attn.: Frank Gesualdo, 7
Becker Farm Road, 2nd Floor, Roseland, NJ 07068
Email: scholarship@njasse.org
http://nj.asse.org/scholarship/
Purpose: To aid New Jersey students who are majoring in industrial
hygiene, occupational safety, environmental science or a related subject.
Eligibility: Applicants must be New Jersey residents who are enrolled
at an accredited New Jersey college or university and must be graduate
students or rising undergraduate juniors or seniors. They must be
majoring in industrial hygiene, occupational safety, environmental
science or a related subject and must be involved in extracurricular
activities pertaining to occupational safety. They must have a major
GPA of 2.5 or higher on a four-point scale. Selection is based on the
overall strength of the application.
Target applicant(s): College students. Graduate school students. Adult
students.
Minimum GPA: 2.5
Amount: $1,000.
Number of awards: 2.
Deadline: April 15; November 15.
How to apply: Applications are available online. An application form,
transcript and one reference letter are required.
Exclusive: Visit www.UltimateScholarshipBook.com and enter code
NE188923 for updates on this award.

(1890) · Tennessee Funeral Directors Association Memorial Scholarship

Tennessee Funeral Directors Association
Scholarship Committee, 1616 Church Street, Suite A, Nashville, TN
37203
Phone: 615-321-8792
Email: office@tnfda.org
http://www.tnfda.org
Purpose: To aid funeral service and mortuary science students who are
residents of Tennessee.
Eligibility: Applicants must be U.S. citizens and legal residents of
Tennessee. They must be enrolled full time in a funeral service or
mortuary science program at a school that has been accredited by the
American Board of Funeral Service Education (ABFSE). They must
have completed one term of their program and must have at least one
term remaining in their program. They must have plans to practice in
Tennessee after graduating. Selection is based on the overall strength
of the application.
Target applicant(s): College students. Adult students.
Amount: Varies.
Number of awards: Varies.
Deadline: Varies.
How to apply: Applications are available online. An application form,
transcript, copies of federal income tax forms, one recommendation
letter and a personal essay are required.
Exclusive: Visit www.UltimateScholarshipBook.com and enter code
TE189023 for updates on this award.

(1891) · Tennessee HOPE Access Grant

Tennessee Student Assistance Corporation
404 James Robertson Parkway, Suite 1510, Parkway Towers,
Nashville, TN 37243
Phone: 800-342-1663

Email: tsac.aidinfo@tn.gov
https://www.tn.gov/collegepays/financial-aid.html
Purpose: To support students who do not qualify for the Tennessee
HOPE Grant.
Eligibility: Applicants must be entering freshmen who have a minimum
GPA of 2.75. They must also have either an ACT score between 18
and 20 or an SAT score between 860 and 970. Independent students or
the parents of dependent students must have an adjusted gross income
under $36,000.
Target applicant(s): High school students.
Minimum GPA: 2.75
Amount: Up to $1,250 per semester.
Number of awards: Varies.
Deadline: February 1; September 1.
How to apply: Applications are available through completion of the
FAFSA.
Exclusive: Visit www.UltimateScholarshipBook.com and enter code
TE189123 for updates on this award.

(1892) · Tennessee HOPE Lottery Scholarship

Tennessee Student Assistance Corporation
404 James Robertson Parkway, Suite 1510, Parkway Towers,
Nashville, TN 37243
Phone: 800-342-1663
Email: tsac.aidinfo@tn.gov
https://www.tn.gov/collegepays/financial-aid.html
Purpose: To support undergraduate students in Tennessee.
Eligibility: Applicants must be entering freshmen and either have at
least a 3.0 GPA, a score of 21 on the ACT or a score of 980 on the
SAT. GED students must also score at least a 525 on the GED test.
Home-schooled students and some private school students must meet
additional requirements. Applicants must be Tennessee residents for at
least one year prior to the application deadline.
Target applicant(s): High school students.
Minimum GPA: 3.0
Amount: Up to $6,000.
Number of awards: Varies.
Scholarship may be renewable.
Deadline: Varies.
How to apply: Applications are available through completion of the
FAFSA.
Exclusive: Visit www.UltimateScholarshipBook.com and enter code
TE189223 for updates on this award.

(1893) · Tennessee Need-Based Supplemental Aspire Awards

Tennessee Student Assistance Corporation
404 James Robertson Parkway, Suite 1510, Parkway Towers,
Nashville, TN 37243
Phone: 800-342-1663
Email: tsac.aidinfo@tn.gov
https://www.tn.gov/collegepays/financial-aid.html
Purpose: To supplement the Tennessee HOPE Scholarship.
Eligibility: Applicants must have a minimum ACT score of 21 or SAT
score of 980. Entering freshmen may substitute a GPA of 3.0 or higher.
GED students must also have a GED test score of 525 or higher. Family
adjusted gross income may not be more than $36,000.
Target applicant(s): High school students. College students. Adult
students.
Minimum GPA: 3.0

Amount: $750 per semester.
Number of awards: Varies.
Scholarship may be renewable.
Deadline: Varies.
How to apply: Applications are available online. A Free Application for Federal Student Aid (FAFSA) is required.
Exclusive: Visit www.UltimateScholarshipBook.com and enter code TE189323 for updates on this award.

(1894) · Tennessee Student Assistance Awards

Tennessee Student Assistance Corporation
404 James Robertson Parkway, Suite 1510, Parkway Towers, Nashville, TN 37243
Phone: 800-342-1663
Email: tsac.aidinfo@tn.gov
https://www.tn.gov/collegepays/financial-aid.html
Purpose: To aid Tennessee students.
Eligibility: Applicants must be Tennessee residents who have applied for federal aid and have an Expected Family Contribution of $2,100 or less. They must be enrolled at least half time at an eligible Tennessee institution of higher learning and maintain satisfactory academic progress. They may not be in default on a loan or owe a refund on any grant previously received for education.
Target applicant(s): High school students. College students. Adult students.
Amount: Up to $4,000.
Number of awards: Varies.
Scholarship may be renewable.
Deadline: Varies.
How to apply: Applications are available online. A Free Application for Federal Student Aid (FAFSA) is required.
Exclusive: Visit www.UltimateScholarshipBook.com and enter code TE189423 for updates on this award.

(1895) · Texas 4-H Opportunity Scholarship Program - Baccalaureate Scholarships

Texas 4-H Youth Development Foundation
4180 Highway 6, College Station, TX 77845
Phone: 979-845-1211
Email: texas4h@ag.tamu.edu
https://texas4-h.tamu.edu/
Purpose: To support Texas 4-H members who are planning to pursue a bachelor's degree.
Eligibility: Students must be high school seniors who have actively participated in a Texas 4-H program during the current year and at least two of the three previous years. They must have formally applied to a Texas college or university, and they must meet the school's admission requirements. Applicants must have a score of at least 1350 on the SAT or 19 on the ACT. Students must provide information about their 4-H achievements, financial need, community service participation and leadership skills.
Target applicant(s): High school students.
Amount: $3,000-$20,000.
Number of awards: Varies.
Deadline: February 15.
How to apply: Applications are available online.
Exclusive: Visit www.UltimateScholarshipBook.com and enter code TE189523 for updates on this award.

(1896) · Texas Association FCCLA Regional Scholarship

Family, Career and Community Leaders of America - Texas Association
1107 West 45th Street, Austin, TX 78756
Phone: 512-306-0099
Email: fccla@texasfccla.org
https://www.texasfccla.org/scholarships
Purpose: To aid Texas students who are planning to major in family and consumer sciences.
Eligibility: Applicants must be members of Texas Association, Family, Career and Community Leaders of America (FCCLA). They must be planning to major in family and consumer sciences in college. Selection is based on the overall strength of the application.
Target applicant(s): High school students.
Amount: $1,000.
Number of awards: 5.
Deadline: March 15.
How to apply: Applications are available online. An application form, transcript, personal essay and standardized test scores are required.
Exclusive: Visit www.UltimateScholarshipBook.com and enter code FA189623 for updates on this award.

(1897) · Texas Broadcast Education Foundation Scholarships

Texas Association of Broadcasters
502 E. 11th Street, Suite 200, Austin, TX 78701
Phone: 512-322-9944
Email: craig@tab.org
https://www.tab.org/scholarships
Purpose: To support promising Texas students.
Eligibility: Applicants must be TAB student members or attend a TAB member college or university. All eligible applicants must have a GPA of 3.0 or higher and enroll full-time in a program that emphasizes radio or television broadcasting or communications at a college or university in Texas.
Target applicant(s): High school students. College students. Graduate school students. Adult students.
Minimum GPA: 3.0
Amount: $3,000-$5,000.
Number of awards: 9.
Deadline: Varies.
How to apply: Applications are available online. An application form is required.
Exclusive: Visit www.UltimateScholarshipBook.com and enter code TE189723 for updates on this award.

(1898) · Texas Elks State Association Scholarship Program

Texas Elks State Association (TESA)
1963 FM 1586, Gonzales, TX 78629
Phone: 830-875-2425
Email: txelks@gvec.net
http://www.texaselks.org
Purpose: To support Texas students.
Eligibility: Applicants must be seniors in Texas high schools who are not in the top 5 percent of their class. They must be U.S. citizens and Texas residents.
Target applicant(s): High school students.
Amount: $1,250.

Number of awards: 6.
Scholarship may be renewable.
Deadline: February 26.
How to apply: Applications are available online. An application form, transcript, SAT or ACT scores, applicant statement and parent statement are required.
Exclusive: Visit www.UltimateScholarshipBook.com and enter code TE189823 for updates on this award.

(1899) · Texas Elks State Association Teenager of the Year Contest

Texas Elks State Association (TESA)
1963 FM 1586, Gonzales, TX 78629
Phone: 830-875-2425
Email: txelks@gvec.net
http://www.texaselks.org
Purpose: To support outstanding high school students.
Eligibility: Applicants must be graduating high school seniors from Texas. Selection criteria include SAT/ACT scores, honors and awards, participation and leadership in extracurricular activities and neatness and organization of application.
Target applicant(s): High school students.
Amount: $500-$1,500.
Number of awards: 6.
Deadline: February 26.
How to apply: Applications are available online. An application form and documentation of awards and activities are required.
Exclusive: Visit www.UltimateScholarshipBook.com and enter code TE189923 for updates on this award.

(1900) · Texas Elks State Association Vocational Grant Program

Texas Elks State Association (TESA)
1963 FM 1586, Gonzales, TX 78629
Phone: 830-875-2425
Email: txelks@gvec.net
http://www.texaselks.org
Purpose: To support students pursuing vocational education.
Eligibility: Applicants must be U.S. citizens and Texas residents 18 years of age or older. They must plan to enroll full-time in a two-year or less vocational or technical program that results in a certificate, diploma or associates degree.
Target applicant(s): High school students. College students. Adult students.
Amount: Varies.
Number of awards: Varies.
Deadline: March 12.
How to apply: Applications are available online. An application form, personal statement, letter from parent or other person with knowledge of family background, letter of recommendation and grade or work records for previous two years are required.
Exclusive: Visit www.UltimateScholarshipBook.com and enter code TE190023 for updates on this award.

(1901) · Texas Fifth-Year Accounting Student Scholarship Program

Texas Higher Education Coordinating Board
1200 East Anderson Lane, Austin, TX 78752
Phone: 512-427-6101

Email: pamela.harris@thecb.state.tx.us
http://www.collegeforalltexans.com
Purpose: To aid Texas students who are preparing for careers as certified public accountants (CPAs).
Eligibility: Applicants must be Texas residents who are enrolled at an accredited, non-profit postsecondary institution located in Texas. By the time of award disbursement, they must have completed at least 120 credit hours of college coursework with at least 15 of those being from accounting courses. They must plan to take the exam to become a certified public accountant (CPA), and they must demonstrate financial need. Selection is based on the overall strength of the application.
Target applicant(s): College students. Adult students.
Amount: Up to $5,000.
Number of awards: Varies.
Deadline: Varies.
How to apply: Applications are available from the applicant's college financial aid office or department of accounting. An application form and supporting materials are required.
Exclusive: Visit www.UltimateScholarshipBook.com and enter code TE190123 for updates on this award.

(1902) · Texas History Essay Scholarship

Sons of the Republic of Texas
1717 8th Street, Bay City, TX 77414
Phone: 979-245-6644
http://www.srttexas.org/community.html
Purpose: To aid high school students and promote awareness of Texas history.
Eligibility: Applicants must be graduating seniors. They must submit an essay exploring the relevance of Texas history in the building of the state. Selection is based on research, originality and organization.
Target applicant(s): High school students.
Amount: $2,000-$4,000.
Number of awards: 3.
Deadline: January 31.
How to apply: Applications are available online. An application form and essay are required.
Exclusive: Visit www.UltimateScholarshipBook.com and enter code SO190223 for updates on this award.

(1903) · Texas International Fishing Tournament Inc. Scholarship

Texas International Fishing Tournament
P.O. Box 2715, South Padre Island, TX 78597
Phone: 956-943-8438
Email: info@tift.org
https://www.tift.org/p/about/scholarships
Purpose: To support college level anglers in their pursuit of completing undergraduate studies.
Eligibility: Applicants must be a college undergraduate (freshman through senior), have at least a 2.25 GPA and have been involved with the Texas International Fishing Tournament. Selection is based on past involvement with T.I.F.T., academic achievement and an essay.
Target applicant(s): College students. Adult students.
Minimum GPA: 2.25
Amount: $2,000.
Number of awards: Varies.
Scholarship may be renewable.
Deadline: March 1.
How to apply: Applications are available online.

Exclusive: Visit www.UltimateScholarshipBook.com and enter code TE190323 for updates on this award.

(1904) · Texas Occupational Therapy Association Scholarships

American Occupational Therapy Foundation
Attn: Jeanne Cooper, 4720 Montgomery Lane, Suite 202, Bethesda, MD 20814
Phone: 240-292-1034
Email: jcooper@aotf.org
https://www.aotf.org/Scholarships
Purpose: To aid Texas occupational therapy students.
Eligibility: Applicants must be members of the Texas Occupational Therapy Association (TOTA). They must be Texas residents who are enrolled in an occupational therapy certificate, associate's or professional degree program at an accredited Texas school. Selection is based on the overall strength of the application.
Target applicant(s): College students. Adult students.
Amount: Varies.
Number of awards: 2.
Deadline: October 31.
How to apply: Applications are available by request from Jeanne Cooper, who is the scholarship coordinator at the American Occupational Therapy Association. An application form and supporting materials are required.
Exclusive: Visit www.UltimateScholarshipBook.com and enter code AM190423 for updates on this award.

(1905) · Texas Oratorical Contest

American Legion, Department of Texas
P.O. Box 140527, Austin, TX 78714
Phone: 512-472-4138
Email: programs@txlegion.org
http://www.txlegion.org
Purpose: To enhance high school students' experience with and understanding of the U.S. Constitution. The contest will help develop students' leadership skills and civic appreciation, as well as the ability to deliver thoughtful, insightful orations regarding U.S. citizenship and its inherent responsibilities.
Eligibility: Applicants must be high school students under the age of 20 who are U.S. citizens or legal residents and residents of the state. Students first give an oration within their state and winners compete at the national level. The oration must be related to the Constitution of the United States focusing on the duties and obligations citizens have to the government. It must be in English and be between three and five minutes. There is also an assigned topic which is posted on the website, and it should be between three and five minutes.
Target applicant(s): High school students.
Amount: $500-$18,000.
Number of awards: Varies.
Deadline: December 17.
How to apply: Application information is available online or by contacting the local post.
Exclusive: Visit www.UltimateScholarshipBook.com and enter code AM190523 for updates on this award.

(1906) · Texas Public Educational Grant

Texas Higher Education Coordinating Board
1200 East Anderson Lane, Austin, TX 78752
Phone: 512-427-6101
Email: pamela.harris@thecb.state.tx.us
http://www.collegeforalltexans.com
Purpose: To assist Texas students who have financial need.
Eligibility: Applicants must attend a public college or university in Texas and demonstrate financial need. Individual institutions determine additional eligibility criteria. Selection is based on financial need.
Target applicant(s): High school students. College students. Graduate school students. Adult students.
Amount: Varies.
Number of awards: Varies.
Deadline: Varies.
How to apply: Application is made by completing the FAFSA and contacting your school's financial aid office.
Exclusive: Visit www.UltimateScholarshipBook.com and enter code TE190623 for updates on this award.

(1907) · Thaddeus Colson and Isabelle Saalwaechter Fitzpatrick Memorial Scholarship

Community Foundation of Louisville
Waterfront Plaza, West Tower, 325 West Main Street, Suite 1110, Louisville, KY 40202
Phone: 502-585-4649
Email: ebonyo@cflouisville.org
https://www.cflouisville.org/scholarships/
Purpose: To aid female undergraduates in Kentucky who are majoring in environment-related subjects.
Eligibility: Applicants must be female Kentucky residents who are attending a public college or university in Kentucky. They must be full-time undergraduate students who are rising sophomores, juniors or seniors and be majoring in a subject that is related to the environment (such as agriculture, horticulture, environmental engineering, biology or environmental studies). They must have a GPA of 3.0 or higher. Selection is based on the overall strength of the application.
Target applicant(s): College students. Adult students.
Minimum GPA: 3.0
Amount: Up to $4,500.
Number of awards: Varies.
Deadline: March.
How to apply: Applications are available online. An application form and supporting materials are required.
Exclusive: Visit www.UltimateScholarshipBook.com and enter code CO190723 for updates on this award.

(1908) · Thomara Latimer Cancer Foundation Scholarship

Thomara Latimer Cancer Foundation
Franklin Plaza Center, 29193 Northwestern Highway #528, Southfield, MI 48034
Phone: 248-557-2346
Email: info@thomlatimercares.org
http://www.thomlatimercares.org
Purpose: To aid African-American students in Michigan who are preparing for careers in medicine or a related field.
Eligibility: Applicants must be African-American students between the ages of 17 and 30, have a minimum 3.0 GPA and be Michigan residents who are enrolled at or have been accepted to an accredited postsecondary institution. They must be studying or planning to study allied health, medicine, nursing, occupational therapy, physical therapy, physician assisting or a related subject. Selection is based on the overall strength of the application.

Target applicant(s): High school students. College students. Graduate school students. Adult students.
Minimum GPA: 3.0
Amount: Varies.
Number of awards: Varies.
Deadline: January.
How to apply: Applications are available online. An application form, official transcript, personal essay, two recommendation letters and proof of college acceptance or enrollment are required.
Exclusive: Visit www.UltimateScholarshipBook.com and enter code TH190823 for updates on this award.

(1909) · Thomas E. Desjardins Memorial Scholarship

Institute of Transportation Engineers - New England Section
Email: rod.emery@jacobs.com
http://www.neite.org
Purpose: To aid New England civil engineering students who are interested in transportation engineering.
Eligibility: Applicants must be civil engineering undergraduates or graduate students who are enrolled at an accredited postsecondary institution in Connecticut, Maine, Massachusetts, New Hampshire, Rhode Island or Vermont. They must demonstrate an interest in transportation engineering through their coursework or extracurricular activities. Selection is based on academic merit, character and extracurricular activities.
Target applicant(s): College students. Graduate school students. Adult students.
Amount: Varies.
Number of awards: 2.
Deadline: September.
How to apply: Applications are available by request from the New England section of the Institute of Transportation Engineers. An application form and supporting materials are required.
Exclusive: Visit www.UltimateScholarshipBook.com and enter code IN190923 for updates on this award.

(1910) · Tongan Cultural Society Scholarship

Hawaii Community Foundation - Scholarships
827 Fort Street Mall, Honolulu, HI 96813
Phone: 888-731-3863
Email: scholarships@hcf-hawaii.org
https://www.hawaiicommunityfoundation.org/
Purpose: To support students of Tongan ancestry.
Eligibility: Applicants must attend school in Hawaii and must maintain a minimum 2.7 GPA.
Target applicant(s): High school students. College students. Graduate school students. Adult students.
Minimum GPA: 2.7
Amount: Varies.
Number of awards: Varies.
Deadline: January 31.
How to apply: To apply, register online, complete the online application and select the scholarships to which you wish to apply. In addition, mail the supporting materials: printed confirmation page from the online application, personal statement, copy of Student Aid Report (SAR) available at www.fafsa.ed.gov and official transcript.
Exclusive: Visit www.UltimateScholarshipBook.com and enter code HA191023 for updates on this award.

(1911) · TOPS Performance Award

Louisiana Office of Student Financial Assistance
605 N. Fifth Street, Baton Rouge, LA 70802
Phone: 800-259-5626 x1012
Email: custserv@la.gov
https://mylosfa.la.gov/students-parents/scholarships-grants/tops/
Purpose: To aid Louisiana student residents.
Eligibility: Applicants must be Louisiana residents, U.S. citizens, apply during their senior year in high school, use the award at a Louisiana college or university, have a minimum 3.0 GPA and have a minimum ACT score of 23 or an equivalent SAT score.
Target applicant(s): High school students.
Minimum GPA: 3.0
Amount: Tuition plus $400 stipend.
Number of awards: Varies.
Scholarship may be renewable.
Deadline: July 1.
How to apply: The application is the Free Application for Federal Student Aid (FAFSA). ACT or SAT scores must also be reported.
Exclusive: Visit www.UltimateScholarshipBook.com and enter code LO191123 for updates on this award.

(1912) · TOPS Tech Award

Louisiana Office of Student Financial Assistance
605 N. Fifth Street, Baton Rouge, LA 70802
Phone: 800-259-5626 x1012
Email: custserv@la.gov
https://mylosfa.la.gov/students-parents/scholarships-grants/tops/
Purpose: To assist Louisiana resident students.
Eligibility: Applicants must be Louisiana residents, apply during their senior year in a public high school and pursue an industry-based occupational or vocational credential in a public college or university that meets certain standards. They must also have a minimum 2.5 GPA, score at least 15 on the English and Mathematics subsections of the ACT PLAN Assessment, have at least minimum passing scores in English and Mathematics on the GEE and have prepared a five-year education and career plan.
Target applicant(s): High school students.
Minimum GPA: 2.5
Amount: Up to full tuition.
Number of awards: Varies.
Scholarship may be renewable.
Deadline: July 1.
How to apply: Applications are available online or from guidance counselors.
Exclusive: Visit www.UltimateScholarshipBook.com and enter code LO191223 for updates on this award.

(1913) · Towards EXcellence, Access and Success (TEXAS) Grant Program

Texas Higher Education Coordinating Board
1200 East Anderson Lane, Austin, TX 78752
Phone: 512-427-6101
Email: pamela.harris@thecb.state.tx.us
http://www.collegeforalltexans.com
Purpose: To assist Texas students who have financial need.
Eligibility: Applicants must be Texas residents and high school graduates. They must demonstrate financial need by having an Expected Family Contribution (EFC) of $4,000 or less. They must be enrolled at a public, non-profit Texas college or university and cannot

have earned more than 30 semester credits at the time of application submission. Those who have earned an associate's degree at a Texas two-year institution and who intend to enroll in a Texas bachelor's degree program within 12 months of graduation are also eligible. Selection is based on financial need.

Target applicant(s): High school students. College students. Adult students.
Amount: Full tuition and fees.
Number of awards: Varies.
Scholarship may be renewable.
Deadline: March 15.
How to apply: Application is made by completing the FAFSA.
Exclusive: Visit www.UltimateScholarshipBook.com and enter code TE191323 for updates on this award.

(1914) · Township Officials of Illinois Scholarship

Township Officials of Illinois
3217 Northfield Drive, Springfield, IL 62702
Phone: 217-744-2212
Email: bryantoi@toi.org
http://www.toi.org
Purpose: To promote the ideas of quality local government and civic duty and to recruit young people into the TOI.
Eligibility: Applicants must be high school seniors attending an Illinois college or university in the fall and must have a minimum 3.0 GPA.
Target applicant(s): High school students.
Minimum GPA: 3.0
Amount: $1,500.
Number of awards: 7.
Deadline: May 21.
How to apply: Applications are available online in January.
Exclusive: Visit www.UltimateScholarshipBook.com and enter code TO191423 for updates on this award.

(1915) · Treacy Foundation Scholarship

Treacy Foundation
P.O. Box 1479, Helena, MT 59624
Email: director@treacyfoundation.org
https://treacyfoundation.org/scholarships/
Purpose: To reward starting freshman and sophomore students from the states of Montana, Idaho and North Dakota.
Eligibility: Applicants must be either a starting freshman or sophomore. Students must be residents of either Montana, Idaho or North Dakota.
Target applicant(s): High school students. College students. Adult students.
Amount: $2,000.
Number of awards: Varies.
Scholarship may be renewable.
Deadline: May 1.
How to apply: Applications are available online.
Exclusive: Visit www.UltimateScholarshipBook.com and enter code TR191523 for updates on this award.

(1916) · Tuition Aid Grant

New Jersey Higher Education Student Assistance Authority
P.O. Box 540, Trenton, NJ 08625
Phone: 800-792-8670
Email: clientservices@hesaa.org
http://www.hesaa.org
Purpose: To support New Jersey students who are unable to pay the full cost of tuition.
Eligibility: Students must be residents of New Jersey for at least 12 months prior to college enrollment, enroll in an approved New Jersey school and remain in school full-time in an undergraduate program. Applicants cannot have any previous degrees, and they cannot be enrolled in theology or divinity programs.
Target applicant(s): High school students. College students. Adult students.
Amount: Up to full tuition.
Number of awards: Varies.
Scholarship may be renewable.
Deadline: September 15.
How to apply: Applications are available through completion of the FAFSA.
Exclusive: Visit www.UltimateScholarshipBook.com and enter code NE191623 for updates on this award.

(1917) · Tuition Assistance Program (TAP)

New York State Higher Education Services Corporation (HESC)
99 Washington Avenue, Albany, NY 12255
Phone: 888-697-4372
Email: scholarships@hesc.ny.gov
http://www.hesc.ny.gov
Purpose: To assist New York resident students in attending in-state postsecondary institutions.
Eligibility: Applicants must be U.S. citizens or eligible noncitizens, be legal residents of New York State, study full-time at an eligible New York State postsecondary institution as undergraduate or graduate students, meet income eligibility requirements and maintain a "C" average in college.
Target applicant(s): High school students. College students. Graduate school students. Adult students.
Minimum GPA: 2.0
Amount: Up to $5,165.
Number of awards: Varies.
Scholarship may be renewable.
Deadline: Varies.
How to apply: Complete the Free Application for Federal Student Aid (FAFSA), include a New York school on the application and then complete the Express TAP Application.
Exclusive: Visit www.UltimateScholarshipBook.com and enter code NE191723 for updates on this award.

(1918) · Tuition Equalization Grant Program

Texas Higher Education Coordinating Board
1200 East Anderson Lane, Austin, TX 78752
Phone: 512-427-6101
Email: pamela.harris@thecb.state.tx.us
http://www.collegeforalltexans.com
Purpose: To assist students with financial need who are attending private, non-profit colleges or universities in Texas.
Eligibility: Applicants must be Texas residents or nonresident National Merit Finalists. They must be enrolled at a private, non-profit Texas institution in a first associate's, bachelor's, master's or doctoral degree program. Applicants cannot be athletic scholarship recipients and must demonstrate financial need. Applicants must maintain at least a 2.5 GPA and must complete 24 credit hours per year. Selection is based on financial need.
Target applicant(s): High school students. College students. Graduate school students. Adult students.

Minimum GPA: 2.5
Amount: Up to $3,497.
Number of awards: Varies.
Deadline: January 15.
How to apply: Application is made by completing the FAFSA.
Exclusive: Visit www.UltimateScholarshipBook.com and enter code TE191823 for updates on this award.

(1919) · Tuition Reduction for Non-Resident Nursing Students

Maryland Higher Education Commission
Office of Student Financial Assistance, 6 North Liberty Street, Baltimore, MD 21201
Phone: 800-974-1024
Email: osfamail@mhec.state.md.us
https://mhec.maryland.gov
Purpose: To support non-resident nursing students who are attending college in Maryland.
Eligibility: Applicants cannot be residents of the state of Maryland, but they must be enrolled in a two-year or four-year undergraduate nursing program in Maryland. Students must agree to work full-time at a Maryland hospital after graduation, for a period of four years for full-time students and two years for part-time students.
Target applicant(s): High school students. College students. Adult students.
Amount: Varies.
Number of awards: Varies.
Scholarship may be renewable.
Deadline: Rolling.
How to apply: Applications are available online.
Exclusive: Visit www.UltimateScholarshipBook.com and enter code MA191923 for updates on this award.

(1920) · Tuition Waiver for Foster Care Recipients

Maryland Higher Education Commission
Office of Student Financial Assistance, 6 North Liberty Street, Baltimore, MD 21201
Phone: 800-974-1024
Email: osfamail@mhec.state.md.us
https://mhec.maryland.gov
Purpose: To assist students who have resided in foster care in attending a public college.
Eligibility: Applicants must be under age 25 and have been in an out-of-home placement when they graduated from high school or have lived in foster care on their 14th birthday and subsequently been adopted.
Target applicant(s): High school students. College students.
Amount: Up to full tuition.
Number of awards: Varies.
Scholarship may be renewable.
Deadline: March 1.
How to apply: Students may apply by filing the FAFSA and contacting the financial aid office at the institution they plan to attend.
Exclusive: Visit www.UltimateScholarshipBook.com and enter code MA192023 for updates on this award.

(1921) · Tuttle Services Inc. Tiny Rauch Scholarship

Associated General Contractors of Ohio
1755 Northwest Boulevard, Columbus, OH 43212
Phone: 614-486-6446
Email: parker@agcohio.com
https://agcohio.com/workforce-development/agc-scholarships/
Purpose: To support students who are residents of Ohio pursuing degrees in construction-related fields or employees of Tuttle Services Inc. or immediate family.
Eligibility: Applicants must be a U.S. citizens and undergraduate students in at least the second year of a two-year, four-year or five-year degree seeking program. The minimum GPA requirement is 2.5. Selection is based on the overall strength of the application.
Target applicant(s): College students. Adult students.
Minimum GPA: 2.5
Amount: $1,000.
Number of awards: 1.
Deadline: March 5.
How to apply: Applications are available online. An application form, official college transcripts and essay are required and must be mailed.
Exclusive: Visit www.UltimateScholarshipBook.com and enter code AS192123 for updates on this award.

(1922) · Tweet Coleman Aviation Scholarship

American Association of University Women - Honolulu Branch
1888 Kalakaua Avenue, Suite C312-359, Honolulu, HI 96815
Phone: 808-537-4702
Email: info@aauwhonolulu.org
http://honolulu-hi.aauw.net/scholarships/
Purpose: To aid females in the state of Hawaii in earning a Federal Aviation Administration (FAA) Pilot Certificate.
Eligibility: Applicants must be a female living in Hawaii (only residence is Hawaii) or stationed in Hawaii with the military. Applicants must also be a college graduate (associate degree or higher) or currently enrolled in a college or university in Hawaii. Women from out of state attending a college in Hawaii are eligible. Selection is based on the overall strength of the application.
Target applicant(s): College students. Adult students.
Amount: Varies.
Number of awards: Varies.
Deadline: May 1.
How to apply: Applications are available by online request. An application form and supporting materials are required.
Exclusive: Visit www.UltimateScholarshipBook.com and enter code AM192223 for updates on this award.

(1923) · Twenty-first Century Scholars Program

State Student Assistance Commission of Indiana
W462 Indiana Government Center South, 402 West Washington Street, Indianapolis, IN 46204
Phone: 888-528-4719
Email: grants@ssaci.state.in.us
http://www.in.gov/che/
Purpose: To support Indiana middle school students from families with low to moderate incomes.
Eligibility: Applicants must be in 7th or 8th grade at a school recognized by the Indiana Department of Education. Students must be below the maximum income requirements, be wards of the state or county or be in foster care. Scholarship funds may only be used at eligible Indiana colleges or technical schools.
Target applicant(s): Junior high students or younger.
Minimum GPA: 2.5
Amount: Up to full tuition.
Number of awards: Varies.
Scholarship may be renewable.

Deadline: Varies.
How to apply: Applications are available at Indiana middle schools.
Exclusive: Visit www.UltimateScholarshipBook.com and enter code ST192323 for updates on this award.

(1924) · Two-year or Associate Degree Program

New Hampshire Charitable Foundation
37 Pleasant Street, Concord, NH 03301-4005
Phone: 603-225-6641
Email: info@nhcf.org
https://www.nhcf.org/how-can-we-help-you/
Purpose: To support New Hampshire students who are attending a two-year or short-term training program.
Eligibility: Applicants must have completed high school or earned a GED and plan to attend a short-term training program. Students will need to submit a copy of the Student Aid Report received from submitting the FAFSA. Preference is given to those who have successfully completed prior educational work or who are entering professions in the STEM fields such as: computer science, advanced manufacturing, clinical health care, engineering, engineering technology, graphic design (CAD), etc.
Target applicant(s): College students. Adult students.
Amount: $100-$3,500.
Number of awards: Varies.
Deadline: December 15.
How to apply: Applications are available online.
Exclusive: Visit www.UltimateScholarshipBook.com and enter code NE192423 for updates on this award.

(1925) · Tyler/Grandmaison MELMAC Scholarship

MELMAC Education Foundation
188 Whitten Road, Augusta, ME 04330
Phone: 866-622-3066
Email: info@melmacfoundation.org
http://www.melmacfoundation.org
Purpose: To assist Maine students and encourage them to continue their college education beyond the first year.
Eligibility: Applicants must be Maine high school students nominated by their school's principal. They must be accepted to a college or university and demonstrate exceptional financial need. They must face challenges or obstacles in their pursuit of an education and be committed to public service.
Target applicant(s): High school students.
Amount: $1,500.
Number of awards: Varies.
Deadline: Varies.
How to apply: Applications are made on the student's behalf by his or her high school principal.
Exclusive: Visit www.UltimateScholarshipBook.com and enter code ME192523 for updates on this award.

(1926) · Unitil Scholarship Fund

Unitil
Attn.: Kristen Anderson/Scholarship Committee, 6 Liberty Lane West, Hampton, NH 03842
Phone: 603-772-0775
http://unitil.com/our-community/unitil-scholarship-fund
Purpose: To support students who live in Maine, New Hampshire or Massachusetts.

Eligibility: Applicants must attend school and reside in one of the cities or towns in Unitil service territories and must have a declared major or concentration in science, technology, math or engineering.
Target applicant(s): College students. Adult students.
Amount: $5,000.
Number of awards: 6.
Deadline: March 15.
How to apply: Applications are available online.
Exclusive: Visit www.UltimateScholarshipBook.com and enter code UN192623 for updates on this award.

(1927) · University Journalism Scholarships

Ohio News Media Foundation
1335 Dublin Road, Suite 216-B, Columbus, OH 43215
Phone: 614-486-6677
Email: ariggs@ohionews.org
https://www.ohionews.org/aws/ONA/pt/sp/foundation
Purpose: To support students pursuing a journalism-related major at an Ohio college or university.
Eligibility: Applicants must be enrolled in an Ohio college or university and be majoring in a journalism-related field such as journalism, advertising or marketing. Students must have at least a 2.5 GPA and write an essay as part of their application showcasing their writing skill along with including work samples related to degree.
Target applicant(s): College students. Adult students.
Minimum GPA: 2.5
Amount: $2,000.
Number of awards: 2.
Deadline: May 24.
How to apply: Applications are available online.
Exclusive: Visit www.UltimateScholarshipBook.com and enter code OH192723 for updates on this award.

(1928) · Upper Midwest Chapter Scholarships

National Academy of Television Arts and Sciences-Upper Midwest Foundation
7319 Hunters Run, Eden Prairie, MN 55346
Phone: 952-474-7126
Email: info@midwestemmys.org
https://midwestemmys.org/student-awards/scholarships/
Purpose: To aid students interested in television, broadcasting and electronic media careers.
Eligibility: Applicants must be high school seniors who live in Minnesota, North Dakota, South Dakota, Iowa or Wisconsin. They must have applied or been accepted to a college or university that offers a broadcasting, television or other electronic media curriculum and intend to pursue one of these fields. A GPA of 3.0 or higher is preferred, but not required.
Target applicant(s): High school students.
Amount: $1,500.
Number of awards: Varies.
Deadline: February 1.
How to apply: Applications are available online. An application form is required.
Exclusive: Visit www.UltimateScholarshipBook.com and enter code NA192823 for updates on this award.

(1929) · Urban Scholars Award

New Jersey Higher Education Student Assistance Authority
P.O. Box 540, Trenton, NJ 08625

Phone: 800-792-8670

Email: clientservices@hesaa.org

http://www.hesaa.org

Purpose: To support New Jersey high school seniors from urban or economically depressed areas.

Eligibility: Applicants must be New Jersey residents for at least 12 months prior to college enrollment, and they must enroll full-time in an approved state college. Students must show outstanding academic achievement in high school through SAT scores and transcripts. Applicants must have a minimum 3.0 GPA and be in the top five percent of their class.

Target applicant(s): High school students.

Minimum GPA: 3.0

Amount: Varies.

Number of awards: Varies.

Scholarship may be renewable.

Deadline: Varies.

How to apply: Applications are available from high school guidance counselors.

Exclusive: Visit www.UltimateScholarshipBook.com and enter code NE192923 for updates on this award.

(1930) · Utah Association of Independent Insurance Agents Scholarship

Utah Association of Independent Insurance Agents

4885 South 900 East, Suite 302, Salt Lake City, UT 84117

Phone: 801-269-1200

Email: info@uaiia.org

https://www.utahia.org/Education/Pages/Scholarships/

Purpose: To aid college-bound Utah high school seniors.

Eligibility: Applicants must be Utah high school seniors. They must have a GPA of 3.0 or higher and must be active in extracurricular activities. Selection is based on the overall strength of the application.

Target applicant(s): High school students.

Minimum GPA: 3.0

Amount: Varies.

Number of awards: At least 3.

Deadline: April.

How to apply: Applications are available online. An application form, transcript and applicant photo are required.

Exclusive: Visit www.UltimateScholarshipBook.com and enter code UT193023 for updates on this award.

(1931) · Utah Young Humanitarian Award

Youthlinc

1166 East Brickyard Road, Salt Lake City, UT 84106

Phone: 801-467-4417

https://www.youthlinc.org/young-humanitarian-award/

Purpose: To reward outstanding humanitarian service.

Eligibility: Applicants must be U.S. citizens, legal residents or have DACA status and be either Utah high school juniors or seniors or be enrolled as a full-time undergraduate student at an accredited college or university in Utah.

Target applicant(s): High school students. College students. Adult students.

Amount: Up to $5,000.

Number of awards: 10.

Deadline: March 1.

How to apply: Applications are available online.

Exclusive: Visit www.UltimateScholarshipBook.com and enter code YO193123 for updates on this award.

(1932) · Valedictorian Program Tuition Waiver

Massachusetts Department of Higher Education

Office of Student Financial Assistance, 454 Broadway, Suite 200, Revere, MA 02151

Phone: 617-727-9420

Email: osfa@osfa.mass.edu

https://www.mass.edu/osfa/programs/programs.asp

Purpose: To provide comprehensive financial aid to Massachusetts valedictorians.

Eligibility: Applicants must be designated as a valedictorian by a public or private high school in the state of Massachusetts, and they must be residents of the state for at least one year prior to the beginning of the school year. Students must enroll in a Massachusetts public college and meet individual requirements for the program imposed by the school. They cannot owe refunds on previous financial aid or have any defaulted government loans.

Target applicant(s): High school students.

Amount: Full tuition.

Number of awards: Varies.

Scholarship may be renewable.

Deadline: Varies.

How to apply: Applications are available at college financial aid offices.

Exclusive: Visit www.UltimateScholarshipBook.com and enter code MA193223 for updates on this award.

(1933) · VCTA Virginia's Future Leaders Scholarship Program

Virginia Cable Telecommunications Association

1001 E. Broad Street, Suite 210, Richmond, VA 23219

Phone: 804-780-1776

Email: kvoxland@vcta.com

https://www.vcta.com/

Purpose: To support Virginia students seeking higher education.

Eligibility: Applicants must be Virginia residents. They must be attending or plan to attend a Virginia two- or four-year undergraduate program. Financial need is required.

Target applicant(s): High school students. College students. Adult students.

Amount: Varies.

Number of awards: Varies.

Deadline: March 30.

How to apply: Applications are available online.

Exclusive: Visit www.UltimateScholarshipBook.com and enter code VI193323 for updates on this award.

(1934) · Vermont Incentive Grants

Vermont Student Assistance Corporation

Scholarships, P.O. Box 2000, Winooski, VT 05404

Phone: 888-253-4819

http://www.vsac.org/pay/student-aid-options/scholarships/vsac-assisted-scholarships

Purpose: To assist Vermont students who are attending college full-time.

Eligibility: Applicants must be Vermont residents who are accepted into or enrolled in an undergraduate degree program, a certificate program, a Doctor of Veterinary Medicine degree program or a University of Vermont College of Medicine degree program. They must attend or

plan to attend school full-time. Applicants who have earned a bachelor's degree previously are ineligible. Selection is based on financial need.
Target applicant(s): High school students. College students. Adult students.
Amount: Varies.
Number of awards: Varies.
Deadline: Varies.
How to apply: Applications are available online. An application form and a completed FAFSA are required.
Exclusive: Visit www.UltimateScholarshipBook.com and enter code VE193423 for updates on this award.

(1935) · Vermont Oratorical Contest

American Legion, Department of Vermont
P.O. Box 396, 126 State Street, Montpelier, VT 05601-0396
Phone: 802-223-7131
Email: alvthq@myfairpoint.net
http://www.vtlegion.org
Purpose: To enhance high school students' experience with and understanding of the U.S. Constitution. The contest will help develop students' leadership skills and civic appreciation, as well as the ability to deliver thoughtful, insightful orations regarding U.S. citizenship and its inherent responsibilities.
Eligibility: Applicants must be high school students under the age of 20 who are U.S. citizens or legal residents and residents of the state. Students first give an oration within their state and winners compete at the national level. The oration must be related to the Constitution of the United States focusing on the duties and obligations citizens have to the government. It must be in English and be between eight and ten minutes. There is also an assigned topic which is posted on the website, and it should be between three and five minutes.
Target applicant(s): High school students.
Amount: Up to $18,000.
Number of awards: Varies.
Deadline: December 4.
How to apply: Applications are available from district representatives.
Exclusive: Visit www.UltimateScholarshipBook.com and enter code AM193523 for updates on this award.

(1936) · Vermont Sheriffs' Association Scholarship

Vermont Student Assistance Corporation
Scholarships, P.O. Box 2000, Winooski, VT 05404
Phone: 888-253-4819
http://www.vsac.org/pay/student-aid-options/scholarships/vsac-assisted-scholarships
Purpose: To aid Vermont residents who are studying to become police officers.
Eligibility: Applicants must be Vermont residents. They must be enrolled in a law enforcement degree program at an accredited school that has been approved for federal Title IV funding. They must have plans to become police officers. Selection is based on academic merit, essay and financial need.
Target applicant(s): College students. Adult students.
Amount: $1,000.
Number of awards: 1.
Deadline: February 11.
How to apply: Applications are available online. An application form, official transcript, personal essay and financial aid information are required.
Exclusive: Visit www.UltimateScholarshipBook.com and enter code VE193623 for updates on this award.

(1937) · Vernon T. Swain, P.E./Robert E. Chute, P.E. Scholarship

Maine Society of Professional Engineers
Colin C. Hewett, P.E., Chairman, Scholarship Committee, P.O. Box 318, Winthrop, ME 04364
Email: chewett@ahgeng.com
http://www.mespe.org
Purpose: To aid Maine students who are preparing for careers in engineering.
Eligibility: Applicants must be Maine residents who are graduating high school seniors. They must have plans to enroll in an ABETEAC-accredited degree program in engineering and to pursue a career in engineering. Applicants have to have applied to at least one school that offers engineering degrees. These are the minimum acceptable standardized test scores: SAT Math 600, SAT Writing 500, SAT Critical Reading 500, ACT Math 29, ACT English 25, PAA Quantitative 750 and PAA Verbal 640. Selection is based on standardized test scores, GPA, personal essay, recommendations, extracurricular activities and work experience.
Target applicant(s): High school students.
Amount: At least $2,500.
Number of awards: 2.
Deadline: March 19.
How to apply: Applications are available online. An application form, official transcript, personal statement, two recommendation letters and official SAT or ACT scores are required.
Exclusive: Visit www.UltimateScholarshipBook.com and enter code MA193723 for updates on this award.

(1938) · Veterans Tuition Awards

New York State Higher Education Services Corporation (HESC)
99 Washington Avenue, Albany, NY 12255
Phone: 888-697-4372
Email: scholarships@hesc.ny.gov
http://www.hesc.ny.gov
Purpose: To assist veterans in obtaining higher education.
Eligibility: Applicants must be veterans from New York State who have been honorably discharged and served in Indochina between December 22, 1961 and May 7, 1975, the Persian Gulf on or after August 2, 1990 or Afghanistan on or after September 11, 2001. Applicants must also have applied for the Tuition Assistant Program if studying full-time and the Federal Pell Grant whether studying full-time or part-time, unless enrolled in a vocational training program.
Target applicant(s): College students. Graduate school students. Adult students.
Amount: Up to full tuition.
Number of awards: Varies.
Scholarship may be renewable.
Deadline: June 30.
How to apply: Applications are available from your institution's financial aid office or by phone from HESC.
Exclusive: Visit www.UltimateScholarshipBook.com and enter code NE193823 for updates on this award.

(1939) · VHSL Achievement Award

Virginia High School League
1642 State Farm Boulevard, Charlottesville, VA 22911
https://www.vhsl.org/scholarships/
Purpose: To support students who have made outstanding achievements in sports, academics or courageousness.

Eligibility: Students must be from a Virginia high school in Group 1A through 6A. Applicants must show participation in VHSL activities and other school or community activities. They must have at least a 3.0 GPA.
Target applicant(s): High school students.
Minimum GPA: 3.0
Amount: $1,500.
Number of awards: 19.
Deadline: April 16.
How to apply: Applications are available online.
Exclusive: Visit www.UltimateScholarshipBook.com and enter code VI193923 for updates on this award.

(1940) · Victoria S. and Bradley L. Geist Foundation

Hawaii Community Foundation - Scholarships
827 Fort Street Mall, Honolulu, HI 96813
Phone: 888-731-3863
Email: scholarships@hcf-hawaii.org
https://www.hawaiicommunityfoundation.org/
Purpose: To support students who have been in the Hawaii foster care system.
Eligibility: Applicants must be residents of Hawaii. Students must not have been legally adopted before the age of 18.
Target applicant(s): High school students. College students. Adult students.
Amount: Varies.
Number of awards: Varies.
Scholarship may be renewable.
Deadline: January 31.
How to apply: Applications are available online. In addition, mail the supporting materials: confirmation letter from a case worker, personal statement and official transcript.
Exclusive: Visit www.UltimateScholarshipBook.com and enter code HA194023 for updates on this award.

(1941) · Vietnam Veterans' Scholarship

New Mexico Higher Education Department
2044 Galisteo Street, Suite 4, Santa Fe, NM 87505-2100
Phone: 505-476-8400
Email: cesaria.tapia1@state.nm.us
https://hed.state.nm.us/financial-aid
Purpose: To support Vietnam veterans who are attending college in New Mexico.
Eligibility: Applicants must have been honorably discharged from the armed forces, and they must have received a Vietnam campaign medal for serving in Vietnam anytime between August 5, 1964 and the official end of the war. Students must be attending either a public school or one of the following private schools in New Mexico: the College of Santa Fe, St. John's College or the College of the Southwest. They must have been New Mexico residents when entering the armed forces or have lived in the state for at least 10 years.
Target applicant(s): College students. Graduate school students. Adult students.
Amount: Full tuition.
Number of awards: Varies.
Scholarship may be renewable.
Deadline: Varies.
How to apply: Applications are available at college financial aid offices.
Exclusive: Visit www.UltimateScholarshipBook.com and enter code NE194123 for updates on this award.

(1942) · Virginia Commonwealth Award

State Council of Higher Education for Virginia
101 N. 14th Street, 10th Floor, James Monroe Building, Richmond, VA 23219
Phone: 804-225-2600
Email: communications@schev.edu
http://www.schev.edu
Purpose: To assist Virginia students.
Eligibility: Undergraduate applicants must be admitted to a Virginia public two- or four-year college or university, be enrolled at least half-time, be residents of Virginia, be U.S. citizens or eligible noncitizens and demonstrate financial need. Graduate applicants must be enrolled full-time in an eligible Virginia graduate degree program. The selection process varies by school.
Target applicant(s): High school students. College students. Graduate school students. Adult students.
Amount: Up to full tuition.
Number of awards: Varies.
Scholarship may be renewable.
Deadline: Varies.
How to apply: Application instructions are available by request from the student's financial aid office.
Exclusive: Visit www.UltimateScholarshipBook.com and enter code ST194223 for updates on this award.

(1943) · Virginia Daughters of the American Revolution Scholarships

Virginia Daughters of the American Revolution
DAR Scholarship Committee, Brenda B. Atkinson, State Chairman, 4040 Snowgoose Circle, Roanoke, VA 24018-4865
Phone: 757-479-4167
Email: gandbatkinson@cox.net
https://www.virginiadar.org/about/#scholarships
Purpose: To support Virginia high school students in pursuing higher education.
Eligibility: Applicants must be high school seniors and U.S. citizens who are sponsored by a Virginia DAR chapter. They may pursue an undergraduate degree in any field except nursing at any Virginia college or university.
Target applicant(s): High school students.
Amount: $2,500.
Number of awards: 4.
Deadline: January 12.
How to apply: Applications are available online. An application form, letter of sponsorship, written statement, transcript, financial need form and letter of recommendation are required.
Exclusive: Visit www.UltimateScholarshipBook.com and enter code VI194323 for updates on this award.

(1944) · Virginia Guaranteed Assistance Program

State Council of Higher Education for Virginia
101 N. 14th Street, 10th Floor, James Monroe Building, Richmond, VA 23219
Phone: 804-225-2600
Email: communications@schev.edu
http://www.schev.edu
Purpose: To provide a financial incentive for economically disadvantaged students to consider attending college.
Eligibility: Applicants must have graduated from a Virginia high school with at least a 2.5 GPA, and they must be enrolled full-time in

a two-year or four-year college in the state. Students must be classified as dependents. Preference will be given to students with the greatest financial need.
Target applicant(s): High school students. College students. Adult students.
Minimum GPA: 2.5
Amount: Up to full tuition.
Number of awards: Varies.
Scholarship may be renewable.
Deadline: Varies.
How to apply: Applications are available at college financial aid offices.
Exclusive: Visit www.UltimateScholarshipBook.com and enter code ST194423 for updates on this award.

(1945) · Virginia High School League Charles E. Savedge Journalism Scholarship

Virginia High School League
1642 State Farm Boulevard, Charlottesville, VA 22911
https://www.vhsl.org/scholarships/
Purpose: To support student journalists in Virginia.
Eligibility: Applicants must be active members of a high school newspaper, yearbook or other publication. Students must be in their senior year and have plans to study journalism in college.
Target applicant(s): High school students.
Amount: $500.
Number of awards: 1.
Deadline: March 1.
How to apply: Applications are available online.
Exclusive: Visit www.UltimateScholarshipBook.com and enter code VI194523 for updates on this award.

(1946) · Virginia Part-Time Assistance Program

State Council of Higher Education for Virginia
101 N. 14th Street, 10th Floor, James Monroe Building, Richmond, VA 23219
Phone: 804-225-2600
Email: communications@schev.edu
http://www.schev.edu
Purpose: To assist part-time Virginia students who have financial need.
Eligibility: Applicants must be Virginia residents. They must attend a school in Virginia's community college system part-time (one to eight credit hours per term) and must demonstrate financial need. Selection is based on financial need.
Target applicant(s): High school students. College students. Adult students.
Amount: Up to full tuition.
Number of awards: Varies.
Deadline: Varies.
How to apply: Applications are available from the student's financial aid office. An application form and supporting materials are required.
Exclusive: Visit www.UltimateScholarshipBook.com and enter code ST194623 for updates on this award.

(1947) · Virginia PTA Annual Citizenship Essay Project

Virginia PTA
1027 Wilmer Avenue, Richmond, VA 23227
Phone: 804-264-1234
Email: info@vapta.org
http://www.vapta.org

Purpose: To promote citizenship awareness among Virginia students.
Eligibility: Applicants must be Virginia students in kindergarten through 12th grade who are attending a school that has a PTA or PTSA chapter in good standing. They must submit an essay on a sponsor-determined topic relating to citizenship. Selection is based on essay originality, clarity and grammar.
Target applicant(s): Junior high students or younger. High school students.
Amount: $50-$250.
Number of awards: 12.
Deadline: February 1.
How to apply: Entry forms are available online. An entry form and essay are required.
Exclusive: Visit www.UltimateScholarshipBook.com and enter code VI194723 for updates on this award.

(1948) · Virginia Sheriffs' Institute Scholarship

Virginia Sheriffs' Institute
951 East Byrd Street, Suite 905, Richmond, VA 23219
Phone: 804-225-7152
Email: vsavsi@virginiasherrifs.org
http://vasheriffsinstitute.org
Purpose: To aid Virginia criminal justice students.
Eligibility: Applicants must be residents of an eligible Virginia locality. They must be accepted or enrolled at a Virginia college or university and must be majoring in or planning to major in criminal justice. Selection is based on the overall strength of the application.
Target applicant(s): High school students. College students. Adult students.
Amount: Varies.
Number of awards: Varies.
Deadline: May 1.
How to apply: Applications are available online. An application form, transcript, letter of recommendation from applicant's local sheriff, personal essay, proof of college acceptance (incoming freshmen only) and standardized test scores (incoming freshmen only) are required.
Exclusive: Visit www.UltimateScholarshipBook.com and enter code VI194823 for updates on this award.

(1949) · Virginia Tuition Assistance Grant Program

State Council of Higher Education for Virginia
101 N. 14th Street, 10th Floor, James Monroe Building, Richmond, VA 23219
Phone: 804-225-2600
Email: communications@schev.edu
http://www.schev.edu
Purpose: To assist Virginia students who are attending eligible private postsecondary institutions in Virginia.
Eligibility: Applicants must be Virginia residents and enrolled full-time as undergraduate, graduate or professional school students at an eligible private, non-profit Virginia postsecondary institution. Applicants who are enrolled in a religious or theological degree program are ineligible as are graduate students who are enrolled in a degree program that is not related to health care. Selection is based on the overall strength of the application.
Target applicant(s): High school students. College students. Graduate school students. Adult students.
Amount: $1,600-$3,200.
Number of awards: Varies.
Scholarship may be renewable.
Deadline: July 31.

How to apply: Applications are available by request from the student's college financial aid office. An application form and supporting materials are required.

Exclusive: Visit www.UltimateScholarshipBook.com and enter code ST194923 for updates on this award.

(1950) · Vocational Nurse Scholarship

Health Professions Education Foundation
400 R Street, Suite 460, Sacramento, CA 95811
Phone: 916-326-3640
Email: stran@oshpd.ca.gov
https://oshpd.ca.gov/loans-scholarships-grants/scholarships/
Purpose: To aid California vocational nursing students.
Eligibility: Applicants must be accepted or enrolled in an accredited California vocational nurse (VN) degree program and must be enrolled full-time. They must maintain a GPA of 2.0 or higher while enrolled in the degree program and must commit to two years of practice in an underserved area of California after graduation. Selection is based on academic merit, stated career goals, community involvement, work experience and financial need.
Target applicant(s): College students. Adult students.
Minimum GPA: 2.0
Amount: Up to $4,000.
Number of awards: Varies.
Deadline: February 22.
How to apply: Applications are available online. An application form, personal statement, official transcript, two recommendation letters and financial information are required.
Exclusive: Visit www.UltimateScholarshipBook.com and enter code HE195023 for updates on this award.

(1951) · W.P. Black Scholarship Fund

Greater Kanawha Valley Foundation
1600 Huntington Square, 900 Lee Street, East, Charleston, WV 25301
Phone: 304-346-3620
Email: shoover@tgkvf.org
https://tgkvf.org/scholarships/available-scholarships/
Purpose: To aid West Virginia students.
Eligibility: Applicants must be residents of West Virginia who are full-time students, have a minimum 2.5 GPA, have a minimum ACT score of 20, be of good moral character and demonstrate significant financial need.
Target applicant(s): High school students. College students. Adult students.
Minimum GPA: 2.5
Amount: $2,000.
Number of awards: 62.
Scholarship may be renewable.
Deadline: February 1.
How to apply: Applications are available online.
Exclusive: Visit www.UltimateScholarshipBook.com and enter code GR195123 for updates on this award.

(1952) · Wallace S. and Wilma K. Laughlin Foundation Trust Scholarships

Nebraska Funeral Directors Association
Wallace S. and Wilma K. Laughlin Foundation Trust, 521 First Street, P.O. Box 10, Milford, NE 68405
Phone: 402-761-2217
Email: staff@nefda.org
https://www.nefda.org/scholarship-information
Purpose: To aid Nebraska students of mortuary science.
Eligibility: Applicants must be residents of Nebraska and must be graduating seniors at a Nebraska high school or they must be graduates of a Nebraska high school. They must be entering or current students of mortuary science, reside in Nebraska for at least three years after completing their mortuary science degree programs and intend to practice mortuary science. Selection is based on applicant interview.
Target applicant(s): High school students. College students. Adult students.
Amount: At least $1,000.
Number of awards: Varies.
Deadline: June.
How to apply: Applications are available online. An application form, transcript, recommendation letter and proof that all pre-mortuary science state requirements have been met are required.
Exclusive: Visit www.UltimateScholarshipBook.com and enter code NE195223 for updates on this award.

(1953) · Walter Schoenknecht Tourism and Travel Scholarship Grant

Connecticut Commission on Culture and Tourism
One Constitution Plaza, Second Floor, Hartford, CT 06103
Phone: 860-256-2725
Email: rosemary.bove@ct.gov
https://portal.ct.gov/DECD/Content/Tourism/03_Partner_Office/Apply-for-College-Scholarship
Purpose: To aid Connecticut travel, tourism and hospitality students.
Eligibility: Applicants must be Connecticut residents. They must be enrolled in a degree program in hospitality, travel or tourism at an accredited college or university. Selection is based on the overall strength of the application.
Target applicant(s): College students. Adult students.
Amount: $1,000.
Number of awards: 1.
Deadline: March.
How to apply: Applications are available by request from the Connecticut Commission on Culture and Tourism. An application form and supporting materials are required.
Exclusive: Visit www.UltimateScholarshipBook.com and enter code CO195323 for updates on this award.

(1954) · Warner Norcross + Judd Diversity Paralegal and Legal Secretarial Scholarship

Grand Rapids Community Foundation
185 Oakes Street SW, Grand Rapids, MI 49503
Phone: 616-454-1751
Email: rbishop@grfoundation.org
http://www.grfoundation.org
Purpose: To aid Michigan minority students who are preparing for careers as paralegals or legal secretaries.
Eligibility: Applicants must be Michigan residents. They must be minority students who are enrolled in a paralegal or legal secretary degree program at an accredited school. They must demonstrate financial need. Selection is based on the overall strength of the application. Applicants who are not residents of Michigan may still apply if attending a Michigan law school.
Target applicant(s): College students. Adult students.
Amount: Varies.

Number of awards: Varies.
Deadline: April 1.
How to apply: Applications are available online. An application form and supporting materials are required.
Exclusive: Visit www.UltimateScholarshipBook.com and enter code GR195423 for updates on this award.

(1955) · Washington BPW Foundation Mature Woman Educational Scholarship

Washington Business and Professional Women's Foundation
Attn: Scholarship Committee Chairman, S. Tellock, 1914 NW 87th Circle, Vancouver, WA 98665
Phone: 360-714-8901
Email: WSBPW_Foundation@bpwwa.org
http://bpwwafoundation.org/apply-for-a-scholarship/
Purpose: To assist non-traditional female students.
Eligibility: Applicants must be female students age 30 or older who are pursuing retraining or continuing education. Students must be U.S. citizens and Washington state residents for at least two years and must be accepted into a program at an accredited Washington state institution of higher learning or enrolled in an accredited online program from a Washington state school. They must demonstrate scholastic ability and financial need.
Target applicant(s): College students. Adult students.
Amount: $500.
Number of awards: Varies.
Deadline: May 15.
How to apply: Applications are available online. An application form, essay, proof of income, financial aid and expense estimates, three letters of recommendation, transcript and proof of acceptance or enrollment are required.
Exclusive: Visit www.UltimateScholarshipBook.com and enter code WA195523 for updates on this award.

(1956) · Washington College Grant

Washington Student Achievement Council
P. O. Box 43430, Olympia, WA 98504-3430
Phone: 360-753-7850
Email: aies@wsac.wa.gov
https://wsac.wa.gov/
Purpose: To assist low-income students to pursue undergraduate degrees or train for new careers.
Eligibility: Applicants must be Washington residents who have a family income of 100 percent or less of the state median and be pursuing a certificate, associate's degree or bachelor's degree. Students can use the financial aid at Washington's eligible institutions, including public two- and four-year colleges and universities and many accredited private/ independent colleges, universities and career schools in the state, as well as for approved apprenticeship programs.
Target applicant(s): High school students. College students. Adult students.
Amount: Varies.
Number of awards: Varies.
Deadline: Varies.
How to apply: Eligible students who have filed a Free Application for Federal Student Aid (FAFSA) are considered.
Exclusive: Visit www.UltimateScholarshipBook.com and enter code WA195623 for updates on this award.

(1957) · Washington Health Corps

Washington Student Achievement Council
P. O. Box 43430, Olympia, WA 98504-3430
Phone: 360-753-7850
Email: aies@wsac.wa.gov
https://wsac.wa.gov/
Purpose: To attract health professionals to work in rural and under served communities in Washington state.
Eligibility: Applicants must be employed, or be under contract to be employed, at an eligible site, provide proof of eligible student debt and sign a contract to serve a minimum of two or three years. A full list of eligible professions can be found on the Washington Health Corps website.
Target applicant(s): College students. Adult students.
Amount: Up to $75,000.
Number of awards: Varies.
Scholarship may be renewable.
Deadline: Varies.
How to apply: Applications are available online.
Exclusive: Visit www.UltimateScholarshipBook.com and enter code WA195723 for updates on this award.

(1958) · Washington Oratorical Contest

American Legion, Department of Washington
P.O. Box 3917, Lacey, WA 98509
Phone: 360-491-4373
Email: americanismchairman@americanism-alwa.org
http://www.walegion.org/index.php?id=8
Purpose: To enhance high school students' experience with and understanding of the U.S. Constitution. The contest will help develop students' leadership skills and civic appreciation, as well as the ability to deliver thoughtful, insightful orations regarding U.S. citizenship and its inherent responsibilities.
Eligibility: Applicants must be high school students under the age of 20 who are U.S. citizens or legal residents and residents of the state. Students first give an oration within their state and winners compete at the national level. The oration must be related to the Constitution of the United States focusing on the duties and obligations citizens have to the government. It must be in English and be between eight and ten minutes. There is also an assigned topic which is posted on the website, and it should be between three and five minutes.
Target applicant(s): High school students.
Amount: Up to $5,000.
Number of awards: Varies.
Deadline: January 31.
How to apply: Application information is available online.
Exclusive: Visit www.UltimateScholarshipBook.com and enter code AM195823 for updates on this award.

(1959) · Washington State Auto Dealers Association Bright Future Scholarship

Washington State Auto Dealers Association (WSADA) Scholarship Program
c/o College Planning Network, 43 Bentley Place, Port Townsend, WA 98368
Phone: 206-433-6300
Email: info@wsada.org
http://www.wsada.org/community/scholarships
Purpose: To provide financial assistance for business majors.

Eligibility: Applicants must be high school seniors enrolled in a Washington State public or private high school, or are home-schooled and reside in Washington State. Students must plan to use their scholarship within the 12 months following the award by enrolling in any public or private school, vocational institution, community college or four-year college or university.

Target applicant(s): High school students.

Amount: $2,500.

Number of awards: 5.

Deadline: June 30.

How to apply: Applications available online and must also include two letters of reference, a resume and an essay.

Exclusive: Visit www.UltimateScholarshipBook.com and enter code WA195923 for updates on this award.

(1960) · Washington State College Bound Scholarship

Washington Student Achievement Council
P. O. Box 43430, Olympia, WA 98504-3430
Phone: 360-753-7850
Email: aies@wsac.wa.gov
https://wsac.wa.gov/

Purpose: To provide an incentive for students and their families who might not consider college due to financial concerns.

Eligibility: Applicants must be Washington students in the seventh or eighth grades who are eligible for free or reduced-price lunch, and they must sign a pledge to participate in the program. The student's family income must be 65 percent or less of the state's median income when he or she graduates high school, and his or her GPA must be 2.0 or higher in order to receive the scholarship.

Target applicant(s): Junior high students or younger.

Minimum GPA: 2.0

Amount: Full tuition at public rates, some fees and $500 for books.

Number of awards: Varies.

Scholarship may be renewable.

Deadline: June 30.

How to apply: Applications are available online.

Exclusive: Visit www.UltimateScholarshipBook.com and enter code WA196023 for updates on this award.

(1961) · Washington State Governors' Scholarship for Foster Youth

College Success Foundation
1605 NW Sammamish Road, Suite 100, Issaquah, WA 98027
Phone: 425-416-2000
Email: info@collegesuccessfoundation.org
http://www.collegesuccessfoundation.org

Purpose: To assist Washington state youth in an open dependency court order.

Eligibility: Applicants must be high school seniors, have a minimum 2.0 GPA, have resided in Washington for at least three years prior to graduation and plan to enroll full-time in an eligible Washington public or private college or university.

Target applicant(s): High school students.

Minimum GPA: 2.0

Amount: $2,000-$4,000.

Number of awards: 40-50.

Deadline: January 31.

Exclusive: Visit www.UltimateScholarshipBook.com and enter code CO196123 for updates on this award.

(1962) · Washington State PTA Scholarship

Washington State PTA
2003 65th Avenue West, Tacoma, WA 98466-6215
Phone: 253-565-2153
Email: wapta@wastatepta.org
http://www.wastatepta.org

Purpose: To provide financial assistance to graduates of Washington public high schools.

Eligibility: Applicants must meet maximum household income requirements and be entering their freshman year of college. Academic performance and community service are also considered.

Target applicant(s): High school students.

Minimum GPA: 3.2

Amount: $2,500.

Number of awards: 4.

Deadline: March 1.

How to apply: Applications are available online.

Exclusive: Visit www.UltimateScholarshipBook.com and enter code WA196223 for updates on this award.

(1963) · Washington Women In Need

Washington Women In Need
232 5th Avenue South, Kirkland, WA 98033
Email: programs@wwin.org
https://www.wwin.org

Purpose: To empower women in Washington State to achieve economic stability through higher education and living wage careers.

Eligibility: Applicants must be female or identify as female Washington residents and U.S. citizens or permanent residents admitted to an approved and accredited Washington state college or university. Students must demonstrate financial need and exhibit qualities reflective of the WWIN program. Applicants must be 18 years of age or older and pursuing and undergraduate degree.

Target applicant(s): College students. Adult students.

Amount: $5,000.

Number of awards: Varies.

Scholarship may be renewable.

Deadline: April 10.

How to apply: Applications are available online.

Exclusive: Visit www.UltimateScholarshipBook.com and enter code WA196323 for updates on this award.

(1964) · West Virginia Engineering, Science and Technology Scholarship

West Virginia Higher Education Policy Commission PROMISE Scholarship
1018 Kanawha Boulevard, East, Suite 700, Charleston, WV 25301
Phone: 304-558-2101
Email: canderson@hepc.wvnet.edu
https://secure.cfwv.com

Purpose: To assist West Virginia students interested in obtaining a degree in engineering, science or technology and committed to the pursuit of a career in West Virginia.

Eligibility: Applicants must be enrolled or accepted for enrollment at time of application. Students must agree to work full-time in an engineering, science or technology field in West Virginia for one year for each year the scholarship was received or begin an approved program of community service related to specific fields. Applicants must demonstrate financial need.

Target applicant(s): High school students. College students. Adult students.
Minimum GPA: 3.0
Amount: Varies.
Number of awards: Varies.
Scholarship may be renewable.
Deadline: March 1.
How to apply: Applications are available online.
Exclusive: Visit www.UltimateScholarshipBook.com and enter code WE196423 for updates on this award.

(1965) · West Virginia Higher Education Grant

West Virginia Higher Education Policy Commission
1018 Kanawha Boulevard, East, Suite 700, Charleston, WV 25301
Phone: 304-558-2101
Email: jacob.abrams@wvhepc.edu
http://www.wvhepc.edu/
Purpose: To assist West Virginia students who have financial need.
Eligibility: Applicants must be U.S. citizens or permanent residents and West Virginia residents who have lived in the state for at least 12 months before the application submission date. They must be high school graduates or GED recipients who are enrolled full-time in an undergraduate degree program at a participating postsecondary institution located in West Virginia or Pennsylvania. They must demonstrate financial need. Applicants who have earned a bachelor's degree previously are ineligible. Selection is based on financial need.
Target applicant(s): College students. Adult students.
Amount: Up to $2,700.
Number of awards: Varies.
Scholarship may be renewable.
Deadline: July 1.
How to apply: Application is made by completing the FAFSA.
Exclusive: Visit www.UltimateScholarshipBook.com and enter code WE196523 for updates on this award.

(1966) · West Virginia PROMISE Scholarship

West Virginia Higher Education Policy Commission PROMISE Scholarship
1018 Kanawha Boulevard, East, Suite 700, Charleston, WV 25301
Phone: 304-558-2101
Email: canderson@hepc.wvnet.edu
https://secure.cfwv.com
Purpose: To assist outstanding West Virginia high school students who are planning to attend college in the state.
Eligibility: Applicants must be West Virginia residents and high school seniors or GED recipients who are planning to attend a West Virginia postsecondary institution. They must have a GPA of 3.0 or higher or a GED score of 2500 or higher. Applicants must also have a combined reading and math SAT score of 1020 or higher or a composite ACT score of 22 or higher. Selection is based on academic merit and financial need.
Target applicant(s): High school students.
Minimum GPA: 3.0
Amount: Up to $4,750.
Number of awards: Varies.
Scholarship may be renewable.
Deadline: March.
How to apply: Applications are available online. An application form, supporting materials and a completed FAFSA are required.
Exclusive: Visit www.UltimateScholarshipBook.com and enter code WE196623 for updates on this award.

(1967) · West Virginia PTA Scholarship

West Virginia PTA
P.O. Box 3557, Parkersburg, WV 26103-3557
Phone: 304-420-9576
http://www.westvirginiapta.org/scholarship
Purpose: To support graduating seniors of West Virginia in pursuing post-secondary education.
Eligibility: A minimum GPA of 2.0 is required. Applicants must submit official transcripts, letters of recommendation and an essay describing their educational goals. Selection is primarily based on academic achievement, extracurricular involvement and community service.
Target applicant(s): High school students.
Minimum GPA: 2.0
Amount: $500.
Number of awards: Varies.
Deadline: December 31.
How to apply: Applications are available online.
Exclusive: Visit www.UltimateScholarshipBook.com and enter code WE196723 for updates on this award.

(1968) · Willa S. Bellamy Scholarship

Government Finance Officers Association of South Carolina
Attn.: Scholarship Committee, P.O. Box 8840, Columbia, SC 29202
Phone: 803-252-7128
Email: scholarship@gfoasc.org
http://gfoasc.org/
Purpose: To aid South Carolina students who are interested in government finance careers.
Eligibility: Applicants must be South Carolina residents who are rising undergraduate sophomores, juniors or seniors at an accredited public college or university located in South Carolina. They must be majoring in accounting, finance or business administration with a concentration in accounting or finance. They must have a GPA of 3.0 or higher and must be full-time students. Selection is based on the overall strength of the application.
Target applicant(s): College students. Adult students.
Minimum GPA: 3.0
Amount: $1,500.
Number of awards: 1.
Deadline: April 7.
How to apply: Applications are available online. An application form, transcript and one recommendation letter are required.
Exclusive: Visit www.UltimateScholarshipBook.com and enter code GO196823 for updates on this award.

(1969) · Willard H. Erwin, Jr. Scholarship

Greater Kanawha Valley Foundation
1600 Huntington Square, 900 Lee Street, East, Charleston, WV 25301
Phone: 304-346-3620
Email: shoover@tgkvf.org
https://tgkvf.org/scholarships/available-scholarships/
Purpose: To aid West Virginia state college and university students.
Eligibility: Applicants must be undergraduate students who are enrolled at a state-run college or university located in West Virginia. They must demonstrate financial need. Preference will be given to sophomores, juniors, seniors, part-time students, full-time students and health care finance students. Selection is based on the overall strength of the application.
Target applicant(s): College students. Adult students.

Amount: $600.
Number of awards: 1.
Scholarship may be renewable.
Deadline: February 15.
How to apply: Applications are available online. An application form, transcript, one recommendation letter and income tax information are required.
Exclusive: Visit www.UltimateScholarshipBook.com and enter code GR196923 for updates on this award.

(1970) · William A. Crawford Minority Teacher Scholarship

State Student Assistance Commission of Indiana
W462 Indiana Government Center South, 402 West Washington Street, Indianapolis, IN 46204
Phone: 888-528-4719
Email: grants@ssaci.state.in.us
http://www.in.gov/che/
Purpose: To support students in Indiana who are pursuing degrees in teaching, special education, physical therapy or occupational therapy.
Eligibility: Applicants must be enrolled or planning to enroll in college full-time. Students must have at least a 2.0 GPA, and financial need may be considered. Preference will be given to black and Hispanic students. Students must agree to work in the state of Indiana for a period of time after graduation.
Target applicant(s): High school students. College students. Adult students.
Minimum GPA: 2.0
Amount: Varies.
Number of awards: Varies.
Scholarship may be renewable.
Deadline: August 31.
How to apply: Applications are available at the financial aid office of attending institution.
Exclusive: Visit www.UltimateScholarshipBook.com and enter code ST197023 for updates on this award.

(1971) · William and Gertrude Fradkin Memorial Scholarship

Los Alamos National Laboratory Foundation
1112 Plaza del Norte, Espanola, NM 87532
Phone: 505-753-8890
Email: tony@lanlfoundation.org
http://www.lanlfoundation.org
Purpose: To support students of northern New Mexico enrolled in or attending a post-secondary institution of higher learning.
Eligibility: Applicants must be permanent residents of northern New Mexico with a minimum GPA of 3.25 and a minimum ACT score of 19 or minimum combined math and critical reading SAT score of 930. Applicants must be enrolled in or currently attending a post-secondary institution of higher learning. Selection is based upon academic success, ability to utilize critical thinking skills and leadership skills. Financial need is also considered but not a requirement for eligibility.
Target applicant(s): High school students. College students. Adult students.
Minimum GPA: 3.25
Amount: $1,000.
Number of awards: Varies.
Deadline: January 18.

How to apply: Applications are available online. An application form, transcripts, SAT and ACT scores, two letter of recommendation, a 250-word essay and wallet-size photograph are required.
Exclusive: Visit www.UltimateScholarshipBook.com and enter code LO197123 for updates on this award.

(1972) · William and Sara Jenne' Scholarship

Montana State Elks Association
Robert J. Byers, Attn: Scholarship, P.O. Box 1274, Polson, MT 59860
Phone: 406-849-5276
Email: robert058@centurytel.net
http://www.mtelks.org
Purpose: To support undergraduate students in Montana.
Eligibility: Students must have completed one year of college or technical school with at least 30 semester hours, and they must have at least a 2.0 GPA. Applicants must show financial need and good character.
Target applicant(s): College students. Adult students.
Minimum GPA: 2.0
Amount: Varies.
Number of awards: Varies.
Deadline: June 1.
How to apply: Applications are available online.
Exclusive: Visit www.UltimateScholarshipBook.com and enter code MO197223 for updates on this award.

(1973) · William D. and Jewell Brewer Scholarship

American Legion, Department of Michigan
212 N. Verlinden Avenue, Ste. A, Lansing, MI 48915
Phone: 517-371-4720 x11
Email: programs@michiganlegion.org
http://www.michiganlegion.org
Purpose: To support Michigan students who are the sons, daughters or grandchildren of veterans.
Eligibility: Applicants must be sons, daughters or grandchildren of war-time veterans, residents of Michigan, have a minimum 2.5 GPA and plan to attend a college or university. Scholarships are based on financial need, academic standing and applicants' goals. Applicants must also provide proof of a parent's military service record. They should send scholarship information to the county district committee person.
Target applicant(s): High school students. College students. Graduate school students. Adult students.
Minimum GPA: 2.5
Amount: $500.
Number of awards: Varies.
Deadline: January 4.
How to apply: Applications are available online.
Exclusive: Visit www.UltimateScholarshipBook.com and enter code AM197323 for updates on this award.

(1974) · William G. Saletic Scholarship

Independent Colleges of Washington
600 Stewart Street, Suite 600, Seattle, WA 98101
Phone: 206-623-4494
Email: info@icwashington.org
https://icwashington.org/page/scholarships
Purpose: To provide financial assistance to students who are studying politics or history at an independent college of Washington.
Eligibility: Applicants must be juniors or seniors who are studying or majoring in politics or history. Students attending Gonzaga University,

Heritage University, Pacific Lutheran University, Saint Martin's University, Seattle Pacific University, Seattle University, University of Puget Sound, Walla Walla University, Whitman College or Whitworth University are eligible.
Target applicant(s): College students. Adult students.
Amount: $1,250.
Number of awards: 1.
Deadline: March.
How to apply: Applications are available online or from your school's financial aid office.
Exclusive: Visit www.UltimateScholarshipBook.com and enter code IN197423 for updates on this award.

(1975) · William James and Dorothy Bading Lanquist Fund

Hawaii Community Foundation - Scholarships
827 Fort Street Mall, Honolulu, HI 96813
Phone: 888-731-3863
Email: scholarships@hcf-hawaii.org
https://www.hawaiicommunityfoundation.org/
Purpose: To support students who are majoring in physical sciences and related fields.
Eligibility: Applicants must be residents of Hawaii and be able to demonstrate financial need. Applicants must attend full-time an accredited, two or four year, not-for-profit institution in the U.S. (including U.S. territories) in an undergraduate or graduate level program in Physical Sciences (excluding Biological and Social Sciences). Applicants must have a minimum 3.0 GPA.
Target applicant(s): High school students. College students. Graduate school students. Adult students.
Minimum GPA: 3.0
Amount: Varies.
Number of awards: Varies.
Deadline: January 31.
How to apply: To apply, register online, complete the online application and select the scholarships to which you wish to apply. In addition, mail the supporting materials: printed confirmation page from the online application, personal statement, copy of Student Aid Report (SAR) available at www.fafsa.ed.gov and official transcript.
Exclusive: Visit www.UltimateScholarshipBook.com and enter code HA197523 for updates on this award.

(1976) · William L. Boyd, IV, Effective Access to Student Education Program

Florida Department of Education
Office of Student Financial Assistance, State Scholarship and Grant Programs, 325 West Gaines Street, Suite 1314, Tallahassee, FL 32399-0400
Phone: 888-827-2004
Email: osfa@fldoe.org
http://www.floridastudentfinancialaid.org
Purpose: Provides monetary assistance to Florida undergraduate college students enrolled at eligible, private, non-profit Florida schools.
Eligibility: Applicants must attend an eligible private, nonprofit Florida college or university, be Florida residents and not be in default on any state or federal grant, loan or scholarship. Requirements vary by institution.
Target applicant(s): High school students. College students. Adult students.
Amount: $3,000.
Number of awards: Varies.

Scholarship may be renewable.
Deadline: Varies.
How to apply: Contact your financial aid office.
Exclusive: Visit www.UltimateScholarshipBook.com and enter code FL197623 for updates on this award.

(1977) · Winifred R. Reynolds Educational Scholarship

Denver Foundation
55 Madison, 8th Floor, Denver, CO 80206
Phone: 303-300-1790
Email: information@denverfoundation.org
https://denverfoundation.org/scholarships/scholarship-opportunities/
Purpose: To support graduate students pursuing a degree related to early childhood education.
Eligibility: Applicants must have financial need, be residents of Colorado and have a 3.5 GPA for the graduate work they have completed. Students must be pursuing a graduate degree in early childhood education, child development or an equivalent field.
Target applicant(s): College students. Graduate school students. Adult students.
Minimum GPA: 3.5
Amount: $1,500-$7,000.
Number of awards: Varies.
Scholarship may be renewable.
Deadline: April 16.
How to apply: Applications are available online.
Exclusive: Visit www.UltimateScholarshipBook.com and enter code DE197723 for updates on this award.

(1978) · Wisconsin Amusement and Music Operators Scholarships

Wisconsin Amusement and Music Operators
P.O. Box 259506, Madison, WI 53725
Phone: 800-827-8011
Email: info@wamo.net
http://wamo.net/
Purpose: To assist students of Wisconsin technical schools.
Eligibility: Applicants must be enrolled in or accepted for a minimum of six credits or plan to attend one of the 16 Wisconsin Technical College campuses. They must be family members, employees or players of a WAMO member business. They must have a recommendation from a WAMO member.
Target applicant(s): High school students. College students. Adult students.
Amount: Varies.
Number of awards: Varies.
Deadline: Open.
How to apply: Applications are available online. Two copies of application form, a transcript and two letters of recommendation are required.
Exclusive: Visit www.UltimateScholarshipBook.com and enter code WI197823 for updates on this award.

(1979) · Wisconsin Broadcasters Association Foundation Student Scholarship Program

Wisconsin Broadcasters Association
Linda Baun, WBA Foundation, 44 E. Mifflin Street, Suite 900, Madison, WI 53703
Phone: 608-255-2600

Email: contact@wi-broadcasters.org
https://www.wbafoundation.org/
Purpose: To assist broadcasting students.
Eligibility: Applicants must attend a public or private college or university, a broadcast or media school or Wisconsin technical college. They must major in broadcasting, communications or a related field and have completed 60 credits by the application deadline. Students must have graduated from a Wisconsin high school or be attending a Wisconsin institution of higher learning. They must plan a career in radio or television broadcasting and must not have previously won a WBA scholarship.
Target applicant(s): College students. Adult students.
Amount: $1,000-$2,000.
Number of awards: 4.
Deadline: November.
How to apply: Applications are available online. An application form, transcript, essay and two letters of recommendation are required.
Exclusive: Visit www.UltimateScholarshipBook.com and enter code WI197923 for updates on this award.

(1980) · Wisconsin Higher Education Grant
State of Wisconsin Higher Educational Aids Board
P.O. Box 7885, Madison, WI 53707
Phone: 608-267-2206
Email: heabmail@wisconsin.gov
http://heab.state.wi.us
Purpose: To assist Wisconsin students who have financial need.
Eligibility: Applicants must be Wisconsin residents and certificate- or degree-seeking undergraduate students with financial need who are enrolled at least part-time. They must be attending a Wisconsin technical college, tribal college or University of Wisconsin system institution. Selection is based on financial need.
Target applicant(s): High school students. College students. Adult students.
Amount: $250-$3,000.
Number of awards: Varies.
Scholarship may be renewable.
Deadline: Varies.
How to apply: Application is made by completing the FAFSA.
Exclusive: Visit www.UltimateScholarshipBook.com and enter code ST198023 for updates on this award.

(1981) · Wisconsin National Guard Tuition Grant
Wisconsin Department of Military Affairs
WIAR-G1-ED, P.O. Box 8111, Madison, WI 53708-8111
Phone: 608-242-3159
Email: karen.behling@wisconsin.gov
http://dma.wi.gov
Purpose: To help Wisconsin National Guard members with their education.
Eligibility: Applicants must be Wisconsin National Guard enlisted members and warrant officers in good standing who do not have a bachelor's degree. Recipients may use the grant at any campus of the University of Wisconsin System, a public institution of higher education under the Minnesota-Wisconsin student reciprocity agreement or an accredited institution of higher education in Wisconsin.
Target applicant(s): High school students. College students. Adult students.
Minimum GPA: 2.0
Amount: Full tuition.
Number of awards: Varies.

Scholarship may be renewable.
Deadline: 90 days after completion of course/term.
How to apply: Applications are available online and are due no later than 90 days after the end of each course or term.
Exclusive: Visit www.UltimateScholarshipBook.com and enter code WI198123 for updates on this award.

(1982) · Wisconsin Oratorical Scholarship Program
American Legion, Department of Wisconsin
2930 American Legion Drive, P.O. Box 388, Portage, WI 53901-0388
Phone: 608-745-1090
Email: info@wilegion.org
https://wilegion.org/oratorical-scholarships/
Purpose: To enhance high school students' experience with and understanding of the U.S. Constitution. The contest will help develop students' leadership skills and civic appreciation, as well as the ability to deliver thoughtful, insightful orations regarding U.S. citizenship and its inherent responsibilities.
Eligibility: Applicants must be high school students under the age of 20 who are U.S. citizens or legal residents and residents of the state. Students first give an oration within their state and winners compete at the national level. The oration must be related to the Constitution of the United States focusing on the duties and obligations citizens have to the government. It must be in English and be between eight and ten minutes. There is also an assigned topic which is posted on the website, and it should be between three and five minutes.
Target applicant(s): High school students.
Amount: Up to $5,000.
Number of awards: Varies.
Deadline: Varies.
How to apply: Application information is available by contacting the local American Legion Post.
Exclusive: Visit www.UltimateScholarshipBook.com and enter code AM198223 for updates on this award.

(1983) · Wisconsin Veterans Education Reimbursement Grants
Wisconsin Department of Veterans Affairs
201 West Washington Avenue, P.O. Box 7843, Madison, WI 53707-7843
Phone: 800-947-8387
Email: WDVAWeb@dva.wisconsin.gov
http://www.dva.state.wi.us
Purpose: To support Wisconsin veterans.
Eligibility: Applicants must be Wisconsin residents and must have served in the U.S. armed forces in active duty for two consecutive years, completed their initial active service obligations, accumulated at least 90 days of active duty during wartime or have received or become qualified to receive an expeditionary or service medal. Students must have received an honorable discharge and be working toward a degree or certificate. A minimum 2.0 GPA is required. Funds are awarded upon course completion.
Target applicant(s): College students. Adult students.
Minimum GPA: 2.0
Amount: Up to full tuition.
Number of awards: Varies.
Deadline: No later than 60 days after the start of classes.
How to apply: Applications are available online. An application form is required.

Exclusive: Visit www.UltimateScholarshipBook.com and enter code WI198323 for updates on this award.

(1984) · Wisconsin Women in Government Undergraduate Scholarship

Wisconsin Women in Government Inc.
P.O. Box 2543, Madison, WI 53701
Phone: 608-848-2321
Email: info@wiscwomeningovernment.org
http://wiscwomeningovernment.org/
Purpose: To aid Wisconsin women who are planning for careers in government and public service.
Eligibility: Applicants must be female Wisconsin residents who are undergraduate students at a participating Wisconsin college or university. They must be interested in government, public service or political careers and demonstrate financial need. Selection is based on academic merit, leadership, initiative, communication skills, extracurricular activities and commitment to public service.
Target applicant(s): College students. Adult students.
Minimum GPA: 2.0
Amount: Up to $3,000.
Number of awards: Varies.
Scholarship may be renewable.
Deadline: June.
How to apply: Applications are available online. An application form, transcript, two recommendation letters and financial aid information are required.
Exclusive: Visit www.UltimateScholarshipBook.com and enter code WI198423 for updates on this award.

(1985) · WISE Scholarship

Anderson Sobel Cosmetic Surgery
1632 116th Avenue NE, Suite A, Bellevue, WA 98004
Phone: 425-453-9060
Email: womeninstemscholarship@gmail.com
https://www.andersonsobelcosmetic.com/wise-scholarship/
Purpose: To support women in Washington to pursue STEM education.
Eligibility: Applicants must be female Washington residents pursuing a degree in a STEM-related field at an accredited institution.
Target applicant(s): High school students. College students. Graduate school students. Adult students.
Amount: $3,500.
Number of awards: 1.
Deadline: January 7.
How to apply: Applications are available online.
Exclusive: Visit www.UltimateScholarshipBook.com and enter code AN198523 for updates on this award.

(1986) · Workforce Shortage Student Assistance Grant Program

Maryland Higher Education Commission
Office of Student Financial Assistance, 6 North Liberty Street, Baltimore, MD 21201
Phone: 800-974-1024
Email: osfamail@mhec.state.md.us
https://mhec.maryland.gov
Purpose: To support students in Maryland who plan to work in jobs which are needed on a statewide or regional basis.

Eligibility: Applicants must be currently enrolled or planning to enroll in a Maryland postsecondary school. Dependent students must have parents who also live in Maryland. Eligible majors are chosen to address current state or regional needs and usually include the following: child care, human services, teaching, nursing, physical and occupational therapy and public service. Students must agree to begin working within that employment field within one year of graduation at a rate of one year for every year that the scholarship was granted.
Target applicant(s): High school students. College students. Graduate school students. Adult students.
Amount: Up to $19,000.
Number of awards: Varies.
Scholarship may be renewable.
Deadline: July 1.
How to apply: Applications are available online in January.
Exclusive: Visit www.UltimateScholarshipBook.com and enter code MA198623 for updates on this award.

(1987) · World Trade Center Memorial Scholarship

New York State Higher Education Services Corporation (HESC)
99 Washington Avenue, Albany, NY 12255
Phone: 888-697-4372
Email: scholarships@hesc.ny.gov
http://www.hesc.ny.gov
Purpose: To support the families and dependents of those who were injured or died as a result of the attacks on September 11, 2001.
Eligibility: Applicants must be full-time undergraduate students. Students must attend school in the state of New York, but they may be residents of any state or country.
Target applicant(s): College students. Adult students.
Amount: Up to full tuition plus room and board.
Number of awards: Varies.
Scholarship may be renewable.
Deadline: June 30.
How to apply: Applications are available online.
Exclusive: Visit www.UltimateScholarshipBook.com and enter code NE198723 for updates on this award.

(1988) · WTS Minnesota Chapter Scholarships

Women's Transportation Seminar (WTS) - Minnesota Chapter
University of Minnesota, 200 Center for Transportation Studies, 511 Washington Avenue SE, Minneapolis, MN 55455
Email: Lyssa.Leitner@co.washington.mn.us
https://www.wtsinternational.org/chapters/minnesota/scholarships
Purpose: To aid women who are pursuing higher education in a transportation-related subject.
Eligibility: Applicants must be women who are enrolled in an undergraduate or graduate degree program that is related to transportation. They either must be attending a school located in Minnesota, or must be North Dakota, South Dakota or Iowa students who have lived in Minnesota at some point during the past five years. They must have plans to pursue a career in the transportation field, and must have a GPA of 3.0 or higher. Selection is based on academic merit, transportation-related activities and career goals.
Target applicant(s): College students. Graduate school students. Adult students.
Minimum GPA: 3.0
Amount: $500-$2,000.
Number of awards: 3.
Deadline: December.

How to apply: Applications are available online. An application form, official transcript, proof of enrollment, one letter of recommendation and a personal essay are required.

Exclusive: Visit www.UltimateScholarshipBook.com and enter code WO198823 for updates on this award.

(1989) · Xello High School Scholarship

Wisconsin School Counselor Association
2820 Walton Commons, Suite 103, Madison, WI 53718
Phone: 608-204-9825
Email: nechodomk@gmail.com
https://www.wscaweb.org/awards-scholarships/scholarships/
Purpose: To support Wisconsin students.
Eligibility: Applicants must be seniors at a public or private Wisconsin high school. They must plan to attend an institution of higher learning in the school year following graduation.
Target applicant(s): High school students.
Amount: $500.
Number of awards: 4.
Deadline: December.
How to apply: Applications are available online. An application form and essay are required.
Exclusive: Visit www.UltimateScholarshipBook.com and enter code WI198923 for updates on this award.

(1990) · You've Got a Friend in Pennsylvania Scholarship

American Radio Relay League Foundation
225 Main Street, Newington, CT 06111-1494
Phone: 860-594-0348
Email: foundation@arrl.org
http://www.arrl.org/scholarship-program
Purpose: To support Pennsylvania students who are involved in amateur radio.
Eligibility: Applicants must have an amateur radio license in General Class or higher and an active American Radio Relay League membership. Applicants must have an "A" or equivalent GPA.
Target applicant(s): High school students. College students. Adult students.
Minimum GPA: 3.6
Amount: $1,000.
Number of awards: 1.
Deadline: December 31.
How to apply: Applications are available online.
Exclusive: Visit www.UltimateScholarshipBook.com and enter code AM199023 for updates on this award.

(1991) · Zagunis Student Leader Scholarship

National Association for Campus Activities
13 Harbison Way, Columbia, SC 29212
Phone: 803-732-6222
Email: info@naca.org
https://www.naca.org/FOUNDATION/Pages/Scholarships.aspx
Purpose: To provide financial assistance to student leaders.
Eligibility: Applicants must be current undergraduate or graduate students who hold a significant campus leadership position, demonstrate significant leadership skills and abilities and make significant contributions through on- or off-campus volunteering. Students must attend school in Kentucky, Michigan, Ohio, West Virginia or western Pennsylvania.

Target applicant(s): College students. Graduate school students. Adult students.
Minimum GPA: 3.0
Amount: Varies.
Number of awards: Varies.
Deadline: November 30.
How to apply: Applications are available online.
Exclusive: Visit www.UltimateScholarshipBook.com and enter code NA199123 for updates on this award.

MEMBERSHIP

(1992) · 4-H Youth in Action

National 4-H Council
7100 Connecticut Avenue, Chevy Chase, MD 20815
Phone: 301-961-2800
Email: youthinaction@4-h.org
https://4-h.org/parents/4-h-youth-in-action-awards/
Purpose: To recognize dynamic young leaders among 4-H members.
Eligibility: Applicants must be current or former 4-H members between the ages of 15-19 years old. Students must create a one-minute video relating to their leadership in one of the 4-H pillar areas and provide the following: several short essays, photos supporting their entry and proof of 4-H involvement. One award will be given in each of four pillar areas: agriculture, civic engagement, healthy living and STEM.
Target applicant(s): High school students. College students.
Amount: $5,000.
Number of awards: 4.
Deadline: March 29.
How to apply: Applications are available online.
Exclusive: Visit www.UltimateScholarshipBook.com and enter code NA199223 for updates on this award.

(1993) · AFSA Financial Aid Scholarships

American Foreign Service Association (AFSA)
2101 East Street NW, Washington, DC 20037
Phone: 202-944-5504
Email: dec@afsa.org
http://www.afsa.org/afsa-scholarships
Purpose: To provide financial aid to university students who are the children or dependents of Foreign Service employees.
Eligibility: Applicants must be dependents of U.S. government Foreign Service employees with a minimum 2.0 GPA. Students must attend or plan to attend full-time an undergraduate U.S. college, university, community college, art school, conservatory or other post-secondary institution. Applicants must submit applications, transcripts and financial need reports. Recipients must complete their undergraduate degree within four years and must demonstrate financial need.
Target applicant(s): High school students. College students. Adult students.
Minimum GPA: 2.0
Amount: $3,000-$5,000.
Number of awards: Varies.
Scholarship may be renewable.
Deadline: March 15.
How to apply: Applications are available after November 1.
Exclusive: Visit www.UltimateScholarshipBook.com and enter code AM199323 for updates on this award.

(1994) · AFSA/AAFSW Merit Awards

American Foreign Service Association (AFSA)
2101 East Street NW, Washington, DC 20037
Phone: 202-944-5504
Email: dec@afsa.org
http://www.afsa.org/afsa-scholarships
Purpose: To recognize the academic and artistic achievements of high school seniors who are the children or dependents of Foreign Service employees.
Eligibility: Applicants must be dependents of U.S. government Foreign Service employees who are members of AFSA or AAFSW. Students must be high school seniors with a minimum 2.0 GPA. Applicants can also submit an art entry under the categories of visual arts, musical arts, drama, dance or creative writing. Awards are based on GPA, SAT scores, a two-page essay, letters of recommendation and extra-curricular activities.
Target applicant(s): High school students.
Minimum GPA: 2.0
Amount: $500-$2,500.
Number of awards: Varies.
Deadline: March 15.
How to apply: Applications are available online after November 1.
Exclusive: Visit www.UltimateScholarshipBook.com and enter code AM199423 for updates on this award.

(1995) · AFSCME Family Scholarship

American Federation of State, County and Municipal Employees (AFSCME), AFL-CIO
Attn: Education Department, 1625 L Street NW, Washington, DC 20036-5687
Phone: 202-429-5080
Email: education@afscme.org
https://www.afscme.org/members/scholarships
Purpose: To offer financial assistance to the dependents of AFSCME members.
Eligibility: Applicants must be graduating high school seniors who are the daughters, sons or financially dependent grandchildren of AFSCME members who intend to enroll in a full-time, four-year degree program in any accredited college or university. Applicants should submit applications, essays, transcripts, test scores and recommendation letters. Selection is based on information provided on the application form, high school transcript, SAT/ACT scores and a required essay.
Target applicant(s): High school students.
Amount: $2,000.
Number of awards: 10.
Scholarship may be renewable.
Deadline: December 31.
How to apply: Applications are available online and by written request.
Exclusive: Visit www.UltimateScholarshipBook.com and enter code AM199523 for updates on this award.

(1996) · AGCO Corporation FFA Scholarship

National FFA Organization
P.O. Box 68960, 6060 FFA Drive, Indianapolis, IN 46268-0960
Phone: 888-332-2668
Email: scholarships@ffa.org
https://www.ffa.org/participate/grants-and-scholarships/
Purpose: To support students in select majors who are in the FFA.
Eligibility: Applicants must be current FFA members and high school seniors or college students planning to enroll or currently enrolled full-time. They must have one of the following undergraduate majors: agronomy, crop science, general agriculture, agricultural communications, education, journalism, extension, public relations, business management, economics, sales and marketing, engineering, mechanization, agriculture power and equipment or welding. Students only need to complete the online application one time to be considered for all FFA-administered scholarships. The application requires information about the student's activities and a 1,000-word essay. Awards may be used for books, supplies, tuition, fees and room and board. Students must show financial need and evidence of community service participation.
Target applicant(s): High school students. College students.

Amount: $2,000.
Number of awards: 12.
Deadline: January 14.
How to apply: Applications are available online.
Exclusive: Visit www.UltimateScholarshipBook.com and enter code NA199623 for updates on this award.

(1997) · Allan Jerome Burry Scholarship

United Methodist Church
Office of Loans and Scholarships, P.O. Box 340007, Nashville, TN 37203-0007
Phone: 615-340-7342
Email: umscholar@gbhem.org
https://www.gbhem.org/loans-scholarships/scholarships/
Purpose: To support students in ministry or chaplaincy programs who are members of the United Methodist Church.
Eligibility: Applicants must be college undergraduates who show evidence of financial need, leadership qualities, academic excellence and church participation. They must have a GPA of 3.0 or higher. Students must have been active members of the United Methodist Church for at least three years and be nominated by the campus chaplain or minister.
Target applicant(s): College students. Adult students.
Minimum GPA: 3.0
Amount: $1,000.
Number of awards: Varies.
Deadline: March 24.
How to apply: Applications are available from campus ministers or chaplains.
Exclusive: Visit www.UltimateScholarshipBook.com and enter code UN199723 for updates on this award.

(1998) · ALPA Scholarship Program

Air Line Pilots Association
1625 Massachusetts Avenue NW, Suite 800, Washington, DC 20036
Phone: 703-689-2270
Email: Yvonne.Willits@alpa.org
http://www.alpa.org
Purpose: To support the children of medically retired, long-term disabled or deceased pilot members of the Air Line Pilots Association.
Eligibility: Applicants must be pursuing a baccalaureate degree. Selection is based on academic achievements and financial need. The award is renewable for four years with a minimum 3.0 GPA.
Target applicant(s): High school students. College students. Adult students.
Minimum GPA: 3.0
Amount: $12,000.
Number of awards: 1.
Scholarship may be renewable.
Deadline: April 1.
How to apply: Applications are available by mail.
Exclusive: Visit www.UltimateScholarshipBook.com and enter code AI199823 for updates on this award.

(1999) · American Association of State Troopers (AAST) Scholarship

American Association of State Troopers (AAST) Inc.
1949 Raymond Diehl Road, Tallahassee, FL 32308
Phone: 800-765-5456
http://www.statetroopers.org
Purpose: To support dependents of AAST trooper members.
Eligibility: Applicants must be a dependent (child by natural birth, child legally adopted, stepchild or claimed dependent on income tax) of a trooper member. Student AAST member parent must have been a member in good standing for two consecutive years prior to application deadline.
Target applicant(s): High school students. College students. Adult students.
Minimum GPA: 3.0
Amount: $500.
Number of awards: 1.
Scholarship may be renewable.
Deadline: July 31.
How to apply: Applications are available online.
Exclusive: Visit www.UltimateScholarshipBook.com and enter code AM199923 for updates on this award.

(2000) · American Legion Eagle Scout of the Year

American Legion
Attn.: Americanism and Children and Youth Division, P.O. Box 1055, Indianapolis, IN 46206
Phone: 317-630-1249
Email: acy@legion.org
http://www.legion.org
Purpose: To provide scholarships for Eagle Scouts.
Eligibility: Applicants must have received the Eagle Scout Award, be active members of their religious institutions, have received the appropriate Boy Scouts religious emblem, demonstrate citizenship, be at least 15 years old and be high school students. Nominations are due March 1.
Target applicant(s): High school students.
Amount: $2,500-$10,000.
Number of awards: 4.
Deadline: March 1.
How to apply: Applications are available online.
Exclusive: Visit www.UltimateScholarshipBook.com and enter code AM200023 for updates on this award.

(2001) · AMVETS National Ladies Auxiliary Scholarship

AMVETS National Ladies Auxiliary Headquarters
Attn: Scholarship Officer, 4647 Forbes Boulevard, Lanham, MD 20706
Phone: 301-459-6255
http://amvetsaux.org/scholarships/
Purpose: To promote educational opportunities for students interested in or involved with a national service organization.
Eligibility: Applicants must be a current member of or the child or grandchild of a current member of the AMVETS Ladies Auxiliary. Students must be at least sophomores at an accredited college or university.
Target applicant(s): College students. Adult students.
Amount: $750-$1,000.
Number of awards: 7.
Deadline: July 1.
How to apply: Applications are available by mail.
Exclusive: Visit www.UltimateScholarshipBook.com and enter code AM200123 for updates on this award.

(2002) · ARA Scholarship

ARA Scholarship Foundation Inc.
ARA Scholarship Advisor, 109 Defiant Way, Grass Valley, CA 95945
Phone: 703-385-1001
Email: arascholar@sbcglobal.net
http://www.a-r-a.org
Purpose: To support the children of Automotive Recyclers Association (ARA) members.
Eligibility: Applicants must be high school seniors and/or planning to attend college full-time and have earned a minimum 3.0 GPA in their last educational program. Applicants must also be the children of employees of a Direct Member of ARA who were hired at least one year prior to March 15 of the application year. Scholarships are based on academic merit, not financial need.
Target applicant(s): High school students. College students. Graduate school students. Adult students.
Minimum GPA: 3.0
Amount: Varies.
Number of awards: Varies.
Scholarship may be renewable.
Deadline: March 15.
How to apply: Applications are available online and by email request.
Exclusive: Visit www.UltimateScholarshipBook.com and enter code AR200223 for updates on this award.

(2003) · Arthur M. and Berdena King Eagle Scout Contest

National Society, Sons of the American Revolution
1000 South Fourth Street, Louisville, KY 40203
Phone: 502-589-1776
Email: sdelong1@san.rr.com
https://www.sar.org/education/
Purpose: To reward exceptional students who have reached the status of Eagle Scout.
Eligibility: Applicants must have reached Eagle Scout status, must currently be registered in an active unit and can't have reached their 19th birthday during the year of application. Applicants can apply multiple years as long as they are under the age limit, but the maximum award amount is $10,000. Applicants usually apply at the chapter level. Applicants will be required to submit an essay and four-generation ancestor chart with their application.
Target applicant(s): Junior high students or younger. High school students.
Amount: $1,000-$10,000.
Number of awards: 4.
Deadline: December 31.
How to apply: Applications are available online.
Exclusive: Visit www.UltimateScholarshipBook.com and enter code NA200323 for updates on this award.

(2004) · Association of Flight Attendants Annual Scholarship

Association of Flight Attendants
501 Third Street NW, Washington, DC 20001
Phone: 202-434-1300
Email: info@afacwa.org
http://www.afacwa.org/
Purpose: To provide financial assistance to the children of members of the AFA.

Eligibility: Applicants must be the dependents of AFA members in good standing. Applicants must also be in the top 15 percent of their class, have or expect to have excellent SAT/ACT scores, demonstrate financial need and provide a 300-word essay along with the completed application.
Target applicant(s): High school students.
Amount: Up to $5,000.
Number of awards: 1.
Scholarship may be renewable.
Deadline: April 10.
How to apply: Applications are available online.
Exclusive: Visit www.UltimateScholarshipBook.com and enter code AS200423 for updates on this award.

(2005) · Assured Life Association National Scholarship

Assured Life Association
Scholarship Committee, P.O. Box 3169, Englewood, CO 80155
Phone: 800-777-9777 x 3773
Email: scholarship@assuredlife.org
http://assuredlife.org
Purpose: To support students seeking a college education.
Eligibility: Applicants must be certificate holders or children or grandchildren of certificate holders of Assured Life Association of Greenwood Village, Colorado. Students must be seniors in high school, undergraduates or graduates students taking at least 12 credit hours. Applicants are required to submit a 250- to 500-word essay on the given topic.
Target applicant(s): High school students. College students. Graduate school students. Adult students.
Amount: $500-$2,500.
Number of awards: 60-70.
Deadline: March 15.
How to apply: Applications are available online and must include an official transcript, a current list of extracurricular activities, a recent photo of the applicant and the certificate information of the certificate holder.
Exclusive: Visit www.UltimateScholarshipBook.com and enter code AS200523 for updates on this award.

(2006) · Bernard Rotberg Memorial Scholarship Fund

Jewish War Veterans of the USA
1811 R Street NW, Washington, DC 20009
Phone: 202-265-6280
Email: jwv@jwv.org
https://jwvusafoundation.org/
Purpose: To provide scholarships for descendants of members of the Jewish War Veterans of the USA.
Eligibility: Applicants must be a direct descendant of a JWV member in good standing. Candidates must also have been accepted to an accredited college, university or nursing school, be in the upper 25 percent of their class and be active in activities at school and within the Jewish community.
Target applicant(s): High school students.
Amount: $1,000.
Number of awards: 1.
Deadline: May 22.
How to apply: Applications are available online and should be submitted by the applicant's school to the department commander in the local post.
Exclusive: Visit www.UltimateScholarshipBook.com and enter code JE200623 for updates on this award.

(2007) · Boys and Girls Clubs of America National Youth of the Year Award

Boys and Girls Clubs of America
1275 Peachtree Street NE, Atlanta, GA 30309
Phone: 404-487-5700
Email: info@bgca.org
https://www.bgca.org/programs/youth-of-the-year
Purpose: To reward club members who demonstrate good academic performance, perform services for both their club and community and who are active in both family and spiritual life.
Eligibility: Applicants must be a member of a BGCA and be selected by their local club to compete for the regional and national scholarships. Regional and national awards are renewable up to four years.
Target applicant(s): High school students.
Amount: $5,000-$25,000.
Number of awards: Varies.
Scholarship may be renewable.
Deadline: Varies.
How to apply: Contact your local club for more information.
Exclusive: Visit www.UltimateScholarshipBook.com and enter code BO200723 for updates on this award.

(2008) · Carroll C. Hall Memorial Scholarship

Tau Kappa Epsilon Educational Foundation
7439 Woodland Drive, Suite 100, Indianapolis, IN 46278
Phone: 317-872-6533
Email: tkeogc@tke.org
https://www.tke.org/foundation/scholarships
Purpose: To reward a member of Tau Kappa Epsilon for outstanding academic achievement and for leadership within the organization, campus or community.
Eligibility: Applicants must have a minimum 3.0 GPA and be undergraduates seeking a degree in education or science with the intention of pursuing a career in teaching or the sciences.
Target applicant(s): High school students. College students. Adult students.
Minimum GPA: 3.0
Amount: $400.
Number of awards: 1.
Deadline: March 15.
How to apply: Applications are available online.
Exclusive: Visit www.UltimateScholarshipBook.com and enter code TA200823 for updates on this award.

(2009) · Catholic United Financial College Tuition Scholarship

Catholic United Financial
Scholarship Program, 3499 Lexington Avenue North, St. Paul, MN 55126
Phone: 800-568-6670
Email: engage@catholicunited.org
http://www.catholicunitedfinancial.org
Purpose: To reward members of the Catholic United Financial.
Eligibility: Applicants must be members of the Catholic United Financial for at least two years prior to the date of application, have completed high school and be entering their first or second year in any accredited college, university, state college or technical college other than a private, non-Catholic college/university. Those attending a Catholic college are eligible for a $300 award and those attending a non-Catholic college are eligible for a $500 award.

Target applicant(s): High school students. College students. Adult students.
Amount: $300-$500.
Number of awards: Varies.
Deadline: April 30.
How to apply: Applications are available online.
Exclusive: Visit www.UltimateScholarshipBook.com and enter code CA200923 for updates on this award.

(2010) · Chairman's Award

National Association of Blacks in Criminal Justice
1801 Fayetteville Street, 106 Whiting Criminal Justice Building, P.O. Box 20011-C, Durham, NC 27707
Phone: 919-683-1801
Email: Office@NABCJ.org
https://nabcj.org/
Purpose: To support an individual who has shown leadership, dedication and made contributions to NABCJ at the chapter or regional level.
Eligibility: Applicants must be nominated by a member of NABCJ.
Target applicant(s): College students. Adult students.
Amount: Varies.
Number of awards: 1.
Deadline: March 15.
How to apply: Nomination applications are available online.
Exclusive: Visit www.UltimateScholarshipBook.com and enter code NA201023 for updates on this award.

(2011) · Champions for Christ Scholarship

Champions for Christ Foundation
P.O. Box 786, Greenville, SC
Phone: 864-294-0800
http://championsforchrist.us/
Purpose: To support students going into full-time Christian ministry.
Eligibility: Applicants must be enrolled at a U.S. educational institution. Selection is based on the overall strength of the application.
Target applicant(s): College students. Adult students.
Amount: Varies.
Number of awards: Varies.
Deadline: November 1.
How to apply: Applications are available online.
Exclusive: Visit www.UltimateScholarshipBook.com and enter code CH201123 for updates on this award.

(2012) · Charles R. Walgreen Jr. Leadership Award

Tau Kappa Epsilon Educational Foundation
7439 Woodland Drive, Suite 100, Indianapolis, IN 46278
Phone: 317-872-6533
Email: tkeogc@tke.org
https://www.tke.org/foundation/scholarships
Purpose: To honor Charles R. Walgreen's support of Tau Kappa Epsilon by recognizing academic achievement in members.
Eligibility: Applicants must be initiated Tau Kappa Epsilon members in good standing and full-time students. They must have a GPA of at least 3.0 and demonstrate leadership in their chapter, campus and community. Applicants must also include a statement describing how they have benefited from TKE membership.
Target applicant(s): High school students. College students. Adult students.
Minimum GPA: 3.0

Amount: $1,400.
Number of awards: 1.
Deadline: March 15.
How to apply: Applications are available online.
Exclusive: Visit www.UltimateScholarshipBook.com and enter code TA201223 for updates on this award.

(2013) · Charlie Logan Scholarship Program for Dependents

Seafarers International Union of North America
Seafarers Health and Benefits Plan, Scholarship Program, 5201 Auth Way, Camp Springs, MD 20746
Phone: 301-899-0675
http://www.seafarers.org
Purpose: To offer scholarships to the dependents of members of the SIU.
Eligibility: Applicants must be the dependent children or spouses of members of the Seafarers International Union. The union member must be eligible for the Seafarer's Plan and must have credit for three years with an employer who is obligated to make a contribution to the Seafarer's Plan on behalf of the employee. Recipients may attend any U.S. accredited institution. Selection is based upon review of secondary school records, SAT or ACT test scores, college transcripts, if any, character references, extracurricular activities and autobiography.
Target applicant(s): High school students. College students. Adult students.
Amount: $20,000.
Number of awards: 5.
Scholarship may be renewable.
Deadline: April.
How to apply: Applications are available by written request.
Exclusive: Visit www.UltimateScholarshipBook.com and enter code SE201323 for updates on this award.

(2014) · Chi Epsilon Scholarship

Chi Epsilon
c/o Dr. Robert L. Henry, University of Texas at Arlington, Box 19316, Arlington, TX 76019
Phone: 817-272-2752
Email: xehq@chi-epsilon.org
http://www.chi-epsilon.org/XEWebGeneral2/Members/ScholarshipApps.aspx
Purpose: To reward undergraduate students who are members of Chi Epsilon.
Eligibility: Applicants must be members of the Chi Epsilon, Civil Engineering Honor Society.
Target applicant(s): College students. Adult students.
Amount: $2,000-$3,500.
Number of awards: Varies.
Deadline: February 1.
How to apply: Applications are available online.
Exclusive: Visit www.UltimateScholarshipBook.com and enter code CH201423 for updates on this award.

(2015) · Community College Transition Award

National Society of Collegiate Scholars (NSCS)
2000 M Street NW, Suite 600, Washington, DC 20036
Phone: 202-265-9000
Email: nscs@nscs.org
https://nscs.org/nscs-scholarships/
Purpose: To aid NSCS members in attaining their goals and to recognize their achievements in academics, leadership and service.
Eligibility: Applicants must be outstanding community college students transferring to a four-year college. Selection is based on the overall strength of the application.
Target applicant(s): College students. Adult students.
Amount: $1,000.
Number of awards: 10.
Deadline: May 13.
How to apply: Applications are available online.
Exclusive: Visit www.UltimateScholarshipBook.com and enter code NA201523 for updates on this award.

(2016) · Community Service Award

Golden Key International Honour Society
Scholarship Program Administrators, Golden Key Scholarships/Awards, 1040 Crown Pointe Parkway, Suite 900, Atlanta, GA 30338
Phone: 800-377-2401
Email: awards@goldenkey.org
https://www.goldenkey.org/scholarships-awards/overview/
Purpose: To recognize a Golden Key member for "outstanding and impactful service to the community."
Eligibility: Applicants must be undergraduate or graduate Golden Key members who are currently enrolled in a degree program. Selection is based on amount of service, impact of service and outside extracurricular involvement. To qualify, applicants much have 100 hours of community service through a nonprofit organization. Applicants must provide an essay of up to 500 words describing the community service project, recommendation letters and list of extracurricular activities.
Target applicant(s): College students. Graduate school students. Adult students.
Amount: $2,000.
Number of awards: Up to 10.
Deadline: June 23 and December 31.
How to apply: Applications are available online.
Exclusive: Visit www.UltimateScholarshipBook.com and enter code GO201623 for updates on this award.

(2017) · CWA Joe Beirne Foundation Scholarship

Communications Workers of America
Attn.: George Kohl, 501 Third Street NW, Washington, DC 20001
Phone: 202-434-1100
Email: kadams@cwa-union.org
http://www.cwa-union.org
Purpose: To provide scholarships for CWA members and their families.
Eligibility: Applicants may be Communications Workers of America (CWA) members, their spouses, their children or their grandchildren. Applicants must be high school graduates or at least high school students who will graduate during the year in which they apply. Winners are selected by a lottery drawing. This is a two-year scholarship.
Target applicant(s): High school students. College students. Graduate school students. Adult students.
Amount: $4,000.
Number of awards: 16.
Scholarship may be renewable.
Deadline: April 30.
How to apply: Contact a CWA Local or write (referencing CWA local number, member name and Social Security number) for an application. Applications are available online.
Exclusive: Visit www.UltimateScholarshipBook.com and enter code CO201723 for updates on this award.

(2018) · David B. Durkee Memorial Scholarship Program

Bakery Confectionary Tobacco Workers and Grain Millers (BCTGM) International Union
Scholarship Program, 10401 Connecticut Avenue, Kensington, MD 20895-3961
Phone: 301-933-8600
http://www.bctgm.org
Purpose: To provide scholarships for the members and families of members of BTGCM.
Eligibility: Applicants must be members of the BCTGM in good standing or the children of such members. The scholarships are also open to office employees and children of those employed at the International Union office. Applicants must be high school students who will be attending an accredited college, technical college or vocational school for the first time, high school graduates who have never attended college or BCTGM members who have never applied to the program before who are currently enrolled or planning to begin or resume their studies in the fall. All applicants are required to take the SAT or an equivalent, such as the ACT.
Target applicant(s): High school students. College students. Graduate school students. Adult students.
Amount: $5,000.
Number of awards: 5.
Deadline: January 31.
How to apply: Applications are available through your local BCTGM union office.
Exclusive: Visit www.UltimateScholarshipBook.com and enter code BA201823 for updates on this award.

(2019) · Delta Gamma Foundation Scholarship

Delta Gamma Foundation
3250 Riverside Drive, P.O. Box 21397, Columbus, OH 43221
Phone: 614-481-8169
Email: dgscholarships08@aol.com
http://www.deltagamma.org
Purpose: To support student members.
Eligibility: Applicants must be initiated members of Delta Gamma, have maintained a 3.0 GPA and have completed three semesters or five quarters of college coursework. Applicants should also be active participants in chapter, campus and community leadership activities. Awards are based on academic achievement and participation in activities.
Target applicant(s): College students. Adult students.
Minimum GPA: 3.0
Amount: Varies.
Number of awards: Varies.
Deadline: March 1.
How to apply: Applications are available online.
Exclusive: Visit www.UltimateScholarshipBook.com and enter code DE201923 for updates on this award.

(2020) · Delta Phi Epsilon Educational Foundation Scholarship

Delta Phi Epsilon Educational Foundation
16A Worthington Drive, Maryland Heights, MO 63043
Phone: 314-275-2626
Email: fausbury@dphie.org
http://www.dphie.org
Purpose: To reward members of Delta Phi Epsilon.

Eligibility: Applicants must be members or the sons or daughters of members of Delta Phi Epsilon who are applying for undergraduate or graduate study. The award is based on service and involvement, academics and financial need. Applicants should submit transcripts, letters of introduction and financial need, autobiographical sketches, two recent photos, at least two letters of recommendation and the contact information of the financial aid director for the school.
Target applicant(s): High school students. College students. Graduate school students. Adult students.
Amount: Varies.
Number of awards: Varies.
Deadline: December 31.
How to apply: Applications are available online.
Exclusive: Visit www.UltimateScholarshipBook.com and enter code DE202023 for updates on this award.

(2021) · Diller Teen Tikkun Olam Awards

Helen Diller Family Foundation
121 Steuart Street, San Francisco, CA 94105
Phone: 415-512-6432
Email: DillerTeenAwards@sfjcf.org
https://www.dillerteenawards.org/
Purpose: To assist Jewish teens who have demonstrated leadership and participation in community service projects that exemplify the value of tikkun olam (repair of the world).
Eligibility: Applicants must be Jewish teens, U.S. residents and between 13 and 19 years old. Two references and an application form are required. Teens' projects can help either the Jewish community or the general community as long as they have not been remunerated for their services. Teens may be nominated by any community member who knows the importance of their project—except family members—or may also nominate themselves.
Target applicant(s): Junior high students or younger. High school students. College students.
Amount: $36,000.
Number of awards: Up to 15.
Deadline: January 7.
How to apply: Applications are available online.
Exclusive: Visit www.UltimateScholarshipBook.com and enter code HE202123 for updates on this award.

(2022) · Diocese of the Armenian Church of America (Eastern) Scholarships

Diocese of the Armenian Church of America (Eastern)
630 Second Avenue, New York, NY 10016
Phone: 212-686-0710
Email: mariab@armeniandiocese.org
https://armenianchurch.us/scholarships/
Purpose: To support young Armenian Church members who are seeking higher education.
Eligibility: Applicants must be Armenian Americans who are currently attending or plan to attend a four-year college or university. Preference is given to applicants who are U.S. citizens and are active in the Armenian Church.
Target applicant(s): High school students. College students. Adult students.
Amount: Varies.
Number of awards: Varies.
Deadline: May 14.
How to apply: Applications are available from the Diocese of the Armenian Church of America (Eastern).

Exclusive: Visit www.UltimateScholarshipBook.com and enter code DI202223 for updates on this award.

(2023) · Donald A. and John R. Fisher Memorial Scholarship

Tau Kappa Epsilon Educational Foundation
7439 Woodland Drive, Suite 100, Indianapolis, IN 46278
Phone: 317-872-6533
Email: tkeogc@tke.org
https://www.tke.org/foundation/scholarships
Purpose: To recognize academic achievement and leadership in honor of father and son members Donald A. and John R. Fisher.
Eligibility: Applicants must be initiated Tau Kappa Epsilon members in good standing and full-time students with a GPA of at least 3.0. They must demonstrate outstanding leadership in their chapter, campus and community. Applicants must also include a statement describing how they have benefited from TKE membership.
Target applicant(s): College students. Adult students.
Minimum GPA: 3.0
Amount: $800.
Number of awards: 1.
Deadline: March 15.
How to apply: Applications are available online.
Exclusive: Visit www.UltimateScholarshipBook.com and enter code TA202323 for updates on this award.

(2024) · Elizabeth Ahlemeyer Quick/Gamma Phi Beta Scholarship

National Panhellenic Conference Foundation
3901 W. 86th Street, Suite 398, Indianapolis, IN 46268
Phone: 317-872-3185
Email: dani@npcwomen.org
https://www.npcwomen.org/foundation/
Purpose: To support collegiate members of the National Panhellenic Conference.
Eligibility: Applicants must be members of an NPC member group in good standing, be nominated by their College Panhellenics and have displayed outstanding service. Students must be rising full-time juniors or seniors in college with a 3.0 or higher GPA.
Target applicant(s): College students. Adult students.
Minimum GPA: 3.0
Amount: $2,000.
Number of awards: 1.
Deadline: March 15.
How to apply: Applications are available online. An application form, transcript and two letters of recommendation are required.
Exclusive: Visit www.UltimateScholarshipBook.com and enter code NA202423 for updates on this award.

(2025) · Emergency Educational Fund Grants

Elks National Foundation Headquarters
2750 North Lakeview Avenue, Chicago, IL 60614
Phone: 773-755-4732
Email: scholarship@elks.org
https://www.elks.org/scholars/
Purpose: To assist children of deceased and incapacitated Elks.
Eligibility: Applicants must be the children of deceased or incapacitated Elks who were/are members in good standing for at least one year, unmarried, under 23 years old and full-time undergraduate students at a U.S. school. Applicants must also demonstrate financial need.
Target applicant(s): High school students. College students.
Amount: Up to $5,000.
Number of awards: Varies.
Scholarship may be renewable.
Deadline: November 1.
How to apply: Applications are available from the local Elks Lodge or by phone or e-mail request.
Exclusive: Visit www.UltimateScholarshipBook.com and enter code EL202523 for updates on this award.

(2026) · Emmett J. Doerr Memorial Scout Scholarship

National Catholic Committee on Scouting
Attn: Elizabeth Olivas/Emmett J. Doerr Memorial Scout Scholarship, P.O. Box 934, Rociada, NM 87742
Phone: 972-580-2114
Email: nccs@scouting.org
http://www.nccs-bsa.org/index.php/college-scholarship
Purpose: To help scouts in a Boy Scouts of America program with their college education.
Eligibility: Applicants must be practicing Catholics and full-time high school seniors who hold a leadership role in their scouting unit and are actively involved with a Scout Troop, Varsity Scout Team, Venturing Crew or Sea Scout Ship. Students must have provided service to their community, school, scouting and home parish and earned the Ad Altare Dei, Pope Pius XII Religious Award or Light is Life (Eastern Rite) Religious Emblem. Applicants must also have earned the Eagle Scout, Summit Award or Quartermaster Award.
Target applicant(s): High school students.
Amount: Up to $5,000.
Number of awards: 7.
Deadline: March 1.
How to apply: Applications are available online. An application form, official high school transcript, four letters of recommendation and a photo are required.
Exclusive: Visit www.UltimateScholarshipBook.com and enter code NA202623 for updates on this award.

(2027) · Eugene C. Beach Memorial Scholarship

Tau Kappa Epsilon Educational Foundation
7439 Woodland Drive, Suite 100, Indianapolis, IN 46278
Phone: 317-872-6533
Email: tkeogc@tke.org
https://www.tke.org/foundation/scholarships
Purpose: To reward a member of Tau Kappa Epsilon for outstanding academic achievement and leadership within the chapter, campus and community.
Eligibility: Applicants must have a minimum GPA of 3.0.
Target applicant(s): College students. Adult students.
Minimum GPA: 3.0
Amount: $300.
Number of awards: 1.
Deadline: March 15.
How to apply: Applications are available online.
Exclusive: Visit www.UltimateScholarshipBook.com and enter code TA202723 for updates on this award.

(2028) · Fadel Educational Foundation Annual Award Program

Fadel Educational Foundation
Phone: 484-694-1783
http://www.fadelfoundation.org
Purpose: To support Muslim U.S. citizens and permanent residents.
Eligibility: Applicants must be non-incarcerated students pursuing higher education. Selection is based on need and merit. Applicants should provide application forms, two teacher recommendation forms, one masjid official recommendation letter and financial need reports.
Target applicant(s): High school students. College students. Graduate school students. Adult students.
Amount: Up to $3,500.
Number of awards: Varies.
Deadline: May 29.
How to apply: Applications are available online.
Exclusive: Visit www.UltimateScholarshipBook.com and enter code FA202823 for updates on this award.

(2029) · FEEA Scholarship Program

Federal Employee Education and Assistance Fund
1641 Prince Street, Alexandria, VA 22314
Phone: 202-554-0007x102
https://feea.org/our-programs/scholarships/
Purpose: The FEEA scholarship program aids current, civilian, federal and postal employees and their dependents and spouses.
Eligibility: Applicants must be current civilian, federal and postal employees and their dependents, including spouses. Applicants must also be enrolled or plan to enroll in an accredited post secondary school, have a minimum 3.0 GPA and may be high school seniors, college students or graduate students.
Target applicant(s): High school students. College students. Graduate school students. Adult students.
Minimum GPA: 3.0
Amount: Up to $5,000.
Number of awards: At least 200.
Deadline: March 24.
How to apply: Applications are available online or by sending a self-addressed and stamped envelope.
Exclusive: Visit www.UltimateScholarshipBook.com and enter code FE202923 for updates on this award.

(2030) · First in the Family Scholarship

National Society of Collegiate Scholars (NSCS)
2000 M Street NW, Suite 600, Washington, DC 20036
Phone: 202-265-9000
Email: nscs@nscs.org
https://nscs.org/nscs-scholarships/
Purpose: To aid NSCS members with achieving their goals and to recognize their academic, service and leadership achievements.
Eligibility: Applicants must be the first person in their family to attend college. Selection is based on the overall strength of the application.
Target applicant(s): College students. Adult students.
Amount: Varies.
Number of awards: Varies.
Deadline: November.
How to apply: Applications are available online.
Exclusive: Visit www.UltimateScholarshipBook.com and enter code NA203023 for updates on this award.

(2031) · Fleet Reserve Association Scholarship

Fleet Reserve Association (FRA)
FRA Scholarship Administrator, 125 N. West Street, Alexandria, VA 22314
Phone: 800-372-1924
Email: news-fra@fra.org
https://www.fra.org/fra/Web/Events_and_Programs/7_12th_Grade_Essay_Contest/Web/Content/Essay_Contest.aspx
Purpose: To provide financial support for post-secondary education to FRA members and their dependents and grandchildren.
Eligibility: Applicants must be either FRA members or the dependents or grandchildren of an FRA member who is in good standing or was in good standing at time of death. Applicants are judged on the basis of leadership skills, financial need, academic record and character.
Target applicant(s): High school students. College students. Graduate school students. Adult students.
Amount: Up to $5,000.
Number of awards: Varies.
Deadline: April 15.
How to apply: Applications are available online.
Exclusive: Visit www.UltimateScholarshipBook.com and enter code FL203123 for updates on this award.

(2032) · Ford Motor Company Fund and Ford Trucks Built Ford Tough - FFA Scholarship Program

National FFA Organization
P.O. Box 68960, 6060 FFA Drive, Indianapolis, IN 46268-0960
Phone: 888-332-2668
Email: scholarships@ffa.org
https://www.ffa.org/participate/grants-and-scholarships/
Purpose: To provide educational assistance to FFA members.
Eligibility: Applicants must be high school seniors who plan to pursue a two- or four-year degree in any major. They must apply online and obtain a signature and dealer code from a local participating Ford Truck dealer. If there is no participating Ford dealer in the applicant's area, he or she may obtain a signature from any local Ford dealer and be eligible for one of five national scholarships.
Target applicant(s): High school students.
Amount: $1,000.
Number of awards: Up to 500.
Deadline: January 14.
How to apply: Applications are available online.
Exclusive: Visit www.UltimateScholarshipBook.com and enter code NA203223 for updates on this award.

(2033) · Fourth Degree Pro Deo and Pro Patria Scholarships

Knights of Columbus
Department of Scholarships, 1 Columbus Plaza, New Haven, CT 06510-3326
Phone: 203-752-4000
Email: info@kofc.org
http://www.kofc.org
Purpose: To provide aid to members or the children of members of the Knights of Columbus.
Eligibility: Applicants must be members or the children of current or deceased members of the Knights of Columbus or, in some cases, be members of the Columbian Squires. Applicants must be entering their freshmen year at a U.S. Catholic college.
Target applicant(s): High school students.

Amount: $1,500.
Number of awards: Varies.
Scholarship may be renewable.
Deadline: April 1.
How to apply: Applications are available by mail.
Exclusive: Visit www.UltimateScholarshipBook.com and enter code KN203323 for updates on this award.

(2034) · Frank S. Land Scholarships

DeMolay Foundation
10200 NW Ambassador Drive, Kansas City, MO 64153
Phone: 800-336-6529
Email: demolay@demolay.org
https://demolay.org/
Purpose: To reward DeMolay members.
Eligibility: Applicants must be active male members of DeMolay and be under the age of 21. DeMolay is an organization with more than 1,000 chapters in the world that helps prepare young men ages 12 to 21 to "lead successful, happy and productive lives." The group aims to help members develop civic awareness, personal responsibility and leadership skills.
Target applicant(s): Junior high students or younger. High school students. College students.
Amount: Varies.
Number of awards: Varies.
Deadline: April 15.
How to apply: Applications are available online.
Exclusive: Visit www.UltimateScholarshipBook.com and enter code DE203423 for updates on this award.

(2035) · Gaston/Nolle Scholarships

Alpha Chi
1210 East Race Avenue, Searcy, AR 72143-4656
Phone: 501-593-4810
Email: scholarships@alphachihonor.org
http://www.alphachihonor.org
Purpose: To assist Alpha Chi members who are entering their senior year of undergraduate study.
Eligibility: Applicants must be members of Alpha Chi who are enrolled full-time in a bachelor's degree program.
Target applicant(s): College students. Adult students.
Amount: $2,000-$3,000.
Number of awards: 12.
Deadline: February 15.
How to apply: Application requirements are available online, and applicants must be nominated by the faculty sponsor.
Exclusive: Visit www.UltimateScholarshipBook.com and enter code AL203523 for updates on this award.

(2036) · GCSAA Legacy Awards

Golf Course Superintendents Association of America
1421 Research Park Drive, Lawrence, KS 66049
Phone: 800-472-7878
Email: mwright@gcsaa.org
https://www.gcsaa.org/education/scholarships
Purpose: To support the children and grandchildren of GCSAA members.
Eligibility: The applicant's parents or grandparents must have been GCSAA members for five or more consecutive years. Applicants must

also be full-time college students or high school seniors already accepted into a postsecondary school.
Target applicant(s): High school students. College students. Adult students.
Amount: $1,500.
Number of awards: Varies.
Deadline: April 15.
How to apply: Applications are available by contacting Pam Smith, 800-472-7878, x3678.
Exclusive: Visit www.UltimateScholarshipBook.com and enter code GO203623 for updates on this award.

(2037) · GEICO Award

National Society of Collegiate Scholars (NSCS)
2000 M Street NW, Suite 600, Washington, DC 20036
Phone: 202-265-9000
Email: nscs@nscs.org
https://nscs.org/nscs-scholarships/
Purpose: To aid NSCS members in attaining their goals and to recognize their achievements in academics, service and leadership.
Eligibility: Applicants must be college undergraduates. Selection is based on the overall strength of the application.
Target applicant(s): College students. Adult students.
Amount: $1,000.
Number of awards: 25.
Deadline: August 26.
How to apply: Applications are available online.
Exclusive: Visit www.UltimateScholarshipBook.com and enter code NA203723 for updates on this award.

(2038) · GEICO Graduate Award

National Society of Collegiate Scholars (NSCS)
2000 M Street NW, Suite 600, Washington, DC 20036
Phone: 202-265-9000
Email: nscs@nscs.org
https://nscs.org/nscs-scholarships/
Purpose: To aid NSCS members and alumni in attaining their goals and to recognize their achievements in academics, service and leadership.
Eligibility: Applicants must be current or accepted graduate students. Selection is based on the overall strength of the application.
Target applicant(s): Graduate school students. Adult students.
Amount: $2,500.
Number of awards: 2.
Deadline: July 1.
How to apply: Applications are available online.
Exclusive: Visit www.UltimateScholarshipBook.com and enter code NA203823 for updates on this award.

(2039) · George Heller Memorial Scholarship Fund of the SAG-AFTRA Foundation

Screen Actors Guild - American Federation of Television and Radio Artists
5757 Wilshire Boulevard, 7th Floor, Los Angeles, CA 90036
Phone: 855-724-2387
Email: sagaftrainfo@sagaftra.org
https://sagaftra.foundation/assistance/scholarship-programs/
Purpose: To support AFTRA members and their children.
Eligibility: Applicants must be AFTRA members in good standing with five years of membership or the children of members. Scholarships are

awarded based on academic achievement and financial need and can be used to study any academic field or for professional training in the performing arts at an accredited higher education institution.
Target applicant(s): High school students. College students. Graduate school students. Adult students.
Amount: Up to $2,500.
Number of awards: Up to 15.
Deadline: May 31.
How to apply: Applications are available online.
Exclusive: Visit www.UltimateScholarshipBook.com and enter code SC203923 for updates on this award.

(2040) · Girls Incorporated Lucile Miller Wright Scholars Program

Girls Inc.
120 Wall Street, 18th Floor, New York, NY 10005-3902
Phone: 212-509-2000
Email: communications@girlsinc.org
http://www.girlsinc.org
Purpose: To support young members of Girls Incorporated.
Eligibility: Applicants must be young women who are in their junior or senior year of high school and members of a Girls Incorporated affiliate.
Target applicant(s): High school students.
Amount: $5,000-$20,000.
Number of awards: Varies.
Deadline: Varies.
How to apply: Applications are available by written request.
Exclusive: Visit www.UltimateScholarshipBook.com and enter code GI204023 for updates on this award.

(2041) · Glass, Molders, Pottery, Plastics and Allied Workers Memorial Scholarship Fund

International Scholarship and Tuition Services Inc.
GMP Memorial Scholarship Fund, 1321 Murfreesboro Road, Suite 800, Nashville, TN 37217
Phone: 855-670-4787
Email: contactus@applyists.com
http://www.gmpiu.org
Purpose: To provide financial assistance to the children of members.
Eligibility: Applicants must be children, step-children or legally-adopted children of Glass, Molders, Pottery, Plastics and Allied Workers members.
Target applicant(s): High school students. College students. Adult students.
Amount: $2,000-$4,000.
Number of awards: 10.
Scholarship may be renewable.
Deadline: January.
How to apply: Applications are available by written request or by contacting your local union office.
Exclusive: Visit www.UltimateScholarshipBook.com and enter code IN204123 for updates on this award.

(2042) · Golden Key Graduate Scholar Award

Golden Key International Honour Society
Scholarship Program Administrators, Golden Key Scholarships/Awards, 1040 Crown Pointe Parkway, Suite 900, Atlanta, GA 30338
Phone: 800-377-2401
Email: awards@goldenkey.org
https://www.goldenkey.org/scholarships-awards/overview/
Purpose: To support Golden Key members' graduate studies at accredited universities in the U.S. or abroad.
Eligibility: Applicant must be a Golden Key member, be enrolled in a graduate program or an undergraduate who will be enrolled in a graduate program in the next academic year. Selection is based on future academic and career goals, as well as how the applicant plans to create change in the future. Applicants must display academic achievement, leadership, service and involvement with the local Golden Key chapter.
Target applicant(s): College students. Graduate school students. Adult students.
Amount: $10,000.
Number of awards: Varies.
Deadline: December 15.
How to apply: Applications are available online.
Exclusive: Visit www.UltimateScholarshipBook.com and enter code GO204223 for updates on this award.

(2043) · Golden Key Undergraduate Achievement Scholarship

Golden Key International Honour Society
Scholarship Program Administrators, Golden Key Scholarships/Awards, 1040 Crown Pointe Parkway, Suite 900, Atlanta, GA 30338
Phone: 800-377-2401
Email: awards@goldenkey.org
https://www.goldenkey.org/scholarships-awards/overview/
Purpose: To aid degree-seeking Golden Key members.
Eligibility: Applicants must be Golden Key members who are enrolled in an undergraduate degree program with a 3.5 minimum GPA. Selection is based on academic achievement, leadership skills and service to the community.
Target applicant(s): College students. Adult students.
Minimum GPA: 3.5
Amount: $5,000.
Number of awards: Varies.
Deadline: December.
How to apply: Applications are available online. An application form, official transcript, resume, personal statement and one recommendation letter are required.
Exclusive: Visit www.UltimateScholarshipBook.com and enter code GO204323 for updates on this award.

(2044) · Guistwhite Scholarships

Phi Theta Kappa Honor Society
1625 Eastover Drive, Jackson, MS 39211
Phone: 601-987-5741
Email: scholarship.programs@ptk.org
http://www.ptk.org
Purpose: To aid Phi Theta Kappa members who plan to pursue bachelor's degrees.
Eligibility: Applicants must be active members of Phi Theta Kappa who will remain enrolled at a community college through December of the application year. They must have completed at least 30 semester credits (or 45 quarter credits) over the past five years and must have maintained a GPA of 3.5 or higher on a four-point scale over the past five years. Students must have plans to transfer to a four-year postsecondary institution during the calendar year following the submission of the scholarship application and must have junior status at the time of transfer. Applicants must have a community college record that is free of any disciplinary action and must not have a criminal record. Selection is based on academic merit and Phi Theta Kappa participation.

Target applicant(s): College students. Adult students.
Minimum GPA: 3.5
Amount: $5,000.
Number of awards: Up to 15.
Deadline: December 1.
How to apply: Applications are available online. An application form, official transcript, two recommendation letters and personal essay are required.
Exclusive: Visit www.UltimateScholarshipBook.com and enter code PH204423 for updates on this award.

(2045) · Harvey and Laura Alpert Scholarship Award

International Flight Services Association (IFSA)
1100 Johnson Ferry Road, Suite 300, Atlanta, GA 30342
Phone: 678-298-1187
Email: cellery@kellencompany.com
https://ifsa.apex.aero/foundation/
Purpose: To aid hospitality students who are relatives of members of the International Flight Services Association.
Eligibility: Applicants must be hospitality management students who have completed at least 32 credits in their degree program and have a minimum 3.0 GPA. They must have a family member who is a member of the International Flight Services Association (IFSA). Selection is based on academic achievement and stated career goals.
Target applicant(s): College students. Adult students.
Minimum GPA: 3.0
Amount: $5,000.
Number of awards: 2.
Deadline: June 4.
How to apply: Applications are available online. An application form, official transcript, personal essay and three recommendation letters are required.
Exclusive: Visit www.UltimateScholarshipBook.com and enter code IN204523 for updates on this award.

(2046) · Helen B. and Lewis E. Goldstein Scholarship Fund

Jewish Community Federation and Endowment Fund
121 Steuart Street, San Francisco, CA 94105
Phone: 415-777-0411
https://jewishfed.org/how-we-help/scholarships/college-scholarships
Purpose: To support Jewish students who pursue continuing education.
Eligibility: Applicants must be Jewish undergraduate or graduate students currently enrolled at an accredited four-year institution in the U.S. Preference is given to immigrants and students enrolled in a professional school. Applicants must demonstrate academic merit.
Target applicant(s): College students. Graduate school students. Adult students.
Amount: Up to $10,000.
Number of awards: 1.
Deadline: March 31.
How to apply: Applications are available online.
Exclusive: Visit www.UltimateScholarshipBook.com and enter code JE204623 for updates on this award.

(2047) · Hites Transfer Scholarship

Phi Theta Kappa Honor Society
1625 Eastover Drive, Jackson, MS 39211
Phone: 601-987-5741

Email: scholarship.programs@ptk.org
http://www.ptk.org
Purpose: To aid Phi Theta Kappa members who intend to transfer to a four-year postsecondary institution.
Eligibility: Applicants must be Phi Theta Kappa members who are in good standing, have a GPA of 3.5 or higher and have completed 50 or more semester credits over the past five years. They must be enrolled at an accredited community college through March of the application year, have plans to transfer to a four-year postsecondary institution in the fall and have plans to pursue a bachelor's degree on a full-time basis. Applicants cannot have a criminal record. Selection is based on the overall strength of the application.
Target applicant(s): College students. Adult students.
Minimum GPA: 3.5
Amount: $7,500.
Number of awards: Up to 10.
Deadline: December 1.
How to apply: Applications are available online. An application form and supporting documents are required.
Exclusive: Visit www.UltimateScholarshipBook.com and enter code PH204723 for updates on this award.

(2048) · Hoard's Dairyman FFA Scholarship

National FFA Organization
P.O. Box 68960, 6060 FFA Drive, Indianapolis, IN 46268-0960
Phone: 888-332-2668
Email: scholarships@ffa.org
https://www.ffa.org/participate/grants-and-scholarships/
Purpose: To support FFA members working toward four-year degrees in agricultural journalism or dairy science.
Eligibility: Applicants specializing in agricultural communications are preferred. Selection is based on the overall strength of the application.
Target applicant(s): High school students. College students.
Amount: $1,000.
Number of awards: 1.
Deadline: January 14.
How to apply: Applications are available online.
Exclusive: Visit www.UltimateScholarshipBook.com and enter code NA204823 for updates on this award.

(2049) · Howard Coughlin Memorial Scholarship Fund

Office and Professional Employees International Union
80 Eighth Avenue, Suite 610, New York, NY 10011
Phone: 212-367-0902
Email: stoffice@opeiu.org
http://www.opeiu.org
Purpose: To offer scholarships to OPEIU members and their children.
Eligibility: Applicants must either be members of OPEIU in good standing, or the children, stepchildren or legally adopted children of an OPEIU member in good standing or associate members. Applicants must also be high school seniors, high school graduates entering a college, university or a recognized technical or vocational post-secondary school as full-time students or presently in a college, university or a recognized technical or vocational post-secondary school as a full-time or part-time student. Part-time scholarships are defined as a minimum of three credits and no more than two courses. Selection is based on transcripts, high school class rank and SAT/ACT scores or evidence of an equivalent exam by a recognized technical or vocational post-secondary school.
Target applicant(s): High school students. College students. Adult students.
Amount: $662-$6,500.

Number of awards: 19.
Scholarship may be renewable.
Deadline: March 31.
How to apply: Applications are available at the local union office, at the secretary-treasurer's office of the International Union or online.
Exclusive: Visit www.UltimateScholarshipBook.com and enter code OF204923 for updates on this award.

(2050) · IAM Scholarship

International Association of Machinists and Aerospace Workers Scholarship Program, 9000 Machinists Place, Room 204, Upper Marlboro, MD 20772-2687
Phone: 301-967-4708
Email: scholarship@iamaw.org
https://www.goiam.org/news/departments/hq/scholarships/
Purpose: To offer scholarships to members of the International Association of Machinists and Aerospace Workers (IAM) and their children.
Eligibility: Applicants must be an IAM member who has two years of continuous good standing membership or the child of a member who has two years of continuous good standing membership. Applicants may be entering college or vocational/technical school as a freshman or at a higher level with some college credits already completed. Grades, attitude, references, test scores, activities and participation in local lodge are considered in selecting scholarship recipients.
Target applicant(s): High school students. College students. Adult students.
Amount: $1,000-$2,000.
Number of awards: Varies.
Deadline: February 12.
How to apply: Applications are available by written request.
Exclusive: Visit www.UltimateScholarshipBook.com and enter code IN205023 for updates on this award.

(2051) · IFSA Foundation Scholarship Award

International Flight Services Association (IFSA)
1100 Johnson Ferry Road, Suite 300, Atlanta, GA 30342
Phone: 678-298-1187
Email: cellery@kellencompany.com
https://ifsa.apex.aero/foundation/
Purpose: To aid students whose parents are members of the International Flight Services Association.
Eligibility: Applicants must be the children of International Flight Services Association (IFSA) members who are enrolled or planning to enroll at an accredited college or university. They must be attending or planning to attend school on an at least part-time basis and have a GPA of 3.0 or higher on a four-point scale. Selection is based on academic achievement and the applicant's interest in pursuing higher education.
Target applicant(s): High school students. College students. Adult students.
Minimum GPA: 3.0
Amount: Varies.
Number of awards: Varies.
Deadline: June 4.
How to apply: Applications are available online. An application form, official transcript, three recommendation letters, a personal essay and proof of college acceptance or enrollment are required.
Exclusive: Visit www.UltimateScholarshipBook.com and enter code IN205123 for updates on this award.

(2052) · Induction Recognition Award

National Society of Collegiate Scholars (NSCS)
2000 M Street NW, Suite 600, Washington, DC 20036
Phone: 202-265-9000
Email: nscs@nscs.org
https://nscs.org/nscs-scholarships/
Purpose: To help NSCS members achieve their goals and recognize their academic, service and leadership achievements.
Eligibility: Applicants must be new college undergraduate members who attend their induction ceremony and become actively involved in their chapter. Selection is based on the overall strength of the application.
Target applicant(s): College students. Adult students.
Amount: Varies.
Number of awards: Varies.
Deadline: December.
How to apply: Applications are available online.
Exclusive: Visit www.UltimateScholarshipBook.com and enter code NA205223 for updates on this award.

(2053) · International Association of Machinists and Aerospace Workers Scholarship for Members' Children

International Association of Machinists and Aerospace Workers Scholarship Program, 9000 Machinists Place, Room 204, Upper Marlboro, MD 20772-2687
Phone: 301-967-4708
Email: scholarship@iamaw.org
https://www.goiam.org/news/departments/hq/scholarships/
Purpose: To offer scholarships to children of the members of the IAM.
Eligibility: The applicant's parent member must have two years of continuous good standing membership, and applicants must be in their senior year of high school. Selection is based on grades, attitude, references, test scores and activities outside of school.
Target applicant(s): High school students.
Amount: $1,000-$2,000.
Number of awards: Varies.
Deadline: February 12.
How to apply: Applications are available by written request.
Exclusive: Visit www.UltimateScholarshipBook.com and enter code IN205323 for updates on this award.

(2054) · ISF Policy Scholarship Program

Islamic Scholarship Fund
1935 Addison Street, Suite A, Berkeley, CA 94704
Phone: 650-995-6782
Email: contact@islamicscholarshipfund.org
https://islamicscholarshipfund.org/policy-scholarship/
Purpose: To aid Muslim students in pursuing degrees in humanities, social sciences, liberal arts and law.
Eligibility: Applicants must be accepted by or attend a top-ranked four-year college or university for undergraduate or graduate studies. They must be practicing Muslims and U.S. citizens or permanent residents. They must have college junior standing or higher and maintain a minimum GPA of 3.0. Applicants should be active members of their communities. Selection is based on academic record, school and extracurricular activities, extenuating circumstances and a personal interview.
Target applicant(s): College students. Graduate school students. Adult students.
Minimum GPA: 3.0

Amount: $3,000-$5,000.
Number of awards: Varies.
Deadline: March 30.
How to apply: Applications are available online.
Exclusive: Visit www.UltimateScholarshipBook.com and enter code IS205423 for updates on this award.

(2055) · Islamic Society of North America Scholarships

Islamic Society of North America
6555 S. County Road 750 E, Plainfield, IN 46168
Phone: 317-839-8157
http://www.isna.net/scholarships/
Purpose: To reward students for their academic performance and community development work.
Eligibility: Applicants must be U.S. citizens or permanent residents attending a U.S. based accredited college or university. Students must be actively engaged in their community.
Target applicant(s): High school students. College students. Graduate school students. Adult students.
Amount: Varies.
Number of awards: Varies.
Deadline: Varies.
How to apply: Applications are available online.
Exclusive: Visit www.UltimateScholarshipBook.com and enter code IS205523 for updates on this award.

(2056) · J. Robert Ashcroft National Youth Scholarship

Assemblies of God
1445 North Boonville Avenue, Springfield, MO 65802-1894
https://colleges.ag.org/
Purpose: To provide financial assistance to college-bound seniors who attend Assemblies of God churches.
Eligibility: Applicants must be high school seniors who attend an Assemblies of God church, either in the United States or abroad as dependents of Assemblies of God missionaries or chaplains. Applicants must also attend an institution of higher learning that is endorsed by the Assemblies of God the fall immediately following their high school graduation.
Target applicant(s): High school students.
Amount: $2,000-$8,000.
Number of awards: 3.
Deadline: February.
How to apply: Applications are available online. Applications must be sent to their AG District Council first, and the top candidates are then sent to us for review.
Exclusive: Visit www.UltimateScholarshipBook.com and enter code AS205623 for updates on this award.

(2057) · James B. Carey Scholarship

International Union of Electronic, Electrical, Salaried, Machine and Furniture Workers-Communications Workers of America
2701 Dryden Road, Dayton, OH 45439
Phone: 937-298-9984
https://www.iue-cwa.org/scholarships
Purpose: To support students who are or are related to IUE-CWA members or employees.
Eligibility: Applicants must have IUE-CWA membership either directly or through a parent or grandparent. Students must be at undergraduate level at an accredited college.

Target applicant(s): High school students. College students. Adult students.
Amount: $1,000.
Number of awards: 9.
Deadline: March 31.
How to apply: Applications are available online.
Exclusive: Visit www.UltimateScholarshipBook.com and enter code IN205723 for updates on this award.

(2058) · James E. Breining Scholarship Award

Explorers Learning for Life
1325 West Walnut Hill Lane, P.O. Box 152225, Irving, TX 75015-2225
Phone: 855-806-9992
Email: exploring@lflmail.org
http://www.exploring.org/scholarships/
Purpose: To encourage Law Enforcement Explorers to attend college.
Eligibility: Applicants must be active Law Enforcement Explorers in good standing who demonstrate a meaningful contribution to society, impeccable character and ethics and leadership abilities in both Law Enforcement Exploring and the community. Award given in even numbered years.
Target applicant(s): High school students. College students. Adult students.
Amount: At least $1,500.
Number of awards: Varies.
Deadline: June 15.
How to apply: Applications are available online.
Exclusive: Visit www.UltimateScholarshipBook.com and enter code EX205823 for updates on this award.

(2059) · John Kelly Labor Studies Scholarship Fund

Office and Professional Employees International Union
80 Eighth Avenue, Suite 610, New York, NY 10011
Phone: 212-367-0902
Email: stoffice@opeiu.org
http://www.opeiu.org
Purpose: To offer scholarships to OPEIU members and associate members.
Eligibility: Applicants must be members of OPEIU in good standing or associate members for at least two years, and applicants must be either undergraduate or graduate students in one of the following areas of study: labor studies, industrial relations, union leadership and administration or non-degree programs sponsored by the National Labor College at the George Meany Center or similar institution. The selections shall be based on recommendations of an academic scholarship committee.
Target applicant(s): College students. Graduate school students. Adult students.
Amount: $3,250.
Number of awards: 10.
Deadline: March 31.
How to apply: Applications are available by phone or written request from the local union office, at the secretary-treasurer's office of the International Union or online.
Exclusive: Visit www.UltimateScholarshipBook.com and enter code OF205923 for updates on this award.

(2060) · John L. Dales Scholarship Fund

Screen Actors Guild Foundation
5757 Wilshire Boulevard, Suite 124, Los Angeles, CA 90036

Phone: 323-549-6649
Email: dlloyd@sag.org
https://sagaftra.foundation/
Purpose: To award scholarships to the families of the SAG.
Eligibility: Applicants must be a member of the Screen Actors Guild or a child of a member of the Screen Actors Guild. Transitional scholarships are open to members under the age of 26 must have been a member of the Screen Actors Guild for five years and have a lifetime earnings of $30,000. The parent of an applicant must have ten vested years of pension credits or a lifetime earnings of $150,000 earned in the Guild's jurisdiction. Children of members are eligible for standard scholarships and must also be under age 26. Applicants must submit an essay of 350 to 750 words on a topic of their choice. The award may be used during college or graduate school.
Target applicant(s): High school students. College students. Graduate school students.
Amount: Varies.
Number of awards: Varies.
Deadline: May 31.
How to apply: Applications are available online.
Exclusive: Visit www.UltimateScholarshipBook.com and enter code SC206023 for updates on this award.

(2061) · John W. McDevitt (Fourth Degree) Scholarship Fund

Knights of Columbus
Department of Scholarships, 1 Columbus Plaza, New Haven, CT 06510-3326
Phone: 203-752-4000
Email: info@kofc.org
http://www.kofc.org
Purpose: To provide financial assistance to college students who are Knights of Columbus members or family members of a member.
Eligibility: Applicants must be a Knights of Columbus member, or the wife, widow or child of a member in good standing. New applicants must also be entering their freshman year at a Catholic college or university.
Target applicant(s): High school students.
Amount: $1,500.
Number of awards: Varies.
Scholarship may be renewable.
Deadline: April 1.
How to apply: Applications are available by mail.
Exclusive: Visit www.UltimateScholarshipBook.com and enter code KN206123 for updates on this award.

(2062) · Jones-Laurence Award for Scholastic Achievement

Sigma Alpha Epsilon (SAE)
Dave Sandell, Sigma Alpha Epsilon Foundation Scholarships, 1856 Sheridan Road, Evanston, IL 60201-3837
Phone: 800-233-1856 x234
Email: dsandell@sae.net
http://www.sae.net
Purpose: To improve scholarship among active Sigma Alpha Epsilon members.
Eligibility: Applicants must be brothers of Sigma Alpha Epsilon in good standing and either must have junior standing or higher or must be pursuing full-time graduate study. This award is merit-based, with an emphasis on combining academic excellence, leadership, service and campus involvement. Applicants are nominated by their chapters and have a minimum 3.8 GPA.

Target applicant(s): College students. Graduate school students. Adult students.
Minimum GPA: 3.8
Amount: $2,000.
Number of awards: 2.
Deadline: March 1.
How to apply: Applications are available online.
Exclusive: Visit www.UltimateScholarshipBook.com and enter code SI206223 for updates on this award.

(2063) · Junior Member Loyalty Scholarship

American Legion Auxiliary
3450 Founders Road, Indianapolis, IN 46268
Phone: 317-569-4500
Email: alahq@alaforveterans.org
https://www.legion-aux.org/scholarships
Purpose: To reward American Legion Auxiliary Junior members who retain their membership into adulthood.
Eligibility: Applicants must have been Junior members of the American Legion Auxiliary, held membership in the American Legion Auxiliary for the past three consecutive years and be a paid member for the current membership year. Students must be traditional college students with no interruption in education in at least the first semester of college but have not obtained a bachelor's degree. Applicants must have a minimum 3.0 GPA.
Target applicant(s): College students. Adult students.
Minimum GPA: 3.0
Amount: $2,500.
Number of awards: 10.
Deadline: March 1.
How to apply: Applications are available online.
Exclusive: Visit www.UltimateScholarshipBook.com and enter code AM206323 for updates on this award.

(2064) · Kiwanis Children's Fund Scholarship

Circle K International
3636 Woodview Trace, Indianapolis, IN 46268
Email: scholarships@kiwanis.org
https://www.kiwanis.org/programs/youth/scholarships
Purpose: This scholarship is in memory of Harry S. Himmel, deceased President Emeritus of the Kiwanis International Foundation. Recipients should demonstrate dedication and leadership within the organization.
Eligibility: Applicants must be Key Club or Circle K members who appear on the international roster, are currently enrolled in college or are college-bound and have completed 100 service hours with the organization. Key Club members must have also held an elected officer position within the organization.
Target applicant(s): High school students. College students. Adult students.
Minimum GPA: 3.0
Amount: $500.
Number of awards: 2.
Deadline: February 1.
How to apply: Applications are available online.
Exclusive: Visit www.UltimateScholarshipBook.com and enter code CI206423 for updates on this award.

(2065) · Kyutaro and Yasuo Abiko Memorial Scholarship

Japanese American Citizens League (JACL)
1765 Sutter Street, San Francisco, CA 94115
Phone: 415-921-5225
Email: jacl@jacl.org
http://www.jacl.org
Purpose: To aid National Japanese American Citizens League (JACL) members who are pursuing higher education.
Eligibility: Applicants must be National JACL members who are enrolled as full-time undergraduates at a U.S. institution of higher learning. Preference will be given to applicants who are studying agriculture or journalism. Selection is based on the overall strength of the application.
Target applicant(s): High school students. College students. Adult students.
Amount: Varies.
Number of awards: Varies.
Deadline: April 1.
How to apply: Applications are available online. An application form, official transcript, personal statement, one recommendation letter and proof of JACL membership are required.
Exclusive: Visit www.UltimateScholarshipBook.com and enter code JA206523 for updates on this award.

(2066) · Legacy Award

Elks National Foundation Headquarters
2750 North Lakeview Avenue, Chicago, IL 60614
Phone: 773-755-4732
Email: scholarship@elks.org
https://www.elks.org/scholars/
Purpose: To assist the descendants of Elk members.
Eligibility: Applicants must be children or grandchildren (including step-children/grandchildren and legal wards) of Elk members in good standing and be high school seniors planning to attend accredited U.S. postsecondary institutions (with the exception of some non-U.S. Elks Lodges). Applicants must also take or have taken the SAT or ACT. The selection committee will evaluate applicants on the core values of knowledge, charity, community and integrity. Financial need is not a consideration.
Target applicant(s): High school students.
Amount: $4,000.
Number of awards: 300.
Deadline: February 7.
How to apply: Applications are available from local Elks Lodges, online or by written request.
Exclusive: Visit www.UltimateScholarshipBook.com and enter code EL206623 for updates on this award.

(2067) · Lillian and Arthur Dunn Scholarship

National Society Daughters of the American Revolution
Committee Services Office, Attn.: Scholarships, 1776 D Street NW, Washington, DC 20006-5303
Phone: 202-628-1776
Email: scholarships@dar.org
https://www.dar.org/national-society/scholarships/general-information
Purpose: To assist the children of members with their education.
Eligibility: Applicants must be sons or daughters of current women members of NSDAR, must be U.S. citizens and plan to attend an accredited U.S. college or university. All applicants must obtain a letter of sponsorship from their local DAR chapter.
Target applicant(s): High school students. College students. Adult students.
Amount: $2,500.
Number of awards: 2.
Scholarship may be renewable.
Deadline: January 31.
How to apply: Applications are available by written request with a self-addressed, stamped envelope.
Exclusive: Visit www.UltimateScholarshipBook.com and enter code NA206723 for updates on this award.

(2068) · Literacy Grants

Honor Society of Phi Kappa Phi
7576 Goodwood Boulevard, Baton Rouge, LA 70806
Phone: 800-804-9880
Email: awards@phikappaphi.org
http://www.phikappaphi.org
Purpose: To award grants to Phi Kappa Phi members and chapters to offer literacy programs.
Eligibility: The project leader must be a member of Phi Kappa Phi. Previous winners have provided books and book bags to literacy programs, organized literacy fairs and conducted research on literacy.
Target applicant(s): College students. Graduate school students. Adult students.
Amount: Up to $2,500.
Number of awards: Varies.
Deadline: April 1.
How to apply: Applications are available online.
Exclusive: Visit www.UltimateScholarshipBook.com and enter code HO206823 for updates on this award.

(2069) · Maids of Athena Scholarships

American Hellenic Education Progressive Association
1909 Q Street NW, Suite 500, Washington, DC 20009
Phone: 202-232-6300
Email: ahepa@ahepa.org
https://ahepa.org/education/
Purpose: To support members of the Maids of Athena.
Eligibility: Students must demonstrate financial need and academic achievement. Applicants must be high school seniors, college undergraduates or graduate students. Selection is based on academic achievement, financial need and participation in the organization.
Target applicant(s): High school students. College students. Graduate school students. Adult students.
Amount: Varies.
Number of awards: Varies.
Deadline: May 31.
How to apply: Applications are available online.
Exclusive: Visit www.UltimateScholarshipBook.com and enter code AM206923 for updates on this award.

(2070) · Margaret Jerome Sampson Scholarship

Phi Upsilon Omicron Inc.
National Office, P.O. Box 50970, Bowling Green, KY 42102-4270
Phone: 270-904-1340
Email: national@phiu.org
http://www.phiu.org

Purpose: To aid Phi Upsilon Omicron members who are working toward bachelor's degrees in family and consumer sciences.

Eligibility: Applicants must be Phi Upsilon Omicron (Phi U) members. They must be full-time students who are enrolled in a family and consumer sciences degree program at the baccalaureate level. Preference will be given to applicants who are majoring in food and nutrition or dietetics. Selection is based on academic merit, participation in Phi U and stated career goals.

Target applicant(s): College students. Adult students.

Amount: $5,650.

Number of awards: Up to 8.

Deadline: March 1.

How to apply: Applications are available online. An application form, three recommendation letters, an official transcript and a financial statement are required.

Exclusive: Visit www.UltimateScholarshipBook.com and enter code PH207023 for updates on this award.

(2071) · Martin Luther King, Jr. Memorial Scholarship

California Teachers Association (CTA)
CTA Human Rights Department, P.O. Box 921, Burlingame, CA 94011-0921
Phone: 650-697-1400
https://www.cta.org/for-educators/scholarships-awards

Purpose: To encourage ethnic minority students to become teachers and support the continuing education of ethnic minority teachers.

Eligibility: Applicants must be African American, American Indian/Alaska Native, Asian/Pacific Islander or Hispanic students pursuing a teaching-related career in public education. Candidates must also be active members of the California Teachers Association or Student California Teachers Association or the dependents of an active, retired-life or deceased California Teachers Association member.

Target applicant(s): High school students. College students. Graduate school students. Adult students.

Amount: Up to $4,000.

Number of awards: Varies.

Deadline: February 12.

How to apply: Applications are available online.

Exclusive: Visit www.UltimateScholarshipBook.com and enter code CA207123 for updates on this award.

(2072) · Mary E. Bivins Religious Scholarship

Mary E. Bivins Foundation
2311 West 16th Avenue, Amarillo, TX 79102
Phone: 806-379-9400
Email: info@bivinsfoundation.org
https://www.bivinsfoundation.org/scholarship/scholarship-program/

Purpose: To assist students pursuing Christian ministry.

Eligibility: Applicants must be graduate students pursuing a master degree in a field which prepares them to preach the Christian religion.

Target applicant(s): Graduate school students. Adult students.

Amount: $3,500.

Number of awards: 1.

Deadline: February 25.

How to apply: Applications are available online.

Exclusive: Visit www.UltimateScholarshipBook.com and enter code MA207223 for updates on this award.

(2073) · Michael Hakeem Memorial College Essay Contest

Freedom from Religion Foundation
P.O. Box 750, Madison, WI 53701
Phone: 608-256-8900
Email: info@ffrf.org
https://ffrf.org/outreach/awards

Purpose: To assist current college students who write an essay about freedom from religion.

Eligibility: Applicants must write a four- to five-page essay on the provided topic. Recent topic choices have been, "Why I am an atheist/agnostic/unbeliever," "Growing up a freethinker" or "Rejecting religion." More details about the topic are available online.

Target applicant(s): High school students. College students.

Amount: $200-$3,500.

Number of awards: Varies.

Deadline: June 30.

How to apply: There is no application form. In addition to the essay, applicants must submit a one-paragraph biography and should not include a resume.

Exclusive: Visit www.UltimateScholarshipBook.com and enter code FR207323 for updates on this award.

(2074) · Michael J. Quill Scholarship Fund

Transport Worker Union of American, AFL-CIO
Michael J. Quill Scholarship Fund, 501 3rd Street NW, 9th Floor, Washington, DC 20001
Phone: 202-719-3900
http://www.twu.org

Purpose: To provide financial assistance to the dependents of TWU members.

Eligibility: Applicants must be high school seniors and may be the children of present, retired or deceased TWU members in good standing or meet other eligibility requirements. Recipients are selected by a public drawing.

Target applicant(s): High school students.

Amount: $4,800.

Number of awards: 15.

Scholarship may be renewable.

Deadline: April 26.

How to apply: Applications are available from local unions and the union publication. They're also available online.

Exclusive: Visit www.UltimateScholarshipBook.com and enter code TR207423 for updates on this award.

(2075) · Modern Woodmen of America Scholarship

Modern Woodmen of America
1701 1st Avenue, P.O. Box 2005, Rock Island, IL 61204
Phone: 309-786-6481
Email: memberservice@modern-woodmen.org
https://learnmore.scholarsapply.org/impact/

Purpose: To support beneficial members of Modern Woodmen.

Eligibility: Applicants must be high school seniors and be beneficial members of Modern Woodmen for at least two years. Applicants should be in the upper half of their graduating class. There are national, regional and one-time awards.

Target applicant(s): High school students.

Amount: Varies.

Number of awards: Varies.

Deadline: February 7.

How to apply: Applications are available online.
Exclusive: Visit www.UltimateScholarshipBook.com and enter code MO207523 for updates on this award.

(2076) · Moris J. and Betty Kaplun Essay Contest

Kaplun Foundation
Essay Contest Committee, P.O. Box 234428, Great Neck, NY 11023
Email: info@kaplunfoundation.org
http://www.kaplunfoundation.org
Purpose: To reward essays about Jewish-related topics.
Eligibility: Applicants must be in grades 7 through 12. Grades 7 through 9 are level one, and grades 10 through 12 are level two. Applicants must submit essays on Jewish-related topics listed on the website, and essays must be typed, double-spaced and a minimum of 250 words. Level one essays may not be more than 1,000 words. Level two essays may not be more than 1,500 words. A recent level one topic has been, "What person of importance to the Jewish people, past or present, would you like to meet and why?" A recent level two topic has been, "Antisemitism plagues all Jews regardless of religious adherence. How do you see yourself reacting to it?"
Target applicant(s): Junior high students or younger. High school students.
Amount: $750-$1,800.
Number of awards: 12.
Deadline: March.
How to apply: Essays must be submitted by mail.
Exclusive: Visit www.UltimateScholarshipBook.com and enter code KA207623 for updates on this award.

(2077) · Mortar Board National Foundation Fellowship

Mortar Board National Foundation
1200 Chambers Road, #201, Columbus, OH 43212
Phone: 614-488-4094
Email: mortarboard@mortarboard.org
http://www.mortarboard.org
Purpose: To support Mortar Board members pursuing post-graduate degrees who exemplify the tenets of scholarship, leadership and dedication to service at their college Alma Mater.
Eligibility: Applicants must be current or former members of Mortar Board entering a post-graduate degree program who have not previously been awarded a Mortar National Foundation Fellowship. They must complete the online application, submit two letters of recommendation and a current, official transcript. Fellowship recipients must be ready to begin and complete the year of post-graduate study upon acceptance of the fellowship award.
Target applicant(s): College students. Adult students.
Amount: $3,000-$5,000.
Number of awards: 12.
Deadline: March 15.
How to apply: Applications are available online.
Exclusive: Visit www.UltimateScholarshipBook.com and enter code MO207723 for updates on this award.

(2078) · Mortin Scholarship

Triangle Education Foundation
Chairman, Scholarship and Loan Committee, 120 S. Center Street, Plainfield, IN 46168-1214
Phone: 317-837-9641
Email: TEF@Triangle.org
http://www.triangleef.org/
Purpose: To help deserving active members of Triangle Fraternity in completing their education.
Eligibility: Applicants must be active members of the Triangle Fraternity enrolled in a course of study leading to a degree. Applicants must have at least a 3.0 GPA, have completed at least two full academic years of school and be undergraduates in the year following their application. Selection is based on financial need, grades and participation in campus and Triangle activities.
Target applicant(s): College students. Adult students.
Minimum GPA: 3.0
Amount: $2,500.
Number of awards: 1.
Deadline: March 1.
How to apply: Applications are available online.
Exclusive: Visit www.UltimateScholarshipBook.com and enter code TR207823 for updates on this award.

(2079) · National Eagle Scout Association Scholarship

National Eagle Scout Association, Boy Scouts of America
1325 West Walnut Hill Lane, P.O. Box 152079, Irving, TX 75015-2079
Phone: 972-580-2000
Email: nesa@scouting.org
https://nesa.org/for-eagle-scouts/scholarships/
Purpose: To support Eagle Scouts.
Eligibility: Applicants must be Eagle Scouts who have received credentials from the national office. Students must demonstrate active participation in school, Scouting activities and community service.
Target applicant(s): High school students.
Amount: $5,000.
Number of awards: Varies.
Scholarship may be renewable.
Deadline: February 12.
How to apply: Applications are available online. An application form, transcript and letter of recommendation from a scout leader are required.
Exclusive: Visit www.UltimateScholarshipBook.com and enter code NA207923 for updates on this award.

(2080) · National FFA Combined Scholarship

National FFA Organization
P.O. Box 68960, 6060 FFA Drive, Indianapolis, IN 46268-0960
Phone: 888-332-2668
Email: scholarships@ffa.org
https://www.ffa.org/participate/grants-and-scholarships/
Purpose: To provide financial assistance to students who have livestock backgrounds and are seeking degrees in animal science, agricultural education and agribusiness.
Eligibility: Applicants must be current FFA members and high school seniors or college students planning to enroll or currently enrolled full-time. Students only need to complete the online application one time to be considered for all FFA-administered scholarships. The application requires information about the student's activities and a 1,000-word essay. Awards may be used for books, supplies, tuition, fees and room and board.
Target applicant(s): High school students. College students.
Amount: $400.
Number of awards: 1.
Deadline: January 14.
How to apply: Applications are available online.
Exclusive: Visit www.UltimateScholarshipBook.com and enter code NA208023 for updates on this award.

(2081) · National Honor Society Scholarship

National Honor Society
c/o National Association of Secondary School Principals, 1904 Association Drive, Reston, VA 20191
Phone: 703-860-0200
Email: nhs@nhs.us
https://www.nhs.us/students/the-nhs-scholarship
Purpose: To recognize NHS members.
Eligibility: Applicants must be senior National Honor Society members. Applicants must demonstrate character, scholarship, service and leadership.
Target applicant(s): High school students.
Amount: $3,200-$25,000.
Number of awards: 600.
Deadline: December 1.
How to apply: Application forms are available from your local NHS chapter adviser.
Exclusive: Visit www.UltimateScholarshipBook.com and enter code NA208123 for updates on this award.

(2082) · National Leadership Council (NLC) Award

National Society of Collegiate Scholars (NSCS)
2000 M Street NW, Suite 600, Washington, DC 20036
Phone: 202-265-9000
Email: nscs@nscs.org
https://nscs.org/nscs-scholarships/
Purpose: To help NSCS members attain their goals and to recognize their achievements in academics, service and leadership.
Eligibility: Applicants must be college undergraduates. Selection is based on the overall strength of the application.
Target applicant(s): College students. Adult students.
Amount: $1,500.
Number of awards: 2.
Deadline: January 8.
How to apply: Applications are available online.
Exclusive: Visit www.UltimateScholarshipBook.com and enter code NA208223 for updates on this award.

(2083) · National Presbyterian College Scholarship

Presbyterian Church (USA)
100 Witherspoon Street, Louisville, KY 40202
Phone: 800-728-7228 x5224
Email: finaid@pcusa.org
https://www.presbyterianmission.org/what-we-do/grants-scholarships/
Purpose: To recognize young students preparing to enter as full-time incoming freshmen in one of the participating colleges related to the Presbyterian Church.
Eligibility: Applicants must be members of the Presbyterian Church, U.S. citizens or permanent residents and high school seniors planning to attend a participating college related to PCUSA. Applicants must also demonstrate financial need and take the SAT or ACT exam no later than December 15 of their senior year in high school. Applicants must have recommendations from both their church pastors and high school guidance counselors.
Target applicant(s): High school students.
Minimum GPA: 3.0
Amount: Up to $1,500.
Number of awards: 25-30.
Scholarship may be renewable.

Deadline: May 17.
How to apply: Applications are available online.
Exclusive: Visit www.UltimateScholarshipBook.com and enter code PR208323 for updates on this award.

(2084) · National Propane Gas Foundation

National Propane Gas Foundation
1899 L Street, NW, Suite 350, Washington, DC 20036
Phone: 202-355-1328
Email: jcasey@npga.org
https://www.npga.org/organization/scholarship-fund/
Purpose: To support the educational opportunities of dependent children of employees of National Propane Gas Association (NPGA) member companies.
Eligibility: Applicants must be high school seniors or undergraduate students and have a 2.6 or higher GPA. Selection is based on academic achievement, letters of recommendation, extra curricular activity involvement, employment experience and financial need.
Target applicant(s): High school students. College students. Adult students.
Minimum GPA: 2.6
Amount: $1,000-$2,000.
Number of awards: Varies.
Deadline: February 15.
How to apply: Applications are only available online. In addition to the application form, students must submit an official transcript and have two letters of recommendation mailed directly to NPGA.
Exclusive: Visit www.UltimateScholarshipBook.com and enter code NA208423 for updates on this award.

(2085) · NESA Hall/McElwain Merit Scholarships

National Eagle Scout Association, Boy Scouts of America
1325 West Walnut Hill Lane, P.O. Box 152079, Irving, TX 75015-2079
Phone: 972-580-2000
Email: nesa@scouting.org
https://nesa.org/for-eagle-scouts/scholarships/
Purpose: To assist Eagle Scouts.
Eligibility: Applicants must have received credentials from the national office. They must be graduating high school seniors or college freshmen, sophomores or juniors. A minimum SAT score of 1200 or ACT score of 28 is required. Applicants must have demonstrated leadership ability in scouting and a record of participation in activities outside of scouting.
Target applicant(s): High school students. College students. Adult students.
Amount: $5,000.
Number of awards: Varies.
Deadline: January 31.
How to apply: Applications are available online. An application form, transcript and letter of recommendation from a scout leader are required.
Exclusive: Visit www.UltimateScholarshipBook.com and enter code NA208523 for updates on this award.

(2086) · NESA Lawrence S. and Mabel Cooke Scholarship

National Eagle Scout Association, Boy Scouts of America
1325 West Walnut Hill Lane, P.O. Box 152079, Irving, TX 75015-2079
Phone: 972-580-2000
Email: nesa@scouting.org

https://nesa.org/for-eagle-scouts/scholarships/
Purpose: To provide scholarship funds for students who have earned the rank of Eagle Scout in the Boy Scouts of America.
Eligibility: Applicants must be high school seniors who plan to enroll as full-time college students at a four-year, non-military college or university and have achieved the rank of Eagle Scout in the Boy Scouts program. Students must demonstrate academic performance, financial need and active participation in school and Scouting activities.
Target applicant(s): High school students.
Amount: $6,250-$12,000.
Number of awards: Varies.
Scholarship may be renewable.
Deadline: January 31.
How to apply: Applications are available online.
Exclusive: Visit www.UltimateScholarshipBook.com and enter code NA208623 for updates on this award.

(2087) · NIADA Scholarship
National Independent Automobile Dealers Association
2521 Brown Boulevard, Arlington, TX 76006-5203
Phone: 817-640-3838
Email: rachel@niada.com
http://www.niada.com
Purpose: To support high school seniors with academic achievement and ties to NIADA members.
Eligibility: Applicants must be the son, daughter or grandchild of a NIADA member, have an excellent high school academic record and have high SAT or ACT scores. Applications, transcripts, test scores and a maximum of five recommendation letters are required.
Target applicant(s): High school students.
Amount: $3,500.
Number of awards: 4.
Deadline: March 12.
How to apply: Applications are available online and should be submitted to the state association.
Exclusive: Visit www.UltimateScholarshipBook.com and enter code NA208723 for updates on this award.

(2088) · Non-Traditional Student Scholarship
American Legion Auxiliary
3450 Founders Road, Indianapolis, IN 46268
Phone: 317-569-4500
Email: alahq@alaforveterans.org
https://www.legion-aux.org/scholarships
Purpose: To support students resuming formal schooling after an interruption.
Eligibility: Applicants must be members of The American Legion, the American Legion Auxiliary or Sons of The American Legion and be undergraduate students who are enrolled in at least six hours per semester or four hours per quarter. Applicants must also be students resuming formal schooling after an interruption or who have had at least one year of college schooling and need financial assistance to continue their degree. Selection is based on financial need, scholastic achievement, character and goals.
Target applicant(s): College students. Adult students.
Amount: $2,000.
Number of awards: 5.
Deadline: March 1.
How to apply: Applications are available online.
Exclusive: Visit www.UltimateScholarshipBook.com and enter code AM208823 for updates on this award.

(2089) · Opportunity Scholarships for Lutheran Laywomen
Women of the Evangelical Lutheran Church in America
8765 W. Higgins Road, Chicago, IL 60631
Phone: 800-638-3522 x2730
Email: women.elca@elca.org
http://www.womenoftheelca.org
Purpose: To assist Lutheran women in studying for careers other than ordained ministry.
Eligibility: Applicants must be U.S. citizens, members of the Evangelical Lutheran Church in America (ELCA) and at least 21 years of age. They must also have had an interruption in education of two years or more since graduating from high school. There are four scholarships awarded with individual criteria including for women of color; for women studying for ELCA service abroad; graduate students preparing for careers in Christian service and for undergraduate, graduate, professional or vocational study.
Target applicant(s): College students. Graduate school students. Adult students.
Amount: Varies.
Number of awards: Varies.
Deadline: April 5.
How to apply: Applications are available online.
Exclusive: Visit www.UltimateScholarshipBook.com and enter code WO208923 for updates on this award.

(2090) · Owens-Bell Award
National Association of Blacks in Criminal Justice
1801 Fayetteville Street, 106 Whiting Criminal Justice Building, P.O. Box 20011-C, Durham, NC 27707
Phone: 919-683-1801
Email: Office@NABCJ.org
https://nabcj.org/
Purpose: To reward an individual NABCJ member for outstanding chapter development and leadership.
Eligibility: Applicants must be nominated by a member of NABCJ.
Target applicant(s): High school students. College students. Adult students.
Amount: Varies.
Number of awards: 1.
Deadline: March 15.
How to apply: Nomination applications are available online.
Exclusive: Visit www.UltimateScholarshipBook.com and enter code NA209023 for updates on this award.

(2091) · Palmer Scholarship
National Eagle Scout Association, Boy Scouts of America
1325 West Walnut Hill Lane, P.O. Box 152079, Irving, TX 75015-2079
Phone: 972-580-2000
Email: nesa@scouting.org
https://nesa.org/for-eagle-scouts/scholarships/
Purpose: To support Boy Scouts who have achieved Eagle Scout rank.
Eligibility: Applicants must be registered Boy Scouts with an Eagle rank and demonstrate active participation in school, Scouting activities and community service.
Target applicant(s): High school students.
Amount: $2,500.
Number of awards: 3.
Scholarship may be renewable.

Deadline: February 12.

How to apply: Applications are available online.

Exclusive: Visit www.UltimateScholarshipBook.com and enter code NA209123 for updates on this award.

(2092) · Phi Delta Kappa International Scholarship Grants for Prospective Educators

Phi Delta Kappa International

P.O. Box 7888, Bloomington, IN 47407

Phone: 812-339-1156

Email: scholarships@pdkintl.org

https://pdkintl.org/scholarship-overview/

Purpose: To aid future and current education majors who are affiliated with Phi Delta Kappa (PDK) or Educators Rising.

Eligibility: Applicants must be high school seniors who are planning to major in education in college or current undergraduates who are majoring in education. They must have a connection to Phi Delta Kappa (PDK) or Educators Rising. Selection is based on the overall strength of the application.

Target applicant(s): High school students. College students. Adult students.

Amount: Varies.

Number of awards: Varies.

Deadline: April 4.

How to apply: Applications are available online. An application form and supporting materials are required.

Exclusive: Visit www.UltimateScholarshipBook.com and enter code PH209223 for updates on this award.

(2093) · Phi Kappa Phi Fellowship

Honor Society of Phi Kappa Phi

7576 Goodwood Boulevard, Baton Rouge, LA 70806

Phone: 800-804-9880

Email: awards@phikappaphi.org

http://www.phikappaphi.org

Purpose: To provide fellowships for Phi Kappa Phi members entering their first year of graduate or professional studies.

Eligibility: Applicants may enter any professional or graduate field and must not have completed one full term of graduate study. Selection is based on academic achievement, service, leadership, letters of recommendation, personal statement and career goals.

Target applicant(s): College students. Graduate school students. Adult students.

Amount: $5,000-$15,000.

Number of awards: 57.

Deadline: April 1.

How to apply: Applications are available online.

Exclusive: Visit www.UltimateScholarshipBook.com and enter code HO209323 for updates on this award.

(2094) · Presbyterian Church USA Student Opportunity Scholarships

Presbyterian Church (USA)

100 Witherspoon Street, Louisville, KY 40202

Phone: 800-728-7228 x5224

Email: finaid@pcusa.org

https://www.presbyterianmission.org/what-we-do/grants-scholarships/

Purpose: To aid students pursuing disciplines that further the mission of the Presbyterian Church.

Eligibility: Applicants must be members of the Presbyterian Church (USA) who have completed their first year of college. They must be enrolled full-time and have a GPA of 2.5 or greater. Students must be pursuing a bachelor's degree in education, health service/science, religious studies, sacred music or social service/sciences. Financial need is required. Preference is given to members of racial and ethnic minorities.

Target applicant(s): College students. Adult students.

Minimum GPA: 2.5

Amount: Up to $2,000.

Number of awards: Varies.

Scholarship may be renewable.

Deadline: May 17.

How to apply: Applications are available by mail or email.

Exclusive: Visit www.UltimateScholarshipBook.com and enter code PR209423 for updates on this award.

(2095) · Priscilla R. Morton Scholarship

United Methodist Church

Office of Loans and Scholarships, P.O. Box 340007, Nashville, TN 37203-0007

Phone: 615-340-7342

Email: umscholar@gbhem.org

https://www.gbhem.org/loans-scholarships/scholarships/

Purpose: To help students who are members of the United Methodist Church.

Eligibility: Applicants must be active, full members of the United Methodist Church for at least a year before applying and enrolled or planning to enroll in an accredited institution working towards a degree full-time. The scholarship may be used for undergraduate, graduate or professional study. Applicants should provide application forms, transcripts, references, membership proof and essays. Applicant should prove financial need. Preference is given to students who enroll at a United Methodist-related college, university, seminary or theological school.

Target applicant(s): High school students. College students. Graduate school students. Adult students.

Minimum GPA: 3.5

Amount: Varies.

Number of awards: Varies.

Deadline: March.

How to apply: Applications are available online.

Exclusive: Visit www.UltimateScholarshipBook.com and enter code UN209523 for updates on this award.

(2096) · Religious Liberty Essay Scholarship Contest

Baptist Joint Committee for Religious Liberty (BJC)

Essay Contest, 200 Maryland Avenue, NE, Washington, DC 20002

Phone: 202-544-4226

Email: cwatson@bjconline.org

https://bjconline.org/contest/

Purpose: To reward students who have written outstanding essays on religious liberty.

Eligibility: Applicants must be high school juniors or seniors. Students must submit an essay relating to religious freedom. Selection is based on the overall strength of the essay.

Target applicant(s): High school students.

Amount: $500-$2,000.

Number of awards: 3.

Deadline: March.

How to apply: Applications are available online.
Exclusive: Visit www.UltimateScholarshipBook.com and enter code BA209623 for updates on this award.

(2097) · Rev. Dr. Karen Layman Gift of Hope Scholarship

United Methodist Church
Office of Loans and Scholarships, P.O. Box 340007, Nashville, TN 37203-0007
Phone: 615-340-7342
Email: umscholar@gbhem.org
https://www.gbhem.org/loans-scholarships/scholarships/
Purpose: To support United Methodist students who are leaders in the church.
Eligibility: Applicants must have been full, active members and leaders in the United Methodist Church for at least three years. They must be U.S. citizens, permanent residents or members of the Central Conferences. Students must be enrolled in a full-time undergraduate degree program at an accredited U.S. institution with a GPA of 3.0 or higher.
Target applicant(s): High school students. College students. Adult students.
Minimum GPA: 3.0
Amount: $1,000.
Number of awards: Varies.
Deadline: March 24.
How to apply: Applications are available online. An application form, transcript, essay and three letters of recommendation are required.
Exclusive: Visit www.UltimateScholarshipBook.com and enter code UN209723 for updates on this award.

(2098) · Richard F. Walsh, Alfred W. DiTolla, Harold P. Spivak Foundation Award

International Alliance of Theatrical Stage Employees, Artists and Allied Crafts of the U.S.
207 West 25th Street, 4th Floor, New York, NY 10001
http://iatse.net/member-benefits/scholarship-foundation
Purpose: To provide scholarships for the children of IATSE members.
Eligibility: Applicants must be the sons or daughters of IATSE members in good standing, be high school seniors and apply for admission to an accredited college or university full-time leading towards a bachelor's degree.
Target applicant(s): High school students.
Amount: $10,000.
Number of awards: 5.
Scholarship may be renewable.
Deadline: December 31.
How to apply: Applications are available by written request (through an online form).
Exclusive: Visit www.UltimateScholarshipBook.com and enter code IN209823 for updates on this award.

(2099) · Robert G. Porter Post-Secondary Scholarships

American Federation of Teachers
555 New Jersey Avenue NW, Washington, DC 20001
Phone: 202-879-4400
https://www.aft.org/member-benefits/scholarships/robert-g-porter-scholars-program
Purpose: To provide scholarships to AFT members' dependents.

Eligibility: Applicants must be graduating high school seniors. The award is merit-based and will consider academics, community service and performance on the required labor-related essay. Applicants' parents or guardians must be AFT members for at least one year.
Target applicant(s): High school students.
Amount: $1,000-$2,000.
Number of awards: 14.
Scholarship may be renewable.
Deadline: March 31.
How to apply: Applications are available by written request.
Exclusive: Visit www.UltimateScholarshipBook.com and enter code AM209923 for updates on this award.

(2100) · Robert G. Porter Scholars Program for Members

American Federation of Teachers
555 New Jersey Avenue NW, Washington, DC 20001
Phone: 202-879-4400
https://www.aft.org/member-benefits/scholarships/robert-g-porter-scholars-program
Purpose: To provide grants to AFT members.
Eligibility: Applicants must be AFT members who have been in good standing for at least one year and intend to pursue courses in their field of work. Applicants must submit an essay on a labor-related topic.
Target applicant(s): Graduate school students. Adult students.
Amount: $1,000.
Number of awards: 10.
Deadline: March 31.
How to apply: Applications are available by written request.
Exclusive: Visit www.UltimateScholarshipBook.com and enter code AM210023 for updates on this award.

(2101) · Rust Scholarship

Triangle Education Foundation
Chairman, Scholarship and Loan Committee, 120 S. Center Street, Plainfield, IN 46168-1214
Phone: 317-837-9641
Email: TEF@Triangle.org
http://www.triangleef.org/
Purpose: To help deserving active members of Triangle Fraternity in completing their education.
Eligibility: Applicants must be active members of the Triangle Fraternity who have completed at least two full academic years of school and will be undergraduates in the school year following their application. Selection is based on financial need, grades and participation in campus and Triangle activities. Preference is given to applicants in engineering and the hard sciences. Applicants must have at least a 3.0 GPA.
Target applicant(s): College students. Adult students.
Minimum GPA: 3.0
Amount: $6,000.
Number of awards: 1.
Deadline: March 1.
How to apply: Applications are available online.
Exclusive: Visit www.UltimateScholarshipBook.com and enter code TR210123 for updates on this award.

(2102) · S. Frank Bud Raftery Scholarship

IUPAT International Office
7234 Parkway Drive, Hanover, MD 21076

Phone: 410-564-5900
Email: mail@iupat.org
https://iupat.org/member-information/scholarships/
Purpose: To provide scholarships for the children of IUPAT members.
Eligibility: Applicants must be the children or legally-adopted dependents of an IUPAT member in good standing. Selection is based on a 1,000- to 2,000-word essay on a subject chosen by the IUPAT.
Target applicant(s): High school students. College students. Adult students.
Amount: $2,000.
Number of awards: 10.
Deadline: January 31.
How to apply: Applications are available by written request.
Exclusive: Visit www.UltimateScholarshipBook.com and enter code IU210223 for updates on this award.

(2103) · Sam Rose Memorial Scholarship

Ladies Auxiliary of the Fleet Reserve Association
Gini Larson PNP, National Scholarship Chairman, 2187 Capeheart Street, Ingleside, TX 78362-6222
Phone: 361-442-5707
Email: lovedduck@aol.com
http://www.la-fra.org
Purpose: To support the descendants of Fleet Reserve Association members.
Eligibility: Applicants must have a deceased father or grandfather who was a member of the Fleet Reserve Association or was eligible for membership at the time of death.
Target applicant(s): High school students. College students. Adult students.
Amount: Varies.
Number of awards: Varies.
Deadline: April 15.
How to apply: Applications are available online.
Exclusive: Visit www.UltimateScholarshipBook.com and enter code LA210323 for updates on this award.

(2104) · Sandra Jo Hornick Scholarship

Kappa Delta Pi Educational Foundation
3707 Woodview Trace, Indianapolis, IN 46268-1158
Phone: 800-284-3167
Email: foundation@kdp.org
http://www.kdp.org
Purpose: To aid Kappa Delta Pi members who are studying education.
Eligibility: Applicants must be active members of Kappa Delta Pi. They must be undergraduate students who are majoring in education. Selection is based on the overall strength of the application.
Target applicant(s): College students. Adult students.
Amount: $1,000.
Number of awards: 2.
Deadline: April 29.
How to apply: Applications are available online. An application form, transcript, one reference letter, a personal essay and the applicant's Kappa Delta Pi membership number are required.
Exclusive: Visit www.UltimateScholarshipBook.com and enter code KA210423 for updates on this award.

(2105) · Service Employees International Union Scholarships

Service Employees International Union
c/o Scholarship Program Administrators Inc., P.O. Box 23737, Nashville, TN 37202-3737
Phone: 800-424-8592
http://www.seiu.org
Purpose: To give financial assistance to members of the SEIU and their children.
Eligibility: For the $1,000 scholarship, applicants must be members or the children of members of SEIU who have been in good standing for at least three years. Applicants must also be enrolled in an accredited college or university and should not have completed more than one year of college. For the $1,500 scholarship, applicants must be members or the children of members of SEIU returning full time to an accredited college or university as a sophomore, junior or senior or attending an accredited community college, trade or technical school. All applicants must read a report online and answer questions.
Target applicant(s): High school students. College students. Adult students.
Amount: $1,000-$1,500.
Number of awards: Varies.
Deadline: March.
How to apply: Applications are available online.
Exclusive: Visit www.UltimateScholarshipBook.com and enter code SE210523 for updates on this award.

(2106) · Shasta Head Start Alumni Scholarship

Shasta Head Start Child Development Inc.
375 Lake Boulevard, Suite 100, Redding, CA 96003
http://www.shastaheadstart.org
Purpose: To support students who were once participants of Head Start and are now pursuing a higher education.
Eligibility: Applicants must have been members of a Head Start program who are now high school seniors enrolling in post-secondary institutions. Students must have a 3.0 GPA and have shown an interest in the welfare of the children and families in their community.
Target applicant(s): High school students.
Minimum GPA: 3.0
Amount: $1,000.
Number of awards: 1.
Deadline: April 16.
How to apply: Applications are available online.
Exclusive: Visit www.UltimateScholarshipBook.com and enter code SH210623 for updates on this award.

(2107) · Sheet Metal Workers' International Scholarship Fund

Sheet Metal Workers' International Association
1750 New York Avenue NW, 6th Floor, Washington, DC 20006-5389
Phone: 202-662-0858
Email: scholarship@smart-union.org
https://smart-union.org/sheet-metal-scholarship-fund/
Purpose: To provide scholarships for members of the SMWIA and their families.
Eligibility: Applicants must be SMWIA members, covered employees, or dependent spouses or children under the age of 25 of SMWIA members or covered employees. Applicants must also be full-time students or accepted to be full-time students at an accredited college or

university. Only qualified applicants from local unions that participate in the one-cent check off are eligible for these four-year scholarships. Selection is based on information on SMWIA membership, including information on the local union's jurisdiction and family member's SMWIA membership, high school transcript, SAT/ACT scores or college transcript if already enrolled in college, an essay on the importance of SMWIA to the applicant's family and a letter of recommendation.
Target applicant(s): High school students. College students.
Amount: $6,000.
Number of awards: 34.
Scholarship may be renewable.
Deadline: February 15.
How to apply: Applications are available by email and written request.
Exclusive: Visit www.UltimateScholarshipBook.com and enter code SH210723 for updates on this award.

(2108) · Shropshire Scholarship

Civitan
Civitan International Foundation, P.O. Box 130744, Birmingham, AL 35213-0744
Phone: 205-591-8910
Email: civitan@civitan.org
http://www.civitan.org
Purpose: The Shropshire Scholarship assists deserving Civitan members who will pursue careers that further the ideals of Civitan International, such as working toward world peace and unity, fighting for justice and building better citizenship.
Eligibility: Applicants must be a Civitan, Campus Civitan or Junior Civitan and must have been a member for at least two years, be enrolled in a college or university and pursue careers which help further the ideals of Civitan International.
Target applicant(s): High school students. College students. Graduate school students. Adult students.
Amount: $1,000.
Number of awards: Varies.
Deadline: January.
How to apply: Applications are available online.
Exclusive: Visit www.UltimateScholarshipBook.com and enter code CI210823 for updates on this award.

(2109) · Sigma Phi Epsilon Balanced Man Scholarship

Sigma Phi Epsilon Fraternity (National)
310 South Boulevard, Richmond, VA 23220
Phone: 804-353-1901
Email: scholarships@sigep.net
http://sigep.org/scholarships
Purpose: To reward students who balance academics with healthy living.
Eligibility: Applicants must be male incoming freshmen or current undergraduates at one of the universities offering the scholarship. Students must exhibit academic excellence, leadership skills and a commitment to health and well-being.
Target applicant(s): High school students. College students. Adult students.
Amount: Varies.
Number of awards: Varies.
Deadline: June 1.
How to apply: Applications are available online.
Exclusive: Visit www.UltimateScholarshipBook.com and enter code SI210923 for updates on this award.

(2110) · Spirit of Youth Scholarship for Junior Members

American Legion Auxiliary
3450 Founders Road, Indianapolis, IN 46268
Phone: 317-569-4500
Email: alahq@alaforveterans.org
https://www.legion-aux.org/scholarships
Purpose: To assist Junior members of the American Legion Auxiliary.
Eligibility: Applicants must be or have been Junior members of the American Legion Auxiliary for three years, be high school seniors, have a minimum 3.0 GPA and demonstrate character. Selection is based on character/leadership (30 percent), essay/application (30 percent) and scholarship (40 percent).
Target applicant(s): High school students.
Minimum GPA: 3.0
Amount: $5,000.
Number of awards: 5.
Scholarship may be renewable.
Deadline: March 1.
How to apply: Applications are available online.
Exclusive: Visit www.UltimateScholarshipBook.com and enter code AM211023 for updates on this award.

(2111) · Stanfield and D'Orlando Art Scholarship

Unitarian Universalist Association
24 Farnsworth Street, Boston, MA 02210
Phone: 617-742-2100
Email: uufp@uua.org
http://www.uua.org/giving/awards
Purpose: To help graduate and undergraduate Unitarian Universalist artists.
Eligibility: Applicants must be preparing for a career in fine arts which includes painting, drawing, photography and sculpture. Applicants must submit applications, transcripts, recommendations, slide portfolios and a list of works.
Target applicant(s): College students. Graduate school students. Adult students.
Amount: Varies.
Number of awards: Varies.
Deadline: February 15.
How to apply: Applications are available online.
Exclusive: Visit www.UltimateScholarshipBook.com and enter code UN211123 for updates on this award.

(2112) · Stanley A. Doran Memorial Scholarship

Fleet Reserve Association (FRA)
FRA Scholarship Administrator, 125 N. West Street, Alexandria, VA 22314
Phone: 800-372-1924
Email: news-fra@fra.org
https://www.fra.org/fra/Web/Events_and_Programs/7_12th_Grade_Essay_Contest/Web/Content/Essay_Contest.aspx?hkey=707c4b42-2eb8-4992-9d57-31b8bd14c68a
Purpose: To provide financial aid to the dependents of FRA members.
Eligibility: Applicants must be the dependent children of a member in good standing of the FRA or a member who was in good standing at time of death. Recipients are selected on the basis of academic achievement, leadership skills, financial need and character.
Target applicant(s): High school students. College students. Graduate school students. Adult students.

Amount: Up to $5,000.
Number of awards: Varies.
Deadline: April 15.
How to apply: Applications are available online.
Exclusive: Visit www.UltimateScholarshipBook.com and enter code FL211223 for updates on this award.

(2113) · Starfleet Scholarships
STARFLEET Scholarship Program
c/o Tammy Wilcox, Director, 316 Dublin Road, Asheboro, NC 27203
Email: scholarships@sfi.org
http://sfi.org
Purpose: To assist members of the International Star Trek Fan Association.
Eligibility: Applicants must have been members of Starfleet for at least one year prior to applying and must be attending or planning to attend a community college, four-year college, technical school, junior college or graduate school. Awards are given in the categories of medicine, engineering, performing arts, international studies, business, science, education, writing, law enforcement and general studies.
Target applicant(s): High school students. College students. Graduate school students. Adult students.
Amount: $1,000.
Number of awards: Varies.
Deadline: June 15.
How to apply: Applications are available online. An application form, a personal essay, three letters of recommendation and a transcript are required.
Exclusive: Visit www.UltimateScholarshipBook.com and enter code ST211323 for updates on this award.

(2114) · Student Activist Scholarships
American Atheists
P.O. Box 158, Cranford, NJ 07016
Phone: 908-276-7300
Email: scholarship@athiests.org
http://www.atheists.org
Purpose: To support Atheist students who are activists.
Eligibility: Applicants must be high school seniors or college students who are Atheists, have a minimum 2.5 GPA and be student activists. The award is based on the level of activism and requires a 500- to 1,000-word essay. In addition to the scholarship, the winner will receive a free trip to the American Atheists National Convention.
Target applicant(s): High school students. College students. Graduate school students. Adult students.
Minimum GPA: 2.5
Amount: $500-$1,000.
Number of awards: 5.
Deadline: June 15.
How to apply: Applications are available online.
Exclusive: Visit www.UltimateScholarshipBook.com and enter code AM211423 for updates on this award.

(2115) · Student CTA (SCTA) Scholarship in Honor of L. Gordon Bittle
California Teachers Association (CTA)
CTA Human Rights Department, P.O. Box 921, Burlingame, CA 94011-0921
Phone: 650-697-1400
https://www.cta.org/for-educators/scholarships-awards
Purpose: To support members of the Student California Teachers Association.
Eligibility: Applicants must be planning to work in public education and have a minimum 3.5 high school GPA or show high academic achievement in college coursework, explaining any special circumstances affecting their grades. Scholarships are based on a personal statement, school and community activities and letters of recommendation.
Target applicant(s): High school students. College students. Graduate school students. Adult students.
Minimum GPA: 3.5
Amount: $5,000.
Number of awards: Up to 3.
Deadline: January 29.
How to apply: Applications are available online.
Exclusive: Visit www.UltimateScholarshipBook.com and enter code CA211523 for updates on this award.

(2116) · Tall Club International Scholarship
Tall Clubs International Foundation Inc.
c/o Carolyn Goldstein, 1555 CR 2103, Weimar, TX 78962
Phone: 888-468-2552
Email: tci-scholarships@tall.org
http://www.tall.org
Purpose: To support students of tall stature.
Eligibility: Applicants must be high school seniors under the age of 21 attending or planning to attend a two- or four-year institution of higher learning for their first year of college. Female applicants must meet the height requirement of 5'10" and male applicants must meet the requirement of 6'2". Applicants must live within the geographic area of a participating club.
Target applicant(s): High school students.
Amount: Up to $1,000.
Number of awards: Varies.
Deadline: March 1.
How to apply: Applications are available by emailing the closest TCI club.
Exclusive: Visit www.UltimateScholarshipBook.com and enter code TA211623 for updates on this award.

(2117) · Tau Beta Pi Scholarships
Tau Beta Pi Association
Attn.: D. Stephen Pierre Jr., P.E., P.O. Box 2697, Knoxville, TN 37901-2697
Phone: 865-546-4578
Email: fellowships@tbp.org
http://www.tbp.org
Purpose: To assist members who are studying engineering.
Eligibility: Applicants must be undergraduate members of Tau Beta Pi and be juniors at the time of application who are planning to remain in or return to school for a senior year of full-time study in engineering.
Target applicant(s): College students. Adult students.
Amount: $2,000.
Number of awards: Varies.
Deadline: April 1.
How to apply: Applications are available online.
Exclusive: Visit www.UltimateScholarshipBook.com and enter code TA211723 for updates on this award.

(2118) · Terrill Graduate Fellowship

Phi Sigma Kappa International Headquarters
2925 E. 96th Street, Indianapolis, IN 46240
Phone: 317-573-5420
Email: vershun@phisigmakappa.org
https://phisigmakappa.org/undergrads/programs/scholarships/
Purpose: To award money to graduating senior and alumni members entering graduate school or members already enrolled in graduate school.
Eligibility: Applicants must graduate from college by August of the year during which they apply, plan to begin graduate or professional study during the next academic year or already be in graduate school and have a minimum B GPA for all undergraduate work. Scholarships are awarded based on scholastic performance.
Target applicant(s): College students. Graduate school students. Adult students.
Minimum GPA: 3.0
Amount: $5,000-$10,000.
Number of awards: 2.
Deadline: January 31.
How to apply: Applications are available online.
Exclusive: Visit www.UltimateScholarshipBook.com and enter code PH211823 for updates on this award.

(2119) · Tri Delta Undergraduate Scholarship

Tri Delta
Delta Delta Delta Foundation, 14951 North Dallas Parkway, Suite 500, Dallas, TX 75254
Phone: 817-633-8001
Email: info@trideltaeo.org
http://www.tridelta.org
Purpose: To offer scholarships to undergraduate members.
Eligibility: Applicants must be undergraduates enrolled full-time in good standing with the organization. Selection is based on academic achievement, chapter involvement, campus/community involvement, financial need and future promise.
Target applicant(s): College students. Adult students.
Amount: Varies.
Number of awards: Varies.
Deadline: March 1.
How to apply: Applications are available online.
Exclusive: Visit www.UltimateScholarshipBook.com and enter code TR211923 for updates on this award.

(2120) · Truckload Carriers Association Scholarship Fund

Truckload Carriers Association
c/o TCA Scholarship Fund, 555 East Braddock Road, Alexandria, VA 22314
Phone: 703-838-1950
Email: TCA@truckload.org
http://www.truckload.org
Purpose: To support college students affiliated with the trucking industry.
Eligibility: Applicants must attend or plan to attend college, be in good standing and be the children, grandchildren or spouses of an employee of a trucking company; applicants may also be the children, grandchildren or spouses of an independent contractor or independent contractors affiliated with a trucking company and attending a four-year college.
Target applicant(s): High school students. College students. Adult students.

Minimum GPA: 3.3
Amount: $2,000-$6,250.
Number of awards: Varies.
Deadline: May 1.
How to apply: Applications are available online.
Exclusive: Visit www.UltimateScholarshipBook.com and enter code TR212023 for updates on this award.

(2121) · Tuition Exchange Scholarships

Tuition Exchange
3 Bethesda Metro Center, Suite 700, Bethesda, MD 20814
Phone: 202-518-0135
Email: info@tuitionexchange.org
http://www.tuitionexchange.org
Purpose: To assist the children or other family members of the faculty and staff at participating colleges and universities to encourage employment of parents and guardians in higher education.
Eligibility: Eligibility varies by institution. Applicants must be family members of the home institution where they are applying. However specific details about employment status, years of service or other requirements are determined solely by the home institution.
Target applicant(s): High school students. College students. Adult students.
Amount: Up to full tuition.
Number of awards: 7,500.
Scholarship may be renewable.
Deadline: Varies.
How to apply: Applications are available from the liaison officer at the home institution.
Exclusive: Visit www.UltimateScholarshipBook.com and enter code TU212123 for updates on this award.

(2122) · UCC Seminarian Scholarship

United Church of Christ
Pat Lyden, Associate Director Grant and Scholarship Administration, 700 Prospect Avenue, Cleveland, OH 44115
Phone: 216-736-2166
Email: scholarships@ucc.org
http://www.ucc.org/scholarships
Purpose: To support members of the United Church of Christ who are preparing for ministry.
Eligibility: Applicants must be members of a United Church of Christ congregation for at least one year prior to receipt of the scholarship. They must be currently enrolled in an ATS accredited seminary in a course of study to become an ordained minister, and they must maintain at least a B average to receive and keep the scholarship. Applicants should be able to show that they have demonstrated leadership abilities in a church or academic environment. Students must also agree to serve the United Church of Christ or one of its partners after the completion of their studies.
Target applicant(s): High school students. College students. Graduate school students. Adult students.
Minimum GPA: 3.0
Amount: Varies.
Number of awards: 5.
Scholarship may be renewable.
Deadline: March 1.
How to apply: Applications are available by mail.
Exclusive: Visit www.UltimateScholarshipBook.com and enter code UN212223 for updates on this award.

(2123) · UFCW Scholarship Program

United Food and Commercial Workers Union
Scholarship Program - Education Office, 1775 K Street NW,
Washington, DC 20006
Email: cfscholarship@ufcw.org
http://www.ufcw.org
Purpose: To provide financial assistance for members of the UFCW and their children.
Eligibility: Applicants must be members of good standing of the UFCW with a membership of one continuous year or more or the unmarried children of a member. Applicants must also be graduating high school in the year of the competition and be less than 20 years old. Academic achievement, community involvement and essays are part of the selection process.
Target applicant(s): High school students.
Amount: Up to $2,000.
Number of awards: Varies.
Scholarship may be renewable.
Deadline: July 24.
How to apply: Applications are available online.
Exclusive: Visit www.UltimateScholarshipBook.com and enter code UN212323 for updates on this award.

(2124) · UMWA-Lorin E. Kerr Scholarships

United Mine Workers of America/BCOA T.E.F.
18354 Quantico Gateway Drive, Suite 200, Triangle, VA 22172
Phone: 703-291-2400
Email: info@umwa.org
https://umwa.org/
Purpose: To offer scholarships to UMWA members and their families.
Eligibility: Applicants must be UMWA members or dependents who pursue undergraduate degrees. Selection is based on academic potential and financial need.
Target applicant(s): High school students. College students. Adult students.
Amount: $2,500.
Number of awards: 2.
Deadline: February 12.
How to apply: Applications are available online.
Exclusive: Visit www.UltimateScholarshipBook.com and enter code UN212423 for updates on this award.

(2125) · Undergraduate Scholarship

Delta Sigma Pi
330 South Campus Avenue, Oxford, OH 45056-2405
Phone: 513-523-1907
Email: centraloffice@dspnet.org
http://www.deltasigmapi.org
Purpose: To assist student members.
Eligibility: Applicants must be members in good standing of Delta Sigma Pi with at least one semester or quarter of undergraduate studies remaining. Applicants are judged on scholastic achievement, financial need, fraternal service, service activities, letters of recommendation and overall presentation of required materials.
Target applicant(s): College students. Adult students.
Amount: $500-$3,800.
Number of awards: 15.
Deadline: June 1.
How to apply: Applications are available online.

Exclusive: Visit www.UltimateScholarshipBook.com and enter code DE212523 for updates on this award.

(2126) · Undergraduate Scholarships

American Baptist Churches USA
P.O. Box 851, Valley Forge, PA 19482-0851
Phone: 800-222-3872
Email: financialaid.web@abc-usa.org
http://abhms.org/ministries/developing-leaders/education-scholarships/
Purpose: To support American Baptist students pursuing educational opportunities.
Eligibility: Applicants must be members of an American Baptist church for at least one year before applying for aid, be enrolled at an accredited educational institution in the U.S. or Puerto Rico, be U.S. citizens and retain a 2.75 GPA to remain eligible for the scholarships.
Target applicant(s): High school students. College students. Adult students.
Minimum GPA: 2.75
Amount: Varies.
Number of awards: Varies.
Scholarship may be renewable.
Deadline: April 30.
How to apply: Applications are available by request.
Exclusive: Visit www.UltimateScholarshipBook.com and enter code AM212623 for updates on this award.

(2127) · Union Plus Scholarship

Union Plus
1100 1st Street NE, Suite 850, Washington, DC 20002
Email: scholarships@unionplus.org
http://www.unionplus.org
Purpose: To help the families of union members.
Eligibility: Applicants must be members of unions participating in a Union Plus program or the spouses or children of such union members. Applicants must be accepted to or attending an undergraduate course of study at an accredited college or university, community college or recognized technical or trade school. Selection is based on academic ability, social awareness, financial need and appreciation of labor. Minimum 3.0 GPA is required.
Target applicant(s): High school students. College students. Graduate school students. Adult students.
Minimum GPA: 3.0
Amount: $500-$4,000.
Number of awards: Varies.
Deadline: January 31.
How to apply: Applications are available online.
Exclusive: Visit www.UltimateScholarshipBook.com and enter code UN212723 for updates on this award.

(2128) · United Agribusiness League and United Agricultural Benefit Trust Scholarships

United Agribusiness League
54 Corporate Park, Irvine, CA 92606-5105
Phone: 800-223-4590
Email: membership@unitedag.org
https://www.unitedag.org
Purpose: To aid undergraduate students who are affiliated with the United Agribusiness League (UAL) or the United Agricultural Benefit Trust (UABT).

Eligibility: Applicants must be current undergraduate students at an accredited college or university and must be affiliated with the United Agribusiness League (UAL) or the United Agricultural Benefit Trust (UABT) through a member or an employee of a member. They must have a GPA of 2.5 or higher. Selection is based on the overall strength of the application.

Target applicant(s): College students. Adult students.

Minimum GPA: 2.5

Amount: Varies.

Number of awards: Varies.

Deadline: December 31.

How to apply: Applications are available online. An application form, three reference letters, a personal essay and a resume are required.

Exclusive: Visit www.UltimateScholarshipBook.com and enter code UN212823 for updates on this award.

(2129) · United Methodist General Scholarship

United Methodist Church

Office of Loans and Scholarships, P.O. Box 340007, Nashville, TN 37203-0007

Phone: 615-340-7342

Email: umscholar@gbhem.org

https://www.gbhem.org/loans-scholarships/scholarships/

Purpose: To support students who are members of a United Methodist Church.

Eligibility: Applicants must be active, full members of a United Methodist Church for at least one year prior to applying, be admitted to a full-time degree program in an accredited college or university and have a minimum 2.5 GPA. Students must also be U.S. citizens or permanent residents and be undergraduate, graduate or doctoral students. Supporting documents are due by May 1.

Target applicant(s): College students. Graduate school students. Adult students.

Minimum GPA: 2.5

Amount: $500-$2,000.

Number of awards: Varies.

Deadline: March 24.

How to apply: Applications are available online.

Exclusive: Visit www.UltimateScholarshipBook.com and enter code UN212923 for updates on this award.

(2130) · United Transportation Union Scholarships

United Transportation Union Insurance Association

UTUIA Scholarship Program, 24950 Country Club Boulevard, Suite 340, North Olmsted, OH 44070-5333

http://www.utuia.org

Purpose: To provide financial aid to the children and grandchildren of UTU/UTUIA members.

Eligibility: Applicants must be at least high school seniors or the equivalent and be age 25 or less. Applicants must also be UTU or UTUIA-insured members, the children or grandchildren of a UTU or UTUIA-insured member or the children of a deceased UTU or UTUIA-insured member. UTU or UTUIA-insured members must be U.S. residents. Applicants must be accepted for admittance or already enrolled for at least 12 credit hours per quarter or semester at a recognized institution of higher learning (university, college or junior college, nursing or technical school offering college credit). Scholarships are awarded on the basis of chance, not grades. A UTUIA scholar, however, is expected to maintain a satisfactory academic record to keep the scholarship for the full four years.

Target applicant(s): High school students. College students.

Amount: $2,000.

Number of awards: 50.

Scholarship may be renewable.

Deadline: April 30.

How to apply: Applications are available from the UTU news or by written request.

Exclusive: Visit www.UltimateScholarshipBook.com and enter code UN213023 for updates on this award.

(2131) · Utility Workers Union of America Scholarships

Utility Workers Union of America

1300 L Street NW, Suite 1200, Washington, DC 20005

Phone: 202-899-2851

Email: rfarley@aflcio.org

http://uwua.net/

Purpose: To offer scholarships to the children of UWUA members.

Eligibility: Applicants must be the sons or daughters of active Utility Workers Union members. Recipients are selected from those who participate in the National Merit Scholarship Competition by taking the PSAT/NMSQT as high school juniors, complete high school and are enrolled in a regionally accredited college in the United States.

Target applicant(s): High school students.

Amount: $500-$2,000.

Number of awards: Varies.

Scholarship may be renewable.

Deadline: March 31.

How to apply: Applications are available online.

Exclusive: Visit www.UltimateScholarshipBook.com and enter code UT213123 for updates on this award.

(2132) · VantagePoint Public Employee Memorial Scholarship Fund

ICMA-RC VantagePoint

ICMA-RC VantagePoint Public Employee Memorial Scholarship Fund, Scholarship Management Services, One Scholarship Way, Saint Peter, MN 56082

Phone: 202-962-8085

Email: anna.owen@vantagescholar.org

http://www.icmarc.org/

Purpose: To support spouses and children of local and state employees including police officers, firefighters and government workers who died in the line of duty.

Eligibility: Applicants must be spouses or children of local or state governmental employees who died in the line of duty and must be able to supply written documentation from the deceased's past employer stating such. At the time of application, individuals must be attending or planning to attend a two-year or four-year college or a vocational school and may be studying at the undergraduate, graduate or technical level. Selection is based on academic performance, community and school involvement, leadership, honors, work experience, goals, letter of recommendation and financial need.

Target applicant(s): High school students. College students. Graduate school students. Adult students.

Amount: Up to $10,000.

Number of awards: Varies.

Deadline: March 15.

How to apply: Applications are available online.

Exclusive: Visit www.UltimateScholarshipBook.com and enter code IC213223 for updates on this award.

(2133) · VFW Scout of the Year Scholarship

Veterans of Foreign Wars
406 W. 34th Street, Kansas City, MO 64111
Phone: 816-968-1117
Email: kharmer@vfw.org
https://www.vfw.org/community/youth-and-education
Purpose: To reward an outstanding Boy Scout, Venture Scout, Sea Scout or Girl Scout.
Eligibility: Applicants must have received the Eagle Scout Award, the Girl Scout Gold Award, the Venture Silver Award or the Sea Scout Quartermaster Award and demonstrated practical citizenship. Applicants must also have reached their 15th birthday and be enrolled in high school.
Target applicant(s): High school students.
Amount: Up to $5,000.
Number of awards: 3.
Deadline: March 1.
How to apply: Applications are available online.
Exclusive: Visit www.UltimateScholarshipBook.com and enter code VE213323 for updates on this award.

(2134) · Vocations Scholarship Funds

Knights of Columbus
Department of Scholarships, 1 Columbus Plaza, New Haven, CT 06510-3326
Phone: 203-752-4000
Email: info@kofc.org
http://www.kofc.org
Purpose: To support theology students on their path to the priesthood.
Eligibility: Applicants must be males studying with ecclesiastical approval at a major seminary for a diocese or religious institute in the United States, its territories and Canada. The Father Michael J. McGivney Vocations Scholarship Fund awards scholarships based on financial need, and applicants must provide proof of need. The Bishop Thomas V. Daily Scholarships Fund awards recipients on the basis of merit, and applicants must submit their most recent transcript and two letters of recommendation. Both funds give preference to Knights of Columbus members and their sons, but membership is not required.
Target applicant(s): High school students. College students. Graduate school students. Adult students.
Amount: $2,500.
Number of awards: Varies.
Scholarship may be renewable.
Deadline: June 1.
How to apply: Applications are available from seminary rectors and diocesan vocations directors starting in February.
Exclusive: Visit www.UltimateScholarshipBook.com and enter code KN213423 for updates on this award.

(2135) · Walter L. Mitchell Memorial Scholarship Awards

International Chemical Workers Union Council/UFCW
Research and Education Department, Walter L. Mitchell Memorial Scholarship Awards, 1655 West Market Street, Akron, OH 44313
Phone: 330-926-1444
http://www.icwuc.org
Purpose: To offer scholarships to the children or step-children of members of the UFCW.
Eligibility: Applicants must be children or step-children of members of at least a year who intend to enter college the fall following application.

Recipients are selected on the basis of biographical information, ACT/SAT scores and high school records.
Target applicant(s): High school students.
Amount: $1,500.
Number of awards: 12.
Deadline: March 5.
How to apply: Applications are available online.
Exclusive: Visit www.UltimateScholarshipBook.com and enter code IN213523 for updates on this award.

(2136) · Warren Poslusny Award for Outstanding Achievement

Sigma Alpha Epsilon (SAE)
Dave Sandell, Sigma Alpha Epsilon Foundation Scholarships, 1856 Sheridan Road, Evanston, IL 60201-3837
Phone: 800-233-1856 x234
Email: dsandell@sae.net
http://www.sae.net
Purpose: To recognize collegians who have demonstrated outstanding leadership and service and have exemplified a dedication to the values established by the founders of Sigma Alpha Epsilon.
Eligibility: Applicants must be brothers of Sigma Alpha Epsilon in good standing, have a minimum 3.0 GPA and either must have junior standing or higher or must be pursuing full-time graduate study. This award is merit-based, with an emphasis on combining academic excellence, leadership, service and campus involvement.
Target applicant(s): College students. Graduate school students. Adult students.
Minimum GPA: 3.0
Amount: $1,000-$3,000.
Number of awards: 9.
Deadline: March 1.
How to apply: Contact the coordinator of educational programs and services.
Exclusive: Visit www.UltimateScholarshipBook.com and enter code SI213623 for updates on this award.

(2137) · Wenderoth Undergraduate Scholarship

Phi Sigma Kappa International Headquarters
2925 E. 96th Street, Indianapolis, IN 46240
Phone: 317-573-5420
Email: vershun@phisigmakappa.org
https://phisigmakappa.org/undergrads/programs/scholarships/
Purpose: To give financial aid to college sophomore and junior members.
Eligibility: Applicants must be sophomores or juniors in college for the year that the scholarship will apply to, have completed two semesters or three quarters of study and have a minimum B GPA. Scholarships are awarded on the basis of academic accomplishments and essays.
Target applicant(s): College students. Adult students.
Minimum GPA: 3.0
Amount: $2,500-$5,000.
Number of awards: 2.
Deadline: January 31.
How to apply: Applications are available online.
Exclusive: Visit www.UltimateScholarshipBook.com and enter code PH213723 for updates on this award.

(2138) · William C. Doherty Scholarship Fund

National Association of Letter Carriers
100 Indiana Avenue NW, Washington, DC 20001-2144
Phone: 202-393-4695
Email: nalcinf@nalc.org
https://www.nalc.org/member-benefits/benefits-for-members/scholarships
Purpose: To offer scholarships to the children of members of the Letter Carriers Union.
Eligibility: Applicants must be the children or legally adopted children of an active, retired or deceased letter carrier and high school seniors. Applicants' parents must be members in good standing at least one year prior to applying. Selection is based on SAT/ACT scores, high school transcript and questionnaire.
Target applicant(s): High school students.
Amount: $4,000.
Number of awards: 5.
Scholarship may be renewable.
Deadline: December 31.
How to apply: Preliminary applications are available online.
Exclusive: Visit www.UltimateScholarshipBook.com and enter code NA213823 for updates on this award.

(2139) · Women in Aviation International Scholarship

Women in Aviation International
1864 Dayton Germantown Pike, Unit 4, Germantown, OH 45327
Phone: 937-839-4647
Email: dwallace@wai.org
http://www.wai.org
Purpose: To assist students pursuing aviation and aerospace education.
Eligibility: Applicants must be members of Women in Aviation International. Students must write a resume and an essay and provide two recommendation letters.
Target applicant(s): High school students. College students. Adult students.
Amount: Varies.
Number of awards: Varies.
Deadline: October 12.
How to apply: Applications are available online.
Exclusive: Visit www.UltimateScholarshipBook.com and enter code WO213923 for updates on this award.

(2140) · Women in Sports Media Scholarship/Internship Program

Association for Women in Sports Media
7742 Spalding Drive #377, Norcross, GA 30092
Email: awsminternship@gmail.com
http://awsmonline.org/internships-scholarships
Purpose: To encourage females interested in sports media careers.
Eligibility: Applicants must be female students working full-time toward a graduate or undergraduate degree with the goal of becoming a sports writer, editor, broadcaster or public relations representative. Applicants must submit a resume, an essay on a memorable experience in sports or sports media, three references, two letters of recommendation and up to five samples of their work. Application fee is waived for AWSM members.
Target applicant(s): College students. Graduate school students. Adult students.
Amount: $1,000 plus paid internship.
Number of awards: Varies.

Deadline: October.
How to apply: Applications are available online.
Exclusive: Visit www.UltimateScholarshipBook.com and enter code AS214023 for updates on this award.

(2141) · Women in United Methodist History Writing Award

General Commission on Archives and History, The United Methodist Church
P.O. Box 127, 36 Madison Avenue, Madison, NJ 07940
Phone: 973-408-3189
Email: research@gcah.org
http://www.gcah.org/research/grants-and-awards
Purpose: To reward research and writing on the history of women in The United Methodist Church.
Eligibility: Applicants must submit completed, original manuscripts no longer than 20 double-spaced, typewritten pages with footnotes and bibliography about the history of women in the United Methodist Church or its antecedents.
Target applicant(s): High school students. College students. Graduate school students. Adult students.
Amount: $500.
Number of awards: 1.
Deadline: December 31.
How to apply: Send manuscript to the General Secretary at the address listed.
Exclusive: Visit www.UltimateScholarshipBook.com and enter code GE214123 for updates on this award.

(2142) · Young Christian Leaders Scholarship

Young Christian Leaders
144 Woodbury Road, Woodbury, NY 11797
Phone: 516-693-5790
Email: info@yclscholarship.org
http://www.yclscholarship.org
Purpose: To support emerging young Christian students.
Eligibility: Applicants must be a high school senior or full-time current college student who is a permanent resident of New York, New Jersey or Connecticut and is an active member of their local church (college students who attend school away from their home will be evaluated on an individual basis). A minimum 3.0 GPA is required. The scholarship is awarded on a monthly basis with a deadline of the 15th of each month.
Target applicant(s): High school students. College students.
Minimum GPA: 3.0
Amount: $1,000.
Number of awards: 12.
Deadline: 15th of each month.
How to apply: Applications are available online.
Exclusive: Visit www.UltimateScholarshipBook.com and enter code YO214223 for updates on this award.

(2143) · Youth of the Year Award

National Exchange Club
3050 West Central Avenue, Toledo, OH 43606
Phone: 419-535-3232
Email: info@nationalexchangeclub.org
http://www.nationalexchangeclub.org
Purpose: To recognize students who excel in academics, leadership and community service.

Eligibility: Applicants are chosen by their local Exchange Clubs. The process begins with Youth of the Month Awards. At the end of the year, a Youth of the Year nominee is selected from Youth of the Month winners. Applicants are judged based on participation in activities, community service, special achievements/awards, grades and a required essay. To be eligible to win, applicants must be able to attend national convention to accept the award.
Target applicant(s): High school students.
Amount: Varies.
Number of awards: Varies.
Deadline: Varies.
How to apply: Applications are available online.
Exclusive: Visit www.UltimateScholarshipBook.com and enter code NA214323 for updates on this award.

(2144) · Youth Partners Accessing Capital
Alpha Kappa Alpha Educational Advancement Foundation Inc.
5656 S. Stony Island Avenue, Chicago, IL 60637
Phone: 800-653-6528
Email: akaeaf@akaeaf.net
https://akaeaf.org/scholarships
Purpose: To provide financial assistance to Alpha Kappa Alpha members with exceptional academic achievement or extreme financial need.
Eligibility: Applicants must be Alpha Kappa Alpha members who are in their sophomore year of college or higher with a GPA of 3.0 or higher. They must have either high academic achievement or extreme financial need, and they must participate in leadership, volunteer, civic or campus activities.
Target applicant(s): College students. Adult students.
Minimum GPA: 3.0
Amount: Varies.
Number of awards: Varies.
Deadline: April 15.
How to apply: Applications are available online.
Exclusive: Visit www.UltimateScholarshipBook.com and enter code AL214423 for updates on this award.

(2145) · A.T. Anderson Memorial Scholarship
American Indian Science and Engineering Society
4263 Montgomery Boulevard, NE, Suite 200, Albuquerque, NM 87109
Phone: 505-765-1052
http://www.aises.org/scholarships
Purpose: To provide scholarships for Native American and Alaskan Native students majoring in science, engineering, math and technology.
Eligibility: Applicants must be full-time undergraduate or graduate students at an accredited college or university. Students must be enrolled citizens or a decedents of an enrolled citizen of a federal or state recognized American Indian Tribe or Alaska Native Village; or Native Hawaiian or decedent from a Native Hawaiian; or Pacific Islander or decedent from Pacific Islander; or Indigenous person of Canada and members of AISES. A minimum GPA of 3.0 is required.
Target applicant(s): High school students. College students. Graduate school students. Adult students.
Minimum GPA: 3.0
Amount: $1,000-$2,000.
Number of awards: Varies.
Deadline: May 31.
How to apply: Applications are available online.
Exclusive: Visit www.UltimateScholarshipBook.com and enter code AM214523 for updates on this award.

(2146) · AAUW Educational Foundation Career Development Grants
American Association of University Women (AAUW) Educational Foundation
Dept. 60, 301 ACT Drive, Iowa City, IA 52243-4030
Phone: 319-337-1716 x60
Email: aauw@act.org
http://www.aauw.org
Purpose: To support college-educated women who need additional training to advance their careers, re-enter the workforce or change careers.
Eligibility: Applicants must be U.S. citizens, hold a bachelor's degree and enroll in courses at a regionally-accredited program related to their professional development, including two- and four-year colleges, technical schools and distance learning programs and have earned the degree at least five years prior to application. Special preference is given to women of color, AAUW members and women pursuing their first advanced degree or credentials in a nontraditional field.
Target applicant(s): College students. Adult students.
Amount: $2,000-$12,000.
Number of awards: Varies.
Deadline: November 15.
How to apply: Applications are available online from August 1-November 15.
Exclusive: Visit www.UltimateScholarshipBook.com and enter code AM214623 for updates on this award.

(2147) · Abe and Esther Hagiwara Student Aid Award
Japanese American Citizens League (JACL)
1765 Sutter Street, San Francisco, CA 94115
Phone: 415-921-5225
Email: jacl@jacl.org

http://www.jacl.org

Purpose: To aid students who otherwise would have to delay or terminate their education due to lack of financing.

Eligibility: Applicants must be National JACL members and must be attending a college, university, trade school, business school or any other institution of higher learning. A personal statement, letter of recommendation, academic performance, work experience and community involvement are considered. Applicants should have extreme financial need.

Target applicant(s): High school students. College students. Graduate school students. Adult students.

Amount: Varies.

Number of awards: Varies.

Deadline: March 1.

How to apply: Applications are available online.

Exclusive: Visit www.UltimateScholarshipBook.com and enter code JA214723 for updates on this award.

(2148) · Achievers in Technology Program

Sankofatech
3560 Webstar Avenue, Bronx, NY 10467
Email: ait@sankofatech.org
https://sankofatech.org/ait/

Purpose: To support students of African descent who are interested in technology careers.

Eligibility: Applicants must be entering a U.S. college or university as a first-year student and demonstrate an interest in pursuing a tech career. Students must be of African descent and come from a low-income household.

Target applicant(s): High school students.

Amount: $2,000.

Number of awards: 6.

Deadline: May 15.

How to apply: Applications are available online.

Exclusive: Visit www.UltimateScholarshipBook.com and enter code SA214823 for updates on this award.

(2149) · Actuarial Diversity Scholarship

Actuarial Foundation
475 N. Martingale Road, Suite 600, Schaumburg, IL 60173-2226
Phone: 847-706-3581
Email: scholarships@actfnd.org
http://www.actuarialfoundation.org/scholarships/

Purpose: To promote diversity through an annual scholarship program for African American, Hispanic and Native American Indian students and encourage academic achievements by awarding scholarships to full-time undergraduate and graduate students pursuing a degree in the actuarial profession.

Eligibility: Applicants must have at least one birth parent who is a member of one of the minority groups listed and a minimum GPA of 3.0. High school seniors must have a minimum ACT math score of 28 or SAT math score of 620. An award will be provided in the recipient's name to any accredited U.S. educational institution to cover educational expenses. An application, a personal statement, a letter of recommendation and official or unofficial school transcripts are accepted.

Target applicant(s): High school students. College students. Graduate school students. Adult students.

Minimum GPA: 3.0

Amount: $1,000-$4,000.

Number of awards: Varies.

Scholarship may be renewable.

Deadline: July 15.

How to apply: Applications are available online.

Exclusive: Visit www.UltimateScholarshipBook.com and enter code AC214923 for updates on this award.

(2150) · Ada I. Pressman Memorial Scholarship

Society of Women Engineers
130 East Randolph Street, Suite 3500, Chicago, IL 60601
Phone: 877-793-4636
Email: scholarships@swe.org
https://swe.org/scholarships/

Purpose: To support female engineering students.

Eligibility: Applicants may major in any type of engineering. They must be U.S. citizens and must be college sophomores, juniors, seniors or graduate students. A GPA of 3.0 or higher is required.

Target applicant(s): College students. Graduate school students. Adult students.

Minimum GPA: 3.0

Amount: $5,000.

Number of awards: 9.

Deadline: February 15.

How to apply: Applications are available online. An application form is required.

Exclusive: Visit www.UltimateScholarshipBook.com and enter code SO215023 for updates on this award.

(2151) · Admiral Grace Murray Hopper Memorial Scholarships

Society of Women Engineers
130 East Randolph Street, Suite 3500, Chicago, IL 60601
Phone: 877-793-4636
Email: scholarships@swe.org
https://swe.org/scholarships/

Purpose: To support women in engineering.

Eligibility: Applicants must be females who are enrolled in their freshman year at an accredited engineering or computer science program. They must have a GPA of 3.5 or higher.

Target applicant(s): College students. Adult students.

Minimum GPA: 3.5

Amount: $1,500.

Number of awards: 3.

Deadline: May 1.

How to apply: Applications are available online. An application form is required.

Exclusive: Visit www.UltimateScholarshipBook.com and enter code SO215123 for updates on this award.

(2152) · Adolph Van Pelt Scholarship

Association on American Indian Affairs
Lisa Wyzlic, Director of Scholarship Programs, 966 Hungerford Drive, Suite 12-B, Rockville, MD 20850
Phone: 240-314-7155
Email: lw.aaia@indian-affairs.org
https://www.indian-affairs.org/whatwedo.html

Purpose: To assist Native American/Alaska Native undergraduate students based on merit and financial need.

Eligibility: Applicants must be full-time students and provide proof of tribal enrollment, a Certificate of Indian Blood (showing 1/4 Indian blood) and an essay on educational goals.

Target applicant(s): High school students. College students. Adult students.
Minimum GPA: 2.5
Amount: Varies.
Number of awards: Varies.
Scholarship may be renewable.
Deadline: May 31.
How to apply: Applications are available online.
Exclusive: Visit www.UltimateScholarshipBook.com and enter code AS215223 for updates on this award.

(2153) · Afro-Academic, Cultural, Technological and Scientific Olympics (ACT-SO)

National Association for the Advancement of Colored People
c/o Poise Foundation, Two Gateway Center, Suite 1700, 603 Stanwix Street, Pittsburgh, PA 15222
Phone: 412-281-4967
Email: info@poisefdn.org
http://www.poisefoundation.org/scholarships-overview/
Purpose: To recognize and reward the academic and cultural achievements of African American high school students.
Eligibility: Students must be in grades 9 through 12, 19 years of age or younger and of African-American descent. They must compete in one of 26 categories including business, sciences, humanities and performing and visual arts. Winners receive scholarships, internships and apprenticeships.
Target applicant(s): High school students.
Amount: Varies.
Number of awards: Varies.
Deadline: April 1.
How to apply: Applications are available from the NAACP.
Exclusive: Visit www.UltimateScholarshipBook.com and enter code NA215323 for updates on this award.

(2154) · AGBU US Graduate Scholarship

Armenian General Benevolent Union (AGBU)
55 East 59th Street, 7th Floor, New York, NY 10022-1112
Phone: 212-319-6383
Email: scholarship@agbu.org
http://www.agbu.org
Purpose: To support graduate students of Armenian heritage.
Eligibility: Applicants must be of Armenian heritage, be a full-time student at a U.S. college/university and have earned a minimum 3.5 GPA in undergraduate study.
Target applicant(s): Graduate school students. Adult students.
Minimum GPA: 3.5
Amount: $5,000.
Number of awards: 3.
Scholarship may be renewable.
Deadline: April 30.
How to apply: Applications are available online.
Exclusive: Visit www.UltimateScholarshipBook.com and enter code AR215423 for updates on this award.

(2155) · Agnes Jones Jackson Scholarship

National Association for the Advancement of Colored People
c/o Poise Foundation, Two Gateway Center, Suite 1700, 603 Stanwix Street, Pittsburgh, PA 15222
Phone: 412-281-4967

Email: info@poisefdn.org
http://www.poisefoundation.org/scholarships-overview/
Purpose: To reward NAACP members with financial need.
Eligibility: Students must be members of the NAACP, U.S. citizens and attending an accredited U.S. college. Undergraduates must attend college full-time, while graduates may be full- or part-time students. High school seniors and undergraduates must have a minimum 2.5 GPA while graduate students must have a minimum 3.0 GPA. Applicants must demonstrate financial need according to the formula in the application form.
Target applicant(s): High school students. College students. Graduate school students.
Minimum GPA: 2.5 for high school seniors and undergraduate students, 3.0 for graduate students
Amount: Up to $3,000.
Number of awards: 20-40.
Scholarship may be renewable.
Deadline: June 18.
How to apply: Applications are available online.
Exclusive: Visit www.UltimateScholarshipBook.com and enter code NA215523 for updates on this award.

(2156) · Agnes Missirian Scholarship

Armenian International Women's Association
65 Main Street, #3A, Watertown, MA 02472
Phone: 617-926-0171
Email: aiwainc@aol.com
http://aiwainternational.org/
Purpose: To honor the memory of Professor Agnes Missirian and assist Armenian women in obtaining higher education.
Eligibility: Applicants must be full-time students at accredited colleges or universities who are females of Armenian descent. They must be juniors, seniors or graduate students. Awards are based on financial need and merit.
Target applicant(s): College students. Graduate school students. Adult students.
Amount: $2,000.
Number of awards: Varies.
Deadline: April 19.
How to apply: Applications are available online.
Exclusive: Visit www.UltimateScholarshipBook.com and enter code AR215623 for updates on this award.

(2157) · AHEPA Educational Foundation National Scholarship Program

American Hellenic Education Progressive Association
1909 Q Street NW, Suite 500, Washington, DC 20009
Phone: 202-232-6300
Email: ahepa@ahepa.org
https://ahepa.org/education/
Purpose: To assist Hellenic students.
Eligibility: Applicants must be members of the AHEPA family or be related to someone who is a member. Students must be of Hellenic descent and/or Phil-Hellene, the son or daughter of a member in good standing of AHEPA, the Maids of Athena, the Daughters of Penelope or the Sons of Pericles.
Target applicant(s): High school students. College students. Graduate school students. Adult students.
Minimum GPA: 3.0
Amount: $2,000.
Number of awards: 1.

Deadline: March.
How to apply: Applications are available online.
Exclusive: Visit www.UltimateScholarshipBook.com and enter code AM215723 for updates on this award.

(2158) · AICPA Fellowship for Minority Doctoral Students

American Institute of Certified Public Accountants
220 Leigh Farm Road, Durham, NC 27707-8110
Phone: 919-402-4500
Email: scholarships@aicpa.org
https://www.aicpa.org
Purpose: To support minority students who demonstrate significant potential to become accounting educators.
Eligibility: Applicants must be minority full-time students who have applied to a doctoral program or have been accepted to a doctoral program and plan to pursue the CPA exam.
Target applicant(s): Graduate school students. Adult students.
Amount: $12,000.
Number of awards: 25.
Deadline: May 30.
How to apply: Applications are available online.
Exclusive: Visit www.UltimateScholarshipBook.com and enter code AM215823 for updates on this award.

(2159) · AICPA Scholarship for Minority Accounting Students

American Institute of Certified Public Accountants
220 Leigh Farm Road, Durham, NC 27707-8110
Phone: 919-402-4500
Email: scholarships@aicpa.org
https://www.aicpa.org
Purpose: To encourage minority students to become certified public accountants (CPAs).
Eligibility: Applicants must be African-American, Native American, Latino or Asian American students who are majoring in accounting. They must be full-time students who have completed at least 30 credits overall and at least six credits in accounting. They must have a GPA of 3.0 or higher and must have plans to become a certified public accountant (CPA). Selection is based on academic merit, leadership, volunteer experience and commitment to becoming a CPA.
Target applicant(s): College students. Graduate school students. Adult students.
Minimum GPA: 3.0
Amount: Up to $5,000.
Number of awards: Varies.
Scholarship may be renewable.
Deadline: March 1.
How to apply: Applications are available online. An application form and a personal essay are required.
Exclusive: Visit www.UltimateScholarshipBook.com and enter code AM215923 for updates on this award.

(2160) · AISES Intel Scholarship

American Indian Science and Engineering Society
4263 Montgomery Boulevard, NE, Suite 200, Albuquerque, NM 87109
Phone: 505-765-1052
http://www.aises.org/scholarships
Purpose: To support the advancement of AISES (American Indian Science and Engineering Society) members who are American Indian, Alaska Natives or Native Hawaiians working towards degrees in the STEM disciplines (science, technology, engineering and math).
Eligibility: Applicants must be AISES members who are also members of an enrolled citizen or a decedent of an enrolled citizen of a federal or state recognized American Indian Tribe or Alaska Native Village; or Native Hawaiian or decedent from a Native Hawaiian; or Pacific Islander or decedent from Pacific Islander; or Indigenous person of Canada. They must also be enrolled as full-time undergraduate or graduate students at a four-year academic institution or at a two-year institution working towards an academic degree. Students must major in one of the following fields: chemistry, computer science, computer engineering, electrical engineering, electrical and computer engineering, mechanical engineering, neuroscience, physics, chemical engineering or material engineering or science. The minimum GPA requirement is 3.0. Selection is based upon the quality of the application.
Target applicant(s): College students. Graduate school students. Adult students.
Minimum GPA: 3.0
Amount: $5,000-$10,000.
Number of awards: Varies.
Deadline: May 31.
How to apply: Applications are available online. An application form, official transcripts, an essay, two letters of recommendation, tribal enrollment documentation and resume are required.
Exclusive: Visit www.UltimateScholarshipBook.com and enter code AM216023 for updates on this award.

(2161) · Allogan Slagle Memorial Scholarship

Association on American Indian Affairs
Lisa Wyzlic, Director of Scholarship Programs, 966 Hungerford Drive, Suite 12-B, Rockville, MD 20850
Phone: 240-314-7155
Email: lw.aaia@indian-affairs.org
https://www.indian-affairs.org/whatwedo.html
Purpose: To assist Native American/Alaska Native undergraduate and graduate students from tribes that are not recognized by the federal government.
Eligibility: Applicants must submit a financial need analysis form, Certificate of Indian Blood or documents proving their lineal descent, proof of tribal enrollment, essay, two letters of recommendation, current financial aid award letter, transcripts and class schedule.
Target applicant(s): High school students. College students. Graduate school students. Adult students.
Minimum GPA: 2.5
Amount: Varies.
Number of awards: Varies.
Deadline: May 31.
How to apply: Applications are available online.
Exclusive: Visit www.UltimateScholarshipBook.com and enter code AS216123 for updates on this award.

(2162) · American Chemical Society Scholars Program

American Chemical Society
Christie Robinson, Training and Development Director, Rubber Division, ACS, 411 Wolf Ledges Parkway, Suite 201, Akron, OH 44311
Phone: 800-227-5558
Email: crobinson@rubber.org

http://www.acs.org

Purpose: To encourage minority students to pursue careers in the sciences and to help them acquire the skills necessary for success in these fields.

Eligibility: Applicants must be African American, Hispanic/Latino or American Indian and graduating high school seniors or college freshmen, sophomores or juniors enrolled full-time at an accredited institution. Students must major in chemistry, biochemistry, chemical engineering or a chemically-related science and plan to work in a chemistry-related field. Those entering pre-med programs or pursuing pharmacy degrees are not eligible. A minimum GPA of 3.0 or "B" or better with high academic achievement in chemistry or science is required. Students must also demonstrate financial need through the Free Application for Federal Student Aid (FAFSA).

Target applicant(s): High school students. College students. Adult students.

Minimum GPA: 3.0

Amount: Up to $5,000.

Number of awards: Varies.

Scholarship may be renewable.

Deadline: March.

How to apply: Applications are available online.

Exclusive: Visit www.UltimateScholarshipBook.com and enter code AM216223 for updates on this award.

(2163) · American Indian Nurse Scholarship

National Society of the Colonial Dames of America

2715 Q Street NW, Washington, DC 20007-3071

Phone: 202-337-2288

Email: dames@nscda.org

https://nscda.org/ains/

Purpose: To support students who have American Indian heritage who are pursuing a degree in health care.

Eligibility: Applicants must be a quarter American Indian and enrolled in a tribe. Students must be a high school graduate and be enrolled in an accredited institution's nursing or health care program. Applicants are expected to graduate in two years if pursuing an associate's degree or four years if pursuing a bachelor's degree. Graduate students may apply. Students must maintain the scholastic average required by the school. Applicants must have a career goal related to the needs of the Indian people.

Target applicant(s): College students. Graduate school students. Adult students.

Amount: $1,500.

Number of awards: 2.

Scholarship may be renewable.

Deadline: June 1 (fall); December 1 (spring).

How to apply: Applications are available online.

Exclusive: Visit www.UltimateScholarshipBook.com and enter code NA216323 for updates on this award.

(2164) · American Indian Services Scholarship

American Indian Services

3115 East Lion Lane, Suite 320, Salt Lake City, UT 84121

Phone: 801-375-1777

Email: scholarship@americanindianservices.org

https://americanindianservices.org/

Purpose: To support Native American students in pursuing post-secondary education.

Eligibility: Applicant must be an enrolled member of a U.S. Federally Recognized American Indian or Alaska Native Tribe or lineal descendant

of a base roll member. A minimum GPA of 2.25 is required. Students must be undergraduate students who have earned fewer than 150 credits.

Target applicant(s): College students. Adult students.

Minimum GPA: 2.25

Amount: Varies.

Number of awards: Varies.

Deadline: February 1, April 1, July 1, November 1.

How to apply: Applications are available online.

Exclusive: Visit www.UltimateScholarshipBook.com and enter code AM216423 for updates on this award.

(2165) · Anne Maureen Whitney Barrow Memorial Scholarship

Society of Women Engineers

130 East Randolph Street, Suite 3500, Chicago, IL 60601

Phone: 877-793-4636

Email: scholarships@swe.org

https://swe.org/scholarships/

Purpose: To support female engineering students.

Eligibility: Applicants must be enrolled in an accredited engineering or computer science program. A minimum GPA of 3.5 is required.

Target applicant(s): High school students. College students. Adult students.

Minimum GPA: 3.5

Amount: $8,000.

Number of awards: 1.

Scholarship may be renewable.

Deadline: February 15 (all others), May 1 (freshmen).

How to apply: Applications are available online.

Exclusive: Visit www.UltimateScholarshipBook.com and enter code SO216523 for updates on this award.

(2166) · ARS Undergraduate Scholarship

Armenian Relief Society of Eastern USA (ARS)

80 Bigelow Avenue, Suite 200, Watertown, MA 02472

Phone: 617-926-3801

https://arseastusa.org/

Purpose: To support students of Armenian descent who are attending a four-year college.

Eligibility: Applicant must be of Armenian descent. Applicants must be an undergraduate student who has completed at least one college semester at an accredited four-year college or university in the United States or enrolled in a two-year college and transferring to a four-year college or university as a full time student in the fall. A letter from an Armenian community leader or representative that attests to the applicant's activity or contributions to the Armenian Community is required.

Target applicant(s): College students. Adult students.

Amount: $1,000.

Number of awards: 12.

Deadline: April 1.

How to apply: Applications are available online.

Exclusive: Visit www.UltimateScholarshipBook.com and enter code AR216623 for updates on this award.

(2167) · ASA Scholarships

Armenian Students' Association of America

333 Atlantic Avenue, Warwick, RI 02888

Phone: 401-461-6114

Email: asa@asainc.org
http://www.asainc.org
Purpose: To provide scholarships for students of Armenian descent.
Eligibility: Applicants must be college sophomores or beyond in the year of application and be of Armenian descent.
Target applicant(s): High school students. College students. Graduate school students. Adult students.
Amount: Varies.
Number of awards: Varies.
Deadline: March 15.
How to apply: Request forms for applications are available online.
Exclusive: Visit www.UltimateScholarshipBook.com and enter code AR216723 for updates on this award.

(2168) · Asian and Pacific Islander American Scholarships

Asian and Pacific Islander American Scholarship Fund
2025 M Street NW, Suite 610, Washington, DC 20036
Phone: 202-986-6892
Email: info@apiasf.org
http://www.apiasf.org
Purpose: To provide financial assistance to Asian and Pacific Island Americans.
Eligibility: Applicants must be of Asian or Pacific Islander ethnicity as defined by the U.S. Census, and they must be legal citizens, nationals or permanent residents of the United States. Citizens of the Marshall Islands, Micronesia and Palau are also eligible. Applicants must be enrolling full-time as a first-year degree-seeking student in an accredited college or university in the U.S. They must have a GPA of 2.7 or higher or have earned a GED, and they must apply for federal financial aid.
Target applicant(s): High school students.
Minimum GPA: 2.7
Amount: $2,500-$20,000.
Number of awards: Varies.
Deadline: January 26.
How to apply: Applications are available online.
Exclusive: Visit www.UltimateScholarshipBook.com and enter code AS216823 for updates on this award.

(2169) · Association of Cuban Engineers Scholarship Foundation Scholarships

Association of Cuban-American Engineers Scholarship Foundation
P.O. Box 941436, Miami, FL 33194-1436
Phone: 305-597-9858
https://www.cubanamericanengineers.com/students/applications-for-scholarships-and-membership/
Purpose: To help undergraduate and graduate students of Hispanic heritage who are pursuing degrees in engineering.
Eligibility: Applicants must be U.S. citizens or legal residents of Hispanic heritage who have completed at least 30 units of coursework towards a bachelor's degree or higher in engineering at an ABET-accredited institution located in the United States or Puerto Rico. They must have a GPA of 3.0 or higher and must be current, full-time students (carrying 12 or more semester hours if an undergraduate and 6 or more semester hours as a graduate student). Selection is based on the overall strength of the application.
Target applicant(s): College students. Graduate school students. Adult students.
Minimum GPA: 3.0
Amount: Varies.

Number of awards: Varies.
Deadline: January 31.
How to apply: Applications are available online. An application form, official transcript and financial aid award letter are required.
Exclusive: Visit www.UltimateScholarshipBook.com and enter code AS216923 for updates on this award.

(2170) · B.J. Harrod Scholarships

Society of Women Engineers
130 East Randolph Street, Suite 3500, Chicago, IL 60601
Phone: 877-793-4636
Email: scholarships@swe.org
https://swe.org/scholarships/
Purpose: To aid female engineering students.
Eligibility: Applicants may major in any type of engineering at an accredited institution of higher learning. They must be freshmen and have a GPA of 3.5 or higher.
Target applicant(s): College students. Adult students.
Minimum GPA: 3.5
Amount: $3,000.
Number of awards: 1.
Deadline: May 1.
How to apply: Applications are available online. An application form is required.
Exclusive: Visit www.UltimateScholarshipBook.com and enter code SO217023 for updates on this award.

(2171) · B.K. Krenzer Reentry Scholarship

Society of Women Engineers
130 East Randolph Street, Suite 3500, Chicago, IL 60601
Phone: 877-793-4636
Email: scholarships@swe.org
https://swe.org/scholarships/
Purpose: To support reentering female engineering students.
Eligibility: Applicants must have been out of school and out of the job market for at least two years. They must enroll in an accredited engineering or computer science program. A GPA of 3.0 or higher is required. Preference is given to degreed engineers.
Target applicant(s): College students. Adult students.
Minimum GPA: 3.0
Amount: $3,250.
Number of awards: 1.
Deadline: February 15 (all others); May 1 (Freshmen).
How to apply: Applications are available online. An application form is required.
Exclusive: Visit www.UltimateScholarshipBook.com and enter code SO217123 for updates on this award.

(2172) · Bechtel Corporation Scholarship

Society of Women Engineers
130 East Randolph Street, Suite 3500, Chicago, IL 60601
Phone: 877-793-4636
Email: scholarships@swe.org
https://swe.org/scholarships/
Purpose: To support female engineering students.
Eligibility: Applicants must be enrolled in an accredited engineering program in their sophomore, junior or senior year. They must be SWE members. A minimum GPA of 3.0 is required.
Target applicant(s): College students. Adult students.
Minimum GPA: 3.0

Amount: $5,000.
Number of awards: 4.
Deadline: February 15.
How to apply: Applications are available online. An application form is required.
Exclusive: Visit www.UltimateScholarshipBook.com and enter code SO217223 for updates on this award.

(2173) · Bee's Fund Microgrants

Stonewall Community Foundation
1270 Broadway, Suite 501, New York, NY 10001
Phone: 212-457-1341
Email: scholarships@stonewallfoundation.org
https://stonewallfoundation.org
Purpose: To support lesbian, bisexual, transgender and queer women as well as non-binary and gender nonconforming individuals who have lost family support because of their sexual orientation or gender identity.
Eligibility: Applicants must be between 16 and 26 years old and reside in the United States. Students must not hold a bachelor's degree and have the support of a 501(c)(3) organization that can accept the grant on their behalf. Applicants must be lesbian, bisexual, transgender and queer women as well as non-binary and gender nonconforming individuals who have lost family support because of their sexual orientation or gender identity.
Target applicant(s): High school students. College students. Adult students.
Amount: Up to $650.
Number of awards: Varies.
Deadline: Varies.
How to apply: Applications are available online.
Exclusive: Visit www.UltimateScholarshipBook.com and enter code ST217323 for updates on this award.

(2174) · Berbeco Senior Research Fellowship

United Negro College Fund (UNCF)
1805 7th Street NW, Washington, DC 20001
Phone: 800-331-2244
https://scholarships.uncf.org/
Purpose: To encourage African Americans to conduct independent research internationally.
Eligibility: Applicants must be college juniors who attend United Negro College Fund (UNCF) member colleges or universities. The need-based award is for students to work on their senior thesis or research projects outside the U.S. during the summer between their junior and senior years.
Target applicant(s): College students. Adult students.
Minimum GPA: 2.5
Amount: Up to $6,000.
Number of awards: Varies.
Deadline: April.
How to apply: Applications are available online.
Exclusive: Visit www.UltimateScholarshipBook.com and enter code UN217423 for updates on this award.

(2175) · BIPOC Scholarship

Point Foundation
P.O. Box 60108, Los Angeles, CA 90060
Phone: 323-580-5058
Email: info@pointfoundation.org
http://www.pointfoundation.org
Purpose: To support students who are members of black, indigenous and people of color (BIPOC) communities who identify as LGBTQ.
Eligibility: Applicants must be members of black, indigenous and people of color (BIPOC) communities who identify as LGBTQ. Students must be enrolled in community college, four-year college or university or graduate program maintaining a full-time or part-time course load. Applicants must demonstrate a proven commitment to furthering their education.
Target applicant(s): High school students. College students. Graduate school students. Adult students.
Amount: $1,500.
Number of awards: 1.
Deadline: May 17.
How to apply: Applications are available online.
Exclusive: Visit www.UltimateScholarshipBook.com and enter code PO217523 for updates on this award.

(2176) · Burlington Northern Santa Fe (BNSF) Foundation Scholarship

American Indian Science and Engineering Society
4263 Montgomery Boulevard, NE, Suite 200, Albuquerque, NM 87109
Phone: 505-765-1052
http://www.aises.org/scholarships
Purpose: To provide a four-year scholarship for an American Indian student attending an accredited four-year college or university in a state where Burlington Northern Santa Fe operates.
Eligibility: Applicants must reside in one of the following states: Arizona, California, Colorado, Kansas, Minnesota, Montana, New Mexico, North Dakota, Oklahoma, Oregon, South Dakota, Texas, Arkansas, Louisiana, Utah, Nevada, Wyoming, Illinois, Missouri, Nebraska, Wisconsin, Iowa or Washington. Students must also major in one of the following areas: business, engineering, math, medicine/health administration, natural/physical sciences, technology or education and belong to AISES. Applicants must be full-time undergraduate or graduate students at an accredited college or university with a 3.0 minimum GPA.
Target applicant(s): High school students. College students. Graduate school students. Adult students.
Minimum GPA: 3.0
Amount: $2,500 for 4 years.
Number of awards: Varies.
Scholarship may be renewable.
Deadline: May 31.
How to apply: Applications are available online.
Exclusive: Visit www.UltimateScholarshipBook.com and enter code AM217623 for updates on this award.

(2177) · Cafe Bustelo El Cafe Del Futuro Scholarship

Hispanic Association of Colleges and Universities (HACU)
8415 Datapoint Drive, Suite 400, San Antonio, TX 78229
Phone: 210-692-3805
Email: scholarship@hacu.net
http://www.hacu.net/hacu/scholarships.asp
Purpose: To support students who are of Latino heritage.
Eligibility: Applicants must be at least 18 years old, a U.S. citizen or permanent legal resident and be of Latino descent. Students must be enrolled full-time in an undergraduate or graduate level program at a four-year HACU-member institution in the United States, Washington, DC, or Puerto Rico. Students will submit a 500-word essay on the topic

outlined on the website pertaining to Latino heritage, goals and future community service.
Target applicant(s): College students. Graduate school students. Adult students.
Amount: $5,000.
Number of awards: 25.
Deadline: July 6.
How to apply: Applications are available online.
Exclusive: Visit www.UltimateScholarshipBook.com and enter code HI217723 for updates on this award.

(2178) · California Chafee Grant for Foster Youth

California Student Aid Commission
Specialized Programs Operations Branch - Chafee, P.O. Box 419029, Rancho Cordova, CA 95741-9029
Phone: 888-224-7268
Email: studentsupport@csac.ca.gov
http://www.csac.ca.gov/
Purpose: To provide educational assistance for students who have been in foster care in California.
Eligibility: Applicants must be current or former foster youth who are under 22 years of age as of July 1 of the award year. Dependency must have been established by the court between the ages of 16 and 18. Financial need is required. Applicants must enroll at least half-time in a program that is at least one academic year long, and they must attend class regularly and maintain good grades.
Target applicant(s): High school students. College students.
Amount: Up to $5,000.
Number of awards: Varies.
Scholarship may be renewable.
Deadline: Varies.
How to apply: Applications are available online and applicants must also complete a FAFSA.
Exclusive: Visit www.UltimateScholarshipBook.com and enter code CA217823 for updates on this award.

(2179) · Casey Family Scholarship

Casey Family
23811 Chagrin Boulevard, Suite 210, Cleveland, OH 44122
Phone: 571-203-0270
Email: info@fc2success.org
http://www.fc2success.org/our-programs/information-for-students/
Purpose: To support foster care students pursuing a higher education.
Eligibility: Applicants must have been in foster care for the year prior to their 18th birthday; or have been adopted or placed into legal guardianship from foster care after their 16th birthday; or they must have been orphaned for at least one year at the time of their 18th birthday. Students must have been accepted into an accredited post-secondary school. Applicants must have been in foster care or orphaned while living in the United States.
Target applicant(s): High school students. College students. Graduate school students. Adult students.
Amount: Up to $10,000.
Number of awards: Varies.
Scholarship may be renewable.
Deadline: Rolling.
How to apply: Applications are available online.
Exclusive: Visit www.UltimateScholarshipBook.com and enter code CA217923 for updates on this award.

(2180) · Catching the Dream Native American Scholarship Fund

Catching the Dream
Attn.: Scholarship Affairs Office, 8200 Mountain Road NE, Suite 103, Albuquerque, NM 87110
Phone: 505-262-2351
Email: nscholarsh@aol.com
http://www.catchingthedream.org
Purpose: To support American Indian students pursuing higher education.
Eligibility: Applicants must be undergraduate or graduate students who are 1/4 or more American Indian, enrolled in a U.S. tribe and attend or plans to attend an accredited institution on a full-time basis. Students must excel academically, have received high ACT or SAT scores and demonstrate a strong commitment to the Indian community. Selection is based on the strength of the overall application.
Target applicant(s): College students. Adult students.
Amount: $5,000.
Number of awards: Varies.
Deadline: March 15 (Summer); April 30 (Fall); September 15 (Spring).
How to apply: Applications are available online.
Exclusive: Visit www.UltimateScholarshipBook.com and enter code CA218023 for updates on this award.

(2181) · CBC Spouses Performing Arts Scholarship

Congressional Black Caucus Foundation
1720 Massachusetts Avenue NW, Washington, DC 20036
Phone: 202-263-2800
Email: info@cbcfinc.org
https://www.cbcfinc.org/scholarships/
Purpose: To support students who are pursuing careers in performing arts.
Eligibility: Applicants must be African American students who have at least a 2.5 GPA, and they must be enrolled or accepted into a full-time undergraduate degree program. Applicants must show leadership qualities and community service participation.
Target applicant(s): High school students. College students. Adult students.
Minimum GPA: 2.5
Amount: Up to $3,000.
Number of awards: Up to 10.
Deadline: April.
How to apply: Applications are available online.
Exclusive: Visit www.UltimateScholarshipBook.com and enter code CO218123 for updates on this award.

(2182) · CHCI United Health Foundation Scholar-Intern Program

Congressional Hispanic Caucus Institute Inc.
300 M Street SE, 5th Floor, Suite 510, Washington, DC 20003
Phone: 202-543-1771
Email: shernandez@chci.org
http://www.chci.org
Purpose: To reward Latino students who are interested in careers in the healthcare industry.
Eligibility: Applicants must be Latinos focused on the healthcare industry who are currently enrolled full-time at an accredited community college, four-year university or graduate or professional program. Students must have at least one more full year of their program remaining

when they apply, must have a minimum 3.0 GPA and must demonstrate financial need.
Target applicant(s): College students. Graduate school students. Adult students.
Minimum GPA: 3.0
Amount: $2,500-$5,000.
Number of awards: Varies.
Deadline: February 15.
How to apply: Applications are available online.
Exclusive: Visit www.UltimateScholarshipBook.com and enter code CO218223 for updates on this award.

(2183) · Cherokee Nation Directed Studies Scholarship

Cherokee Nation
P.O. Box 948, Tahlequah, OK 74465
Phone: 918-453-5000
Email: communications@cherokee.org
https://cherokee.org/all-services/education-services/college-resources/
Purpose: To aid Cherokee college students.
Eligibility: Applicants must be citizens of the Cherokee Nation and reside in the Cherokee Nation jurisdictional area. They must be enrolled full-time in a graduate or upper-level undergraduate degree program. They must agree to work for the Cherokee Nation for two years following graduation. Selection is based on the overall strength of the application.
Target applicant(s): College students. Graduate school students. Adult students.
Amount: Full tuition, books and fees.
Number of awards: Varies.
Deadline: June 15.
How to apply: Applications are available online. An application form and supporting materials are required.
Exclusive: Visit www.UltimateScholarshipBook.com and enter code CH218323 for updates on this award.

(2184) · Cherokee Nation Scholarship - Graduate

Cherokee Nation
P.O. Box 948, Tahlequah, OK 74465
Phone: 918-453-5000
Email: communications@cherokee.org
https://cherokee.org/all-services/education-services/college-resources/
Purpose: To aid graduate students who are members of the Cherokee Nation.
Eligibility: Applicants must be citizens of the Cherokee Nation. They must be graduate students who are attending a not-for-profit educational institution. Selection is based on the overall strength of the application.
Target applicant(s): Graduate school students. Adult students.
Amount: Varies.
Number of awards: Varies.
Deadline: June 15.
How to apply: Applications are available online. An application form and supporting materials are required.
Exclusive: Visit www.UltimateScholarshipBook.com and enter code CH218423 for updates on this award.

(2185) · Cherokee Nation Scholarship - Undergraduate

Cherokee Nation
P.O. Box 948, Tahlequah, OK 74465

Phone: 918-453-5000
Email: communications@cherokee.org
https://cherokee.org/all-services/education-services/college-resources/
Purpose: To aid undergraduate students who are members of the Cherokee Nation.
Eligibility: Applicants must be citizens of the Cherokee Nation. They must be undergraduate students who are attending a not-for-profit educational institution. Selection is based on the overall strength of the application.
Target applicant(s): College students. Adult students.
Amount: Varies.
Number of awards: Varies.
Deadline: June 15.
How to apply: Applications are available online. An application form and supporting materials are required.
Exclusive: Visit www.UltimateScholarshipBook.com and enter code CH218523 for updates on this award.

(2186) · Chief Manuelito Scholarship Program

Office of Navajo Nation Scholarship and Financial Assistance
P.O. Box 1870, Window Rock, AZ 86515
Phone: 928-871-7444
http://www.onnsfa.org
Purpose: The scholarship was created to help high-achieving Navajo students.
Eligibility: Students must be enrolled members of the Navajo nation, submit a Certificate of Indian Blood, attend a regionally-accredited school and complete a FAFSA form. Students must also complete a Navajo Government course (available online).
Target applicant(s): High school students. College students. Adult students.
Amount: $7,000.
Number of awards: Varies.
Scholarship may be renewable.
Deadline: June 25.
How to apply: Applications are available online and must be submitted to your agency, which is listed online.
Exclusive: Visit www.UltimateScholarshipBook.com and enter code OF218623 for updates on this award.

(2187) · Citizen Potawatomi Nation Tribal Scholarship

Citizen Potawatomi Nation
1601 S. Gordon Cooper Drive, Shawnee, OK 74801
Phone: 405-275-3121
Email: college@potawatomi.org
https://www.potawatomi.org/services/
Purpose: To assist Citizen Potawatomi Nation tribal members who are pursuing higher education.
Eligibility: Applicants must be Citizen Potawatomi Nation tribal members who are enrolled full or part-time in an undergraduate or graduate academic degree program at an accredited, not-for-profit postsecondary institution. Selection is based on the overall strength of the application.
Target applicant(s): High school students. College students. Graduate school students. Adult students.
Amount: $750-$2,000 per semester.
Number of awards: Varies.
Scholarship may be renewable.
Deadline: February 15 (spring), June 15 (summer), September 15 (fall).

How to apply: Applications are available online. An application form, proof of enrollment, federal tax return information and transcript are required.

Exclusive: Visit www.UltimateScholarshipBook.com and enter code CI218723 for updates on this award.

(2188) · Colgate-Palmolive Make the U Educational Grant

Hispanic Heritage Foundation Colgate-Palmolive Haz la U
1001 Pennsylvania Ave NW, Washington, DC 20004
Email: info@hispanicheritage.org
https://www.colgate.com/en-us/make-the-u

Purpose: To support Latino students who excel in the classroom and their community by providing them with funds to further their education.

Eligibility: Applicants must have Latino heritage, have a minimum 3.0 GPA and be graduating high school seniors. Students must be role models in their communities and must also be permanent residents, DACA, U.S. citizens or eligible non-citizens.

Target applicant(s): High school students.

Minimum GPA: 3.0

Amount: $2,000-$10,000.

Number of awards: 31.

Deadline: November 14.

How to apply: Applications are available online.

Exclusive: Visit www.UltimateScholarshipBook.com and enter code HI218823 for updates on this award.

(2189) · Conference of Minority Transportation Officials (COMTO) National Scholarship

Conference of Minority Transportation Officials
100 M Street SE, Suite 917, Washington, DC 20003
Phone: 202-857-8065
Email: info@comto.org
https://members.comtonational.org/page/scholarshipapp

Purpose: To support graduating high school students whose parents are COMTO members and college or graduate students who are studying fields related to transportation.

Eligibility: Applicants must have at least a 3.0 GPA. High school students must be accepted into a college or technical school, and their parents must have been COMTO members in good standing for at least the past year. College students must have at least 60 credits, and graduate students must have at least 15 credits.

Target applicant(s): High school students. College students. Graduate school students. Adult students.

Minimum GPA: 3.0

Amount: $4,500.

Number of awards: Varies.

Deadline: May 21.

How to apply: Applications are available online.

Exclusive: Visit www.UltimateScholarshipBook.com and enter code CO218923 for updates on this award.

(2190) · Congressional Black Caucus Spouses Education Scholarship

Congressional Black Caucus Foundation
1720 Massachusetts Avenue NW, Washington, DC 20036
Phone: 202-263-2800
Email: info@cbcfinc.org

https://www.cbcfinc.org/scholarships/

Purpose: To support students who are pursuing undergraduate or graduate degrees.

Eligibility: Applicants must be African American students attending or planning to attend school on a full-time basis. Students must have at least a 2.5 GPA, and they must demonstrate leadership and community service participation.

Target applicant(s): High school students. College students. Graduate school students. Adult students.

Minimum GPA: 2.5

Amount: Varies.

Number of awards: Varies.

Deadline: April 30.

How to apply: Applications are available online.

Exclusive: Visit www.UltimateScholarshipBook.com and enter code CO219023 for updates on this award.

(2191) · Congressional Black Caucus Spouses Visual Arts Scholarship

Congressional Black Caucus Foundation
1720 Massachusetts Avenue NW, Washington, DC 20036
Phone: 202-263-2800
Email: info@cbcfinc.org
https://www.cbcfinc.org/scholarships/

Purpose: To support students who are pursuing careers in visual arts.

Eligibility: Applicants must be African American students, have at least a 2.5 GPA and be enrolled at or accepted into a full-time undergraduate degree program. Applicants must show leadership qualities and community service participation.

Target applicant(s): High school students. College students. Adult students.

Minimum GPA: 2.5

Amount: Up to $3,000.

Number of awards: Varies.

Deadline: April.

How to apply: Applications are available online.

Exclusive: Visit www.UltimateScholarshipBook.com and enter code CO219123 for updates on this award.

(2192) · Development Fund for Black Students in Science and Technology

Development Fund for Black Students in Science and Technology
2705 Bladensburg Road NE, Washington, DC 20018
http://www.dfbsstscholarship.org/dfb_sch.html

Purpose: To support African-American students studying scientific fields.

Eligibility: Applicants must be U.S. citizens or permanent residents and undergraduate African-American students at a Historically Black College majoring in a technical field such as engineering or math. Students must demonstrate financial need and provide an essay along with their application materials.

Target applicant(s): High school students. College students. Adult students.

Amount: Up to $3,000.

Number of awards: 1.

Deadline: June 15.

How to apply: Applications are available online.

Exclusive: Visit www.UltimateScholarshipBook.com and enter code DE219223 for updates on this award.

(2193) · Displaced Homemaker Scholarship

Association on American Indian Affairs
Lisa Wyzlic, Director of Scholarship Programs, 966 Hungerford Drive, Suite 12-B, Rockville, MD 20850
Phone: 240-314-7155
Email: lw.aaia@indian-affairs.org
https://www.indian-affairs.org/whatwedo.html
Purpose: To provide assistance to Native American/Alaska Native undergraduate men and women in any curriculum who would be unable to complete college due to family responsibilities.
Eligibility: Applicants must be full-time students able to prove financial need, proof of tribal enrollment and Certificate of Indian Blood (showing 1/4 Indian blood). Applicants must be 35 years old or older.
Target applicant(s): College students. Adult students.
Minimum GPA: 2.5
Amount: $1,500.
Number of awards: Varies.
Deadline: May 31.
How to apply: Applications are available online.
Exclusive: Visit www.UltimateScholarshipBook.com and enter code AS219323 for updates on this award.

(2194) · Distinguished Young Women Scholarship Program

Distinguished Young Women
751 Government Street, Mobile, AL 36602
Phone: 251-438-3621
Email: lynne@ajm.org
http://distinguishedyw.org/scholarships/
Purpose: To provide scholarship opportunities and encourage personal development for high school girls through a competitive pageant stressing academics and talent as well as self-expression and fitness.
Eligibility: Teen girls are selected from state competitions to participate in a national pageant. Contestants are judged on a combination of scholastics, personal interview, talent, fitness and self-expression. Applicants should be a high school student at least in their sophomore year. Students must be U.S. citizens, have never been married and have never been pregnant.
Target applicant(s): High school students.
Amount: Varies.
Number of awards: Varies.
Deadline: Varies.
How to apply: Applications are available online.
Exclusive: Visit www.UltimateScholarshipBook.com and enter code DI219423 for updates on this award.

(2195) · Diversity Advocacy Council Scholarship

American Society for Clinical Laboratory Science
Alpha Mu Tau Scholarship, Attn: Joe Briden, AMTF Scholarship Coordinator, 7809 S. 21st Drive, Phoenix, AZ 85041-7736
Phone: 571-748-3770
Email: awards@ascls.org
http://www.ascls.org
Purpose: To assist minority students in becoming clinical laboratory scientists and clinical laboratory technicians.
Eligibility: Applicants must be minority students accepted to an NAACLS-accredited Clinical Laboratory Science/Medical Technology program or a Clinical Laboratory Technician/Medical Laboratory Technician program. They must also demonstrate financial need.

Target applicant(s): High school students. College students. Graduate school students. Adult students.
Amount: Varies.
Number of awards: 2.
Deadline: April 1.
How to apply: Applications are available online.
Exclusive: Visit www.UltimateScholarshipBook.com and enter code AM219523 for updates on this award.

(2196) · Dr. Ivy M. Parker Memorial Scholarship

Society of Women Engineers
130 East Randolph Street, Suite 3500, Chicago, IL 60601
Phone: 877-793-4636
Email: scholarships@swe.org
https://swe.org/scholarships/
Purpose: To aid female undergraduates who are majoring in engineering.
Eligibility: Applicants must be full-time students who are enrolled in an ABET-accredited engineering program. They must be rising juniors or seniors who have a GPA of 3.0 or higher on a four-point scale. Applicants cannot be currently receiving another scholarship awarded by the Society of Women Engineers (SWE), and they cannot be receiving full funding from another source (such as an employee reimbursement program or the U.S. military). Selection is based on academic merit and financial need.
Target applicant(s): College students. Adult students.
Minimum GPA: 3.0
Amount: $1,500.
Number of awards: 1.
Deadline: February 15.
How to apply: Applications are available online. An application form, official transcript and two letters of recommendation are required.
Exclusive: Visit www.UltimateScholarshipBook.com and enter code SO219623 for updates on this award.

(2197) · Dr. Juan Andrade, Jr. Scholarship

United States Hispanic Leadership Institute
431 S. Dearborn Street, Suite 1203, Chicago, IL 60605
Phone: 312-427-8683
http://www.ushli.org
Purpose: To support Hispanic students in pursuing post-secondary education.
Eligibility: Applicants must be enrolled or accepted for enrollment as a full-time student at an accredited educational institution in the U.S. Students must have demonstrated financial need and at least one parent of Hispanic ancestry. Applicants must submit letters of recommendation, grade transcripts, a resume and several essays.
Target applicant(s): High school students. College students. Adult students.
Amount: $500-$1,000.
Number of awards: Varies.
Deadline: November 30.
How to apply: Applications are available online.
Exclusive: Visit www.UltimateScholarshipBook.com and enter code UN219723 for updates on this award.

(2198) · Drs. James and Wanda Trefil Science Scholarship

Kosciuszko Foundation
15 East 65th Street, New York, NY 10021-6595
Phone: 212-734-2130

http://www.thekf.org
Purpose: To support American students of Polish descent.
Eligibility: Applicants must be U.S. citizens or legal permanent residents of Polish descent who are full-time undergraduate freshmen, sophomores or juniors at the time of application. Students must have a minimum GPA of 3.5 and be pursuing a major in physics, chemistry, biology, astronomy, earth science or another similar area.
Target applicant(s): College students. Adult students.
Minimum GPA: 3.5
Amount: $5,000.
Number of awards: 1.
Deadline: January 15.
How to apply: Applications are available online.
Exclusive: Visit www.UltimateScholarshipBook.com and enter code KO219823 for updates on this award.

(2199) · Edie Windsor Coding Scholarship

Lesbians Who Tech
Email: edie@lesbianswhotech.org
https://lesbianswhotech.org/codingscholarship/
Purpose: To inspire future generations of LGBTQ, technical women and non-binary individuals.
Eligibility: Applicants must identify as part of the LGBTQ, non-binary or transgender communities. Students must be interested in coding as a future career.
Target applicant(s): High school students. College students. Adult students.
Amount: Varies.
Number of awards: Varies.
Deadline: Varies.
How to apply: Applications are available online.
Exclusive: Visit www.UltimateScholarshipBook.com and enter code LE219923 for updates on this award.

(2200) · EDSA Diversity Scholarships

Landscape Architecture Foundation
1129 20th Street NW, Suite 202, Washington, DC 20036
Phone: 202-331-7070
Email: scholarships@lafoundation.org
https://www.lafoundation.org/what-we-do/scholarships
Purpose: To aid minority students of landscape architecture.
Eligibility: Applicants must be members of an ethnic, cultural or racial minority. They must be landscape architecture students who are in the final two years of their undergraduate degree program or who are graduate students of landscape architecture. Selection is based on the overall strength of the application.
Target applicant(s): College students. Graduate school students. Adult students.
Amount: $5,000.
Number of awards: 2.
Deadline: February 1.
How to apply: Applications are available online. An application form, personal essay, three work samples, two recommendation letters and an applicant photo are required.
Exclusive: Visit www.UltimateScholarshipBook.com and enter code LA220023 for updates on this award.

(2201) · Education Scholarship

Polish Roman Catholic Union of America
984 North Milwaukee Avenue, Chicago, IL 60642-9981

Phone: 800-772-8632
Email: scholarships@prcua.org
https://www.prcua.org/scholarships/
Purpose: To support students of the Polish American community in their higher education pursuits.
Eligibility: Applicants must have completed their freshman year of undergraduate studies and be sophomores, juniors and seniors enrolled full-time in undergraduate study or those students enrolled in graduate or professional degree programs. Students must be citizens of the United States or permanent residents with a minimum 3.0 GPA on a 4.0 scale or a minimum 4.0 on a 5.0 scale. An essay submission on a provided prompt is required.
Target applicant(s): College students. Graduate school students. Adult students.
Minimum GPA: 3.0
Amount: $500-$2,000.
Number of awards: Varies.
Deadline: June 1.
How to apply: Applications are available online.
Exclusive: Visit www.UltimateScholarshipBook.com and enter code PO220123 for updates on this award.

(2202) · Education Support Award

Patsy Takemoto Mink Education Foundation
P.O. Box 769, Granby, MA 01033
http://patsyminkfoundation.org
Purpose: To support low-income mothers in pursuing post-secondary education.
Eligibility: Applicants must be at least 17 years old. Selection is primarily based on demonstration of financial need, personal circumstances, educational and professional goals and community involvement.
Target applicant(s): High school students. College students. Adult students.
Amount: $5,000.
Number of awards: 5.
Deadline: August 1.
How to apply: Applications are available online.
Exclusive: Visit www.UltimateScholarshipBook.com and enter code PA220223 for updates on this award.

(2203) · Elizabeth and Sherman Asche Memorial Scholarship

Association on American Indian Affairs
Lisa Wyzlic, Director of Scholarship Programs, 966 Hungerford Drive, Suite 12-B, Rockville, MD 20850
Phone: 240-314-7155
Email: lw.aaia@indian-affairs.org
https://www.indian-affairs.org/whatwedo.html
Purpose: To provide financial assistance to American Indians who are seeking undergraduate or graduate degrees in public health or science.
Eligibility: Applicants must be American Indians who are studying full-time in public health or science programs. They must be full-time students and must not be enrolled in a technical or trade program or seminary. The scholarship is open to undergraduate and graduate students.
Target applicant(s): High school students. College students. Graduate school students. Adult students.
Minimum GPA: 2.5
Amount: $1,500.
Number of awards: Varies.

Deadline: June.
How to apply: Applications are available online.
Exclusive: Visit www.UltimateScholarshipBook.com and enter code AS220323 for updates on this award.

(2204) · ESA Foundation Scholarship Program

Entertainment Software Association Foundation
575 7th Street NW, Suite 300, Washington, DC 20004
Phone: 202-223-2400
Email: esafinfo@theesa.com
https://www.esafoundationscholars.com/how-to-apply.html
Purpose: To support female and minority students working on degrees toward a career in computer and video game arts.
Eligibility: Applicants must be female or minority students, U.S. citizens and current full-time college students or graduating high school seniors enrolled or accepted in a full-time program at a four-year college or university in the U.S. A minimum 2.75 GPA is required. Selection is based on the overall strength of the application.
Target applicant(s): High school students. College students. Adult students.
Minimum GPA: 2.75
Amount: $3,000.
Number of awards: Up to 30.
Deadline: April.
How to apply: Applications are available online.
Exclusive: Visit www.UltimateScholarshipBook.com and enter code EN220423 for updates on this award.

(2205) · Eugene and Elinor Kotur Scholarship Trust Fund

Ukrainian Fraternal Association
371 N. 9th Avenue, Scranton, PA 18504-2005
Phone: 570-342-0937
http://www.members.tripod.com/~ufa_home
Purpose: To support Ukrainian students.
Eligibility: Applicants must be in their sophomore year of college or higher at one of 30 participating schools. They must be of Ukrainian descent and have been members of the Ukrainian Fraternal Association for two years.
Target applicant(s): College students. Graduate school students. Adult students.
Amount: At least $1,000.
Number of awards: Varies.
Deadline: Varies.
How to apply: Applications are available by mail or phone.
Exclusive: Visit www.UltimateScholarshipBook.com and enter code UK220523 for updates on this award.

(2206) · Florence Young Memorial Scholarship

Association on American Indian Affairs
Lisa Wyzlic, Director of Scholarship Programs, 966 Hungerford Drive, Suite 12-B, Rockville, MD 20850
Phone: 240-314-7155
Email: lw.aaia@indian-affairs.org
https://www.indian-affairs.org/whatwedo.html
Purpose: To provide financial assistance to Native Americans who are working toward a master's degree in art, public health or law.
Eligibility: Applicants must be full-time students from the continental U.S. or Alaska.
Target applicant(s): Graduate school students. Adult students.

Amount: Varies.
Number of awards: Varies.
Deadline: May 31.
How to apply: Applications are available online.
Exclusive: Visit www.UltimateScholarshipBook.com and enter code AS220623 for updates on this award.

(2207) · Foundation Scholarships

CIRI Foundation
3600 San Jeronimo Drive, Suite 256, Anchorage, AK 99508-2870
Phone: 800-764-3382
Email: tcf@thecirifoundation.org
http://www.thecirifoundation.org
Purpose: To provide financial aid for Alaska Natives.
Eligibility: Applicants must be qualified Alaska Native beneficiaries who plan to attend or are currently attending undergraduate or graduate institutions. There are a number of awards based on field of study or career goal. Applicants must submit applications, proof of eligibility, reference letter, transcripts, purpose statements and proof of enrollment.
Target applicant(s): High school students. College students. Graduate school students. Adult students.
Amount: Up to $20,000.
Number of awards: Varies.
Scholarship may be renewable.
Deadline: June 1.
How to apply: Applications are available online.
Exclusive: Visit www.UltimateScholarshipBook.com and enter code CI220723 for updates on this award.

(2208) · Full Circle Scholarship

American Indian College Fund
8333 Greenwood Boulevard, Denver, CO 80221
Phone: 303-426-8900
https://collegefund.org/#n
Purpose: To support American Indian and Alaska Native students seeking undergraduate and graduate degrees.
Eligibility: Applicants must be enrolled full-time in a certificate, associate's, bachelor's or graduate program at an accredited tribal, public or private college or university. Students must be registered as an enrolled member of a federal or state recognized tribe or a descendant of at least one grandparent or parent who is an enrolled tribal member. Applicants must have a minimum 2.0 GPA.
Target applicant(s): College students. Graduate school students. Adult students.
Minimum GPA: 2.0
Amount: Varies.
Number of awards: Varies.
Deadline: May 31.
How to apply: Applications are available online.
Exclusive: Visit www.UltimateScholarshipBook.com and enter code AM220823 for updates on this award.

(2209) · GAHCC Foundation Scholarship

Hispanic Scholarship Consortium
314 E. Highland Mall Boulevard #103, Austin, TX 78752
Phone: 512-368-2956
https://www.hispanicscholar.org/
Purpose: To support Hispanic graduating seniors who are pursuing a degree in science, technology, engineering or mathematics.

Eligibility: Applicants must be enrolled full-time. A minimum GPA of 3.0 is required. Selection is based on the overall strength of the application.
Target applicant(s): High school students. College students. Adult students.
Minimum GPA: 3.0
Amount: $2,000.
Number of awards: 1.
Scholarship may be renewable.
Deadline: April 30.
How to apply: Applications are available online.
Exclusive: Visit www.UltimateScholarshipBook.com and enter code HI220923 for updates on this award.

(2210) · Gates Scholarship

Gates Foundation
P.O. Box 10500, Fairfax, VA 22031
Phone: 877-690-4677
https://www.thegatesscholarship.org/scholarship
Purpose: To provide outstanding minority students with opportunities to complete their undergraduate college educations.
Eligibility: Applicants must be U.S. citizens or permanent residents who are high school seniors with a minimum GPA of 3.3. Students must be African-American, American Indian/Alaska Native, Asian and Pacific Islander American and/or Hispanic American, plan to enroll in a four-year degree program and be Pell-eligible.
Target applicant(s): High school students.
Minimum GPA: 3.3
Amount: Varies.
Number of awards: 300.
Deadline: September 15.
How to apply: Applications are available online.
Exclusive: Visit www.UltimateScholarshipBook.com and enter code GA221023 for updates on this award.

(2211) · GEM MS Engineering Fellowship Program

National GEM Consortium
1430 Duke Street, Alexandria, VA 22314
Phone: 703-562-3646
Email: info@gemfellowship.org
http://www.gemfellowship.org
Purpose: To provide fellowships for minority engineering and computer science students pursuing master's degrees.
Eligibility: Applicants must be college seniors or graduate students majoring in engineering or computer science and be members of one of the following minority groups: African American, Native American or Latino or other Hispanic American. Students must also be U.S. citizens or permanent residents, have a minimum 2.8 GPA and agree to intern for two summers with a GEM employer.
Target applicant(s): College students. Graduate school students. Adult students.
Minimum GPA: 2.8
Amount: $8,000.
Number of awards: Varies.
Deadline: October 1.
How to apply: Applications are available online. The deadline for Part I is October 1, and the deadline for part II is November 13.
Exclusive: Visit www.UltimateScholarshipBook.com and enter code NA221123 for updates on this award.

(2212) · General Society of Mayflower Descendants (GSMD) Scholarship

General Society of Mayflower Descendants
P.O. Box 3297, Plymouth, MA 02361
Phone: 508-746-3188
Email: scholarships@themayflowersociety.org
https://www.themayflowersociety.org/blog/scholarships
Purpose: To assist high school seniors who are Mayflower descendants.
Eligibility: Applicants must plan to attend a four-year college or university or a two-year community college and must obtain a valid GSMD membership number. Recipients typically are in the top 10 percent of their class and score in the 75th percentile or higher on the SAT or ACT.
Target applicant(s): High school students.
Amount: $2,500-$5,000.
Number of awards: 3.
Deadline: March 15.
How to apply: Applications are available online.
Exclusive: Visit www.UltimateScholarshipBook.com and enter code GE221223 for updates on this award.

(2213) · Gentlemen Showcase

Network of Enlightened Women
1360 East Capitol Street NE, Washington, DC 20003
Phone: 423-838-4477
Email: info@enlightenedwomen.org
http://enlightenedwomen.org
Purpose: To recognize and honor young gentlemen across the country.
Eligibility: Individuals nominated must be at least 18 years of age and not more than 40 years of age. Nominees must be enrolled in undergraduate or graduate programs and provide a student email address.
Target applicant(s): High school students. College students. Graduate school students. Adult students.
Amount: $250-$500.
Number of awards: 4.
Deadline: January 30.
How to apply: Applications are available online.
Exclusive: Visit www.UltimateScholarshipBook.com and enter code NE221323 for updates on this award.

(2214) · George Choy Memorial/Gay Asian Pacific Alliance (GAPA) Scholarship

Horizons Foundation
550 Montgomery Street, Suite 700, San Francisco, CA 94111
Phone: 415-398-2333
Email: info@horizonsfoundation.org
https://www.horizonsfoundation.org/
Purpose: To assist Bay Area gay, lesbian, bisexual and transgender Asian and Pacific Islander graduating high school students.
Eligibility: Applicants should have at least 25 percent Asian/Pacific Islander ancestry, in the process of applying to or currently attending a college, university or vocational school and reside in one of the nine Bay Area counties (Alameda, Contra Costa, Marin, San Francisco, San Mateo, Santa Clara, Napa, Sonoma or Solano). Preference is given to those who are lesbian, gay, bisexual or transgender or who are involved in the LGBT community.
Target applicant(s): High school students. College students. Adult students.
Minimum GPA: 2.75
Amount: Up to $1,000.

Number of awards: Varies.
Deadline: June 6.
How to apply: Applications are available by phone.
Exclusive: Visit www.UltimateScholarshipBook.com and enter code HO221423 for updates on this award.

(2215) · Goldie Bateson Scholarship

Ladies Professional Golf Association
100 International Golf Drive, Daytona Beach, FL 32124-1092
Phone: 386-274-6200
Email: info@lpgafoundation.org
http://www.lpga.com/lpga-foundation/scholarships
Purpose: To support junior age females who play golf or have an interest in learning the game of golf.
Eligibility: Applicants must be between 7 and 17 years of age and have an interest in playing golf or be currently involved in golf. Students must reside within one of the LPGA T&CP Midwest Section States. Selection is based on the personal essay and letters of recommendation.
Target applicant(s): Junior high students or younger. High school students.
Amount: $250.
Number of awards: 10.
Deadline: February.
How to apply: Applications available online and include a personal essay and two letters of recommendation.
Exclusive: Visit www.UltimateScholarshipBook.com and enter code LA221523 for updates on this award.

(2216) · Google Generation Google Scholarship

Google Inc.
1600 Amphitheatre Parkway, Mountain View, CA 94043
https://buildyourfuture.withgoogle.com/scholarships/
Purpose: To encourage students who are aspiring computer scientists to become leaders in their field.
Eligibility: Applicants must either be a graduating high school senior or be currently enrolled as an undergraduate or graduate student. Students must be enrolled as computer science or computer engineering majors, exhibit strong leadership skills and demonstrate a passion for computer science and technology. Applicants must be from an underrepresented group in computer science such as African American, Hispanic, American Indian or Filipino/Native Hawaiian/Pacific Islander.
Target applicant(s): High school students. College students. Graduate school students. Adult students.
Amount: $10,000.
Number of awards: Varies.
Deadline: December (university), Varies (high school).
How to apply: Applications are available online.
Exclusive: Visit www.UltimateScholarshipBook.com and enter code GO221623 for updates on this award.

(2217) · Harriet Fitzgerald Scholarship

Sunflower Initiative
P.O. Box 378, Bedford, VA 24523
https://www.thesunflowerinitiative.com/scholarship/
Purpose: To support female students seeking post-secondary education.
Eligibility: Applicants must be female and planning to start her undergraduate education at a women's college in the following academic year. Women who have already completed a semester of college or more are not eligible. A minimum 3.7 GPA and either a SAT composite score of 1900 (old scoring through 2016) or 1350 (new scoring since 2016) OR an ACT composite score of 27 or higher with no single ACT score below 25 are required.
Target applicant(s): High school students.
Minimum GPA: 3.7
Amount: $10,000.
Number of awards: 1.
Deadline: February 1.
How to apply: Applications are available online.
Exclusive: Visit www.UltimateScholarshipBook.com and enter code SU221723 for updates on this award.

(2218) · Health Professions Pre-Graduate Scholarship Program

Indian Health Service
Scholarship Program Office, 5600 Fishers Lane, Mail Stop: OHR (11E53A), Rockville, MD 20857
Phone: 301-443-6197
Email: dawn.kelly@ihs.gov
http://www.ihs.gov
Purpose: To aid Native Americans and Alaska Natives who are enrolled in selected health-related pre-professional degree programs.
Eligibility: Applicants must be U.S. citizens who are enrolled in or accepted into a pre-medicine, pre-dentistry, pre-optometry, pre-podiatry or other health-related pre-professional degree program. Applicants must have plans to work in the Native American or Alaska Native community as a health care provider in the chosen field of study. Selection is based on academic achievement, recommendation letters and the applicant's stated career goals. Applicant must have a minimum 2.0 GPA.
Target applicant(s): High school students. College students. Adult students.
Minimum GPA: 2.0
Amount: Full tuition and fees.
Number of awards: Varies.
Scholarship may be renewable.
Deadline: Varies.
How to apply: Applications are available online. An application form, course curriculum outline, two recommendation forms, proof of Native American/Alaska Native status, an official transcript, proof of acceptance into an academic program and other supporting documents are required.
Exclusive: Visit www.UltimateScholarshipBook.com and enter code IN221823 for updates on this award.

(2219) · Health Professions Preparatory Scholarship Program

Indian Health Service
Scholarship Program Office, 5600 Fishers Lane, Mail Stop: OHR (11E53A), Rockville, MD 20857
Phone: 301-443-6197
Email: dawn.kelly@ihs.gov
http://www.ihs.gov
Purpose: To aid Native Americans and Alaska Natives who are preparing for careers in one of the health professions.
Eligibility: Applicants must be U.S. citizens accepted into or enrolled in a compensatory or pre-professional general education course of study at an accredited college or university. The applicant must be studying or have plans to study a subject that has been designated as a priority career category by the Indian Health Service. Applicants must plan to serve Native American or Alaska Native communities as a professional healthcare provider after completing the necessary training. Selection is based on academic achievement, recommendation letters and stated career goals.

Target applicant(s): College students. Adult students.
Minimum GPA: 2.0
Amount: Varies.
Number of awards: Varies.
Scholarship may be renewable.
Deadline: March.
How to apply: Applications are available online. An application form, two letters of recommendation, proof of Native American or Alaska Native status, an official transcript, proof of acceptance into a postsecondary educational program and other supporting documents are required.
Exclusive: Visit www.UltimateScholarshipBook.com and enter code IN221923 for updates on this award.

(2220) · Helene M. Overly Memorial Graduate Scholarship

Women's Transportation Seminar (WTS) International
1701 K Street NW, Suite 800, Washington, DC 20006
Phone: 202-955-5085
Email: membership@wtsinternational.org
https://www.wtsinternational.org/resources/scholarships
Purpose: To support women pursuing careers in the transportation industry with their higher education expenses.
Eligibility: Applicants must be women enrolled in graduate studies in transportation or the related fields of engineering, planning, finance or logistics. Selection is based on the applicant's academic record, transportation-related activities or job skills and specific transportation goals.
Target applicant(s): Graduate school students. Adult students.
Amount: $10,000.
Number of awards: 1.
Deadline: Varies.
How to apply: Applications are available through a local chapter.
Exclusive: Visit www.UltimateScholarshipBook.com and enter code WO222023 for updates on this award.

(2221) · Henry Salvatori Scholarship

Order Sons of Italy in America (OSIA)
219 E Street NE, Washington, DC 20002
Phone: 202-547-2900
Email: scholarships@osia.org
https://www.osia.org/sif
Purpose: To support students who demonstrate exceptional leadership, distinguished scholarship and respect for the principles upon which our nation was founded.
Eligibility: Applicants must be U.S. citizens of Italian descent who are graduating high school seniors who are planning to attend an undergraduate program at a four-year, accredited college or university for the upcoming fall semester. Students must write an essay as part of the application process.
Target applicant(s): High school students.
Amount: Varies.
Number of awards: 1.
Deadline: February 28.
How to apply: Applications are available online.
Exclusive: Visit www.UltimateScholarshipBook.com and enter code OR222123 for updates on this award.

(2222) · Herbert Lehman Education Fund Scholarship

NAACP Legal Defense and Educational Fund Inc.
40 Rector Street, 5th Floor, New York, NY 10006
Phone: 212-965-2200
Email: scholarships@naacpldf.org
http://www.naacpldf.org/scholarships
Purpose: To support African American students who are attending college for the first time.
Eligibility: Applicants must have a strong academic record and clear educational goals, and they must show leadership potential through involvement in school and extracurricular activities. Students must show good character through positive recommendations from teachers, employers or community representatives.
Target applicant(s): High school students. College students. Adult students.
Amount: $2,000.
Number of awards: Varies.
Scholarship may be renewable.
Deadline: April 1.
How to apply: Applications are available by sending a written request.
Exclusive: Visit www.UltimateScholarshipBook.com and enter code NA222223 for updates on this award.

(2223) · Higher Education Grant

Bureau of Indian Education
Tony L. Dearman, Director, 1849 C Street NW, Mailstop 4657
MIB, Washington, DC 20240
Phone: 202-208-6123
https://www.bie.edu/
Purpose: To assist American Indian and Alaska Native students obtaining their undergraduate degrees.
Eligibility: Applicants must be members of a tribe or at least one-quarter degree Indian blood descendants of members of an American Indian tribe, be accepted into a college or another similar institution that provides an associate's or bachelor's degrees and show financial need.
Target applicant(s): High school students. College students. Adult students.
Amount: Varies.
Number of awards: Varies.
Deadline: June 1.
How to apply: Applications are available through tribes.
Exclusive: Visit www.UltimateScholarshipBook.com and enter code BU222323 for updates on this award.

(2224) · Hispanic Heritage Youth Awards

Hispanic Heritage Awards Foundation
1001 Pennsylvania Avenue NW, Washington, DC 20004
Phone: 202-861-9797
Email: contact@hispanicheritageawards.org
http://hispanicheritage.org/
Purpose: To promote Hispanic excellence and recognize the contributions of Hispanic American youth.
Eligibility: Applicants must be high school seniors who are U.S. citizens or permanent residents, reside in Atlanta, Chicago, Dallas, Houston, Los Angeles, Miami, New York City, Philadelphia, Phoenix, San Diego, San Jose and Washington, DC and have Hispanic parentage (Hispanic parentage can be one parent of Mexican, Central American, Cuban, Puerto Rican, South American, Spanish or Caribbean Hispanic descent). Selection criteria include achievement in the applicant's discipline, involvement in community, ability to overcome adversity and character.

The disciplines are: Academic Excellence, Sports, the Arts, Literature/Journalism, Mathematics, Leadership/Community Service and Science and Technology.

Target applicant(s): High school students.

Minimum GPA: 3.0

Amount: Varies.

Number of awards: Varies.

Deadline: November 14.

How to apply: Applications are available by request.

Exclusive: Visit www.UltimateScholarshipBook.com and enter code HI222423 for updates on this award.

(2225) · Hispanic Scholarship Fund

Hispanic Scholarship Fund (HSF)

1411 W. 190th Street, Suite 700, Gardena, CA 90248

Phone: 877-473-4636

Email: info@hsf.net

https://www.hsf.net/

Purpose: To support students of Hispanic heritage.

Eligibility: Applicants must be high school seniors, entering college students or current college undergraduate or graduate students who are of Hispanic heritage and U.S. citizens or permanent residents. Students must have a GPA of 3.0 or higher and plan to enroll full-time in a degree program at a two- or four- year accredited institution in the U.S., Puerto Rico, the Virgin Islands or Guam in the upcoming academic year. Applicants must also apply for federal financial aid and be pursuing their first undergraduate or graduate degree.

Target applicant(s): High school students. College students. Graduate school students. Adult students.

Minimum GPA: 3.0

Amount: $500-$5,000.

Number of awards: Varies.

Deadline: February 14.

How to apply: Applications are available online.

Exclusive: Visit www.UltimateScholarshipBook.com and enter code HI222523 for updates on this award.

(2226) · Honeywell International Inc. Scholarships

Society of Women Engineers

130 East Randolph Street, Suite 3500, Chicago, IL 60601

Phone: 877-793-4636

Email: scholarships@swe.org

https://swe.org/scholarships/

Purpose: To aid female students planning to pursue undergraduate degrees in computer science and engineering.

Eligibility: Applicants must be female U.S. citizens. They must be rising undergraduate sophomores, juniors or seniors and must plan to major in computer science, computer engineering, electrical engineering, chemical engineering, manufacturing engineering, mechanical engineering, architectural engineering, aerospace engineering, industrial engineering or materials science and engineering. Applicants must demonstrate financial need. Selection is based on the overall strength of the application. Minimum 3.5 GPA required.

Target applicant(s): College students. Adult students.

Minimum GPA: 3.5

Amount: $5,000.

Number of awards: 3.

Deadline: February 15.

How to apply: Applications are available online. An application form and supporting documents are required.

Exclusive: Visit www.UltimateScholarshipBook.com and enter code SO222623 for updates on this award.

(2227) · Hopi Scholarship Program

Hopi Tribe Grants and Scholarship Program

P.O. Box 123, Kykotsmovi, AZ 86039

Phone: 800-762-9630

Email: heef@hopieducationfund.org

http://www.hopieducationfund.org

Purpose: To help Hopi students with academic achievement.

Eligibility: Applicants must be enrolled members of the Hopi tribe, be high school graduates or have earned a GED, have been accepted to a regionally accredited college and plan to attend full-time and have completed the Free Application for Federal Student Aid. Students must be in top 10 percent of their high school class or score 930 on the SAT or 21 on the ACT as entering freshmen; have a minimum 3.0 GPA as undergraduates or have a minimum 3.2 GPA as graduate, post graduate or professional degree students. Applications, statements of goals, financial needs analysis, proof of Hopi enrollment and transcripts are required.

Target applicant(s): High school students. College students. Graduate school students. Adult students.

Minimum GPA: 3.0 for undergraduate students, 3.2 for graduate students

Amount: $3,000.

Number of awards: Varies.

Deadline: July 15, October 15, December 15.

How to apply: Applications are available by mail.

Exclusive: Visit www.UltimateScholarshipBook.com and enter code HO222723 for updates on this award.

(2228) · Howard County PFLAG Academic Scholarship

PFLAG Columbia-Howard County, Maryland

Attention: Scholarship Committee, P.O. Box 1479, Columbia, MD 21044

Phone: 443-718-0474

Email: info@pflagmd.org

http://www.pflaghoco.org/

Purpose: To support outstanding gay, lesbian, bisexual and transgendered students and their straight allies.

Eligibility: Applicants must be Maryland residents who are attending or plan to attend an institution of higher learning during the upcoming academic year. They must not be receiving a scholarship or other assistance that pays their tuition in full. Prior Howard County PFLAG scholarship recipients may not apply.

Target applicant(s): High school students. College students. Adult students.

Amount: $2,000.

Number of awards: 1.

Deadline: May 31.

How to apply: Applications are available online. An application form, questionnaire, transcript and two letters of recommendation are required.

Exclusive: Visit www.UltimateScholarshipBook.com and enter code PF222823 for updates on this award.

(2229) · Hubertus W.V. Wellems Scholarship for Male Students

National Association for the Advancement of Colored People
c/o Poise Foundation, Two Gateway Center, Suite 1700, 603 Stanwix Street, Pittsburgh, PA 15222
Phone: 412-281-4967
Email: info@poisefdn.org
http://www.poisefoundation.org/scholarships-overview/
Purpose: To aid male students who are studying certain math and science subjects at the undergraduate and graduate levels.
Eligibility: Applicants must be U.S. citizens who are high school seniors, undergraduates or graduate students. They must be enrolled in or plan to enroll in a mathematics, chemistry, physics or engineering degree program at an accredited four-year institution of higher learning located in the U.S. Undergraduate applicants must be full-time students. High school seniors and undergraduate students must have a GPA of 2.5 or higher, and graduate students must have a GPA of 3.0 or higher. All applicants must demonstrate financial need. Selection is based on the overall strength of the application.
Target applicant(s): High school students. College students. Graduate school students. Adult students.
Minimum GPA: 2.5 for high school seniors and undergraduate students, 3.0 for graduate students
Amount: Up to $3,000.
Number of awards: 20-40.
Deadline: July 31.
How to apply: Applications are available online. An application form, personal essay, official transcript and two letters of recommendation are required.
Exclusive: Visit www.UltimateScholarshipBook.com and enter code NA222923 for updates on this award.

(2230) · Ida M. Pope Memorial Scholarship

Hawaii Community Foundation - Scholarships
827 Fort Street Mall, Honolulu, HI 96813
Phone: 888-731-3863
Email: scholarships@hcf-hawaii.org
https://www.hawaiicommunityfoundation.org/
Purpose: To assist female students of Hawaiian ancestry in obtaining higher education.
Eligibility: Applicants must attend an accredited college or university and have a GPA of 3.5 or higher. Students must also major in health, science, education, counseling or social work.
Target applicant(s): High school students. College students. Adult students.
Minimum GPA: 3.5
Amount: Varies.
Number of awards: Varies.
Deadline: January 31.
How to apply: To apply, register online, complete the online application and select the scholarships to which you wish to apply. In addition, mail the supporting materials: printed confirmation page from the online application, personal statement, copy of Student Aid Report (SAR) available at www.fafsa.ed.gov and official transcript.
Exclusive: Visit www.UltimateScholarshipBook.com and enter code HA223023 for updates on this award.

(2231) · Jackie Robinson Foundation Scholarship Program

Jackie Robinson Foundation
3 W. 35th Street, 11th Floor, New York, NY 10001
Phone: 212-290-8600
Email: general@jackierobinson.org
http://www.jackierobinson.org
Purpose: To help minority students who have shown leadership skills in their communities.
Eligibility: Applicants must be minority high school seniors with demonstrated financial need, leadership potential and academic achievement and who have already been accepted to a four-year college or university. Students must also be U.S. citizens and have a minimum SAT score of 1000 or composite ACT score of 22.
Target applicant(s): High school students.
Amount: Up to $28,000.
Number of awards: Varies.
Deadline: January 12.
How to apply: Applications are available online.
Exclusive: Visit www.UltimateScholarshipBook.com and enter code JA223123 for updates on this award.

(2232) · Japanese American Citizens League Entering Freshman Awards

Japanese American Citizens League (JACL)
1765 Sutter Street, San Francisco, CA 94115
Phone: 415-921-5225
Email: jacl@jacl.org
http://www.jacl.org
Purpose: To recognize and encourage education as a key to greater opportunities among JACL members.
Eligibility: Applicants must be National JACL members and must be planning to attend a college, university, trade school, business school or any other institution of higher learning at the undergraduate level. A personal statement, letter of recommendation, academic performance, work experience and community involvement will all be considered.
Target applicant(s): High school students.
Amount: Varies.
Number of awards: Varies.
Deadline: March 1.
How to apply: Applications are available through local JACL chapters, regional offices, National JACL Headquarters and website.
Exclusive: Visit www.UltimateScholarshipBook.com and enter code JA223223 for updates on this award.

(2233) · Japanese American Citizens League Graduate Awards

Japanese American Citizens League (JACL)
1765 Sutter Street, San Francisco, CA 94115
Phone: 415-921-5225
Email: jacl@jacl.org
http://www.jacl.org
Purpose: To provide monetary assistance for graduate studies to JACL members.
Eligibility: Applicants must be National JACL members and must attend a college or university at the graduate level. A personal statement, letter of recommendation, academic performance, work experience and community involvement are considered.
Target applicant(s): Graduate school students. Adult students.
Amount: Varies.

Number of awards: 7.

Deadline: April 1.

How to apply: Applications are available online and by sending a self-addressed, stamped envelope.

Exclusive: Visit www.UltimateScholarshipBook.com and enter code JA223323 for updates on this award.

(2234) · Japanese American Citizens League Law Scholarships

Japanese American Citizens League (JACL)

1765 Sutter Street, San Francisco, CA 94115

Phone: 415-921-5225

Email: jacl@jacl.org

http://www.jacl.org

Purpose: To help JACL members who are studying law.

Eligibility: Applicants must be National JACL members and must be studying law at a college or university. A personal statement, letter of recommendation, academic performance, work experience and community involvement will all be considered.

Target applicant(s): Graduate school students. Adult students.

Amount: Varies.

Number of awards: 4.

Deadline: April 1.

How to apply: Applications are available online and by sending a self-addressed, stamped envelope.

Exclusive: Visit www.UltimateScholarshipBook.com and enter code JA223423 for updates on this award.

(2235) · Japanese American Citizens League Undergraduate Awards

Japanese American Citizens League (JACL)

1765 Sutter Street, San Francisco, CA 94115

Phone: 415-921-5225

Email: jacl@jacl.org

http://www.jacl.org

Purpose: To recognize and encourage education as a key to greater opportunities among JACL members.

Eligibility: Applicants must be National JACL members and must be attending a college, university, trade school, business school or any other institution of higher learning at the undergraduate level. A personal statement, letter of recommendation, academic performance, work experience and community involvement will all be considered.

Target applicant(s): College students. Adult students.

Amount: Varies.

Number of awards: 8.

Deadline: April 1.

How to apply: Applications are available through local JACL chapters, regional offices, National JACL Headquarters and website.

Exclusive: Visit www.UltimateScholarshipBook.com and enter code JA223523 for updates on this award.

(2236) · Jeannette Rankin Women's Scholarship Fund

Jeannette Rankin Foundation

1 Huntington Road, Suite 701, Athens, GA 30606

Phone: 706-208-1211

Email: info@rankinfoundation.org

http://www.rankinfoundation.org

Purpose: To support the education of low-income women 35 years or older.

Eligibility: Applicants must be women 35 years of age or older, plan to obtain an undergraduate or vocational education and meet maximum household income guidelines.

Target applicant(s): College students. Adult students.

Amount: Varies.

Number of awards: Varies.

Scholarship may be renewable.

Deadline: February 26.

How to apply: Applications are available online or by sending a self-addressed and stamped envelope to the foundation.

Exclusive: Visit www.UltimateScholarshipBook.com and enter code JE223623 for updates on this award.

(2237) · Judith Resnik Memorial Scholarship

Society of Women Engineers

130 East Randolph Street, Suite 3500, Chicago, IL 60601

Phone: 877-793-4636

Email: scholarships@swe.org

https://swe.org/scholarships/

Purpose: To help female undergraduates who are majoring in astronautical, aeronautical or aerospace engineering.

Eligibility: Applicants must be rising undergraduate sophomores, juniors or seniors and have a GPA of 3.0 or higher on a four-point scale. They must be enrolled in an ABET-accredited degree program in aeronautical engineering, aerospace engineering or astronautical engineering. They cannot be receiving a renewable scholarship from the Society of Women Engineers. Applicants who are receiving full funding from another source (such as the U.S. military or an employee reimbursement plan) are ineligible. Selection is based on the overall strength of the application.

Target applicant(s): College students. Adult students.

Minimum GPA: 3.0

Amount: $4,000.

Number of awards: 1.

Deadline: February 15; May 1 (freshmen).

How to apply: Applications are available online. An application form, official transcript and two recommendation letters are required.

Exclusive: Visit www.UltimateScholarshipBook.com and enter code SO223723 for updates on this award.

(2238) · Julianne Malveaux Scholarship

National Association of Negro Business and Professional Women's Clubs Inc.

1806 New Hampshire Avenue NW, Washington, DC 20009-3298

Phone: 202-483-4206

Email: info@nanbpwc.org

http://www.nanbpwc.org

Purpose: To award scholarships to college students majoring in journalism, economics or a related field.

Eligibility: Applicants must be enrolled as sophomores or juniors at an accredited college or university and have a minimum 3.0 GPA. Students may major in related fields such as public policy or creative writing.

Target applicant(s): College students. Adult students.

Minimum GPA: 3.0

Amount: Varies.

Number of awards: Varies.

Deadline: March 1.

How to apply: Applications are available online.

Exclusive: Visit www.UltimateScholarshipBook.com and enter code NA223823 for updates on this award.

(2239) · Kenneth W. Payne Student Prize

Association for Queer Anthropology (AQA)
Email: payne.prize@gmail.com
http://queeranthro.org/awards/the-kenneth-w-payne-student-prize/
Purpose: To encourage LGBT students interested in any of the four fields of anthropology.
Eligibility: Applicants must undergraduates or graduate students who are members of the LGBT community. Students must be studying any of the four fields of anthropology. Research papers as well as visual media are eligible for submission for this competition.
Target applicant(s): College students. Graduate school students. Adult students.
Amount: $500.
Number of awards: 1.
Deadline: June 1.
How to apply: Applications are available online.
Exclusive: Visit www.UltimateScholarshipBook.com and enter code AS223923 for updates on this award.

(2240) · Knights of Lithuania Scholarship Program

Knights of Lithuania Scholarship Program
c/o Mikalina Tambasco, Committee Chair, 14 Pine Avenue, Johnstown, NY 12095
Phone: 518-705-1165
Email: mikalina@hotmail.com
http://knightsoflithuania.com/scholarship/
Purpose: To assist Lithuanian-Americans in obtaining higher education.
Eligibility: Applicants must be members of the Knights of Lithuania for at least two years. They must receive recommendations from their council president or vice president, a pastor or spiritual adviser and a former teacher in addition to a separate character reference.
Target applicant(s): High school students. College students. Graduate school students. Adult students.
Amount: Varies.
Number of awards: Varies.
Deadline: June 16.
How to apply: Applications are available online.
Exclusive: Visit www.UltimateScholarshipBook.com and enter code KN224023 for updates on this award.

(2241) · Korean Ancestry Grant

William Orr Dingwall Foundation
P.O. Box 57088, Washington, DC 20037
Email: kag@dingwallfoundation.org
http://www.dingwallfoundation.org
Purpose: To aid students of Asian ancestry.
Eligibility: Applicants must be of Asian ancestry and have at least one Asian grandparent. They must be entering or current undergraduate students. Preference will be given to applicants of Korean ancestry. Selection is based on the overall strength of the application.
Target applicant(s): High school students. College students. Adult students.
Amount: Up to $10,000.
Number of awards: At least 7.
Scholarship may be renewable.
Deadline: April 1.
How to apply: Applications are available online. An application form, official transcript, personal statement and two recommendation letters are required.

Exclusive: Visit www.UltimateScholarshipBook.com and enter code WI224123 for updates on this award.

(2242) · LAGRANT Scholarship Program

LAGRANT Foundation
633 W. 5th Street, 48th Floor, Los Angeles, CA 90071
Phone: 323-469-8680
http://www.lagrantfoundation.org
Purpose: To support minority students who are seeking degrees in advertising, graphic design, marketing or public relations.
Eligibility: Applicants must be African American/Black, Asian American/Pacific Islander, Hispanic/Latino or Native American/Alaskan Native. Students must be U.S. citizens, permanent residents, AB-540 students or DACA recipients. Applicants must be full-time students at an accredited four-year institution in the U.S. A minimum 3.0 GPA or higher is required. Students must submit an essay with their application.
Target applicant(s): College students. Graduate school students. Adult students.
Minimum GPA: 3.0
Amount: $2,500-$3,750.
Number of awards: 50.
Deadline: February 28.
How to apply: Applications are available online.
Exclusive: Visit www.UltimateScholarshipBook.com and enter code LA224223 for updates on this award.

(2243) · Larry Whiteside Scholarship

National Association of Black Journalists
1100 Knight Hall, Suite 3100, College Park, MD 20742
Phone: 301-405-7520
Email: iwashington@nabj.org
https://nabjonline.org/student-services/
Purpose: To assist students who are planning for careers in sports journalism.
Eligibility: Applicants must be student members of the National Association of Black Journalists (NABJ). They must be graduate students or rising undergraduate juniors or seniors at an accredited four-year institution who are planning to pursue careers in sports journalism. They must be majoring in journalism or communications or must have demonstrated an interest in journalism by working for a media outlet. They must have a major GPA of 2.5 or higher. Selection is based on the overall strength of the application.
Target applicant(s): College students. Graduate school students. Adult students.
Minimum GPA: 2.5
Amount: $3,000.
Number of awards: 1.
Deadline: December 31.
How to apply: Applications are available online. An application form, resume, official transcript, personal essay, three writing samples and three references are required.
Exclusive: Visit www.UltimateScholarshipBook.com and enter code NA224323 for updates on this award.

(2244) · Lillian Moller Gilbreth Memorial Scholarship

Society of Women Engineers
130 East Randolph Street, Suite 3500, Chicago, IL 60601
Phone: 877-793-4636
Email: scholarships@swe.org
https://swe.org/scholarships/

Purpose: To aid female students who are majoring in engineering.
Eligibility: Applicants must be rising undergraduate juniors or seniors who are enrolled in an ABET-accredited engineering degree program. They must have a GPA of 3.0 or higher on a four-point scale. Applicants cannot be receiving full academic funding from another source, and they cannot be receiving another renewable SWE scholarship at the time of award disbursement. Selection is based on the overall strength of the application.
Target applicant(s): College students. Adult students.
Minimum GPA: 3.0
Amount: $14,500.
Number of awards: 1.
Scholarship may be renewable.
Deadline: February 15.
How to apply: Applications are available online. An application form, official transcript and two letters of recommendation are required.
Exclusive: Visit www.UltimateScholarshipBook.com and enter code SO224423 for updates on this award.

(2245) · Live Your Dream Awards Program
Soroptimist International of the Americas
1709 Spruce Street, Philadelphia, PA 19103
Phone: 215-893-9000
Email: siahq@soroptimist.org
https://www.soroptimist.org/our-work/live-your-dream-awards/
Purpose: To assist women entering or re-entering the workforce with educational and skills training support.
Eligibility: Applicants must be attending or been accepted by a vocational/skills training program or an undergraduate degree program. Applicants must be the women heads of household who provide the primary source of financial support for their families and demonstrate financial need. Applicants must submit their application to the appropriate regional office.
Target applicant(s): High school students. College students. Adult students.
Amount: Up to $16,000.
Number of awards: Varies.
Deadline: November 15.
How to apply: Applications are available online.
Exclusive: Visit www.UltimateScholarshipBook.com and enter code SO224523 for updates on this award.

(2246) · Lockheed Martin Corporation Scholarship
Society of Women Engineers
130 East Randolph Street, Suite 3500, Chicago, IL 60601
Phone: 877-793-4636
Email: scholarships@swe.org
https://swe.org/scholarships/
Purpose: To aid female students who are planning to pursue higher education in engineering.
Eligibility: Applicants must be undergraduate students who are majoring in computer science, computer engineering, software engineering or electrical engineering. Students must have a minimum 3.2 GPA. Selection is based on the overall strength of the application.
Target applicant(s): College students. Adult students.
Minimum GPA: 3.2
Amount: $2,000.
Number of awards: 8.
Deadline: February 15.
How to apply: Applications are available online. An application form and supporting materials are required.

Exclusive: Visit www.UltimateScholarshipBook.com and enter code SO224623 for updates on this award.

(2247) · Louise Moritz Molitoris Leadership Scholarship for Undergraduates
Women's Transportation Seminar (WTS) International
1701 K Street NW, Suite 800, Washington, DC 20006
Phone: 202-955-5085
Email: membership@wtsinternational.org
https://www.wtsinternational.org/resources/scholarships
Purpose: To aid female undergraduates who are pursuing transportation-related degrees.
Eligibility: Applicants must be currently enrolled in a transportation-related degree program, have a GPA of 3.0 or higher and have plans to pursue a career in the field of transportation. Selection is based on academic merit, proven leadership in transportation-related activities and stated career goals.
Target applicant(s): College students. Adult students.
Minimum GPA: 3.0
Amount: $5,000.
Number of awards: 1.
Deadline: Varies.
How to apply: Applications are available from local WTS chapters by request. An application form and supporting materials are required.
Exclusive: Visit www.UltimateScholarshipBook.com and enter code WO224723 for updates on this award.

(2248) · Lucy Kasparian Aharonian Scholarship
Armenian International Women's Association
65 Main Street, #3A, Watertown, MA 02472
Phone: 617-926-0171
Email: aiwainc@aol.com
http://aiwainternational.org/
Purpose: To aid female students of Armenian descent who are studying selected subjects.
Eligibility: Applicants must be full-time undergraduate juniors, undergraduate seniors or graduate students who are enrolled at an accredited postsecondary institution. They must be pursuing a degree in architecture, computer science, engineering, mathematics or technology. Selection is based on academic merit and financial need.
Target applicant(s): College students. Graduate school students. Adult students.
Amount: $1,000.
Number of awards: 1.
Deadline: April 19.
How to apply: Applications are available online. An application form and supporting materials are required.
Exclusive: Visit www.UltimateScholarshipBook.com and enter code AR224823 for updates on this award.

(2249) · LULAC General Awards
League of United Latin American Citizens
1133 19th Street NW, Suite 1000, Washington, DC 20036
Phone: 202-835-9646
Email: scholarships@lnesc.org
https://www.lnesc.org
Purpose: To provide assistance to Latino students who are seeking or plan to seek degrees.
Eligibility: Students must have applied to or be enrolled in a two- or four-year college or graduate school and be U.S. citizens or legal

residents. Grades and academic achievement may be considered, but emphasis is placed on motivation, sincerity and integrity as demonstrated by the interview and essay.

Target applicant(s): High school students. College students. Graduate school students. Adult students.

Amount: $250-$1,000.

Number of awards: Varies.

Deadline: March 31.

How to apply: Applications are available online.

Exclusive: Visit www.UltimateScholarshipBook.com and enter code LE224923 for updates on this award.

(2250) · LULAC Honors Awards

League of United Latin American Citizens
1133 19th Street NW, Suite 1000, Washington, DC 20036
Phone: 202-835-9646
Email: scholarships@lnesc.org
https://www.lnesc.org

Purpose: To provide assistance to Latino students of all levels of education.

Eligibility: Applicants must be U.S. citizens or legal residents, have applied to or attend a college or graduate school and have a GPA of 3.0 or better. Applicants who are entering freshmen must also have an ACT score of 23 or higher or an SAT score of 1100 or higher.

Target applicant(s): High school students. College students. Graduate school students. Adult students.

Minimum GPA: 3.0

Amount: $500-$2,000.

Number of awards: Varies.

Deadline: March 31.

How to apply: Applications are available from LULAC.

Exclusive: Visit www.UltimateScholarshipBook.com and enter code LE225023 for updates on this award.

(2251) · MAES Scholarship Program

Society of Mexican American Engineers and Scientists Inc. (MAES)
711 W. Bay Area Boulevard, Suite #206, Webster, TX 77598-4051
Phone: 281-557-3677
Email: execdir@maes-natl.org
http://mymaes.org/programs/

Purpose: To assist Hispanic students in the fields of science and engineering.

Eligibility: Applicants must be current Hispanic MAES student members who are full-time undergraduate and graduate students in an accredited U.S. college or university majoring in science or engineering. Community college applicants must be enrolled in majors that are transferable to a four-year institution offering bachelor's degrees. There are various scholarships in the program. Some sponsors require students to be U.S. citizens or permanent residents. Awards are based on financial need, academic achievement, personal qualities, strengths and leadership abilities. Applicants should submit applications, financial information, recommendations and transcripts.

Target applicant(s): High school students. College students. Graduate school students. Adult students.

Amount: Varies.

Number of awards: Varies.

Deadline: April 30.

How to apply: Applications are available online.

Exclusive: Visit www.UltimateScholarshipBook.com and enter code SO225123 for updates on this award.

(2252) · MagellanTV Women in STEM Scholarship

MagellanTV LLC
415 Mission Street, San Francisco, CA 94105
Email: connect@magellantv.com
https://www.magellantv.com/scholarships

Purpose: To support female students in pursuit of education in the STEM (Science, Technology, Engineering, Mathematics) fields.

Eligibility: Applicants must be females or identify as females who are 18 years of age or older and U.S. citizens or permanent legal residents of the United States. Students must be accepted to or enrolled as a full-time student at an accredited college or university with a minimum 3.0 GPA. An essay or video submission on a provided prompt is required.

Target applicant(s): High school students. College students. Graduate school students. Adult students.

Minimum GPA: 3.0

Amount: $1,000.

Number of awards: 5.

Deadline: September 1.

How to apply: Applications are available online.

Exclusive: Visit www.UltimateScholarshipBook.com and enter code MA225223 for updates on this award.

(2253) · Malcolm X Scholarship for Exceptional Courage

United Negro College Fund (UNCF)
1805 7th Street NW, Washington, DC 20001
Phone: 800-331-2244
https://scholarships.uncf.org/

Purpose: To assist students who attend UNCF member colleges and universities and have overcome extreme circumstances and hardships.

Eligibility: Applicants must be African American students, have a minimum 2.5 GPA, complete the Free Application for Federal Student Aid (FAFSA) and have unmet financial need that is verified by the college or university financial aid office. Students are encouraged to complete the UNCF General Scholarship application to be matched with scholarships for which they meet the criteria. Academic excellence and leadership on campus and in the community are also required.

Target applicant(s): College students. Adult students.

Minimum GPA: 2.5

Amount: $4,000.

Number of awards: Varies.

Deadline: October.

How to apply: Applications are available online.

Exclusive: Visit www.UltimateScholarshipBook.com and enter code UN225323 for updates on this award.

(2254) · MALDEF Law School Scholarship

Mexican American Legal Defense and Educational Fund
634 South Spring Street, Los Angeles, CA 90014
Phone: 213-629-2512
Email: lawscholarships@maldef.org
http://maldef.org

Purpose: To support law school students in funding their education.

Eligibility: Applicants must be enrolled full-time at an accredited U.S. law school. Selection is primarily based on demonstration of academic achievement, extracurricular involvement, financial need and commitment to the advancement of Latino civil rights. Students must submit transcripts, letters of recommendation and a personal statement.

Target applicant(s): College students. Graduate school students. Adult students.

Amount: $5,000.
Number of awards: Varies.
Deadline: February 26.
How to apply: Applications are available online.
Exclusive: Visit www.UltimateScholarshipBook.com and enter code ME225423 for updates on this award.

(2255) · Marcus Garvey Scholarship

Malcolm Frierson Foundation
P.O. Box 271221, Flower Mound, TX 75027
Email: mfrierson@gmail.com
https://www.malcolmfrierson.com/
Purpose: To encourage students who identify as being of African descent and who demonstrate leadership and service.
Eligibility: Applicants must identify as being of African descent and plan on enrolling as a first-time student at an accredited U.S. college or university. Students must have a minimum high school GPA of 3.0 and demonstrate leadership and commitment to service.
Target applicant(s): High school students. College students. Adult students.
Minimum GPA: 3.0
Amount: $1,000.
Number of awards: 1.
Deadline: July 1.
How to apply: Applications are available online.
Exclusive: Visit www.UltimateScholarshipBook.com and enter code MA225523 for updates on this award.

(2256) · Margaret McNamara Education Grants

Margaret Mcnamara Memorial Fund
Margaret McNamara Education Grants, 1818 H Street NW, MSN J2-202, Washington, DC 20433
https://www.mmeg.org/
Purpose: To provide financial assistance to women from developing countries who are currently studying to earn a undergraduate or graduate degree in the U.S. or Canada.
Eligibility: Applicants must be citizens of low or middle income country, have a proven track record of professional or volunteer services towards improving well-being of women and children and be U.S. or Canadian residents at the time of application. Students must be at least 25 years of age.
Target applicant(s): College students. Graduate school students. Adult students.
Amount: $4,000-$12,000.
Number of awards: Varies.
Deadline: January 15.
How to apply: Applications are available online.
Exclusive: Visit www.UltimateScholarshipBook.com and enter code MA225623 for updates on this award.

(2257) · Marilynn Smith Scholarship

Ladies Professional Golf Association
100 International Golf Drive, Daytona Beach, FL 32124-1092
Phone: 386-274-6200
Email: info@lpgafoundation.org
http://www.lpga.com/lpga-foundation/scholarships
Purpose: To support female high school senior golf participants who wish to play competitive golf in college.
Eligibility: Applicants must have played at least 50 percent of their high school team's schedule or played competitive junior golf for the past two years. Students must also be a U.S. citizen or legal resident, have a 3.2 GPA or higher, be accepted to attend a college or university and plan on playing competitive golf while attending college. Selection is based on the personal essay, letters of reference and financial need.
Target applicant(s): High school students.
Minimum GPA: 3.2
Amount: $5,000.
Number of awards: 5.
Deadline: April.
How to apply: Applications are available online and must include the official application form, three letters of reference, official high school transcript and the personal essay.
Exclusive: Visit www.UltimateScholarshipBook.com and enter code LA225723 for updates on this award.

(2258) · Mark Ando and Ito Family Scholarship

Far West Athletic Trainers' Association/District 8
Ned Bergert, Committee Chair
Phone: 714-501-3858
Email: nhbergert@gmail.com
http://www.fwatad8.org/
Purpose: To aid students of Asian descent in California, Hawaii and Nevada who are pursuing higher education in athletic training.
Eligibility: Applicants must be District 8 student members of the National Athletic Trainers' Association (NATA) who are of Asian descent. They must be enrolled in an undergraduate- or graduate-level athletic training program. Community college applicants and all other applicants must have a GPA of 3.2 or higher on a four-point scale. Non-community college undergraduates must be sponsored by a certified athletic trainer and must have junior standing. All applicants must have plans to pursue a career in athletic training. Selection is based on academic merit, extracurricular activities, leadership potential and athletic training achievement.
Target applicant(s): College students. Graduate school students. Adult students.
Minimum GPA: 3.2
Amount: Varies.
Number of awards: Varies.
Deadline: May 15.
How to apply: Applications are available online. An application form, an official transcript and a personal essay are required.
Exclusive: Visit www.UltimateScholarshipBook.com and enter code FA225823 for updates on this award.

(2259) · Mary Gunther Memorial Scholarship

Society of Women Engineers
130 East Randolph Street, Suite 3500, Chicago, IL 60601
Phone: 877-793-4636
Email: scholarships@swe.org
https://swe.org/scholarships/
Purpose: To aid students who plan to major in engineering.
Eligibility: Applicants must be female rising undergraduate freshmen, sophomores, juniors or seniors who intend to major in engineering at an ABET-accredited school. They must be full-time students who have a GPA of 3.5 or higher on a four-point scale. Preference will be given to students majoring in architectural engineering or environmental engineering. Selection is based on the overall strength of the application.
Target applicant(s): High school students. College students. Adult students.
Minimum GPA: 3.5
Amount: $3,000.

Number of awards: 4.
Deadline: February 15; May 1.
How to apply: Applications are available online. An application form, transcript, proof of college acceptance and two recommendation letters are required.
Exclusive: Visit www.UltimateScholarshipBook.com and enter code SO225923 for updates on this award.

(2260) · Mary Quan Moy Ing Memorial Scholarship

Asian American Journalists Association
1301 K Street, NW, 300W, 3rd Floor, Washington, DC 20005
https://www.aaja.org/news-and-resources/scholarships-internships/
Purpose: Monetary assistance is awarded to a high school senior pursuing college studies that lead to a journalism career.
Eligibility: Applicants must be high school seniors intending to major in journalism. Applicants must also demonstrate a commitment to the field of journalism, sensitivity to Asian American issues as demonstrated by community involvement, journalistic ability, scholastic ability and financial need.
Target applicant(s): High school students.
Amount: $2,000.
Number of awards: 1.
Deadline: April 21.
How to apply: Applications are available online.
Exclusive: Visit www.UltimateScholarshipBook.com and enter code AS226023 for updates on this award.

(2261) · Mary R. Norton Memorial Scholarship Award for Women

ASTM International
100 Barr Harbor Drive, P.O. Box C700, West Conshohocken, PA 19428-2959
Phone: 610-832-9585
Email: awards@astm.org
https://www.astm.org/memstudent23.html
Purpose: To aid female students who are pursuing graduate studies in materials science or physical metallurgy.
Eligibility: Applicants must be full-time undergraduate seniors or first-year graduate students. They must be enrolled in or planning to enroll in a graduate program in physical metallurgy or materials science, with an emphasis on the relationship between properties and microstructures. Selection is based on faculty recommendation and personal statement.
Target applicant(s): College students. Graduate school students. Adult students.
Amount: $1,000.
Number of awards: 1.
Deadline: Varies.
How to apply: Applications are available online. An application form, one faculty recommendation, personal statement and transcripts are required.
Exclusive: Visit www.UltimateScholarshipBook.com and enter code AS226123 for updates on this award.

(2262) · Mas Family Scholarships

Jorge Mas Canosa Freedom Foundation
Attn: Mas Family Scholarships, P.O. Box 14-1898, Coral Gables, FL 33114-1898
Phone: 305-507-7323
Email: jmcff@jmcff.org
http://jmcff.org/

Purpose: To aid undergraduate and graduate students of Cuban descent who are studying selected subjects.
Eligibility: Applicants must be majoring in or have plans to major in business, communications, economics, engineering, international relations or journalism. They must demonstrate leadership potential and a commitment to success in a democratic, free enterprise society. Selection is based on academic merit, personal essay, leadership ability, professional potential and character.
Target applicant(s): High school students. College students. Graduate school students. Adult students.
Minimum GPA: 3.5
Amount: Varies.
Number of awards: Varies.
Scholarship may be renewable.
Deadline: February 19.
How to apply: Applications are available online. An application form, official transcript, SAT scores, personal essay, three recommendation forms, proof of Cuban descent, proof of college acceptance (for incoming freshmen only), cost of tuition statement and statement of financial need are required.
Exclusive: Visit www.UltimateScholarshipBook.com and enter code JO226223 for updates on this award.

(2263) · Maureen L. and Howard N. Blitman, P.E., Scholarship

National Society of Professional Engineers
1420 King Street, Alexandria, VA 22314-2794
Phone: 703-684-2885
Email: students@nspe.org
https://www.nspe.org/resources/students/scholarships
Purpose: To encourage minority students to pursue careers in engineering.
Eligibility: Applicants must be African-American, Hispanic or Native American high school seniors who have been accepted into an accredited engineering program at a four-year institution. Students are evaluated based on academic achievement, community involvement and recommendations and must have a minimum 3.5 GPA.
Target applicant(s): High school students.
Minimum GPA: 3.5
Amount: $5,000.
Number of awards: 1.
Deadline: April 1.
How to apply: Applications are available online.
Exclusive: Visit www.UltimateScholarshipBook.com and enter code NA226323 for updates on this award.

(2264) · MCCA Lloyd M. Johnson, Jr. Scholarship Program

Minority Corporate Counsel Association (MCCA)
1111 Pennsylvania Avenue, NW, Washington, DC 20004
Phone: 202-739-5901
Email: contactus@applyists.com
http://www.mcca.com/resources/scholarship-program/
Purpose: To support first-year entering law students.
Eligibility: Applicants must be diverse students entering their first year of law school full-time at an accredited institution. They must have a GPA of at least 3.2 and demonstrate financial need.
Target applicant(s): College students. Graduate school students. Adult students.
Minimum GPA: 3.2

Amount: $10,000.
Number of awards: Up to 10.
Scholarship may be renewable.
Deadline: June 1.
How to apply: Applications are available online.
Exclusive: Visit www.UltimateScholarshipBook.com and enter code MI226423 for updates on this award.

(2265) · Medicus Student Exchange

Swiss Benevolent Society of New York
Scholarship Committee, 500 Fifth Avenue, Room 1800, New York, NY 10110
Email: scholarship@sbsny.org
https://www.sbsny.org/
Purpose: To provide need and merit-based scholarships for students from Swiss-American backgrounds.
Eligibility: Applicants or one of their parents must be a Swiss national. The Medicus grant for study in Switzerland is only open to U.S. residents and is a need-based award. Applicants must be college juniors or seniors or graduate-level students accepted to a Swiss university or the Federal Institute of Technology.
Target applicant(s): College students. Graduate school students. Adult students.
Amount: Varies.
Number of awards: Varies.
Deadline: March 31.
How to apply: Applications are available online.
Exclusive: Visit www.UltimateScholarshipBook.com and enter code SW226523 for updates on this award.

(2266) · Michael Jackson Scholarship

United Negro College Fund (UNCF)
1805 7th Street NW, Washington, DC 20001
Phone: 800-331-2244
https://scholarships.uncf.org/
Purpose: To assist students majoring in communications, English or performing arts.
Eligibility: Applicants must be African American students at a UNCF member college or university majoring in communications, English or performing arts. Applicants must have a GPA of at least 3.0 and demonstrate financial need.
Target applicant(s): High school students. College students. Adult students.
Minimum GPA: 3.0
Amount: Up to $5,000.
Number of awards: Varies.
Deadline: October.
How to apply: Applications are available online.
Exclusive: Visit www.UltimateScholarshipBook.com and enter code UN226623 for updates on this award.

(2267) · Minority Affairs Committee Award for Outstanding Scholastic Achievement

American Institute of Chemical Engineers - (AIChE)
120 Wall Street, Floor 23, New York, NY 10005-4020
Phone: 800-242-4363
Email: awards@aiche.org
https://www.aiche.org/community/awards
Purpose: Recognizes outstanding achievements by a chemical engineering student who serves as a role model for minority students.

Eligibility: Applicants must be ethnic minorities, major in chemical engineering and be undergraduate students.
Target applicant(s): College students. Adult students.
Amount: $1,000.
Number of awards: 10.
Deadline: July 15.
How to apply: Applications are available online or by telephone or written request.
Exclusive: Visit www.UltimateScholarshipBook.com and enter code AM226723 for updates on this award.

(2268) · Minority Scholarship

National Strength and Conditioning Association (NSCA)
Foundation
1885 Bob Johnson Drive, Colorado Springs, CO 80906
Phone: 800-815-6826
http://www.nsca.com/foundation/
Purpose: To encourage minorities to enter the field of strength and conditioning.
Eligibility: Applicants must be African American, Hispanic, Asian American or Native American students working toward a graduate degree related to strength and conditioning. Students must be NSCA members for one year before applying and be pursuing careers in strength and conditioning. Applications are evaluated based on grades, courses, experience, honors, recommendations and involvement in the community and with NSCA.
Target applicant(s): High school students. College students. Graduate school students. Adult students.
Amount: $1,500.
Number of awards: Varies.
Deadline: October 15.
How to apply: Applications are available with membership.
Exclusive: Visit www.UltimateScholarshipBook.com and enter code NA226823 for updates on this award.

(2269) · Minority Scholarship Award for Physical Therapy Students

American Physical Therapy Association
1111 North Fairfax Street, Alexandria, VA 22314
Phone: 703-684-2782
Email: honorsandawards@apta.org
https://www.apta.org/for-students/scholarships-awards
Purpose: To aid minority physical therapy students.
Eligibility: Applicants must be U.S. citizens or legal permanent residents. They must be African-American, Hispanic, Native American, Pacific Islander, Native Hawaiian or Alaska Native. They must be in the final year of an accredited or developing professional physical therapist program at the time of award disbursement. Students must demonstrate academic excellence, service to minority affairs and career potential. Selection is based on the overall strength of the application.
Target applicant(s): Graduate school students. Adult students.
Amount: Varies.
Number of awards: Varies.
Deadline: December 1.
How to apply: Applications are available online. An application form, official transcript, personal essay and three letters of reference are required.
Exclusive: Visit www.UltimateScholarshipBook.com and enter code AM226923 for updates on this award.

(2270) · Minority Scholarship Awards for College Students

American Institute of Chemical Engineers - (AIChE)
120 Wall Street, Floor 23, New York, NY 10005-4020
Phone: 800-242-4363
Email: awards@aiche.org
https://www.aiche.org/community/awards
Purpose: To aid minority students who are majoring in chemical engineering.
Eligibility: Applicants must be members of a minority group that is underrepresented in the field of chemical engineering (African-American, Latino, Native American, Alaska Native or Pacific Islander). They must be student members of the American Institute of Chemical Engineers (AIChE) and must be undergraduates who are majoring in chemical engineering. Selection is based on academic merit, stated career goals, AIChE participation and financial need.
Target applicant(s): College students. Adult students.
Amount: $1,000.
Number of awards: Varies.
Deadline: July 15.
How to apply: Applications are available online. An application form and supporting materials are required.
Exclusive: Visit www.UltimateScholarshipBook.com and enter code AM227023 for updates on this award.

(2271) · Minority Scholarship Awards for Incoming College Freshmen

American Institute of Chemical Engineers - (AIChE)
120 Wall Street, Floor 23, New York, NY 10005-4020
Phone: 800-242-4363
Email: awards@aiche.org
https://www.aiche.org/community/awards
Purpose: To offer financial aid to minority students in chemical engineering.
Eligibility: Applicants must be members of a minority group (i.e. African American, Hispanic, Native American or Alaskan Native) that is underrepresented in chemical engineering. Applicants must also be high school graduates during the academic year of application and plan to enroll in a four-year college or university. Applicants are encouraged to major in science or engineering. Selection is also based on academic record, reason for choosing science or engineering, work or activities and financial need.
Target applicant(s): High school students.
Amount: $1,000.
Number of awards: 10.
Deadline: July 15.
How to apply: Applications are available online or by telephone or written request.
Exclusive: Visit www.UltimateScholarshipBook.com and enter code AM227123 for updates on this award.

(2272) · Minority Serving Institution Grants

Council on International Educational Exchange (CIEE)
300 Fore Street, Portland, ME 04101
Phone: 207-553-4000
Email: studyinfo@ciee.org
http://www.ciee.org
Purpose: To aid underrepresented students who wish to study abroad.
Eligibility: Applicants must be CIEE Study Center participants. They must be students who are self-identified as being from a group that is underrepresented in study abroad programs. Selection is based on the overall strength of the application.
Target applicant(s): College students. Adult students.
Amount: Up to $2,000.
Number of awards: Varies.
Deadline: April 1 (summer and fall) and October 15 (winter/spring).
How to apply: Applications are available online. An application form, financial aid information and an essay are required.
Exclusive: Visit www.UltimateScholarshipBook.com and enter code CO227223 for updates on this award.

(2273) · Morgan Stanley Richard B. Fisher Scholarship Program

Morgan Stanley
1585 Broadway, New York, NY 10036
Email: richardbfisherprogram@morganstanley.com
https://www.morganstanley.com/people-opportunities/insight-program/north-america/morgan-stanley-richard-b-fisher-scholarship-program-north-america
Purpose: To assist minority students with outstanding academic achievement.
Eligibility: Applicants must be African American, Hispanic, Native American or LGBT current juniors at an accredited four-year college. The award includes a summer internship.
Target applicant(s): College students. Adult students.
Amount: $15,000.
Number of awards: Varies.
Deadline: February 15.
How to apply: Applications are available by email.
Exclusive: Visit www.UltimateScholarshipBook.com and enter code MO227323 for updates on this award.

(2274) · Morris K. Udall Scholarship

Morris K. Udall Foundation
130 S. Scott Avenue, Tucson, AZ 85701-1922
Phone: 520-901-8500
Email: info@udall.gov
http://www.udall.gov
Purpose: To aid students committed to careers related to the environment, tribal public policy or Native American health care.
Eligibility: Students must be juniors or sophomores studying full-time for an associate's or bachelor's degree at an accredited two- or four-year institution. They must be U.S. citizens, nationals or permanent residents and be committed to a career related to the environment, tribal public policy or Native American health care. Students must be nominated by a college or university faculty representative and must have a grade point average equivalent to a "B" or higher. Selection is based on demonstrated commitment to the environment, tribal public policy or Native American healthcare. Selection is also based on potential of applicant to make significant contributions, leadership, character, desire to make a difference and demonstration of diverse interests and activities.
Target applicant(s): College students. Adult students.
Minimum GPA: 3.0
Amount: Up to $5,000.
Number of awards: 50.
Scholarship may be renewable.
Deadline: March 2.
How to apply: Applications are available online. An application form, essay, college transcript(s) and three recommendation letters are required.

Exclusive: Visit www.UltimateScholarshipBook.com and enter code MO227423 for updates on this award.

(2275) · Mutual of Omaha Actuarial Scholarship for Minority Students

Mutual of Omaha
Mutual of Omaha Plaza, Strategic Staffing - Actuarial Recruitment, Omaha, NE 68175
Phone: 402-351-3300
http://www.mutualofomaha.com
Purpose: To support undergraduate students who are preparing for actuarial careers.
Eligibility: Applicants must be African-American, Native American, Hispanic, Asian American or from another underrepresented minority group. They must be U.S. citizens, permanent residents, temporary residents, asylees or refugees and must be full-time undergraduate students who have completed 24 or more credit hours (including 18 or more graded hours). They must be pursuing a degree in mathematics or an actuarial-related subject and must have a GPA of 3.4 or more. Applicants must have plans to pursue a career in an actuarial field and must have passed at least one actuarial exam. Scholarship recipients must be willing to complete a summer internship at the Mutual of Omaha offices in Omaha. Selection is based on the overall strength of the application.
Target applicant(s): High school students. College students. Adult students.
Minimum GPA: 3.4
Amount: $5,000.
Number of awards: Varies.
Scholarship may be renewable.
Deadline: October 20.
How to apply: Applications are available online. An application form, personal statement, one recommendation letter and a resume are required.
Exclusive: Visit www.UltimateScholarshipBook.com and enter code MU227523 for updates on this award.

(2276) · NAHJ General Scholarships - Rubén Salazar Fund

National Association of Hispanic Journalists
Scholarship Committee, 1050 Connecticut Avenue NW, 10th Floor, Washington, DC 20036
Phone: 202-662-7145
Email: nahj@nahj.org
http://nahj.org
Purpose: To support Hispanic students who plan to enter the broadcast journalism field.
Eligibility: Applicants must be high school seniors, college undergraduate or graduate students who plan to pursue careers in English or Spanish-language broadcast journalism.
Target applicant(s): High school students. College students. Graduate school students. Adult students.
Amount: $1,000-$2,000.
Number of awards: Varies.
Deadline: February.
How to apply: Applications are available online.
Exclusive: Visit www.UltimateScholarshipBook.com and enter code NA227623 for updates on this award.

(2277) · NAHN Scholarship

National Association of Hispanic Nurses
1500 Sunday Drive, Suite 102, Raleigh, NC 27607
Phone: 919-573-5443
Email: info@thehispanicnurses.org
https://www.nahnnet.org
Purpose: To aid Hispanic nursing students who demonstrate the potential to make contributions to the nursing profession and who will act as positive role models for other nursing students.
Eligibility: Applicants must be members of the NAHN and be enrolled in a diploma, associate, baccalaureate, graduate or practical/vocational nursing program.
Target applicant(s): College students. Graduate school students. Adult students.
Minimum GPA: 3.0
Amount: Varies.
Number of awards: Varies.
Deadline: June 15.
How to apply: Applications are available online or by mail.
Exclusive: Visit www.UltimateScholarshipBook.com and enter code NA227723 for updates on this award.

(2278) · NANBPWC National Scholarships

National Association of Negro Business and Professional Women's Clubs Inc.
1806 New Hampshire Avenue NW, Washington, DC 20009-3298
Phone: 202-483-4206
Email: info@nanbpwc.org
http://www.nanbpwc.org
Purpose: To provide assistance to African American students who wish to pursue higher education.
Eligibility: Applicants must be graduating African American high school seniors with a GPA of 3.0 or higher. A 300-word essay is required.
Target applicant(s): High school students.
Minimum GPA: 3.0
Amount: Varies.
Number of awards: Varies.
Deadline: April 15.
How to apply: Applications are available online.
Exclusive: Visit www.UltimateScholarshipBook.com and enter code NA227823 for updates on this award.

(2279) · National and District Scholarships

American Hellenic Education Progressive Association
1909 Q Street NW, Suite 500, Washington, DC 20009
Phone: 202-232-6300
Email: ahepa@ahepa.org
https://ahepa.org/education/
Purpose: To support projects furthering the goals of AHEPA: studies concerning Hellenism, Hellenic culture or Greek-American life.
Eligibility: Applicants must be high school seniors, college students, post-graduate students or adult students of Greek descent.
Target applicant(s): High school students. College students. Graduate school students. Adult students.
Amount: Up to $2,000.
Number of awards: Varies.
Scholarship may be renewable.
Deadline: March.
How to apply: Applications are available online.

Exclusive: Visit www.UltimateScholarshipBook.com and enter code AM227923 for updates on this award.

(2280) · National Association of Black Accountants National Scholarship Program

National Association of Black Accountants
7249-A Hanover Parkway, Greenbelt, MD 20770
Phone: 301-474-NABA
Email: memberservices@nabainc.org
https://www.nabainc.org/scholarship
Purpose: To support African Americans and other minorities in the accounting and finance professions.
Eligibility: Applicants must be ethnic minorities currently enrolled as full-time undergraduates in accounting, finance or business or as graduate students in a Master's of Accountancy program. Applicants must also be NABA members and have a minimum 3.5 major GPA and 3.3 cumulative GPA.
Target applicant(s): College students. Graduate school students. Adult students.
Minimum GPA: 3.3
Amount: $1,500-$5,000.
Number of awards: 50.
Deadline: January 31.
How to apply: Applications are available online.
Exclusive: Visit www.UltimateScholarshipBook.com and enter code NA228023 for updates on this award.

(2281) · National Foster Parent Association (NFPA) Youth Scholarship

National Foster Parent Association (NFPA)
14508 Owen-Tech Boulevard, Suite 129, Austin, TX 78728
Phone: 800-557-5238
Email: scholarships@nfpaonline.org
https://nfpaonline.org/Scholarships
Purpose: To support foster youth.
Eligibility: Applicants must be foster children, adopted children or biological children of currently licensed foster parents who are high school seniors planning to attend a college or university.
Target applicant(s): High school students.
Amount: $500.
Number of awards: Up to 6.
Deadline: April 4.
How to apply: Applications are available online.
Exclusive: Visit www.UltimateScholarshipBook.com and enter code NA228123 for updates on this award.

(2282) · National Gymnastics Foundation Men's Scholarship

USA Gymnastics
Men's Scholarship Program, 132 E. Washington Street, Suite 700, Indianapolis, IN 46204
Phone: 317-237-5050
Email: dmcintyre@usagym.org
https://www.usagym.org/pages/men/pages/scholarship_program.html
Purpose: To support competitive USA Gymnastics athlete members by helping to fund college or post-secondary education.
Eligibility: Applicants must be USA Gymnastics members and pursuing college or post-secondary education.

Target applicant(s): High school students. College students. Adult students.
Amount: Varies.
Number of awards: Varies.
Deadline: May 15.
How to apply: Applications are available online.
Exclusive: Visit www.UltimateScholarshipBook.com and enter code US228223 for updates on this award.

(2283) · National Hispanic Health Professional Student Scholarship

National Hispanic Health Foundation
The New York Academy of Medicine, 1216 Fifth Avenue, Room 457, New York, NY 10029
Phone: 212-419-3686
Email: nhhf@nhmafoundation.org
http://www.nhmafoundation.org
Purpose: To support Hispanic students who are planning to pursue careers in health care.
Eligibility: Applicants must be students who are fully enrolled in a postsecondary degree program in medical (allopathic or osteopathic), dentistry, pharmacy, PA, public health or health policy or nursing. Undergraduate BSN students are also eligible to apply. Selection is based on academic achievement, leadership skills and commitment to improving health care in the Hispanic community.
Target applicant(s): Graduate school students. Adult students.
Amount: $5,000.
Number of awards: 15-20.
Deadline: September 24.
How to apply: Applications are available online. An application form and supporting materials are required.
Exclusive: Visit www.UltimateScholarshipBook.com and enter code NA228323 for updates on this award.

(2284) · National Italian American Foundation Scholarship

National Italian American Foundation
1860 19th Street NW, Washington, DC 20009
Phone: 202-387-0600
Email: scholarships@niaf.org
https://www.niaf.org/programs/scholarships/
Purpose: To support Italian American students.
Eligibility: Applicants must be Italian American students who demonstrate outstanding academic achievement and must either be a member or child of a member. Applicants must also plan to be or currently be enrolled in an accredited institution of higher education, have a minimum 3.5 GPA and be U.S. citizens or permanent residents.
Target applicant(s): High school students. College students. Adult students.
Minimum GPA: 3.5
Amount: $2,500-$12,000.
Number of awards: Varies.
Deadline: March 1.
How to apply: Applications are available online.
Exclusive: Visit www.UltimateScholarshipBook.com and enter code NA228423 for updates on this award.

(2285) · National Medical Fellowships Emergency Scholarship Fund

National Medical Fellowships Inc.
347 Fifth Avenue, Suite 510, New York, NY 10016
Phone: 212-483-8880
Email: scholarships@nmfonline.org
https://nmfonline.org/about-our-scholarships-and-awards/programs/
Purpose: To aid minority medical students who are in need of emergency funding.
Eligibility: Applicants must be African-American, Latino, Native American, Alaska Natives, Native Hawaiians, Vietnamese or Cambodian. They must be third- or fourth-year medical students who are in need of immediate, emergency funding for living expenses and/or tuition. Selection is based on the overall strength of the application.
Target applicant(s): Graduate school students. Adult students.
Amount: Up to $5,000.
Number of awards: Varies.
Deadline: Varies.
How to apply: Applications are available by request. An application form, two personal essays, financial information and one letter of support are required.
Exclusive: Visit www.UltimateScholarshipBook.com and enter code NA228523 for updates on this award.

(2286) · National Scholarship

National Association of Negro Business and Professional Women's Clubs Inc.
1806 New Hampshire Avenue NW, Washington, DC 20009-3298
Phone: 202-483-4206
Email: info@nanbpwc.org
http://www.nanbpwc.org
Purpose: To award scholarships to aspiring business and professional college or university students.
Eligibility: Applicants must be African American graduating high school seniors and have a minimum 3.0 GPA. Students must submit a transcript, an application form, two letters of recommendation and an essay that is at least 300 words on "Why is education important to me?"
Target applicant(s): High school students.
Minimum GPA: 3.0
Amount: Varies.
Number of awards: Varies.
Deadline: April 15.
How to apply: Applications are available online.
Exclusive: Visit www.UltimateScholarshipBook.com and enter code NA228623 for updates on this award.

(2287) · Native American Education Grant

Presbyterian Church (USA)
100 Witherspoon Street, Louisville, KY 40202
Phone: 800-728-7228 x5224
Email: finaid@pcusa.org
https://www.presbyterianmission.org/what-we-do/grants-scholarships/
Purpose: To aid Alaska Natives and Native Americans pursuing full-time post-secondary education.
Eligibility: Applicants must be U.S. citizens who are high school graduates or G.E.D. recipients and demonstrate financial need and must have a minimum 2.5 GPA. Applicants must present proof of tribal membership, and preference will be given to active members of the Presbyterian Church. Students are selected based on the availability of funds and best match to donor restrictions. The deadline for students applying to renew the grant is May 1. Awards for new students will be offered on a funds available basis after May 1.
Target applicant(s): College students. Adult students.
Minimum GPA: 2.5
Amount: Up to $1,500.
Number of awards: Varies.
Scholarship may be renewable.
Deadline: May 17.
How to apply: Applications are available online.
Exclusive: Visit www.UltimateScholarshipBook.com and enter code PR228723 for updates on this award.

(2288) · Native American Scholarship

International Order of the King's Daughters and Sons
Director, P.O. Box 1040, Chautauqua, NY 14722
Email: headquarters@iokds.org
https://iokds.org/scholarships/
Purpose: To support Native American students with their post-secondary education.
Eligibility: Applicants must be Native Americans enrolled or planning to enroll at a technical school, vocational school, college or university for undergraduate studies. Students must provide a tribal registration number.
Target applicant(s): High school students. College students. Adult students.
Amount: $1,000.
Number of awards: 1.
Deadline: April 1.
How to apply: Applications are available online.
Exclusive: Visit www.UltimateScholarshipBook.com and enter code IN228823 for updates on this award.

(2289) · NativeVision Scholarships

NativeVision
Johns Hopkins Center for American Indian Health, 415 North Washington Street, 4th Floor, Baltimore, MD Baltimore
Phone: 410-955-6931
Email: mhammen@jhu.edu
http://www.nativevision.org/Scholarship_Recipients/Scholarship_Recipients.html
Purpose: To support Native American students with their educational expenses.
Eligibility: Applicants must be Native American students entering their first year of college.
Target applicant(s): High school students.
Amount: $5,000.
Number of awards: 2.
Deadline: May 28.
How to apply: Applications are available online.
Exclusive: Visit www.UltimateScholarshipBook.com and enter code NA228923 for updates on this award.

(2290) · NCTA and AWMF Scholarship

Alliance for Women in Media
2365 Harrodsburg Road, Suite A325, Lexington, KY 40504
Phone: 202-750-3664
Email: info@allwomeninmedia.org
https://allwomeninmedia.org/foundation/scholarships/

Purpose: To support female undergraduate and graduate students studying media, journalism, English, communications and related fields.
Eligibility: Applicants must be attending an accredited college or university in the United States in the fall of application year. Students must submit a 750- to 1,000-word essay on a suggested topic.
Target applicant(s): College students. Graduate school students. Adult students.
Amount: $5,000.
Number of awards: 1.
Deadline: May 1.
How to apply: Applications are available online.
Exclusive: Visit www.UltimateScholarshipBook.com and enter code AL229023 for updates on this award.

(2291) · NCWIT Award for Aspirations in Computing

National Center for Women and Information Technology (NCWIT)
University of Colorado, Campus Box 322 UCB, Boulder, CO 80309
Phone: 303-735-6671
Email: aspirations@ncwit.org
http://www.ncwit.org
Purpose: To recognize young women who are interested in technology-related pursuits.
Eligibility: Applicants must be U.S. residents and be female high school students. They must be interested in technology-related subjects. Selection is based on aptitude for computing and internet technology, leadership skills, academic merit and educational goals.
Target applicant(s): High school students.
Amount: $500.
Number of awards: Varies.
Deadline: November 5.
How to apply: Applications are available online. An application form and supporting materials are required.
Exclusive: Visit www.UltimateScholarshipBook.com and enter code NA229123 for updates on this award.

(2292) · NeW Essay Contest

Network of Enlightened Women
1360 East Capitol Street NE, Washington, DC 20003
Phone: 423-838-4477
Email: info@enlightenedwomen.org
http://enlightenedwomen.org
Purpose: To support female, conservative students who write about women's achievements and women moving forward.
Eligibility: Applicants must be female high school seniors or college students currently enrolled in an undergraduate institution in the United States. An essay on a provided prompt is required to be submitted.
Target applicant(s): High school students. College students. Adult students.
Amount: $500.
Number of awards: 2.
Deadline: May 2.
How to apply: Applications are available online.
Exclusive: Visit www.UltimateScholarshipBook.com and enter code NE229223 for updates on this award.

(2293) · New York Ramblers Scholarship

New York Ramblers Soccer Club
2 Gold Street, Apartment 21C, New York, NY 10038
Email: committee@nyramblers.com
https://nyramblers.com/scholarship/

Purpose: To support undergraduate student athletes of all sports who are members or allies of the LGBTQIA2S+ community.
Eligibility: Applicants must be open and self-identified lesbian, gay, bisexual, transgender, queer or intersex persons or a demonstrated and committed ally to the community. Students must be between the ages of 15 and 21 years of age and athletes in any sport or athletic activity. Applicants must be graduating high school students who plan to attend a recognized undergraduate college or university in the United States or are already matriculated U.S. undergraduate college students.
Target applicant(s): High school students. College students.
Amount: Varies.
Number of awards: Varies.
Deadline: June 1.
How to apply: Applications are available online.
Exclusive: Visit www.UltimateScholarshipBook.com and enter code NE229323 for updates on this award.

(2294) · NMF National Alumni Council Scholarship Program

National Medical Fellowships Inc.
347 Fifth Avenue, Suite 510, New York, NY 10016
Phone: 212-483-8880
Email: scholarships@nmfonline.org
https://nmfonline.org/about-our-scholarships-and-awards/programs/
Purpose: To support minority medical students demonstrating community service dedication.
Eligibility: Applicants must be fourth-year medical students at an accredited U.S. medical school and members of an underrepresented minority group. Students must demonstrate community service and leadership potential.
Target applicant(s): Graduate school students. Adult students.
Amount: $5,000.
Number of awards: 8.
Deadline: July 5.
How to apply: Applications are available online.
Exclusive: Visit www.UltimateScholarshipBook.com and enter code NA229423 for updates on this award.

(2295) · NOAA Educational Partnership Program Undergraduate Scholarships

NOAA Educational Partnership Program - Office of Education
Herbert C Hoover Building, 14th Street and Constitution Ave NW, Room 6863, Washington, DC 20230
Phone: 202-482-3384
Email: EPP.USP@noaa.gov
https://www.noaa.gov/office-education
Purpose: To aid undergraduates who are attending a minority-serving institution and are pursuing undergraduate degrees in subjects related to the atmospheric, oceanic or environmental sciences.
Eligibility: Applicants must be U.S. citizens and full-time undergraduates who are in the second year of a four-year degree program or in the third year of a five-year degree program. They must be attending an accredited minority-serving institution (MSI), and they must have a GPA of 3.2 or higher on a four-point scale. Applicants must be majoring in a discipline that is related to environmental, atmospheric or oceanic sciences. Selection is based on relevant coursework completed, stated career goals, recommendations and extracurricular activities.
Target applicant(s): College students. Adult students.
Minimum GPA: 3.2
Amount: Varies.

Number of awards: Varies.
Scholarship may be renewable.
Deadline: January.
How to apply: Applications are available online. An application form, two personal essays, two recommendation letters and an official transcript are required.
Exclusive: Visit www.UltimateScholarshipBook.com and enter code NO229523 for updates on this award.

(2296) · Northrop Grumman/HENAAC Scholars Program

Great Minds in STEM (HENAAC)
602 Monterey Pass Road, Monterey Park, CA 91754
Phone: 323-262-0997
Email: jcano@greatmindsinstem.org
http://www.greatmindsinstem.org
Purpose: To aid Hispanic undergraduates who are studying naval architecture, computer science, computer engineering, electrical engineering or systems engineering.
Eligibility: Applicants must be undergraduates who have completed at least one academic year of college and must have a minimum 3.0 GPA. They must demonstrate leadership experience. Selection is based on the overall strength of the application.
Target applicant(s): College students. Adult students.
Minimum GPA: 3.0
Amount: Up to $10,000.
Number of awards: Varies.
Deadline: May 28.
How to apply: Applications are available online. An application form, personal essay, transcript, letters of recommendation and resume are required.
Exclusive: Visit www.UltimateScholarshipBook.com and enter code GR229623 for updates on this award.

(2297) · OCA/UPS Gold Mountain Scholarship

OCA (formerly Organization of Chinese Americans)
1322 18th Street NW, Washington, DC 20036
Phone: 202-223-5500
Email: oca@ocanational.org
https://www.ocanational.org/scholarships
Purpose: To support first generation Asian American students.
Eligibility: Applicants must be Asian Pacific Americans who intend to begin college in the fall of the year of application and must demonstrate significant financial need. Applicants must also be the first in their family to attend college and have a minimum 3.0 GPA.
Target applicant(s): High school students.
Minimum GPA: 3.0
Amount: $2,000.
Number of awards: 15.
Deadline: May 31.
How to apply: Applications are available online or by written request.
Exclusive: Visit www.UltimateScholarshipBook.com and enter code OC229723 for updates on this award.

(2298) · Olive Lynn Salembier Memorial Reentry Scholarship

Society of Women Engineers
130 East Randolph Street, Suite 3500, Chicago, IL 60601
Phone: 877-793-4636
Email: scholarships@swe.org
https://swe.org/scholarships/
Purpose: To aid female engineering students.
Eligibility: Applicants must be females who have been out of the engineering work force and out of school for a minimum of two years prior to reentry, Applicants must have a GPA of 3.0 or higher on a four-point scale except for first year reentry. Selection is based on the overall strength of the application.
Target applicant(s): High school students. College students. Graduate school students. Adult students.
Minimum GPA: 3.0
Amount: $1,500.
Number of awards: 1.
Deadline: February 15.
How to apply: Applications are available online. An application form and supporting materials are required.
Exclusive: Visit www.UltimateScholarshipBook.com and enter code SO229823 for updates on this award.

(2299) · P.E.O. International Peace Scholarship

P.E.O. International
3700 Grand Avenue, Des Moines, IA 50312
Phone: 515-255-3153
http://www.peointernational.org
Purpose: Women from countries other than the U.S. or Canada are assisted in their graduate studies within North America.
Eligibility: Applicants must be female, attend a North American graduate school or Cottey College and be from a country other than the U.S. or Canada. Eligibility must be established by submitting an eligibility form between August 15 and December 15.
Target applicant(s): College students. Graduate school students. Adult students.
Amount: Up to $12,500.
Number of awards: Varies.
Scholarship may be renewable.
Deadline: December 15.
How to apply: Applicants must first submit an eligibility form, available online. If found eligible, students will be mailed application materials.
Exclusive: Visit www.UltimateScholarshipBook.com and enter code P.229923 for updates on this award.

(2300) · P.E.O. Program for Continuing Education

P.E.O. International
3700 Grand Avenue, Des Moines, IA 50312
Phone: 515-255-3153
http://www.peointernational.org
Purpose: To assist women whose education has been interrupted.
Eligibility: Applicants must be women who are resuming studies to improve their marketable skills due to changing demands in their lives. They must have financial need and cannot use the funds to pay living expenses or repay educational loans. They must be sponsored by a P.E.O. chapter and be citizens and students of the United States or Canada. They must have had at least two consecutive years as a non-student in their adult lives and be able to complete their educational goals in two consecutive years or less. Doctoral degree students are not eligible.
Target applicant(s): College students. Graduate school students. Adult students.
Amount: $3,000.
Number of awards: Varies.
Deadline: 10 weeks before the start of classes.

How to apply: Applications are available from your local P.E.O. Chapter. An application form, income and expense statement and chapter recommendation are required. See website to locate nearest P.E.O. Chapter.

Exclusive: Visit www.UltimateScholarshipBook.com and enter code P.230023 for updates on this award.

(2301) · P.O. Pistilli Undergraduate Scholarship for Advancement in Computer Science and Electrical Engineering

Design Automation Conference/Association for Computing Machinery
Professor Andrew B. Kahng, P.O. Pistilli Scholarship Director, Department of Computer Science and Engineering, UCSD, 9500 Gilman Drive #0404, La Jolla, CA 92093
Phone: 858-822-4884
Email: abk@cs.ucsd.edu
http://www.dac.com

Purpose: To promote professions in electrical engineering, computer engineering and computer science among underrepresented groups.

Eligibility: Applicants must be high school seniors who are from an underrepresented group (African American, Hispanic, Native American, women or disabled). Students must have a minimum 3.0 GPA, have demonstrated high achievement in math and science courses and have financial need. Applicants must also intend to pursue a career in electrical engineering, computer engineering or computer science.

Target applicant(s): High school students.
Minimum GPA: 3.0
Amount: $4,000.
Number of awards: Up to 7.
Scholarship may be renewable.
Deadline: June 15.

How to apply: Applications are available online. An application form, three letters of recommendation, an official transcript, a personal letter, a copy of tax returns and a copy of the FAFSA are required.

Exclusive: Visit www.UltimateScholarshipBook.com and enter code DE230123 for updates on this award.

(2302) · Paumanauke Native American Indian Scholarship

Paumanauke Native American Festival Inc.
2005 Merrick Road, Suite 221, Attn.: Tony Moon Hawk Langhorn, Merrick, NY 11566
Email: info@paumanauke.org
http://www.paumanauke.org

Purpose: To encourage Native American Indians to finish their college educations.

Eligibility: Applicants must be members of a Native American Indian tribe who are enrolled full-time at a college, university or other accredited post-secondary institution. Selection is based on the overall strength of the application.

Target applicant(s): College students. Graduate school students. Adult students.
Amount: $500.
Number of awards: 6.
Deadline: June 1.

How to apply: Applications are available online.

Exclusive: Visit www.UltimateScholarshipBook.com and enter code PA230223 for updates on this award.

(2303) · Pega Scholars Program

Pega Scholars Program
Scholarship America, One Scholarship Way, Saint Peter, MN 56082
Phone: 507-931-1682
Email: pegascholars@scholarshipamerica.org
https://learnmore.scholarsapply.org/pegascholars

Purpose: To support future technologists from diverse communities around the globe.

Eligibility: Applicants must be current high school or secondary school graduates or current university students pursuing a degree in computer science, technology or a related field. Students must plan to enroll in part-time or full-time undergraduate study at a two-, three- or four-year accredited institution. Applicants must reside in one of the following countries: USA, Canada, Brazil, United Kingdom, The Netherlands, India or Australia. Students must self-identify with one or more of the following: women; LGBTQIA+; person with disability; military veteran; Indigenous; Native American or Alaskan Native; Asian American; Black; African American; Hispanic or Latino/Latina; Native Hawaiian or other Pacific Islander.

Target applicant(s): High school students. College students. Adult students.
Amount: $1,500.
Number of awards: 10.
Deadline: September 30.

How to apply: Applications are available online.

Exclusive: Visit www.UltimateScholarshipBook.com and enter code PE230323 for updates on this award.

(2304) · Performing Arts Scholarship

Armenian General Benevolent Union (AGBU)
55 East 59th Street, 7th Floor, New York, NY 10022-1112
Phone: 212-319-6383
Email: scholarship@agbu.org
http://www.agbu.org

Purpose: To support students of Armenian descent who demonstrate exceptional artistic accomplishment.

Eligibility: Applicants must be full-time undergraduate and graduate students of Armenian descent worldwide who are pursuing studies in the field of performing arts and enrolled in highly selective colleges and universities. Students must have a minimum 3.5 GPA and submit examples of their artistic experience in the form of audio/visual recordings.

Target applicant(s): College students. Graduate school students. Adult students.
Minimum GPA: 3.5
Amount: Up to $5,000.
Number of awards: Varies.
Deadline: June 1.

How to apply: Applications are available online.

Exclusive: Visit www.UltimateScholarshipBook.com and enter code AR230423 for updates on this award.

(2305) · Phyllis G. Meekins Scholarship

Ladies Professional Golf Association
100 International Golf Drive, Daytona Beach, FL 32124-1092
Phone: 386-274-6200
Email: info@lpgafoundation.org
http://www.lpga.com/lpga-foundation/scholarships

Purpose: To support a female high school senior golf participant of a recognized minority background in pursuit of a college education.

Eligibility: Applicants must have a 3.0 GPA and be a U.S. citizen or legal resident. Students must also have been accepted to a college or university and plan to play competitive golf at the collegiate level. Selection is based on financial need.
Target applicant(s): High school students.
Minimum GPA: 3.0
Amount: $5,000.
Number of awards: 2.
Deadline: April.
How to apply: Applications available online.
Exclusive: Visit www.UltimateScholarshipBook.com and enter code LA230523 for updates on this award.

(2306) · Point Community College Scholarship
Point Foundation
P.O. Box 60108, Los Angeles, CA 90060
Phone: 323-580-5058
Email: info@pointfoundation.org
http://www.pointfoundation.org
Purpose: To support LGBTQ students attending a community college.
Eligibility: Applicants must be LGBTQ, be enrolled or intending to enroll in an accredited community college in the U.S. and intend to transfer to a bachelor's degree program. Students are assessed on academic performance, leadership skills, financial need, personal goals and the applicant's involvement in the LGBTQ community. Consideration is also given to students who have lost the social support of their families and/or communities as a result of revealing their sexual orientation, gender identity or gender expression.
Target applicant(s): High school students. College students. Adult students.
Amount: $2,000-$4,800.
Number of awards: 34.
Deadline: May 3.
How to apply: Applications are available online.
Exclusive: Visit www.UltimateScholarshipBook.com and enter code PO230623 for updates on this award.

(2307) · Point Flagship Scholarship
Point Foundation
P.O. Box 60108, Los Angeles, CA 90060
Phone: 323-580-5058
Email: info@pointfoundation.org
http://www.pointfoundation.org
Purpose: To support LGBTQ students pursuing an undergraduate or graduate degree.
Eligibility: Applicants must be LGBTQ and be at least seniors in high school and enrolled or intending to enroll in an accredited college or university in the U.S. Students are assessed on academic performance, leadership skills, financial need, personal goals and the applicant's involvement in the LGBTQ community. Consideration is also given to students who have lost the social support of their families and/or communities as a result of revealing their sexual orientation, gender identity or gender expression. Point Scholarships are awarded on a "last provider" basis, meaning that Point fills in the gaps and provides funds not provided by other scholarships, grants, loans, work/study programs, etc. It is the responsibility of those selected as Point Scholars to annually secure as much other funding as possible.
Target applicant(s): High school students. College students. Adult students.
Amount: $3,000.
Number of awards: 1.

Scholarship may be renewable.
Deadline: January 26.
How to apply: Applications are available online.
Exclusive: Visit www.UltimateScholarshipBook.com and enter code PO230723 for updates on this award.

(2308) · Polish National Alliance Scholarship
Polish National Alliance
Educational Department, 6100 Cicero Avenue, Chicago, IL 60646
Phone: 800-621-3723
Email: pna@pna-znp.org
http://www.pna-znp.org
Purpose: To assist members of the Polish National Alliance with their undergraduate studies.
Eligibility: Applicants must be college sophomores, juniors or seniors and have been paying members in good standing with the Polish National Association for at least three years and must have a minimum 3.0 GPA. If the applicant has been in good standing with the PNA for at least two years, his or her parents must have been paying PNA members for at least five years.
Target applicant(s): College students. Adult students.
Minimum GPA: 3.0
Amount: Varies.
Number of awards: Varies.
Scholarship may be renewable.
Deadline: June 15.
How to apply: Applications are available by email at mary.srodon@pna-znp.org.
Exclusive: Visit www.UltimateScholarshipBook.com and enter code PO230823 for updates on this award.

(2309) · PRSA Diversity Multicultural Scholarship
Public Relations Student Society of America
33 Maiden Lane, 11th Floor, New York, NY 10038
Phone: 212-460-1474
Email: prssa@prsa.org
https://prssa.prsa.org/scholarships-and-awards/
Purpose: To aid minority communications students.
Eligibility: Applicants must be of African-American, Latino, Asian, Native American, Alaska Native or Pacific Islander descent. They must be undergraduates of at least junior standing who are majoring in communications at an accredited four-year institution. They must be full-time students who have a GPA of 3.0 or higher on a four-point scale. Selection is based on the overall strength of the application.
Target applicant(s): College students. Adult students.
Minimum GPA: 3.0
Amount: $1,500.
Number of awards: 2.
Deadline: May 31.
How to apply: Applications are available online. An application form, official transcript, essay and one recommendation letter are required.
Exclusive: Visit www.UltimateScholarshipBook.com and enter code PU230923 for updates on this award.

(2310) · Que Llueva Cafe Scholarship
Chicano Organizing and Research in Education
P.O. Box 160144, Sacramento, CA 95816
Email: jdelrazo@ca-core.org
http://www.ca-core.org

Purpose: To aid undocumented Latino students who wish to attend college.

Eligibility: Applicants must be graduating high school seniors, high school graduates or GED recipients who are legally undocumented residents of the U.S. They must have plans to enroll at an accredited postsecondary institution located in the U.S. or Puerto Rico. They must show academic promise and demonstrate financial need. Selection is based on the overall strength of the application.

Target applicant(s): High school students.

Amount: Varies.

Number of awards: Varies.

Deadline: July.

How to apply: Applications are available online. An application form, transcript, one letter of recommendation, a personal essay and a financial need statement are required.

Exclusive: Visit www.UltimateScholarshipBook.com and enter code CH231023 for updates on this award.

(2311) · Religious Studies Scholarship

Armenian General Benevolent Union (AGBU)
55 East 59th Street, 7th Floor, New York, NY 10022-1112
Phone: 212-319-6383
Email: scholarship@agbu.org
http://www.agbu.org

Purpose: To support graduate students of Armenian descent who are pursuing religious studies.

Eligibility: Applicants must be graduate students of Armenian descent worldwide who are pursuing religious studies. Students must be enrolled in full-time degree programs at seminaries or highly selective colleges or universities with a minimum 3.0 GPA.

Target applicant(s): Graduate school students. Adult students.

Minimum GPA: 3.0

Amount: Up to $5,000.

Number of awards: Varies.

Deadline: June 1.

How to apply: Applications are available online.

Exclusive: Visit www.UltimateScholarshipBook.com and enter code AR231123 for updates on this award.

(2312) · Richard R. Tufenkian Memorial Scholarship

Armenian Educational Foundation Inc.
600 W. Broadway, Suite 130, Glendale, CA 91204
Phone: 818-242-4154
Email: aef@aefweb.org
http://www.aefweb.org

Purpose: To support Armenian undergraduate students.

Eligibility: Applicants must be full-time undergraduate students of Armenian descent at U.S. universities, have a minimum 3.0 GPA, demonstrate financial need and be involved in the Armenian community. Tax returns, transcripts, two reference letters, essays and applications are required.

Target applicant(s): High school students. College students. Adult students.

Minimum GPA: 3.0

Amount: $3,000.

Number of awards: 3.

Deadline: June 30.

How to apply: Applications are available online.

Exclusive: Visit www.UltimateScholarshipBook.com and enter code AR231223 for updates on this award.

(2313) · Ron Brown Scholar Program

CAP Charitable Foundation
Ron Brown Scholar Program, 1160 Pepsi Place, Suite 206, Charlottesville, VA 22901
Phone: 434-964-1588
Email: franh@ronbrown.org
http://www.ronbrown.org

Purpose: To award scholarships to academically talented, highly motivated African American high school seniors.

Eligibility: Applicants must be African American collegebound high school seniors. Selection is based on academic promise, leadership, communication skills, school and community involvement and financial need.

Target applicant(s): High school students.

Amount: $40,000.

Number of awards: Varies.

Scholarship may be renewable.

Deadline: January 9.

How to apply: Applications are available online.

Exclusive: Visit www.UltimateScholarshipBook.com and enter code CA231323 for updates on this award.

(2314) · Ruth D. Peterson Fellowship for Racial and Ethnic Diversity

American Society of Criminology
1314 Kinnear Road, Suite 212, Columbus, OH 43212-1156
Email: ronet@udel.edu
https://www.asc41.com

Purpose: To encourage minorities to study criminology or criminal justice.

Eligibility: Applicants must be African American, Asian American, Latino or Native American. Recipients must have been accepted into a doctoral studies program. Selection is based on curriculum vitae, college transcripts, financial need, references and letter describing career plans, experiences and interest in criminology.

Target applicant(s): Graduate school students. Adult students.

Amount: $6,000.

Number of awards: 3.

Deadline: March 1.

How to apply: Applications are available by written request.

Exclusive: Visit www.UltimateScholarshipBook.com and enter code AM231423 for updates on this award.

(2315) · Scholarships for Social Justice

Higher Education Consortium for Urban Affairs
2233 University Avenue W, Suite 210, St. Paul, MN 55114
Phone: 651-287-3300
Email: hecua@hecua.org
https://hecua.org/logistics/scholarships/

Purpose: To support students from low-income families, students from ethnic minorities and students who are the first in their families to attend college.

Eligibility: Students must have submitted an application to one of HECUA's semester programs, and they must be enrolled at an HECUA member institution. A list of member institutions is available online.

Target applicant(s): College students. Adult students.

Amount: $1,500.

Number of awards: Varies.

Deadline: April 15 (fall), December 1 (spring).

How to apply: Applications are available online. An essay, letter of recommendation and Student Aid Report from completing the Free Application for Federal Student Aid are required.

Exclusive: Visit www.UltimateScholarshipBook.com and enter code HI231523 for updates on this award.

(2316) · Sequoyah Graduate Scholarships

Association on American Indian Affairs

Lisa Wyzlic, Director of Scholarship Programs, 966 Hungerford Drive, Suite 12-B, Rockville, MD 20850

Phone: 240-314-7155

Email: lw.aaia@indian-affairs.org

https://www.indian-affairs.org/whatwedo.html

Purpose: To provide graduate fellowships for students of American Indian and Alaskan Native heritage.

Eligibility: Applicants must be full-time students who can provide proof of tribal enrollment and an essay on educational goals.

Target applicant(s): Graduate school students. Adult students.

Amount: $1,500.

Number of awards: Varies.

Deadline: May 31.

How to apply: Applications are available online.

Exclusive: Visit www.UltimateScholarshipBook.com and enter code AS231623 for updates on this award.

(2317) · Sharon D. Banks Memorial Undergraduate Scholarship

Women's Transportation Seminar (WTS) International

1701 K Street NW, Suite 800, Washington, DC 20006

Phone: 202-955-5085

Email: membership@wtsinternational.org

https://www.wtsinternational.org/resources/scholarships

Purpose: To help women pursuing transportation careers with their higher education expenses.

Eligibility: Applicants must be women enrolled in undergraduate programs related to transportation studies. Selection is based on the applicant's academic record, transportation-related activities, job skills and specific transportation goals.

Target applicant(s): College students. Adult students.

Amount: $5,000.

Number of awards: Varies.

Deadline: Varies.

How to apply: Applications are available through a local chapter.

Exclusive: Visit www.UltimateScholarshipBook.com and enter code WO231723 for updates on this award.

(2318) · SHPE Scholarship Program

Society of Hispanic Professional Engineers

13181 Crossroads Parkway North, Suite 450, City of Industry, CA 91746

Phone: 323-725-3970

Email: scholarships@shpe.org

https://www.shpe.org/students

Purpose: To aid Hispanic students who are majoring in STEM related fields.

Eligibility: Applicants must be members of the Society of Hispanic Professional Engineers (SHPE). They must be graduating high school seniors, current undergraduates or entering graduate students who are pursuing degrees in STEM related fields. They must have a GPA of 2.75 or higher. Selection is based on the overall strength of the application.

Target applicant(s): High school students. College students. Graduate school students. Adult students.

Minimum GPA: 2.75

Amount: Varies.

Number of awards: Varies.

Deadline: April 30.

How to apply: Applications are available online. An application form, official transcript, resume, personal statement and two recommendation letters are required.

Exclusive: Visit www.UltimateScholarshipBook.com and enter code SO231823 for updates on this award.

(2319) · Snapology STEM Studies Scholarship

Snapology

1699 Washington Road, Pittsburgh, PA 15228

Phone: 412-780-2996

Email: scholarship@snapology.com

https://www.snapology.com/scholarships

Purpose: To support female students in STEM studies.

Eligibility: Applicants must be female graduating high school seniors and be enrolling at an accredited institution to pursue a STEM education. Applicants must demonstrate academic achievement and financial need.

Target applicant(s): High school students.

Amount: $1,000.

Number of awards: 1.

Deadline: April 30.

How to apply: Applications are available online.

Exclusive: Visit www.UltimateScholarshipBook.com and enter code SN231923 for updates on this award.

(2320) · St. Andrew's Society of Washington, DC Scholarship

St. Andrew's Society of Washington, DC

Chairman, Scholarships Committee, P.O. Box 7849, Washington, DC 20044

Email: scholarships@saintandrewsociety.org

http://www.saintandrewsociety.org/scholarships/

Purpose: To assist students of Scottish birth or descent.

Eligibility: Applicants must be of Scottish birth or descent and be able to cite their Scottish descent. U.S. citizens must be permanent residents of the District of Columbia, Delaware, Maryland, New Jersey, North Carolina, West Virginia, Pennsylvania or Virginia. Students must also demonstrate financial need and academic achievement. Attention will be given to work that enhances the "knowledge of Scottish history or culture."

Target applicant(s): College students. Graduate school students. Adult students.

Amount: Varies.

Number of awards: Varies.

Deadline: April 30.

How to apply: Applications are available online.

Exclusive: Visit www.UltimateScholarshipBook.com and enter code ST232023 for updates on this award.

(2321) · Stantec Equity and Diversity Scholarship

Stantec

International Scholarship and Tuition Services Inc. (ISTS), 1321 Murfreesboro Road, Suite 800, Nashville, TN 37217

Email: askstantec@stantec.com
https://www.stantec.com/en/about/community-engagement/
scholarships/equity-diversity-scholarship
Purpose: To support the creation of a critical mass of talented students that will fully represent the STEAM fields.
Eligibility: Applicants must be enrolled in a college, university or post-secondary institution in pursuit of a bachelor's degree and pursuing a STEAM (science, technology, engineering, arts and mathematics) major. Students must be a historically underrepresented population/group such as BIPOC (Black, Indigenous, and People of Color), members of the LGBTQ2+ community, people with disabilities, veterans and first-generation college students.
Target applicant(s): High school students. College students. Adult students.
Amount: $1,500-$10,000.
Number of awards: 100.
Deadline: November 18.
How to apply: Applications are available online.
Exclusive: Visit www.UltimateScholarshipBook.com and enter code ST232123 for updates on this award.

(2322) · Student Relief Fund

Ascend: Pan-Asian Leaders in Finance and Accounting
247 West 30th Street, 12th Floor, New York, NY 10001
Phone: 212-248-4888
Email: scholarships@ascendleadership.org
http://www.ascendleadership.org/
Purpose: To support Ascend student members with their unexpected financial burdens.
Eligibility: Applicants must be currently enrolled as a full-time students and be Ascend student members. An essay on a provided prompt is required to be submitted.
Target applicant(s): High school students. College students. Graduate school students. Adult students.
Amount: $1,000.
Number of awards: 1.
Deadline: July 15.
How to apply: Applications are available online.
Exclusive: Visit www.UltimateScholarshipBook.com and enter code AS232223 for updates on this award.

(2323) · SWE Exelon Corporation Scholarship

Society of Women Engineers
130 East Randolph Street, Suite 3500, Chicago, IL 60601
Phone: 877-793-4636
Email: scholarships@swe.org
https://swe.org/scholarships/
Purpose: To aid female students who plan to major in electrical engineering or mechanical engineering.
Eligibility: Applicants must be female and must be rising undergraduate freshmen who are planning to major in electrical engineering or mechanical engineering at an ABET-approved college or university. They must plan to enroll on a full-time basis and must have a GPA of 3.5 or higher on a four-point scale.
Target applicant(s): High school students.
Minimum GPA: 3.5
Amount: $5,000.
Number of awards: 5.
Deadline: May 1.

How to apply: Applications are available online. An application form, transcript, two recommendation letters and proof of college acceptance are required.
Exclusive: Visit www.UltimateScholarshipBook.com and enter code SO232323 for updates on this award.

(2324) · SWE Past Presidents Scholarship

Society of Women Engineers
130 East Randolph Street, Suite 3500, Chicago, IL 60601
Phone: 877-793-4636
Email: scholarships@swe.org
https://swe.org/scholarships/
Purpose: To aid female engineering students.
Eligibility: Applicants must be U.S. citizens and be graduate students or undergraduate sophomores, juniors or seniors. They must be enrolled in an ABET-accredited engineering degree program and have a GPA of 3.0 or higher on a four-point scale. Selection is based on the overall strength of the application.
Target applicant(s): College students. Graduate school students. Adult students.
Minimum GPA: 3.0
Amount: $5,500.
Number of awards: 1.
Deadline: February 15.
How to apply: Applications are available online. An application form and supporting materials are required.
Exclusive: Visit www.UltimateScholarshipBook.com and enter code SO232423 for updates on this award.

(2325) · Taiwanese American Scholarship Fund

Taiwanese American Scholarship Fund
P.O. Box 60074, Pasadena, CA 91116-6074
Email: kfan@apcf.org
https://tascholarshipfund.org/
Purpose: To assist Taiwanese American students with financial need.
Eligibility: Applicants must be U.S. citizens or permanent residents and direct blood descendants of a Taiwanese citizen. Students must also be high school seniors or first-year college students planning to attend a university or college as full-time 1st or 2nd year students in the United States, have a minimum 3.0 GPA and have a household income level below the federal, state or county low-income level.
Target applicant(s): High school students. College students. Adult students.
Minimum GPA: 3.0
Amount: $5,000.
Number of awards: 10.
Scholarship may be renewable.
Deadline: April 1.
How to apply: Applications are available online.
Exclusive: Visit www.UltimateScholarshipBook.com and enter code TA232523 for updates on this award.

(2326) · TE Connectivity African Heritage Scholarship

TE Connectivity African Heritage Scholarship
Scholarship America, One Scholarship Way, Saint Peter, MN 56082
Phone: 507-931-1682
Email: teconnectivity-african-heritage@scholarshipamerica.org
https://te.com/scholarships
Purpose: To support African American students pursuing degrees in STEM and related fields.

Eligibility: Applicants must be college sophomores who self-identify as black or African American or multiracial. Students must be pursuing a degree in Science, Technology, Engineering, Mathematics (STEM), operations management, supply chain, finance or information technology. Applicants must demonstrate financial need and have a minimum 3.0 GPA.
Target applicant(s): College students. Adult students.
Minimum GPA: 3.0
Amount: Up to $22,500.
Number of awards: 14.
Deadline: August 30.
How to apply: Applications are available online.
Exclusive: Visit www.UltimateScholarshipBook.com and enter code TE232623 for updates on this award.

(2327) · TheDream.US Scholarship

TheDream.US
One Scholarship Way, Saint Peter, MN 56082
Phone: 507-931-1682
Email: TheDream.US@applyISTS.com
http://thedream.us
Purpose: To support immigrant students in pursuing post-secondary education.
Eligibility: Applicants must be graduating seniors who intend to enroll full-time in an associate's or bachelor's degree program at one of TheDream.US Partner Colleges. Students must have come to the U.S. before their 16th birthday and must demonstrate significant unmet financial need.
Target applicant(s): High school students.
Minimum GPA: 2.5
Amount: Up to $33,000.
Number of awards: Varies.
Scholarship may be renewable.
Deadline: February 25.
How to apply: Applications are available online.
Exclusive: Visit www.UltimateScholarshipBook.com and enter code TH232723 for updates on this award.

(2328) · Thurgood Marshall College Scholarship Fund

Thurgood Marshall Scholarship Fund
901 F Street NW, Suite 300, Washington, DC 20004
Phone: 202-507-4851
Email: deshuandra.walker@tmcf.org
https://tmcf.org/our-scholarships
Purpose: To provide support to the nation's 47 historically black public colleges and universities by offering merit-based scholarships.
Eligibility: Applicants must be currently enrolled or planning to enroll as full-time students at one of the 47 TMSF member schools and have a minimum 3.0 high school GPA. Applicants must demonstrate a commitment to academic excellence and community service and show financial need. Winners need to maintain a 3.0 GPA for the duration of the scholarship. Applicants must submit a head shot photograph, letters of recommendation, essay and resume.
Target applicant(s): High school students. College students. Graduate school students. Adult students.
Minimum GPA: 3.0
Amount: $3,100.
Number of awards: Varies.
Scholarship may be renewable.
Deadline: Varies.
How to apply: Applications are available through the member schools.

Exclusive: Visit www.UltimateScholarshipBook.com and enter code TH232823 for updates on this award.

(2329) · Traub-Dicker Rainbow Scholarship

Stonewall Community Foundation
1270 Broadway, Suite 501, New York, NY 10001
Phone: 212-457-1341
Email: scholarships@stonewallfoundation.org
https://stonewallfoundation.org
Purpose: To support lesbian women in pursuing post-secondary education.
Eligibility: Applicants must be incoming or current college students in any year of study, including graduate school. Selection is primarily based on demonstration of academic achievement, community service and desire to make a difference.
Target applicant(s): High school students. College students. Graduate school students. Adult students.
Amount: $3,000.
Number of awards: Varies.
Deadline: June 11.
How to apply: Applications are available online.
Exclusive: Visit www.UltimateScholarshipBook.com and enter code ST232923 for updates on this award.

(2330) · Tribal College and University (TCU) Scholarships

American Indian College Fund
8333 Greenwood Boulevard, Denver, CO 80221
Phone: 303-426-8900
https://collegefund.org/#n
Purpose: To support American Indian and Alaska Native students pursuing undergraduate and graduate degrees at tribal colleges.
Eligibility: Applicants must be American Indian and Alaska Native college students seeking undergraduate and graduate degrees at tribal colleges. Scholarships are awarded by each Tribal College or University. Students should contact their school's financial aid office to learn more.
Target applicant(s): High school students. College students. Graduate school students. Adult students.
Amount: Varies.
Number of awards: Varies.
Deadline: May 31.
How to apply: Applications are available online.
Exclusive: Visit www.UltimateScholarshipBook.com and enter code AM233023 for updates on this award.

(2331) · Truman D. Picard Scholarship

Intertribal Timber Council
Attn.: Education Committee, 1112 NE 21st Avenue, Suite 4, Portland, OR 97232-2114
Phone: 503-282-4296
Email: intertribaltimbercouncil@gmail.com
http://www.itcnet.org/about_us/scholarships.html
Purpose: To promote the field of natural resources.
Eligibility: Applicants must be high school seniors or college students and must pursue the natural resources field. Applicants must submit a resume, letters of reference, validated enrollment in Tribe/Native Alaska Corporation and a letter about their interest in natural resources, educational background, academic achievements and financial need.
Target applicant(s): High school students. College students. Graduate school students. Adult students.

Amount: $2,000-$2,500.
Number of awards: Varies.
Deadline: March 13.
How to apply: There is no official application form.
Exclusive: Visit www.UltimateScholarshipBook.com and enter code IN233123 for updates on this award.

(2332) · U.S. Lacrosse Native American Scholarships

Tewaaraton Foundation
1135 16th Street NW, Washington, DC 20036
Phone: 202-255-1485
Email: sarah@tewaaraton.com
http://www.tewaaraton.com
Purpose: To acknowledge and reward students' academic and athletic achievement in the sport of lacrosse.
Eligibility: Applicants must be a member of the Iroquois community, enrolled in a secondary school and in good academic standing. Scholarships are awarded based on academic achievement, athletic performance and ambition.
Target applicant(s): High school students.
Amount: $5,000.
Number of awards: 2.
Deadline: April.
How to apply: Applications are available online. An application form, an essay, two letters of recommendation, a high school transcript and a photograph of the applicant are required.
Exclusive: Visit www.UltimateScholarshipBook.com and enter code TE233223 for updates on this award.

(2333) · United Parcel Service Scholarship for Minority Students

Institute of Industrial and Systems Engineers
3577 Parkway Lane, Suite 200, Norcross, GA 30092
Phone: 800-494-0460
Email: bcameron@iienet.org
http://www.iise.org/
Purpose: To help minority undergraduate students in industrial engineering.
Eligibility: Applicants must be full-time undergraduate minority students enrolled in a college in the United States, Canada or Mexico with an accredited industrial engineering program, have at least a 3.4 GPA, major in industrial engineering and be active members. Students may not apply directly for this scholarship and must be nominated. The award is based on academic ability, character, leadership, potential service to the industrial engineering profession and financial need.
Target applicant(s): College students. Adult students.
Minimum GPA: 3.4
Amount: $4,000.
Number of awards: 1.
Deadline: November 15.
How to apply: Nomination forms are available online.
Exclusive: Visit www.UltimateScholarshipBook.com and enter code IN233323 for updates on this award.

(2334) · Upakar Foundation Indian American Community College Scholarship

Upakar Foundation
9015 Shady Grove Court, Gaithersburg, MD 20877
Email: upakarfoundation@hotmail.com
http://www.upakar.org/
Purpose: To support Indian-American graduating seniors in pursuing post-secondary education at a community college.
Eligibility: Applicants must have been born in India or have at least one parent born in India. Students must be U.S. citizens or U.S. Green Card holders. A minimum GPA of 3.6 is required.
Target applicant(s): High school students.
Minimum GPA: 3.6
Amount: Varies.
Number of awards: Varies.
Scholarship may be renewable.
Deadline: April 30.
How to apply: Applications are available online.
Exclusive: Visit www.UltimateScholarshipBook.com and enter code UP233423 for updates on this award.

(2335) · UPS Hallmark Scholarship

U.S. Pan Asian American Chamber of Commerce
1329 18th Street NW, Washington, DC 20036
Phone: 800-696-7818
Email: info@uspaacc.com
https://celebrasianconference.com/scholarships
Purpose: To provide financial assistance to Asian American students.
Eligibility: Applicants must be high school seniors at least 16 years of age who are of Asian or Pacific heritage. They must be U.S. citizens or permanent residents and plan to enroll full-time at an accredited college or university in the United States in the fall following graduation. A minimum GPA of 3.3 is required, and applicants should demonstrate academic excellence, leadership, community service involvement and financial need.
Target applicant(s): High school students.
Minimum GPA: 3.3
Amount: Varies.
Number of awards: 2.
Deadline: May 15.
How to apply: Applications are available online.
Exclusive: Visit www.UltimateScholarshipBook.com and enter code U.233523 for updates on this award.

(2336) · William and Charlotte Cadbury Award

National Medical Fellowships Inc.
347 Fifth Avenue, Suite 510, New York, NY 10016
Phone: 212-483-8880
Email: scholarships@nmfonline.org
https://nmfonline.org/about-our-scholarships-and-awards/programs/
Purpose: To reward minority medical students with outstanding achievement.
Eligibility: Applicants must be senior minority medical students at an accredited U.S. medical school. Students must demonstrate outstanding academic achievement, leadership and community service.
Target applicant(s): Graduate school students. Adult students.
Amount: $5,000.
Number of awards: 1.
Deadline: Varies.
How to apply: Applications are available online.
Exclusive: Visit www.UltimateScholarshipBook.com and enter code NA233623 for updates on this award.

(2337) · William Wrigley Jr. Scholarship/Internship

United Negro College Fund (UNCF)
1805 7th Street NW, Washington, DC 20001
Phone: 800-331-2244
https://scholarships.uncf.org/
Purpose: To support African American engineering, business and chemistry students with scholarships and paid internships.
Eligibility: Applicants must be sophomores or juniors at a UNCF member college or university. They must demonstrate financial need and have a GPA of at least 2.5.
Target applicant(s): College students. Adult students.
Minimum GPA: 2.5
Amount: Up to $5,000.
Number of awards: Varies.
Deadline: October 28.
How to apply: Applications are available online.
Exclusive: Visit www.UltimateScholarshipBook.com and enter code UN233723 for updates on this award.

(2338) · Working Parent College Scholarship Award

Job-Applications.com
6615 Promway Street, North Canton, OH 44720
http://www.job-applications.com/scholarships
Purpose: To assist working parents with costs for post-secondary education.
Eligibility: Applicants must be part- or full-time students at an accredited U.S. post-secondary institution, have a minimum 3.0 GPA and have worked an average of at least 12 hours per week for the previous four weeks. Students must also be the residential parent of at least one minor child, be a legal U.S. resident and be at least 18 years old.
Target applicant(s): College students. Adult students.
Minimum GPA: 3.0
Amount: $1,000.
Number of awards: 1.
Deadline: August 13.
How to apply: Applications are available online. An essay is required.
Exclusive: Visit www.UltimateScholarshipBook.com and enter code JO233823 for updates on this award.

(2339) · Worthy Women's Professional Studies Scholarship

Worthy
551 5th Avenue, 20th Floor, New York, NY 10176
Phone: 888-222-0208
Email: scholarships@worthy.com
https://www.worthy.com/about/scholarship
Purpose: To assist women who have enrolled in continuing education professional studies to pursue their passion.
Eligibility: Applicants must be a permanent resident of the U.S., identify as a female, be over the age of 30 and be enrolled in a continuing education professional studies program. A 300- to 500-word essay is required on one of three provided topics.
Target applicant(s): College students. Adult students.
Amount: $1,000-$2,500.
Number of awards: 3.
Deadline: December 6.
How to apply: Applications are available online. A 300- to 500-word essay on one of three topics provided is required.
Exclusive: Visit www.UltimateScholarshipBook.com and enter code WO233923 for updates on this award.

(2340) · Young Women in Public Affairs Award

Zonta International
1211 West 22nd Street, Suite 900, Oak Brook, IL 60523
Phone: 630-928-1400
Email: zontaintl@zonta.org
http://www.zonta.org
Purpose: To encourage young women to participate in politics and public service.
Eligibility: Applicants must be young women between the ages of 16 and 19. District award winners receive at least $1,000, and international award winners receive $4,000. Selection is based on volunteerism, volunteer leadership and dedication to "advancing the status of women worldwide." Club deadlines vary. The April 1 deadline is the date by which applications must be received by the District Governor.
Target applicant(s): High school students.
Amount: $1,000-$4,000.
Number of awards: Varies.
Deadline: Varies.
How to apply: Applications are available online or from your local Zonta Club.
Exclusive: Visit www.UltimateScholarshipBook.com and enter code ZO234023 for updates on this award.

DISABILITY / ILLNESS

(2341) · #RAREis Scholarship

#RAREis Scholarship Fund
Scholarship America, One Scholarship Way, Saint Peter, MN 56082
Phone: 507-931-1682
Email: rareis@scholarshipamerica.org
https://learnmore.scholarsapply.org/rareis/
Purpose: To support students diagnosed with a rare disease.
Eligibility: Applicants must be U.S. residents who have been diagnosed by a physician as having any form of rare disease regardless of treatment status and provide a diagnosis verification form. Students must be at least 17 years of age and plan to enroll full-time or part-time in undergraduate or graduate study at an accredited two- or four-year college, university or vocational-technical/trade school. An essay submission on a provided prompt is required.
Target applicant(s): High school students. College students. Graduate school students. Adult students.
Amount: $5,000.
Number of awards: 35.
Deadline: August.
How to apply: Applications are available online.
Exclusive: Visit www.UltimateScholarshipBook.com and enter code #R234123 for updates on this award.

(2342) · AbbVie Immunology Scholarship

AbbVie Immunology Scholarship
Scholarship America, One Scholarship Way, Saint Peter, MN 56082
Phone: 507-931-0651
Email: abbvieimmunology@scholarshipamerica.org
https://abbvieimmunologyscholarship.com/
Purpose: To support students who are living with chronic inflammatory diseases.
Eligibility: Applicants must be legal residents of the U.S. who have been diagnosed with one of the following conditions: ankylosing spondylitis, Crohn's disease, hidradenitis suppurativa, juvenile idiopathic arthritis, psoriasis, psoriatic arthritis, rheumatoid arthritis, ulcerative colitis or uveitis. Students must plan to enroll full-time in an undergraduate or graduate level program at an accredited college, university or technical school in the U.S. for the upcoming school year.
Target applicant(s): High school students. College students. Graduate school students. Adult students.
Amount: Up to $15,000.
Number of awards: Varies.
Deadline: December.
How to apply: Applications are available online.
Exclusive: Visit www.UltimateScholarshipBook.com and enter code AB234223 for updates on this award.

(2343) · American Council of the Blind Scholarships

American Council of the Blind
Scholarship Program, 1703 North Beauregard Street, Suite 420, Alexandria, VA 22311
Phone: 202-467-5081
Email: info@acb.org
http://www.acb.org
Purpose: To reward outstanding blind students.
Eligibility: Students must be legally blind in both eyes and admitted full-time to a post-secondary academic or vocational program. A minimum GPA of 3.3 is required, except in extenuating circumstances. Students who work full-time and attend school part-time may apply for the John Hebner Memorial Scholarship. Scholarship recipients are expected to attend a national convention if they are over 18.
Target applicant(s): High school students. College students. Graduate school students. Adult students.
Minimum GPA: 3.3
Amount: $2,000-$7,500.
Number of awards: Up to 20.
Deadline: February 14.
How to apply: Applications are available online and by phone.
Exclusive: Visit www.UltimateScholarshipBook.com and enter code AM234323 for updates on this award.

(2344) · Anne Ford Scholarship Program

National Center for Learning Disabilities
1220 L Street NW, Suite 100, Box #168, Washington, DC 20005
Phone: 301-966-2234
Email: afscholarship@ncld.org
http://www.ncld.org
Purpose: To provide financial assistance to high school seniors with learning disabilities who plan to pursue undergraduate degrees.
Eligibility: Applicants must be U.S. citizens who are academically successful in public or private secondary schools and with an identified learning disability. Students must have a minimum 3.0 GPA. Financial need is considered.
Target applicant(s): High school students.
Minimum GPA: 3.0
Amount: $10,000.
Number of awards: 2.
Deadline: April 10.
How to apply: Applications are available online.
Exclusive: Visit www.UltimateScholarshipBook.com and enter code NA234423 for updates on this award.

(2345) · Baer Reintegration Scholarship

Baer Reintegration Scholarship
P.O. Box 259, Lafayette Hill, PA 19444
Phone: 800-809-8202
Email: baerscholarships@reintegration.com
http://www.reintegration.com
Purpose: To provide aid to students with schizophrenia or similar disorders who are seeking to advance themselves academically and vocationally.
Eligibility: Applicants must have been diagnosed with schizophrenia, schizophreniform, schizoaffective disorder or bipolar disorder, be undergoing medical treatment for their disease(s) and be involved in other rehabilitative efforts, such as working part-time or volunteering with a civic organization.
Target applicant(s): High school students. College students. Graduate school students. Adult students.
Amount: Varies.
Number of awards: Varies.
Deadline: January.
How to apply: Applications are available online or by phone, mail or email.
Exclusive: Visit www.UltimateScholarshipBook.com and enter code BA234523 for updates on this award.

(2346) · BMO Capital Markets Lime Connect Equity Through Education Scholarship

Lime Connect
590 Madison Avenue, 21st Floor, New York, NY 10022
Phone: 212-521-4469
https://www.limeconnect.com/programs/page/scholarships
Purpose: To support undergraduate and graduate students with disabilities in pursuing a career in financial services.
Eligibility: Applicants must be enrolled full-time in a finance, business, engineering, mathematics, physics, statistics or related program in the U.S. or Canada. Students must submit university transcripts, resume, an essay explaining their career goals and a letter of recommendation. Selection is based on the overall strength of the application.
Target applicant(s): College students. Graduate school students. Adult students.
Amount: $10,000.
Number of awards: 1.
Deadline: February 14.
How to apply: Applications are available online.
Exclusive: Visit www.UltimateScholarshipBook.com and enter code LI234623 for updates on this award.

(2347) · Boomer Esiason Foundation General Academic Scholarship

Boomer Esiason Foundation
c/o Chris McEwan, 483 10th Avenue, Suite 300, New York, NY 10018
Phone: 646-292-7930
Email: jcahillbef@aol.com
http://www.esiason.org/cf-living/scholarships
Purpose: To provide assistance to students with cystic fibrosis.
Eligibility: Applicants may be pursuing undergraduate or graduate degrees. They must demonstrate financial need. Selection is based on scholastic achievement, character, leadership, community service and financial need. Scholarships are awarded in April, July, September and December of each year.
Target applicant(s): High school students. College students. Graduate school students. Adult students.
Amount: $500-$2,500.
Number of awards: 10-15.
Deadline: March 27, June 26, September 25, December 21.
How to apply: Applications are available online. An application form, recent photo, letter from doctor, essay, transcript, tuition breakdown and W2 from both parents are required.
Exclusive: Visit www.UltimateScholarshipBook.com and enter code BO234723 for updates on this award.

(2348) · Bristol-Myers Squibb Scholarship for Cancer Survivors

Bristol-Myers Squibb
Scholarship America, One Scholarship Way, Saint Peter, MN 56082
Phone: 507-931-1682
Email: cancer-survivors@scholarshipamerica.org
https://learnmore.scholarsapply.org/cancer-survivors/
Purpose: To assist cancer survivors pursue post-secondary education.
Eligibility: Applicants must be cancer survivors age 25 years or younger. Students must be high school seniors or post-secondary undergraduates with at least a 3.5 grade point average. Applicants must plan to enroll as full-time students at an accredited college, university, vocational or technical school.

Target applicant(s): High school students. College students.
Minimum GPA: 3.5
Amount: $10,000.
Number of awards: Up to 25.
Deadline: April 1.
How to apply: Applications are available online.
Exclusive: Visit www.UltimateScholarshipBook.com and enter code BR234823 for updates on this award.

(2349) · Cancer for College Scholarships

Cancer for College
981 Park Center Drive, Vista, CA 92081
Phone: 760-599-5096
Email: applications@cancerforcollege.org
https://www.cancerforcollege.org/
Purpose: To support current and former cancer patients and amputees.
Eligibility: Applicants must be U.S. residents. They must be enrolled in an accredited university, community college or trade school. Recipients must agree to attend regional events and be available for interviews and media coverage.
Target applicant(s): High school students. College students. Adult students.
Amount: $1,000-$5,000.
Number of awards: Varies.
Scholarship may be renewable.
Deadline: January 31.
How to apply: Applications are available online. An application form, summary of cancer treatment, personal statement, details of college financing and two letters of recommendation are required.
Exclusive: Visit www.UltimateScholarshipBook.com and enter code CA234923 for updates on this award.

(2350) · Challenge Met Scholarship

American Radio Relay League Foundation
225 Main Street, Newington, CT 06111-1494
Phone: 860-594-0348
Email: foundation@arrl.org
http://www.arrl.org/scholarship-program
Purpose: To provide assistance to amateur radio operators with learning disabilities.
Eligibility: Applicants must be licensed amateur radio operators who are accepted to or enrolled in a two- or four-year college, technical school or university. Preference is given to students with documented learning disabilities who are putting forth effort.
Target applicant(s): High school students. College students. Adult students.
Amount: $500.
Number of awards: 1.
Deadline: December 31.
How to apply: Applications are available online.
Exclusive: Visit www.UltimateScholarshipBook.com and enter code AM235023 for updates on this award.

(2351) · Disabled Student Scholarship

Disability Care Center
2875 South Orange Avenue #500, Orlando, FL 32806
Phone: 888-504-0035
Email: scholarship@disabilitycarecenter.org
http://www.disabilitycarecenter.org/giving-back/scholarships/

Purpose: To support students who have a physical or mental impairment who are pursuing a college education.

Eligibility: Applicants must have a medically diagnosed physical or mental impairment that interferes with everyday activities or quality of life and can provide a physician's statement regarding their impairment. A minimum GPA of 2.5 is required. Students must be a legal resident of the U.S. and enrolled full time for the upcoming fall semester. Applicants will need to submit a short essay describing an obstacle or hardship incurred due to their medical condition, how the student overcame that obstacle, how it influence the student's life and how it will impact them in the future. Selection is based on the essay.

Target applicant(s): High school students. College students. Adult students.

Minimum GPA: 2.5

Amount: $500.

Number of awards: 1.

Deadline: August 1.

How to apply: Applications are available online and must also include proof of college acceptance or college ID, proof of registration for the fall semester, copy of most recent transcript, proof of U.S. citizenship, a physician's letter and the essay.

Exclusive: Visit www.UltimateScholarshipBook.com and enter code DI235123 for updates on this award.

(2352) · Duane Buckley Memorial Scholarship

American Council of the Blind
Scholarship Program, 1703 North Beauregard Street, Suite 420, Alexandria, VA 22311
Phone: 202-467-5081
Email: info@acb.org
http://www.acb.org

Purpose: To assist students who work to overcome challenges.

Eligibility: Applicants must be legally blind college freshmen. A letter of recommendation, autobiographical sketch and copies of transcripts are required.

Target applicant(s): College students. Adult students.

Amount: $1,000.

Number of awards: 1.

Deadline: February 15.

How to apply: Applications are available online.

Exclusive: Visit www.UltimateScholarshipBook.com and enter code AM235223 for updates on this award.

(2353) · Elizabeth Nash Foundation Scholarship Program

Elizabeth Nash Foundation
P.O. Box 1260, Los Gatos, CA 95031-1260
Email: info@elizabethnashfoundation.org
http://www.elizabethnashfoundation.org

Purpose: To support students with cystic fibrosis.

Eligibility: Applicants must be current or entering graduate or undergraduate students at an accredited U.S. institution of higher learning. They must be U.S. citizens, and they must be pursuing a bachelor's degree or higher. Selection criteria include scholastic achievement, character, leadership, community service, service to cystic fibrosis-related causes and financial need.

Target applicant(s): High school students. College students. Graduate school students. Adult students.

Amount: $1,000-$2,500.

Number of awards: Varies.

Deadline: April 13.

How to apply: Applications are available online. An application form, essay, letter of recommendation, documentation of cystic fibrosis diagnosis, transcript, copy of FAFSA and details of tuition costs are required.

Exclusive: Visit www.UltimateScholarshipBook.com and enter code EL235323 for updates on this award.

(2354) · Eric Dostie Memorial College Scholarship

NuFACTOR
41093 County Center Drive, Temecula, CA 92591
Phone: 800-323-6832
Email: info@kelleycom.com
http://www.kelleycom.com

Purpose: To assist students who suffer from hemophilia or related bleeding disorders as well as their immediate families.

Eligibility: Applicants must be individuals with hemophilia or related to said individuals, enrolled full-time in an accredited college or university and demonstrate academic achievement, financial need and a history of community service.

Target applicant(s): High school students. College students. Adult students.

Amount: $1,000.

Number of awards: 10.

Deadline: March 1.

How to apply: Applications are available after November 1 by telephone or mail.

Exclusive: Visit www.UltimateScholarshipBook.com and enter code NU235423 for updates on this award.

(2355) · Fred Scheigert Scholarships

Council of Citizens with Low Vision International
1155 15th Street NW, Suite 1004, Washington, DC 20005
Phone: 800-733-2258
Email: ncclv@yahoo.com
http://www.cclvi.org

Purpose: To provide educational assistance for students with low vision.

Eligibility: Applicants must be registered in a full-time undergraduate or graduate course of study at a college, trade or vocational school. They must have a GPA of 3.2 or higher. Those with extenuating circumstances may be exempt from these requirements. Applicants must have 20/70 or worse vision in the better eye with the best possible correction, or a field of vision of 30 degrees or less.

Target applicant(s): High school students. College students. Graduate school students. Adult students.

Minimum GPA: 3.2

Amount: $3,000.

Number of awards: 3.

Deadline: March 15.

How to apply: Applications are available online.

Exclusive: Visit www.UltimateScholarshipBook.com and enter code CO235523 for updates on this award.

(2356) · George H. Nofer Scholarship for Law and Public Policy

Alexander Graham Bell Association for the Deaf and Hard of Hearing
Youth and Family Programs Manager, 3417 Volta Place NW, Washington, DC 20007
Phone: 202-337-5220
Email: financialaid@agbell.org

http://www.agbell.org

Purpose: To assist graduate students with a moderate to profound hearing loss.

Eligibility: Applicants must attend or be accepted to attend full-time an accredited law school or a master's or doctoral program in public policy or public administration and must use spoken language as the primary mode of communication. Students must also have a pre-lingual and bilateral hearing loss. Applications are available online.

Target applicant(s): Graduate school students. Adult students.

Amount: $5,000.

Number of awards: Up to 3.

Deadline: April 12.

How to apply: Applications are available online.

Exclusive: Visit www.UltimateScholarshipBook.com and enter code AL235623 for updates on this award.

(2357) · Graeme Clark Scholarship

Cochlear Americas

The Graeme Clark Scholarship, 13059 East Peakview Avenue, Centennial, CO 80111

Phone: 303-790-9010

http://www.cochlearamericas.com

Purpose: To support cochlear implant recipients.

Eligibility: Applicants must have received a Nucleus cochlear implant. They may be high school seniors, current college students or students who have been accepted into an institution of higher learning. Students must pursue a minimum of a three-year undergraduate degree at an accredited university. Criteria for selection include academic achievement and commitment to leadership and humanity. A minimum GPA of 2.5 is required for all applicants.

Target applicant(s): High school students. College students. Adult students.

Minimum GPA: 2.5

Amount: $2,000.

Number of awards: Varies.

Deadline: September 30.

How to apply: Applications are available online. An application form, transcript, proof of university admission, list of activities and awards, personal statement, proof of age and citizenship and three letters of reference are required.

Exclusive: Visit www.UltimateScholarshipBook.com and enter code CO235723 for updates on this award.

(2358) · Guthrie-Koch PKU Scholarship

National PKU News

6869 Woodlawn Avenue NE #116, Seattle, WA 98115

Phone: 206-525-8140

Email: scholarship@pkunews.org

https://pkunews.org/guthrie-koch-scholarship/

Purpose: In honor of the doctor who created the newborn screening test for PKU, the scholarship gives support to bright students living with PKU.

Eligibility: Students must have PKU, follow the diet and attend an accredited school. Financial need is considered along with academic excellence.

Target applicant(s): High school students. College students.

Amount: Varies.

Number of awards: Varies.

Deadline: February 1.

How to apply: Applications are available online after July 1 each year.

Exclusive: Visit www.UltimateScholarshipBook.com and enter code NA235823 for updates on this award.

(2359) · HIV-Positive Scholarship

STDcheck.com

Phone: 800-456-2323

https://www.stdcheck.com/scholarship-application.php

Purpose: To support students who are HIV-positive.

Eligibility: Applicants must be U.S. citizens who are currently enrolled or will be enrolled the following semester full-time at an accredited college or university in the U.S. Students will need to provide proof that they are HIV-positive. Applicants must also submit an essay on how HIV was contracted, how it has affected their life and what they wish those living without HIV knew about living with the virus. The scholarship is awarded monthly.

Target applicant(s): High school students. College students. Adult students.

Amount: $250-$5,000.

Number of awards: Varies.

Deadline: Varies.

How to apply: Applications are available online and must include the essay, proof of HIV-positive status and an official transcript.

Exclusive: Visit www.UltimateScholarshipBook.com and enter code ST235923 for updates on this award.

(2360) · Incight Scholarship

Incight Education

P.O. Box 82056, Portland, OR 97282

Phone: 971-244-0305

Email: questions@incight.org

https://www.incight.org/scholarship

Purpose: To support students with physical or learning disabilities who are residents of Oregon, Washington or California.

Eligibility: Applicants must have a documented disability that may include physical, learning or cognitive. Students must also attend a trade school, college or university on a full-time basis. Recipients are placed with internships related to their field of study.

Target applicant(s): High school students. College students. Graduate school students. Adult students.

Amount: $500-$2,500.

Number of awards: Varies.

Scholarship may be renewable.

Deadline: April 15.

How to apply: Applications are available online.

Exclusive: Visit www.UltimateScholarshipBook.com and enter code IN236023 for updates on this award.

(2361) · Jaime Guttenberg All Abilities Scholarship

Orange Ribbons for Jaime

5944 Coral Ridge Drive, Suite 301, Coral Springs, FL 33076

Phone: 561-750-1500

Email: info@orangeribbonsforjaime.org

https://orangeribbonsforjaime.org/

Purpose: To support students with a diagnosis of a special need or disability.

Eligibility: Applicants must have a diagnosis of a special need or disability such as, but not limited to autism, down's syndrome, cerebral palsy or limb deficiency. Students must have a high school diploma and be applying to any post-high school program such as, but not limited to,

university, college, technical school, trade school or vocational training. A writing submission on a provided topic is required.
Target applicant(s): High school students.
Amount: Varies.
Number of awards: Varies.
Deadline: March.
How to apply: Applications are available online.
Exclusive: Visit www.UltimateScholarshipBook.com and enter code OR236123 for updates on this award.

(2362) · Kevin Child Scholarship

National Hemophilia Foundation
7 Penn Plaza, Suite 1204, New York, NY 10001
http://www.hemophilia.org
Purpose: To support students who have been diagnosed with hemophilia A or B.
Eligibility: Applicants must be high school seniors or enrolled undergraduate students.
Target applicant(s): High school students. College students. Adult students.
Amount: $1,000.
Number of awards: 1.
Deadline: August 2.
How to apply: Applications are available online.
Exclusive: Visit www.UltimateScholarshipBook.com and enter code NA236223 for updates on this award.

(2363) · L.I.F.E. Scholarship

Lupus Inspiration Foundation For Excellence
P.O. Box 64088, Tucson, AZ 85728
Email: life4lupuscholarship@gmail.com
http://www.lifescholarship.org
Purpose: To support students diagnosed with lupus in pursuing post-secondary education.
Eligibility: Applicants must be enrolled for a minimum of six credits for the upcoming fall semester after the award is granted. A minimum GPA of 3.0 is required. Selection is primarily based on extracurricular involvement, community service and leadership ability.
Target applicant(s): High school students. College students. Adult students.
Minimum GPA: 3.0
Amount: $500.
Number of awards: Varies.
Deadline: July 1.
How to apply: Applications are available online.
Exclusive: Visit www.UltimateScholarshipBook.com and enter code LU236323 for updates on this award.

(2364) · Lighthouse Guild Scholarships

Lighthouse Guild
Scholarship Awards, 15 West 65th Street, New York, NY 10023
Phone: 212-769-7801
Email: scholars@lighthouseguild.org
https://www.lighthouseguild.org/
Purpose: To assist blind or partially-sighted collegiate or college-bound students.
Eligibility: Applicants must be legally blind. Visual requirements include a best corrected visual acuity of 20/200 or less in the better eye and/or a visual field of less than 20 degrees in the better eye and be in one of three categories: college-bound high school student, undergraduate

college student or graduate student. They must also be U.S. citizens and residents and attend an accredited college or university in the U.S. or its territories. Selection is based on academic and personal achievements.
Target applicant(s): High school students. College students. Graduate school students. Adult students.
Amount: Up to $10,000.
Number of awards: Up to 17.
Deadline: March 31.
How to apply: Applications are available online.
Exclusive: Visit www.UltimateScholarshipBook.com and enter code LI236423 for updates on this award.

(2365) · Lime Connect Pathways Scholarship for High School Seniors with Disabilities

Lime Connect
590 Madison Avenue, 21st Floor, New York, NY 10022
Phone: 212-521-4469
https://www.limeconnect.com/programs/page/scholarships
Purpose: To support high school seniors with disabilities.
Eligibility: Applicants must be current high school seniors in the U.S. or Canada and have or consider themselves to have a visible or invisible disability. Students must be accepted to, or applied and awaiting acceptance to, a four-year university or college in the U.S. or Canada and intend to enroll full-time.
Target applicant(s): High school students.
Amount: $1,000.
Number of awards: Varies.
Deadline: May 31.
How to apply: Applications are available online.
Exclusive: Visit www.UltimateScholarshipBook.com and enter code LI236523 for updates on this award.

(2366) · Little People of America Scholarships

Little People of America
250 El Camino Real, Suite 218, Tustin, CA 92780
Phone: 888-572-2001
Email: info@lpaonline.org
http://www.lpaonline.org
Purpose: To aid those affected by dwarfism.
Eligibility: Applicants may be junior high, high school or college students who have been involved with Little People of America. Preference is given in the following order: LPA members with medically diagnosed dwarfism, immediate family members of LPA members diagnosed with dwarfism and non-LPA members with dwarfism.
Target applicant(s): Junior high students or younger. High school students. College students. Graduate school students. Adult students.
Amount: $250-$1,000.
Number of awards: 3.
Deadline: May 31.
How to apply: Applications are available online. An application form, personal statement and three letters of recommendation are required.
Exclusive: Visit www.UltimateScholarshipBook.com and enter code LI236623 for updates on this award.

(2367) · Living With Dyslexia Scholarship

Gemm Learning
877 Post Road E., Suite 2, Westport, CT 06880
Phone: 203-292-5410
https://www.gemmlearning.com/about/scholarship-opportunities

Purpose: To support students with dyslexia in pursuing post-secondary education.

Eligibility: Applicants must be enrolled or planning on enrolling at a U.S. or Canada based educational institution. Students must submit an essay explaining what it's like to live with dyslexia. Selection is based on the overall strength of the submission.

Target applicant(s): High school students. College students. Adult students.

Amount: $1,000.

Number of awards: 1.

Deadline: October 31.

How to apply: Applications are available online.

Exclusive: Visit www.UltimateScholarshipBook.com and enter code GE236723 for updates on this award.

(2368) · MAPDA Scholarship

Mothers Against Prescription Drug Abuse
2308 Mt. Vernon Avenue, Suite 753, Alexandria, VA 22301
Phone: 603-513-8017
Email: whitney.taylor@mapda.net
https://mapda.net/scholarships

Purpose: To support students in recovery as they rebuild their lives.

Eligibility: Applicants must be U.S. citizens and recently admitted or currently enrolled in classes at a junior college or vocational school. Students must submit signed documentation which verifies successful completion of a full course of treatment from one of the accredited treatment facilities and verification of current regular attendance at a recovery support system or peer support group.

Target applicant(s): High school students. College students. Adult students.

Amount: $1,500.

Number of awards: 5.

Deadline: Rolling.

How to apply: Applications are available online.

Exclusive: Visit www.UltimateScholarshipBook.com and enter code MO236823 for updates on this award.

(2369) · Marion Huber Learning Through Listening Awards

Learning Ally
20 Roszel Road, Princeton, NJ 08540
Phone: 800-221-4792
Email: naa@LearningAlly.org
https://www.learningally.org/

Purpose: To assist learning-disabled high school seniors.

Eligibility: Applicants must demonstrate leadership skills, scholarship and a desire to help others and attend a two- or four-year college or vocational school. Students must have a specific learning disability and be registered with RFB&D for at least one year prior to the application deadline.

Target applicant(s): High school students.

Minimum GPA: 3.0

Amount: $2,000-$6,000.

Number of awards: 6.

Deadline: December 31.

How to apply: Applications are available online.

Exclusive: Visit www.UltimateScholarshipBook.com and enter code LE236923 for updates on this award.

(2370) · Mary P. Oenslanger Scholastic Achievement Awards

Learning Ally
20 Roszel Road, Princeton, NJ 08540
Phone: 800-221-4792
Email: naa@LearningAlly.org
https://www.learningally.org/

Purpose: Assistance for graduate study is awarded to blind college senior students or graduate students who have shown leadership skills, scholarship and a desire to help others.

Eligibility: Applicants must be blind or visually impaired, Learning Ally members and college seniors and graduate students.

Target applicant(s): College students. Graduate school students. Adult students.

Minimum GPA: 3.0

Amount: $1,000-$6,000.

Number of awards: 9.

Deadline: December 31.

How to apply: Applications are available online.

Exclusive: Visit www.UltimateScholarshipBook.com and enter code LE237023 for updates on this award.

(2371) · Michael A. Hunter Memorial Scholarship Fund

Orange County Community Foundation
4041 MacArthur Boulevard, Suite 510, Newport Beach, CA 92660
Phone: 949-553-4202
Email: cmontesano@oc-cf.org
https://www.oc-cf.org/grants-scholarships-overview/scholarships/

Purpose: To support those who have been affected by leukemia as they pursue an education.

Eligibility: Applicants must be high school seniors or current college students who are leukemia patients and/or are the children of non-surviving leukemia patients. Applicants must be full-time students with a GPA of at least 3.0 and demonstrate financial need. They must submit an essay describing how leukemia has impacted their life, a doctor's note verifying the leukemia diagnosis and two letters of recommendation.

Target applicant(s): High school students. College students. Adult students.

Minimum GPA: 3.0

Amount: $2,000-$5,000.

Number of awards: Varies.

Deadline: March 16.

How to apply: Applications are available online.

Exclusive: Visit www.UltimateScholarshipBook.com and enter code OR237123 for updates on this award.

(2372) · Mike Hylton and Ron Niederman Scholarships

BioMatrix
3300 Corporate Avenue, Suite 104, Weston, FL 33331
Phone: 877-337-3002
https://www.biomatrixsprx.com/bleeding-disorders-scholarships

Purpose: To support men with hemophilia or von Willebrand disease and their families.

Eligibility: Students must provide proof of diagnosis by a physician. Applicants must submit an essay and two letters of recommendation.

Target applicant(s): High school students. College students. Adult students.

Amount: $1,000.

Number of awards: 2.
Deadline: August 1.
How to apply: Applications are available online.
Exclusive: Visit www.UltimateScholarshipBook.com and enter code BI237223 for updates on this award.

(2373) · Millie Brother Scholarship

Children of Deaf Adults, International
Dr. Jennie E. Pyers, Assistant Professor of Psychology, Wellesley College, 106 Central Street, SCI480, Wellesley, MA 02481
Phone: 781-283-3736
Email: scholarships@coda-international.org
https://coda-international.org/about/scholarships/
Purpose: To assist hearing children of deaf parents to pursue post-secondary educational opportunities.
Eligibility: Applicants must be graduating high school seniors and the hearing children of deaf parents. Applicants must submit a transcript, letters of recommendation and essay. Essays should describe applicants' Coda experience and future career goals.
Target applicant(s): High school students. College students. Graduate school students. Adult students.
Amount: $3,000.
Number of awards: 2.
Deadline: May 7.
How to apply: Applications are available online.
Exclusive: Visit www.UltimateScholarshipBook.com and enter code CH237323 for updates on this award.

(2374) · Millie Gonzales Memorial Scholarships

BioMatrix
3300 Corporate Avenue, Suite 104, Weston, FL 33331
Phone: 877-337-3002
https://www.biomatrixsprx.com/bleeding-disorders-scholarships
Purpose: To support women with hemophilia or von Willebrand Disease.
Eligibility: Students must provide proof of diagnosis by a physician. Applicants must submit an essay and two letters of recommendation.
Target applicant(s): High school students. College students. Adult students.
Amount: $1,000.
Number of awards: 1.
Deadline: August 1.
How to apply: Applications are available online.
Exclusive: Visit www.UltimateScholarshipBook.com and enter code BI237423 for updates on this award.

(2375) · National Collegiate Cancer Foundation Scholarship

National Collegiate Cancer Foundation
4858 Battery Lane, #216, Bethesda, MD 20814
Phone: 240-515-6262
Email: info@collegiatecancer.org
http://www.collegiatecancer.org
Purpose: To provide financial assistance to college students who have been diagnosed with cancer.
Eligibility: Applicants must demonstrate financial need. Selection is based on financial need, quality of essay and recommendations, demonstrating a "will win" attitude and overall story of cancer survivorship.

Target applicant(s): High school students. College students. Graduate school students. Adult students.
Amount: $1,000.
Number of awards: Varies.
Deadline: May 21.
How to apply: Applications are available online.
Exclusive: Visit www.UltimateScholarshipBook.com and enter code NA237523 for updates on this award.

(2376) · National Federation of the Blind Scholarship

National Federation of the Blind
200 East Wells Street, Baltimore, MD 21230
Phone: 410-659-9314
Email: scholarships@nfb.org
https://nfb.org
Purpose: The National Federation of the Blind offers thirty scholarships to exceptional blind scholars.
Eligibility: Applicants must be legally blind and pursue a full-time postsecondary study in the following semester in the U.S. One scholarship may be given to a part-time student. There are no additional restrictions for most of the scholarships. However, a few require study in certain fields or other special traits. Awards are based on academic excellence, community service and financial need. Applicants must reside in the United States or Puerto Rico and attend college in the United States or Puerto Rico. Students make one application for any of the 30 awards; the members of the NFB Scholarship Committee choose the 30 winners and decide which person will receive which award. Legally blind means one is blind in both eyes according to the legal definition, which is available on the organization's website.
Target applicant(s): High school students. College students. Graduate school students. Adult students.
Amount: $3,000-$12,000.
Number of awards: 30.
Deadline: March 31.
How to apply: Applications are available online.
Exclusive: Visit www.UltimateScholarshipBook.com and enter code NA237623 for updates on this award.

(2377) · National MS Society Scholarship Program

National Multiple Sclerosis Society
733 Third Avenue, New York, NY 10017
Phone: 800-344-4867
http://www.nationalmssociety.org
Purpose: To provide educational opportunities for students affected by multiple sclerosis.
Eligibility: Applicants must be high school seniors or graduates who have MS, or who have a parent with MS and will be attending college for the first time. They must be U.S. citizens or legal residents who plan to enroll in an undergraduate program at an accredited institution of higher learning. Applicants must take at least six credit hours per semester, and the courses taken must lead to a degree, license or certificate.
Target applicant(s): High school students.
Amount: $1,000-$3,000.
Number of awards: Up to 400.
Deadline: January.
How to apply: Applications are available online.
Exclusive: Visit www.UltimateScholarshipBook.com and enter code NA237723 for updates on this award.

(2378) · National Scholarship Competition for Disabled College Students

disABLEDperson Inc.
P.O. Box 230636, Encinitas, CA 92023
Phone: 760-420-1269
Email: info@disabledperson.com
https://www.disabledperson.com/scholarships/info
Purpose: To support disabled students in pursuing their undergraduate studies.
Eligibility: Applicants must be enrolled full-time in an two- or four-year college. Students must provide proof of disability through the Disability Student Services department at their school. Applicants must also include an essay with their application. Selection is based on the overall strength of the application.
Target applicant(s): College students. Adult students.
Amount: $2,000.
Number of awards: 1.
Deadline: March.
How to apply: Applications are available online.
Exclusive: Visit www.UltimateScholarshipBook.com and enter code DI237823 for updates on this award.

(2379) · NFMC Hinda Honigman Award for the Blind

National Federation of Music Clubs (NC)
Bobbye Guyton, 2400 Coronado Drive, Hoover, AL 35226
Phone: 205-822-6117
Email: rag2400@aol.com
http://www.nfmc-music.org/competitions-awards/
Purpose: To support blind instrumentalists or vocalists.
Eligibility: Applicants must be between the ages of 16 and 25, be an instrumentalist or vocalist and submit an affidavit from an ophthalmologist stating that they are blind. Applicants must also be affiliated with the National Federation of Music Clubs.
Target applicant(s): High school students. College students. Graduate school students. Adult students.
Amount: $500-$1,500.
Number of awards: 2.
Deadline: February 1.
How to apply: Applications are available online.
Exclusive: Visit www.UltimateScholarshipBook.com and enter code NA237923 for updates on this award.

(2380) · Northwestern Mutual Childhood Cancer Survivor Scholarship

Northwestern Mutual Foundation
Scholarship America, One Scholarship Way, Saint Peter, MN 56082
Phone: 507-931-1682
Email: nmsurvivors@scholarshipamerica.org
https://learnmore.scholarsapply.org/nmsurvivors
Purpose: To support students who have survived cancer and are pursuing a college education.
Eligibility: Applicants must be U.S. citizens who are cancer survivors and age 25 and under. Students must be planning to enroll for full-time undergraduate study at an accredited college, university or technical school for the upcoming school year. Applicants must have at least a 2.5 GPA and have need of financial assistance.
Target applicant(s): High school students. College students.
Minimum GPA: 2.5
Amount: $5,000.
Number of awards: 25.
Scholarship may be renewable.
Deadline: February 2.
How to apply: Applications are available online.
Exclusive: Visit www.UltimateScholarshipBook.com and enter code NO238023 for updates on this award.

(2381) · Northwestern Mutual Foundation Childhood Cancer Sibling Scholarship

Northwestern Mutual Foundation Childhood Cancer Sibling Scholarship
Scholarship America, One Scholarship Way, Saint Peter, MN 56082
Phone: 507-931-1682
Email: nmsibling@scholarshipamerica.org
https://learnmore.scholarsapply.org/nmsibling
Purpose: To support students whose siblings have been affected by cancer.
Eligibility: Applicants must be U.S. citizens ages 25 or younger and siblings of individuals who have been affected by pediatric cancer, whether they have survived, passed away or are currently in treatment. Students must have a minimum 2.5 GPA, demonstrate financial need and plant to enroll full-time for undergraduate study.
Target applicant(s): High school students. College students.
Minimum GPA: 2.5
Amount: $5,000.
Number of awards: 25.
Scholarship may be renewable.
Deadline: February 2.
How to apply: Applications are available online.
Exclusive: Visit www.UltimateScholarshipBook.com and enter code NO238123 for updates on this award.

(2382) · Optimist International Communications Contest

Optimist International
4494 Lindell Boulevard, St. Louis, MO 63108
Phone: 314-371-6000
Email: programs@optimist.org
http://www.optimist.org
Purpose: To reward students based on their communications performance.
Eligibility: Applicants must be students up to grade 12 in the U.S. and Canada, to CEGEP in Quebec and to grade 13 in the Caribbean who are recognized by their schools as deaf or hard of hearing.
Target applicant(s): High school students.
Amount: $2,500.
Number of awards: Varies.
Deadline: Varies.
How to apply: Contact your local Optimist Club.
Exclusive: Visit www.UltimateScholarshipBook.com and enter code OP238223 for updates on this award.

(2383) · P. Buckley Moss Endowed Scholarship

P. Buckley Moss Foundation for Children's Education
74 Poplar Grove Lane, Mathews, VA 23109
Phone: 800-430-1320
Email: foundation@mossfoundation.org
http://mossfoundation.org
Purpose: To support students with learning disabilities to pursue visual arts education.

Eligibility: Applicants must be graduating high school seniors with a language-related learning disability who are enrolling in an accredited two- or four-year college or university. Students must be pursuing a career in the visual arts and demonstrate financial need.
Target applicant(s): High school students.
Amount: $1,000.
Number of awards: 1.
Deadline: March 31.
How to apply: Applications are available online.
Exclusive: Visit www.UltimateScholarshipBook.com and enter code P.238323 for updates on this award.

(2384) · Paul and Ellen Ruckes Scholarship

American Foundation for the Blind Scholarship Committee
1000 Fifth Avenue, Suite 350, Huntington, WV 25701
Phone: 800-232-5463
Email: afbinfo@afb.net
http://www.afb.org
Purpose: To support visually impaired engineering, computer science, life sciences or physical sciences students.
Eligibility: Applicants must be U.S. citizens who are blind or visually impaired. They must be undergraduate or graduate students who are majoring in computer science, life sciences, physical sciences or engineering. Selection is based on the overall strength of the application.
Target applicant(s): High school students. College students. Graduate school students. Adult students.
Amount: $2,000.
Number of awards: 2.
Deadline: February 15.
How to apply: Applications are available online. An application form, official transcript, personal statement, two reference letters, proof of college acceptance, proof of U.S. citizenship and proof of legal blindness are required.
Exclusive: Visit www.UltimateScholarshipBook.com and enter code AM238423 for updates on this award.

(2385) · Rudolph Dillman Memorial Scholarship

American Foundation for the Blind Scholarship Committee
1000 Fifth Avenue, Suite 350, Huntington, WV 25701
Phone: 800-232-5463
Email: afbinfo@afb.net
http://www.afb.org
Purpose: To aid blind or visually impaired students who are preparing for careers in the rehabilitation or education of the blind or visually impaired.
Eligibility: Applicants must be U.S. citizens who are blind or visually impaired. They must be undergraduate or graduate students who are preparing for careers in the education or rehabilitation of visually impaired or blind people. Previous recipients of this award are ineligible. Selection is based on the overall strength of the application.
Target applicant(s): College students. Graduate school students. Adult students.
Amount: $2,500.
Number of awards: 4.
Deadline: February 15.
How to apply: Applications are available online. An application form, official transcript, personal essay, two recommendation letters, proof of legal blindness and proof of U.S. citizenship are required.
Exclusive: Visit www.UltimateScholarshipBook.com and enter code AM238523 for updates on this award.

(2386) · Salix Gastrointestinal Health Scholars Award

Salix Pharmaceuticals
400 Somerset Corporate Boulevard, Bridgewater, NJ 08807
Phone: 908-927-1190
Email: karen.paff@salix.com
https://www.salix.com/scholarship
Purpose: To support students living with gastrointestinal disease.
Eligibility: Applicants must be undergraduates, graduate students, working parents or single parents who have been diagnosed with gastrointestinal disease. Students must have applied to, been accepted to or be currently attending a qualifying institution in pursuit of an undergraduate, vocational/technical or graduate degree. An essay submission on a provided topic is required.
Target applicant(s): High school students. College students. Graduate school students. Adult students.
Amount: Up to $10,000.
Number of awards: 10.
Deadline: May 31.
How to apply: Applications are available online.
Exclusive: Visit www.UltimateScholarshipBook.com and enter code SA238623 for updates on this award.

(2387) · Scholarships for Survivors

Patient Advocate Foundation
421 Butler Farm Road, Hampton, VA 23666
Phone: 800-532-5274
Email: scholarship@patientadvocate.org
http://www.patientadvocate.org
Purpose: This group of scholarships seeks to assist students who have been diagnosed with cancer or another life-threatening illness.
Eligibility: Students must be under the age of 25 and have been diagnosed with or be actively treated for their life-threatening illness in the past five years. If awarded a scholarship, the student must maintain a 3.0 GPA, be enrolled full time and perform 20 hours of community service each year.
Target applicant(s): High school students. College students. Graduate school students.
Minimum GPA: 3.0
Amount: $3,000.
Number of awards: 12.
Scholarship may be renewable.
Deadline: March 9.
How to apply: Applications are available online.
Exclusive: Visit www.UltimateScholarshipBook.com and enter code PA238723 for updates on this award.

(2388) · Sertoma Scholarship for Students Who Are Hard of Hearing or Deaf

Sertoma Inc.
1912 E. Meyer Boulevard, Kansas City, MO 64132
Phone: 816-333-8300
Email: infosertoma@sertomahq.org
http://www.sertoma.org
Purpose: The organization's focus is to concentrate on communicative disorders.
Eligibility: Applicants must be entering or continuing as full-time undergraduates in the U.S., show proof that they have a clinically significant (40dB) bilateral hearing loss and have a minimum 3.2 GPA for all high school and college courses.

Target applicant(s): High school students. College students. Adult students.
Minimum GPA: 3.2
Amount: $1,000.
Number of awards: Varies.
Deadline: March 30.
How to apply: Applications are available online.
Exclusive: Visit www.UltimateScholarshipBook.com and enter code SE238823 for updates on this award.

(2389) · Soozie Courter Hemophilia Scholarship Program

Pfizer
Hemophilia Scholarship Program, 235 East 42nd Street, New York, NY 10017
Phone: 888-999-2349
http://www.hemophiliavillage.com
Purpose: To provide financial assistance to students with hemophilia.
Eligibility: Applicants must be high school seniors or graduates, GED recipients or college or vocational school students who have been diagnosed with hemophilia A or B.
Target applicant(s): High school students. College students. Adult students.
Amount: $2,500-$4,000.
Number of awards: 15.
Deadline: June 11.
How to apply: Applications are available online.
Exclusive: Visit www.UltimateScholarshipBook.com and enter code PF238923 for updates on this award.

(2390) · Student Award Program of FSD

Foundation for Science and Disability
503 N.W. 89 Street, Gainesville, FL 32607
http://stemd.org
Purpose: To support students with disabilities in completing a science project or thesis in any field of mathematics, science, medicine, engineering or computer science.
Eligibility: Applicants must be graduate students or senior undergraduates who have been accepted to graduate school. Students must submit two letters of recommendation and an essay outlining their professional goals and aspirations and the purpose for which the grant would be used. Selection is based on the overall strength of the application.
Target applicant(s): College students. Graduate school students. Adult students.
Amount: $1,000.
Number of awards: 1.
Deadline: December 1.
How to apply: Applications are available online.
Exclusive: Visit www.UltimateScholarshipBook.com and enter code FO239023 for updates on this award.

(2391) · Susanna DeLaurentis Memorial Scholarship

Susanna DeLaurentis Charitable Foundation
SDCF, P.O. Box 11208, Elkins Park, PA 19027
Phone: 215-635-9405
http://thesusannafoundation.org/scholarships/apply.php
Purpose: To support graduating seniors who have faced chronic disease or other serious health issues in pursuing post-secondary education.

Eligibility: Applicants must submit high school transcripts, verification of health condition from a medical professional, a letter of recommendation and a personal statement. Selection is primarily based on academic achievement and extracurricular involvement.
Target applicant(s): High school students.
Amount: $1,000.
Number of awards: 1.
Deadline: April 15.
How to apply: Applications are available online.
Exclusive: Visit www.UltimateScholarshipBook.com and enter code SU239123 for updates on this award.

(2392) · Tony Coelho Media Scholarship

American Association of People with Disabilities (AAPD)
2013 H Street, NW, 5th Floor, Washington, DC 20006
Phone: 800-840-8844
Email: scholarship@aapd.com
http://www.aapd.com
Purpose: To support students with disabilities pursuing a career in the entertainment industry.
Eligibility: Applicants must be second year associate's degree students, undergraduate students in their sophomore year or higher or graduate students with disabilities who are interested in pursuing a career in the communications, media or entertainment industry.
Target applicant(s): College students. Graduate school students. Adult students.
Amount: $5,625.
Number of awards: 8.
Deadline: May 20.
How to apply: Applications are available online.
Exclusive: Visit www.UltimateScholarshipBook.com and enter code AM239223 for updates on this award.

(2393) · TPA Scholarship Trust for the Hearing Impaired

TPA Scholarship Trust for the Deaf and Near Deaf
2041 Exchange Drive, Saint Charles, MO 63303
Phone: 314-371-0533
Email: support@tpahq.org
http://www.tpahq.org
Purpose: To provide financial aid to children and adults who are deaf or hearing impaired and who need assistance in obtaining mechanical devices, treatment or specialized education.
Eligibility: Applicants must suffer from deafness or hearing impairment. Completed applications must be returned to the Trust by the end of each quarter. Applications are reviewed on the last day of each quarter and recipients will be notified within 30 days of the decision.
Target applicant(s): Junior high students or younger. High school students. College students. Graduate school students. Adult students.
Amount: Varies.
Number of awards: Varies.
Deadline: March 31, June 30, September 30, December 31.
How to apply: Applications are available by written request or online.
Exclusive: Visit www.UltimateScholarshipBook.com and enter code TP239323 for updates on this award.

(2394) · UCB Family Epilepsy Scholarship Program

UCB Family Epilepsy Scholarship Program
1421 East Broad Street, Suite 340, Fuquay-Varina, NC 27526

Phone: 866-825-1920
Email: ucbepilepsyscholarship@summitmedcomm.com
https://ucbepilepsyscholarship.com
Purpose: To provide financial assistance to people with epilepsy who wish to obtain higher education.
Eligibility: Applicants must be U.S. citizens or legal and permanent residents who have epilepsy, or family members or caregivers of persons with epilepsy. They must be graduating high school in the year of application or have already graduated and be enrolled in or awaiting acceptance from a U.S. institution of higher learning. They must have demonstrated academic achievement, participate in extracurricular activities and be positive role models.
Target applicant(s): High school students. College students. Graduate school students. Adult students.
Amount: $5,000-$10,000.
Number of awards: 33.
Deadline: March 1.
How to apply: Applications are available online.
Exclusive: Visit www.UltimateScholarshipBook.com and enter code UC239423 for updates on this award.

(2395) · Vitality Medical's Student Disability Scholarship

Vitality Medical
Attn.: Vitality Medical Scholars, 7910 S. 3500 E., Suite C, Salt Lake City, UT 84121
Phone: 800-397-5899
http://www.vitalitymedical.com/scholarship
Purpose: To encourage outstanding students who make an impact on their school and community.
Eligibility: Applicants must be a high school senior or currently enrolled undergraduate student. Students should be 16 years old or older and have at least a 3.0 GPA. Applicants do not have to have a disability to enter. A poem and personal statement on how using disability aids have added vitality to your life are required.
Target applicant(s): High school students. College students. Adult students.
Minimum GPA: 3.0
Amount: $500.
Number of awards: varies.
Deadline: September 15.
How to apply: Application information available online. Poem, personal statement and transcript must be submitted by mail.
Exclusive: Visit www.UltimateScholarshipBook.com and enter code VI239523 for updates on this award.

(2396) · Wells Fargo Scholarship Program for People with Disabilities

Wells Fargo Scholarship Program for People with Disabilities, Scholarship America
One Scholarship Way, Saint Peter, MN 56082
Phone: 844-402-0357
Email: pwdscholarship@scholarshipamerica.org
https://learnmore.scholarsapply.org/pwdscholarship/
Purpose: To support students with disabilities in the career path of their choice.
Eligibility: Applicants must have an identified disability, a long-term or recurring issue that impacts one or more major life activities. Students must be either high school seniors or current undergraduate students enrolled full- or half-time at an accredited two- or four-year college or university in the U.S. A GPA of 3.0 or higher is required.

Target applicant(s): High school students. College students. Adult students.
Minimum GPA: 3.0
Amount: Up to $2,500.
Number of awards: Up to 35.
Scholarship may be renewable.
Deadline: June 30.
How to apply: Applications are available online.
Exclusive: Visit www.UltimateScholarshipBook.com and enter code WE239623 for updates on this award.

(2397) · William and Dorothy Ferrell Scholarship

Association for Education and Rehabilitation of the Blind and Visually Impaired
AER Scholarship Committee, 1703 N. Beauregard Street, Suite 440, Alexandria, VA 22311
Phone: 703-671-4500
Email: scholarships@aerbvi.org
https://aerbvi.org/resources/aer-scholarships/
Purpose: To assist visually-impaired students who plan to assist others who are visually impaired.
Eligibility: Applicants must be legally blind, with a vision of 20/200 or less in the best eye or 20 degrees or less in the visual field. Applicants must also study in college or a similar institution in the field of services for the blind or visually impaired. Scholarships are only awarded in even-numbered years.
Target applicant(s): College students. Graduate school students. Adult students.
Amount: $1,000.
Number of awards: 2.
Deadline: Varies.
How to apply: Applications are available online or by phone request.
Exclusive: Visit www.UltimateScholarshipBook.com and enter code AS239723 for updates on this award.

Scholarship Indexes

What would you rather do: read the description of every single scholarship in this book or use an index to quickly zero in on scholarships that fit you? That's what we thought, which is why we put together a set of indexes that make it easy for you to find the perfect scholarships. We strongly recommend that you use all of the indexes. This is because every scholarship can be categorized in numerous ways and often the decision is unavoidably subjective. So to make sure that you don't miss out on a great scholarship, spend the time to consult each of the following indexes:

GENERAL CATEGORY INDEX

This is one of the most useful indexes since it organizes the scholarships by common fields of study or career areas. It does not list any state specific scholarships since there is another index just for state of residence.

BIOLOGICAL SCIENCES/LIFE SCIENCES

Also See Scholarships Listed Under:
Agriculture/Horticulture/Animals
Chemistry
Forestry/Wildlife
Medicine/Nursing/Health Profession

Angus Foundation Scholarships • 807
Annual University Scholarship • 809
AOS Student and Postdoctoral Research Awards • 815
ASABE Foundation Engineering Scholarship • 819
Astronaut Scholarship • 837
Barry M. Goldwater Scholarship and Excellence in Education Program • 846
C. Bertrand and Marian Othmer Schultz Collegiate Scholarship • 1311
Charles H. Bussmann Undergraduate Scholarship • 867
Davidson Fellows Scholarships • 109
DNA Day Essay Contest • 891
Drs. James and Wanda Trefil Science Scholarship • 2198
Gaige Fund Award • 932
GEM MS Engineering Fellowship Program • 2211
George A. Hall / Harold F. Mayfield Grant • 941
Gorgas Scholarship Competition • 1468
Graduate Research Fellowship Program • 950
Hertz Foundation's Graduate Fellowship Award • 964
HSA Research Grants • 969
International Women's Fishing Association Scholarship • 979
Jean Theodore Lacordaire Prize • 987
John C. Bajus Scholarship • 992
John Henry Comstock Graduate Student Awards • 993
LabRoots Scholarship • 1008
Libbie H. Hyman Memorial Scholarship • 1020
Louis Agassiz Fuertes Award • 1026
Ludo Frevel Crystallography Scholarships • 1029
MAES Scholarship Program • 2251
Mollie Butler Memorial Scholarship • 1054
MTS Student Scholarship for Two-Year, Technical, Engineering and Community College Students • 1057
MTS Student Scholarship for Undergraduate Students • 1058
National Garden Clubs Scholarship • 1072
NDSEG Fellowship Program • 1085
NIH Undergraduate Scholarship Program • 1092
Novus Biologicals Scholarship Program • 1093
Paros-Digiquartz Scholarship • 1105
Paul A. Stewart Grants • 1107
Payzer Scholarship • 1109
Raney Fund Award • 1130
Regeneron Science Talent Search • 1132
Science Ambassador Scholarship • 1157
Student Research Scholarships • 1182
William F. Helms Internship Program • 1221
William J. Adams, Jr. and Marijane E. Adams Scholarship • 1222
Youth Incentive Award • 1226

BUSINESS/MANAGEMENT

Also See Scholarships Listed Under:
Accounting/Finance
Marketing
Leadership

Actuarial Diversity Scholarship • 2149
Adult Students in Scholastic Transition (ASIST) • 527
Alice L. Haltom Educational Fund Scholarship • 534
Allied Van Lines Scholarship • 535
Alpha Kappa Psi Scholarships • 536
Betsy Plank/PRSSA Scholarship • 549
CardRates.com Financial Futures Scholarship • 560
Executive Women International Scholarship Program • 586
FOARE Scholarship Program • 589
Francis X. Crowley Scholarship • 591
Fund for American Studies Internships • 596
Gary Yoshimura Scholarship • 600
Harry A. Applegate Scholarship • 607
Henry Belin du Pont Dissertation Fellowship • 609
Hermine Solt Student Scholarship • 1500
Humane Studies Fellowships • 182
IMA Memorial Education Fund Scholarship • 618
James A. Turner, Jr. Memorial Scholarship • 627
Jane M. Klausman Women in Business Scholarship Fund • 629
Joe Perdue Scholarship • 633
John W. Rogers Memorial Scholarship • 1567
Jungle Scholar • 638
Lawrence G. Foster Award for Excellence in Public Relations • 646
MBA Fellowship • 659
National Academic Scholarships • 673
National Association of Black Accountants National Scholarship Program • 2280
National Scholarship • 2286
National Scholarship Program • 677
North American Van Lines Logistics Scholarship • 686
NSA Scholarship Foundation • 689
Office Supply Scholarship • 485
Risk Management Association Foundation Scholarship • 711
Ritchie-Jennings Memorial Scholarship • 712
SSPI Scholarship Program • 727
Stuart Cameron and Margaret McLeod Memorial Scholarship • 731
Summer Graduate Research Fellowships • 340
TechChecks Business Leadership Scholarship • 738
Undergraduate Scholarship • 2125
Vern and Elaine Clark Outdoor Advertising Industry • 752
Virtual Business Scholarship • 754
WIIT Charitable Trust Scholarship • 756

CHEMISTRY

Also See Scholarships Listed Under:
Biological Sciences/Life Sciences
Engineering
Medicine/Nursing/Health Professions
Sciences/Physical Sciences

AACT National Candy Technologists John Kitt Memorial Scholarship Program • 765
American Chemical Society Scholars Program • 2162
AMS Graduate Fellowships • 802
Analytical Chemistry Scholarship • 806
Astronaut Scholarship • 837
Composites Division/Harold Giles Scholarship • 874
David R. Jones IV Scholarship • 886
Davidson Fellows Scholarships • 109
Donald F. and Mildred Topp Othmer Scholarships • 892
Gladys Anderson Emerson Scholarship • 945
Gorgas Scholarship Competition • 1468
Graduate Research Fellowship Program • 950
Hubertus W.V. Wellems Scholarship for Male Students • 2229
Industrial Electrolysis and Electrochemical Engineering Division H.H. Dow Memorial Student Award • 973
John J. McKetta Scholarship • 994
Larson Aquatic Research Support (LARS) • 1011
Minority Affairs Committee Award for Outstanding Scholastic Achievement • 2267
Minority Scholarship Awards for Incoming College Freshmen • 2271
National Association for Surface Finishing Scholarships • 1067
NDSEG Fellowship Program • 1085
Polymer Modifiers and Additives Division Scholarships • 1120
Regeneron Science Talent Search • 1132
Robert E. Dougherty Educational Foundation Scholarship Award • 1144
Rubber Division Undergraduate Scholarship • 1149
Society of Plastics Engineers (SPE) Foundation Scholarships • 1167
Student Poster Session Awards • 1180
Ted and Ruth Neward Scholarship • 1185
Thermoforming Division Memorial Scholarships • 1189
Undergraduate Award for Excellence in Chemistry • 1205

COMMUNICATIONS

Also See Scholarships Listed Under:
English/Writing
Journalism/Broadcasting

AFCEA Ralph W. Shrader Diversity Scholarships • 780
ARRL Foundation General Fund Scholarship • 542
Bill Gove Scholarship • 413
Bill, W2ONV, and Ann Salerno Memorial Scholarship • 550
Bodie McDowell Scholarship • 553
Carole J. Streeter, KB9JBR, Scholarship • 561
Cavett Robert Scholarship • 418
CCNMA Scholarships • 1338
Charles Clarke Cordle Memorial Scholarship • 563
Charles N. Fisher Memorial Scholarship • 564
Dayton Amateur Radio Association Scholarship • 573
Distinguished Service Award for Students • 575

DMI Milk Marketing Scholarship • 890
Donald Riebhoff Memorial Scholarship • 576
Dr. James L. Lawson Memorial Scholarship • 577
Edmond A. Metzger Scholarship • 583
FOWA Scholarship for Outdoor Communicators • 590
Fred R. McDaniel Memorial Scholarship • 593
Fund for American Studies Internships • 596
Hispanic Heritage Youth Awards • 2224
IFEC Scholarships Award • 616
IRARC Memorial, Joseph P. Rubino, WA4MMD, Scholarship • 623
John Bayliss Radio Scholarship • 634
Julianne Malveaux Scholarship • 2238
K2TEO Martin J. Green, Sr. Memorial Scholarship • 640
L. Phil and Alice J. Wicker Scholarship • 643
L.B. Cebik, W4RNL and Jean Cebik, N4TZP Memorial Scholarship • 644
Mary Lou Brown Scholarship • 658
Massachusetts Student Broadcaster Scholarship • 1638
Media Fellows Program • 660
Mississippi Association of Broadcasters Scholarship Program • 1670
NCTA and AWMF Scholarship • 2290
New England FEMARA Scholarships • 684
Optimist International Communications Contest • 2382
Optimist International Oratorical Contest • 690
Paul and Helen L. Grauer Scholarship • 693
PHD Scholarship • 696
Print and Graphics Scholarship • 493
Ray, NRP and Katie, WKTE Pautz Scholarship • 707
Richard W. Bendicksen, N7ZL, Memorial Scholarship • 710
SSPI Scholarship Program • 727
Student with a Disability Scholarship • 733
TLMI Four Year College Degree Scholarship Program • 740
Tom and Judith Comstock Scholarship • 742
YASME Foundation Scholarship • 760
Youth Scholarship • 761

COMPUTER AND INFORMATION SCIENCE
Also See Scholarships Listed Under:
Engineering
Mathematics
Sciences/Physical Sciences
Admiral Grace Murray Hopper Memorial Scholarships • 2151
AFCEA Ralph W. Shrader Diversity Scholarships • 780
AFCEA ROTC Scholarships • 15
Anne Maureen Whitney Barrow Memorial Scholarship • 2165
AOC Scholarships • 813
Association of Information Technology Professionals (AITP) Scholarships • 835
Astronaut Scholarship • 837
ATLANT Women in Fintech • 838
Davidson Fellows Scholarships • 109
Evolve IP Scholarship • 913
Future Leaders in Tech Scholarship • 930
GAHCC Foundation Scholarship • 2209
Google Generation Google Scholarship • 2216

Google SVA Scholarship • 167
Graduate Research Fellowship Program • 950
HIMSS Foundation Scholarship • 965
Intertech Foundation STEM Scholarship • 980
Jungle Scholar • 638
Mary V. Munger Scholarship • 1035
Michigan Council of Women in Technology University Scholarship • 1652
MIE Solutions • 1049
National Academic Scholarships • 673
National Space Club Keynote Scholar • 1074
NCWIT Award for Aspirations in Computing • 2291
Northrop Grumman/HENAAC Scholars Program • 2296
Outstanding Undergraduate Researchers Award Program • 1103
PixelPlex Bi-Annual STEM Scholarship • 1118
Pretty Photoshop Actions Bi-annual Scholarship • 1125
Raymond Davis Scholarship • 1131
Regeneron Science Talent Search • 1132
Science Ambassador Scholarship • 1157
SMART Scholarship • 1163
STANLEY Technology Scholarship Program • 1172
Stokes Educational Scholarship Program • 329
Susan Miszkowicz Memorial Scholarship • 1183
VIP Women in Technology Scholarship • 1216
Way Scholarship • 1219

CONSTRUCTION TRADES
Also See Scholarships Listed Under:
Vocational/Technical
AAGS Joseph F. Dracup Scholarship Award • 767
AGC Graduate Scholarships • 782
AGC of Ohio Scholarships • 1242
AGC Undergraduate Scholarships • 783
American Fire Sprinkler Association High School Senior Scholarship Contest • 31
Associated General Contractors of Minnesota Scholarships • 1283
Complete Water Solutions Scholarship • 873
Connecticut Building Congress Scholarships • 1372
Delta Faucet Company Scholarships • 888
Geneva Rock Scholarship • 940
Herman J. Smith Scholarship • 1498
Independence Excavating, A DiGeronimo Company Scholarship • 1527
IRF Fellowship Program • 983
Kilbourn-Sawyer Memorial Scholarship • 1584
Kokosing Construction Co. Scholarship • 1587
Lee S. Evans Scholarship • 1016
NAWIC Founders' Undergraduate Scholarship • 1077
NAWIC Granite State Chapter Scholarships • 1694
NPCA Educational Foundation Scholarships • 1094
Path to Pro Scholarship • 1106
PHCC Educational Foundation Scholarship • 1114
Pulte Group Build Your Future Scholarship Program • 1126

Roofing Industry Scholarship - Melvin Kruger Endowed Scholarship • 1147
Sandra Imprescia Essay Scholarship • 1154
Shook Construction Harry F. Gaeke Memorial Scholarship • 1849
Tuttle Services Inc. Tiny Rauch Scholarship • 1921
Undergraduate Scholarship and Construction Trades Scholarship • 1207
Yanmar/SAE Scholarship • 1225

CULINARY ARTS
Also See Scholarships Listed Under:
Food Services
Hospitality/Travel/Tourism
American Culinary Federation Scholarships • 538
IFEC Scholarships Award • 616
IFSEA Worthy Goal Scholarship • 617
John Schwartz Scholarship • 1566
Ray and Gertrude Marshall Scholarship • 706

DENTISTRY
Also See Scholarships Listed Under:
Medicine/Nursing/Health Professions
ADHA Institute Scholarship Program • 779
Colgate Bright Smiles, Bright Futures Minority Scholarships • 871
Crest Oral-B Laboratories Dental Hygiene Scholarships • 878
Dr. Esther Wilkins Scholarship • 896
Irene Woodall Graduate Scholarship • 982
Karla Girts Memorial Community Outreach Scholarship • 1006
NHSC Scholarship • 1091

DISABILITY
Also See Scholarships Listed Under:
Academics/General
#RAREis Scholarship • 2341
AbbVie Immunology Scholarship • 2342
American Council of the Blind Scholarships • 2343
Anne Ford Scholarship Program • 2344
Baer Reintegration Scholarship • 2345
BMO Capital Markets Lime Connect Equity Through Education Scholarship • 2346
Boomer Esiason Foundation General Academic Scholarship • 2347
Bristol-Myers Squibb Scholarship for Cancer Survivors • 2348
Cancer for College Scholarships • 2349
Challenge Met Scholarship • 2350
Disabled Student Scholarship • 2351
Duane Buckley Memorial Scholarship • 2352
Elizabeth Nash Foundation Scholarship Program • 2353
Eric Dostie Memorial College Scholarship • 2354
Fred Scheigert Scholarships • 2355
George H. Nofer Scholarship for Law and Public Policy • 2356
Graeme Clark Scholarship • 2357
Guthrie-Koch PKU Scholarship • 2358
HIV-Positive Scholarship • 2359
Incight Scholarship • 2360
Jaime Guttenberg All Abilities Scholarship • 2361
Kevin Child Scholarship • 2362
L.I.F.E. Scholarship • 2363
Lighthouse Guild Scholarships • 2364

DEED Funding Opportunities • 887
Delaware Solid Waste Authority John P. "Pat" Healy Scholarship • 1389
Desk and Derrick Educational Trust • 889
Donald F. and Mildred Topp Othmer Scholarships • 892
Dorothy M. and Earl S. Hoffman Award • 894
Dr. Ivy M. Parker Memorial Scholarship • 2196
Dr. James L. Lawson Memorial Scholarship • 577
Duane M. Hanson Scholarship • 897
Dwight D. Gardner Scholarship • 899
E. Noel Luddy Scholarship • 900
E.J. Sierieja Memorial Fellowship • 901
East Asia and Pacific Summer Institutes • 902
Ed and Charlotte Rodgers Scholarships • 1413
Edmond A. Metzger Scholarship • 583
Edward D. Hendrickson/SAE Engineering Scholarship • 903
Elizabeth McLean Memorial Scholarship • 906
Elson T. Killam Memorial Scholarship • 908
EngineerGirl Essay Contest • 910
Engineering Undergraduate Scholarship • 911
Engineers Foundation of Ohio General Fund Scholarship • 1425
F.W. Beich Beichley Scholarship • 916
Francis X. Crowley Scholarship • 591
Frank and Dorothy Miller ASME Auxiliary Scholarships • 926
Fred M. Young, Sr./SAE Engineering Scholarship • 927
Fred R. McDaniel Memorial Scholarship • 593
GAHCC Foundation Scholarship • 2209
Garland Duncan Scholarships • 933
Gary Wagner, K3OMI, Scholarship • 935
GEM MS Engineering Fellowship Program • 2211
Gilbreth Memorial Fellowship • 943
Giuliano Mazzetti Scholarship • 944
Gordon Rankin Corrosion Engineering Scholarship • 948
Graduate Research Award (GRA) • 949
Graduate Research Fellowship Program • 950
Harold and Inge Marcus Scholarship • 956
Henry Adams Scholarship • 962
Hertz Foundation's Graduate Fellowship Award • 964
Holly Cornell Scholarship • 966
Honeywell International Inc. Scholarships • 2226
Hubertus W.V. Wellems Scholarship for Male Students • 2229
IBTTA Scholarship Program • 971
IIE Council of Fellows Undergraduate Scholarship • 972
Industrial Electrolysis and Electrochemical Engineering Division H.H. Dow Memorial Student Award • 973
Industrial Electrolysis and Electrochemical Engineering Division Student Achievement Awards • 974
Injection Molding Division Scholarship • 975
Institute of Electrical and Electronics Engineers Life Members' Fellowship in Electrical History • 976
International Gas Turbine Institute Scholarship • 977
ISPE/M.E. Amstutz Memorial Award • 1545

J.R. Popalisky Scholarship • 1547
Jill S. Tietjen P.E. Scholarship • 988
John and Elsa Gracik Scholarships • 990
John and Muriel Landis Scholarship • 991
John J. McKetta Scholarship • 994
John L. Imhoff Scholarship • 995
John S. Marshall Memorial Scholarship • 997
John S.W. Fargher, Jr. Scholarship • 998
John V. Wehausen Graduate Scholarship • 999
Kenneth Andrew Roe Scholarship • 1007
LabRoots Scholarship • 1008
Larson Aquatic Research Support (LARS) • 1011
Lee Magnon Memorial Scholarship • 1015
Lewis C. Hoffman Scholarship • 1019
Light Metals Division Scholarship • 1021
Lillian Moller Gilbreth Memorial Scholarship • 2244
Lisa Zaken Award For Excellence • 1022
Lockheed Martin Corporation Scholarship • 2246
Lockheed Martin STEM Scholarship Program • 1023
Long-Term Member Sponsored Scholarship • 1025
Louise Moritz Molitoris Leadership Scholarship for Undergraduates • 2247
Lowell H. and Dorothy Loving Undergraduate Scholarship • 1027
Mackinac Scholarship • 1615
MAES Scholarship Program • 2251
Mandell and Lester Rosenblatt Undergraduate Scholarship • 1030
Marliave Fund • 1031
Marvin Mundel Memorial Scholarship • 1033
Mary Gunther Memorial Scholarship • 2259
Mary V. Munger Scholarship • 1035
Materials Processing and Manufacturing Division Scholarship • 1037
Maureen L. and Howard N. Blitman, P.E., Scholarship • 2263
Melvin J. Schiff Fellowship Fund • 1041
Melvin R. Green Scholarships • 1042
Meredith Thoms Memorial Scholarship • 1043
Michael Kidger Memorial Scholarship • 1046
Michigan Engineering Scholarships • 1653
Minority Affairs Committee Award for Outstanding Scholastic Achievement • 2267
Minority Scholarship Awards for College Students • 2270
Minority Scholarship Awards for Incoming College Freshmen • 2271
MTI Bert Krisher Memorial Scholarship • 1056
Myrtle and Earl Walker Scholarship • 1060
N.G. Kaul Memorial Scholarship • 1061
NACE Eastern Area Scholarship • 1062
NACE Foundation Academic Scholarship • 1063
NACE Past Presidents Scholarship • 1064
NACE Sandia Mountain Section Scholarship • 1689
NAPA Research and Education Foundation Scholarship • 1066
National Environmental Health Association Graduate Scholarship • 1070
National Space Club Keynote Scholar • 1074
NDSEG Fellowship Program • 1085
Nellie Yeoh Whetten Award • 1087

Northrop Grumman/HENAAC Scholars Program • 2296
Old Guard Oral Presentation Competition • 1099
Olive Lynn Salembier Memorial Reentry Scholarship • 2298
Operations and Power Division Scholarship • 1101
P.O. Pistilli Undergraduate Scholarship for Advancement in Computer Science and Electrical Engineering • 2301
Payzer Scholarship • 1109
Petroleum Division College Scholarships • 1113
Plastics Pioneers Association Scholarships • 1119
Polymer Modifiers and Additives Division Scholarships • 1120
PPG Protective and Marine Coatings Academic Scholarship • 1121
Presidents Scholarship of the Institute of Industrial Engineers • 1124
Ralph K. Hillquist Honorary SAE Scholarship • 1129
Raymond Davis Scholarship • 1131
Regeneron Science Talent Search • 1132
Reuben Trane Scholarship • 1134
RMEL Foundation Scholarships • 1142
Robert B. Oliver ASNT Scholarship • 1143
Robert E. Dougherty Educational Foundation Scholarship Award • 1144
Robert E. Thunen Memorial Scholarships • 1145
Robert N. and Helen H. Herbert Undergraduate Scholarship • 1146
Russell and Sigurd Varian Award • 1150
Rust Scholarship • 2101
Salvatore J. Monte Thermoplastic Materials and Foams Division Scholarship • 1152
Samuel Fletcher Tapman ASCE Student Chapter/Club Scholarship • 1153
Schonstedt Scholarship in Surveying • 1156
Science Ambassador Scholarship • 1157
SEE Education Foundation Scholarships • 1159
SMART Scholarship • 1163
Society of Exploration Geophysicists (SEG) Scholarship • 1165
Society of Manufacturing Engineers Directors Scholarship • 1166
Society of Plastics Engineers (SPE) Foundation Scholarships • 1167
Society of Vacuum Coaters Foundation Scholarship • 1168
SPIE Optics and Photonics Education Scholarship • 1169
SSPI Scholarship Program • 727
STEEL Engineering Education Link Initiative • 1173
Steel Intern Scholarships • 1174
Steinman Scholarship • 1175
Stokes Educational Scholarship Program • 329
Structural Materials Division Scholarship • 1178
Student Cash Grant Program • 1179
Student Poster Session Awards • 1180
Susan Miszkowicz Memorial Scholarship • 1183
SWE Exelon Corporation Scholarship • 2323
SWE Past Presidents Scholarship • 2324
Tau Beta Pi Scholarships • 2117

Tau Beta Pi/Society of Automotive Engineers Engineering Scholarship • 1184
Ted and Ruth Neward Scholarship • 1185
Theodore D. Harrington Scholarship • 1187
Thermoforming Division Memorial Scholarships • 1189
Thermoplastic Elastomers Special Interest Group Scholarship • 1190
Thomas E. Powers/Detroit Section Scholarship • 1191
Thomas M. Stetson Scholarship • 1192
Thomas R. Camp Scholarship • 1193
Tilford Fund • 1194
TMC/SAE Donald D. Dawson Technical Scholarship • 1196
TMS Best Paper Contest • 1197
TMS Technical Division Student Poster Contest • 1198
TMS/International Symposium of Superalloys Scholarships • 1199
Trent R. Dames and William W. Moore Fellowship • 1201
Tuskegee Airmen Scholarship Foundation Scholarships • 1202
Undergraduate Engineering Scholarships • 1206
United Parcel Service Scholarship for Female Students • 1212
United Parcel Service Scholarship for Minority Students • 2333
Vernon T. Swain, P.E./Robert E. Chute, P.E. Scholarship • 1937
Vertical Flight Foundation Technical Scholarships • 1215
Walter B. Sinnott Scholarship • 1218
William J. Adams, Jr. and Marijane E. Adams Scholarship • 1222
Yanmar/SAE Scholarship • 1225
Youth Scholarship • 761

ENGLISH/WRITING
Also See Scholarships Listed Under:
Academics/General
Education/Teaching
Communications
Journalism/Broadcasting
Library Science
ACES Copy Editing Scholarships • 398
ACES Education Fund Scholarship • 399
Amy Lowell Poetry Travelling Scholarship • 408
Anthem Essay Contest • 409
Atlas Shrugged Essay Contest • 411
Bill Gove Scholarship • 413
Cavett Robert Scholarship • 418
Clauder Competition Prize • 420
Crossword Hobbyist Crossword Scholarship • 104
CTA César E. Chávez and Dolores Huerta Education Award Program • 1379
Davidson Fellows Scholarships • 109
Disney/ABC Television Writing Program • 425
Feldco Windows, Siding and Doors Scholarship • 434
Global Citizen Scholarship • 162
Heinlein Society Scholarship Program • 444
Henry Salvatori Scholarship • 2221
Hispanic Heritage Youth Awards • 2224
Huntington Fellowships • 613

Huntington-British Academy Fellowships for Study in Great Britain • 614
ILA Jeanne S. Chall Research Fellowship • 452
John F. Kennedy Profile in Courage Essay Contest • 636
Julianne Malveaux Scholarship • 2238
Mensa Foundation Scholarship Program • 231
Minnesota Academic Excellence Scholarship • 1663
Moris J. and Betty Kaplun Essay Contest • 2076
National High School Poetry Contest/Easterday Poetry Award • 476
National Peace Essay Contest • 479
New York Life Award • 482
Optimist International Essay Contest • 486
Patriot's Pen Youth Essay Contest • 488
Platt Family Scholarship Prize Essay Contest • 489
Prize in Ethics Essay Contest • 494
Ruth Lilly and Dorothy Sargent Rosenberg Poetry Fellowship Program • 496
Scholastic Art and Writing Portfolio Award • 498
Student Activist Scholarships • 2114
SuperCollege Scholarship • 341
Taylor/Blakeslee University Fellowships • 507
The Fountainhead Essay Contest • 508
United States Hispanic Leadership Institute Denny's Hungry for Education • 362
Voice of Democracy Audio Essay Contests • 375
We the Students Essay Contest • 382

ETHNIC AND AREA STUDIES
Also See Scholarships Listed Under:
Foreign Language
Social Science/History
Bridging Scholarships for Study Abroad in Japan • 414
Carl A. Ross Student Paper Award • 417
Council on International Educational Exchange (CIEE) Scholarships • 422
DAAD/AICGS Research Fellowship Program • 424
Dumbarton Oaks Fellowships • 429
Fellowships/Grants to Study in Scandinavia • 436
Finlandia Foundation National Student Scholarships Program • 438
Fulbright Grants • 151
Gilman International Scholarship • 441
IACI/NUI Visiting Fellowship in Irish Studies • 448
International Scholarships • 455
ItaliaRail Study Abroad in Italy Scholarship • 457
John O. Crane Memorial Fellowship • 463
Junior Fellowships • 465
Marshall Memorial Fellowship • 223
Marshall Scholar • 224
National Italian American Foundation Scholarship • 2284
Study Abroad Europe Scholarship • 506

FOOD SERVICES
Also See Scholarships Listed Under:
Culinary Arts
Hospitality/Travel/Tourism
Asparagus Club, Thomas K. Zaucha Scholarship • 543
Bob Richardson Legacy Scholarship • 552

California Restaurant Association Educational Foundation Scholarship for High School Seniors • 1325
California Restaurant Association Educational Foundation Scholarships for Undergraduate Students • 1326
Charlie and Becky Bray Legacy Scholarship • 565
FMS Solutions Holdings LLC Legacy Scholarship • 588
IFEC Scholarships Award • 616
IFSEA Worthy Goal Scholarship • 617
James Beard Foundation Scholarship • 628
Kimberly-Clark Corporation Legacy Scholarship • 641
Mondelez International Legacy Scholarship • 667
Nancy Curry Scholarship • 671
Peter and Jody Larkin Legacy Scholarship • 695
Roger Collins Leadership Scholarship • 713
Schwan's Food Service Scholarship • 718
Women Grocers of America (WGA) Mary Macey Scholarship(s) • 759

FOREIGN LANGUAGE
Also See Scholarships Listed Under:
Ethnic and Area Studies
ACL/NJCL National Greek Examination Scholarship • 400
ACL/NJCL National Latin Examination Scholarships • 401
Babbel Language Scholarship • 412
Bridging Scholarships for Study Abroad in Japan • 414
Council on International Educational Exchange (CIEE) Scholarships • 422
Fellowships for Regular Program in Greece • 435
Language Grants • 466
Leif and Inger Sjoberg Award • 468
Nadia Christensen Prize • 475
National Junior Classical League (NJCL) Scholarships • 477
National Latin Exam Scholarship • 478
Stokes Educational Scholarship Program • 329
Student Translation Award • 505

FORESTRY/WILDLIFE
Also See Scholarships Listed Under:
Agriculture/Horticulture/Animals
Biological Sciences/Life Sciences
AOS Student and Postdoctoral Research Awards • 815
Apprentice Ecologist Initiative Youth Scholarship Program • 818
ASF Olin Fellowships • 824
Campus Safety Health and Environmental Management Association Scholarship • 862
Federal Junior Duck Stamp Program and Scholarship Competition • 433
George A. Hall / Harold F. Mayfield Grant • 941
Gloria Barron Wilderness Society Scholarship • 946
John Mabry Forestry Scholarship • 996
John Wright Memorial Scholarship • 1000
Louis Agassiz Fuertes Award • 1026
Masonic-Range Science Scholarship • 1036
Minnesota Division Izaak Walton League Scholarship • 1664
National Garden Clubs Scholarship • 1072
Paul A. Stewart Grants • 1107

Actuarial Diversity Scholarship • 2149
AFCEA Ralph W. Shrader Diversity Scholarships • 780
AFCEA ROTC Scholarships • 15
Alice T. Schafer Mathematics Prize • 793
Astronaut Scholarship • 837
Barry M. Goldwater Scholarship and Excellence in Education Program • 846
Biographies of Contemporary Women in Mathematics Essay Contest • 854
Collegiate Inventors Competition • 872
Curtis E. Huntington Memorial Scholarship • 880
Davidson Fellows Scholarships • 109
Frank and Brennie Morgan Prize for Outstanding Research in Mathematics by an Undergraduate Student • 925
GAHCC Foundation Scholarship • 2209
Gertrude Cox Scholarship For Women In Statistics • 942
Graduate Research Fellowship Program • 950
Hispanic Heritage Youth Awards • 2224
Hubertus W.V. Wellems Scholarship for Male Students • 2229
LabRoots Scholarship • 1008
Learner Education Women in Mathematics Scholarship • 1014
Mary Rhein Memorial Scholarship • 1034
Minnesota Academic Excellence Scholarship • 1663
Moody's Mega Math Challenge • 1055
National Space Club Keynote Scholar • 1074
NDSEG Fellowship Program • 1085
Paradigm Challenge • 1104
Payzer Scholarship • 1109
Regeneron Science Talent Search • 1132
Science Ambassador Scholarship • 1157
SMART Scholarship • 1163
Stokes Educational Scholarship Program • 329

MEDICINE/NURSING/HEALTH PROFESSIONS
Also See Scholarships Listed Under:
Biological Sciences/Life Sciences
Chemistry
Dentistry
AAMA Student Essay Competition • 768
Academic Education Award • 771
Academy of Nutrition and Dietetics Foundation Student Scholarship • 772
ADEA/Crest Oral-B Scholarships for Dental Hygiene Students Pursuing Academic Careers • 776
ADEA/GlaxoSmithKline Consumer Healthcare Preventive Dentistry Scholarships • 777
ADEA/Sigma Phi Alpha Linda Devore Scholarship • 778
AHIMA Foundation Merit Scholarships • 784
Alice W. Rooke Scholarship • 794
Alpha Mu Tau Fraternity Undergraduate Scholarships • 795
AMBUCS Scholars • 796
American Indian Nurse Scholarship • 2163
AMT Student Scholarship • 805
Annual NBNA Scholarships • 808
AORN Foundation Scholarship Program • 814
Arc of Washington State Trust Fund Stipend Award • 1272

Association of Food and Drug Officials Scholarship Award • 834
AUA Foundation Research Scholars Program • 839
Avacare Medical Scholarship • 842
Bart Kamen Memorial FIRST Scholarship • 847
Benton-Meier Scholarships • 851
Bill Kane Scholarship, Undergraduate • 853
BrightLife Direct Physical Therapy Scholarship • 856
BSN Scholarship • 859
Campus Safety Health and Environmental Management Association Scholarship • 862
CHAHRM Scholarship • 1343
Charlotte McGuire Scholarship • 868
ChiroHealthUSA Foxworth Family Scholarship • 869
Critical Care Scholarship Program • 1377
CTAHPERD Gibson-Laemel Scholarship • 1380
Dorothy Budnek Memorial Scholarship • 893
Eight and Forty Lung and Respiratory Nursing Scholarship Fund • 904
Elekta Radiation Therapy Scholarship • 905
ENA Foundation Undergraduate Scholarship • 909
Foundation for Neonatal Research and Education Scholarships • 922
Foundation for Surgical Technology Medical Mission Scholarship • 923
Foundation for Surgical Technology Scholarships • 924
Frances A. Mays Scholarship Award • 1448
GoodRx Pharmacy Innovation Scholarship • 947
Graduate Student Scholarship • 953
H.M. Muffly Memorial Scholarship • 1481
Harriet Hayes Austin Memorial Scholarship for Nursing • 1485
Harry J. Harwick Scholarship • 958
Health Careers Scholarship • 959
Health Professions Pre-Graduate Scholarship Program • 2218
Health Professions Preparatory Scholarship Program • 2219
Health Research and Educational Trust Pathway Scholarship • 1494
Healthline and Prevention Institute Stronger Scholarship • 960
HIMSS Foundation Scholarship • 965
Illinois Association for Health, Physical Education, Recreation and Dance Scholarships • 1522
International Student Scholarship • 978
Iowa Physician Assistant Society Scholarship • 1537
Irene and Daisy MacGregor Memorial Scholarship • 981
Jack E. Barger, Sr. Memorial Nursing Scholarship • 1548
Jackson Laboratory Scholarship • 985
Jane Delano Student Nurse Scholarship • 986
Jean Lee/Jeff Marvin Collegiate Scholarships • 1556
Jimmy A. Young Memorial Education Recognition Award • 989
John D. and Virginia Riesch Scholarship • 1563
Kappa Delta Phi • 1004
Karen O'Neil Memorial Scholarship • 1005

Leaders Scholarship • 1013
Linda Craig Memorial Scholarship Presented by St. Vincent Sports Performance • 1602
Margaret A. Pemberton Scholarship • 1622
Margaret A. Stafford Nursing Scholarship • 1623
MARILN Professional Scholarship Award • 1624
Medical Scrubs Collection • 1038
Medical Student Research Scholarship • 1039
Medical Student Training in Aging Research (MSTAR) Program • 1040
MGMA Midwest Section Scholarship • 1044
MGMA Western Section Scholarship • 1045
Michael Moody Fitness Scholarship • 1047
Migrant Health Scholarships • 1050
Minority Fellowship Program • 1051
Minority Scholarship Award for Physical Therapy Students • 2269
Minority Student Scholarship • 1052
MLA Scholarship • 665
Murse World Scholarship • 1059
NAHN Scholarship • 2277
Naomi Brack Student Scholarship • 1065
National Hispanic Health Professional Student Scholarship • 2283
National Student Nurses' Association Scholarship • 1075
NBRC/AMP Gareth B. Gish, MS, RRT Memorial and William F. Miller, MD Postgraduate Education Recognition Awards • 1078
NBRC/AMP William W. Burgin, Jr. MD and Robert M. Lawrence, MD Education Recognition Award • 1079
NCAPA Endowment Annual Student Grants • 1080
NCPA Foundation Presidential Scholarship • 1082
NEHA/AAS/APU Scholarship Awards • 1086
New Century Scholars Doctoral Scholarship • 1088
NFMC Dorothy Dann Bullock Music Therapy Award and the NFMC Ruth B. Robertson Music Therapy Award • 1090
NHSC Scholarship • 1091
NIH Undergraduate Scholarship Program • 1092
NMF National Alumni Council Scholarship Program • 2294
Nurse Candidate Program • 1096
Nurse Corps Scholarship Program • 1097
Osmosis Raise the Line Scholarship • 1102
Past Presidents' Parley Nursing Scholarships • 1780
Phoebe Pember Memorial Scholarship • 1115
Physician Assistant Foundation Scholarship • 1116
Predoctoral Research Training Fellowship • 1123
Resident Research Scholarship • 1133
Richard J. Stull Student Essay Competition in Healthcare Management • 1136
Richard L. Davis, FACMPE - Managers Scholarship • 1138
Richard L. Davis, FACMPE/Barbara B. Watson, FACMPE - National Scholarship • 1139
Robert G. Porter Post-Secondary Scholarships • 2099
Ruth Abernathy Presidential Scholarship • 1151
Scholarships for Disadvantaged Students • 1155

Americorps National Civilian Community Corps • 36

Americorps Vista • 37

Arthur M. and Berdena King Eagle Scout Contest • 2003

Bonner Scholars Program • 57

Caring Community Scholarship • 68

Coca-Cola Scholars Program • 87

Colorado Council Volunteerism and Community Service Scholarship • 1362

Connecticut Domestic Violence Information Center's Good Samaritan Scholarship • 92

Future Community Leaders Scholarship • 152

Gloria Barron Prize for Young Heroes • 163

Grungo Colarulo Giving Back to the Community • 169

Hispanic Heritage Youth Awards • 2224

Horatio Alger National Scholarship Program • 181

Imagine America High School Scholarship Program • 619

James M. and Erma T. Freemont Foundation Scholarship Program • 195

James M. and Virginia M. Smyth Scholarship • 196

Japanese American Citizens League Entering Freshman Awards • 2232

Japanese American Citizens League Undergraduate Awards • 2235

Markley Scholarship • 221

National Honor Society Scholarship • 2081

Navin Narayan College Scholarship • 257

Newman Civic Fellow Awards • 266

Pedro Zamora Young Leaders Scholarship • 280

Pilot Pen G2 Overachievers Student Grant • 283

Prudential Emerging Visionaries • 290

Samuel Huntington Public Service Award • 303

Sodexo STOP Hunger Scholarship • 320

Student Activist Awards • 332

SuperCollege Scholarship • 341

Thurgood Marshall College Scholarship Fund • 2328

Truman Scholar • 355

United States Senate Youth Program • 747

Urban Fellows Program • 364

White House Fellows Program • 385

Women's Overseas Service League Scholarships for Women • 393

RACE/ETHNICITY/GENDER/FAMILY STATUS
Also See Scholarships Listed Under:
Academics/General

A.T. Anderson Memorial Scholarship • 2145

AAUW Educational Foundation Career Development Grants • 2146

Abe and Esther Hagiwara Student Aid Award • 2147

Achievers in Technology Program • 2148

Actuarial Diversity Scholarship • 2149

Ada I. Pressman Memorial Scholarship • 2150

Admiral Grace Murray Hopper Memorial Scholarships • 2151

Adolph Van Pelt Scholarship • 2152

Adult Students in Scholastic Transition (ASIST) • 527

Afro-Academic, Cultural, Technological and Scientific Olympics (ACT-SO) • 2153

AGBU US Graduate Scholarship • 2154

Agnes Jones Jackson Scholarship • 2155

Agnes Missirian Scholarship • 2156

AHEPA Educational Foundation National Scholarship Program • 2157

AICPA Fellowship for Minority Doctoral Students • 2158

AICPA Scholarship for Minority Accounting Students • 2159

AISES Intel Scholarship • 2160

Alice T. Schafer Mathematics Prize • 793

Alice W. Rooke Scholarship • 794

Allogan Slagle Memorial Scholarship • 2161

American Chemical Society Scholars Program • 2162

American Indian Nurse Scholarship • 2163

American Indian Services Scholarship • 2164

AMS Minority Scholarship • 803

Anne Maureen Whitney Barrow Memorial Scholarship • 2165

Annual NBNA Scholarships • 808

ARS Undergraduate Scholarship • 2166

ASA Scholarships • 2167

Asian and Pacific Islander American Scholarships • 2168

Association of Cuban Engineers Scholarship Foundation Scholarships • 2169

Auxiliary Legacy Scholarship • 841

AWAF Scholarships • 1286

B.J. Harrod Scholarships • 2170

B.K. Krenzer Reentry Scholarship • 2171

Bechtel Corporation Scholarship • 2172

Bee's Fund Microgrants • 2173

Berbeco Senior Research Fellowship • 2174

Biographies of Contemporary Women in Mathematics Essay Contest • 854

BIPOC Scholarship • 2175

Burlington Northern Santa Fe (BNSF) Foundation Scholarship • 2176

Cafe Bustelo El Cafe Del Futuro Scholarship • 2177

California Chafee Grant for Foster Youth • 2178

Casey Family Scholarship • 2179

Catching the Dream Native American Scholarship Fund • 2180

CBC Spouses Performing Arts Scholarship • 2181

CHCI United Health Foundation Scholar-Intern Program • 2182

Cherokee Nation Directed Studies Scholarship • 2183

Cherokee Nation Scholarship - Graduate • 2184

Cherokee Nation Scholarship - Undergraduate • 2185

Chief Manuelito Scholarship Program • 2186

Citizen Potawatomi Nation Tribal Scholarship • 2187

Colgate-Palmolive Make the U Educational Grant • 2188

Conference of Minority Transportation Officials (COMTO) National Scholarship • 2189

Congressional Black Caucus Spouses Education Scholarship • 2190

Congressional Black Caucus Spouses Visual Arts Scholarship • 2191

Development Fund for Black Students in Science and Technology • 2192

Displaced Homemaker Scholarship • 2193

Distinguished Young Women Scholarship Program • 2194

Diversity Advocacy Council Scholarship • 2195

Dr. Ivy M. Parker Memorial Scholarship • 2196

Dr. Juan Andrade, Jr. Scholarship • 2197

Drs. James and Wanda Trefil Science Scholarship • 2198

Edie Windsor Coding Scholarship • 2199

EDSA Diversity Scholarships • 2200

Education Scholarship • 2201

Education Support Award • 2202

Elizabeth and Sherman Asche Memorial Scholarship • 2203

ESA Foundation Scholarship Program • 2204

Eugene and Elinor Kotur Scholarship Trust Fund • 2205

Florence Young Memorial Scholarship • 2206

Foundation Scholarships • 2207

Full Circle Scholarship • 2208

GAHCC Foundation Scholarship • 2209

Gates Scholarship • 2210

GEM MS Engineering Fellowship Program • 2211

General Society of Mayflower Descendants (GSMD) Scholarship • 2212

Gentlemen Showcase • 2213

George Choy Memorial/Gay Asian Pacific Alliance (GAPA) Scholarship • 2214

Girls Incorporated Lucile Miller Wright Scholars Program • 2040

Gladys Anderson Emerson Scholarship • 945

Goldie Bateson Scholarship • 2215

Google Generation Google Scholarship • 2216

Harriet Fitzgerald Scholarship • 2217

Health Professions Pre-Graduate Scholarship Program • 2218

Health Professions Preparatory Scholarship Program • 2219

Helene M. Overly Memorial Graduate Scholarship • 2220

Henry Sachs Foundation Scholarship • 1496

Henry Salvatori Scholarship • 2221

Herbert Lehman Education Fund Scholarship • 2222

Higher Education Grant • 2223

Hispanic Heritage Youth Awards • 2224

Hispanic Scholarship Fund • 2225

Honeywell International Inc. Scholarships • 2226

Hopi Scholarship Program • 2227

Howard County PFLAG Academic Scholarship • 2228

Hubertus W.V. Wellems Scholarship for Male Students • 2229

Ida M. Pope Memorial Scholarship • 2230

Jackie Robinson Foundation Scholarship Program • 2231

Japanese American Citizens League Entering Freshman Awards • 2232

Japanese American Citizens League Graduate Awards • 2233

Japanese American Citizens League Law Scholarships • 2234

FIELD OF STUDY INDEX

This index organizes the scholarships by fields of study. It lists both general areas of study (in bold) as well as specific areas of study. If you cannot find a specific area of study that matches your major simply look at the scholarships under the closest matching general area.

In addition to this index be sure to use the Career Index since many scholarships are targeted to specific careers but do not have specific field of study requirements.

ACCOUNTING
See: *BUSINESS, MANAGEMENT AND MARKETING*

ACTING
See: *VISUAL AND PERFORMING ARTS*

ACTUARIAL SCIENCE
See: *BUSINESS, MANAGEMENT AND MARKETING*

ADULT DEVELOPMENT AND AGING
See: *FAMILY AND CONSUMER SCIENCES / HUMAN SCIENCES*

ADVERTISING
See: *COMMUNICATION AND JOURNALISM*

AEROSPACE, AERONAUTICAL AND ASTRONAUTICAL ENGINEERING
See: *ENGINEERING*

AFRICAN STUDIES
See: *AREA, ETHNIC, CULTURAL AND GENDER STUDIES*

AGRICULTURAL / BIOLOGICAL ENGINEERING AND BIOENGINEERING
See: *ENGINEERING*

AGRICULTURE AND RELATED SCIENCES
AGCO Corporation FFA Scholarship • 1996
ASEV Scholarships • 823
ASF Olin Fellowships • 824
Bunge North America FFA Scholarship • 860
Careers in Agriculture Scholarship Program • 863
Carville M. Akehurst Memorial Scholarship • 864
Dairy Student Recognition Program • 881
Emily M. Hewitt and Stephen K. Stocking Memorial Scholarship • 1423
FarmAid FFA Scholarship • 917
Feeding Tomorrow General Education Scholarships/Freshman Scholarships • 919
Good Eats Scholarship Fund • 1467
Hoard's Dairyman FFA Scholarship • 2048
Iowa 4-H and FFA Livestock Show Competition • 1531
Iowa Pork Foundation Scholarship • 1538
Ivomec Generations of Excellence Internship and Scholarship Program • 1546
Kansas Agricultural Aviation Association Scholarship • 1573
Lois Britt Pork Industry Memorial Scholarship Program • 1024
Mabel Mayforth Scholarship • 1614
Mollie Butler Memorial Scholarship • 1054

National Garden Clubs Scholarship • 1072
NCGA William C. Berg Academic Excellence in Agriculture Scholarship • 1081
NDS / Klussendorf / McKown Scholarships • 1084
Novus Biologicals Scholarship Program • 1093
Ohio Turfgrass Foundation Scholarships • 1748
Oregon Farm Bureau Memorial Scholarships • 1766
R. Flake Shaw Scholarship • 1799
South Carolina Farm Bureau Foundation Scholarships • 1861
Spring Meadow Nursery Scholarship • 1170
Thaddeus Colson and Isabelle Saalwaechter Fitzpatrick Memorial Scholarship • 1907
USDA/1890 National Scholars Program • 1213
William F. Helms Internship Program • 1221
Yanmar/SAE Scholarship • 1225

AGRICULTURE AND RELATED SCIENCES -- AGRICULTURAL AND FOOD PRODUCTS PROCESSING
E.H. Marth Food Protection and Food Science Scholarship • 1408
Iowa Pork Foundation Scholarship • 1538
Undergraduate Scholarships • 1208

AGRICULTURE AND RELATED SCIENCES -- AGRICULTURAL BUSINESS AND MANAGEMENT
DMI Milk Marketing Scholarship • 890
Iowa Pork Foundation Scholarship • 1538
National Potato Council Scholarship • 1073

AGRICULTURE AND RELATED SCIENCES -- ANIMAL SCIENCES
Iowa Pork Foundation Scholarship • 1538
Louis Agassiz Fuertes Award • 1026
National Dairy Shrine/Iager Dairy Scholarship • 1069
National FFA Combined Scholarship • 2080

AGRICULTURE AND RELATED SCIENCES -- APPLIED HORTICULTURE AND HORTICULTURAL BUSINESS SERVICES
Emily M. Hewitt and Stephen K. Stocking Memorial Scholarship • 1423
Harold Bettinger Scholarship • 957
James F. Davis Memorial Scholarship • 1552
Joseph Shinoda Memorial Scholarship • 1569
LEAF Scholarships • 1592
Loy McCandless Marks Scholarship in Tropical Horticulture • 1028
National FFA Combined Scholarship • 2080
National Foliage Foundation General Scholarships • 1071
Nurseries Foundation Award • 1098
Perennial Plant Association Scholarship • 1111
Perfect Plants Nursery Scholarship • 1112
Rain Bird Intelligent Use of Water Scholarship • 1128
Retail Chapter Awards • 1813
Timothy S. and Palmer W. Bigelow, Jr. Scholarship • 1195
Usrey Family Scholarship • 1214

AGRICULTURE AND RELATED SCIENCES -- FOOD SCIENCE AND TECHNOLOGY
AACT National Candy Technologists John Kitt Memorial Scholarship Program • 765
Asparagus Club, Thomas K. Zaucha Scholarship • 543
Association of Food and Drug Officials Scholarship Award • 834
Bob Richardson Legacy Scholarship • 552
Charlie and Becky Bray Legacy Scholarship • 565
E.H. Marth Food Protection and Food Science Scholarship • 1408
FMS Solutions Holdings LLC Legacy Scholarship • 588
Graduate Scholarships • 951
Iowa Pork Foundation Scholarship • 1538
Kimberly-Clark Corporation Legacy Scholarship • 641
Mondelez International Legacy Scholarship • 667
Peter and Jody Larkin Legacy Scholarship • 695
Phyllis V. Roberts Scholarship • 1795
Roger Collins Leadership Scholarship • 713
Undergraduate Scholarships • 1208
Women Grocers of America (WGA) Mary Macey Scholarship(s) • 759

AGRONOMY AND CROP SCIENCE
See: *AGRICULTURE AND RELATED SCIENCES*

AIRLINE / COMMERCIAL / PROFESSIONAL PILOT AND FLIGHT CREW
See: *TRANSPORTATION AND MATERIALS MOVING*

AMERICAN HISTORY
See: *HISTORY*

ANIMAL SCIENCES
See: *AGRICULTURE AND RELATED SCIENCES*

ANTHROPOLOGY
See: *SOCIAL SCIENCES*

APPLIED HORTICULTURE AND HORTICULTURAL BUSINESS SERVICES
See: *AGRICULTURE AND RELATED SCIENCES*

AQUACULTURE
See: *AGRICULTURE AND RELATED SCIENCES*

ARCHEOLOGY
See: *SOCIAL SCIENCES*

ARCHITECTURE (BARCH, BA / BS, MARCH, MA / MS, PHD)
See: *ARCHITECTURE AND RELATED SERVICES*

ARCHITECTURE AND RELATED SERVICES
AIA/Architects Foundation Diversity Advancement Scholarship • 785
Alabama Concrete Industries Association Scholarships • 1245
ASCA/AISC Student Design Competition • 820
Associated General Contractors of Minnesota Scholarships • 1283
AWAF Scholarships • 1286
Byers Scholarship • 1310
Carville M. Akehurst Memorial Scholarship • 864
Chairish Design Your Future Scholarship • 866
Connecticut Building Congress Scholarships • 1372

BIOLOGICAL AND BIOMEDICAL SCIENCES -- BIOLOGY / BIOLOGICAL SCIENCES, GENERAL
AACT National Candy Technologists John Kitt Memorial Scholarship Program • 765
Creative Biolabs • 877
NOAA Educational Partnership Program Undergraduate Scholarships • 2295
NYWEA Major Environmental Career Scholarship • 1743
Thermo Fisher Scientific Antibody Scholarship • 1188
USDA/1890 National Scholars Program • 1213
William F. Helms Internship Program • 1221

BIOLOGICAL AND BIOMEDICAL SCIENCES -- BIOTECHNOLOGY
American Chemical Society Scholars Program • 2162
Joseph P. and Helen T. Cribbins Scholarship • 203

BIOLOGICAL AND BIOMEDICAL SCIENCES -- BOTANY / PLANT BIOLOGY
Mabel Mayforth Scholarship • 1614
USDA/1890 National Scholars Program • 1213

BIOLOGICAL AND BIOMEDICAL SCIENCES -- ENTOMOLOGY
Jean Theodore Lacordaire Prize • 987
John Henry Comstock Graduate Student Awards • 993
Youth Incentive Award • 1226

BIOLOGICAL AND BIOMEDICAL SCIENCES -- MARINE BIOLOGY AND BIOLOGICAL OCEANOGRAPHY
Charles H. Bussmann Undergraduate Scholarship • 867
International Women's Fishing Association Scholarship • 979
John C. Bajus Scholarship • 992
Libbie H. Hyman Memorial Scholarship • 1020
MTS Student Scholarship for Two-Year, Technical, Engineering and Community College Students • 1057
MTS Student Scholarship for Undergraduate Students • 1058
NOAA Educational Partnership Program Undergraduate Scholarships • 2295
Paros-Digiquartz Scholarship • 1105
Rockefeller State Wildlife Scholarship • 1829
Zale Parry Scholarship • 396

BIOLOGICAL AND BIOMEDICAL SCIENCES -- MICROBIOLOGICAL SCIENCES AND IMMUNOLOGY
Creative Biolabs • 877
NYWEA Major Environmental Career Scholarship • 1743

BIOLOGICAL AND BIOMEDICAL SCIENCES -- ZOOLOGY / ANIMAL BIOLOGY
George A. Hall / Harold F. Mayfield Grant • 941
Libbie H. Hyman Memorial Scholarship • 1020
Louis Agassiz Fuertes Award • 1026

BIOLOGY / BIOLOGICAL SCIENCES, GENERAL
See: BIOLOGICAL AND BIOMEDICAL SCIENCES

BIOMEDICAL / MEDICAL ENGINEERING
See: ENGINEERING

BIOTECHNOLOGY
See: BIOLOGICAL AND BIOMEDICAL SCIENCES

BOTANY / PLANT BIOLOGY
See: BIOLOGICAL AND BIOMEDICAL SCIENCES

BROADCAST JOURNALISM
See: COMMUNICATION AND JOURNALISM

BUSINESS, MANAGEMENT AND MARKETING
AGCO Corporation FFA Scholarship • 1996
American Legion Auxiliary, Department of California $1,000 Scholarships • 1261
American Legion Auxiliary, Department of California $2,000 Scholarships • 1262
Betsy Plank/PRSSA Scholarship • 549
Burlington Northern Santa Fe (BNSF) Foundation Scholarship • 2176
Hermine Solt Student Scholarship • 1500
IBTTA Scholarship Program • 971
James A. Turner, Jr. Memorial Scholarship • 627
Jane M. Klausman Women in Business Scholarship Fund • 629
Joe Perdue Scholarship • 633
Jungle Scholar • 638
Lambeth Family Scholarship • 1588
Lawrence G. Foster Award for Excellence in Public Relations • 646
Mas Family Scholarships • 2262
MBA Fellowship • 659
National Academic Scholarships • 673
National Association of Black Accountants National Scholarship Program • 2280
National Scholarship • 2286
NSA Scholarship Foundation • 689
TechChecks Business Leadership Scholarship • 738
TE Connectivity African Heritage Scholarship • 2326
Ted Rollins ECO Scholarship • 1186
Washington State Auto Dealers Association Bright Future Scholarship • 1959
William Wrigley Jr. Scholarship/Internship • 2337

BUSINESS, MANAGEMENT AND MARKETING -- ACCOUNTING
AICPA Fellowship for Minority Doctoral Students • 2158
AICPA Foundation Scholarship for Future CPAs • 528
AICPA Foundation Two-year Transfer Scholarship • 529
AICPA John L. Carey Scholarship • 530
AICPA Scholarship for Minority Accounting Students • 2159
AICPA/Robert Half Student Scholarship • 531
Alice L. Haltom Educational Fund Scholarship • 534

ASWA Seattle Chapter Scholarship • 1284
AWSCPA Scholarship • 545
Candon, Todd and Seabolt Scholarship Fund • 1328
CardRates.com Financial Futures Scholarship • 560
CHAHRM Scholarship • 1343
Hawaii Society of Certified Public Accountants Scholarship Fund • 1493
IBTTA Scholarship Program • 971
Laurels Fund Scholarship • 645
PAVE Student Design Competition • 694
Pennsylvania Society of Tax and Accounting Professionals Scholarships • 1790
Risk Management Association Foundation Scholarship • 711
Ritchie-Jennings Memorial Scholarship • 712
TACTYC Accounting Scholarship • 735
Washington State Auto Dealers Association Bright Future Scholarship • 1959
Willa S. Bellamy Scholarship • 1968
William (Bill) Ezzell Scholarship • 757

BUSINESS, MANAGEMENT AND MARKETING -- ACTUARIAL SCIENCE
Actuarial Diversity Scholarship • 2149
Mutual of Omaha Actuarial Scholarship for Minority Students • 2275
Nebraska Actuaries Club Scholarship • 1698

BUSINESS, MANAGEMENT AND MARKETING -- BUSINESS ADMINISTRATION AND MANAGEMENT, GENERAL
BMO Capital Markets Lime Connect Equity Through Education Scholarship • 2346
CardRates.com Financial Futures Scholarship • 560
George Mason Business Scholarship Fund • 1459
IBTTA Scholarship Program • 971
PixelPlex Bi-Annual STEM Scholarship • 1118
Richard D. Wiegers Scholarship • 1818
Richard E. Bangert Business Award • 1819
Risk Management Association Foundation Scholarship • 711
Virtual Business Scholarship • 754
Washington State Auto Dealers Association Bright Future Scholarship • 1959
Willa S. Bellamy Scholarship • 1968

BUSINESS, MANAGEMENT AND MARKETING -- CONSTRUCTION MANAGEMENT
Associated General Contractors of Minnesota Scholarships • 1283
Herman J. Smith Scholarship • 1498
Kilbourn-Sawyer Memorial Scholarship • 1584
Maple Flooring Manufacturers Association Scholarship • 657
NAPA Research and Education Foundation Scholarship • 1066

BUSINESS, MANAGEMENT AND MARKETING -- FINANCE, GENERAL
BMO Capital Markets Lime Connect Equity Through Education Scholarship • 2346
Candon, Todd and Seabolt Scholarship Fund • 1328

National Association for Surface Finishing Scholarships • 1067
Robert B. Oliver ASNT Scholarship • 1143
STEEL Engineering Education Link Initiative • 1173

ENGINEERING -- NUCLEAR ENGINEERING
ANS Incoming Freshman Scholarships • 811
Operations and Power Division Scholarship • 1101

ENGINEERING -- POLYMER / PLASTICS ENGINEERING
Composites Division/Harold Giles Scholarship • 874
Injection Molding Division Scholarship • 975
Plastics Pioneers Association Scholarships • 1119
Polymer Modifiers and Additives Division Scholarships • 1120
Richard Goolsby Scholarship Fund • 1820
Salvatore J. Monte Thermoplastic Materials and Foams Division Scholarship • 1152
Ted and Ruth Neward Scholarship • 1185
Thermoforming Division Memorial Scholarships • 1189
Thermoplastic Elastomers Special Interest Group Scholarship • 1190
Thomas E. Powers/Detroit Section Scholarship • 1191

ENGINEERING SCIENCE
See: ENGINEERING

ENGLISH LANGUAGE AND LITERATURE
ACES Copy Editing Scholarships • 398
Bill Gove Scholarship • 413
Cavett Robert Scholarship • 418
Davidson Fellows Scholarships • 109
Heinlein Society Scholarship Program • 444
Huntington Fellowships • 613
Huntington-British Academy Fellowships for Study in Great Britain • 614
ILA Jeanne S. Chall Research Fellowship • 452
Iowa Scholarship for the Arts • 1539
Julianne Malveaux Scholarship • 2238
Michael Jackson Scholarship • 2266
Minnesota Academic Excellence Scholarship • 1663
NCTA and AWMF Scholarship • 2290
Oratorical Contest Scholarship • 1764
PenSPRA Scholarship • 1793
Playwright Discovery Award • 490
Ruth Lilly and Dorothy Sargent Rosenberg Poetry Fellowship Program • 496

ENTOMOLOGY
See: BIOLOGICAL AND BIOMEDICAL SCIENCES

ENTREPRENEURSHIP / ENTREPRENEURIAL STUDIES
See: BUSINESS, MANAGEMENT AND MARKETING

ENVIRONMENTAL / ENVIRONMENTAL HEALTH ENGINEERING
See: ENGINEERING

ENVIRONMENTAL DESIGN / ARCHITECTURE
See: ARCHITECTURE AND RELATED SERVICES

ENVIRONMENTAL SCIENCE
See: NATURAL RESOURCES AND CONSERVATION

EQUESTRIAN / EQUINE STUDIES
See: AGRICULTURE AND RELATED SCIENCES

EUROPEAN HISTORY
See: HISTORY

EUROPEAN STUDIES / CIVILIZATION
See: AREA, ETHNIC, CULTURAL AND GENDER STUDIES

FAMILY AND CONSUMER SCIENCES / HUMAN SCIENCES
Arc of Washington State Trust Fund Stipend Award • 1272
Association of Food and Drug Officials Scholarship Award • 834
IEHA Scholarship • 615
IFSEA Worthy Goal Scholarship • 617

FAMILY AND CONSUMER SCIENCES / HUMAN SCIENCES -- CHILD DEVELOPMENT
Arc of Washington State Trust Fund Stipend Award • 1272
Scholars for Excellence in Child Care • 1841
Winifred R. Reynolds Educational Scholarship • 1977

FAMILY AND CONSUMER SCIENCES / HUMAN SCIENCES -- FOODS, NUTRITION AND RELATED SERVICES
Health Research and Educational Trust Pathway Scholarship • 1494
Phyllis V. Roberts Scholarship • 1795
Undergraduate Scholarships • 1208

FAMILY PRACTICE NURSE / NURSE PRACTITIONER
See: HEALTH PROFESSIONS AND RELATED CLINICAL SCIENCES

FASHION / APPAREL DESIGN
See: VISUAL AND PERFORMING ARTS

FINANCE, GENERAL
See: BUSINESS, MANAGEMENT AND MARKETING

FINE / STUDIO ARTS, GENERAL
See: VISUAL AND PERFORMING ARTS

FINNISH AND RELATED LANGUAGES, LITERATURES AND LINGUISTICS
See: FOREIGN LANGUAGES, LITERATURES AND LINGUISTICS

FIRE PROTECTION
See: SECURITY AND PROTECTIVE SERVICES

FISHING AND FISHERIES SCIENCES AND MANAGEMENT
See: NATURAL RESOURCES AND CONSERVATION

FOOD SCIENCE AND TECHNOLOGY
See: AGRICULTURE AND RELATED SCIENCES

FOODS, NUTRITION AND RELATED SERVICES
See: FAMILY AND CONSUMER SCIENCES / HUMAN SCIENCES

FOREIGN LANGUAGES, LITERATURES AND LINGUISTICS
Fellowships for Regular Program in Greece • 435
Finlandia Foundation National Student Scholarships Program • 438
Language Grants • 466
Leif and Inger Sjoberg Award • 468
Minnesota Academic Excellence Scholarship • 1663
Nadia Christensen Prize • 475
Student Translation Award • 505

FOREIGN LANGUAGES, LITERATURES AND LINGUISTICS -- JAPANESE LANGUAGE AND LITERATURE
Bridging Scholarships for Study Abroad in Japan • 414
Language Grants • 466

FOREIGN LANGUAGES, LITERATURES AND LINGUISTICS -- LATIN LANGUAGE AND LITERATURE
ACL/NJCL National Latin Examination Scholarships • 401
Fellowships for Regular Program in Greece • 435
National Junior Classical League (NJCL) Scholarships • 477

FOREIGN LANGUAGES, LITERATURES AND LINGUISTICS -- MODERN GREEK LANGUAGE AND LITERATURE
ACL/NJCL National Greek Examination Scholarship • 400
Fellowships for Regular Program in Greece • 435
National Junior Classical League (NJCL) Scholarships • 477

FORENSIC SCIENCE AND TECHNOLOGY
See: SECURITY AND PROTECTIVE SERVICES

FORESTRY
See: NATURAL RESOURCES AND CONSERVATION

FRENCH LANGUAGE AND LITERATURE
See: FOREIGN LANGUAGES, LITERATURES AND LINGUISTICS

FRENCH STUDIES
See: AREA, ETHNIC, CULTURAL AND GENDER STUDIES

FUNERAL SERVICE AND MORTUARY SCIENCE, GENERAL
See: PERSONAL AND CULINARY SERVICES

GENETICS, GENERAL
See: BIOLOGICAL AND BIOMEDICAL SCIENCES

GEOGRAPHY
See: SOCIAL SCIENCES

GEOLOGICAL AND EARTH SCIENCES / GEOSCIENCES
See: PHYSICAL SCIENCES

GERMAN LANGUAGE AND LITERATURE
See: FOREIGN LANGUAGES, LITERATURES AND LINGUISTICS

GERMAN STUDIES
See: AREA, ETHNIC, CULTURAL AND GENDER STUDIES

587

GRAPHIC DESIGN
See: VISUAL AND PERFORMING ARTS

HEALTH AND MEDICAL ADMINISTRATIVE
SERVICES
*See: HEALTH PROFESSIONS AND RELATED
CLINICAL SCIENCES*

HEALTH AND PHYSICAL EDUCATION,
GENERAL
*See: PARKS, RECREATION, LEISURE AND FIT-
NESS STUDIES*

HEALTH PROFESSIONS AND RELATED
CLINICAL SCIENCES
A.T. Anderson Memorial Scholarship • 2145
AAMA Student Essay Competition • 768
Advanced Practice Healthcare Scholarship
Program • 1238
Allied Healthcare Scholarship Program • 1252
American Indian Nurse Scholarship • 2163
American Legion Auxiliary, Department of
California $2,000 Scholarships • 1262
Associate Degree Nursing Scholarship Program
• 1281
Avacare Medical Scholarship • 842
Bachelor of Science Nursing Scholarship Program
• 1287
Benton-Meier Scholarships • 851
Boeing Company STEM Scholarship • 1302
Burlington Northern Santa Fe (BNSF) Founda-
tion Scholarship • 2176
Campus Safety Health and Environmental Man-
agement Association Scholarship • 862
Carole J. Streeter, KB9JBR, Scholarship • 561
CHAHRM Scholarship • 1343
CHCI United Health Foundation Scholar-Intern
Program • 2182
Critical Care Scholarship Program • 1377
Elizabeth and Sherman Asche Memorial Scholar-
ship • 2203
Fellowship Award • 920
Florence Young Memorial Scholarship • 2206
Graduate Student Scholarship • 953
Health Professions Pre-Graduate Scholarship
Program • 2218
Health Professions Preparatory Scholarship
Program • 2219
Health Research and Educational Trust Pathway
Scholarship • 1494
Ida M. Pope Memorial Scholarship • 2230
International Student Scholarship • 978
Jimmy A. Young Memorial Education Recogni-
tion Award • 989
Kaiser Permanente Health Care Career Scholar-
ship • 1572
Maple Flooring Manufacturers Association
Scholarship • 657
Medical Scrubs Collection • 1038
Migrant Health Scholarships • 1050
Minority Fellowship Program • 1051
Minority Student Scholarship • 1052
Murse World Scholarship • 1059
NAHN Scholarship • 2277
National Hispanic Health Professional Student
Scholarship • 2283

NBRC/AMP Gareth B. Gish, MS, RRT Memo-
rial and William F. Miller, MD Postgraduate
Education Recognition Awards • 1078
NBRC/AMP William W. Burgin, Jr. MD and
Robert M. Lawrence, MD Education Recogni-
tion Award • 1079
NCPA Foundation Presidential Scholarship •
1082
NFMC Dorothy Dann Bullock Music Therapy
Award and the NFMC Ruth B. Robertson Music
Therapy Award • 1090
Novus Biologicals Scholarship Program • 1093
Oliver Joel and Ellen Pell Denny Healthcare
Scholarship Fund • 1760
Presbyterian Church USA Student Opportunity
Scholarships • 2094
RevPart STEM Scholarship • 1135
Robanna Fund • 1824
Ruth Abernathy Presidential Scholarship • 1151
Scholarships for Disadvantaged Students • 1155
Sharps Scholarship Program • 1161
SNMTS Paul Cole Scholarship • 1164
Student Research Awards • 1181
Ted Brickley/Bernice Shickora Scholarship •
1889
Tocris Scholarship • 1200
Welch Scholars Grant • 1220

HEALTH PROFESSIONS AND RELATED
CLINICAL SCIENCES -- ATHLETIC
TRAINING / TRAINER
Maple Flooring Manufacturers Association
Scholarship • 657
Mark Ando and Ito Family Scholarship • 2258
Michael Moody Fitness Scholarship • 1047

HEALTH PROFESSIONS AND RELATED
CLINICAL SCIENCES -- CHIROPRACTIC
(DC)
ChiroHealthUSA Foxworth Family Scholarship
• 869
Chiropractic Education Assistance Scholarship
• 1349
Cora Aguda Manayan Fund • 1374
Dr. Hans and Clara Zimmerman Foundation
Health Scholarships • 1404
Dr. William S. Boyd Scholarship • 1406

HEALTH PROFESSIONS AND RELATED
CLINICAL SCIENCES -- CLINICAL /
MEDICAL LABORATORY SCIENCE AND
ALLIED PROFESSIONS
Alpha Mu Tau Fraternity Undergraduate Schol-
arships • 795
Diversity Advocacy Council Scholarship • 2195
Foundation for Surgical Technology Scholarships
• 924

HEALTH PROFESSIONS AND RELATED
CLINICAL SCIENCES -- COMMUNICATION
DISORDERS, GENERAL
New Century Scholars Doctoral Scholarship •
1088
Sertoma Communicative Disorders Scholarship
• 1160

HEALTH PROFESSIONS AND RELATED
CLINICAL SCIENCES -- DENTAL SUPPORT
SERVICES AND ALLIED PROFESSIONS
1Dental Scholarship • 8
ADEA/Crest Oral-B Scholarships for Dental Hy-
giene Students Pursuing Academic Careers • 776
ADEA/Sigma Phi Alpha Linda Devore Scholar-
ship • 778
ADHA Institute Scholarship Program • 779
AMT Student Scholarship • 805
Colgate Bright Smiles, Bright Futures Minority
Scholarships • 871
Cora Aguda Manayan Fund • 1374
Crest Oral-B Laboratories Dental Hygiene
Scholarships • 878
Dr. Esther Wilkins Scholarship • 896
Dr. Hans and Clara Zimmerman Foundation
Health Scholarships • 1404
John Dawe Dental Education Fund • 1564
Karla Girts Memorial Community Outreach
Scholarship • 1006
Sigma Phi Alpha Undergraduate Scholarship •
1162

HEALTH PROFESSIONS AND RELATED
CLINICAL SCIENCES -- DENTISTRY (DDS,
DMD)
1Dental Scholarship • 8
ADEA/GlaxoSmithKline Consumer Healthcare
Preventive Dentistry Scholarships • 777
Cora Aguda Manayan Fund • 1374
Dr. Hans and Clara Zimmerman Foundation
Health Scholarships • 1404
Health Professions Pre-Graduate Scholarship
Program • 2218
John Dawe Dental Education Fund • 1564
Michael Moody Fitness Scholarship • 1047
NHSC Scholarship • 1091

HEALTH PROFESSIONS AND RELATED
CLINICAL SCIENCES -- DIETETICS /
DIETITIAN
Academy of Nutrition and Dietetics Foundation
Student Scholarship • 772
Sister Helen Marie Pellicer Scholarship • 1852

HEALTH PROFESSIONS AND RELATED
CLINICAL SCIENCES -- EMERGENCY
MEDICAL TECHNOLOGY / TECHNICIAN
(EMT PARAMEDIC)
Alpha Mu Tau Fraternity Undergraduate Schol-
arships • 795
Health Research and Educational Trust Pathway
Scholarship • 1494

HEALTH PROFESSIONS AND RELATED
CLINICAL SCIENCES -- FAMILY PRACTICE
NURSE / NURSE PRACTITIONER
AMT Student Scholarship • 805
Annual NBNA Scholarships • 808
Cora Aguda Manayan Fund • 1374
Dr. Hans and Clara Zimmerman Foundation
Health Scholarships • 1404
Margaret A. Pemberton Scholarship • 1622
Margaret A. Stafford Nursing Scholarship • 1623
MARILN Professional Scholarship Award • 1624
NHSC Scholarship • 1091
Nurse Corps Scholarship Program • 1097

Nursing Education Scholarship Program • 1741
Osmosis Raise the Line Scholarship • 1102
Predoctoral Research Training Fellowship • 1123
Stephanie Carroll Memorial Scholarship • 1176
Tuition Reduction for Non-Resident Nursing Students • 1919

HEALTH PROFESSIONS AND RELATED CLINICAL SCIENCES -- HEALTH AND MEDICAL ADMINISTRATIVE SERVICES

AHIMA Foundation Merit Scholarships • 784
Harry J. Harwick Scholarship • 958
Health Research and Educational Trust Pathway Scholarship • 1494
HIMSS Foundation Scholarship • 965
Leaders Scholarship • 1013
Richard J. Stull Student Essay Competition in Healthcare Management • 1136
Richard L. Davis, FACMPE - Managers Scholarship • 1138
Richard L. Davis, FACMPE/Barbara B. Watson, FACMPE - National Scholarship • 1139

HEALTH PROFESSIONS AND RELATED CLINICAL SCIENCES -- LICENSED PRACTICAL / VOCATIONAL NURSE TRAINING (LPN, LVN, CERT., DIPL, AAS)

AMT Student Scholarship • 805
Annual NBNA Scholarships • 808
Cora Aguda Manayan Fund • 1374
Dr. Hans and Clara Zimmerman Foundation Health Scholarships • 1404
Margaret A. Pemberton Scholarship • 1622
MARILN Professional Scholarship Award • 1624
Nursing Education Scholarship Program • 1741
Predoctoral Research Training Fellowship • 1123
Stephanie Carroll Memorial Scholarship • 1176
Tuition Reduction for Non-Resident Nursing Students • 1919
Vocational Nurse Scholarship • 1950

HEALTH PROFESSIONS AND RELATED CLINICAL SCIENCES -- MEDICINE AND PRE-MEDICINE STUDIES

AGBU US Graduate Scholarship • 2154
Annual University Scholarship • 809
Bart Kamen Memorial FIRST Scholarship • 847
Cora Aguda Manayan Fund • 1374
Dr. and Mrs. Arthur F. Sullivan Fund • 1401
Dr. Hans and Clara Zimmerman Foundation Health Scholarships • 1404
Health Professions Pre-Graduate Scholarship Program • 2218
John D. and Virginia Riesch Scholarship • 1563
Medical Student Research Scholarship • 1039
National Medical Fellowships Emergency Scholarship Fund • 2285
NHSC Scholarship • 1091
NMF National Alumni Council Scholarship Program • 2294
Osmosis Raise the Line Scholarship • 1102
Resident Research Scholarship • 1133
Steve Dearduff Scholarship Fund • 1876
Student Award Program of FSD • 2390
Tutor the People Pre-Med Scholarship • 1203
Visiting Medical Student Scholar • 1217
William and Charlotte Cadbury Award • 2336

HEALTH PROFESSIONS AND RELATED CLINICAL SCIENCES -- MUSIC THERAPY / THERAPIST

Health Research and Educational Trust Pathway Scholarship • 1494
Music Committee Scholarship • 1684
NFMC Gretchen E. Van Roy Music Education Scholarship • 685

HEALTH PROFESSIONS AND RELATED CLINICAL SCIENCES -- NURSE / NURSING ASSISTANT / AIDE AND PATIENT CARE ASSISTANT

Albert E. and Florence W. Newton Nursing Scholarship • 1246
AMT Student Scholarship • 805
Annual NBNA Scholarships • 808
Cora Aguda Manayan Fund • 1374
Dr. Hans and Clara Zimmerman Foundation Health Scholarships • 1404
Margaret A. Stafford Nursing Scholarship • 1623
Nursing Education Scholarship Program • 1741
Predoctoral Research Training Fellowship • 1123
Stephanie Carroll Memorial Scholarship • 1176
Tuition Reduction for Non-Resident Nursing Students • 1919

HEALTH PROFESSIONS AND RELATED CLINICAL SCIENCES -- NURSING ADMINISTRATION (MSN, MS, PHD)

H.M. Muffly Memorial Scholarship • 1481
Health Research and Educational Trust Pathway Scholarship • 1494
Nightingale Awards of Pennsylvania Scholarship • 1717
Nursing Incentive Scholarship Fund • 1742
South Carolina Nurses Foundation Nurses Care Scholarship • 1863
Stephanie Carroll Memorial Scholarship • 1176

HEALTH PROFESSIONS AND RELATED CLINICAL SCIENCES -- NURSING SCIENCE (MS, PHD)

H.M. Muffly Memorial Scholarship • 1481
Health Research and Educational Trust Pathway Scholarship • 1494
Jane Delano Student Nurse Scholarship • 986
Margaret A. Pemberton Scholarship • 1622
Margaret A. Stafford Nursing Scholarship • 1623
MARILN Professional Scholarship Award • 1624
Michael Moody Fitness Scholarship • 1047
Nightingale Awards of Pennsylvania Scholarship • 1717
South Carolina Nurses Foundation Nurses Care Scholarship • 1863
Stephanie Carroll Memorial Scholarship • 1176

HEALTH PROFESSIONS AND RELATED CLINICAL SCIENCES -- NURSING/ REGISTERED NURSE (RN, ASN, BSN, MSN)

Albert E. and Florence W. Newton Nursing Scholarship • 1246
AMT Student Scholarship • 805
Annual NBNA Scholarships • 808
Annual University Scholarship • 809
Army Nurse Corps Association Scholarships • 44
Cora Aguda Manayan Fund • 1374

Dr. Hans and Clara Zimmerman Foundation Health Scholarships • 1404
H.M. Muffly Memorial Scholarship • 1481
Harriet Hayes Austin Memorial Scholarship for Nursing • 1485
Health Research and Educational Trust Pathway Scholarship • 1494
Jack E. Barger, Sr. Memorial Nursing Scholarship • 1548
Jane Delano Student Nurse Scholarship • 986
John D. and Virginia Riesch Scholarship • 1563
Licensed Vocational Nurse to Associate Degree Nursing Scholarship • 1598
Margaret A. Pemberton Scholarship • 1622
Margaret A. Stafford Nursing Scholarship • 1623
MARILN Professional Scholarship Award • 1624
McLean Scholarship for Nursing and Physician Assistant Majors • 1644
Naomi Brack Student Scholarship • 1065
Nightingale Awards of Pennsylvania Scholarship • 1717
NROTC Nurse Corps Scholarship • 270
Nurse Candidate Program • 1096
Nurse Corps Scholarship Program • 1097
Nursing Education Scholarship Program • 1741
Nursing Incentive Scholarship Fund • 1742
Osmosis Raise the Line Scholarship • 1102
Phoebe Pember Memorial Scholarship • 1115
Predoctoral Research Training Fellowship • 1123
Ruth Lutes Bachmann Scholarship • 1837
South Carolina Nurses Foundation Nurses Care Scholarship • 1863
Stephanie Carroll Memorial Scholarship • 1176
Tuition Reduction for Non-Resident Nursing Students • 1919
Workforce Shortage Student Assistance Grant Program • 1986

HEALTH PROFESSIONS AND RELATED CLINICAL SCIENCES -- OCCUPATIONAL THERAPY / THERAPIST

AMBUCS Scholars • 796
BrightLife Direct Physical Therapy Scholarship • 856
Health Research and Educational Trust Pathway Scholarship • 1494
Jaime Guttenberg Helping Hands Scholarship • 626
Kappa Delta Phi • 1004
Laura N. Dowsett Fund • 1589
Texas Occupational Therapy Association Scholarships • 1904

HEALTH PROFESSIONS AND RELATED CLINICAL SCIENCES -- OPTOMETRY (OD)

Health Professions Pre-Graduate Scholarship Program • 2218
Health Research and Educational Trust Pathway Scholarship • 1494

HEALTH PROFESSIONS AND RELATED CLINICAL SCIENCES -- PHARMACY (PHARMD (USA), PHARMD OR BS / BPHARM (CANADA))

Annual University Scholarship • 809
Cora Aguda Manayan Fund • 1374
Dr. Hans and Clara Zimmerman Foundation Health Scholarships • 1404

PERSONAL AND CULINARY SERVICES -- FUNERAL SERVICE AND MORTUARY SCIENCE, GENERAL

Dennis Schoepp Memorial Scholarship • 1391

Memorial Classic Golf Tournament Scholarship • 661

National Scholarship Program • 677

Shipley Rose Buckner Memorial Scholarship • 1847

Tennessee Funeral Directors Association Memorial Scholarship • 1890

Wallace S. and Wilma K. Laughlin Foundation Trust Scholarships • 1952

PHARMACOLOGY
See: BIOLOGICAL AND BIOMEDICAL SCIENCES

PHARMACY (PHARMD (USA), PHARMD OR BS / BPHARM (CANADA))
See: HEALTH PROFESSIONS AND RELATED CLINICAL SCIENCES

PHARMACY TECHNICIAN / ASSISTANT
See: HEALTH PROFESSIONS AND RELATED CLINICAL SCIENCES

PHILOSOPHY AND RELIGIOUS STUDIES

Mary E. Bivins Religious Scholarship • 2072

Presbyterian Church USA Student Opportunity Scholarships • 2094

PHOTOGRAPHY
See: VISUAL AND PERFORMING ARTS

PHOTOJOURNALISM
See: COMMUNICATION AND JOURNALISM

PHYSICAL SCIENCES

A.T. Anderson Memorial Scholarship • 2145

AFCEA Ralph W. Shrader Diversity Scholarships • 780

AFCEA ROTC Scholarships • 15

AMS Graduate Fellowship in the History of Science • 801

AMS Graduate Fellowships • 802

AMS Minority Scholarship • 803

AMS Senior Named Scholarships • 804

ASNE Scholarship Program • 831

Astronaut Scholarship • 837

BAFTX Undergraduate Award • 1289

Battery Division Student Research Award • 848

Boeing Company STEM Scholarship • 1302

Burlington Northern Santa Fe (BNSF) Foundation Scholarship • 2176

Chuck Reville, K3FT Memorial Scholarship • 870

Collegiate Inventors Competition • 872

Computational Science Graduate Fellowship • 875

Davidson Fellows Scholarships • 109

East Asia and Pacific Summer Institutes • 902

Elizabeth and Sherman Asche Memorial Scholarship • 2203

Ezoe Memorial Foundation Academic Scholarship • 915

Father James B. Macelwane Annual Award in Meteorology • 918

Fellowship Award • 920

Freshman Undergraduate Scholarship • 928

GAHCC Foundation Scholarship • 2209

GeneTex Scholarship Program • 939

Gladys Anderson Emerson Scholarship • 945

Gorgas Scholarship Competition • 1468

Graduate Research Fellowship Program • 950

Heinlein Society Scholarship Program • 444

Hertz Foundation's Graduate Fellowship Award • 964

Horkheimer/Smith Youth Service Award • 967

Ida M. Pope Memorial Scholarship • 2230

Institute of Electrical and Electronics Engineers Life Members' Fellowship in Electrical History • 976

John J. McKetta Scholarship • 994

LabRoots Scholarship • 1008

Lambeth Family Scholarship • 1588

Lockheed Martin STEM Scholarship Program • 1023

MAES Scholarship Program • 2251

Mikkelson Foundation Scholarship • 1659

Minnesota Academic Excellence Scholarship • 1663

Minority Affairs Committee Award for Outstanding Scholastic Achievement • 2267

NDSEG Fellowship Program • 1085

Novus Biologicals Scholarship Program • 1093

Paul and Ellen Ruckes Scholarship • 2384

Payzer Scholarship • 1109

PixelPlex Bi-Annual STEM Scholarship • 1118

R&D Systems Scholarship Program • 1127

RBC Wealth Management Colorado Scholarship • 1808

RevPart STEM Scholarship • 1135

Ridgeline International Community Scholarship • 1141

SMART Scholarship • 1163

Snapology STEM Studies Scholarship • 2319

Society of American Military Engineers, Albuquerque Post Scholarship • 1858

Stantec Equity and Diversity Scholarship • 2321

Student Award Program of FSD • 2390

TE Connectivity African Heritage Scholarship • 2326

Tech High School Alumni Association/W.O. Cheney Merit Scholarship • 1886

Unitil Scholarship Fund • 1926

West Virginia Engineering, Science and Technology Scholarship • 1964

William James and Dorothy Bading Lanquist Fund • 1975

WISE Scholarship • 1985

Women in STEM Scholarship/BHW Scholarship • 1223

PHYSICAL SCIENCES -- CHEMISTRY

AACT National Candy Technologists John Kitt Memorial Scholarship Program • 765

AISES Intel Scholarship • 2160

American Chemical Society Scholars Program • 2162

David R. Jones IV Scholarship • 886

Hubertus W.V. Wellems Scholarship for Male Students • 2229

Industrial Electrolysis and Electrochemical Engineering Division H.H. Dow Memorial Student Award • 973

Kathryn D. Sullivan Earth and Marine Science Fellowship • 1580

National Association for Surface Finishing Scholarships • 1067

National Foundation Scholarships • 674

Robert E. Dougherty Educational Foundation Scholarship Award • 1144

Rubber Division Undergraduate Scholarship • 1149

Thermo Fisher Scientific Antibody Scholarship • 1188

Thomas E. Powers/Detroit Section Scholarship • 1191

Undergraduate Award for Excellence in Chemistry • 1205

William Wrigley Jr. Scholarship/Internship • 2337

PHYSICAL SCIENCES -- GEOLOGICAL AND EARTH SCIENCES / GEOSCIENCES

Graduate Student Research Grants • 952

Kathryn D. Sullivan Earth and Marine Science Fellowship • 1580

Leo Bourassa Scholarship • 1596

Marliave Fund • 1031

NYWEA Major Environmental Career Scholarship • 1743

Society of Exploration Geophysicists (SEG) Scholarship • 1165

Tilford Fund • 1194

Trent R. Dames and William W. Moore Fellowship • 1201

Undergraduate Student Research Grants: South-Central Section • 1209

Worthy Women's Professional Studies Scholarship • 2339

PHYSICAL SCIENCES -- PALEONTOLOGY

Florence C. and Robert H. Lister Fellowship • 587

PHYSICAL SCIENCES -- PHYSICS, GENERAL

AISES Intel Scholarship • 2160

BMO Capital Markets Lime Connect Equity Through Education Scholarship • 2346

Herbert Levy Memorial Scholarship • 963

Hubertus W.V. Wellems Scholarship for Male Students • 2229

Kathryn D. Sullivan Earth and Marine Science Fellowship • 1580

NOAA Educational Partnership Program Undergraduate Scholarships • 2295

Northrop Grumman Scholarship • 1739

Peggy Dixon Two-Year Scholarship • 1110

Rubber Division Undergraduate Scholarship • 1149

Shuichi, Katsu and Itsuyo Suga Scholarship • 1850

Society of Exploration Geophysicists (SEG) Scholarship • 1165

Society of Vacuum Coaters Foundation Scholarship • 1168

SPS Future Teacher Scholarship • 726

SPS Leadership Scholarships • 1171

Thomas E. Powers/Detroit Section Scholarship • 1191

PHYSICAL THERAPY / THERAPIST
See: HEALTH PROFESSIONS AND RELATED CLINICAL SCIENCES

CAREER INDEX

This index organizes the scholarships by common career fields. If you cannot find your specific career listed simply look at the scholarships under the closest matching career area.

In addition to this index be sure to use the Major Index since many scholarships are targeted to fields of study but do not have specific career requirements.

BIOLOGISTS

ASABE Foundation Engineering Scholarship • 819

ASF Olin Fellowships • 824

Barry M. Goldwater Scholarship and Excellence in Education Program • 846

C. Bertrand and Marian Othmer Schultz Collegiate Scholarship • 1311

Carroll C. Hall Memorial Scholarship • 2008

Fellowship Award • 920

Gaige Fund Award • 932

National Garden Clubs Scholarship • 1072

Nebraska Academy of Sciences High School Scholarships • 1697

NIH Undergraduate Scholarship Program • 1092

Paul A. Stewart Grants • 1107

Raney Fund Award • 1130

Student Research Scholarships • 1182

RELATED CAREER (FORESTRY / FISHING / WILDLIFE)

Arkansas Game and Fish Commission Conservation Scholarship • 1277

Clair A. Hill Scholarship • 1354

Gloria Barron Wilderness Society Scholarship • 946

RELATED CAREER (ENVIRONMENTAL SCIENCE)

Len Assante Scholarship Fund • 1018

Morris K. Udall Scholarship • 2274

RELATED CAREER (SCIENTIST)

ANS Graduate Scholarship • 810

ANS Undergraduate Scholarship • 812

Battery Division Student Research Award • 848

Burlington Northern Santa Fe (BNSF) Foundation Scholarship • 2176

Horkheimer/Smith Youth Service Award • 967

Industrial Electrolysis and Electrochemical Engineering Division Student Achievement Awards • 974

John and Muriel Landis Scholarship • 991

John J. McKetta Scholarship • 994

Language Grants • 466

Minority Affairs Committee Award for Outstanding Scholastic Achievement • 2267

National Space Club Keynote Scholar • 1074

BIOMEDICAL SCIENCES / BIOTECHNOLOGY

Barry M. Goldwater Scholarship and Excellence in Education Program • 846

Carroll C. Hall Memorial Scholarship • 2008

NIH Undergraduate Scholarship Program • 1092

RELATED CAREER (BIOLOGISTS)

ASABE Foundation Engineering Scholarship • 819

ASF Olin Fellowships • 824

C. Bertrand and Marian Othmer Schultz Collegiate Scholarship • 1311

Gaige Fund Award • 932

National Garden Clubs Scholarship • 1072

Nebraska Academy of Sciences High School Scholarships • 1697

Paul A. Stewart Grants • 1107

Raney Fund Award • 1130

Student Research Scholarships • 1182

RELATED CAREER (DOCTOR (MEDICINE))

Advanced Practice Healthcare Scholarship Program • 1238

Alice W. Rooke Scholarship • 794

Allied Healthcare Scholarship Program • 1252

American Legion Auxiliary, Department of California $2,000 Scholarships • 1262

Associate Degree Nursing Scholarship Program • 1281

Bachelor of Science Nursing Scholarship Program • 1287

Benton-Meier Scholarships • 851

Burlington Northern Santa Fe (BNSF) Foundation Scholarship • 2176

Dr. Ralph E. White Graduating Senior Scholarship • 1405

Fellowship Award • 920

Foundation for Surgical Technology Medical Mission Scholarship • 923

Health Careers Scholarship • 959

Irene and Daisy MacGregor Memorial Scholarship • 981

Language Grants • 466

Loan Assistance Repayment Program Primary Care Services • 1604

Medical Student Training in Aging Research (MSTAR) Program • 1040

Minority Fellowship Program • 1051

Morris K. Udall Scholarship • 2274

NAHN Scholarship • 2277

Thomara Latimer Cancer Foundation Scholarship • 1908

TOPSS Competition for High School Psychology Students • 744

Washington Health Corps • 1957

BUSINESS AND MANAGEMENT

American Legion Auxiliary, Department of California $1,000 Scholarships • 1261

American Legion Auxiliary, Department of California $2,000 Scholarships • 1262

Betsy Plank/PRSSA Scholarship • 549

Burlington Northern Santa Fe (BNSF) Foundation Scholarship • 2176

Executive Women International Scholarship Program • 586

Harry A. Applegate Scholarship • 607

Joe Perdue Scholarship • 633

Language Grants • 466

Lawrence G. Foster Award for Excellence in Public Relations • 646

Media Fellows Program • 660

National Scholarship • 2286

Nebraska Academy of Sciences High School Scholarships • 1697

NSA Scholarship Foundation • 689

Office Supply Scholarship • 485

PRSA-Hawaii/Roy Leffingwell Public Relations Scholarship • 1798

Steven J. Finkel Service Excellence Scholarship • 730

RELATED CAREER (ACCOUNTING / FINANCE / BANKING)

Goldberg-Miller Public Finance Scholarship • 604

IMA Memorial Education Fund Scholarship • 618

John W. Rogers Memorial Scholarship • 1567

Julianne Malveaux Scholarship • 2238

National Academic Scholarships • 673

Stuart Cameron and Margaret McLeod Memorial Scholarship • 731

Student Relief Fund • 2322

Texas Fifth-Year Accounting Student Scholarship Program • 1901

CHEMISTS

Analytical Chemistry Scholarship • 806

Barry M. Goldwater Scholarship and Excellence in Education Program • 846

C. Bertrand and Marian Othmer Schultz Collegiate Scholarship • 1311

Carroll C. Hall Memorial Scholarship • 2008

John J. McKetta Scholarship • 994

Minority Affairs Committee Award for Outstanding Scholastic Achievement • 2267

NIH Undergraduate Scholarship Program • 1092

RELATED CAREER (SCIENTIST)

ANS Graduate Scholarship • 810

ANS Undergraduate Scholarship • 812

ASABE Foundation Engineering Scholarship • 819

ASF Olin Fellowships • 824

Battery Division Student Research Award • 848

Burlington Northern Santa Fe (BNSF) Foundation Scholarship • 2176

Fellowship Award • 920

Gaige Fund Award • 932

Horkheimer/Smith Youth Service Award • 967

Industrial Electrolysis and Electrochemical Engineering Division Student Achievement Awards • 974

John and Muriel Landis Scholarship • 991

Language Grants • 466

National Space Club Keynote Scholar • 1074

Nebraska Academy of Sciences High School Scholarships • 1697

Raney Fund Award • 1130

CLERGY

Truman Scholar • 355

Vocations Scholarship Funds • 2134

RELATED CAREER (SOCIAL SERVICES)

Allied Healthcare Scholarship Program • 1252

Language Grants • 466

COMPUTER HARDWARE ENGINEERS

Language Grants • 466

RELATED CAREER (COMPUTERS / INFORMATION TECHNOLOGY)

Achievers in Technology Program • 2148

ESA Foundation Scholarship Program • 2204

National Academic Scholarships • 673

National Space Club Keynote Scholar • 1074

P.O. Pistilli Undergraduate Scholarship for Advancement in Computer Science and Electrical Engineering • 2301

VIP Women in Technology Scholarship • 1216

RELATED CAREER (ENGINEERING)

AIAA Foundation Undergraduate Scholarship Program • 786

LANDSCAPE ARCHITECTS

AWAF Scholarships • 1286
Carville M. Akehurst Memorial Scholarship • 864

RELATED CAREER (ARCHITECTURE / DESIGN)
American Architectural Foundation and Sir John Soane's Museum Foundation Traveling Fellowship • 798
National Garden Clubs Scholarship • 1072
Robert E. Thunen Memorial Scholarships • 1145

LEGAL

AALL Educational Scholarships • 523
American Legion Auxiliary, Department of California $1,000 Scholarships • 1261
American Legion Auxiliary, Department of California $2,000 Scholarships • 1262
Charles T. Stoner Law Scholarship • 74
George A. Strait Minority Scholarship • 601
LexisNexis / John R. Johnson Memorial Scholarship Endowment • 650
LimNexus Scholarship • 651
Mary Church Terrell Award • 225
University of California Public Policy and International Affairs Law Fellowship • 748

RELATED CAREER (POLICE / FIRE / LAW ENFORCEMENT)
Language Grants • 466
Sheryl A. Horak Memorial Scholarship • 317
Vermont Sheriffs' Association Scholarship • 1936

LIBRARY SCIENCES

AALL Educational Scholarships • 523
Begun Scholarship • 548
Bound to Stay Bound Books Scholarship • 555
CLA Scholarship for Minority Students in Memory of Edna Yelland • 567
Frederic G. Melcher Scholarship • 594
George A. Strait Minority Scholarship • 601
Leadership for Diversity Scholarship • 1591
LexisNexis / John R. Johnson Memorial Scholarship Endowment • 650
Paraprofessional Scholarship • 1773

MANUFACTURING / OPERATIONS

AFS Wisconsin Past President Scholarship • 1240
Giuliano Mazzetti Scholarship • 944
Robert E. Thunen Memorial Scholarships • 1145

RELATED CAREER (BUSINESS AND MANAGEMENT)
American Legion Auxiliary, Department of California $1,000 Scholarships • 1261
American Legion Auxiliary, Department of California $2,000 Scholarships • 1262
Betsy Plank/PRSSA Scholarship • 549
Burlington Northern Santa Fe (BNSF) Foundation Scholarship • 2176
Executive Women International Scholarship Program • 586
Joe Perdue Scholarship • 633
Language Grants • 466
Lawrence G. Foster Award for Excellence in Public Relations • 646
Media Fellows Program • 660
National Scholarship • 2286
Nebraska Academy of Sciences High School Scholarships • 1697
NSA Scholarship Foundation • 689

Steven J. Finkel Service Excellence Scholarship • 730

MARKETING

Betsy Plank/PRSSA Scholarship • 549
Harry A. Applegate Scholarship • 607
Language Grants • 466
Lawrence G. Foster Award for Excellence in Public Relations • 646
Media Fellows Program • 660
National Scholarship • 2286
PRSA-Hawaii/Roy Leffingwell Public Relations Scholarship • 1798

RELATED CAREER (BUSINESS AND MANAGEMENT)
American Legion Auxiliary, Department of California $1,000 Scholarships • 1261
American Legion Auxiliary, Department of California $2,000 Scholarships • 1262
Burlington Northern Santa Fe (BNSF) Foundation Scholarship • 2176
Executive Women International Scholarship Program • 586
Joe Perdue Scholarship • 633
Nebraska Academy of Sciences High School Scholarships • 1697
NSA Scholarship Foundation • 689
Steven J. Finkel Service Excellence Scholarship • 730

MATHEMATICIANS

Barry M. Goldwater Scholarship and Excellence in Education Program • 846
Biographies of Contemporary Women in Mathematics Essay Contest • 854
Burlington Northern Santa Fe (BNSF) Foundation Scholarship • 2176
Gertrude Cox Scholarship For Women In Statistics • 942
National Space Club Keynote Scholar • 1074

RELATED CAREER (ACADEMIA)
Henry Belin du Pont Dissertation Fellowship • 609
Herbert Hoover Presidential Library Association Travel Grant Program • 610
Language Grants • 466
Robert E. Thunen Memorial Scholarships • 1145
Summer Graduate Research Fellowships • 340

RELATED CAREER (PHYSICISTS)
AIAA Foundation Undergraduate Scholarship Program • 786
ANS Graduate Scholarship • 810
ANS Undergraduate Scholarship • 812
C. Bertrand and Marian Othmer Schultz Collegiate Scholarship • 1311
Carroll C. Hall Memorial Scholarship • 2008
John and Muriel Landis Scholarship • 991

RELATED CAREER (ACCOUNTING / FINANCE / BANKING)
Goldberg-Miller Public Finance Scholarship • 604
IMA Memorial Education Fund Scholarship • 618
John W. Rogers Memorial Scholarship • 1567
Julianne Malveaux Scholarship • 2238
National Academic Scholarships • 673
NSA Scholarship Foundation • 689

Stuart Cameron and Margaret McLeod Memorial Scholarship • 731
Student Relief Fund • 2322
Texas Fifth-Year Accounting Student Scholarship Program • 1901

MECHANICS

Language Grants • 466

RELATED CAREER (TRANSPORTATION AND TRUCKING)
Allied Van Lines Scholarship • 535
Helene M. Overly Memorial Graduate Scholarship • 2220
Louise Moritz Molitoris Leadership Scholarship for Undergraduates • 2247
North American Van Lines Logistics Scholarship • 686
Ohio Section Scholarships • 1746
Sharon D. Banks Memorial Undergraduate Scholarship • 2317
WTS Minnesota Chapter Scholarships • 1988

RELATED CAREER (AVIATION / AEROSPACE / SPACE)
AIAA Foundation Undergraduate Scholarship Program • 786
Aviation Distributors and Manufacturers Association Scholarship Program • 843
Aviation Insurance Association Education Foundation Scholarship • 844
Daedalian Foundation Scholarship Program • 107
Dan L. Meisinger Sr. Memorial Learn to Fly Scholarship • 882
David Arver Memorial Scholarship • 885
Dutch and Ginger Arver Scholarship • 898
Full-Time Employee Student Scholarship • 929
Garmin Scholarship • 934
John R. Lillard VAOC Scholarship • 1565
Johnny Davis Memorial Scholarship • 1001
Lawrence C. Fortier Memorial Scholarship • 1012
Lee Tarbox Memorial Scholarship • 1017
Mid-Continent Instruments and Avionics Scholarship • 1048
National Aviation Explorer Scholarships • 1068
Pioneers of Flight • 1117
Richard Lee Vernon Aviation Scholarship • 1140
SSPI Scholarship Program • 727
Tuskegee Airmen Scholarship Foundation Scholarships • 1202
Tweet Coleman Aviation Scholarship • 1922
UAA Janice K. Barden Aviation Scholarship • 1204

RELATED CAREER (METAL WORK / MACHINIST / WELDING)
AFS Twin City Memorial Scholarship • 1239
AFS Wisconsin Past President Scholarship • 1240
STEEL Engineering Education Link Initiative • 1173

RELATED CAREER (MANUFACTURING / OPERATIONS)
Giuliano Mazzetti Scholarship • 944
Robert E. Thunen Memorial Scholarships • 1145

603

Medical Student Training in Aging Research (MSTAR) Program • 1040

Minority Fellowship Program • 1051

NAHN Scholarship • 2277

NIH Undergraduate Scholarship Program • 1092

TOPSS Competition for High School Psychology Students • 744

TRANSPORTATION AND TRUCKING

Allied Van Lines Scholarship • 535

Helene M. Overly Memorial Graduate Scholarship • 2220

Louise Moritz Molitoris Leadership Scholarship for Undergraduates • 2247

North American Van Lines Logistics Scholarship • 686

Ohio Section Scholarships • 1746

Sharon D. Banks Memorial Undergraduate Scholarship • 2317

WTS Minnesota Chapter Scholarships • 1988

VETERINARIAN

Fellowship Award • 920

RELATED CAREER (FORESTRY / FISHING / WILDLIFE)

Arkansas Game and Fish Commission Conservation Scholarship • 1277

ASF Olin Fellowships • 824

Clair A. Hill Scholarship • 1354

Gloria Barron Wilderness Society Scholarship • 946

National Garden Clubs Scholarship • 1072

Nebraska Academy of Sciences High School Scholarships • 1697

RELATED CAREER (MEDICAL RESEARCHER / TECH)

AUA Foundation Research Scholars Program • 839

Elekta Radiation Therapy Scholarship • 905

Thomara Latimer Cancer Foundation Scholarship • 1908

WRITER

Disney/ABC Television Writing Program • 425

Julianne Malveaux Scholarship • 2238

Playwright Discovery Award • 490

Summer Graduate Research Fellowships • 340

Taylor/Blakeslee University Fellowships • 507

RELATED CAREER (JOURNALISM)

BEA National Scholarships in Broadcasting • 546

Bob East Scholarship • 551

Bob Eddy Scholarship Program • 1300

Bohdan Kolinsky Memorial Sports Journalism Scholarship • 1304

Carole Simpson Scholarship • 562

CCNMA Scholarships • 1338

College Photographer of the Year • 569

Ed Bradley Scholarship • 582

FOWA Scholarship for Outdoor Communicators • 590

Iowa Newspaper Association Scholarships • 1534

Lou and Carole Prato Sports Reporting Scholarship • 654

Marshall E. McCullough Scholarship • 1032

Mary Quan Moy Ing Memorial Scholarship • 2260

NAHJ General Scholarships - Rubén Salazar Fund • 2276

National Press Club Scholarship for Journalism Diversity • 676

Overseas Press Club Foundation Scholarships/Fellowships • 692

RTNDA President's Scholarship • 716

Vincent Chin Scholarship • 753

RELATED CAREER (MEDIA / RADIO / TELEVISION / INTERNET)

CBC Spouses Performing Arts Scholarship • 2181

Idaho State Broadcasters Association Scholarships • 1517

John Bayliss Radio Scholarship • 634

Massachusetts Student Broadcaster Scholarship • 1638

Tony Coelho Media Scholarship • 2392

Upper Midwest Chapter Scholarships • 1928

Wisconsin Broadcasters Association Foundation Student Scholarship Program • 1979

Youth Scholarship • 761

RELATED CAREER (ENTERTAINMENT INDUSTRY)

Career Center • 416

Steven J. Finkel Service Excellence Scholarship • 730

INTERESTS / HOBBIES INDEX

This index lists awards that are geared toward students who are active in specific pastimes and hobbies.

AMATEUR RADIO

ARRL Foundation General Fund Scholarship • 542

Bill, W2ONV, and Ann Salerno Memorial Scholarship • 550

Carole J. Streeter, KB9JBR, Scholarship • 561

Central Arizona DX Association Scholarship • 1339

Challenge Met Scholarship • 2350

Charles Clarke Cordle Memorial Scholarship • 563

Charles N. Fisher Memorial Scholarship • 564

Chuck Reville, K3FT Memorial Scholarship • 870

Dayton Amateur Radio Association Scholarship • 573

Donald Riebhoff Memorial Scholarship • 576

Dr. James L. Lawson Memorial Scholarship • 577

Edmond A. Metzger Scholarship • 583

Fred R. McDaniel Memorial Scholarship • 593

Gary Wagner, K3OMI, Scholarship • 935

IRARC Memorial, Joseph P. Rubino, WA4M-MD, Scholarship • 623

Irving W. Cook, WA0CGS, Scholarship • 1543

K2TEO Martin J. Green, Sr. Memorial Scholarship • 640

L. Phil and Alice J. Wicker Scholarship • 643

L.B. Cebik, W4RNL and Jean Cebik, N4TZP Memorial Scholarship • 644

Louisiana Memorial Scholarship • 1611

Mary Lou Brown Scholarship • 658

Mississippi Scholarship • 1672

New England FEMARA Scholarships • 684

Paul and Helen L. Grauer Scholarship • 693

PHD Scholarship • 696

Ray, NRP and Katie, WKTE Pautz Scholarship • 707

Richard W. Bendicksen, N7ZL, Memorial Scholarship • 710

Six Meter Club of Chicago Scholarship • 1854

Tom and Judith Comstock Scholarship • 742

YASME Foundation Scholarship • 760

ANIMALS

Arizona National Livestock Show Scholarship • 1275

ASHA Youth Scholarships • 825

Federal Junior Duck Stamp Program and Scholarship Competition • 433

Junior Showmanship Scholarship Program • 1003

Marshall E. McCullough Scholarship • 1032

Rover Sitter Scholarship • 301

Scholars Helping Collars Scholarship • 306

ART / DESIGN

Adobe Creativity Scholarships • 403

Antonio Cirino Memorial Award • 1271

Archibald Rutledge Scholarship Program • 1273

Art Scholarship • 1279

SPECIAL CIRCUMSTANCES

This index lists a variety of special circumstances that are used as eligibility limits for these scholarships.

World Trade Center Memorial Scholarship • 1987

SINGLE PARENT
Live Your Dream Awards Program • 2245

SPOUSE KILLED FROM WORK-RELATED INJURY
VantagePoint Public Employee Memorial Scholarship Fund • 2132

SPOUSE LAW ENFORCEMENT OFFICER KILLED IN LINE OF DUTY
California Law Enforcement Personnel Dependents Grant Program • 1322
John F. Duffy Scholarship/Grant Program • 199
VantagePoint Public Employee Memorial Scholarship Fund • 2132

SPOUSE OF FIREFIGHTER KILLED IN THE LINE OF DUTY
California Law Enforcement Personnel Dependents Grant Program • 1322
VantagePoint Public Employee Memorial Scholarship Fund • 2132

SUBSTANCE ABUSE, OVERCAME
Ho'omaka Hou - A New Beginning Fund • 1507
MAPDA Scholarship • 2368

TALL
Tall Club International Scholarship • 2116

TRANSGENDER
Bee's Fund Microgrants • 2173
BIPOC Scholarship • 2175
Edie Windsor Coding Scholarship • 2199
Kenneth W. Payne Student Prize • 2239
New York Ramblers Scholarship • 2293
Pega Scholars Program • 2303

UNCF MEMBER COLLEGE AND UNIVERSITY
Berbeco Senior Research Fellowship • 2174
Malcolm X Scholarship for Exceptional Courage • 2253
Michael Jackson Scholarship • 2266
William Wrigley Jr. Scholarship/Internship • 2337

UPWARD BOUND
Dell Scholars Program • 112

STATE OF RESIDENCE INDEX

This index lists awards that are restricted to students who are residents of the state or territory or who are planning to study in the state or territory.

ALABAMA
Alabama Concrete Industries Association Scholarships • 1245
Charles Clarke Cordle Memorial Scholarship • 563
Crumley Roberts Next Step Scholarship • 1378
Curwen-Guidry-Blackburn Scholarship Fund • 106
Dixie Boys Baseball Scholarship Program • 117
Dixie Youth Scholarship Program • 119
Don't Wait to Reach Your Potential Scholarship for Alabama Teens • 1396
Ed and Charlotte Rodgers Scholarships • 1413
Educational Training Voucher Programs for Foster Youth • 1418
Family District 1 Scholarships • 1435
Gorgas Scholarship Competition • 1468
Jimmy Rane Foundation Scholarships • 1558
NACA South Student Leadership Scholarships • 1688
NACE Eastern Area Scholarship • 1062
Northrop Grumman Scholarship • 1739
Regions Riding Forward Scholarship Essay Contest • 1812
Smith Scholarship Program • 1857

ALASKA
Arc of Washington State Trust Fund Stipend Award • 1272
Atsuhiko Tateuchi Memorial Scholarship • 1285
Lori Rhett Memorial Scholarship • 1606
Mary Lou Brown Scholarship • 658
MGMA Western Section Scholarship • 1045
Red Boucher Scholarship • 1810
Richard D. Johnson Memorial Post-Secondary Scholarship • 1817

ARIZONA
Alisa's Angels Scholarship • 1248
Arizona BPW Foundation Annual Scholarships • 1274
Arizona National Livestock Show Scholarship • 1275
Burlington Northern Santa Fe (BNSF) Foundation Scholarship • 2176
Central Arizona DX Association Scholarship • 1339
Charles N. Fisher Memorial Scholarship • 564
Educational Training Voucher Programs for Foster Youth • 1418
Kappa Delta Phi • 1004
MGMA Western Section Scholarship • 1045
Shari Simon Greenberg Community Scholarships of the Simon Youth Foundation • 315
Theodore D. Harrington Scholarship • 1187

ARKANSAS
Academic Challenge Scholarship • 1229
American Legion Department of Arkansas High School Oratorical Scholarship Program • 1264
Arkansas Cheer Coaches Association Cheer Classics Team of Excellence • 1276

Arkansas Game and Fish Commission Conservation Scholarship • 1277
Arkansas Service Memorial Scholarship Endowment • 1278
Burlington Northern Santa Fe (BNSF) Foundation Scholarship • 2176
Curwen-Guidry-Blackburn Scholarship Fund • 106
Dixie Boys Baseball Scholarship Program • 117
Dixie Youth Scholarship Program • 119
Fred R. McDaniel Memorial Scholarship • 593
Governor's Distinguished Scholarship • 1471
Jimmy Rane Foundation Scholarships • 1558
Lee Magnon Memorial Scholarship • 1015
Markley Scholarship • 221
MFA Foundation Scholarships • 1649
R. Preston Woodruff, Jr. Scholarships • 1800
Regions Riding Forward Scholarship Essay Contest • 1812

CALIFORNIA
ACEC Scholarship • 1235
Advanced Practice Healthcare Scholarship Program • 1238
Allied Healthcare Scholarship Program • 1252
Alyssa McCroskey Memorial Scholarship • 1254
American Association of Japanese University Women Scholarship Program • 1256
American Legion Auxiliary, Department of California $1,000 Scholarships • 1261
American Legion Auxiliary, Department of California $2,000 Scholarships • 1262
American Legion Auxiliary, Department of California $500 Scholarships • 1263
Associate Degree Nursing Scholarship Program • 1281
Atsuhiko Tateuchi Memorial Scholarship • 1285
AWAF Scholarships • 1286
Bachelor of Science Nursing Scholarship Program • 1287
Begun Scholarship • 548
Betty Bacon Memorial Scholarship • 1294
Burlington Northern Santa Fe (BNSF) Foundation Scholarship • 2176
Cal Grant A • 1312
Cal Grant B • 1313
Cal Grant C • 1314
Cal Grant Entitlement Award • 1315
California - Hawaii Elks Association Vocational Grants • 558
California - Hawaii Elks Major Project Undergraduate Scholarship Program for Students with Disabilities • 1316
California Chafee Grant for Foster Youth • 2178
California Council of the Blind Scholarships • 1317
California Fee Waiver Program for Children of Veterans • 1318
California Fee Waiver Program for Dependents of Deceased or Disabled National Guard Members • 1319
California Fee Waiver Program for Recipients of the Medal of Honor and Their Children • 1320
California Freethought Day High School Essay Scholarship • 1321
California Law Enforcement Personnel Dependents Grant Program • 1322

American Legion Department of Florida General Scholarship • 1265

Curwen-Guidry-Blackburn Scholarship Fund • 106

Dixie Boys Baseball Scholarship Program • 117

Dixie Youth Scholarship Program • 119

Excellence in Service Award • 1430

Family District 1 Scholarships • 1435

First Generation Matching Grant Program • 1438

Florida Bright Futures Scholarship Program • 1440

Florida Engineers in Construction Scholarship • 1441

Florida Governor's Black History Month Essay Contest • 1442

Florida Oratorical Contest • 1443

Florida Student Assistance Grant Program • 1444

FOWA Scholarship for Outdoor Communicators • 590

James F. Davis Memorial Scholarship • 1552

Jimmy Rane Foundation Scholarships • 1558

Jose Marti Scholarship Challenge Grant • 1568

Kappa Delta Phi • 1004

Lloyd F. Hutt Scholarship • 1603

NACA South Student Leadership Scholarships • 1688

NACE Eastern Area Scholarship • 1062

Northrop Grumman Scholarship • 1739

Regions Riding Forward Scholarship Essay Contest • 1812

Rosewood Family Scholarship Program • 1834

Roy W. Likins Scholarship • 1835

Shari Simon Greenberg Community Scholarships of the Simon Youth Foundation • 315

Sister Helen Marie Pellicer Scholarship • 1852

Southern Scholarship Foundation Scholarship • 1866

William L. Boyd, IV, Effective Access to Student Education Program • 1976

GEORGIA

Ben W. Fortson, Jr., Scholarship • 1292

Charles Clarke Cordle Memorial Scholarship • 563

Curwen-Guidry-Blackburn Scholarship Fund • 106

Dixie Boys Baseball Scholarship Program • 117

Dixie Youth Scholarship Program • 119

Family District 1 Scholarships • 1435

Georgia Oratorical Contest • 1460

Georgia Press Educational Foundation Scholarships • 1461

Georgia Thespians Achievement Scholarships • 1462

Georgia Tuition Equalization Grant • 1463

Greenhouse Scholars Scholarship • 1476

HOPE Scholarship Program • 1509

James M. and Virginia M. Smyth Scholarship • 196

Jimmy Rane Foundation Scholarships • 1558

Judge William F. Cooper Scholarship • 1570

NACA South Student Leadership Scholarships • 1688

NACE Eastern Area Scholarship • 1062

Nancy Penn Lyons Scholarship Fund • 1691

Regions Riding Forward Scholarship Essay Contest • 1812

Steve Dearduff Scholarship Fund • 1876

Tech High School Alumni Association/W.O. Cheney Merit Scholarship • 1886

HAWAII

Allan Eldin and Agnes Sutorik Geiger Scholarship Fund • 1250

Alma White - Delta Kappa Gamma Scholarship • 1253

Ambassador Minerva Jean Falcon Hawaii Scholarship • 1255

American Institute of Graphic Arts (AIGA) Honolulu Chapter Scholarship Fund • 1259

Atsuhiko Tateuchi Memorial Scholarship • 1285

Ben and Vicky Cayetano Scholarship Fund • 1291

Bick Bickson Scholarship Fund • 1295

Blossom Kalama Evans Memorial Scholarship Fund • 1298

Booz Allen Hawaii Scholarship Fund • 1305

California - Hawaii Elks Association Vocational Grants • 558

California - Hawaii Elks Major Project Undergraduate Scholarship Program for Students with Disabilities • 1316

Candon, Todd and Seabolt Scholarship Fund • 1328

Clem Judd, Jr., Memorial Scholarship • 1356

Community Scholarship Fund • 1368

Cora Aguda Manayan Fund • 1374

Doris and Clarence Glick Classical Music Scholarship • 1398

Dr. Edison and Sallie Miyawaki Scholarship Fund • 1402

Dr. Hans and Clara Zimmerman Foundation Education Scholarship • 1403

Dr. Hans and Clara Zimmerman Foundation Health Scholarships • 1404

Edward Payson and Bernice Piilani Irwin Scholarship • 1420

Eizo and Toyo Sakumoto Trust Scholarship • 1421

Ellison Onizuka Memorial Scholarship Fund • 1422

Esther Kanagawa Memorial Art Scholarship • 1429

F. Koehnen Ltd. Scholarship Fund • 1434

George Mason Business Scholarship Fund • 1459

Good Eats Scholarship Fund • 1467

Hawaii Community Foundation Scholarships • 1489

Hawaii High School Athletic Association Hall of Honor • 1490

Hawaii Pizza Hut Scholarship Fund • 1491

Hawaii Rotary Youth Foundation Scholarship • 1492

Hawaii Society of Certified Public Accountants Scholarship Fund • 1493

Henry A. Zuberano Scholarship • 1495

Hideko and Zenzo Matsuyama Scholarship Fund • 1501

Ho'omaka Hou - A New Beginning Fund • 1507

Johanna Drew Cluney Fund • 1560

John and Anne Clifton Scholarship • 1562

John Dawe Dental Education Fund • 1564

Laura N. Dowsett Fund • 1589

Mamoru and Aiko Takitani Foundation Scholarship • 1621

Marion Maccarrell Scott Scholarship • 1625

Mark Ando and Ito Family Scholarship • 2258

MGMA Western Section Scholarship • 1045

Mildred Towle Scholarship - Study Abroad • 1660

Mildred Towle Scholarship for African-Americans • 1661

Outrigger Duke Kahanamoku Scholarship • 1770

Paulina L. Sorg Scholarship • 1783

PRSA-Hawaii/Roy Leffingwell Public Relations Scholarship • 1798

R.W. Bob Holden Scholarship • 1801

Raymond F. Cain Scholarship Fund • 1805

Ritchie M. Gregory Fund • 1821

Robanna Fund • 1824

Rosemary and Nellie Ebrie Fund • 1833

Shirley McKown Scholarship Fund • 1848

Shuichi, Katsu and Itsuyo Suga Scholarship • 1850

Tongan Cultural Society Scholarship • 1910

Tweet Coleman Aviation Scholarship • 1922

Ukulele Festival Hawaii's College Scholarship Program • 513

Victoria S. and Bradley L. Geist Foundation • 1940

William James and Dorothy Bading Lanquist Fund • 1975

IDAHO

Arc of Washington State Trust Fund Stipend Award • 1272

GEAR UP Idaho Scholarship 2 • 1456

Governor's Cup Scholarship • 1470

Idaho State Broadcasters Association Scholarships • 1517

Lori Rhett Memorial Scholarship • 1606

Mary Lou Brown Scholarship • 658

MGMA Western Section Scholarship • 1045

Theodore D. Harrington Scholarship • 1187

Treacy Foundation Scholarship • 1915

ILLINOIS

American Legion Scholarship Award • 1266

Americanism Essay Scholarship • 1268

Boy Scout and Eagle Scout Scholarship • 1306

Burlington Northern Santa Fe (BNSF) Foundation Scholarship • 2176

Cathay Bank Foundation Scholarship • 1336

Community Banker Association of Illinois Annual Essay Scholarship Program • 1367

Dan L. Meisinger Sr. Memorial Learn to Fly Scholarship • 882

Edmond A. Metzger Scholarship • 583

Golden Apple Scholars of Illinois (Illinois Scholars Program) • 1465

Greenhouse Scholars Scholarship • 1476

Illinois AMVETS Ladies Auxiliary Memorial Scholarship • 1518

Illinois AMVETS Ladies Auxiliary Worchid Scholarship • 1519

Illinois AMVETS Sad Sacks Nursing Scholarship • 1520

Illinois AMVETS Service Foundation Scholarship • 1521

Tennessee Need-Based Supplemental Aspire Awards • 1893
Tennessee Student Assistance Awards • 1894

TEXAS
A.D. Osherman Scholarship Fund • 1228
BAFTX Graduate Scholarship • 1288
BAFTX Undergraduate Award • 1289
Beginning Teacher Scholarships • 1290
Bob C. Powers Scholarship • 1299
Burlington Northern Santa Fe (BNSF) Foundation Scholarship • 2176
Career Colleges and Schools of Texas Scholarship Program • 1332
Cathay Bank Foundation Scholarship • 1336
Collegiate Scholarship • 1360
Courageous Heart Scholarship • 1376
Curwen-Guidry-Blackburn Scholarship Fund • 106
Dixie Boys Baseball Scholarship Program • 117
Dixie Youth Scholarship Program • 119
Don't Mess with Texas Scholarship • 1395
Early Starters Award • 1412
Exemption for Highest Ranking High School Graduate • 1431
Exemption for Texas Veterans (Hazelwood Exemption) • 1432
Fred R. McDaniel Memorial Scholarship • 593
H-E-B Scholarships for UIL Participants • 1479
Herman J. Smith Scholarship • 1498
Houston Livestock Show and Rodeo Scholarships • 1511
Ivomec Generations of Excellence Internship and Scholarship Program • 1546
James M. and Virginia M. Smyth Scholarship • 196
Jimmy Rane Foundation Scholarships • 1558
Lee Magnon Memorial Scholarship • 1015
Markley Scholarship • 221
Mary E. Bivins Religious Scholarship • 2072
Moody Scholar Program • 1681
North Texas State Fair Association Scholarship • 1738
Ray Anthony Peacock Scholarship • 1804
Regions Riding Forward Scholarship Essay Contest • 1812
Richard A. Brown Memorial Scholarship for Students • 1816
Shari Simon Greenberg Community Scholarships of the Simon Youth Foundation • 315
Susan Howard Community Service Award • 1881
Technical Certification Scholarship • 1887
Texas 4-H Opportunity Scholarship Program - Baccalaureate Scholarships • 1895
Texas Broadcast Education Foundation Scholarships • 1897
Texas Elks State Association Scholarship Program • 1898
Texas Elks State Association Teenager of the Year Contest • 1899
Texas Elks State Association Vocational Grant Program • 1900
Texas Fifth-Year Accounting Student Scholarship Program • 1901
Texas History Essay Scholarship • 1902

Texas International Fishing Tournament Inc. Scholarship • 1903
Texas Occupational Therapy Association Scholarships • 1904
Texas Oratorical Contest • 1905
Texas Public Educational Grant • 1906
Tom and Judith Comstock Scholarship • 742
Towards EXcellence, Access and Success (TEXAS) Grant Program • 1913
Tuition Equalization Grant Program • 1918

UTAH
ACLU of Utah Youth Activist Scholarship • 1236
Burlington Northern Santa Fe (BNSF) Foundation Scholarship • 2176
Daniels Scholarship Program • 1383
MGMA Western Section Scholarship • 1045
New Century Scholarship • 1702
Northrop Grumman Scholarship • 1739
Sterling Scholar Awards of Utah • 1875
Theodore D. Harrington Scholarship • 1187
Utah Association of Independent Insurance Agents Scholarship • 1930
Utah Young Humanitarian Award • 1931

VERMONT
Clauder Competition Prize • 420
Dr. James L. Lawson Memorial Scholarship • 577
FMC Skaters Scholarship • 145
Kilbourn-Sawyer Memorial Scholarship • 1584
Mabel Mayforth Scholarship • 1614
Martin Devlin Scholarship • 1627
NACE Eastern Area Scholarship • 1062
New England FEMARA Scholarships • 684
New England Regional Student Program • 1703
Part-Time Grants • 1776
Stephen Phillips Memorial Scholarship Fund • 1874
Thomas E. Desjardins Memorial Scholarship • 1909
Timothy S. and Palmer W. Bigelow, Jr. Scholarship • 1195
Vermont Incentive Grants • 1934
Vermont Oratorical Contest • 1935
Vermont Sheriffs' Association Scholarship • 1936

VIRGINIA
Carville M. Akehurst Memorial Scholarship • 864
Collegiate Shooting Scholarship Program • 1361
Dixie Boys Baseball Scholarship Program • 117
Dixie Youth Scholarship Program • 119
Frances A. Mays Scholarship Award • 1448
Gary Wagner, K3OMI, Scholarship • 935
Granville P. Meade Scholarship • 1474
Jimmy Rane Foundation Scholarships • 1558
John R. Lillard VAOC Scholarship • 1565
L. Phil and Alice J. Wicker Scholarship • 643
Leo Bourassa Scholarship • 1596
Mary Macon McGuire Scholarship • 1633
Middle School Essay Contest • 1657
NACA South Student Leadership Scholarships • 1688
NACE Eastern Area Scholarship • 1062
Northrop Grumman Scholarship • 1739
Phyllis V. Roberts Scholarship • 1795
VCTA Virginia's Future Leaders Scholarship Program • 1933

VHSL Achievement Award • 1939
Virginia Commonwealth Award • 1942
Virginia Daughters of the American Revolution Scholarships • 1943
Virginia Guaranteed Assistance Program • 1944
Virginia High School League Charles E. Savedge Journalism Scholarship • 1945
Virginia Part-Time Assistance Program • 1946
Virginia PTA Annual Citizenship Essay Project • 1947
Virginia Sheriffs' Institute Scholarship • 1948
Virginia Tuition Assistance Grant Program • 1949

WASHINGTON
American Indian Endowed Scholarship • 1258
Arc of Washington State Trust Fund Stipend Award • 1272
ASWA Seattle Chapter Scholarship • 1284
Atsuhiko Tateuchi Memorial Scholarship • 1285
Burlington Northern Santa Fe (BNSF) Foundation Scholarship • 2176
Cathay Bank Foundation Scholarship • 1336
Edmund F. Maxwell Foundation Scholarship • 1414
Incight Scholarship • 2360
John Schwartz Scholarship • 1566
Kaiser Permanente Health Care Career Scholarship • 1572
Lambeth Family Scholarship • 1588
Lori Rhett Memorial Scholarship • 1606
Mary Lou Brown Scholarship • 658
MGMA Western Section Scholarship • 1045
Northwest Danish Association Scholarships • 1740
Opportunity Grant • 1763
Richard E. Bangert Business Award • 1819
Shari Simon Greenberg Community Scholarships of the Simon Youth Foundation • 315
Smart Choices Scholarship Program • 1855
State Work Study • 1873
Theodore D. Harrington Scholarship • 1187
Washington BPW Foundation Mature Woman Educational Scholarship • 1955
Washington College Grant • 1956
Washington Oratorical Contest • 1958
Washington State Auto Dealers Association Bright Future Scholarship • 1959
Washington State College Bound Scholarship • 1960
Washington State Governors' Scholarship for Foster Youth • 1961
Washington State PTA Scholarship • 1962
Washington Women In Need • 1963
WISE Scholarship • 1985

WEST VIRGINIA
Carville M. Akehurst Memorial Scholarship • 864
Gary Wagner, K3OMI, Scholarship • 935
Greater Kanawha Valley Foundation Scholarship Program • 1475
Higher Education Adult Part-Time Student (HEAPS) Grant Program • 1505
Independence Excavating, A DiGeronimo Company Scholarship • 1527
Jimmy Rane Foundation Scholarships • 1558

MILITARY RELATED INDEX

Most of the awards in this index require that you have a parent, grandparent or spouse who has served in the military. There are also awards if you want to enter the armed services or if you have served.

ETHNICITY AND RACE INDEX

This index lists awards for members of minority and non-minority ethnic groups.

AFRICAN-AMERICAN

CLA Scholarship for Minority Students in Memory of Edna Yelland • 567

Cora Aguda Manayan Fund • 1374

Diversity Advocacy Council Scholarship • 2195

EDSA Diversity Scholarships • 2200

ESA Foundation Scholarship Program • 2204

George A. Strait Minority Scholarship • 601

Google Generation Google Scholarship • 2216

Jackie Robinson Foundation Scholarship Program • 2231

Jimmy A. Young Memorial Education Recognition Award • 989

Leadership for Diversity Scholarship • 1591

Martin Luther King, Jr. Memorial Scholarship • 2071

Minority Fellowship Program • 664

Minority Scholarship • 2268

Minority Serving Institution Grants • 2272

OCA/UPS Gold Mountain Scholarship • 2297

UPS Hallmark Scholarship • 2335

GREEK

AHEPA Educational Foundation National Scholarship Program • 2157

Family District 1 Scholarships • 1435

National and District Scholarships • 2279

HAWAIIAN

AISES Intel Scholarship • 2160

Asian and Pacific Islander American Scholarships • 2168

Atsuhiko Tateuchi Memorial Scholarship • 1285

Blossom Kalama Evans Memorial Scholarship Fund • 1298

Clem Judd, Jr., Memorial Scholarship • 1356

Diversity Advocacy Council Scholarship • 2195

EDSA Diversity Scholarships • 2200

ESA Foundation Scholarship Program • 2204

Google Generation Google Scholarship • 2216

Ida M. Pope Memorial Scholarship • 2230

Jackie Robinson Foundation Scholarship Program • 2231

Jimmy A. Young Memorial Education Recognition Award • 989

Leadership for Diversity Scholarship • 1591

Louis B. Russell Scholarship • 1609

Martin Luther King, Jr. Memorial Scholarship • 2071

Minorities and Women Educational Scholarship • 663

Minority Fellowship Program • 664

Minority Scholarship Award for Physical Therapy Students • 2269

Minority Serving Institution Grants • 2272

National Medical Fellowships Emergency Scholarship Fund • 2285

NMF National Alumni Council Scholarship Program • 2294

OCA/UPS Gold Mountain Scholarship • 2297

Pega Scholars Program • 2303

UPS Hallmark Scholarship • 2335

William and Charlotte Cadbury Award • 2336

HISPANIC / LATINO

Actuarial Diversity Scholarship • 2149

AICPA Fellowship for Minority Doctoral Students • 2158

AICPA Scholarship for Minority Accounting Students • 2159

American Chemical Society Scholars Program • 2162

AMS Minority Scholarship • 803

Association of Cuban Engineers Scholarship Foundation Scholarships • 2169

Cafe Bustelo El Cafe Del Futuro Scholarship • 2177

Carole Simpson Scholarship • 562

CCNMA Scholarships • 1338

CHCI United Health Foundation Scholar-Intern Program • 2182

CLA Scholarship for Minority Students in Memory of Edna Yelland • 567

Colgate-Palmolive Make the U Educational Grant • 2188

Diversity Advocacy Council Scholarship • 2195

Dr. Juan Andrade, Jr. Scholarship • 2197

Ed Bradley Scholarship • 582

EDSA Diversity Scholarships • 2200

ESA Foundation Scholarship Program • 2204

GAHCC Foundation Scholarship • 2209

Gates Scholarship • 2210

GEM MS Engineering Fellowship Program • 2211

George A. Strait Minority Scholarship • 601

Google Generation Google Scholarship • 2216

Healthline and Prevention Institute Stronger Scholarship • 960

Hispanic Heritage Youth Awards • 2224

Hispanic Scholarship Fund • 2225

Holly Cornell Scholarship • 966

Jackie Robinson Foundation Scholarship Program • 2231

James B. Morris Scholarship • 1551

Jimmy A. Young Memorial Education Recognition Award • 989

Jose Marti Scholarship Challenge Grant • 1568

Kansas Ethnic Minority Scholarship • 1576

LAGRANT Scholarship Program • 2242

Leadership for Diversity Scholarship • 1591

Legal Opportunity Scholarship Fund • 649

Louis B. Russell Scholarship • 1609

LULAC General Awards • 2249

LULAC Honors Awards • 2250

MAES Scholarship Program • 2251

MALDEF Law School Scholarship • 2254

Martin Luther King, Jr. Memorial Scholarship • 2071

Maureen L. and Howard N. Blitman, P.E., Scholarship • 2263

MBA Fellowship • 659

MCCA Lloyd M. Johnson, Jr. Scholarship Program • 2264

Minorities and Women Educational Scholarship • 663

Minority Affairs Committee Award for Outstanding Scholastic Achievement • 2267

Minority Fellowship Program • 664

Minority Scholarship • 2268

Minority Scholarship Award for Physical Therapy Students • 2269

Minority Scholarship Awards for College Students • 2270

Minority Scholarship Awards for Incoming College Freshmen • 2271

Minority Serving Institution Grants • 2272

Minority Student Scholarship • 1052

MLA Scholarship for Minority Students • 666

Morgan Stanley Richard B. Fisher Scholarship Program • 2273

Mutual of Omaha Actuarial Scholarship for Minority Students • 2275

NAHJ General Scholarships - Rubén Salazar Fund • 2276

NAHN Scholarship • 2277

National Association of Black Accountants National Scholarship Program • 2280

National Hispanic Health Professional Student Scholarship • 2283

National Medical Fellowships Emergency Scholarship Fund • 2285

NMF National Alumni Council Scholarship Program • 2294

NOAA Educational Partnership Program Undergraduate Scholarships • 2295

Northrop Grumman/HENAAC Scholars Program • 2296

P.O. Pistilli Undergraduate Scholarship for Advancement in Computer Science and Electrical Engineering • 2301

Pega Scholars Program • 2303

Phyllis G. Meekins Scholarship • 2305

PRSA Diversity Multicultural Scholarship • 2309

Que Llueva Cafe Scholarship • 2310

Rosewood Family Scholarship Program • 1834

Ruth D. Peterson Fellowship for Racial and Ethnic Diversity • 2314

SHPE Scholarship Program • 2318

United Parcel Service Scholarship for Minority Students • 2333

Warner Norcross + Judd Diversity Paralegal and Legal Secretarial Scholarship • 1954

William A. Crawford Minority Teacher Scholarship • 1970

William and Charlotte Cadbury Award • 2336

ITALIAN

Henry Salvatori Scholarship • 2221

National Italian American Foundation Scholarship • 2284

Sons of Italy Grand Lodge of California College Scholarship • 1859

Sons of Italy Grand Lodge of California Italian Language Study Grant • 1860

JAPANESE

Abe and Esther Hagiwara Student Aid Award • 2147

Asian and Pacific Islander American Scholarships • 2168

Atsuhiko Tateuchi Memorial Scholarship • 1285

Diversity Advocacy Council Scholarship • 2195

EDSA Diversity Scholarships • 2200

Eizo and Toyo Sakumoto Trust Scholarship • 1421

ESA Foundation Scholarship Program • 2204

George A. Strait Minority Scholarship • 601

Jackie Robinson Foundation Scholarship Program • 2231

Japanese American Citizens League Entering Freshman Awards • 2232

RELIGION INDEX

This index lists awards from various churches and religious organizations.

Allan Jerome Burry Scholarship • 1997
Catholic United Financial College Tuition Scholarship • 2009
CCA Christian Cheer Nationals • 72
Champions for Christ Scholarship • 2011
Diller Teen Tikkun Olam Awards • 2021
Education Scholarship • 2201
Emmett J. Doerr Memorial Scout Scholarship • 2026
Fadel Educational Foundation Annual Award Program • 2028
Helen B. and Lewis E. Goldstein Scholarship Fund • 2046
ISF Policy Scholarship Program • 2054
Islamic Society of North America Scholarships • 2055
J. Robert Ashcroft National Youth Scholarship • 2056
Michael Hakeem Memorial College Essay Contest • 2073
Moris J. and Betty Kaplun Essay Contest • 2076
National Presbyterian College Scholarship • 2083
Native American Education Grant • 2287
Opportunity Scholarships for Lutheran Laywomen • 2089
Otto M. Stanfield Legal Scholarship • 691
Presbyterian Church USA Student Opportunity Scholarships • 2094
Priscilla R. Morton Scholarship • 2095
Rev. Dr. Karen Layman Gift of Hope Scholarship • 2097
Stanfield and D'Orlando Art Scholarship • 2111
Student Activist Awards • 332
Student Activist Scholarships • 2114
UCC Seminarian Scholarship • 2122
Undergraduate Scholarships • 2126
United Methodist General Scholarship • 2129
Vocations Scholarship Funds • 2134
Women in United Methodist History Writing Award • 2141
Young Christian Leaders Scholarship • 2142

DISABILITY INDEX

This index lists awards for students with physical, hearing, vision, mental and learning disabilities. It also includes awards for students who have been afflicted with certain illnesses.

#RAREis Scholarship • 2341
AbbVie Immunology Scholarship • 2342
Alyssa McCroskey Memorial Scholarship • 1254
American Council of the Blind Scholarships • 2343
Anne Ford Scholarship Program • 2344
Baer Reintegration Scholarship • 2345
Betty Bacon Memorial Scholarship • 1294
BMO Capital Markets Lime Connect Equity Through Education Scholarship • 2346
Boomer Esiason Foundation General Academic Scholarship • 2347
Bristol-Myers Squibb Scholarship for Cancer Survivors • 2348
California - Hawaii Elks Major Project Undergraduate Scholarship Program for Students with Disabilities • 1316
California Council of the Blind Scholarships • 1317
Cancer for College Scholarships • 2349
CAPED Excellence Scholarship • 1329
Challenge Met Scholarship • 2350
Dick Griffiths Memorial Scholarship • 1393
Disabled Student Scholarship • 2351
Duane Buckley Memorial Scholarship • 2352
Elizabeth Nash Foundation Scholarship Program • 2353
Eric Dostie Memorial College Scholarship • 2354
Fred Scheigert Scholarships • 2355
George H. Nofer Scholarship for Law and Public Policy • 2356
Graeme Clark Scholarship • 2357
Guthrie-Koch PKU Scholarship • 2358
Harry Alan Gregg Foundation Grants • 1486
HIV-Positive Scholarship • 2359
Incight Scholarship • 2360
Jaime Guttenberg All Abilities Scholarship • 2361
Kathern F. Gruber Scholarship Program • 206
Kevin Child Scholarship • 2362
L.I.F.E. Scholarship • 2363
Lighthouse Guild Scholarships • 2364
Lime Connect Pathways Scholarship for High School Seniors with Disabilities • 2365
Little People of America Scholarships • 2366
Living With Dyslexia Scholarship • 2367
Marion Huber Learning Through Listening Awards • 2369
Mary P. Oenslanger Scholastic Achievement Awards • 2370
Michael A. Hunter Memorial Scholarship Fund • 2371
Mike Hylton and Ron Niederman Scholarships • 2372
Millie Brother Scholarship • 2373
Millie Gonzales Memorial Scholarships • 2374
National Collegiate Cancer Foundation Scholarship • 2375
National Federation of the Blind Scholarship • 2376

National MS Society Scholarship Program • 2377
National Scholarship Competition for Disabled College Students • 2378
New Jersey State Elks Special Children's Committee Scholarship • 1706
NFMC Hinda Honigman Award for the Blind • 2379
Northwestern Mutual Childhood Cancer Survivor Scholarship • 2380
OK-AHEAD Scholarship • 1749
Optimist International Communications Contest • 2382
P. Buckley Moss Endowed Scholarship • 2383
Paul and Ellen Ruckes Scholarship • 2384
Pega Scholars Program • 2303
Rudolph Dillman Memorial Scholarship • 2385
Salix Gastrointestinal Health Scholars Award • 2386
Scholarships for Survivors • 2387
Sertoma Scholarship for Students Who Are Hard of Hearing or Deaf • 2388
Soozie Courter Hemophilia Scholarship Program • 2389
Steve Fasteau Past Presidents' Scholarship • 1877
Student Award Program of FSD • 2390
Student with a Disability Scholarship • 733
Susan Bunch Memorial Scholarship • 1880
Susanna DeLaurentis Memorial Scholarship • 2391
Tony Coelho Media Scholarship • 2392
TPA Scholarship Trust for the Hearing Impaired • 2393
UCB Family Epilepsy Scholarship Program • 2394
Vitality Medical's Student Disability Scholarship • 2395
Wells Fargo Scholarship Program for People with Disabilities • 2396
William and Dorothy Ferrell Scholarship • 2397

MEMBERSHIP INDEX

If you or your parents or grandparents are members of any of the groups in this index, you may qualify for a scholarship.

Air Line Pilots Association
ALPA Scholarship Program • 1998
Alpha Chi
Gaston/Nolle Scholarships • 2035
Alpha Kappa Alpha Educational Advancement Foundation Inc.
Alpha Kappa Alpha Financial Need Scholars • 28
Educational Advancement Foundation Merit Scholarship • 134
Youth Partners Accessing Capital • 2144
Alpha Kappa Psi Foundation
Alpha Kappa Psi Scholarships • 536
American Association of Airport Executives
AAAE Foundation Scholarship • 764
American Association of State Troopers (AAST) Inc.
American Association of State Troopers (AAST) Scholarship • 1999
American Criminal Justice Association
ACJA/Lambda Alpha Epsilon Scholarship • 13
Student Paper Competition • 333
American Culinary Federation
American Culinary Federation Scholarships • 538
Ray and Gertrude Marshall Scholarship • 706
American Dental Hygienists' Association (ADHA) Institute for Oral Health
ADHA Institute Scholarship Program • 779
Colgate Bright Smiles, Bright Futures Minority Scholarships • 871
Crest Oral-B Laboratories Dental Hygiene Scholarships • 878
Dr. Esther Wilkins Scholarship • 896
Irene Woodall Graduate Scholarship • 982
Karla Girts Memorial Community Outreach Scholarship • 1006
Sigma Phi Alpha Undergraduate Scholarship • 1162
American Federation of State, County and Municipal Employees (AFSCME), AFL-CIO
AFSCME Family Scholarship • 1995
American Federation of Teachers
Robert G. Porter Post-Secondary Scholarships • 2099
Robert G. Porter Scholars Program for Members • 2100
American Federation of Teachers (AFT) Michigan
Rollie Hopgood Future Teachers Scholarship • 1830
American Foreign Service Association (AFSA)
AFSA Financial Aid Scholarships • 1993
AFSA National Essay Contest • 16
AFSA/AAFSW Merit Awards • 1994
American Foundation
Angus Foundation Scholarships • 807
American Health Information Management Association (AHIMA) Foundation
AHIMA Foundation Merit Scholarships • 784
American Hellenic Education Progressive Association
AHEPA Educational Foundation National Scholarship Program • 2157
Family District 1 Scholarships • 1435
Maids of Athena Scholarships • 2069

National and District Scholarships • 2279
American Holistic Nurses Association
Charlotte McGuire Scholarship • 868
American Jersey Cattle Association
Cedarcrest Farms Scholarship • 865
American Legion
American Legion Eagle Scout of the Year • 2000
Eight and Forty Lung and Respiratory Nursing Scholarship Fund • 904
National Oratorical Contest • 249
American Legion Auxiliary
Children of Warriors National Presidents' Scholarship • 77
Junior Member Loyalty Scholarship • 2063
Non-Traditional Student Scholarship • 2088
Spirit of Youth Scholarship for Junior Members • 2110
American Legion, Department of Florida
American Legion Department of Florida General Scholarship • 1265
Florida Oratorical Contest • 1443
American Legion, Department of Illinois
Boy Scout and Eagle Scout Scholarship • 1306
American Occupational Therapy Foundation
Kappa Delta Phi • 1004
Mary Eileen Dixey Scholarship • 1631
Ohio State Association/AOTF Scholarships • 1747
Texas Occupational Therapy Association Scholarships • 1904
American Ornithologists' Union
AOS Student and Postdoctoral Research Awards • 815
American Quarter Horse Foundation
American Quarter Horse Foundation (AQHF) Youth Activities Scholarship • 799
American Radio Relay League Foundation
ARRL Foundation General Fund Scholarship • 542
Bill, W2ONV, and Ann Salerno Memorial Scholarship • 550
Carole J. Streeter, KB9JBR, Scholarship • 561
Central Arizona DX Association Scholarship • 1339
Challenge Met Scholarship • 2350
Charles Clarke Cordle Memorial Scholarship • 563
Charles N. Fisher Memorial Scholarship • 564
Dayton Amateur Radio Association Scholarship • 573
Donald Riebhoff Memorial Scholarship • 576
Dr. James L. Lawson Memorial Scholarship • 577
Edmond A. Metzger Scholarship • 583
Fred R. McDaniel Memorial Scholarship • 593
Gary Wagner, K3OMI, Scholarship • 935
IRARC Memorial, Joseph P. Rubino, WA4MMD, Scholarship • 623
Irving W. Cook, WA0CGS, Scholarship • 1543
K2TEO Martin J. Green, Sr. Memorial Scholarship • 640
L. Phil and Alice J. Wicker Scholarship • 643
L.B. Cebik, W4RNL and Jean Cebik, N4TZP Memorial Scholarship • 644
Louisiana Memorial Scholarship • 1611
Mary Lou Brown Scholarship • 658
Mississippi Scholarship • 1672
New England FEMARA Scholarships • 684

Paul and Helen L. Grauer Scholarship • 693
PHD Scholarship • 696
Ray, NRP and Katie, WKTE Pautz Scholarship • 707
Richard W. Bendicksen, N7ZL, Memorial Scholarship • 710
Six Meter Club of Chicago Scholarship • 1854
Tom and Judith Comstock Scholarship • 742
YASME Foundation Scholarship • 760
You've Got a Friend in Pennsylvania Scholarship • 1990
American Red Cross Youth
Navin Narayan College Scholarship • 257
American Society of Civil Engineers (ASCE)
Samuel Fletcher Tapman ASCE Student Chapter/Club Scholarship • 1153
Trent R. Dames and William W. Moore Fellowship • 1201
American Society of Civil Engineers-Michigan Section
Mackinac Scholarship • 1615
Marvin L. Zuidema Scholarship Award • 1628
American Society of Mechanical Engineers (ASME)
ASME Auxiliary Lucy and Charles W. E. Clarke Scholarship • 829
ASME Foundation Scholarships • 830
Berna Lou Cartwright Scholarship • 852
F.W. Beich Beichley Scholarship • 916
Frank and Dorothy Miller ASME Auxiliary Scholarships • 926
Garland Duncan Scholarships • 933
International Gas Turbine Institute Scholarship • 977
John and Elsa Gracik Scholarships • 990
Kenneth Andrew Roe Scholarship • 1007
Melvin R. Green Scholarships • 1042
Old Guard Oral Presentation Competition • 1099
American Society of Radiologic Technologists Foundation (ASRT)
Elekta Radiation Therapy Scholarship • 905
AMVETS National Headquarters
AMVETS National Scholarships for Entering College Freshman • 38
AMVETS National Scholarships for Veterans • 39
AMVETS National Ladies Auxiliary Headquarters
AMVETS National Ladies Auxiliary Scholarship • 2001
Ancient and Accepted Scottish Rite of Freemasonry Southern Jurisdiction
Shepherd Scholarship • 316
Appaloosa Horse Club
Appaloosa Youth Association Art Contest • 816
Appaloosa Youth Association Essay Contest • 817
Larry Williams Photography and AYA Photo Contest • 1010
Youth Program • 1227
ARA Scholarship Foundation Inc.
ARA Scholarship • 2002
ASME International Petroleum Technology Institute
Petroleum Division College Scholarships • 1113
Association for Women in Sports Media
Women in Sports Media Scholarship/Internship Program • 2140
Association of Flight Attendants
Association of Flight Attendants Annual Scholarship • 2004

INDEX BY SPONSOR

AMERICAN INDIAN SERVICES
American Indian Services Scholarship • 2164

AMERICAN INSTITUTE FOR CONTEMPORARY GERMAN STUDIES - (AICGS)
DAAD/AICGS Research Fellowship Program • 424

AMERICAN INSTITUTE FOR FOREIGN STUDY
International Scholarships • 455

AMERICAN INSTITUTE OF AERONAUTICS AND ASTRONAUTICS
AIAA Foundation Undergraduate Scholarship Program • 786

AMERICAN INSTITUTE OF ARCHITECTS
AIA/Architects Foundation Diversity Advancement Scholarship • 785
American Architectural Foundation and Sir John Soane's Museum Foundation Traveling Fellowship • 798
Payette Sho-Ping Chin Memorial Academic Scholarship • 1108

AMERICAN INSTITUTE OF CERTIFIED PUBLIC ACCOUNTANTS
AICPA Fellowship for Minority Doctoral Students • 2158
AICPA Foundation Scholarship for Future CPAs • 528
AICPA Foundation Two-year Transfer Scholarship • 529
AICPA John L. Carey Scholarship • 530
AICPA Scholarship for Minority Accounting Students • 2159
AICPA/Robert Half Student Scholarship • 531
AWSCPA Scholarship • 545
William (Bill) Ezzell Scholarship • 757

AMERICAN INSTITUTE OF CHEMICAL ENGINEERS - (AIChE)
Donald F. and Mildred Topp Othmer Scholarships • 892
John J. McKetta Scholarship • 994
Minority Affairs Committee Award for Outstanding Scholastic Achievement • 2267
Minority Scholarship Awards for College Students • 2270
Minority Scholarship Awards for Incoming College Freshmen • 2271

AMERICAN INSTITUTE OF INDIAN STUDIES
Junior Fellowships • 639

AMERICAN INSTITUTE OF MINING, METALLURGICAL AND PETROLEUM ENGINEERS (AIME)
John S. Marshall Memorial Scholarship • 997

AMERICAN INSTITUTE OF WINE AND FOOD - PACIFIC NORTHWEST CHAPTER
John Schwartz Scholarship • 1566

AMERICAN JERSEY CATTLE ASSOCIATION
Cedarcrest Farms Scholarship • 865

AMERICAN KENNEL CLUB
Junior Showmanship Scholarship Program • 1003

AMERICAN LEGION
American Legion Eagle Scout of the Year • 2000
American Legion Legacy Scholarships • 33

Eight and Forty Lung and Respiratory Nursing Scholarship Fund • 904
National Oratorical Contest • 249

AMERICAN LEGION AUXILIARY
Children of Warriors National Presidents' Scholarship • 77
Junior Member Loyalty Scholarship • 2063
Non-Traditional Student Scholarship • 2088
Spirit of Youth Scholarship for Junior Members • 2110

AMERICAN LEGION AUXILIARY, DEPARTMENT OF CALIFORNIA
American Legion Auxiliary, Department of California $1,000 Scholarships • 1261
American Legion Auxiliary, Department of California $2,000 Scholarships • 1262
American Legion Auxiliary, Department of California $500 Scholarships • 1263
Continuing/Re-entry Students Scholarship • 1373
Past Department Presidents' Junior Scholarship Award • 1779
Past Presidents' Parley Nursing Scholarships • 1780

AMERICAN LEGION AUXILIARY, DEPARTMENT OF NEW YORK
Mary Ann K. Murtha Memorial Scholarship • 1629
New York Legion Auxiliary Department Scholarship • 1709
New York Legion Auxiliary District Scholarships • 1710
Raymond T. Wellington, Jr. Memorial Scholarship • 1807

AMERICAN LEGION BASEBALL
American Legion Baseball Scholarship • 32

AMERICAN LEGION, DEPARTMENT OF ALASKA
Richard D. Johnson Memorial Post-Secondary Scholarship • 1817

AMERICAN LEGION, DEPARTMENT OF ARKANSAS
American Legion Department of Arkansas High School Oratorical Scholarship Program • 1264

AMERICAN LEGION, DEPARTMENT OF CALIFORNIA
California Oratorical Contest • 1324

AMERICAN LEGION, DEPARTMENT OF COLORADO
Colorado Oratorical Contest • 1364

AMERICAN LEGION, DEPARTMENT OF CONNECTICUT
American Legion - Connecticut Oratorical Contest • 1260

AMERICAN LEGION, DEPARTMENT OF FLORIDA
American Legion Department of Florida General Scholarship • 1265
Florida Oratorical Contest • 1443

AMERICAN LEGION, DEPARTMENT OF GEORGIA
Georgia Oratorical Contest • 1460

AMERICAN LEGION, DEPARTMENT OF ILLINOIS
American Legion Scholarship Award • 1266
Americanism Essay Scholarship • 1268
Boy Scout and Eagle Scout Scholarship • 1306
Illinois Oratorical Program Scholarships • 1525

AMERICAN LEGION, DEPARTMENT OF INDIANA
Indiana Oratorical Contest • 1530

AMERICAN LEGION, DEPARTMENT OF IOWA
Iowa Oratorical Contest • 1535

AMERICAN LEGION, DEPARTMENT OF KANSAS
Albert M. Lappin Scholarship • 1247
Charles W. and Annette Hill Scholarship • 1345
Hugh A. Smith Scholarship Fund • 1514
Kansas Oratorical Contest • 1577
Music Committee Scholarship • 1684
Paul Flaherty Athletic Scholarship • 1782
Rosedale Post 346 Scholarship • 1832
Ted and Nora Anderson Scholarships • 1888

AMERICAN LEGION, DEPARTMENT OF MAINE
Children and Youth Scholarships • 1348
Daniel E. Lambert Memorial Scholarship • 1382
James V. Day Scholarship • 1555

AMERICAN LEGION, DEPARTMENT OF MICHIGAN
Guy M. Wilson Scholarship • 1478
Michigan Oratorical Contest • 1654
William D. and Jewell Brewer Scholarship • 1973

AMERICAN LEGION, DEPARTMENT OF MINNESOTA
Minnesota Oratorical Contest • 1667

AMERICAN LEGION, DEPARTMENT OF MISSOURI
Missouri Oratorical Contest • 1675

AMERICAN LEGION, DEPARTMENT OF NEBRASKA
Oratorical Contest Scholarship • 1764

AMERICAN LEGION, DEPARTMENT OF NEW JERSEY
New Jersey Oratorical Contest • 1705
Safety Essay Contest • 1838

AMERICAN LEGION, DEPARTMENT OF NEW YORK
New York Oratorical Contest • 1711

AMERICAN LEGION, DEPARTMENT OF NORTH CAROLINA
North Carolina Oratorical Contest • 1730

AMERICAN LEGION, DEPARTMENT OF NORTH DAKOTA
Hattie Tedrow Memorial Fund Scholarship • 1488

AMERICAN LEGION, DEPARTMENT OF PENNSYLVANIA
Pennsylvania American Legion Essay Contest • 1784
Pennsylvania Oratorical Contest • 1789

AMERICAN LEGION, DEPARTMENT OF TEXAS
Texas Oratorical Contest • 1905

AMERICAN LEGION, DEPARTMENT OF VERMONT
Vermont Oratorical Contest • 1935

AMERICAN LEGION, DEPARTMENT OF VIRGINIA
Middle School Essay Contest • 1657

AMERICAN LEGION, DEPARTMENT OF WASHINGTON
Washington Oratorical Contest • 1958

AMERICAN LEGION, DEPARTMENT OF WISCONSIN
Americanism and Government Scholarship Program • 1267
Eagle Scout of the Year • 1409
Schneider-Emanuel American Legion Scholarship • 1840
Wisconsin Oratorical Scholarship Program • 1982

AMERICAN SOCIETY OF LANDSCAPE ARCHITECTS
Karen Ann Shopis-Fox Memorial Scholarship • 1579

AMERICAN SOCIETY OF MECHANICAL ENGINEERS (ASME)
ASME Auxiliary Lucy and Charles W. E. Clarke Scholarship • 829
ASME Foundation Scholarships • 830
Berna Lou Cartwright Scholarship • 852
F.W. Beich Beichley Scholarship • 916
Frank and Dorothy Miller ASME Auxiliary Scholarships • 926
Garland Duncan Scholarships • 933
International Gas Turbine Institute Scholarship • 977
John and Elsa Gracik Scholarships • 990
Kenneth Andrew Roe Scholarship • 1007
Melvin R. Green Scholarships • 1042
Old Guard Oral Presentation Competition • 1099

AMERICAN SOCIETY OF NAVAL ENGINEERS
ASNE Scholarship Program • 831

AMERICAN SOCIETY OF RADIOLOGIC TECHNOLOGISTS FOUNDATION (ASRT)
Elekta Radiation Therapy Scholarship • 905

AMERICAN SOCIETY OF WOMEN ACCOUNTANTS - SEATTLE CHAPTER
ASWA Seattle Chapter Scholarship • 1284

AMERICAN SOCIOLOGICAL ASSOCIATION MINORITY FELLOWSHIP PROGRAM
Minority Fellowship Program • 664

AMERICAN SPEECH-LANGUAGE-HEARING FOUNDATION
Graduate Student Scholarship • 953
International Student Scholarship • 978
Minority Student Scholarship • 1052
New Century Scholars Doctoral Scholarship • 1088
Student with a Disability Scholarship • 733

AMERICAN STATISTICAL ASSOCIATION
Gertrude Cox Scholarship For Women In Statistics • 942

AMERICAN TRANSLATORS ASSOCIATION
Student Translation Award • 505

AMERICAN VACUUM SOCIETY
Dorothy M. and Earl S. Hoffman Award • 894
Graduate Research Award (GRA) • 949
Nellie Yeoh Whetten Award • 1087
Russell and Sigurd Varian Award • 1150

AMERICAN WATER WORKS ASSOCIATION
Abel Wolman Fellowship • 769
Academic Achievement Award • 770
American Water Scholarship • 800
Bryant L. Bench Carollo Engineers Inc. Scholarship • 858
Holly Cornell Scholarship • 966
Larson Aquatic Research Support (LARS) • 1011
Thomas R. Camp Scholarship • 1193

AMERICAN WATER WORKS ASSOCIATION - FLORIDA SECTION
Roy W. Likins Scholarship • 1835

AMERICAN WATER WORKS ASSOCIATION - MICHIGAN SECTION
Raymond J. Faust Scholarship • 1806

AMERICAN WATER WORKS ASSOCIATION - MISSOURI SECTION
J.R. Popalisky Scholarship • 1547

AMERICAN WATER WORKS ASSOCIATION - NEW YORK SECTION
Walter B. Sinnott Scholarship • 1218

AMERICAN WELDING SOCIETY FOUNDATION
James A. Turner, Jr. Memorial Scholarship • 627

AMERICAN-ARAB ANTI-DISCRIMINATION COMMITTEE
Jack G. Shaheen Mass Communications Scholarship • 625

AMERICAN-SCANDINAVIAN FOUNDATION
Fellowships/Grants to Study in Scandinavia • 436
Leif and Inger Sjoberg Award • 468
Nadia Christensen Prize • 475

AMERICANS UNITED FOR SEPARATION OF CHURCH AND STATE
AU Student Essay Contest • 50

AMERICORPS
Americorps National Civilian Community Corps • 36
Americorps Vista • 37

AMVETS NATIONAL HEADQUARTERS
AMVETS National Scholarships for Entering College Freshman • 38
AMVETS National Scholarships for Veterans • 39

AMVETS NATIONAL LADIES AUXILIARY HEADQUARTERS
AMVETS National Ladies Auxiliary Scholarship • 2001

ANCHOR SCHOLARSHIP FOUNDATION
Anchor Scholarship Foundation Scholarship • 40

ANCIENT AND ACCEPTED SCOTTISH RITE OF FREEMASONRY SOUTHERN JURISDICTION
Shepherd Scholarship • 316

ANDERSON SOBEL COSMETIC SURGERY
WISE Scholarship • 1985

ANNE FRANK CENTER USA
Spirit of Anne Frank Awards • 324

ANTHONY MUÑOZ FOUNDATION
Anthony Muñoz Scholarship Fund • 1270

ANTI-DEFAMATION LEAGUE MIDWEST
Our First Amendment Freedoms Art and Essay Contest • 1769

ANTIBODIES-ONLINE INC.
Annual University Scholarship • 809

APARTMENT GUIDE/RENTPATH LLC
Apartment Guide Scholarship • 41

APPALACHIAN STUDIES ASSOCIATION
Carl A. Ross Student Paper Award • 417

APPALOOSA HORSE CLUB
Appaloosa Youth Association Art Contest • 816
Appaloosa Youth Association Essay Contest • 817
Larry Williams Photography and AYA Photo Contest • 1010
Youth Program • 1227

APPRAISAL INSTITUTE EDUCATION TRUST
AIERF Graduate Scholarship • 532
AIERF Undergraduate Scholarship • 533
Minorities and Women Educational Scholarship • 663

ARA SCHOLARSHIP FOUNDATION INC.
ARA Scholarship • 2002

ARC OF WASHINGTON STATE
Arc of Washington State Trust Fund Stipend Award • 1272

ARIZONA BUSINESS AND PROFESSIONAL WOMEN'S FOUNDATION
Arizona BPW Foundation Annual Scholarships • 1274

ARIZONA NATIONAL LIVESTOCK SHOW
Arizona National Livestock Show Scholarship • 1275

ARKANSAS CHEER COACHES ASSOCIATION
Arkansas Cheer Coaches Association Cheer Classics Team of Excellence • 1276

ARKANSAS COMMUNITY FOUNDATION
Arkansas Service Memorial Scholarship Endowment • 1278

ARKANSAS DEPARTMENT OF HIGHER EDUCATION
Academic Challenge Scholarship • 1229
Governor's Distinguished Scholarship • 1471

ARKANSAS GAME AND FISH COMMISSION
Arkansas Game and Fish Commission Conservation Scholarship • 1277

ARKANSAS STUDENT LOAN AUTHORITY
R. Preston Woodruff, Jr. Scholarships • 1800

ARMED FORCES COMMUNICATIONS AND ELECTRONICS ASSOCIATION (AFCEA)
AFCEA Ralph W. Shrader Diversity Scholarships • 780
AFCEA ROTC Scholarships • 15

ARMED SERVICES YMCA
Armed Services YMCA Annual Essay Contest • 42

ARMENIAN EDUCATIONAL FOUNDATION INC.
Richard R. Tufenkian Memorial Scholarship • 2312

ARMENIAN GENERAL BENEVOLENT UNION (AGBU)
AGBU US Graduate Scholarship • 2154
Helen C. Evans Scholarship • 961
Performing Arts Scholarship • 2304
Religious Studies Scholarship • 2311

ARMENIAN INTERNATIONAL WOMEN'S ASSOCIATION
Agnes Missirian Scholarship • 2156
Lucy Kasparian Aharonian Scholarship • 2248

ARMENIAN RELIEF SOCIETY OF EASTERN USA (ARS)
ARS Undergraduate Scholarship • 2166

INTERNATIONAL ASSOCIATION OF FIRE CHIEFS
FOUNDATION
   IAFC Foundation Scholarship • 183

INTERNATIONAL ASSOCIATION OF FIRE FIGHTERS
   W. H. Howie McClennan Scholarship • 376

INTERNATIONAL ASSOCIATION OF MACHINISTS AND
AEROSPACE WORKERS
   IAM Scholarship • 2050
   International Association of Machinists and
   Aerospace Workers Scholarship for Members'
   Children • 2053

INTERNATIONAL ASSOCIATION OF PLUMBING AND
MECHANICAL OFFICIALS (IAPMO)
   IAPMO Essay Scholarship Contest • 184

INTERNATIONAL BRIDGE, TUNNEL AND TURNPIKE
ASSOCIATION FOUNDATION
   IBTTA Scholarship Program • 971

INTERNATIONAL CENTRE FOR DIFFRACTION DATA
   Ludo Frevel Crystallography Scholarships • 1029

INTERNATIONAL CHEMICAL WORKERS UNION
COUNCIL/UFCW
   Walter L. Mitchell Memorial Scholarship Awards
   • 2135

INTERNATIONAL EXECUTIVE HOUSEKEEPERS
ASSOCIATION (IEHA) EDUCATION FOUNDATION
   IEHA Scholarship • 615

INTERNATIONAL FACILITY MANAGEMENT ASSOCIATION
   International Facility Management Association
   Foundation Scholarship Program • 621

INTERNATIONAL FLIGHT SERVICES ASSOCIATION (IFSA)
   Harvey and Laura Alpert Scholarship Award •
   2045
   IFSA Foundation Scholarship Award • 2051

INTERNATIONAL FOOD SERVICE EXECUTIVES
ASSOCIATION
   IFSEA Worthy Goal Scholarship • 617

INTERNATIONAL FOODSERVICE EDITORIAL COUNCIL
(IFEC)
   IFEC Scholarships Award • 616

INTERNATIONAL FURNISHINGS AND DESIGN
ASSOCIATION (IFDA)
   IFDA Leaders Commemorative Scholarship •
   450
   IFDA Student Member Scholarship • 451
   Part-Time Student Scholarship • 487
   Ruth Clark Furniture Design Scholarship • 495
   Tricia LeVangie Green/Sustainable Design
   Scholarship • 511
   Vercille Voss IFDA Graduate Student Scholar-
   ship • 516

INTERNATIONAL HOUSEWARES ASSOCIATION
   Student Design Competition • 504

INTERNATIONAL INSOLVENCY INSTITUTE
   Prize in International Insolvency Studies • 702

INTERNATIONAL LITERACY ASSOCIATION
   ILA Jeanne S. Chall Research Fellowship • 452

INTERNATIONAL MILITARY COMMUNITY EXECUTIVES'
ASSOCIATION (IMCEA) HEADQUARTERS -
SCHOLARSHIPS
   IMCEA Scholarships • 188

INTERNATIONAL ORDER OF THE KING'S DAUGHTERS
AND SONS
   Health Careers Scholarship • 959
   Native American Scholarship • 2288

INTERNATIONAL ROAD FEDERATION
   IRF Fellowship Program • 983

INTERNATIONAL SCHOLARSHIP AND TUITION SERVICES
INC.
   Glass, Molders, Pottery, Plastics and Allied
   Workers Memorial Scholarship Fund • 2041

INTERNATIONAL SOCIETY OF AUTOMATION
   Educational Foundation Scholarship • 584

INTERNATIONAL SOCIETY OF EXPLOSIVES ENGINEERS
   SEE Education Foundation Scholarships • 1159

INTERNATIONAL SURFING ASSOCIATION
   Individual Scholarship Program • 190

INTERNATIONAL TECHNOLOGY AND ENGINEERING
EDUCATORS ASSOCIATION
   FTEE Scholarship: Undergraduate Major in
   Technology and Engineering Education • 595
   International Technology Engineering Educators
   Association Scholarship - FTEE/Undergraduate
   • 622
   Litherland/FTEE Scholarship • 652
   Maley/FTEE Teacher Professional Development
   Scholarship • 656

INTERNATIONAL TRUMPET GUILD
   International Trumpet Guild Conference Scholarship • 456

INTERNATIONAL UNION OF ELECTRONIC, ELECTRICAL,
SALARIED, MACHINE AND FURNITURE WORKERS-
COMMUNICATIONS WORKERS OF AMERICA
   James B. Carey Scholarship • 2057

INTERNATIONAL WATER, SANITATION AND HYGIENE
FOUNDATION
   Sandra Imprescia Essay Scholarship • 1154

INTERNATIONAL WOMEN'S FISHING ASSOCIATION
   International Women's Fishing Association
   Scholarship • 979

INTERNATIONALSTUDENT.COM
   Travel Video Contest • 353

INTERSCHOLASTIC EQUESTRIAN ASSOCIATION
   IEA Founders College Scholarship Awards • 185
   IEA Zone Specific Scholarships • 186
   National Sportsmanship Award • 251

INTERTECH FOUNDATION
   Intertech Foundation STEM Scholarship • 980

INTERTRIBAL TIMBER COUNCIL
   Truman D. Picard Scholarship • 2331

INVESTOR'S PODCAST
   Corporate Culture Scholarship • 94

IOTA SIGMA PI (ISP) ND
   Gladys Anderson Emerson Scholarship • 945
   Undergraduate Award for Excellence in Chemis-
   try • 1205

IOWA 4-H FOUNDATION
   Iowa 4-H College Scholarships • 1532

IOWA ARTS COUNCIL
   Iowa Scholarship for the Arts • 1539

IOWA AUTOMOBILE DEALERS FOUNDATION FOR
EDUCATION
   IAD Foundation Scholarships • 1515

IOWA CHEERLEADING COACHES' ASSOCIATION
   ICCA Scholarships • 1516

IOWA COLLEGE STUDENT AID COMMISSION
   All Iowa Opportunity Scholarship • 1249
   Future Ready Iowa Grant • 1453
   Future Ready Iowa Last-Dollar Scholarship •
   1454
   Iowa Tuition Grants • 1541
   Iowa Vocational-Technical Tuition Grants •
   1542
   Kibbie Grant (Iowa Skilled Workforce Shortage
   Tuition Grant) • 1583

IOWA FOUNDATION FOR AGRICULTURAL
ADVANCEMENT
   Iowa 4-H and FFA Livestock Show Competition
   • 1531
   Russ Brannen/KENT FEEDS Memorial Beef
   Scholarship • 1836
   Schlutz Family Beef Breeding Scholarship • 1839

IOWA GOLF ASSOCIATION
   Ann Griffel Scholarship • 1269
   Herman Sani Scholarship • 1499

IOWA HIGH SCHOOL MUSIC ASSOCIATION
   Leo H. Grether Memorial Scholarship • 1597

IOWA NEWSPAPER ASSOCIATION
   Iowa Newspaper Association Scholarships • 1534

IOWA PGA FOUNDATION
   Iowa PGA Foundation Charlie Burkart Scholarship • 1536

IOWA PHYSICIAN ASSISTANT SOCIETY
   Iowa Physician Assistant Society Scholarship •
   1537

IOWA PORK PRODUCERS ASSOCIATION
   Iowa Pork Foundation Scholarship • 1538

IOWA PTA
   H.L. Taylor Scholarship Program • 1480

IOWA STATE ARCHERY ASSOCIATION
   ISAA Scholarship Program • 1544

IOWA STUDENT LOAN EDUCATION LENDING
   Iowa Financial Know-How Challenge: Senior
   Scholarship • 1533
   Iowa Student Loan Midwest Senior Scholarship
   • 192

IOWA THESPIAN CHAPTER
   Iowa Thespian Chapter Board Senior Scholarships • 1540

IRISH-AMERICAN CULTURAL INSTITUTE (IACI)
   IACI/NUI Visiting Fellowship in Irish Studies
   • 448

ISLAMIC SCHOLARSHIP FUND
   ISF Policy Scholarship Program • 2054

Kit C. King Graduate Scholarship Fund • 642
NPPF Still and Multimedia Scholarship • 687
NPPF Television News Scholarship • 688
Reid Blackburn Scholarship • 708

NATIONAL PROPANE GAS FOUNDATION
National Propane Gas Foundation • 2084

NATIONAL RADIO ASTRONOMY OBSERVATORY (NRAO)
GBT Student Support Program • 936
Graduate Summer Student Research Assistantship • 954
Undergraduate Summer Student Research Assistantship • 1211

NATIONAL RIFLE ASSOCIATION
Collegiate Shooting Scholarship Program • 1361
George Montgomery/NRA Youth Wildlife Art Contest • 158
Jeanne E. Bray Memorial Scholarship • 198

NATIONAL ROOFING FOUNDATION (NRF)
Roofing Industry Scholarship - Melvin Kruger Endowed Scholarship • 1147

NATIONAL SCHOLASTIC SURFING ASSOCIATION
National Scholarship Program • 250

NATIONAL SCIENCE FOUNDATION
Graduate Research Fellowship Program • 950

NATIONAL SCIENCE FOUNDATION EAST ASIA AND PACIFIC SUMMER INSTITUTES
East Asia and Pacific Summer Institutes • 902

NATIONAL SCULPTURE SOCIETY
National Sculpture Society Scholarship • 480

NATIONAL SECURITY AGENCY (NSA)
Stokes Educational Scholarship Program • 329

NATIONAL SECURITY EDUCATION PROGRAM INITIATIVE, ADMINISTERED BY INSTITUTE OF INTERNATIONAL EDUCATION
Boren Scholarships • 554

NATIONAL SOCIETY DAUGHTERS OF THE AMERICAN REVOLUTION
Alice W. Rooke Scholarship • 794
Irene and Daisy MacGregor Memorial Scholarship • 981
Lillian and Arthur Dunn Scholarship • 2067

NATIONAL SOCIETY OF ACCOUNTANTS SCHOLARSHIP PROGRAM
NSA Scholarship Foundation • 689

NATIONAL SOCIETY OF COLLEGIATE SCHOLARS (NSCS)
Community College Transition Award • 2015
First in the Family Scholarship • 2030
GEICO Award • 2037
GEICO Graduate Award • 2038
Induction Recognition Award • 2052
National Leadership Council (NLC) Award • 2082

NATIONAL SOCIETY OF PROFESSIONAL ENGINEERS
Auxiliary Legacy Scholarship • 841
Maureen L. and Howard N. Blitman, P.E., Scholarship • 2263
Steinman Scholarship • 1175

NATIONAL SOCIETY OF PROFESSIONAL SURVEYORS (NSPS/AAGS)
AAGS - NSPS Scholarships • 766
AAGS Joseph F. Dracup Scholarship Award • 767
Lowell H. and Dorothy Loving Undergraduate Scholarship • 1027
Nettie Dracup Memorial Scholarship • 683
Schonstedt Scholarship in Surveying • 1156
Tri State Surveying and Photogrammetry Kris M. Kunze Memorial Scholarship • 745

NATIONAL SOCIETY OF THE COLONIAL DAMES OF AMERICA
American Indian Nurse Scholarship • 2163

NATIONAL SOCIETY, SONS OF THE AMERICAN REVOLUTION
Arthur M. and Berdena King Eagle Scout Contest • 2003
George S. and Stella M. Knight Essay Contest • 159
Joseph S. Rumbaugh Historical Oration Contest • 637

NATIONAL SPACE CLUB
National Space Club Keynote Scholar • 1074
Olin E. Teague Scholarship • 1100

NATIONAL SPEAKERS ASSOCIATION
Bill Gove Scholarship • 413
Cavett Robert Scholarship • 418

NATIONAL SPORTING CLAYS ASSOCIATION
NSCA Scholarship • 272

NATIONAL STRENGTH AND CONDITIONING ASSOCIATION (NSCA) FOUNDATION
Challenge Scholarship • 73
GNC Nutritional Research Grant • 165
Graduate Research Grant - Master and Doctoral • 168
High School Scholarship • 180
Minority Scholarship • 2268
Women's Scholarship • 1224

NATIONAL STUDENT NURSES' ASSOCIATION
National Student Nurses' Association Scholarship • 1075

NATIONAL WILD TURKEY FEDERATION (NWTF)
Dr. James Earl Kennamer Scholarship • 126

NATIVEVISION
NativeVision Scholarships • 2289

NAVAL ENLISTED RESERVE ASSOCIATION
Naval Enlisted Reserve Association Scholarships • 254

NAVAL HELICOPTER ASSOCIATION
Naval Helicopter Association Scholarship • 255

NAVAL SEA CADET CORPS
NSCC Scholarship Funds • 273

NAVAL SERVICE TRAINING COMMAND OFFICER DEVELOPMENT
NROTC Scholarship Program • 271

NAVAL SPECIAL WARFARE FOUNDATION
UDT-SEAL Scholarship • 359

NAVY EXCHANGE
Next Gen Scholars Award • 267

NAVY LEAGUE FOUNDATION
Capt. Winifred Quick Collins, USN (Ret) Scholarship • 64
Gladys Ann Smith Greater Los Angeles Women's Council Scholarship • 161
Planning Systems Incorporated and Engineering Scholarship • 284
Subic Bay-Cubi Point Scholarship 2 • 339

NAVY MEDICINE PROFESSIONAL DEVELOPMENT CENTER
Nurse Candidate Program • 1096

NAVY SUPPLY CORPS FOUNDATION INC.
Navy Supply Corps Foundation Scholarship • 259

NAVY WIVES CLUBS OF AMERICA (NWCA)
Judith Haupt Member's Child Scholarship • 205
Mary Paolozzi Member's Scholarship • 226
Navy/Marine Corps/Coast Guard (NMCCG) Enlisted Dependent Spouse Scholarship • 263
Pauline Langkamp Memorial Scholarship • 279

NEA FOUNDATION
Learning and Leadership Grants • 647
Student Achievement Grants • 732

NEBRASKA ACADEMY OF SCIENCES INC.
C. Bertrand and Marian Othmer Schultz Collegiate Scholarship • 1311
Nebraska Academy of Sciences High School Scholarships • 1697

NEBRASKA ACTUARIES CLUB
Nebraska Actuaries Club Scholarship • 1698

NEBRASKA COORDINATING COMMISSION FOR POSTSECONDARY EDUCATION
Access College Early Scholarship • 1232

NEBRASKA DEPARTMENT OF VETERANS' AFFAIRS
NDVA Waiver of Tuition • 1696

NEBRASKA FUNERAL DIRECTORS ASSOCIATION
Wallace S. and Wilma K. Laughlin Foundation Trust Scholarships • 1952

NEMETSCHEK VECTORWORKS
Vectorworks Design Scholarship • 515

NETWORK OF ENLIGHTENED WOMEN
Gentlemen Showcase • 2213
NeW Essay Contest • 2292

NEVADA OFFICE OF THE STATE TREASURER
Governor Guinn Millennium Scholarship Program • 1469

NEVADA WOMEN'S FUND
Nevada Women's Fund Scholarships • 1701

NEW ENGLAND BOARD OF HIGHER EDUCATION
New England Regional Student Program • 1703

NEW ENGLAND WATER WORKS ASSOCIATION
Elson T. Killam Memorial Scholarship • 908
Francis X. Crowley Scholarship • 591

NEW HAMPSHIRE CHARITABLE FOUNDATION
Certificate, License or Other Industry-Recognized Credential • 1340
Four-year or Bachelor's Degree Program • 1446
Master's, Ph.D. or Other Advanced Degree Program • 1640
Medallion Fund • 1645

651

TMC/SAE Donald D. Dawson Technical Scholarship • 1196
Yanmar/SAE Scholarship • 1225

SOCIETY OF BROADCAST ENGINEERS
Youth Scholarship • 761

SOCIETY OF EXPLORATION GEOPHYSICISTS
Society of Exploration Geophysicists (SEG) Scholarship • 1165

SOCIETY OF HISPANIC PROFESSIONAL ENGINEERS
SHPE Scholarship Program • 2318

SOCIETY OF MANUFACTURING ENGINEERS EDUCATION FOUNDATION
Giuliano Mazzetti Scholarship • 944
Myrtle and Earl Walker Scholarship • 1060
Society of Manufacturing Engineers Directors Scholarship • 1166

SOCIETY OF MEXICAN AMERICAN ENGINEERS AND SCIENTISTS INC. (MAES)
MAES Scholarship Program • 2251

SOCIETY OF NAVAL ARCHITECTS AND MARINE ENGINEERS (SNAME)
David A. O'Neil Scholarship • 883
John V. Wehausen Graduate Scholarship • 999
Mandell and Lester Rosenblatt Undergraduate Scholarship • 1030
Robert N. and Helen H. Herbert Undergraduate Scholarship • 1146

SOCIETY OF NUCLEAR MEDICINE AND MOLECULAR IMAGING
SNMTS Paul Cole Scholarship • 1164

SOCIETY OF PHYSICS STUDENTS
Herbert Levy Memorial Scholarship • 963
Peggy Dixon Two-Year Scholarship • 1110
SPS Future Teacher Scholarship • 726
SPS Leadership Scholarships • 1171

SOCIETY OF PLASTICS ENGINEERS
Composites Division/Harold Giles Scholarship • 874
Injection Molding Division Scholarship • 975
Plastics Pioneers Association Scholarships • 1119
Polymer Modifiers and Additives Division Scholarships • 1120
Salvatore J. Monte Thermoplastic Materials and Foams Division Scholarship • 1152
Society of Plastics Engineers (SPE) Foundation Scholarships • 1167
Ted and Ruth Neward Scholarship • 1185
Thermoforming Division Memorial Scholarships • 1189
Thermoplastic Elastomers Special Interest Group Scholarship • 1190
Thomas E. Powers/Detroit Section Scholarship • 1191

SOCIETY OF SATELLITE PROFESSIONALS INTERNATIONAL (SSPI)
SSPI Scholarship Program • 727

SOCIETY OF VACUUM COATERS FOUNDATION
Society of Vacuum Coaters Foundation Scholarship • 1168

SOCIETY OF WOMEN ENGINEERS
Ada I. Pressman Memorial Scholarship • 2150
Admiral Grace Murray Hopper Memorial Scholarships • 2151
Anne Maureen Whitney Barrow Memorial Scholarship • 2165
B.J. Harrod Scholarships • 2170
B.K. Krenzer Reentry Scholarship • 2171
Bechtel Corporation Scholarship • 2172
Brill Family Scholarship • 857
Cummin's Inc. Scholarship • 879
Dr. Ivy M. Parker Memorial Scholarship • 2196
Elizabeth McLean Memorial Scholarship • 906
Honeywell International Inc. Scholarships • 2226
Jill S. Tietjen P.E. Scholarship • 988
Judith Resnik Memorial Scholarship • 2237
Lillian Moller Gilbreth Memorial Scholarship • 2244
Lockheed Martin Corporation Scholarship • 2246
Mary Gunther Memorial Scholarship • 2259
Mary V. Munger Scholarship • 1035
Meredith Thoms Memorial Scholarship • 1043
Northrop Grumman Scholarship • 1739
Olive Lynn Salembier Memorial Reentry Scholarship • 2298
Susan Miszkowicz Memorial Scholarship • 1183
SWE Exelon Corporation Scholarship • 2323
SWE Past Presidents Scholarship • 2324

SODEXO FOUNDATION
Sodexo STOP Hunger Scholarship • 320

SOLIANT CONSULTING
Soliant's Sunrise Scholarship • 321

SONS OF THE REPUBLIC OF TEXAS
Texas History Essay Scholarship • 1902

SONS OF UNION VETERANS OF THE CIVIL WAR
Sons of Union Veterans of the Civil War Scholarships • 322

SOROPTIMIST INTERNATIONAL OF THE AMERICAS
Live Your Dream Awards Program • 2245

SOUTH CAROLINA COMMISSION ON HIGHER EDUCATION
Legislative for Future Excellence (LIFE) Scholarship Program • 1593
Lottery Tuition Assistance Program • 1608
Palmetto Fellows Scholarship Program • 1772
South Carolina Hope Scholarship • 1862
State Need-based Grants • 1871

SOUTH CAROLINA FARM BUREAU FOUNDATION
South Carolina Farm Bureau Foundation Scholarships • 1861

SOUTH CAROLINA NURSES FOUNDATION INC.
South Carolina Nurses Foundation Nurses Care Scholarship • 1863

SOUTH CAROLINA SPACE GRANT CONSORTIUM
Kathryn D. Sullivan Earth and Marine Science Fellowship • 1580

SOUTH CAROLINA STATE DEPARTMENT OF EDUCATION
Archibald Rutledge Scholarship Program • 1273

SOUTH CAROLINA TUITION GRANTS COMMISSION
South Carolina Tuition Grants Program • 1864

SOUTH DAKOTA BOARD OF REGENTS
Marlin R. Scarborough Memorial Scholarship • 1626
South Dakota Free Tuition for Veterans and Others Who Performed War Service • 1865

SOUTHEASTERN THEATRE CONFERENCE INC.
Marian A. Smith Costume Award • 472

SOUTHERN BOWLING CONGRESS
Curwen-Guidry-Blackburn Scholarship Fund • 106

SOUTHERN SCHOLARSHIP FOUNDATION
Southern Scholarship Foundation Scholarship • 1866

SPECIALTY EQUIPMENT MARKET ASSOCIATION
Specialty Equipment Market Association (SEMA) Memorial Scholarship • 725

SPIE, THE INTERNATIONAL SOCIETY FOR OPTICAL ENGINEERING
SPIE Optics and Photonics Education Scholarship • 1169

SPORTS IN ACTION
H-E-B Scholarships for UIL Participants • 1479

SPORTS UNLIMITED
Sports Unlimited Scholarship • 326

ST. ANDREW'S SOCIETY OF WASHINGTON, DC
St. Andrew's Society of Washington, DC Scholarship • 2320

STAMPS FAMILY CHARITABLE FOUNDATION INC.
Stamps Scholars • 327

STANLEY BLACK AND DECKER
DEWALT Trades Scholarship • 574

STANLEY TECHNOLOGY SCHOLARSHIP PROGRAM
STANLEY Technology Scholarship Program • 1172

STANTEC
Stantec Equity and Diversity Scholarship • 2321

STARFLEET SCHOLARSHIP PROGRAM
Starfleet Scholarships • 2113

STATE COUNCIL OF HIGHER EDUCATION FOR VIRGINIA
Virginia Commonwealth Award • 1942
Virginia Guaranteed Assistance Program • 1944
Virginia Part-Time Assistance Program • 1946
Virginia Tuition Assistance Grant Program • 1949

STATE OF WISCONSIN HIGHER EDUCATIONAL AIDS BOARD
Academic Excellence Scholarship • 1230
Talent Incentive Program Grant • 1884
Wisconsin Higher Education Grant • 1980

STATE STUDENT ASSISTANCE COMMISSION OF INDIANA
Adult Student Grant • 1237
Frank O'Bannon Grant Program • 1450
Twenty-first Century Scholars Program • 1923
William A. Crawford Minority Teacher Scholarship • 1970

STDCHECK.COM
HIV-Positive Scholarship • 2359

STEPHEN PHILLIPS MEMORIAL SCHOLARSHIP FUND
Stephen Phillips Memorial Scholarship Fund • 1874

STONEWALL COMMUNITY FOUNDATION
Bee's Fund Microgrants • 2173
Traub-Dicker Rainbow Scholarship • 2329

STOSSEL IN THE CLASSROOM
Private Frontier Essay Contest • 287
Private Frontier Video Contest • 288

STRIDE BANK
May T. Henry Scholarship Fund • 1642

STUDENT INSIGHTS
Student View Scholarship • 336

STUDENT VETERANS OF AMERICA
Google SVA Scholarship • 167

STUDY ABOARD EUROPE
Study Abroad Europe Scholarship • 506

STUDY.COM
Study.com Academic Awards • 338

STUTTGART ARKANSAS CHAMBER OF COMMERCE
Chick and Sophie Major Memorial Duck Calling Contest • 1347

SUNFLOWER INITIATIVE
Harriet Fitzgerald Scholarship • 2217

SUPERCOLLEGE.COM
SuperCollege Scholarship • 341

SURFERS' ENVIRONMENTAL ALLIANCE
Benjamin J. Keiser Memorial Coastal Engineering Scholarship • 850
SEA Environmental Studies Scholarship • 1158

SURVEYING AND MAPPING SOCIETY OF GEORGIA
Ben W. Fortson, Jr., Scholarship • 1292

SUSAN THOMPSON BUFFETT FOUNDATION
Susan Thompson Buffett Foundation Scholarship Program • 1882

SUSANNA DELAURENTIS CHARITABLE FOUNDATION
Susanna DeLaurentis Memorial Scholarship • 2391

SUTLIFF & STOUT LAW SCHOOL SCHOLARSHIP
Sutliff & Stout Law School Scholarship • 734

SWISS BENEVOLENT SOCIETY OF NEW YORK
Medicus Student Exchange • 2265

TACO BELL FOUNDATION
Live Mas Scholarship • 215

TAG AND LABEL MANUFACTURERS INSTITUTE INC.
TLMI Four Year College Degree Scholarship Program • 740
TLMI Two-Year College or Technical Degree Program Scholarship • 741

TAILHOOK ASSOCIATION
Tailhook Educational Foundation Scholarship • 344

TAIWANESE AMERICAN SCHOLARSHIP FUND
Taiwanese American Scholarship Fund • 2325

TALL CLUBS INTERNATIONAL FOUNDATION INC.
Tall Club International Scholarship • 2116

TAMPA BAY BUCCANEERS FOUNDATION
Tampa Bay Buccaneers Foundation Girls in Football Scholarship • 345

TAU BETA PI ASSOCIATION
Tau Beta Pi Scholarships • 2117

TAU KAPPA EPSILON EDUCATIONAL FOUNDATION
Carroll C. Hall Memorial Scholarship • 2008
Charles R. Walgreen Jr. Leadership Award • 2012
Donald A. and John R. Fisher Memorial Scholarship • 2023
Eugene C. Beach Memorial Scholarship • 2027

TE CONNECTIVITY AFRICAN HERITAGE SCHOLARSHIP
TE Connectivity African Heritage Scholarship • 2326

TEACHERS OF ACCOUNTING AT TWO-YEAR COLLEGES
TACTYC Accounting Scholarship • 735

TECHCHECKS
TechChecks Business Leadership Scholarship • 738

TED ROLLINS
Ted Rollins ECO Scholarship • 1186

TELLURIDE ASSOCIATION
Telluride Association Summer Programs • 348

TENNESSEE FUNERAL DIRECTORS ASSOCIATION
Tennessee Funeral Directors Association Memorial Scholarship • 1890

TENNESSEE STUDENT ASSISTANCE CORPORATION
Aspire Award • 1280
Christa McAuliffe Scholarship • 1350
General Assembly Merit Scholarship • 1457
Ned McWherter Scholars Program • 1699
Tennessee HOPE Access Grant • 1891
Tennessee HOPE Lottery Scholarship • 1892
Tennessee Need-Based Supplemental Aspire Awards • 1893
Tennessee Student Assistance Awards • 1894

TEWAARATON FOUNDATION
U.S. Lacrosse Native American Scholarships • 2332

TEXAS 4-H YOUTH DEVELOPMENT FOUNDATION
Collegiate Scholarship • 1360
Courageous Heart Scholarship • 1376
Technical Certification Scholarship • 1887
Texas 4-H Opportunity Scholarship Program - Baccalaureate Scholarships • 1895

TEXAS ASSOCIATION OF BROADCASTERS
Texas Broadcast Education Foundation Scholarships • 1897

TEXAS CATTLEWOMEN
Ivomec Generations of Excellence Internship and Scholarship Program • 1546

TEXAS COMPUTER EDUCATION ASSOCIATION
Richard A. Brown Memorial Scholarship for Students • 1816

TEXAS ELKS STATE ASSOCIATION (TESA)
Texas Elks State Association Scholarship Program • 1898
Texas Elks State Association Teenager of the Year Contest • 1899

Texas Elks State Association Vocational Grant Program • 1900

TEXAS HIGHER EDUCATION COORDINATING BOARD
Exemption for Highest Ranking High School Graduate • 1431
Exemption for Texas Veterans (Hazelwood Exemption) • 1432
Texas Fifth-Year Accounting Student Scholarship Program • 1901
Texas Public Educational Grant • 1906
Towards EXcellence, Access and Success (TEXAS) Grant Program • 1913
Tuition Equalization Grant Program • 1918

TEXAS INTERNATIONAL FISHING TOURNAMENT
Texas International Fishing Tournament Inc. Scholarship • 1903

TEXAS RETIRED TEACHERS FOUNDATION
Beginning Teacher Scholarships • 1290

THEDREAM.US
TheDream.US Scholarship • 2327

THERMO FISHER SCIENTIFIC
Thermo Fisher Scientific Antibody Scholarship • 1188

THIRD MARINE DIVISION ASSOCIATION
Memorial Scholarship Fund • 230

THOMARA LATIMER CANCER FOUNDATION
Thomara Latimer Cancer Foundation Scholarship • 1908

THOMAS J. WATSON FELLOWSHIP
Watson Travel Fellowship • 379

THUNEN SCHOLARSHIP COMMITTEE
Robert E. Thunen Memorial Scholarships • 1145

THURGOOD MARSHALL SCHOLARSHIP FUND
Thurgood Marshall College Scholarship Fund • 2328

TIMOTHY S.Y. LAM FOUNDATION
Timothy S.Y. Lam Foundation Education Scholarships • 739

TOCRIS BIOSCIENCE
Tocris Scholarship • 1200

TOMBOW
Tombow's Create Your Best Work Art Scholarship • 510

TOOL, DIE AND MACHINING ASSOCIATION OF WISCONSIN
Edward L. Simeth Scholarships • 1419

TOPEKA COMMUNITY FOUNDATION
Harriet Hayes Austin Memorial Scholarship for Nursing • 1485

TOWNSHIP OFFICIALS OF ILLINOIS
Township Officials of Illinois Scholarship • 1914

TPA SCHOLARSHIP TRUST FOR THE DEAF AND NEAR DEAF
TPA Scholarship Trust for the Hearing Impaired • 2393

TRANSPORT WORKER UNION OF AMERICAN, AFL-CIO
Michael J. Quill Scholarship Fund • 2074

USA Gymnastics
National Gymnastics Foundation Men's Scholarship • 2282

USA Racquetball
USAR Scholarship • 367

USA Roller Sports
USA Roller Sports Scholarship Fund • 365

USA Water Ski and Wake Sports Foundation
George Blair Ambassador Scholarship • 157
Jean Downes Scholarship • 197
Southern Region/Elmer Stailing Scholarship • 323
Tim Olson Memorial Scholarship • 350
USA Water Ski and Wake Sports Foundation Scholarships • 366

Utah Association of Independent Insurance Agents
Utah Association of Independent Insurance Agents Scholarship • 1930

Utah System of Higher Education
New Century Scholarship • 1702

Utility Workers Union of America
Utility Workers Union of America Scholarships • 2131

VA Mortgage Center
VA Essay Scholarship • 373

Verified Scholarships
$1,000 All Star Verified Scholarship • 1

Vermont Student Assistance Corporation
Kilbourn-Sawyer Memorial Scholarship • 1584
Part-Time Grants • 1776
Vermont Incentive Grants • 1934
Vermont Sheriffs' Association Scholarship • 1936

Vertical Flight Foundation
Vertical Flight Foundation Technical Scholarships • 1215

Veterans Caucus of the American Academy of Physician Assistants
Veterans Caucus Scholarship • 374

Veterans of Foreign Wars
Patriot's Pen Youth Essay Contest • 488
VFW Scout of the Year Scholarship • 2133
Voice of Democracy Audio Essay Contests • 375

Veterans of Foreign Wars Teacher of the Year Award
Teacher of the Year Award • 737

Virginia Association for Health, Physical Education, Recreation and Dance
Frances A. Mays Scholarship Award • 1448

Virginia Cable Telecommunications Association
VCTA Virginia's Future Leaders Scholarship Program • 1933

Virginia Daughters of the American Revolution
Virginia Daughters of the American Revolution Scholarships • 1943

Virginia Department of Aviation
John R. Lillard VAOC Scholarship • 1565

Virginia Department of Education
Granville P. Meade Scholarship • 1474

Virginia High School League
VHSL Achievement Award • 1939
Virginia High School League Charles E. Savedge Journalism Scholarship • 1945

Virginia Lakes and Watersheds Association
Leo Bourassa Scholarship • 1596

Virginia PTA
Virginia PTA Annual Citizenship Essay Project • 1947

Virginia Sheriffs' Institute
Virginia Sheriffs' Institute Scholarship • 1948

Visionary Integration Professionals
VIP Women in Technology Scholarship • 1216

Vitality Medical
Vitality Medical's Student Disability Scholarship • 2395

Volunteer Florida
Florida Governor's Black History Month Essay Contest • 1442

Volunteer Forever Inc.
Travel Scholarship • 352

Volunteers for Outdoor Colorado
Grossman Scholarship • 1477

WAFP Scholarship Committee
E.H. Marth Food Protection and Food Science Scholarship • 1408

Warrell Corp
AACT National Candy Technologists John Kitt Memorial Scholarship Program • 765

Washington Business and Professional Women's Foundation
Washington BPW Foundation Mature Woman Educational Scholarship • 1955

Washington Crossing Foundation
National Washington Crossing Foundation Scholarship • 678

Washington Interscholastic Activities Association (WIAA)
Smart Choices Scholarship Program • 1855

Washington Media Scholars Foundation
Media Fellows Program • 660

Washington State Auto Dealers Association (WSADA) Scholarship Program
Washington State Auto Dealers Association Bright Future Scholarship • 1959

Washington State Board for Community and Technical Colleges
Opportunity Grant • 1763

Washington State PTA
Washington State PTA Scholarship • 1962

Washington Student Achievement Council
American Indian Endowed Scholarship • 1258
State Work Study • 1873
Washington College Grant • 1956
Washington Health Corps • 1957

Washington State College Bound Scholarship • 1960

Washington Women In Need
Washington Women In Need • 1963

Way.com
Way Scholarship • 1219

Wealth By Health Steps For Change Foundation
Steps For Change Scholarship • 328

Wells Fargo Scholarship Program for People with Disabilities, Scholarship America
Wells Fargo Scholarship Program for People with Disabilities • 2396

Wells Fargo Veterans Scholarship Program, Scholarship America
Wells Fargo Veterans Scholarship Program • 383

Welsh Pony and Cob Society
Mollie Butler Memorial Scholarship • 1054

West Virginia Higher Education Policy Commission
Higher Education Adult Part-Time Student (HEAPS) Grant Program • 1505
West Virginia Higher Education Grant • 1965
West Virginia Engineering, Science and Technology Scholarship • 1964
West Virginia PROMISE Scholarship • 1966

West Virginia PTA
West Virginia PTA Scholarship • 1967

Western Digital Scholarship Program
Western Digital Scholarship Program • 384

White House
White House Fellows Program • 385

Wilderness Society
Gloria Barron Wilderness Society Scholarship • 946

William Orr Dingwall Foundation
Korean Ancestry Grant • 2241

William Randolph Hearst Foundation
United States Senate Youth Program • 747

Wilson Ornithological Society
George A. Hall / Harold F. Mayfield Grant • 941
Louis Agassiz Fuertes Award • 1026
Paul A. Stewart Grants • 1107

Wine Country Gift Baskets
Spirit of Giving Scholarship • 325

Winfield Solutions LLC
Careers in Agriculture Scholarship Program • 863

Winston-Salem Foundation
Oliver Joel and Ellen Pell Denny Healthcare Scholarship Fund • 1760

Wisconsin Amusement and Music Operators
Wisconsin Amusement and Music Operators Scholarships • 1978

Wisconsin Broadcasters Association
Wisconsin Broadcasters Association Foundation Student Scholarship Program • 1979

Wisconsin Department of Military Affairs
Wisconsin National Guard Tuition Grant • 1981

SCHOLARSHIP NAME INDEX

NFMC Gretchen E. Van Roy Music Education Scholarship • 685
NFMC Hinda Honigman Award for the Blind • 2379
NFMC Lynn Freeman Olson Composition Awards • 483
NFMC Wendell Irish Viola Award • 484
NHSC Scholarship • 1091
NIADA Scholarship • 2087
Nicholas Virgilio Haiku and Senryu Contest • 268
Nightingale Awards of Pennsylvania Scholarship • 1717
NIH Undergraduate Scholarship Program • 1092
Nissan Scholarship • 1718
NJ Student Tuition Assistance Reward Scholarship • 1719
NJ Student Tuition Assistance Reward Scholarship II • 1720
NJCDCA Scholarship • 1721
NJSCA High School Scholarship • 1722
NMASBO Scholarship • 1723
NMF National Alumni Council Scholarship Program • 2294
NNM American Society of Mechanical Engineers Scholarship • 1724
NOAA Educational Partnership Program Undergraduate Scholarships • 2295
Non Commissioned Officers Association Scholarships • 269
Non-Traditional Student Scholarship • 2088
Norman and Ruth Good Educational Endowment • 1725
Norman S. and Betty M. Fitzhugh Fund • 1726
North American Van Lines Logistics Scholarship • 686
North Carolina 4-H Development Fund Scholarships • 1727
North Carolina Community College Grant • 1728
North Carolina Education Lottery Scholarship • 1729
North Carolina Oratorical Contest • 1730
North Dakota Academic Scholarship • 1731
North Dakota Career and Technical Education Scholarship • 1732
North Dakota Career Builders Scholarship • 1733
North Dakota Dollars for Scholars • 1734
North Dakota Scholars Program • 1735
North Dakota School Counseling Association • 1736
North Dakota State Student Incentive Grant • 1737
North Texas State Fair Association Scholarship • 1738
Northrop Grumman Scholarship • 1739
Northrop Grumman/HENAAC Scholars Program • 2296
Northwest Danish Association Scholarships • 1740
Northwestern Mutual Childhood Cancer Survivor Scholarship • 2380
Northwestern Mutual Foundation Childhood Cancer Sibling Scholarship • 2381
Novus Biologicals Scholarship Program • 1093

NPCA Educational Foundation Scholarships • 1094
NPFDA Scholarships • 1095
NPPF Still and Multimedia Scholarship • 687
NPPF Television News Scholarship • 688
NROTC Nurse Corps Scholarship • 270
NROTC Scholarship Program • 271
NSA Scholarship Foundation • 689
NSCA Scholarship • 272
NSCC Scholarship Funds • 273
Nurse Candidate Program • 1096
Nurse Corps Scholarship Program • 1097
Nurseries Foundation Award • 1098
Nursing Education Scholarship Program • 1741
Nursing Incentive Scholarship Fund • 1742
NYWEA Major Environmental Career Scholarship • 1743
OCA/UPS Gold Mountain Scholarship • 2297
Odenza Marketing Group Scholarship • 274
ODS Youth Interscholastic Merit Scholarship • 275
Office Supply Scholarship • 485
Ohio Classical Conference Scholarship for Prospective Latin Teachers • 1744
Ohio Newspaper Women's Association (ONWA) Annual Scholarship • 1745
Ohio Section Scholarships • 1746
Ohio State Association/AOTF Scholarships • 1747
Ohio Turfgrass Foundation Scholarships • 1748
OK-AHEAD Scholarship • 1749
Oklahoma Foundation for Excellence Academic All-State Scholarships • 1750
Oklahoma Hall of Fame Scholarship • 1751
Oklahoma Rural Rehabilitation Corporation Scholarships • 1752
Oklahoma Schools Insurance Group (OSIG) Scholarship • 1753
Oklahoma Society of Land Surveyors Scholarships • 1754
Oklahoma State Fair Inc. Scholarship Program • 1755
Oklahoma Tuition Aid Grant Program (OTAG) • 1756
Oklahoma Tuition Equalization Grant Program (OTEG) • 1757
Oklahoma Youth with Promise Scholarship Fund • 1758
Oklahoma's Promise • 1759
Old Guard Oral Presentation Competition • 1099
Oleg Fastovsky Outstanding Citizenship Scholarship • 276
Olin E. Teague Scholarship • 1100
Olive Lynn Salembier Memorial Reentry Scholarship • 2298
Oliver Joel and Ellen Pell Denny Healthcare Scholarship Fund • 1760
One Earth Award • 277
One Family Scholars Program • 1761
Operations and Power Division Scholarship • 1101
Opportunity Award • 1762
Opportunity Grant • 1763
Opportunity Scholarships for Lutheran Laywomen • 2089

Optimist International Communications Contest • 2382
Optimist International Essay Contest • 486
Optimist International Oratorical Contest • 690
Oratorical Contest Scholarship • 1764
Oregon Army National Guard • 1765
Oregon Farm Bureau Memorial Scholarships • 1766
OROS Scholarship • 1767
Osher Scholarship • 1768
Osmosis Raise the Line Scholarship • 1102
Otto M. Stanfield Legal Scholarship • 691
Our First Amendment Freedoms Art and Essay Contest • 1769
Outrigger Duke Kahanamoku Scholarship • 1770
Outstanding Undergraduate Researchers Award Program • 1103
Overseas Press Club Foundation Scholarships/Fellowships • 692
Owens-Bell Award • 2090
P. Buckley Moss Endowed Scholarship • 2383
P.E.O. International Peace Scholarship • 2299
P.E.O. Program for Continuing Education • 2300
P.O. Pistilli Undergraduate Scholarship for Advancement in Computer Science and Electrical Engineering • 2301
Page Education Foundation Grants • 1771
Palmer Scholarship • 2091
Palmetto Fellows Scholarship Program • 1772
Paradigm Challenge • 1104
Paraprofessional Scholarship • 1773
Paraprofessional Teacher Preparation Grant • 1774
Paros-Digiquartz Scholarship • 1105
Part-Time Grant • 1775
Part-Time Grants • 1776
Part-Time Student Scholarship • 487
Part-Time TAP Program • 1777
Part-Time Tuition Aid Grant • 1778
Past Department Presidents' Junior Scholarship Award • 1779
Past Presidents' Parley Nursing Scholarships • 1780
Path to Pro Scholarship • 1106
Patriot's Pen Youth Essay Contest • 488
Patty and Melvin Alperin First Generation Scholarship • 1781
Paul A. Stewart Grants • 1107
Paul and Daisy Soros Fellowships for New Americans • 278
Paul and Ellen Ruckes Scholarship • 2384
Paul and Helen L. Grauer Scholarship • 693
Paul Flaherty Athletic Scholarship • 1782
Paulina L. Sorg Scholarship • 1783
Pauline Langkamp Memorial Scholarship • 279
Paumanauke Native American Indian Scholarship • 2302
PAVE Student Design Competition • 694
Payette Sho-Ping Chin Memorial Academic Scholarship • 1108
Payzer Scholarship • 1109
Pedro Zamora Young Leaders Scholarship • 280
Pega Scholars Program • 2303
Peggy Dixon Two-Year Scholarship • 1110

Pennsylvania American Legion Essay Contest • 1784

Pennsylvania Business Education Association Scholarship • 1785

Pennsylvania Educational Gratuity Program • 1786

Pennsylvania Knights Templar Educational Foundation Scholarships • 1787

Pennsylvania Land Surveyors' Foundation Scholarship • 1788

Pennsylvania Oratorical Contest • 1789

Pennsylvania Society of Tax and Accounting Professionals Scholarships • 1790

Pennsylvania State Bowling Association Scholarship Program • 1791

Pennsylvania State Grant Program • 1792

PenSPRA Scholarship • 1793

Perennial Plant Association Scholarship • 1111

Perfect Plants Nursery Scholarship • 1112

Performing Arts Scholarship • 2304

Peter and Jody Larkin Legacy Scholarship • 695

Petroleum Division College Scholarships • 1113

PG&E Better Together STEM Scholarship Program • 1794

PGA WORKS Golf Management University Scholarship • 281

PHCC Educational Foundation Scholarship • 1114

PHD Scholarship • 696

Phi Delta Kappa International Scholarship Grants for Prospective Educators • 2092

Phi Delta Kappa Scholarship Grant for Prospective Educators • 697

Phi Kappa Phi Fellowship • 2093

Phoebe Pember Memorial Scholarship • 1115

Phyllis G. Meekins Scholarship • 2305

Phyllis V. Roberts Scholarship • 1795

Physician Assistant Foundation Scholarship • 1116

Pierre and Patricia Bikai Fellowship • 698

Pilot International Scholarship • 282

Pilot Pen G2 Overachievers Student Grant • 283

Pinnacol Foundation Scholarship Program • 1796

Pioneers of Flight • 1117

PixelPlex Bi-Annual STEM Scholarship • 1118

Plan NH Scholarship and Fellowship Program • 1797

Planning Systems Incorporated and Engineering Scholarship • 284

Plastics Pioneers Association Scholarships • 1119

Platt Family Scholarship Prize Essay Contest • 489

Playwright Discovery Award • 490

Point Community College Scholarship • 2306

Point Flagship Scholarship • 2307

Polish National Alliance Scholarship • 2308

Polymer Modifiers and Additives Division Scholarships • 1120

Pony Alumni Scholarship • 285

Porch Skilled Trade and Technology Scholarships • 699

Poster Contest for High School Students • 491

Power of Parents Scholarship • 286

PPG Protective and Marine Coatings Academic Scholarship • 1121

Predoctoral Fellowship Program • 1122

Predoctoral Fellowships for Historians of American Art to Travel Abroad • 700

Predoctoral Research Training Fellowship • 1123

Presbyterian Church USA Student Opportunity Scholarships • 2094

Presidential Scholarships • 701

Presidents Scholarship of the Institute of Industrial Engineers • 1124

Pretty Photoshop Actions Bi-annual Scholarship • 1125

Princess Grace Awards • 492

Print and Graphics Scholarship • 493

Priscilla R. Morton Scholarship • 2095

Private Frontier Essay Contest • 287

Private Frontier Video Contest • 288

Prize in Ethics Essay Contest • 494

Prize in International Insolvency Studies • 702

Project Vote Smart National Internship Program • 703

Project Yellow Light/Hunter Garner Scholarship • 289

Prospective Educator Scholarships • 704

PRSA Diversity Multicultural Scholarship • 2309

PRSA-Hawaii/Roy Leffingwell Public Relations Scholarship • 1798

Prudential Emerging Visionaries • 290

Pulte Group Build Your Future Scholarship Program • 1126

Pursuing a Positive Impact Scholarship • 291

Que Llueva Cafe Scholarship • 2310

Quill and Scroll Student Scholarships • 705

R&D Systems Scholarship Program • 1127

R. Flake Shaw Scholarship • 1799

R. Preston Woodruff, Jr. Scholarships • 1800

R.W. Bob Holden Scholarship • 1801

Race Entry Student Scholarship • 292

Rae Lee Siporin Award • 1802

Rain Bird Intelligent Use of Water Scholarship • 1128

Ralph K. Hillquist Honorary SAE Scholarship • 1129

Ranelius Scholarship Program • 1803

Raney Fund Award • 1130

Rawhide Scholarship • 293

Ray and Gertrude Marshall Scholarship • 706

Ray Anthony Peacock Scholarship • 1804

Ray, NRP and Katie, WKTE Pautz Scholarship • 707

Raymond Davis Scholarship • 1131

Raymond F. Cain Scholarship Fund • 1805

Raymond J. Faust Scholarship • 1806

Raymond T. Wellington, Jr. Memorial Scholarship • 1807

RBC Wealth Management Colorado Scholarship • 1808

Reach Higher Montana Scholarships • 1809

RealtyHop Scholarship • 294

Red Boucher Scholarship • 1810

Regeneron Science Talent Search • 1132

Regional University Baccalaureate Scholarship • 1811

Regions Riding Forward Scholarship Essay Contest • 1812

Reid Blackburn Scholarship • 708

Reiff Law Firm Legal Scholarship • 709

Religious Liberty Essay Scholarship Contest • 2096

Religious Studies Scholarship • 2311

RentHop Apartment Scholarship • 295

Resident Research Scholarship • 1133

Retail Chapter Awards • 1813

Return 2 College Scholarship • 296

Reuben Trane Scholarship • 1134

Rev. Dr. Karen Layman Gift of Hope Scholarship • 2097

RevPart STEM Scholarship • 1135

Rhode Island Foundation Association of Former Legislators Scholarship • 1814

Rhodes Scholar • 297

RI Promise • 1815

Richard A. Brown Memorial Scholarship for Students • 1816

Richard D. Johnson Memorial Post-Secondary Scholarship • 1817

Richard D. Wiegers Scholarship • 1818

Richard E. Bangert Business Award • 1819

Richard F. Walsh, Alfred W. DiTolla, Harold P. Spivak Foundation Award • 2098

Richard Goolsby Scholarship Fund • 1820

Richard J. Stull Student Essay Competition in Healthcare Management • 1136

Richard Jensen Scholarship • 1137

Richard L. Davis, FACMPE - Managers Scholarship • 1138

Richard L. Davis, FACMPE/Barbara B. Watson, FACMPE - National Scholarship • 1139

Richard Lee Vernon Aviation Scholarship • 1140

Richard R. Tufenkian Memorial Scholarship • 2312

Richard W. Bendicksen, N7ZL, Memorial Scholarship • 710

Ridgeline International Community Scholarship • 1141

RISE Financial Progress Scholarship • 298

Risk Management Association Foundation Scholarship • 711

Ritchie M. Gregory Fund • 1821

Ritchie-Jennings Memorial Scholarship • 712

RMEL Foundation Scholarships • 1142

Road to Safety Scholarship Contest • 1822

Rob Branham Scholarship • 1823

Robanna Fund • 1824

Robert B. Oliver ASNT Scholarship • 1143

Robert D. Blue Scholarship • 1825

Robert E. Dougherty Educational Foundation Scholarship Award • 1144

Robert E. Thunen Memorial Scholarships • 1145

Robert G. Porter Post-Secondary Scholarships • 2099

Robert G. Porter Scholars Program for Members • 2100

Robert N. and Helen H. Herbert Undergraduate Scholarship • 1146

Robert R. Robinson Memorial Scholarship • 1826

Roberta B. Willis Scholarship - Need and Merit-Based Award • 1827

Roberta B. Willis Scholarship - Need-Based Award • 1828

Rockefeller State Wildlife Scholarship • 1829

Roger Collins Leadership Scholarship • 713

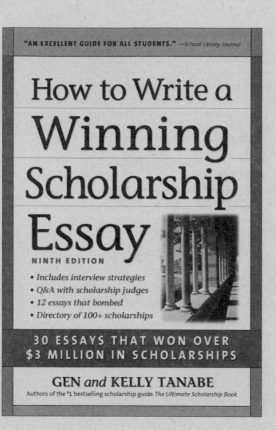

YOU WIN OR LOSE A SCHOLARSHIP WITH YOUR ESSAY AND INTERVIEW. LEARN TO ACE BOTH!

- Complete instructions on crafting a powerful scholarship essay

- 30 money-winning essays that won $3 million in scholarships

- Scholarship judges reveal what separates winners from runner-ups

- 12 essays that bombed and how to avoid these mistakes

- Master the interview with sample questions and answers

ISBN: 978-1-61760-176-7

$17.99

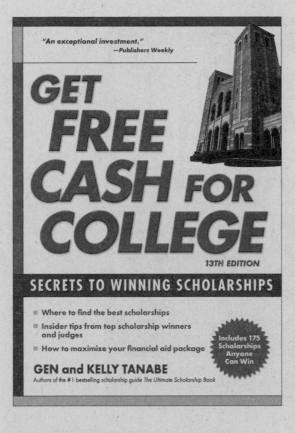

GET THE MONEY YOU NEED
TO PAY FOR COLLEGE!

- Insider tips from top scholarship winners and judges

- Secrets to writing applications and essays that win

- Where to find the best scholarships

- Techniques for maximizing your financial aid package

ISBN13: 978-1-61760-174-3

$19.99

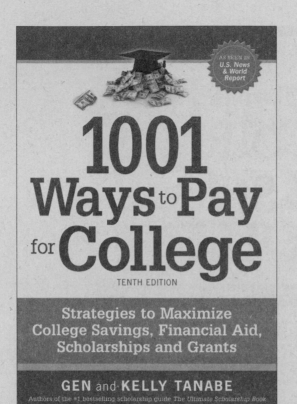

EVERY CONCEIVABLE WAY TO PAY FOR COLLEGE

- Where to find the best scholarships

- Pay in-state tuition even if you're an out-of-state student

- Jump-start your college savings

- Get your share of the $242 billion in financial aid available

- Have your state pay for your college education

- Get your student loans forgiven

- And much, much more!

ISBN: 978-1-61760-166-8

$19.99

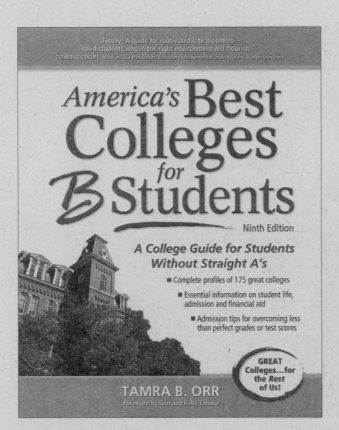

A COLLEGE GUIDE FOR STUDENTS WITHOUT STRAIGHT A'S

- Complete profiles of 175 great colleges that welcome students like you

- Information on academics, majors and what the colleges seek

- Admission tips for overcoming less than perfect grades or test scores

- Inside advice from students, counselors and admission officers

SBN: 978-1-61760-168-2

$19.99

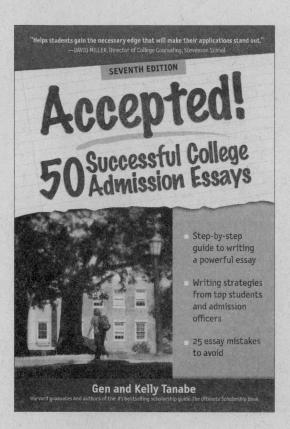

WRITE THE COLLEGE ADMISSION ESSAY THAT GETS YOU IN!

- 50 successful college essays—learn from the best

- Admission officers reveal exactly what colleges want to see in your admission essays

- 25 essay mistakes to avoid

- Complete instructions on crafting a powerful essay

- How to recycle your essay to save time

- Write the essay that will get you into your dream college

ISBN: 978-1-61760-157-6

$14.99

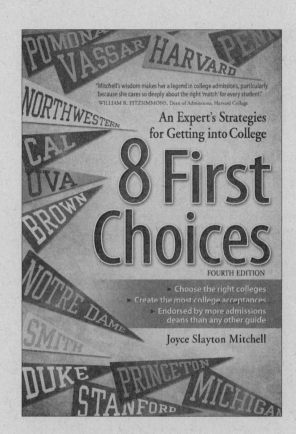

AN EXPERT'S STRATEGIES FOR GETTING INTO COLLEGE

- Choose the right colleges
- Create the most college acceptances
- Endorsed by more admissions deans than any other guide

ISBN: 978-1-61760-163-7

$14.99

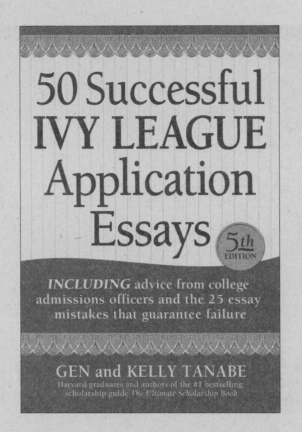

CRAFT A WINNING ESSAY FOR AN IVY LEAGUE COLLEGE

- How to select the best topic
- What Ivy League admissions officers want to see in your essay
- The 25 mistakes that guarantee failure
- The top tips from Ivy League students

ISBN: 978-1-61760-156-9

$14.99

APPLY FOR THE ALL STAR VERIFIED SCHOLARSHIP

The All Star Verified Scholarship assists students with tuition or room and board. The merit-based scholarship is open to 9th-12th grade high school, college or graduate students including adult learners.

Visit **www.verifiedscholarships.com/scholarship-program** to apply.

GET MORE TOOLS AND RESOURCES AT SUPERCOLLEGE.COM

Visit **www.supercollege.com** for more free resources on college admission, scholarships and financial aid. And, apply for the SuperCollege Scholarship.

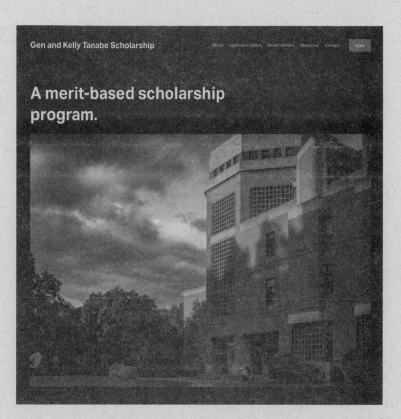

APPLY FOR THE GEN AND KELLY TANABE SCHOLARSHIP

The Gen and Kelly Tanabe Scholarship is a merit-based program that helps students fulfill their dreams of a higher education. The program is open to 9th-12th grade high school, college, or graduate students including adult learners. Visit **www.gkscholarship.com** to apply.

ABOUT THE AUTHORS

Harvard graduates and husband and wife team Gen and Kelly Tanabe are the founders of SuperCollege and award-winning authors of 14 books including: *Get Free Cash for College, 1001 Ways to Pay for College, How to Write a Winning Scholarship Essay, The Ultimate Guide to America's Best Colleges, Get into Any College, Accepted! 50 Successful College Admission Essays, 501 Ways for Adult Students to Pay for College* and *Accepted! 50 Successful Business School Admission Essays*.

Together, Gen and Kelly were accepted to every school to which they applied, including all the Ivy League colleges and won over $100,000 in merit-based scholarships. They were able to graduate from Harvard debt-free.

Gen and Kelly give workshops across the country and write the nationally syndicated "Ask the SuperCollege Experts" column. They have made hundreds of appearances on television and radio and have served as expert sources for *USA Today*, the *New York Times, U.S. News & World Report, New York Daily News, San Jose Mercury News, Chronicle of Higher Education, CNN* and *Seventeen*.

Gen grew up in Waialua, Hawaii. A graduate of Waialua High School, he was the first student from his school to be accepted at Harvard, where he graduated magna cum laude with a degree in both History and East Asian Studies.

Kelly attended Whitney High School, a nationally ranked public high school in her hometown of Cerritos, California. She graduated magna cum laude from Harvard with a degree in Sociology.

The Tanabes approach financial aid from a practical, hands-on point of view. Drawing on the collective knowledge and experiences of students, they provide real strategies students can use to pay for their education.

Gen and Kelly live in Belmont, California with their sons Zane and Kane.